TO

THE TWO

MRS. JOHN TASKER HOWARDS,

MY WIFE AND MY MOTHER,

this book is lovingly inscribed

PREFACE

THE author of a book on American music may well approach his task with fears as to the outcome, knowing that no matter how thorough he may try to be, his work will be incomplete in many respects. Yet it has seemed that a book like this is called for, to bring information about the music that has been written in this country; one that will be both historical and contemporary, look facts fairly in the face, avoid chauvinism, and present the honest opinion of the writer. This book is an account of the music that has been written in America; not a history of musical activities, except, of course, where we must have some idea of the conditions that have produced the composers of each era.

The student of American music will find many paths open to him. There is an abundance of source material, gathered by such tireless research workers as Oscar G. Sonneck and others who have worked in our libraries and historical societies. Mr. Sonneck's source books on our early secular music, concerts, and opera, though written a quarter of a century ago, are still surprisingly complete. While discoveries have been made since his books were published, little has been found that would prove any of his findings wrong. Mr. Sonneck carried his studies up to 1800, and beyond that date the student must do his own research, in newspapers, musical journals, diaries, from concert programs, and from printed music. It is of interest to note that a fund has been established as a memorial to Mr. Sonneck, which, it is hoped, will provide for a complete compilation of all musical records of New York, Boston, and Philadelphia for the years 1800 to 1850; a mammoth task, but one that will be of inestimable value.

Material for the present volume has been gathered from a wide variety of sources, as listed in the bibliography. Mr. Sonneck's compilations were, of course, invaluable. Private collectors have generously opened their collections, and descendants and relatives of our early composers have been kind in showing material that has added fresh data to the information previously available. Contemporary musical journals of various periods have likewise yielded an amazing wealth of information.

An outline serialization of much of the material in this book has appeared in *Voice of the Air;* and other material has appeared in the form of articles in *The Musical Digest* and *The Musical Quarterly.* I acknowledge the kindness of their editors in granting permission to include this matter.

Many individuals have also been helpful in my task. Among the descendants and relatives of composers—Mr. Edward Hopkinson, great grandson of Francis Hopkinson; Mr. Hobart Hewitt and Miss Carrie W. Hewitt, grandson and great granddaughter of James Hewitt; Mrs. James Spurr Whitman, granddaughter of Oliver Shaw; Mr. Howard Van Sinderen, husband of the late Minna Mason Van Sinderen, who was the daughter of William Mason and grand-daughter of Lowell Mason and George James Webb; Mrs. Edward MacDowell; Mrs. Ethelbert Nevin; Mrs. Horatio Parker; as well as many friends and associates of MacDowell, Parker, Nevin, Paine, and others, who have given valuable information, impressions, and anecdotes.

Those in charge of the libraries to which I have gone for reference and study have done much to make my work pleasant and easier. Dr. Otto Kinkeldey, who was head of the Music Division of the New York Public Library until he became librarian of Cornell University; Miss Dorothy Lawton and her assistants at the 58th Street Music Library in New York; Mr. Walter R. Whittlesey, and Mr. W. Oliver Strunk of the Library of Congress; Mr. Richard G. Appel, of the Public Library of the City of Boston; as well as those at the many state libraries who have helped me in finding books referring to music and musicians in their states.

Among the private collectors who have given access to their treasures, I am particularly grateful to Mr. Arthur Billings Hunt of Brooklyn, Mr. Joseph Muller of Closter, New Jersey, and Mr. George Fischer of New York City.

I wish also to acknowledge the kindness of the book publishers who have granted me permission to quote from their copyright publications, as indicated in the text.

Music publishers have been helpful in supplying information about the composers of the music in their catalogues; and I should like to save a large portion of my gratitude for the contemporary composers, who have responded most graciously to requests for data. If I have failed to put any of them in the place they feel they should have, I hope they will forgive me and credit it to ignorance rather than to malice.

And lastly I wish to acknowledge my debt to many friends who have helped in suggestions and criticism, and in many cases with recollections of the happenings chronicled in these pages; among them my erstwhile music teacher and lifelong friend, Paul Tidden; my friend and neighbor, Osbourne McConathy; Professor Homer A. Watt of New York University, who has been helpful in introducing me to specialists in several fields; J. Walker McSpadden, who has been my friend and adviser as well as my publisher's editor. Many others, too, whom I should like to mention; but space forbids.

So here is the book. I let it go from me with misgivings, but at least I know that I have tried to state the case of the American composer honestly. And I have the feeling that his music is better qualified to speak for him than any single writer of a book on American music.

J. T. H.

Glen Ridge, New Jersey.
January, 1931.

PREFACE TO
THIRD EDITION

In 1939, when *Our American Music* had been in circulation for eight years, two supplementary chapters were added to tell briefly of the developments and the many new composers that had appeared in that comparatively short time. And now, after six more years, it is not only desirable, but necessary, to revise the book completely, to adjust certain viewpoints to changing conditions, to re-evaluate, to add to the discussion of composers included in the original volumes the many works they have composed more recently, and also to include the several hundred composers who became recognized after 1931.

Since the first appearance of *Our American Music* many specialists have been busy with research into the early days of America's music life, some of them carrying on the work of Oscar G. Sonneck in examining the beginnings of our secular music and concert life; others in the backgrounds of the psalmody and hymnology of New England, some into folk music, many into regional history, and a dozen or more into jazz and contemporary manifestations of twentieth-century phenomena. Consequently, our scholars know infinitely more about the backgrounds of American music than was known even fifteen years ago. Evidence of this is in the addition of more than three hundred titles to the Bibliography at the end of our book, most of them of works published in recent years.

In order that *Our American Music* might have the benefit of this varied research, certain chapters and sections of the book have been submitted to specialists in several fields, who have checked the accuracy of all statements in the light of recent discoveries, and have suggested additional text material to amplify what was already presented in the book. Accordingly, my thanks and sincere appreciation for invaluable assistance go to Henry Wilder Foote for his contributions on early New England psalmody, the later hymn-tune composers, and on certain phases of our contemporary church music; to William Treat

Upton for his help in the sections on early secular music and on Anthony Philip Heinrich and William Henry Fry; to Richard S. Hill for the latest information on the origins of our national airs, particularly *The Star-Spangled Banner;* to Hans Nathan for the benefit of his studies in Negro minstrel shows, Negro minstrel music, singing families of the mid-nineteenth century, and for material on Daniel Decatur Emmett; to George Pullen Jackson for his contribution on the "White Spirituals" and folk hymnody and their effect on the present-day gospel songs; to Fletcher Hodges, Junior, for a review of the chapter on Stephen Foster; and to Sigmund Spaeth for amplifying the material on popular songs to cover more adequately the period between the Civil War and the 1890's.

Several institutions and individuals have been particularly helpful. The Americana Collection of the Music Division of the New York Public Library, of which the author is curator, has naturally been a rich mine of information, and a clearing ground for many matters which required examination and sifting. The staff of the Music Division has had an indispensable part in the preparation of these pages. My thanks are due to them and particularly to Miss Anita Goldstein, who has given unsparingly of her time in attending to innumerable details of preparation.

Likewise, the staff of the Music Library on 58th Street have been highly co-operative and helpful in locating information on many individuals included in these pages. Thanks are due also to Mr. Daniel McNamara of the staff of the American Society of Composers, Authors and Publishers for supplying information on composers who are members of that society.

It is a pleasure further to express my appreciation of the willingness of my publishers to spare no pains in making this revised edition of *Our American Music* as thorough and comprehensive as it could be made, and of the interest and sympathetic co-operation offered by Mr. Robert L. Crowell and his editorial staff. And lastly, but by no means least, my heartfelt thanks are offered to Miss Ava Yeargain, for her invaluable assistance in research and in the actual preparation of several chapters, as well as in proofreading.

J. T. H.

Glen Ridge, New Jersey, 1946.

PREFACE TO
FOURTH EDITION

AND now another ten years have gone by since the 1946 edition was supplemented by two chapters covering the eight-year period of 1946–54. Since then a careful record has been kept of all events in American music as they were reported in the newspapers and music journals. From these the chronicle has been brought up to date, new composers have been added, and the recent scores of older composers have been described.

In writing of these more recent developments, the author appears in the role of chronicler and historian rather than as critic. Instead of offering his own opinion of contemporary works, he has continued and enlarged upon the method that was begun in former editions of the book: citing by direct quotation the judgments of contemporary critics on the occasions of first performances of new works. In some instances later opinions are quoted when certain works have been revived or have remained continuously in the repertory. We can thus learn how these pieces have weathered the years of their existence.

One important feature of this fourth edition is the bringing up to date of the bibliography. No additions had been made to it since 1946. The number of books and articles that have been issued during the ensuing eighteen years have been astounding, and at the author's request Mr. Karl Kroeger has selected and added the most important new material. Mr. Kroeger occupies the position at the New York Public Library that the author filled for fifteen years, that of Curator of the Americana Collection, and his predecessor is most grateful to him for making the bibliography comprehensive.

J. T. H.

July, 1964.

Contents

PAGE

Introduction   xix

PART I—1620–1800

EUTERPE IN THE WILDERNESS

CHAPTER

I. Early Days   3
1. New England Psalmody   3
2. Early Church Organs   17
3. Early Secular Music in New England   20
4. Philadelphia, New York, and the South   24

II. Our First Composers   37
1. Francis Hopkinson (1737–1791)   37
2. James Lyon (1735–1794)   44
3. William Billings and His "Fuguing Pieces" (1746–1800)   49

III. The Latter Eighteenth Century   58
1. New England   58
2. Post-Revolutionary Immigrants in New York and Philadelphia   71

PART II—1800–1860

EUTERPE CLEARS THE FOREST

IV. Our First National Airs   113
1. Yankee Doodle   113
2. Hail Columbia   118
3. The Star-Spangled Banner   121
4. America   126

V. The Turn of the Century   129
1. Foreign and Native Artists   129
2. Lowell Mason (1792–1872) and the Return of the Native Composer   136
3. Mason's Contemporaries   141

CHAPTER   PAGE
VI. OUR NINETEENTH-CENTURY BACKGROUND IN SECULAR MUSIC   150
    1. Concert Life   150
    2. Early Song Writers   158
    3. Singing Families   173
    4. Minstrel Shows and Their Songs   176
    5. Stephen Collins Foster (1826–1864)   184
    6. Rampant Virtuosi   198
    7. Louis Moreau Gottschalk (1829–1869)   205

VII. THE FOREIGN INVASION OF 1848   211

VIII. THE AWAKENING OF A NATIONAL CONSCIOUSNESS   226
    1. Anton Philip Heinrich (1781–1861)   226
    2. William Henry Fry (1815[?]–1864)   238
    3. George F. Bristow (1825–1898)   247

PART III—1860 TO THE PRESENT

EUTERPE BUILDS HER AMERICAN HOME

IX. SONGS OF THE CIVIL WAR   255
    1. *Dixie* and *The Battle Hymn*   255
    2. Other War Songs   260

X. THE SPREAD OF MUSICAL CULTURE   269
    1. Westward Expansion   269
    2. William Mason (1829–1908)   274
    3. Theodore Thomas (1835–1905)   280
    4. Other Teachers and Composers of the Period   289

XI. THE PARENTS OF OUR CONTEMPORARIES   294
    1. The Grandfathers   294
    2. The Boston Group   306
    3. Edward MacDowell (1861–1908)   323
    4. Links with the Past   344

XII. TWENTIETH CENTURY COMPOSERS   364
    1. Composers Born in the 1870's   364
    2. Composers Born in the 1880's   389
    3. From the 1890's   424
    4. From the 1900's   478
    5. From the 1910's   530
    6. Composers Born After 1920   588

CHAPTER		PAGE
XIII.	COMPOSERS BEST KNOWN FOR THEIR SHORTER WORKS	621
	1. Composers of Songs and Short Pieces	621
	2. Art Songs	629
	3. Choral Pieces and Part-Songs	633
	4. Folk Song Settings	635
	5. Instrumental Pieces	638
XIV.	LATTER-CENTURY AND PRESENT-DAY RELIGIOUS MUSIC	644
	1. Dudley Buck (1839–1909) and His Successors	644
	2. Twentieth-Century Religious Music	651
	3. Folk Hymns and the Gospel Song	663
XV.	OUR FOLK MUSIC	670
	1. The Music of the North American Indian	670
	2. Negro Folk Music	680
	3. Other Sources of Folk Songs	690
XVI.	OUR LIGHTER MUSICAL MOMENTS	701
	1. Yesterday	701
	2. Yesterday—The Musical Theatre	711
	3. Ragtime and After	720
	4. Twentieth-Century War Songs	726
	5. The Twentieth-Century Musical Theatre	729
	6. Twentieth-Century Popular Song Composers	749
XVII.	CONCLUSION	755
	BIBLIOGRAPHY	769
	INDEX	847

List of Illustrations

FACING PAGE

Title Page of the *Bay Psalm Book*   10

Two Pages from Thomas Walter's Singing Book (1721)   11

Francis Hopkinson   42

Frontispiece of Billings' Sixth and Last Book, *The Continental Harmony* (1794), Showing a "Tune" Engraved on a Circle   43

James Hewitt   74

Alexander Reinagle   75

Benjamin Carr   75

An Early Nineteenth-Century Broadside of *Yankee Doodle*   106

Francis Scott Key   107

Lowell Mason   138

Characteristic Mid-Century Title Pages   139

Stephen Collins Foster   170

Foster's Own Account of His Income from Royalties (1857)   171

Daniel Decatur Emmett   234

Julia Ward Howe   234

George F. Root   235

Henry Clay Work   235

Theodore Thomas   266

Going to the Peace Jubilee   267

George W. Chadwick   298

Arthur Foote   298

Horatio Parker   299

Mrs. H. H. A. Beach   299

Edward MacDowell   330

FACING PAGE

Original Manuscript of MacDowell's *Told at Sunset*, No. 10 of His *Woodland Sketches*   331

Edgar Stillman Kelley   362

Walter Damrosch   362

John Alden Carpenter   363

Henry K. Hadley   363

Deems Taylor   394

Charles Wakefield Cadman   394

Ernest Bloch   395

Louis Gruenberg   395

Howard Hanson   490

George Gershwin   490

Aaron Copland   491

Virgil Thomson   491

William Schuman   522

Paul Creston   522

Morton Gould   523

Leonard Bernstein   523

Ethelbert Nevin   586

Oley Speaks   587

Albert Hay Malotte   587

Victor Herbert   618

Jerome Kern   618

Richard Rodgers   619

Irving Berlin   619

INTRODUCTION

BEFORE beginning this account of Our American Music, it will be wise if the reader and the author agree as to just what American music is and, likewise, who is an American composer. It may be argued that all such classifications are arbitrary, and that the author is privileged to make his own distinctions. Nevertheless, we will get along much better, and be happier, if we can agree.

Shall we insist that music must be nationalistically American? We shall have to settle this at the start, for it will make a vast difference in our contents. And if we limit ourselves to those things that we can agree are American, we probably will need to write no book at all; for even though we may each have our own ideas on the subject, I doubt if any two of them are alike. And, moreover, even if we do agree, we must omit all composers who have written principally in the manner of other nations, and perhaps whatever may be considered *universal* or *cosmopolitan* in its style or idiom. Under such a rule, Tschaikowsky might conceivably be barred from a book on Russian music. So why not say right here that music written by Americans will be our American music, at least for the purpose of our discussion? Then, if we are careful to point out Americanisms as we find them, we can give the composers responsible for them an A double plus, or whatever merit mark we choose.

Then who is the American composer? Many think he must be born in this country; that those who urge the adoption of foreign residents as Americans do so because we have so few natives. That a French-born composer is always a Frenchman; a German-born, a German. Maybe so, and the day may come when we no longer lengthen our list with foreigners. But our case is a little different. We have all adopted America, even those of us who let our ancestors do our immigrating for us. And shall we be like college boys in treating newcomers as freshmen, just because our ancestors had the idea first?

You may say that the Constitution requires the president of the country to be a native-born citizen; but there can be only a few presidents, and we have room for many composers. You and I know many native Americans whose families have been here for generations, but whose temperaments and points of view are as foreign as those of their cousins who stayed at home. Of course, it is obvious that mere residence will not make an American, and we cannot call a composition American merely because its composer has had a part of his physical existence in this country. If that were allowable, the *New World Symphony* would have been written while Dvořák was an American composer. No; visitors are welcome, but they are not Americans.

It must be a case of extended residence, to all intents permanent; the adopted composer may go home to visit, but he mustn't stay away too long. And it must be something more subtle and subjective than citizenship. Legal naturalization may make a citizen, but it does not in itself make an American. The foreigner must become one of us, become identified with our life and institutions. And also he must make his reputation here. He must come to us in his formative years, not as an established artist.

Try this definition: a composer is an American if, by birth or choice of permanent residence, he becomes identified with American life and institutions before his talents have had their greatest outlet; and through his associations and sympathies he makes a genuine contribution to our cultural development.

These specifications would admit Charles Martin Loeffler, who came here at the beginning of his career; Ernest Bloch, who received his first important recognition in this country; Percy Grainger, who came to us as a well-established pianist, but most of whose composing was yet to be accomplished; the more recent composers Lukas Foss, Alexei Haieff, Nikolai Lopatnikoff, Gian-Carlo Menotti, Bernard Wagenaar; and, among the composers of lighter music, Victor Herbert, Rudolf Friml, Sigmund Romberg, and Jule Styne. The definition obviously does not include many of those who were widely discussed and internationally known composers before political events drove them from Europe. Arnold Schoenberg, Igor Stravinsky, Darius Milhaud, Sergei Rachmaninoff, Ernst Křenek, Kurt Weill, Paul Hindemith, and dozens of others have taken up residence in this country and in many cases become Americans by naturalization.

Our nation may well be proud of this fact, but it does not seem appropriate to include them in this volume as musical products of the United States.

The music of America's three hundred years seems naturally to fall into three periods, but not according to centuries. Dating its existence in this country from the settlement of Plymouth in 1620, the first period would include the one hundred and eighty years to 1800, to a time when our independence was established and we had begun to be a nation, and we were beginning to absorb the first immigration of those foreigners who came to our land of freedom after we had become the United States of America. There were the early psalmodists in New England, but none who were known to have written music of their own until the time of William Billings, in the latter part of the eighteenth century. There was secular music in New York, Philadelphia, and the South, but no composers we know of until Francis Hopkinson appeared. Yet we shall find that there were certain factors in our early musical life, barren as it was, that have had an influence on the music of our day. Euterpe did indeed come to a wilderness, but she made the best of her situation.

The next period, in which Euterpe seems to have made up her mind to stay with us, extends from 1800 to 1860. The foreigners who had come in the 1780's and 1790's, because of the French revolution and because they had heard of America's freedom, were becoming Americans. The native composer, who had been forced to the background by the coming of skilled Europeans, came forward again with more confidence. Lowell Mason appeared, with his contemporary hymn writers. Concert life and operas became more firmly established. The new Western cities demanded some music. The minstrel show became a favorite diversion, and Stephen Foster wrote melodies that have become folk songs.

Then another tide of immigration swept our shores, which had the same effect that the latter eighteenth-century coming of foreigners had had fifty years before. The revolutions in Central Europe made America a refuge for hundreds of Germans in the years around 1848. When they came here they took over a large part of our musical life, and many Americans were content to sit back and listen rather than put their less developed talents in competition with the foreigners.

And so the second period ended, as the first had finished, with aliens in the foreground.

The third period reaches from 1860 to the present day. Euterpe makes a home with us. As at the beginning of the century, in the second period, most of the foreigners became Americans. Moreover, we were beginning to be nationally conscious in our music. And we began to produce composers who were important: John K. Paine and Dudley Buck among the first. Then MacDowell—Chadwick, Foote, Parker, and the rest of the Boston group; Ethelbert Nevin, with his lilting tunes and his *Rosary*. All of this right down to our own day, when we have passed through a phase of arguing about the nationalistic character of our music and considering that feature to be of prime importance; when the term "modern music" is considered a bit archaic; when twelve-tone composers are a dime a dozen; when the prefix *neo-* is applied to classicists and Romantics; when the eclectics are helping themselves to idioms both contemporary and old-fashioned; when the development of jazz has gone through all those colorfully named phases we remember so well—hot jazz, sweet jazz, swing, boogie-woogie, be-bop, cool jazz, progressive jazz, and every other sort of jazz. But perhaps most important, we have come to a period when our musical life is on a par with that of any other country in the world; when we have the finest of symphony orchestras in our large cities; the finest teachers of the world in our conservatories or in their own private studios; and the finest performers gracing our concert stages.

But more of this in its proper place. The division into periods has been arbitrary, and there has been some chronological overlapping. For example, the first national airs are included in the second section, yet two of them—*Yankee Doodle* and *Hail Columbia*—first appeared in the eighteenth century. It has seemed better to include all of these national songs in one chapter, and to consider that the earliest of them bridged the century and the first two periods.

And now we go to the first act of our pageant. There will be much to amuse us, and, I trust, to interest us. But I ask one favor of you: smile and laugh if you wish, but *with* not *at* the friends we shall meet. For when we think of their handicaps, the few tools they had to work with, talent rises to genius. But enough of the sermon. Raise the curtain and meet Euterpe in the Wilderness.

PART ONE

1620–1800

EUTERPE IN THE WILDERNESS

CHAPTER ONE

Early Days

I. NEW ENGLAND PSALMODY

THE history of American music, meaning the music of what is now the United States, should logically start with the psalm singing of the New England colonists, not because it was the first music known on the North American continent, but rather because it was the earliest music of which we have any satisfactory record, and of which any extended account can be written.

The folk music of the American Indians was probably in existence long before the coming of the colonists, and no doubt the Negroes who were brought from Africa in the first slave ship in 1619 used song as an outlet for their emotions; but recognition of folk music has been a comparatively modern fashion, and it seems more appropriate to discuss it in other than a chronological place which is wholly problematical. The earliest European music to be heard upon either coast of North America north of the Spanish settlements was the French psalmody sung by the Huguenots on the Carolina Coast in 1572, before their brief settlement was wiped out by the Spaniards; and the English psalmody sung by Drake's seamen during their stay of several weeks in June, 1579, at what is now known as Drake's Bay on the California Coast, as described in Francis Fletcher's *The World Encompassed by Sir Francis Drake*.

Aside from these brief episodes the first recorded use of music on this continent, north of the Spanish domain, was that of the Pilgrims at Plymouth. The settlement at Jamestown preceded that at Plymouth by eleven years, it is true, but the Virginia planters have left no record of singing, though it is not unreasonable to assume that in spite

of the miseries they endured they may at times have plucked up courage to sing popular "catches" round their campfires, and psalms in
their houses of worship. In contrast to our lack of information about
the Jamestown settlement, we do have definite knowledge of the
music the New England settlers brought with them from England,
and contemporary documents tell of their methods of singing. We
are, therefore, able to follow the course of musical development in the
Northern colonies from the earliest days.

The first century of New England's history was in many respects a
musical wilderness, but probably little if any more so than in the other
colonies. The England from which the first settlers emigrated was a
land noted for its singing, and there is no reason to suppose that only
those persons emigrated who were unmusical. The Puritans, of course,
held strictly to psalmody as the only music suitable for use in worship,
and discountenanced lewd and indecent songs, of which there were
plenty in the seventeenth century, as tending to "the nourishment of
vice and the corruption of faith," but there is adequate evidence that
many of them appreciated good music and that some brought musical
instruments with them to this country.[1]

But the hard conditions of pioneer life, with its heavy labor, left no
leisure for the fine arts, and in all the colonies the second and third
generations grew up without the cultural background their English
fathers had enjoyed. This was undoubtedly the principal cause of the
musical impoverishment that existed until more stable conditions
made possible the revival of interest in music early in the eighteenth
century.

When the Pilgrims crossed from Holland in the *Mayflower* in 1620
they brought with them Henry Ainsworth's *Book of Psalmes*, prepared by him in 1612 for the congregations of Separatists who fled
from England to Holland. His book included thirty-nine psalm-tunes,
about half being taken from English psalm books, the rest being the
longer and finer French and Dutch tunes in a considerable variety of
meters. Ainsworth's *Psalter* was superior, musically, to any English
psalm book then available.[2]

[1] H. W. Foote, *Three Centuries of American Hymnody*, chap. III (1940); also
Foote, "Musical Life in Boston in the Eighteenth Century," *Proceedings of the Antiquarian Society, New Series*, XLIX, 293–313.

[2] Waldo S. Pratt, *The Music of the Pilgrims*, Boston, 1921.

The Plymouth Pilgrims undoubtedly had a love for music, for a contemporary account of their sailing from Leyden tells of the ceremony that attended their departure. In *Hypocrisie Unmasked* Edward Winslow wrote:

They that stayed at Leyden feasted us that were to go at our pastor's house . . . ; where we refreshed ourselves, after tears, with singing of Psalms, making joyful melody in our hearts as well as with the voice, there being many of our congregation very expert in music; and indeed it was the sweetest melody that ever mine ears heard.

Ainsworth's *Book of Psalmes* remained in use at Plymouth until 1692, when it was abandoned in favor of the *Bay Psalm Book*, because the children of the emigrant generation were no longer able to sing the longer and more involved tunes their fathers had loved.

The Puritans of the Massachusetts Bay Colony brought with them the psalm book that had been produced by English Protestant exiles in Geneva on the model of the *French Genevan Psalter* of 1562. The English book was first printed in the same year by John Day under the title *The Whole Booke of Psalmes, collected into English Meter by T. Sternhold, I. Hopkins and others; conferred with the Ebrue, with apt Notes to sing them withal, Faithfully perused and alowed according to th' ordre appointed in the Queenes maiesties Iniunctions: Very mete to be used of all sortes of people privately for their solace and comfort; laying apart all ungodly Songes and Ballades, which tende only to the nourishment of Vyce & corruption of Youth.*

It is necessary to know something about this book, and its various editions, if we are to understand the Psalmody of New England. Commonly called *Sternhold and Hopkins* and later known as the *Old Version*—after the appearance in 1696 of Tate and Brady's *New Version* of the metrical psalms, the book had been quickly adopted into popular and universal use in Elizabethan England. Its verse, which later generations came to regard as crude and barbarous, was cast in the popular ballad meters and was probably as good as England could have produced at the period. At any rate, it pleased the people for whom it was written. Sternhold and Hopkins' book was promptly introduced into the worship of the Church of England, and only slowly gave way to the *New Version* nearly a century and a half later.

Musically it was inferior to the *French Genevan Psalter*. Yet at times it has a simple dignity and solemnity, often combined with sweetness.

Three other musical editions followed John Day's first *Sternhold and Hopkins*; Damon's in 1579; Este's in 1592; and Allison's in 1599. Este printed his tunes in four-part settings arranged by distinguished musicians, and Allison's collection of psalm-tunes has been called by a competent authority, "on the whole the best that ever appeared." They were followed by Thomas Ravenscroft's *Psalter* in 1621, containing ninety-seven tunes, by far the best English selection available in the seventeenth century, with which the Puritans in New England were quite familiar, as will presently appear. Ravenscroft acknowledges his indebtedness to outstanding musicians of his own or the immediately preceding generation, including Dowland, Farnaby, Morley, Tallis, and Tomkins.

The only early psalm-tune that appeared in these books which is still familiar to churchgoers is the *Old Hundredth*. This melody is attributed to Louis Bourgeois, the music editor of Calvin's *Genevan Psalters*, and first appeared in 1551, set to the 38th Psalm. It was taken over by the English Puritans and was attached to William Kethe's version of the 100th Psalm in John Day's edition of *Sternhold and Hopkins*, with a slightly different ending from the Genevan form, and so passed into all the later psalm books. The original words began,

> All people that on earth do dwell
> Sing to the Lord with cheerful voyce;
> Him serve with mirth, his praise forth tell,
> Come ye before Him and rejoice.

Our forefathers called it a "lively and jocund tune," because they sang it with some quick notes which well expressed the sentiment of the words—not with the slow and solemn tread of even notes into which the tune was flattened out in the eighteenth century, and to which we are accustomed when we sing the *Doxology*. Some modern hymnbooks have revived the original form of the tune, to the original words. A few other psalm-tunes from the sixteenth and seventeenth centuries have also been restored to recent hymnbooks, notably *St. Florian, Dundee, Dunfermline, Windsor,* and *Old 120th* from English and Scottish sources; and *Toulon* (*Old 124th*), *L'Omnipotent*, *Donne Secours*, and *St. Michael* from Genevan sources.

In John Day's edition of *Sternhold and Hopkins*, and in Ainsworth, the music of the psalms was printed with the words, a single melody line to be sung in unison, a single note to each syllable, after the Genevan fashion. A large proportion of the tunes are in the minor key, which our forefathers do not appear to have found depressing, as so many moderns do.

But to return to New England: the Puritans brought with them to the Massachusetts Bay Colony copies of *Sternhold and Hopkins*, probably in most cases with Ravenscroft's settings.[3] But they were dissatisfied with the words they found in it. To understand their dissatisfaction we must go back to Calvin's teaching. He held that the only words suitable for singing in worship were those taken from Scripture, the inspired Word of God, put into metrical verse in the most accurate translation possible. But the New England ministers were good enough Hebraists to realize that in many places the metrical versions they found in *Sternhold and Hopkins* were quite inaccurate. As Cotton Mather puts it in his Magnolia:

About the year 1639, the New English Reformers, considering that their churches enjoyed the ordinances of Heaven in their spiritual purity, were willing that the ordinance of singing Psalms should be restored among them unto a share in that purity. Though they blessed God for the religious endeavors of them who translated the psalms into the metre usually annexed, at the end of the Bible, yet they beheld in the translation, variations of, not only the text, but the very sense of the Psalmist, that it was an offence unto them.

They therefore appointed a committee of thirty divines to prepare a new and more "close-fitting" translation, each of whom "took a portion to be translated." The work, however, appears to have been done almost entirely by the Reverend Richard Mather of Dorchester, and the Reverend Thomas Welde and the Reverend John Eliot of Roxbury, all of whom had studied at Emmanuel College, Cambridge. This is indicated by Cotton Mather, who says that they "were of so

---

[3] John Endicott's copy of Ravenscroft's *Psalter*, with his autograph, is now owned by the Massachusetts Historical Society.

different a Genius for their Poetry that Mr. Shephard of Cambridge on the Occasion addressed them to this Purpose,

> You Roxbury Poets, keep clear of the Crime
> Of missing to give us a very good Rhime;
> And you of Dorchester, your verses lengthen,
> But with the Text's own words, you will them strengthen.

Today the verses of these Roxbury and Dorchester "poets" seem uncouth enough, although careful examination reveals lines of rugged beauty. But it is essential to remember that their aim was not smoothly flowing verse so much as close accuracy of translation. In that they succeeded well. Their book was printed in 1640 in the little press at Cambridge, and was the first book to appear in the English-speaking colonies of North America. It was popularly known as the *Bay Psalm Book*, but its actual title was *The Whole Booke of Psalmes faithfully translated into English Metre. Whereunto is prefixed a discourse declaring not only the lawfullnes, but also the necessity of the heavenly Ordinance of Singing Scripture Psalmes in the Churches of God.* Richard Mather wrote the preface in which he states the case for psalm singing. "The singing of Psalmes, though it breathe forth nothing but holy harmony, and melody; yet such is the subtilty of the enemie, and the enmity of our nature against the Lord, and his wayes, that our hearts can find matter of discord in this harmony and crochets of dirision in this holy melody." And he concludes: "If . . . the verses are not always so smooth and elegant as some may desire or expect, let them consider that God's Altar needs not our pollishings . . . for we have respected rather a plaine translation, and so have attended Conscience rather than Elegance, fidelity rather than poetry, in translating the Hebrew words into English language, and David's poetry into English meetre: that soe we may sing in Sion the Lord's songs of praise according to his own will; until hee take us from hence, and wipe away all our tears, and bid us entre our masters joye to sing eternall Halleluiahs."

Only ten copies of the original edition survive, not three of them perfect. In 1651 a revised edition was brought out, edited by Henry Dunster and Richard Lyon, with considerable improvements in the versification. This revised edition bore the title *The Psalms, Hymns*

*and Spiritual Songs of the Old and New Testaments, faithfully trans-
lated into English meter for the use, edification and comfort of the
Saints, in publick and private, especially in New England.* The two
books have been commonly regarded as successive editions of what was
universally called *The Bay Psalm Book.*

The early edition contained no music, probably for lack of anyone
capable of engraving the plates, but all included an "Admonition"
about the tunes to which the psalms might be sung, which reads (in
part) as follows:

The verses of these psalmes may be reduced to six kinds [metres], the first
whereof may be sung in very neere fourty common tunes; as they are
collected out of our chief musicians, by Tho. Ravenscroft. The second kinde
may be sung in three tunes, as Ps. 25, 50 and 67 in our English psalme books.
The third may be sung indifferently, as ps. the 51, 100, and ten command-
ments, in our English psalme books, which these tunes aforesaid, comprehend
almost this whole book of psalmes, as being tunes most familiar to us. . . .

Altogether some fifty tunes are referred to in either Ravenscroft's
Psalter or other English psalm books. It is important to remember
that although the editors were unable to print music in the *Bay Psalm
Book,* they did recommend to its users the best collections of tunes
which the time afforded.

The ninth edition, 1698, inserted thirteen tunes at the back of the
book and is the earliest known book with music printed in the English
colonies. The tunes were doubtless those in frequent use at the time—
*Oxford, Litchfield, Low-Dutch, York, Windsor, Cambridge, St.
David's, Martyn, Hackney, 119th Psalm Tune, 100th Psalm Tune,
115th Psalm Tune,* and *148th Psalm Tune.* Most are in common
meter, but *Cambridge* is short meter, the *100th Psalm Tune* is long
meter, and the *148th Psalm Tune* is six, six, six, six, four, four, four,
four.

The music was copied inaccurately from some unidentified English
source. It was crudely engraved on wood in diamond-shaped notes in
two-part harmony, without bars except at the end of each line. In later
editions, well-made copper plates were used.

The *Bay Psalm Book* soon came into wide use, not only in New
England but, in its 1651 form, as far south as Philadelphia. It even

had some use in England and Scotland where, according to the historian Thomas Prince, it was well esteemed. Twenty-seven editions were printed in New England, the last in 1762, and some twenty more in Great Britain, the last in 1754. Of the many versions of metrical psalms, only those of *Sternhold and Hopkins*, of *Tate and Brady*, the *Scottish Psalter*, and that of *Watts* were reprinted and used more widely.

Evidently not all of the early Bostonians favored singing, even of psalms, for in 1647 the Reverend John Cotton found it advisable to publish a treatise entitled:

Singing Psalms a Gospel Ordinance: or a Treatise wherein are handled these 4 particulars:

1. Touching the duty itself.
   (Singing of Psalmes with a lively voyce, is an holy Duty of God's Worship now in the dayes of the New Testament)
2. Touching the Matter to be Sung.
   (We hold and believe that not only the Psalmes of David, but any other spirituall songs recorded in Scripture, may lawfully be sung in Christian Churches)
3. Touching the Singers.
   1. Whether one be to sing for all the rest; or the whole congregation?
   2. Whether women; as well as men; or men alone?
   3. Whether carnall men and Pagans may be permitted to sing with us, or Christians alone, and Church members?
4. Touching the Manner of Singing.
   (It will be a necessary helpe, that the words of the Psalme, be openly read beforehand, line after line, or two lines together, so that they who want either books or skill to reade, may know what is to be sung, and joyne with the rest in the duties of singing.)

This document shows the nature of the discussions that were taking place in regard to music. Some complained that psalms should not be sung because the tunes were uninspired by God, and that God could not take delight in praises when sinful man had had a hand in making the melody. Some even went so far as to scoff at the Puritan ministers who called on the people to sing one of "Hopkins Jiggs, and so hop into the Pulpit." Cotton replied by calling all such "Cathedrall Priests of an Anti-Christian spirit," and by pointing out that "they that had

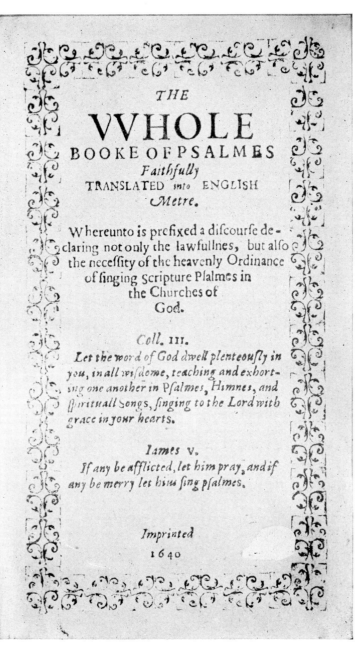

THE

VVHOLE

BOOKE OF PSALMES
Faithfully
TRANSLATED *into* ENGLISH
Metre.

Whereunto is prefixed a difcourfe declaring not only the lawfullnes, but alfo
the neceffity of the heavenly Ordinance
of finging Scripture Pfalmes in
the Churches of
God.

Coll. III.
*Let the word of God dwell plenteoufly in
you, in all wifdome, teaching and exhort-
ing one another in Pfalmes, Himnes, and
fpirituall Songs, finging to the Lord with
grace in your hearts.*

Iames V.
*If any be afflicted, let him pray, and if
any be merry let him fing pfalmes.*

Imprinted
1640

Title Page of the *Bay Psalm Book* (1640)
(See pages 7–10)

(1)

SOME BRIEF
And very plain INSTRUCTIONS
For *Singing* by *NOTE*.

USICK is the Art of modulating Sounds, either with the Voice, or with an Inſtrument. And as there are Rules for the right Management of an Inſtrument, ſo there are no leſs for the well ordering of the Voice. And tho' Nature it ſelf ſuggeſts unto us a Notion of Harmony, and many Men, without any other Tutor, may be able to ſtrike upon a few Notes tolerably tuneful ; yet this bears no more Proportion to a Tune compoſed and ſung by the Rules of Art than the vulgar Hedge-Notes of every Ruſtic does to the Harp of

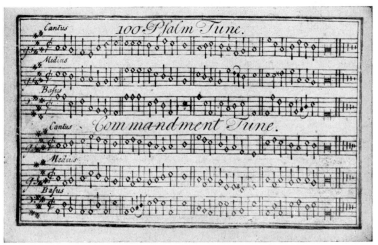

Two Pages from Thomas Walter's Singing Book (1721)
(See page 13)

a hand in making Melody of the English *Psalms* were men of a better spirit than the Ahab."

The lack of music in the *Bay Psalm Book*, the inability of many in the congregations to read not only music but printed English as well, led to the continuation of the earlier English practice of "lining out" the psalms, which was done in England by the parish clerk. In New England it was led by a deacon acting as precentor, whose duty it was to "set the tune," and who would sing the psalm, line by line, pausing for the congregation to repeat the line he had just sung. If the precentor had a good ear for music, and a good sense of pitch, well and good; otherwise the results were far from musical. It was probably this practice, more than any other factor, that brought congregational singing to its deplorable condition at the beginning of the eighteenth century. Tunes would be pitched too high or too low; the leader would take it upon himself to alter the tune, to add embellishments. By the end of the seventeenth century there was great confusion in regard to the tunes themselves, and in the manner of singing them.

George Hood, in his *History of Music in New England*, gives a vivid description of conditions at this time:

When the Puritans first came to their wilderness-home, they cultivated music even in their College. [Harvard, founded in 1636.] Their songs of praise were conducted with decorum, if not with ability; and a laudable pride, if such can be, inspired them still to improve their purity and excellence. . . .

But soon after their settlement, the Colonies were disturbed by contentions and party strife. . . . Troubles came upon troubles in rapid succession. The genius of discord settled upon the land. . . .

Music dwells not in scenes of contention; she flies the abode of anarchy and confusion, and seeks a home in the land of peace. . . .

The few music-books, that had from time to time found their way into the Colonies, were rapidly decreasing; and the few they had were unlike. The cultivation of music was neglected, until in the latter part of the seventeenth, and at the commencement of the eighteenth century, the congregations throughout New England were rarely able to sing more than three or four tunes. The knowledge and use of notes, too, had so long been neglected, that the few melodies sung became corrupted, until no two individuals sang them alike. . . .

The declining state of music had been so gradual and imperceptible, that the very confusion and discord were grateful to their ears; and a melody sung in time and in tune, was really offensive. At this stage of affairs, some of the best men of the day, seeing the need of reform, resolved to set about the work. This they did; and about the year 1720, several excellent and spirited discourses from the best divines, were published and scattered among the people. . . .

One might think, that a duty so obvious and practical, would find none but friends to its best performance. But it was not so. No sooner had the cry for reform been heard, than it was opposed by a large party in almost every church; and opposed with a virulence of feeling, and tenacity of attachment to their old customs, that seemed to defy their best efforts. Objections were urged even by serious, well informed persons, which, however trifling and pitiful they may seem to us, were to them important and solemn. The idea of learning to sing by note, or to sing a melody correctly, had something in it little less fearful in itself, or in its effects, than witchcraft and its scenes, through which they had just passed.

The principal objections were:

1. That it was a new way;—an unknown tongue.
2. That it was not so melodious as the usual way.
3. That there were so many tunes, one could never learn them.
4. That the new way made disturbances in churches, grieved good men, exasperated them and caused them to behave disorderly.
5. That it was popish.
6. That it would introduce instruments.
7. That the names of the notes were blasphemous.
8. That it was needless, the old way being good enough.
9. That it was only a contrivance to get money.
10. That it required too much time to learn it, made the young disorderly, and kept them from the proper influence of the family, &c., &c.

Here was a controversy as violent as that between the fundamentalists and the modernists in the Protestant Church of our day. That which had been good enough for their fathers was good enough for the New Englanders of the early eighteenth century. The agitation among the ministers for improvement in singing did not actually commence until 1720, but previous to that time the Reverend John Tufts, a minister of Newburyport, had published *A very plain and easy introduction to the whole Art of Singing Psalm Tunes*. There is evidence that the first edition of this work was published in 1712, though no copies appear to be in existence. The book must have had a wide circulation, for the edition of 1744 is marked as the eleventh printing.

This was the first instruction book on singing compiled in the English colonies. The author endeavored to give a musical notation that would be simpler to read and to understand, but really succeeded only in making it more complicated and difficult. Letters instead of notes were used on the staff, and the time was marked by placing one or more dots on the right side of the letter. The tunes were given in three parts, *Cantus, Medius,* and *Base.* Thirty-seven tunes were included in the book, in arrangements possibly copied from John Playford's *Whole Book of Psalms,* published in England in 1677.

John Tufts's book was followed in 1721 by another instruction book —*Grounds and Rules of Musick explained: or an introduction to the Art of Singing by Note,* by the Reverend Thomas Walter of Roxbury, Massachusetts. In addition to the instructions for singing by note, Walter's book contained some "Rules for Tuning the Voice." Some of the directions were a bit vague; especially the guide for distinguishing between "flat" and "sharp" keys. The author obviously refers to *minor* and *major* modes:

Tunes are said to be upon a flat Key, or a sharp Key. To know whether your Tune be upon a flat Key or a sharp Key, this is the general Rule. If the two Notes above the last Note of your Tune be whole Notes [evidently meaning whole *tones*] it is upon a sharp Key; but if the two Notes above, be one an whole Note, and the other an half Note, then it is a flat Key.

In Walter's book the tunes were given in three parts, in arrangements probably taken from Playford. The work enjoyed a number of editions.

The Reverend Thomas Symmes of Bradford, Massachusetts, was one of the parsons who fought for better singing. He published two sermons and an essay: *The Reasonableness of Regular Singing, or Singing by Note* (1720); *Prejudice in Matters of Religion* (1722); and *Utile Dulci; or Joco-Serious Dialogue* (1723). In these discourses the Reverend Doctor Symmes argued the case in detail, and sought to answer the objections of those who wanted the "old way" of lining out psalms. In the *Dialogue* he disputes the statement that reading by note is a "new way":

That which is now called the *Usual* way, in opposition to singing by note, is but a defective imitation of the *regular* way. . . . Your usual way of singing is but of yesterday, an upstart novelty, a deviation from the regular, which is the only scriptural good way of singing; much older than our fathers or fathers' grandfathers.

The beauty and harmony of singing consists very much in a just timing and turning the notes; every singer keeping the exact pitch the tune is set in, according to the part he sings. Now you may remember, that in our congregation we us'd frequently to have some people singing a note or two, after the rest had done. And you commonly strike the notes not together, but one after another, one being half way thro' the second note, before his neighbor has done with the first. Now this is just as melodious to a well-tuned musical ear, as Æsop was beautiful to a curious eye.

The author then proceeded to refute the argument that reading by note would lead to the use of instruments, and the accusation that it was a scheme to get money:

Since you make a noise (Tho' no pleasant one) about instrumental musick, I'll give you an unanswerable argument, that may put you out of all pain about it: And that is, that, truly, it's too chargeable a piece of worship ever to obtain amongst us; and you may depend upon it, that such as are not willing to be at the cost of a bell, to call the people together on Lord's day, and of a man to ring it . . . will never be so extravagant as to lay out their cash . . . to buy organs, and pay an artist for playing on them. . . . And in the mean time, pray be easy and assure yourself, that singing by Rule (note), wont in our day introduce instrumental musick, much less Quaker-ism and Popery. I promise you, your usual way of singing would much sooner dispose me to fall into them. Because the Quakers don't sing at all and I should be out of the noise of it; and the Papists sing much better when they sing by Rule.

As to getting money by it—why the singing master is not worthy of his reward for his pains in teaching our children to sing, as well as the School Dame or school master for teaching our children to read, write and cypher, I can't device. For Musick is as real and lawful and ingenious an art as either of the others.

In 1723 a tract was issued anonymously, entitled:

Cases of Conscience about singing Psalms, briefly considered and resolved. An Essay by several ministers of the Gospel, for the satisfaction of their pious and conscientious brethren, as to sundry Questions and Cases of Conscience, concerning the singing of Psalms, in the public worship of God, under the present Evangelical constitution of the Church-state.

Such questions as the following were discussed:

Whether you do believe that singing in the worship of God ought to be done skilfully?

Whether you do believe that skilfullness in singing may ordinarily be gained in the use of outward means, by the blessing of God?

Is it possible for Fathers of forty years old and upward to learn to sing by rule? And ought they to attempt at that age to learn?

Do you believe that it is Lawful and Laudable for us to change the customary way of singing, for a more uniform and regular way of singing the Psalms?

Whether they who purposely sing a tune differently from that which is appointed by the pastor or elder to be sung, are not guilty of acting disorderly, and of taking God's name in vain also, by disturbing the order of the sanctuary?

Fortunately, the progressive spirits in the clergy eventually won their battle. Singing societies were gradually established throughout New England, in which the meager instruction that was available was faithfully given. Finally, some of the churches allowed the first seats in the gallery to be reserved for the best singers, who were to lead in singing the psalms, and from this, church choirs eventually developed. Many pastors later found that these choirs grew into something more than they had bargained for. The singers' sense of their importance was often troublesome.

The lining out of psalms was not abandoned without many a bitter struggle, and in some cases the deacons whose functions were usurped by singing from note refused to give up their duties. Some of them had literally to be sung down by the congregations.

The *Bay Psalm Book* reigned supreme in the New England churches for three generations, as did *Sternhold and Hopkins* among the Presbyterians and Episcopalians in the other colonies, but with the revival of singing towards the end of the first quarter of the eighteenth century, other influences began to seep into colonial church life which brought a slow decline in the popularity of both books. This decline was caused by the appearance of Tate and Brady's *New Version* of the psalms in 1696, followed in 1711 by Watts's *Hymns* and in 1719 by his *Psalms of David Imitated*. The literary quality of the psalms and hymns in these books was far superior to that of the earlier version, more pleasing to ears which had become accustomed to the style of Addison and Pope. And with the words came new tunes which were fresh and interesting in contrast to the well-worn old psalm-tunes.

On March 16, 1720–21, Samuel Sewall noted in his *Diary*,

At night Dr. Mather preaches in the School-House to the young musicians from Rev. 14.3,—no man could learn that Song. House was full, and the singing extraordinarily Excellent, such as has hardly been heard before in Boston. Sang four times out of Tate and Brady.

This entry refers to the first singing school established in Boston. Tate and Brady provided words and tunes which were not yet admitted to the churches but were permissable in the schoolhouse. But it was inevitable that they should eventually gain admission to the churches, not only in Boston but elsewhere, though often against opposition.

Watts was well known in Boston as a theologian as well as a religious poet, and corresponded with Cotton Mather, who approved of his verses for private devotional reading. But it was George Whitefield, the English religious leader, who chiefly promoted the use of Watts's *Hymns and Psalms*. Whitefield made his great evangelistic tour of the colonies from 1739 to 1741. He was a great believer in singing. When Jonathan Edwards returned to his charge at Northampton, Massachusetts, after an absence, he found that his congregation, under Whitefield's influence, had turned to Watts's hymns "and sang nothing else, and neglected the Psalms entirely." A compromise was arranged, which included the use of both the older psalms and of Watts's hymns. In Virginia the noted preacher, the Reverend Samuel Davies, who in 1753, at the age of thirty, succeeded Jonathan Edwards as president of the College of New Jersey (Princeton), was also an ardent advocate of Watts. From the middle of the century on, the use of Watts's hymns and psalms spread rapidly, superseding the use of the *Bay Psalm Book* and of *Sternhold and Hopkins*, until by 1800, Watts completely dominated the hymnody in most churches.

In 1755 there was issued in Newburyport an American edition of William Tans'ur's *A Complete Melody in Three Parts* (1755). Tans'ur was a contemporary English psalmodist and musician of probable German origin. The publication of his work in the colonies was important, for it was the authority used by many of our early composers. Tans'ur helped to introduce some of the fine English hymn-tunes that were contained also in Watts, among them Crofts's *Hanover* and *St. Anne*. Tans'ur's own tune *St. Martin's* is still sung at Harvard commencements to a version of the 78th Psalm based on *Tate and Brady*, and is included in a few modern hymnbooks. By the end of the century a considerable number of the new English tunes were well established, of which Hatton's *Duke Street*, Knapp's *Wareham*, Miller's *Rockingham*, and the anonymous *Truro* are still in common use.

One more of the eighteenth-century colonial psalm books should be mentioned, if only because it was engraved by Paul Revere. This was *A Collection of the Best Psalm Tunes*, which was published by Josiah Flagg of Boston in 1764. The tunes were announced as "from the most approved authors, fitted to all measures, and approved by the best masters in Boston, New England; the greater part of them never before printed in America." Whether any of the new tunes were composed by Americans we cannot know, for the names of the authors are not given. Flagg was active in other fields than psalmody; he formed and trained a military band and often organized concerts. We shall meet him again in later pages.

2. EARLY CHURCH ORGANS

Organs had been unknown in the colonies in the seventeenth century, and even in England were to be found only in cathedrals, college chapels, and the larger parish churches, so that probably the majority of the colonists of the early period, coming from rural districts or small towns, had but slight acquaintance with them. Furthermore, organs were costly, cumbersome to ship, and it may be doubted if there were any persons in the colonies prior to 1700 capable of playing one. At the Smithsonian Institution there is an organ said to have been imported in 1700 for St. Peter's Church at Port Royal, Virginia, but the claim cannot be substantiated, and this particular instrument probably dates from at least a half a century later. The German Pietists who settled in the Wissahickon Valley, now a part of Philadelphia, had a small organ which in 1703 was borrowed for use in *Gloria Dei* (Swedish) Church in Philadelphia. A year later they were joined by an English organ builder, Dr. Christopher Witt, who built one or more organs for private use, the first to be constructed in this country. One of these was probably the instrument purchased in 1728 for Christ Church in Philadelphia. The first organ constructed by a native-born colonist was the work of young Edward Bromfield, Junior, of Boston, who was graduated from Harvard in 1742 and died in 1746 at the age of twenty-three. He left it not quite complete, but his contemporaries greatly admired his skill and ingenuity.

The first organ imported into New England was that owned by Thomas Brattle of Boston. He procured the organ as early as 1711, for on May 29 of that year the Reverend Joseph Green noted in his *Diary:*

I was at Mr. Thomas Brattle's; heard ye organ and saw strange things in a microscope.

When Brattle died in 1713 he bequeathed the organ to the Brattle Square Church, of which he was a leading member, but, foreseeing a possible, or probable, rejection of his gift, he provided that in such case it should go to King's Chapel. He further stipulated that the church which accepted the organ should "procure a sober person that can play skilfully thereon with a loud noise." The organ went to King's Chapel where it was set up a year later, and Mr. Enstone was imported from London to play it. It was supplanted by a better organ in 1756, and was sold to St. Paul's Church, Newburyport, Massachusetts, whence it went eighty years later to St. John's Church, Portsmouth, New Hampshire, where it still exists in usable condition.

Brattle's organ, when set up in King's Chapel, was the first to be permanently installed in a colonial church. The second church in the colonies to install an organ seems to have been the Dutch Reformed Church of New York; to which Governor Burnet gave an organ in 1724; the third was Christ Church, Philadelphia, already referred to; the fourth was Trinity Church, Newport, Rhode Island, which in 1733 received one from Bishop Berkeley. In 1736, Trinity Church and Christ Church, Boston, each imported an organ. In 1737, Trinity Church, New York, set up an organ built for it by Johann Gottfried Klemm, a Moravian organ builder. Bruton Parish Church at Williamsburg, Virginia, got one in 1755, and St. Michael's, Charleston, South Carolina, imported one in 1768. It will be noted that most of these organs were installed in Episcopal churches. Their congregations generally included a large proportion of newcomers from England, and their clergymen, if not of English birth, had gone to England for ordination, and naturally sought to introduce the latest Anglican practices. Even with them, however, the increase in the number of organs was slow, because of the cost of the instruments and the difficulty of procuring organists.

Other Protestant groups moved even more slowly. An anonymous writer who signed himself "A Presbyterian" in 1763 printed a tart pamphlet in Philadelphia deploring the low state of singing, and arguing that it could be improved by the introduction of organs. The Congregational Church in Providence, Rhode Island, set up an organ in 1770, as noted by Ezra Stiles in his *Diary*, July 10:

Last month an Organ of 200 Pipes was set up in the Meeting-house of the first Congregational Church in Providence; and for the first time it was played upon in Divine Service last Ldsday, as Mr. Rowland the pastor tells me. This is the first organ in a dissentive presby. Chh. in America except Jersey College, [Princeton] or Great Britain.

And under date of May 16, 1785, Ezra Stiles notes:

They have lately determined to set up an Organ in Dr. Chauncey's Meetghouse being the old Brick or first Chh. in Bo. founded in 1629. The Doctor was against it, but Mr. Clark, his colleague, and the Congregn. in general were for it. This spring the Meetghouse was repaired and Dr. C. preached a consecrn. and farewell sermon on acct. of his great age. The people eager to get an organ waited on the Dr. who told them that it would not be long before he was in his grave,—he knew that before his head was cold there they would have an organ—and they might do as they pleased.

The venerable Dr. Chauncey reflects the conservatism of old age, resisting innovations. But in his own lifetime he had seen the slow change from very poor singing without any instrumental accompaniment, to the use of tuning forks for the benefit of choirs, and then to the introduction of the bass viol which came into fairly general use by the end of the eighteenth century, and was to linger in some churches down to nearly the middle of the nineteenth. As late as 1800 there are said to have been less than twenty church organs in all New England, and no more, in proportion to the population, in other parts of the country.

3. EARLY SECULAR MUSIC IN NEW ENGLAND

Secular amusements did not have much chance to flourish in early New England. In the diary of Samuel Sewall, one of the first justices of Boston, we find an entry under the date of *Thorsday, Novr. 12, 1685:*

. . . the ministers of this Town (Boston) Come to the Court and Complain against a Dancing Master who seeks to set up here and hath mixt Dances; and 'tis reported he should say that by one play he could teach more Divinity than Dr. Willard or the Old Testament. Mr. Moodey said 'twas not the time for N.E. to dance. Mr. Mather struck at the Root, speaking against mixt dances.

This dancing master intended to fight it out, for on December 17:

. . . Mr. Stepney, the Dncing Master, desired a Jury, so he and Mr. Shrimpton Bound in 50 lbs. to Janr. Court. Said Stepney is ordered not to keep a Dancing School; if he does will be taken in contempt and be proceeded with accordingly.

The odds were too great, and on the following July 28:

. . . Francis Stepney the Dancing Master runs away for Debt. Several attachments out after him.

Evidently Stepney had a poor reputation on other grounds than wanting to open a dancing school.

Another quotation from Sewall refers to dancing (Friday, May 27, 1687):

. . . Between 5 and 6 Father Walker is taken with a Lethargy. . . . His speech came to him something between 6 and 7. . . . He overheard some discourse about the May-Pole, and told what the manner was in England to dance about it with Musick, and that 'twas to be feared such practices would be here . . .

Early in the next century dancing schools were permitted.

There was little instrumental music in New England in the seventeenth century. Drums and trumpets were used to summon people to church until bells became available—or to sound an alarm or in connection with military training. Jew's-harps were imported in quantities for trade with the Indians who delighted in them. A few of the early emigrants brought music books and small musical instruments with them, but most of them had to turn their possessions into cash in England to pay for their voyage and for equipment for pioneer life. Moreover, shipping space was too limited to allow transportation of luxuries. But Nathaniel Rogers of Rowley, dying in 1664, left a "treble Violl" and the Reverend Edmund Browne, who died in 1678, left a "bass vyol," some books of music, and the reputation of being a good musician. Tutor Wigglesworth of Harvard, about 1650, caught an idle student "in the forenoon with ill company playing musick, though I had solemnly warned him but yesterday of letting his spirit go after pleasures." The implication is that the boy was idling with undesirable companions when he ought to have been studying.

Seaborn Cotton, son of the Reverend John Cotton, who himself became a minister, left a student's commonplace book in which he copied out the words of several well-known English ballads and a bar of music jotted down as a memorandum of a tune. In 1661 the Reverend Leonard Hoar wrote from London to his nephew Josiah Flynt, a freshman at Harvard, who had asked him for a fiddle. The letter contains sensible advice and ends:

Musick I had almost forgot. I suspect you seek it both to soon and to much. This be assured of that if you be not excellent at it its worth nothing at all. And if you be excellent it will take up so much of your mind and time that you will be worth little else: and when all that excellence is obtained your acquest will prove little or nothing of real profit to you unlesse you intend to take upon you the trade of fidling. Howbeit hearing your mother's desires were for it for your sisters, for whom it is more proper and they also have more leizure to look after it: For them I say I had provided the instruments desired. But I cannot now attend to sending them being hurrying away from London.

The writer of this letter clearly did not disapprove of music as such, but he knew that his nephew had to earn a living in the world and that the "trade of fidling" would not suffice, though music would be a pleasant pastime for the girls.

By the end of the seventeenth century people were beginning to import larger instruments. On December 1, 1699, Samuel Sewall, always a lover of music, notes in his *Diary* that he went to a shop to inquire about repairs to his wife's virginals. In 1716, Edward Enstone, the recently arrived organist for King's Chapel, advertised in the *Boston News-Letter:*

This is to give notice that there is lately just come over from England a choice collection of Instruments, consisting of Flageolets, Flutes, Haut-boys, Bass-Viols, Violins, Bows, Strings, Reeds for Haut-Boys, Books of Instruction for all these Instruments, Books of Ruled Paper. To be sold at The Dancing School of Mr. Enstone in Sudbury Street near The Orange Tree, Boston. Note: Any person may have all instruments of Musick mended, or Virginalls and Spinnets Strung and Tuned at a reasonable Rate, and likewise may be taught to Play on any of these instruments above mentioned; dancing taught by a true and easier method than has been heretofore.

The growing interest in instrumental music led to public concerts by groups of amateur musicians. It should be remembered that concerts to which the public was admitted for a price did not occur even in London until late in the seventeenth century, and were at first held in taverns. The first authentic record of a public concert in any of the English-speaking colonies is an advertisement which appeared in the *Boston News-Letter* of December 16 and 23, 1731, as follows:

On Thursday, the 30th of this instant December, there will be performed a "concert of Music" on Sundry instruments At Mr. Pelham's great Room, being the house of the late Doctor Noyes near Sun Tavern. Tickets to be delivered at the place of Performance at "Five Shillings" each. The concert to begin exactly at Six o'clock, and no Tickets will be delivered after Five the day of Performance. N.B. There will be no admittance after Six.

This concert antedates by only three and a half months the first concert given in Charleston, South Carolina, and it is, of course, possible that there were earlier concerts in either place of which no record has survived.

The Mr. Pelham, in whose "great Room" the concert was held, was Peter Pelham, the engraver, who had emigrated to America from

London in 1726. He was an excellent maker of mezzotints and a painter of sorts, but the demand for such work was too limited to support him, and he resorted to teaching and other occupations to gain a livelihood. He later married the widow Copley, and thus became the stepfather of John Singleton Copley.

In 1732 or 1733 the first European musician of note visited Boston. He was Karl Theodor Pachelbel, son of a noted German organist related to the family of Johann Sebastian Bach, and himself well trained. It would be pleasant to believe that he was the first European artist to be heard in Boston, but there is no record of the programs or the performers at the two concerts which were held in the town in each of the two years mentioned. When Pachelbel left he took with him Peter Pelham's son by his first wife, Peter Junior. He went to Newport, where he assisted in setting up the organ which Bishop Berkeley had given to Trinity Church, and thence to New York and Charleston, where he stayed for some years. We shall learn presently of his giving New York its first recorded concert. Peter Pelham Junior did not return to Boston till 1743, and advertised on May 30 of that year in the *Boston Evening Post* that after "nine years under the Tuition of an accomplish'd Professor in the Art of Musick" he was prepared to give lessons on the harpsichord and in the "Rudiments of Psalmody, Hymns, Anthems, etc." He became the first organist of Trinity Church in Boston, where he remained until 1749. He then went to Virginia and in 1755 became the first organist at Bruton Parish Church in Williamsburg, where he served with distinction for forty years.

A few years after Pelham Senior's concert, the Boston selectmen felt justified in according the use of Faneuil Hall to such gentlemen as William Sheafe, Samuel Deblois, and Thomas Hancock for "concerts of Musick." By 1754 the city had a Concert Hall at the corner of Hanover and Court streets, where concerts of "Vocal and instrumental Musick to consist of Select Pieces by the Masters" were given. There is evidence that Thomas Dipper may have inaugurated a regular series of subscription concerts in the late fifties or early sixties, and it has been definitely established that Boston enjoyed such affairs in 1766.

Boston was not friendly to theatrical entertainments. As early as 1686 a play had been suppressed, and Increase Mather had published

his "Testimony against profane and superstitious customs." Again, in
1714, we hear of Judge Sewall protesting against the acting of a play
in the Council Chamber. In 1750, two young Englishmen, assisted by
amateur friends, gave a performance of Otway's *Orphan* in a Boston
Coffee House. This so horrified the good citizens that a law was passed
absolutely prohibiting "public stage plays, interludes and other theatrical entertainments," as "tending to discourage industry and fru-
gality, and greatly to increase impiety."

And yet, as the days of the Revolution approached, New England
was growing artistically, and slowly acquiring cultural traits that made
its life richer. It was in such a scene that New England's first composer
made his appearance—the tanner-musician William Billings, the first
American composer to make music his profession.

4. PHILADELPHIA, NEW YORK, AND THE SOUTH

It is to be regretted that records of musical life during the early
years of the Southern colonies, and of Pennsylvania and New York,
are not as complete as those of New England, for further information
would help in estimating the relative importance of each colony's contribution. The New England psalmodists, and their successors in the
latter eighteenth century, have probably exerted a deeper influence on
one branch of our present music—hymnology—than any of the Pennsylvania Germans, the Dutch in New York, or even the few professional musicians who migrated to this country before 1750. Nevertheless, it seems unwise to dismiss altogether, as some historians have
done, certain elements in our early music, even though they have had
no obvious influence on the future of the nation. The Germans and
Swedes who came to the neighborhood of Philadelphia when William
Penn first proclaimed his "glorious new world," and the Moravians
who later settled in Bethlehem, enjoyed a musical life far in advance
of anything in contemporary New England. These were settlements
established for religious motives, and many of their beliefs were
fanatical, yet there was not the suspicion that any kind of music was
the invention of the devil, to be shunned as worldly and frivolous.
Good singing in church was required, and insisted upon. One pastor,

the Reverend Andreas Sandel (Swedish), imposed a fine of six shillings on certain members of his congregation for "untimely singing."

It was in 1694 that a German band of pietists took up their dwelling beside the Wissahickon River, eight miles from Philadelphia. These people were German mystics who believed that the end of the world was near at hand, and who renounced marriage as sinful, believing that their one love should be the Lord Jesus Christ. The leader of the hermits was Johann Kelpius, a highly educated man, the son of a pastor at Dendorf, Germany. Not only did these Germans sing hymns, but they accompanied their singing with instrumental music, and brought instruments with them when they first landed in this country. As early as 1708, Kelpius wrote abroad for two clavichords "with additional strings."

The Wissahickon hermits evidently acquired a reputation for singing soon after their arrival, for in 1700 they were invited to act as choristers and to furnish instrumental music at the dedication of the new Swedish church *Gloria Dei* near Philadelphia. Kelpius is mentioned as the composer of nineteen of the hymns used by the hermits, but he probably was the author of only the words, for the same writer who mentions his authorship speaks of another as the first "composer" on American soil.

The *Gloria Dei* Church is important musically, as it may have been the first American church equipped with an organ.[1] Some authorities believe that Kelpius brought with him from Europe the organ that was installed in that church. At any rate, it was present three years later when Justus Falckner was ordained as its minister, and not only was music supplied by Jonas, the regular organist, but the neighboring mystics furnished music on the viol, hautboy, trumpets, and kettledrums. Falckner was the first German minister ordained in this country, and was the author of several of the fine hymns of his congregation.

Two years before he was awarded the pastorate of the *Gloria Dei* Church, Falckner wrote a letter to Heinrich Muhlen of Holstein, asking for assistance for his church. The letter tells of conditions in the colony, and provides an interesting contrast to the attitude of New Englanders regarding music:

[1] See pages 17–18.

. . . I will take occasion to mention that many others besides myself, who know the ways of the land, maintain that music would contribute much towards a good Christian service. It would not only attract and civilize the wild Indians, but it would do much good in spreading the Gospel truths among the sects and others by attracting them. Instrumental music is especially serviceable here. Thus a well-sounding organ would perhaps prove of great profit, to say nothing of the fact that the Indians would come running from far and near to listen to such unknown melody, and upon that account might become willing to accept our language and teaching, and remain with people who had such agreeable things; for they are said to come ever so far to listen to one who plays even a reed-pipe: such an extraordinary love have they for any melodious and ringing sound. Now as the melancholy, saturnine, stingy Quaker spirit has abolished all such music, it would indeed be a novelty here, and tend to attract many of the young people away from the Quakers and sects to attend services where such music was found, even against the wishes of their parents. This would afford a good opportunity to show them the truth and their error.

. . . And it may be assumed that even a small organ-instrument and music in this place would be acceptable to God, and prove far more useful than many hundreds in Europe where there is already a superfluity of such things.

There are in Europe masters enough who would build such instruments, and a fine one can be secured for 300 or 400 thalers. Then if an experienced organist and musician could be found, who would undertake so far a journey, he would be very welcome here. In case this could not be, if we only had an organ, some one or other might be found who had knowledge thereof.

Robert R. Drummond, in *Early German Music in Philadelphia*, claims that CONRAD BEISSEL was the first composer of music in America. This statement seems plausible, for Beissel was associated with the *Ephrata Cloister* in the early part of the century. At this famous sisterhood they sang hymns and chorals in four, five, six, and seven parts, while congregations in other parts of the country were singing in unison. The first edition of the *Ephrata* hymn collection was published by Benjamin Franklin in 1730. Over a thousand of these hymns have been attributed to Beissel.

The history of music in Philadelphia is a record of continual struggle with the Quakers in the early years, for the Friends were opposed to music of any sort. Plays, games, lotteries, music, and dancing were classed alike, and the meetings advised all members against either attending such diversions or being in any way connected with them. Arrayed against the Quakers and the Presbyterians were the members of the Church of England, who consistently championed lighter amusements. Though musical entertainments, and especially dramatic offerings, were often presented in an apologetic tone, they nevertheless existed. As early as 1710 there is record of a dancing master in Philadelphia, and dancing was taught in boarding schools in 1728. Although the earliest public concert of which there is record was given by John Palma in 1757, it seems hardly possible that some were not given before this time. Before 1750, Philadelphians enjoyed no theatrical diversions, except for an "agreeable comedy or tragedy" which Benjamin Franklin's *Pennsylvania Gazette* (our *Saturday Evening Post*) advertised in 1742 as acted "by changeable figures two feet high" every evening "at the Sign of the Coach and Horse, against the State House"; and a performance by live actors of Addison's *Cato* in 1749.

In 1750 (the year of Boston's antitheatre law), the Kean and Murray Company from London tried to give a performance in Plumstead's Warehouse, but the Recorder of the city reported that

certain persons had lately taken upon them to act plays in this city, and he was informed intended to make a frequent practice thereof, which, it was feared, would be attended with very mischievous effects.

Whereupon the Philadelphia authorities requested the Magistrates "to take the most effective measures for suppressing this disorder." The Kean and Murray Company departed for New York and the Quaker element was undisturbed by such shocking possibilities for about four years. In 1754 a company headed by Lewis Hallam, which had already entertained New York and several Southern cities, and which was later to be known as the famous American Company, attempted a Philadelphia season, lasting from April to June. The Quaker city then had its first opportunity to hear ballad-operas. Even though the players obeyed the condition that "nothing indecent or immoral should be presented," the season ended in failure, and no regular players appeared again for five years. In 1759, David Douglass, manager of the reorganized Hallam Company, obtained the Governor's permission to erect a theatre on "Society Hill," and a season of plays and ballad-operas was offered which lasted from June to December. In the meantime, however, the Quakers, Lutherans, and Presbyterians forced through the local Assembly an act against "the idle persons and strollers who have come into this Province from foreign parts in the character of players." The Governor was forced to sanction the measure, and though the King set it aside in Council less than a year later, Philadelphia heard no more operas until 1766.

Douglass returned in that year, and from then until the Revolution, the Southwark Theatre on Society Hill saw regular seasons by the American Company, unmolested by the authorities, even though attacks by its opponents were at times insulting. In 1767, Douglass announced for performance a work that would have been the first American Opera, had it been given. This was advertised as "a new comic opera *The Disappointment, or The Force of Credulity,*" but withdrawn "as it contains personal reflections." It seems that certain prominent Philadelphians had been hunting for treasure reputed hidden by a Captain Blackbeard, and either the gentlemen themselves, or their friends, had convinced Mr. Douglass that it would be wiser not to present the satire. The libretto was subsequently printed, and copies are still in existence. The composer of the music is unknown, and the librettist used a pen name, Andrew Barton.

Bethlehem, Pennsylvania, was settled in 1741 by the Moravians, and since its first year to the present day it has been a musical center which few cities of its size can rival. It is claimed that the first copies of many of Haydn's quartets and symphonies to reach this country were brought to Bethlehem. It is believed that *The Creation* and *The Seasons* had their American premières in the little Pennsylvania town. In 1742 the first *Singstunde* was held in Bethlehem, and a few years later the *Collegium Musicum* was founded, remaining in existence until 1820, when it was succeeded by the Philharmonic Society. In the Moravian Archives at Bethlehem are manuscript copies of six trios and three symphonies by Mozart, dated 1785, when the composer was only twenty years old.

A letter from a little girl attending the boarding school at Bethlehem in 1787, states that she was taught music, vocal and instrumental. "I play the guitar twice a day; am taught the spinet and forte piano, and sometimes I play the organ"—an exceedingly well-rounded musical education for eighteenth-century America.

If a group of manuscripts now in the Archives of the Moravian Church had been dated, we would know exactly where to place a group of Bethlehem composers chronologically. These men lived in Bethlehem in the latter part of the eighteenth century, and their works show a musicianship far in advance of composers in other parts of the country. Most of the works are for instrumental combinations beyond the facilities or ability of colonial contemporaries.

One of the composers, JOHN ANTES, was born in 1740 at Fredericktop, Pennsylvania, where the Moravians had established a preaching station. He made an intensive study of music, and learned to perform on all the stringed instruments. Later in life he went abroad, and was dispatched as a missionary to Egypt. On his return to Europe he became acquainted with Haydn, who is said to have performed some of his works.

Another, DAVID MORITZ MICHAEL (1751–1825), was born and died in Germany but lived for many years at Bethlehem and Nazareth. Some of his works are in the Archives at Bethlehem: A *Parthie*, for wind instruments—two clarinets, two horns, and bassoon; a Suite, for wind instruments (for the same combination); and *Die Wasserfahrt* (The Boat Ride), a programmatic Suite for two clarinets, two bassoons, two horns.

JOHN FREDERICK PETER (1746–1813) left behind him six quintets, for two violins, two violas, and violoncello. These interesting quintets are "the oldest known chamber music works composed in the States." Peter was an organist and violinist of the Moravian congregation.

From an American standpoint, it must be admitted that these composers and their works are not of importance, even though they are superior in workmanship to those of our first native composers. That the works themselves were influenced entirely by the German school would not in itself make them unimportant, but the fact that they were not known very far beyond Bethlehem's limits prevents the possibility of their exerting any marked influence on our musical life. The Moravians at Bethlehem were complete unto themselves, and well might they be musically; there was little mingling with other colonies with whom they would have little in common. Consequently, the most advanced musical settlement did the least for the cultural advancement of the country as a whole.

Several of the Southern cities have claims as pioneers in musical activity. Charleston, South Carolina, not only runs a close second to Boston in fostering the first public concert in America, but enjoys the distinction of having what is generally considered the first musical society formed in America—the St. Cecilia Society, founded in 1762, and remaining in existence until 1912.

The activities of the St. Cecilia Society may be judged from entries in Josiah Quincy's *Journal of a Voyage to South Carolina* (1772). His accounts show that the society was in the habit of engaging professional musicians at good-sized fees:

The concert-house is a large, inelegant building, situated down a yard. . . . The music was good—the two bass viols and French horns were grand. One Abercrombie, a Frenchman just arrived, played the first violin, and a solo incomparably better than any one I ever heard. He cannot speak a word of English, and has a salary of five hundred guineas a year from the St. Cecilia Society. There were upwards of two hundred and fifty ladies present, and it was called no great number. In loftiness of headdress, these ladies stoop to the daughters of the North,—in richness of dress, surpass them,—in health and floridity of countenance, vail to them. In taciturnity during the performances, greatly before our ladies; in noise and flirtation after the music is over, pretty much on a par.

Another item tells of a musical evening in Charleston:

Dined with the Sons of St. Patrick. While at dinner six violins, two hautboys, etc. After dinner, six French horns in concert:—most surpassing music. Two solos on the French horn, by one who is said to blow the finest horn in the world. He has fifty guineas for the season from the St. Cecilia Society.

Charleston witnessed, in 1735, the first recorded performance of an opera in America, the ballad-opera *Flora, or Hob in the Well*. This inaugurated three regular theatrical seasons in the South Carolina city, after which the theatre was turned over to dancing masters for a number of years. It was reopened for plays and opera in 1754.

Williamsburg, Virginia, presented a gay contrast to bleak New England. While the Boston divines were arguing the case of church singing, a real playhouse was in use in Williamsburg, the first known to have existed in America. Records show that it was there as early as 1722, possibly earlier. It was here that George Washington, ever a lover of the theatre, saw his first play on Virginia soil, and the little city also had the honor of being the first to welcome Lewis Hallam's London Company of comedians (1752), which later became the American Company. Williamsburg was treated to regular seasons by the best players in the country.

When the Kean and Murray Company opened the new theatre in Upper Marlborough, Maryland, with *The Beggar's Opera* (1752), an orchestra was used for the first time in an American performance of the opera. The South was by no means behind in its share of musical development during the eighteenth century. If it should be disproved that Johann Kelpius brought with him the organ that was used in the *Gloria Dei* Church, the Episcopal church at Port Royal, Virginia, has the distinction of owning the first pipe organ brought to this country from Europe (1700).

Though it lagged behind the South in musical development, New York at least kept pace with other important cities. Its first concerts date from 1736, according to existing records, though some may have been given which antedate the "*Consort* of Musick, Vocal and Instrumental, for the benefit of Mr. Pachelbel, the Harpsichord Part performed by himself. The songs, Violins and German Flutes by private Hands" (January 21, 1736). Mr. Pachelbel, of course, was the Karl Theodor Pachelbel who came to Boston in 1732 or 1733, and after moving to Newport and to New York, lived for a number of years in Charleston.

Ballad-operas were probably performed in New York from 1732 on, and when the Kean and Murray Company opened a theatre in Nassau Street in 1750, music lovers of the city were treated to a repertory that included seven of them. After this troupe had played two seasons in New York, the Hallam Company arrived and opened the first theatre built for the purpose in the city. According to custom the patrons were entertained with dancing and singing between the acts of such favorites as *Damon and Phillida* and the *Conscious Lovers*. The young Hallams would perform a *Punch's Dance* or sing *As Chloe Came into the Room*, Mr. Hulett would oblige with a hornpipe, and

Mr. Love with *The Quaker's Sermon* on the violin and a solo on the hautboy. As the years passed, New York experienced some opposition to the theatre. Personal possessions brought by the audience had a habit of disappearing, and rather than blaming the unknown sneak thieves who came with the audience, the public turned against the management and the actors. In 1764 a mob wrecked a theatre that David Douglass, successor to Hallam as manager of the American Company, had built in Chapel Street.

In 1767, Douglass brought the American Company back to New York and opened the new John Street Theatre. There was still considerable antagonism to the theatre, and the actors, many of them musicians, were forced to add to their incomes by giving concerts. The theatrical season of 1773 was the last the colonial cities enjoyed until after the Revolution, for in October, 1774, the newly formed Continental Congress, because of the coming struggle with England, found it advisable to pass a resolution which was respectfully observed:

That we will discourage every species of extravagance and dissapation, especially horse-racing, and all kinds of gaming, cock-fighting, exhibition of shows, plays and other expensive diversions and entertainments.

Following Mr. Pachelbel's recital in 1736, New Yorkers were treated to increasingly frequent concerts. Such musicians as Charles Love, of Hallam's theatrical company; William Hulett, an actor, dancing master, and musician who was one of Hallam's violinists; Alexander Dienval, who taught the "violin, German Flute, hautboy, French horn, bass violin, tenor violin, etc., in the newest and best method" offered concerts for their own benefit and for charity. In 1760 the Messrs. Hulett and Dienval established New York's first series of subscription concerts, which were held regularly each season until 1767, when they were discontinued for six years. In 1765, Hulett, in association with a Mr. Leonard, established New York's first open-air summer concerts in Ranelagh Gardens, where "after the concert a small firework will be play'd off, which will continue 'till ten: the whole to be managed with the utmost regularity." Competition soon appeared in concerts in the "King's Arms Garden in the Broadway," and in the biweekly concerts of vocal and instrumental music in the "Vaux Hall Gardens," "newly fitted up with a very good long Room, convenient for a ball or turtle entertainment." A *Harmonic Society* existed in New York in 1774, and its members were active in concerts both for the society and for themselves. In that year New Yorkers had their first glimpse of French and Italian *virtuosi*. The star of the occasion was a Mr. Caze, who had the assistance of the "gentlemen of the Harmonic Society." (Amateurs were designated "gentlemen.") The program was as follows:

1st Act

A grand Orchestry's Symphony
A French Ariette will be sung accompanied with the guitar and violin.
Mr. Caze will play his own composed music, on the violin with Mr. Zedtwitz.
A Concert on the Flute
A Sonada on the Spanish Guitar
The first Act to end with a March

2nd Act

A Grand Orchestry's Symphonie
A French Ariette accompany'd with the Mandolin and Violin
A Solo on the Violin
A Duo on Mandoline and Violin
A Sonada of the Salterio; and d'Exaudet's Minuet with echoes.
The Concert to finish with a March of the grand Orchestry.
After the Concert there will be a ball.

Music lovers of early Gotham were often troubled by disturbing elements at concerts. Frequently protests would appear in the press, and one who signed himself "X.Y.Z." wrote to the New York *Weekly Post Boy* (1764):

It is a very just observation that a gentleman is to be known by his politeness—this qualification, wherever it is to be found, convinces us that it's possessor has seen the world and has had his manners formed by a good education. . . .

I am led into this short reflection by a circumstance, I can scarcely think of without indignation. What I mean is the strange behaviour at the Concert, of a certain set of males and females to whom . . . I will give the soft appelation of gentlemen and ladies. I am a dear lover of music and can't bear to be disturbed in my enjoyment of an entertainment so polite and agreeable.

How great then is my disappointment and vexation, when instead of a modest and becoming silence nothing is heard during the whole performance, but laughing and talking very loud, sqawling, overturning the benches, etc. Behaviour more suited to a *broglio* than a musical entertainment.

What is meant by so ill-timed an interruption I know not: for . . . I cannot conceive that either the audience or the gentlemen performers are under any obligations to bear these impertinences—and I have authority to assure those offenders against decency that . . . the managers and performers will be forced . . . to the disagreeable necessity of insisting on their absenting themselves from a place where they do nothing but give offence or . . . of hiring the adjacent room for the convenience of such whose conduct will not bear the eye of the public. . . .

In 1753 a man who was to exert a profound influence on the city's musical life came to New York: WILLIAM TUCKEY (1708–1781), an Englishman who had been Vicar Choral of the Bristol Cathedral, and clerk of the Parish. Tuckey not only established himself in New York as an organist, choirmaster, concert artist, and composer, but he made the great contribution of organizing and directing the first performance of Handel's *Messiah* in America. In 1770 he led an orchestra and chorus in the overture and sixteen numbers from the oratorio. *The Messiah* was not performed in Germany until 1772, two years after Tuckey brought it to New York.

When Tuckey first came to New York he was appointed a clerk of Trinity Church at a salary of twenty-five pounds per annum. (Small pay in comparison with the reputed salaries of the St. Cecilia Society in Charleston.) His next step was to convince the vestry of Trinity that music should be taught to the pupils of the Charity School, which the church had established in 1739. In this way he developed a choir to sing in the church services. Before long the Trinity Choir was famous, even outside of New York. In 1762, Tuckey resolved to extend his choral efforts beyond the church, and he advertised for volunteers for a chorus. Four years later the newspapers contained an account of one of Mr. Tuckey's *rehearsals* and the announcement of a forthcoming concert.

The musician was sometimes considered worthy of his hire in early New York, for Tuckey was paid fifteen pounds for playing the organ at the dedication of the "new Episcopal Chapel called *St. Paul's*" in 1766. He was active as a concert artist, and two years after coming to America announced a concert in conjunction with William Cobham, musician and dealer in "bear skins, spotted ermin, white and yellow flannels. . . ." The concert was announced in the New York *Weekly Post Boy*, December 15, 1755:

For the benefit of Messrs. Cobham and Tuckey, at the New Exchange on Monday the 29 instant; will be a *Concert* of Vocal and Instrumental musick. Among a variety of select pieces, both vocal and instrumental, will be performed, the celebrated dialogue between *Damon and Chloe*, compos'd by Mr. Arne. A two part song, in praise of a Soldier, by the late famous Mr. Henry Purcell. *An Ode on Masonry* never perform'd in this country, nor ever in England, but once in publick. And a Solo on the German flute, by Mr. Cobham.

Tickets to be had of Mr. Cobham, in Hanover Square; of Mr. Tuckey near Mr. Willet's, at the New York Arms; and at the King's Arms; and at the new Printing Office in Beaver Street at 5 *s* each.

To begin precisely at six o'clock. After the concert there will be a *Ball* for the ladies.

The *Ode on Masonry* may have been a composition by Tuckey. Although his only works extant today are those in psalm collections, we know that his music was widely known in his time. His *Thanksgiving Anthem* was sung before His Excellency General Amherst, on his return to New York from the conquest of Canada, in 1760. His *Anthem from the 97th Psalm* was performed at a "Grand Concert of Sacred Music for the benefit of the Pennsylvania Hospital and the Poor," and again in 1787 at the First Uranian Concert in Philadelphia. This anthem, subsequently known as *Liverpool*, was anonymously included in James Lyon's *Urania*, a collection of psalm tunes discussed in a later chapter.

It is through his advertisements for subscriptions that we know what Tuckey wrote. In the *New York Mercury* of March 11, 1771, appeared the following:

Proposals for publishing Two select pieces of Church music.

    1st. An Hymn (by way of an anthem) consisting of Solos, Duets, one Trio and Chorus; together with a Psalm Tune, adapted for any charitable church collection. . . .

2nd. A performance adapted for a *funeral*, consisting of three Dirges (for chorus), the words part of the burial service; together with an Anthem and a Psalm Tune suitable on the solemnity of a funeral or interment of any person of note, etc. The whole never yet perform'd being very lately set to music by *William Tuckey*. . . .

Although Tuckey labored hard to establish regular choral singing in America, the time was not yet ripe for his efforts. He accomplished some very remarkable things, when we consider what he had to contend with, but the tools he needed were not yet at hand.

An account of early music in the colonies must necessarily be superficial in a book that aims to deal with the whole subject of American music. The student who wishes to study closely the conditions in the pre-Revolutionary days must seek works that deal more specifically with those times. It has been necessary to review this period as thoroughly as space will allow, so that as we approach the work of our first native composers—Hopkinson, Lyon, and Billings—we will know what lies back of them, and what equipment their musical public possessed for receiving their work. Unless we are familiar with the conditions that produced these first makers of music, our attitude toward their efforts will be wholly unsympathetic. O. G. Sonneck, one of the foremost authorities on our early musical life, wrote that nobody composed in a musical wilderness, no matter how valueless the compositions may be, if not forced to do so by latent creative powers. With this warning, and apology if you must, we turn our attention to those believed to be the first of our composers born in America.

CHAPTER TWO

Our First Composers

1. FRANCIS HOPKINSON (1737–1791)

IT IS only from circumstantial evidence that we are able to determine who may have been our *first* native composer. Just as Francis Hopkinson was unknown to our first music historians, so may some forgotten composer be overlooked by those writing about American music today. John Antes of Bethlehem may be a possible candidate, should any manuscripts of his be discovered that bear a date prior to 1759; but the only works by Antes of which we know definitely are the string quartets he is said to have written in Europe. Some think that the problematical connection of John Barnard with the tune *Mear* gives him a claim. This matter is discussed in the section on James Lyon.

As matters stand, the evidence that Hopkinson's manuscript song *My Days Have Been So Wondrous Free* was written in 1759, and that James Lyon's psalm collection *Urania* was issued at the earliest in 1761, establishes Hopkinson as the first native composer whose works are extant today. It is altogether fitting that Hopkinson should be our first composer, for this charming musical amateur was one of the signers of the Declaration of Independence, an intimate friend of George Washington, and a man who lent his talents and best efforts to helping our nation establish itself. Among the public offices that Hopkinson held were those of the first Secretary of the Navy, and Judge of the Admiralty from Pennsylvania. In addition to his musical talents, he was a satirist, poet, inventor, and painter. Throughout the War of the Revolution he wrote satirical articles in support of his political faith. *The Battle of the Kegs* is a famous historical document. During the Constitutional Convention, his *History of a New*

Roof influenced some of the most distinguished men of the time.
In one of his letters to his wife, John Adams thus described Hopkinson:

> He is one of your pretty, little, curious, ingenious men. His head is not
> bigger than a large apple. I have not met with anything in natural history
> more amusing and entertaining than his personal appearance, yet he is
> genteel and well bred, and is very social.

Hopkinson was born in Philadelphia, September 21, 1737. Little
is known of his childhood, except that the love of music was traditional
in the Hopkinson family, and the young Francis must have been introduced to its delights at an early age. He was a member of the first class
to receive the Bachelor's degree from the College of Philadelphia in
1757 (now the University of Pennsylvania), and he was later awarded
degrees of Master of Arts and Doctor of Laws. He was admitted to
the Bar in 1761.

His first public office was that of secretary to a conference between
the Governor and the Indians of the Lehigh region. He was made
secretary of the Library Company of Philadelphia in 1759. In 1766
he visited England, and in 1768 he married Ann Borden of Bordentown, New Jersey. His house in Bordentown is still standing.

He was always active in public affairs. He was made Collector of
the Port of Newcastle in 1772, and in 1774 he was appointed to a seat
in the Provincial Council of New Jersey. In 1776 he resigned all
offices that would demand allegiance to King George III, and became
a delegate to the Continental Congress. He signed the Declaration of
Independence, and he was appointed by Congress to "execute the business of the navy under their direction."

In 1779 he was made Judge of the Admiralty from Pennsylvania.
He was active in the debates of the convention of 1787 that framed
the Constitution of the United States. According to some authorities
he was the designer of the United States flag. George E. Hastings, his
most comprehensive biographer, presents an interesting discussion of
this claim.[1] Hopkinson lived until 1791, when he died of apoplexy on
May 9.

---

[1] George E. Hastings, *The Life and Letters of Francis Hopkinson*, Chicago: The
University of Chicago Press.

Conjecture must supply the names of Hopkinson's music teachers, for there were several with whom he could have studied in early Philadelphia. John Beals, "musick master from London," was in Philadelphia from 1749 to 1758. Charles Love, the musician from Hallam's theatrical company, gave music lessons; and in 1757, John Palma's services may have been available. A piece by Palma—*Lesson*—was copied in Hopkinson's own handwriting in his manuscript book. It is fairly certain that Hopkinson studied later with James Bremner, who came to Philadelphia in 1763 and became an active influence in the musical life of the city. When Bremner died in 1780, Hopkinson composed an *Ode* to his memory.

From his own correspondence we may guess that Hopkinson was the center of the musical life in Philadelphia. A talented harpsichordist, he was a member of a group of amateurs and professionals who met at each other's houses, and also gave subscription concerts in public. Hopkinson conducted at the harpsichord; James Bremner, Stephen Forrage, and John Schneider would play the strings in company with Governor John Penn; and wind instruments were furnished by Schneider, Ernst Barnard, George D'Eissenburg (French horn), and John Stadler (German flute). From Hopkinson's library, which is still in the possession of his descendants in Philadelphia, we learn something of the music played at these concerts. The works of Handel were well represented. The Italians, Pergolesi, Giardini, Scarlatti, Corelli, Vivaldi; the English Arne and Purcell were favorites. The group was familiar with the best music of its day.

Philadelphia enjoyed a musical life that extended to the home; households that wished to enjoy music could do so undisturbed by Quaker influences. In this respect the Pennsylvania capital was distinctive. *Soirées* of chamber music were frequent occurrences, and music for its own sake was not disturbed by the virtuoso influence that was later to dominate America's musical life.

Hopkinson's career as a composer started when he was seventeen, when he wrote an *Ode on Music*, the words later printed anonymously in the *American Magazine*. He was always closely associated with the College of Philadelphia, even after graduation, for at various of the commencements he accompanied the choruses and instrumental music on the harpsichord, and on several occasions composed the Odes. When

his teacher James Bremner temporarily relinquished the post of organist at Christ Church, Hopkinson filled the vacancy. The vestry minutes
(1770) contained the following entry:

> Mr. church-warden Hopkinson having been so obliging as to perform on
> the organ at Christ Church during the absence of Mr. Bremner, the late
> organist, the vestry unanimously requested of him a continuance of this kind
> office, until an organist should be appointed, or as long as it should be con-
> venient and agreeable to himself. Mr. Hopkinson cheerfully granted this
> request.

His musical activities in the church were not confined to playing the
organ, for he was familiar with the best of the psalmodists and taught
singing to the children of the church.

As an inventor, he is chiefly known for his improved method of
quilling the harpsichord. There are several references to this invention in his correspondence with Thomas Jefferson, whom he asked to
introduce the idea to foreign manufacturers; and in his letters to
Robert Bremner, the noted English music publisher, probably a relative of James Bremner.

A work that was probably the most important of Hopkinson's efforts
was *The Temple of Minerva*—undoubtedly from his pen—although
no record has been found of the musical setting. Since this "oratorial
entertainment" was somewhat operatic in type, it has claim to consideration as the first American opera. The libretto was first printed
anonymously in *Freeman's Journal* in Philadelphia, December 19,
1781, and the work was performed in the same year "by a company
of gentlemen and ladies in the hotel of the minister of France in the
presence of his Excellency General Washington and his lady." When
the libretto was again printed six years later in the *Columbian Magazine* it was signed "H.," and this fact, added to Sonneck's discovery of
a fragment of the manuscript in the second volume of Hopkinson's
collected poems and prose, seems to establish the authorship.

The Temple of Minerva was in effect an allegorical-political opera
or dramatic cantata, consisting of an overture, arias, ensembles, and
choruses in praise of the American alliance with France.

The earliest of Hopkinson's works are contained in a manuscript
book of *Songs*, which was in the possession of the Hopkinson family

until it was acquired by the Library of Congress in Washington. In addition to *My Days Have Been So Wondrous Free*, there are three other songs composed by *F. H.* in the volume: *The Garland, Oh! Come to Mason Borough's Grove,* and *With Pleasure Have I Past My Days*, as well as two religious compositions: *The 23ᵈ Psalm* and *An Anthem from the 114ᵗʰ Psalm*. Possibly there are also unsigned works of his.

Hopkinson was probably the compiler of *A Collection of Psalm Tunes with a Few Anthems, Some of them Entirely New for the use of the United Churches of Christ Church and St. Peter's Church in Philadelphia.*

His most ambitious published work was the collection of *Seven Songs* (actually eight), *for the harpsichord or forte piano,* which was issued in Philadelphia in 1788. An advertisement in the *Federal Gazette* states:

These songs are composed in an easy, familiar style, intended for young practitioners on the harpsichord or forte piano, and is the first work of this kind attempted in the United States.

The collection was dedicated to the composer's friend George Washington, then about to enter upon his first term as President. In his letter to Washington, Hopkinson shows himself to be a thoroughly modest person, with no exalted ideas of his greatness as a composer. He was aware of the fact that he was probably the first American composer:

. . . With respect to this little Work, which I now have the honor to present to your notice, I can only say, that it is such as a Lover, not a Master, of the Arts can furnish. I am neither a profess'd poet, nor a Profess'd Musician; and yet venture to appear in those characters united [Hopkinson wrote the words as well as the music of the songs]; for which I confess, the censure of Temerity may justly be brought against me.

If these Songs should not be so fortunate as to please the young Performers for whom they are intended, they will at least not occasion much Trouble in learning to perform them; and this will, I hope, be some Alleviation of their Disappointment.

However small the Reputation may be that I shall derive from this Work, I cannot I believe, be refused the Credit of being the first Native of the

United States who has produced a Musical Composition. If this attempt should not be too severely treated, others may be encouraged to venture on a path, yet untrodden in America, and the Arts in succession will take root and flourish amongst us. . . .

To which Washington replied with his characteristic humor and good grace:

. . . But, my dear Sir, if you had any doubts about the reception which your work would meet with—or had the smallest reason to think that you should meet with any assistance to defend it—you have not acted with your usual good judgment in the choice of a coadjutator, for, . . . what alas! can I do to support it? I can neither sing one of the songs, nor raise a single note on any instrument to convince the unbelieving.

But I have, however, one argument which will prevail with persons of true estate (at least in America)—I can tell them that *it is the production of Mr. Hopkinson.*

The titles of the songs, as well as their poetic and musical content, show the influence of the contemporary English style: *Come, fair Rosina, come away; My love is gone to sea; Beneath a weeping willow's shade; Enraptur'd I gaze, when my Delia is by; See, down Maria's blushing cheek; O'er the hills far away, at the birth of the morn; My gen'rous heart disdains, the slave of love to be;* and the eighth of the group, added after the title page announcing *seven* had been engraved, *The trav'ler benighted and lost, o'er the mountains pursues his lone way.* Hopkinson thought that the last song, "if played very slow, and sung with Expression," was "forcibly pathetic—at least in my Fancy." Its pathos was corroborated by Thomas Jefferson in acknowledging receipt of the songs:

I will not tell you how much they have pleased us, nor how well the last of them merits praise for it's pathos, but relate a fact only, which is that while my elder daughter was playing it on a harpsichord, I happened to look toward the fire & saw the younger one all in tears. I asked her if she was sick? She said "no; but the tune was so mournful."

Hopkinson's dedication of his *Seven Songs* to George Washington was altogether appropriate, even though Washington replied that he could "neither sing one of the songs, nor raise a single note on any instrument to convince the unbelieving." By that statement he contradicted the later belief that he was himself a musician, but he was

Francis Hopkinson
(See pages 37–44)

Frontispiece of Billings' Sixth and Last Book, *The Continental Harmony* (1794), Showing a "Tune" Engraved on a Circle

(See page 53)

nevertheless an active patron and friend of music. He loved the fine things of life, and as a gentleman of culture he had the rare gift of knowing how to get the most from his leisure. He was a frequent attendant at concerts, and he was a lover of the theatre, where he heard the ballad-operas of the day. At Mount Vernon there is still preserved the harpsichord he bought for Nelly Custis. The music books which belonged to Martha and Nelly Custis, some now at Mount Vernon and others in private hands, contain the standard music of the time, and also the work of some of the composers resident in America.

During the Revolutionary War, Hopkinson had penned another musical tribute to George Washington—a *Toast*, which celebrated the fact that Washington was commander-in-chief of the Continental Forces, and expressed confidence that "Our arms shall in battle with conquest be crowned, While virtue and he's on our side." The words of the *Toast* were printed in the *Pennsylvania Packet* of April 8, 1778, and twenty-one years later, in 1799, Benjamin Carr published both words and music in a music-sheet that contained also "a favorite new patriotic song in favor of Washington" entitled *Brother Soldiers All Hail*. The latter was not a work by Hopkinson, however. Prior to the bicentennial celebration of Washington's birth in 1932, a manuscript book in Hopkinson's handwriting came to light, which contained the *Toast*, words and music, and also the *Ode* to James Bremner which Hopkinson had composed when Bremner died in 1780. The words of this *Ode* appeared in the *Miscellaneous Essays* of Hopkinson, volume III, page 184.

At about this time, in 1931 and 1932, Hopkinson manuscripts began to appear in amazing numbers in Philadelphia. Many works described by Sonneck, but never before found, began to appear. Musical numbers from the *Temple of Minerva*, and odes of which only the words were known but which presumably had had musical settings, came to light in the possession of dealers and in the hands of private collectors who had enthusiastically purchased them. Several manuscript copies of *My Days Have Been So Wondrous Free* appeared in various collections. Careful examination of the newly discovered manuscripts revealed several matters that aroused suspicion. One was the dedication of one of the compositions to Benjamin Carr, who actually had come to this country in 1793, two years after Hopkinson's death. Another startling discovery was that the melody of one of the compositions was almost identical with that of Rubinstein's *Melody in F*. It was highly improbable that Hopkinson could have written such a melody, for its interval structure was entirely unlike that of the characteristic style Hopkinson used. A number of the suspected manuscripts were submitted to experts who pronounced them forgeries, basing their decision on the fact that they were made with a steel pen. Only quill pens were used in Hopkinson's day.

Eventually the manuscripts were traced to the same source, and it became apparent that they were the work of a convicted forger, a man who has since served prison sentences on other charges. Unfortunately, there are probably a number of these forgeries still in the hands of private collectors who bought them in good faith and are unaware of their origin. It is my opinion, however, that the manuscript book containing the *Toast* and the *Ode to the Memory of James Bremner* is genuine, and that even though this book came to light in Philadelphia at about the same time the forged manuscripts were appearing, it is in no way connected with the spurious items. The source of the genuine book has been satisfactorily traced to Hopkinson's time, having once been the property of Michael Hillegas (1729–1804), the first Treasurer of the United States.

It is, of course, as students of history, rather than as music critics, that we should view Hopkinson's works, though they are possessed of a freshness and ingenuous point of view that lends them considerable charm. Their importance lies not in any impress they may have had on later composers, for they did not have enough originality to exert any influence in themselves. It is rather as an indication of the existing vogue in the colonies that they are interesting, and to the historian, important. A study of Hopkinson's life and writings shows that music was appreciated and enjoyed in the colonies; and that the people of that time had access to the best of contemporary music literature.

2. JAMES LYON (1735–1794)

Like Hopkinson, our second native composer was also an amateur. James Lyon was chiefly a psalmodist, and he runs Hopkinson a close race as first composer. In fact, those who claim that he is the first are able to make a fairly good case. Yet when Hopkinson claimed to be the first American composer he was undoubtedly not only aware of Lyon's existence, but was well acquainted with him, and it is not to be supposed that a man of Hopkinson's standing would make such a claim lightly without being sure of his ground.

Lyon was a mild-mannered Presbyterian minister, who was so color blind that once when he journeyed a considerable distance to procure some black cloth for a ministerial frock, his wife discovered that the cloth was as scarlet as the coats of the British officers. He was born in Newark, "East New Jersey," July 1, 1735, during the turbulent days when the colony was under a royal governor, and just a few years before it was redivided into east and west sections. It is known that his father was Zopher Lyon, "Yeoman of the Town of Newark," and that he was orphaned at an early age. In 1750, Isaac Lyon and John Crane were appointed "guardians of the Body and Estate of James Lyon above fourteen years of age until he shall be the age of twenty-one."

It was during his college days that Lyon first left record of being a composer, for at the Commencement of 1759 at Nassau Hall (now Princeton), when President Samuel Davies had delivered a Latin oration that won the "applause of his numerous and learned auditors," and the "young gentlemen" had "performed the customary exercises with uncommon Facility and Correctness, the whole ceremony concluded with an ODE, set to music by Mr. James Lyon, one of the students."

Next, we hear of him as a candidate for a Master's degree at the College of Philadelphia, and in 1761 we learn of one of his works performed on the same program with an *Ode* by Hopkinson. The Pennsylvania *Gazette* (1761) stated:

On Saturday last the public COMMENCEMENT was held in the College of this City, before a vast Concourse of People of all Ranks. Besides the usual Exercises (which gave great satisfaction to the Audience) there was performed an elegant Anthem composed by James LYON, of New Jersey College, and in the afternoon an *Ode*, sacred to the Memory of our late Gracious Sovereign George II, written and set to Music in very grand and Masterly Taste by Francis Hopkinson, Esq. A.M. of the College of this City.

It was while Lyon was in Philadelphia that he produced his *Urania, or A Choice Collection of Psalm-Tunes, Anthems and Hymns*, although he may have left the city before it was finally published. He became a Presbyterian minister and went first to Nova Scotia; but, unable to support himself and his family on the meager salary the frontier church afforded, he accepted a call to the new settlement of Machias, Maine, where he remained, with a few brief interruptions, until his death, October 12, 1794.

That he returned to New Jersey at least once is indicated by the diary of a Southerner named Fithian, who spent his vacations in Cohansie, New Jersey. Fithian's diary affords a meager portrait of the minister-composer. Under date of April 22, 1774:

> Rode to the stage early for the Papers, thence I went to Mr. Hunter's where I met with that great master of music, Mr. Lyon. He sung at my request, & sings with his usual softness and accuracy—he is about publishing a new book of Tunes which are to be chiefly of his own Composition.

And on the following day:

> At home drawing off some of Mr. Lyon's Tunes, & revising my Own Exercises. . . . Afternoon according to Appointment I visited Mr. Lyon at Mr. Hunter's. He sings with great accuracy. I sung with him many of his Tunes & had much conversation on music, he is vastly fond of music & musical genius's. We spent the Evening with great satisfaction to me.

After Lyon's first year in Machias, the parish invited him to remain, and raised his salary to eighty-four pounds per annum, with a hundred pounds as an additional settlement. When we learn later that the parish was at one time in arrears some nine hundred pounds of the dominie's salary, we can appreciate what devotion to the cause persuaded Lyon to remain. Sometimes he and his family had to live almost entirely on fish that he caught with his own hands in the waters of Machias Bay.

Because of his residence in Nova Scotia, Lyon was familiar with the geography of the country, and when the Revolution broke out, he wrote to Washington asking permission to lead an expedition for conquering the province. With his offer he outlined a wholly practical plan of attack. The Canadian historian J. J. Bulmer admits that it was fortunate for the British that Washington rejected the scheme.

There is at hand convincing evidence to contradict the early historians who stated that *Urania* was a failure which almost ruined its publishers. Comparison of the few copies in existence today shows three separate editions, with a fourth possibly printed in New England. In many ways the collection was the most progressive of any that had yet been issued in the colonies. It was printed first in 1761, and contained six original works by Lyon, in addition to what may have been the first appearance in the colonies of the tune of our *America*, the English *God Save the King*. In *Urania* it was called *Whitefield's Tune*, to be sung to the words, "Come, Thou Almighty King."

The first tune in the book was the famous *Mear*. Some have claimed that this is an American tune, composed by a pastor of Marblehead, Massachusetts—John Barnard—in 1727. If this were true, Barnard would be the first American composer of whose works we have definite knowledge; but evidence seems to show that it was probably an English tune. There is no definite proof that Barnard was a composer of music, though he did publish a psalm book in 1752, with his own metrical version of the psalms and a neatly engraved collection of forty-nine tunes. The confusion probably arises from the fact that there was another John Barnard, an Englishman, who published a psalm book (presumably in England) in 1727. *Mear* is a fine old tune and it has come down to our own time through eighteenth- and nineteenth-century hymnbooks, set to a variety of texts. If it could be proved that it was of American origin it would be most important, for it is one of the few tunes sung in the early days that has survived to our time.

The other tunes in *Urania* were psalm-tunes, hymns, and anthems by such English writers as Arnold, Green, Knapp, and Evison. William Tuckey's *Liverpool* was included. The original works by Lyon were settings of the 8th, 23rd, and 95th Psalms; *Two Celebrated Verses by Sternhold and Hopkins*; an *Anthem taken from the 150th Psalm*; and the *104th Psalm* [translated] *by Dr. Watts*.

The fact that Fithian referred to a new book of tunes by Lyon, *chiefly of his own composition*, indicates that Lyon did not stop composing when he went to Maine, even though his later work was evidently never published. Possibly the later tunes were the ones that found their way into the collections of other psalmodists. *A Marriage*

Hymn by James Lyon appears in Daniel Bayley's *New Universal Harmony;* Simeon Jocelin's *Chorister's Companion* (1788) contained *Psalm 17th, Lyon;* the fourth edition of Andrew Law's *Rudiments of Music* (1792) included *Psalm 19, Lyon.* John Stickney's *Gentleman and lady's musical companion* (1774), and Elias Mann's *Massachusetts collection of sacred harmony* (1807), contained an ode, *Friendship: the words from Dr. Watts' lyric poems—set to music by the Rev. James Lyon.*

Frédéric L. Ritter, one of the first historians of American music, in his *Music in America,* takes occasion to be somewhat patronizing in his review of *Urania.* While Lyon's work is undoubtedly crude and primitive, it certainly is in advance of its few predecessors, and superior to some that came later. After quoting Lyon's *directions for singing,* Ritter exclaims sarcastically: "A great help that must have been to inexperienced singers!"

Well, here are the directions, and while it must be admitted that they give little technical help, they contain much common sense, and lay down some principles which were shamelessly disregarded by eighteenth-century singers:

1. In learning the 8 notes, get the assistance of some person well acquainted with the Tones and Semitones.

2. Choose that part which you can sing with the greatest Ease, and make yourself Master of that first.

(Surely Mr. Ritter could not quarrel with such a sound principle!)

3. Sound all high Notes as soft as possible, but low ones hard and full.

(True, exceptions could be found to this rule, but its observance would at least prevent the "Squeaking above, or Grumbling below" that the *Bay Psalm Book* deplored.)

4. Pitch your Tune so that the highest and lowest Notes may be sounded distinctly.

(Thoroughly sound—the obviousness of this rule was made necessary by the contemporary manner of singing.)

Lyon's exposition of the *Keys in Music* was much clearer than that of Thomas Walter. The rules of transposition are correct as far as they go, but less complete. Lyon had at least familiarized himself with the best sources available in his time. He did not copy from the faulty, incorrect Tans'ur, who had led other colonial psalmists astray. He was an able musician for his time and surroundings, a scholar, and a man who exerted a wholesome and thoroughly dignified influence not only on his contemporaries but on those who were to follow in the immediate future.

3. WILLIAM BILLINGS, AND HIS "FUGUING PIECES" (1746–1800)

In 1770, the year in which Beethoven was born, and when Bach had been at rest for twenty years, William Billings of Boston produced *The New England Psalm Singer*, and announced his musical declaration of independence from the chafing restrictions of simplicity in psalm tunes and hymns. For, as he proclaimed in a later work, this collection contained some of his "fuguing pieces . . . more than twenty times as powerful as the old slow tunes. Each part striving for mastery and victory. The audience entertained and delighted, their minds surprisingly agitated and extremely fluctuated, sometimes declaring for one part and sometimes for another. Now the solemn bass demands their attention; next the manly tenor; now the lofty counter; now the volatile treble. Now here, now there, now here again! O ecstatic! Rush on, you sons of harmony!"

Such an imagination, and such enthusiasm should surely have produced masterworks, but alas, no—merely the crude attempts of a tanner to produce something different, a striving for effects he could imagine, but for which he lacked the necessary equipment. A picturesque character was Billings, blind in one eye, an arm withered, legs of different length, and a rasping voice to add color to his slovenly appearance. And yet here was the musical enthusiast who was so wrapped up in the making of melody that he gave up his business of tanning to become the first American composer to make music his profession. And as a result died in poverty. He did have the satisfaction of recognition, however, for contemporary New England had never seen the like of him before, and as he devoted the major part of his efforts to music of the church, he was not set aside as a freak, but became a man honored in his own time, and hailed by many as a genius.

Billings was born in Boston, October 7, 1746. Music secured an early hold on him, and no doubt his tannery suffered because so much of his time was spent in chalking music exercises on the walls and on the hides with which he worked. He was self-taught, and most of his knowledge in music was gained from faulty treatises by Tans'ur and others. Like many another novice, Billings refused to be daunted by his lack of technique. Rules hampered him, and he was frank in saying so. And though, when he rushed into print with his *New England Psalm Singer*, he was loud in the praises of his brain-child, or "Reuben" as he called it, he found occasion to apologize for his first-born when he issued his second book *The Singing Master's Assistant* some eight years later.

In the Preface to the first book, Billings thus addressed his patrons:

To all musical Practitioners:

Perhaps it may be expected by some, that I could say something concerning rules for composition; to these I answer that *Nature is the best Dictator*, for all the hard dry studied rules that ever were prescribed will not enable any person to form an Air any more than the bare knowledge of the four and twenty letters, and strict Grammatical rules will qualify a scholar for composing a piece of Poetry. . . . It must be Nature; Nature must lay the Foundation, Nature must give the Thought. . . .

I have read several Authors Rules on Composition, and find the strictest of them make some exception, as thus, they say that two 8vos or two 5ths may not be taken together rising or falling, unless one be Major and the other Minor; but rather than spoil the Air, they will allow that Breach to be made, and this Allowance gives great Latitude to young Composers, for they may always make that Plea and say, if I am not allowed to transgress the Rules of composition I shall certainly spoil the Air, and cross the Strain that Fancy dictated. . . .

For my own part, as I don't think myself confined to any Rules for Composition laid down by any that went before me, neither should I think (were I to pretend to lay down rules) that any who comes after me were any ways obligated to adhere to them any further than they should think proper: so in fact I think it is best for every composer to be his own learner. Therefore, upon this consideration, for me to dictate, or to pretend to prescribe Rules of this Nature for others, would not only be very unnecessary but also a very great piece of Vanity.

The Motto of the book left no doubt as to its merits:

> Out of the mouths of babes and sucklings
> Hast Thou perfected praise.

Eight years tempered the composer's estimate, and in his second book, which became known as *Billings' Best*, he set forth this confession:

KIND READER—

No doubt you (do or ought to) remember that about eight years ago, I published a Book entitled, *The New England Psalm Singer*, &c. And truly a most masterly and inimitable performance, I then thought it to be. Oh! how did my foolish heart throb and beat with tumultuous joy! With what impatience did I wait on the Book-Binder, while stitching the sheets and putting on the covers, with what extacy did I snatch the yet unfinished Book out of his hands, and pressing to my bosom, with rapturous delight how lavish was I in enconiums on this infant production of my own Numb-Skull. Welcome, thrice welcome, thou legitimate offspring of my brain, go forth my little book, go forth and immortalize the name of your Author; may your sale be rapid and may you speedily run through ten thousand Editions, may you be a welcome guest in all companies and what will add tenfold to thy dignity, may you find your way into the Libraries of the Learned. Thou art my Reuben, my first born; the beginning of my Strength, the Excellency of my Dignity, and the Excellency of my power. But to my great mortification I soon discovered it was Reuben in the sequel, and Reuben all over, for unstable as water, it did not excel: and since I have begun to play the Critic, I will go through with my Criticisms, and endeavour to point out its beauties as well as deformities, and it must be acknowledged, that many of the pieces are not so ostentatious, as to send forth their own praises; for it has been judiciously observed, that the oftener they are sounded, the more they are abased. After impartial examination, I have discovered that many pieces were never worth my printing or your inspection; therefore in order to make you ample amends for my former intrusion, I have selected and corrected some of the Tunes which were most approved of in that book and have added several new peices [sic] which I think to be very good ones. . . .

Billings did not take kindly to one particular criticism of his "Reuben." It seems that some of his readers had considered the arrangement of tunes too simple; the constant succession of thirds and sixths proved cloying. There was none of the seasoning of discord. This criticism annoyed Billings, and in his second book he resolved to go all the way and show his critics what he could do in the field of dissonance. He included his *Jargon*, which we may consider the first of our present *modernistic* compositions, antedating Schoenberg and Stravinsky by at least a century and a half, and in one respect altogether worthy of them. There was a complete absence of concord, and the composer accomplished exactly what he was after. The words commence, "Let horrid Jargon split the air, And rive the nerves asunder—." *Jargon* also shows that Billings, sometimes given to literary bombast, could upon occasion be a humorist. It was accompanied by a *Manifesto* to the *Goddess of Discord*, which read:

In order to do this piece justice, the concert must be made of vocal and instrumental music. Let it be performed in the following manner, viz: Let an Ass bray the base, let the filing of a saw carry the tenor, let a hog who is extremely weak squeal the counter, and let a cart-wheel, which is heavy-loaded, and that has long been without grease, squeak the treble; and if the concert should appear to be too feeble you may add the cracking of a crow, the howling of a dog, the squalling of a cat, and what would grace the concert yet more, would be the rubbing of a wet finger upon a window glass. This last mentioned instrument no sooner salutes the drum of the ear, but it instantly conveys the sensation to the teeth; and if all these in conjunction should not reach the cause, you may add this most inharmonious of all sounds, "Pay me what thou owest."

To which his critics replied by hanging two cats by their tails to the sign—BILLINGS MUSIC—which swung outside his door.

Billings's best-known tune was *Chester*. It was popular in his own time, and was in wide use well into the nineteenth century. Always an enthusiast, he became one of the most fervent patriots during the War of the Revolution, and used his gifts for patriotic songs. He wrote new words for *Chester*, and the song became the *Over There* of the Revolution, with its fiery verses shouted by every soldier:

> Let tyrants shake their iron rod,
> And Slav'ry clank her galling chains,
> We fear them not, we trust in God,
> New England's God forever reigns.

Howe and Burgoyne and Clinton, too,
With Prescott and Cornwallis join'd,
Together plot our overthrow,
In one Infernal league combin'd.

When God inspired us for the fight,
Their ranks were broke, their lines were forc'd,
Their Ships were Shelter'd in our sight,
Or swiftly driven from our Coast.

The Foe comes on with haughty Stride,
Our troops advance with martial noise,
Their Vet'rans flee before our Youth,
And Gen'rals yield to beardless boys.

What grateful Off'ring shall we bring,
What shall we render to the Lord?
Loud Hallelujahs let us Sing,
And praise his name on ev'ry Chord.

Not only did Billings claim God exclusively for New England, but he paraphrased the Scriptures, and changed the locale of some of the psalms. The 137th Psalm became his *Lamentation over Boston,* when the city was occupied by British troops:

By the rivers of Watertown, we sat down;
Yea we wept as we remembered Boston.

Billings published six collections altogether. In addition to the first two there were: *Music in Miniature* (1779); *The Psalm Singer's Amusement* (1781); *The Suffolk Harmony* (1786); and *The Continental Harmony* (1794). The last lays down the rudiments of music in the form of a dialogue between *Scholar* and *Master*. Again we find major and minor discussed as *sharp* and *flat* keys, but this time in an exposition of the relations of the keys to the two sexes:

Scholar: Sir, I do not well understand you, for you have but just given it as your opinion, that the two keys were to most equally pleasing.

Master: When I spoke in that manner, I meant to confine the observation to the male sex: but you may take it for granted that the female part of the creation are much the greater lovers of music: for I scarcely ever met with one but what was more or less entertained with musical sounds, and I am very positive that nine-tenths of them are much more pleased with a flat, than a sharp air; and I make no doubt, but that the musical world (if upon reading what I have now asserted, they should be induced to make some observations that way) must unavoidably fall into my opinion.

Among Billings's secular works was a choral piece entitled *Modern Music*. As a rhymster he proved himself something of a predecessor of W. S. Gilbert:

> We are met for a concert of modern invention
> To tickle the ear is our present intention
>
> .   .   .   .   .   .
>
> Through common and treble we jointly have run
> We'd give you their essence compounded in one;
> Although we are strongly attached to the rest,
> Six-four is the movement that pleases us best.
> And now we address you as friends to the Cause
> Performers are modest and write their own laws.
> Although we are sanguine and clap at the Ban,
> 'Tis the part of the hearers to clap their applause.

Billings's works were widely used and his reputation extended throughout the states, for programs of concerts in Philadelphia and other cities show his anthems in abundance. His anthem from the second of Solomon's Songs, *The Rose of Sharon*, seems to have been a favorite. At the First Uranian Concert in Philadelphia (1787), Billings was represented with three works; Lyon and Tuckey with one each. In Boston, at a *Concert of Sacred Musick* "projected by the Musical Societies" to rebuild the Hollis Street Meeting House, two of Billings's anthems were sung, and the concert concluded with the *Hallelujah* Chorus from *The Messiah*, "accompanied by kettle-drums."

Although he was respected, Billings was often the object of practical jokes. Probably his deformities provoked the jibes of the thoughtless. Once a local jokester called on him, and after a long preamble in which he flattered the composer by assuming that he could answer any musical question, asked whether snoring was to be classed as vocal or instrumental music. In spite of the fact that he was the protégé of Governor Samuel Adams and Dr. Pierce, and was termed an "extraor-dinary genius" by many a contemporary writer, Billings found it difficult to provide for his wife and six children. There are records of several attempts to improve the finances of the needy Billings family. *The Columbian Centinel* of December 8, 1790, announced its gratification

in hearing that a number of benevolent characters are determined to bring forward a Concert of Sacred Musick for the benefit of Mr. William Billings of this town—whose distress is real, and whose merit in that science, is generally acknowledged.

The pieces to be performed will consist of a great, and, it is expected, a pleasant variety, and whilst the charitable will rejoice in this opportunity to exercise their benevolence, the amateurs of musick, will no doubt be abundantly gratified.

Again, in 1792, when Billings was about to publish his last volume, the *Massachusetts Magazine* stated:

The distressed situation of Mr. Billings' family has so sensibly operated on the minds of the committee as to induce their assistance in the intended publication.

When he died on the twenty-ninth of September, 1800, there was no money to provide a tombstone. He lies in an unmarked grave in the little graveyard on the Boston Common.

Billings made a lasting contribution to our musical life by his activities in forming singing societies and church choirs. He was the chief agent in the second revival of singing in New England, midway between that of the 1720's and that led by Lowell Mason a little more than a century later. The singing class that he formed in Stoughton, Massachusetts, became in 1786 the Stoughton Musical Society, and continued an active existence until it grew into the oldest singing society in America. Billings's introduction of the pitch-pipe eventually did away with the faulty pitching of tunes that had caused so much poor singing in churches. His use of the violoncello in church services was a daring innovation.

Those who look for real fugues in Billings's "fuguing" pieces will be disappointed, for they are, of course, not fugues at all—they are merely primitive attempts at imitative counterpoint. It is to be doubted whether any contemporary musicians in the colonies knew what a fugue really was. Tans'ur, one of the accepted authorities of the time, thus explained the *canon* and *fugue:*

To compose a Canon, you must first prick down your Fuge (or such a Quantity of Notes as you would have to lead your Point) in *one* Part; and then carry the same Notes forward, and prick them down in another Part, either in the Unison, 3rd, 4th, 5th, or 6th etc. above, or below the leading Part.

A Canon is a perpetual Fuge, i.e. Parts always flying one before another; the following parts repeating the very same Notes (either in Unison, or higher, or lower) as the leading Part, and because it is carried on by so strict a Rule, it is called a Canon; which is the superlative, or highest Degree of Musical Composition.

A single Fuge or Imitation, is when Parts imitate one another.

A Double Fuge, is when two or several Points, or Fuges fall in, one after the other.

No indeed, we must not be too hard on Billings if this was the extent of his training. And while he was undoubtedly clumsy and crude, Billings exerted an influence on music in New England, and the other colonies too, that has had a lasting effect. The man was vital, and while he probably copied the forms of contemporary English church musicians, he did have a spark of originality. He fanned into life the smouldering musical interest of New England, and consequently really established in the young United States of America a definite interest in music, crude and imitative though it was.

In 1790 his career was at its peak. There were scarcely any psalm collections published which did not contain many of his works. His music was more popular with Americans than that of foreign composers—chauvinism was unnecessary to secure appreciation of this American composer. After 1790 his influence outside of the church lessened. The coming of foreign musicians after the Revolution exposed the primitive character of Billings's music, and as the years progressed, his name appeared less frequently on concert programs. His Revolutionary song *Chester* survived to the latter part of the nineteenth century, but to the early twentieth century he was largely a legendary figure, except in isolated instances. George Pullen Jackson found that Billings's "fuges," and those of his contemporaries and followers, had remained very much alive for a century and a half among the numerous "Sacred

Harp" singers in the rural South, but music lovers and churchgoers in the urban centers of the East and North knew of him only by reading about him.[1]

In recent years there has been renewed interest in Billings's music, and something in the nature of a revival has occurred, bringing with it modern publications of many of his tunes and some of his "fuguing" pieces. They are sung in concert and on radio programs, particularly on those designed to show the early history of American music. And modern music lovers have found that there is indeed something vital in this music of our early composer—something sincere, rugged, and altogether expressive of the age in which he lived.

[1] Cf. George Pullen Jackson, *White Spirituals in the Southern Uplands*, Chapel Hill, N.C.: University of North Carolina Press, 1933.

CHAPTER THREE

The Latter Eighteenth Century

I. NEW ENGLAND

THE closing years of the eighteenth century were somewhat more friendly to music in New England, for Puritanism was relaxing its fear and hatred of lighter diversions. Piety was still demanded by churchmen, yet music had firmly established itself as a proper part of divine worship. Secular music was gaining a foothold.

The Revolution halted musical progress less in New England than in other sections of the country, for after the field of military operations moved from Boston, musicians resumed their activities. Concerts were frequent occurrences, and as music teachers became more numerous, the audiences grew more discriminating. Owing to the difficulty of travel, there was not the opportunity for keeping in close touch with musical events in other cities; each musical center was a unit which had to rely principally on its own resources. The stagecoach, springless and uncomfortable, was about the only mode of travel by land for those who could not go on horseback. So it was something of an event when our colonial cities had a chance to become acquainted with each other's musicians. Only ten per cent of the population of the colonies lived in cities when Washington was inaugurated; the rest were farmers. Land was abundant, while money and labor for manufacturing were scarce.

There were two distinct groups among the contemporaries and successors of William Billings: those who caught the spirit of his lively "fuguing pieces," and others who were violently opposed to their style as trivial and undignified. Clergymen were often in sympathy with the latter group, for they began to realize that the pendulum in favor of popular music had swung a little too far, and that some of the music sung in church was little suited to divine worship. It must be admitted that the parsons who took this stand were probably right. Had their opposition been against true contrapuntal choral music, against the lofty part-writing of a Bach or Handel, the controversy would have been a different matter. But we can well sympathize with those who hated to see their worship halted by the meaningless repetitions of Billings's "fuges." It is difficult to see how his florid anthems could have been conducive to worship.

John Hubbard, a professor at Dartmouth College, a number of years later (1807) crystallized the sentiment against frivolous church music. In one of his essays he wrote:

From the midnight revel, from the staggering bacchanal, from the profane altar of Comus, they have stolen the prostituted Air, and with sacrilegious hands have offered it in the Temple of *Jehovah*. . . . Such profanation must wound every feeling heart. Devotion ever assumes a dignity. It cannot delight in the tinkling bustle of unmeaning sounds. The air of a catch, a glee, a dance, a march, a common ballad is very improper for the worship of the Most High. . . .

This, of course, is one side of a time-honored controversy which survives to our own day. Nonliturgical worship has frequently allowed of the introduction of music that seems to sensitive ears unsuitable. Bach made *Chorales* of airs of questionable origin, but when he chose them, and passed his magic hands over their stately phrases, it was impossible to question their adaptability to sacred uses. In our generation evangelical hymns, and many of the tunes of our hymnbooks are open to the same charge leveled against the music of Billings's time.

Among Billings's contemporaries was ANDREW LAW (1748–1821), a man of good education, and a church music composer of taste and discrimination. Law was opposed to the overflorid style, and because of his comparatively simple arrangements of his own and others' tunes, he never achieved the popularity of Billings. He spent his life in various parts of the country; some of his publications were issued in Philadelphia, but he was born and died in Connecticut, and belongs primarily to New England.

Law was one of our first writers on music. In a series of *Essays on Music* he announced his intention of publishing reviews of contemporary music publications. In one of these he vigorously attacked a work which had had the boldness to designate itself as a collection of *Classi-cal Church Music.* "What," asked the critic, "is implied by the word classical? . . . Can music, published in an altered and mutilated state, contrary to the true principles of the art . . . be called classical? Can the use of terms derived from foreign languages make it classical? . . . Or can turning churches into theatres, and ministers into comedians, make the music classical?"

Law published his first collection, a *Select Number of Plain Tunes,* in 1767, but his first works to attract much attention were his *Select Harmony* (1778), and *Collection of Best Tunes and Anthems* (1779). In his works he attempted two innovations, one of which was successful. This was setting the melody in the soprano rather than in the tenor. The idea was borrowed from English arrangers of the time, but Law was its principal exponent in this country. The other experiment was the substitution of "character notes" for the usual symbols. Character notes had four differently shaped heads—square, oval, triangular, and diamond shaped, and corresponded respectively to the four old English note names, *fa, sol, la,* and *mi,* then in general use in this land. (The *do-re-mi* system had not yet arrived on these shores.) At first Law used these notes without any staff lines at all, placing them merely on different levels relative to an imaginary line or lines. This shape-note system did not survive long in New England, but it did spread to other parts of the country, to the Midwest and the South. We shall hear more of it in the discussion of folk hymnody in Chapter XIII.

The most popular tune that Law composed was *Archdale.*

In one important respect OLIVER HOLDEN (1765–1844) should be considered the outstanding composer of this time: he was the first American to produce a melody that has been used continuously from his own time to the present day. This is *Coronation,* set to the words *All Hail the Power of Jesus' Name,* which has needed no discovery by historians, no revival, to make it known to later generations. If lasting value is the criterion by which music is to be judged, the palm goes to Holden, and an account of American music which has survived on its own merits must start with him.

He was born in Shirley, Massachusetts, in 1765, and at an early age moved to Charlestown, where he first became a carpenter. He spent his leisure hours in composing, and finally became a singing teacher. As a musician, he was about equal to Billings in equipment, but because of his associations, and more cautious nature, he did not go as far afield as his older contemporary.

A year after his first publication *The American Harmony* (1792), Holden announced an ambitious scheme which does not seem to have met with enough response to warrant starting—the publication of *The Massachusetts Musical Magazine*. An advertisement in the *Massachusetts Spy* (Worcester, March 14, 1793) gave the details:

Proposal, for printing by Subscription, in monthly numbers, a new work, to be entitled *The Massachusetts Musical Magazine*, intended principally to furnish Musical Societies and other Practitioners in that pleasing art, with a choice and valuable collection of odes, anthems, dirges and other favorite pieces of musick. Principally original American compositions. By Oliver Holden, author of the American Harmony.

As a work of this kind has never been attempted in this part of the Union, and as many have expressed a wish to see such a publication, it is presumed that it will be found exceedingly useful, and meet a very general acceptance with all those who wish to possess themselves of a valuable collection of tunes, which are not to be found in musick books calculated only for schools and publick worship. . . .

As the price is set so exceedingly low the editor flatters himself that little persuasion will be necessary to effect a speedy and extensive subscription; . . .

Coronation was first printed in Holden's *Union Harmony* (1793). His other sacred books included the *Charlestown Collection* (1803), and *Plain Psalmody* (1800).

At the time of Washington's death, Holden was one of the many composers who lent their talents to commemorating the father of the nation. According to the newspapers, the "tributory honors" to George Washington, announced at the Old South Meeting House in Boston in January, 1800, were to conclude with the singing of *From Vernon's Mount Behold the Hero Rise*, the music by Oliver Holden. In February of the same year the Mechanics' Association of Boston requested him to write a cantata on the subject of Washington. He provided a *Dirge, or Sepulchral Service*, in which the first "Solemn Recitative" began: "Lo! sorrow reigneth, and the nation mourns."

Aside from *Coronation*, Holden's most important work was done in association with Samuel Holyoke and Hans Gram. This was the editing and compiling of *The Massachusetts Compiler* (1795), which was in many ways the most progressive work on psalmody to appear in the United States before 1800. It contained the "theoretical and practical elements of sacred vocal music, together with a musical dictionary." In 1797, Isaiah Thomas, the publisher, engaged Holden as editor and reviser of the *Worcester Collection* which, he presumed, would be "pleasing to its patrons." Holden lived until 1844.

SAMUEL HOLYOKE (1762–1820), coeditor with Holden in *The Massachusetts Compiler*, was the son of a clergyman from Boxford, Massachusetts. A versatile musician, with perhaps less natural talent than some of his contemporaries, he was nevertheless active in musical affairs. Holyoke was an avowed opponent of the Billings school, and in his first publication *Harmonia Americana* (1791), he made the following statement:

Perhaps some may be disappointed that fuguing pieces are in general omitted. But the principal reason why few were inserted was the trifling effect produced by that sort of music; for the parts, falling in, one after another, each conveying a different idea, confound the sense, and render the performance a mere jargon of words.

He was active in promoting choral concerts in and around Boston, especially in Salem, and on the programs he included some of the best music of the times. His fame rests chiefly on the hymn-tune *Arnheim*. Others of his works were the following collections:

The Columbian repository of sacred harmony. Selected from European and American authors with many new tunes not before published. Including the whole of Dr. Watts' psalms and hymns, to each of which a tune is adapted and some additional tunes suited to the particular metres in Tate and Brady's, and Dr. Belknap's collection of psalms and hymns. (Date unknown, probably 1800 or 1802.)

The Christian harmonist; containing a set of tunes adapted to all the metres. . . . To which are added, hymns on particular subjects . . . two anthems, and a funeral dirge . . . designed for the use of the Baptist Churches of the U.S.A. (1804.)

Vocal Companion. . . . (1807.)

Instrumental Assistant. . . . (Date unknown.)

As with Holden, the death of Washington called Holyoke's musical pen into play. The library of Harvard University possesses a copy of

Hark from the tombs, etc. and *Beneath the honors*, etc. Adapted from Dr. Watts, and set to music, by Samuel Holyoke, A.M. Performed at Newburyport, 2nd January, 1800. The day on which the citizens unitedly expressed their unbounded veneration for the memory of our beloved Washington. . . .

Holyoke had not waited for Washington's death to extol him in music, for in September, 1790 the *Massachusetts Magazine* had printed his song *Washington*. This journal issued a number of Holyoke's compositions, among them *The Pensive Shepherd* (words by J. Lathrop); *Sally, a Pastoral*; and *Terraminta*, words from *The Apollo*.

The third editor of the *Massachusetts Compiler* was a foreigner, HANS GRAM, who settled in Boston some time before 1790, where he acted as organist of the Brattle Square Church. Gram enjoys the distinction of being the composer of the first orchestral score published in the United States. The Bethlehem group left behind them works for orchestral combinations, but they were all in manuscript. Gram's work was scored for strings, two clarinets, and two E-flat horns. It was entitled *The Death Song of an Indian Chief*, and was printed on a flyleaf in the *Massachusetts Magazine* of March, 1791. It is from the contents of this magazine that we know what Gram composed. Among the songs was one that bore the title *A Shape Alone let others Prize*. There were also *A Hunting Song* and *Till Noah's Time*, "A favorite song. Translated from the Danish by Mr. Hans Gram. The air a Gothick composition." Gram was a good musician, and was no doubt principally responsible for the superiority of the harmonizations in the *Compiler*.

Among the lesser composers of the day, DANIEL READ (1757–1836) was author of several collections: *The American Singing Book; or a new and easy guide to the art of psalmody* (1785); and *The Columbian Harmonist* (1807). Read was by trade originally a comb maker. He was clumsy as a harmonist and fond of "fuguing pieces."

TIMOTHY SWAN (1757–1842) was a New Englander who composed some tunes that survived him by many years, some in use today: *China, Poland, Ocean*, and *Pownall*. One of his works, *The Songster's Assistant* (1800), has a novel decoration; a canon for two voices engraved on a staff in the form of a French horn.

JACOB KIMBALL (1761–1826) left the practice of law to become a musician, and died in the Almshouse at Topsfield, Massachusetts. He was one of the "fuge" writers. In 1793 he published his *Rural Harmony*, and was coeditor with Holyoke in compiling the *Essex Harmony* (1800).

JACOB FRENCH (1754–?), produced the *New American Melody* (1789); *Psalmodist's Companion* (1793), and *Harmony of Harmony* (1802), the latter containing five parts: 1. The ground work or principles of music: by way of question and answer. 2. The gamut . . . with observations on music. 3. A complete set of psalm-tunes. 4. A number of pieces set to particular psalms and hymns, together with odes, fuguing and flying pieces. 5. A number of anthems.

Secular music, and the giving of concerts, was with a few exceptions largely in the hands of foreign residents. One of the exceptions was JOSIAH FLAGG (1738–1794), who has been mentioned in a previous chapter as a psalmodist, and compiler of *A Collection of the Best Psalm Tunes* (1764). Flagg was familiar with the best music of his time, and being an energetic person he was possessed of ambitions. As early as 1771 he promoted a concert of "vocal and instrumental musick accompanied by French horns, hautboys, etc. by the band of the 64th Regiment." The program included works of both Handel and Bach. Two years later he left Boston, and in the announcement of a final concert, in which there would be "upwards of 50 performers," he expressed the hope that the receipts would be sufficient to enable him to leave the Province "in an independant manner." Evidently the career of concert manager was precarious in those days! Where Flagg spent the following years until his death in 1794 is not known, but his widow was in Boston in the following year, for we learn that Mr. Stone, the flutist, organized a concert for her benefit. Evidently her want had been caused by the misdeeds of her "vile miscreant son," the surgeon dentist Josiah Flagg, junior. The proceeds of the concert were $102, which, when the *Columbian Centinel* "considered the disadvantages unavoidably attending the business, must be considered as handsome." Mrs. Flagg and her daughters publicly thanked their friends for their efforts in their behalf, and in their announcement took pains to say that they "carried on the business of riveting and mending China and glass, and needle work of all kinds."

Flagg's program of vocal and instrumental music in 1771 contained a *Hunting Song* by W. S. MORGAN, a musician from abroad who provided color if little else of importance to Boston's musical life immediately preceding the Revolution. Morgan was evidently a good musician, but also something of a rascal. He had come to Boston in 1770, and had advertised himself as a "pupil of Signior Giardini" who intended "instructing ladies and gentlemen on the harpsichord, violin, etc., on the easiest terms and by the most approv'd methods." A year later he appeared before the Boston public in one of the subscription concerts of William Turner, a concert manager and dancing teacher. Morgan soon became involved with the sheriff, and Turner befriended him, not only by paying the board bill which was the cause of the trouble, but also by supporting him for the next six months. Morgan then went to Newport to become the organist of Trinity Church, but he got into trouble again and Turner was obliged to find him a job, this time in Portsmouth, New Hampshire. Then the ungrateful Morgan notified Turner that if he did not help him further, he would ally himself with Turner's newly arrived concert rival David Propert. Whereupon the exasperated Mr. Turner sent an officer to Morgan's house with a writ in which he "requested my just due, and desir'd he would settle with me and pay the balance or at least give security for it." This caused a postponement of the Propert concert, but Turner, probably not wishing to appear in the capacity of legally hindering a rival's concert, withdrew his complaint, and the concert was held on April 26, 1773.

Morgan appears again as a composer, this time for orchestra, when a concert was announced in 1774 "to conclude with a grand Military Symphony accompanied by kettle drums, etc. compos'd by Mr. Morgan." The last we hear of him is when he announced a concert for his own benefit in 1775, "when will be performed a Concert of Vocal and Instrumental Music; between the parts of which will be delivered (gratis) several comic Lectures on various subjects."

Josiah Flagg introduced the London organist and composer WILLIAM SELBY (1738–1798), who was largely responsible for the rapid progress of music in Boston during the following years. Soon after his arrival (about 1771), Selby was appointed organist of King's Chapel, and the vestry ordered a public collection for his benefit. During the Revolution he found it necessary to turn to other activities for a livelihood, and in his shop near Broomfield's Lane he advertised himself as selling "Port, Teneriffe, Malaga Wines, Tea, Brown and Loaf sugar, logwood, English soap, etc."

In 1782, Selby advertised for subscriptions to a work which seems never to have been issued, a monthly publication of music under the title *The New Minstrel,* each number to consist of "at least one composition for the harpsichord, piano forte or spinnet, one for the guitar, and one for the German flute, also of one song in French, and two songs in the English language." The advertisement for subscriptions gives a picture of conditions at the time:

Mr. Selby conceives that he need not urge the literary and other benefits which might arise from a due encouragement of works of the above kind. At this age of general civilization, at this aera of the acquaintance with a nation far gone in politeness and fine arts—even the stern patriot and lover of his country's glory, might be addressed on the present subject with not less propriety than the man of elegance and taste.

The promptness of this young country in those sciences which were once thought peculiar only to riper age, has already brought upon her the eyes of the world.

She has pushed her researches deep into philosophy and her statesmen and generals equalled those of the Roman name.

And shall those arts which make her happy be less courted than those arts which have made her great? Why may she not be "In song unequall'd as unmatch'd in war?"

A cry has gone forth against all amusements which are but a step from Gothism. The raisers of such a cry being unacquainted with distinctions, and little considering that "indulgences are only vices when pursued at the expence of some virtue" and that where they intrench on *No* virtue, they are innocent, and have in every age been acknowledged by almost all moralists.

When he first came to Boston, Selby was concerned chiefly with instrumental music. In many of his concerts he appeared as composer. At his initial appearance with Flagg he performed his *Concerto on the Organ,* and he featured his Harpsichord Concerto (probably a transcription of the same piece) on two of Morgan's benefit programs. Gradually his interest seemed to center in choral music, and through his efforts in organizing choral concerts in Boston, he can well be considered an indirect founder of the *Handel and Haydn Society*, which has played such an important part in the musical life of New England from the early nineteenth century.

One of Selby's concerts, September 22, 1773, on the anniversary of George III's coronation, shows the type of music he presented. The instrumental pieces were furnished by the Sixty-fourth Regiment Band, conducted by Morgan, and the choral music was probably performed by the Choir of King's Chapel. Handel was represented with three works: an overture, the *Hallelujah* Chorus, and the *Grand Coronation Anthem in 22 Parts*. In addition to songs, an organ concerto, and a sinfonia by unnamed composers, there was a *Glee in three parts, composed in the year 1600*. Morgan contributed a solo on the violin. In appealing to his public for support, Selby advertised that

Mr. Selby having been at great pains and expence to have this concert performed elegantly, humbly hopes to be patronized by his friends and the public.

In the spring of 1782, when Selby was again acting as organist at King's Chapel (he held the position until his death in 1798), he announced a concert of *Musica Spiritualis*, for the benefit of the poor of Boston. In 1786 came the mammoth event which marked the peak of his career. A *Musical Society* in which Selby seems to have been the moving spirit, sponsored a festival concert from which the proceeds would be devoted to much-needed prison relief. The *Massachusetts Gazette* printed a long announcement containing a program that was in truth stupendous for those days. Works of Handel and Bach, and compositions by Selby himself were performed.

The success of this concert encouraged the musical society and Selby to attempt in the following year another "Spiritual Concert for the benefit of those who have seen better days." An equally mammoth program, however, failed to draw an equally large audience.

When Washington visited Boston during his inaugural tour in 1789, the concerts arranged in his honor featured Selby's compositions. Although his name gradually disappeared from concert programs after 1793, he lived until 1798 in Boston, where he died at the age of fifty-nine.

It is chiefly because of his compositions that this book is concerned with Selby, and while his works have not survived, and his chief value was the stimulation he afforded to the musical life of Boston, he was exceedingly active as a composer. The Sonneck-Upton *Bibliography of Early Secular American Music* gives the titles of the following works:

Apollo, and the Muse's musical compositions . . . consisting of anthems in four parts, with symphonies for the organ,—Voluntaries or fuges for the organ or harpsichord—Sonatas or lessons for the harpsichord or pianoforte—Songs set for the voice and harpsichord or pianoforte, also, transposed for the German flute and guittar—A piece with variations for the harpsichord or pianoforte, in concert with the violin and guittar. —A concerto for the organ or harpsichord, with instrumental parts— A sonata for two violins and violoncello.

The Lovely Lass, a song, words by Mr. Brown.
Ode for the New Year.
An Ode in honor of General Washington.
Ode on the Anniversary of Independence.
On Musick, a song.
Ptalæmon to Pastora, "a new air."
The Rural Retreat, a song.

In addition, there were numerous sacred compositions, the anthems *O be Joyful in the Lord, Jubilate Deo, Now the King Eternal*, and others.

Another colorful figure from abroad was the blind organist and pianist JOHN L. BERKENHEAD who arrived in 1795, and from 1796 to 1804 was organist at Trinity Church in Newport. When he first arrived in Boston a concert was announced for his benefit at the Universal Meeting House. The advertisement said that

> Tho' he mourns a prison'd sense
> [he] Has music in his soul.

At the concert for Josiah Flagg's widow the program featured Berkenhead's playing of his own piece *The Demolition of the Bastile for piano forte or harpsichord*. There are records of many performances of this work by the composer—its name changed to the *Abolition of the Bastile* on a later occasion. He composed songs and instrumental pieces, and it is known that he traveled among near-by New England towns giving concerts with his associates. The *Columbian Centinel* of February 21, 1798 gave a glimpse of his entertainments:

Dr. Berkenhead and Co. entertained the inhabitants of Salem with a "Concert" on Thursday evening. Washington Hall was well filled. Mrs. Berkenhead, though indisposed, sang with feeling and taste; Mrs. Spencer with emphasis and correctness; and Mr. Spencer was loudly applauded and repeatedly *encored* by the gallery boys! The Bastile by the Doctor, was admirably played on an elegant harpsichord, belonging to a respectable family in that town.

It seems that Mrs. Berkenhead, even when sick, was easier to listen to than Mrs. Spencer.

Evidently Dr. Berkenhead had one lamentable weakness that called upon him the wrath of the vestry of Trinity Church. On his way to the church the organist was in the habit of calling upon a friend who had some excellent Scotch whiskey. He became confused in the order of his program after one of these visits, and the clerk called out, "Mr. Berkenhead, you are playing the wrong tune!" Undaunted, the bibulous Mr. Berkenhead calmly pulled apart the curtains in front of him and called the clerk a liar. In his next contract the vestry specified that his tenure of office was to exist "during good behavior and punctual attendance."

At the close of the century, Boston definitely accepted the theatre as at least permissible, and attendance had become a matter of individual conscience rather than one of law. The eighteenth-century theatre is closely associated with music, for a large proportion of the repertoire of the early companies was devoted to the English type of ballad-opera; plays interspersed with music, generally compiled from miscellaneous sources.

The Boston anti-theatre law of 1750 was for a number of years rigidly observed, but gradually the more venturesome made sporadic attempts to lure patrons to their exhibitions. Various terms were used to get around the law: "readings," "moral lectures," were advertised, rather than plays. In 1769, the ballad-opera *Love in a Village* was "read," and in 1770 a Mr. Joan (probably James Juhan, a Frenchman) gave a "reading" of *The Beggar's Opera*.

In 1775, the year of Bunker Hill, theatrical entertainment was offered by a number of officers and ladies, the proceeds devoted to distressed soldiers, their widows and children. Obviously the newly established Massachusetts government, independent of the King, could do nothing about such entertainments, but when Washington compelled Howe to evacuate Boston in the spring of the following year, the Boston authorities were free to regulate their own diversions. Consequently, there are practically no records of dramatic entertainments in the Hub during the following twelve years.

In 1778 a systematic agitation for repeal of the law of 1750 began. Subterfuges were again employed to fool the authorities. A Mr. and Mrs. Smith gave some "Moral Lectures" at Concert Hall, one of them being a "dialogue on the horrid crime of murder, from Shakespeare's *Macbeth*." Then followed a series of petitions to the Legislature, which were refused in spite of the growing strength of those who wanted their drama called by its right name. At length defiance of the law became systematic. A "New Exhibition Room" was opened, offering "a Gallery of Portraits, songs, feats of tumbling and ballet pantomime," and "Lectures Moral and Entertaining."

This was unmolested for several months, but at last Governor Hancock felt the necessity for respect of the law, and started legal action against the offenders. Though he never closed the theatrical speak-easy, he curtailed its repertoire considerably. In the spring of 1793 the anti-theatre law was talked to death in the Legislature, and though the necessary two-thirds majority never actually voted for repeal, sentiment in favor of the theatre was too strong for the authorities to attempt further enforcement.

After this the New Federal Street Theatre was built, and later the Haymarket, where Bostonians were treated regularly each season to comedies, tragedies, and ballad-operas. During the ensuing seven years the repertoire of the Federal Street Theatre embraced over ninety ballad-operas, and the Haymarket more than sixty.

The history of the theatre in Boston is important because it played a large part in introducing several musicians who were to become leading influences in the city's musical development; men like Gottlieb Graupner and the Van Hagens, father and son.

And so the century closes with Puritan Boston still stern, but sometimes smiling.

2. POST-REVOLUTIONARY IMMIGRANTS IN NEW YORK AND PHILADELPHIA

During the Revolution, matters musical were almost negligible in Philadelphia, and those in New York were largely in the hands of the British. The British officers and their Tory friends, who refused to consider the rebellion as serious an affair as it finally proved to be, sought lighter diversions, and Howe's *Thespians*, and other groups composed principally of military persons, gave plays, and often concerts. When the British evacuated Philadelphia in 1778, a number of professional actors tried to attract the members of the Congress and the people of Philadelphia to plays at the Southwark Theatre, but Congress discouraged this attempt by another resolution to supplement that of 1774, and the local legislature followed suit with an anti-theatre law.

In New York, the gallant Major André was the moving spirit among the military players, and officiated as manager, actor, and scene painter—the latter a somewhat harrowing occupation when a number of years later, in a play based on the André episode, a back-drop painted by André himself was used to depict the scene of his execution. Officers of the Army and Navy, and colonial sympathizers to the British cause, were subscribers to several regular concert series which prospered from 1781 until the last British regulars left the city in 1783. No doubt the unfortunate war sufferers (generally British) had their troubles considerably lightened by the proceeds.

In 1783, when Washington proclaimed hostilities at an end and retired to Mount Vernon where he hoped to enjoy the peace and quiet he was soon to be denied, musical activities came to life and assumed fresh vigor. Philadelphia started immediately with a series of *City Concerts* inaugurated by John Bentley, which continued under changing managements almost regularly for ten years. Then interest in the theatre and the establishment of summer concerts proved competition too strong to surmount. Postwar subscription concerts in New York were established in 1785 by William Brown, and they continued under different managements until 1796, when conditions similar to those in Philadelphia proved too discouraging.

Immediately after the war theatrical affairs were largely in the hands of the reorganized American Company, which reopened the John Street Theatre in New York in 1785, and in 1798 erected the famous Park Theatre in Park Row. In Philadelphia the American Company encountered much opposition because of the Quakers' energy in urging enforcement of the antitheatre law of 1778. As a result, Philadelphia paralleled Boston in witnessing "Lectures, properly diversified with music, scenery and other decorations, spectaculum vitæ," and other subterfuges calculated to hide forbidden fruit. One play, *The Gamester*, was offered as a "serious and moral lecture in five parts, on the sin of gambling," and *Hamlet* was introduced between the parts of a concert as a "moral and instructive tale called *Filial Piety, Exemplified in the History of the Prince of Denmark*." It was not until 1789 that the theatre law was repealed, and the old Southwark Theatre reopened officially with plays called by their proper names. Thereafter, the city enjoyed regular visits of the American Company, until the opening in 1794 of the Chestnut Street Theatre by the newly formed Wignell and Reinagle Company. This became Philadelphia's own company, and was the center of its theatrical life.

During these years a factor that has always been predominant in American music became increasingly apparent. Before the war, America had enjoyed the presence of a number of foreign musicians, and from 1783 scores of them appeared in the newly established United States. From their arrival they took largely into their own hands the management and performance of our musical affairs. Of course, this immigration offered advantages as well as disadvantages to the cause of American music, and it is difficult, if not impossible, to weigh the gains and drawbacks, and determine intelligently whether our musical life was eventually the gainer or the loser. We shall see that similar events occurred in the middle of the following century. Would our Billingses, our Hopkinsons, and Lyons have sowed the seeds of a truly national school of music, which would have gained in background and in craftsmanship, if its growth had been uninterrupted by the coming of skilled, thoroughly trained musicians whose knowledge and talents paled the glories of our native composers? Or would the crude yet native spark of creative genius have become sterile on virgin soil, where there was not the opportunity for exchange of ideas in a cultured environment?

Whether it was to our advantage or not, the musicians came, and as nearly all of them were active as composers as well as performers, they were the principal source of our late eighteenth-century secular music. Their concerts form the catalogue of the bulk of the music written in this country from the close of the Revolution to the early eighteen hundreds.

PETER ALBRECHT VAN HAGEN was a Hollander of German descent. Born of a musical family, he had been active in the musical life of Rotterdam before he settled in Charleston, South Carolina, in 1774. Having offered the inhabitants of that city a "Grand Concert of Vocal and Instrumental Music," he advertised for pupils in organ, harpsichord, pianoforte, violin, violoncello, and viola, and proposed to teach "the manner of composition to any that are inclined to be instructed therein." This list of subjects was subsequently put to shame when the family moved to New York fifteen years later, and Mr. Van Hagen advertised that he sold instruments of all sorts, and taught at six dollars a month (twelve lessons) and a guinea entrance fee, any or all of the following:

> violin, harpsichord, tenor, violoncello, German flute,
> hautboy, clarinet, bassoon, and singing.

Van Hagen's New York debut occurred in October, 1789, when he introduced to the public his son Peter Junior, eight years of age. According to the program, the father played two concertos on the violin and one on the tenor, while the boy rendered a vocal selection and played a concerto on the pianoforte. Peter Senior showed his versatility by playing a "solo upon iron nails, called Violin Harmonika."

Mrs. Van Hagen was also a musician, and in addition to participating in the family's concerts, she taught pupils. Her advertisement (1792) described her abilities:

Mrs. Van Hagen, lately from Amsterdam, respectfully informs the ladies of this city that she intends to teach the theory and practice of music on the harpsichord and Piano Forte with thoroughbass, if desired: also, the principles of vocal music and singing according to the most approved method and present taste in Europe.

As she has been for several years organist in the churches at Namur, Middleburg, Vlissingen and Bergen op den zoom, she also teaches on that instrument, as well church music, as lessons, sonatas, concertos, etc.

Mrs. Van Hagen hopes from her theoretic knowledge and successful experience in the science of music, to be as fortunate in the progress of her pupils in this city, as she has been in some of the first families in Holland.

As motives of delicacy may induce parents to commit the tuition of young ladies in this branch of education to one of their own sex, and the female voice from its being in unison, is better adapted to teach them singing than that of the other sex, which is an octave below, she flatters herself that she shall be indulged with their approbation and the protection of a respectable public.

In the same year the entire family presented a concert at which Mother Van Hagen played a "Forte Piano Sonata" and a "Forte Piano Concerto," Papa Van Hagen rendered a Tenor Concerto, little Peter played a Violin Concerto, and his sister, "Miss Van Hagen, *about* 13 years old," sang a "Song Duetto" with her little brother, and a trio with her mother and Peter, Junior.

In 1792, Van Hagen, Senior, joined with Henri Capron and George Saliment in the management of the annual New York subscription concerts, and in the following fall, when Capron had gone to Philadelphia, he gave three subscription concerts on his own account, with the assistance of several amateurs from a St. Cecilia Society, organized a year earlier. Again the entire family joined forces to make the affairs a success. In succeeding years Van Hagen was active in the management of the so-called "City Concerts," until the family departed for Boston in 1796. Here, in partnership with his son, he opened a Musical Magazine and Warranted Piano Forte Warehouse at 62 Newbury Street. He became leader of the Haymarket Theatre orchestra, and organist of Stone Chapel. He ultimately withdrew from the firm, which had begun to publish music in 1797, and his son continued the business alone.

As a composer, Van Hagen the elder left behind him records of having written music principally for the theatre, arrangements for ballad-operas that were performed at the theatres in Boston. To *The Adopted Child, or The Baron of Milford Castle,* for which Thomas Atwood had composed the original score, Van Hagen wrote entirely new music. For *The Battle of Hexham; Columbus, or The Discovery of America;* and *Zorinski, or Freedom to the Slaves,* he merely supplied some incidental music, and fitted the orchestral accompaniments to the instrumentation

James Hewitt (from a Painting Made in England When He Was
Twenty-One, a Year Before He Came to America)

(See pages 81–90)

Benjamin Carr
(See pages 96–101)

Alexander Reinagle (from a Drawing by Joseph
Muller after a Painting in the Possession of the Family)
(See pages 75–81)

of the Boston theatres. Of his original compositions, the *Federal Overture* was advertised for performance at the Haymarket Theatre in 1797, and his *Funeral Dirge* on the death of General Washington was published in 1800.

PETER VAN HAGEN, JUNIOR (1781–1837) must have been born in this country, presumably in Charleston, and was therefore doubly entitled to consideration as an American composer. Some of his works are preserved in the library of Harvard University, all of them issued by the Van Hagen publishing firm. There is a patriotic song *Adams and Washington*, whose words expressed the national state of mind when a state of war existed with France in 1798:

> Columbia's brave friends with alertness advance
> Her rights to support in defiance of France.
> To volatile fribbles we never will yield
> While John's at the helm, and George rules the field.

Others of his published songs were *Anna, Gentle Zephyr, May Morning, Pride of our Plains,* and *To Arms, Columbia*. He also composed an *Overture* which was played at the Haymarket in Boston.

One of the most prolific composers of the late eighteenth century was ALEXANDER REINAGLE (1756–1809), a man not only active in musical affairs both in New York and Philadelphia, but one who exerted an influence that made for high standards. Born of Austrian parents in England (1756), Reinagle inherited his love of music from his father. His early musical education was received in Scotland, where he studied with Raynor Taylor who followed him to America in 1792, and of whom we shall hear more later. From his correspondence with Karl Philipp Emanuel Bach, it was apparent that Reinagle was one of the younger Bach's intimate friends. No doubt he was well acquainted with other prominent Europeans of the time.

His activities in this country, centered largely in Philadelphia, were concerned with giving concerts and composing; and with managing a theatrical company in conjunction with Thomas Wignell. He first landed in New York in 1786, where he announced that "Mr. Reinagle, member of the Society of Musicians in London, gives lessons on the pianoforte, harpsichord and violin." New Yorkers did not offer the encouragement and patronage he needed, and he soon departed for

Philadelphia. As early as the autumn of 1786 he was busy with concerts in the Pennsylvania city.

On September 21 he assisted in a concert for Henri Capron's benefit
by contributing a song, and a sonata on the pianoforte. In October he
announced a benefit concert of his own, and showed himself something
of a modern by opening and closing the program with works of Haydn.
He joined forces with Capron, William Brown, and Alexander Juhan
in the management of the season's subscription concerts, and gave the
musical public of Philadelphia an adequate idea of his musicianship and
high ideals. In the following season he continued the subscription concert management with Brown.

After he had been in Philadelphia but a year, Reinagle was the first
to introduce four-hand piano music to America. At a concert for Juhan's
benefit, he played with Juhan a Piano Sonata for four hands by Haydn.
No less a celebrity graced this concert than General Washington, soon
to be elected President; and when Reinagle gave a concert of his own
three weeks later, Washington was again in the audience. Reinagle was
the harpsichord teacher of Washington's step-granddaughter Nelly
Custis.

By this time Reinagle had become interested in the theatre. Although
the antitheatre law had not yet been repealed in Philadelphia, the Old
American Company had reopened the Southwark Theatre with its
moral lectures, and Reinagle became associated with the troupe, probably as harpsichordist. It must have been this connection that caused
his return to New York late in 1788, where he was no doubt associated
with the company's brilliant season at the John Street Theatre in 1789.
New York had become the capital of the new government. Washington, always fond of the theatre and other amusements, was in constant
attendance.

In September, 1788, Reinagle joined Capron, who had also left
Philadelphia, in reviving New York's subscription concerts, which had
been dormant since the war, except for the only partially successful
series by William Brown two years earlier. In the following season
three more concerts were offered by Reinagle and Capron, in September and October. At the first of these a chorus by Reinagle was sung.
This work has been the subject of an interesting controversy. The advertisement of the concert contained the following information:

After the first act will be performed a Chorus, to the words that were sung, as Gen. Washington passed the bridge at Trenton—the Music now composed by Mr. Reinagle.

In 1789 the piece was published under the following heading:

Chorus sung before Gen. Washington as he passed under the triumphal arch raised on the bridge at Trenton, April 21st, 1789. Set to music and dedicated by permission to Mrs. Washington by A. Reinagle. . . .

Superficially, it would appear that Reinagle had written the music that had been sung at the Trenton ceremonies as Washington passed on his way to his inauguration as our first president; and casual students have so interpreted it. The concert advertisement speaks of "music *now* composed by Mr. Reinagle," and in the scoring of the published version there are significant differences with contemporaneous accounts of how the piece was sung. This discredits the theory that Reinagle composed the original music for the welcome to Washington, and indicates that the music later used in the concert and subsequently published was a new setting of the words that had been sung at Trenton, beginning:

Welcome, mighty chief! Once more. . . .

After the second series of New York concerts, Reinagle returned to Philadelphia, perhaps because the Old American Company had gone there to celebrate the repeal of the antitheatre law by reopening the Southwark Theatre. He was active in subscription concerts, and from the music that was played it would appear that he had a hand in the management. There were works of Haydn and Gossec, as well as the inevitable Pleyel and Stamitz.

The Philadelphia City Concerts of 1791–92 were under the joint management of Reinagle and J. C. Moller. Capron joined them the following season, when eight concerts were given at intervals of several weeks from December to March. Sonneck, in *Early Concert Life in America*, made some comments on the character of the programs:

In view of programs like these, I believe, the customary good-natured or ill-natured smile worn by historians in stumbling accidentally across an isolated eighteenth century program in our country will have to be cancelled once for ever. Though several of the composers who figured on these programs have since passed into (perhaps unmerited) oblivion, they were prominent masters in those days, and names like Haydn, Grétry, Bach, and Mozart are still household names in every musical community. If the arrangement of the "Plans" seems a trifled checkered at times to us moderns who fail to find the same or worse faults in the programs of our own time, we should not forget that the City Concerts ran strictly on European lines and contained no oddities which could not easily be duplicated by quoting European programs.

Meanwhile, Reinagle had become increasingly interested in matters theatrical and operatic, and had formed a partnership with Thomas Wignell, a brilliant English actor and singer who had been connected with the Old American Company since 1785. In 1791, Reinagle and Wignell commenced carrying out their plans for building a new theatre of their own in Chestnut Street, which would be the home for a permanent company that Wignell had recruited from abroad. So great was the competition the Wignell and Reinagle company offered to later visits of the American Company, that the older organization left the field to the newcomers after a final season in 1794. Although the Chestnut Street Theatre was actually ready a year before it was officially opened, the yellow fever epidemic that raged in Philadelphia in the winter of 1793 caused postponement of any but necessary gatherings. Though the company was not yet assembled when the plague subsided, Reinagle felt that he should no longer deny the public a chance to see the new playhouse, and he opened its doors with a "grand concert of vocal and instrumental music" on the second of February, 1793. In February of the following year it commenced its career as a theatre with a performance of *The Castle of Andalusia.*

Although Reinagle was in charge of the music and the orchestral department, George Gillingham, an English violinist who had sat with Reinagle in the orchestra of the Handel Commemoration at Westminster Abbey in 1784, was brought from England as conductor of the orchestra. Durang's *History of the Stage in Philadelphia* has the following picture of Reinagle:

Who that once saw old manager Reinagle in his official capacity, could ever forget his dignified person. He presided at his piano forte, looking the very personification of the patriarch of music—investing the science of harmonious sounds, as well as the dramatic school, with a moral influence, reflecting and adorning its salutary uses with high respectability and polished manners. His appearance was of the reverent and impressive kind, which at once inspired the universal respect of the audience.

Such was Reinagle's imposing appearance, that it awed the disorderly of the galleries, or the fop of annoying propensities, and impertinent criticism of the box lobby into decorum.

It was inspiring to behold the polished Reinagle saluting from his seat (before the grand square piano forte in the orchestra) the highest respectability of the city, as it entered the boxes to take seats. It was a scene before the curtain that suggested a picture of the master of private ceremonies receiving his invited guests at the fashionable drawing room.

Mr. Reinagle was a gentleman and a musician. His compositions evinced decided cleverness and originality, and some of his accompaniments to the old opera music were much admired by good judges.

William McKoy, in an article written twenty years after Reinagle's death in Poulson's *Daily Advertiser,* tells of the musician's participation in the performances:

Mr. Reinagle, one of the Managers, and a Professor of Music, used to be seen, but only on particular occasions, seated at the Piano Forte, then standing against the stage, in the rear of the band for the mere purpose of touching a few notes solo, by way of accompaniment to the silvery tones of Mrs. Wignell. . . . Mr. Reinagle, while thus enjoying the effect of her inimitable chant, exhibited to the audience a head not unlike that of Louis the XIV but divested of the simplicity, bushy, powdered hair, large high forehead, and round full face, illuminated by silver mounted spectacle glasses, a perceptible smirk at all times about the mouth, and an extraordinary depth of dimple in his cheek, while sitting there and surveying the irritability of Mr. Gillingham, the Leader of the Band, on his being obliged to leave the music of Handel and Mozart, and strike off into the "President's March. . . ."

Wignell died in 1803, and his widow continued the management of the Chestnut Street Theatre with Reinagle. During his later years, Reinagle managed a theatre in Baltimore, where he died September 21, 1809. He was married and had two sons, Thomas and Hugh, the latter a scenic painter who was named for Reinagle's brother, an eminent cellist.

Reinagle composed much music, and some of it has been preserved. His more important works seem not to be in existence, and it is not altogether fair to judge his abilities by the scattered pieces which are now in libraries and in private collections. The Library of Congress has a collection of *Sonatas for the Pianoforte* by Reinagle, which are probably the best of his works now extant. These sonatas, in manuscript, are in the manner of Philipp Emanuel Bach and the early Haydn, and at the same time show that Reinagle had some individuality of style and unquestionable taste.

Like the other composers of the day who were associated with the theatre, Reinagle made many arrangements of music used in ballad-operas, pantomimes, and so on: *Auld Robin Gray* (1795); *Blue Beard* (1799); *Columbus* (1797); *La Foret Noire* (1794); *Harlequin Shipwreck'd* (1795); *Harlequin's Invasion* (1795); *The Italian Monk* (1797); *The Mountaineers* (1796); *The Naval Pillar* (1800); *Pierre de Provence* (1796); *The Purse* (1795); *Robin Hood* (1794); *Sicilian Romance* (1795); *Spanish Barber* (1794); *The Witches of the Rocks* (1796). Copies of these arrangements are now practically nonexistent, but their titles indicate what was probably one of Reinagle's most significant contributions to the music of his time.

The most important of Reinagle's original works were a *Miscellaneous Quartett*, played at several of the City Concerts in Philadelphia in 1791, and the *New Miscellaneous Quartett*, offered in the same season; a *Concerto on the Improved Pianoforte with Additional Keys* (1794); *Preludes in three classes, for the improvement of practitioners on the piano forte* (1794); songs for the play *Slaves in Algiers* (1794); music for the musical farce *Savoyard, or the Repentant Seducer* (1797); *Monody on the Death of the much lamented, the late Lieutenant-General of the Armies of the United States*, composed by Reinagle in association with Raynor Taylor (1799); *Collection of favorite songs, divided into two books; The basses rendered easy and natural for the pianoforte or harpsichord* (probably 1789); *Masonic Overture* (1800); music written with Taylor to Richard Brinsley Sheridan's adaptation of Kotzebue's *Pizarro; The Volunteers*, Reinagle's "comic opera in two acts (written by Mrs. Rowson)," performed in Philadelphia, January 21, 1795; the much admired song in *The Stranger* (I Have a Silent Sorrow), a song *Rosa;* and *America, Commerce and Freedom*, published in 1794, and supposedly sung by Mr. Darley, Junior, a famous singer of that time, in the ballet pantomime of *The Sailor's Landlady*. This became widely used as a patriotic song.

Reinagle's *Federal March* was performed in the "grand procession," in Philadelphia, July 4, 1788, which celebrated the signing of the Constitution by a sufficient number of states to make it effective.

JAMES HEWITT (1770–1827) was one of the most important of the late century immigrants. He had an interesting background, he was himself a prime factor in the musical life of New York and Boston, and he established a line of descendants who are still carrying on the family tradition of music. John Hill Hewitt, his eldest son, was a ballad composer whom we shall meet later.

In September of the year 1792 the New York *Daily Advertiser* gave to the citizens of Gotham the promising information that James Hewitt, Jean Gehot, B. Bergmann, William Young, and a gentleman named Phillips, "professors of music from the Opera house, Hanover-square and professional Concerts under the direction of Haydn, Pleyel, etc., London," had arrived in town, and that they would give a concert on the twenty-first of the month at Corre's Hotel, at which "they humbly hoped to experience the kind patronage of the ladies and gentlemen, and public in general."

Inasmuch as Hewitt, Gehot, and Bergmann were violinists, Phillips played the violoncello and Young the flute, they provided among themselves the nucleus of an orchestra that was no doubt amplified by assistant performers. The program is one of the most interesting that has been preserved from this period. It shows that the members of this little group were possessed of imagination, whatever else they may have offered. The standard works were an Overture by Haydn, a *Quartetto* by Pleyel, and a Symphony and Flute *Quartetto* by Stamitz. Mr. Phillips contributed a Violoncello Concerto of his own, and the remainder of the program was devoted to two works of major proportions by Hewitt and Gehot.

Of these, the first was Hewitt's *Overture in 9 movements, expressive of a battle,* which pictured successively: 1. *Introduction,* 2. *Grand March; the army in motion,* 3. *The Charge for the attack,* 4. *A National Air,* 5. *The Attack commences, in which the confusion of an engagement is heard,* 6. *The Enemy surrender,* 7. *The Grief of those who are made prisoners,* 8. *The Conqueror's quickmarch,* and 9. *The Finale.* It is probable that Hewitt composed this *Overture* before he left England, no doubt inspired by the vogue of Kotzwara's *Battle of*

Prague, an insipid though highly popular piece written as early as 1788. But the other new work on the Hewitt-Gehot-Bergmann program must have been written on American soil, and while Hewitt's *Overture* represented a series of incidents he probably never experienced himself, Gehot's *Overture* told the story of their journey to America, and was therefore not only programmatic, but autobiographical as well.

This was the *Overture in 12 movements, expressive of a voyage from England to America.* The titles of the several movements afford a miniature history, as follows: 1. *Introduction,* 2. *Meeting of the adventurers, consultation and their determination on departure,* 3. *March from London to Gravesend,* 4. *Affectionate separation from their friends,* 5. *Going on board, and pleasure at recollecting the encouragement they hope to meet with in a land where merit is sure to gain reward,* 6. *Preparation for sailing, carpenter's hammering, crowing of the cock, weighing anchor, etc.,* 7. *A Storm,* 8. *A Calm,* 9. *Dance on the deck by the passengers,* 10. *Universal joy on seeing land,* 11. *Thanksgiving for safe arrival,* 12. *Finale.*

Immediately following their benefit concert, Messrs. Hewitt, Gehot, Bergmann, and Young decided to enter the subscription concert field in New York, which at that time was controlled by the Van Hagens. Although they announced a promising program for October 4, and advertised for a series of twelve concerts, they soon learned that their terms were too high and their series too long for the spending habits of New Yorkers. Consequently, they announced a postponement with this reason for the delay:

to obtain the celebrated singers, Mrs. Pownall (late Mrs. Wrighten) and Mrs. Hodgkinson, both recently of England, and as they were determined to engage the first singers in America, they have spared no expence nor trouble (by separate journeys to Philadelphia, etc. etc.) to gratify the amateurs of music.

Meanwhile, the Van Hagens, stirred by the thought of competition, had given their three subscription concerts in the fall of 1792, and Gehot had left his comrades to go to Philadelphia where he participated in the City Concerts of 1792–93, then managed by Reinagle and Capron. Gehot probably settled definitely in Philadelphia and later became a violinist in the orchestra of Wignell and Reinagle's Company. Although he is probably identical with a Gehot who published over thirty-six quartets, trios, and similar numbers; a *Complete Instructor of Every Musical Instrument;* and other educational works in London prior to 1790, the only composition, other than the *Overture,* of which we know in this country was the Quartet played at the City Concert in Philadelphia, December 1, 1792, and a few songs. John R. Parker's musical Reminiscences in the *Euterpeiad* (1822) tell that he died in obscurity and poverty.

It was not until January, 1793 that Hewitt, with Bergmann and Phillips, finally launched the subscription concerts and gave a series of six at Corre's Hotel, lasting until April 6. Young, too, had dropped out and had accompanied or followed Gehot to Philadelphia, where a few years later he was sentenced to death for having killed a constable who came to arrest him for his debts. The programs of the 1793 concerts were interesting for a number of reasons. Not only did they offer, as promised, the vocal talents of Mrs. Pownall and Mrs. Hodgkinson —singers from the Old American Company—and several works by Phillips and Hewitt (including a repetition of the *Battle* Overture), together with the accustomed list of Pleyel and Stamitz; they also included works of Vanhall and Haydn played from manuscript. On the program of the fifth concert (March 25), America probably heard its first performance of what was termed Haydn's *Passion of our Saviour,* identical with the famous *Seven Words,* composed for the Cathedral of Cadiz in 1785, and later performed in London as the *Passione Instrumentale.*

In the following winter the competition in subscription concerts continued. Capron, returning from Philadelphia, joined forces with Hewitt in promoting three "City" Concerts at the City Tavern in December and January, while Phillips took charge of the ball at a series which the Van Hagens offered as the "Old City" Concerts in Corre's Hotel in January and February. Bergmann remained with Hewitt. While the Van Hagen series emphasized the virtuoso element, offering Mr. and Mrs. Hodgkinson and Mr. Prigmore as vocalists, and numerous solos by the infant prodigy *Master* Van Hagen, the Hewitt concerts were more devoted to instrumental music. The songs of Mrs. Pownall and Madame de Seze, plus an occasional duet with Capron, were the only vocal offerings. Haydn was well represented on each of the programs.

Hewitt probably effected a merger with his rivals in the following season, for the series of three concerts in 1795 were offered by Mr. and Mrs. Van Hagen, Hewitt, and Saliment. Then Hewitt withdrew from the City Concerts, and devoted himself largely to his duties as leader of the orchestra of the Old American Company. His activities were by no means exclusively confined to any single undertaking, for he appeared as conductor of a band at Joseph Delacroix's celebrated summer concerts, held in the house and garden of "the late alderman Bayard," and called "Vaux Hall Gardens," where the two shillings admission entitled the patron "to a glass of ice cream punch," and the privilege of witnessing the fireworks "made by the celebrated Mr. Ambrose." He also had conducted the orchestra when in 1793, Mrs. Melmoth "from the Theatres Royal of London and Dublin" presented "*Select Extracts*, from the most eminent authors, recited by particular request." Evidently Hewitt was called upon to organize and conduct orchestras for occasions of all sorts.

He was born in Dartmoor, England, June 4, 1770. His father was Captain John Hewitt of the British Navy, a generous and brave man, who later followed his son James to America, where he lived until he was killed by a fall from his chaise in 1804, at the age of one hundred and one years. James entered the navy when he was a lad, but resigned as a midshipman when he saw the cruel treatment of the sailors on board his man-of-war. He was musically talented and his father decided to give him a musical education. Family accounts say that he studied under Viotti, but according to Grove's Dictionary, Viotti did not come to London until 1792; so if Hewitt actually took lessons from him it could hardly have been in London, as Hewitt was in New York in September of that year.

His progress was rapid, for before he came to New York he was leader of the Court Orchestra during the reign of George III. He was intimate with the Prince of Wales, and the future George IV presented him with an Amati cello, valued at five hundred dollars.

In 1790, Hewitt married a Miss Lamb, but his wife and their infant child died a year later, and in 1792, Hewitt came to America. According to the directories, he lived in New York almost continuously until

1812. He was connected with the orchestra of the Old American Company, he was for a time organist of Trinity Church, he conducted the orchestras at various outdoor summer resorts in town—Delacroix' Vaux Hall, Columbia and Mount Vernon Gardens. From 1805 to 1809 he was director of all the military bands in the city and commanded the Third Company of artillery.

About 1798, Hewitt purchased the New York branch of Carr's Musical Repository, and established a publishing business which was carried on by his son until the middle of the next century. On December 10, 1795, Hewitt married a second time. His bride was Eliza King, and the ceremony was performed at Trinity Church by Bishop Moore. Eliza was the daughter of Sir John King of the Royal British Army, who had come to America to settle some estates that had been bequeathed to his wife. Had Hewitt attended properly to securing the property in his wife's behalf, his descendants would have been wealthy. But Hewitt was never a good business man.

His second wife was an accomplished woman. She had been educated in Paris, and was there during the French Revolution. At the time of the Reign of Terror she was confined for safety in the Bastille with her mother. She saw the guillotine in action and would often recount its gruesome work with a shudder. She knew Napoleon Bonaparte when he was first making a name for himself.

Hewitt and his wife had six children, whom we shall meet in later chapters. His wife survived him by many years, living until 1865, when she died at the home of her youngest son in Burlington, New Jersey.

In 1812 the Hewitt family moved to Boston, where Hewitt took charge of the music at the Federal Street Theatre. He was also organist of Boston's Trinity Church. His name appears in the Boston directories until 1816, and in 1818 it reappears in New York. He must have traveled somewhat during the next few years. He was in Boston for a year—about 1820. Parker's *Euterpeiad* refers to a grand oratorio he conducted in Augusta, Georgia, in 1821, and in biographical data regarding his son, there are references to Southern theatrical companies in which James Hewitt was interested. Under date of 1826 there is a note that he was succeeded by George Gillingham as musical director at the Park Theatre in New York. Presumably he resigned because of ill health, though there are references to a subsequent connection with the Chatham Theatre.

Hewitt died in 1827 in Boston. For a time he had been estranged from his wife, and while she lived in Boston with their son James L. Hewitt, he was boarding in New York. There is in existence a series of letters written to this son late in 1826 and in January, 1827, which show that he was very ill at the time they were written. These last letters are interesting. They speak of his work, his financial and personal affairs. Some references throw light on the surgery of the period.

Dec. 27, 1826—This day at 12 o'clock closes the 6 weeks since the operation was performed, and I am at present no better for it.

Jan. 26, 1827—In a conversation I've had with Dr. Mott, he acknowledged the Lachrymal duct was cut but not so as to destroy its usefulness—but that is not the complaint, my present sufferings are from some part of the Jaw being left which was injured at the finishing of the operation before he closed the wound (he had been cutting away part of my nose) I heard him say to his assistant that there appeared some small part yet but he thought it would be of no consequence and did not wish to continue my sufferings—therefore had the wounds closed. . . . My sufferings are great and my death slow, but certain. I hope my dear James you will be here to receive my last breath. I feel the want of home—tho every kind attention is paid me here—yet my heart longs once more to behold my family.

In an undated letter he refers to his manuscripts:

In the large Red Box my clothes. In the smaller Red Box all manuscripts which I think you had better be careful of, they may eventually be of value to you. Among those Mans Books you may find music worth your printing. A Box for the whole of the Theatrical music, should you wish to pack it, is in the cellar, but I believe they have burnt the lids.

He had neglected looking after his own father's property as well as that belonging to his wife:

I did mean, if it pleased God to have spared my life, to have made secret inquiries respecting my father's affairs. Is it to be supposed that he could live here thirty years without some means? there are persons to whom he has lent money which has never been paid. What has become of the acknowledgments, and previous to his death he was known to have plenty of money. On his deathbed . . . he had something of consequence to communicate! Be assured there is something wrong, which if it had pleased God, my dear

James to have suffered me to have lived, I should have endeavoured to have found out.

A number of Hewitt's works are preserved in libraries, and while they represent his less important efforts, they nevertheless show that he was important in the development of American music. Many of his songs were early forerunners of our modern sentimental ballads. While none of these descended to the mawkish depths that our popular songs were to achieve in the next century, they do show "heart" tendencies that are prophetic. *The Music of the Harp of Love, The Wounded Hussar, When the Shades of Night Pursuing* (these three in the New York Public Library), and *How Happy Was My Humble Lot*—a favorite ballad sung by Mrs. Oldmixon and Miss Broadhurst (preserved in the Library of Congress)—are illustrative of this trend.

A year after his arrival, and immediately following the first series of subscription concerts, Hewitt advertised for subscriptions to a book of songs which he had written and compiled in association with Mrs. Pownall. The announcement contained the following details:

Flatter'd by the unbounded applauses which the songs of the Primrose Girl, Jemmy of the Glen, etc. [the latter was by Mrs. Pownall], have met with in this city and Philadelphia, M. A. Pownall and J. Hewitt, are induced to publish them (with four others entirely new) arranged for the Harpsichord and Pianoforte. A work which they hope will do credit to themselves and give satisfaction to those Ladies and Gentlemen who will please to honor them by becoming subscribers.

The book was published a year later and was advertised to contain, in addition to the other songs, *Song of the Waving Willow* and the celebrated French national air *La Carmagnole*. It actually contained, however, along with the several songs by Mrs. Pownall, Hewitt's songs *A Rural Life* and *The Primrose Girl;* also his adaptation of *La Chasse* and a *Canzonet* by Jackson of Exeter. Apparently *The Waving Willow* and *La Carmagnole* dropped out.

In addition to the *Overture* "expressive of a battle," Hewitt composed another *Overture*, "to conclude with the representation of a Storm at Sea," and an *Overture de Demophon, Arrangé pour le fortipiano par Jacques Hewitt.* The latter may be found in the Boston Public Library and in the Hopkinson collection at Philadelphia.

The Library of Congress has recently acquired two interesting Hewitt items. One is a set of *Three Sonatas for the Pianoforte*, Opus 5, published probably in 1796, four years after he came to America. The other is *The 4th of July—A Grand Military Sonata for the Pianoforte*, published some time between 1801 and 1811. In the collection of Joseph Muller, at Closter, New Jersey, I found a setting by Hewitt of the *Star-Spangled Banner*. Purely manufactured music, technically sound, but awkward to sing. Hewitt, like others, no doubt deplored the singing of our anthem to an English drinking song, and tried to provide a setting composed on native soil.[1] Mr. Muller's collection contained also a sonata by Hewitt [2]—*The Battle of Trenton*, published anonymously in 1797 and dedicated to "General Washington." This is interesting because of its similarity to the Battle Overture Hewitt presented at his first concert in New York, both of them reflective of the vogue of Kotzwara's *The Battle of Prague*, which was known in England in 1788, and performed for the first time in America in 1794. *The Battle of Trenton* has an elaborate program:

Introduction—The Army in motion—General Orders—Acclamation of the Americans—Drums beat to Arms.

Attack—cannons—bomb. Defeat of the Hessians—Flight of the Hessians —Begging Quarter—The Fight Renewed—General Confusion—The Hessians surrender themselves prisoners of War—Articles of Capitulation Signed—Grief of Americans for the loss of their companions killed in the engagement.

Yankee Doodle—Drums and Fifes—Quick Step for the Band—Trumpets of Victory—General Rejoicing.

The most important work that Hewitt wrote for the theatre was his score for the opera *Tammany*, produced in New York in 1794 under the auspices of the Tammany Society, the ancestor of the present Tam-

---

[1] The Boston Public Library has had a copy of this rare piece for several years. In 1930 a third copy appeared in the possession of C. A. Strong and C. J. Nagy of Philadelphia. Muller's copy, however, is undoubtedly from the first edition, as it bears Hewitt's imprint as publisher. The Strong-Nagy and Boston Library copies were published by J. A. & W. Geib of New York, somewhere between 1818 and 1821. The first edition was probably published by Hewitt in 1816.

[2] The Muller copy is now in the Americana Music Collection of the New York Public Library; others are in the Huntington Library in California, the Library of Congress, and in the private collection of Malcolm N. Stone, West Englewood, New Jersey.

many Hall. The libretto was written by Mrs. Anne Julia Hatton, a sister of Mrs. Siddons, and wife of a musical instrument maker in New York. In those days feeling between the Federalists and anti-Federalists ran high, and Mrs. Hatton was an ardent supporter of the anti-Federalists, who at that time were favoring support of the French Revolution. The powerful Tammany Society was also anti-Federalist, so Mrs. Hatton based her opera plot on the legend of the society's patron, the Indian Chief Tammany.

Because its presentation was largely political it was but to be expected that it would arouse a storm of controversy. The anti-Federalists hailed it with fervor and the Federalists denounced it in hostile terms as a "wretched thing," and "literally a mélange of bombast." Although the complete libretto and the score were never published we may gain an idea of its underlying theme by reading the prologue, supplied by another poet, R. B. Davis:

> Secure the Indian roved his native soil,
> Secure enjoy'd the produce of his toil,
> Nor knew, nor feared a haughty master's pow'r
> To force his labors, or his gains devour.
> And when the slaves of Europe here unfurl'd
> The bloody standard of their servile world,
> When heaven, to curse them more, first deign'd to bless
> Their base attempts with undeserved success,
> He knew the sweets of liberty to prize,
> And lost on earth he sought her in the skies;
> Scorned life divested of its noblest good,
> And seal'd the cause of freedom with his blood.

One writer went so far as to accuse the promoters of *Tammany* of attracting an audience by circulating a rumor that a party had been gathered to hiss the performance, and evidently there was considerable disturbance.

It is not known whether any of Hewitt's music from *Tammany* was published, although there did appear proposals for printing the "Overture with the songs, chorus's, etc., etc., to Tammany as composed and adapted to the pianoforte by Mr. Hewitt." Others of the operas to which he composed music were as follows: *Columbus* (1799); *The Mysterious Marriage, or The Heirship of Rosselva* (1799); *The Pa-*

triot, or Liberty Asserted (1794), "founded on the well-known story of William Tell, the Swiss patriot, who shot an apple from his son's head at the command of Tyrant Grislor who first gave liberty to the cantons of Switzerland"; the New York production of *Pizarro, or The Spaniards in Peru* (1800), (it will be remembered that Reinagle composed music for this work); *Robin Hood, or Sherwood Forest* (1800) (also by Reinagle); *The Spanish Castle, or The Knight of the Guadalquivir* (1800); and *The Wild Goose Chase* (1800).

Of the remaining two "Professors of Music from Hanoversquare, London," Phillips, as far as he has been traced, remained in New York, where in addition to his work as a cellist, he handled the terpsichorean features of concerts and parties, for, as he announced at the first concert in America, he had been connected abroad (probably in London) with the Pantheon and City Balls, and was qualified to introduce new English dances which, "if the ladies and gentlemen request, will be performed by a concert band." Bergmann became a member of the theatre orchestra which Hewitt conducted, but remained in New York only until 1795, after which he appeared at various times in Charleston, South Carolina and Boston. That he went directly from New York to Charleston is evident by the fact that he arranged the orchestral accompaniments for the presentation at the City Theatre, April 26, 1796, of a *pasticcio, The Doctor and Apothecary*.

A prominent member of the group who led musical affairs of Philadelphia well into the following century was RAYNOR TAYLOR (1747–1825), an older man than his pupil Reinagle, yet one who outlived him by sixteen years. Taylor was born in England in 1747 and was educated as a child in the King's Singing School at the Chapel Royal. The choirboys attended Handel's funeral in a body in 1759, and young Raynor, leaning too close to the grave, accidentally let his hat fall, so that it was buried with the remains of the great composer. "Never mind," consoled a friend, "he left you some of his brains in return."

In 1765, Taylor became organist in a church at Chelmsford, near London, but his interest in theatrical matters procured him the position of music director at Sadler's Wells Theatre in London, the playhouse made famous to our generation by Pinero's play *Trelawney of the Wells*. He had also made an enviable reputation as a ballad composer by the time he followed his friends to America in 1792.

When he arrived in Baltimore he sought to establish himself as a "music professor, organist, and teacher of music in general," and he announced his debut as a performer, when for the evening of October 17 he proposed

to perform a musical entertainment on a new plan, the whole of which will be entirely original, and his own composition. In the course of it many songs will be sung by his pupil, Miss Huntley, late of the theatre Royal, Covent Garden, a young lady, whose performance has been highly approved both in London and America.

With this and similar entertainments Taylor proceeded to introduce to America a species of extravaganza, or musical olio, which bordered on our present vaudeville or revue skits.

Taylor then settled in Annapolis, where in October, 1792, he had been appointed organist of St. Anne's Church. The parishioners evi‑ dently had no objection to their organist's being an entertainer, and on January 24 and February 28, 1793, he again engaged Miss Huntley for two of his burlesque entertainments. The program for January 24 con‑ sisted of three parts, the first devoted to a selection of comic and pas‑ toral songs. The second part presented a "Dramatic proverb (per‑ formed in London with great applause) being a burletta, in one act, called *The Gray Mare's Best Horse.*"

This sketch consisted of *A Breakfast scene a month after marriage*, a duet by Mr. Taylor and Miss Huntley. Next the *Mock wife in a vio‑ lent passion*, a solo number by Miss Huntley. This was followed by *A Father's advice to his son-in-law, Giles the countryman's grief for the loss of a scolding wife*, and the *Happy Miller*, performed by Mr. Tay‑ lor; then, in order, *Dame Pliant's obedience to her husband*, by Miss Huntley; a duet, the *Obedient wife, determined to have her own way*; and finally, two more duets, *New married couple reconciled*, and *All parties happy.*

The third part of the show was a burlesque on Italian opera, called *Capocchio and Dorinna*. In this presentation Mr. Taylor and Miss Huntley appeared in costume, Taylor portraying *Signor Capocchio*, an Italian singer and director of the opera; Miss Huntley, *Signora Dorinna*, an Italian actress. There were recitatives, airs, and duets, probably parodies of the Italian style, which offered a contrast to the

English type of ballad-opera, in which the main action was carried by dialogue between songs. The entertainment was further lengthened by "a piece on the Grand Pianoforte, preceding each part, by Mr. Taylor."

Affairs at Annapolis did not progress smoothly for Taylor. Those who had offered to guarantee his salary as organist did not make good their promises with actual money, and the employment of a collector failed to bring forth what was due him. So by the end of May he publicly thanked the families who had employed him as a music teacher and departed for Philadelphia. Here he became organist of St. Peter's Church, and held that position for almost the rest of his life. He lived until 1825, and was one of the leading spirits in founding the Musical Fund Society of Philadelphia in 1820. His brilliant powers of improvisation helped him as an organist, and no doubt lent an added charm to his entertainments.

Shortly after he went to Philadelphia he presented, on January 18 and 28 (1794) two more of his entertainments: the first, *An Ode to the New Year*, "with a variety of other pieces, consisting of songs, duets and trios, pastoral, serious and comic, entirely original," and the second similar to his entertainments in Maryland, consisting of

The Poor female ballad singer, a pathetic song; Hunting song; Algerian captive; Sailor's song; Ding Dong Bell, or the Honeymoon expired, being the courtship and wedding of Ralph and Fan; Character of smart Dolly, a laughing song; Rustic courtship or the unsuccessful love of poor Thomas, a crying song with duet, trio, etc.

In 1796, Taylor offered for his own benefit a concert at Oeller's Hotel, April 21. The program consisted of music from the Handelian school, and works of his own which occupied the entire second half of the concert. The announcement afforded a full description of the orchestra that was to be used. Though it would be small in a modern symphony hall, it was large for the time. The *concertino*, or small band of soloists, was constituted as follows:

First violin and leader of the band .... Mr. Gillingham
Principal violoncellos .... Mr. Menel
Double bass .... Mr. Demarque
Principal hautboy .... Mr. Shaw
Tenor .... Mr. Berenger

Bassoon and trumpet .... Mr. Priest
Horns .... Messrs. Grey and Homman
Violins .... Messrs. Daugel, Bouchony, Stewart and Schetky

With the supplementary band, or *ripieno*, the orchestra assumed large proportions. Of Taylor's own works on the program, the most important were a *New Overture,* and a *Divertimento* for orchestra, and his Violin Concerto, played by George Gillingham. In addition, there were a number of vocal numbers, sung by Miss Huntley.

In 1814, when the Vauxhall Garden in Philadelphia was opened in May for concerts and other entertainments, Taylor was engaged as organist for the opening night, and Gillingham was conductor of the orchestra. This garden was a popular resort in the summer, and even though smoking was not permitted "in or near the temple," the music and the temple and garden, "brilliantly illuminated with variegated lamps," seemed amply to justify the dollar admission. One of the entertainments for Lafayette was held at the Vauxhall Garden, when he paid us his second visit in 1825.

In the New York Public Library there are three anthems by Taylor, written and published before he came to America. These were printed in the *Cathedral Magazine* in London: *Hear my crying, O God* (Psalm 61), for two voices; *Hear, O Lord, and Consider my Complaint* (Psalm 17); and, *I will give thanks unto the Lord.* In the same library there are several songs and the libretto of a melodrama *The Rose of Arragon, or The Vigil of St. Mark,* published in 1822, for which Taylor had written music.

In addition to the Violin Concerto and instrumental works, there is a *Sonata for the pianoforte, with an accompaniment for violin,* published in 1797, "price one dollar, to be had at the music stores," and a "new symphony," which was advertised for performance at the Federal Street Theatre in Boston during the same year. As we have seen from his entertainments, Taylor composed many songs, sentimental and humorous, most of them either lost or unpublished. The Hopkinson collection in Philadelphia possesses a manuscript piece for piano *The Bells*; and printed copies of *The Wounded Sailor* and *The Philadelphia Hymn.* The Yale library at New Haven has two songs published in Carr's *Musical Miscellany—The Merry piping lad,* "a ballad in the Scot's taste," and *The Wand'ring village maid.* The Boston Public Library has a copy of Taylor's arrangement for piano, four hands, of the famous *President's March*.

Capitalizing his experience at Sadler's Wells in London, Taylor did some writing for the theatre after he came to America. In 1795 his *La Petite Piedmontese, or The Travellers Preserved*, a "serious panto-mimical ballet," was produced in Philadelphia. Two years later he supplied the music for a production of Colman's play *The Iron Chest*, which was given in Baltimore. He wrote a "serious pantomime," *La Bonne Petite Fille or The Shipwrecked Mariner Preserved*, which was performed at Philadelphia, Baltimore, and Boston. He collaborated with Reinagle in music for the Philadelphia presentation of *Pizarro, or The Spaniards in Peru* (1800), as well as in the composition of the *Monody* on the death of Washington (1799). There is also record of an educational work by Taylor, published at Carr's Musical Repository in 1797: *Divertimenti, or familiar lessons for the pianoforte, to which is prefixed a Ground for the Improvement of Young Practitioners*.

VICTOR PELISSIER first appeared in Philadelphia in 1792. This accomplished French musician had been the first horn player at the theatre in Cape François, and though his participation in concerts was largely confined to playing the French horn, his association with the orchestra of the Old American Company (which he joined a year after his arrival) led him to compose many scores for its productions, and to act as arranger and adapter of foreign ballad-operas.

Pelissier has been described as short in stature, and so nearsighted that he was almost blind. It was said that he was always a cheery person, whose thoughts were as fully occupied by notes as any banker or broker in Wall Street. Some historians have claimed that his opera *Edwin and Angelina* (presented in New York, December 19, 1796) was the first work of its kind composed in America, but it is evident that such was not the case. It is probably true that Pelissier's score, a setting of lyrics to a libretto by Elihu Hubbard Smith, had been accepted several years before Carr's *Archers* was produced April 18, 1796, but neither is entitled to the distinction. Hewitt's *Tammany* was produced in 1794, and Hopkinson's "oratorial entertainment," *The Temple of Minerva* (1781), has as much right to be considered an opera as these later works. There is not at hand sufficient evidence to designate any of the early operas as the first written on American soil.

Smith, the librettist, adapted *Edwin and Angelina* from Goldsmith. Its deliciously romantic plot was highly illogical and offered the audience many surprises. It was designed for audiences who delighted in a sentimentality that overcame stage villainy. And it at least afforded the popular actors of the day ample opportunity to display their vocal gifts in the dozen or more lyrics. Whether the libretto or the music was at fault, the work did not meet with sufficient success to warrant a second performance.

Pelissier's next work was a "piece, in one act, never performed in America," called *Ariadne Abandoned by Theseus, in the Isle of Naxos.* This was a melodrama of unknown authorship. Of the music the advertisement said:

Between the different passages spoken by the actors, will be Full Orchestral Music, expressive of each situation and passion. The music composed and managed by Pelissier.

The New York production of *Ariadne Abandoned* occurred in 1797, and it was played in Boston soon after.

In the same year John Hodgkinson produced in Boston a patriotic spectacle *The Launch, or Huzza for the Constitution*, "the Musick selected from the best Composers, with new Orchestra parts by Pelissier." The advance bulletins told that

The whole will conclude with a striking Representation of Launching the New Frigate Constitution. Boats passing and repassing on the Water. View of the River of Charleston, and the neighboring country. . . .

Two years later (1799) Pelissier offered two more scores. The first was music for William Dunlap's *Sterne's Maria, or The Vintage.* Dunlap later wrote in his *History of the American Theatre*, that though "the piece pleased and was pleasing," it was "not sufficiently attractive to keep the stage after the original performers in it were removed by those fluctuations common in theatrical establishments." Three of Pelissier's songs from *Sterne's Maria* are still in existence. In his own collection of *Columbian Melodies* (published in 1811) appeared *I laugh, I sing; Hope, gentle hope;* and *Ah! why on Quebec's bloody plain*, all from the score of the opera.

Pelissier wrote music for the performance of a "splendid allegorical, musical drama, never exhibited," called *The Fourth of July; or Temple of American Independence,* presented in New York on July 4, 1799. It was thus described in the newspaper advertisement:

[there] will be displayed (among other scenery, professedly intended to exceed any exhibition yet presented by the Theatre) a view of the lower part of Broadway, Battery, Harbor, and Shipping taken on the spot.

After the shipping shall have been saluted, a military Procession in perspective will take place, consisting of all the uniform Companies of the City, Horse, Artillery and Infantry in their respective plans, according to the order of the March.

The whole to conclude with an inside view of the *Temple of Independence* as exhibited on the Birthday of Gen. Washington. Scenery and Machinery by Mr. Ciceri—Music by Mr. Pelessier.

In 1800, Pelissier supplied music and accompaniments for the *Castle of Otranto,* which had been altered from the *Sicilian Romance.* He also arranged orchestral accompaniments for many other performances in New York, and adapted the music of other composers to the requirements of the Old American Company orchestra. In fact, he did for New York what Reinagle was doing in Philadelphia. Among the works adapted or arranged by Pelissier were: *The Deserter* (1795), with Benjamin Carr; *The Flitch of Bacon* (1796); *La Foret Noire* (1795); *Harlequin Pastry Cook* (1794); *The Haunted Tower* (1795); *Inkle and Yarico* (1796); *The Jubilee* (1800); *Lock and Key* (1799); *Maid of the Mill* (1796); *The Mountaineers* (1796); *My Grandmother* (1796); *The Mysterious Monk* (1796); *Poor Vulcan* (1796); *Robinson Crusoe* (1796); *Rosina* (1796); *The Siege of Belgrade* (1796); *The Son-in-Law* (1798); *Sophia of Brabant* (1794); *The Virgin of the Sun* (1800); *The Waterman* (1796); *Zorinski* (1798).

The only purely instrumental works by Pelissier, of which there is record, are a *Quartet* and a few occasional pieces, including a *Waltz* contained in his *Columbian Melodies,* and reprinted in a modern arrangement in the present author's *A Program of Early American Piano Music.*[3]

Like Hewitt and Taylor, BENJAMIN CARR (1768–1831) was one of the musicians who bridged the turn of the century, arriving in this

[3] New York, J. Fischer & Bro., 1931.

country in the post-revolutionary days, when concert activities were re-awakening from their early beginnings. He lived to see musical affairs in a far more advanced stage than when he had come. Carr, who arrived in Philadelphia in 1793, achieved distinction as composer, opera and concert singer, choral conductor, organist, pianist, and music publisher and dealer. He was an Englishman of breeding and culture. Born in 1768, he had received his musical education from the foremost church musicians of England, and had participated in a number of concert ventures in London.

A full-length biography of Benjamin Carr would make good reading. The man was many sided, and in his sixty-two years of life he saw much, and gave to those around him many times the value of what he absorbed. When he came to Philadelphia his first venture was the establishment of Carr's Musical Repository, claimed to be the first music store in Philadelphia. It seems, however, that this honor must be shared with the firm of Moller and Capron who opened their Philadelphia store this same summer (1793)—in fact, probably a few months earlier than Carr. Carr's activities as music publisher were important to American music, for it was through his establishment that many of the works of contemporary composers were issued, both in Philadelphia and in New York. Carr's *Musical Miscellany*, and the *Musical Journal for the Pianoforte* (distributed from Baltimore by J. Carr) were to the early nineteenth century what our modern publishers' trade-marked editions are to us today. A year after its establishment in Philadelphia, a branch of the firm was started in New York. Later this was sold to James Hewitt.

Carr's participation in concerts commenced soon after his arrival. In the spring of 1794 he appeared with Reinagle, Gillingham, and Menel as one of the directors of a series of "Amateur and Professional Concerts" at Oeller's Hotel in Philadelphia. Tickets for the concerts were sold at the Repository. On each of the four programs Carr appeared only as a singer. In the following December he made his debut as an opera singer, appearing at New York in the Old American Company's production of Arne's *Love in a Village*. The *New York Magazine's* review of the performance had this to say of Carr:

Mr. Carr made on this occasion his first appearance on our stage; and we confess, to us a very prepossessing first appearance. Good sense and modesty, united to a perfect knowledge of his profession as a musician, and a pleasing and comprehensive voice are not the only qualifications which this young gentleman possesses for the stage; he speaks with propriety, and we doubt not but practice will make him a good actor, in addition to his being an excellent singer.

In February of the following year he was engaged by Hewitt and the Van Hagens, who had dropped their competition and formed a temporary merger, as a vocalist at the City Concerts in New York. In the following December he rendered a vocal solo, and appeared as an instrumentalist by playing a pianoforte sonata. During the ensuing years his name appears frequently on Philadelphia concert programs as a vocalist, and occasionally as an instrumentalist. In 1797 he was one of the principal singers at Mrs. Grattan's "Ladies' Concerts," which this feminine impresario presented because "necessity obliges her to make this effort for the maintenance of her infant family," and for which "any subscriber on paying his subscription, will have a right to demand tickets for the unmarried part of his family."

But in spite of his evident popularity, Carr was least important as a singer. His work as church organist and his interest in choral matters, as well as his activities as a pianist, kept him in the center of Philadelphia's musical life, and finally led to his part in founding the Musical Fund Society in 1820. This organization has been to Philadelphia what the Handel and Haydn Society has been to Boston. In 1816 a musician named Charles Hupfield, and several others, endeavored to establish a society to meet each week for regular practice. It was difficult to keep a large enough group of musicians together for concerted playing, and finally it was decided to give concerts for the relief of needy musicians; "decayed musicians" they were called in the articles of incorporation. The prime object of the society was to "reform the state of neglect into which the beautiful art of music had fallen."

The first concert of the Musical Fund Society, at which Carr was one of the choral conductors, was given April 24, 1821, and repeated May 8. In addition to a number of choral works, for which Carr arranged the orchestral accompaniments, the program marked what has been claimed for many years as the first American performance of Beethoven's First Symphony. It now seems probable that the first American performance of this symphony was that given at Lexington,

Kentucky, November 12, 1817, under the direction of Anton Philip Heinrich. (In each case possibly only the first movement, however.)

But it is as a composer that we are chiefly concerned with Carr, and fortunately many of his works are extant. His music, like that of Hewitt and others of his contemporaries, represents a tendency that is definitely apparent in our music of today. Students of the *sob-song* will find its beginnings in this eighteenth–nineteenth-century literature. Yet for all this, Carr did not always descend to sentimentality, and in his editing of standard works he showed himself a capable musician, with powers of discretion.

He has been known for the production of his opera *The Archers, or Mountaineers, of Switzerland,* erroneously termed "the first American opera." This work was produced by the Old American Company in New York, April 18, 1796, and belongs to the English ballad-opera type. Carr's score to this adaptation of Schiller's *Wilhelm Tell* antedates Rossini's setting by thirty-three years. The piece met with gratifying success and was repeated on numerous occasions. Of the music to this drama only a few pieces have been preserved, but so charming as to cause regret at the loss of the others. The *Rondo* from the Overture to *The Archers* was copyrighted in 1813 as No. 7 of the *Musical Miscellany,* and an extremely graceful song *Why, Huntress, Why* appeared in Carr's *Musical Journal.* There is also *A Fragment* (There liv'd in Altdorf City fair) to be found in the second book of *Elegant Extracts* for the German flute or violin (1796); and a *March in The Archers* occurs in *Military Amusement* (1796) which presumably comes from this opera.

Like many of his colleagues, Carr composed a piece in honor of Washington when the national hero died in 1799. The *Dead March and Monody* was first performed at the Lutheran Church in Philadelphia. When published it was advertised as "being part of the music selected for funeral honors to our late illustrious cheif [sic] General George Washington. Composed for the occasion and respectfully dedicated to the Senate of the United States by their obedt. humble servt. B. Carr. . . ."

Carr's songs and ballads have survived him in abundance, and the New York Public Library, and the private collection of Mr. Arthur Billings Hunt in Brooklyn, New York, are among those possessing many of these historically valuable pieces. Taken from their rather thin, tinkling setting in the accompaniment, and arranged in the manner of our modern ballad songs, these lyrics are in many cases quite as effective in their climaxes as the lyric ballads of today. Carr showed his experience on the concert platform. *Ellen, Arise* is singularly effective; sopranos must have won great applause with its high *A*. *The Soldier's Dream* is somewhat bombastic, but *Mary Will Smile* and the *Hymn of Eve* are Handelian in the chaste simplicity of their melodic line. *Noah's Dove* is altogether a charming song, with a compelling power in its sequential phrases. He wrote a song that has so far escaped the notice of those who sponsor toothpaste radio programs. *Thy Smiles are all Decaing* [sic], *Love,* is its charming title, and in its verses the hero swears that he will continue to love his lady, even though her smiles do actually decay, her "lip shed its sweetness," her "form lose its fleetness."

Mr. Muller's collection at Closter had a curious Carr item; a lengthy piece for the piano called *The History of England, from the close of the Saxon Heptarchy to the Declaration of American Independence, in familiar verse, adapted to music by B. Carr, Op. XI.* An explanatory note under the title reads as follows:

The following Poetical sketch of events, so intimately connected with our own History, being adapted to Music of the most familiar kind, has been consider'd by several, as a means of improvement for Juvenile Students in History and Music. A Publication of this nature has already appeared in England; but unfit for the purpose intended—the Poetry being mere doggerel, and the Music (tho good) extraneous in its modulation and too difficult of execution to be of service to young pupils, a literary friend has kindly supplied new Poetry—The idea being of using known airs of appropriate title and character for the vocal parts, as well as illustrative symphonies, is taken from T. Carr's Composition to, and arrangement of Roscoe's beautiful little Poem of the Butterfly's Ball.

N.B.—Should this humble effort to combine improvement in other branches of education with the practice of music be received with approbation, other matters of the same kind may be given in some future numbers.

To the biographer, the most interesting and helpful relics of Benjamin Carr are three manuscript books, in his own handwriting. One of these, devoted to sacred music, is in the New York Public Library;

the other two, chiefly secular, are in Mr. Hunt's possession. These books were evidently used by Carr not only for original composition, but also for editing the works of others for publication.

He also published instrumental pieces, a collection of Masses, Litanies, Hymns, Anthems, Psalms, and Motets, and did additional writing for the stage in Philadelphia and New York productions.

After his death in 1831, the Musical Fund Society erected a monument to his memory in St. Peter's Church, Philadelphia. The inscription is a testimonial to his achievements and to his character:

BENJAMIN CARR

a distinguished professor of music
died May 24, 1831, aged 62 years.

Charitable, without ostentation,
faithful and true in his friendship,
with the intelligence of a man
he united the simplicity of a child.

In testimony of the high esteem in which he
was held, this monument is erected by
his friends and associates of the
Musical Fund Society of Philadelphia.

There were many other early immigrants who played an active part in our musical life at this time, and who wrote music of which we have definite knowledge. One of these, H. B. VICTOR, dates back to the Revolution, for he arrived in Philadelphia in 1774. Announcing that he had been "musician to her late Royal Highness, the Princess of Wales, and organist at St. George in London," he offered to instruct the "musical gentry in general . . . on the harpsichord, forte piano, violin, German flute, etc. and in the thorough bass both in theory and practice." The versatile gentleman then sought to startle his public by advertising a concert at which he would play two instruments of his own invention: the one a "Tromba doppia con tympana," on which he was to play first and second trumpet and a pair of annexed kettledrums with the feet, all at once; the other, a "Cymbaline d'amour" which resembled "the musical glasses played by harpsichord keys, never subject to come out of tune."

But it is not as a freak that Victor is most interesting. In 1778 he advertised for publication a work which was a forerunner of our modern
courses or *methods*. This was *A New Composition of Music, consisting
of four separate books, viz.:*

The *Compleat Instructor* for the violin, flute, guitar and harpsichord.
Containing the easiest and best method for learners to obtain a proficiency;
with some useful directions, lessons, graces, etc. *By H. B. Victor.*

To which is added, A favourite collection of airs, marches, minuets, etc.,
now in vogue; with some useful pieces for two violins, etc. etc.

JOHN BENTLEY has already been mentioned as the manager of the
Philadelphia City Concerts in 1783. In 1785 he became harpsichordist
of the Old American Company, and "selected and composed" the music
for several of their productions: *Genii of the Rock, The Cave of Enchantment,* and *The Touchstone.* He also figured in the Old American
Company as an occasional pantomimist.

Through a controversy which was aired in the newspapers, and which
is strikingly similar to the Turner-Morgan dispute in Boston, Bentley's
name is associated with WILLIAM BROWN, the composer who published
Three Rondos for the Pianoforte or Harpsichord, "composed and
humbly dedicated to the Honorable Francis Hopkinson, Esqr."

This Brown, something of a trouble-maker, was the first of the musicians to appear in New York after the war, and in August, 1783, he
gave New York the last concert it was to hear during the British regime.
He then went to Philadelphia, where he offered two concerts at the
City Tavern in October, "having been prevailed upon by several gentlemen to continue his stay in Philadelphia, and being inclined to gratify them." In addition to benefit concerts he seems to have participated in Bentley's Subscription Concerts, for in the *Pennsylvania Journal* of February 12, 1785, both Bentley and Henri Capron saw fit to
tell the public their side of a dispute to which Brown had probably
been treating his friends verbally. It seems that Brown had accused
Bentley and Capron of declining to assist at his benefit concerts. Bentley addressed his "card" directly to *Mr. Brown:*

. . . And first, Sir, allow me to enquire, whether at any time, you desired
my assistance at your concert; nay, whether by refusing the loan of the

harpsichord usually lent, you did not give me room to suppose it was neither wished nor expected?

That you raised an opinion in the public that I occasioned the absence of two performers, is certain; but as truth is contrary to that opinion, I must request you to declare the grounds upon which so invidious an insinuation was founded? The gentlemen alluded to, for reasons which I have no right to control, objected to any further correspondence with Mr. Brown, on footing of favour.

. . . here let me recall to your remembrance your own conduct upon our first acquaintance. Did you not live free of every expence in my house for the whole of last winter, and some months after the concerts were closed? Did this induce you to perform without a premium . . . ? No, Sir, You were supported at my cost; your demand of three pounds for every night's performance was paid; and . . . you were ungrateful enough to traduce me in private, and to attempt my ruin with a most respectable character, whose friendship I had essentially experienced. . . .

Mr. Capron's card appeared above Mr. Bentley's in the same paper:

Mr. Capron being informed that the motives maliciously assigned for his absenting himself from Mr. Brown's benefit concert, may operate to his prejudice; and being solicitous on all occasions to evince the highest respect for the public, he begs leave to observe that he would chearfully have contributed his abilities to the entertainment of the evening, had Mr. Brown condescended to make the request.

. . . In truth Mr. Capron has acquitted himself of every obligation to Mr. Brown, and . . . he could never be again induced to enter into an intercourse of favours: . . . surely it is sufficient triumph . . . that every concert for the benefit of that Gentleman opens a scene of considerable profit, while the only opportunity which the public has had to assist Mr. Capron, scarcely supplied the means to defray his expenses.

If Brown was personally a troublesome character, his abilities as a flutist and musician must have been of a high order, for Capron soon again engaged him for concerts, and later Brown joined Reinagle and Capron in the management of the Subscription Concerts.

HENRI CAPRON was one of the most prominent of the French musicians who came to the United States. He first appeared in Philadelphia (1785), and soon became active in the management of subscription concerts both in Philadelphia and New York. As a cellist he was a

member of the Old American Company orchestra. Among his compositions were a *New Contredance*, a particularly attractive *Favorite Song*
(*Softly as the breezes blowing*) and a "new song" *Delia*. After spending the years 1788 to 1792 in New York he settled permanently in
Philadelphia in 1794, where he became the principal of a French boarding school. In 1793 he kept a music store in Philadelphia with JOHN
CHRISTOPHER MOLLER, a composer, organist, pianist, and editor, who
had appeared in New York as a harpsichordist in 1790.

Moller came to Philadelphia immediately after his concerts in New
York, and took part in the City Concerts both as manager and performer. On many of his programs he appeared with his daughter, a
musical prodigy. In addition to being organist of Zion Church in Philadelphia, he entered partnership with Capron in the music store, and
combined with it a music school. In 1796, Moller moved back to New
York and took Hewitt's place in the management of the City Concerts
with the Van Hagens. When Van Hagen left for Boston, Moller made
an unsuccessful attempt to continue the subscription series.

He was a talented musician, and his compositions had considerable
merit. The New York Library possesses the violin part of six *Sonatas
for the forte piano or harpsichord, with a violin or violoncello accompaniment*, which Moller composed and published in London before
coming to America. *Moller and Capron's Monthly Numbers*, a collection of music published in 1793, of which four issues are still extant,
contained several compositions of Moller, among them a graceful
though innocuous *Sinfonia* and a *Rondo*. He wrote also an *Overture*,
and a *Quartetto* for "harmonica [this was Benjamin Franklin's *ar-
monica*, or musical glasses], two tenors, and violoncello." In addition
there was a *Duetti*, for piano and clarinet, advertised for performance
at one of the 1792 City Concerts in Philadelphia.

ALEXANDER JUHAN (1765–1845) "junior, master of music," who
appeared in Philadelphia in 1783, was probably the son of a James
Juhan, who had come to Charleston as a music teacher in 1771, and
who had announced himself in 1786 at Philadelphia as the maker of
the "Great North American Forte Piano." Some authorities link Juhan
the elder with the Mr. *Joan* who gave the "reading" of *The Beggar's
Opera* in Boston in 1770. Alexander Juhan (believed to have been
born in Halifax and brought to Boston in 1768) was a violinist who

was for a time one of the managers of the City Concerts in Philadelphia, and as a composer he advertised in Charleston (where he lived
for a year or two before his return to Philadelphia in 1792) for subscriptions to *A Set of Six Sonatas*, for the pianoforte or harpsichord,
"three with an accompaniment for the flute or violin, and three with
out"; and a book of twelve songs, with an accompaniment for the same
instrument.

Juhan's career provides interest because of his part in another of
the controversies that seemed often to trouble the peace of early American music. This time the dispute was based partly on artistic rather than
on wholly personal grounds. The trouble came from Juhan's position
as conductor of the orchestra at the concerts of ANDREW ADGATE
(? –1793), a Philadelphian who founded in 1784 an *Institution for
the Encouragement of Church Music*, and in the following year established a *Free School for Spreading the Knowledge of Vocal Music*
—which developed into the *Uranian Academy* in 1787.

Adgate was to Philadelphia what Tuckey had been to New York,
and what Selby was to Boston. The elaborate "plan" of the Uranian
Society, published five days after the Constitutional Convention had
first assembled, was the first document on record that urged the necessity and advantage of having music "form a part of every system of
education." Philadelphia heard a number of Mr. Adgate's "Vocal
Music Concerts" during 1784 and 1785, at which such musicians as
Brown and Juhan furnished instrumental numbers. On May 4, 1786,
the year of Selby's mammoth concert for prison relief in Boston (January 10), Adgate, no doubt spurred by the review of the Boston concert that had appeared in the *Pennsylvania Herald*, offered Philadelphians *A Grand Concert of Sacred Music*, for the benefit of the Pennsylvania Hospital, Philadelphia Dispensary, and the Poor, for whom
there has, hitherto, been no regular provision made. There was a chorus
of two hundred and thirty voices, and an orchestra of fifty pieces conducted by Mr. Juhan. Aside from Handel's *Hallelujah* Chorus, and
an Anthem by A. Williams (probably Aaron Williams, an English
psalmodist), the vocal numbers were principally devoted to American
composers—Lyon, Billings, and Tuckey.

The *Pennsylvania Packet*, in its extended review of the concert, had
this to say of the conducting:

To the skill and attention of Mr. Adgate, in training and instructing the voices, and of Mr. Juhan, in arranging and leading the instruments, may be attributed that forcible and uniform effect so manifestly produced throughout the exhibition.

Juhan evidently had a different opinion of Mr. Adgate's share in the proceedings, for in the following year, prior to the first concert of the new Uranian Society, he wrote to the *Pennsylvania Packet* (April 5, 1787):

. . . the subscriber thinks it his duty to state the reasons that have induced him to decline any part in the concert, intended to be performed . . . the 12th instant.

The applause of some . . . has certainly so far elevated the subscriber in his own opinion that he rates himself superior to the instruction of a person, who, with little knowledge in the theory, is confined in the practice of music to the humble province of Solfa. . . .

Another and very forcible reason for the subscriber's conduct upon this occasion, is the neglect of consulting the principal performers as to the pieces of music, and the arrangement of the band. . . . It would surely therefore have improved the general effect of the entertainment and could not have been considered as a very extraordinary indulgence, had those who were best able to determine upon the respective powers of the performers, been invited to select the music and to suggest what could be attempted with the greatest probability of success. . . .

Juhan's "card" closed with the statement that his work at Adgate's concerts had entailed great sacrifices, interfered with his teaching, and the necessary exertions had injured his health. Adgate's reply was printed in the same paper, two days later:

Before the Plan of the Uranian Academy was drawn . . . I mentioned to Mr. Juhan that I had it in view to establish an institution, at which the poor might be instructed in church music, free of expense; and, as the first measure, . . . to have a concert performed. . . . I introduced the subject that I might have the opportunity of consulting him thereon and engaging him as a principal in carrying the concert into effect. His answer to my proposition . . . was immediate and unequivocal! *"We have agreed not to play any more for the poor."* This peremptory declaration . . . foreclosed effectually all consultation. I believed Mr. Juhan, and, in consequence, took my measures, independently of him, as well as I was able . . . he had an

THE YANKEE'S RETURN FROM CAMP.

FATHER and I went down to camp,
  Along with Captain Gooding;
There we see the men and boys
  As thick as hasty-pudding.

CHORUS.

Yankee doodle keep it up,
  Yankee doodle dandy;
Mind the music and the step,
  And with the girls be handy.

And there we see a thousand men,
  As rich as 'Squire David;
And what they wasted every day,
  I wish it could be saved.
    Yankee doodle, &c.

The 'lasses they eat every day,
  Would keep a house a winter;
They have as much that I'll be bound,
  They eat it when they're a mind to.
    Yankee doodle, &c.

And there we see a swamping gun,
  Large as a log of maple,
Upon a duced little cart,
  A load for father's cattle.
    Yankee doodle, &c.

And every time they shoot it off,
  It takes a horn of powder;
It makes a noise like father's gun,
  Only a nation louder.
    Yankee doodle, &c.

I went as nigh to one myself,
  As 'Siah's under-pinning;
And father went as nigh again,
  I thought the deuce was in him.
    Yankee doodle, &c.

Cousin Simon grew so bold,
  I thought he would have cock'd it;
It scar'd me so I streak'd it off,
  And hung by father's pocket.
    Yankee doodle, &c.

But Captain Davis has a gun,
  He kind of clap'd his hand on't;
And stuck a crooked stabbing iron,
  Upon the little end on't.
    Yankee doodle, &c.

And there I see a pumpkin shell,
  As big as mother's bason;
And every time they touch'd it off,
  They scamper'd like the nation.
    Yankee doodle, &c.

I see a little barrel too,
  The heads were made of leather,
They knock'd upon it with little clubs,
  And call'd the folks together.
    Yankee doodle, &c.

And there was Captain WASHINGTON,
  And gentlefolks about him;
They say he's grown so tarnal proud,
  He will not ride without 'em.
    Yankee doodle, &c.

He got him on his meeting clothes,
  Upon a slapping stallion;
He set the world along in rows,
  In hundreds and in millions.
    Yankee doodle, &c.

The flaming ribbons in their hats,
  They look'd so tearing fine, ah,
I wanted plaguily to get,
  To give to my Jemima.
    Yankee doodle, &c.

I see another snarl of men,
  A digging graves, they told me,
So tarnal long, so tarnal deep,
  They 'tended they should hold me.
    Yankee doodle, &c.

It scar'd me so, I hook'd it off,
  Nor stopp'd, as I remember;
Nor turn'd about till I got home,
  Lock'd up in mother's chamber.
    Yankee doodle, &c.

Sold, wholesale and retail, by L. DEMING, No. 62, Hanover Street, 2d door from Friend st. Boston.

An Early Nineteenth-Century Broadside of *Yankee Doodle*
(See pages 113–118)

Francis Scott Key

(See pages 122–124)

undoubted right to be the sole judge of what would contribute most essentially to his *interest* and *health*.

Consequently, the Uranian Concert, on April 12, was given without the assistance of either Mr. Juhan or Mr. Brown, who, known to be troublesome, may have been in league with Juhan in the dispute. The program again contained works of Tuckey, Lyon, and Billings, as well as those of Handel, Arne, and Arnold. Further Uranian concerts and "concerts of sacred music for benevolent purposes" may be traced through the following years. Adgate died in 1793 during the yellow fever epidemic, and left behind him several publications: *Lessons for the Uranian Society* and *Uranian Instructions* (1785–87); *Select Psalms and Hymns* (1787); *Rudiments of Music* (1788); *Selection of Sacred Harmony* (1788).

The violinist who took Juhan's place as soloist at the First Uranian Concert was PHILIP PHILE (? –1793), a composer who played a concerto of his own on the occasion. Phile had come to Philadelphia before 1784, when he appeared in a concert advertised for his benefit. Soon he was associated with the Old American Company orchestra, and until his death in 1793 he was to be found either in New York or Philadelphia, participating in concerts and in the orchestras of the theatres. Phile is important historically because of his authorship of the famous *President's March*, now known as the musical setting of *Hail Columbia*, the words by Joseph Hopkinson, son of Francis Hopkinson. Phile also wrote a piece called *Harmony Music*, which was announced for performance at Gray's Gardens, a Philadelphia summer retreat where the Concerts of "harmonial music" were rendered by two clarinets, two French horns, two bassoons, and one flute.

The name of PHILIP ROTH (? –1804) is linked with that of Phile, because Roth was formerly supposed by some to have been the composer of the *President's March*. Roth's residence in America dates back to 1771, when he appeared in a concert for the benefit of John M'Lean in Philadelphia. He was presented as "Master of the Band belonging to his Majesty's Royal Regiment of North British Fusiliers," and his contribution to the program was an *Overture*, composed for the occasion. From 1785 to 1804, the year of his death, he lived in Philadelphia as a music teacher. His advertisements showed that he was fully as versatile as any of his colleagues, for he taught all kinds of Instrumental Music in the shortest manner [short cuts to knowledge are not altogether a purely twentieth century demand], viz: Harpsichord or Piano Forte, Guitar, Flute, Hautboy, Clarinet, Bassoon, French Horn, Harp and Thorough-Bass, which is the Ground of Music. . . .

William McKoy described him as

of middle size and height. His face was truly German in expression; dark grey eyes and bushy eyebrows, round pointed nose, prominent lips, and parted chin. He took snuff immoderately, having his ruffles and vest usually sprinkled with grains of rappee. He was considered an eccentric and a kind of drole.

GEORGE SCHETKY (1776–1831) was a Scotch musician who, according to Madeira, was a nephew of Reinagle. Madeira said that he came to Philadelphia to live with his uncle in 1792. This date is incorrect, for Schetky appeared as a cellist on Philadelphia concert programs as early as 1787. About 1800 he was in partnership with Carr in the music publishing business, and later became one of the prominent founders of the Musical Fund Society. His name appears frequently on concert programs of this period as the author of the military band arrangement of Kotzwara's *Battle of Prague*.

MRS. MARY ANN POWNALL (1751–1796), who had been known in England as Mrs. Wrighten, was one of the most popular actresses and singers in the Old American Company. She first came to Boston in 1792, for the American Company was playing at the Federal Street Theatre that season. She had splendid dramatic and vocal gifts and was also prolific as a composer. She wrote both words and music of many songs that were featured in concerts and in operas and plays. Among them were *Advice to the Ladies of Boston*, and *Address to the Ladies of Charleston; Jemmy of the Glen* (copy in the Library of Congress); *Mrs. Pownal's Adres* (sic), in behalf of French musicians, "delivered on her benefit concert night to a very crowded audience: to which are added, Pastoral songs; written by herself at an early period of life," *On by the spur of valeur; Kiss me now or never; Poor Tom Bowling; Italian Song; My Poll and my partner Joe; A smile from the girl of my heart; 'Bly the Colin* and *Cottage Boy*.

Mrs. Pownall also paid homage to the President with a song, *Wash-*

ington. The New York Library possesses a copy of *Primroses,* "a favorite song by Mrs. Pownall, with additions and alterations by a lady." She died in Charleston in 1796, following the shock she received when her daughter eloped with a pantomimist named Alexander Placide.

A violoncellist and composer named DEMARQUE may have been one of the musicians who fled with Pelissier from Cape François and arrived in America in 1793. At any rate, he first appeared in that year as a concert artist in Baltimore, and soon afterwards became a prominent member of the Wignell and Reinagle orchestra at the Chestnut Street Theatre in Philadelphia. He also played in the City Theatre Orchestra in Charleston. Demarque wrote several pieces for the cello, one of them a Concerto, and he also composed music for several pantomimes: *The Elopement, Harlequin Shipwreck'd,* the *Miraculous Mill,* and *Rural Revels.*

Nor may we forget JOHN HENRY SCHMIDT, the Dutch organist, composer, and music dealer, who first came to New York in 1793, and was later organist at St. Peter's in Philadelphia. Whether or not he was the same Mr. Smith who had offered lectures in Philadelphia in 1788, "interspersed with music and singing," he nevertheless composed a Sonata which he advertised with this comprehensive announcement:

His [Schmidt's] easy Sonata for beginners, consisting in a larghetto, minuet and trio, and Yankee Doodle, turned into a fashionable rondo, may be had of him at No. 50 Green street, where he has furnished rooms to let.

As the century closes, the flirtation and the courtship end. Euterpe enters the trials of early married life, for America has definitely taken her to its bosom and knows her charms. In the wilderness she will clear the forest.

Her way has not been easy. The early New Englanders would admit her only to their churches, and then only upon pledge of what they considered the utmost decorum. Philadelphians loved her, but the Quakers would have none of her themselves, and tried to interfere in her friendship with their broader-minded neighbors.

But youth will have its way, and even though it was necessary for new arrivals to point out Euterpe's perennial charms and beauty, Hopkinson the aristocrat, Lyon the clergyman, and Billings the tanner who awakened Boston, all contrived to keep the Goddess on native soil. And then Selby in Boston, Tuckey in New York, and Adgate in Philadelphia showed the joys of choral music. Reinagle, Carr, Hewitt, Taylor, and their fellows came from Europe to tell of Euterpe's doings abroad, and to show how her gifts might be used. These are names and faces we shall meet in later chapters, for their lives and influence do not end in this century, though it was in the eighteenth century that they were most important, for their coming hastened Euterpe's conquest of America.

PART TWO

1800–1860

EUTERPE CLEARS THE FOREST

CHAPTER FOUR

Our First National Airs

I. YANKEE DOODLE

OUR early national airs have survived in spite of the many unkind things that have been said about them. It is easy to pick flaws in any one of them, yet they are all so vital that they fire our emotions and force us to sing with the crowd. Relegate *Yankee Doodle* to the category of jingle, *Hail Columbia* to mere bombast, and cry against the impossibly wide vocal range of the *Star-Spangled Banner*, yet the songs persist. They were not intended as national anthems when they were written; no patriotic organizations commissioned their composers to write them, and none of their authors realized how far his influence would reach.

Many pretty stories are attached to our national ballads, some of them so fanciful that it is a pity to explode them. Yet tireless researchers have been at work, and it becomes a duty to consult them and to select between the true and the false, where possible. *Yankee Doodle* has caused more quarrels between historians and scholars than any of our songs, for this impertinent, jolly little tune has thumbed its nose at many a dignified sage, and grayed hundreds of hairs by hiding its origin.

The controversy has covered about everything a song can possess— its name, its words, and its tune, and as yet little has been settled. When O. G. Sonneck was chief of the Music Division of the Library of Congress, he was commissioned to examine all of the traditions regarding the origin of *Yankee Doodle*, as well as our other airs, and to decide which were right and which were wrong. As far as *Yankee Doodle* was concerned, he summed up his examination of all available evidence by writing: "The origin of *Yankee Doodle* remains as mysterious as ever, unless it be deemed a positive result to have eliminated almost every theory thus far advanced and thus by the process of elimination to have paved the way for an eventual solution of the 'puzzle.' " [1] Sonneck may not have been altogether pessimistic—he apparently expected further evidence to turn up. Unfortunately, the almost forty years that have passed since his report was published have produced nothing conclusive.

Today the term *Yankee* means a New Englander, a term of whimsical approval when used by his friends, and one of derision when uttered by his less enthusiastic countrymen from the South. Exactly where the word came from and what it meant is a mystery, though there are plenty to tell of their theories. Some would have it the Indians' corruption of the word "English," or if you prefer French, "Anglais." Even Washington Irving's satirical *Diedrich Knickerbocker's History of New York* has been taken seriously when it suggests that

the simple aborigines of the land . . . discovering that they [the settlers] were a lively, good-humoured race of men . . . gave them the name of *Yanokies*, which . . . signifies silent men—a waggish appellation, since shortened into the familiar epithet of *Yankees*, which they retain unto the present day.

Friends of the *Yankees* claim that back in 1713 the word was used as a superlative of excellence. A "Yankee" horse or a "Yankee" team denoted the last word in fine horse flesh. One etymologist has gone so far as to claim that the word *Yankee* was a corruption of "Yorkshire." But whether it meant good or evil, and from whatever source it may have been derived, it was a far from complimentary term when used by the British just before the Revolution. It was hurled at the colonists with the utmost scorn by the British commanding officer at the Boston Massacre.

Doodle is not quite so baffling, though the reader may still choose the theory that pleases him best, and have as good a chance at winning as his neighbor. The term may be traced in English dramatic literature as far back as 1629, when one of the characters in *The Lover's Melancholy* shouts, "Vanish, doodles, vanish!" Possibly the word is a corruption of *do little*, and means a simpleton or a silly. Another theory holds that it is derived from "tootle," which, in turn, springing from

[1] *Report on The Star-Spangled Banner, Hail Columbia, America, Yankee Doodle.* Washington, Library of Congress, 1909.

the "tooting" into German flutes that was such a popular occupation of eighteenth-century gentlemen, would indicate that *Yankee Doodle* was a purely instrumental tune at first, and that the many different sets of words were added later. In other words, the *Yankee Doodle* was the Yankee air that was "tootled" on the flute. This theory has some logic to support it. Most of the early printed versions had no words, and the very diversity of the later verses suggests that it was first known as an instrumental air.

Theories regarding the origin of the tune are more numerous than those pertaining to the title. Few have survived critical examination. The legend that it was sung in the time of Charles I and of Cromwell cannot be proved; the tunes from these times bear no relation to our *Yankee Doodle*. The lines

> Lucy Locket lost her locket
> Kitty Fisher found it

show an early nineteenth-century *use* of the tune, rather than its origin. It could hardly have been composed during the Revolution for it is one of the tunes mentioned in Andrew Barton's *The Disappointment*, in 1767. Suppositions that it is of Spanish, Dutch, Hungarian, and German origin are highly improbable. The burden of proof is on the claimants.

While there are contemporary references to *Yankee Doodle* as early as 1767, its first known appearance in print did not occur until 1782, when it appeared in James Aird's *Selection of Scotch, English, Irish and Foreign Airs, for the fife, violin or German flute,* published in Glasgow. The discovery of this first printed version was made by Mr. Frank Kidson, who believes that the tune may be of American origin, for the same volume contains several "Virginia" airs, a *Negro Jig,* and other tunes from America. It was probably first printed in America as part of Benjamin Carr's popular *Federal Overture,* composed in 1794 and published in 1795. The *Overture* was a potpourri of such airs as *Yankee Doodle, La Carmagnole, Caira,* the *Marseillaise Hymn, Oh, Dear, What Can the Matter Be,* and others.

Several stories center around the French-Indian War, principally with the army of General Amherst. An early account from *Farmer & Moore's Literary Journal* (1824) tells the following story:

. . . the British army lay encamped in the summer of 1755, on the eastern bank of the Hudson, a little south of the city of Albany. . . . In the early part of June the eastern troops (Colonial) began to pour in, company after company, and such a motley assemblage of men never before thronged together on such an occasion. It would . . . have relaxed the gravity of an anchorite to have seen the descendants of the Puritans making through the streets of our ancient city to take their station on the left of the British army, some with long coats, some with short coats, and some with no coats at all. . . . Their march, their accoutrements, and the whole arrangement of their troops furnished material of amusement to the wits of the British army. Among the club of wits that belonged to the British army there was a physician attached to the staff, by the name of *Doctor Schackburg*, who combined with the science of the surgeon the skill and talents of a musician. To please Brother Jonathan he composed a tune, and, with much gravity, recommended it to the officers as one of the most celebrated airs of martial musick. The joke took, to the no small amusement of the British Corps. Brother Jonathan exclaimed that it was a "nation fine," and in a few days nothing was heard in the Provincial camp but "Yankee Doodle"!

With characteristic thoroughness, Sonneck analyzed this theory in his report, tracing Dr. Shuckburg's (this is the proper spelling) probable whereabouts throughout this entire period. He found it extremely unlikely that Shuckburg was either in Albany in the summer of 1755, or attached to General Amherst's army. It is possible, however, that the Doctor was with General Abercrombie's division when it was encamped on the Van Rensselaer estate near Albany, in 1758, and it is plausible that he should have written humorous *Yankee Doodle* verses to an existing familiar tune. Which of the many sets of verses he wrote cannot be determined.

There is one fact in the history of *Yankee Doodle* that may be accepted without reservation. It was used by the British to make fun of the Yankees, and later adopted by the Yankees it taunted as their own song. One of the favorite pastimes of the British troops was to gather in front of the New England churches and sing *Yankee Doodle* as the congregations were singing their psalms. When Lord Percy's troops marched out of Boston on an April night in 1775, bound for Lexington to aid in the capture of John Hancock and Samuel Adams, they kept step to the strains of *Yankee Doodle*. When the colonials routed British troops at Concord, they immediately appropriated the song as their own, and since then it has been the exclusive property of Americans.

Tradition has it that when Cornwallis surrendered at Yorktown and the British band played *The World Turned Upside Down*, the American band replied with *Yankee Doodle*. Unfortunately, this incident is apparently mentioned only in later accounts, and its truth cannot be established by any contemporary evidence that has as yet come to light. As for the British playing *The World Turned Upside Down*, that story was widely circulated by John Fiske in *The American Revolution*, published in 1891, so it, too, is in the realm of legend. A poem with that title appeared in *The Gentleman's Magazine* in 1767 (vol. 36, page 140), stating that it was to be sung to the old English air *Derry Down*. Unfortunately, the verses do not fit satisfactorily any known version of that tune.

It is probable that the lines containing *Yankee* and *Doodle* did not appear in England until considerably after 1770, though they were fairly current in America by 1767. The verse that is best known today:

> Yankee Doodle came to town
> Riding on a pony
> Stuck a feather in his cap
> And called it macaroni

may have had an origin which had nothing to do with the *Yankee Doodle* of colonial America. Katharine Elwes Thomas, in *The Real Personages of Mother Goose*,[2] states that the original Yankee Doodle was Prince Rupert. Accordingly, if the Yankee Doodle of the Macaroni was actually from Mother Goose, then he had no connection with our tune until much later. And if "Yankee" used to be "Nanky," then the jingle is not even the origin of the title.

About 1775, when John Hancock was the bane of the British, this verse appeared:

> Yankee Doodle came to town
> For to buy a firelock:
> We will tar and feather him
> And so we will John Hancock.

An accompanying illustration shows a broadside of *Yankee Doodle* printed in Boston about 1835. For many years this was the current ver-

[2] New York: Lothrop, Lee & Shepard, 1930.

sion of *Yankee Doodle,* and some writers connect it with Dr. Shuckburg. It is not likely that this doggerel goes back as far as 1758, and
Sonneck inclined to the belief that it originated in the vicinity of the
"Provincial Camp" (near Cambridge) in 1775 and 1776. George
Washington's arrival at this camp July 2, 1775, after he had been appointed commander-in-chief of the American Army, would account for
the reference to *Captain* Washington.

But whatever the controversies, whatever words were sung at certain
times, and whatever the real origin of the tune, the description contained in one of the stanzas is indisputable:

> It suits for feasts, it suits for fun;
> And just as well for fighting.

2. HAIL COLUMBIA

While *Yankee Doodle* was associated principally with the Revolution, *Hail Columbia* had its origin in the war we almost had with
France in 1798. The French Revolution had broken out nine years
before, and in 1793, France was at war with England and Prussia. The
anti-Federalist party in America favored our supporting the French,
but President Washington kept us neutral. When John Adams was
inaugurated in 1797, matters had come to a crisis. The French government had so insulted our ministers and violated our rights, that by
1798 an actual state of war existed with France, though it was never
formally declared by Congress.

It was at this time that *Hail Columbia* came into being. The words
were written by JOSEPH HOPKINSON, a young man of twenty-eight, the
son of Francis Hopkinson, our first native composer. Hopkinson has
told the story of the song himself:

"Hail Columbia" was written in the summer of 1798, when war with
France was thought to be inevitable. Congress was then in session in Philadelphia, debating upon that important subject, and acts of hostility had
actually taken place. The contest between England and France was still
raging, and the people of the United States were divided into parties for the
one side or the other, some thinking that policy and duty required us to
espouse the cause of "republican France" as she was called, while others were

for connecting ourselves with England, under the belief that she was the great preservative power of good principles and safe government. The violation of our rights by both belligerents was forcing us from the wise and just policy of President Washington, which was to do equal justice to both but to part with neither, and to preserve an honest and strict neutrality between them. The prospect of a rupture with France was exceedingly offensive to the portion of the people who espoused her cause, and the violence of the spirit of party had never risen higher, I think not so high, in our country, as it did at that time upon that question.

The theatre was then open in our city [Philadelphia]. A young man belonging to it [Gilbert Fox], whose talent was high as a singer, was about to take a benefit. I had known him when he was at school. On this acquaintance he called on me one Saturday afternoon, his benefit being announced for the following Monday. His prospects were very disheartening; but he said that if he could get a patriotic song adapted to the "President's March" he did not doubt a full house; that the poets of the theatrical corps had been trying to accomplish it, but had not succeeded. I told him I would try what I could do for him. He came the next afternoon, and the song, such as it is, was ready for him. The object of the author was to get up an American spirit which should be independent of, and above the interests, passion and policy of both belligerents, and look and feel exclusively for our honor and rights. No allusion is made to France or England, or the quarrel between them, or to the question of which was most in fault in their treatment of us. Of course the song found favor with both parties, for both were American, at least neither could disown the sentiments and feelings it indicated. Such is the history of this song, which has endured infinitely beyond the expectation of the author, as it is beyond any merit it can boast of except that of being truly and exclusively patriotic in its sentiment and spirit.

The advertisements of the benefit were designed to arouse the curiosity of the public:

Mr. Fox's night. On Wednesday Evening, April 25. By Desire will be presented . . . a Play, interspersed with Songs in three Acts, called *The Italian Monk* . . . after which an entire *New Song* (written by a Citizen of Philadelphia) to the tune of the "President's March" will be sung by Mr. Fox; accompanied by the Full Band and the following *Grand Chorus:*

> Firm united let us be
> Rallying around our Liberty
> As a band of brothers join'd
> Peace and Safety we shall find!

Two days after the performance, Benjamin Carr, then a music publisher in Philadelphia, advertised publication of the song:

. . . the very New Federal Song, written to the tune of the President's March, by J. Hopkinson, Esq. And sung by M. Fox, at the New Theatre with great applause, ornamented with a very elegant portrait of the President.

For many years there was a lively controversy as to which of existing editions was the first, particularly since some of them were "ornamented with a very elegant portrait" of George Washington, and others with an eagle. In 1920 a copy was discovered bearing a portrait of John Adams, and since he was President in 1798, this is undoubtedly the first edition. In recent years several other first-edition copies have been discovered and are now deposited in the Library of Congress, the Historical Society of Pennsylvania, and in several private collections, including that of Mr. Arthur Billings Hunt of Brooklyn, New York, who was the first to discover the original edition.

There have been many controversies also on the origin of the *President's March*, but its date and authorship have been satisfactorily established. It is generally accepted that the *March* was composed in honor of George Washington's becoming President in 1789, and all authorities are agreed that it dates before 1793.

Its authorship is even clearer and more definite than the date of its origin, although there have been several claimants to the honor. For example, William McKoy in 1829 stated that the *March* was composed by a German teacher of music in Philadelphia, named Johannes Roat, or Roth, "the seat of the Federal Government . . . being removed to Philadelphia and in honour of the new President Washington, then residing at No. 190 High Street."

He undoubtedly referred to the Philip Roth we discussed in a previous chapter, but Roth lived until 1804, after the song was famous. According to present knowledge, he never claimed authorship of the piece. Moreover, Philadelphia did not become the seat of the Government until 1790 and, if a new march had been played in honor of General Washington when he was accorded "an elegant Entertainment of 250 covers at the City Tavern" in Philadelphia on April 20 (1789), some of the newspapers would certainly have mentioned the fact.

The other composer who appears to have a claim is Philip Phile, who died in Philadelphia in 1793. For many years the claim in Phile's behalf was as difficult to prove as that of Roth, but a number of years ago the collection of former Governor Pennypacker of Pennsylvania yielded an unnumbered page, torn from an engraved music collection, bearing two marches. One of these was the *President's March* by Phile, the other a *March* by Moller. This music-sheet was issued about 1793, and it seems to establish Phile's authorship of the *President's March* beyond reasonable doubt.

3. THE STAR-SPANGLED BANNER

Up to the time of the Spanish-American War, *Hail Columbia* shared honors with the *Star-Spangled Banner* as one of our national anthems, and it was not until Admiral Dewey officially designated the *Star-Spangled Banner* that *Hail Columbia* lost its place. From that time, the Army and Navy regulations have included a statement that when an occasion arose on which the national anthem of the United States was required, *The Star-Spangled Banner* should be played. These regulations, however, governed only the Armed Forces, not the civilian population, and the confusion continued until the Seventy-first Congress, during its Third Session, passed Public No. 823 which designated as our national anthem "the composition consisting of the words and music known as *The Star-Spangled Banner*." This bill was signed by President Hoover on March 3, 1931, the day before he left office.

Our national anthem had a dramatic birth. During the War of 1812, one of the principal stratagems of the British had been to blockade Chesapeake Bay. Reinforcements arrived from England in August, 1814, intending that the major portion of the fleet would be moved around for the attack on New Orleans. Before departing, however, the British wished to teach the upstarts a lesson. Washington was attacked and easily taken, since nothing but untrained militia defended it. After burning many public buildings, including the Capitol, they returned to their boats in the bay.

On their way to Washington, Dr. Beanes, a leading physician of Upper Marlborough, Maryland, proved to be something of a "collaborationist," lavishly entertaining some British officers, who in return had his property protected from marauding soldiers. After the main body of troops had safely passed Upper Marlborough on their way back to their ships, Dr. Beanes turned his coat back again, and had three stragglers arrested. Unfortunately for him, he turned it a little too soon. The British learned of his "treachery" and sent a detachment back to release their men and take Dr. Beanes prisoner. Friends attempted to get him released, but he was unceremoniously loaded on the ships for a trip to Halifax.

Knowing that a young lawyer named FRANCIS SCOTT KEY (1779–1843) was an acquaintance of Dr. Beanes and that he had influential connections in Washington, the friends asked Key to intercede. He left Washington on September 2, armed with a letter to Colonel John S. Skinner, the cartel agent for the United States who was stationed in Baltimore. Boarding an unidentified sloop, the party reached the British fleet off the mouth of the Potomac on September 7. Encouraged by their easy success in Washington, the British had meanwhile decided to attack Baltimore. The city had been one of the most ardent proponents of the war in the first place and had served as one of the chief bases for privateers who had been taking the place of our practically nonexistent Navy.

Key and Skinner finally prevailed on the British to release Dr. Beanes, but all three, together with their crew of fourteen, were held on the British ships for fear they might reveal the plans for the new attack. The fleet started up the bay on the eighth, arriving off Baltimore harbor during Sunday church services on the eleventh. Troops were landed on North Point, and early the next morning they started along the northern shore of the harbor to attack Baltimore from the side. To support the land attack, a group of small bombing vessels were moved up the harbor to make a frontal attack on Fort McHenry.

Unfortunately for the British, their burning of the Capitol had so electrified all the large cities along the eastern coast that the citizens, from beggars to bankers, had pitched in to build fortifications and trenches surrounding their cities. Consequently, Key and his friends, who had been put aboard their own flag-of-truce ship under guard with orders not to attempt to land, had the thrill of watching a far more stubborn resistance than that which had been put up on the outskirts of Washington. Since Key had taken a conspicuous part in that engagement, he knew from personal experience what it was like to retreat before the British, and he also knew what would happen to Baltimore if the city was taken.

All during the night of the thirteenth he stayed on deck watching the rockets arching about the Fort and exploding in mid-air. He knew that some small boats were going to try to sneak past Fort McHenry under cover of darkness, and when the firing ceased around one o'clock on the fourteenth, he had no way of telling whether their mission had been successful. As time wore on, the tension became terrific, until as the dawn crept out of the East, he gradually saw the outlines of the fort through the drizzle and mist, and suddenly discovered that the flag was still flying. This was too much for his emotional nature. Inspired by his countrymen's triumph he took an envelope from his pocket and feverishly wrote the words of the *Star-Spangled Banner*, adapting them to one of the most popular songs of the period, *To Anacreon in Heaven*. The next day a printer struck off a handbill with the poem; it was sung that night in a tavern, a week later it was printed in a Baltimore newspaper, and since then its career has been history.

This story, in effect, has never been disputed; controversies have been confined to such details as to who the printer was, who first sang it and where, and what has become of the envelope on which Key wrote his first sketches. The manuscript preserved in the Walters Art Gallery in Baltimore is probably the first complete copy the author made from his first notes. It is obviously not the draft he made on the flag-of-truce ship.

Copies of the handbill, or broadside, are still in existence. It bore the title *Defence of Fort McHenry*, and following a brief description of the circumstances under which the poem was written, designates the tune to which it is sung—*To Anacreon in Heaven*. Recently, through the research of Virginia Larkin Redway, it has been established that the first sheet-music edition of the song was published by Joseph Carr of Baltimore, father of Benjamin Carr, and was arranged by a younger son Thomas. Probably this edition was issued not later than October 19, 1814, or about a month after the bombardment. According to the papers of the Carr family, now in the possession of descendants, Key called on Carr and requested him to arrange the song and adapt his words to the music. Presumably the title of the song was agreed upon at that meeting, for the Carr edition is entitled *The Star-Spangled Banner*.[1]

It has been claimed that Key had no music in mind, and that either the printer or some early singer discovered that its meter would match the tune, accent for accent. It is hard to see how these legends ever grew, since it is preposterous to suppose that anyone would just happen to write a verse in such a complicated verse structure. They have now been disproved quite definitely. Not only was the Anacreontic Song one of the three most parodied melodies of the period (nearly a hundred sets of verses, mostly patriotic, have been found in the songsters of that day, but Key had written another parody earlier and sung it himself at a dinner in honor of Stephen Decatur early in December, 1805. Key used several ideas from this earlier poem in *The Star-Spangled Banner*, and thus there can be no doubt that the tunes were intended to be the same.

The authorship of the tune has never been satisfactorily established, although a vast amount of research has been conducted over a period of more than half a century. For a time during the last century the music of *To Anacreon in Heaven* was widely credited to the English scholar and composer SAMUEL ARNOLD (1740–1803), presumably because he was the director of the symphony concerts which took up the first three hours of the meetings of the Anacreontic Society. In 1873, William Chappell advanced a theory, later adopted by other scholars —notably Oscar George Theodore Sonneck—that the composer was actually JOHN STAFFORD SMITH (1750–1836). The evidence is much too complex to present, let alone analyze, here, but it will be sufficient to state that for a time it was quite generally accepted. Closer examination of the evidence, however, reveals it to be extremely equivocal, and there are a growing number of people who suspect that the attribution was mistaken. It is entirely possible that the author of the words simply adapted them to an earlier melody whose source has not yet been located. Ralph Tomlinson, a lawyer of Lincoln's Inn and one of the presidents of the Anacreontic Society in London, is regularly given as the author of the words in all the early editions of the song, but no composer is ever mentioned. In itself, this would be a little startling in case the music had been specifically written for the song by men of the

[1] Joseph Muller, *The Star-Spangled Banner*, New York: G. A. Baker & Co., 1935.

standing of Arnold or Smith. Whatever the origin of the tune, Tomlinson made a very competent, if not exactly inspired, job of the words. They are addressed to Anacreon, the famous lyric poet of Greece around 500 B.C., whose verses became increasingly popular during the course of the eighteenth century. Inspired by love and wine, his poems sometimes advise continence—a practice he may have followed himself, since he lived to his eighty-fifth year, only to choke to death on a grape seed. The song begins:

> To Anacreon in Heaven, where he sat in full glee,
>   A few sons of harmony sent a petition,
> That he their inspirer and patron would be; . . .

And each of its six stanzas end with an adaptation of the couplet:

> And, besides, I'll instruct ye, like me, to intwine
> The myrtle of Venus with Bacchus's vine.

Just when the song reached these shores cannot be definitely established, since the country depended largely on imported songbooks for its music. It was not included in any of the fifteen extant songsters which were printed here between 1786 and 1794, but one parody—"The genius of France from his star begem'd throne"—appeared in a New York newspaper in 1793. *To Anacreon* was included in two songsters published in 1795, and its popularity seems to have increased rapidly after that date. Whatever implications of conviviality the song may have had in England were soon combined with expressions of patriotism, and new parodies were constantly being written for Fourth of July banquets and for dinners in honor of military heroes. A few sample first lines are:

"Ye sons of Columbia, determined to keep"
"To Columbia, who gladly reclin'd at her ease"
"Ye sons of Columbia, unite in the cause"
"Brave sons of Columbia, your triumph behold."
"In years which are past, when America fought"
"Columbians, arise; let the cannon resound"
"When our sky was illuminated by freedom's bright dawn"
"Hark! the trumpet of war from the East sounds alarm."
"Of the victory won over tyranny's power"

In June, 1798, the Massachusetts Charitable Fire Society, at its banquet in Boston, sang a song it had commissioned Robert Treat Paine to write for the occasion. This was *Adams and Liberty*, to the tune *To Anacreon in Heaven*. Paine is said to have received $750 for his copyright to the song. The author's name was originally Thomas, and he is frequently confused with the early patriot and freethinker of the same name. As a young man he was much struck with the stage and its gayer ways. His father, Robert Treat Paine, a signer of the Declaration of Independence, disapproved, and there was an estrangement. When an older brother, who also bore the name Robert Treat, died, Thomas took his brother's name in an effort to get back into the good graces of his family. The reconciliation lasted only a few months, however, and eventually he died in drunken destitution. It was not to be expected that *Adams and Liberty* would have long life. No song with a title referring to a single president could become a permanent national anthem.

One more set of verses is worthy of comment—*The Battle of the Wabash*. The battle was the famous engagement at Tippecanoe that made William Henry Harrison famous (November 4, 1811). A music-sheet containing this poem gives also the words and music of *To Anacreon in Heaven*, and facing the first page of music, the verses of the *Star-Spangled Banner* are printed under the title *Fort McHenry, or The Star-Spangled Banner*. This is the only known music-sheet on which the words of both *To Anacreon in Heaven* and *The Star-Spangled Banner* are printed.

4. AMERICA

The song *America* is unique among our early national airs; its origin is associated with no war, and it voices no belligerent sentiments. In this regard it is truly our national *hymn*. The complaint that its tune is British in origin may be viewed from two sides. Before the Revolution it belonged to our British colonial ancestors as fully as it did to their brothers in the mother country. After we were independent of England, our fathers kept the English language and their English customs. Why should they have abandoned their English anthem, so long as it dropped its allusion to their former monarch?

New verses were plenteous: *God Save America, God Save George Washington, God Save the Thirteen States, God Save the President.* A pioneer suffragette in 1795 went so far as to write a poem called *Rights of Woman,* which began

> God save each female's right
> Show to her ravish'd sight
> Woman is free.

Traditions about the origin of the tune are numerous. It has been claimed that it was taken from a Swiss hymn, written to celebrate the victory of ancient Geneva over the troops of the Duke of Savoy in the early seventeenth century, and was some years later arranged by Dr. John Bull (1563–1628), the English composer. Some say that early in the eighteenth century the French musician Lully made it into a French patriotic song in honor of Louis XIV, and that Handel arranged it as a song in praise of the Elector of Hanover who became George I of England. These are merely legends, but the fact remains that the tune is used in many countries.

It is probable that it was really written by Henry Carey (1685?–1743), the English composer of *Sally in our Alley.* Carey sang the song, with the words "God Save Great George our King," at a tavern in Cornhill in 1740 on the occasion of a dinner party held to celebrate Admiral Vernon's capture of Porto Bello. He announced that the words and music were his own, and it is probable that they were, for he would have had a hard time escaping detection had he stolen so striking a melody.[1]

The words of *America* date from 1831, and were written by Samuel Francis Smith (1808–1895). Smith claimed that when he wrote his poem he did not realize the tune was that of the British national anthem. On several occasions he told of writing *America:*

The origin of my hymn, "My Country 'tis of Thee" is briefly told. In the year 1831, Mr. William C. Woodbridge returned from Europe, bringing a quantity of German music-books, which he passed over to Lowell Mason. Mr. Mason, with whom I was on terms of friendship, one day turned them over to me, knowing that I was in the habit of reading German works, say-

---

[1] In James Lyon's *Urania,* 1761, the melody appears as *Whitefield's* tune, set to the words *Come, Thou Almighty King.*

ing, "Here, I can't read these, but they contain good music, which I should be glad to use. Turn over the leaves, and if you find anything particularly good, give me a translation or imitation of it, or write a wholly original song, —anything, so I can use it."

Accordingly, one leisure afternoon, I was looking over the books, and fell in with the tune of "God Save the King," and at once took up my pen and wrote the piece in question. It was struck out at a sitting, without the slightest idea that it would ever attain the popularity it has since enjoyed. I think it was first written in the town of Andover, Mass., in February, 1832. The first time it was sung publicly was at a children's celebration of American independence, at the Park Street Church, Boston, I think, July 4, 1832. If I had anticipated the future of it, doubtless I would have taken more pains with it. Such as it is, I am glad to have contributed this mite to the cause of American freedom.

Smith recalled two of his dates incorrectly. Woodbridge returned from Europe in 1829, not in 1831, and the Independence Day celebration at which *America* was first sung occurred in 1831, not in 1832. The program of the event is in the collection of the American Antiquarian Society of Worcester, Massachusetts, and in the Chapin Library at Williams College. Furthermore, an account of the affair was printed in the *Christian Watchman* of July 8, 1831.

At any rate, *America* was written by a young clergyman who had no idea he was writing a national hymn, but whose sentiments proved so expressive of our ideals that they have been an inspiration to generations of peace-loving Americans.

CHAPTER FIVE

The Turn of the Century

I. FOREIGN AND NATIVE ARTISTS

In many respects the beginning of the nineteenth century forms a dividing line in the history of our musical development, just as it marks a division in our political and economic history. The year that saw the downfall of the Federalist party and the election of Thomas Jefferson witnessed many changes in administrative policies. It was a year when the ambitions of Napoleon Bonaparte threatened the well-being of the young United States; it was only because his problems in Continental Europe were all he could handle that he made a treaty with us in 1801, one of the last acts of Adams's administration. Then followed the closing of the Mississippi's mouth by Spain, the final purchase of the Louisiana Territory from Napoleon (for $15,000,000), the Burr-Hamilton duel, the Lewis and Clark Expedition, and the constant disputes with England over the impressment of our seamen, which finally led to the War of 1812. Eventful years, forcing our new constitutional government to prove its stability at the very outset of its career.

The first years of the century still saw the foreigners who had migrated to our shores in control of our musical life, but with a difference. The Hewitts, the Carrs, Van Hagens, and Reinagles had become thoroughly naturalized—they, too, were American musicians. Young when they came, they had made their reputations principally in America; this was their home, and their foreign origin was in the background. Their descendants today may cite several generations of American ancestors.

Among the important foreigners was GOTTLIEB GRAUPNER (1767–1836), who came to America shortly after 1790, but whose life in Boston, where his influence was most felt, was chiefly in the nineteenth century. Graupner has been called the "Father of American Orchestral Music," and while there were others who did much to develop orchestra playing in this country, Graupner is most assuredly entitled to credit for true pioneer work.

His full name was Johann Christian Gottlieb Graupner; born in Hanover, October 6, 1767, the son of Johann Georg Graupner, oboist in the regiment of Colonel von Groten from Andreasberg. Gottlieb himself became an excellent oboist and played in a Hanoverian regiment when he was twenty years old. Receiving an honorable discharge in 1788, he went to London, and, like Hewitt, played in Haydn's orchestra when Salomon brought the great composer to London in 1791. After a few years in England, Graupner sought new fields. He went first to Prince Edward Island, and finally came to Charleston, South Carolina. Here he married, in 1796, a singer named Mrs. Catherine Comerford Hillier, known to the public as Mrs. Heelyer. It may be possible that Graupner had been in America prior to landing in Charleston, for a manuscript biography in the Boston Public Library written by a descendant, Mrs. George Whitefield Stone, speaks of his leaving London in June, 1792, and making an American debut in Boston, December 15, 1794. As the same document speaks of his returning to London *February* 4, 1794, and remaining until *August* 15, 1795, it is apparent that there is some confusion of dates. It was probably Mrs. Graupner who made the 1794 debut at the Boston Theatre.

The biography describes Graupner as a tall, somewhat austere man of precise speech and manner, who became white haired before he reached middle age. He had received a thorough musical education, and was able to perform on every known musical instrument, with the oboe and double bass as favorites. As a skilled oboist he was much in demand; good players on the oboe were rare in those days, though the tradition that Graupner was the only oboist in the country is hardly accurate.

There is record of a concert in Charleston in November, 1795, when Graupner played a concerto on the oboe between the performance of the drama and the farce that followed it. The summer of 1797 found Mrs. Graupner acting in Salem, Massachusetts, and in the autumn appearing with the Solee theatrical company in New York. In the spring of 1798 both Mr. and Mrs. Graupner were in Salem, and shortly afterwards the family settled in Boston, where Graupner was to play an active part in the city's musical life until his death in 1836.

Among his other activities, Graupner kept a music store and published considerable music of his own and others' composition. He advertised that he had "pianofortes for sale and to let, and that private instruments would be tuned in town and in country." An old newspaper clipping describes his place of business:

> Gottlieb Graupner's music store, hall, and house, No. 6 Franklin Street, was four doors on the left from Washington Street. This was a place of great resort for young and old, teachers, pupils, and music lovers. Mr. Graupner's name was an honored one in the musical history of Boston. He was an eminent teacher of the piano-forte and of all orchestral instruments. He struck the first blow in the cause of true musical art, and continued the strife until a taste for good music, and a fair understanding of its intrinsic value was established in Boston.

Although it is known that Graupner composed music, there is little extant today. No doubt he wrote some of the oboe concertos that he performed at concerts, and *Columbia's Bold Eagle*, "a patriotic song, words by a gentleman of Salem—music by Mr. Graupner," was on the program of a concert in Salem in 1799. He was a pioneer in compiling educational works for the pianoforte, and in 1819 wrote and published his *Rudiments of the art of playing the pianoforte, containing the elements of music*, as well as "remarks on fingering, with examples, 30 fingered lessons, and a plain direction for tuning."

In 1810, Graupner started a small organization that was to be his greatest contribution to the future music of Boston. This was the Philharmonic Society, at first a social meeting where a number of musicians gathered regularly to practice Haydn's symphonies and other works for their own delight. Aside from nondescript theatre orchestras and the bands that gathered together for special concerts, there had been few organizations that met regularly for playing symphonic music. Graupner played the oboe. The first violinist was Louis Ostinelli, the Italian who married James Hewitt's daughter Sophia. Two clarinetists were members—Thomas Granger and Louis Schaffer, though Schaffer probably played the cello at the meetings. Francis Mallet, a vocalist, could play the contrabass, and he became a useful member. The professionals were assisted by amateurs of the city. The orchestra lived for at least fourteen years, for the last concert announcement did not appear until November 24, 1824. Parker's *Euterpeiad and Musical Intelligencer*, one of our early musical journals, spoke of the organization in 1821:

The Concerts of this Society are chiefly instrumental; the music is always heard with attention and oft times delight. The orchestra consists of nearly all the gentlemen of the profession in town, and its members are principally amateurs both vocal and instrumental; its support is derived from an annual assessment of ten dollars upon its members, who gain admission by ballot. The public Concerts are always fully attended by a large assemblage of ladies and gentlemen, introduced by members who possess certain privileges of admission on public nights.

Graupner became an American citizen in 1808. In 1821 he was saddened by the death of his wife, who was but forty-nine years old at the time. He later married again, for at the settlement of his will after his own death in 1836, his widow, Mary H. Graupner, inherited the estate of $975.

Aside from his more serious achievements it is possible that Graupner was also the originator of one of our lighter musical diversions—the minstrel songs that were so popular in the middle and later nineteenth century. A New York newspaper in 1889 offered the following information and surmises:

The Beginning of Negro Minstrelsy—the Banjo-Opera a Generation Ago.—In the current number of Harper's Magazine, Mr. Lawrence Hutton essays to trace the history of Negro minstrelsy in America, and succeeds in bringing together a large number of interesting facts in connection with early music and theatricals. In one respect the most surprising of these facts is the one stated on the authority of Mr. Charles White, an old Ethiopian comedian, which credits a Mr. Graupner with being the father of Negro song. This Graupner is said to have sung "The Gay Negro Boy," in character, accompanying himself on the banjo, at the end of the second act of "Oroonoko," on December 30th, 1799, at the Federal Street Theatre, Boston. This was Gottlieb Graupner, a hautboist. . . . In Boston, he led the orchestra of the old Federal Street Theatre, kept a music shop, played the oboe, the double-bass, and nearly every other instrument; gave lessons in music, organized the Philharmonic Society, and joined in the first call for the organization of the Handel & Haydn Society in March 1815. . . . Mr. Graupner's sojourn in Charleston suggests where he, a German, became acquainted with the banjo, and also offers evidence on the question mooted by Mr. Hutton, whether or not the banjo was common among slaves of the south.

Graupner, together with Thomas Smith Webb and Asa Peabody, signed the invitation that was issued in March, 1815, for a meeting to consider "the expediency of forming a society for cultivating and improving a correct taste in the performance of sacred music, and also to introduce into more general practice the works of Handel, Haydn and other eminent composers." Sixteen responded to the call and in April of the same year an organization was formed, with Webb as president, that became the *Handel and Haydn Society* of Boston, today one of the largest, and, with the exception of the Stoughton Musical Society, the oldest living musical organization in the United States. The first concert was held in the Stone Chapel on Christmas night in 1815, and one critic wrote that there was nothing to compare with it; that the Society was the wonder of the nation. The Handel and Haydn was not only influential in raising the standards of choral music in New England, but it led the way to the formation of similar organizations throughout the country.

One of the earliest organists of the Society was GEORGE K. JACKSON (1745–1823), a schoolmate of Raynor Taylor; born in Oxford, England. He came to America in 1796, landing at Norfolk, Virginia, and living in turn in Alexandria, Virginia; Baltimore; Philadelphia; Elizabeth, New Jersey; and New York, before he finally settled in Boston in 1812. He soon became active as a teacher, and at various times held the position of organist in several Boston churches—Brattle Square, King's Chapel, Trinity, and St. Paul's. Together with Mr. and Mrs. Graupner, Mallet, and other musicians, he organized performances of oratorios and concerts of choral music.

Before Dr. Jackson left England he had published *A treatise on practical thorough bass*. It was he who was largely responsible for Lowell Mason's start in music, for when he was organist of the Handel and Haydn Society, the manuscript of Mason's first collection of hymns and anthems was brought to his attention. Seeing its merits immediately, Jackson recommended that the Society publish it. Mason himself was anxious that his name should not appear, and Jackson was mentioned as the chief compiler. He had, moreover, added a number of his own compositions and arrangements to the collection.

Jackson had eleven children. He has been described as somewhat undemonstrative, though mentally keen. He was probably a ponderous person, for General Henry K. Oliver remembered him as "a very incarnation of obesity. . . . Like Falstaff he 'larded the lean earth as he walked along.'" When he died in 1823 he left an even smaller estate than Graupner was to leave thirteen years later. Metcalf, in his *American Writers and Compilers of Sacred Music*, says that the total inventory consisted of $98.86, including one hundred and twenty-nine volumes of old music books valued at six cents each.

BENJAMIN CROSS (1786–1857), one of the founders of the Philadelphia Musical Fund Society, was a contemporary of Benjamin Carr, and was active in Philadelphia as a teacher and singer. He was one of the conductors of the Society, and also appeared as a concert pianist, sometimes playing his own compositions. At some New York concerts in 1839 he played his pianoforte "Fantasia—Introducing two Irish airs"; a Potpourri, "introducing airs from *La Dame Blanche, Masaniello,* and *Fra Diavolo*"; and other pieces.

A New England musician whose importance has sometimes been overlooked was OLIVER SHAW (1779–1848), significant because he was prominent at a time when the country was commencing to reassert itself in music; when it had absorbed the foreigners and the new ideas they had brought with them, and was again turning its attention to its native-born music makers. Shaw was one of those who paved the road for Lowell Mason.

He was born March 13, 1779, in Middleboro, Massachusetts, the son of John Shaw and Hannah Heath. When he was a young lad he accidentally shoved the blade of a penknife into his right eye. Later the family moved to Taunton and the father went to sea. When Oliver was seventeen he attended the Bristol Academy at Taunton, and shortly after graduation he joined his father in his sea-faring enterprises. When he was twenty-one he was stricken with yellow fever. While not fully recovered he helped in taking nautical observations from the sun. This so affected his remaining eye, weakened from sickness, that the young man soon became totally blind.

It was this affliction that probably turned him to music, for otherwise he might have continued his maritime career. Wondering where to turn for a living, he came in touch with John L. Berkenhead, the blind organist of Newport, who gave him music lessons. Here was a profession he might follow in spite of his blindness. His progress was rapid, and he later went to Boston to study with Graupner. He also took clarinet lessons from Granger, and when he finally settled in Providence in 1807, he went there as a thoroughly trained musician.

Employing a little boy to lead him to the homes of his pupils he gave many music lessons, and he became the organist of the First Congregational Church. In 1809 he gathered a group of fellow musicians, among them Thomas Webb (who later moved to Boston), and founded the Psallonian Society, formed by its founders "for the purpose of improving themselves in the knowledge and practice of sacred music and inculcating a more correct taste in the choice and performance of it." The society lasted until 1832, and in its twenty-three years gave thirty-one concerts. In 1812, Shaw married Sarah Jencks and raised a family of two sons and five daughters.

As a composer he devoted himself almost entirely to sacred music. Among his hymn-tunes were *Taunton*, *Bristol*, *Weybosset*, and others. One of his most popular sacred songs was *Mary's Tears*, "a favorite song from Moore's sacred melodies; sung at the oratorio performed by the Handel & Haydn Society in Boston, July 5th, 1817, in presence of the President of the United States." (Monroe.) The program also contained his duet *All things bright and fair are thine*.

Others of his sacred melodies were: *Arrayed in clouds of golden light*; *The missionary angel*; *There is an hour of peace and rest*; *There's nothing true but heaven*; *To Jesus the crown of my hope*, and others which are significant because they show the trend of nonliturgical church music toward the ballad type of sentiment.

Shaw also compiled several collections of sacred music: *Melodia sacra*, "or Providence selection of sacred musick—from the latest European publications; with a number of original compositions"; and *The social sacred melodist* (1835). His secular compositions included the *Bangor March*, the *Bristol March*, and *Gov. Arnold's March*; the songs *Sweet Little Ann, Love's last words, The Blue Bird,* and the *Death of Commodore O. H. Perry.* In 1807, H. Mann of Dedham, published Shaw's

> *For the Gentlemen:* A favourite selection of instrumental music . . . for schools and musical societies. Consisting principally of marches, airs, minuets, etc. Written chiefly in four parts, viz: two clarinets, flute and bassoon; or two violins, flute and violoncello.

These are the men who appeared at the opening of the century to join those who had bridged its turn. Some of them were of foreign birth and some were natives, but together they helped finish the foundation on which Lowell Mason, in one direction, and others in their own fields, cultivated the beginnings of a native art.

2. LOWELL MASON (1792–1872) AND THE RETURN OF THE NATIVE COMPOSER

Early in the nineteenth century there arose a group of native composers who carried on the tradition of New England's church music. After Billings, there had been a reaction against his "lively, fuguing pieces." Music for the church again assumed a more stately character. Singing schools had helped in developing singers who could sing at least correctly in church, and conditions were favorable to the development of a style of music in some respects individual in character. Immediately following the time of Tuckey, Selby, and Adgate, who gave American composers a place on their programs, the foreign immigration had diverted the attention of the musical public from native composers, and the music of Billings and his contemporaries was forced to the background. After two or three decades, this alien element was absorbed, and our church music, at least, fell to the hands of men better educated musically than the early New Englanders, men who had opportunity to study abroad, and were thoroughly grounded in considerably more than the rudiments of the art. From all this sprang the *hymnology* of the American Protestant church, which, though it has had its ignoble products, has formed a contribution to the sacred song of the entire world. Born chiefly in New England, it is nevertheless the expression of the American people at large. In some ways the hymn-tunes of Lowell Mason and his colleagues are as much folk songs as the melodies of Stephen Foster.

Lowell Mason appeared at a time when American *hymnology*, with its origin in the psalmody of the Puritans, was beginning to develop in two distinct directions. One branch was expressed in the dignified, stately type of hymn-tune which appears in the better collections today; the other found its outlet in the gospel song, used effectively in camp-meetings, revivalist campaigns, and in many Sunday Schools. Mason was identified with the better type.

We know Mason principally as the composer of *Bethany* (for *Nearer My God to Thee*); *Olivet* (for *My Faith Looks Up to Thee*); *Missionary Hymn* (for *From Greenland's Icy Mountains*); and of a great number of other hymn-tunes, most of which have now dropped out of use, but his influence has been felt in other directions, equally important. He was the pioneer in music teaching in the public schools, and the teachers' conventions that he organized have been the parents of our annual music festivals and our summer normal schools for teachers. They bridged the work of the old-fashioned traveling singing teacher and modern music schools. Mason was the chief factor in the third revival of singing in New England, and because of his abilities and personality, and because of greatly improved methods of communication, his influence spread far and wide across the country. Few single American musicians have ever exerted so wide an influence in the improvement of musical taste and standards as did Lowell Mason over a period of forty years.

Mason is one of the few pioneers who profited by his work. Royalties from the sale of his collections netted him a handsome fortune, and during his lifetime he was recognized and honored. For his services to education New York University awarded him the honorary degree of Doctor of Music in 1855, the first ever granted in America.

His American ancestry dated back seven generations. Robert Mason, born in England in 1590, had landed at Salem with John Winthrop in 1630. Lowell Mason was born in Medfield, Massachusetts, January 8, 1792, the son of Johnson Mason and Catharine Hartshorn. Although his parents did not want him to become a musician they encouraged the boy's early fondness for music, and saw to it that his talent was cultivated. When he was twenty he left home for Savannah, Georgia, for he had heard of a position in a bank that was open to him. In his spare hours he studied music, and found an instructor to help him—a man named F. L. Abel. He soon began to try his hand at composition, and wrote some hymn-tunes, and anthems. In the fourteen years in Savannah he led several church choirs, and acted as organist in the Independent Presbyterian Church.

During these years he worked at the compilation of a hymn collection. Some of the tunes he selected from William Gardner's *Sacred Melodies*, and others he wrote himself. He took the bulky manuscript and offered it to several publishers in Philadelphia and Boston, and was turned down by all of them. He was about to lay it aside when someone suggested that he submit it to George K. Jackson, at that time organist of the Handel and Haydn Society of Boston. Jackson saw its merits and recommended it highly, with the result that it was published as the *Boston Handel & Haydn Society's Collection of Sacred Music*. It became popular immediately, and its many editions totaled 50,000 copies during the following thirty-five years, netting Mason and the Society $30,000 apiece.

Mason still had no thought of making music his profession, and he was so afraid that being known as a musician might hurt his standing as a banker, that he did not allow his name to appear on the collection. Later editions acknowledged his work in the preface.

All this was in 1822. When he had arranged the details of publication he returned to Savannah, where he stayed for five more years. He had married Abigail Gregory in 1817, and had the responsibility of a growing family, a family that still has its impress on American musical life. Of the four sons, Daniel Gregory and Lowell, Junior founded the publishing business of Mason Brothers in New York, which continued until 1869. Lowell, with his younger brother Henry, then founded the firm of Mason & Hamlin, which first made organs and then pianos. The youngest son, William, became one of the most influential musicians in America during the last half of the nineteenth century.

When he was thirty-seven years old, Lowell Mason accepted an offer to return to Boston, and was guaranteed an income of $2,000 a year to lead the music in three churches, six months in each. He soon asked to be released from the contract and for a short time went back to

Lowell Mason
(See pages 136–141)

Characteristic Mid-Century Title Pages

(See pages 176–181, 163)

banking. But not for long. Music asserted itself as his chief interest, and he gave it his entire time, largely as a reformer. He was honored with the presidency of the Handel and Haydn Society for several years, beginning in 1827, but declined re-election in 1831 that he might give his whole attention to the establishment of music teaching in the public schools. Mason was among the first to preach the doctrine that every child has a right to receive elementary instruction in music at public expense. And he was the man who gained them that right.

At this time the public schools were first becoming recognized as an American institution, and the Boston schools were a fertile field for Mason to work in. Such a revolutionary doctrine was not welcomed immediately by the school board; Mason had to conduct many experiments to prove that his ideas were sound.

By 1829 he had studied the Pestalozzian methods of teaching which W. C. Woodbridge, author of school geographies, had brought back from Europe. Having learned what the system had accomplished in other subjects, he determined to apply its principles to music teaching. Accordingly, in conjunction with George J. Webb, Samuel A. Eliot, and others, he founded the Boston Academy of Music in 1832 to try his ideas. Sessions were held in the rooms of the Bowdoin Street Church and later at the Odeon. Children were taught free of charge, if they would promise to attend for the entire year. In the first year there were 1,500 pupils. Mason himself taught 400 of them, and Webb took care of 150.

In a few years the school board began to be impressed, and some of its members saw that they were wrong in fearing that music study would divert the pupils from their regular tasks. Those who studied music had an added zeal for other subjects. The board passed a resolution that "one school from each district be selected for the introduction of systematic instruction in vocal music." In 1836 the introduction of music into the schools was formally authorized, but the board forgot to appropriate any money. Even this failed to stop Mason. He taught without pay for an entire year, and bought music and materials for the pupils from his own pocket. A year of this was too much for the public conscience, and in 1838 the board went the whole way and appropriated the necessary funds.

It was while he was conducting the classes at the Academy of Music that Mason started his music conventions. If he was to spread his ideas, there must be teachers trained to do the work. The first was held in 1834. Twelve teachers came. By 1838 there were 134, coming from ten states, and in 1849 the attendance had grown to 1,000. The meetings generally lasted for two weeks. Those who came were taught to sing chiefly by rote, and then went home and became teachers. Meager instruction, but considerably more than they had ever had before. Moreover, the results were so successful that Mason spent much of his time traveling around the country in answer to the demand for "conventions" elsewhere. He would often go as far west as Rochester, New York, a real journey in the days of early railroading, to meet choruses of 500 voices, many of them teachers who had traveled a hundred miles to attend.

By 1850, Mason's pioneer work in Boston was finished. He had made the Hub a self-developing musical city, not largely dependent, like New York, on musical culture from abroad. The Academy passed out of existence in 1847 because its mission had been fulfilled. In 1850, Mason went to Europe for two years, and lectured in England on his application of the Pestalozzian method to music teaching. In 1853 he returned and established his headquarters in New York, where with George F. Root and William B. Bradbury he established the New York Normal Institute for training teachers. He bought a home on the side of the Orange Mountains in New Jersey which he named *Silver-spring*, and he continued his activities until his death at the age of eighty, August 11, 1872.

Mason had opposition in his lifetime, and even after his work had borne fruit in Boston the intelligentsia of the day said that he and his fellow writers of hymn-tunes were degrading and cheapening music. From certain standpoints this may be true; Mason was no Handel or Bach; his tunes incline to the sentimental and their appeal is to the emotions rather than the intellect. But compare what had been before him with what he left, and then decide whether he cheapened and degraded it. Mason was the first who preached music for the masses. The festivals that grew from his conventions may have been a sorry contrast to modern performances in both program and execution, but think of the thousands who participated in making music far better than anything they had ever heard before.

It has been estimated that over a million copies of Mason's books have been sold; one collection alone brought him $100,000. The best known were the *Boston Handel & Haydn Collection* (1822); *Juvenile Psalmodist* (1829); *Juvenile Lyre* (1830); *Sabbath School Songs* (1836); *Boston Academy Collection of Church Music* (1836); *Lyra Sacra* (1837); *Boston Anthem Book* (1839); *The Psaltery* (1845); *Cantica Laudis* (1850); *New Carmina Sacra* (1852); and *The Song Garden* (1866).

3. MASON'S CONTEMPORARIES

Among Mason's contemporaries and associates, THOMAS HASTINGS (1784–1872) deserves a prominent place. He was a few years older than Mason and like his colleague enjoyed long life. Between the two men there was one marked difference. With Mason, music was first, and he appreciated its power to make worship more beautiful. Hastings was a pious soul who believed that music should be used to exemplify the teachings of the gospel, occupying an entirely subordinate place. Moreover, Hastings was not the musician that Mason was.

Hastings was born in Washington, Connecticut, October 15, 1784. His father, Seth Hastings, combined the professions of country doctor and farmer. Thomas and his two brothers were complete albinos, with absolutely white hair from childhood. When Thomas was twelve the family moved to Clinton, New York, and the boy obtained all the education he ever had in the country schools. His experience was practical, however, for at eighteen he was leading a village choir. He started to compile hymn collections when he was about thirty years old, and in 1816 an editor named Solomon Warriner suggested that they merge his own *Springfield Collection* with Hastings's *Utica Collection*. The joint product was called *Musica Sacra*.

Hastings moved to Utica in 1828 and was active in a Handel and Haydn Society of that city. For several years he edited a weekly religious paper *The Western Recorder*, and expressed his views on church music in many of his editorials. He had already published an *Essay on Musical Taste*, in which his ideas were considered radical and advanced. The essay was widely read, and a new edition was printed in 1853.

In 1832, Hastings settled in New York, where he later became associated with Mason in the New York Normal Institute. For a number of years he was choirmaster of the Bleecker Street Presbyterian Church. His works were widely used, and his influence was second only to Mason's. In 1858, New York University paid him the same honor it had accorded Mason three years earlier, and conferred on him the degree of Doctor of Music.

Hastings is supposed to have written the words of six hundred hymns, and to have composed over a thousand tunes. He issued fifty volumes of music altogether. While modern hymnals contain many of his hymns, the best known is the famous tune *Toplady*, sung to Augustus Toplady's words, *Rock of Ages, cleft for me*. Many of his tunes appeared under nom de plumes, for Hastings was one of the first American composers to believe that a foreign name impressed the American public. He once wrote: "I have found that a foreigner's name went a great way, and that very ordinary tunes would be sung if 'Palestrina' or 'Pucitto' were over them, while a better tune by Hastings would go unnoticed." A number of his hymns were composed by "Kl—f," and there is reason to suppose that those signed "Zol—ffer" are from his pen. Hastings died in New York, May 15, 1872, eighty-eight years old. He was active until three years before his death.

It may be that the good die young, but if devotion to church music is any sign of virtue, Mason and Hastings disproved the theory by their eighty and eighty-eight years of life. To support the argument of his elders, their young associate, George James Webb (1803–1887), decided that the average was what he wanted, and lived for eighty-four years.

Webb was an Englishman who came to Boston in 1830. The son of a landowner with an estate near Salisbury, England, he was born June 24, 1803. His father was a singer, and his mother a cultured amateur musician. He received his first musical instruction from his mother before he was seven years old, and when he attended a boarding school near his home he studied music with Alexander Lucas. He became proficient in playing both the piano and violin, and by the time he was sixteen decided to make music his career.

To continue his education he went to Falmouth where he studied with an organist, and soon succeeded his teacher at the organ. After a few years in Falmouth he decided to try America, for many friends had told him of its opportunities. He had booked passage for New York, but the captain of a boat sailing for Boston persuaded young Webb to come with him. He went to the New England city and within a few weeks was engaged as the organist of the Old South Church and, what was most important, met Lowell Mason.

Mason needed a man like Webb, for he was beginning to formulate his plans for teaching children. Webb accordingly became one of the organizers of the Boston Academy of Music, and took charge of the secular music courses, while Mason devoted himself to the church music department. His talents as a choral conductor led to his becoming president of the Handel and Haydn Society for three years, and with Mason he was influential in promoting better choral music throughout the country.

Webb also cultivated instrumental music at the Academy, and organized an orchestra that gave regular concerts, following in the footsteps of Graupner's Philharmonic group. This orchestra existed for fourteen years, and when the Academy had served its purpose and ceased to exist in 1847, a Musical Fund Society was organized by Tom Comer, and Webb later became conductor of its orchestra. He held the position until 1852 when he resigned because of other duties, though he remained president of the society which continued until 1855. As an orchestral conductor he was an important link in Boston's musical life; he formed the bridge between Graupner's pioneer efforts and the future work of Zerrahn with the orchestra of the Harvard Musical Association.

In 1871, Webb followed Mason to New York and established his home in Orange, New Jersey. He taught vocal pupils in New York and in the summers conducted normal courses for teachers at Binghamton, New York. He died in Orange, October 7, 1887.

Only one of Webb's many compositions has survived to our day, the famous tune sung to the words, *Stand Up, Stand Up for Jesus*. This originally appeared as a secular song, then as a setting to *The Morning Light is Breaking*, a hymn by Samuel Francis Smith, author of *America*. At first the tune was called *Goodwin*, but it is known today by the name of its composer, *Webb*.

Webb wrote many sacred songs and cantatas, and compiled many collections of hymn-tunes, a number of them in association with Lowell

Mason. Among these were *The Massachusetts Collection of Psalmody*, published in 1840 by the Handel and Haydn Society, *Cantica Ecclesiastica*, consisting largely of English anthems (1859), and a number of collections for young singers—*The American Glee Book* and others. The connection with the Mason family was further strengthened when Lowell Mason's son William married Webb's daughter Mary.

He also wrote many secular songs, some published in 1830, the year of his arrival in America. *Art Thou Happy, Lovely Lady* was published in that year by C. Bradlee in Boston. An announcement at the end of the voice and piano copy stated that "the orchestral accompaniment may be had on application to the publisher." There were a number of songs in these early Boston years—*I'll Meet, Sweet Maid, with Thee; Homeward Bound; Oh, Go Not to the Field of War* ("as sung by Miss George with rapturous applause"); *When I Seek My Pillow;* and many others. There was also a *Boston Cotillons*, for piano, "composed and dedicated to the ladies of Boston." Between the graceful phrases of music are printed directions for the dancers. "Right and left four—balance and turn partners—half promenade—half right and left." And again, "First Lady balance to 2nd Gent; turn the next—balance to next, turn partners and come in the center—four Gent: hands around the Lady—turn partners."

Mr. Howard Van Sinderen, husband of Minna Mason Van Sinderen, daughter of William Mason and granddaughter of Lowell Mason and Webb, very kindly placed at my disposal some of Webb's manuscripts —a number of sacred and secular songs, showing careful workmanship. Most interesting is the *Ode to the 4th July, 1832*, for soli and chorus. Also the cantata *Song of Death*, to words selected from Burns. One of the manuscripts has on one side the outline of a song, with merely the start of an accompaniment; and on the other side a penciled canon, which may have been a sketch for a choral piece, or merely an exercise for his own routine.

Among the members of the Mason group was WILLIAM BATCHELDER BRADBURY (1816–1868), a younger man than Mason, but one who was imbued with his ideas and well equipped to help carry them out. Bradbury, like Mason, was successful in his work with children; he loved them and understood them and they responded readily to his teaching. His forte was music for Sunday Schools, and he was the author and compiler of books with colorful titles. There was the *Golden* series: *Bradbury's Golden Shower of Sunday School Melodies; Bradbury's Golden Chain of Sabbath School Melodies; The Golden Censer* (a musical offering to the Sabbath Schools of children's hosannas to the Son of David); as well as *Bright Jewels for the Sunday School* and *Musical Gems for School and Home*. The suggestion of gold and jewels had its point for the author, too, for the books made him a fortune. His handling of children would have won the approval of the most modern of psychologists. In his later years his home in Bloomfield, New Jersey, lay directly opposite the town school. Bradbury had fruit trees which he prized highly. Every year he protected his orchard from schoolboy raids by sending baskets of cherries, apples, and pears to the pupils.

He was born in York, Maine, October 6, 1816. His parents were musical and he had advantages of training in his youth. By the time he was fourteen he could play every instrument known to York. When he went to Boston he took lessons in harmony from Sumner Hill and became a pupil of Lowell Mason. In 1836, when he was twenty, Mason recommended him to the authorities in Machias, Maine, where he taught for a year and a half. After this, Bradbury went to St. John's, New Brunswick. Then he divided his time between Boston and northeastern points for a few years, and finally moved to New York in 1840, where he became the organist of the Baptist Tabernacle. As a disciple of Lowell Mason he started music conventions in New Jersey, the first held in Somerville in 1851. When Mason came to New York, Bradbury joined his former teacher in founding the New York Normal Institute. By this time he had added considerably to his musical background. He spent almost two years in Europe, after leaving the Baptist Tabernacle in 1847, and studied with Moscheles, Hauptmann, Wenzl, and Böhme.

In 1854 he formed a partnership with his brother for manufacturing pianos, and the firm that produced the Bradbury piano was highly successful. Bradbury was a natural money-maker, but overwork brought on an ailment of the lungs which caused his death at his New Jersey home, January 7, 1868. His best-known hymn-tunes were: *He Leadeth Me; Woodworth* (*Just as I am, without one plea*); and *Bradbury* (*Saviour, like a shepherd lead me*).

Church music and songs for Sunday Schools were in great demand in the early and middle nineteenth century, and many of the composers who wrote them made large sums of money. Most of these musicians are known to us by an occasional hymn-tune; their ambitious collections have been replaced by modern editions.

SILVANUS BILLINGS POND (1792–1871) was born in Worcester, Massachusetts, became a piano maker in Albany, New York, and moved to New York City in 1832, where he entered the publishing house of Firth & Hall. In 1848 the firm became Firth, Pond & Company and was one of the principal publishers of Stephen Foster's songs. In 1863, Pond left the Firth interests and established the business now known as William A. Pond & Company. He wrote many Sunday School songs, some secular songs, and compiled the *United States Psalmody*.

CHARLES ZEUNER (1795–1857) was a German who came to Boston in 1824. Baptized *Heinrich Christopher*, he changed his name to *Charles*, possibly to seem more like an American. He is best known today for his *Missionary Chant*, which is contained in many hymnbooks. For seven years he was organist of the Handel and Haydn Society. After thirty years in Boston he moved to Philadelphia, where he held the position of organist in several prominent churches. Unfortunate moodiness and eccentricities of temperament made it difficult for him to get along with others, and a mental ailment culminated in death by his own hand when he was sixty-two years old.

Zeuner's largest composition was an oratorio, *The Feast of Tabernacles*, which was published and performed in Boston. Tradition has it that Zeuner demanded $3,000 when he offered the manuscript to the Handel and Haydn Society. The Society felt this was too much. When the work was later given eight performances by the Boston Academy of Music at the Odeon, it resulted in complete failure financially. The hot-tempered Zeuner broke into the Academy one night and destroyed all copies of the work that he could find, including the manuscript.

Several years later a correspondent of *Dwight's Journal of Music* wrote as follows:

I doubt if Zeuner is appreciated. There is hardly a great composition for church or stage which one person at least would rather hear than Zeuner's "Feast of Tabernacles," the oratorio which after a few performances in Boston some years since he withdrew—there is too much reason to fear—forever!

For long life HENRY KEMBLE OLIVER (1800–1885) ranks with Mason, Hastings, and Webb. He lived to be eighty-five years old. He is known best as the composer of the hymn-tune *Federal Street*, sometimes sung to Oliver Wendell Holmes's *Lord of All Being, Throned Afar*, but originally written for Miss Steele's hymn *So fades the lovely blooming flower*.

Oliver was truly a man of parts, and a dominant factor in the business and cultural interests of nineteenth-century New England. Although he was a choirmaster and organist, music was his avocation. In middle life he was Adjutant-General of Massachusetts for four years, superintendent of the Atlantic Cotton Mills in Lawrence for ten years, mayor of Lawrence for a year, treasurer of Massachusetts during the Civil War, and for ten years chief of the state's Department of Labor. He was active in musical organizations, some of which he organized and managed himself. He was born in Beverly, Massachusetts, and died in Salem, where he had lived for many years.

He published several volumes of hymn-tunes: *Oliver's Collection of Hymn and Psalm Tunes;* and with Tuckerman and Bancroft *The National Lyre: a new collection of sacred music*.

BENJAMIN FRANKLIN BAKER (1811–1889) was Lowell Mason's successor as teacher of music in the Boston schools. He was a singer and director of church choirs in Salem and Boston, and participated in the work of the music conventions. From 1841 to 1847 he was vice-president of the Handel and Haydn Society. He founded a Boston Music School in 1851, acted as its principal and took charge of the vocal department. When the school went out of business in 1868, Baker retired from active work.

Although Baker was himself a composer, one of his most interesting works was the *Haydn Collection of Church Music*, in which the tunes were selected and arranged from the works of Haydn, Handel, Mozart, Beethoven, Weber, Rossini, Mendelssohn, Cherubini, and others. In like manner the *Classical Chorus Book* contained anthems, motets, and hymns arranged from the works of Mozart, Beethoven, and so on. He was the author of a treatise on *Thorough Bass and Harmony*, and wrote three cantatas: *The Storm King, The Burning Ship*, and *Camillus the Conqueror*.

Baker spent his whole life in New England. He was born in Wenham, Massachusetts, and died in Boston.

ISAAC BAKER WOODBURY (1819–1858), like General Oliver, was born in Beverly, Massachusetts. In his early life he was apprenticed to a blacksmith, and devoted his spare time to music. At thirteen he went to Boston for study, and when he was nineteen went to Europe and studied in Paris and London. When he came back to America he taught in Boston, and joined the Bay State Glee Club, which traveled through New England. In 1851 he went to New York and became editor of the *New York Musical Review*. Because of ill health he went again to Europe, and later decided to spend his winters in the South. The rigors of one of these trips proved too much for him, and he died in Columbia, South Carolina, in 1858, thirty-nine years of age.

In his lifetime, Woodbury's music was used in churches more than that of any of his contemporaries, and though little of it is heard today, a number of his tunes are still found in our hymnbooks. Certainly he had the benefit of a good advertising man, for in Dwight's staid *Journal of Music* this advertisement appeared in 1853:

125,000 Copies in Two Seasons!

Live Music Book!

The Dulcimer

A Collection of Sacred Music

by I. B. Woodbury

The "learn-music-at-home" idea had an early advocate in Woodbury, for one of his works was called *Woodbury's Self-Instructor in Musical Composition and Thorough Bass*. With B. F. Baker he compiled the *Boston Musical Education Society's Collection of Church Music* (1842) and *The Choral* (1845). One of his first songs was a ballad *He Doeth All Things Well*, or *My Sister*. He sold this for ten dollars to George P. Reed of Boston, who published it in 1844. Another of his songs which had wide use was *The Indian's Lament*, with its first line: "Let me go to my home in the far distant West."

Metcalf has given a sympathetic portrait of Woodbury: [1]

Gentleness was the characteristic of the man and his music. His compositions were for the church, the fireside and the social circle. He wrote with
remarkable fluency and it was surprising how much he could accomplish in
a short space of time. . . . He had a beautiful voice and sang various styles,
but excelled in the ballad and descriptive music. For sport he was fond of
hunting and duck-shooting. And in a letter to his paper he wrote that even
in winter it was his daily custom to ride on horseback, or, when Old Boreas
blew cold, in his carriage, among the leafless trees or the evergreen pines.

[1] From *American Writers and Compilers of Hymn Tunes;* copyright, 1925, by
Frank J. Metcalf. Quoted by permission of the Abingdon Press.

CHAPTER SIX

Our Nineteenth-Century Background in Secular Music

I. CONCERT LIFE

CITY dwellers in the early nineteenth century had plenty of musical entertainment. Both foreign and native artists found it profitable to offer their services for public and private occasions. Sometimes the concerts were for the benefit of the artists themselves, and sometimes for charity. Old newspapers ran advertisements of such affairs as a "Vocal Concert for the benefit of the Respectable Aged and Indigent Female Assistance Society" (New York, 1839) and others to raise funds for equally worthy objects. In New York the concerts were held at the City Hotel, Niblo's Gardens, the Lyceum, the Apollo, or the Broadway Tabernacle. Even Davies' Hot Pie House was not without its musical affairs; the New York *Herald* of January 7, 1839, told its readers that

A musical party will meet this evening, at 8 o'clock, at Davies' Hot Pie House, No. 14 John Street. A professor will preside at the Piano Forte. Admission 12½ cents.

Some of the artists made impressive claims. Signor de Begnis, first buffo singer from the Italian Opera House in London, promised that at one of his concerts he would sing six hundred words and three hundred bars of music in the short space of four minutes. Many of the concerts assumed mammoth proportions. At a "Great Union Performance of Sacred Music," in the Broadway Tabernacle (New York, 1839) the New York Sacred Music Society was assisted by choirs from twenty surrounding towns, one thousand singers in all.

Each of the three leading cities had a group of serious musicians in whom the better musical life centered, and who cultivated a following and did much to raise standards. Benjamin Carr, Raynor Taylor, Hupfeld, Cross, and others in Philadelphia formed a group that culminated in the Musical Fund Society. In Boston, Graupner, Ostinelli, Mallet, Granger, and others founded a Philharmonic Society; Graupner, Peabody, and Thomas Webb the Handel and Haydn Society; and Mason and George Webb the Boston Academy of Music.

New York, too, had its musicians, and though they were forced to compromise with the public taste, they kept their own standards high and did much for the cultivation of good music. The eighteenth century had seen musical organizations in New York. James Hewitt with his English friends had formed a Philharmonic Society which flourished for a number of years; the Germans had founded the Concordia, and the Euterpean Society celebrated its forty-eighth anniversary in 1847. There was also a New York Sacred Music Society, directed by U. C. Hill, which presented *The Messiah* in 1831, and Mendelssohn's *St. Paul* in 1838. In 1839 a "Musical Solemnity" was held in the memory of Daniel Schlesinger, a thoroughly trained musician who had made his home in New York at the time of his death; and from this concert, largely orchestral in character, the idea of a permanent professional orchestra was born. With Hill as the motivating spirit, the Philharmonic Society of New York was founded in 1842, an orchestra which is today acknowledged one of the finest in the world. An account of the men who formed the Philharmonic is the history of New York's musical life in the first half of the century.

Ureli Corelli Hill (1802–1875) deserves credit, above all others, for forming the Society and for maintaining its existence in its first years. H. E. Krehbiel, in his monograph *The Philharmonic Society of New York*,[1] presents a brief sketch of Hill:

He was not a New Yorker, but a Connecticut Yankee, and the strangeness of his Christian name suggests the idea that some of his mental peculiarities were an inheritance. In all probability his father was fond of the violin. . . .

Yankee "push," energy, shrewdness, enthusiasm, industry, pluck, self-

---

[1] H. E. Krehbiel; *The Philharmonic Society of New York*, Novello, Ewer & Co.

reliance, and endurance were all present in the composition of Hill's character. It seems incontestable from the evidence that his natural gifts as a musician were not great. When he went to study with Spohr in 1835, he had already occupied a prominent position in the musical life of the city for some years. He could plan and could organize. Obstacles had no terror for him; he thought that patience and industry would surmount them. He did achieve wonderful things with the crude material at his disposal, but though he labored hard he never overcame the limitations which nature had set for him as an executant.

He remained over two years with Spohr, and when he returned he gave great vogue to that master's "School for the Violin," and became the most popular and successful violin teacher in the city. He was of the stuff that pioneers are made of, and filled with a restless energy. Despite his achievements as a conductor of amateur and professional bodies, he was continually looking for new fields to conquer. He had some of the spirit of the New England convention leader, and would have been supremely happy had he been able to count his performers by the hundreds or thousands, instead of scores. But with all his eagerness he inculcated a taste for good music, and his pupils bless his memory.

His fate was a melancholy one. Though he could earn money he could not keep it. He sought his fortunes out West, five years after the foundation of the Philharmonic, and was gone three or four years, only to find that the best field for his energies was New York. Once the Society helped him with a loan of practically all the money in the sinking fund, and had to wait long for its return.

He played in the orchestra until 1873, and was then retired because of old age, being seventy. For a while, he played as an extra at Wallack's Theatre, but was unable to maintain himself there. Some operations in New Jersey real estate had proved abortive. He tried to get up a concert for a daughter in Jersey City, and was shocked at the lack of interest in his enterprise displayed by the musical profession.

Then, the painful conviction was forced on him that he "lagged superfluous on the stage." At his home in Paterson, N.J., on September 2, 1875, he killed himself by taking morphine. In a letter of explanation and farewell he wrote these words:

"To live and be a beggar and a slave is a little too much for me, maugre I am an old man. Look at all of us! Is it not heartrending to contemplate? Ha, ha! the sooner I go the better. O, merciful father, take good care of my wife and family! Blessings on all they have done for me."

In the first five seasons of the Philharmonic, Hill conducted five of the concerts. The first program, presented at the Apollo Rooms, December 7, 1842, shows that the standards of the group were high though their performances may have been ragged. Hill conducted the orchestra in Beethoven's Fifth Symphony, Weber's Overture to *Oberon*, and an Overture in D by Kalliwoda. Five instrumentalists played the Hummel D Minor Quintette, and the vocal numbers, rendered by Madame Otto and C. E. Horn, consisted of selections from *Oberon*, Beethoven's *Fidelio*, Mozart's *Belmont and Constantia*, and a duet from Rossini's *Armida*. There is further discussion of the early Philharmonic performances in our chapter on Theodore Thomas.

The program of the first concert stated that "the vocal music will be directed by Mr. Timm." HENRY CHRISTIAN TIMM (1811–1892) was one of the first competent pianists who lived in New York. Born in Hamburg, Germany in 1811, he had settled in New York in 1835, and after giving a concert at the Park Theatre had immediately come into public favor. His debut was followed by an unsuccessful concert tour through New England, and to make a living he became second horn player in the Park Theatre Orchestra. Next he went South as conductor of an opera troupe that traveled for six months, and settled in Baltimore where he had a position as organist. He soon returned to New York, and became chorus master and trombone player for a company organized by C. E. Horn, who had leased the new National Opera House. When the theatre burned down, Timm became organist of St. Thomas's Church in New York, and later played at the Unitarian Church, where he remained for eighteen years. He lived until he was eighty-one years old, when he died in New York in 1892.

Timm was active in the formation of the Philharmonic, and was its president from 1847 to 1864. From contemporary accounts he was an excellent pianist. One legend has it that he could play scales with a full wine glass on the back of his hand without spilling a drop. The New York correspondent of Dwight's *Journal* in Boston described him as "the most elegant of our pianists," and in reviewing a concert in November, 1852, said:

The next instrumental piece was the first movement of Hummel's Concerto in B minor, the piano-forte by Mr. Timm. How finely that gentleman plays you need not be told. The deeply melancholy character of the music was admirably conveyed in the performance of both pianist and orchestra, and was doubly effective from its contrast to the Symphony (Beethoven's 8th).

Timm was also something of a composer. He wrote a grand Mass, part-songs, and made many transcriptions for two pianos, which he played in concerts with his colleagues.

DANIEL SCHLESINGER (1799–1839), whose memorial concert was largely responsible for forming the Philharmonic, was a German pianist who came to New York in 1836. He was an excellent musician, pupil of Ferdinand Ries and Moscheles, and if he had been spared he would undoubtedly have proved a powerful influence in this country.

Concert notices of the time tell something of Schlesinger's activities. On one occasion he played a Hummel concerto with orchestra; on another he joined his colleague Scharfenberg in playing the Rondo and Variations for two pianos by Henri Herz; and with Scharfenberg and another pianist, Czerny's "Grand Trio Concertante, for six hands on two pianos."

At the memorial concert after his death in 1839—"The Musical Tribute to the Memory of the late Daniel Schlesinger"—held at the Broadway Tabernacle in 1839, an orchestra of sixty performers, the Concordia (a chorus of forty amateurs of which he had been the director), and distinguished *virtuosi* played a program that included his *Grand Overture, Full Orchestra, Composed expressly for the London Philharmonic Society;* and the *Adagio and Finale of the celebrated Quatuor in C minor, for piano, tenor, violin and violoncello.*

WILLIAM SCHARFENBERG (1819–1895) was also a German. U. C. Hill met him when he went to Cassel to take lessons from Spohr. Hill painted an enthusiastic picture of the opportunities for young musicians in America, and finally persuaded the young German to come here. He arrived in New York in 1838 and made his debut as a pianist under Hill's auspices.

Scharfenberg at once took a leading position among the musicians of the city, for he had only one rival as a pianist, Daniel Schlesinger, and the latter died a few months after Scharfenberg came. Moreover, it was a rivalry, as Krehbiel wrote, that was "sweetened by a most un-selfish and friendly interest on the part of the elder musician." Excerpts from Dwight's *Journal* afford descriptions of Scharfenberg and his colleagues. May 1, 1852:

> The Philharmonic Orchestra is admirably drilled. The members are all inspired by the same sympathies,—mostly Germans, they believe in the German Composers, who would not regret to sit among the audience and hear their own immortality so assured. Mr. Timm . . . is President; Mr. Scharfenberg, whose delicate and polished style evinces the student of the best classics only, is vice-president. They assist in the orchestra, taking very humble parts. Mr. Scharfenberg, I think, played the cymbals. . . .
>
> Mr. Scharfenberg played a Concerto of Mendelssohn's with the orchestra. I wish he were more impassioned. Yet his reverence for the master is very beautiful, and the quiet, uncompromising purity of his style is sure to secure your most judicious approval. Later in the evening he and Mr. Timm played a Grand Duo of Mendelssohn's upon the Bohemian march from "Preciosa." It was effective, but not striking. In fact, neither of the piano performances were strictly interesting. They were learned and skillful rather than inspired. But the audience made it a point of honor to listen silently, and recognized by their applause the admirable performance, although there was no great enthusiasm for the works.

And from Newport, Rhode Island, August 28, 1852:

> The lover of music has great privileges here. Besides the many concerts, always of a high order, there is sometimes at the hotels, but constantly in private circles, a great variety of choice music. In Mr. Scharfenberg's little cozy parlor, Beethoven, Chopin and Mendelssohn, Spohr, and other worthy associates, are daily worshipped by a few of the true worshippers. . . .

Scharfenberg was active in the Philharmonic Society from the start. In its third season he was secretary; in the ninth, vice-president; and from 1863 to 1866, president. He also formed, in 1845, the music publishing firm Scharfenberg & Luis, whose store on Broadway was headquarters for the Philharmonic. The business lasted until 1866, when Scharfenberg left to live temporarily in Havana. On his return he became associated as reader and editor with the publisher who was to become one of the foremost in America, Gustave Schirmer. Although Scharfenberg was something of a composer on his own account, it was as editor that he made his great contribution, and hundreds of the volumes in the Schirmer *Library of Classics* were annotated and prepared by his careful pen. He enjoyed long life, and died in 1895 at the age of seventy-six in Quogue, Long Island.

CHARLES EDWARD HORN (1786–1849) belongs both in this chapter and the next. He was a serious musician, singer, pianist, and composer; as a ballad singer and composer he was influential in shaping a type of song popular to our own day. Unlike Scharfenberg and Timm, Horn had made a reputation abroad before he came here. He was the son of Karl Friedrich Horn, a German musician who came to London in 1782 and became the vogue as a teacher among the English nobility. The father was appointed music master in ordinary to Queen Charlotte and the princesses, and was organist at St. George's Chapel at Windsor from 1824 until his death in 1830.

The son Charles was born in St. Martin's-in-the-Fields, and received most of his musical training from his father. By the time he came to America in 1833, at the age of forty-seven, he had been one of the composers at the Vauxhall, director of music at the Olympia, and was highly popular as an opera singer (although his voice was poor, and useful principally because of its enormous range). He had composed and produced twenty-two operas, some, like his setting of Moore's *Lalla Rookh*, highly successful.

When Horn came to New York he first produced English operas at the Park Theatre, where he met with great success. During the following years he was active in theatrical affairs, concert appearances with his wife, who was also a singer, and he found time to write and produce an oratorio *The Remission of Sin*. When he directed this work in London some years later he presented it under the brief, but alluring, title *Satan*. In 1842 he was one of the founders of the Philharmonic and sang at its first concert. Shortly after this a severe illness cost him the use of his voice, and he was obliged to give up singing. With a man named Davis, he established a publishing house called Davis & Horn. His partner withdrew after a year, and Horn continued the business alone.

In 1843, Horn returned to England for four years, and acted as musical director at the Princess Theatre in London. When he came back to America in 1847 he settled in Boston, where he was elected conductor of the Handel and Haydn Society. In 1848 he went to England for a few months to produce another of his oratorios, *Daniel's Predic-*

tion, and when he went back to Boston in June of the same year he was re-elected conductor of the Handel and Haydn. He performed these duties for the ensuing season only, for he died in 1849.

In the year 1839, Horn made almost thirty concert and recital appearances in New York City. First, there were the six *Soirées Musicales* that were offered by Mr. and Mrs. Horn on the Thursday of each alternate week during February, March, and April. Then he appeared in a number of concerts for charity; at the affair for the benefit of "Indigent Females"; at the Schlesinger Memorial; at a "Grand Sacred Concert" at the Broadway Tabernacle; and at a benefit for his partner Davis. He participated in many recitals offered by his colleagues—Knight, Russell, Signor Rapetti, Signora Maroncelli, and others.

Many of the songs on the programs were composed by Horn, but he often presented works by Purcell, Beethoven, Rossini and like composers, as well as songs by his colleagues Joseph Knight and Henry Russell. At the first and second of the *Soirées Musicales,* half of the programs were devoted to Handel's *Acis and Galatea.* Horn appeared not only as a singer; many concert programs bore the line, "Mr. C. E. Horn will preside at the pianoforte." With Henry Russell, also a singer, he played the *Zampa* Overture of Herold as a piano duet, and on several occasions he played duets with Scharfenberg. At one of his *soirées* he conducted an orchestra that numbered Scharfenberg and U. C. Hill among its members. The same program presented a solo and chorus from his oratorio *The Remission of Sin*—"Oh, myriads of immortal spirits."

Horn paid many musical tributes to America in his music, and he made several attempts to adapt what seemed to him to be Americanisms. On many of his programs there were excerpts from his *National Melodies of America,* a song cycle set to poems of George P. Morris, at one time editor of the New York *Home Journal* in conjunction with N. P. Willis. In his settings, Horn used supposedly native melodies. The first, *Northern Refrain,* was based on the "carol of the sweeps of the city of New York"; *Meeta,* and *Near the Lake, Where Drooped the Willow* were made from Negro airs. One of Horn's most popular songs was *Cherry Ripe.* Many were tenderly sentimental—*All Things Love Thee, So Do I; Tell Her She Haunts Me Yet* ("the words by a young lady of Louisville"); *Do You Remember, Mary?; Dark Eyed One;*

Child of Earth with the Golden Hair, and others. In some of his songs he caught the old English spirit of merriment—*Thru the Streets of New York, Blithely and Gay; How Roses Came Red; If Maidens Would Marry;* and a setting of *I Know a Bank Whereon the Wild Thyme Grows.* The majority of his larger works were composed and published in London, though a number had been reprinted in New York before he came to this country.

2. EARLY SONG WRITERS

Sigmund Spaeth once wrote that the history of American manners, morals, tastes, and absurdities is largely written in our songs. Famous historical events have always been commemorated musically, but our lighter ballads have gone further; in intimate fashion they tell of what we were thinking, and how we were consoling ourselves at the time they were written.

The last chapter discussed early nineteenth-century concerts, and musical organizations of a fairly serious character. The popular concerts and recitals of the day, bordering often on entertainments, were closely associated with songs and ballads that have either survived to our time, or have at least formed a definite link in the evolutionary chain of our popular music.

Some of these concert programs were devoted exclusively to ballads, some to operatic selections, and others to a mixture of light orchestral pieces, instrumental solos, and contemporary ballads. The New York *Musical Review* gave an account of an anniversary concert given by the Euterpean Society at the City Hotel, January 30, 1839, in which the "orchestra was superior to that we have heard in New York, in respect to the amount of *talent* it contained." For this, it said, "much praise is due to the Society, which consists of amateurs, and especially to Mr. Quin, the leader, who is also an amateur, for the manner in which the overtures were got up."

The orchestra consisted of amateurs, with the first desks occupied by professionals. There were six first violins, five second violins, four tenors (violas), three cellos, and two contrabasses. The wind section consisted of two clarinets, two oboes, two bassoons, four horns, and two trumpets. Drums, cymbals, and kettledrums formed the percussion group. Mr. and Mrs. Horn were the vocalists, and U. C. Hill and William Scharfenberg were among the professional instrumentalists.

A compilation of New York newspaper references to music in the year 1839, made by Miss Kathleen Munro, shows that there were at least seventy concerts. Of these, ten were devoted to sacred music, some of them performances by the New York Sacred Music Society with the assistance of church choirs from surrounding towns. Ten offered operatic selections from the Italian repertoire, presented by the Seguins and such visiting artists as Madame Albini, Madame Vellani, and Signora Maroncelli. Six were chiefly instrumental recitals, one given by Baron Rudolph de Fleur, pianist of His Majesty the Emperor of Russia. Fourteen were a mixture of vocal and instrumental selections. The largest classification was that of the ballad concerts; there were at least thirty of them. The Horns were the most prominent of the recitalists, and not only offered their own ballad concerts, but participated in those given by others, and in concerts and recitals of various types.

Two of the most prominent singers of the time were visiting Englishmen who were also ballad composers. The name of Joseph Philip Knight will be immortal, among bassos particularly, for *Rocked in the Cradle of the Deep*, which he wrote when he visited America in 1839. Henry Russell can be forgiven much for his setting of Morris's *Woodman, Spare That Tree*.

JOSEPH PHILIP KNIGHT (1812–1887) was a prolific ballad composer and singer who became eventually a clergyman of the Church of England, and was ordained by the Bishop of Exeter to the charge of St. Agnes in the Scilly Isles. At the age of sixteen he had studied harmony under Crofe, at one time organist of Bristol Cathedral. The single year he spent in the United States, 1839, was one of the most productive of his career.

At the concert for the benefit of the Indigent Female Assistance Society it was announced that "Mr. J. P. Knight will make his first appearance in this country, and will sing four of his most popular songs." Two of these songs were written by himself: *Oh Lord, I Have Wandered*, and *The Veteran*. Three days later, March 1, he sang his setting of T. H. Bayly's *She Wore a Wreath of Roses*, in which the unfortunate heroine is introduced, first wearing roses, then orange blossoms, and finally a widow's somber cap.

Knight made nine appearances in New York in the first half of the year, and returned to the city in the fall for another series of concerts. For October 9, the newspapers announced a Grand Concert at which "Mr. Knight, in addition to his most popular songs, will introduce three of his latest compositions, which have never yet been heard in public." These were *Cupid, 'mid the Roses Playing, Twenty Years Ago,* and most important of all, *Rocked in the Cradle of the Deep.* His American visit also inspired *Oh, Fly to the Prairie,* and *The Old Year's Gone, and the New Year's Come.*

The song that did much to establish Knight's vogue as a song writer was *The Grecian Daughter,* to words by Thomas Haynes Bayly, composer and writer of *Long, Long Ago.* The verses were prophetic of the coming school of self-pity:

> Oh! never heed my mother dear,
> The silent tears I shed;
> Indeed I will be happy here,
> Then ask me not to wed.
> By day you shall not see me weep,
> Nor nightly murmur in my sleep;
> But ask me not to be a bride,
> For when my own dear Lara died,
> I kiss'd his brow, I breath'd a vow,
> Ah! bid me not to break it now.

HENRY RUSSELL (1812–1900) spent more time in America than Knight; he was here for nearly nine years—1833 to 1841. He had a keen sense of dramatic values and platform effectiveness. A master of hokum, he could draw cheers from his audiences at will. He was well educated musically, and at one time he had been a pupil of Rossini in Naples. Although of Jewish extraction, he came to America as organist of the First Presbyterian Church in Rochester, New York, and then traveled extensively as a concert singer.

Russell was very busy in New York during the year that Knight was in this country, and the two often appeared on the same programs. He must have been a drawing card, for his appearance was generally featured. On February 25, the Board of Managers of the New York Sacred Music Society had "the honor to state that they had prevailed on Mr. Russell to remain in town for this occasion, when he will perform his celebrated Sacred Songs of *The Skeptic's Lament, Wind of the Winter's Night, The Maniac, The Charter Oak*," and others. The performance was "intended to surpass that of any other occasion." Three days later the committee of the concert for Indigent Females felt "happy to announce that Mr. H. Russell had kindly volunteered his services." His participation in Mr. Davis's benefit (March 1) was announced as "Mr. Henry Russell's Last Appearance in New York." Like many other farewell appearances it was followed by concerts March 5 and May 24.

After a number of Russell's concerts in the fall of 1839, Mrs. Horn, giving a concert of her own, advertised that she had "the pleasure of announcing the valuable services of Mr. H. Russell, who has politely postponed his departure for the South." Whether he lacked funds for traveling, or just decided he didn't want to go, the latter part of December found him still in New York, giving a series of concerts with the Seguins.

John Hill Hewitt gave an account of Russell in his book *Shadows on the Wall:*

He spent much of his time in Baltimore, though New York was his headquarters. In person he was rather stout, but not tall. His face was prepossessing, of the Hebrew cast, dark and heavy whiskers and curly hair. He was an expert at wheedling audiences out of applause, and adding to the effect of his songs by a brilliant pianoforte accompaniment. With much self-laudation he used often to describe the wonderful influence of his descriptive songs over audiences.

On one occasion he related an incident connected with "Woodman, Spare that Tree." He had finished the last verse. . . . The audience were spellbound for a moment, and then poured out a volume of applause that shook the building to its foundation. In the midst of this tremendous evidence of their boundless gratification, a snowy-headed gentleman, with great anxiety depicted in his venerable features, arose and demanded silence. He asked, with a tremulous voice: "Mr. Russell, in the name of Heaven, tell me, was the tree spared?" "It was, sir," replied the vocalist. "Thank God! Thank God! I breathe again!" and then he sat down, perfectly overcome by his emotions. This miserable bombast did not always prove a clap-trap; in many instances it drew forth hisses.

Russell's voice was a baritone of limited register; the few good notes he possessed he turned to advantage. His "Old Arm Chair," for instance, has but five notes in its melodic construction. . . .

Russell once called on me and asked me to write him a song on an "Old Family Clock" (he was remarkably fond of the prefix *old*; a wag of a poet once sent him some words addressed to an "Old Fine-tooth Comb"). I wrote the words. He then changed his mind, and employed me, promising good pay, to write a descriptive song on the "Drunkard," to stir up the temperance people. I pleased him much by beginning the song in this way: "The *old* lamp burned on the *old* oaken stool." He made a taking affair of it; and he made money on it too, but I never even got his promise to pay. . . .

The Old Arm Chair was published in 1840, and is one of our very early mother songs.

> I love it! I love it, and who shall dare
> To chide me for loving that old Arm chair.
>
> 'Tis bound by a thousand bands to my heart
> Not a tie will break, not a link will start,
> Would ye learn the spell, a mother sat there.

A few years later Russell decided that the idea was good for another song, especially if it drew a moral from the first. Accordingly, he published *Oh! Weep Not*, a companion to *The Old Arm Chair*, copies of which sold for six and a fourth cents.

> Oh! Weep not, oh! weep not, nor idly sigh
> Thy tears can recall not the days gone by.
>
> But neglect not the precepts, forget not the prayer
> Which thy mother taught thee from her old arm chair.

This custom of following a successful song with a companion, or sequel, was prevalent at the time. When Bayly had scored a success with *Oh, No, We Never Mention Her*, he may have decided that he had been a bit hard on the lady, and presented her side of the story to the public with *She Never Blamed Him, Never*, "answer to the admired ballad *Oh, No, We Never Mention Her*." Instead of "blaming him,"

> She sighed when he caressed her
> For she knew that they must part;
> She spoke not when he press'd her
> To his young and panting heart;

The banners waved around her
And she heard the bugles sound—
They pass'd—and strangers found her
Cold and lifeless on the ground.

In one respect times were changing. In the eighteenth century, songs were sung by certain artists with "unbounded" applause. As competition became keen they were announced as sung with "rapturous" applause—which must have proved emotionally wearing to the audience.

The songs that belong to Russell's American period were *The Brave Old Oak*; *The Charter Oak*; *The Old Bell*; *The Ivy Green*; *Our Way Across the Mountain, Ho*; *Woodman, Spare That Tree*; *The Wreck of the Mexico*; *A Life on the Ocean Wave*; *I Love the Man with a Generous heart*; *Those Locks, Those Ebon Locks*, and many others, including *The Old Sexton*, the gravedigger who sings, as he "gathers them in": "and their final rest is here, down here on the earth's dark breast."

Although he was a favorite with the public, Russell had his critics, for there were some who did not fall victim to his theatrical charms. One reviewer in Boston wrote that the only item Russell had omitted from his program was the "old boot jack." His methods were not designed for Americans alone, for when he returned to England, he continued the same kind of concerts, and the same ways of getting publicity. If he had his tongue in his cheek here, he at least failed to remove it when he went home. Dwight's *Journal* of April 16, 1853 contained the following item, under the heading "Miscellaneous."

A Life on the Ocean Wave! Ho, ho, etc. Mr. Henry Russell, a great charlatan, has put forth a scheme for ameliorating the condition of the poor, by advertising in the program of a week's entertainment, just concluded at the Strand Theatre, that he will each evening present a ticket to every person at entrance, which will entitle them to a chance of obtaining a free passage to America The drawing will take place after his entertainment.

He lived to be eighty-eight years old. In 1889, *A Life on the Ocean Wave* was made the official march of the Royal marines, and *Cheer, Boys, Cheer* has for many years been the only air played by British regimental fife and drum corps when a regiment goes abroad. His sons achieved fame on their own account. One, Henry Russell, was an impresario, and the other, Landon Ronald, an eminent British composer.

And now for the rest of the Hewitt family, the sons and daughters of the James Hewitt who came to New York in 1792. Few of the songs of JOHN HILL HEWITT (1801–1890), his eldest son, are sung today, but they were once so popular that their composer became a decided influence in shaping the style of our lighter ballads. His life was so varied, and his exploits so colorful, that he occupies a unique position in both the musical and literary history of America. Any man who won a poetry contest against Edgar Allan Poe warrants mention as a curiosity, if for no other reason. Hewitt has been termed the "Father of the American ballad." Obviously, this is too great a claim, for English influences have been too pronounced for us to grant that title to any of our native composers.

In the letters of his father, written just before his death to his younger son James Lang Hewitt, the elder Hewitt expressed his concern over the ways of John, the rolling stone:

> John I am still uneasy about. When you see him, or write, tell him his father in his latter moments did not forget him—left him his blessing, with the hope that he will turn his mind to one particular object, that he may get thro the World respected.

And a few weeks later:

> In the *Weekly Mirror* and *Advertiser* of here [New York] I see the last two papers that have poetry of John's. Very pretty, but he ought to write to me.

In an undated document addressed to James L., in which the father disposes of his worldly goods, there is another reference to John:

> . . . there is a reserve in my character which others have said was pride. No—it has been that I should not force myself into others' company. John unfortunately has this latter—it is right for a young man to be in some degree reserved—but in case of business that must in a great degree be laid aside, as it is necessary to have some degree of effrontery to get on in the world. This I am afraid will keep John, with all his talents, poor like myself. It is a fact that a man with independence, without talent, will make a fortune, while the modest man, let his talents be ever so great, will be kept in the background.

John, as we shall see, never let modesty deter him in later life.

This eldest son of James Hewitt was born in Maiden Lane, New York, July 11, 1801. When he was eleven the family moved to Boston, and the boy was placed in the public schools. Later he was apprenticed to a sign painter, but he disliked the work so much that he ran away. He then entered the employ of a commission firm named Lock and Andrews, and stayed with them until they failed a few years later. By this time the family had moved back to New York, and in 1818, John secured an appointment to West Point. Various legends have sprung up regarding his career at the military academy, one to the effect that he was breveted a second lieutenant after successfully completing three years of study. Another story tells that at the end of four years he was graduated, but resigned his commission immediately afterwards. Still another connects him with a plot of the Southern cadets to get control of the Academy and blow up the superintendent in 1820.

None of these accounts is accurate. The records of the War Department show that Hewitt was admitted to the academy from New York on September 21, 1818. When he was a member of the graduating class in 1822 he was turned back to the next line class because of deficiency in studies, and did not return the following year. There is no record of his participation in any disturbance.

At the time of his death in 1890, an obituary notice in the Baltimore *American* said that among his fellow cadets were Beauregard, Robert E. Lee, Polk, Johnson, and Jackson. While at the academy he had studied music with Willis, the leader of the West Point band, and when he left and went South, he turned to music teaching as the pleasantest way to earn a living. He also started his editorial work, and became associated with newspapers in the various cities in which he lived. Soon after leaving West Point he married his first wife Estelle Mangin, who bore him seven children.

Shortly after his marriage, Hewitt's father persuaded him to join a theatrical company he was organizing to tour the South. The venture ended in failure, and the company was burned out in a fire in Augusta, Georgia. He stayed in Augusta for a short while and then went to Columbia, South Carolina, where he taught music, composed, and commenced the study of law. From Columbia he went to Greenville, and

established a newspaper called the *Republican*. Meeting with reverses
he returned to Augusta.

It was about this time (1825) that he composed his first song *The
Minstrel's Return from the War*. On the original manuscript of this
song, now at the Library of Congress, the composer in later years penciled the following memorandum:

> This song, as crude as it is, was one of my first musical efforts. It was
> composed in 1825 in the village of Greenville, S.C. now a city of 10,000
> souls. When I returned to the North, I took this book with me to Boston. My
> brother James was a music publisher. I gave him a copy to publish—he did
> it very reluctantly—did not think it worthy of a copyright. It was eagerly
> taken up by the public, and established my reputation as a ballad composer.
> It was sung all over the world—and my brother, not securing the right, told
> me that he missed making at least $10,000.

He returned to the North because of his father's death in 1827. He
remained for a short while in Boston, and worked on the staff of the
Massachusetts Journal. He soon departed for the South again, intending to go back to Georgia, but a visit to Baltimore determined him to
stay in that city, where he spent the greater part of his long life.

In Baltimore he immediately became active in newspaper work, music, and matters theatrical. He was also achieving some contemporary
fame as both composer and poet. He became the editor of the *Visitor*,
and when that paper sponsored a literary contest, he entered a poem
under a nom de plume. He called it *The Song of the Wind*, and it was
awarded the prize over Edgar Allan Poe's *The Coliseum*. In his book
of memories, *Shadows on the Wall*, Hewitt told the story of the contest:

> The proprietors of the journal . . . offered two premiums; one of $100
> for the best story, another of $50 for the best poem. I was editor of the paper
> at the time. The committee on the awards . . . decided that Poe's weird
> tale entitled "A Manuscript Found in a Bottle" should receive first premium.
> There were two poems selected from the four-score offered, as worthy of the
> second award. They were "The Coliseum" by Poe, and "The Song of the
> Wind," by myself. The judges were brought to a stand, but, after some
> debate, agreed that the latter should receive the second prize, as the author
> of the former had already received the first. This decision did not please Poe,
> hence the "little unpleasantness" between us.

Poe received his money with many thanks; I preferred a silver goblet, which is now in my family.

The opening lines of Hewitt's poem were as follows:

> Whence come ye with your odor-laden wings,
>   Oh, unseen wanderer of the summer night?
> Why, sportive, kiss my lyre's trembling strings,
>   Fashioning wild music, which the light
> Of listening orbs doth seem in joy to drink?
>   Ye wanton 'round my form and fan my brow,
> While I hold converse with the stars that wink
>   And laugh upon the mirror stream below.

The "little unpleasantness" between Poe and Hewitt had had fuel to feed it several years before the contest. When a volume of Poe's poems, *Al Aaraaf, Tamerlane and Minor Poems*, had appeared three years earlier (1829), Hewitt, as reviewer for the *Minerva*, admiring "the richness and smoothness of Thomas Moore and the grandeur of Byron," took occasion to assail the uneven and irregular rhythm of the comparatively unknown poet, whom with all his "brain cudgelling," he could not compel himself to understand "line by line, or the sum total."

The result of the contest, added to previous insults, was a little too much for the moody Poe. The next time he met Hewitt on the street, he accused him of using underhand methods as editor of the *Visitor* to win the prize. Words resulted in blows, but they were separated before any serious damage was done. Hewitt never forgave Poe for achieving fame; they parted as friends outwardly, but in *Shadows on the Wall* he expressed his real opinion:

Poe was not the poet he was said to be; he added but little to the literary reputation of our country. His "Raven" to be sure, gained him vast renown (particularly after he had rested in the grave for nearly 26 years!); but the idea was not original—it was taken from the old English poets. The "Manuscript Found in a Bottle" a composition which won several prizes, was only a new version of the "Rhyme of an Ancient Mariner."

For many years tributes to Poe have called forth reminders of the contest from Hewitt's admirers. When the University of Virginia unveiled the Poe monument, a correspondent of the New York *Herald* asked if it "would not be well to recognize the talents of one who was contemporary with Poe, and whose poetic genius won the prize over the very poem, the 'Coliseum,' quoted in the editorial column of the New York *Herald* of October 2!" The underrated genius complex went to extremes among Hewitt's admirers; there was even a tradition that he had sold ten of his song manuscripts to Stephen Foster, one of them *Old Folks at Home*.

In 1840, Hewitt moved to Washington, where he established and edited a paper called the *Capitol*. Five years later he went to Norfolk, Virginia, and then returned to Baltimore in 1847. Shortly after this he was offered a position as music teacher at the Chesapeake Female College in Hampton, Virginia. He went there and stayed for nine years. In Hampton his wife died.

When John Brown's raid made it apparent that northern Virginia would be an active scene for future hostilities between North and South, Hewitt left Hampton for Chambersburg and later went to Richmond. When Virginia seceded from the Union, he offered his services to the Confederacy, but he was then over sixty and was not accepted for active military service. Because of his West Point training, Jefferson Davis appointed him to the thankless task of drill master of raw recruits.

In 1863 he went to Savannah, Georgia, and married a former pupil, Mary Alethea Smith. Four more children were subsequently added to the family.

After the war, Hewitt returned to Baltimore and remained there for the rest of his long life. He became one of the characters of the city, and when he died at the age of eighty-nine, Baltimore felt that it had lost one of its links with the past. He had seen Fulton's first steamboat on the Hudson, he was present when the first dispatch was sent over Morse's telegraph line between Baltimore and Washington, and he was a passenger on the first train of cars that had been pulled out of Baltimore by a locomotive.

Hewitt composed over three hundred songs. *The Minstrel's Return from the War* brought him a reputation early in life. This was followed by another song which his brother James published, and had the foresight (or was it hindsight?) to copyright. This song was *The Knight of the Raven Black Plume*, agreeable both in words and music. The opening phrase is akin to Mendelssohn's *On Wings of Song,* undoubtedly a mere coincidence, as Hewitt could hardly have been familiar with Mendelssohn's song at the time. *On Wings of Song* was probably written in 1834; Hewitt's song was published before 1835. Others of his songs were *The Mountain Bugle; Take Me Home; Our Native Land; All Quiet Along the Potomac; Rock Me to Sleep, Mother;* and *Where the Sweet Magnolia Blooms. Take Me Home to the Sunny South* expressed the Southern sentiment after the war.

Although his greatest success was in a narrative type of ballad, Hewitt's oratorio *Jephtha* was given successfully in Washington, Georgetown, Norfolk, and Baltimore. When it was presented at the Broadway Tabernacle in New York with a chorus of two hundred and an orchestra of fifty, it was roughly handled by the critics. The composer also published several cantatas: *Flora's Festival; The Fairy Bridal; The Revellers;* and *The Musical Enthusiast.* His operas were *Rip Van Winkle; The Vivandière; The Prisoner of Monterey;* and *The Artist's Wife.*

In 1838, N. Hickman of Baltimore published a volume of Hewitt's miscellaneous poems. Many of these possess true imagery, and show genuine talent. *Shadows on the Wall,* the book of memories published in 1877, contains many of his later poems. His connections with theatrical enterprises led him to write plays, several of which were produced: *Washington; The Scouts; The Jayhawker; The Marquis in Petticoats; The Log Hut;* and *Plains of Manassas.*

The musical tradition of the Hewitt family has survived to the present generation. HORATIO DAWES HEWITT, the eldest son of John Hill Hewitt, was a musician and composer as well as a music critic. Born in Baltimore, he spent much of his life there, though he lived at various times in New Orleans and St. Louis, owning music stores in both cities. He composed a comic opera and many songs that enjoyed success. He survived his father by only four years, and died in Baltimore in 1894.

Of the brothers of John Hill Hewitt, JAMES LANG HEWITT, born in 1807, devoted his life to the music publishing business which had originally been started by his father when the latter bought Benjamin Carr's New York branch of the Musical Repository in 1798. He first appeared as a publisher on his own account when he joined J. A. Dickson at 34 Market Street, Boston, in 1825. After his father's death he moved back to New York, and became one of the prominent dealers and publishers of the city until the late 1840's. He died in 1853.

The third son of James Hewitt, HORATIO NELSON HEWITT, continued the music business in Boston for a number of years and later moved to New York. The youngest son, GEORGE WASHINGTON HEWITT, was trained as a musician and after a disastrous publishing venture in Philadelphia, settled in Burlington, New Jersey. He was a prolific composer, and his salon pieces for piano were much in demand. His son HOBART DOANE HEWITT, born in 1852, lived for many years in Burlington as a teacher of violin and piano. He died there in 1932. At one time associated with the publishing firm of Theodore Presser in Philadelphia, he published many compositions.

Both of James Hewitt's daughters were musicians. SOPHIA HENRIETTE, the eldest, married Louis Ostinelli, the violinist, who was one of the group that formed the Philharmonic Society with Graupner in Boston. Her daughter ELIZA OSTINELLI became a well-known opera singer after studying at the Conservatory at Naples. At one time she was a prominent prima donna in Europe. She married the Italian Count Biscaccianti, a cellist.

Sophia was organist of the Handel and Haydn Society from 1820 to 1829. She had been brought before the public as a pianist when she was only seven years old, in New York. She also sang and appeared occasionally at the New York concerts of the Euterpean Society. Parker's *Euterpeiad* of May 11, 1822, gave the following estimate of her performances on the piano:

> Her playing is plain, sensible and that of a gentlewoman; she neither takes by storm, nor by surprise, but she generally wins upon the understanding, while the ear, though it never fills the other senses with ecttacy [sic] drinks in full satisfaction.

Sophia died in Portland, Maine, in 1846. Her younger sister ELIZA never married, but was a music teacher, first in Boston, and then in Burlington where she lived with her brother.

There were many other song writers in the first half of the nineteenth century who contributed to our ballad literature. JOHN C. BAKER was perhaps best known for his song *Where can the soul find rest?* From this account, the soul has a long search. First the winds are consulted:

Stephen Collins Foster (from a Painting by Marie Goth in the Stephen Foster
Conservatories, Carmel, Indiana)

(See pages 184–198)

Foster's Own Account of His Income from
Royalties (1857)

(See page 195)

Tell me, ye winged winds, that round my pathway roar,
Do ye not know some spot, where mortals weep no more,
Some lone and pleasant dell, some valley in the West,
Where free from toil and pain, the weary soul may rest?

Chorus

The loud winds dwindled to a whisper low
And sighed for pity as it answered, No! No!

The second and third verses address the "mighty deep" and the "serenest moon," with no better results. Finally the bard goes to head-quarters and finds the answer:

Tell me, my secret soul, oh! tell me hope and faith,
Is there no resting place from sorrow, sin, and death;
Is there no happy spot where mortals may be bless'd
Where grief may find a balm, and weariness a rest?

Chorus

Faith, Hope, and Love, best boons to mortals giv'n
Wav'd their bright wings and whispered, "Yes, in Heav'n."

THOMAS BRICHER was organist of the Bowdoin Street Church in Boston in the fifties. Among his contributions to balladry were *Oh! Home of My Boyhood, My Own Country Home;* and *Our Fathers' Old Halls,* "as sung at the concerts of the Boston Musical Institute."

To WILLIAM CLIFTON we owe one of the most complete examples of noble resignation—*The Last Link is Broken* (published about 1840):

The last link is broken that bound me to thee,
And the words I have spoken have rendered me free;
That bright glance misleading on others may shine,
Those eyes smil'd unheeding when tears burst from mine:
If my love was deem'd boldness that error is o'er,
I've witnessed thy coldness and prize thee no more.

Refrain

I have not lov'd lightly, I'll think on thee yet,
I'll pray for thee nightly till life's sun has set

If FREDERICK WILLIAM NICHOLLS CROUCH (1808–1896) had post-poned writing *Kathleen Mavourneen* for twelve years we might have been able to claim it as an American song. Crouch was an Englishman who came here in 1849 at the age of forty, and lived here until his death in 1896. An excellent cellist, he had been a member of the Drury Lane Theatre in London, and had taught singing. *Kathleen Mavourneen* was first published in 1839, and scored an immediate success.

The composer came to America as cellist in the Astor Place Theatre in New York. Later he went to Boston. Next to Portland, Maine, where he gave an excellent series of chamber music concerts; then to Phila-delphia as conductor of a series of Saturday concerts, and afterwards to Washington, where he started an unsuccessful music school. At the time of the Civil War he was in Richmond, and joined the Confederate Army as a trumpeter. If Stonewall Jackson, on a forced march, had not ordered burned all superfluous baggage of officers and troops, Crouch would have published his manuscript notes as a history of the Civil War. After the war he settled in Baltimore as a singing teacher, and many years later died in Portland. Among the songs he wrote in America was *The Blind Piper,* published in Philadelphia in 1856. He was also the composer of two operas, *Sir Roger de Coverley* and *The Fifth of November.*

Many of the songs of the day were published anonymously, and it is difficult to determine which were of American origin, and which were reprinted by American publishers from British editions. A great variety of subjects were treated. Love predominates, of course, and sometimes such renunciation of worldly joys as was expressed in *I Will Be a Nun:*

> I've been long enough in mischief, 'tis sufficient I have done
> And my Mother's often told me that I must be a Nun.
>
> My Mother now is satisfied; and men must let me be,
> The Nuns will surely like to have a Novice mild as me.

Sometimes the songs dealt with more practical subjects, such as the *Multiplication Table,* published by John G. Klemm in Philadelphia, which covered all items up to twelve times twelve.

3. SINGING FAMILIES

An institution which had a profound effect on the song literature of the nineteenth century was that of the "singing family." These singing-family troupes traveled far and wide, and the songs they sang became the popular songs of the American people. They were at the height of their popularity from the early 1840's to the 1860's, and many of them offered instrumental as well as vocal music.

The best known of the troupes were the Alleghanians, Amphions, Bakers, Barkers, Bohannas, Browns, Burdetts, Cheneys, Foxes, Gibsons, Harmoneons, Hutchinsons, Moravians, Orpheans, the Peak and Berger Families of Bell Ringers, and Father Kemp's Old Folks. Each troupe usually consisted of four singers, including one or two women. They called themselves "families," and in such songs as *Our Home Is on the Mountain Brow* (Alleghanians) or *Will You Come to My Mountain Home* (Orphean Family), they tried to convey the atmosphere of the American outdoors. Some of them did come from the mountains—the Hutchinson and the Baker Families of New Hampshire, and the Cheney Family of Vermont. These groups did not sing what we would now call folk songs, but rather "ballads" of every description—sentimental, dramatic, comic, and realistic. They often wrote their own verses and sometimes even their own tunes. They gave their performances in whatever buildings were available—concert halls, churches, and even barns. In their style of singing they differed noticeably from that of Italian opera which then dominated American musical taste. They sang their songs in simple harmonizations, sometimes improvised, and with closely blended voices. They enunciated their words most clearly, though with utter informality.

The best known of the early troupes was the Hutchinson Family, whose members had a farm in Milford, New Hampshire. About 1842 they began to make concert tours, first as a trio, and soon as a quartet consisting of the brothers Judson, John, and Asa, and their sister Abby. For some time they accompanied their songs with two violins and a cello, and occasionally a guitar. Later, however, they sang without instrumental accompaniment. In early years they styled themselves "Aeolian Vocalists," a name which they soon replaced with that of "The Hutchinson Family."

Giving concerts was not the sole concern of the Hutchinsons. Their aim was to serve a progressive cause—that of abolitionism. Mincing no words on this explosive issue of their time, they made many friends and many enemies. Their reputation steadily increased. They counted among their admirers John Greenleaf Whittier, Henry W. Longfellow, William Lloyd Garrison, Frederick Douglas, and many others. Besides abolitionism, the Hutchinsons advocated temperance, religious socialism, revivalism, and even spiritualism. As their theme song they adopted a tune which was popular around 1840—*You Will See Your Lord a-Coming*—a hymn of the Second Adventists. The Hutchinsons wrote their own words for it:

> We have come from the mountains,
> Of the "Old Granite State."
> We're a band of brothers
> And we live among the hills.

> With a band of music,
> We are passing round the world.
> We have left our aged parents,
> In the "Old Granite State."

> We obtain'd their blessing,
> And we bless them in return.
> Good old-fashioned singers,
> They can make the air resound.

> Equal liberty is our motto
> In the "Old Granite State."
> We despise oppression,
> And we cannot be enslaved.

The songs the Hutchinsons sang ran into the dozens. One of their antislavery songs was called *Get Off the Track*, and it began:

> Ho, the car Emancipation
> Rides majestic through our nation.

Though the singing mountain families became an American institution, their roots were in Europe. In the 1830's, when interest in folk music was rampant in Europe, small ensembles of folk singers and instrumentalists from the Bavarian, Austrian, and Swiss Alps roamed the continent, yodling and fiddling their native music in beer gardens as well as in theatres and concert halls. One of the first of these ensembles —the first, at least, to gain wide recognition—was a vocal group, the brothers Felix, Anton, and Franz Rainer, and their sister Maria. They were originally cattle dealers at Fuegen in the Ziller Valley of the Tyrol. In 1824 they went on their first concert tour and met with instantaneous success. When they appeared in London during the season 1827–28, they became literally the rage of the town, and through the active support of the composer-pianist Ignace Moscheles, they entered the most exclusive circles of society.

A little more than ten years later, during the fall of 1839, another Rainer Family arrived in New York, consisting at first only of distant relatives of the older group. Soon, however, they were joined by Franz Rainer, and they stayed in the United States for four years, giving concerts with hardly an interruption in New York, in Southern cities, in the Northeast, and in Canada. During the season 1840–41 they made Boston their headquarters, and it did not take them long to arouse the enthusiasm of New England audiences. Local musicians, including Lowell Mason, praised them for the perfect blending of their voices and the unanimity and simplicity of their expression. They were held up as models by music educators who were working to stimulate the interest of the average American in the pleasures of choral singing.

The success of the Rainers encouraged Americans to form similar ensembles. Thus, the Hutchinsons were sometimes called the "New Hampshire Rainers," and they started out by imitating the Tyrolese mountain style of singing, and by having "Alpine" songs in their repertoire, such as *The Vulture of the Alps*, and *The Lament of the Alpine Shepherd Boy*. The Hutchinsons' song *We Are Happy and Free* was nothing but an adaptation of the *Grand March* of the Rainers. They were, however, keenly conscious of the competition of foreign troupes, and at the beginning of their career they printed the following lines on their programs:

> When foreigners approach your shores,
> You welcome them with open doors.
> Now we have come to seek our lot,
> Shall native talent be forgot?

4. MINSTREL SHOWS AND THEIR SONGS

Negro minstrelsy—the impersonation of Negroes in action and song by white men—was more characteristically American. It developed about the late 1820's and lasted approximately to the turn of the century, though it degenerated after the Civil War. At that time Negro minstrelsy began to lose its "Negroid" flavor and to develop in the direction of a sumptuous vaudeville show. It was then that the term "show business" originated.

American theatrical performances in the 1820's and 1830's generally offered a variety of features in one evening: short dramas and farces, dances, and songs. Black-face acts came to be included, and two types of Negro impersonators developed: one, in ragged clothes, fashioned after the Southern plantation hand; the other portraying the Northern Negro, the dandy, who, with ridiculous effect, tried to emulate the white man.

It has been claimed that Gottlieb Graupner may have been the first of the black-face singers, but the men who first popularized the type were Thomas Dartmouth ("Daddy") Rice, Bob Farrel, and George Washington Dixon. Rice is said to have started the idea more or less spontaneously by borrowing an old Negro's clothes, and imitating his singing of the *Jim Crow* song.

Rice literally whipped his audiences into a frenzy, in America and in England. He must have been an actor of great imagination. He sang the first part of *Jim Crow* in a more or less static pose:

> Come listen all you gals and boys,
> I'm just from Tuckyhoe;
> I'm going to sing a leetle song,
> My name's Jim Crow.

But in the refrain:

> Wheel about and turn about,
> And do jis so;
> Eb'ry time I wheel about,
> I jump Jim Crow

he used grotesque gestures and steps of a style which would delight the modern American painter Thomas Benton.

The other early type of impersonation was that of the "Broadway swell." He swaggered about the stage in his modish coat, his "long-tail blue," as he called it, his silk hat, his walking cane, his lorgnon, and told his audience how successful he was with the ladies. Either in the refrain or during the instrumental music between stanzas he did a few dance steps. The name of one of these dandies was *Zip Coon*, whose song— generally entitled *Turkey in the Straw*—is still sung. No Negro minstrel, or "Ethiopian Delineator," as he figured on playbills, forgot to make his quips about the political issues of his time.

In the late thirties, the solo black-face banjoist and the solo "Negro dancer" became popular. Joe Sweeny and Billy Whitlock were famous banjoists who tapped out the rhythm while they played and sang. John Diamond was one of the best-known dancers. His "Negro breakdowns" were a mixture of Irish and Scotch jigs with Negroid gestures and steps. These dances were popular among the Western boatmen and backwoodsmen long before they were performed on the stage. They were characterized by comic jumps and a heel-and-toe technique which anticipated modern tap dancing.

From the early forties on, small ensembles of "Negro" performers appeared in ever increasing numbers on the theatrical stage and in the circus ring. Some of the teams consisted of a banjoist and a dancer (such as Whitlock and Diamond), or two dancers who also sang and acted. Soon banjoists, fiddlers, singers, and dancers formed trios in various combinations.

Some comic scenes were included and were called "Negro extravaganzas." There were also Negro plays which were longer and had a larger cast, figuring as "Ethiopian Opera." They were the successors of the English ballad-opera and the forerunners of our modern musical comedies. They included spoken conversation and a great deal of music—songs with choral refrains, duets, and dances. Popular minstrel songs were mostly used, though occasionally vocal or instrumental excerpts were borrowed from real operas. T. D. Rice is credited with having written the two well-known "Ethiopian operas"—*O Hush, or The Virginny Cupids* and *Bone Squash*. Female roles were played by men who made a specialty of impersonating "Negro wenches."

At the beginning of 1843, the first minstrel band—an early "jazz band"—made its appearance, and along with it came the first real minstrel show. Many companies have claimed to have originated the idea, but the Virginia Minstrels were without doubt the first to make a success. "Old Dan Emmit" (later "Emmett," the composer of *Dixie*) was the "leader" of the band. He played the fiddle, Billy Whitlock the banjo, Frank Brower the bones (a kind of linked castanets), and Dick Pelham the tambourine. When they performed they sat in a semicircle with the bone and tambourine players at the ends. Their program consisted of songs and choral refrains, banjo solos, Negro dances, comic stump speeches, jokes, and comic repartee. Scraping, thumping, rattling, and jingling, they produced a merry and humorously incongruous sound. There was no body to the tone of the ensemble, since all instruments were fairly high pitched and the banjoist played no chords. Instead, he picked his tunes, as was the custom with minstrel music, and when he had warmed up, he would invent variants and variations by adding notes of the open strings, especially the highest one.

The first full-length show of the Virginia Minstrels was given March 7, 1843 at the Masonic Temple in Boston. This event may be considered the official beginning of the "minstrel show," even though many other bands appeared only a few weeks after the Virginia Minstrels had made their New York debut, probably on February 6, 1843, at the Bowery Amphitheatre. Some of these companies were the Columbia Minstrels, Kentucky Minstrels, Alabama Minstrels, Kentucky Rattlers, Missouri Minstrels, Ethiopian Serenaders, and the Congo Minstrels.

Most of these bands performed as "Northern Darkies" in the first part of their show and as "Southern Darkies" in the second. This division led in the fifties to the almost complete elimination of "Negroid" features in the first part and to the introduction of sentimental salon music.

The banjo, the fiddle, and the bones were used by the real plantation Negroes. Whether the tambourine was indigenous with them is uncertain, though they might have borrowed it from their white masters. In combination with the fiddle, it was well known to Western river boatmen; and these rivermen served the early minstrels as models just as much as the Negroes did. Some minstrel bands included the triangle, and another Negro instrument—the jawbone of an ass, ox, or horse, whose loose teeth rattled as the players struck it with a stick, or simply shook it.

The size of the minstrel band steadily increased during the 1840's, until towards the end of the fifties, it often numbered a dozen players. The old instruments, with the exception of the jawbone, were still in use, but regular orchestral instruments had been added. Among the prominent minstrel companies of the fifties were the Christy Minstrels, White's Serenaders, Bryant's Minstrels, and others. From the sixties on, a trend towards large ensembles set in and resulted in mammoth companies which had to be transported from town to town in special railroad cars. The imaginative primitiveness of early minstrelsy had disappeared forever.

For songs, the Negro minstrels laid their hands on anything they thought would serve their purposes. They borrowed from folk music, mainly that of the British Isles, and even from the popular Italian operas of their time, adapting their own Negro words to these tunes. But they also created a music of their own which after a few decades turned out to be more indigenously American than any compositions of more learned composers. In its October issue of 1845, the serious New York magazine *The Knickerbocker* suggested that the creators of Negro minstrel songs be considered "our only truly national poets."

Negro minstrel songs of the 1820's and 1830's are clearly indebted to foreign sources. Some show unmistakably the style of eighteenth-century opera buffa—*Bonja Song* and *Coal Black Rose*. *Jim Crow* is a characteristic variant of an English song from English eighteenth-century opera. *Zip Coon* cannot hide its Irish origin. One of the least derivative and perhaps the most original of minstrel songs of the 1830's is *Sich a Gitting Upstairs*. Its tune possesses a true folk vigor and jaunti-ness. Its first stanza reads:

> On a Suskehanna raft I come down de bay
> And I danc'd and I frolick'd, and fiddled all de way,
> Sich a gitting up stairs I never did see
> Sich a gitting up stairs I never did see.

In the late 1840's the production and publication of minstrel songs increased. A characteristic style now evolved. Scotch and Irish elements, plus features typical of banjo music, were blended into something that bore the flavor of the American scene. It possessed nonchalant humor, brevity, sturdiness, and the inflection of Negro dialect or everyday slang. How much the slaves contributed to this style is hard to say. If they stimulated the white composer at all, it was more in rhythm than in melody. But the short, recurrent phrases of minstrel tunes, characteristic of all primitive music, appealed so much to them that they took these tunes over enthusiastically and completely identified themselves with them. Many of these early minstrel songs are still sung today in the backwoods. Among the best are *Old Dan Tucker, Dandy Jim, 'Twill Nebber Do to Gib It Up So, Ole Pee Dee, Jonny Boker, Old Gray Goose, I'm Gwine Ober de Mountains, O Lud Gals Gib Me Chaw Terbackur, Ole Bull and Old Dan Tucker,* and *De Boatmen's Dance.* A most characteristic song was *Ole Dad,* published in Boston in 1844. Its first two stanzas read:

> I'be sung so much ob Dandy Jim,
> Ob course you knows all about him;
> I'be heard it sed when I was a lad,
> 'Twas a wise child knew his own old dad.

(Refrain)

> Old Dad!
> Old Dad!
> Old Dad he took a swim all along,
> He dive like a fedder an he swim like a stone.

> One day my daddy took a swim,
> Him hung he clothes on a hick'ry limb,
> He could not swim an dibe berry bad,
> So dat was de last ob my old dad.

> Old Dad!

The refrain, along with its accompaniment, really anticipates jazz in its partly somber, partly sensual tone, its slangy, rhythmic shouts followed by brief, "hot" instrumental passages, and in its latent syncopations.

Many of these songs cannot be traced to any author or composer, though almost all Negro minstrels were capable of writing their own literary and musical material. Many of the texts and some of the tunes were composed by Dan Emmett. He is usually credited with *Old Dan Tucker,* but he wrote only its words. During the late 1840's, Stephen Foster composed his humorous, nonsentimental minstrel songs. Though skillful, they follow traditional patterns. *Oh, Susanna* is indebted to *Gwine Long Down* (published by Emmett in 1844, though not composed by him); *Nelly Bly* to *Clare de Kitchen* of the early 1830's; and *Camptown Races* to *Picayune Butler.*

Banjo jigs and variants of songs, full of tricky syncopations, were a part of the imaginative music of Negro minstrelsy. One of the best collections that covers the 1840's and 1850's is Phil Rice's *Correct Method for the Banjo,* Boston, 1858.

The most prominent minstrel song composers of the 1850's and 1860's were Stephen Foster and Dan Emmett. While Foster wrote his plaintive "plantation melodies" for the first part of the minstrel show (which was hardly "Negroid" in character), Emmett composed humorous walk-arounds for the "plantation festival" at the end of the show. Foster's songs were performed by soloists; Emmett's by the entire company.

The name DANIEL DECATUR EMMETT (1815–1904) was once on the lips of thousands of Americans, but for years it became almost forgotten. Little is generally known today of Emmett's activities as a musician, comedian, and composer, for *Dixie* is the only one of his numerous songs that has survived. If it were not for a recent movie, *Dixie* would hardly be associated with Emmett's name. Nevertheless, he actually composed some of the most popular songs of the forties, fifties, and sixties. In the forties it was *'Twill Nebber Do to Gib It Up So, I'm Gwine Ober de Mountains,* and *Old Dan Tucker.* In the fifties his *Root, Hog or Die* and *Jordan Is a Hard Road to Trabel* were great favorites; and in the late fifties and sixties his plantation "walk-arounds" were performed by practically all minstrel companies and were heard in towns and villages all over the United States. Some of the best-known "walk-arounds" were *Billy Patterson; Johnny Roach; What o' Dat; Black Brigade; High Daddy;* and *Dixie's Land.*

Many minstrel songs consist of two sections of about equal length, the second being the refrain, which was usually sung in chorus. The first section is not a mere introduction as it is in modern "popular" songs; it is just as expressive as the refrain itself. Emmett's songs frequently follow the same pattern. The first part of his "walk-arounds" is definitely Negroid in form; it consists of solo passages alternating with recurrent choral ejaculations. Yet if one looks for what we recognize today as Negroid features he is apt to be disappointed. It is true that Emmett asserted: "In the composition of a 'walk-around' (by this I mean the style of music and character of the words) I have always strictly confined myself to the habits and crude ideas of the slaves of the South," but the result was a white man's creation, flavored by not only the Negro's language, manners, and gait, but even more by banjo music and Irish and Scottish influences.

A few quotations may illustrate at least Emmett's literary ideas, his humor, and the form of his songs. The first example is taken from *De Wild Goose Nation*, published in 1844. Only the words of the song are by Emmett:

> Away down south in de wild goose nation,
> I first come to life mong de rest ob creation;
> Dar's where I used to hab de old times ober,
>
> I'd go to bed dead drunk and get up sober;
> I first begin to peep,
> And den I 'gin to creep;
> In de year ob our Lord eighteen hundred fast asleep.

The following stanza from *Jordan Is a Hard Road to Trabel*, published in 1853, is a sample of a later style:

> David and Goliath both had a fight
> A cullud man come behind 'em.
> He hit Goliath on de head wid a bar of soft soap
> And it sounded to de oder side ob Jordan.
>
> (Refrain)   So take off your coat, boys,
> And roll up your sleeves,
> For Jordan is a hard road to trabel.
> So take off your coat, boys,
> And roll up your sleeves,
> For Jordan is a hard road to trabel, I believe.

The third example is from the walk-around *Sandy Gibson's, or Chaw Roast Beef*, which abounds in nonsense rhymes.

(solo)   In eighteen hundred and forty-four
(chorus)   Oh, hurry up,
(solo)   We used to swim in close to shore;
(chorus)   Fare y'e well, ladies all
(solo)   But when we got beyond the reef,
(chorus)   Oh, hurry up,
(solo)   The boys all holler out "chaw roast beef!"
(chorus)   Fare y'e well, ladies all.

(Entire company)
    Sandy, old Sandy, Sandy, old Sandy clam,
    Makry, old Makry, Makry, old Makry ham,
    Den jis before de break ob day
    "Chaw roast beef!"
    Dem boys dey stole our clothes away,
    "Chaw roast beef!"
    De Jack takes ten, an' de ten takes de nine
    And we "chaw roast beef" for de rail-road line.

Dan Emmett (or Emmit, as he called himself in early years) spent his childhood in Mount Vernon, a little frontier town in Ohio. He was born there on October 29, 1815. In this struggling, hard-working community his education could hardly be more than elementary. He had his first jobs as a printer with local newspapers. Music was his pastime. He joined the Army at the age of eighteen, pretending to be twenty-one, and there received the only formal musical training he ever got in his life: instruction in reading music and in fifing and drumming. He was stationed in Kentucky, and later in Missouri. Since he showed talent, he was employed as fifer in the "Field Music." After fourteen months in the Army, he probably worked as printer in wintertime and traveled with circuses in summertime, playing in the band. In about 1838 or 1839 he wrote his first Negro lyrics, and in 1840 he learned the banjo. During the next season he appeared for the first time as a black-face singer and banjoist in the circus ring. He afterwards went to New York and performed there, successfully, in trios and duos in variety shows and circuses. As mentioned above, he established his reputation as a "Negro delineator" when he became the "leader" of the Virginia Minstrels, a troupe that made history in the American theatre.

After having traveled with his band through the British Isles, Emmett returned and carried on chiefly as a solo banjoist and singer, always appearing with prominent minstrel companies. In the early fifties he was a member of "White's Serenaders." In the late fall of 1858 he joined "Bryant's Minstrels," the finest troupe of their time, as a composer, black-face instrumentalist, vocalist, and comedian. During the eight years he stayed with them, he wrote his best songs, including *Dixie*. The story of that song is given in Chapter IX. In the middle fifties and the early sixties, Emmett appeared in Chicago, and made numerous tours. In Chicago, as well as in New York, he owned minstrel theatres, but he always gave them up after a while. He was not a good business man. When he left the Bryants, his career was practically at an end. The type of minstrelsy which he represented was fast becoming out of date. He moved to Chicago where the fire of 1871 ruined him completely, and in 1888 he retired with his wife to a little cottage just outside Mount Vernon, Ohio. A few years earlier and again in the nineties he traveled for a while with mammoth minstrel companies, but he was nothing more than a museum piece. In Mount Vernon he eked out a living by doing manual labor and occasionally selling a manuscript copy of *Dixie*. In the last years of his life he was supported by the Actors' Fund of New York. On June 28, 1904, he passed away. Many newspapers ran a notice of his death, but public interest in his person lasted hardly longer than a day.

5. STEPHEN COLLINS FOSTER (1826–1864)

I

Stephen Foster provided one of the summits of American music. Today he could offer his work without apology or without reservation, for time has proved its worth. Foster was one of the greatest melodists we have yet produced, and some of his simplest songs are among the most beautiful that have ever been written, anywhere. He accomplished what many a better-trained musician has failed to do: he wrote melodies that can be understood by everybody—so poignant, so direct in their appeal that they grow in our affections the more we hear them.

Father Time has had the privilege of correcting John S. Dwight, who once wrote in his *Journal of Music* (1853):

We wish to say that such tunes [*Old Folks at Home*], although whistled and sung by everybody, are erroneously supposed to have taken a deep hold of the popular mind; that the charm is only *skin-deep*; that they are hummed and whistled *without musical emotion*, whistled "for lack of thought"; that they persevere and haunt the morbidly sensitive nerves of deeply musical persons, so that they too hum and whistle them involuntarily, hating them even while they hum them; that such melodies become catching, idle habits, and are not popular in the sense of musically inspiring, but that such and such a melody *breaks out* every now and then, like a morbid irritation of the skin.

A less musical writer in the *Albany State Register* (1852) was more tolerant:

We confess to a fondness for negro minstrelsy. There is something in the melodious "Uncle Ned" that goes directly to the heart, and makes Italian trills seem tame. . . . God bless that fine old colored gentleman, who we have been so often assured has

"Gone where the good niggers go."

Old Folks at Home the *last* negro melody, is on everybody's tongue, and consequently in everybody's mouth. Pianos and guitars groan with it, night and day; sentimental young ladies sing it; sentimental young gentlemen warble it in midnight serenades; volatile young "bucks" hum it in the midst of their business and their pleasures; boatmen roar it out stentorially at all times; all the bands play it; amateur flute players agonize over it at every spare moment; the street organs grind it out at every hour; the "singing stars" carol it on the theatrical boards, and at concerts; the chamber maid sweeps and dusts to the measured cadence of *Old Folks at Home*; the butcher's boy treats you to a strain or two of it as he hands in the steaks for dinner; the milk-man mixes it up strangely with the harsh ding-dong accompaniment of his tireless bell; there is not a "live darkey," young or old, but can whistle, sing, dance and play it, and throw in "Ben Bolt" for seasoning; indeed at every hour, at every turn, we are forcibly impressed with the interesting fact, that—

"Way down upon de Swanee Ribber
    Far, far away,
  Dere's whar my heart is turnin' ebber
  Dere's whar de old folks stay."

Old Folks at Home had been published less than a year when this was written.

In some respects, Foster was akin to Schubert. He had a natural gift of melody that shone because of its simplicity. Schubert with all his natural genius lacked the power of self-criticism and produced hundreds of works that are forgotten today. From a little over two hundred of Foster's published works only fifty or so are sung nowadays, but these fifty are so potent in their charm that they have long since earned their composer's immortality. His limitations were his power; the few chords he used made his songs direct and simple, and always natural. Had he been a trained musician, his charm might have vanished.

Many legends have grown around Stephen Foster, many of them untrue. Unfortunately, they are still being perpetuated by motion pictures, radio programs, and by magazine writers who do not take the trouble to learn facts. Up to a quarter century ago, this was understandable, and pardonable, for very little had been written about Foster which was based on contemporary documents. In 1920, Harold Vincent Milligan issued a biography of Foster which was more complete than any that had been issued before, not excepting the short biography Stephen's brother Morrison had written in 1896. Yet, while Milligan had the benefit of consultation with several members of the Foster family, only a small number of the Foster family letters and documents were available at that time.

It was not for another decade that a systematic attempt was made to gather together everything in existence pertaining to Stephen Foster. This task was undertaken with distinguished success by Josiah K. Lilly of Indianapolis, who had long been a lover of Foster's songs and who determined to collect and make available to posterity, all first editions (and later editions, too) of Foster's songs, and all the material regarding his life that could be found. Assisted by Fletcher Hodges, Junior, and an able staff, Mr. Lilly achieved his object on a scale that even he had not dreamed of when he began his collection. For several years the material was housed in a stone building in Indianapolis, which was appropriately named "Foster Hall." Then, when it had become truly comprehensive, and had been fully catalogued and indexed, it was given by Mr. Lilly to the Stephen Foster Memorial of the University of Pittsburgh, where it is now available to the public as the "Foster Hall Collection," and is still directed by Mr. Hodges as curator.

Foster Hall has issued a number of publications of its own, most notably a complete set of reproductions of the first editions of every known Foster composition. The collection has also been the main source of information for subsequent writings on Foster, including my own *Stephen Foster, America's Troubadour*, and it has sponsored the writing and publication of the most extensive work on the Foster family to date, *Chronicles of Stephen Foster's Family*, by Evelyn Foster Morneweck, a niece of the composer.

II

Foster's life was altogether tragic. It represented a disintegration that ended almost literally in the gutter. From a parentage of aristocrats on one side, and hardy pioneers on the other, a weakling who lacked the stamina to fight life's battles was produced. Stephen's family loved him, did all in their power to protect and shield him, and yet failed to understand him. Pioneer surroundings are rarely kind to artistic souls, and Stephen was probably born too soon, for it never occurred to the Fosters that the young man's indolence, and his dreaming ways, were in fact his very strength. In the family letters there were many references to the boy's "strange talent for music," but not once was there the thought that the talent should be cultivated. There were few music teachers near at hand, and such diversions were not for able-bodied men. It may be that the world would have been the loser if a musically trained Stephen Foster had not been satisfied to write songs of the utmost simplicity—but his own fate might have been less tragic.

He was born in Lawrenceville, Pennsylvania, near Pittsburgh, on July 4, 1826, the day John Adams and Thomas Jefferson died. He spent his boyhood around Pittsburgh and Allegheny, attended the local schools, and academies at Athens and Towanda, near his eldest brother's home at the time. At seventeen he wrote his first published song *Open thy Lattice, Love*. In 1846 he went to Cincinnati to act as bookkeeper for his brother Dunning, and there he met W. C. Peters, a music publisher his family had known in Pittsburgh. He virtually made Peters a present of *Old Uncle Ned*, *Oh! Susanna*, and two other songs, which were published as *Songs of the Sable Harmonists*. The publisher is said to have made ten thousand dollars from the songs. This determined Foster to give up the bookkeeping he disliked so heartily, and to make a business of song writing.

Orders began to come to him for songs, and he made a contract with Firth, Pond & Company of New York through which he received a royalty on every copy published. The common belief that Foster did not receive adequate payment for his works is not altogether true—from some he gained many hundreds of dollars. Later, when dissipation had reduced him to a vagabond, he was exploited by unscrupulous publishers. Because he needed money, he had to accept anything that was offered him, but in his better days he dealt chiefly with reputable firms who gave him the benefit of what his compositions earned.

In 1851, E. P. Christy, of Christy's Minstrels, asked Foster to write songs for him which he could sing before they were published. One of these was *Old Folks at Home,* and a clause in the agreement specified that the printed copies were to name Christy as the composer. Morrison Foster said that Christy paid five hundred dollars for this privilege, but this, as we shall find later, was greatly exaggerated. Foster reserved the publishing rights, and had the royalties on the sales.

Except for possible visits to Louisville and Bardstown, Kentucky, Stephen Foster had never been south of the Ohio River when *Old Folks at Home* was published. His idea of Negro singing had been gained from colored church services and from minstrel shows. The name of the *Swanee River* had been suggested by a brother who found the name on the map, and Foster used it because it sounded better than the "Pedee" he had used originally. In 1852 he did take a trip through the South, and observed many incidents of Southern life.

III

When Stephen was six his mother wrote:

. . . Stephen has a drum and marches about with a feather in his hat and a girdle round his waist, whistling "Auld Lang Syne." There still remains something perfectly original about him.

When he was ten he himself wrote to his father:

I wish you to send me a commic songster for you promised to. If I had my pensyl I could rule my paper or if I had the money to buy black ink but if I had my whistle I would be so taken with it I do not think I would write a tall. . . .

This same year he went on a shopping trip with his mother to the music store of Smith & Mellor in Pittsburgh. He picked a flageolet from the counter, and in a few minutes amazed clerks and customers by playing *Hail Columbia*.

Brother Morrison wrote, years later: [1]

Melodies appeared to dance through his head continually. Often at night he would get out of bed, light a candle and jot down some notes of melody on a piece of paper, then retire to bed and to sleep.

And yet to his adoring family these countless indications of talent never once suggested a solution for the boy's future. His musical inclinations troubled them. In 1840 his mother wrote, with apparent relief:

He is not so much devoted to music as he was; other studies seem to be elevated in his opinion; he reads a great deal and fools about none at all.

It is not hard to understand why Stephen's family did not take his love for music seriously. Colonel William Barclay Foster, his father, was a man of practical affairs. A love of pioneering, and disregard of its dangers, left little room for softer pleasures. He had settled in Pittsburgh when it was a border settlement, twenty days from Philadelphia by pack horse and wagon. Finding employment with Anthony Beelen and Ebenezer Denny, merchants "in dry goods, hardware, groceries, stationery, perfumery, china, glass and queensware," he made himself valuable by taking charge of the firm's shipments of furs, pelts, flour, salt, and other products of the neighboring country (including whiskey), and seeing that they reached New Orleans safely by way of the huge flatboats that navigated the rivers. Sometimes he would return overland, with frequent encounters with Indians. Often he would sail from New Orleans to New York, through the heart of the Spanish Main and its pirates. In New York and Philadelphia he bought goods for the Pittsburgh store, carrying them over the mountains on six-horse wagons.

---

[1] Morrison Foster, *Biography, Songs and Musical Compositions of Stephen Collins Foster.*

In Philadelphia he met Eliza Tomlinson, daughter of an aristocratic family from Wilmington. In 1807 they were married, and spent their honeymoon on the three-week horseback trip to Pittsburgh. William Foster became so valuable to his employers that they gave him a partnership. He became a substantial citizen, and acquired wealth which he placed at the disposal of his country when the national treasury was depleted in the War of 1812. In 1814 he bought a large tract of a hundred and seventy-one acres about two miles out of the city. This he named Lawrenceville. Part of the land he donated as a burial ground for soldiers; thirty acres were sold to the government for an arsenal, and on a spot overlooking the river he built the "White Cottage" that became the Foster homestead.

IV

With the exception of Stephen, the baby of the family, the Foster children were like their father, well equipped to fight frontier battles. The eldest son, William Barclay Foster, Junior, was about twenty years older than Stephen, and became a civil engineer who helped build the Pennsylvania Railroad by taking charge of the most difficult part of the work—the section that crossed the Allegheny Mountains. The other three sons, Henry, Dunning, and Morrison all became successful men of business, so where was there thought for a musician when Stephen came to manhood?

"Little Stephy" was loved and petted. Brother William was like a father, and when the boy was in his early teens he took him to live with him in Towanda, that he might go to the Academy at Athens. But Stephen found little anywhere to hold his interest for long. He was generous, he was loving, he had his longings, but while he was in the most important years of his life there was no one who understood, who could show him where to turn.

Only one of the many relatives seemed to have any conception of Stephen's temperament. Uncle John Struthers lived in a log house in Youngstown, Ohio. The visits to Uncle Struthers were glorious—the old man let the boy do as he pleased, and told him stories of Indians and hunting that fired his imagination. The uncle prophesied that Stephen would become "something famous." Pity he could not point out where that fame would lie!

The outward, self-created standards of business success and solid citizenship were all the Fosters knew, and inability to meet those standards was failure. All sorts of occupations were suggested, and some of them tried. When he dropped out of Jefferson College after a few dismal days, his father wrote to William:

I regret extremely that Stephen has not been able to appreciate properly your generous exertions in his behalf by availing himself of the advantages of a college education, which will cause him much regret before he arrives at my age and he will no doubt express these regrets in much sorrow to you, should you both live long after I shall be no more. He is at school now with Mr. Moody, a first rate teacher of mathematics in Pittsburgh, and it is a source of comfort to your mother and myself that he does not appear to have any evil propensities to indulge; he seeks no associates and his leisure hours are all devoted to musick, for which he possesses a strange talent.

It was not until the songs he had written as a diversion became popular beyond even the publisher's hopes, that Stephen, grown to manhood, realized that here was his occupation. Too late to learn how to write with the mind as well as the heart, he had nothing in him that would cultivate his gifts so that they would grow to something bigger. He could acquire no background that would withstand the ravages of early success. The "evil propensities" his father had feared became realities, and Stephen had nothing with which to fight them.

His marriage was not altogether a success, though he worshiped his wife and little daughter. Jane Denny McDowell was the daughter of one of Pittsburgh's physicians. She was an amateur singer and had been a member of the "Stephen Foster Quartet" which gathered for singing at the Foster home. For this group Foster wrote some of his earliest songs. Stephen and Jane were married July 22, 1850, and lived for several years with Stephen's parents.

There were apparently two separations. In 1853, for some reason, not clear from the family correspondence on the subject, Stephen left Jane and lived alone in New York. The fact that there was some sort of estrangement is indicated by a letter written by Stephen's sister Henrietta, which expressed concern for "poor Stephy," who had "had trouble enough already." By the summer of 1854, however, the little family came together again, and for a few months they lived in a rented house in Hoboken, New Jersey. By October they were back in Allegheny. At this time Stephen was not the inveterate drinker he later became; so dissipation could not have been the cause of the first separation. His wife and little girl were with him part of the time he lived in New York from 1860 to 1864, but he lived alone at the time of his death. When news of his passing reached Pittsburgh his wife came to New York with Morrison to bring the body back home.

There were probably a number of reasons for partings. It is not unlikely that love for his parents, the "Old Folks at Home," was so uppermost in his heart that his wife felt a neglect that was not consciously intended. Stephen was not fitted for the harness of a marriage that demanded his whole being. He was a dreamer, thoroughly impractical, wholly improvident, and probably difficult at the breakfast table. How could he have been an ideal husband?

v

He was never business man enough to realize the full commercial value of his best songs. The gift to Peters was quite in keeping with his methods. Common law copyright was not established in those days, and many of the early songs of which Foster gave manuscript copies to minstrel performers were published by others. Sometimes they were copyrighted by those who had no right to them.

It was in 1849 that Foster made a contract with Firth, Pond & Company which protected his interests. The letter from the firm gives the details:

Your favor of the 8th instant is received and we hasten to reply.

We will accept the proposition therein made, viz., to allow you two cents upon every copy of your future publications issued by our house, after the expenses of publication are paid, and of course it is always our interest to push them as widely as possible. From your acquaintance with the proprietors or managers of different bands of "Minstrels," and from your known reputation, you can undoubtedly arrange with them to sing them and thus introduce them to the public in that way, but in order to secure the copyright exclusively for our house, it is safe to hand such persons printed copies only, of the pieces, for if manuscript copies are issued, particularly by the author, the market will be flooded with spurious issues in a short time.

The next paragraph contained advice that Foster would have done well to follow:

It is also advisable to compose only such pieces as are likely both in the sentiment and melody to take the public taste. Numerous instances can be cited of composers whose reputation has greatly depreciated from the fact of their music becoming too popular and as a natural consequence they write too much and too fast and in a short time others supersede them.

The minstrel troupes did indeed spread the popularity of Foster's songs. Some were well known to the public before they were published. For a number of years E. P. Christy had the official privilege of being the first to sing his works. Existing letters show what arrangements were made. On June 12, 1851, Foster wrote to the singer:

I have just received a letter from Messrs. Firth, Pond & Co. stating that they have copy-righted a new song of mine ("Oh! boys, carry me 'long") but will not be able to issue it for some little time yet, owing to other arrangements. This will give me time to send you the m.s. and allow you the privilege of singing it for at least two weeks, and probably a month before it is issued, or before any other band gets it (unless they catch it up from you). If you will send me 10 $ immediately for this privilege, I pledge myself, as a gentleman of the old school, to give you the m.s. I have written to F. P. & Co. not to publish till they hear from me again. This song is certain to become popular, as I have taken great pains with it. If you accept my proposition I will make it a point to notify you hereafter when I have a new song and send you the m.s. on the same terms, reserving to myself in all cases the exclusive privilege of publishing. Thus it will become notorious that your hand brings out all the new songs. You can state in the papers that the song was composed expressly for you. I make this proposition because I am sure of the song's popularity.

Eight days later Foster acknowledged receipt of the check and forwarded the manuscript with the following explanation:

I regret that it is too late to have the name of your band on the title page, but I will endeavor to place it (alone) on future songs, and will cheerfully do anything else in my humble way to advance your interest.

There are many references to arrangements with Christy. Some of these disprove Morrison Foster's statement that Stephen received $500 from Christy for *Old Folks at Home*. John Mahon published some reminiscences of Foster in the New York *Clipper* (1877). He tells of meeting him in 1861, "a short man, who was very neatly dressed in a blue swallow-tailed coat, high silk hat." At Mahon's home they talked of many things:

. . . my wife asked Stephen if he knew "The Old Folks at Home."

"I should think I ought to," he replied, "for I got $2,000 from Firth, Pond & Co. for it."

"Why," said I, "how could that be? Was not E. P. Christy the author and composer?"

"Oh, no," he replied, laughing, "Christy paid me $15 for allowing his name to appear as the author and composer. I did so on condition that after a certain time his name should be superseded by my own. One hundred thousand copies of the first edition were soon sold, for which I received a royalty of two cents a copy. . . ."

Foster had himself suggested to Christy that the minstrel's name be given as composer of *Old Folks at Home*. When he wrote it there was some public prejudice against Negro songs, and Foster preferred to remain in the background. In his biography of Foster,[2] Milligan publishes the following letter, written by Foster to Christy, May 25, 1852, less than six months after *Old Folks at Home* was first copyrighted:

As I once intimated to you, I had the intention of omitting my name on my Ethiopian songs, owing to the prejudice against them by some, which might injure my reputation as a writer of another style of music, but I find that by my efforts I have done a great deal to build up a taste for the Ethiopian songs among refined people by making the words suitable to their taste, instead of the trashy and really offensive words which belong to songs of that order. Therefore I have concluded to reinstate my name on my songs and to pursue the Ethiopian business without fear or shame and lend all my energies to making the business live, at the same time that I will wish to establish my name as the best Ethiopian song-writer. But I am not encouraged in undertaking this so long as "The Old Folks at Home" stares me in the face with another's name on it. As it was at my own solicitation that you allowed your name to be placed on the song, I hope that the above reasons will be sufficient explanation for my desire to place my own name on it as author and composer, while at the same time I wish to leave the name of your band on the title page. This is a little matter of pride in myself which it will certainly be to your interest to encourage. On the receipt of your free consent to this proposition, I will, if you wish, willingly refund the money which you paid me on that song, though it may have been sent me for other

[2] Harold V. Milligan, *Stephen Collins Foster*, G. Schirmer, Inc.

considerations than the one in question, and I promise in addition to write you
an opening chorus, in my best style, free of charge, and in any other way in
my power to advance your interests hereafter. I find I cannot write at all
unless I write for public approbation and get credit for what I write. As we
may probably have a good deal of business with each other in our lives, it is
best to proceed on a sure basis of confidence and good understanding, therefore I hope you will appreciate an author's feelings in the case and deal with
me with your usual fairness. Please answer immediately.

It is easy to sympathize with Stephen Foster in his making this request, but it must have placed Christy in an exceedingly embarrassing
position. For eight months the minstrel had been receiving the applause
of nightly audiences for a song he had claimed as his own, so it is not
surprising that he apparently refused to acknowledge Foster's authorship. At any rate, it was not until 1879, when the first term of copyright expired, and fifteen years after Stephen's death, that his name
appeared on printed copies of the song.

A royalty account in Foster's handwriting, dated January 27, 1857,
gives some interesting data. A footnote at the bottom states:

In the amounts recd. I have included $15 on each of the two songs "Old
folks" and "Farewell Lilly," from E. P. Christy, also $10 on each of the
songs, "Dog Tray," "Oh boys," "Massa's in" & "Ellen Bayne."

There are two columns of figures: one the amount Foster had already received on the songs, the other what he thought they would
bring him in the future. He used the latter estimate to determine the
amount he would ask his publishers for his future rights to the songs.
For those of the songs which were published by Firth, Pond & Company of New York he had received in a little over seven years, $9,-
436.96. From another publisher, F. D. Benteen of Baltimore, he had
received $461.85. These amounts, together with sums received for
miscellaneous items, totaled over $10,000, and made his average in-
come a little over $1,400 a year.

Old Folks at Home headed the estimate Foster made in 1857. In
its five and a quarter years it had yielded $1,647.46; Foster considered
it good for a hundred more. *My Old Kentucky Home*, only three and
a half years old, had brought $1,372.06. This, too, should bring an-
other hundred. *Old Dog Tray*, a youngster of two years, had over a

thousand dollars to its credit, and promised another hundred and fifty.

The account shows that Foster's chief income came from a few of his songs—some of the oldest had brought as little as eight dollars alto-gether. *Willie, We Have Missed You* had earned almost $500, and Foster expected that its future would bring an equal amount. *Gentle Annie* was but an infant; her $39.08 should increase to over $500.

Altogether, over a period of eleven years, from the date of his first contract in 1849 with Firth, Pond & Company until he came to New York in 1860, Foster's earnings from songs totaled a little more than $15,000. Unfortunately, more than $3,600 of this amount represented the proceeds from outright sales of further rights in some of his best works, made necessary by the fact that his expenses were higher than his income from royalties.

VI

Soon after Foster sold out his royalty interests. The "profitable offer" that took him to New York in 1860 was possibly an arrangement with Firth, Pond & Company whereby they agreed to pay him $800 a year for twelve songs, and another, which came to little, for six songs at $400 per year from Lee & Walker.[3] Stephen did not have character enough in his last days to keep producing even under the promise of an assured income. He was constantly drawing ahead on his payments, and before he died he took anything he could get for his songs. He would write one in the morning, sell it for a pittance in the afternoon, and have the money spent by evening. He formed a sort of song-writing partnership with George Cooper, who afterwards had a long career as a writer of song lyrics.

Morrison Foster gave only a brief account of his brother's death:

In January, 1864, while at the American Hotel, he was taken with an ague and fever. After two or three days he arose, and while washing him-self he fainted and fell across the wash basin, which broke and cut a gash in his neck and face. He lay there insensible and bleeding until discovered by the chambermaid who was bringing the towels he had asked for to the room. She called for assistance and he was placed in bed again. On recovering his senses he asked that he be sent to a hospital. He was so much weakened by

[3] For further discussion of these arrangements see *Stephen Foster, America's Troubadour* by John Tasker Howard.

fever and loss of blood that he did not rally. On the 13th of January he died peacefully and quietly.

The first indication the family had of Stephen's accident was a letter from Cooper to Morrison Foster, then in Cleveland:

January 12th, 1864

Your brother Stephen I am sorry to inform you is lying in Bellevue Hospital in this city very sick. He desires me to ask you to send him some pecuniary assistance as his means are very low. If possible, he would like to see you in person.

The letter had probably not been delivered when a telegram passed it:

STEPHEN IS DEAD. COME ON.
GEORGE COOPER.

Cooper gave Milligan a detailed and presumably accurate account of Foster's death: [4]

Early one winter morning I received a message saying that my friend had met with an accident; I dressed hurriedly and went to 15 Bowery, the lodging-house where Stephen lived, and found him lying on the floor with a bad bruise on his forehead. Steve never wore any night-clothes and he lay there on the floor, naked and suffering horribly. He had wonderful big brown eyes and they looked up at me with an appeal I can never forget. He whispered, "I'm done for," and begged for a drink, but before I could get it for him, the doctor who had been sent for arrived and forbade it. He started to sew up the gash in Steve's throat, and I was horrified to observe that he was using black thread. "Haven't you any white thread," I asked, and he said no, he had picked up the first thing he could find. I decided the doctor was not much good, and I went down stairs and got Steve a big drink of rum, which I gave him and which seemed to help him a lot. We put his clothes on him and took him to the hospital. In addition to the cut on his throat and the bruise on his forehead, he was suffering from a bad burn on his thigh, caused by the overturning of a spirit lamp used to boil water. This had happened several days before, and he had said nothing about it, nor done anything for it. All the time we were caring for him, he seemed terribly weak and his eyelids kept fluttering. I shall never forget it.

I went back to the hospital to see him, and he said nothing had been done

[4] Harold V. Milligan, *Stephen Collins Foster*, G. Schirmer, Inc.

for him, and he couldn't eat the food they brought him. When I went back again the next day they said "Your friend is dead."

So ended the life of a man who made the world a better place to live in. A man to whom home meant everything, and for whom home was impossible. This longing was the strongest emotion of his nature; and it is as a poet of homesickness that he was greatest. Many times he descended to the banal, but time has not preserved the things that were unworthy of him. When he tried his hand at sentimental love songs, a lesser Stephen Foster sang.

A few of his nonsense songs have survived along with the songs of home. *Oh! Susanna* is still the joyous thing it was when it was written. *De Camptown Races*, in which the "Camptown ladies" chant "doo-dah," is still popular with college boys, young and old. The melodies are vital.

Why try to analyze his tunes, so lovely in their simplicity? Classifying their intervals may well be left to scholars. Foster at his best was inevitable rather than obvious. He was good enough musician to harmonize his songs as they should be harmonized—quite simply. What more can we ask of a man who has touched our hearts?

In 1940 the tributes and memorials to Foster reached a climax in the greatest honor Americans can pay to their great men of the past. In that year Stephen Foster became the first musician to be elected to the Hall of Fame at New York University. In fact, in the election of that year, Foster was the only candidate on whom a majority of the one hundred electors could agree.

6. RAMPANT VIRTUOSI

By the middle of the nineteenth century each of the principal cities of the United States had its music-loving public—small indeed, but no doubt representing as high a percentage of the general population as that which fills our concert halls today. For these music lovers there were a few organizations that provided good music, played by those who loved it for its own sake. Nor was the man on the street neglected, for early in the 1800's bright stars of the musical firmament abroad scented our American dollars and came over here to gather them in abundance. The fact that people will pay any amount to *see* famous artists they have read about in the papers is as old as the hills. Modern press agents may learn much from their grandfathers.

It is not easy to believe that a New York hatter paid several hundreds of dollars for a pair of seats to Jenny Lind's first New York concert merely because he must hear some beautiful music. The hatter became a person, and he sold more hats. Under the leadership of P. T. Barnum advertising became an art, and music profited—in dollars anyway. Some of the artists were sincere, others were tricksters and showmen. The latter made the most money. They all had their share in making the musical history of America, and one should be cautious in making fun of our ancestors for their hero worship, for we are not one whit different today in our attitude towards music and in our box-office habits.

Few of the early *virtuosi* were Americans; most of them were periodical visitors from abroad, but they affected our musical life so deeply that they cannot be ignored. Most important of all was the effect on the newer communities in the West. While New York, Boston, and Philadelphia had resident organizations which attempted the best music of the day, some of the Western cities were too busy clearing land and building houses to give much thought to music; but they had money to spend, and the bright stars of the musical world went among them to get their share of it. The West acquired the listening habit before it learned to make music itself. The eccentricities of some of the *virtuosi,* and more especially their imitators, may have been responsible for a prevalent opinion regarding all musicians. An editorial in the Pittsburgh *Evening Chronicle* (1853) calls a spade a shovel:

A hobby of society at the present day is to be music-mad, and the adulation and toddyism lavished upon every Piano-Forte player of any talent is enough to disgust all sensible people with the instrument forever. From the language of the musical critiques of the Eastern press, one would suppose that there was nothing else worth living for in this life but music, and Piano Forte playing especially, and the musical world, following the key-note, look for the advent of each fresher greater Signor Pound-the-keys with a devotion and religious constancy unparalleled. He makes his advent and the whole town talks. . . . And Signor Pound-the-keys for having rattled and splurged and hammered and tinkled and growled through three or four musical compositions with long-line names, fills his pockets for one night's work with as many dollars as three-fourths of the community earn in a year, while the mustached gentleman who assists him by quavering, quivering and shouting through three or four songs in as many different European languages, which is all gibberish to all of the audience with perhaps the exception of some dozen, pockets one-half as much more.

We think music is an art which deserves fostering and cultivating as much as any other among our people, but we feel no ways backward in saying that from a common-sense point of view, the musical furore which pervades this country for wonderful piano playing and extraordinary effects of vocal powers in foreign languages, like what it is, is thorough humbug.

The Americans are a musical people, but we want to be educated up to the science and so long as nine-tenths of our people do not know even the A.B.C. of music, it is folly for them to listen to the most finished and eloquent combinations of it.

OLE BULL (1810–1880) was the most brilliant violinist of his time. He was a Norwegian who enjoyed international fame, and spent much of his time in America—five visits altogether. Huge audiences were always thrilled by the fire of his playing, but more sober critics called him a trickster. He could play on all four strings of his fiddle at once. His admirers said that his colossal strength enabled him to do it, while sceptics claimed he had a flat bridge. Vast crowds were awed by the way he ended his pieces with the softest of pianissimos. Some who stood in the wings said that at such times his bow never touched the strings at all. William Mason wrote that Ole Bull was a law unto himself. He burst into full blossom without first showing various degrees of growth.

Born in Bergen, Norway, in 1810, he first came to America in 1843. His first tour lasted over two years, and he gave over two hundred concerts in the Eastern states, and in Havana. His box office receipts were about $400,000. When he returned in 1852 he stayed for five years, and went all the way to California with a concert party that included the child prodigy ADELINA PATTI. Early in 1855 he tried his hand at managing an opera company, and took over the Academy of Music in New York. He really tried to make it an American institution, and offered a prize of $1,000 for the "best original grand opera by an American composer, upon a strictly *American subject.*" Foreign adaptations would not be accepted. In his announcement he gave native composers a chance to declare their independence:

The national history of America is rich in themes both for the poet and the musician; and it is to be hoped that this offer will bring to light the musical talent now latent in the country, which only needs a favorable opportunity for its development.

But the Academy closed its doors in March, and none of our latent talents had a chance to show their manuscripts.

It was during his second visit that Ole Bull embarked upon his most ambitious scheme—establishing a colony in Pennsylvania called *Oleana,* where there would arise a New Norway "consecrated to freedom, baptized in independence, and protected by the mighty flag of the Union." He purchased a large tract of land, described in Dwight's *Journal of Music:*

Ole Bull's Norwegian Colony is situated in Potter County, Pa. . . . Ole Bull has built himself a beautiful Norwegian cottage for his summer residence. He proposes to establish a Polytechnic school for this colony for the advancement of the arts and sciences generally, to be conducted by the most scientific men of Europe. His plan is to make it a civil and a military school to be open to the youth of the Union. . . . An armory and a foundry are to be built for practical purposes. . . . The corps when graduated, to be received into the regular army as a new corps. The Government is to have the benefit of the result of all discoveries in the arts and sciences, in return for which he asks the preference in all contracts for cannons, arms, ammunition etc. . . . This idea of the Norwegian is certainly a good one. . . . West Point has become an exclusive and aristocratical institution, and we greatly want an institution as proposed by Ole Bull, for the people at large. . . . His knowledge of the sciences extends vastly beyond horse hair and fiddle strings.

But it was not to be. Bull had fallen victim to a group of frauds who had no title to the land; who sold him what was not theirs. Even the improvements he had already made were a trespass on the property of others, and long litigation followed that almost broke his health, as well as his heart. He returned to Bergen in 1857, and did not come back for ten years.

When he returned in 1867 he gave his first concert in Chicago, and a year later married an American, Sara Chapman Thorpe, in Wisconsin. He spent the summer of 1872 in Norway, and then came back here for his fourth visit, which lasted for a year. His last tour was in the season of 1879–80, with Emma Thursby. His failing health resulted in his death in Norway the following summer.

Bull's compositions are interesting because they represent a translation of everything into his own style. In a way, he was an intense nationalist, as much of a Norwegian as Grieg. The climate of his native country was in his veins—he had a wild, poetic, northern imagination that fired everything he did. He chose many American subjects for the works he played here, but they were probably no more American than Dvořák's *New World Symphony*. He described the Revolution by introducing *Yankee Doodle*, "piped and screamed" alternately with *God Save the King*, "amid discordant tremolos and battle storms of the whole orchestra."

His war horse was the *Polacca Guerriera*, a warlike piece which he played with orchestra with telling effect. Among his tributes to America was the *Grand March to the Memory of Washington*, published in 1845; *Niagara;* and *Solitude of the Prairie*. In his *Musical Memories*,[1] George P. Upton described Bull:

Ole Bull belonged to no school. Perhaps that was another secret of his success, for people neither know nor care about schools, but like a player to be himself. Ole Bull certainly was all that. He imitated certain of Paganini's eccentricities by attempting effects of a bizarre sort, but he was always Ole Bull. . . . He rarely attempted the classical, probably because it is so unyielding in construction that it does not admit of moods or humors, so his repertory was comparatively small. . . . It was impossible to resist the magic of his bow even when you suspected it of sleight-of-hand.

There has been nothing in American history to compare with the furore that JENNY LIND (1820–1887) created in the fifties. But if Americans made fools of themselves, they at least had the comfort of knowing that their English cousins had done so before them. Probably no more curious combination has ever existed than that of Barnum as manager and Jenny Lind as artist. Barnum the showman, who first showed how to work the press, and planted stories of his own as news in any paper he wished; and Lind, the plain little lady with angelic voice, deeply religious by nature, who abandoned opera and stage because it was too immoral. There can be no question of her consummate

---

[1] George P. Upton, *Musical Memories*, A. C. McClurg & Co.

artistry and her exquisite voice. The masses were not alone in worshiping her. Clara Schumann said: "What a great, heaven-inspired being she is! What a pure, true artist soul! Her songs will ever sound in my heart." And Mendelssohn: "She is as great an artist as ever lived and the greatest I have known," though he admitted on a later occasion, "She sings bad music the best."

Barnum had a double motive in bringing Jenny Lind to America. He was fairly certain that he would make money by it, even if he did have to guarantee her $1,000 each for a hundred and fifty concerts, pay all her expenses, and deposit $187,500 in cash with his London bankers as security for fulfilment of the contract. He confessed the other motive himself:

Inasmuch as my name has long been associated with "humbug," and the American public suspect that my capacities do not extend beyond the power to exhibit a stuffed Monkey-skin or a dead mermaid, I can afford to lose fifty thousand dollars in such an enterprise as bringing to this country, in the zenith of her life and celebrity, the greatest musical wonder in the world. . . .

And so the man who managed Tom Thumb, who had made a fortune by charging two shillings for a look at a horse with his tail where his head should be, sold Jenny Lind to the American public as extensively as he sold his circus years later.

She had fears of Barnum that she never quite overcame. A rival manager who bid for her American tour told her that Barnum would put her in a box and exhibit her about the United States at twenty-five cents admission. Because Barnum was sensitive about his reputation as a showman, Jenny capitalized his inferiority complex by altering the contract in her own favor on every possible occasion.

Her first concert in America was given at Castle Garden, New York on the eleventh of September, 1850. Its program was in many ways typical of the period. Singers or instrumentalists rarely gave recitals. The star of the occasion would make two or three appearances, and the rest of the evening was generally devoted to music of the orchestra, and of assisting artists. Despite her lavish contributions to charity, Jenny Lind made $100,000 from her two years in America. She toured both East and West, and conquered wherever she went. She did little

to raise musical standards by presenting good music, but she did allow
Americans to hear a voice and artistry that were very nearly perfect.

There were other famous singers. MARIA MALIBRAN, daughter of
the Manuel García who gave New York its first taste of Italian opera,
had been here with her father in 1825, and had stayed two years.
HENRIETTE SONTAG, who had made a great success in opera and a
sensation in concert, was in America when Jenny Lind was with us.
Sontag went to Mexico City in 1854, where she died of cholera.

Among pianists, HENRI HERZ was largely responsible for the fondness of variations, fantasias, and florid runs and trills that permeated
nineteenth-century piano music. Herz was a Viennese who spent most
of his life in Paris. After several successful years as a pianist, writer,
and teacher, he joined a piano maker in Paris, and lost a fortune. To
repair his losses he came to America in 1845, and toured the United
States (going all the way to California), Mexico, and the West Indies.
He was here for six years. His brilliancy and bravura were immense,
but he lacked solider qualities. He knew what the public wanted, and
he was able to give it to them. He dazzled foreigners as well as Americans. He once wrote that Parisians could understand and appreciate
nothing but variations.

Herz was known to Americans by his compositions long before he
actually came. Schlesinger and Scharfenberg often played the *Rondo
and Variations for Two Pianos*, as well as the *Bravura Variations on
the Romance of Joseph*. There were also *Grand Variations* for the harp
and piano, and other "grand duos." When he died in 1888, Herz had
written eight piano concertos, and over two hundred piano pieces, all
forgotten today.

SIGISMUND THALBERG, who came in 1856–57, was a pianist of more
thorough musicianship than Herz, but he, too, won by display. Upton [2]
remembers his playing as

almost entirely confined to his own operatic fantasies, like the "Moise" and
"Lucia." . . . The melody of the aria stood out very clearly in the midst
of a most dazzling display of scales, arpeggios, shakes, and coruscations of
every sort, and the whole keyboard was none too big for the exhibition of his
elegant and absolutely perfect technic. But there was no more soul in it than
there is in the head of a kettledrum. It was simply marvellous mechanism.

[2] George P. Upton, *Musical Memories*, A. C. McClurg & Co.

. . . It was rather a pyrotechnic display, with the rockets left out, for Thalberg never soared. The real attraction of his work was its elegance and its clearness, even in the most intricate mazes with which he enclosed a melody. He had a host of imitators, and the Thalberg fantasies were all the rage for a time. Every little piano thumper tackled them. But Thalberg, his school of virtuosity, and his fantasies are now only memories. The fantasies to-day are empty as last year's birds' nests.

7. LOUIS MOREAU GOTTSCHALK (1829–1869)

Gottschalk was a native American, but he had spent so much time abroad, and had achieved such a substantial foreign reputation, that he was regarded as a foreigner by the great majority of Americans— and was accordingly most successful. He combined the attractions of pianist-composer and *beau ideal*. He was the first of our matinee idols.

He was born in New Orleans in 1829, the son of Edward Gottschalk, an English Jew who had studied medicine in Leipzig, and Aimée Marie de Braslé, a Creole. Because of his precocious talent, the little boy was given music lessons when he was three years old. When he was only six, he was able to substitute for the organist of one of the churches, and at eight he gave a public concert for the benefit of one of the violinists from the French opera in New Orleans.

When he was thirteen he went to Paris, and studied with Hallé, Stamaty, and Maledan. Through his aunt, La Comtesse de Lagrange, he was admitted to the exclusive social circles of Paris, and in many countries he became the favorite of royalty and the aristocracy. He started his career as composer in his early youth, and several of his most popular pieces, including the *Bananier* and *Bamboula*, were written when he was fifteen. He became a pupil of Berlioz, who said of him:

Gottschalk is one of the very small number who possess all the different elements of a consummate pianist—all the faculties which surround him with an irresistible prestige, and give him a sovereign power. He is an accomplished musician—he knows just how far fancy may be indulged in expression. He knows the limits beyond which any liberties taken with the rhythm produce only confusion and disorder, and upon these limits he never encroaches. There is an exquisite grace in his manner of phrasing sweet melodies and throwing light touches from the higher keys. The boldness, the brilliancy, and the originality of his playing at once dazzles and astonishes, and the infantile naïveté of his smiling caprices, and charming simplicity with which he renders simple things, seem to belong to another individuality distinct from that which marks his thundering energy—thus the success of M. Gottschalk before an audience of musical cultivation is assured.

Chopin predicted that he would become a "king of pianists." After concert tours through France and Spain, he returned to America, where he made his debut in Niblo's Garden, New York, February 10, 1853. The resulting sensation was almost comparable to Jenny Lind's reception a year and a half before. Perhaps the highest tribute was an offer from Barnum for $20,000 a year and all expenses. This Gottschalk refused, no doubt with scorn. He commenced his tours of other cities, and in the winter of 1855–56 gave eighty concerts in New York alone.

After this he spent six years in the West Indies. In 1862 he came back to the States, and for three more years toured his native America. In 1865 he went to South America, and lived there for his few remaining years. He died in Rio de Janeiro in 1869.

Some of Gottschalk's music is played today and much of it is still in print. *The Last Hope* may belong to the Victorian era, with its saccharine melody punctuated with runs that delighted many an aspiring pianist at pupils' recitals, but its restful phrases are still useful as movie music. *The Dying Poet* may have achieved its vogue because of its title, but it was effective, nevertheless. *Pasquinade* represented Gottschalk in a capricious mood, and in such he was at his best. There was true individuality in *The Banjo, Le Bananier, Bamboula, Dance Ossianique,* and others of their kind. Gottschalk in many ways was a forerunner of Ethelbert Nevin—at heart and by necessity a sentimentalist, he was a composer of *salon* music *par excellence.* And we must never forget that he was the first American composer and pianist to make a foreign reputation; he achieved an international rank that would satisfy the most ardent propagandists for American music today.

To know the man himself, it is a simple matter to piece together contemporary accounts. Gottschalk never married, but it is certain that his erotic nature led him into many love affairs. Women literally flung themselves at him. There are records of ladies of the audience rushing to the piano in a body, seizing his white gloves, tearing them to bits and fighting over the pieces for souvenirs. When he practiced on the second floor of a piano store in New Orleans, women fought for places on the stairs where they could listen, maybe catch a glimpse of him, and, if they were lucky, actually touch him. One of his biographies was written by Octavia Hensel. Her friendship with Gottschalk, which she presents in the third person, is described in terms of such fervor, and her opinions are offered with such bias and such scorn for adverse criticism of her hero, that one is tempted to suspect her own relations with him. She refers to slanders which were circulated when Gottschalk left for South America, never to return. He wrote that it was best to ignore them:

It is beneath my dignity as a man of honor to notice such slanders. Surely my friends can never credit them; and, if believed by those who are not my friends, I only pray kind heaven had given them better minds. A man whose nature allowed him to commit so dishonourable an act could also lie, and disown it! Let the story of my whole life be told, every act scrutinized; and, if you can find in it anything to prove me capable of such unmanly conduct, cast me from your regard, blot my name forever from your memory.

According to Mme. Hensel, Gottschalk died from natural causes. He was giving a monster festival in Rio de Janeiro. There were to be eight hundred performers, led by the composer. He had been appointed director-general of all the bands of the army, navy, and national guards. Several new works had been composed for the occasion. The festival started at the opera house, November 26, 1869. On the morning after the first program Gottschalk awoke too ill to get up, and had to be carried to the opera house in the evening. He collapsed before the first number, was taken to Tijuca, a neighboring village, and died there December 18.

Contradicting Hensel's account, many stories persist to the effect that Gottschalk was assassinated. If these are true, the assassin and his motive are today a mystery. The composer's body was brought back to New York, and he was buried in Greenwood Cemetery, Brooklyn, where a large monument marks his grave.

He was something of a *poseur*. He always wore white gloves to his concerts, and never took them off until he was on the platform facing his audience. Then, with perfect deliberation, and supreme indifference, he would remove them, one finger at a time, as he calmly surveyed his audience, and nodded to friends in the front rows. He once told George Upton that he did this to compose himself before playing.

Richard Hoffman wrote in his *Recollections:* [1]

I have often seen him arrive at a concert in no mood for playing, and declare that he would not appear; that an excuse might be made, but that he would not play. He cared no more for the public than if he had been in a private drawing-room where he could play or not as he pleased, but a little coaxing and a final *push* would drive him onto the stage, and after a few moments the fire would kindle and he would play with all the brilliancy which was so peculiarly his own.

There was a genial, friendly side of his nature that he showed to his friends. William Mason in his *Memories of a Musical Life* [2] published a note he once received from him:

If you have nothing to do, come and spend the evening with me on Sunday next. No formality. Smoking required, impropriety allowed, and complete liberty, with as little music as possible. I was going to mention that we will have a glass of wine and chicken salad.

Your friend,

GOTTSCHALK.

He had a sense of humor, and was delighted when an engraver printed the title page of a revised edition of *The Last Hope* as "The Latest Hops."

To know Gottschalk as a pianist it is best to read contemporary criticisms, and recollections by those who heard him. These indicate that he was really an excellent pianist, a sound musician, who could have played the best in music if he had wished, but who sensed what the vast public most wanted to hear, and gave it to them with a vengeance. No artistic conscience stood between him and material success. He craved applause, and used the surest means of gaining it. In Boston, the intolerant Dwight, who had fallen under the spell of Ole Bull's bow, perhaps unwillingly, steeled himself to Gottschalk's charms, and wrote what he thought of him, or possibly what he thought he ought to think of him:

[1] Richard Hoffman, *Some Musical Recollections of Fifty Years*, Charles Scribner's Sons.

[2] William Mason, *Memories of a Musical Life*, Century Co.

. . . It *was* great execution. But what is execution without some thought and meaning in the combinations to be executed? . . .

Skilful, graceful, brilliant, wonderful, we own his playing was. But players less wonderful have given us far deeper satisfaction . . . of what use were all these difficulties? . . . Why all that rapid tossing of handfuls of chords from the middle to the highest octaves, lifting the hand with such conscious appeal to our eyes? To what end all those rapid octave passages? since, in the intervals of easy execution, in the seemingly quiet impromptu passages, the music grew so monotonous and commonplace: the same little figure repeated and repeated, after listless pauses, in a way which conveyed no meaning, no sense of musical progress, but only the appearance of fastidiously critical scale-practising.

The New York papers, musical and unmusical, were loud in their praise. The *Tribune* even went so far as to make comparisons with Beethoven which were not altogether flattering to Beethoven; Gottschalk, a young man, went beyond the old fogies of classical music. The *Home Journal* said that his playing had the effect of an orchestra, and quoted a lady of the audience who said that he had the dexterity of Jaell, the power of de Meyer, and the taste of Herz—all of which was intended as a compliment.

Richard Hoffman [3] wrote:

. . . Thalberg and Gottschalk joined forces and played some duets for two pianos at the Niblo concerts. One in particular, on themes from "Trovatore" composed by both of them . . . was wonderfully effective and created the most tremendous furore and excitement. A remarkable double shake which Thalberg played in the middle of the piano, while Gottschalk was playing all over the keyboard in the "Anvil Chorus," produced the most prodigious volume of tone I have ever heard from the piano. . . . Possessed of the languid, emotional nature of the tropics, his music recalled the land of his birth and the traits of his people.

William Mason can be trusted for a sound opinion: [4]

I knew Gottschalk well, and was fascinated by his playing, which was full of brilliancy and bravura. His strong, rhythmic accent, his vigor and dash, were exciting and always aroused enthusiasm. He was the perfection of his

[3] Richard Hoffman, *Some Musical Recollections of Fifty Years*, Charles Scribner's Sons.

[4] William Mason, *Memories of a Musical Life*, Century Company.

school, and his effects had the effervescence and sparkle of champagne. He was far from being an interpreter of chamber or classical music, but notwithstanding this some of the best musicians of the strict style were frequently to be seen among his audience. . . . He first made his mark through his arrangement of Creole melodies. They were well defined rhythmically, and he played them with absolute rhythmic accuracy. . . . He did not care for the German school, and on one occasion, after hearing me play Schumann . . . he said, "Mason, I do not understand why you spend so much of your time over music like that; it is stiff and labored, lacks melody, spontaneity, and naïveté. It will eventually vitiate your musical taste and bring you into an abnormal state."

Although an enthusiastic admirer of Beethoven's symphonies and other orchestral works, he did not care for the pianoforte sonatas, which he said were not written in accordance with the nature of the instrument. It has been said that he could play all the sonatas by heart, but I am quite sure . . . that such was not the fact. . . .

George Upton [5] tells a different story:

Gottschalk was a great lover of Beethoven's music, especially the sonatas. How well I remember the last time I saw him! We spent an afternoon together in 1864, and he played for me in his dreamy way the so-called "Moonlight" sonata of Beethoven, some of Mendelssohn's "Midsummer Night's Dream" music, and his "Lieder ohne Worte," running from one piece to the other with hardly a pause except to light a fresh cigar or interview the Merry Widow Cliquot. I remember asking him why he didn't play that class of music in his concerts. He replied: "Because the dear public don't want to hear me play it. People would rather hear my 'Banjo' or 'Ojos Creollos,' or 'Last Hope.' Besides, there are plenty of pianists who can play that music as well or better than I can, but none of them can play my music half so well as I can. And what difference will it make a thousand years hence, anyway?"

If he had played any other sonata but the "Moonlight," it would be easier to credit his love for the Beethoven Sonatas.

[5] George P. Upton, *Musical Memories*, A. C. McClurg & Co.

CHAPTER SEVEN

The Foreign Invasion of 1848

THE middle of the nineteenth century saw hundreds of foreign musicians migrating to America. Many of them came in 1848 because they were reduced to poverty by the series of revolutions in Central Europe which had reached their climax in that year. It was natural that they should seek America, where gold had been discovered in California, the war with Mexico had just ended in victory for the United States, and the country was about to have one of its most prosperous periods.

It is difficult to determine precisely what the effect of this invasion has been. Some think that American composers were forced to give way to the Germans and Austrians, and that American music would be a more vital thing today if it had not been shoved aside by foreigners. In many ways the experience of the latter eighteenth century was repeated. This mid-century immigration was the second of the foreign invasions.

It is obvious that the immigrants did not kill American music. They may have increased our ancestors' love of a foreign label, and thus made it harder for Americans of average ability to earn a living. Yet Stephen Foster's career was just starting when they came, and Lowell Mason was at the height of his fame. Moreover, many of the newcomers were highly skilled musicians who helped to raise our musical standards.

It is not with foreign *virtuosi* that this chapter is concerned. The brilliant soloists who reaped a harvest at the box office were mostly visitors—the immigrants we are now discussing were musicians who came here to live, to play in our orchestras, to teach, and to take an active part in our everyday musical life. Living among us they exerted a far more powerful influence than those who merely dazzled us at occasional concerts.

The most important group of musicians who came from Europe was an orchestra of about twenty-five members called the Germania Society. There had been a few well-trained foreign orchestras who attempted concerts here from 1846, but none of them had been able to get a foothold. The Germania was the first orchestra in America whose members made it their principal business to play together, and rehearsed daily. The Philharmonic in New York, and the few orchestral societies in other cities gave only a few concerts a year, and the players were all engaged in other musical pursuits. The Germanians' playing was better than any that Americans had heard before. They did not achieve great financial success—Boston was the only city that gave adequate support to their concerts—but they did manage to hold together for six years, and in that time played in all our principal cities.

They brought to America some music we had never heard before—theirs was the first performance of Wagner's Overture to *Tannhäuser*. Native orchestras had tried Mendelssohn's *Midsummer Night's Dream* music, but none before the Germanians had played it with the necessary finesse and lightness. When the orchestra finally disbanded, its members settled in various of our cities, joined other organizations, and continued their activities separately.

When the little band first came to New York in 1848, it made a modest beginning. It was booked to appear as part of the bill at Niblo's Astor Place Theatre. In a small advertisement in the *Tribune* and other newspapers of October 5, William Niblo respectfully announced that the *Lady of Lyons* would be performed that evening,

after which the Grand Instrumental Concert by the Germanic Music Society, consisting of 25 performers, from Berlin, directed and conducted by Herr Lenschow.

The performance was to conclude with the farce *The Secret*.

In a few days the Germanians started their own concerts at the Broadway Tabernacle. The *Tribune* had a music critic who deplored concessions to public taste:

. . . the company seemed to excel particularly in the execution of light waltzes and polkas. . . . We should be glad to hear more of the old classi-

cal compositions of Beethoven, Mozart, and Weber, which they are capable
of giving with such power and expression.

In the same issue the Germanians had a paid advertisement, which
gave their own ideas of how their concerts should be reviewed:

. . . Selections from Donizetti, Strauss, Auber, Rossini and others were
greeted by the audience with perfect enthusiasm. The march by Lenschow
was a gem. . . . The prompt and efficient manner of the conductor presented [surely a careless compositor was responsible for this "s," instead of
"v"] those too common vexatious delays, so that the concert was finished at
an early hour. The modest and gentlemanly deportment of the whole band
was the subject of general remark. An overwhelming house is expected at
their next concert. . . .

The Germanians did make concessions to the apparent taste of the
public, and for their early programs, at least, put together some potpourris to satisfy the demand for descriptive fantasias. Thomas Ryan, in
his *Recollections of an Old Musician*,[1] describes *Up Broadway:*

It was supposed to be a graphic tone-picture of sights and sounds seen
and heard from Castle Garden to Union Square, which was at that time the
boundary of New York's bustling life.

This potpourri began with a musical picture of Castle Garden. . . .
Moving up . . . you next came to Barnum's Museum, with "Barnum's
Band" of six or eight brass instruments, which . . . played all day long on
a high balcony outside his Museum on Broadway, nearly opposite the Astor
House. It was side-splitting to hear the imitation of this brass band. . . .

. . . a fireman's parade with brass band came next. Naturally it was
preceded by a violent ringing of firebells, and a rushing down a side street
with the machine. When that noise died away, music from the open door
of a dance hall was heard; with of course all its accompaniments—the
rhythm of dancing feet, and the calling out of the figures. Then . . . we
passed by a church whence came the sound of organ music and the chanting
of a service by a number of voices. After that we heard in the distance a faint
kind of Turkish patrol music; then a big *crescendo* and sudden *fortissimo*
introduced us to Union Square and its life; and two brass bands in two
different keys prepared our nerves for the usual collision and fight between
two opposing fire companies. Finally, fireworks were touched off, the *Star-*

[1] Thomas Ryan, *Recollections of an Old Musician*, E. P. Dutton & Co.

Spangled Banner was played, and the potpourri ended, sending every one home in smiling good humor.

All of this, remember, was in America, around 1850. Surely there is nothing new.

CARL LENSCHOW resigned after a year or so of conducting the Germanians, and settled in Baltimore. He was succeeded in 1850 by CARL BERGMANN (1821–1876) who had joined the orchestra as cellist a few months before. Bergmann was a talented and capable musician, an inspired conductor, and something of a composer. It was he who arranged the *Broadway* potpourri. When the Germanians disbanded in 1854, he went to New York, and a year later became one of the conductors of the Philharmonic Society. For ten years he alternated with Theodor Eisfeld as director, and from 1866 to 1876 was the sole conductor of the orchestra. At his death in 1876 he was succeeded by Theodore Thomas.

Bergmann was responsible for one of the pinnacles of the Philharmonic's career; his methods of conducting and his interpretations are still a tradition. Toward the end of his life he went to pieces physically and morally, and the directors had to force his resignation. He died soon after.

Boston was the scene of most of the Germanians' triumphs, for Boston had a group of music lovers who enjoyed the classics. During several seasons the orchestra made the city its winter headquarters; in 1852–53 it gave a series of twenty subscription concerts there. In these concerts were played six symphonies by Beethoven, two by Mozart, one each by Haydn and Mendelssohn. Alfred Jaell played a number of piano concertos with the orchestra; Ole Bull engaged the band for his Boston concerts; it toured with Jenny Lind.

On November 27, 1852, the Germanians gave Boston, and America, its first hearing of *Tannhäuser* when they played its *Finale*. Dwight the critic, lover of the classics and champion of the romanticists Mendelssohn and Schumann, could never swallow Wagner, and he wrote:

. . . an arranged Finale from Richard Wagner's Tannhauser agreeably disappointed us in being less strange than the fame of this bold innovator had led us to expect. . . . The melody was beautiful, not particularly original, but rather *Spohr*-ish.

It later proved most important to New England that CARL ZER-
RAHN (1826–1909), flute player of the Germanians, decided to make
Boston his home when the orchestra disbanded. Until his death in 1909,
at the age of eighty-three, he was one of the most influential of Boston's
many musicians. From 1855 to 1863 he conducted one of the several
orchestras known in Boston by the name of Philharmonic. From 1865
to 1882 he led the concerts of the Harvard Musical Association. For
forty-two years (1854–1895), he was conductor of the Handel and
Haydn Society, and the other choral organizations which prospered
under his direction included the Worcester, Massachusetts, Music Festivals, which he conducted for thirty years.

There were others who settled here. THOMAS RYAN, an Irishman
who came in 1844 at the age of seventeen, lived in New England until
he died in 1903. In 1849 he became an early member of the Mendelssohn Quintette Club, one of our first chamber music organizations.
This club traveled through the country for fifty years. It was most
important in the middle of the century, for it was then that it acted
as musical missionary. Ryan played viola and clarinet. The first violinist was August Fries, a German who came to Boston in 1847. His
brother Wulf Fries was cellist. Wulf played with the club until 1870,
and from 1875 until his death in 1902 was one of New England's best-
known teachers. Francis Riha, the second violinist, had come to America in 1846 with the ill-fated Steyermark Orchestra. Edward Lehmann
played viola when Ryan played the clarinet, and flute when Ryan
played the viola.

The club jumped into immediate favor. William Schultze, who had
been first violinist of the Germanians, succeeded August Fries as first
violin of the Quintette Club in 1859. He was with it for almost twenty
years. In 1854 Carl Meisel took Riha's place as second violin. Ryan
and Wulf Fries were still with the club when it disbanded in 1895.

Dwight wrote of them in 1852:

Dear especially and justly to the lovers of good classic music is this fraternity of five young artists. . . . To them we owe our *sphere* of periodical
communion with the great German masters in their most select and genial
moods. . . . No society has ever given us such a series of good programs.
. . . Think how much of Haydn, Mozart, Beethoven, and Mendelssohn
—of the masters, who used to seem so far off, unapproachable to us novices

in music—they have this winter opened to us in their eight subscription concerts.

One more word, since now is the time for it. We earnestly trust that the Messrs. Fries, Riha, Ryan and Lehmann will not abandon the high ground they have taken, from any dismay at a momentary fluctuation in their outward success. Recent rehearsals, the programme of that last "extra" concert, together with paragraphs in newspapers congratulating us that the Club were henceforth to "play more miscellaneous music," have been ominous. There is but one ground on which such a Society can stand and outlive temporary discouragements, and that is the ground of almost strict adherence to classic chamber compositions, in their original forms. Mr. Ryan's *arrangements* of things like the "Invitation to the Dance," movements of pianoforte sonatas, &c. are certainly clever and creditable to him; but such things are never as satisfactory as the originals to hear, and they crowd out of the programme too many genuine works, which it seems due to our musical culture that we should have every chance to hear. Classic music is the peculiar field of this little Club; if they enter other fields, the weakness of a mere quintette enables them but poorly to compete with popular orchestras and bands.

THEODOR EISFELD (1816–1882) was in America for only eighteen years (1848–1866), but he did much for our musical life, especially in New York. When he arrived he had been director of the Court Theatre at Wiesbaden, and of the Concerts Viviennes in Paris. For fifteen years (until 1864), he was a conductor of the Philharmonic Society in New York, alternating with Bergmann in later years. In 1851 he commenced a series of chamber music concerts which, like the Mendelssohn Quintette Club, did real pioneer work. The first program offered Haydn's Quartet in B flat, Mendelssohn's D Minor Trio, and Beethoven's Quartet in F. In 1857, Eisfeld became the first conductor of the Brooklyn Philharmonic Society, and from 1864 shared the directorship with Theodore Thomas, until he returned to Wiesbaden in 1866. His health had suffered greatly from exposure and shock when he had been one of the few survivors of the burning of the ship *Austria*, in midocean in 1858.

Eisfeld was something of a composer. One of his works was played by the orchestra at a Jenny Lind concert. One newspaper critic became poetic in reviewing it:

Mr. Eisfeld's "Concert Polonaise" was a spirited, refreshing orchestral piece. It moved on with a triumphant and intoxicating wealth of harmony, worthy to clothe the noble rhythmic outline of the Polonaise form, like a young Bacchus crushing red grapes with every step.

OTTO DRESEL (1826–1890) was the pianist at the first of the Eisfeld *soirées*. He was one of the musicians who came in 1848. He had been a pupil of Hiller and Mendelssohn, and was an intimate friend of Robert Franz. Apthorp, in *Musicians and Music Lovers*,[2] coupled Franz and Dresel in a splendid tribute:

In both of these men was found in the highest perfection . . . the sense of musical beauty, the keenest sense for beauty of expression, beauty of form, proportion and color. They were staunch, life-long friends; their agreement on musical subjects was as complete as their friendship; they both worked together toward the same end; though they lived long apart, neither gave anything to the world without the ordeal of its passing through the other's criticism; they died within two years of each other.

In 1852, Dresel moved to Boston, where he lived until his death in Beverly, Massachusetts, in 1890. Forty-two of his sixty-four years were spent in America. He became the leading pianist of Boston, and gave chamber music concerts similar to Eisfeld's in New York. Under "Local Intelligence," Dwight's *Journal* announced his coming:

With great pleasure we announce the arrival of Mr. OTTO DRESEL, a pianist and composer of the highest order, who formerly in New York held rank with Timm, Rackeman and Scharfenberg. We have truly needed such an artist and such a teacher among us. Those who have read the papers upon Chopin in our columns, will rejoice in the opportunity of hearing his most delicate and deep music from the hands of an authentic, passionate interpreter. Mr. Dresel, too, is equally at home in the works of Bach, Beethoven, Mozart, Mendelssohn, Schumann, Robert Franz, &c., which as well as his own tone poems, he possesses in his mind and fingers. Mr. Dresel is a gentleman of superior culture and refinement. He is not a mere finger virtuoso, but one who makes the piano a means and not an end. His intention is to reside in Boston and give instruction; and to no one can we more confidently commend those who would become initiated into the genuine and enduring

[2] William F. Apthorp, *Musicians and Music Lovers*, Charles Scribner's Sons.

classics, old and new, that have been written for our common parlor instruments.

Dresel's works have not had the immortality of those of his friend Franz. He was a musician of the head rather than the heart, and of the two the heart is more often required. Maybe he was too severe a critic of his own work. His few piano pieces and songs were highly praised in their composer's day, and his unpublished *In Memoriam,* to words by Longfellow, had several performances in its original form as a ballad for soprano and orchestra. The Civil War inspired his *Army Hymn,* to a poem by Oliver Wendell Holmes, for soli, chorus, and orchestra. There were also a Piano Trio and a Quartet for piano and strings, often played at his chamber music concerts.

Julius Eichberg (1824–1893) did not come to America until 1856, but when he went to Boston in 1859 he started a career as conductor and educator that lasted until 1893. For years he was supervisor of music in the Boston Public Schools, and his chamber music, and *études* and pieces for the violin were much used. We know Eichberg today as a composer of operettas. *The Doctor of Alcantara* is still a favorite, and the patriotic chorus *To Thee, O Country* is widely sung.

We have had references to Dwight's *Journal of Music,* and perhaps there is no more fitting place than this to introduce its founder and editor John S. Dwight (1813–1893), who was at the height of his career during the foreign immigration. He was so much the friend of classic music that he was often assailed as a *Germanophile* by those who wanted American musicians to have a better chance. Dwight was needed just at the time he was most effective, though the cause of American music may have suffered at his pen. He was the foe of humbug, of charlatanism, and though he made some grave errors, he generally knew what he was talking about.

Dwight was born in Boston in 1813, and after being graduated from Harvard in 1832, he became a Unitarian minister. But his heart was in music and teaching, and after a few years in the ministry, he became a teacher of music and Latin at the Brook Farm community. In 1837, with a group of five contemporaries, he founded the *Harvard Musical Association,* for the purpose of raising the standard of musical taste at the University, preparing the way for a professorship of music, and collecting a library that would contain music and musical literature in all its branches. These aims were all realized, and the association's *soirées*, and later its orchestral concerts, were a regular part of the musical life of Boston. It is still in active existence.

It was the moral backing of the Harvard Musical Association that led Dwight to establish his *Journal of Music* in 1852. He was editor, publisher, and proprietor for six years. In 1858 the Oliver Ditson Company took it over, and retained Dwight as editor. In 1878 it was sold to other publishers and was discontinued in 1881. Dwight probably never had more than five or six hundred subscribers until he went with Ditson, but he was an influence, nevertheless. Musicians read his paper and courted his praises.

An account of Jullien's career in America may well belong in the chapter on *virtuosi*, for Jullien was certainly a prima donna conductor. Yet many of the men in his orchestra, such musicians as the Mollenhauer brothers, stayed here when Jullien returned. Louis Antoine Jullien (1812–1860) could almost have taught Barnum some tricks, and maybe he did, though he did not come here until three years after Jenny Lind. His father was a bandmaster, and the son was familiar with instruments and music from the cradle. As a youth he studied composition with Le Carpentier and Halévy at the Paris Conservatoire. In 1836, when he was twenty-four, he left the Conservatoire without graduating, and soon became a conductor of dance music. In 1840 he appeared in London as conductor of the *Concerts d'été* at the Drury Lane Theatre. He had an orchestra of ninety-eight and a chorus of twenty-four. Then came the *Concerts d'hiver*, and the *Concerts de société*, and Jullien began to be the fashion.

His aim was always to popularize music, and to do this he used the largest band, the best performers, and the most attractive pieces. When he had attained vogue, he played whole symphonies on a program, and sometimes two in an evening. Jullien would have made a fortune in our movie palaces. Almost eighty years ago he did what our movie conductors do today—presented music with showmanship. And if good music could be made theatrical it would and does appeal to the masses.

Jeweled baton, white gloves, both contributed to the effect. None of these details was assumed for the benefit of Americans alone—they were part of his stock in trade both here and abroad. When he came in 1853 he had considerable foreign reputation, and his advance agents did much to excite the curiosity of New Yorkers. One newspaper was playful:

Jullien's "monster" ophicleid is exhibited in Broadway, and there is much talk of his *Monster drum*, used in his concerts when great, *striking* effects are required, and played upon, it is said, by a drummer at each end. This has not yet arrived, it probably will take two ships to bring it. But Jullien has a bigger drum than that at his command; namely the great *press* drum, which stretches its sheep skin over the whole land, and is a wonderful *E pluribus unum* made up of a vast number of all sorts of drums, including *snare* drums, *side* drums, *bass* drums, humdrums and doldrums. This is the great drum suspended over Jullien's orchestra, one end of it in Europe, the other (now the loudest) in America; and Jullien is the king of the drummers thereupon.

Jullien was an apostle of the bigger and better idea. His preliminary advertisements occupied nearly an entire column on the front pages of the newspapers for an entire week:

CASTLE GARDEN
M. JULLIEN

has the honor to announce that his first series of

GRAND CONCERTS
VOCAL AND INSTRUMENTAL

In the United States of America
will commence on

MONDAY EVENING, Aug. 29, 1853,

and be continued

EVERY EVENING
For
ONE MONTH ONLY

.   .   .   .

Encouraged by his European success, M. JULLIEN has been induced to introduce his musical entertainments to the American public, well assured that such patronage as it may be considered they merit will be liberally awarded. With this view, he has engaged CASTLE GARDEN. When the improvements now in progress are completed, from both its natural and artificial advantages Castle Garden will form the most perfect

SALLE DE CONCERT
IN THE WORLD

M. JULLIEN'S Orchestra will be complete in every department and will include many of the most distinguished Professors, selected from the Royal Opera Houses of London, Paris, Vienna, Berlin, St. Petersburg, Brussels, etc.

. . . .

The selections of music, in addition to those of a lighter character, will embrace the grander compositions of the great masters, the gradual introduction of which, with their complete and effective style of performance, cannot fail, it is believed, to contribute to the enhancement of musical taste.

GENERAL ARRANGEMENTS

The programme (which will be changed every evening) will be selected from a Repertoire of

TWELVE HUNDRED PIECES

and will include a Classical Overture and two Movements of a Symphony by one of the great masters, a grand Operatic Selection, together with Quadrilles, Waltzes, Mazurkas, Polkas, Schottisches, Tarantelles, Galops, etc.

. . . .

In addition to the above general arrangements, M. JULLIEN will each evening, introduce one of his celebrated NATIONAL QUADRILLES, as the English, Irish, Scotch, French, Russian, Chinese, Indian, Hungarian, Polish, &c.: and at the beginning of the second week will be produced the

AMERICAN QUADRILLE

which will contain all the

NATIONAL AIRS

and embrace no less than

TWENTY SOLOS AND VARIATIONS,

for twenty of M. JULLIEN'S solo performers, and conclude with a

TRIUMPHAL FINALE

The American Quadrille has been composed by M. JULLIEN since his arrival in America, and is now in active preparation. Several other new Quadrilles, Waltzes, Polkas, &c. will also be introduced during the season.

And the amazing part was that it was all true. The audiences saw a good show, and they heard some good music along with the clap-trap, all played perfectly. Whatever Jullien's faults may have been, he was a musician and he knew how to conduct an orchestra. The New York *Courier and Enquirer* knew what it was talking about when it said:

Monsieur Jullien is a humbug; which may be news to our readers, but it is not news to M. Jullien. Let us not be misunderstood. M. Jullien is not a pitiful humbug, or a timorous humbug, or worse than all, an unsuccessful humbug; he is a splendid, bold, and dazzlingly successful humbug; one who merits his great success almost as much as if he had not employed the means by which he has achieved it. M. Jullien, having blazoned himself and his principal artists in infernal scarlet and black all over the town, for some months—having issued an infinite series of portraits of himself, and ruined the prospectus of the Art Union by establishing several free galleries of portraits of his colleagues,—having occupied (and handsomely paid for) a large portion of valuable space in our columns and those of our principal contemporaries by informing them of what they knew perfectly well before or did not want to know at all,—having brought over from England forty and odd orchestral performers, when we could hardly support those who were already here, and created a dearth in the musician market by recklessly buying up the services of sixty more . . . having done all this, he sends us a vast and ponderous card of admission printed in scarlet and gold. . . .

. . . Exactly in the middle of the vast orchestra was a crimson platform edged with gold, and upon this was a music stand, formed by a fantastic gilt figure supporting a desk, and behind the stand a carved arm chair decorated in white and gold, and tapestried with crimson velvet, a sort of throne for the musical monarch. He steps forward, and we see those ambrosial whiskers and moustaches which Punch has immortalized; we gaze upon that immaculate waistcoat, that transcendent shirt front, and that unutterable cravat which will be read about hereafter; the monarch graciously and gracefully accepts the tumultuous homage of the assembled thousands, grasps his sceptre, and the violins wail forth the first broken phrase of the overture to *Der Freyschutz*. The overture is splendidly performed.

. . . Other conductors use their batons to direct their orchestras. Not so with M. Jullien. His band is so well drilled at rehearsal that it conducts itself at performances, while he uses his baton to direct the audience. He does everything with that unhappy bit of wood, but put it to its legitimate purpose of beating time. . . . The music is magnificent, and so is the humbug, as M. Jullien caps its climax by subsiding into his crimson gilded throne, over-whelmed by his exertions, a used up man. . . .

. . . The discipline of his orchestra is marvellous. He obtains from fifty strings a pianissimo which is scarcely audible and he makes one hundred instruments stop in the midst of a fortissimo which seems to lift the roof, as if a hundred men dropped dead at the movement of his hand . . .

Jullien started a custom which modern jazz bands claim as their own. He arranged airs from *Masaniello,* and other works, so that the men in the orchestra sang as they played.

Even Dwight capitulated when Jullien went to Boston, though his New York correspondent had warned him that he was extravagant and foppish as compared to Bergmann, and that Anna Zerr, his soloist, "shame to say, had stooped to pick up one night and sang 'Old Folks at Home' for the b'hoys; one would as soon think of picking up an apple-core in the street." Probably Dwight forgave the quadrilles and galops for the way in which Jullien played the *Scherzo* from Mendelssohn's *Scotch* Symphony, or the *Allegretto* from Beethoven's A Major Symphony. He wrote:

Jullien *can* play the best kind of music . . . if he makes a colossal toy of the orchestra in his quadrilles and polkas, he has also his Beethoven, his Mendelssohn and Mozart nights, in which he proves his love and power of interpreting the finest works. . . . We were present last week at his Mendelssohn night, and never before have we so felt the power and beauty of the A minor or Scotch Symphony.

The climax of Jullien's American career came when he was playing at the Crystal Palace in New York. One night the program announced a piece called *Night, or The Firemen's Quadrille.* He had always gone after vivid effects. If his music pictured a battle he used everything but real cannon. Even Handel once said that he would introduce the dis-charge of artillery into his choruses if he could. Pat Gilmore, the band-master, did actually use heavy guns for the first beat of each measure in the national anthems at the Boston Peace Jubilee in 1869, but he had more room outside the hall than Jullien had in New York, and there were fewer horses to be frightened. Jullien had to content himself with his monster drum.

Before the *Firemen's Quadrille* commenced, the audience was warned that something unusual might happen. Jullien loved to spring a surprise, but a lot of fainting women might be too much of a good thing. Wiping his brow with his gorgeous silk handkerchief, he arose from his throne and faced his men. The piece started quietly, like a nocturne or lullaby. A hush through the house made the suspense more thrilling. Then the music picked up a bit, the violins fluttered as they told of the awesome mystery of darkness. You could almost see ghosts. Suddenly the clang of firebells was heard outside. Flames burst from the ceiling. Three companies of firemen rushed in, dragging their hoses behind them. Real water poured from the nozzles, glass was broken. Some of the women fainted, and the ushers were rushing here and there yelling that it was all part of the show. And all the while the orchestra was playing at a tremendous fortissimo.

When Jullien thought they had had enough, he signaled for the firemen to go, and in a glorious blare of triumph the orchestra burst into the *Doxology*. Those of the audience who were conscious joined in the singing.

Such was Monsieur Jullien. When he went back to Europe in 1854 he may have had some money in his pocket, but he didn't know how to keep it. When Covent Garden burned in 1856, the manuscripts of all his famous quadrilles were lost. In 1857 he sank between five and six thousand pounds in an opera venture. Then he toured the British provinces with a small orchestra.

His hard luck was too much for him; it got on his nerves, and he finally ended in a madhouse, where he died in 1860. Maybe he belonged there all the time, but he at least practiced insanity in the grand manner.

It is not because of his showmanship and his playing that we are chiefly concerned with Jullien, though they were highly important in cultivating American concertgoers. It is principally because Jullien was shrewd enough to play works by native American composers during his visit. He gave them a hearing and at the same time crystallized the beginning of a controversy that has not yet ended, and which will probably never end. At this time a few of our composers began to be conscious of their nationality, and to feel slighted over the recognition they were not receiving. And after all, this was probably the most important result of the foreign invasion of 1848. It made the American composer conscious of himself, and if at first he had to fight for his existence with poor equipment and meager talents, the very contrast afforded by his foreign rivals made an issue of his rights.

CHAPTER EIGHT

The Awakening of a National Consciousness

1. ANTON PHILIP HEINRICH (1781–1861)

WE are anxious today to make an important person of the American composer. He must have international standing and at the same time be a nationalist. He must appeal to music lovers throughout the world, and yet choose native subjects for his musical ideas. He must be both Wagner and Grieg. Whether he is here or not, we must make a place for him, and secure his recognition in advance. If he doesn't exist, we must create him by hothouse methods. We want bigger and better composers in this country. All of which sounds like a twentieth-century idea, a final awakening to the fact that our composers haven't had a fair chance. Seventy-five years have passed since Ole Bull hoped that his offer of a thousand dollars for an American opera "would bring to light the musical talent now latent in this country, which only needs a favorable opportunity for its development." And he was careful to specify that it be the work of an American composer, upon a strictly American subject.

Even Ole Bull, in 1855, was only repeating what had been said before, for there were a few brave apostles of the American composer from the beginning of the century. Strange to say, one of the first who felt he should be encouraged because he was an American composer was a foreigner, a Bohemian named Anton Philip Heinrich. He called himself Anthony when he came to America.

Histories of American music have quite neglected Father Heinrich, and if he is to be judged on the lasting merits of his work, he is hardly entitled to much of a place among our composers. Yet he is highly important, not alone as an eccentric, but because he was one of the first to seek for nationalism, and to capitalize his limitations. In his own mind, these limitations were geographical, not flaws in his own powers of expression.

Heinrich was born to wealth, and subsequent reverses turned him to the music he loved as a source of livelihood. Had he only had talent equal to his ardor, his life story would have satisfied the most romantic of biographers; for there are scenes in garrets, interviews with royalty, and disappointments that sing the old, old song of genius starving for want of recognition. The only thing missing is the genius. His friends hailed him as the Beethoven of America, but the only similarity was that he may have written as many notes.

Some years ago the Library of Congress acquired a whole trunkful of Heinrich's manuscripts, his own copies of his published works, and his personal scrapbook. Sonneck catalogued these works with his accustomed thoroughness, and in his notes called attention to the various duplications of similar material in separate works. Through Heinrich's own data on his manuscripts it is possible to piece together the principal facts of his life.

He was born in Bohemia in 1781. As a young man he became an officer in a large banking house. His business called for traveling, and once when he was in Malta he bought a Cremona violin, which he learned to play. On a visit to this country he married an American in Boston, a lady "abundantly rich in beauty, accomplishments and qualities of a noble heart," who died in 1814. A few years later Heinrich came to America and settled in Philadelphia, where he was director of music at the Southwark Theatre. It was at about this time that news reached him that his banking house had failed, and he was reduced to poverty. He went to Kentucky, and for a while gave violin lessons in Louisville, and then lived among the Indians at Bardstown. Parker's *Euterpeiad* (April 13, 1822) tells of his reverses:

The author but a few years since was merely an amateur and a prosperous merchant whom sudden misfortune transformed into a professor, the only character in which he expected to gain honest livelihood . . . this transformation had not taken place until he was verging on forty.

It was in 1820 that he published his *Dawning of Music in Kentucky, or the Pleasures of Harmony in the Solitudes of Nature*. In his preface to this work he stated his position as an American composer:

In presenting this work to the world, the Author observes, that he has been actuated much less by any pecuniary interest, than zeal, in furnishing a Volume of various *Musical Compositions,* which, it is hoped, will prove both useful and entertaining.

The many and severe animadversions, so long and repeatedly cast on the talent for Music in this Country, has been one of the chief motives of the Author, in the exercise of his abilities, and should he be able, by this effort, to create but one single *Star* in the *West,* no one would ever be more proud than himself, to be called an *American Musician.*—He however is fully aware of the dangers which, at the present day, attend talent on the crowded and difficult road of eminence; but fears of just criticism, by *Competent Masters,* should never retard the enthusiasm of genius, when ambitious of producing works more lasting than the *Butterfly-effusions* of the present age. —He, therefore, relying on the candour of the public, will rest confident that justice will be done, by due comparisons with the works of other Authors (celebrated for their merit, especially as regards Instrumental *execution*) but who have never, like him, been thrown, as it were, by *discordant events,* far from the emporiums of musical science, into the isolated wilds of nature, where he invoked his Muse, tutored *only* by ALMA MATER.

So much for Heinrich's own opinion of himself and his work. Parker's *Euterpeiad* quite agreed with him. Under the head of *Criticism* appeared the following review:

In attending to other duties we fear we have too long neglected the pleasing task of recommending the above *American production* to the favorable notice of the public. . . . It is . . . with great satisfaction that we feel ourselves authorized to say, that whoever has the will and ability to overstep the fence and unveil the hidden treasure, will be no less surprised than delighted with his discovery. With what success the first attempt of this kind was made in Boston, and to whom the honor of it belongs, has already been stated in our former numbers; and we can only add now that the vigour of thought, variety of ideas, originality of conception, classical correctness, boldness and luxurance of imagination, displayed throughout this volume, are . . . extraordinary. . . . His genius . . . triumphs over everything. —He may, therefore, justly be styled the *Beethoven* of America, and as such he is actually considered by the few who have taken the trouble to ascertain his merits. . . .

In another paragraph the writer holds that one of the melodies "is a strain that would do credit to the Beethoven of Europe."

In 1827, Heinrich went to London, presumably to study music. By 1832 he was back in America, this time in Boston as organist of the Old South Church. Another trip to Europe followed shortly, and penciled notes on his manuscripts tell of incidents during his travels and sojourns. In 1834 he was in London, playing in the orchestra of the Drury Lane Theatre for thirty-six shillings a week. There were frequent trips to the Continent, and in 1835 he suffered a severe illness. Notes on one of his manuscripts (*The Jager's Adieu*) are dated London, November 24, 1835:

Composed and arranged under severe bodily affliction, and at the time of finishing this work, I was under the painful necessity of becoming a patient in the London Hospital. . . . Later, during the above year, I was also laid up very sick, in the Hospital of the Merciful friars at Buda (Hungary) and at Vienna, "im Spital der Barmherzigen brüder."

When he was in Grätz in 1836 he had a performance of his symphony *The Combat of the Condor*. Things didn't go too well.

The gentlemen of the orchestra went this introductory movement twice very handsomely through, namely on the 25th of May, 1836. On the 7th of June another rehearsal took place, but having obtained only a few violin performers, and those mostly strangers to their parts, there was great deficiency in the effect. The actual concert took place on the 10th of June following, when this first movement met with public introduction; however, as there were by far too few violin performers and basses, and again some new gentlemen, not enlisted before, the author must confess that he suffered by it.

In 1837 he was in Bordeaux, where he suffered more misfortune:

After having been severely robbed in the Hotel de la Paix, Rue Chapeau rouge, kept by a Mr. Sansot, I retired for consolation to a solitary garret in the boarding house of Madamoiselle Jouano, Rue devise Ste. Catharine no. 7, and wrote this work [*The Columbiad, Grand American national chivalrous symphony*]. I finished at the same place "The Condor," and my instrumental phantasy "Pocahonta." The Muses had not favoured me with a pianoforte, in fact, since two years, I have been so situated, as constantly travelling about, that practical music is estranged to me, but I trust notwithstanding, that at some day or other, this work and those other productions alluded to will be found worthy of public patronage, especially in the United

States, and should I not live, to derive any benefit from these works may my daughter Antonia, the child of my sorrows, be benefitted by them or should she be in prosperity, may they then serve to some other charitable purpose. I have travelled so far through France without letters of introduction and without holding a special converse with any human being, that after my disaster in the "Hotel de la Paix," not to mention other disappointments and misfortunes on my journey, I found it necessary to seclude myself for a few weeks at Bordeaux and find diversion and comfort in these compositions. May the blessings of Heaven rest upon them, and on my daughter Antonia, who alas! is far distant from me, and whom my eyes, as yet, have never beheld.

When his wife died in 1814, he had left his infant daughter with a relative at Grund, near Rumburg. When he came to Europe she had disappeared. When he went back to America in 1837 he found that she had followed him, and they eventually discovered each other.

From this year until his death in 1861, Heinrich spent most of his time in and around New York. There were a couple of years abroad shortly before he died, but he devoted himself principally to the business of being an American musician. In 1840 he solicited subscriptions to his *Jubilee*, "a grand national song of triumph, composed and arranged for a full orchestra and a vocal chorus—in two parts, commemorative of events from the landing of the Pilgrim fathers to the consummation of American liberty." In publishing this work he asked for the support of "statesmen, legislators, and other distinguished citizens." He spent several years in lining up his patrons for the piece, and journeyed to Washington to get the names of high government officials. It may be that this is the work that he wished to dedicate to the President. He asked John Hill Hewitt to introduce him, and Hewitt described the incident in *Shadows on the Wall:*

The eccentric Anthony Philip Heinrich . . . visited Washington while I was in that city, with a grand musical work of his, illustrative of the greatness and glory of this republic, the splendor of its institutions and the indomitable bravery of its army and navy. This work Heinrich wanted to publish by subscription. He had many names on his list; but, as he wished to dedicate it to the President of the United States, and also to obtain the signatures of the Cabinet and other high officials, he thought it best to call personally and solicit their patronage.

He brought with him a number of letters of introduction, among them one to myself from my brother, a music-publisher in New York. . . . I tendered him the hospitalities of my house . . . promising him to go the rounds with him the following morning and introduce him to President Tyler.

Poor Heinrich! I shall never forget him. He imagined he was going to set the world on fire with his "Dawning of Music in America"; but alas! it met with the same fate as his "Castle in the Moon" and "Yankee Dood-liad."

Two or three hours of patient hearing did I give to the most complicated harmony I ever heard, even in my musical dreams. Wild and unearthly passages, the pianoforte absolutely groaning under them, and "the old man eloquent," with much self-satisfaction, arose from the tired instrument, and with a look of triumph, asked me if I had ever heard music like that before? I certainly had not.

At a proper hour we visited the President's mansion, and . . . were shown into the presence of Mr. Tyler, who received us with his usual urbanity. I introduced Mr. Heinrich as a professor of exalted talent and extraordinary genius. The President after learning the object of our visit, which he was glad to learn was not to solicit an office, readily consented to the dedication, and commended the undertaking. Heinrich was elated to the skies, and immediately proposed to play the grand conception. . . .

We were shown into the parlor. . . . The composer labored hard to give full effect to his weird production; his bald pate bobbed from side to side, and shone like a bubble on the surface of a calm lake. At times his shoulders would be raised to the line of his ears, and his knees went up to the key-board, while the perspiration rolled in large drops down his wrinkled cheeks. . . .

The composer labored on, occasionally explaining some incomprehensible passage, representing, as he said, the breaking up of the frozen river Niagara, the thaw of the ice, and the dash of the mass over the mighty falls. Peace and plenty were represented by soft strains of pastoral music, while the thunder of our naval war-dogs and the rattle of our army musketry told of our prowess on sea and land.

The inspired composer had got about half-way through his wonderful production, when Mr. Tyler arose from his chair, and placing his hand gently on Heinrich's shoulder, said:

"That may all be very fine, sir, but can't you play us a good old Virginia reel?"

Had a thunderbolt fallen at the feet of the musician, he could not have been more astounded. He arose from the piano, rolled up his manuscript, and taking his hat and cane, bolted toward the door, exclaiming:

"No, sir; I never plays dance music!"

I joined him in the vestibule . . . As we proceeded along Pennsylvania Avenue, Heinrich grasped my arm convulsively, and exclaimed:

"Mein Gott in himmel! de peebles vot made Yohn Tyler Bresident ought to be hung! He knows no more apout music than an oyshter!"

Heinrich was active among the New York musicians of the forties and fifties. He was the chairman of the first meeting of the Philharmonic Society, although there is no record of any further connection with the orchestra. On June 16, 1842, a "Grand Musical Festival" at the Broadway Tabernacle was devoted largely to his works. At this time he lived at 41 Liberty Street. A note on his *Warrior's March to the Battlefield* states that it was

Finished on the 1st of May 1845 at my lodgings, say: desolated garret in Liberty Street no. 41, where I had dwelt for many years *quasi* in solitude, wrote many things etc. etc. but which lodging I was obliged leaving, with much melancholy, the house going to be pulled down, as Music had no charms for the proprietor of the building, but more the hammer's din, in order to destroy the composer's garret, to make room for cocklofts and commercial stores. I loved thee dearly cherished and sequestered attic, notwithstanding many sorrows and inconveniences which I experienced there, but where my imagination wandered free and independent.

William Mason, in his *Memories*,[1] gives a picture of Heinrich at about this time:

. . . there lived in New York an elderly German musician who had somehow gained the cognomen of Father Heinrich. During a visit which he made to Boston . . . I was presented to him as a youth of some musical promise. He immediately showed me one of his pianoforte pieces in manuscript, and said:

"Young man, I am going to test your musical talent and intelligence and see if you appreciate in any degree the importance of a proper observance of dynamics in musical interpretation."

He had placed the open pages of the Mss. on the pianoforte desk, and I was glancing over them in close scrutiny.

"I wish to tell you before you begin to play that I have submitted this piece

[1] William Mason, *Memories of a Musical Life*, The Century Co.

to one or two of the best musicians in New York and they have failed to bring out the intended effects in an important phrase. . . ."

About half way down the 2nd page I discovered a series of sforzando marks over several notes of the inner parts, and immediately determined to bring out these notes with all possible force. . . . On coming to the passage referred to I put a tremendous emphasis on the tones marked sforzando, playing all the other voices by contrast quite softly. To my boyish satisfaction I found I had hit the mark. The excitement and pleasure of Father Heinrich was excessive and amusing. "Bravo, bravo!" he cried; "you have great talent, and have done what none of our best musicians in New York have accomplished."

When Jenny Lind came in 1850, Heinrich tried to call her attention to his works. If he could only get the "nightingale" to sing some of his songs, his fortunes were made. He was ready when she arrived. One of the works could be played by her orchestra as a feature number—*Jenny Lind and the Septinarian*, "an artistic perplexity" (he wasn't quite seventy yet, but that made little difference). The first part was "Jenny Lind's Journey across the ocean, a grand divertissement for the orchestra"; the second was "Jenny Lind's maelstrom on the ship-wreck of a book, a phantasy for the pianoforte." Then there was *Barnum: invitation to Jenny Lind, the museum polka.*

He didn't get very far with Jenny Lind. After she married Gold-schmidt he tried to see her husband about his works. He sent him a whole volume of songs. Receiving no reply he wrote him a couple of letters, asking when he could see him. Goldschmidt returned the volume of music without comment, and enclosed a pair of tickets to one of Jenny Lind's concerts. Heinrich called this the greatest insult of his artistic career.

The Philharmonic also offended his dignity. He had enough works scored for orchestra to fill the Society's programs for an entire season. The committee was a little too slow in considering his music to please Heinrich, and when he was finally informed that they would give him a performance, he withdrew his application, and continued to enjoy the sweets of martyrdom.

In 1853 came a triumphant moment in Heinrich's career. He was given a Grand Valedictory Concert at Metropolitan Hall. Nearly all of the prominent musicians took part. The orchestra, "a numerous and powerful one," was under the direction of Theodor Eisfeld and Heinrich himself. Mme. Otto was the principal vocalist. H. C. Timm presided at the pianoforte. Advance information spread to Boston, where Dwight's *Journal* told its readers that the

enthusiastic veteran is to have a concert, for the production of those strange and elaborate works of his. He has gone on in his solitary attic, composing oratorios, operas, symphonies, and songs, merely composing, not publishing [this is not altogether accurate] till he has accumulated several large chests full of original compositions, his only wealth. May the devoted old servant of St. Cecilia be cheered by a full house, and may some of that inspiration, which has sustained his long labors appear in his works and be felt by his audience.

The program was lengthy, and of course the majority of the works were by Heinrich. The opening number was for orchestra—*The Wildwood Troubadour, a musical Auto-Biography*. This "festive ouverture" was in four movements, representing the "Genius of Harmony slumbering in the forest shades of America."

After songs by Wallace, Loder and Hobbs, there came another of Heinrich's orchestral works, *The New England Feast of Shells*, a "Divertimento Pastorale Oceanico." This opened with an *Andante* movement—"The home Adieus of the Nymphs and Swains departing to the Maritime Festival." Then an *Andantino*—"The fanciful curvetings of the Mermaids in the ocean surf" (Yes, in New England!). The *Finale Brillante*—told of "The romantic 'Love Feast,' resulting in the destruction of the 'bivalves' at the 'sacrifice of shells,' *vulgate* 'Clam Bake.'"

The second part of the concert commenced with a tribute to England—*National Memories*, a "Grand British Symphony, by gracious acceptance, dedicated to H.B.M. Queen Victoria." Then came arias by Mozart and Weber, and a Quintette from Heinrich's Oratorio *The Pilgrim Fathers*. The closing selection was intended as a climax—*The Tower of Babel, or Language Confounded*. This consisted of two parts—first, the *Sinfonia canonicale*, and then the *Coda fugato*, representing "The Dispersion, which will be characterized by a gradual cessation of melodies, and consecutive retirement of each individual performer." Heinrich may have had his doubts about the endurance of the audience,

Daniel Decatur Emmett
(See pages 181–184, 255–258)

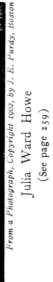

Julia Ward Howe
(See page 259)

Henry Clay Work

(See pages 166-168)

George F. Root

(See pages 164-166)

for the program adds: "If time permits, the whole Symphony will be given; if not, the *Dispersion* alone."

In 1857 he went to Europe again, and spent a season in Prague and in Dresden. A note on the manuscript of *Der Felsen von Plymouth* is dated Prague, April, 1859:

The foregoing musings were chiefly written during the winter season of 1858 & 1859 in a desolate, comfortless chamber, without any fire whatsoever, during great sufferings of cold, as without the aid and solace of a pianoforte. The wanderer leaves now his winter-quarter for more genial climes, on his musical experimental tour, under the banner: *Hope on, hope ever.*

He eventually came back to America, and lived to see his eightieth birthday in New York. He was very ill at the time and died two months later—May 3, 1861.

Detailed review of Heinrich's music from a critical standpoint is difficult. His works are marked by extravagance, repetition, and a constant striving for the grand manner. Yet, in spite of his eccentricities (musical and otherwise), there must have been something very appealing about the man himself and even something akin to native genius in his music. He might well take a real pride and pleasure in a letter he received from the well-known German composer Heinrich Marschner (May 10, 1849), which, in translation, read in part as follows:

Although you are sometimes tempted through your originality, to offer the performers too great difficulties, and to require of the human voice too extensive a compass: still the originality, and the deeply poetic ideas, which are developed in your compositions, repay the painstaking to master them; and are a splendid testimonial of German talent in the West. Remain assured of my most perfect esteem, and may you be gladdened long yet with the applause of every lover of the art. This wish is from my heart.

And another distinguished musician and critic of that day, Joseph Leopold Zvonar of Prague, in reviewing Heinrich's concert in that city (May 3, 1857) wrote of Heinrich's musical personality as "so absolutely untouched by any fundamental art culture such as is obtained through the study of theory and musical literature, but forced to rely solely upon its own exceedingly sensitive and innately expressive spirit. That the effect is often surprising and strange is easily understood,"

Zvonar continued, "yet it cannot be denied that on occasion we find not only true spiritual essence, but also its eminently worthy expression. Then, too, there are moments showing a well-disciplined, consistent, logically correct musical diction, and a carefully worked out and originally conceived instrumentation; all of which places the really artistic personality of our worthy countryman in a very advantageous light."

The statement in Dwight's *Journal* that Heinrich merely composed in his attic, and did not publish his works, is hardly accurate when the Library of Congress collection contains nearly two hundred printed pieces. Many of these are pianoforte editions of the manuscript orchestral works. There are a number of duplications under different titles; the composer had a habit of reworking his material.

His works were played in his time. Scharfenberg featured the *Pocahontas* Waltz at a number of his recitals and Mrs. Ostinelli (Sophia Hewitt) played *Paganini's Incantation* at a concert in Boston.

Heinrich's importance in a history of American music lies in his treatment of nationalistic material. Others had taken the Indian as a subject for musical description, but Heinrich was the first to use the red man as a theme for orchestral works on a large scale. In this he was truly a pioneer. The *Indian Carnival or The Indian's festival of dreams* was a "Sinfonia eratico fantachia" [sic] for orchestra, with a score of sixty-four pages. He used its theme for a *Toccata* for piano, published in 1849. His *Indian Fanfares* (published for piano, but recommended as quick-steps for military band) comprised *The Comanche revel, The Sioux galliarde,* and *The Manitou air dance. The Mastodon* was programmatic. The score of this "grand symphony in three parts" occupies three volumes. The movements are: *Black Thunder, the patriarch of the Fox tribe; The Elkhorn pyramid, or the Indians' offering to the spirit of the prairies;* and *Shenandoah, a celebrated Indian chief.*

Manitou mysteries, or the voice of the Great Spirit was described on the manuscript title page as a "Gran sinfonia misteriosa indiana." *Pushmataha, a venerable chief of a Western tribe of Indians,* was a fantasia for thirty-three instruments. A note at the end states that "the author composed this fantasia under peculiar circumstances which have given it great wildness. An arrangement from the score for the pianoforte will be found at the end. The composer begs, that no decision on its merits will be made, unless performed by a master."

In at least one of his works Heinrich claimed that he was transcrib-
ing authentic voices of nature. He explained this phenomenon in a note
on the manuscript score of *The wild wood spirits' chant, or Scintilla-
tions of Yankee doodle, forming a grand national heroic fantasia scored
for a powerful orchestra in forty-four parts, designed as introductory
to the second part of the oratorio of the Pilgrim fathers, entitled The
consummation of American liberty. Composed and inscribed as a legacy
to his adopted country, the land of Washington, by Anthony Philip
Heinrich.* The note was as follows:

There is no fact better authenticated than that poets, (who were grave
historians in ancient times), heard, or feigned to hear, the voices of spirits,
and the music of the spheres, and men have always believed that "myriads
of beings walk the earth unseen by mortal eyes."—But, whether that be fact
or fable, the author has himself heard the *genii of music,* (if any credence is
to be given to his imagination) in an American forest—and although strange
vicissitudes have chased him since, and as the storms of more than sixty
winters have left their chill upon him, yet, the impressions of that ethereal
music were so deep, and his recollections so vivid, that by the help of sketch-
ings *scored* upon that mystic ground in the State of Kentucky, then the abode
of Sylphs and Naiads, he has been able to *note* down that music on these
pages, as he heard it from an invisible hand.

When he dedicated a work to the Musical Fund Society of Philadelphia, he chose a subject appropriate to that city—*The treaty of William
Penn with the Indians*—*Concerto grosso*—*An American national dramatic divertisement, for a full orchestra, comprising 6 different characteristic movements, united in one.*

He considered it entirely appropriate to use foreign languages in
titles and programs of works on American subjects, and occasionally to
indulge in a confusion of tongues. Hence *Der Felsen von Plymouth,
oder die Landung der Pilgrim Väter in Neu-England,* and the published *Storia d'un violino of the premier violon to His Majesty Andrew
the 1st, King of the Yankee Doodles.* . . . "Composto dal General
Jackson's primo fiddler."

Heinrich liked to make gestures, especially magnanimous tributes to
such colleagues as Beethoven and Mendelssohn. *To the spirit of Beethoven* was a "monumental symphony for a grand orchestra—an echo
from America to the inauguration of Beethoven's monument at Bonn."

The tomb of genius was a "sinfonia sacra, for grande orchestra, to the memory of Mendelssohn-Bartholdy."

The account of Heinrich's music could continue for many pages, but lack of space forces us to leave that task to his biographer. We may laugh both at and with the dear old man, principally at him, I fear, and yet he had a real idea in his poor eccentric head, an idea that others more talented than he have failed to carry out. We must respect him for what he tried to do, and never forget that he was the first to make the attempt. That he failed to accomplish his ends was unfortunate, in many ways tragic, but the important fact is that Heinrich was the first to attempt American nationalism in the larger forms of musical composition.

2. WILLIAM HENRY FRY (1815[?]–1864)

William Henry Fry is important as the composer of the first publicly performed grand opera by a native American. He is equally important as one of the first who fought the battle of the American composer; not wisely perhaps, but bravely. A curious combination, this Fry, the son of the publisher of the *National Gazette*, well educated, and a discriminating critic who let his patriotism get the better of his judgment. Modern societies for the spread of American music might well take Fry as their patron saint.

Fry was educated principally along literary lines, but he had an overwhelming love for music. His older brother had piano lessons, and William taught himself to play by following the instructions he heard given to his brother. After he had composed an overture at fourteen years of age, he studied theory and composition with Leopold Meignen, the Philadelphia musician and publisher who had studied at the Paris Conservatoire. Before he was twenty, Fry had written three more overtures; one of them won him a gold medal, and a performance by a "Philharmonic Society" that existed in Philadelphia.

Grand opera was heard frequently in the principal American cities by the time Fry reached manhood. New Orleans had started its operatic career with Paisiello's *Barber of Seville* in 1810, and during following seasons enjoyed three or four operas a week. New York heard *Der Frieschütz*, in 1825. Soon after this, in the same year, Manuel García brought his family and troupe to New York, and gave seventy-nine performances in a year's time at the Park and Bowery Theatres. Other companies had followed. Rossini and Boïeldieu were favorites, even though their works were adapted to the capacities of resident and traveling companies. In 1832, Lorenzo da Ponte was living in New York— the Italian poet who had written the libretto to Mozart's *Don Giovanni*. He persuaded Montressor to bring his opera troupe to America.

Arthur Seguin and his wife Ann, distinguished opera singers from England, came to America in 1838 and soon formed their own company. They made extended visits to the cities of the United States and Canada. Filippo Trajetta, an Italian, had come to Boston as early as 1799, and after living in New York and Virginia, settled in Philadelphia as a singing teacher in 1822. He founded an "American Conservatorio," and was an earnest propagandist for Italian opera.

Fry had plenty of opportunity to know the works of Rossini, Bellini, Donizetti, and Auber, so he tried his hand at opera and wrote *Leonora*, a lyrical drama in three acts. The libretto was the work of Fry's brother, Joseph R. Fry, who adapted it from Bulwer's *The Lady of Lyons*. It was produced at the Chestnut Street Theatre, Philadelphia, June 4, 1845, by members of the Seguin troupe, and enjoyed a run of twelve nights. Eighty-four years later, in May of 1929, Dr. Otto Kinkeldey, then music chief at the New York Library, arranged a presentation of excerpts from *Leonora* in concert form. It was presented at a concert of the Pro Musica Society, following a number of works by American moderns. The critics were all present and offered their opinions. Chotzinoff, in the New York *World*, said:

When Mr. Kinkeldey . . . arrived at the music of Mr. Fry's opera the joke seemed to me to be on Pro Musica, for "Leonora," though outmoded, was found to contain tunes the absence of which was the main feature of the modern pieces which preceded the exposure of the operatic antiquity.

Oscar Thompson, in the *Post*, deplored the levity of the audience, and added:

. . . at least one tenor-soprano duet in mellifluous thirds would not have been laughed at, it is fair to assume, if it had been heard in a performance of "Norma," "Puritani" or "Somnambula" at the opera.

Henderson in the *Sun* said that Mr. Fry evidently lived in his time, and probably thought "Norma" the greatest opera ever written. Peyser in the *Telegram* made comparisons with the present:

. . . As much of the music as one heard last evening played the sedulous ape to Bellini, Donizetti, and Auber, besides faintly remembering the neo-Weberian ways of Reissiger tradition. Who shall say that, properly mounted and sung, Fry's ambitious opus would not, in its archaic way, furnish better diversion than "Egyptian Helen"?

The original production in Philadelphia was lavish; the composer paid for it himself. There was a chorus of eighty, and an orchestra of sixty; the settings were the finest that could be built. In true operatic style, the work presented recitatives and arias, ensemble numbers, choruses, coloratura cadenzas, and a climax that was indeed melodramatic.

The libretto was almost too well adapted to musical setting. The regularity of rhythm and meter prevented Fry from achieving much in the way of variety. The Philadelphia performances were given in English, for Fry was one of the first to cry for opera in the native tongue. The Grecian muse spoke Greek. "Shall our American muse chant in a foreign tongue? Forbid it, national sense, pride, ambition." But thirteen years later, when *Leonora* was revived and sung by an Italian company at the New York Academy of Music, practical considerations demanded that it be translated into Italian. Even Fry could compromise with necessity.

As music critic for the *Tribune* he failed to supply a precedent for Deems Taylor in reviewing his own work. He stepped aside and allowed his colleagues to fill his column for him. The *Express* was a bit patronizing:

Our impressions of "Leonora" are of a mixed character. The opera seems to us a study in the school of Bellini. It is full of delicious, sweet music, but constantly recalls the Somnambula and Norma. It is marked by skill in instrumentation, the secret of which the composer seems effectively to have probed. It has many flowing melodies, many pretty effects, much that should encourage its author to renewed efforts; but, like all early efforts, it is full of reminiscences. . . . The peculiarities which most strongly distinguish his production are sweetness of melody and lack of dramatic characterization.

All the characters sing the same sort of music—a love passage or a burst of stormy passion is treated much in the same style. . . . Were Mr. Fry now to write an opera, he would probably rely more on his own strength—he would know when he was composing, and when he was remembering. . . .

The *Times* attempted analysis:

"Leonora" is Mr. Fry's first operatic effort for the public, and like all first works, it contains much that is admirable, and much that might be better. Its principal characteristic is melody. The fertility of Mr. Fry's invention in this respect is remarkable, and it is the more remarkable from the fact that he does not seek his inspiration in the shady and sentimental groves of the minor scale, like most young composers, but in the broad and healthful uplands of the major mode. The best melodies of the opera, orchestral and vocal, are in the long-breathed, deep-chested major. The exceptions to this general rule are, we should suppose, intentional, as in the drinking song, "King Death," where sackcloth and ashes and a touch of brimstone are needed, and in the opening of the second act, where sentimentalism and an oboe are necessary, and elsewhere as occasion demanded. But the prevalent coloring of Mr. Fry's sentimentality is manly; it does not remind you of the greenhorn who trembles when he speaks to a lady, and sits down on his hat in a perspiring tremor. What the literature of the day (especially dramatic literature) lacks, this Opera supplies and illustrates—namely, *abandon*. . . .

A frank acknowledgment of the superabundant merit of one of the first essentials of opera leads us naturally to the contemplation of a fault which is sometimes unpleasantly apparent in Mr. Fry's work. There is a certain suggestiveness in the opening bars of some of the melodies which carries our memory to past pleasures afforded by other composers. . . . It happens, invariably, that the first works of any composer bear certain ear-marks of other hands. It is the case in Mr. Fry's first opera, and it was the case in Mr. Beethoven's first symphony.

The *Musical Review and Gazette* saw little of merit in *Leonora:*

. . . The inexperienced hand can be traced not only in the choruses and *ensemble*-pieces, but in the phrasing of most of the songs of the opera. Almost everything is poorly shaped and put together, and what is still worse, worked closely after the most common pattern. . . .

We have learnt to esteem Mr. Fry in his literary pursuits for the very opposite qualities he displays in his music. . . . Mr. Fry, as *homme de lettres* presents to us a strong-minded individuality, while the music to his opera has not a fathom of individuality whatever. . . . Mr. Fry knows his own language thoroughly, but he has no command over that of music. . . . The whole orchestration of *Leonora* is somewhat like a picture in which trees and houses are daubed in red, and the people make a very green appearance.

. . . it is not a very pleasant task to tell a man whose *literary* ideas we respect and have often made our delight, that he bores us with the poverty of his *musical* ones. . . . Mr. Fry can be passionate and inspired; he seems to be one of those men—of which our country seems to be richer than any other—who attempt everything grand and beautiful; but whether he has on the musical field, the power to finish his attempts successfully, can only be added when he favors us with another opera of more recent composition. *Leonora* makes us fear he has not.

Soon after the Philadelphia production of *Leonora*, Fry went abroad as foreign correspondent for the New York *Tribune*. He stayed in Europe for six years, and though he was unsuccessful in getting *Leonora* produced in Paris, he found much to enjoy. He made the acquaintance of Berlioz, and had the friendship of a number of leading European musicians.

When he returned to America in 1852, he was ready to take up the banner for the American composer. He had had some experiences in Paris which furnished him with ammunition; he had tasted some of the joys of martyrdom. He became music editor of the *Tribune*, and in the winter of 1852–53, he gave New York a series of lectures on music, which, except for the audience, rivaled our present educational series on the radio. Fry's own paper gave him its moral backing, and ran this announcement:

Wm. Henry Fry, Esq., proposes a course of lectures upon the Science and Art of Music, and upon the most colossal scale. Yet imposing as is his programme, it does not seem to us impossible, and of the very great benefit and actual necessity of such an undertaking there is no doubt. Mr. Fry's proposition is nothing less than to give a general, and, to a fair extent, adequate comprehension of the whole subject of musical composition, including its scientific relations, its history, its ethics and its æsthetics.

To accomplish this design, which implies extensive illustration, the following essentials are named: A corps of principal Italian vocalists; a grand chorus of one hundred singers; an orchestra of eighty performers; a military band of fifty performers.

Lectures of this sort are clearly not matters to be lightly undertaken or executed, and ample time is allowed for the preparation, because negotiations must be commenced with artists. Ten lectures are proposed, at five dollars for the course, and ten thousand dollars is the estimated whole expense. The proposal has a lordly air, and it promises such real advantages to the many who love music and yet know nothing about it, that we shall hope for its entire success.

The subscriptions were sold, and the series actually started in Metropolitan Hall, November 30, 1852, with a chorus and an orchestra of eighty.

Mr. Fry [said the *Tribune*] at first labored under considerable embarrassment, but it soon wore off. . . . He began with a glowingly poetic assertion of the universal presence of Music in Nature . . . then explained the elementary ideas and technical expressions and rules of music in a very succinct manner, the orchestra and chorus illustrating as he went along. As an illustration of the ordinary major chord the "Star Spangled Banner" was performed.

The second part of the lecture . . . opened with some specimens of Chinese music. . . . This was followed by the overture to Der Freyschutz which marked all the advance of Christian upon Pagan civilization.

The second lecture . . . indicated . . . a degree of curious learning in the music of China, Siam, India and Europe of the middle ages.

Following lectures covered the human voice, the ballad, the orchestra, church, oratorio, and chamber music, the nature and progress of musical ideas, the "difference between formal and inspired music," the lyrical drama, and the connection between literature and oratory and music.

It was in the last lecture that Fry cut loose and gave his American ideas about music. The *Musical World* reported his statements at length, and if there is a familiar sound in their phrases, kindly remember that they were uttered in 1852. He was reported as saying that there is no taste or love for, or appreciation of, true Art in this country. The public, as a public, know nothing about Art. We pay enormous sums to hear a single voice, or a single instrument, but we will pay nothing to hear a sublime work of Art performed. As a nation we have totally neglected Art. In this country politicians reap all the public applause and emoluments to the exclusion of their betters. Our colleges ignore Art.

Hitherto there has been too much servility on the part of American artists. The American composer should not allow the names of Beethoven, Handel, or Mozart to prove an eternal bugbear to him, nor should he pay them reverence. He should reverence only his Art, and strike out manfully and independently into untrodden realms, just as his nature and inspirations may incite him, else he can never achieve lasting renown.

Until this Declaration of Independence in Art shall be made—until American composers shall discard their foreign liveries and found an American school—and until the American public shall learn to support American artists, Art will not become indigenous to this country, but will only exist as a feeble exotic, and we shall continue to be provincial in Art.

We have some good musical societies, said Fry, and they should devote a portion of their rehearsals to American compositions, and perform the best of them in public. The American public decry native compositions, and sneer at native artists. We now have symphonies, operas, cantatas, and other American compositions which are as good and better than the *first* similar compositions by the much talked of "great masters," and we should listen to these first compositions of American composers with as much respect and as bright anticipations as the people of former days listened to the *first* symphonies of Handel, Beethoven, and Mozart.

An American composer cannot get his works brought out at home unless he has a fortune which will enable him to bear the expense himself. An American composer cannot get his works brought out in Europe at all—not even by paying for it. In Europe, an American artist is spit upon, and finally the whole world over, artists are not and never have been treated as they should be—especially at mealtime. Instead of being assigned seats of honor at the table with other guests they are too often consigned to the kitchen to take their chance with the servants.

When the *Musical World* printed these statements, Fry protested that he had been misquoted in a number of important places. It was not the public, but the *critics* who ignored the existence of American musical works. Nor had he said that an American artist was spit upon in Europe; merely that when he had tried to have an opera produced, he was spit upon because he was an American.

I took the best possible introductions, and offered to pay the expenses of a rehearsal, according to my invariable custom to expect nothing as a favor. I wished the music to be heard simply; given book in hand without dress or decoration, and so pronounced upon—a frightful hazard, but one which I was willing to abide by, in the same way that I had my works performed at my lectures in New York without the necessary aids of the opera house. . . . When I asked for this simple rehearsal—so easily accorded and so fairly required—the director of the opera in Paris said to me: "In Europe we look upon America as an industrial country—excellent for electric telegraphs, but not for art . . . they would think me crazy to produce an opera by an American."

It was when Jullien brought his orchestra to America in 1853 that Fry's symphonies were heard, for Jullien liked new music. He may also have realized that Fry was critic of the *Tribune*. There were four of these symphonies: *Childe Harold, A Day in the Country, The Breaking Heart,* and the *Santa Claus* Symphony. A colleague on the *Tribune* described *Santa* for the public:

We have seen it stated that the composer of Santa Claus intended it for an occasional piece—a sketch, etc. This is not so. He intended it—in regard to instrumentation—as the means of exposing the highest qualities in execution and expression of the greatest players in the world. As to spirit, he designed it in the introductory movement to represent the declamatory style in which he conceives oratorios ought to be written. Next, the verisimilitude which should mark music adapted to festivities from its rollicking traits and abandon. Then, he designed to show all the sexual peculiarities of the orchestra, *dramatically* treated. Likewise the accents of English speech as related to English music. He wished also, to prove as he believes, that the Lullaby, poetically handled, is as sublime as the Madonna and Child, if looked at artistically, and connected with it may be four separate counterpoints, all distinct and all painting different ideas and facts.

Next he wished to connect the music of nature with the tragedy of human life—the latter played by M. Bottesini—and the composer essayed, too, to paint the sublimest music in the world—that of the deity singing the monody of the passing world in the winter's wind. Next, he wished to individualize in music our only remaining fairy,—the character being grotesque, yet withal gentle and melodious, and with the sweetest mission that ever fairy performed. Next he desired to paint the songs of the stars—the fluttering ecstasies of hovering angels—on the purest harmonies of the violins, only to be achieved by artists who have given a life of labor and love and lyrical devotion to extract the transcendental element in their instruments.

Next, he designed to paint the change from starlight to sunlight by poetical analogies and mathematical facts. Then he sought to imitate the mother's cry to her little ones by rousing them on Christmas morning, and by the playing of Bo-peep, which as a little love story, admits of dramatic harmonies. The introduction of toys into the orchestra at this point, may be considered by the thoughtless as a burlesque, but not so did the composer consider it. The divine words, "Suffer little children to come unto me, for of such is the kingdom of Heaven," make the artistic painting of children and their toys, as much of a mission of art as the writing of a hallelujah chorus. The finale, too, of this symphony, where an orchestra of drums is introduced to represent the rolling of the spheres, is among the composer's ideas of the necessity of towering sonority to crown a long work designed to be of religious and romantic character.

With all these preparations for a heaven-storming work that would plunge its creator into immortality, Fry was naturally hurt when Richard Storrs Willis, brother of Nathaniel, dismissed *Santa Claus* with a few lines in the *Musical World* and termed it a composition hardly to be criticized as an earnest work of art. It was rather "a kind of extravaganza which moves the audience to laughter, entertaining them seasonably with imitated snow-storms, trotting horses, sleighbells, cracking whips, etc."

Fry rushed for his pen and wrote a twenty-five-page letter, which Willis published. He said that his piece was the longest "unified" instrumental composition that had ever been written on a single subject, and therefore entitled to an extended review. Any work which began in Heaven "and then swings down to Hell, returns to Heaven and thence to earth to depict the family joys of a Christmas party" was certainly worth more than passing notice.

He pleaded his Americanism:

I think that the American who writes for the mere dignity of musical art, as I understand it, without recompense deserves better treatment at the hands of his countrymen at least. This is more due from an American, as the Philharmonic Society of this city is an incubus on Art, never having asked for or performed a single American composition during the eleven years of its existence.

. . . As the chances for an American to put before the public any work of musical High Art depend, in this country, upon the accidental presence of such [conductors] as M. Jullien . . . there ought to be at least one technical journal in this city where technical criticism and extended analysis of works are habitually rendered.

In replying, Willis made the most of his opportunity:

. . . the length of a piece of music is novel ground, certainly, upon which to base its musical excellence, or its requirement for a very long criticism.

Dwight lent his voice from Boston:

Why . . . is not friend Fry willing practically to submit the merit of the American symphonies to what he himself maintains to be the only true test?—namely to time and the world's impression. . . . Of course the bulk of our public concerts and musical entertainments must consist of pieces of a guaranteed excellence, of works that the world *knows* to be good, sure to give pleasure, sure to inspire and reward attention. It will not do to invite the public to perpetual experimental feasts of possibilities; to assemble a concert audience, like a board of jurors, to listen to long lists of new works and award prizes . . . If a work have genius in it, it will sooner or later make its mark upon the world. . . .

It is of no use to tell us why we ought to like *Santa Claus,* the thing is to make us like it.

3. GEORGE F. BRISTOW (1825–1898)

Fry's reference to the Philharmonic Society drew another man into the controversy—George Frederick Bristow, a native composer who had been one of the first violins of the Philharmonic since the Society was founded in 1842. Bristow wrote to the *Musical World:*

As it is possible to miss a needle in a hay-stack, I am not surprised that Mr. Fry has missed the fact, that during the eleven years the Philharmonic Society has been in operation in this city, it played once, either by mistake or accident, one single American composition, an overture of mine. As one exception makes a rule stronger, so this single stray fact shows that the Philharmonic Society has been as anti-American as if it had been located in London during the Revolutionary War, and composed of native-born British tories. . . .

It appears the society's eleven years of promoting American art have embraced one whole performance of one whole American overture, one whole rehearsal of one whole American symphony, and the performance of an overture by an Englishman stopping here—Mr. Loder—(whom your beautiful correspondent would infer is an American) who, happening to be conductor here, had the influence to have it played. . . .

This drew an official statement from the Philharmonic, as well as Bristow's resignation. The Society had formulated a policy in regard to American compositions at the very beginning, and had included this clause in its constitution (April 23, 1842):

If any grand orchestral compositions such as overtures, or symphonies, shall be presented to the society, they being composed in this country, the society shall perform one every season, provided a committee of five appointed by the government shall have approved and recommended the composition.

H. C. Timm, as president, signed the answer to Bristow's letter, and it was printed in the *Musical World* two weeks after Bristow's challenge:

In your journal of the 4th inst. appears a letter from Mr. Geo. F. Bristow, in which he undertakes to censure the spirit and action of the New York Philharmonic Society in such a remarkable and unjustifiable manner that the Board of Directors feels it a duty to the public and their constituents to make a reply. . . .

Now the society had existed four years before any American composition was suggested to members for performance. . . . During the remaining seven years, several American compositions by either native or adopted citizens of this country were brought to the notice of the Society and performed, as follows:

Overture to Marmion, by George Loder (English), performed twice at concerts.

Overture by H. Saroni (German) performed at public rehearsal.
Overture by F. G. Hansen (German) performed at public rehearsal.
Overture by Theo. Eisfeld (German) performed at public rehearsal.
Overture by Geo. F. Bristow (American) performed at concert.
Indian March by F. E. Miguel (French) performed at public rehearsal.
Descriptive Battle Symphony, by Knaebel (German) at public rehearsal.
Symphony No. 1, by Geo. F. Bristow (American) performed twice at public rehearsal.

Duetto for two cornets, by Dodworth (American) performed at concert.
Serenade by William Mason (American) performed at concert.
Several songs by W. V. Wallace (Irish) performed at concert.
Application was also made by A. P. Heinrich (German) for the performance of several of his compositions, and when he was informed the society was ready, withdrew.

The same issue of the *World* contained this item:

At the regular meeting (March 11, 1854), Mr. Bristow's resignation as one of the Board of Directors and as performing member of the Society was accepted.

Forgiveness followed soon, and Bristow was not absent from the Society's roster for very long. He was connected with the orchestra for almost forty years from its founding. He had a long and honorable career. His father, William Richard Bristow, was an English musician who came to New York in 1824. The son George was born in New York in 1825, and at the age of eleven was playing the violin at the Olympic Theatre. In addition to his work with the Philharmonic, he was conductor of the Harmonic Society from 1851 to 1862. From 1854 until his death in 1898 he was a visiting teacher in the New York public schools.

As director of the Harmonic Society, Bristow did what he could to bring out the works of American composers. In 1852 the society performed *The Waldenses,* an oratorio by Asahel Abbot, who was described as "a phenomenon, . . . a sturdy self-made New Englander who has for some years taught music in New York; but, what is more, can boast himself the composer of an incredible number of oratorios and other scores in great forms."

Dwight had his doubts about Abbot:

He has instructed several of his pupils to be likewise composers of great oratorios. To hear him talk, you would suppose that great oratorios grew on every bush, where he resided. We know nothing of the merit of Mr. Abbot's music, and trust that it will have a fair chance. The "Waldenses," we understand, is one of a series which he designs to sketch in honor of the different races that have struggled for liberty through the last 1600 years.

W. J. Henderson has described Bristow as "a most earnest man, filled with real love for his art, and self sacrificing in labor for its benefit; one of the earliest of the long-suffering band of American composers, who will be remembered always as one who strove to push American music into artistic prominence."

Bristow may be coupled with Fry for another reason than being a pioneer fighter for the rights of the native composer. Fry wrote the first native grand opera to be produced; Bristow composed the second. And what is more, Bristow chose a native subject—Irving's legend of *Rip Van Winkle*. Bristow's opera was produced in New York in 1855, soon after the Fry-Willis controversy, and Bristow's differences with the Philharmonic. It was also the same year that Ole Bull had announced his prize for an American opera during his ill-fated management of the Academy of Music. Fry's *Leonora* had been produced in Philadelphia ten years before, and three years were to pass before it was to have its New York production. It must have been a bitter pill for Fry to see his colleague's work produced before his own. The *Musical World* hinted at a political situation:

Mr. Bristow's grand opera *Rip Van Winkle*, produced at Niblo's on Thursday evening, is the second one composed in this country by an American. As musical intelligence it is due to the reader that we should give the following historical facts. . . . The first opera by an American was *Leonora*, composed by Mr. W. H. Fry, and produced in Philadelphia by the Seguin troupe about ten years ago. . . . Mr. Fry composed several other operas, which have not yet been produced. The managers of all the theatres in New York, as is well known, are in utter fear of a journal whose editor has made war on Mr. Fry and all his productions from the moment *Leonora* appeared. The public is sufficiently acquainted with the causes of this hostility, but is hardly aware that its exercise up to this time, through the acknowledged subserviency of the managers of all the theatres, deprived Mr. Fry of a hearing in New York for any of his operas; though his symphonies through Mr. Jullien, who defied the wrath of the editor in question, have been frequently performed. . . .

This tends to contradict the belief that *Leonora* enjoyed its New York performances because its composer was music critic of the *Tribune*.

Willis, whom Fry had assailed as unfriendly to American composers, was one of the first to welcome *Rip Van Winkle:*

Sebastopol has fallen, and a new American opera has succeeded in New York! The clash of Russian steel with the bristling bayonets of the Allies has not been more fierce and uncompromising than the strife in lyric art between the stronghold of foreign prejudice and the steady and combined attacks of native musicians. It is true, the enemy has long since given evidence of his respect in other departments of art. But chiefly by a blind deference to the pompous pretensions of foreign interpreters of the art divine, has the real strength of our native musical genius been kept in abject abeyance, or suffered to linger in worse than aboriginal obscurity by our chilling reserve, if not studied neglect.

It is, however, neither good nor wise in us, to remain longer insensible to our own sources of power, or to the palpable weakness and misgivings of the enemy. This position may not be questioned, either in view of a proper respect for ourselves, or of a sincere regard to the welfare of the natives of other climes. Indeed, the truest policy for the foreign artist or artisan, is to labor long and largely for the development of the *creative* as well as the executive ability of the community in which he dwells, since hereby he most thoroughly exemplifies the workings of a truly benevolent heart, and most directly contributes to the permanent employment of a larger number of his brother artists.

Rip Van Winkle had a run of four weeks at Niblo's, following its première, September 27, 1855. Comparison of box-office receipts with those of other current attractions shows that it was third in popularity among the New York theatres. On the Monday of the week following its opening, *Rip Van Winkle* drew $700. The Metropolitan Theatre drew $4,500, and the Broadway $1,050. The Italian opera at the Academy of Music was next to *Rip Van Winkle* with $600. Wood's Minstrels and Buckley's Minstrels took in but $300 and $250 apiece.

J. R. Wainwright's libretto to the opera took a few liberties with Irving's story, though it followed the original in its essentials. The librettist introduced imaginary episodes from the Revolution, and conceived a love affair between Rip's daughter Alice and a British officer. This gave opportunity for love duets, as well as soldiers' choruses by both Continental and British troops. In the *Musical World*, Willis discussed the American elements of the score:

But if the subject be quite American, is the music of Mr. Bristow quite American?

Though agreeable and fluent it is somewhat devoid of character. It takes a long time before a nation has adapted art to its own nature. . . . If the English had a genuine form of opera, it is probable that it would serve as a model to composers of this country; as the English have not yet an opera of their own (sui generis), it would be unfair to demand of Mr. Bristow a school of an American stamp. It is from such a point of view that we must judge his work. It would be absurd to demand of one who writes for the stage for the first time a great creation or a masterpiece; for this requires, first of all, experience. If we find in Mr. Bristow's work an appropriate use of the forms of the existing musical drama he will be fully justified.

The opera of *Rip Van Winkle* exhibits an easy flow of melody. This melody is free from effort and spontaneous—an important quality in a dramatic composer. But in none of the arias of Mr. Bristow do we meet with large conception or rich development of ideas; none of them is shaped after a large pattern. The same remark will apply to the choruses. . . .

Mr. Bristow has produced before the public of this city several fragments of symphonies, which evidenced experience of the orchestra. We were rather disappointed, when hearing this opera, to find that the deficient part of his work was precisely the instrumentation. . . . The orchestra of *Rip Van Winkle* is in general inanimate and lifeless, and devoid of that brilliancy which we must meet with in modern opera.

Bristow outlived Fry by many years. Fry died of tuberculosis in the West Indies in 1864, the year his second opera *Notre Dame de Paris* was produced in Philadelphia. It was given later in New York under Thomas. Bristow lived until almost the close of the century. His *Rip Van Winkle* was revived in 1870, and by that time he had heard two more of his symphonies played—the second in 1856 and the third in 1859. In 1874 he presented his *Arcadian* Symphony. There were also two symphonies that were not performed, two string quartets, two oratorios, and two cantatas, some of them published. When he died in 1898 he was at work on another opera, *Columbus*.

It is not because they wrote great or fine music that Heinrich, Fry, and Bristow are important. Some of their writings may even seem ridiculous. Their consciousness of nationality is what is important to the cause of American music, for they were early prophets. In their controversies they went to extremes, and laid themselves open to refutation by those who thought and spoke more calmly. Yet they fired the first cannon in a fight that has never ended.

PART THREE

1860 TO THE PRESENT

EUTERPE BUILDS HER AMERICAN HOME

CHAPTER NINE

Songs of the Civil War

I. DIXIE AND THE BATTLE HYMN

WARS have always produced songs, and people keep on singing them long after thoughts of war have gone from their minds. Generally it is only the inspirational songs that survive, rather than those associated with the actual facts and episodes of the war that gave them birth. The Civil War produced hundreds of songs that could be arranged in proper sequence to form an actual history of the conflict; its events, its principal characters, and the ideals and principles of the opposing sides.

We all know *Dixie* and *The Battle Hymn of the Republic*—these are national songs now, and though they were put to partisan uses in the war days, they may be heard without resentment by descendants of either North or South today. Strangely enough, *Dixie* was written and composed by a *Northerner*, and the tune of *The Battle Hymn of the Republic* was claimed by a Southern composer of popular Sunday School songs—WILLIAM STEFFE.

There have been many myths concerning *Dixie*. At a time when copyrights were not always respected, various composers and authors claimed *Dixie* as their property. Even now there are many people who doubt Daniel Decatur Emmett's authorship.[1] To Southerners it may be an almost irreconcilable fact that *Dixie, their* song since the Civil War, was written by a Northerner. But there can be no doubt whatever that *Dixie* was composed by Emmett. His name is clearly stated on playbills of the earliest performances on the original edition of Firth, Pond & Company of 1860, which was copyrighted on June 21 of that year. His name also appears on the contract of February 11, 1861 which

[1] For an account of Emmett's career, see pp. 181–184.

transferred all of his rights to the publishers for only $300. Moreover, the style of the tune is Emmett's.

In order to minimize Emmett's contribution, some have asserted that his *Dixie* is heavily indebted to other songs. It is true that Irish and Scotch elements have gone into its making. But the result is not a weak, synthetic product, but a lively, original tune that holds its own. A melody, however unique, shows some relation to earlier or contemporary music. What may make it outstanding is the new meaning which has been given to existing material. This is true of *Dixie*.

There are some sources which Emmett, unconsciously, blended into a tune all his own. The opening measures are slightly related to a number of melodies of the British Isles. The refrain, too, might some day be traced back to earlier material, possibly to a Scotch song. It is similar to the refrain of another song by Emmett, *Billy Patterson*, written a few months later than *Dixie*.

Emmett wrote also the words of *Dixie*. Their accents and inflection are in perfect harmony with the melodic line. People who enjoy hunting for sources might be interested in the fact that the expressions "I wish I was in" [name of a Southern state or city] and "Away down South," appear in minstrel songs of the forties. The latter was a Stephen Foster song. The second stanza of *Dixie*, which contains the story of "Old Missus" and "Will de weaber," the "gay deceiber," was inspired by a stanza in *Gumbo Chaff*, a minstrel song of the thirties. It was the custom of minstrel-song writers—as indeed of the minstrels of the Middle Ages—to borrow from each other. Various explanations of the word "Dixie" have been given, but most of them are completely unsatisfactory. The most plausible seems to be the one which derives "Dixie" from "Mason and Dixon's Line." The word "Dixie" does not appear in print before 1860. Though it probably was used before that time, perhaps by the slaves and by white showmen, it was Emmett who established and popularized its meaning as the name of the place where Negroes could live in happiness. A few weeks before it appeared in *Dixie's Land*, it was used by Emmett in the last stanza of his song *Johnny Roach*:

> Gib me de place called "Dixie's Land" [or "Dixie Land"]
> Wid hoe and shubble in my hand;

Whar fiddles ring and banjos play,
I'd dance all night and work all day.

A few months earlier Emmett, in his song *I Ain't Got Time to Tarry*, spoke of the "land of freedom" as the home of the Negroes, without calling it "Dixie," however. This song received its first performance in November, 1858.

On April 4, 1859, *Dixie's Land* was presented for the first time anywhere by the Bryant's Minstrels at Mechanics' Hall on Broadway. It was performed as a Negro "walk-around"; that is, sung and danced by a few soloists in the foreground, and the rest of the company—about six or eight men—in the background of the stage. Appearing at a time when the Southern question was in everybody's mind, *Dixie* was an immediate success. It spread like wildfire all over the nation. Minstrel companies picked it up, and black-face comedians added their own words to the popular tune. From 1860 on, publishers in the North and South issued it in its original form or with its tune varied and its words changed, in piano arrangements and paraphrases—by no means always giving credit to Emmett. The list of *Dixie* editions is a long one. It was perhaps the greatest song success in America up to that time, but the composer realized very little money from it.

On February 18, 1861, *Dixie* was played in Montgomery, Alabama, at the inauguration of Jefferson Davis, and from then on became the symbol of the Confederacy. Its original tempo which was *Allegro* was undoubtedly changed to that of a fiery military quickstep. General Albert Pike wrote the following revolutionary words to the tune in 1861:

Up, lest worse than death befall you!
To arms! To arms! To arms in Dixie.
Lo! all the beacon fires are lighted,
Let all hearts be now united.
To arms! [and so on]

At about the same time the North adapted anti-Southern words to *Dixie*. A stanza of a broadside reads:

Away down south in the land of traitors,
Rattlesnakes and alligators,
Right away come away, right away come away.
Where cotton's king and men are chattles,

> Union-Boys will win the battles.
> Right away [and so on]

The tune was used by the Union Army until 1862 and probably later, though it had never the exclusive popularity which it had in the Confederate Army.

Yet, in spite of its Southern associations, *Dixie* has come to be something more than a song of just one section of our country. There is something indefinably American about the tune; a jauntiness, an impertinence, a carefree spirit that seems to be one of our characteristics as a people. In some ways *Dixie* is one of the few pieces of music that can be said to be American; it represents a state of mind common to all parts of the nation.

The melody of *The Battle Hymn of the Republic* was first popular around Charleston, South Carolina, where it was sung as a hymn to the words:

> Say, brothers, will you meet us?
> Say, brothers, will you meet us?
> Say, brothers, will you meet us?
> On Canaan's happy shore?

and the refrain:

> Glory, glory, hallelujah,
> Glory, glory, hallelujah,
> Glory, glory, hallelujah,
> For ever, evermore!

The tune was rousing and easily remembered. It had a swing that made it a splendid marching song, and it was inevitable that it should spread like fire. The actual date of William Steffe's writing it has never been determined, but it dates back at least to 1856. It became popular in colored churches, with firemen, and especially in the army posts which were beginning to be more fully manned in the years that led up to the war.

In the summer of 1859, John Brown made himself famous and helped to precipitate the actual war by leading his little band in the misguided raid on Harpers Ferry. His hanging was hailed by Northern Abolitionists as martyrdom. About this time, the "Tigers," a battalion of Massachusetts Infantry, was stationed at Fort Warren in Boston Harbor. The men had formed a glee club, and one of their favorite songs was the Sunday School hymn from the South. Many new verses were improvised, some of them far from the accepted Sunday School idea. Rhymes were nonessential, for each line was repeated twice.

One of the men was a Scotchman named John Brown, who was the butt of many jokes, practical and otherwise. The John Brown incident in the South was a brilliant opportunity for the humorists, and a John Brown verse was accordingly improvised:

> John Brown's body lies a-mouldering in the grave,
> John Brown's body lies a-mouldering in the grave,
> John Brown's body lies a-mouldering in the grave,
> His soul is marching on.

then the "Glory hally, hallelujah" refrain.

Other verses were added:

> He's gone to be a soldier in the army of the Lord, *etc.*
> His pet lambs will meet him on the way, *etc.*

and then when the Confederacy was formed:

They will hang Jeff Davis to a tree (later extended to a "sour apple tree" for purposes of rhythm).

Other regiments took up the song, and to Colonel Fletcher Webster's Twelfth Massachusetts Regiment belongs the credit of spreading its fame on the march to the South. As the men passed through New York and other cities, they halted and sang it over and over again.

Edna Dean Proctor tried to save the tune from ribaldry by setting Abolitionist words to it, but with indifferent success. In December, 1861, JULIA WARD HOWE visited Washington. With her husband, Dr. Howe, she saw a skirmish a few miles from the city, and heard the troops go into battle singing *John Brown's Body*. The Reverend James Freeman Clark, a member of the party, asked her why she shouldn't write new words to the song. That night she wrote the lines beginning, "Mine eyes have seen the Glory of the coming of the Lord." Steffe's Sunday School hymn achieved respectability along with immortality as *The Battle Hymn of the Republic*.

2. OTHER WAR SONGS

Historically, the most interesting of the war songs are those which refer to actual episodes, even though their musical value is doubtful, and as songs most of them are forgotten today. In the early days of secession there were a number of doubtful states, especially those along the border. Maryland actually stayed in the Union, but she was a slave-holding state, and Southern sentiment was strong among her people. One of her native sons, JAMES RYDER RANDALL, was living in New Orleans when he heard that Massachusetts troops had been fired on as they passed through Baltimore. He hoped that this episode would swing his native state to the Southern cause, and in a moment of inspiration he wrote his appeal in verses that have ever since been sung to the old German song *O Tannenbaum:*

> Hark to thy wandering son's appeal,
> Maryland, my Maryland! *etc.*

and the second stanza:

> Thou wilt not cower in the dust,
> Maryland, my Maryland! *etc.*

The Northern bards were ready with an answer, and in addition to Maryland, they turned their thoughts to Missouri, another slave state loyal to the Union. To the same tune one of them wrote:

> Arise and join the patriot train,
> Belle Missouri, my Missouri!

The Southern poets also courted Missouri; one of them produced this lyric:

> Missouri! Missouri! bright land of the West
>
>   .   .   .   .
>
> Awake to the notes of the bugle and drum!
> Awake from your peace, for thy tyrant hath come,
> And swear by your honor that your chains shall be riven,
> And add your bright star to our flag of eleven.

In some of the songs the wish was father to the thought; the *Song of the South* bore a caption on its title page—"Kentucky and Tennessee Join Hands." But of course this was not to be; Tennessee joined the Confederacy and Kentucky stayed with the Union.

One song, written before the outbreak of the war, proved to be a powerful propaganda weapon for the Abolitionist movement in the North. This was *Darling Nelly Gray*, composed in 1856 by BENJAMIN RUSSELL HANBY (1833–1867). Hanby's father was a minister whose Ohio home was a station of the underground railroad. One of the slaves whom he helped to escape had found that his own sweetheart had been sold, chained and taken to Georgia. Benjamin Hanby based his song on this episode, and it achieved a tremendous circulation. He composed over eighty songs altogether, but none of them gained the popularity of *Darling Nelly Gray*.

In 1862, when Lincoln issued a call for three hundred thousand more troops, James Sloan Gibbons, an Abolitionist writer, wrote a poem *We are Coming, Father Abraham, three hundred thousand more*. For many years these verses were attributed to William Cullen Bryant, who at one time issued a signed denial of the authorship. The swing of the words made them easily adapted to musical setting and many of the wartime song writers tried their hands at it. Among them was LUTHER ORLANDO EMERSON (1820–1915), a gospel-hymn composer who had already achieved something of a reputation with his *Golden Wreath* collection of songs for schools. Stephen Foster also made a setting of the Father Abraham song.

In the difficult days of the war, when the cause seemed lost to the North, and further financing of operations seemed impossible, one wag wrote a parody on *Father Abraham* which dealt with the new issue of paper currency:

> We're coming, Father Abram
> One hundred thousand more
> Five hundred presses printing us
> From morn till night is o'er;
> Like magic you will see us start
> And scatter thro' the land
> To pay the soldiers or release
> The border contraband.

Chorus

> With our promise to pay
> "How are you, Secretary Chase?"
> Promise to pay,
> Oh, dat's what's de matter.

Many of the Southern songs commemorated historic events. In the first year of the war, General Beauregard ordered that all church and plantation bells in Louisiana should be melted into cannon. This gave birth to a song called *Melt the Bells*, published for the benefit of the Southern Relief Association.

The Southern Girl told of the privations Southerners were willing to endure:

> My homespun dress is plain, I know,
> My hat's palmetto, too,
> But, then, it shows what Southern girls
> For Southern rights will do!
> We've sent the bravest of our land,
> To battle with the foe,
> And we will add a helping hand,
> We love the South, you know.

The Star-Spangled Banner was used for the *Cross of the South:*

> Oh, say, can you see, thro' the gloom and the storm,
> More bright from the darkness, that pure constellation, *etc.*

The second verse had a fling at New England:

> How peaceful and blest was America's soil,
> 'Til betrayed by the guile of the Puritan demon,
> Which lurks under Virtue, and springs from its coil
> To fasten its fangs in the lifeblood of freemen.

The tune of *The Marseillaise* was adapted by A. E. Blackmar, an Ohioan who had engaged in music publishing in New Orleans, where his business suffered when the city was captured by Federal troops:

> Sons of the South, awake to glory,
> A thousand voices bid you rise,
> Your children, wives and grandsires hoary,
> Gaze on you now with trusting eyes, *etc.*

Blackmar wrote a number of Southern war songs, among them *The Sword of Robert E. Lee;* and a tribute to Carolina:

> 'Mid her ruins proudly stands,
>> Our Carolina.
> Fetters are upon her hands,
>> Dear Carolina.
> Yet she feels no sense of shame,
> For upon the scroll of Fame,
> She hath writ a deathless name,
>> Brave Carolina.

Except for *Dixie,* the most popular Southern song was *The Bonnie Blue Flag,* written by HENRY McCARTHY. Its words told the story of secession:

> First gallant South Carolina nobly took the stand,
> Then came Alabama, who took her by the hand; *etc.*

with the refrain:

> Hurrah! Hurrah! for Southern rights, hurrah!
> Hurrah for the bonnie blue flag that bears a single star.

The North was ready with an answer. With words to the same tune it shouted:

> Hurrah! Hurrah! for *equal* rights, hurrah!
> Hurrah for the brave old flag that bears the Stripes and Stars!

Northerners celebrated their victories with songs: *Charleston is Ours* and *Richmond is Ours* were typical. Heroes were commemorated by both sides. Flora Byrne's *Jefferson Davis* shared popularity with *General Beauregard's Grand March,* by Mrs. V. G. Coudin. The North sang the praises of *Jenny Wade, the Heroine of Gettysburg,* in a song beginning "Raise high the monumental pile." The death of Ellsworth was mourned with JOSEPH PHILBRICK WEBSTER's *Brave Men, Behold Your Fallen Chief.*

One group of song writers was shrewd enough to sense the commercial value of sentimental songs that could be sung by both sides. There were hundreds of these lyrics, possibly the most famous of them, *Tenting on the Old Camp Ground,* written by WALTER KITTREDGE after he was drafted in 1862. Pacifists were squelched in Civil War days, as

they have been in all times of war. One of the most sentimental ballads
was Henry Tucker's *Weeping, Sad and Lonely, or When This Cruel
War Is Over.* CHARLES CARROLL SAWYER was the author of the words.
The effect of the song was so mournful that the generals of the Army
of the Potomac had to forbid the troops to sing it—it lowered their
morale. SEPTIMUS WINNER (1827–1902), another song writer who
sometimes appeared under the pen name of Alice Hawthorne, soon
answered the Sawyer-Tucker song with *Yes, I Would the Cruel War
Were Over,* and then stated some conditions:

. . . .

> Would the cruel work were done;
> With my country undivided
> And the battle fought and won.
> Let the contest now before us,
> Be decided by the sword,
> For the war cannot be ended
> Till the Union is restored.

It was Winner, under the Hawthorne pseudonym, who wrote *Listen
to the Mocking Bird* and *Whispering Hope.*

Sawyer reveled in sentimentalism, and his fellow poets often found
it necessary to publish "answers" to his songs. In *Who Will Care for
Mother Now?*, set to music by his publishing partner in Brooklyn,
C. F. Thompson, he told the story of a dying soldier who wondered
what would become of the mother he supported. From Ohio came the
reply: *Do Not Grieve for Thy Dear Mother; answer to Who Will
Take Care of Mother Now.* The idea was that Mother would be all
right, for Heaven would look after her.

Stephen Foster wrote almost a dozen war songs, but they came from
his last years, when his powers were spent and he was grinding out
songs to order. None of them is representative of the real Foster. They
included the *Father Abraham* setting; *Was My Brother in the Battle;
Stand Up for the Flag; We've a Million in the Field; Willie Has Gone
to the War; For the Dear Old Flag I Die;* and several others.

GEORGE FREDERICK ROOT (1820–1895) was one of the most famous
of the composers of Northern war songs. Before the years of the war
he had made a considerable reputation as a writer of gospel hymns and
ballads, but his *Battle Cry of Freedom* and *Tramp, Tramp, Tramp,*

were as popular as anything he wrote. Root's songs fell into three groups: sentimental songs, such as *Hazel Dell* and the ever lovely *There's Music in the Air;* war songs; and finally, sacred songs—*The Shining Shore* and others of the gospel-hymn type.

Root was born in Sheffield, Massachusetts, in 1820. When he was six the family moved to North Reading, a town rich in musical history, not far from Boston. From childhood his ambition was to be a musician, and he made the most of the few opportunities that came his way. As a youth he went to Boston, and through the help of his teacher, B. F. Baker, he soon began to have pupils of his own, and also taught a number of singing schools. He met Lowell Mason, and was asked to help with the music in the Boston public schools, and in the teachers' classes at the Boston Academy of Music.

About 1845 he went to New York, where he became the music teacher at Abbot's Institute for young ladies. He formed a vocal quartet which became popular and sometimes appeared at the concerts of the New York Philharmonic Society. He went to Europe in 1850 for further study, and in 1853, when Lowell Mason had come to New York, he helped to organize the New York Normal Institute.

The vogue of Stephen Foster's songs made Root want to try his hand at song writing, so he had a former pupil, the blind Fanny Crosby, write a few verses for him, and he wrote the music to *Hazel Dell*, *There's Music in the Air*, and *Rosalie, the Prairie Flower*. A friend in Boston, who had started a publishing business, asked Root for a few songs. Instead of a royalty, Root asked six hundred dollars for the six songs he selected. The publisher thought this figure too high, and sent Root a royalty contract instead. *Rosalie* alone paid $3,000 in royalties.

In 1859, Root went to Chicago. His brother had opened a music store there in partnership with C. M. Cady, under the name of Root & Cady. G. F. Root became associated with the business. The fire of 1871 ruined them temporarily, but the firm was soon restored. In 1872, Root was awarded the Doctor of Music degree by the University of Chicago, and he continued his active career until his death in 1895.

When the war broke out, Root, like many other song writers, tried to write war songs. *The First Gun Is Fired* was unsuccessful, but when Lincoln issued his second call for troops, Root read the proclamation and conceived the idea for his *Battle Cry of Freedom*. The song was written hurriedly at Root & Cady's store. Two popular singers of the day, Frank Lombard and his brother Jules, came to the store and asked for a song to sing at a rally to be held that day in the Court House Square. Root gave them his manuscript copy of the *Battle Cry*, and after the Lombards had sung it over they went directly to the meeting and not only sang it as a duet, but had thousands joining in the refrain before the last verse was ended. Then the Hutchinson Family, a traveling troupe of singers, took the song all over the country, and it was soon shouted in camps, on the march, and on the battlefield. *Tramp, Tramp, Tramp, the Boys Are Marching* enjoyed an almost equal success.

These, of course, were Northern songs, expressing Union thoughts, but some of Root's sentimental songs, such as *Just Before the Battle, Mother*, were sung by the people of both North and South. Another of this type was *The Vacant Chair*, to verses that Henry Washburn had written about the death of a lieutenant in the Fifteenth Massachusetts Infantry.

Root was definitely of the Lowell Mason, Webb, and Bradbury school, with strong evangelical tendencies, as far as his sacred music was concerned. Probably his most famous hymn was *The Shining Shore*, with its first line, "My days are gliding swiftly by." He wrote no great music, and nothing in the larger forms, except a few cantatas for mixed voices. George P. Upton described him as a courteous, refined gentleman of the old school, always wearing a genial smile, and the cheeriest of optimists.

It was through Root's persuasion that another song writer, HENRY CLAY WORK (1832–1884), lent his abilities to composing war songs. Work's name is still anathema to the South, for his most famous song, *Marching Through Georgia*, celebrates an event that the South has never condoned—Sherman's march from Atlanta to the sea in 1864. No matter what a person's heritage may be, he must admit that *Marching Through Georgia* glorifies episodes that admittedly had their darker sides. Moreover, it goes into details that cannot fail constantly to reopen old wounds.

And yet the seeming immortality of the song has had its humorous aspects. When the Democratic National Convention was held in New York in 1924, the band leader was told to play an appropriate song

Theodore Thomas
(See pages 280–289)

GOING TO THE PEACE JUBILEE.

Going to the Peace Jubilee (from a Contemporary Cartoon)

(See page 297)

for each state delegation. *Maryland, My Maryland* received almost hysterical applause; *My Old Kentucky Home* made everyone ecstatic, and then when the misguided leader, stronger on geography than history, swung into *Marching Through Georgia,* he was greeted by a silence that turned into hisses and boos noisier than the applause he had heard before.

Work's intense partisanship is understandable. He was born in Connecticut in 1832, and when he was a lad the family moved to Illinois, where the elder Work's antislavery views soon got him into trouble. He helped maintain one of the stations on the famous "underground railway" which helped runaway slaves to escape, and before long he was put in prison for his activities. When he was released in 1845 the family went back to Middletown, poverty stricken.

So young Henry was himself an ardent, fiery Abolitionist. As a boy he thought of little else but music, and when he was very young he sold his first song to Christy's Minstrels—*We're Coming, Sister Mary.* In 1855 he went to Chicago, where he later came to know George Root. He continued his trade as a printer, and often composed the words of his songs as he set up the actual type. There is also a tradition that when he had access to music type he composed his music directly with the type, without first writing out a manuscript copy. If this be true, Work was a good musician; and anyway, it makes a good story.

One of his first war songs was *Kingdom Coming,* which Root & Cady published in 1862. It became popular immediately, and the composer followed it with *Babylon Is Fallen* the next year. *Wake, Nicodemus* was published in 1864, and *Marching Through Georgia* in 1865.

Work was famous for temperance songs, for he was an ardent temperance advocate as well as an Abolitionist. The most famous was *Come Home, Father,* issued by Root & Cady in 1864. Even today we hear the immortal opening lines:

> Father, dear father, come home with me now,
> The clock in the belfry strikes one.

And then the rest of the story, with the other verses telling how the clock strikes *two,* and then *three,* when it is too late for father, dear father, to do any good. Others of his songs were *The Song of a Thousand Years, King Bibber's Army, The Lost Letter, The Ship That Never*

Returned, Phantom Footsteps, and *Grandfather's Clock.* Work lived until 1884, when he died suddenly of heart disease.

These are the principal writers and songs associated with the Civil War. They occupy a unique place in song literature, and in our national history. In many ways the songs are historical documents, for they afford a study of the contemporary state of mind of both sides in a conflict that was probably inevitable.

CHAPTER TEN

The Spread of Musical Culture

1. WESTWARD EXPANSION

ONE of the remarkable features of the development of music in America is the rapidity with which the inland cities have become music centers. Boston has been a center of culture from its earliest days, Philadelphia has had a nucleus of art and music lovers from its beginnings, and New York, as our principal seaport, has enjoyed a cosmopolitan population that would naturally have its percentage of art patrons. The early pioneers who joined the westward marches were hardy men, noted for their ability to endure hardships and for their dogged persistence in overcoming the terrific odds arrayed against them. Like the early settlers in New England and the South, they had little time for softer pleasures. Men who have spent a long day chopping logs for their cabins can hardly be expected to make immediate plans for the formation of a symphony orchestra. For these reasons, the seaboard cities had a long, running start on their Western cousins in musical matters.

Yet, since 1850, from the time when the Midwest pioneers have had a chance to enjoy themselves, they have more than made up for the time they lost. The history of music in the American provinces is yet to be written, but when the facts are gathered and the full truth is told, it will be something of a revelation. In our day, New York still holds its place as the American center of *world* music, for it is the port of entry; but there are other *American* centers. Chicago, Cincinnati, Detroit, St. Louis, Rochester, the Pacific coast towns; in fact, all of our large industrial cities are music centers as well. Some musicians still dread the local tag which may result from living in any city but New

York, or possibly Boston or Philadelphia, but the day is rapidly passing when they need be afraid of being known as merely Cincinnati, Milwaukee, or any other locality's musicians.

Before 1850 there was little music in the West. The Southwest, of course, could be proud of the opera at New Orleans, which dated from the beginning of the century, but this activity was the result of the French element in a city where conditions were far different from the settlements on the frontiers. There is record of a Haydn Society in Cincinnati, formed in 1819, and a Musical Fund Society in St. Louis in 1838. In 1849 a *Saengerfest* was held in Cincinnati, and a *Musikverein* was founded in Milwaukee during the same year. It is significant that these were towns with large German populations.

As a city, Chicago is well past its hundredth birthday, and also its musical centennial. In 1833, the few residents heard their first local musician when Mark Beaubien, public ferryman, played his fiddle for the dancing at his Saguenash Tavern. Moreover, he was accompanied by a piano which his brother had brought to Chicago on a schooner. A year later a Miss Wyeth opened a music school; and the Old Settler's Harmonic Society gave its first concert in the Presbyterian Church. In 1837, Dean and McKenzie opened a theatre where the nine-year-old Joseph Jefferson played in the company. By 1840 entertainments had multiplied. Barnum came with a minstrel troupe, and Henry Russell and other ballad singers made visits.

The short-lived Chicago Sacred Music Society was organized in 1842, and in 1847 a Mozart Society was formed by Frank Lumbard, who was appointed vocal teacher in the public schools in that same year. This, it is well to remember, was only eleven years after Lowell Mason's first experiments in the Boston schools, and but nine years after the Boston authorities had made music a regular part of the school routine. Soon after this came the debut of Richard Hoffman, the first piano virtuoso to visit Chicago, and then other great soloists, vocal and instrumental, included the city on their regular tours. But these beginnings were humble indeed, and the middle of the century found Chicago little advanced in musical culture.

The year 1850 marks two important events in Chicago. In July, theatregoers heard the first performance of a grand opera—*La Sonnambula*, at Rice's Theatre; and in October a Philharmonic Society, which had recently been organized, gave an orchestral concert. This group had been formed by Julius Dyhrenfurth, a German violinist who came to America in 1830, and after giving concerts in the Ohio Valley and in New Orleans and the South, had returned to Germany. He came back in 1847 and settled in Chicago. The orchestra grew from frequent gatherings of German musicians at Dyhrenfurth's home. After they had practiced and played together for a time, they decided to give a few concerts, and advertised for subscriptions to a series of eight programs, one a week. The first presented an orchestral potpourri, a song with vocal quartet accompaniment, a cello solo, a *Chicago Waltz* written by one of the players (Carlino Lenssen), a medley overture of Negro airs, and a chorus from Weber's *Preciosa*.

The Philharmonic under Dyhrenfurth lasted for two seasons, but its career was financially disastrous. Efforts were made to revive the society, and in 1853 it was decided that the band should be legally incorporated. The petition made something of a stir at Springfield, the state capital. Some of the farmer members of the legislature were a bit scornful of such trivialities as musical societies. Their feeling may account for the title of the bill when it was finally passed—"an act to encourage the science of fiddling." In these years two or three conductors tried unsuccessful hands at directing the orchestra, until Carl Bergmann came to Chicago in 1854. He thought of moving from New York permanently. When he was appointed conductor of the Philharmonic there was trouble among the men, and Bergmann hurriedly resigned and left town.

Then this Chicago Philharmonic fell to pieces. A teacher named C. W. Webster tried to bring it together in 1856 but with no good results. Then a trumpet player, Henry Ahner, from the old Germania orchestra came to Chicago and built up a really good orchestra of twenty-six players. He gave concerts for two seasons, which were popular for a time, but later failed to attract an audience. Another ex-Germanian followed Ahner—Julius Unger. He reorganized Ahner's orchestra and gave afternoon concerts. Competition then appeared; a musician with the musical name of J. M. Mozart organized a rival orchestra and drove Unger out of town. Then this Mozart found his own reward in bankruptcy.

Meanwhile, opera troupes were playing regularly at the theatres.

In December of 1859, two companies fought an opera war—an English troupe at McVicker's and an Italian company at Metropolitan Hall. The Englishmen won. In 1865 the Crosby Opera House was built by the enterprising Uranus H. Crosby. The magnificent structure was a combined opera house, art gallery, and studio building. For a year or so it housed lavish productions of opera with the finest singers of the day, but somehow the enterprise fell on evil ways, and before many years had passed it was given over to Humpty Dumpty shows, families of bell ringers, trained animals, acrobats, and pantomimes. In 1871 the opera house was restored to its original purpose and Max Maretzek brought a German troupe to its stage. During the summer and fall it was redecorated, and was about to be reopened when the great fire in October ruined the Crosby Opera House and almost everything else in Chicago. The fire marked the end and the beginning of two distinct epochs in Chicago's career—musical and otherwise.

The year 1860, like 1850, brought two important musical events to Chicago. One was the coming of HANS BALATKA from Milwaukee. Balatka was a Moravian who had been a choral conductor in Vienna. He came to Milwaukee in 1849, where he directed the newly formed *Musikverein*. In 1857 he led the annual Northwestern *Saengerfest* in Chicago, and made such a favorable impression that he was persuaded to live in Chicago. So in 1860 he left Milwaukee, and was soon appointed conductor of the once more reorganized Philharmonic. His first program was given in Bryant Hall, and it contained not only an entire symphony (Beethoven's Second, which the Germanians had played in Chicago on their visit some years before), but also the first performance of a Wagner composition in Chicago—the Chorus from *Tannhäuser*. The Balatka concerts became the fashion, and the conductor a popular idol. This vogue lasted for about six years, and in the seventh season the audiences grew thinner, and the trustees decided it was of no use to go further in debt. There was an attempt to revive the orchestra in 1868 and 1869, but on the twenty-ninth of November, 1869, the day following one of Balatka's concerts, a young conductor from the East, Theodore Thomas, gave a concert with his Central Park Garden Orchestra from New York. The finesse of this band, the new meanings it gave to the music, were something that Chicagoans had never heard before. Thomas's concert sounded the death of the Balatka orchestra, for this man Thomas was later to mean everything to music in Chicago.

Balatka, despite his inability to equal Thomas's success, had a long and honorable career in American music. He lived until 1899 and directed many organizations in Chicago and Milwaukee. He was also something of a composer, and wrote a cantata, many choruses, some songs, and orchestral fantasias. Chicago owes him a great debt—he was really the first to espouse the cause of higher music there. He introduced eight of Beethoven's symphonies; two by Mozart; one by Mendelssohn; and several by Haydn and Schubert.

The other musical event of 1860 created less of a stir than Balatka's coming, but it was significant. Henri DeClerque, a violinist, inaugurated a series of chamber music recitals known as the Briggs House Concerts. The personnel consisted of DeClerque, a second violin, a cello, and a piano. They gave Chicago its first hearing of the chamber music of the classicists and of the romanticists. Again Chicago was only a few years behind the East. The Mendelssohn Quintette Club had been organized in Boston in 1849, the Eisfeld Chamber Music Concerts in New York in 1851, and the Mason-Thomas recitals in New York (of which more in the next chapter) in 1855. Hans Balatka also organized chamber music concerts in 1863, which had the advantage of a complete string quartet, augmented by a piano. It is not to be supposed that these organizations prospered—chamber music has rarely proved a box-office attraction for the general public—but the mere fact that the concerts were given at all is testimony to the fact that there were worthy attempts at music of a high order in places other than the East, at a date not much later than they were first offered in the older centers.

The fact that intensive musical activity seemed to start from 1850 in the West is explained not alone by the theory that the Midwest settlers by this time had opportunity to turn their thoughts to leisure enjoyment, although this may have had much to do with it. The wholesale immigration from Central Europe, which commenced in the late forties, affected the West as well as the East—possibly to an even greater degree. The German musicians who came to this country in 1848, and during the following years, sought many fields, and many of them settled in cities to which their friends had preceded them. We have seen how some of the members of the Germanian Orchestra finally landed in Chicago. It was the same in other cities—Cincinnati, St. Louis, Louisville, Chicago, and Milwaukee.

The *Saengerfest* which was held in Cincinnati in 1849 was the first meeting of the several German singing societies of Midwest cities. From this the North American *Saengerbund* was formed, and its festivals soon grew to large proportions. In 1870 one of them was again held in Cincinnati. A large hall was built to accommodate the two thousand singers and the audience. Cincinnati liked the festival so much that in 1873 the first annual Cincinnati Festival was held under the direction of Theodore Thomas, who conducted the annual concerts for many years.

Of course, the traveling virtuosos and prima donnas, who visited every city of importance in the West, did their part in molding the public taste for music; but brilliant concert stars have always had a box-office value that sometimes has little to do with music. People like to see famous artists, even though they cannot understand or enjoy their music. It is always the resident musical activity that is the better indication of the real musical life of a city, and it is significant that from 1850, hundreds of musicians and teachers found that they could gain a respectable livelihood in various parts of the country.

2. WILLIAM MASON (1829–1908)

Among the musical missionaries who have had a part in developing music in this country, the name of William Mason should always be remembered. Like his father, Lowell Mason, he had the spirit of a pioneer. He distinguished himself in several directions, and in at least two of them he was an influence of prime importance. He sacrificed much to bring chamber music to the public, and to play it so often that people would grow to like it. As a piano teacher, he is in a large part responsible for the really excellent piano playing in this country today. He was among the first of the American teachers to evolve a method for acquiring touch, and the remarkable feature of his work is that Mason evolved by empirical methods certain principles of muscular control that have recently been discovered by scientists after years of patient research. Then, too, he was a prolific composer of piano pieces that had considerable vogue for many years.

William Mason was born in Boston, January 24, 1829. He showed a love for music when he was a little child, and of course his musician father gave him every opportunity to develop his talents. When he was small he had little instruction in piano playing, but he used to practice regularly, and his mother sat by him and helped him as much as she could. He really acquired a remarkable facility.

He became useful to his father as an accompanist, and went with him to many of the music conventions. He also became an organist, and held several church positions before he was out of his teens. He made his first public appearance as a pianist when he was seventeen, at one of the concerts of his father's Boston Academy of Music. In the same year he played the piano part in a series of six chamber music concerts, given by the Harvard Musical Association at the piano warerooms of Jonas Chickering.

He began studying with Henry Schmidt, a violinist who was a careful and able piano teacher as well. It was Schmidt who helped him evolve what has since been known as the Mason "elastic finger touch," accomplished by quietly drawing the finger tips inward toward the palm of the hand. Mason analyzed the playing of the various concert pianists who came to Boston. He learned much from DeMeyer's method of tone production, and spent hours at the piano imitating his manner and style, and striving to acquire the habit of devitalizing the upper arm muscles. He learned to play for hours without tiring, and at length arrived at the conclusion that the secrets of touch and technique lay not so much in the muscles of the fingers as in those of the arm.

Then came the years abroad, when Mason lived among the most celebrated of the world's musicians, and not only gained the finest instruction, but formed rich associations that colored the rest of his long and active life. Armed with introductions from Boston musicians, he sailed in 1849 on the side-wheel steamer *Herrman*. These were the years of the German revolutions, when foreign musicians found it profitable, and in some cases healthier, to come to America. Mason had intended to go directly to Leipzig to study with Moscheles, but his plans had to be postponed because of the insurrections. But the time was well spent, for he was invited to visit Julius Schuberth, the famous music publisher from Hamburg he had met on the steamer. Schuberth took a fancy to one of Mason's pieces, *Les Perles de Rosée*, and when he went to Weimar he showed it to Liszt, who was delighted with it and gladly accepted the young composer's dedication. Schuberth's report of this visit gave Mason courage to try immediately what he had intended to do later, to ask Liszt to take him for a pupil. Liszt replied with a vaguely worded letter, which Mason took for a polite refusal. Several years after, when Mason met him at Weimar, Liszt remarked that he never took pupils for regular lessons, but that those who lived in Weimar had frequent opportunity to hear him and to meet the artists who visited him. Liszt actually meant this as an invitation to study with him, but Mason was a bit too literal to take the remarks as they were intended. When he actually did go to Liszt for study in 1853, he was surprised to learn that Liszt had been wondering why he had not come before.

In the meantime he worked with Moscheles, and studied harmony and counterpoint with Hauptmann. Then he went to Dreyschock in Prague, where he had over one hundred lessons. In 1853 he received an invitation from Sir Julius Benedict in London to play at one of the concerts of the Harmonic Union in Exeter Hall. The praise of the critics was somewhat qualified. The *Times* reviewer wrote:

Mr. William Mason was somewhat foolishly, we think, announced as "the first American pianist who had ever performed before an English audience,"—as if the bare fact of nationality, independent of actual merit, was a matter of any importance. Happily Mr. Mason possesses talent; and although very young, already exhibits promise of excellence. He played the pianoforte part in Weber's Concert Stuck with a great deal of spirit; so well, indeed that we are confident he will play it still better when he has acquired a more perfect command of the instrument. It is in mechanism that Mr. Mason is deficient. This deficiency makes him nervous and uncertain, imparts unsteadiness to his accentuation, and robs his passages of clearness. He has, nevertheless, a light and elastic touch, and evidently understands his author.

The *Chronicle* was no more flattering:

A pianist from New York, Mr. William Mason, who appeared for the first time in London, selected somewhat boldly for his début the single concerto of Weber. His performance was smoothly correct, but tame and uniform. His touch is light, rapid, but it wants delicacy of expression, and there is also a lack of color and verve about his playing. Mr. Mason is, no doubt, an able and accomplished pianist; but more than that is demanded of those who would now-a-days take the place to which he aspires in his art.

It is significant that both accounts, contradictory in many points, should praise his touch.

After the London visit Mason decided to go directly to Liszt at Weimar. There might still be hope of being accepted as a pupil. When he arrived, Liszt remarked that Mason let people wait for him for a long time. Then he told him to go to Leipzig and select a piano; and that he could find pleasant rooms in the same house with Klindworth. So Mason stayed at Weimar for a year and three months, a member of the little group that studied under the wing of one of the greatest pianists of all time. There were only three of them—Karl Klindworth from Hanover, Dionys Bruckner from Munich, and Mason. Joachim Raff was there too, a former pupil, who acted as Liszt's private secretary.

There were no formal lessons. Mason wrote in his memoirs: [1]

His idea was that the pupils whom he accepted should all be far enough advanced to practice and prepare themselves without routine instruction, and he expected them to be ready whenever he gave them an opportunity to play. . . . We constituted, as it were a family, for while we had our own apartments in the city, we all enjoyed the freedom of Liszt's home, and were at liberty to come and go as we liked . . . We were always quite at ease in those lower rooms, but on ceremonial occasions we were invited up-stairs to the drawing room, where Liszt had his favorite Érard. . . . During the entire time I was with him I did not see him give a regular lesson in the pedagogical sense. He would notify us to come up to the Altenburg [Liszt's home]. . . . We would go there, and he would call on us to play. I remember very well the first time I played to him after I had been accepted as a pupil. . . . After I was well started he began to get excited. He made audible suggestions, inciting me to put more enthusiasm into my playing, and occasionally he would push me gently off the chair and sit down at the piano and play a phrase or two himself by way of illustration. He gradually got me worked up to such a pitch of enthusiasm that I put all the grit that was in me into my playing.

All kinds of musicians came to Weimar. The pupils met them all, heard them play, and in turn played for them. Berlioz, Joachim,

[1] William Mason, *Memories of a Musical Life*, Century Co.

Wieniawski, and Rubinstein were welcome visitors. One evening Liszt sent for the "boys" to come up to his house to meet a twenty-year-old composer who was said to be very talented. His name was Brahms, and he was making a concert tour with Rémenyi, the violinist. Brahms was so nervous that he was unable to play his music, so Liszt took the almost illegible manuscripts and played at sight the E-flat Minor Scherzo, and part of the first Sonata. Brahms was delighted. Then someone asked Liszt to play his own Sonata. After he had started, Brahms dozed in his chair, and Liszt rose from the piano and left the room. Soon after this, Brahms had his famous meeting with Schumann, who published an article that established Brahms's fame throughout Europe—to the utter amazement of the Liszt group at Weimar.

There were others whom Mason met, at Weimar and elsewhere. He called on Schumann in 1850. He was received by Wagner in 1852, long before the great composer had been recognized as a towering giant. With these associations, and a background that had been gained by few American musicians of his time, Mason came home in 1854 to take up his life work in his own country.

His first act on landing was to hurry to Boston, to see again the daughter of George James Webb, his father's associate. Mason had met the young lady years before and had never forgotten her. They became engaged, and were married a few years later.

His first musical enterprise was a concert tour, possibly the first of its kind ever undertaken by a pianist alone. Concerts had generally offered a variety of talent. He went as far as Chicago, stopping for recitals at Albany, Troy, Utica, and all the towns along the way. He had a versatile manager, Oliver Dyer, who had been associated with Mason's brothers, Daniel and Lowell, in their music publishing business. Dyer was a newspaper man who could write well, and he prepared a pamphlet about Mason which he distributed among the townsfolk before the concerts. Then he would go to the newspaper editors, and offer to do odd reporting jobs for them. They were so grateful that they would print any advance notices of Mason's concerts that Dyer might give them.

On the way to Chicago, Mason's audiences were none too large, and when they had played two concerts in Chicago, Dyer was all for a speedy return to New York while they still had their carfare. Mason had more courage; he insisted on playing again in each of the towns they had visited, to see if the people had liked his playing well enough to come again. The halls were filled on the return trip.

He always closed his program with improvisations on a theme suggested by the audience. This was a custom started by Ferdinand Hiller, and no doubt it did lighten the proceedings for many of the listeners. All sorts of tunes were suggested, but the climax came when someone suggested that he play *Old Hundred* with one hand, and *Yankee Doodle* with the other. He did it, but he had to mollify the religious element by announcing afterwards that he meant no disrespect to *Old Hundred*.

Mason soon decided that the career of piano virtuoso was not for him. It was for this that he had prepared himself in Europe, and his concert tour had been encouraging. Yet he disliked the constant repetition of the public's favorite pieces, and he had already commenced to take pupils. He found himself singularly well fitted to teach. The occasional engagements with the New York Philharmonic, and the chamber music recitals, would satisfy his desire for public performance.

Probably the immediate reason for starting the chamber music concerts was to introduce the Brahms Grand Trio in B Major, Opus 8. He had for some time wanted to give New York music lovers something of the flavor of Weimar. Every Sunday morning he had heard the Weimar String Quartet in the two lower rooms of Liszt's house, and to Mason this had meant *Go thou and do likewise*. So he gathered a quartet about him. Theodore Thomas was first violin; Joseph Mosenthal, second; George Matzka, viola; and Carl Bergmann, cello. When friction developed between Bergmann and Thomas, Bergmann resigned and Frederick Bergner took his place. Thomas became the leader, and the maker of the programs, a field in which he displayed true genius. The first program was given in Dodworth's Hall, next to Grace Church on Broadway. The major works were the Brahms Trio, and the Schubert D Minor Quartet. There were also solos, vocal and instrumental, but in a few years the concerts were devoted to chamber music exclusively.

The refusal to compromise with public taste represented a real sacrifice. Often there was little left in the cash box after the hall rent was paid; yet in spite of all discouragements, the valiant little group played on for thirteen years. Then Thomas had other interests; he had become an orchestral conductor, and anyway the real missionary work was done. The last concert was given April 11, 1868. Though they played mostly in New York, the Mason-Thomas ensemble went regularly to Farmington, Connecticut, where the music teacher of Miss Porter's School, Karl Klauser, had aroused a real interest in music. There were also frequent concerts in Brooklyn, and in Orange, New Jersey.

Mason's influence as a teacher was tremendous. Many of his pupils, such men as W. S. B. Mathews, William Sherwood, and others, studied with him, became his disciples, and passed his methods on to their own pupils, who in their turn became teachers. His technical works, *Touch and Technic*, and several others, are still available to teachers and students, and they are still being used.

His compositions are not played as much today as they used to be. They belonged to a period of music that has quite definitely passed, and as music they have not had enough vitality to survive their idiom. *Silver Spring*, named for his father's estate in Orange, was highly popular. *Amitié pour Amitié* was a favorite with Liszt, who often played it. The *Ballade* and *Capriccio Fantastico* were well contrived and graceful.

But it is not as a composer that William Mason will be known. His place as a musical missionary, as a champion of the highest standards, and as the foremost piano teacher of his day, seems permanently assured. His span of life turned the century; he lived until 1908, when he died in New York in his eightieth year. He had a life full of many fine things; advantages of his youth that he was able to use; years of activity; and full recognition, by friends and the public, of all he had accomplished.

3. THEODORE THOMAS (1835–1905)

I

Theodore Thomas is an epic figure in American history—one of our great heroes. Compare the state of musical culture at the time of the Civil War with conditions today, and then thank Theodore Thomas for the difference. It is through his efforts that this country is the home of the best in orchestral music, that almost all of our major cities have symphony orchestras of the first rank, and, what is more important, that in each of these cities there is a public that will listen to the finest symphonic works. As for our composers, they can thank Thomas for orchestras to play their music, and to provide an incentive for writing in the larger forms.

It is important that Thomas was a masterful conductor, that he trained his men to standards of performance that had been unknown in this country, but it was more important that his whole career was devoted to carrying out a plan of education shrewdly calculated to develop our taste for good music. Other conductors had been concerned with single programs. Thomas occupied himself with a lifelong *series* of programs, progressively planned to cultivate the public's liking for the best in music literature.

Jullien had tried this, and so had the Germanians, but with one essential difference from the methods of Thomas. Like the early programs that Thomas arranged, theirs offered lighter works to offset the bugbear of the symphonies that appeared on their lists. But their lighter music was generally trash, and Thomas never offered any piece that lacked musical merit, no matter how light it might be. Jullien relied on theatrical methods to draw the crowds—*Firemen's Quadrilles* with real firemen. The Germanians had even produced in classic Boston a *Railroad Gallop*, illustrated by a miniature locomotive that ran around in a circle, with a tuft of black wool fastened to its funnel in lieu of real smoke.

When Thomas made a program he selected lighter pieces—and they were often very light—chiefly for their relations to the heavier works they were paired with. He would play a symphony that was over the heads of all but a few of his listeners. Then he would offer a waltz or light overture in which the themes would have some relation to those of the symphony. He knew that if he could get people to recognize the themes of a symphony, they would grow eventually to like it. Almost all of his programs have been preserved in the second volume of his autobiography; those who plan courses in music appreciation will do well to study them.

There were orchestras before Thomas's time, but the only group that was in any degree permanent was the New York Philharmonic, a band whose members played together more for the love of it than from any artistic results they achieved, or for any notable support they had from the public. In the early days there were from three to five concerts a season, and the public was admitted to some of the rehearsals. If a player had a professional engagement that would bring him real money, he kept it instead of going to rehearsal. Hence, the orchestra was often incomplete, and clarinet or oboe parts would be played on a violin, or a cello would do service for a bassoon. The concerts were held in Apollo Hall. Rough wooden benches were dragged in for the audience, and the music was a pleasant background for conversation. Yet the orchestra played bravely ahead, and as one commentator remarked, the players generally finished their pieces at the same time. Such was the state of musical culture when Thomas began his notable career. Starting with nothing but an inner feeling that people would come to want good music if it was brought to them, he devoted his life to their education. He was our first prophet of good music for the masses, and to him the term "good music" meant *good music.*

The list of positions he held during his lifetime reads like a catalogue of all the organizations in our musical history. And he paid the price of his eminence. When any great man holds a number of offices, and stays in the public eye for many years, he eventually becomes the target for savage attacks from every direction. Thomas was no exception. If all the hostile criticisms were gathered together and printed without comment, we would learn that he was a villain of the deepest hue. Incompetent, arrogant—yes, even dishonest. But when the truth was learned, the hero emerged untarnished and triumphant, greater for the attacks he had ignored.

II

And now for the catalogue of his doings—a long, long list. He was brought to America in 1845 as a lad of ten. His father had been *Stadtpfeifer,* or town musician, in Esens, Germany. There were too many little brothers and sisters to support on the meager income the little town could offer, so America beckoned. When they came to New York things were not much better, so little Theodore had to tuck his violin under his arm and go out to play in all kinds of places—for dances, weddings, theatres, even in saloons where he passed the hat.

He never had much training, but his inordinate curiosity led him into all sorts of artistic adventures, and he had the ability to absorb knowledge for himself. He had the kind of youth that makes great men, or causes the downfall of weaklings.

When he was still in his teens he took a concert trip through the South, all on his own. When he came to a town he would tack up a few handwritten posters announcing a concert by "Master T. T.," the remarkable prodigy. Then he would stand at the door and take in the money until he decided that all who were coming had arrived, rush backstage to change his clothes, and then appear before the audience with his violin.

Among his friends in New York, the Dodworth family did more than anyone else to find him work. These Dodworths deserve a place by themselves in our musical annals. All of them did something musical. Harvey was a cornetist, Allen played the violin. C. Dodworth was a virtuoso on the trombone, and C. R. played the concertina. They had a hall in Broadway next to Grace Church. Here the Mason-Thomas Quintette later gave its matinees. The Dodworths had orchestras for dances, weddings, or banquets. They offered brass bands with uniforms. They kept a music store; all of them were composers. Polkas, quicksteps, marches, and quadrilles flowed easily from their pens. They were one of the mainstays of the early Philharmonic. Whenever young Theodore Thomas needed money, he could count on Harvey Dodworth to find something for him to do; often a half-dollar engagement to play all night for a dance.

When Jullien came in 1853, Thomas was chosen as a first violin. The antics of the conductor disgusted him, but he nevertheless had his first idea of the symphony from playing in this great orchestra. It gave him something to think about—thoughts that later shaped the whole work of his life. He was elected a member of the Philharmonic in 1854, and in the next year the Mason-Thomas chamber concerts began. He traveled with famous soloists—Thalberg and others as a solo violinist. He was appointed concertmaster of the opera house orchestra. In 1858 he was suddenly called to take Anschütz's place as conductor, and led a performance of Halévy's *Jewess*, a score he had never seen before. The retirement of Anschütz became permanent, and Thomas was made conductor.

Conducting was a revelation to him. He was doing well as a violin-ist, looking forward to the career of virtuoso. Yet there was more thrill in leading an orchestra; it could be played as an instrument with subtle changes of color. And what is more important, he could make his life work the development of America's taste for music. He organized an orchestra of his own, and gave his first concert in Irving Hall, New York, May 13, 1862. This was the beginning of new things for musi-cal America.

He soon realized that only a permanent orchestra could give the best results; an orchestra in which the players devoted all of their time to its rehearsals and concerts; a group whose members were under the sole control of their conductor; whose players were not constantly lowering their standards and injuring their tone by playing for dances, and staying out late nights to keep other engagements.

Without a subsidy, he found that the only way to maintain such an orchestra was by having enough concerts each season to keep its mem-bers busy. This meant traveling, and thus the Thomas Highway was finally established. It reached from New England to the Pacific Coast. To all the principal cities of the country, playing in whatever halls the towns offered—churches or railroad stations, it made no difference. For each of these cities this greatest of all program makers adopted his idea of progressive programs—leading gradually from the familiar to the unfamiliar. Always having something on each program that was a little above the heads of most of the audience, but not too far beyond their liking. Then compensating them with something more obviously tuneful. All of this until his work was done, and he was at the end of his career in Chicago, with a subsidized orchestra, backed by the au-thority of his trustees to make no concessions to the public taste, but to reap the benefit of his missionary work by playing only that which belonged on a true symphony program.

III

It sounds as though it had all been an easy and pleasant path. It most decidedly was not. Anyone but a man of iron and steel would have quit after a few years of it. In fact, most of those who tried it were beaten before they began.

In 1862, Thomas was made alternate conductor with Theodore

Eisfeld of the Brooklyn Philharmonic Society. Four years later he became its sole conductor. He also had his own orchestra and concerts. In 1866 he started his summer concerts at Terrace Garden, where he offered light music interspersed with masterworks, and those who came to listen could bring or buy refreshments. Two years later these concerts were moved to the Central Park Garden. In two more years he had the training of his audiences well under way. He remarked in his notebook: "At last the summer programs show a respectable character and we are rid of the cornet! Occasionally a whole symphony is given."

By 1867 his orchestra was truly a permanent one, and on his own resources he was able to guarantee his men a full season's work. The first tour came in 1869, and he dropped his poorly attended New York concerts until a delegation of prominent citizens begged him to give them again. He had visited Chicago, and the Chicago Philharmonic died soon after the citizens had once heard the Thomas orchestra. When other summer organizations, principally bands, gave him competition for his Central Park Garden concerts in New York, he was invited to give them in the old Exposition Hall in Chicago.

In 1873 he was asked to organize and conduct the Cincinnati Festival. Under his direction it grew to be one of the finest musical events in the world. He had charge of the Philadelphia Centennial Concerts in 1876. Their failure was financial rather than artistic. The next year the New York Philharmonic insisted that he be its conductor. He had been offered the position before, but he would not give up his own orchestra. This time he consented, for he was allowed to keep his own band in addition to his new duties. He arranged that his own concerts would be lighter than the programs of the Philharmonic, so that there would be no competition.

In 1878 he was asked to come to Cincinnati to head the newly formed College of Music. He thought he saw a chance to found an institution that would fulfill his ideals and dreams for an educational center, but he endured the task for only a year. He resigned when he found that the backers of the school intended it as a commercial rather than an artistic enterprise. Thomas had no time to waste on purely commercial ventures.

New York, which had had a share in his persecution, welcomed him back, and he was again made conductor of the Philharmonic. The orchestra was in bad shape, its receipts had fallen to their lowest point, and the playing was far from good. Thomas brought it to heights far beyond its former achievements in his first season. More people came to the concerts, and the men made more money. In 1882 he was asked to organize mammoth festivals in New York and in Chicago.

He made a serious blunder in 1885. He was under the impression that America would welcome an American venture in opera producing. He was induced to become conductor of an enterprise presumably sponsored by the wealthiest men of the country. He was led to think that the backers of the newly formed American Opera Company would carry it along even though it might lose money. He was mistaken, for at the end of the first season the deficit frightened these backers away. It was generally agreed that opera had never been given so magnificently in this country, but the company was left to founder, and Thomas, who had been merely a salaried employee (for a long time without the salary), was attacked as a deadbeat who failed to make good his promises.

He had known financial troubles before. When he was invited to give the concerts at the Philadelphia Centennial, the invitation had been entirely honorary. Thomas was expected to give the concerts at his own risk, and take the chances of profit and loss. The people who came to the Exposition came to see, and not to listen. Affairs became so bad that one day the audience included the sheriff, who loved the music of the auction block more than that of the orchestra. Thomas could have evaded all his debts by voluntary bankruptcy, but he preferred an easy conscience, and he paid off every cent he owed, even though it took him twelve years to do it.

Then came more years of traveling with his orchestra. His work was having its effect. The Boston Symphony Orchestra was founded and supported by Major Higginson in 1881, directly as the result of the Thomas concerts in Boston. This took Boston from the Thomas itinerary, but Thomas bore the loss of territory with the knowledge that it was for this he was working. In later years his territory was continually cut by the establishment of permanent orchestras in cities where he had created the desire for them. Yet to his last, weary days, he was continually taking the Chicago Orchestra to towns that had none of their own.

IV

The years after the opera tragedy were bad ones for Thomas. New York seemed to think that he was tarnished with the blame, though his only sin had been to do a good job. There was keen rivalry among the orchestras in New York. Back in 1878 the Symphony Society of New York had been founded as a competitor of both the Philharmonic and Thomas's own orchestra. There were factions. The followers of Leopold and Walter Damrosch, and later of Seidl, taunted those of Thomas, and rivalry was fostered where none might have arisen had the artists been left to arrange things for themselves. When Chicago beckoned in 1891 it found Thomas in a receptive state of mind. He was weary of promises, and here was a group of fifty Chicago business men who had actually signed pledges to contribute a thousand dollars each to make up the deficit that might be incurred by the symphony orchestra they wanted for their city.

A chance to get together the men from his old orchestra, which he had been forced to disband—everything he had dreamed of—yes, he would leave even New York for that. The New York that had turned its back to him, but which was nevertheless his home. He signed the contract, and became Chicago's. New York suddenly awoke to his leaving, and rushed to give him everything Chicago had offered, and more. He had given his word to Chicago, and he went.

For fourteen years he directed the Chicago Orchestra. The splendid concerts of those fourteen seasons are models of program-making for any conductor, anywhere. Standard works and new experiments, both were represented. Always aiming a little beyond the public taste, he was constantly bringing it to a higher level. And yet the hostile press still hounded him. Why ask people to listen to Wagner when they would rather hear *Yankee Doodle?* Who is this Thomas person that disturbs our idea of what we ought to like? And the guarantors continued to pay their share of the deficit without a whimper. And Thomas turned down handsome offers from Boston and elsewhere, because his friends in Chicago had the courage to back him.

1893 brought another failure—one that almost finished his career, bringing torment that would have destroyed a weaker man. He was appointed director of music for the Chicago World's Fair. He immediately set about making plans for an all-summer festival that would show the world what America was doing in music, and America, the music of the world. He arranged for an orchestra of over a hundred, and for an exposition chorus. He invited the leading soloists of the world to appear in the concert hall; he asked the finest orchestras of America and Europe, and the foremost choruses to come and give concerts. It was a mammoth plan, conceived by a man of great vision.

When he accepted the post he had been careful to specify that the musical events of the fair were to be run separately from the exhibits of musical merchandise. This condition looked well on paper, but it was not to be taken seriously by the business men and politicians in charge of the exposition. It happened that Steinway & Sons, whose pianos were played by several of the soloists, was not one of the exhibitors. Those who had spent their good money for exhibit space could see no reason why a piano that was not exhibited should get the free advertising that came from the use of its piano in the concert hall. Thomas saw the justice of this, but the great artists had already been invited to play, and he had always been a firm believer in allowing musicians to choose their own instruments. So in defiance of the ruling against nonexhibited pianos, the proceedings commenced with a concert at which Paderewski played his Steinway.

The storm broke; the autocrat must be in the pay of instrument manufacturers. He was brought up on charges, hostile newspapers slung mud from the river bottom—Thomas was a crook. Even proof that he was innocent, incapable of being bribed, could not still the savage snarling of his enemies. Yet it was impossible to force his resignation, and the concerts proceeded according to the huge schedule. Finally the financial panic of 1893 nearly ruined the fair. People could no longer afford the trip to Chicago, and in August the foes of Theodore Thomas had their revenge by cutting his appropriation for music. Seeing no chance of continuing his plans he resigned, and went East to his summer home in Maine for a chance to cure his hurt. Times improved, people had more money, and the fair was again prosperous. Thomas was invited to come back, but he had had enough, and he felt he couldn't stand much more. He waited to join his friends until it was time for the third season of the Chicago Orchestra.

V

One of the significant features of his program at the Chicago Fair was the invitation to American composers to write works for performance. Those with established reputations—Paine, Chadwick, Foote, Mrs. Beach, Dudley Buck, and others—were definitely commissioned to compose something for the occasion. Other composers were invited to submit works to a committee of judges. Twenty-three were submitted, and seven were chosen.

Thomas was all for the American composer, but he always said that he would never play anything merely because it was American. It must be good music. Study of his programs reveals the fact that as the years progressed he found more and more American works that deserved performance, and he was always the first to welcome them when they came. And it was because of Theodore Thomas that there are orchestras today to play the works of Americans, or of any composers.

When Thomas died January 4, 1905, he had lived to see the last of his dreams fulfilled—the building of a permanent home for his permanent orchestra—and the concert which dedicated Orchestra Hall in Chicago was the greatest triumph of his career. He was still assailed by the press, chiefly because the orchestra did not sound as it had in the great Auditorium where it had been necessary to play much louder. But, though the sound of the orchestra was new to the ears of the public,Thomas went to his end knowing that it would not be long before its tone could be adjusted to the new and better acoustics. He also knew that the young assistant conductor he had selected some years before—Frederick Stock—was fully capable of doing the job, though he must have dearly wanted to do it himself, and thus vindicate his plans and his unfailing judgment.

4. OTHER TEACHERS AND COMPOSERS OF THE PERIOD

There were many others, contemporaries of Mason and Thomas, who did much to shape our musical culture. Some of them came from abroad and some were American born. They all had a hand in making us musical, and in training teachers who are still at work. Some of them wrote music representative of the period, important as a link in the development of our music.

RICHARD HOFFMAN (1831–1909) was an Englishman who came to America when he was sixteen years old. He was the well-trained son of an accomplished musician. He had studied with DeMeyer, Moscheles, Rubinstein and Liszt, and was a talented pianist by the time he arrived in America. He made his debut with the Philharmonic in New York, when he played a Mendelssohn concerto. He played at Jenny Lind's first concert at Castle Garden, and was engaged for her concert tour. In 1854 he introduced Chopin's Concerto in E Minor to the Philharmonic audiences, and was elected an honorary member of the Society. When the Philharmonic gave its fiftieth anniversary concert in 1892, Hoffman was a soloist. Then, when he celebrated the fiftieth anniversary of his own coming to America, his friends gave him a testimonial concert.

As a composer Hoffman was prolific; many of his works were effective transcriptions of popular orchestral works—the Scherzo from Mendelssohn's *Scotch* Symphony, airs from *Trovatore* and other operas. There were also many original works that were considerably used; a *Caprice de Concert; Impromptus; Tarantelles;* and an effective anthem for mixed quartet based on the 137th Psalm—*By the Waters of Babylon.* As a teacher Hoffman stood high in his profession. Though he could command his own terms he accepted many talented pupils for what they could pay. He lived to be honored at an old age, and died in Mount Kisco, New York.

SEBASTIAN BACH MILLS (1838–1898), another English pianist, like his colleague Hoffman, was influential as a teacher. He was always fond of getting showy effects from his pupils, but he was nevertheless careful to play good music on his own programs. For many years he had a reputation for introducing works new to New York. Among them were Chopin's *Fantasia* and F Minor Piano Concerto, Mozart's posthumous Concerto in C, Liszt's E-flat Concerto, and the Weber-Liszt *Polonaise.* He came to New York as a visiting pianist in 1856, and was so warmly received that he made his home in New York, though he made frequent concert trips to Europe. Among his many pupils was Homer Bartlett, of whom we shall hear more later.

He was a prolific composer for the piano, and if most of his pieces were frothy and trivial, that was what the public of the day wanted most from its recital favorites. *Recollections of Home*, the first *Tarantelle*, *Fairy Fingers*, the second *Barcarolle*, were ready favorites. There were also *The Murmuring Fountain*, and transcriptions of favorite melodies—*Home, Sweet Home*, and others.

FRÉDÉRIC LOUIS RITTER (1834–1891), an Alsatian music teacher, is known today principally as the author of the first complete history of music in this country, *Music in America*, written in 1883. This work was useful, because it was truly the first thorough study of the subject. Yet he was not in sympathy with our musical past, and some of his scathing remarks were uncalled for. Moreover, he was not always accurate, and not particularly careful to confirm his statements of fact.

Ritter came to America in 1856, when he went to Cincinnati to organize the Cecilia Choral Society, and a Philharmonic Orchestra. He came to New York in 1861, where he stayed as teacher and conductor of choral societies until he was appointed director of music at Vassar College in 1878. Eventually he returned to Europe, and died in Antwerp in 1891. In addition to his *Music in America*, he was the author of a two-volume *History of Music*, and a volume on *Music in England*. He was also active as a composer, and while he was in this country he published *8 Clavierstücke*; a set of six songs; some sacred songs; and a set of arrangements of Irish melodies. He wrote several treatises on harmony and musical dictation.

Among Ritter's pupils in New York was a youngster from Sandusky, Ohio, ALBERT ROSS PARSONS (1847–1933), a man who lived to be the dean of New York music teachers. When he went abroad in 1867, Parsons studied with Moscheles, Reinecke, and Tausig, and returned to his native country to become one of the leading musicians in New York. He was an organist at some of the principal churches, and head of the piano departments of several leading conservatories. He was an early American apostle of Wagner, and translated several of the great composer's literary efforts—the essay on *Beethoven* and others. He was also a composer of songs and piano pieces.

WILLIAM SMITH BABCOCK MATHEWS (1837–1912), born in New London, New Hampshire, was at one time a pupil of William Mason, and later a collaborator in several of Mason's technical works. All of his musical education was gained in this country, and when he was twenty-three he started his career of teaching, in Georgia and other places in the South. By the time he was thirty he landed in Chicago, and from then to the rest of his life he was a powerful influence in developing the musical life of the Middle West. Shortly before he died he moved to Denver and finished his days in editorial work.

It is principally as a writer on musical subjects that we know Mathews today, though in his time he was active as a musician and teacher. Six years after Ritter had published his *Music in America*, Mathews compiled a second volume on the subject—*One Hundred Years of Music in America*. As an American, it was to be expected that Mathews would have more sympathy with his subject than Ritter; but Mathews leaned too far in the other direction, he failed to keep his sense of values, and his overhasty production lost much of the worth it might easily have possessed.

Another pupil of Mason to distinguish himself as a pianist and teacher was WILLIAM HALL SHERWOOD (1854–1911), son of a clergyman who had founded a musical academy in Lyons, New York. Sherwood had been a boy wonder, and had taught at his father's school from the time he was twelve years old. In 1871 he went to Mason, then to Berlin where he studied with Kullak and others, and finally with Liszt at Weimar. After he had made some successful appearances as a pianist in Germany, he came back to America, and made a concert tour of our principal cities. Then he went as a teacher to the New England Conservatory in Boston, and after subsequent years in New York he went to Chicago in 1889, where eventually he founded the Sherwood Piano School. He was a brilliant pianist, and he was in demand with the orchestras as a soloist. He should always be remembered as one of the first pianists to make a regular practice of including a number of American compositions on each of his concert programs. He was also something of a composer himself, and in his published works for piano there are interesting ventures in chromatic harmonies.

In New England, BENJAMIN JAMES LANG (1837–1909) was an influence of prime importance. Known chiefly as an organist and choral director, he was nevertheless prominent as a teacher of piano, and had for his pupils many young musicians who were to become prominent in later life—Arthur Foote, Ethelbert Nevin, and his own talented daughter, Margaret Ruthven Lang. Lang was born in Salem, and in addition to lessons at home, he traveled abroad to study with Satter and Jaell, and finally with Liszt. He was organist and at one time conductor for the Handel and Haydn Society in Boston, and for years he directed the Apollo Club and the Cecilia Club. Although he wrote a great deal of music, he never published it nor often allowed it to be played, for he felt he would rather be known in other fields than that of composer.

CHAPTER ELEVEN

The Parents of Our Contemporaries

1. THE GRANDFATHERS

THE second half of the century saw our young musical talents flocking to Europe to study with the master teachers of the Continent. Most of them went to Germany, then the musical center of the world. The effect was inevitable; they came home thoroughly saturated with German ideas, and those who were composers wrote their music after the models of the Germans. Although this denied individuality to their own work, the foreign influence at least produced music that was workmanlike, and it led to standards of craftsmanship that American composition must follow in later years. The hymn-tune writers had gone abroad for their education early in the century; now those who had larger ambitions were doing likewise.

The files of Dwight's *Journal of Music* often contained news of the young Americans studying abroad. A correspondent wrote in the issue of June 11, 1853:

At Leipsic I called on Mr. C. C. Perkins, but did not find . . . him at home; but I was informed that he was still pursuing his studies with much diligence and has recently finished another Quartet for stringed instruments, which is considered above par.

In the fall of the same year, the London *Athenæum* announced:

We must take a fresh paragraph to announce the publication at Leipsic of a Quartet by Mr. C. C. Perkins . . . the first American who has devoted himself to classical instrumental composition. So far as we can judge of this Quartet by examining its single parts, the themes appear pleasing—the working of them neat—and the taste of the whole laudable, as eschewing the modern defects calling themselves romanticisms, against which there is reason to warn American musical imagination.

The June 11 issue of Dwight's *Journal* contained an item about another American:

Mr. Parker is still making rapid progress in playing, as well as in composition. It will interest his friends to know that he has also composed a Quartet for strings, which is pronounced very clever. A Quartet is one of the most difficult things to compose, requiring pure musical talent, as well as a thorough knowledge of the power and effects of the several instruments for which it is written. It costs genius and much study to write the parts so that they harmonize effectively and melodiously and are at the same time expressive; comparatively few are written that are worth playing through.

These two young men, CHARLES CALLAHAN PERKINS (1823–1886) and JAMES CUTLER DUNN PARKER (1828–1916), were fellow students in Germany. They were friends of William Mason, who met them on several occasions while he, too, was studying abroad. Perkins was slightly older than Parker. Born in Boston, he had been graduated from Harvard in 1843, and had already been in Italy and Paris to study painting. Music delighted him, and he added its study to his various pursuits. Then he came back to Boston in 1849, and for a year he was both president and director of the Handel and Haydn Society. Soon after this he went back to Europe for further study.

By this time his friend Parker, also a native of Boston and a graduate of Harvard, had decided to give up the career of lawyer for which he had been preparing himself, and he, too, went to Germany to learn to be a musician. He studied with Hauptmann, Richter, and Moscheles, and had a thorough training. One had to be serious minded to win the approval of the classic-minded John S. Dwight.

Perkins and Parker came back to Boston in 1854, to follow different paths. Perkins was never particularly active in music as a profession. He left a few published works: a Quartet, a Trio, and a few pieces for piano and violin, published in Germany. His most important work was as a patron of the fine arts and as a critic. He was one of the chief factors in building the Music Hall in Boston (1851), and his *History of the Handel and Haydn Society*, which he never lived to finish, is an important document for the student of American music history. When he died in 1886, the work was completed by John S. Dwight.

Parker came back from Germany for an active career as a musician, a career that lasted until his death in 1916, when he was eighty-eight years old. He taught piano and composition, and some of his pupils became our leading composers of the next generation. Arthur Whiting was among them, and they all attest to Parker's thorough methods. He was organist of Boston's Trinity Church for twenty-seven years; he played the organ for the Handel and Haydn Society. He was a teacher of piano, organ, and harmony at the New England Conservatory, and for a time at Boston University.

He wrote a great deal of music. Aside from a few instrumental works, and the String Quartet which Dwight's foreign correspondent had said "was pronounced very clever," most of his music was for chorus. For this he had something of a flair, though his sentimental nature led him into paths of sweetness that have kept his works from living. His most significant work was the *Redemption Hymn,* which the Handel and Haydn Society performed in 1877. For many years this cantata was in the standard repertoire of choral societies generally. *The Blind King* (1886) was a secular cantata, and there were other oratorios—*St. John,* and *The Life of Man* (1895). In many ways *The Life of Man* was a better work than the *Redemption Hymn.* Its canons and fugal imitations were well contrived, and lent themselves effectively to the voices of a choir. The seven churches of Asia were pictured by seven voices, each entering in canonic imitation. There were also a few piano pieces and a miscellaneous assortment of church music.

Then there was ELLSWORTH C. PHELPS (1827–1913), a native of Connecticut. From his nineteenth year he was an organist, first at New London, Connecticut, at Syracuse, New York, and from 1857 in Brooklyn, where he was also a teacher of music in the public schools. Phelps composed two symphonies, four symphonic poems, several overtures, two comic operas, and a number of cantatas. He often chose native subjects for his music; one of his symphonies was based on Longfellow's *Hiawatha.*

And there were foreigners, too. MATTHIAS KELLER (1813–1875) came from Germany in 1846. He was a violinist and bandmaster, and after living in Philadelphia and New York he finally landed in Boston.

He became an ardent patriot, and wrote an *American Hymn* for which he himself supplied the words of the text. This hymn, sung by full chorus, supported by grand orchestra, organ, and military band, was a feature of the first concert of Gilmore's Peace Festival in Boston in 1869. This festival and the one that followed it in 1872 deserve a volume by themselves. PATRICK SARSFIELD GILMORE was a bandmaster who had the bigger and better idea with a vengeance. He had conducted festivals in former years, but the affairs in classic Boston were the climax of his career. A coliseum to seat fifty thousand persons was erected. A chorus of ten thousand and an orchestra of one thousand were assembled. Railroads arranged special excursions from all over the country to see and hear "the grandest musical festival ever known in the history of the world." Barnum himself could not have staged the affair one bit more effectively. President Grant, with members of his cabinet, governors of states, army and navy officers, notables of every kind, came to Boston to be present at the Great National Peace Jubilee, "to be held in the city of Boston, to commemorate the restoration of peace throughout the land." Five days were devoted to programs of colossal dimensions. Besides Gilmore, conductors of genuine ability, Zerrahn and others, helped in leading the musical forces. It proved too much for John S. Dwight, who left town to spend the week at his summer home at Nahant, where he hoped he could not hear the cannon used to mark the rhythm of the national airs. But other musicians were not so particular; they helped Pat Gilmore make his party a huge success. Besides the cannon, which were fired by electric buttons on a table in front of the conductor, one hundred real firemen in red shirts helped in the proceedings by pounding real anvils in the Anvil Chorus from *Trovatore*.

Gilmore was only forty in 1869, and he found it hard to rest on his laurels so early in his career. He must have another festival. The idea of peace in America was somewhat old by then, but there had been a war in Europe, so why not an international music festival which he could call a World Peace Jubilee? To add to the international idea, Johann Strauss was brought from Europe to conduct the *Blue Danube*, Franz Abt came from Germany, and the soloists were all to be world famous. This time the size of the chorus would be doubled—twenty thousand would sing. It was here that Gilmore failed. Even Carl

Zerrahn could not keep such a vast body of singers together, and the results were almost calamitous.

But to return to the composers. MAX MARETZEK (1821–1897) was a Moravian who came to America in 1848. Fry had him brought to New York to conduct the opera at the Academy. He was a clever manager, too; successful with his companies in New York, Havana, and Mexico. He wrote two operas: *Hamlet*, and another based on Irving's legend *Sleepy Hollow*.

GEORGE MATZKA, the viola player of the Mason-Thomas chamber music concerts, came to New York in 1852. He was long a member of the Philharmonic, and for a short time in 1876 he acted as conductor. Matzka was a prolific composer; he wrote several overtures, two String Quartets, a Violin Sonata, and many choruses and songs.

ADOLF NEUENDORF (1843–1897) was born in Hamburg, but came to New York when he was twelve, where he studied the violin with Matzka. He was for years a violinist and conductor in theatre orchestras. In 1877 he conducted the first American performance of Wagner's *Die Walküre* at the Academy of Music in New York. When Theodore Thomas went to Cincinnati in 1878, Neuendorf succeeded him as conductor of the Philharmonic, but for one year only, for Thomas returned soon after his troubles with the directors of the college. Neuendorf composed two symphonies and several overtures, but he was best known by his comic operas, a field in which he had real talent. *The Rat Charmer of Hamelin* was a favorite for many years after it was first produced in 1880, and the works that followed it were successful, too: *Don Quixote* (1882), *Prince Woodruff* (1887), and *The Minstrel* (1892).

And so the path is cleared for the first native composer whose fame has endured as a writer in the larger forms, even though his works are seldom heard today. JOHN KNOWLES PAINE (1839–1906) lived to see himself the dean of American composers, and many of his younger brethren, some of them his pupils, making quite a name for themselves. Some say that American music starts with J. K. Paine, and in many ways they are right, for none of those who came before him had done much in the symphonic field. Certainly Fry and Bristow enjoyed but a short fame with their works, and the attention they attracted was based more on the fact that they were among the few Americans who

George W. Chadwick
(See pages 306–310)

Arthur Foote
(See pages 310–313)

Horatio Parker
(See pages 313–319)

Copyright by Pirie MacDonald

Mrs. H. H. A. Beach
(See pages 319–323)

wrote music. As such, they were curiosities who could win a following for the mere fact that they existed at a time when there were few others like them.

And as we grow further from the days of John K. Paine, the venerable father of our composers is relegated to a somewhat similar position. His music was infinitely superior to that of either Fry or Bristow, yet he holds his place in our music history because he stood alone at a time when we had few composers. Compared to his contemporaries, he was and still is a giant. Were he writing today the same music he wrote fifty years ago, he would be lost in the crowd, where hundreds of our present-day composers are writing far better music.

It is not to remove Paine from his pedestal that the critic of today makes reservations in praising his music. The fact that he was the first American composer to win serious consideration abroad is enough to deserve a monument. Yet it is but honest to admit that as a creative artist he was something of a pedant, wholly dominated by European composers of his time. As Daniel Gregory Mason has written,[1] "his *Island Fantasy* was supposed to be inspired by the Isles of Shoals, off Portsmouth, but artistically speaking it was within easy sailing distance of Mendelssohn's *Hebrides*."

Histories of American music written twenty-five and thirty years ago were too close to Paine to be entirely mature in their judgment of his work. Superlatives abound in their accounts of his music. Elson [2] speaks of the first symphony as an "epoch-making" work; to his mind the second symphony has a final movement that is a glorious outburst of thanksgiving almost comparable with the *finale* of the B-flat Symphony by Schumann. He also states that at the Philadelphia Exposition, Paine's *Centennial Hymn* was decidedly more of a success than Wagner's *Centennial March*. But he fails to add that the Wagner march, which had been commissioned by Theodore Thomas, was so unworthy of Wagner that Thomas never quite forgot the insult. Rupert Hughes,[3] writing in 1900, was ecstatic over the second symphony.

It seems wiser today to admit that Paine's music has not had im-

[1] D. G. Mason, *The Dilemma of American Music.* By permission of Macmillan Co., publishers.
[2] L. C. Elson, *The History of American Music*, Macmillan Co.
[3] Hughes & Elson, *American Composers*, L. C. Page & Co.

mortality for the good reason that it really did not deserve it. Concede that its freshness has somewhat wilted, and then proceed to do its composer the honor he merits as the first of our composers to have his works performed repeatedly for many years, and to have them published both here and abroad.

For they were performed often. By 1899 the Boston Symphony Orchestra had played his compositions more than eighteen times. Theodore Thomas gave the first symphony its initial performance in 1876 in Boston. He also commissioned Paine to write a *Centennial Hymn* for the Philadelphia Exposition in 1876, and the *Columbus March and Hymn* for the Chicago World's Fair. He performed his cantata *Song of Promise* at the Cincinnati Festival of 1888. When he was not yet thirty, Paine conducted his Mass at the *Sing Academie* in Berlin. In 1873 he directed the first performance of his oratorio *St. Peter* in his native town of Portland, Maine. A year later it was given by the Handel and Haydn Society in Boston. In 1881 his music for Sophocles's *Œdipus Tyrannus* was played at the Sander's Theatre in Cambridge, Massachusetts, and in 1904 this score won the gold medal at an international concert at the unveiling of the monument to Wagner in Berlin. His *Hymn to the West* was written for the St. Louis World's Fair in 1904, and the Handel and Haydn Society gave it a Boston performance the following year.

He was born in Portland, January 9, 1839. His first teacher was Hermann Kotzschmar, the German who came to America with the Saxonia Band in 1848, and settled in Portland in 1849 where he lived for the remaining sixty years of his life. Paine made his debut as an organist when he was eighteen, and then went to Berlin, where he studied organ, composition, and orchestration under Haupt and other teachers. He toured Germany as an organist, and acquired something of a reputation. Soon after his return to America he was appointed instructor of music at Harvard (1862), and thirteen years later he was honored with a full professorship. Harvard and the University of Pennsylvania ran a close race in creating the first professorships of music. Paine held his chair for thirty years, and then resigned to give all his time to composition. But not for long; he died April 25, 1906, while he was working to complete a symphonic poem based on the life of Abraham Lincoln.

The first symphony was published by Breitkopf and Haertel in Leipzig, but not until 1908, two years after the composer's death. The second symphony was issued by a Boston publisher, Arthur P. Schmidt, who deserves a monument for what he did to publish the larger orchestral works of our early composers. This second symphony is an attempt at program music. It bears the title *Spring*, and its first movement (like that of Raff's spring symphony, written one year before Paine's) is called *Nature's Awakening*. There are two motives, one "Winter" and the other "Awakening." The two conflict, and the strength of Winter fails. The second movement is *The May Night Fantasy*—the bassoon adds to the merriment. Then comes a Romance, *A Promise of Spring*, in rondo form; and the *finale* is a sort of hallelujah on *The Glory of Nature*.

Paine was much given to program music. At heart he was probably a romanticist, academic New Englander though he was. He wrote several symphonic poems inspired by Shakespeare. There was one to *The Tempest*, and an overture to *As You Like It*. The legend of *Poseidon and Aphrodite* inspired an "Ocean Fantasy." The *Island Fantasy* grew from his admiration for two paintings of the Isles of Shoals, New Hampshire, by J. Appleton Brown. The contrasting themes of the music suggest the dangers and the beauty of the sea.

Paine's opera *Azara* never reached dramatic performance, although it had a concert performance with piano accompaniment in 1903, and another in 1907 by the Cecilia Society of Boston, with orchestra, chorus, and soloists, conducted by B. J. Lang. It is said that there was a plan to produce *Azara* at the Metropolitan during Conried's regime, but the idea was abandoned because it was impossible to find a contralto or bass who could sing well enough in English to manage the leading roles.

Paine wrote his own libretto for *Azara*, a fact which may be responsible for its failure to gain performance. The dramatic action is a bit heavy and ponderous, and from a theatrical standpoint not particularly effective. As for the music, Paine knew how to write for voices; and the ballet music and the three Moorish dances from the score were frequently played on orchestral programs. There were traces of Wagner in the music, which show that Paine had changed his opinions of the great German. He was at first firm with the Boston clique that could see nothing of good in Wagner or his work, and his gradual awakening to his error did away with much of the pedantry of his own music.

As a professor, there are many traditions about Paine. Some of his pupils have told me that his teaching was as dry as the dust, and that they could find no inspiration in his classes. Others speak loyally of the grand old man, and what he did for them. Probably if he had not been academic, even to the point of dryness, he would never have been tolerated in a nineteenth-century university. If his courses had not been conducted according to the rigid classroom standards of the day, he might have failed in the same way that MacDowell failed to gain the support of the authorities some years later at Columbia.

List the names of his pupils in composition, and you cannot deny his influence, for good or for bad, on the native music of our day. The roster reads like a Who's Who of composers—Arthur Foote, Louis A. Coerne, Clayton Johns, Frederick S. Converse, John Alden Carpenter, Daniel Gregory Mason, *ad infinitum*.

It was Paine's own idea that he teach at Harvard. Shortly after his return from Europe he had been appointed organist and music director of the university, and he offered to give free of charge, a series of lectures on musical form. There was opposition, chiefly because it was a new idea, but he was finally allowed to lecture. No credit toward a degree was given for attendance, and few students came to hear him. Then Charles Eliot became president, and the lectures were started again in 1870. Paine also offered a course in harmony, which became popular, and then a course in counterpoint. For none of this early work did he receive any salary. In a very few years so many pupils were taking the courses that the work had to be recognized officially. Paine was made an assistant professor in 1873, and two years later he was given a full professorship, and his students were granted credit for their work in the music department.

This has led gradually to the Music School at Harvard, where there are courses in applied music, and in music as one of the arts. The Harvard curriculum has been a model for other universities to follow; and in the same way that Lowell Mason forced music into the public schools, John Knowles Paine was the pioneer in organized music courses in the American colleges. As a frontier composer when there were few of his kind, and as a prophet of music education, Paine's glory can never be dimmed merely because his music does not grip as it did thirty years ago.

There were other composers who came to the front in Paine's lifetime. Among them, WILLIAM WALLACE GILCHRIST (1846–1916), born in Jersey City. Gilchrist lived most of his life in Philadelphia. He had his training there at the hands of Hugh Clarke, the teacher who was appointed professor of music at the University of Pennsylvania in the same year Paine was awarded similar honors at Harvard (1875). Gilchrist was the organizer, and for forty years conductor, of the Philadelphia Mendelssohn Club. He led the old Philadelphia Symphony Orchestra which had been started by men from Gustav Hinrichs's Opera Company, and which was the ancestor of the present Philadelphia Orchestra. He was a vocal teacher and a choirmaster— an active career.

As a composer Gilchrist had an uncanny faculty for winning prizes. He was given a thousand dollars for his Psalm 46 at the 1882 Cincinnati Festival. The judges were Reinecke, Saint-Saëns, and Theodore Thomas. Before that, in 1878, the Abt Male Singing Society of Philadelphia had offered two prizes for choral works, and Gilchrist won both. Soon after this he won three more, awarded by the Mendelssohn Glee Club of New York.

He wrote a Symphony that was played by the Philadelphia Orchestra in 1910 under the composer's direction. Unlike Paine, Gilchrist attempted no program in this work. It was absolute music, pure and simple. The man had a facile technique, and the chief attribute of this symphony was its scholarliness. His second Symphony showed more individuality. He wrote a number of works for small combinations— a Nonet for piano, strings, flute, clarinet, and horn. It was a graceful piece of writing, not without a certain distinction. There was a Quintet for piano and strings, as well as a String Quartet and a Trio. Despite his success in choral fields, Gilchrist was in happier vein when he wrote for instruments. He was less banal, and not led into temptation by the bombastic poems of Mrs. Hemans, and others.

FREDERICK GRANT GLEASON (1848–1903) was a native of New England. Born in Middletown, Connecticut, he was taken to live in Hartford while he was still a boy. His father was an amateur musician, but it was not until the son, at sixteen, had written a *Christmas Oratorio*, without any instruction in harmony or counterpoint, that he was allowed to prepare himself for the profession of musician. He was then put to work with Dudley Buck, and later he went abroad to study with Moscheles, Richter, and others. He came back to Hartford, but when he was thirty he moved west to Chicago, where he spent the rest of his life as one of the city's prominent organists and musicians.

Gleason was a prolific composer. Tinged with Wagnerisms, he yet had something to say for himself. He sometimes had arguments with proofreaders and copyists for his harmonic innovations. He generally knew what he was about, and when copyists wrote "Fifths!" in the margin of his scores, he could reply, "Certainly!" His works were often played by Theodore Thomas, and Thomas never put anything on his programs that did not in his opinion belong there.

Gleason wrote a work for the World's Fair concerts, a *Processional of the Holy Grail*. The connection with Wagner was not altogether confined to the title. There was a symphonic poem *Edris*, based on a novel by Marie Corelli. Thomas played this with the Chicago Orchestra in 1896. He made a setting of *The Culprit Fay*, for chorus. He wrote a Piano Concerto, and his *Auditorium Festival Ode* was performed at the dedication of the Auditorium in Chicago. Another orchestral tone poem *Song of Life* was presented by the Chicago Orchestra in 1900.

Gleason wrote a number of operas; some of them have never been known, for he left a clause in his will that their scores should not be examined until he had been dead for fifty years. One of his operas, *Otho Visconti*, was produced at the College Theatre, Chicago, in 1907. Excerpts from its score had been played before. The overture was performed in Leipzig in 1892, and Thomas presented it at the Chicago World's Fair. In *Montezuma*, another opera, Gleason used the Wagnerian system of leit-motifs. One of its soprano arias was sung in concert on several occasions, but the opera itself was never produced.

Probably Gleason's handicap was that his intellect was not properly balanced by his emotions. He was more of a harmonist than a melodist, and his harmonic combinations were the product of his mind rather than of his feelings. Yet the intellectuals command respect, and Gleason had his place in our music.

In some ways SILAS GAMALIEL PRATT (1846–1916) narrowly missed being another Father Heinrich. He certainly conceived ideas on a no less colossal scale than Heinrich had. But Pratt had a really thorough training, and though he did make himself ridiculous at times, there was something solid beneath all the bombast that he mistook for grandeur. Like others, Pratt wanted to be a nationalist, and turned to native subjects for his titles, if not for his mode of expressing them. The names of his symphonic works read like the chapter headings of a school history: *Paul Revere's Ride;* a *Fantasy* in which hostile themes depict the battles between North and South; *The Battle of Manila;* a *Lincoln* Symphony; and *A Tragedy of the Deep,* on the sinking of the steamship *Titanic.*

He wrote cantatas and operas—one of them *Zenobia, Queen of Palmyra,* first given in concert form in Chicago (1882), and a year later in full dramatic production in both New York and Chicago. *Antonio,* later called *Lucille,* was performed in Chicago in 1887. *The Triumph of Columbus* was intended to be his greatest work. It was written for the fourth centennial of the discovery of America, and produced in New York in 1892.

Pratt was a go-getter who would have warmed the heart of any sales manager. In youth his ambition to be a musician was thwarted by poverty, for as a boy he had to earn his living, and he worked in a music store in Chicago. He kept at his studies in music, and finally saved up enough money to go to Europe. When he was twenty-two he went to Germany and studied the piano under Bendel and Kullak, and composition with Kiel.

He came back to Chicago in 1872, but the effects of the fire were still apparent, and Pratt had to go back behind the counter of the music store. But not for long. He had some pupils, and after a while he gave some concerts, and then went back to Germany. To make up for lost time he practiced hours at a time, so frantically that he injured his wrists permanently. He went to Bayreuth in 1875, met Liszt, and gave a recital of his own pieces at Weimar.

He went to Berlin in 1876, and conducted a performance of his own *Centennial Overture.* Later he played it at the Crystal Palace in London while Grant, former President, was guest of honor. Home again for symphony concerts in Chicago, and the production of *Zenobia.*

Then back to Europe in 1885 for a performance of his *Prodigal Son* Symphony at the Crystal Palace.

For fourteen years after 1888 he lived and taught in New York. Then he moved to Pittsburgh, where he established in 1906 a musical institute. All of his training and all this imagination should have produced something far more lasting than Pratt was able to achieve. Maybe his ambition got the better of him, and he tried too much. If courage and industry were all that were required for immortality, Pratt would have been another Wagner. (In fact, he once generously proclaimed that the immortal Richard was the Silas G. Pratt of Europe.) Unfortunately, more was needed, and stability and the spark of genius were missing from the make-up of a man who had the initiative and the ability to make his work known and heard in high places.

2. THE BOSTON GROUP

John K. Paine lived to see a group of composers active in his native New England—a few men who are generally classed together because they have lived and worked side by side, and because they have something in common artistically. Yet the relationship is one of sympathy and background, rather than of any particular traits of style that mark their music. They were all the product of the same age—a time when the American composer was first having a respectful and interested hearing—and when all the musical world was under the spell of the German romanticists. These New Englanders are often called the Boston classicists, or the New England academics, yet neither term is quite accurate. None of them departed far from accepted paths, nor ventured into startling experiments of his own, yet to call a man an academic or a classicist is, after all, a rather arbitrary pigeonholing. It is safer to group these composers for their geographical kinship, and maybe for comradeship, and to let it go at that.

Paine's mantle as dean of our composers fell upon GEORGE W. CHADWICK (1854–1931). Arthur Foote was a year older, but Chadwick was the more significant. Historically, his importance lies in carrying on where Paine left off. Paine was one of the first to win respect, to write music that was practicable and playable. Chadwick added a spark of genuine inspiration; he had a sense of humor. He makes us chuckle, and he makes us think. And while we are thinking, he warms our emotions—even though he seldom thrills us. He had all of Paine's substance and more—in his scholarship he was indeed an academic—but he added life to the forms he used, and gave us something vital.

Tradition has it that Chadwick wistfully confided to his friends that he determined his career when he turned toward Munich and sought Rheinberger as a master, instead of going to César Franck in Paris. Maybe he had his regrets, for the Belgian was a great teacher, but it is hard to imagine Chadwick's Yankee thoughts robed in the mysticism of a Franck disciple. In many ways Chadwick was typically the American in his music—at any rate, a Yankee. Not from use of folk songs, or by choosing Niagara Falls or the life of George Washington for his subjects (which he didn't), but by something far subtler, something he could never have avoided even if he had tried very hard. Philip Hale described it as "a certain jaunty irreverence, a snapping of the fingers at Fate and the Universe," and it is no doubt this delicious impertinence that is genuinely American. None but a Yankee can say such things and get away with it.

In the spring of 1930 there were at least two festivals to mark Chadwick's fiftieth anniversary as a composer, dating his career from the time when he came back from Germany and his apprenticeship. The New England Conservatory in Boston, where he had been director for thirty-three years, and the Eastman School in Rochester, honored the deacon of our composers with festival concerts of his music. In Boston the final number was the *Rip Van Winkle* Overture which Chadwick had conducted at the May Festival of the Handel and Haydn Society in 1880. The 1930 audience found much of the charm left in a work that the Leipzig *Musikalisches Wochenblatt* had fifty years before found possessed of "interesting traits which reflect an emotional life of personal cast."

Chadwick was born in Lowell, Massachusetts, November 13, 1854. He was of New England stock on both sides of his family tree. Orthodox, devout Congregationalists. His mother died when she gave him birth, and he was placed in the care of relatives until he was three. Then his father married again, and had a wife who could take care of little George. The father was a good musician, and in his spare time taught a singing class and organized a chorus and an orchestra in the neighborhood. He prospered in his business; first a farmer, he had gone to Lowell to become a machinist; then moving down to Lawrence in 1860, when George was six, he started a life and fire insurance company. When Boston was devastated by fire in 1872, the citizens of Lawrence flocked to Chadwick for policies.

Music always held George Chadwick in its spell. The musical gatherings of his relatives were the high spots of his childhood. His older brother Fitz Henry had had piano lessons, so he taught George to play, and together they learned the four-hand arrangements of the Beethoven Symphonies. Then George played the organ in church, and when he was graduated from high school he was allowed to take regular trips to Boston for piano lessons. He went into his father's business, and worked there until he was twenty-one. He had some lessons at the New England Conservatory, and studied harmony with Stephen A. Emery.

In 1876 he decided to teach music himself, and had an appointment as music professor of Olivet College. From this he saved money to go abroad. Then came opposition from his God-fearing father. Teaching was one thing, especially in a college, but to have an out-and-out professional musician in the family was a quite different matter. Anyway, the insurance business was making money, and likely to make considerably more. But George had decided to go, and George went.

He arrived in Berlin in the fall of 1877, and tried studying with Karl August Haupt. But Haupt was not to Chadwick's liking, for he wanted teaching in orchestration, which Haupt confessed he could not give him. He went to Leipzig where he worked with Jadassohn. Others have called Jadassohn's classes a joke, but the teacher took a personal interest in Chadwick, and would often give him lessons at his house. He offered his pupil training in counterpoint that gave him the command of his choral style, a polyphonic freedom that makes voices of orchestral choirs. With Jadassohn for teacher he wrote the *Rip Van Winkle* Overture, and two String Quartets.

Chadwick was not quite satisfied after two years with Jadassohn. He felt there was something more to learn, somewhere, before he went back to Boston. He chose Rheinberger (instead of Franck), and in Munich he learned the power of self-criticism. Rheinberger knew how to build on what Chadwick had already learned, and he gave him what Carl Engel has termed "an orderly idea of strict composition." The straightforwardness of the German pedants was surely more suited to the expression of Yankee ideas than the subtleties of the Frenchmen.

He came back home in 1880, where he rented a studio and hung his sign on the door as teacher. Horatio Parker was one of his first pupils; Sidney Homer and Arthur Whiting soon joined his class. He conducted choral societies, and was a church organist for seventeen years. In 1882 he was made an instructor at the New England Conservatory, and fifteen years later he was asked to be its director. He held that position until his death, April 4, 1931.

Chadwick composed twenty major works for orchestra; eleven of them are published. Of his six chamber music compositions, three have been issued in printed form. This fifty per cent record does credit to the music, and says something in behalf of the American publisher. Orchestral works in Chadwick's prime were scarcely a commercial enterprise. The thirteen dollars he received in 1886 from the Boston Symphony Orchestra, for performance of a movement from his second symphony, established a new precedent.

Three of the orchestral works were symphonies and one was a sinfonietta. All but the first symphony, written in 1882, are published. The overture was a form that offered him a happy chance to express his notions. He composed six of them: *Rip Van Winkle* (1879); *Thalia* (1883); *The Miller's Daughter* (1884); *Melpomene* (1891); *Adonais* (1899); and *Euterpe* (1906). The works that show his jauntiness and carefree spirit most effectively are *A Vagrom Ballad* (No. 4 of his *Symphonic Sketches*, 1907), and the symphonic ballad *Tam o' Shanter* (1917). The *Suite Symphonique* won first prize in the 1911 competition of the National Federation of Music Clubs.

The chamber music list included five string quartets and a piano quintet. The Kneisels played some of these on a number of occasions. Engel [1] wrote of his treatment of the strings:

Chadwick does not lose himself in mere juggling with patterns when he writes for competing strings, nor is he preoccupied with questionable experi-

[1] Carl Engel, *George W. Chadwick* (*Musical Quarterly*, July, 1924).

ments in sonorities that go against the nature of the instrument. He loves a cantilena and is capable of endowing it with enough breath to let it sing its way calmly through all the registers from the E-string of the violin to the C-string of the 'cello.

Chadwick tried his hand at opera, yet his dramatic powers were more devoted to the narratives of his orchestral ballads. The lyric drama *Judith* was performed in concert form at the Worcester Festival in 1901. *Tabasco*, a comic opera, was first given professionally at the Boston Museum in 1894. There are also *The Padrone*, an opera, and *Love's Sacrifice*, an operetta, both to libretti of David Stevens, as well as incidental music to Walter Browne's morality play *Everywoman*.

Chadwick attained distinction as a composer of choral works. His *Dedication Ode* was written for the dedication of the Hollis Street Church in 1886. He made a setting of Harriet Monroe's *Ode* for the opening concert of the World's Fair in Chicago (1893); *Phœnix Expirans* (1892) was written for the Springfield (Massachusetts) Festival, of which he was the conductor for a number of years, as he was of the Worcester Festival also. *Ecce jam Noctis*, for men's voices, organ, and orchestra was written for the Yale commencement exercises in 1897; and the *Noël*, a pastoral for soli, chorus, and orchestra was first produced at the Norfolk (Connecticut) Festival in 1908.

He published over a hundred songs, and his setting of Sidney Lanier's *Ballad of Trees and the Master* ranks as a classic. It is in the folklike ballad that he was happiest as a song writer. Not the lyric ballad of the sentimentalists, but the true ballad that demands musical dramatization.

It is the fashion today to turn our backs to Chadwick and his colleagues, past and present. And it may be true that our recent composers make our earlier writers seem tame by comparison. Yet there is a steadiness in Chadwick's music that is always dependable, a freshness that is a matter of spirit rather than of style or idiom. After all, modernity is youth, and of youthfulness Chadwick had his full share. The man himself was far older than his music.

Arthur William Foote (1853–1937) did not go abroad for study; in fact, it was not until he had been graduated from Harvard, when he was twenty-one, that he definitely made up his mind to be a musician. He had taken J. K. Paine's music courses in college, and had been conductor of the Harvard Glee Club. After he was graduated, he decided to pass a useful summer before going into business, so he had some organ lessons with B. J. Lang. Lang gave him so much encouragement that Foote decided then and there that music should be his profession. For two years more he studied organ and piano with Lang, and in 1876 he started on his own as a piano teacher. He was one of the prominent teachers of the Boston district for over sixty years.

He had shown little interest in music as a boy. He was born in Salem, and his Anglo-Saxon parents were not musically inclined. When he was fourteen, he was given some piano lessons as part of a general education. He soon found that he liked to play, and his curiosity led him to take a few harmony lessons with Stephen Emery before he entered Harvard. Then when he went to college, and found Paine conducting courses in music, he was one of the most eager of the students.

From 1878 until 1910, Foote was organist of the First Unitarian Church in Boston. He helped found the American Guild of Organists, and was at one time its president. Other than these, he held few regular positions, but was active as a free-lance teacher, pianist, and organist, giving many piano recitals and often playing chamber music with the Kneisel, and other quartets. He lived to be eighty-four years old, and only a few months before his death, April 9, 1937, he was present to acknowledge from the platform the applause that greeted the performance of his Suite in E for Strings, by the Boston Symphony.

Like the other composers of his early days, he reflected his likes and dislikes in music of the masters. The Brahmsian flavor of such pieces as his Quintet for piano and strings shows that in the nineties he was a progressive, interested in the thoughts of the post-romanticists. He called himself a conservative, but admiration of Brahms was by no means a conservative matter in the late Victorian era.

In his writing, Foote seems chiefly concerned with harmonic rather than with contrapuntal patterns. His scoring for male voices may owe its success to his glee club days at Harvard, when he acquired a fondness for chords in close formation, in the richness of the lower registers.

He wrote many works in the larger forms, eight for orchestra, five of which were published by Schmidt in Boston. *In the Mountains,* an overture, was first performed by the Boston Symphony under Gericke in 1887. It was repeated the following year. His *Serenade* in E, for strings, and his Suite in D, for string orchestra, had been played a year earlier. Foote took the episode of *Francesca da Rimini* from Dante for his symphonic prologue, probably his most distinguished work. Somewhat programmatic in its development, the music opens with an introduction that seems to be a long, deep sigh, followed by the shrieking and shuddering of the poor damned souls in inferno. The first theme, in its passion, seems to be Francesca's recital of her love story; the other themes and their development weave a dramatic and tragic tale of love and retribution.

Francesca was first performed in Boston in 1893. In the same year Theodore Thomas played the *Serenade* for strings at the World's Fair. Foote said that it was due to the interest of Thomas that his orchestral works were given a hearing. In 1894, Thomas conducted a performance of his Concerto for cello and orchestra (with Bruno Steindel as soloist) at one of the concerts of the Chicago Symphony Orchestra, then in its fourth season. After 1900 he composed only two works for orchestra: a Suite in E, for strings (1910), and *Four Character Pieces after Omar Khayyám* (1912).

Of his eight major works for chamber music combinations, only one is unpublished. Most of them had their first performances at concerts of the Kneisel Quartet; the G Minor Violin Sonata in 1890; the Piano Quartet, Opus 23 in the following year; the String Quartet in E, 1894; the Quintet in 1898, and the Piano Trio in B flat, 1909. In his Sonatas for violin and piano, and in the *Ballade,* Opus 69, Foote wrote in a broad style with an epic, narrative unfolding of theme and development.

There are a number of choral works with orchestra—*The Farewell of Hiawatha,* for men's voices (1886), and others for mixed voices—*The Wreck of the Hesperus* (1888), and *The Skeleton in Armor* (1893). He composed many works for chorus *a cappella* or with piano accompaniment, and a great deal of church music. In his many piano pieces and in his songs he wrote idiomatic music, playable and singable, of generally high taste, showing discretion and restraint in gaining intended effects. He was always sincere and genuine, and rarely if ever the sentimentalist when he was tender. He composed two suites for piano, three pieces for left hand alone, five poems after Omar Khayyám, and some thirty other piano pieces. There are almost one hundred and fifty songs, many from the English poets—Herrick, Marlowe, Shakespeare. Among the best known are *I'm Wearing Awa', The Lake Isle of Innesfree, On the Way to Kew, It Was a Lover and his Lass, O Swallow, Flying South,* and *Irish Folk Song.* He published over thirty works for organ, most important being the Suite in D Major.

Foote followed in the paths of others from abroad greater than himself, but the modest, retiring gentleman nevertheless made a handsome contribution to American music. He was substantial, reliable, workmanlike, and, most important, agreeable. As a writer in *The Art of Music* puts it, "His music is the pure and perfectly formed expression of a nature at once refined and imaginative." He belonged to the Boston of the nineties, where most of the composers of that time worked and met each other for exchange of ideas—Chadwick, Parker, Whiting, MacDowell, Nevin, Mrs. Beach, Converse, Johns, and their artistic parent John K. Paine. He saw the musical idols of one period after another thrown down and broken. Why, in his later years, should he have become excited over Schoenberg or Stravinsky? As an early devotee of Brahms and Wagner, he had his fill of innovations in his youth. He at least had the satisfaction of knowing that confidence in his early Gods was well placed.

If HORATIO WILLIAM PARKER (1863–1919) had been as successful in his symphonic works as he was in his choral writings, he might in his time have been the greatest of our American composers. There are some who think he was, anyway. Certainly he produced outstanding works—the oratorio *Hora Novissima* may be mentioned in the same breath with Franck's *Beatitudes,* and the intelligentsia went so far as to class the opera *Mona* with *Salomé* and *Pelléas et Mélisande.* Parker was a composer who derived from a background of Puritan hymn singing, with a German training superimposed; yet the influences that shaped his style never prevented his being individual. His music was generally his own; even today, some of his passages have a modern sound.

Parker never achieved the popular fame of MacDowell, or some others of our American composers. He wrote few little tunes that may be taught to school children in music memory contests, or small piano pieces that are played by amateurs. His songs and smaller pieces are the least fortunate of his works, and the least distinctive. Besides, his operas are known today only to those who take the trouble to read the scores. That *Mona* was never repeated after four performances in its first season is a blot on the history of New York's Metropolitan Opera House. In many ways it is the finest music drama that has been written in this country.

He was primarily a composer for musicians, yet many of his passages can thrill layman and musician alike. His hatred of anything weak or sentimental made much of his music angular and austere, yet there is a fine emotional appeal in page after page of his scores.

Parker was born of a cultured family. His mother, Isabella Parker, the daughter of a Baptist minister, was a scholar and a musician, organist of the village church at Auburndale, Massachusetts, the town where Horatio was born September 15, 1863. His father, Charles Edward Parker, was an architect. Fine old English stock on both sides of the family, steeped in a New England heritage that had its Puritan phases. As a child Horatio went further than just not being musically inclined—he disliked anything connected with music. His mother often wondered how she could get him to take any interest in it. Suddenly, when he was fourteen, he seemed to wake from his musical sleep and wanted to know all about it, how it was played, and how it was made. He had piano lessons from his mother, and then with local teachers. He started to compose, and in two days set to music fifty poems of Kate Greenaway, later published as songs for school children. At sixteen he was made organist of a church in Dedham, and for its services he wrote hymn-tunes, anthems, and choir services.

About this time Chadwick returned from Europe, and Parker became one of his first pupils. Chadwick writes: [2]

As my pupil he was far from docile. In fact, he was impatient of the restrictions of musical form and rather rebellious of the discipline of counterpoint and fugues. But he was very industrious and did his work faithfully and well. His lessons usually ended with his swallowing his medicine, but with many a wry grimace.

[2] George W. Chadwick, *Horatio Parker*, Yale University Press.

In 1882 he went to Europe, to Rheinberger in Munich, where he studied organ playing and composition at the Royal School of Music. By placing himself wholly in Rheinberger's hands, he acquired a contrapuntal mastery that helped him later to reach the summits of choral writing.

When he came back to America he settled in New York. He was put in charge of the music teaching at the Cathedral School in Garden City; he was organist at St. Andrew's and later at Holy Trinity; and he taught at the National Conservatory of Music in New York, where Antonin Dvořák was director. Seven years later, in 1893, he had a chance to return to his native Boston as organist and choirmaster of Trinity Church, then famous for the sermons of Phillips Brooks. In the next year he was invited to head the Music Department of Yale University at New Haven; and he held that position until his death in 1919.

While at Yale, Parker organized the New Haven Symphony Orchestra, subsidized by the University. For a comparison of our educational facilities with those of England, it is illuminating to read what *The Musical Times* (London, September 1, 1902) had to say about the Music Department at Yale:

Professor Parker teaches counterpoint, composition and instrumentation. He gives lectures on the history of music, and conducts six orchestral concerts every season. An additional orchestral concert is devoted chiefly to the compositions of the students. No anxiety is felt in regard to the financial result of these concerts. The orchestra is supported by the University as a laboratory for the Department of Music, where, as in a chemical laboratory, the students may, by means of their compositions, blow themselves up. Courses in orchestration are offered by the University, and common sense requires that the means of practical exemplification of the results of studies in such courses should be available. Where have we in old England, or even in Auld Reekie, anything to approach such a boon and privilege as is enjoyed by the students in music at Yale?

The same article tells of Parker's relations with the University, concluding its account with this felicitation:

Professor Parker enjoys a vacation of four months every year, and one year in every seven is a Sabbatical Year—twelve months' complete rest from his ordinary vocations! Who will say that his lot is not a happy one?

Nobody! But the poor man must have needed all the summer rest he could get, for his weekly routine would have killed a weaker man far sooner than it eventually killed Horatio Parker. He always had a church position in some city other than New Haven—first, Trinity in Boston, and later, St. Nicholas's in New York. He conducted choral societies in several cities. David Stanley Smith, his assistant at Yale and later his successor, recounts a typical Parker schedule in the *Musical Quarterly*, April, 1930:

Late Saturday afternoon, choir rehearsal in New York; Sunday, service morning and evening; Monday afternoon and evening in Philadelphia for rehearsals of the Eurydice and Orpheus Clubs; night train to New York, thence to New Haven for two classes on Tuesday; Tuesday evening, by trolley to Derby for a rehearsal of the Derby Choral Club, arriving in New Haven at midnight; Wednesday, a lecture on the History of Music and a class in composition; Thursday, again two classes; Thursday evening, rehearsal of the New Haven Oratorio Society; Friday morning, rehearsal of the New Haven Symphony Orchestra; Saturday, off again for New York.

And then Smith adds: "It seems incredible, but through this period Parker composed incessantly. There was always a score in the making." He found some time for recreation. He loved to ride his bicycle, and he played some golf with his friends. Without some out-of-doors life, he could have stood but a few years of such a grind.

Parker was quite the man of the world. Fastidious, immaculate, he commanded a social standing often denied musicians of his time. He had for his friends artists, writers, and men from the several professions—seldom musicians. He was at ease in talking on any subject; he could hold his own in prolonged discussions on topics far removed from music. His friends were fascinated by him; those who were not his friends feared him. His brusque manner frightened the timid, and he despised those who were afraid of him. In this he was something of the bully; he would often wilfully confuse his pupils in class, and then scoff at their confusion. But for those who stood on their two feet and talked back to him he had the profoundest admiration. His manner was a challenge which he expected would be met in kind. The wags of New Haven say it was a pleasure to be insulted by Horatio Parker, he could apologize so handsomely.

His life at home with his wife and daughters was in many ways ideal. His wife had been a fellow pupil abroad—Anna Plössl, the daughter of a Munich banker. Though he later hated the Germans, Parker loved this wife of his. His life was her only interest. When they were first married she taught pupils herself, so that they could meet their daily bills.

These personal traits are apparent in his music. He was intolerant of anything that was too easy, of anything facile. His horror of the obvious made him avoid repeating a phrase whenever he could keep from doing it. If an idea must be repeated, let it be changed in some detail. True enough, he was often trivial, so trivial that we may wonder whether he was not trying to force himself to write in a popular vein against his better judgment. But he was never cheaply superficial; his lighter moments were doubtless more studied and conscious than his more serious, happier efforts.

He wrote over forty works for chorus, religious and secular; two operas; nine pieces for orchestra (one published: an Organ Concerto); four chamber compositions (one, a Suite for trio, published); seven groups of pieces for organ; four for piano; and twelve sets of songs. Added to these, he wrote incidental music for a masque, and for a Yale commencement, and he acted as editor-in-chief for a graded series of songbooks for schools. He felt that when school children sang, they had a right to the best in music.

Hora Novissima was written in 1891–92, his Opus 30. While he was composing it, he was grieving for the loss of a sister and some other members of his family. The work of these years has a background of absolute sincerity where pathos is concerned. For the text of *Hora Novissima* he used the Latin hymn of Barnard de Morlaix; his mother made the English translation. Here, as in so many of his choral works, Parker shows his instinct for massed effects, for fine choral texture, for full development of hymnlike themes. Masculine, vital music, with often the sweep of the inevitable. Fugal writing and chant, contrasted with stunning effect.

Parker submitted *Hora Novissima* and a cantata *The Dream King and His Love*, Opus 31, in a prize contest at the National Conservatory in 1892. He won the prize, but not for *Hora Novissima*—the judges, including Dvořák, liked the *Dream King* better. *Hora Novissima* had its first performance in 1893 by the Church Choral Society of New

York at the Church of Zion and St. Timothy. The next year it was sung by the Handel and Haydn Society in Boston, and later at the Cincinnati Festival. In 1899 it was performed at the Three Choirs Festival at Worcester, England, and it made such an impression on the English audience that Parker was commissioned to write a new work for the Hereford Festival. This produced the *Wanderer's Psalm*; and the *Star Song* was written for the Norwich Festival in 1902.

His fame in England was almost greater than in America. The English have a warm place in their hearts for choral music, and Parker had enough of the Englishman in his blood to write what they liked best. *The Legend of St. Christopher*, sung at Bristol, completed all that was needed for an award of the Doctor of Music degree by Cambridge University in 1902. Like *Hora Novissima*, *St. Christopher* shows largeness of conception, breadth of structure; but it goes further, for it shows Parker trying some experiments in religious drama. He employs the leit-motif in Wagnerian fashion. It was possibly the writing of *St. Christopher* that led him to try opera a few years later.

Like many of his works, *Mona* was written for a definite purpose. Parker was able to do this, generally without sacrificing quality. Commissions, or prize contests, never drew hack work from him. The directors of the Metropolitan Opera House in New York offered a prize of $10,000 for an opera by an American composer, with an English text. Parker heard of the offer and was tempted. His friend Brian Hooker, professor of English at Yale, wrote the libretto—the tale of Mona, princess of Britain in the days of the invasion, torn between her love for the son of the Roman governor and her hatred of the Roman conquerors.

The judges (and his teacher Chadwick was one of them) agreed that no other decision was possible than to give the prize to *Mona*. The opera was produced March 14, 1912. There had been American operas at the Metropolitan before—Converse's *Pipe of Desire* in 1910 and Herbert's *Natoma* a year later (by the Philadelphia-Chicago Company)—but neither had made as profound an impression as *Mona*. The performance was inadequate, but the gravity and vitality of the music, its lovely blending with the words of the text, were apparent to all who heard it. Whatever the reasons, box office or politics, *Mona* was dropped after its first short season, and has never been heard again. Whether Gatti-Casazza and the directors of the opera house gave the work which they themselves had called into being a fair chance, is a question that seems almost to answer itself.

For *Mona* is truly a fine and a great work. Uneven, yes, but its unevenness is almost its charm. It is Parker's own music, rarely synthetic. While it is obviously written by a man who knows his choral writing best, its very churchliness often establishes precisely the right atmosphere. It has telling moments—Mona's narrative of her dream, the love duet, the prelude to the third act, the orchestral passage that follows Mona's killing of her lover. In *Mona*, Parker is Parker, and no one else.

A year or so later he wrote another opera; like *Mona* to a libretto by Hooker. Like *Mona*, it won a $10,000 prize. The work was *Fairyland*, and the prize was offered in 1913 by the National Federation of Music Clubs. The opera was performed six times in Los Angeles at the Federation Biennial in 1915. Lighter than *Mona*, *Fairyland* offers charming, unaffected music.

Of course, Parker was not primarily a composer for the stage, any more than he was a symphonist. His field was the oratorio and the choir loft. His orchestral conception seems often to be confused with his feeling for the tones and color combinations of the organ. His orchestra sometimes comes between his chorus and his hearers. Yet the music itself is large, healthy, alive, and probably enduring. Daniel Gregory Mason has described Parker's music as "so facile, and so voluminous, and on the whole so characterless." With this I cannot agree; at any rate in regard to those things by which we know him best. Undramatic, poor theatre, *Mona* may be; but never characterless. Parker's own character—strong willed, intolerant, individual—is stamped on every page of his major works.

I once asked Mrs. H. H. A. BEACH (1867–1944) if she ever resented being called an American composer. "No," she answered, "but I would rather be called a composer." I might have put it still stronger, and asked if she minded being known as an American woman composer. For whether we are to judge Mrs. Beach for her music alone, or for the added interest of her nationality and sex, the fact remains that she was the outstanding composer among American women, a highly talented and able creative musician.

Mrs. Beach was the youngest of the Boston group, the little sister who accomplished much on her own; who, as a youthful prodigy, caused the intolerant old John S. Dwight to scratch his head and to bow in admiration of her extraordinary gifts. She once fooled Dwight and his friend Otto Dresel. Neither of them could see much good in Brahms. One day the young pianist played them a *Capriccio* that had just come to America. They were enchanted; what was it? who wrote it? "Brahms," said the young Miss Cheney. Dwight and Dresel choked and muttered that it was the best thing he ever wrote.

When Theodore Thomas engaged her to play the Mendelssohn D Minor Concerto with his orchestra in Boston, she had to go to Worcester for rehearsal. Thomas was playing there the day before the Boston concert. She was seventeen at the time, and Thomas thought he would make things easy for her in the last movement. He started the orchestra at a leisurely tempo. At the entrance of the piano, the young artist started at her usual pace, and the startled Thomas had to follow.

Mrs. Beach was born September 5, 1867—Amy Marcy Cheney. Her birthplace was the little village of Henniker, New Hampshire, and her parents were New Englanders of colonial descent. She was musical from babyhood. She could sing songs when she was scarcely more than a year old, and her memory was so accurate that she always remembered a song exactly as she first heard it. She would rebel whenever she heard it sung differently. She was extremely sensitive to melody—anything sad or sentimental upset her. When she must be punished, her mother would play Gottschalk's *Last Hope*, instead of giving her a New England spanking.

Amy started to play the piano when she was four; two years later she had lessons. She insisted on having them from her mother, who was herself a singer and pianist. In a short time the child mastered *études* of Heller and Czerny, the Handel *Harmonious Blacksmith* Variations, several Beethoven Sonatas, some Chopin Waltzes, and Dresel's arrangements of Mendelssohn songs. And she had written some pieces of her own.

When she was eight the family moved to Boston, where instruction continued under various teachers—Ernst Perabo, Junius Hill, Carl Baermann. She had some harmony lessons with Hill when she was fourteen. Then she gave herself some training without outside help. She became so engrossed in her study of instrumentation that she made her own translation of treatises by Berlioz and Gavaert. At about this time her father and mother had to decide between Europe and America for their daughter's final education. They chose America.

She made her first public appearance in Boston when she was sixteen, and played the Moscheles G Minor Concerto with a symphony orchestra. The next year she was soloist with the Boston Symphony, and played the Chopin F Minor. Then she played Mendelssohn with Thomas. In 1885, when she was eighteen, she married Dr. Beach, a physician who achieved distinction as a surgeon and medical authority. Until his death in 1910, Mrs. Beach and her husband lived in Boston.

The year after Dr. Beach died, Mrs. Beach went to Europe to stay for almost four years, playing in concert and introducing her works in Germany. She played her own Piano Concerto with orchestras in Hamburg, Leipzig, and Berlin. Her *Gaelic* Symphony was heard in Hamburg and Leipzig, and she played the piano part of her Quintet, and the Sonata for violin and piano, in various cities. The years abroad were something of a triumph. Foreign critics were more than friendly —many of them reviewed her works with enthusiasm. She achieved an international standing.

Upon her return from abroad she busied herself with composing and playing in concert. She had an energy for work that seemed almost inexhaustible—and yet she was never hasty or feverish. She once wrote me that it seemed as if a century must separate the present from her earlier life, devoted mostly to composition in her own home, with only occasional concert appearances.

"I have literally lived the life of two people," she explained, "one a pianist, the other a writer. Anything more unlike than the state of mind demanded by these two professions I could not imagine! When I do one kind of work, I shut the other up in a closed room and lock the door, unless I happen to be composing for the piano, in which case there is a connecting link. One great advantage, however, in this kind of life, is that one never grows stale, but there is always a continual interest and freshness from the change back and forth.

"My outdoor summer life is another story, and a most delightful one. Life in the woods is my greatest joy, with my friends and all that they have meant to me in these past years."

Mrs. Beach is best known to the layman for her songs—*Ah, Love, but a Day, The Year's at the Spring,* and *Ecstasy.* She composed over a hundred and fifty songs, but these named are the most sung, and in many ways her best song writing, for they are direct, free from the fondness for overelaboration that she often indulged. Musicians know her by her instrumental works. She published the *Gaelic* Symphony, a Piano Concerto, a Violin and Piano Sonata, a Quintet for piano and strings, a Theme and Variations for flute and string quartet, and a Suite for two pianos, founded on old Irish melodies. In addition, there are suites and many individual pieces for piano.

She was fond of writing music for the church. Her first important work (Opus 5) was a Mass, for soli, chorus, orchestra, and organ, which was first performed by the Handel and Haydn Society under Zerrahn in 1892. There are a number of anthems, and a complete Episcopal service.

She was commissioned to write a work for the dedication of the Woman's Building at the Chicago World's Fair, and she composed a *Festival Jubilate* in six weeks. In 1898 she wrote a *Song of Welcome* for the Trans-Mississippi Exposition at Omaha, and in 1915 a *Panama Hymn* for the Panama-Pacific Exposition in San Francisco.

She used folk songs in many of her works—the *Gaelic* Symphony is made from Gaelic themes. Yet she never felt that she was writing nationalistic music when she used national songs. She merely adapted for her own purposes melodies she happened to like. With her, nationalism was something subtler than using Indian or other tunes found in America—Americanism was something that could not be acquired by thinking about it. She used bird calls, Eskimo songs, Balkan themes, anything that happened to appeal to her. But she was not an Eskimo, or a Balkan, and she knew she was not writing Eskimo or Balkan music.

This theory is typical of the common-sense attitude she had in regard to many things, notably her music. She wrote sincerely, according to her thoughts, and she had the technical equipment to express those thoughts fluently. She lived to be seventy-seven years old, and died in New York, December 27, 1944.

3. EDWARD MACDOWELL (1861–1908)

I

In *Lonely Americans*, Rollo Walter Brown calls MacDowell "A Listener to the Winds." An apt characterization, for MacDowell was at heart a romanticist, at his best as a poet of nature. He caught the moods of the forest, the fields, and the ocean. He could express those moods in a way that made us understand what he was talking about. He was the first of the Americans to speak consistently a musical speech that was definitely his own.

It is not an easy matter to appraise MacDowell fairly in his relation to American music, or to the music of the world. Whenever American music is mentioned, the name of MacDowell comes forward immediately as the foremost of our composers. Yet there are many doubters who ask embarrassing questions. Does he loom largest because he was the greatest in his own time, when there were fewer good composers in America? Perhaps he would be less significant in company with those who would be his colleagues if he were living today. And, as for the rest of the musical world, has he held his own with Grieg, with whom he can best be compared, musically and temperamentally?

These are questions on which there can be many opinions. Some think that much music has been written in America since MacDowell's time which is fully as distinctive as that of MacDowell—maybe more distinctive. Since there are hundreds of well-equipped, talented composers today, against the dozen or so of MacDowell's time, we do not hear as much of individuals as we did of MacDowell. And as for Grieg, many feel that the Norwegian's star is constantly rising, while MacDowell's is gradually setting.

MacDowell's reputation today is somewhat in the same situation as that of his lesser brother artist, Nevin. There is always a penalty to be paid for remaining long in the public esteem. When we produce a famous artist in this country he must be idealized by his disciples, and belittled by his opponents. Common-sense appraisal is all too rare in the case of public heroes. And so with MacDowell—he must be a world master in the eyes of some, an overrated Pigmy to others.

Shortly after MacDowell's death, Lawrence Gilman in his revised edition of the biography he had first written in 1905 stated that he knew of no piano sonatas since the death of Beethoven that could compare with the four of MacDowell for passion, dignity, and breadth of style.

Paul Rosenfeld, writing in 1929 on *American Music*, devotes an early chapter to MacDowell.[1] A few quotations will suffice:

Were it not for MacDowell's celtic descent, one might almost be tempted to attribute this group-wide weakness for the odors of sanctity to a racial strain, so many instances arising in which saxondom and snobbery . . . seem almost synonymous. . . . In music, this weakness took the form of sentimentality. The feelings entertained about life by him seem to have remained uncertain; and while fumbling for them he seems regularly to have succumbed to "nice" and "respectable" emotions, conventional, accepted by and welcome to, the best people. It is shocking to find how full of vague poesy he is. Where his great romantic brethren, Brahms, Wagner, and Debussy, are direct and sensitive, clearly and tellingly expressive, MacDowell minces and simpers, maidenly and ruffled. He is nothing if not a daughter of the American revolution. . . .

And still, MacDowell brought something into the world not hitherto present in it; not, at least, as music. Impure in style and weak in spirit though they are; indeed of anything but the first water, a group of his compositions, particularly the ballade-like Norse sonata, certain of the more vigorous Sea Pieces, and the atmospheric Legend and Dirge of the Indian Suite for Orchestra, *actually have musical value* [the italics are mine]. . . . They constitute a beginning. And nature does nothing by bounds.

Somewhere between these two views there must be middle ground. It is surely too much to term MacDowell the composer of the greatest piano sonatas since Beethoven, nor can he be dismissed lightly as a mere beginner, whom we may patronize and pat gently on the back. Moreover, he was far from musically polite to the best people—when he came back from Europe in the late eighties his playing and his compositions were the dismay of many correct Bostonians.

There are a few important points that may be disposed of at the start. MacDowell need never be put forward with the chauvinism he

[1] Paul Rosenfeld, *An Hour with American Music*, J. B. Lippincott & Co.

hated so heartily himself. He is probably the first of our creative musicians for whom we need make no allowances for lack of early training. None of his limitations was caused by his being an American. Whether he shall eventually be judged great or small, he may be considered simply as a composer, without our being kind to him because he was our countryman. And after we have put him under the magnifying glass, stripped him of the idealization that has been wrapped about him by admirers more zealous than wise, he will emerge with several of his banners still flying.

II

If there must be comparisons, and it is often necessary to have a place to hang our opinions, Grieg and MacDowell have enough in common to warrant our looking at them side by side. Their artistic statures are comparable. Each had a style that is easily recognized. Both had a feeling for melodic and harmonic combinations that were individual. Each has had a host of imitators—so many that the terms "MacDowellian" and "Grieg-like" have become generic.

There are, of course, essential differences. One is strong where the other is weak. MacDowell seeks a broader pattern than Grieg in his sonatas, but in seeking breadth he sometimes grows diffuse. Grieg can accomplish more with fewer means. MacDowell is more heroic in his conception; when Grieg grows dramatic he seldom achieves effects that are more than theatrical. In his F Major Violin Sonata, Grieg is compact, to the point, vital in every phrase. In the C Minor there is more abandon, but not the closeknit perfection of the lesser work Grieg's single Piano Sonata cannot compare in breadth of conception with any of the four that MacDowell wrote, yet Grieg shows more control of his medium, a far more distinct utterance.

Both are best as miniaturists. In larger works they come to frequent climaxes, and then make a fresh start. They are short breathed. Their themes are episodic in their treatment and development. Intense individualists, each limited the scope of his appeal.

For MacDowell did indeed pay a high price for his individuality. Markedly original, he guarded his manner of speech jealously. In his latter years he often told his friends that he avoided hearing music, so that he would not be in danger of showing its influence. Possibly this explains the limitations of his own music, for all composers derive from some source. If they are great they add something of their own to the pattern of their predecessors; the fact that they were influenced does not in itself prevent them from saying something new.

It would be interesting to gather statistics that would show how kind the years have been to MacDowell and Grieg. Without them, and it would be impossible to make them accurate, comparison is mere guesswork. Surely the sparkling though shallow Piano Concerto of Grieg is more played today than either of those MacDowell wrote. Probably this may be explained by the fewer difficulties of Grieg's Concerto. MacDowell wrote nothing for orchestra that is heard as often as Grieg's *Peer Gynt* Suites, for the MacDowell orchestral works are not appearing on programs as often as they did twenty years ago. Yet in the field of the piano, MacDowell's pieces seem to be holding their own—especially the smaller ones. The sonatas, particularly the *Tragica*, are considerably played on recital programs, and amateur pianists and pupils still play the *Woodland Sketches*, a few of the virtuoso *études*, the *Sea Pieces*, and many others of a type in which MacDowell was altogether inimitable. Certainly his music today is more familiar to the music-loving public than that of any other American composer of serious music. Whether his works are as familiar as Grieg's is another matter, and not particularly important.

And then, the nationalist question. Was MacDowell an American composer in his idiom? Many say that he was more Celtic than American—his German training with Raff made him follow Teuton models. An obvious contradiction here, for it is apparent to anyone that German training (and he was educated in Paris before he went to Germany) did not kill the obvious Celtic traits in his music. What is an American, anyway? Aren't we all Scotch-Americans, Irish-Americans, English-Americans, German-Americans, Jewish-Americans, or whatever our ancestry may be? MacDowell's ancestry was Scotch—he himself was an American. If he showed Scotch tendencies in his music, was his work any the less American?

In his lectures at Columbia (some of these since published as *Critical and Historical Essays*),[2] MacDowell himself disposed of nationalism in music:

---

[2] Edward MacDowell, *Critical and Historical Essays*, Arthur P. Schmidt Co.

. . . nationalism, so-called, is merely an extraneous thing that has no part in pure art. For if we take any melody, even of the most pronounced national type, and merely eliminate the characteristic turns, affectations, or mannerisms, the theme becomes simply music, and retains no touch of nationality. We may even go further; for if we retain the characteristic mannerisms of dress, we may harmonize a folk song in such a manner that it will belie its origin, and by means of this powerful factor (an essentially modern invention) we may even transform a Scotch song, with all its "snap" and character, into a Chinese song, or give it an Arabian flavour.

Of course, he wrote an *Indian Suite* for orchestra, in which he used Indian themes, but I think he never seriously thought he was writing American music just because he used Indian melodies. He once said to Hamlin Garland: "I do not believe in 'lifting' a Navajo theme and furbishing it into some kind of a musical composition and calling it American music. Our problem is not so simple as all that."

Then again, in a lecture, he said: "What we must arrive at is the youthful optimistic vitality and the undaunted tenacity of spirit that characterizes the American man. That is what I hope to see echoed in American music."

As for the music MacDowell left us, Mr. Rosenfeld is correct in saying that it is not of the first water, if we mean by that the music of a Bach, a Beethoven, a Wagner, or a Brahms. But as one of the best of the lesser poets, MacDowell produced music of the first order, some of it charming, some of it stirring. Within its limitations, it is the work of a truly creative genius. Between the opus numbers 9 and 62, which include the bulk of his published work, there is much that will live for many years to come. Some of his music may have fallen by the wayside, but the best of it is still vital.

III

It is by his piano music that we know him best. There are four Sonatas: the *Tragica*, Opus 45 (1893); the *Eroica*, Opus 50 (1895); the *Norse*, Opus 57 (1900); and the *Keltic*, Opus 59 (1901). The last two were dedicated to Grieg, who acknowledged the dedication of the *Norse* Sonata with a charming attempt at English:

MY DEAR SIR:

Will you permit me in bad English to express my best thanks for your kind letter and for the simpathi you feel for my music. Of course it will be a great honor and pleasure for me to accept your dedication.

Some years ago I thought it possible to shake hands with you in your own country. But unfortunately my delicat health does not seem to agree. At all events, if we are not to meet, I am glad to read in the papers of your artistical success in Amerika.

MacDowell once said that if a composer's ideas do not imperatively demand treatment in the sonata form, if his first theme is not actually dependent upon his second and side themes for its poetic fulfillment, he has composed a potpourri rather than a sonata. Certainly Mac-Dowell has lived up to this principle in his own sonatas, for in each of them the themes are related and dependent on each other. There is always a nobility of conception, and an impatience with the limits of the piano that leads him to seek orchestral effects.

There was no definite program suggested in the *Tragica* Sonata, but the music itself is sufficiently vivid to enable the listener to understand what kind of thoughts the composer was thinking when he wrote it. MacDowell said that in the first three movements he aimed to express tragic details, and in the *Finale* a generalization—"to heighten the darkness of tragedy by making it follow closely on the heels of triumph." He probably wrote the third movement first—the *Largo*; for he played it in Boston at a recital in 1891, two years before the work as a whole was published. There is a beautiful dignity in this movement, a pathos which never sinks to bathos. He shows an artistic kinship with Rachmaninoff; there is a similar feeling for chordal effects between the younger Russian and the American.

The *Eroica* Sonata (dedicated to William Mason) bears the motto "*Flos regum Arthurus.*" Though admittedly program music, Mac-Dowell intended it to be less of an actual depiction of the subject than a commentary. He had in mind the Arthur legend. The first movement was the coming of Arthur. The *Scherzo* suggested a knight in the woods surrounded by elves. MacDowell's conception of Guinevere was the basis of the third movement, and the last was the passing of Arthur.

In the *Norse* Sonata MacDowell attempted to free himself further from the restrictions of form. In painting the barbaric feeling of the Norse sagas he extended the span of his phrases, his chord formations widened, and he achieved a still more epic breadth.

The fourth Sonata was the *Keltic*, to which he attached these lines:

> Who minds now Keltic tales of yore,
> Dark Druid rhymes that thrall;
> Deirdré's song, and wizard lore
> Of great Cuchullin's fall.

MacDowell wrote of this sonata:

Like the third, this fourth sonata is more of a "bardic" rhapsody on the subject than an attempt at actual presentation of it, although I have made use of all the suggestion of tone-painting in my power—just as the bard would have reinforced *his* speech with gesture and facial expression.

And it is true that MacDowell's music does heighten the meaning of the poem. He felt that a poem was far more valuable as a suggestion for instrumental music than as the text of a song, where syllables are generally distorted. As a text for an instrumental work, a poem of four words may contain enough suggestion for four pages of music.

Whether or not MacDowell sacrificed clarity and directness in reaching out so far for the nobler conception, the broader outline, is another matter. Surely he is never as tidy as Grieg—in the *Finale* of the *Tragica* he does not seem to proceed as directly to his goal as Grieg would have gone. Yet mere tidiness is not always inspiring, and Mac-Dowell showed a courage in his sonatas at which we well may wonder. If the sonatas do not thrill posterity, they are none the less the real expression of a truly poetic nature that sought epic forms for its outlet.

The *First Modern Suite*, Opus 10, was MacDowell's first published work. Since it was first issued in Germany in 1883 the composer made a number of revisions, and it still remains one of his well-known works. It has a number of characteristics that mark the later MacDowell, though the intense individualities are missing. The Prelude is probably played the most; its pianistic flow, not too difficult for many amateurs, makes it grateful to the player.

The two Piano Concertos (the first, A Minor, Opus 15, 1884; the second, D Minor, Opus 23, 1890) are both comparatively early works. As such they are brilliant, but they show the influences of his training—

marked fluency and ease, but not the imagination of his later works. It was really not until after 1890 that he showed his true colors— though some of the pieces written before that date have shown healthy life: *The Scotch Poem, The Eagle*, and the song *Menie* rank with his best work. But the *Twelve Virtuoso Studies* in 1894 began to show the real MacDowell as a composer for the piano. The *Novelette*, the *Improvisation*, and the *Polonaise* are among the finest work he has done. The *Woodland Sketches* were first published in 1896. *To a Wild Rose*, and *To a Water Lily* may have haunted him with their popularity, but they are exquisite. The *Sea Pieces* were issued two years later. Here is MacDowell at the height of his powers, lyric and dramatic. He keeps within the limits that prevent his losing his breath, and within a smaller frame he writes pieces that are small only in their length; large in their ideas. The last two opus numbers on his list were the *Fireside Tales* and the *New England Idyls*. The next to the last of the idyls was *From a Log Cabin:*

> A house of dreams untold,
> It looks out over the whispering tree-tops
> And faces the setting sun.

Prophetic lines when we know how near he was to his own tragedy when he wrote them. Maybe he knew it, too, and gave us one of the sincerest bits of contemplation in the literature of music.

MacDowell wrote several major works for orchestra, but it was not his best medium. He liked best to write for piano. He felt that the modern pianoforte had developed to a degree where it would not be likely to change in the future, and whatever he wrote for it would be played the same both in the present and tomorrow. As for the orchestra, a friend, T. P. Currier, in an article in the *Musical Quarterly* (January, 1915), reported him as saying:

> It's one thing to write works for the orchestra, and another to get them performed. There isn't much satisfaction in having a thing played once in two or three years. If I write large works for the piano I can play them myself as often as I like.

Nevertheless, his orchestral works were often performed, even though we do not hear them as much as we would like today. His first purely orchestral piece was a symphonic poem *Hamlet and Ophelia*,

Edward MacDowell
(See pages 323–344)

Original Manuscript of MacDowell's *Told at Sunset*, No. 10 of His
Woodland Sketches

(See page 330)

Opus 22 (1885). Three years later he published another, *Lancelot and Elaine*, Opus 25. *Lamia*, after Keats, was written in 1888–89 but not published until after MacDowell's death. *The Saracens* and *The Lovely Alda*, two fragments after the Song of Roland, were numbered Opus 30 and published in 1891. According to Gilman, MacDowell originally intended these two pieces as movements of a Roland symphony. Four movements of the first Suite for orchestra, Opus 42, were published in 1891; the third piece (*In October*), although written at the same time as the others, was issued as a "supplement" to the Suite in 1893.

After the second (*Indian*) Suite, Opus 48, MacDowell wrote no more for orchestra. It was a fitting climax to his list in this field, for it is a fine work. The *Dirge*, like the *Largo* of the *Tragica* Sonata, has a nobility that makes grandeur in anguish. In explanation of his sources, the composer wrote:

> The thematic material of this work has been suggested for the most part by melodies of the North American Indians. Their occasional similarity to northern European themes seems to the author a direct testimony in corroboration of Thorfinnkarlsefin's Saga.
>
> The opening theme of No. 3 [*In War-time*], for instance, is very similar to the (presumably Russian) one made use of by Rimsky-Korsakow in the 3rd movement of his symphony "Antar."

MacDowell also said of the different movements: "If separate titles . . . are desired, they should be arranged as follows: I. Legend. II. Love song. III. In War-time. IV. Dirge. V. Village festival."

The Suite was first performed by Emil Paur and the Boston Symphony Orchestra (to whom it was dedicated) in New York City, January 23, 1896. MacDowell's own views on nationalism in music show clearly that he did not intend to write American music by using Indian themes, nor did he think that such material could be harmonized in a manner that would make it sound like the originals from which it was taken. He may, of course, have been experimenting; but he was no doubt content to catch the spirit of his theme, the joys and sorrows of a vanishing race. This he did most eloquently; the *Dirge* can rank with the funeral marches of the masters.

Although he was never satisfied with music's ability to match the syllables and inflection of a poem, MacDowell's songs show a rare ability to interpret the spirit and mood of the verses he chose for setting. Something of a poet himself, he was often happiest when he wrote his own poems for his songs, for then he had the music in mind as he fashioned his text. Aside from his choruses, he published over forty songs, some of them masterpieces. Writing in 1900, Henry T. Finck thought that Grieg and MacDowell were the greatest living song writers. But there was Strauss to be reckoned with, and we must remember that Finck never liked Brahms. Yet *Menie* (1889), *Thy Beaming Eyes* (1890), the poignantly emotional setting of Howell's *The Sea* (1893), and the tender treatment of his own poem *The Swan Bent Low to the Lily* (1898), are exquisite songs, created by a man who knew what a good song should be, without compromises with what singers like to sing.

IV

To understand MacDowell fully, to grasp his powers and to appreciate his limitations, it is necessary to know of his life and his personality. With all true geniuses, their character and environment shine through their writings. That is, if their work is sincere; and with MacDowell, whatever he wrote was himself. He cannot be separated from his music.

He had advantages that have not been given to many Americans—either before or after him. His talents were recognized by his parents at the start, and everything was done to foster and train his gifts. While he was still in his formative years he entered the Paris Conservatoire, where two years of rigid training gave him a groundwork that was the basis of everything he accomplished technically. Other Americans had studied abroad, but generally for polishing touches to finish what they had acquired at home. MacDowell had the best, the strictest training from almost the very beginning. Mrs. MacDowell once told me what this training had meant to him:

> One of the most fortunate things that ever came to him was that period with Marmontel at the Paris Conservatory, where he had to learn rapidity and facility in writing notes, although at that time there was no idea of his ever being a composer. But it was part of the routine. They turned out a musician, whether he played the violin, piano, or sang, enormously equipped with a musical education. But the work was terrific.

It meant at eighteen when he went into Raff's composition class, although still the piano was his principal goal, that he outstripped all the other students, most of them men ten or fifteen years older than he. Outstripped them, I mean, in actual mechanical facility. Complicated fugue he could scratch off on the blackboard just as I might write a sentence in a letter. I don't have to think how to spell words, although sometimes I don't spell them correctly, nor did he have to think of the possible combinations that were allowed.

He was born December 18, 1861, in New York City, at 220 Clinton Street. He was the third son of Thomas MacDowell and his wife, Frances Knapp. The father was of Scotch ancestry, the mother Irish. There was a Quaker background, and probably the fact that he himself had not been allowed to become a painter, made his father sympathetic with his boy's extraordinary talents for music. Edward had his first piano lessons when he was eight—principally from a South American, Juan Buitrago. Buitrago was a great friend of Teresa Carreño, and on one of her trips to New York she became interested in the talented boy and gave him some lessons herself. It was a friendship that lasted for many years.

When Edward was fifteen it was decided that he should go abroad for study, and his mother took him to Paris. For a year he worked privately with Marmontel, and then his teacher urged him to enter the competition for a scholarship at the Conservatoire. He won it, and became a regular pupil in 1877. One of his fellow students was a lad with queer ideas—named Debussy. It was about this time that he had to decide between music and painting for his career. So that he could better understand the lectures at the Conservatoire, he attended a class in French given by a teacher who had a nose like Cyrano de Bergerac. It was too great a temptation for young Edward's facile pencil. Behind his textbook he sketched the teacher. The master saw that he was inattentive and demanded to see what he was doing. The drawing was tremblingly produced, and the teacher was overcome by the striking likeness. He took it to a friend, one of the famous French artists, who immediately offered to give the boy free lessons, and to pay for his support while he was teaching him.

Music or painting? It was not an easy choice. Here was a painter saying that he had a great career ahead of him, and Marmontel insisting that he should stick at his music. Yet they had come to Paris for music, he had worked hard and done well, so the family council agreed with Edward that he had better keep to his idea of becoming a pianist.

In the summer of 1878 he decided he had had enough of the Paris Conservatoire. After hearing Nicholas Rubinstein in a concert, he told his mother that he could never learn to play like that if he stayed in Paris. So to Germany to the Stuttgart Conservatory, where things were no more to his liking than they had been in Paris. He would have to forget all he had learned in Paris, and then start over again. A friend suggested Heymann in Frankfort, so to Frankfort they went, and after a few lessons during the summer with Ehlert in Wiesbaden, he entered Heymann's class at the Frankfort Conservatory in the fall. Here MacDowell was eminently happy, for he began to study composition seriously with Joachim Raff. Raff saw the possibilities of his gifts, and it was through his influence that MacDowell eventually decided to become a composer. He also formed a friendship with his teacher that was to be one of his fondest memories.

By 1880 he was a thoroughly trained musician, a finished artist. When Heymann retired from the conservatory in that year, he thought so highly of MacDowell's gifts as a pianist that he recommended him as his successor. But the youth of the young American, and politics, kept him from getting the appointment. He continued his studies with Heymann privately, and began to take pupils himself. Some of them were of the German nobility, who bored him excessively. He was also beginning to compose. The *First Modern Suite* was written between lessons, as a response to a sort of challenge on Raff's part. Raff had been disgusted with his mechanical exercises in composition, and told him to try something real. The Suite was Edward's answer. He wrote the *Second Modern Suite* on the train rides he had to take to visit his pupils.

His first Piano Concerto was also composed to show Raff what he could do. Raff paid him an unexpected call one evening, and abruptly asked him what he had been working on. "A concerto," fibbed MacDowell. "Bring it to the next lesson," said Raff. Fortunately, the next lesson was postponed several weeks, but MacDowell had to sit up late to have it ready when Raff was able to see him.

In 1882, when MacDowell was twenty-one, Raff urged him to call on Liszt at Weimar. Liszt received him cordially. D'Albert was there at the time, and he played the orchestral part of the concerto on a second piano. Liszt told D'Albert that he would have to bestir himself if he did not want to be outdone by the young American. MacDowell left some other manuscripts, and soon had a letter from Liszt telling him that he had recommended the *First Modern Suite* to the General Society of German Musicians. MacDowell was invited to play it at the society's meetings, July 11, 1882. Through Liszt's recommendations the Suite and the first Concerto were published by Breitkopf & Haertel.

But just before this Raff died, and MacDowell was heartbroken. He had grown to love his teacher, who had told him that his music would be played long after his own was forgotten. Raff could not see his pupil's triumph before the august body of German musicians, and it took much of the joy from the great event.

With Liszt's encouragement MacDowell began to give almost all of his time to composition. Conductors of the *kur-orchester*, the little bands at the health resorts, tried his new works at rehearsals, and he was able to gain firsthand experience. In 1884 he returned to America for a visit, and for a more important matter; he was to be married in Waterford, Connecticut, to an American girl who had been his pupil in Germany—Marian Nevins. The wedding took place in July, and the young couple went back to Europe, living first in Frankfort, where MacDowell began his second Concerto. In 1885 they moved to Wiesbaden, where in another year they bought a small cottage near the edge of a wood. He had already finished the second Concerto, and before that he had composed *Hamlet* and *Ophelia*. In the cottage he wrote *Lancelot and Elaine, Lamia, The Saracens, The Lovely Alda,* and a number of piano pieces. Moreover, his friend Carreño was telling America of its young music maker, by playing his works at home.

v

Liszt's death in 1886 was a sad blow. After Raff, it removed a friend who had already done much for him, and could and would do still more. It may have been one of the factors that determined him to return permanently to America in 1888, although he probably wanted to come back to his native country anyway. Rollo Brown claims that he wanted to prove that there is a place for the serious musician in the United States.

He first thought of living in New York, but B. J. Lang helped to persuade him that he would be better off in Boston. So for eight years, from 1888, he lived in the Hub as a composer, teacher, and concert pianist. He was not too anxious to be a pianist, for he had let himself get out of practice, but he was told that he would have to make his works known by playing them, and that if he wanted pupils he would have to establish his reputation as a concert pianist. It meant taking time from his composing, but he did it in spite of the work.

On the whole, the eight years in Boston were happy ones, although it was not until his third season there that he tasted financial success, and his studio was a mecca for pupils. Also, he was not altogether temperamentally fitted for the type of comradeship and social contacts that Americans demand of their famous artists. Delightful to his friends, he was in a shell when he met mere acquaintances. Shy to the extreme, he really suffered among people he did not know well. A brilliant conversationalist when at ease, he was awkward when he did not feel at home. Though he was blessed with a sharp sense of humor, he could never enjoy the back-slapping methods of the heavy-handed.

It is an easy matter to construct what should prove an accurate picture of MacDowell from the many printed memories written by those who knew him. T. P. Currier's recollections in the January, 1915, *Musical Quarterly*, Rollo Brown's chapter in *Lonely Americans*, several passages from Hamlin Garland, and some articles by W. H. Humiston afford intimate portraits of this sensitive, charming aristocrat. Brown calls him "the handsomest thoroughbred that ever stepped up to address a golf-ball." Currier writes of the Boston years:

Gradually the figure of "MacDowell the composer" became a familiar one on the Common's walks and the near-by streets. It is interesting to recall the change in his personal appearance that came about after several months' residence in Boston. For some time he had clung, innocently enough, as it afterward proved, to the high, full-crowned felt hat, the rather fiercely curled moustache, and the goatee. . . . Then suddenly he appeared in a derby hat, which became him extremely well; and shortly afterward the goatee vanished. Commenting one day on these changes as gratifying, to my eye at least, he replied in genuinely injured tones, "Why didn't you say so, long ago?"

And in another place in the article:

He looked strong. And his strength was practically evinced by his surprisingly vital hand-grasp. . . . MacDowell, had he not had an innate aversion to exercise for the mere sake of physical well-being, might easily have had a body to match his uncommonly strong and active brain.

Garland tells of his first meeting with him,[3] in 1894:

MacDowell, who had retreated behind the piano, now came forward to meet me, shyly, boyishly, one hand sliding along the edge of the piano as a child runs a hand along a banister to relieve his embarrassment. He was a glorious young figure. His scintillant, laughing blue eyes, his abundant brown hair and, beyond all, his smile and his jocund voice, delighted me.

The years in Boston were punctuated with concert tours, since his playing, especially of his own music, was much in demand. He enjoyed his independence, and was loath to tie himself down to a regular routine position when he was invited by President Seth Low, and the trustees of Columbia University, to come to New York and take charge of the new department of music, in 1896. Yet there were several reasons that were worth considering. A guaranteed income, a chance to put into effect some of his ideas for the education of American youth, and an opportunity to give musical training of the first order to some who could not afford to pay for it elsewhere. And so he notified the trustees of his acceptance, and from the fall of 1896 he occupied the Robert Center chair of music at Columbia, endowed with a fund of a hundred thousand dollars by its benefactors. Maybe he had his own doubts of the outcome, but few of his friends realized the fatal mistake he was making.

For it really was a fatal mistake. He was not temperamentally fitted for an organization job. He was an individualist, he did not understand university procedure. As Finck remarked after his resignation, it is never wise to harness Pegasus. Though he was a brilliant teacher for brilliant pupils, lecturing and teaching the less intelligent was for him hopeless drudgery.

[3] "Roadside Meetings of a Literary Nomad," by Hamlin Garland: *The Bookman,* March, 1930.

The first years at Columbia went well enough. Seth Low wanted him because he was an individualist, and it was to the glory of the University to have him there. MacDowell worked like a slave—lecturing on the history and aesthetics of music, and teaching classes in harmony and composition—correcting exercises with meticulous care, consulting with students, and attending to matters of routine. For a season or so he conducted New York's Mendelssohn Glee Club. In a year he had an assistant—Leonard McWhood, who had been his pupil. In 1899, Gustav Hinrichs was engaged to conduct the student orchestra and chorus. And all the while MacDowell was planning and dreaming of what a university music department should be, especially in its relation to teaching other branches of the fine arts.

VI

Exactly what happened to puncture this state of affairs, I do not know. Probably there were a number of factors that led to the final disaster. There are, of course, printed records of the controversy, newspaper accounts, letters, and records of trustee meetings. But most of the discussions that led up to the break were held verbally between President Butler and MacDowell, and the really inside story may never be known. Maybe there is no inside story. Possibly the printed records are, after all, complete.

I have consulted all the documents in the case, read the contemporary newspaper reports and comments, and talked to his assistants and a number of his associates and pupils. Probably there is something to be said on both sides of the controversy, though partisans have held that MacDowell was shamefully treated. The two points of view are briefly expressed by Butler's statement that MacDowell had resigned because he wanted more time to compose, and MacDowell's retort that he was leaving because he felt his work had been futile, and that he could see no chance for conducting the kind of department with which he would care to be associated at Columbia.

When Seth Low became the first mayor of Greater New York, Nicholas Murray Butler succeeded him as president of the University in 1902. From then on, MacDowell was never comfortable. Low had understood him and sympathized with his plans, but MacDowell felt that the new administration had ideas of its own. He had visualized a department of fine arts at Columbia that would embrace not only Belles Lettres and music, but architecture, painting, and sculpture, too. No doubt Butler wanted this, but MacDowell claimed he had dismissed his ideas as impractical. When he was absent on his sabbatical year in the season of 1902–3, Butler started a reorganization according to his own ideas. Possibly either MacDowell's or Butler's plan would have achieved the same goal in the end, but each had his own way of doing things. And as Currier wrote of MacDowell in the *Musical Quarterly:*

He was not fitted by nature to cope with situations where change, or interference with plans he had set his heart on, might have seemed advisable. He could not argue. Either he must do what he wanted to do in his own way, or not at all.

When he resumed his work at Columbia in the fall of 1903, MacDowell was highly nervous; the strain of work and worry was telling on his health. Maybe his perspective was clouded. After Christmas holidays at his summer retreat in Peterboro, New Hampshire, and after much discussion with his wife, he concluded to resign, and he so informed President Butler early in January. I think he had no hard feelings. He was merely discouraged, he felt he could not do the job he had planned, and therefore decided to quit. His assistant McWhood testifies that when MacDowell told him he was resigning, he pledged McWhood to absolute secrecy. He knew that his resignation would attract attention, and he wanted to give Butler a chance to choose a successor before the president's office was swamped with the applications that would be sure to pour in.

Yet MacDowell was in a state of mind that needed only a spark to send it into flame. Somehow the news of his resignation leaked out, and two student reporters called on him. At first he wouldn't talk. But then they chided him for being a quitter, and that was too much. He had to let off steam, and evidently he did, with a fury. When he had finished, he made the naïve request that nothing of the interview be printed—but who could expect youthful reporters to miss such a scoop? They made for the office of the *Evening Post* as fast as they could get there.

The afternoon of February 3, 1904, was fateful, for on the front page of the *Post* appeared this headline:

MACDOWELL TO RESIGN

Unable to Obtain the Reorganization of Work Which He Thinks Necessary

Then followed some details of his criticism. The next morning the papers had more of the MacDowell affair. The *Times* said that he called college graduates "barbarians." "During the time of his service, he had had only three pupils with whom he was entirely satisfied." The *World* had this headline:

COLLEGE MEN BOORS, SAYS PROFESSOR

No Idealism Left in Columbia, and MacDowell Will Give Up Department of Music

And so the lid was off. If it had not been for this interview, and its publicity, the affair might never have become public, and Mac-Dowell might have retired quietly to recover from the hurt he had sustained. Anyway, there would never have been the recriminations that followed.

VII

Butler answered MacDowell a few days later, in the *Times*. In a lengthy statement, he printed a letter he had received from Mac-Dowell, stating that the interviews were incorrect and unauthorized. He had forbidden the student reporters to give one word of his conversation to the press. (There was, however, no denial that the interview had taken place.) Butler then went on to explain that MacDowell's resignation had been wholly unexpected, that it was prompted by the composer's wish to have all his time and strength for composition. That MacDowell had been a delightful colleague, and the University was losing him with the greatest regret. Moreover, the trustees had offered him a research professorship which would carry with it no duties, and MacDowell was now considering this offer. In addition, the School of Fine Arts was under consideration. Professor MacDowell was now at work upon a paper outlining the status of music in universities in general, and from this paper the University hoped to obtain valuable suggestions. MacDowell's answer came two days later, in the *Post* of February 10.

President Butler has evidently misunderstood my interview with him when he affirms that my sole object in resigning from Columbia was to have more time to write: he failed to explain the circumstances which led to my resignation. . . . There is certainly individual idealism in all universities, but the general tendency of modern education is toward materialism.

Then followed a copy of the report he was sending to the trustees.

It is with some chagrin that I have to report the small results my efforts have brought to the development of art at Columbia. The reason for this is obvious. Few colleges in the United States consider the fine arts (except "Belles Lettres" and architecture) worthy of serious consideration.

.   .   .   .

I have tried to impress the "powers that be" with the necessity of allowing no student to enter the university without some knowledge of the fine arts. Such knowledge may be very general, and not technical. This would force upon the preparatory school the admission of fine arts to its curriculum. . . .

In order to bring to a focus the art elements existing in Columbia I proposed that music be taken out of the faculty of philosophy and architecture out of the School of Mines, and with Belles Lettres form a faculty of fine arts, to complete which, painting and sculpture would be indispensable.

Owing to my inability to persuade rich men of New York into endowing a chair of painting and sculpture, the scheme, though approved by the "powers that be," was not realized. . . . The outcome of all this was the establishment of a division in fine arts during my absence last year. In this Division of Fine Arts the inclusion of Belles Lettres and Music, including kindergarten, etc., at Teachers College, seemed ill-advised. To me, expansion in this direction, before a focus be attained, means a swamping of Columbia's individuality. The Division of Fine Arts thus acquires somewhat the nature of a co-educational department store, and tends toward materialism rather than idealism.

The research professorship offered me by the president, consisted of my lending to Columbia the use of my name, with no duties, and no salary. I immediately refused it as I was unwilling to associate my name with a policy I could not approve of.

.   .   .   .

For seven years I have put all my energy and enthusiasm in the cause of art at Columbia, and now at last, recognizing the futility of my efforts, I have resigned the chair of music in order to resume my own belated vocation.

More fuel for the flames. The authorities at the College were out-raged. A professor whose resignation had not yet taken effect had given an official report to the press. At their next meeting the trustees accepted the resignation, and put on record an official reprimand. They regarded "Professor MacDowell's act in making public an official re-port, as an offense against propriety, a discourtesy to the Board, and a breach of that confidence which the Board always seeks to repose in every officer of the University."

MacDowell wrote a letter which he sent to each of the trustees individually. He said in part:

My letter to the trustees was a condensed repetition of a long conversa-tion I had with President Butler. My aims and ideas he dismissed as being impossible and revolutionary. He, knowing all this, prints a plausible letter calculated to make the public think that my own work was my sole reason for leaving the University. My only means of righting this was an immediate protest. . . . As to my "breach of confidence which the Board always seeks to repose in every officer of the University," I beg to say that the officers seek to repose this same trust in members of the Board; and Mr. Butler's misleading communication to the press was a far graver breach of this confidence than my using the only means in my power to correct this statement.

Nor did the matter rest here. Some time later in the spring Presi-dent Butler announced McWhood's advancement to an adjunct pro-fessorship, stating that the promotion was well earned, as McWhood had for some time borne the burden of the teaching in the department. Maybe Butler meant merely to explain that McWhood was qualified to assume greater responsibilities, but it was an unfortunate way of putting it. MacDowell himself had tried to secure promotion for his assistant some time before, and there had been no funds to provide for it. In view of this, Butler's announcement stung MacDowell deeply. To his mind he was being called a shirker, and a shirker he never was. He sent the trustees a comparative schedule, showing ex-actly how many classes both he and McWhood had conducted each week. He felt that McWhood had been disloyal to him, and he told him so in no uncertain terms. McWhood has explained his part of the affair in a paper read before the Music Teachers' National Association in 1923. Butler's statement, he said, was wholly a surprise to him. It certainly did put him in an uncomfortable position, for MacDowell was in a frame of mind to think the worst of him.

June came, and after commencement it was all over. But not for MacDowell. He was not the kind who could shrug his shoulders, and turn placidly to his job of composing. He brooded and brooded. They had said he neglected his duties; all sorts of interpretations were being put on the entire affair. To make things worse, he was knocked down by a cab on the streets and injured. He lay awake nights—thinking restless thoughts.

VIII

For a year he did some private teaching, but in the spring of 1905 the end came, as far as he was concerned. His mind refused to do any more thinking, and he gradually sank into a state where he looked vacantly out of the window, staring blankly, comprehending nothing. For over two years his was a body without a mind, until he quietly passed away at the Westminster Hotel in New York, January 23, 1908.

The Columbia affair is almost forgotten today. The University is proud of the fact that MacDowell was its first professor of music, and recently the position he occupied has been named the Edward Mac-Dowell Chair of Music. Nor is it my purpose to recount these details of a past controversy merely to make interesting reading. To my mind, the events at Columbia were prompted by a nature that is clearly reflected in MacDowell's music. Impulsive, hasty, yet generous and sensitive, he sometimes lost his sense of perspective. His music reaches out for great heights. It often achieves them, yet it frequently stops for breath on the way to the summit. There was no compromise either in his music or in MacDowell. He must be himself. He was at a loss in adapting his ideas to the ways of others, even though both were after the same object. They must take the same road, or one of them must stay at home.

And finally a brighter side. A dream of MacDowell's that has been realized through the efforts of his wife, who knew it would please him if she built what he had vaguely planned. The listener to the winds had found a place where he could hear the sounds of nature more distinctly than anywhere else; where he had the quiet to write them down in his music. With his wife he had discovered Peterboro, in the lower New Hampshire hills, and there they had bought an eighty-acre farm soon after he had gone to Columbia. He built a log cabin, his "house of dreams untold," where he went early in the summer mornings to write his *Fireside Tales,* his *New England Idyls.* He often thought of having other artists share his retreat, and he talked of the artist colony they would some day found at Peterboro.

Mrs. MacDowell has made the fulfillment of this idea her life work. Her concert tours, playing her husband's music, have been undertaken for the distinct purpose of raising funds to maintain the colony at Peterboro. Today it is the summer refuge of artists, composers, poets, and writers who come to do their work in the spot where MacDowell wrote his last two Sonatas, his *Sea Pieces,* and his later miniatures.

4. LINKS WITH THE PAST

GEORGE TEMPLETON STRONG (1856–1948), a close friend of Mac-Dowell, was one of the first of our composers who decided to live permanently in Europe. When MacDowell came home he tried to persuade Strong to live here, too, but after trying Boston for a year as a teacher at the New England Conservatory (1891–92), Strong was so discouraged by the failure of American composers to find recognition in their own country that he went back to Europe for good.

He was born in New York, May 26, 1856, of musical parents. His father was president of the New York Philharmonic for four years, and an amateur organist. Strong went to Leipzig in 1879, and studied with Jadassohn. He became a Liszt disciple, and often visited the great musician at Weimar. Then he went to Wiesbaden, where he saw much of the young MacDowell, and finally settled in Vevey, Switzerland.

He wrote three symphonies, each with a title: *In the Mountains, Sintram,* and *An der See.* He composed two *American Sketches* for violin and orchestra, and a symphonic poem *Undine.* The Suite for orchestra, *Die Nacht,* is in four movements: *At Sunset; Peasants' Battle March;* the shadowy, atmospheric *In Deep Woods;* and the spooky *Awakening of the Forest-Spirits.* Most important are his two works for soli, male chorus, and orchestra: *Wie ein fahrender Hornist sich ein Land erblies,* and *Die verlassene Mühle.* Later orchestral works are a symphonic poem *Le Roi Arthur,* a somber, gloomy, tragic piece of rich and heavy texture, and an *Elegie* for cello and orchestra.

In 1935, the Philadelphia Orchestra played Strong's *Chorale on a Theme by Hassler,* beautifully textured music, exquisitely scored for strings. On October 21, 1939, the composer, at the age of eighty-three, had the pleasure of sitting by the radio in Geneva, Switzerland, and hearing his *Die Nacht* played by the National Broadcasting Symphony Orchestra under Toscanini.

Strong composed much piano music, running from the style of Debussy and Ravel to the outdoor spirit of America, as expressed in the Suite *Au pays des Peaux-Rouges,* with its *Le Cow-boy humoriste* and *Chant de guerre.* His songs are effective, a number of them written to cynical texts of his own.

ARTHUR BIRD (1856–1923) was another who preferred to live abroad. He was born in Cambridge, Massachusetts, July 23, 1856, and died in Berlin, December 22, 1923. His last visit to America was in 1886, and after that he lived in Germany for the rest of his life. He studied composition with Urban and spent a year with Liszt at Weimar. He wrote a Symphony which he called *Karnevalszene;* three Suites for orchestra; two *Decimettes* for wind instruments, which won the Paderewski prize in 1901; some ballet music, and a comic opera; and numerous piano pieces and songs.

EDGAR STILLMAN KELLEY (1857–1944) really belonged to the Chadwick, Foote, and Parker group, for he dated from the time when the American composer had to work hard to make himself heard. He also reflected the German models of his student days abroad. Yet he showed a venturesome nature, and his experiments in tone color led him to discoveries interesting to his listeners, as well as to himself. One of his early works was his Chinese orchestral suite—*Aladdin.* He listened to native music in San Francisco's Chinatown, and he used oboes, muted trumpets, and mandolins to imitate the Chinese instruments. When he wrote his *New England* Symphony he based his themes on bird notes, Indian songs, and Puritan psalm tunes. For incidental music to the New York production of *Ben Hur,* in 1899, he used Greek modes.

His best-known work is his oratorio *The Pilgrim's Progress*, with text by Elizabeth Hodgkinson, based on Bunyan's allegory. It was first performed at the Cincinnati Festival of 1918, and has since been given by the New York Oratorio Society, at the Worcester Festival, and at choral festivals in England, as well as many others in America. His symphonic poem *The Pit and the Pendulum* was first heard at the Cincinnati Festival of 1925, and was shortly afterwards repeated in Portland, Oregon, where it was awarded the prize in the annual contest of the National Federation of Music Clubs. *Alice in Wonderland*, a symphonic suite, was composed for the Norfolk (Connecticut) Festival of 1919.

Kelley was born in Sparta, Wisconsin, April 14, 1857. He studied first in Chicago with Clarence Eddy, and then went to Stuttgart to work at the Conservatory. He came back to America and settled first in San Francisco, where he was organist, teacher, and music critic on one of the papers. He went east in 1890 to conduct a comic opera company. In 1892 he produced an operetta of his own—*Puritania*. It ran over one hundred nights at the Tremont Theatre in Boston. In the season of 1901–2 he was acting professor at Yale University while Horatio Parker was absent on his sabbatical year; then for eight years he was in Berlin, teaching piano and composition.

In 1910 he was awarded a Fellowship in Musical Composition by the Western College at Oxford, Ohio, and he was invited to make his home and do his work on its campus.

Kelley's eightieth birthday, in 1937, was the occasion of a widely observed celebration, and during the following months his works were given many performances throughout the country. An Edgar Stillman Kelley Society was formed to underwrite publication of works by younger American composers. Among the "younger" composers whose pieces were selected was Dr. Kelley himself, and a work of his was chosen which had lain unfinished for many years—his First Symphony. This was a programmatic composition which he called *Gulliver*. The first movement had been completed years before, and the other movements had been sketched, but it was not until his seventy-eighth year that the composer finished the work and scored it.

The first movement of *Gulliver* tells of the voyage and shipwreck. In the second movement "Gulliver Sleeps and Dreams," and in the third the Lilliputians appear playing their national anthem. This becomes a double fugue when they enmesh the "Man Mountain" with their ropes. The *finale* is a hornpipe which celebrates Gulliver's rescue and his homeward journey. The première of the Symphony was given by the NBC Symphony Orchestra conducted by Walter Damrosch over a large network of radio stations, April 15, 1937.

Kelley's music has always been widely played. The *Ben Hur* score was performed five thousand times in English-speaking countries. His Piano Quintet and the String Quartet, Opus 25, are known in both Europe and America, and the *New England Symphony* is a standard item in the repertoire of our symphony societies.

Kelley lived to the venerable age of eighty-seven years, and up to the time of his death, November 12, 1944, was active in spite of failing health. Every winter he could be seen in New York where he and his wife, who was long active in Music Club Federation circles, would receive their friends at their hotel.

He had definite ideas on nationalism, and he tried to carry them out in his music. He once expressed his views in the following words:

The American composer should apply the universal principles of his art to the local and special elements of the subject-matter as they appeal to him, and then, consciously or unconsciously, manifest his individuality, which will involve the expression of mental traits and moral tendencies peculiar to his European ancestry, as we find them modified by the new American environment.

FRANK VAN DER STUCKEN (1858–1929) was said to be the first orchestral conductor to present all-American programs. He did this first in New York in the eighties, and then he gave one in Paris at the 1889 exposition. Van der Stucken was a prolific composer and an able conductor. He was in much demand for festivals.

He was born in Texas, October 15, 1858, of German and Belgian parents. Educated chiefly in Europe, his music teachers included Reinecke and Grieg. He came to New York in 1884 and made his debut in Steinway Hall. Then he was made conductor of a male choral society, the Arion, and he directed orchestral concerts. In 1895 he went to Cincinnati, to become the director of the College of Music and the conductor of the new symphony orchestra. When Thomas died in 1905, Van der Stucken succeeded him as conductor of the Cincinnati Festival, and he held the position regularly until 1912. He conducted many festivals abroad, for after 1908 he lived mostly in Europe, and died in Hamburg, August 18, 1929.

Some of Van der Stucken's early music was performed first in Europe, when he was a young man of hardly twenty-five. Liszt presented his prologue to Heine's tragedy *William Ratcliff* at Weimar, and his incidental music to Shakespeare's *Tempest* was played at Breslau. He had a fine talent for orchestration; his scores sparkle with subtle effects. He composed a Symphonic Prologue *Pax Triumphans*, in which peace is indeed triumphant, though noisy; a Festival March *Louisiana*; other shorter pieces for orchestra; and a *Festival Hymn* for men's voices and orchestra. He also wrote a number of songs and piano pieces.

CHARLES MARTIN LOEFFLER (1861–1935) was one of the picturesque figures in American music. There are many who denied his Americanism; not because he was born in Alsace, but because his music is so akin to the Frenchmen of Debussy's time that it is really not American at all. Yet to some all things are American; and if Loeffler, in his musical journeys around the world, picked something from France, a bit from Russia, and maybe a blossom or two from the banks of the Rhine, who shall say that he was any the less American for sampling whatever he found? Especially since he wrought it all with such exquisite perfection, and turned everything he touched to jewels and gold.

Loeffler lived the life of a recluse at Medfield, Massachusetts, twenty miles from Boston. Paul Rosenfeld believed that his many years in Boston had made his work sterile; that the brilliant musician succumbed to the correct manners and inhibitions of New England. Rosenfeld even went so far as to compare his music to the dead Queen of Castile, whose remains were swathed in royal robes, and hung with gold and precious stones.[1] But there are others who were dazzled by the jewels, and who felt the pulse within. The musical refinement and the brilliance of Loeffler were not any too common among the American composers of past decades.

[1] In *An Hour with American Music*. Philadelphia: J. B. Lippincott Company, 1929.

Loeffler first came to America in the summer of 1881. He had an unusual background. He was born in Alsace, January 30, 1861, had lived in Russia and had been one of Joachim's favorite violin pupils. He studied in Paris with Massart, pupil of Kreutzer, and played in Pasdeloup's orchestra. He was engaged for the private orchestra of Baron Paul von Derweis, who spent his summers at his castle near Lake Lugano and his winters at Nice. Whenever the court moved from summer to winter quarters, three special trains were needed to carry the family, the guests, the tutors for the children, the servants and the horses, the orchestra of seventy, and the mixed choir of forty-eight singers. Loeffler was a favorite with the Baron, and he was often asked to help in the performance of chamber music by members of the family.

Loeffler was in New York for about a year, playing in Damrosch's orchestra, and sometimes with Theodore Thomas. Then Major Higginson asked him to come to Boston to play in the Boston Symphony, which had just finished its first season. He shared the first desk with Listemann, the concertmaster. When Franz Kneisel succeeded Listemann, Loeffler played side by side with Kneisel until 1903. Then he resigned, gave up playing his violin in public, and decided to devote the rest of his life to composition, and to his farm at Medfield where he lived until his death, May 20, 1935.

Spiritually, Loeffler was a mystic, a deep student of medieval culture and thought. He was an authority on Gregorian plain song; the church modes of the Middle Ages. Living in the twentieth century, he seemed a wanderer searching for a place where pious mystics would speak his language. Not finding it, he lived in his dreams. There he polished his music until it was refined to a purity that would satisfy his sense of the exquisite. Even though Rosenfeld found him sterile, and his style chosen from many sources, he was frank to admit the skill with which he fashioned his music.

Loeffler published practically nothing until he had finished his career as a violinist. Many of his works had been performed, but he had kept them all in manuscript. In 1891 the Boston Symphony played his Suite for violin and orchestra, *Les Veillées de l'Ukraine* (after Gogol); in 1894 his *Fantastic Concerto* for cello and orchestra; and in

1895 his *Divertimento* for violin and orchestra. He had also written a number of songs and chamber music works which were performed by the Kneisels and others.

His first published orchestral works were the dramatic poem *La Morte de Tintagiles* (after Maeterlinck), and a symphonic fantasy based on a poem by Rollinat, *La Villanelle du Diable*. They were issued in 1905, though *La Morte de Tintagiles* had been written first in 1897 and revised in 1900, and *La Villanelle* in 1901.

Loeffler's most frequently played work is the *Pagan Poem*. It is based on the eighth Eclogue of Virgil, in which a Thessalian girl tries to become sorceress, to draw her truant lover home. The piece was first written in 1901, as chamber music for piano, two flutes, oboe, clarinet, English horn, two horns, three trumpets, viola, and double bass. Loeffler arranged the score for two pianos and three trumpets, and it was played in 1903 at the home of the famous Mrs. Jack Gardner. Then Loeffler remodeled the work and expanded it to symphonic proportions, for piano and large orchestra. It was first played by the Boston Symphony in 1907 and published in 1909.

The three trumpets are treated *obbligati*—they suggest the refrain of the sorceress: *Ducite ab urbe domum, mea carmina, ducite Daphnim* (Draw from the city, my songs, draw Daphnis home). First they are heard offstage, then nearer and nearer until they finally come onto the stage, and the orchestra voices the triumph of the sorceress in an outburst of exultant passion. Loeffler's dark, brooding music brings the odor of strange incense, the magic incantations. It paints a vivid picture of the lovesick sorceress, chanting her desirous songs.

The plain chant, Gregorian influence is most apparent in the *Music for Four String Instruments* (published in 1923); and in the Symphony *Hora Mystica*, written for the Norfolk (Connecticut) Festival of 1916, and still in manuscript. Loeffler supplied explanatory notes for the symphony:

The mood is one of religious meditation and adoration of nature. A lonely pilgrim winds his way through a land of ever-changing enchantments, a land where clouds move like a procession of nuns over the hills or descend upon a lake, changing it into a mysterious gray sea—a land where shepherds still pipe to their flocks. From far away comes a curious tolling of church-bells. At last the wanderer stands before the cathedral of a Benedictine monastery, contemplating its beauty—even the grotesque beauty of the gargoyles, placed on the house of worship to ward off evil spirits. In the church, with its rose-window still aglow with the last evening light, the office of compline—known to the Benedictine monks as Hora Mystica—is tendered to God, and peace descends into the soul of the pilgrim.

The Library of Congress, under the provisions of the Elizabeth Sprague Coolidge Foundation, commissioned and published Loeffler's *Canticum Fratris Solis,* a remarkable setting for solo voice and chamber orchestra of the "Canticle of the Sun" by St. Francis. It was first performed in Washington at the first chamber music festival at the Library of Congress in 1925. Again Loeffler used old church modes, and sometimes definite liturgical motives. It is rare music, a truly distinguished work.

Another commission from Mrs. Coolidge produced a *Partita* for violin and piano. In 1930 for the Cleveland Orchestra Loeffler composed an *Evocation,* for orchestra, women's chorus, and speaking voice. This was first performed in Cleveland, February 5, 1931, and was published in the same year by the Juilliard Foundation. After a subsequent performance of this work by the Boston Symphony, a reviewer in *Musical America* (April 10, 1933) wrote that "its luminous clarity, delicate coloring, and fine workmanship are a constant delight."

Besides his songs (to poems of Verlaine, Baudelaire, Rossetti, Poe, Yeats), Loeffler composed and published two rhapsodies for oboe, viola, and piano (*L'étang* and *La Cornemuse*); a chorus for women's voices *By the Rivers of Babylon;* an eight-part chorus for mixed voices *a cappella, For One who Fell in Battle;* a *Poem* for orchestra; and an orchestral poem *Memories of my Childhood* ("Life in a Russian Village").

Much has been written about Loeffler's work, but there are few portraits of the man himself. Carl Engel provided as intimate an account of him as probably can be found, in the *Musical Quarterly* of July, 1925. He treated his subject with sympathy and understanding.

When this volume was first published, in 1931, WALTER DAM-ROSCH (1862–1950) frankly stated that he had abandoned all ambitions as a composer, that his other activities as conductor and musical ambassador and missionary were enough, and that a rival conductor was probably right in calling his first opera *The Scarlet Letter* the "Nibelungen of New England." After Dr. Damrosch's retirement from the conductorship of the New York Symphony Society, and when his Friday afternoon broadcasts for school children had become more or less a routine matter, he apparently changed his mind, for the list of works he has recently composed and produced would do credit to the industriousness of a far younger man.

First there was the *Abraham Lincoln Song*, for baritone solo, chorus, and orchestra which was performed at the Metropolitan Opera House, April 3, 1936, and broadcast over an NBC network. The following year brought an opera *The Man Without a Country*, to a libretto which Arthur Guiterman had adapted from Edward Everett Hale's story. This was produced by the Metropolitan Opera Company during its 1937 spring season. Then he rewrote his earlier opera *Cyrano de Bergerac*, which originally had been produced at the Metropolitan in 1913. In its revised form the opera was produced in Carnegie Hall, New York, by the Philharmonic-Symphony Society, with soloists and the Oratorio Society Chorus, under the composer's direction, February 21, 1941.

Next came another opera, a fantasy in one-act entitled *The Opera Cloak*, produced by the New Opera Company at the Broadway Theatre, New York, November 4, 1942. Virgil Thomson called the work "literate music, clear music, but rather dull music" which "would have made a pleasant eight-minute skit for the International Ladies' Garment Workers." [2] Most recently, in 1943, Damrosch made a setting of Robert Nathan's poem *Dunkirk*, for baritone solo, male chorus, and small orchestra. This work was first performed by the National Broadcasting Symphony, May 2, 1943, with Thomas L. Thomas as soloist.

Damrosch had a long and honored career in America. Born in Breslau, Germany, January 30, 1862, he came to New York with his family when he was nine years old. His father, Leopold Damrosch, had come to America, first to conduct the New York Männergesangverein Arion, a male chorus. In 1874 he organized the New York Oratorio Society, and in 1878, after a season with the Philharmonic, he was made conductor of the newly founded Symphony Society of New York. The elder Damrosch became a bitter rival of Theodore Thomas,

---

[2] New York *Herald Tribune*, November 4, 1942.

and the orchestra war of the late seventies and eighties added spice to table conversation and to the columns of the musical journals. And bitterness, too.

When his father died in 1885, Walter succeeded him as conductor of the Oratorio Society and the New York Symphony. He had been his father's assistant as conductor of German opera at the Metropolitan, and in 1894 he organized his own company, which gave German operas in New York and in other cities for five years. For two years after 1900 he was conductor of German operas at the Metropolitan. For the season of 1902–3 he conducted the Philharmonic, and when the Symphony Society was reorganized the following year he again assumed its leadership. In 1928 the orchestra was merged with the Philharmonic, and for a season Damrosch was one of the conductors of the combined orchestras. In 1929 he resigned to devote all of his time to radio broadcasting, giving weekly orchestral concerts in the evening, and a children's series, with explanatory remarks, in school hours. Damrosch died in New York, December 22, 1950.

During his conductorship of the Symphony Society, Damrosch introduced many new works which have since proved to be masterpieces —among them Tschaikowsky's Fifth and Sixth Symphonies, and Brahms's Fourth. He also directed the first American performances of several operas: Saint-Saëns' *Samson and Delilah*, Tschaikowsky's *Eugen Onegin*, and Wagner's *Parsifal*. He was a pioneer in welcoming the works of American composers to his programs, and it was he who commissioned George Gershwin to compose his Piano Concerto.

The Scarlet Letter, based on Hawthorne's novel, was Damrosch's first opera, and he produced it with his own company in Boston in 1896. It was thoroughly Wagnerian in conception, with leit-motives and everything else that goes with a post-romantic German music drama.

Cyrano, the opera after Rostand's play, was originally produced at the Metropolitan Opera House in New York in 1913. A comic opera *The Dove of Peace*, to a libretto by Wallace Irwin, was produced in 1912 in New York and Philadelphia. Damrosch also wrote incidental music to the Greek dramas *Iphigenia in Aulis*, *Medea*, and *Electra*, for performances in California in 1915. His Sonata for violin and piano bears the title *At Fox Meadow*. In his songs he achieved more individuality and better success than in his work in larger forms—particularly in setting ballads of the dramatic type: Kipling's *Danny Deever*, and others.

Yet, as I have remarked elsewhere: "Walter Damrosch does not need the role of composer for immortality, and it is not necessary that one admire him as a creative artist in order to do him high honor. His name will go on the roll with that of Theodore Thomas, as belonging to one who has done more than his share in helping to make America musical." [3]

HENRY FRANKLIN BELKNAP GILBERT (1868–1928) possessed a genuine talent which created music with a spontaneity and a raciness that makes it sparkle. Gilbert was not recognized for many years, and his association with Arthur Farwell and others of the composers who thought in nationalistic terms was no doubt one of the reasons that he was heard at all. Although his setting of Stevenson's *Pirate Song* ("Fifteen Men on a Dead Man's Chest") had been made popular by David Bispham, and his work for soprano and orchestra, *Salammbô's Invocation to Tanith*, had had a single performance by the Russian Symphony Orchestra in New York, it was not until 1911, when Gilbert was forty-two years old, that he was really brought to the attention of the musical public. In April of that year the Boston Symphony played his *Comedy Overture on Negro Themes*. It may have disturbed the audience, but those who heard it knew that it was something new. As Olin Downes remarked, "There were some who thought that the opening was undignified, and stopped thinking at that place."

The *Overture* had originally been intended as a prelude to an operetta based on the *Uncle Remus* tales of Joel Chandler Harris. Gilbert actually completed his sketches of the operetta and then found that the exclusive stage rights had been granted to another composer. So he could use only the overture, which he rescored for a larger orchestra. The first theme was a Negro melody from the Bahamas; the second a tune sung by the roustabouts of the Mississippi steamboats—*I'se G'wine to Alabammy, Oh*; and the middle section was a witty, rollicking fugue on the *Old Ship of Zion*. The genuine treatment of this material caused Gilbert to be talked about, and two years later he

[3] In *Our Contemporary Composers.*

was invited to write an orchestral work for the Litchfield County Festival in Norfolk, Connecticut.

For this occasion he wrote his *Negro Rhapsody*, which pictures first a Negro "Shout," alternating a savage dance tune and a spiritual; then a glorification of the spiritual in which the barbaric is supposed to fall away and the nobler elements take its place. It is interesting to contrast this final triumph of the spiritual with the reversion to paganism depicted in John Powell's rhapsody, discussed elsewhere in this volume.

Five songs of the Louisiana Creole Negroes were the basis of Gilbert's *Dance in the Place Congo*. First written as an orchestral piece, the composer later composed a ballet scenario, and the work was finally performed at the Metropolitan in New York, March 23, 1918. It is one of the best of Gilbert's works. The tropical grace of the Creole tunes is subtly emphasized, but the gloomy, tragic note of the slave dances in the old Place Congo of New Orleans forms a weird and fantastic background. First comes the Bamboula, then some light moments rising to frenzy, interrupted at last by the booming of the great bell that summoned the slaves back to their quarters. Then a pause and a cry of despair.

When Gilbert first hit upon the idea of using native themes is not known. Possibly he talked with Farwell about the example set for American composers by Dvořák, and by MacDowell with his *Indian Suite*. At any rate, Gilbert turned to the Negroes while others looked to the Indians and produced his *Americanesque*, an orchestral work based on three minstrel tunes—*Zip Coon* ("Turkey in the Straw"), *Dearest May*, and *Don't Be Foolish, Joe* (1903).

Gilbert was born in Somerville, Massachusetts, September 26, 1868. He studied first at the New England Conservatory, and then became MacDowell's first American pupil. During his student years, from 1889 to 1892, he earned his living playing the violin for dances and in theatres. This hack work disgusted him, and he determined to keep his music apart from the routine of getting money to feed himself. Olin Downes, in the *Musical Quarterly* of January, 1918, has told how he first became real estate agent, then a foreman in a factory, a raiser of silkworms, and finally a bread and pie cutter in a restaurant at the Chicago World's Fair. There he met a Russian prince who had been a friend of Rimsky-Korsakoff, and who, when he recovered from "the unconventional advances of the bread and pie cutter, was able to impart interesting information about this composer and other members of the 'Neo-Russian' school."

Gilbert was always interested in composers who used folk songs in their music, and his journeys after 1895, when he inherited a small sum of money, took him wherever he could find material and kindred spirits. He was so stirred when he heard of the première of Charpentier's *Louise* in Paris, knowing that it tended toward the use of popular themes, that he worked his way to Europe on a cattle boat to hear the first performance.

He left some works not based on American folk songs. In his *Symphonic Prelude* to Synge's drama *Riders to the Sea,* he makes use of a fragment of an old Irish melody. This was first written for small orchestra, to be played at some performances of the drama by the Twentieth Century Club of Boston in 1904. Later he expanded the work, scoring it for full orchestra, and it was performed at the music festival of the MacDowell Memorial Association in Peterboro, September, 1914. He also composed a one-act opera that has not yet been performed—*Fantasy in Delft,* with the scene laid in the Dutch town of Delft in the seventeenth century. Gilbert died in Cambridge, Massachusetts, May 19, 1928.

ARTHUR BATELLE WHITING (1861–1936) made his home and headquarters in New York from 1895 until the time of his death, July 20, 1936, but through his place of birth and early training and associations, he belonged to the Boston Group. He was born in Cambridge, Massachusetts, June 20, 1861, the nephew of George E. Whiting (1842–1923), composer and organist. He had his first instruction at the New England Conservatory—piano with Sherwood, and harmony, counterpoint, and composition with Maas and Chadwick. From 1883 to 1885 he was abroad, studying with Rheinberger in Munich. Then back to Boston for ten years, where he lived and worked among his New England colleagues. In 1895 he moved to New York, and after 1907 was active in giving chamber music concerts in our universities—Harvard, Yale, Princeton, Columbia.

As a composer, Whiting wrote little compared to his Boston contemporaries, but in spite of his small output he showed a genuine talent, which had its native characteristics. He was either a severe self-critic, or he wrote only when he felt that he had something definite to say. His principal works were a Concert Overture, a Suite for horns and strings, a Concerto, and a Fantasy for piano and orchestra. In his later years he wrote a String Quartet (1929), and he published a Dance Pageant *The Golden Cage,* with the music scored for small orchestra. The libretto was adapted from the poems of William Blake by C. C. Smith. He composed a number of small works, anthems, songs, and piano pieces, and made some transcriptions for piano of the toccatas and suites of Bach and Handel.

All his life Whiting was a man of wit and humor, the coiner of epigrams that have become traditions among musicians. He spared no one at whom he might level a gibe—Hale described him as "a man with a very pretty knack at sarcasm." It may be that this keen, acrid sense of humor kept him from taking anything too seriously, including himself, and that it was responsible for his comparatively small list of compositions.

The *Indian Dances* of CHARLES SANFORD SKILTON (1868–1941) have been played all over the country in their scoring for large orchestra, and in arrangements for smaller combinations in theatres, on phonograph records, and over the radio. Skilton wisely avoided over-elaboration and development. He used the resources of the modern orchestra to emphasize primitive effects, and wherever it was required, he employed the monotonous insistence of the percussion to sharpen the constant recurrence of drum rhythms.

Skilton was a New Englander by birth—he was born in Northampton, Massachusetts, August 16, 1868. He graduated from Yale University, and then after teaching in a school at Newburgh, New York, he went abroad to study music at the Berlin Hochschule. When he returned to America he studied further with Harry Rowe Shelley and Dudley Buck, and held several teaching positions, until he went to Kansas in 1903 to take charge of music at the state university. He held that position until his death, March 12, 1941.

Skilton first became interested in Indian music in 1915, when an Indian pupil offered to trade tribal songs, which he would sing to Skilton, for lessons in harmony. After that Skilton paid many visits to the near-by Indian school—Haskell Institute. His first works on

Indian themes were the *Deer Dance* and the *War Dance*, originally written for string quartet, and later expanded to orchestral form. These comprised the first part of his *Suite Primeval*. The second part was published four years later, consisting of four movements, all based on primitive songs: *Sunrise Song* (Winnebago); *Gambling Song* (Rogue River); *Flute Serenade* (Sioux); and *Moccasin Game* (Winnebago).

Skilton composed Indian operas. One, the three-act *Kalopin*, is based on the New Madrid Earthquake of 1811 and the legendary causes attributed to it by the Chickasaw and Choctaw Indians. The Indians believed that the disaster was the punishment sent by the great spirit because Kalopin, the young Chickasaw chief, went to another tribe for his bride. Skilton treated this as an allegory, representing the overwhelming of the Indians by the white race, just as the Indian village was overwhelmed by earthquake and flood.

Kalopin has not yet had a public performance, but a one-act opera by Skilton, *The Sun Bride*, was given a radio production over a network of the National Broadcasting Company in the spring of 1930. The plot is based on the sun-worshiping beliefs of the Pueblo Indians of Arizona. The composer used as one of the motives the Winnebago Sunrise Song found in the *Suite Primeval*. He also used a Chippewa melody. Exotic rhythms help to bring out the Indian locale and story, and in spite of a conventional melodiousness, the Indian atmosphere is effectively suggested.

Skilton composed other music than that founded on Indian sources. One of his first scores was the incidental music and choral odes for a performance of Sophocles's *Electra* given at Smith College, Northampton. His oratorio *The Guardian Angel* was performed under the auspices of the Kansas Federation of Music Clubs, which provided for its publication. His orchestral works include a *Legend*, first performed by the Minneapolis Orchestra in 1927, an Overture, *Mount Oread*, and an Overture in E which was performed at the American Composers' Concerts in Rochester, March 28, 1934.

CARL BUSCH (1862–1943) gained distinction for carrying into his music the spirit of the Western prairies, and for incorporating Indian material into his compositions. He was born in Bjerre, Denmark, March 29, 1862, and his early training was in the country of his birth, at the University of Copenhagen, and with Hartmann and Gade. In 1886 he went to Paris to study with Godard, and in the following year he came to America. He settled in Kansas City and was active there until the time of his death, December 19, 1943, as a composer, teacher, and conductor of various choral and orchestral organizations, many of which he himself founded.

Busch generally chose American subjects for his works. A piece for military band is entitled *Chant from the Great Plains; Ozarka* is a Suite for orchestra; *Minnehaha's Vision* is based on an episode from Longfellow's *Hiawatha*. He made many settings of actual Indian melodies, for voice, for piano, and for orchestra; for example, the *Four Indian Tribal Melodies*. He also composed two Symphonies; a symphonic prologue *The Passing of Arthur;* an *Elegy* for string orchestra; a String Quartet; and many cantatas, anthems, songs, and small pieces. In 1912 he was knighted by the Danish government.

HENRY HOLDEN HUSS (1862–1953) was a composer of the elder contemporary group who wrote music of considerable charm in the romantic mold, even though he seemed to lack enough of the power of self-criticism to give his works endurance. His Sonata for violin and piano is spirited and playable; in turn, rhythmically full of life, lyrical, and capricious. His Quartet for strings, Opus 31, has been performed by the Kneisel and Berkshire Quartets, and is published by the Society for the Publication of American Music.

Huss was a pupil of Rheinberger. Born in Newark, New Jersey, June 21, 1862, a descendant of the Bohemian patriot and martyr John Huss, he studied first with his father and later under Boise and Rheinberger abroad. Most of his life was spent in New York, teaching and giving joint recitals with his wife, the former Hildegard Hoffmann, a soprano.[4]

He wrote two works for piano and orchestra—a Rhapsody and a Concerto in B Major. He played them with orchestras both abroad and at home. There are several Quartets, a Trio, the Violin Sonata, and a Sonata for cello and piano, as well as a number of piano pieces and about thirty published songs. He wrote several works for chorus, one of them a *Festival Sanctus* for chorus, orchestra, and organ.

ROSSETTER GLEASON COLE (1866–1952) was a pupil of Max Bruch in Germany and of Middelschulte at home. He was born in Michigan,

[4] Huss died in New York, September 17, 1953.

February 5, 1866, and for many years he lived in Chicago as a teacher, composer, organist, and lecturer. As a composer he published over ninety works. His style was possibly influenced more by the music of César Franck than by that of any other composer; but he nevertheless succeeded in evolving something of a personal idiom. He felt that American music must grow on individual rather than on nationalistic lines.

His *Symphonic Prelude* for orchestra was first performed by the Chicago Symphony under Stock in 1916, and repeated in 1918. An overture, *Pioneer*, was written in commemoration of the Illinois State Centennial (1918), and dedicated to the memory of Abraham Lincoln. It was first performed in 1919, the composer conducting. A *Heroic Piece* for orchestra and organ was first played at a special concert of the Chicago Symphony in 1924.

Cole has written three choral works—*The Passing of Summer*; *The Broken Troth*, a cantata for women's voices; and *The Rock of Liberty*, a Pilgrim ode, composed for the tercentenary of the landing of the Pilgrims. His Sonata for violin and piano was first performed in Germany in 1892, and then in America by Theodore Spiering in 1897. It is an early work, conventional and long, though melodic and musical. The *Ballade* for cello and orchestra was introduced in Minneapolis in 1909.

Like David Stanley Smith, Cole composed an opera on the *Merrymount* theme several years before Howard Hanson's opera was produced in 1934. Cole accordingly changed the name of his opera to *The Maypole Lovers*. Although the opera has not been produced in its original form, an orchestral suite from its score was performed by the Chicago Symphony Orchestra, January 9 and 10, 1936.

Louis Victor Saar (1868–1937) was a Hollander who came to America in 1894 as an accompanist at the Metropolitan Opera House. He was born in Rotterdam, December 10, 1868. His family had been distantly related to Schubert. While he was in New York he taught at the National Conservatory and at the Institute of Musical Art. From 1906 to 1917 he was head of the theory and composition courses at the College of Music in Cincinnati; from 1917 to 1933 he held a similar position at the Chicago Musical College; and at the time of his death, November 23, 1937, he headed the theory department at the St. Louis Institute of Music. His orchestral works include a *Rococo*

Suite (1915); a Suite, *From the Mountain Kingdom of the Great Northwest* (1922); and *Along the Columbia River* (1924).

HENRY LAWRENCE FREEMAN (1869–1954), a Negro composer who wrote fifteen operas, was born in Cleveland, Ohio, October 9, 1869. In addition to composing he taught at Wilberforce University in Chicago, at the Salem School of Music, and at his own Freeman School of Music. In 1923 he founded the Freeman School of Grand Opera and in 1920 he organized a Negro Opera Company.

All of his operas were based on Negro, Oriental, or Indian themes; they include *The Martyr* (1893); *Valdo* (1906); *Zuluki* (dated 1898); *African Kraal* (1903); *The Octoroon* (1904); *The Tryst* (1912); *The Plantation* (1914); *Athalia* (1916); *Vendetta* (1923); *American Romance*, a jazz opera composed in 1927; *Voodoo* (1928); *Leah Kleschna* (1930); *Uzziah* (1931); and a tetralogy entitled *Zululand*, comprising *Nada, the Lily* (1941–44), *Allah* (1947), *The Zulu King* (1934), and *The Slave* (1932).

MAX BENDIX (1866–1945) was born in Detroit, Michigan, March 28, 1866; a violinist and composer, he served as concertmaster and assistant conductor for Theodore Thomas from 1886 to 1889. He composed a Violin Concerto; incidental music for the play *Experience* and for Jane Cowl's production of *Romeo and Juliet*; music for the ballet that Fokine arranged for the play *Johannes Kreisler*; a Valse-Caprice for orchestra entitled *Pavlova*; *The Sisters*, a ballad for soprano and orchestra; and many songs.

ELEANOR EVEREST FREER (1864–1942), born in Philadelphia, May 14, 1864, composed ten operas, including *The Court Jester* (1926) and *The Legend of the Piper* (1928). An ardent supporter of American composers, she founded the American Opera Society of Chicago. In addition to operas she composed vocal quartets and trios, about a hundred and fifty songs, and many piano pieces.

PAOLO GALLICO (1868–1955), born in Trieste, Italy, May 13, 1868, composed an oratorio, *The Apocalypse*, that won the $500 prize of the National Federation of Music Clubs in 1921. His orchestral works include *Euphorion*, *Rhapsodie Mondial*, and *Rhapsodie Montereyan*. He also composed an instrumental Sextet; an opera, *Harlequin*; songs; and piano pieces. He died in New York.

WILLIAM J. MCCOY (1848–1926), born at Crestline, Ohio, March

15, 1848, composed an opera, *Egypt;* a Symphony in F; an Overture, *Yosemite; The Najads Idyl;* a Prelude for orchestra; *Introduction and Valse Concertante,* for flute and orchestra; miscellaneous chamber music; music for the plays of the San Francisco Bohemian Club; choral works; and many songs.

PAUL FRIEDRICH THEODORE MIERSCH (1868–1956) was born in Dresden, Germany, January 8, 1868, and came to America in 1886. His works include a Cello Concerto; a Violin Concerto; *Indian Rhapsody* for orchestra; a String Quartet; numerous songs; and pieces for violin and for cello.

HENRY SCHOENFELD (1857–1936), born in Milwaukee, Wisconsin, October 4, 1857, was one of the earliest composers to utilize the resources of American Indian music. He composed a grand opera, *Atala, or The Love of Two Savages; Suite Caractéristique* for string orchestra; an Indian pantomime, *Wachicanta;* and *Two Indian Legends* for orchestra. His *Rural Symphony* won a $500 prize offered by the National Conservatory in New York in 1892.

EDMUND SEVERN (1862–1942), born in Nottingham, England, December 10, 1862, was brought to America at the age of four. A violinist, conductor, and composer, he wrote a *Festival Overture;* two tone poems, *Lancelot and Elaine* and *Héloïse and Abélard;* a Suite for orchestra, *From Old New England;* an orchestral *Fantasy* on *The Tempest;* a Violin Concerto; three String Quartets; a Trio; a Sonata for violin and piano; and many violin pieces.

HUMPHREY JOHN STEWART (1856–1932), for nearly half a century a prominent organist of San Francisco, was born in London, May 22, 1856, and came to California when he was thirty years old. His compositions include three operas: *His Majesty* (1890); *The Conspirators* (1900); and *King Hal* (1911). He also wrote a sacred music drama, *The Hound of Heaven* (1924); two orchestral Suites: *Montezuma* and *Scenes in California;* a Mass; and many organ pieces and songs.

GUSTAV STRUBE (1867–1953), founder and conductor from 1916 to 1930 of the Baltimore Symphony Orchestra, was born in Bellenstedt, Germany, March 3, 1867. He immigrated to America in 1891, and after twenty-two years as violinist with the Boston Symphony settled in Baltimore, where he was associated with the Peabody Conservatory until four years before his death. His compositions include

Walter Damrosch
(See pages 351–354)

Edgar Stillman Kelley
(See pages 345–347)

John Alden Carpenter
(See pages 168-172)

Henry K. Hadley
(See pages 372-374)

three Symphonies; four symphonic poems; three Overtures; two Rhapsodies and four Preludes for orchestra; two Violin Concertos; symphonic music for chamber orchestra; a wind Quintet; a Trio; a String Quartet; Sonatas for cello, for viola, and for violin; an opera, *The Captive*; and smaller pieces for violin.

MAX WILHELM KARL VOGRICH (1852–1916), born in Transylvania, January 24, 1852, came to America in 1878. He composed three operas that were produced abroad; two Symphonies; a Violin Concerto; cantatas and choruses; church music; songs; and instrumental pieces.

ARNOLD VOLPE (1869–1940), born in Kovno, Lithuania, July 9, 1869, studied with Leopold Auer in St. Petersburg and emigrated from Europe to America in 1898. He founded the Young Men's Symphony Orchestra in New York in 1902, the Volpe Symphony Orchestra in 1904, and the summer concerts at the Lewisohn Stadium in New York in 1918, conducting the first two seasons himself. After conducting the Washington, D.C., Opera Company from 1919 to 1922 and directing the Kansas City Conservatory from 1922 to 1925, he settled in Florida in 1926, where he founded and conducted until his death the University of Miami Symphony Orchestra. He composed a Mazurka for violin and orchestra; a String Quartet; songs; and violin pieces.

ADOLF WEIDIG (1867–1931), born in Hamburg, Germany, November 28, 1867, came to the United States in 1892. He composed two Symphonies; a Suite for string orchestra; three String Quartets; a String Quintet; a Trio; several Suites for violin and piano; songs; and choruses.

CHAPTER TWELVE

Twentieth Century Composers

I. COMPOSERS BORN IN THE 1870'S

IN the first section of this chapter we shall find most of the composers writing in a more or less conventional post-romantic idiom, although we shall also meet the Impressionists John Alden Carpenter and Edward Burlingame Hill, the Nationalists Arthur Farwell and Frederick Ayres, and, most remarkable of all, a pioneer who even in his own day was far in advance of the most radical Europeans and largely ignorant of their music. Since this man's work, totally unknown until at his own expense he published his First Piano Sonata and a book of songs in 1919, is now the most widely discussed and frequently performed of any compositions of men born in this decade, it seems fitting to consider him first.

CHARLES E. IVES (1874–1954) is still a controversial figure, but his reckless courage in experimenting with polyharmonies and polyrhythms, strong dissonances, atonality, and rhythmic intricacies, long before Stravinsky, Schoenberg, and equally famous European revolutionaries had forsaken the conventional idiom, has become more and more widely acknowledged.

Ives believed that the old and new are either parts of the same substance or are nonexistent and that the apostles of each are usually taken up with abusing each other or getting in their own way. And he pointed out, truly enough, that while each examines and appreciates the other to some extent, the radicals fight in a bigger way than their opponents: they generally pay homage to the old, while many of the conservatives either ignore the new or deride it. And as for the manner of speech, he wrote:

If idioms are more to be born than to be selected, then the things of life and human nature that a man has grown up with—(not that one man's experience is better than another's, but that it is *his*)—may give him something better in his substance and manner than an overlong period of superimposed idiomatic education which quite likely doesn't fit his constitution. My father used to say, "If a poet knows more about a horse than he does about heaven, he might better stick to the horse, and some day the horse may carry him into heaven."

Ives was born in Danbury, Connecticut, October 20, 1874. His father was a musician, teacher of the violin, piano, and theory, who played in the town brass band, led the village choir, conducted the music at camp meetings, and directed the local choral society. He was also a student of acoustics and made experiments with musical instruments, tonal combinations, and tone divisions. The young Charles studied with his father, and after the senior Ives's death he had lessons from Dudley Buck and Harry Rowe Shelley and from Horatio Parker at Yale.

For a time Charles Ives was an organist at Danbury, New Haven, and New York, but in 1898 he entered business and kept his music as an avocation until his retirement in 1930. He had intended to devote his retirement entirely to composing, but failing health made him virtually an invalid. Even though he lived twenty-four years longer, the vast bulk of his work was completed before 1930. He died in New York on May 19, 1954.

The dates of Ives's compositions show how much of a pioneer he was. In his eight-part setting of the *64th Psalm* (1898) the sopranos and altos sing in the key of C major and the tenors and basses in G minor. *Over the Pavements*, composed in 1913 for chamber orchestra, was written in the omnibus tonality of C-F sharp. These early essays in polytonality make it clear that Ives's experiments were not suggested by the works of others, but were entirely his own empirical attempts to record the musical impressions of his youth, such as the effect of two bands, each playing a different piece simultaneously, at different ends of the village green; reed organs out of tune; country fiddlers; soldiers and bands marching, some out of step and trying to get in pace with the others.

Ives's first work to be published, in 1919, was his second Sonata,

Concord, Massachusetts, 1840–60, with its four movements named *Emerson, Hawthorne, The Alcotts,* and *Thoreau.* It was accompanied by an essay printed in a separate volume. The composer stated that his Sonata was an attempt "to present one person's impression of the spirit of transcendentalism that is associated with the minds of Concord over half a century ago. This is undertaken in impressionistic pictures of Emerson and Thoreau, a sketch of the Alcotts, and a scherzo supposed to reflect a lighter quality often found in the fantastic side of Hawthorne."

When the Sonata first was distributed, most musicians were astonished by its appalling technical difficulties, bizarre beyond serious consideration. Part of it was played at the 1928 Salzburg Festival, but it was not publicly performed in this country until John Kirkpatrick presented it in Town Hall, New York, January 20, 1939. The next day Lawrence Gilman wrote in the New York *Herald Tribune:*

This sonata is exceptionally great music—it is, indeed, the greatest music composed by an American, and the most deeply and essentially American in impulse and implication. It is wide-ranging and capacious. It has passion, tenderness, humor, simplicity, homeliness. It has imaginative and spiritual vastness. It has wisdom and beauty, and profundity, and a sense of the encompassing terror and splendor of human life and destiny—a sense of those mysteries that are both human and divine.

Not all members of the audience agreed with Gilman's extraordinary praise. Many felt that the work lacked organization and that it was not sufficiently articulate. But almost everyone present felt that he had heard something moving and vital.

In the years following Kirkpatrick's performance of the *Concord* Sonata Ives's fame grew steadily. Others of his works were performed, and he was recognized as one of our most important composers. After years of absolute neglect he was hailed by enthusiasts as a genius unparalleled in the history of American music. Some, less enthusiastic but still appreciative, considered him a primitive, akin to our earlier pioneer William Billings or, in a larger sphere, to the Russian Mussorgski. Some called him the "Grandma Moses" of American music.

There can be no doubting the inherent greatness in Ives's music. Whatever his methods and technical limitations, his thoughts were great thoughts and his massive sonorities were expressive of a lofty, mountainous idealism. Yet there was with all this an iconoclastic urge to smash false idols of the past, an urge that took the form of impish jokes which often cannot help but mar the real seriousness of his intention and the rugged vigor of his music.

Following a performance of Ives's Second Symphony by the New York Philharmonic on October 3, 1958, Paul H. Lang devoted an article to him in the New York *Herald Tribune* of October 12, discussing the alleged primitivism of Ives's work. He wrote in part:

Many an American musician of today . . . smiles indulgently at this homespun New England revolutionary. He feels a little embarrassed by the "primitive quaintness" of Ives, yet secretly he also feels the greatness hidden there. . . . Ives is the symbolic representation of the American composer. . . . Far from being a "primitive," [his] was an entirely modern, complex, and cultivated mind, which the specifically American conditions prevented from developing in an orderly and natural way. It could not develop because at the turn of the century the nation would not accept an American composer on his own terms. It must have been the realization that this kind of musical ambition had no chance that made Ives into a musical hermit. I am convinced that both in his music and in his attitude he wanted to exemplify the fate of an American composer whose background was pure Connecticut, untempered by German education. . . . He could have become the Walt Whitman of music, but in his life there were no Emersons and Carlyles to take his side, and posterity, though paying him homage, tries to reduce his status to that of a musical roadside curiosity. If our performers do not stop at the innocuous Second Symphony but play his great works, we shall discover an American composer compared to whom many of those who were born when Ives quit composing appear as primitives, indeed.

Though he composed no more after 1930, Ives's output was enormous. Sorting out the accumulation of his manuscripts was a mammoth task, for he had a habit of reworking his compositions and using the same material in different works. An expert librarian was assigned to the job, and after Ives's death his manuscripts, fully catalogued, were given to Yale University. Many have been published and are available for performance.

For orchestra there are five numbered Symphonies, composed respectively in 1896–98; 1897–1902; 1901–4; 1910–16; and the Fifth,

1911–16, only partially completed. The Second Symphony was first performed in New York, February 22, 1951, four years after a performance of the Third Symphony (New York, May 5, 1947) had won for Ives the Pulitzer Prize of that year. *Three Places in New England*, an orchestral set, was composed in 1903–14 and had its première in New York with the Chamber Orchestra of Boston, January 10, 1931. In 1935 it was published by the C. C. Birchard Company of Boston and was probably the first of Ives's compositions to be issued by a commercial publisher. The Fourth Symphony was introduced by Leopold Stokowski and the American Orchestra in New York in 1965, fifty years after it had been composed; the work was enthusiastically received by critics and by the public.

Other orchestral works include a *Robert Browning* Overture composed in 1911 and first performed October 14, 1956, by the Orchestra of the Air under Leopold Stokowski. *Lincoln, the Great Commoner*, for chorus and orchestra, based on a poem by Edwin Markham, was composed in 1912 and given its première by the Orchestra of America in New York, February 10, 1960. A work composed in 1904, 1912, and 1913, entitled *Holidays*, is also designated a Symphony, its four movements commemorating *Washington's Birthday*, *Decoration Day*, *Fourth of July*, and *Thanksgiving*. These symphonic movements are generally performed separately. A First Piano Sonata, composed in 1909, preceded by ten years the publication of the *Concord* Sonata. This earlier work has jazzy, syncopated passages written well before jazz was widely known. There is also a long list of chamber works and choral music.

CARL RUGGLES (1876———), Ives's junior by only a year and a half, has much in common with him. He has the same disregard for recognition and writes his music as he himself wants it, even though it might never be performed. Unlike Ives, Ruggles has composed relatively few works. In recent years he has spent much of his time painting abstract pictures at his home in Arlington, Vermont. This occupation has proved more profitable than music, for his paintings are said to bring as much as $800 apiece. He continues to compose, however, using for music paper large mural-sized sheets on which he draws notes with crayons of different colors.

It is probably Ruggles's severe self-criticism that has limited his musical output. He is said to have destroyed the score of his one-act opera, *The Sunken Bell* (the only opera he has composed), after the Metropolitan had accepted it and set a performance date. His music is powerfully dissonant and often atonal, but he resents the suggestion that he used a Schoenbergian or any other fixed formula.

When Ruggles's symphonic Suite *Men and Mountains* was first performed in New York, December 7, 1924, and even twelve years later when it was played in revised form for larger orchestra, its granitic dissonance was too strong for the average concertgoer, even though many musicians perceived its vitality and rugged strength. Yet in 1958, when Leonard Bernstein played the work on a program of the New York Philharmonic, the public was ready for it. What Lawrence Gilman had called "a strange, torrential, and disturbing discourse" sounded almost romantic, sweeping, and spacious; Robert Sabin reviewed the concert for *Musical America* (November, 1958), writing of *Men and Mountains*, "It has a rugged simplicity of line, for all its dissonance and complex plan of structure, that is truly eloquent. And the second section, the 'Lilacs' for strings alone, like some of the music of Charles Ives, has a curious gnomic sweetness. One senses a profound love of nature in it and attachment to old, well-loved places and people."

Ruggles was born in Marion, Massachusetts, March 11, 1876. He studied with Walter Spalding and John K. Paine at Harvard, and for some years lived in Minnesota, where in 1912 he organized and conducted the Winona Symphony Orchestra. From 1937 until the time of his retirement to Vermont he was instructor in modern composition at the University of Miami in Florida. In 1954 he was elected to the National Institute of Arts and Letters.

Ruggles's earliest orchestral work to be performed was originally entitled *Men and Angels*. Scored for five trumpets and one bass trumpet, it was premièred in New York, December 17, 1922. It was later revised for strings and brass, retitled *Angels*, and in that form played under the composer's baton in Miami in 1939. *Portals*, for string orchestra, was performed on January 24, 1926, in New York, and *Sun Treader*, for large orchestra, based on a poem by Robert Browning, in Paris, February 25, 1932.

In 1949 the New York Philharmonic under Leopold Stokowski

gave the first performance of Ruggles's *Organum.* Henry Cowell wrote in the *Musical Quarterly* (April, 1950):

Rather to the surprise of both composer and conductor, the work achieved a real popular success. Audiences have gained wide experience since the twenties, when all dissonant music sounded alike and horrible to them. Nowadays, the audience of the New York Philharmonic discriminates. It hissed and tore paper resoundingly this winter at the rather cerebral music of Anton Webern; but it applauded Ruggles vociferously. The difference obviously lies in the fact that Ruggles' web of chromatic, atonal sound is felt fully and vitally by the composer, to a point of extraordinary contagion; the music is full of verve. It is rich, full-blooded, super-romantic, urgent.

In addition to orchestral compositions Ruggles has composed *Polyphonic Composition* for three pianos (1940) and *Evocations* (1945), four chants for piano.

JOHN PARSONS BEACH (1877–1953), a year and a half younger than Ruggles and another of the pioneers to branch into radical paths, was born in Gloversville, New York, October 11, 1877, trained at the New England Conservatory of Music in Boston, and studied fugue with André Gédalge in Paris. Beach's orchestral works include *Asolani* (1926), a series of three pieces; *New Orleans Street Cries* (1927); and the ballets *Phantom Satyr* (1925) and *Mardi Gras* (1926). His chamber music includes *Native Landscapes* for flute, oboe, clarinet, and piano (1917); a *Poem* for string quartet (1920); *Angelo's Letter,* for tenor or baritone and chamber orchestra; and a *Concert for Six Instruments* (1929). He published a number of piano pieces and songs and composed, in addition to ballets, short stage works: *Pippa's Holiday* (1915), a theatre scene for soprano and orchestra from Browning's *Pippa Passes;* and *Jornida and Jornidel* (1926), a short opera from Grimm's fairy tale.

The music of ARTHUR FICKENSCHER (1871–1954) may be of largely historical interest today, but he was a pioneer experimenter with intervals smaller than the semitone, dividing the octave into sixty microtones and inventing an instrument, the "Polytone," which will sound these tones in accurate intonation. Born in Aurora, Illinois, March 9, 1871, Fickenscher studied at the Munich Conservatory and after graduation served as assisting pianist with famous singers, including David Bispham and Schumann-Heink. From 1920 to 1924 he headed the music department of the University of Virginia.

His orchestra works include *Willowwave and Wellaway* (1924); *Day of Judgment* (1927); *Variations on a Theme in Medieval Style* (1931); and *Out of the Gay Nineties* (1934). His most important experimental work was his *Evolutionary Quintet*, developed from a Violin Sonata and an orchestral Scherzo that he had composed in the 1890's. The manuscripts of the original pieces were burned in the San Francisco earthquake of 1906, and he reconstructed the material from memory in the form of a Quintet for piano and strings.

After these radicals we may now consider two men, forward-looking for their time, who may loosely be classed as Impressionists. JOHN ALDEN CARPENTER (1876–1951) evidenced an occasional predilection for contemporary subjects that caused Walter Damrosch to call him the most American of our composers. In his ballet *Skyscrapers* Carpenter sought to portray our age of rivets and mechanism, and in *Krazy Kat* the exaggerated humor and slapstick caricature of newspaper comic strips.

Born in Park Ridge, Illinois, February 28, 1876, Carpenter had his first lessons from his mother, a talented amateur singer, and subsequently studied with John K. Paine at Harvard, with Edward Elgar in England, and with Bernard Ziehn in Chicago. For many years he was entitled to amateur standing as a musician: until his retirement in 1936 he was vice-president of George B. Carpenter & Company, Chicago merchants in mill, railway, and vessel supplies. Yet for all his business interests, he found enough time for music to become one of the most important of our composers.

Carpenter's first important orchestral work, the widely-played Suite *Adventures in a Perambulator* (1915) describes the sensations of a baby wheeled along the sidewalks by his nurse: the child sees *The Policeman, The Hurdy-Gurdy, The Lake,* and *Dogs.* It is witty, sparkling music, and the composer was skillful in evoking the sounds of the street organ and of barking dogs. A *Concertino* for piano and orchestra (1916), written a year later, suggests a light-hearted conversation between the piano and orchestra—two friends who have traveled different paths and have become a little garrulous over their separate experiences. The following year a Symphony was played in

Norfolk, Connecticut, and in 1920 *A Pilgrim Vision*, for orchestra, composed for the tercentenary Mayflower celebration, was introduced in Philadelphia.

On December 23, 1919, *The Birthday of the Infanta*, Carpenter's first ballet score, was performed by the Chicago Opera Company. It was followed by the two ballets which more than any others of his works established him as a nationalist composer: *Krazy Kat*, first produced in Chicago, December 23, 1921, a pioneer experiment in using the jazz idiom, with scenario and action based on George Herriman cartoons; and *Skyscrapers*, first produced at the Metropolitan Opera House in New York on February 19, 1926—Carpenter's most advanced score, in some ways radical for its time, with no attempt to spare the listener the cacophony of city streets. In condensed version the score was often played as an orchestral piece. The jazz element was again apparent in *Patterns*, a one-movement work for orchestra and piano obbligato that was first performed by the Boston Symphony in 1932. A year later Carpenter produced *Sea Drift*, inspired (like Delius's work of the same title and the *Sea Symphony* of Vaughan Williams) by the sea poems of Walt Whitman. It was first performed in 1934 by the New York Philharmonic-Symphony under Werner Janssen.

Danza, introduced by the Chicago Symphony in 1935, is perhaps a less important piece than others of Carpenter's works, but it is charming and suggestive of the Spanish influence that appears every once in a while in his music. Two years later, in 1937, Zlato Balakovič played Carpenter's Concerto for violin and orchestra with the Chicago Symphony.

In 1940 Carpenter composed a Symphony in One Movement for the fiftieth anniversary of the Chicago Symphony. The work was based on the principal theme of the 1917 Symphony and was described by Francis Perkins in the New York *Herald Tribune* (November 23, 1940) as "sincere and appealing music, generous in melodic content, well knit and concise in form, ably wrought in its scoring and in its employment of ideas." Carpenter's Symphony No. 2 was introduced October 22, 1942, by the New York Philharmonic-Symphony under Bruno Walter. Virgil Thomson called it "rich man's music, gentleman's composition. . . . Mr. Carpenter has been to Harvard and Paris."

. . . His mind is cultivated and adult. He writes with force and some charm. This work is well woven, contrapuntally alive; it has no empty spots in it. . . . The whole is opulent and comfortable, intelligent, well organized, cultured and firm without being either ostentatious or unduly modest." (New York *Herald Tribune*, October 23, 1942.) Later orchestral works include a symphonic poem, *The Anxious Bugler* (1943); a symphonic Suite, *The Seven Ages* (1945); and *Carmel Concerto* (1948).

Carpenter's chamber compositions include a Sonata for violin and piano (1912) and two compositions that had first performances at the Library of Congress in Washington: a String Quartet (1928) and a Quintet for piano and strings (1935). In 1931 the United States George Washington Bicentennial Committee asked Carpenter to compose an Ode for the forthcoming celebration in 1932. The composer responded with *Song of Faith*, for chorus and orchestra, to his own text, based on Washington's writings and speeches. Ten years later, in 1941, Carpenter composed *Song of Freedom*, for chorus and orchestra.

It was perhaps in his songs that Carpenter showed most distinctly his leanings toward French Impressionism. He was especially happy with the texts of Rabindranath Tagore, whose spirit he seemed to catch more faithfully than did any other composer. His settings of poems from *Gitanjali* abound in sensitivity and Oriental warmth of color. *Water Colors*, settings of four Chinese poems, are well named, for they deal in tints rather than colors. Carpenter suggests the Chinese lute in the accompaniment, and subtly brings out the drollery that lurks in the verses. In quite different spirit, similar in type to the *Adventures in a Perambulator*, are his *Improving Songs for Anxious Children*.

Although EDWARD BURLINGAME HILL (1872–1960) was a New Englander thoroughly steeped in Boston traditions, he avoided the academic inhibitions that limited the expressiveness of his contemporaries. He was interested in the Impressionist school, and for the most part his work followed French models, though with characteristic clarity of design and elegance of expression.

Born in Cambridge, Massachusetts, September 9, 1872, Hill studied music with John Knowles Paine at Harvard, the university of which his grandfather had been president and where his father had been a chemistry professor. After graduation Hill worked with Widor in Paris and with Chadwick in Boston. In 1908 he became a teacher at Harvard, and from 1928 to 1939 he served as chairman of the division of music. From 1934 until his retirement in 1941 he was James E. Ditson Professor of Music.

Hill's two *Stevensoniana Suites* for orchestra had their premières in New York: No. 1 in 1918 and No. 2 in 1923. The second, inspired by poems from Robert Louis Stevenson's *A Child's Garden of Verses,* was the more frequently performed. Hill based a symphonic poem on Poe's *The Fall of the House of Usher* and another on Amy Lowell's poem *Lilacs.* The Poe piece was first performed in 1920, *Lilacs* in 1927. The latter is perhaps Hill's finest work in the Impressionist idiom.

Hill subsequently confined himself to absolute music in which he showed an occasional tendency toward mild polytonality. The Boston Symphony introduced his orchestral works of this period, including the First Symphony (1928); an *Ode* composed for the orchestra's fiftieth anniversary (1930); the Second Symphony (1931); a *Concertino* for piano and orchestra (1932) that exhibited certain traits derived from jazz; two Sinfoniettas (1933 and 1936), the second an orchestral arrangement of Hill's String Quartet; the Third Symphony (1937); the Concerto for violin and orchestra (1938); the *Concertino* for strings (1940); *Music for English Horn and Orchestra* (1945); and *Prelude for Orchestra* (1953).

Others of Hill's works include a Sonata for clarinet (or violin) and piano (1926–27); a Sextet for wind instruments and piano (1934); a Quintet for piano and strings (1938); a Sonata for two clarinets (1938); a Quintet for clarinet and string quartet (1945); a Sonata for bassoon and piano (1948); a Sonatina for cello and piano (1949); and a Sonatina for violin and piano (1951).

ARTHUR FARWELL (1872–1952) attempted to achieve a nationalistic American music through the use of American Indian melodies. Joining with other composers of similar aim, he became a founder of the Wa-Wan Press, which welcomed works by American composers that were unacceptable to commercial publishers, and was especially hospitable to compositions developing in interesting fashion any folk music heard on American soil. Through the press Farwell helped to launch a number of his fellow-composers, and from 1901 to 1912 he raised money for Wa-Wan by lecturing and teaching. Feeling that the work was accomplished, he then transferred Wa-Wan's catalogue to the firm of G. Schirmer.

Born in St. Paul, Minnesota, April 23, 1872, Farwell heard a symphony concert for the first time when he went to Boston to study at the Massachusetts Institute of Technology. The pull of music soon proved too strong, and he gave up the idea of becoming an engineer to study composition, initially in Boston and subsequently with Humperdinck and Pfitzner in Germany and with Guilmant in Paris. He returned to America in 1899 and was successively lecturer on music at Cornell University, editor on the staff of *Musical America,* and Supervisor of Municipal Music for the City of New York. In 1915 he succeeded David Mannes as director of the Music School Settlement in New York, and a year later he organized the New York Community Chorus. He then taught at the University of California in Los Angeles, at Berkeley, and at Michigan State College. He retired from teaching in 1939.

The opus numbers of Farwell's compositions run to one hundred and three. His Indian compositions include *Dawn,* an orchestral score premièred at the St. Louis Exposition in 1904; *The Domain of Hurakan,* named for the wind god of the Central American Indians; and various characteristic pieces for piano. He also composed a *Fugue Fantasia* for piano and numerous settings of Negro, cowboy, and prairie melodies.

Among Farwell's innovations was the "symphonic song-suite," a form that can be compared to the chorale-prelude of the Reformation. The first such composition was *Mountain Song:* its movements were based on song-themes and the audience sang the songs whenever the form of the piece demanded. The same pattern was repeated in *Symphonic Hymn on March! March!* and *Symphonic Song on Old Black Joe.* Farwell's later works include *The Hako,* for string quartet (1922); a Violin Sonata (1928); and an orchestral Suite after Dunsany's play, *Gods of the Mountains* (1929). The Third (1905) of the six *Symbolist Studies* for orchestra was played by the Philadelphia Orchestra in a revision for two pianos and orchestra, and the

Sixth (1931) won first prize in a competition of the National Federation of Music Clubs and was performed on CBS radio May 28, 1939.

FREDERICK AYRES (1876–1926) was another composer interested in Indian music, although he may not have actually used its melodies in his work. Born Frederick Ayres Johnson in Binghamton, New York, March 17, 1876, he had an academic education at Cornell University and then studied composition with Edgar Stillman Kelley and Arthur Foote. For a number of years he lived at Colorado Springs and became a musical spokesman for the Rocky Mountain section. He composed an Overture, *From the Plains;* a String Quartet; two Trios; a Sonata for violin and piano; a Sonata for cello; and a song cycle, *The Seeonee Wolves.*

Without doubt the most widely played composer of his time, HENRY KIMBALL HADLEY (1871–1937) demonstrated generosity to his colleagues when, during his three seasons as conductor of the Manhattan Symphony in the early 1930's, he presented thirty-six American works, of which only eight were his own. During his last years he founded the National Association for American Composers and Conductors which, among other services, sponsors the Henry Hadley Memorial Library of works by contemporary Americans, deposited in the New York Public Library.

Born in Somerville, Massachusetts, December 20, 1871, Hadley studied composition at the New England Conservatory with Emery and Chadwick. At twenty-two he toured the country as conductor of the Laura Schirmer–Mapleson Opera Company. He made two trips abroad, the first to study composition with Mandyczewski in Vienna and the second to compose and conduct at the Stadt Theatre of Mayence, where in 1909 he produced his one-act opera *Safie.* The same year he became conductor of the Seattle Symphony Orchestra, which he led for five seasons beginning in 1911. In 1920 he was made associate conductor of the New York Philharmonic, and nine years later he organized the Manhattan Symphony Orchestra.

In addition to *Safie,* Hadley's operatic works include the masque *The Atonement of Pan* (1912); *Azora, or The Daughter of Montezuma* (1917); *Bianca* (1918), adapted from a Goldoni play and winner of a $1,000 prize; *Cleopatra's Night* (1920), hailed by critics as the best yet written and retained by the New York Metropolitan

Opera for a second season; and *A Night in Old Paris,* a one-act radio opera presented by NBC in 1933.

Hadley gave subtitles to all his Symphonies but the Third. The First, *Youth and Life,* was first performed in 1897; the Second, *The Four Seasons,* in 1901—it later won the Paderewski Prize; the Third was premièred in Berlin in 1907; the Fourth, *North, East, South, West,* in 1911; and the Fifth, *Connecticut Tercentenary,* in 1935.

Hadley wrote a number of concert Overtures, among them *Hector and Andromache,* performed when the composer was twenty; *In Bohemia* (1901); *Herod* and *Othello,* both performed in 1919; *Youth Triumphant* and *Aurora Borealis* (both 1931); *Academic Overture* and *Alma Mater* (both 1932). His other orchestral works include the tone poem *Salome* (1907); the Rhapsody *The Culprit Fay* (1909), which won the National Federation of Music Clubs' $1,000 prize; *Lucifer,* a symphonic fantasia (1914); the tone poem *The Ocean* (1921); the Oriental Suite *The Streets of Pekin* (1930), introduced by the composer in Tokyo; and *Scherzo Diabolique,* written in 1934 for the Chicago World's Fair. The *Scherzo* is a musical depiction of "the hazards of fast driving, the onrushing myriad headlights of approaching autos, the whirring and whizzing of cars as they pass." In addition Hadley composed three ballet Suites, a Concertstück for cello and orchestra (1937), and a *Concertino* for piano and orchestra.

An effective choral composer, Hadley produced an *Ode to Music* to a poem by Henry Van Dyke; a secular oratorio, *Resurgam* (1923); *Mirtil in Arcadia* (1928); a cantata, *Belshazzar* (1932); and *The Legend of Hani.* In addition to these choral works his vocal compositions include about one hundred and fifty songs. At the time of his death Hadley was a member of the American Academy of Arts and Letters.

DANIEL GREGORY MASON (1873–1953) felt that American music had necessarily to be eclectic and cosmopolitan and that its distinctiveness must be individual rather than national. Taking little pleasure in the Impressionism of Debussy, Ravel, and Scriabin or in the Primitivism of Stravinsky, willing to risk the reactionary label, he turned to the classic Romanticism of Beethoven, Schumann, Brahms, and Franck.

Born in Brookline, Massachusetts, November 20, 1873, he was the grandson of Lowell Mason and the son of the piano manufacturer Henry Mason. At Harvard he attended the music classes of John K. Paine and later studied in Boston with Chadwick, in New York with Percy Goetschius, and in Paris with Vincent d'Indy. After 1900 he was active as lecturer and teacher, and in 1910 he joined the faculty of Columbia University, where he became MacDowell Professor of Music in 1929. He retired in 1940.

Mason's early works include a Sonata for violin and piano, Opus 5; a Quartet for piano and strings, Opus 7; and *Country Pictures* for piano, Opus 9. The Sonata for clarinet (or violin) and piano, composed in 1915, was the first work selected by the Society for the Publication of American Music in 1920. Mason's first work for orchestra, the Symphony No. 1, was introduced by Stokowski and the Philadelphia Orchestra in 1916. A song-cycle for baritone and orchestra, *Russians,* appeared in 1918. The *String Quartet on Negro Themes* (1919), first privately printed, was subsequently withdrawn, revised, and published in its new form by the Society for the Publication of American Music.

Other works include the Prelude and Fugue for piano and orchestra, dedicated to John Powell, who introduced it in Chicago in 1921; *Variations on a Theme of John Powell* (1926), for string quartet; a festival Overture, *Chanticleer* (1928), which proved to be the most widely played of Mason's works; a *Folk-Song Fantasy on the English Air Fanny Blair* (1929); the Symphony No. 2 (1930); *A Lincoln Symphony* (1937); a *Serenade* for string quartet (1932); *Sentimental Sketches* for violin, cello, and piano (1935); and a *Divertimento* for symphonic band.

Mason was widely published as a writer on music, and some of his magazine articles were later incorporated into books. He was the author of a critical-historical series of four volumes: *Beethoven and His Forerunners, The Romantic Composers, From Grieg to Brahms,* and *Contemporary Composers. Tune in America* (1931) was an analysis of musical conditions in this country.

RUBIN GOLDMARK (1872–1936) was the nephew of Karl Goldmark, the Austrian composer of *Sakuntula.* When Dvořák heard the younger Goldmark's Trio at one of the concerts at the National

Conservatory in New York, he exclaimed, "Now there are two Goldmarks!"

Rubin Goldmark was born in New York City, August 15, 1872, and had his academic training at the College of the City of New York and at the University of Vienna. He studied music at the Vienna Conservatory and after his return to New York became a piano pupil of Rafael Joseffy and studied composition with Dvořák at the National Conservatory. He subsequently became a teacher at the Conservatory himself, but in 1894 his health failed and he went to Colorado, where he founded the Colorado College Conservatory. By 1902 his health had improved sufficiently to allow him to return to New York, where he established himself not only as a composer but, perhaps more importantly, as one of our leading teachers of composers. He headed the composition department of the Juilliard School from 1924 until his death; his composition pupils included such widely divergent composers as Frederick Jacobi, Aaron Copland, Nicolai Berezowsky, Bernard Wagenaar, Vittorio Giannini, Paul Nordoff, and George Gershwin.

Goldmark's most widely known work is his *Requiem* for orchestra, suggested by Lincoln's Gettysburg Address. It has an austere grandeur appropriate to its subject, and was first played by the Philharmonic Society of New York in 1919. An earlier work, the *Hiawatha Overture*, was introduced by the Boston Symphony in 1900. *Samson*, a tone poem, was first played in Boston in 1914. In *Negro Rhapsody* (1923) Goldmark tried using Negro folk material; another attempt at catching the American locale, *The Call of the Plains*, was originally composed for violin and piano (1915) and later scored for orchestra (1925). Goldmark also composed a String Quartet, a Piano Trio, a Sonata for violin and piano, and many smaller pieces and songs.

DAVID STANLEY SMITH (1877–1949), born in Toledo, Ohio, July 6, 1877, studied with Horatio Parker at Yale, with Ludwig Thuille in Munich, and with Charles Widor in Paris. He became an instructor at the Yale School of Music in 1903, a professor in 1916, and in 1920 dean, a position in which he succeeded Horatio Parker and which he held for twenty-six years. During the years 1920–46 he was also conductor of the New Haven Symphony. He retired from the music school and from the orchestra in 1946.

Smith's orchestral works include the First Symphony (1912), the Overture *Prince Hal* (1916), a Suite of *Impressions* (1916), the Second Symphony (1918), *Fête Galante* (1920), introduced by the flutist Georges Barrère with the New York Symphony in 1921; a *Cathedral Prelude* for organ and orchestra (1926); the Third Symphony (1931); *1929—A Satire* (1932); *Tomorrow*, an Overture (1933); an *Epic Poem* (1935); and a *Rondo Appassionato* for violin and orchestra.

His imposing catalogue of chamber works includes two Sonatas, one for oboe and piano (1918) and one for violin and piano (1921); *Flowers* (1924), a suite of four pieces for chamber orchestra; and eight String Quartets. He composed a Sinfonietta for strings (1931) and a Sonatina for junior string orchestra (1932). The *Rhapsody of St. Bernard* (1915) and the *Vision of Isaiah* (1927) are large choral pieces, and the unproduced opera *Merrymount* was composed many years before Howard Hanson's work of the same title.

Following his retirement from the Yale School of Music, Smith composed *Credo*, a poem for orchestra (1941); a Requiem (1942); and *Daybreak*, a choral work which opened the Centenary Celebration at the Temple Emanu-El, New York, in 1945.

FREDERICK SHEPHERD CONVERSE (1871–1940) composed the first American opera to be produced by the Metropolitan Opera in New York, the one-act *The Pipe of Desire*. The opera was first produced in Boston in 1906 and four years later at the Metropolitan in New York; it was awarded the Bispham Medal.

Born at Newton, Massachusetts, January 5, 1871, Converse studied composition with John K. Paine at Harvard, with George W. Chadwick, and with Josef Rheinberger at the Royal Academy in Munich. His Symphony in D Minor was played at his graduation from the Academy in 1899. He returned to Boston the same year to teach harmony at the New England Conservatory, shifting to Harvard two years later as instructor in composition and subsequently becoming assistant professor. He resigned in 1907 in order to devote himself to composition, but later returned to the New England Conservatory and in 1931 became dean of the faculty, a position that he held for seven years. He died two years after his retirement.

Converse wielded the fluent technique and contrapuntal facility common to Rheinberger pupils. Though his music generally reflected his academic training and conservative taste, he on one occasion adopted the devices of his more radical colleagues to compose a choice bit of musical humor. In 1924 Arthur Honegger sought to depict the journey of a locomotive in his orchestra piece *Pacific 231*. Whether or not the wide vogue of this composition influenced Converse we cannot know, but at any rate the publicity that heralded the advent of the ten millionth "Flivver" from the Ford production line turned his mind toward the automobile, and the result was *Flivver Ten Million*, first played by the Boston Symphony on April 15, 1927.

The opening movement, *Dawn in Detroit*, depicts the toilers marching to work and the din of automobile construction. *The Birth of the Hero* introduces the flivver, emerging full-fledged from the welter, ready for service. He tries his mettle (the pun is intended) and wanders forth into the great world in search of adventure. *May Night by the Roadside* depicts America's romance; *The Joy Riders*, America's frolic; and *The Collision*, America's tragedy. *Phoenix Americanus* invokes the building theme of the first movement, and the hero, righted though shaken, proceeds on his way with redoubled energy, "typical," to quote the program notes, "of the indomitable American spirit." To depict his flivver's adventures, the composer augmented his orchestra with a muted Ford horn, a wind machine, a factory whistle, and an anvil.

Others of Converse's orchestral works include the *Festival of Pan* (1900); *Endymion's Narrative* (1903); the Overture *Euphrosyne* (1903); *Night and Day* (1905), two tone poems for piano and orchestra; *The Mystic Trumpeter* (1905), an orchestral fantasy; two symphonic poems, *Ormazd* (1912) and *Ave atque Vale* (1917); the Symphony No. 1, performed in 1920 (Converse did not number the Symphony performed in Munich in 1898); the *Fantasia* for piano and orchestra (1922); the Symphony No. 2 (1922); *Song of the Sea* (1924); *Elegiac Poem* (1926); the tone poem *California*, subtitled "Festival Scenes" (1928); *American Sketches* (1935); the Symphony No. 3 (1936); and the Symphony No. 6, introduced posthumously by the Indianapolis Symphony in 1940.

In addition to *The Pipe of Desire* Converse's operas include *The Sacrifice*, produced in 1911, and two unproduced works, *Sinbad the Sailor* (1913) and *The Immigrants* (1914). Converse composed incidental music to three plays of Percy MacKaye: *Jeanne d'Arc, Sanctu-*

ary, and *The Scarecrow*. His music for the last-named was made into a synchronized orchestral accompaniment for the film version of the play, and parts of it served in the Piano Suite *Scarecrow Sketches*.

Converse's choral works include *Job* (1907), the first American oratorio to be performed in Hamburg, and three cantatas: *The Peace Pipe* (1914); *The Answer of the Stars* (1919); and *The Flight of the Eagle* (1930). Other vocal works are the *Ballade* for baritone and orchestra, *La Belle Dame sans Merci* (1902), and *Hagar in the Desert*, a dramatic narrative for low voice and orchestra composed for Madame Schumann-Heink, who sang it in Hamburg in 1908. Converse's chamber music consists of three String Quartets, a Violin Sonata, a Cello Sonata, and a Piano Trio. In 1937 Converse was elected to membership in the American Academy of Arts and Letters.

One of the composers of this decade who sought after new sounds, HENRY EICHHEIM (1870–1942), best known for his study of Oriental music and for his authentic treatment of its melodies, was born in Chicago, January 3, 1870, and was educated at the Chicago Musical College. For a year he was a member of the Theodore Thomas Orchestra, and from 1890 to 1912 he was one of the first violinists of the Boston Symphony. He then resigned to devote himself to composing, recital work, and the study of Oriental music.

His *Oriental Impressions* for orchestra (1922) was an enlargement of a series of *Oriental Sketches* composed for the Pittsfield (Massachusetts) Chamber Music Festival of 1921, by which year the composer had journeyed several times to the Far East, returning from each trip with copious notes and a large collection of native instruments. *Burma*, a symphonic poem, followed in 1926, as incidental music to a play at the New York Neighborhood Playhouse; in its original form it was played in 1927 by the Chicago Symphony. *Java*, an orchestral work calling for a "gamelan" section with forty-five Oriental instruments, was introduced by the Philadelphia Orchestra in 1929. *Bali*, a series of variations on music that Eichheim had heard performed in a temple court at Denpassar, was first performed by the Philadelphia Orchestra in 1933. Following a New York performance of the work Lawrence Gilman [1] pronounced it "a fascinating web of tone, cunningly wrought, perturbing, not easily to be forgotten."

[1] New York *Herald Tribune*, December 6, 1933.

Eichheim's other compositions include a *Korean Sketch* for chamber orchestra and Oriental instruments; a *Japanese Nocturne* (1930), commissioned by Mrs. Elizabeth Sprague Coolidge; and a Sonata for violin and piano (1934).

BERTRAM SHAPLEIGH (1871–1940), another composer interested in Oriental music, was born in Boston, January 15, 1871. The Oriental atmosphere permeates his orchestral Suites *Ramayana* and *Gur Amir* and his tone poem *Mirage*. His other works include a setting of Poe's *The Raven* for chorus and orchestra; two Symphonies; a *Symphonic Prelude*; a poem for cello and orchestra; a String Quartet; a Piano Trio; five one-act operas; two grand operas; considerable church music; and over one hundred songs, many based on Oriental themes.

Two of the composers born in the 1870's were first known as pianists. ERNEST SCHELLING (1876–1939) was at one time one of our leading concert pianists as well as the composer of several colorful orchestral works. Born in Belvidere, New Jersey, July 26, 1876, he made a public appearance as pianist at the Philadelphia Academy of Music at the age of four. At six he was taken to the Paris Conservatory to study with Mathias, a pupil of Chopin, and he later worked with Moszkowski, Pruckner, Leschetizky, Huber, Barth, and finally for four years with Paderewski at the latter's villa in Switzerland. In the summer of 1919 Schelling was injured in an auto accident and was forced to curtail the greater part of his piano career. He then became active as a conductor, particularly of the children's concerts of the New York Philharmonic-Symphony, which he continued till his death.

Schelling was most widely known as a composer for his *Impressions from an Artist's Life* (1915), a set of variations for piano and orchestra in each of which the composer described one of his artist friends, and *A Victory Ball* (1923), a symphonic poem based on Alfred Noyes's poem *A Victory Dance*. Schelling also composed a *Legende Symphonique* (1906); a Symphony in C Minor; a *Suite Fantastique* (1907); a Violin Concerto (1916); a tone poem, *Morocco* (1927); numerous piano pieces; and some chamber music.

RUDOLPH GANZ (1877——), born in Zurich, Switzerland, February 24, 1877, was a pupil of Busoni and conductor of the St. Louis Symphony from 1921 to 1927. A distinguished concert pianist and teacher, he served from 1929 to 1954 as president of the Chicago

Musical College, and from 1938 to 1949 he conducted the Young People's Concerts of the New York Philharmonic-Symphony.

Ganz's compositions include a Symphony; a series of *Animal Pictures;* a Suite of *American Scenes* for orchestra; and a *Konzertstück* for piano and orchestra, which he played with the Chicago Symphony on February 20, 1941. He also composed numerous piano pieces and choral works.

SIGISMOND STOJOWSKI (1870–1946), another pianist, enjoyed the patronage of Paderewski and studied with Delibes. Born in Strzelce, Poland, he came to America in 1905, and except for visits abroad he lived in New York until his death. He was active as a pianist and teacher of pianists. He wrote a Symphony and a Suite for orchestra; two Piano Concertos and a Rhapsody for piano and orchestra; a Violin Concerto; a Cello Sonata; a quantity of chamber music; and many piano pieces. His *Prayer for Poland* was scored for chorus, organ, and orchestra.

Among the composers who were also teachers of their younger colleagues were Howard Brockway and Mortimer Wilson. HOWARD BROCKWAY (1870–1951) was born in Brooklyn, New York, November 22, 1870, and spent the years 1890–95 in Berlin studying piano with Karl Barth and composition with O. B. Boise. While abroad he composed a Sonata for violin and piano and a *Ballade* for piano solo. On February 23, 1895, the Berlin Philharmonic devoted an entire program to Brockway's works, including the Symphony in D, a work that received its American première in 1907 with the Boston Symphony under Karl Muck.

Returning to America, Brockway joined the faculty of the Peabody Conservatory in 1903, where he stayed six years. He later moved to New York, where he was active as a teacher both privately and at the Institute of Musical Art and the Mannes School.

Brockway's orchestral works include his Symphony in D; a *Ballade;* a symphonic Scherzo; and a *Sylvan Suite,* first performed by the Boston Symphony in 1901. Brockway also published many piano and choral works. In 1915 he visited the Kentucky Mountains with the singer Loraine Wyman, collecting the melodies of mountain ballads while Miss Wyman collected the words. Their collaboration resulted in two volumes of exquisitely arranged versions of the songs: *Lonesome Tunes* (1916) and *Twenty Kentucky Mountain Songs.*

MORTIMER WILSON (1876–1932), born at Chariton, Iowa, August 6, 1876, studied in Chicago with Jacobsohn, Gleason, and Middel-schulte, taught theory from 1901 to 1907 at the University School of Music at Lincoln, Nebraska, and spent three years in Leipzig studying with Hans Sitt and Max Reger and teaching pupils of his own. He returned to the United States in 1911 and became a teacher at the Atlanta Conservatory in Georgia, where he also conducted the Atlanta Symphony Orchestra. He settled in New York in 1918.

A composer in the Reger tradition, Wilson could toss complicated counterpoint from his pen as easily as he could talk to his friends; as a result he was an excellent teacher as well as composer. His long list of published works includes a Suite for trio, *From My Youth*, later scored for orchestra; two Sonatas for violin and piano; three Suites for piano (one of them, *In Georgia*, orchestrated by the composer); a Trio; an *Overture "1849"*; a scenic fantasy for orchestra entitled *My Country*; and many shorter pieces. In manuscript he left five Sym-phonies; a *Country Wedding Suite* for orchestra; and an Organ Sonata.

Before the development of sound pictures Douglas Fairbanks en-gaged Wilson to write original scores for his motion pictures, to be played by theater orchestras during the projection. For *The Thief of Bagdad* Wilson composed music on broad lines, with leitmotifs to identify each character and to represent underlying emotions and situations.

MABEL WHEELER DANIELS (1879——) has an honored place among our women composers. Born in Swampscott, Massachusetts, November 27, 1879, she studied composition with George W. Chad-wick and later with Ludwig Thuille in Munich. In 1911 she won two prizes offered by the National Federation of Music Clubs, one for a song, *Villa of Dreams*, and the other for two three-part songs: *Voice of My Beloved* and *Eastern Song*.

Among her best known works are *The Desolate Cry* (1913), a poem for baritone and orchestra; *Peace with a Sword* (1917), for mixed chorus and orchestra; *Songs of Elfland* (1924); *The Holy Star* (1928); *Exultate Deo*, composed for the fiftieth anniversary of Radcliffe College and presented by the Radcliffe Choral Society and the Harvard Glee Club with the Boston Symphony, May 31, 1929; *Deep Forest*, a Prelude for little symphony that was later rescored and performed in its larger form by the Boston Symphony in 1937; *Song of Jael*, a cantata for soli, mixed voices, and orchestra (1940); a *Pastoral Ode*, for flute and strings (1940). In 1956 Miss Daniels's *Psalm of Praise*, composed to commemorate the seventy-fifth anniversary of Radcliffe College, was performed by the Radcliffe Choral Society and the Boston Symphony.

Others of Miss Daniels's orchestral works include *Pirates' Island*, *In the Greenwood*, and *Fairy Scherzo*. She has also composed many songs, including *Glory and Endless Years*, *The Waterfall*, *Lady of Dreams*, *Daybreak*, and *Beyond*. She has also composed a choral work, *June Rhapsody*, and a Violin Sonata.

ARTHUR NEVIN (1871–1943), a younger brother of Ethelbert Nevin, was born in Sewickley, Pennsylvania, April 27, 1871, and was educated at the New England Conservatory in Boston and abroad with Klindworth, Boise, and Humperdinck. For five years he was professor of music at the University of Kansas and for another five director of municipal music in Memphis, Tennessee. He lived his later years in the East. He spent the summers of 1903 and 1904 on the Blackfeet Reservation in Montana, and there heard a legend that he used for an Indian opera entitled *Poia*. President Theodore Roosevelt invited Nevin to give an illustrated talk on his work at the White House in 1907, but in spite of this endorsement and interest, the opera was not performed in America, but at the Royal Opera in Berlin, April 23, 1910. Another opera, composed in 1911 and originally entitled *Twilight*, was produced in Chicago in 1918 under the title *A Daughter of the Forest*.

Nevin's instrumental works include five major orchestral pieces: *Lorna Doone Suite* (1897); *Miniature Suite* (1902); *Springs of Saratoga* (1911); a symphonic poem (1930); and *Arizona* (1935). He also composed a String Quartet in D Minor (1929).

ARNE OLDBERG (1874–1961) was born in Youngstown, Ohio, July 12, 1874. He had his early training in Chicago and then studied abroad, piano under Leschetizky and composition under Rheinberger. In 1899 he became head of the piano department at Northwestern University in Evanston, Illinois, a position he held until his retirement in 1914. Oldberg's orchestral works include two Overtures, *Paola and Francesca* (1908) and *Festival*; an orchestral fantasy, *At Night* (1917); a Rhapsody; a set of *Twelve Variations* for organ and orchestra; a Violin Concerto; two Piano Concertos, of which the Second (introduced in 1932) was awarded a first prize of $1,000 in the 1931 Hollywood Bowl competition; and a symphonic poem, *The Sea*. His chamber works include a String Quartet; two Quintets for piano and strings; a Quintet for piano and woodwinds; a Piano Sonata; and numerous smaller works.

FRANK PATTERSON (1871———), born in Philadelphia, January 5, 1871, studied music with Hugh Clarke at the University of Pennsylvania and with Rheinberger and Thuille in Munich. He achieved a reputation as a theorist, and delved deeply into the subject of tone relationships. For a number of years he was a member of the editorial staff of the *Musical Courier*. He lived for a time in Paris, returning to America before the outbreak of World War II. He was the author of three books: *Practical Instrumentation, How to Write a Good Tune,* and *The Perfect Modernist*.

Patterson composed two produced operas, *The Echo* (1925) and *Beggar's Love* (1929). The latter work had been performed ten years earlier in Los Angeles under its original title, *A Little Girl at Play* (*A Tragedy of the Slums*). In 1931 the Overture to another Patterson opera, *Mountain Blood*, was played at the American Composers' Concerts in Rochester.

There were three other composers from this decade who were concerned chiefly with opera. JOHN ADAM HUGO (1873–1945), born at Bridgeport, Connecticut, was one of the relatively few American composers to have an opera produced by the Metropolitan Opera Company in New York. The work was *The Temple Dancer*, presented March 12, 1919. Hugo also composed a Symphony; two Piano Concertos; a Piano Trio; and many songs and instrumental pieces.

MARY CARR MOORE (1873–1957), a prolific composer of operas, was born in Memphis, Tennessee. Her works include *The Oracle* (1894); *Narcissa* (1912), which won the David Bispham Memorial Medal in 1930; *The Leper* (1912); *Los Rubios* (1931); and *Davide Rizzio* (1932). She also composed choral works, songs, and instrumental pieces.

JOSEPH CARL BREIL (1870–1926) was born in Pittsburgh, Pennsylvania, and composed an opera, *The Legend,* that was produced at the Metropolitan Opera House in New York, April 4, 1919. Among his other operas, *Asra* had a single performance in Los Angeles, November 24, 1925. Breil composed what is said to have been the first score ever written to accompany a motion picture, *Queen Elizabeth*, in 1912. He also composed the music for three comic operas.

BLAIR FAIRCHILD (1877–1933) lived in Paris as an expatriate for the last thirty years of his life. Born in Belmont, Massachusetts, he studied at Harvard and with Giuseppe Buonamici in Florence. After serving in the United States diplomatic corps in Turkey and Persia, he settled in Paris in 1903, where he studied with Charles Widor, taught music, and lived until his death. His works include a ballet, *Dame Lillebule*, produced at the Opéra Comique in Paris in 1921; an orchestral poem, *East and West* (1908); the symphonic poems *Zal*, *Tamineh*, and *Shah Geridoun*; an *Etude Symphonique* for violin and orchestra; a *Rhapsody on Old Hebrew Melodies* for violin and orchestra; a long list of chamber works; choruses; songs; and smaller pieces.

FRANZ CARL BORNSCHEIN (1879–1948), born in Baltimore, Maryland, studied at the Peabody Conservatory and joined its faculty in 1906 as violin teacher and conductor of its orchestra. He was active also as a choral conductor and from 1910 to 1913 was music critic of the Baltimore *Evening Sun*. Bornschein's compositions include a Violin Concerto; a String Quartet; a Quintet; a Sextet for flute and strings; *Three Persian Dances* for orchestra; a symphonic Scherzo, *The Sea God's Daughter* (1924); an orchestral Suite, *The Phantom Canoe* (1916); a symphonic ballad, *Old Louisiana* (1930); and six symphonic poems: *The Rime of the Ancient Mariner*; *A Hero's Espousal*; *Leif Ericson* (1936); *Southern Nights* (1936); *The Mission Road* (1937); and *Ode to the Brave* (1944). He composed many prize-winning choral works, as well as solo songs and instrumental pieces.

The *Southern Rhapsody* of LUCIUS HOSMER (1870–1935) was for many years a standard item on radio and popular orchestra programs. Hosmer also composed a *Northern Rhapsody* and an *Ethiopian Rhapsody*. These pieces are somewhat in the nature of potpourris of familiar melodies, but they are woven together in an integrated form. Born in South Acton, Massachusetts, Hosmer studied with George W. Chadwick. His works include two operas: *The Rose of Alhambra*, produced in New York in 1907, and *The Walking Delegate*; numerous orchestral pieces; piano music; and songs.

HERMAN HANS WETZLER (1870–1943), known widely in his day both as conductor and composer, was born in Frankfurt, Germany, and came to the United States as a child. His orchestral compositions include an Overture to *As You Like It* (1917); a *Symphonic Fantasy; Six Symphonic Movements;* a *Symphonic Dance in Basque Style* (1927); a *Symphonie Concertante* for violin and orchestra (1932); and *Assisi,* a legend for orchestra, written in commemoration of the 700th anniversary of the death of Saint Francis of Assisi and winner of a $1,000 prize offered by the Chicago North Shore Festival Association in 1925. Wetzler also composed a choral Magnificat; a String Quartet; and works for the stage and films.

COURTLANDT PALMER (1872–1951), born in New York City, composed a considerable amount of orchestral and chamber music, including a Piano Concerto; a *Berceuse* for violin and piano; an *Elegie* for cello; and numerous songs and piano pieces.

WILLIAM CLIFFORD HEILMAN (1877–1946), born in Williamsport, Pennsylvania, was a faculty member of the music department of Harvard University from 1905 till 1930. His compositions include an orchestral tone poem, *By the Porta Catania;* a Suite for orchestra; a Trio; a Suite of dances for cello and piano; a Suite for flute and piano; and songs and piano pieces. His choral works include *Night Song; Knew Not the Sun;* and *Among the Garden Ways.*

Philadelphia-born LIONEL BARRYMORE (1878–1954), long distinguished as an actor on stage and screen, was able partially to realize his ambition as a composer. His Preludium and Fugue received its première with the Indianapolis Symphony Orchestra in 1944. Barrymore also composed a symphonic poem, *Beyond the Horizon;* an orchestral piece, *The Woodsman and the Elves;* an *Elegie* for oboe and orchestra; a Concerto for piano and orchestra; *Farewell Symphony,* a one-act opera; *Russian Dances* and *Ballet Viennoise* for orchestra; two songs, *Johnnie Bear* and *Our Prayer;* and several piano pieces.

2. COMPOSERS BORN IN THE 1880'S

CHARLES TOMLINSON GRIFFES (1884–1920), one of the most sensitive and colorful tone poets of the twentieth century, was born in

Elmira, New York, September 17, 1884. He was talented in other fields besides music. He could draw well with pen and ink; he made excellent water color landscapes, and later in life he worked in etchings on copper. When he was in high school, he decided to become a musician, and he went to Berlin to make a concert pianist of himself. It was not until he studied theory with Engelbert Humperdinck that he decided to be a composer. He returned to America in 1908 and took the position of music teacher at the Hackley School in Tarrytown, New York, which he held until his death.

Griffes's work falls into three distinct periods. The first is the student period, when he was under the influence of his German teachers, Rüfer and Humperdinck. In his second period he leaned toward the style of the French Impressionists and also showed a fondness for Russian Orientalism that was to appear as the mysticism of his later works. *The Lake at Evening,* from the *Three Tone Pictures* for piano (1915), shows him in this period, and it also demonstrates his power of musical description. The third period revealed a modern trend: he grasped for something less rigid than the tempered scale, for a medium to sound the overtones he wanted us to hear. This was the period of his Piano Sonata (1921) and his orchestral works. The Sonata evinces the intellectual consistency of a Schoenberg without any sacrifice of poetic conception.

Griffes's tone poem, *The Pleasure Dome of Kubla Khan,* his most important orchestral work, was performed by the Boston Symphony, November 28, 1919, only a few months before the composer's death. The work was based on Coleridge's poem: the lines that describe the "stately pleasure dome," the "sunny pleasure dome with caves of ice, the miracle of strange device." In writing his music Griffes gave his own imagination free rein, depicting the palace and the revelry which might have taken place there. The vague, foggy beginning suggests the sacred river which ran "through caverns measureless to man down to a sunless sea." Then the outlines of the palace gradually rise, "with walls and towers girdled round." Sounds of revelry and dancing rise to a wild climax and suddenly break off. The original mood returns, and we again hear the sacred river and the "caves of ice."

In the orchestration of the *Poem* for flute and orchestra, introduced by Georges Barrère with the New York Symphonic Society, November 16, 1919, Griffes surpassed *Pleasure Dome*. *Poem*, the most mature of his works, ranges in color from the opening grey mood to the Oriental excitement of the dance movement.

Of his piano works, the *Roman Sketches* are the best known. First comes "The White Peacock," who makes his bow with a languorous chromatic theme. "Nightfall" brings the strange sounds of the early evening, an almost oppressive quiet. "The Fountain of Acqua Paola" shows the rise and fall of the water, the shimmering lights of the foam. "Clouds" starts with a lofty chordal passage, suggesting the high and massive cloudbanks. The *Roman Sketches* were published in 1917; the composer himself played them at the MacDowell Club the following year in New York. He later scored "The White Peacock" and a number of his songs for orchestra.

When Griffes's works were first being published, a composer whose fame, like that of Griffes, was to continue growing through the coming half-century came to America from abroad. Unlike Griffes, ERNEST BLOCH (1880–1959) lived to enjoy the recognition he had earned. Though he composed a number of major works before coming to this country at the age of thirty-six, he did not succeed in gaining a reputation abroad, and it was the United States that first recognized his genius and an American publisher, G. Schirmer, who issued his first orchestral works. Since America was the first nation to appreciate Ernest Bloch, it seems highly appropriate to consider him an American composer.

Ernest Bloch was born in Geneva, Switzerland, July 24, 1880. As a child he studied the violin, and at the age of eleven he decided to devote his life to the composing of music. He studied in Brussels, Frankfurt, Munich, and Paris, and returned to his native Geneva when he was twenty-four years old. He had little encouragement from orchestra leaders or others who might play his music, and, since his father was suffering business reverses, Bloch spent much of his time traveling in Germany taking orders for the cuckoo clocks his father made.

On November 30, 1910, his opera *Macbeth* was produced at the Opéra Comique in Paris. The public liked it but the critics did not, and for political reasons it was dropped from the repertory. Bloch then conducted a number of concerts at Lausanne and Neufchâtel, and for a time was professor of composition and aesthetics at the Geneva Conservatory. Again the victim of politics and intrigue, he left the Conservatory to return to composing.

In 1916 Bloch came to America, arriving unknown and unheralded. For a while he conducted the orchestra that played accompaniments for the dancer Maud Allan; when her tour closed in Ohio, Bloch returned to New York without backing or friends. In 1917, however, he was appointed instructor in composition at the David Mannes School, and the Flonzaley Quartet had meanwhile played his First String Quartet in New York. It was cordially received and resulted in an invitation from Karl Muck to conduct the Boston Symphony in a performance of Bloch's own *Trois Poèmes Juifs,* March 23, 1917. In May of that year the Friends of Music in New York, under Artur Bodanzky, presented an entire Bloch program, including *Schelomo,* a Hebrew Rhapsody for cello and orchestra, and the Symphony *Israel.* Two years later, in 1919, Bloch's Suite for viola and piano won the Coolidge Prize at the Berkshire Festival in Massachusetts, and in 1920 the composer was appointed director of the newly-founded Cleveland Institute of Music.

The works that first introduced Bloch to America were written at a time when he was deeply devoted to Jewish cultural tradition, moved by what he himself described as "the vigor and ingenuousness of the Patriarchs, the violence that finds expression in the books of the Prophets, the burning love of justice, the desperation of the preachers of Israel, the sorrow and grandeur of the Book of Job, the sensuality of the Song of Songs."

The passionate intensity of *Schelomo* and the rhapsodic nature of the *Hebrew Poems* marked many of Bloch's works, but these qualities were somewhat tempered in others of his compositions, especially those which might be termed neoclassic in style. To quote Henry Cowell,[1] "Bloch has never ceased to train himself in the techniques of past centuries. . . . He studies as stubbornly as any of the many students to whom he has recommended the same method of work." The neoclassic pattern was evident in such early works as the *First Concerto Grosso* for piano and strings (1925), the Suite for viola and piano (1919), later scored for viola and orchestra, and a Quintet

[1] *Musical Quarterly,* April, 1954.

(1923), in which work Bloch also experimented with quarter-tones.

During the 1920's Bloch paid tribute to his adopted country by composing his epic Rhapsody *America*, a work that was awarded a $3,000 prize by *Musical America* and that was first performed by the New York Philharmonic, December 20, 1928; the next day it was simultaneously performed by orchestras in Chicago, Philadelphia, Boston, and San Francisco. In this work the composer tried to embody the ideals of our nation, described in his own words as the "future credo of all mankind . . . the common purpose of widely diversified races to become one race, strong and great." The entire piece is built upon the theme of an anthem to be sung by chorus and by the audience. From the first bars it appears, in root, dimly, slowly taking shape, "rising, falling, developing, and finally asserting itself" in the last bars of the final movement. There are three parts. First, *1620: The Soil—The Indians—(England)—The Mayflower—The Landing of the Pilgrims*. Indian themes, the trumpet "Call of America," *Old Hundred*, a sea chanty, all combine to tell of the country before and after the Pilgrims landed in Plymouth. The second movement is *1860–1865: Hours of Joy—Hours of Sorrow*. The drama of the North and South; happiness, war, distress, agony. Negro songs; a bit from Stephen Foster; *Pop Goes the Weasel*; then war songs—*John Brown's Body*; *The Battle Cry of Freedom*; *Tramp, Tramp, Tramp*. Intensity paints the strife, yet the America call is heard above the din, and even though it is a "bleeding America," it is still there. The finale is *1926: The Present—The Future*. Speed, noise, jazz, the pomp of material prosperity. An inevitable collapse, and a gradual rebuilding that comes at last to the anthem—the promise that our ideals will save us.

After six years at the Cleveland Institute Bloch moved in 1926 to California, where he taught at the San Francisco Conservatory. During his lifetime Bloch trained many of our finest composers, among them Roger Sessions, Ernst Bacon, Randall Thompson, Douglas Moore, and others who have since come to hold distinguished positions in universities. In his *Musical Quarterly* article [2] Henry Cowell remarks that Bloch's pupils "are remarkable because they all write thoughtfully and well, but differently. . . . Bloch's main thesis has

[2] *Op. cit.*

always been the impossibility of teaching anything important, and the necessity of learning for one's self. His lessons have been for the most part demonstrations of his own preoccupations of the moment and his methods of work, endlessly stimulating to his students' energies and ideas."

In 1930 a music patron and philanthropist offered to provide Bloch with an annual income for ten years so that he could devote himself exclusively to composing. Accepting this offer, Bloch spent most of his time from 1930 to 1939 in Switzerland, returning to this country only for visits. During these years his fame increased abroad, especially in England, where an Ernest Bloch Society was formed to promote recordings and performances of his works, and in Italy where, until the inauguration of the official anti-Semitic policy, he received many performances and widespread appreciation among musicians, critics, and the public.

One of the first Italian performances was the première of a work composed in 1928, *Helvetia,* a symphonic poem that was introduced in Rome in 1933. In 1934 Bloch's *Sacred Service* was performed in Turin. This modern treatment of the Hebrew ritual was composed soon after he returned to Switzerland, and represented a reawakening of his preoccupation with Jewish traditions. In 1936 an Italian publisher issued Bloch's Piano Sonata, and on March 1, 1938, the opera *Macbeth* was performed in Naples for the first time since its original production.

Meanwhile in the United States, *A Voice in the Wilderness,* a six-movement symphonic work with cello obbligato, was introduced in Los Angeles in 1937. *Evocations,* a symphonic Suite, was premièred in San Francisco in 1938, and a Violin Concerto was performed by Joseph Szigeti with the Cleveland Orchestra the same year.

A few years after returning permanently to America in 1939, Bloch settled in Oregon in a small town on the coast. For a few years he taught summer classes at the University of California in Berkeley, but he eventually retired to devote himself once more to composing. He left home only on rare occasions, preferring, to quote Cowell again, "to send his music to speak for him." Eventually, at the age of seventy, he announced that he would compose no more, for he had said all that he had to say. He died in 1959 in Portland, Oregon.

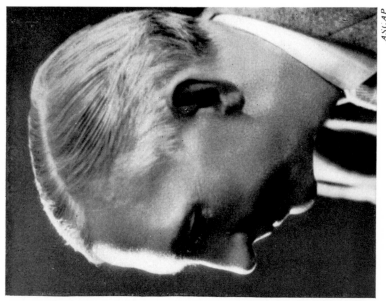

ASCAP

Charles Wakefield Cadman
(See pages 407–411)

ASCAP

Deems Taylor
(See pages 402–407)

Ernest Bloch

Louis Gruenberg

In the works of his last fifteen years Bloch's genius reached its fulfillment with the assimilation of several phases of his creative nature. Of a *Suite Symphonique,* first performed in Philadelphia, October 26, 1945, Olin Downes wrote in the New York *Times,* "It is evident that in this work the passionate and picturesquely Hebraic character of Bloch's earlier music gives place to a more severe and less personal idiom. But the old intensity and emotional grandeur remain, enclosed within the architectonics of later thinking."

A Second String Quartet, winner of the 1947 New York Music Critics' Circle Award, was described by Robert Sabin in *Musical America* as "a work of ripe maturity and artistic wisdom, and in some sense a more complete synthesis than ever before of all the elements of Bloch's musical nature." A Third String Quartet, composed in 1951, was likewise given the New York Music Critics' Circle Award, in 1954. Two neoclassic works were given their first performances by the British Broadcasting Corporation, April 11, 1953: these were *Sinfonia Breve* and *Concerto Grosso No. 2.* Of the latter work Peggy Glanville-Hicks wrote in the New York *Herald Tribune,* "this work has great expressive power, great contrapuntal mastery, and an orchestral expertness that is dazzling."

A few further works were introduced after 1950: a *Scherzo Fantastique* for piano and orchestra (1950); a *Suite Hébraïque* for viola (or violin) and orchestra (1950); Symphony for trombone and orchestra (1956); a Symphony in E flat (1956); a *Suite Modale* (1957); and *Proclamation* for trumpet and orchestra (1957). Contrary to his earlier declaration that he would compose no more, Bloch fulfilled a commission from the University of California by writing a Second Piano Quintet for the May T. Morrison Festival held in Berkeley, April 15, 1958.

Just as it was remarkable to find such a rebelliously independent composer as Charles Ives coming from the 1870's, so it was unusual to find an out-and-out atonalist from the 1880's, writing his advanced music at a time when most of his contemporaries were post-Romanticists or, at their most modern, Impressionists. Georgia-born WALLINGFORD RIEGGER (1885–1961) once confessed that when Scriabin's *Poème d'Extase* had its Berlin première he joined the audience in hissing, just as Philadelphia box holders hissed twenty years later when

Stokowski presented Riegger's own *Study in Sonority*. Born in Albany, Georgia, April 29, 1885, Riegger studied with Percy Goetschius and Alvin Schroeder at New York's Institute of Musical Art and went to Germany to continue his studies at the Berlin Hochschule. He conducted the opera at Würtzberg and Königsberg in 1915 and 1916, and the following year he led the Bluethner Orchestra in Berlin.

Returning to America, he taught theory and cello for four years at the Drake University in Des Moines, Iowa, and in 1922 he won the Paderewski Prize for his Trio in B Minor. In 1923 Riegger's rather conventional *American Polonaise* for orchestra was performed at the Stadium Concerts in New York, and the following year his setting of Keats's *La Belle Dame sans Merci*, for four solo voices and chamber orchestra, was performed at the Pittsfield (Massachusetts) Festival, winning the E. S. Coolidge Prize of that year.

During 1924 and 1925 Riegger taught at the Institute of Musical Art in New York, and then spent the next two years teaching at the Ithaca (New York) Conservatory of Music, where on August 11, 1927, a group of conservatory pupils played his *Study in Sonority*, a bitingly atonal work for ten violins "or any multiple thereof." Returning to New York in 1928, Riegger was engaged for more than thirty years as a composer, as a promoter of the cause of contemporary music and, in order to make a living, as an editor for publishing houses. Reserving his own name for compositions in his advanced style, he used seven different pseudonyms for the more than seven hundred choral arrangements he made for music publishers, of works ranging from the compositions of Palestrina to such popular songs as *Tea for Two*.

In an article in the *Musical Quarterly* of January 1950, Richard Franko Goldman points out that although Riegger was an atonalist, his music does not strictly adhere to the dodecaphonic technique of Schoenberg. Of the *Study in Sonority* Goldman wrote:

> Riegger relied on a purely arbitrary invention, tested only in his ear, of dissonant harmonies of motion and repose . . . and sought in the discovery of new tonalities and textures, both harmonic and contrapuntal, unexplored possibilities of formal structure.

Concerning the influence of Schoenberg on Riegger, Goldman explained that the *Study in Sonority* appears to be (but is not) the work of a man who has spent three years in a thoughtful and by no means parasitical study of Schoenberg. Riegger's acquaintance with Schoenberg's theories was in fact limited at this time to general notions derived from casual readings and to conversations with Adolph Weiss [a Schoenberg pupil]. His approach to atonality . . . was entirely his own. The *Study* is plainly not a twelve-tone piece, although [certain] passages . . . suggest the texture at least of Viennese dodecaphony.

It was not until twenty years after the *Study in Sonority* was first performed that Riegger gained general recognition, when the New York Music Critics' Circle gave their annual award to the Third Symphony (1948), a work that had been commissioned by the Alice M. Ditson Fund of Columbia University. Alfred Frankenstein, in a report to the San Francisco *Chronicle*, called the Symphony "a work of great energy and impact. . . . There is a grand, abrasive quality about it, its orchestration rings clear and hard, like hammers on steel—and at heart it is as romantic as anything of Mahler's." At this time the composer was sixty-three years of age, and it was during the following decade that the general public discovered the qualities that Goldman had attributed to him in his 1950 article—that his music, "striking in its vigorous individuality, has clarity without naïveté, force without bombast, resourcefulness without pedantry, independence without rootlessness, and vitality without boyishness."

Riegger's early works in his new idiom include a Suite for flute solo (1930); Three Canons for flute, oboe, clarinet, and bassoon (1931); Rhapsody for orchestra (1931); *Dichotomy* for orchestra (1932); Scherzo for orchestra (1933); and a *Divertissement* (1933), for flute, harp, and cello.

From 1933 to 1941, Riegger devoted almost all his efforts in composition to music for modern dance groups, feeling that the taxing limitations of the medium stimulated a composer's ingenuity and inventiveness. His first dance score, *Frenetic Rhythms* (1933), was composed for Martha Graham, as were *Evocation* (1933) and *Chronicle* (1936). For the Humphrey-Weidman Group Riegger composed *New Dance* (1935); originally scored for drums and piano four hands, it was later rescored by the composer for orchestra. *Theater Piece* and *With My Red Fires*, also written for the Humphrey-Weidman Group, were performed in 1936. For Charles Weidman alone Riegger composed *Candide* (1937). Other dancers for whom Riegger composed scores include Hanya Holm—*The Cry* (1935) and *Trend* (1937); Helen Tamiris—*Trojan Incident* (1938); Anna Sokolow—*Case History* (1937); Saida Gerrard—*Machine Ballet* (1938); and Eric Hawkins—*Pilgrim's Progress* (1941).

When Riegger's preoccupation with dance ended abruptly in 1941, he had already composed his First String Quartet (1938–39) and had heard it performed by the Galimir Quartet at the composers' colony in Yaddo, New York, in 1940. In 1942 a Canon and Fugue for strings was premièred in Berkeley, California; in 1943 a *Passacaglia and Fugue* for band was performed by the Goldman Band in New York, the composer conducting. Riegger later scored the piece for orchestra, and it was played in that form by the National Symphony in Washington, D.C., in 1944. Riegger's Second String Quartet, composed in 1948, had its première in New York with the New Music Quartet, January 23, 1949; it drew contrasting opinions from two critics of the *Herald Tribune*. Virgil Thomson called it "puckish . . . serene . . . the mature thought of a master workman," while Jay S. Harrison wrote, "The composer has foregone his customary twelve-tone regimen, but his intense atonalism remains. . . . The music's constant drive is wearing. . . . The light of fun never strikes it."

A few months prior to the première of the Second String Quartet, the Third Symphony had been performed at Columbia and had won the Music Critics' Circle Award. Riegger's First Symphony (composed 1935) and Second (1946) have never been performed; the First was never even offered for performance. The success of the Third Symphony, however, opened a new era of recognition for Riegger. Not only did first performances become more frequent, a number of his works became part of the contemporary repertory and were heard repeatedly, and Riegger was kept busy filling commissions.

His later works include *Music for Brass Choir* (1949); a Quintet for piano and strings, commissioned by the University of Michigan (1951); a Concerto for woodwinds and piano (1954); Variations for piano and orchestra (1954), commissioned by the Louisville Orchestra; another set of Variations (1954), for two pianos and orchestra; a *Preamble and Fugue* for orchestra (1956); *Music for Orchestra* (1956); an Overture for orchestra (1956); the Fourth Symphony (1957), commissioned by the Fromm Foundation; a Rhapsody for four cellos (1957); a *Shakespeare Sonnet* for chorus and baritone solo (1957); Variations for violin and orchestra (1959), commissioned by the Louisville Orchestra; a *Festival Overture* (1960), of which Jay S. Harrison wrote in the New York *Herald Tribune* (April 20, 1960) that there was nothing in the piece to "recall Mr. Riegger's more recondite and thorny style," but that it was "bright, perky, tuneful and lavishly scored . . . deftly diatonic, rhythmically four-square"; a Sinfonietta (1960), which P. H. Lang of the New York *Herald Tribune* (November 17, 1960) found "singularly tame, tonal and tolerant for such an advanced musician"; and an *Introduction and Fugue* for cello and symphonic winds, later also published for four cellos or cello orchestra.

During the first quarter of the twentieth century and for perhaps a decade thereafter, it was to be expected that the composers most widely accepted by the concertgoing public would be men whose works followed tradition closely and were comparatively easy to listen to. For this reason the composers of that time who commanded the widest audiences were undoubtedly Deems Taylor and Charles Wakefield Cadman.

For the two decades following the late 1920's, DEEMS TAYLOR (1885——) was a leading figure in the world of music and undoubtedly the most widely played of contemporary American composers. The public was always ready to listen to his warm, rich melodies with their lush harmonic background, and it did not matter too much that there were frequent reminders of Wagner and Puccini. Even though much of his work may have been like old wine in bottles that were none too new, it invariably satisfied.

Taylor was born in New York City, December 22, 1885. After attending the Ethical Culture School, he entered New York University, graduating in 1906. With his fellow student William Le Baron he wrote the music for a series of undergraduate musical comedies. One of them, *The Echo*, was chosen by Charles Dillingham as a starring vehicle for Bessie McCoy, and was produced on Broadway in August of 1910. Although the name of Deems Taylor appeared at the top of the program as composer of the music, so many new songs by a variety of composers were interpolated during rehearsals that by opening night there was not one of Taylor's songs left.

After graduating from college, Taylor did some writing for

Nelson's Encyclopedia and for the *Britannica* and contributed verse and prose items to F.P.A.'s newspaper column. For the latter there was no payment, so it was not surprising that when he was offered a job as assistant editor of the *Western Electric News,* an industrial house organ, and was asked what salary he required, he answered that he didn't care how *much* it was so long as it was regular. After holding this position from 1912 to 1916, he became assistant Sunday editor of the New York *Tribune.* For a short time he was *Tribune* correspondent in France, and from 1917 to 1919 he was associate editor of *Collier's Weekly.*

It was with the first performances of his Suite *Through the Looking Glass* that Taylor began to gain his considerable reputation as a musician. This work, his most widely played, is also his best: he has never surpassed the charm and grace with which he matched Lewis Carroll's wit—half-tender, half-mocking. From the charming *Dedication* and *The Garden of the Live Flowers,* on through the gallant struggle in *Jabberwocky,* in which the hideous creature is slain with a fugue for woodwinds, through the shimmering *Looking Glass Insects,* to the droll and affectionate picture of *The White Knight,* who falls forward when his horse stops and backward when it goes on again, the whole series is presented with brilliance and sparkling humor. Composed for chamber orchestra and first played by Carolyn Beebe's New York Chamber Music Society in 1919, the piece was later scored by the composer for full orchestra, in which form it was first played in 1923. For Miss Beebe's group Taylor had written a piece for eleven instruments, *Portrait of a Lady,* performed in 1918.

For the most part Taylor was self-taught in music, but during the years 1908–11 he had lessons with an obscure musician named Oscar Coon, of whom he drew an affectionate picture in his book *Of Men and Music.* In 1912 Taylor composed a symphonic poem, *The Siren Song,* which won first prize from the National Federation of Music Clubs the following year. However, the work had its first performance in 1922, ten years after it was written. After *Siren Song* Taylor composed a cantata for mixed voices and orchestra, *The Chambered Nautilus,* and a cantata for women's voices, a setting of Alfred Noyes's *The Highwayman* (1914). Taylor's next major work after *Looking Glass* was *Jurgen,* a symphonic poem commissioned by Walter

Damrosch for the New York Symphony Society and introduced in 1925, the year that Taylor composed *Circus Day* for Paul Whiteman's dance band; eight years later he rescored the piece for symphony orchestra.

As Taylor's musical reputation grew, he was appointed music critic of the New York *World*, a position he held until 1925, when he resigned in order to compose an opera commissioned by the New York Metropolitan. Taylor asked Edna St. Vincent Millay to write a libretto for him. She responded with *The King's Henchman*, the story of Aethelwold, sent by King Aedgar of England to fetch Aelfrida for his queen. Inevitably, the henchman falls in love with the king's prospective bride, and tragedy results. Some may have remarked that this was the theme of *Tristan and Isolde*.

The opera was finished in a couple of years, and the première took place on February 17, 1927. It was a gala event. There had been tremendous advance publicity, and the work met with stirring success. The critics were as enthusiastic as the public. In the *Herald Tribune* Lawrence Gilman hailed *The King's Henchman* as "the best American opera we have ever heard," describing the music as "richly textured, mellifluous," and praising its "grace and flexibility." The opera was kept in the Metropolitan repertory for three seasons.

Following the success of *Henchman*, Taylor became editor of *Musical America*, a post he retained from 1927 till 1929. He was then commissioned by the Metropolitan to write a second opera, *Peter Ibbetson*, produced February 7, 1931. For his libretto Taylor himself worked with Constance Collier in adapting a play that she had made from Du Maurier's novel. It may be that the critical fraternity felt that a composer might be forgiven his derivativeness in his first opera, but that in a second he should stand on his own feet. At any rate, *Peter Ibbetson* did not meet with the almost unanimous press acclaim that greeted its predecessor. With the public, however, it became even more popular than *The King's Henchman*, and in its third year at the Metropolitan it was given the honor of performance on the opening night of the season. It was kept in the repertory for a fourth season. During the next decade Taylor composed a third opera, *Ramuntcho*, which was produced by the Philadelphia Opera Company on February 10, 1942.

After the production of his second opera, Taylor turned once more to other activities. For a time he was music critic of the New York *American*, he delivered a series of radio lectures on the history of opera, and in 1933 he began the first of many series of radio programs under commercial sponsorship. In the fall of 1936 he was appointed consultant on music for the Columbia Broadcasting System, and began at that time his Sunday afternoon intermission talks on the broadcasts of the New York Philharmonic-Symphony. These continued for more than five years, and Taylor achieved a high mark in comments on music for the layman. These talks were subsequently published in two books: *Of Men and Music* (1937) and *The Well-Tempered Listener* (1940).

The movies also claimed Taylor's services. In 1940 he acted as commentator and master of ceremonies for Walt Disney's *Fantasia*. He has been a director of the American Society of Composers, Authors, and Publishers for many years, and from 1942 to 1948 he was president of the society. He has been awarded the honorary degrees of Doctor of Music by New York University (1927) and Doctor of Letters by Juniata College (1931), and in 1935 was elected a member of the American Academy of Arts and Letters. He is a trustee of the American Academy in Rome. And as if to show the wide scope of his interests and tastes, he was for many years one of the judges of the Miss America Contest in Atlantic City.

Taylor's orchestral works introduced since 1940 include *Processional* (1941); *Marco Takes a Walk* (1942); *A Christmas Overture* (1944); and *Fanfare for the People of Russia* (1944). In 1945 he was asked to provide an adaptation of *Through the Looking Glass* for the "Alice in Wonderland" episode in the Ringling Barnum and Bailey Circus.

Taylor has been much in demand to provide incidental music for the theatre. He has written scores to *Liliom; The Adding Machine; Beggar on Horseback; Will Shakespeare; Humoresque; Rita Coventry;* Gilbert Miller's production of *Casanova;* and Katherine Cornell's *Lucrece*. From the last two scores Taylor subsequently fashioned the *Casanova Ballet Music* for orchestra, and the *Lucrece Suite* for string quartet. Many of Taylor's shorter works have been widely performed, particularly his song *Captain Stratton's Fancy*, for many years a favorite with baritones. He has also written many short pieces for chorus and a magnificent series of choral arrangements of folk songs, among them a rich, warm setting of the traditional *May Day Carol*.

Although CHARLES WAKEFIELD CADMAN (1881–1946) achieved his greatest commercial success with two songs, he also composed four operas and many orchestral works. In the public mind he was closely associated with American Indian music, for much of the music he wrote from 1909 to 1925 was based on Indian subjects and melodies. Born in Johnstown, Pennsylvania, December 24, 1881, Cadman studied with Leo Oehmler in Pittsburgh and with Luigi von Kunitz. When he was twenty-three several of his songs were accepted by a publisher, but they did not find a ready sale and copies of them rested undisturbed on the publisher's shelves. For a while the same treatment was accorded *At Dawning*, published in 1906, and it remained unheard until John McCormack ran across it and featured it in his concerts. It then became a tremendous success, eventually selling over a million copies. *From the Land of the Sky Blue Water*, based on an Indian melody and set to verses by Nelle Richmond Eberhart, the librettist of his operas and of most of his vocal works, was published in 1909 and, unlike the earlier songs, met with immediate success.

Cadman's opera *Shanewis*, produced at the Metropolitan Opera House in New York in 1918, told the story of an Indian maiden who went to New York for musical training and fell in love with a white man. *The Sunset Trail*, first heard in Denver in 1922, was less a grand opera than its predecessor; in fact, its music seemed better suited to operetta. Mrs. Eberhart's libretto told of an Indian tribe gathered around a campfire, debating whether to submit to the white man or to try further to repulse him.

Cadman's most successful attempt at grand opera, *The Witch of Salem*, performed by the Chicago Civic Opera Association in 1926, dealt with the witch-hunting days of the Massachusetts colony town of Salem. An earlier opera, *The Garden of Mystery*, for which Mrs. Eberhart adapted Hawthorne's story *Rappaccini's Daughter*, did not have its first performance until 1925, when it was produced at New York's Carnegie Hall. It had been composed in 1916.

Cadman's many instrumental compositions include a Trio in D Major; a Piano Sonata; a Sonata in G Major for violin and piano; a

Thunderbird Suite (originally composed for piano and later orchestrated); an *Oriental Rhapsody* for orchestra; and a Quintet entitled *To a Vanishing Race*. In July of 1932 the New York Orchestra, an organization conducted by Modest Altschuler, presented Cadman's *Hollywood Suite*, a work consisting of four contrasting tonal sketches: *Mary Pickford, Charlie Chaplin, To My Mother,* and *Hollywood Bowl. Dance of the Scarlet Sister Mary* dates from the same period. *Dark Dancers of the Mardi Gras* (1933), scored for orchestra and piano obbligato, portrayed the grotesque, fantastic, and exuberant spirit of the annual Mardi Gras carnival; Cadman himself often took the piano part in performances of this work. In addition, there are a *Suite of American Folk-Tunes* (composed in 1937); a symphonic poem, *Pennsylvania* (1940); a Symphony in E Minor; and a tone poem for piano and orchestra entitled *Aurora Borealis*.

Cadman's major choral works include *The Vision of Sir Launfal* (1909), scored for male voices; and the cantatas *Father of Waters* (1928) and *The Far Horizon*. For the National Broadcasting Company Cadman composed the music for a radio play, *The Willow Tree*, performed October 3, 1933.

Like Cadman, there were a number of composers from the 1880's who may be considered nationalists, either because they used actual folk material from our continent, or because they chose American subjects and treated them in a manner that seemed American to them and to their audiences.

Some listeners claim that they hear certain racial traits in the music of ARTHUR SHEPHERD (1880–1958), particularly an Anglo-Celtic flavor that may have resulted from the fact that his parents were English. He himself was born in Paris, Idaho, and had his training at the New England Conservatory in Boston. In Salt Lake City he conducted a theatre orchestra and a symphonic group, and in 1908 he returned to Boston to teach at the New England Conservatory. After three years in the U.S. Army (1917–20) he became an assistant conductor of the Cleveland Orchestra and inaugurated a series of children's concerts. From 1920 to 1950 he was professor of music and chairman of the music division of Western Reserve University, and from 1929 to 1932 he was music critic for the Cleveland *Press*.

His most widely played work, *Horizons* (1929; designated as his

First Symphony), is based partly on original material and partly on such frontier American ballads as *The Dying Cowboy*, *The Old Chisholm Trail*, and *The Dogie Song*. The entire piece is full of the raciness, the adventure, and the spacious life of the plains. Shepherd's career as a recognized composer began in 1902, when his *Ouverture Joyeuse* won the Paderewski Prize. In 1909 he won two prizes awarded by the National Federation of Music Clubs—one for his First Piano Sonata (1907) and the other for a song, *The Lost Child*. Two more Overtures followed: *The Festival of Youth* (1915) and *Overture to a Drama* (1919).

Shepherd's *Fantaisie Humoresque*, for piano and orchestra, was played in Boston in 1918. Then came *Song of the Sea Wind*, for women's voices and orchestra; *City of the Sea*, for baritone, mixed chorus, and orchestra; a Second Piano Sonata (1929); three String Quartets; a *Triptych* for voice and string quartet (1927); two cantatas, *City in the Sea* and *Song of the Pilgrims;* for orchestra a *Choreographic Suite*, described as a series of *Dance Episodes on an Exotic Theme;* the Second Symphony (1940), with the composer himself conducting the Cleveland Orchestra in the première; a Piano Quintet (1941); a *Praeludium Salutorium* (1942), for strings and wind instruments; a *Fantasy on Down East Spirituals* (1946); a Violin Concerto (1946); and *Theme and Variations for Orchestra*. Some of Shepherd's early piano pieces were issued by the Wa-Wan Press: a Mazurka, a Prelude, and *Theme and Variations*.

JOHN POWELL (1882–1963) achieved his greatest distinction with his *Rhapsodie Nègre* for piano and orchestra, a piece that he himself introduced with the Russian Symphony Orchestra in New York, March 23, 1918. He later turned from Negro subjects to American folk music derived from Anglo-Saxon sources, and as founder of the Virginia State Choral Festival was a moving spirit in the annual White Top Mountain Folk Music Festival and a friend to all who are interested in our Appalachian tunes and ballads. Powell studied in America with F. C. Hahr and in Vienna with Leschetizky and Navrátil. In his music he preserved the modal nature of his folk material and strived to fit his style to the innate character of the material itself, avoiding incongruous progressions or extraneous chromaticisms.

For a number of years *Rhapsodie Nègre* was one of the most widely played of the larger works by American composers, with more than fifty performances in New York City in 1929 alone. It was heard from Rome to Amsterdam and was chosen as the representative American work to be performed with soloist on the New York Symphony's tour under Walter Damrosch. The *Rhapsodie*, inspired by Joseph Conrad's *Heart of Darkness*, begins and ends on a primal note, pagan and orgiastic; a note of idealization is felt in the middle section.

Others of Powell's works include the Sonata for violin and piano entitled *Sonata Virginianesque* (1919); the Overture *In Old Virginia* (1921); a *Sonata Noble*, for piano; a Suite for piano, also arranged for orchestra, entitled *At the Fair*; another Suite, *In the South*; a set of *Variations and Double Fugue*; a Concerto for violin and orchestra; *Natchez on the Hill* (1931), one of his most widely played orchestral pieces; *A Set of Three* (1940), an orchestral Suite based on Virginia folk tunes; the Symphony in A, performed in 1947 after numerous revisions, further revised and performed in final form as the principal event of "John Powell Day," celebrated by the Commonwealth of Virginia upon proclamation of the governor, November 5, 1951.

The closeness of various sections of the American population to their Anglo-Saxon heritage has never been more clearly exemplified than in the work of PERCY ALDRIDGE GRAINGER (1882–1961), who did much to stimulate interest in folk music, both through his own transcriptions of British folk songs and by his performances of similar works by American composers, such as David Guion's *Turkey in the Straw* and *The Arkansas Traveler* and Nathaniel Dett's *Juba Dance*. He is best known for his brief settings of folk tunes of the British Isles: *Country Gardens, Irish Tune from County Derry* (sometimes known as *Londonderry Air*), *Mock Morris, Molly on the Shore*, and many others. His orchestral works include *To a Nordic Princess*, written to commemorate his own marriage in California to Ella Viola Ström, a Norwegian. Grainger's *Tribute to Stephen Foster* (1931) is a work of major dimensions, scored in typically unorthodox fashion for five solo voices, solo piano, mixed chorus, orchestra, and musical glasses.

Born in Melbourne, Australia, July 8, 1882, Grainger did not come to America until he was thirty-three years old. Though his early studies were with Kwast and Busoni in Germany, his fundamental musical kinships were with his fellow students Sandby, a Dane, and Cyril Scott, an Englishman. Grainger was a friend and disciple of Edvard Grieg and a leading exponent of his music. After Grieg's death in 1907 Grainger became more closely identified with his Piano Concerto than any other pianist, and he supervised the revised edition of the work.

In 1917 Grainger interrupted his career as a concert pianist, which he had pursued since going to London at the age of eighteen, in order to enlist in the American army, where he played oboe and saxophone in the band and taught in the army music school. Soon afterwards he took out American citizenship papers and made his home in this country. He traveled frequently to other parts of the world—to Scandinavia to collect folk songs, to the Orient, and to Australia and New Zealand. For a short time he was head of the New York University music department.

In addition to his *Tribute* to Foster, Grainger's works for chorus and orchestra include *Marching Song of Democracy* (1916); *The Merry Wedding* (1916); *Father and Daughter*; *The Hunter in His Career*; *The Bride's Tragedy*; and *Love Verses from the Song of Solomon*. For military band he composed a *Children's March* (1918); and for chorus and brass band *I'm Seventeen Come Sunday*, *We Have Fed Our Seas for a Thousand Years*, and *Marching Tune*. For piano as well as for various chamber combinations he composed *Handel in the Strand* (1913), humorous variations on Handel's *Harmonious Blacksmith*; *My Love Is to the Greenwood Gone*; *Walking Tune*; *Hill Song No. 1* and *Hill Song No. 2*; and *Spoon River*.

By playing on his recital programs the *Juba Dance* of R. NATHANIEL DETT (1882–1943), Percy Grainger helped materially to bring this remarkable Negro composer to the attention of the public. Dett did much to acquaint music-lovers with the true flavor of the folk music of his race. The *Juba Dance* that Grainger popularized was part of a piano Suite called *In the Bottoms*.

Dett was born at Drummondsville, Quebec, October 11, 1882. In 1903 he went to Oberlin, Ohio, to study music. After appearing as a concert pianist and holding a number of positions as director of music in colored institutes, he was put in charge of music at Hampton Institute, Virginia, where he remained for eighteen years (1913–31). From

1931 till 1937 he taught privately in Rochester, New York, and at the time of his death he was in Battle Creek, Michigan, where he had organized a Negro WAC chorus and was directing music activities at a USO clubhouse.

Dett's larger works include *Chariot Jubilee* for orchestra and *The Ordering of Moses* for soloists, chorus, and orchestra. The latter work was performed at the Cincinnati Festival of 1937, at the Worcester Festival of 1938, and by the Oratorio Society in New York in 1939.

So much for the nationalists. Turning to those who may be called Impressionists, we find four from the 1880's: Louis Gruenberg, Emerson Whithorne, Marion Bauer, and the German-born Werner Josten.

Louis Gruenberg (1884–1964) has shown himself to be a many-sided composer: first an Impressionist, particularly in his early piano pieces; then an explorer of the possibilities of jazz; and later an exponent of *Gebrauchmusik* in his scoring of motion pictures; and, for a number of years, a composer of operas. His adaptation of Eugene O'Neill's play *The Emperor Jones* stands out as his most significant operatic work. Produced at the Metropolitan in New York, January 7, 1933, with Lawrence Tibbett in the title role, it was called by Olin Downes [3] "the first American opera by a composer whose dramatic instinct and intuition for the theater seem unfailing, and whose musical technique is characterized by a very complete modern knowledge and a reckless mastery of his means."

Gruenberg set himself a tremendously difficult task in making an opera of the play about a Pullman porter who declares himself "emperor" of an island in the West Indies. His music was undeniably effective: the interludial outcries of the chorus, the orchestra comments on the drama, and the dramatic fervor of the spiritual *Standin' in the Need of Prayer* were all in keeping with the intensity of the drama. Yet it seemed to some that O'Neill himself had provided all the music that was necessary with the beat of an offstage drum, accelerating slowly and terrifyingly throughout the action, gradually pounding its way into the listener's consciousness. Gruenberg incorporated this drumbeat into his score, but it is doubtful that the musical elaborations added to the suspense of the drama. Yet his savage music,

[3] New York *Times*, January 8, 1933.

with its explosive detonations, its howls and outcries, succeeded in providing the most finished and theatrically effective American opera that the Metropolitan had produced up to that time.

Gruenberg was born near Brest Litovsk, Russia, August 3, 1884. He was brought to America when he was two years old, and as a child was given piano lessons in New York. He studied piano and composition with Busoni in Berlin and made his debut as a pianist with the Berlin Philharmonic in 1912. He also studied at the Vienna Conservatory and returned to the United States in 1919. Aside from helping to organize the League of Composers in 1922, he devoted most of his time to composing, except for the years 1933–36, when he taught composition at the Chicago Musical College. He later settled in California.

Gruenberg first came into prominence when his symphonic poem *Hill of Dreams* won the Flagler Prize and a resultant performance by the New York Philharmonic in 1921. *The Enchanted Isle*, a symphonic poem, was selected in 1929 for publication by the Juilliard Foundation, and had its first performance the same year at the Worcester (Massachusetts) Festival. In 1930 the first of Gruenberg's five Symphonies was awarded a $5,000 prize by the RCA-Victor recording company; it was premièred by the Boston Symphony in 1934.

Gruenberg's preoccupation with the symphonic treatment of jazz was most pronounced in the 1920's, when he produced *Four Indiscretions* for string quartet (1922); *The Daniel Jazz* for high voice and eight instruments (1925); *Jazzettes* (1926) for violin and piano; and a *Jazz Suite* for orchestra, composed in 1926 and first performed in 1929.

While in Germany, Gruenberg composed two operas: *The Witch of Brocken* (1912) and *The Bride of the Gods* (1913). *Dumb Wife* was composed in 1921. In 1931 the Juilliard School of Music produced Gruenberg's opera *Jack and the Beanstalk*. Describing the work as "a fairy opera for the childlike," the librettist, John Erskine, gave his own interpretation of the story, and made of the cow a philosopher who comments on the situations and on human nature in general. For this satiric fun-making Gruenberg supplied a score marked by a flow of melody that was not apparent in his earlier works. Another opera, *Queen Helen*, was composed in 1936. The following year the

Columbia Broadcasting System produced *Green Mansions,* a radio opera based on the novel by W. H. Hudson. Gruenberg's later stage works include an opera, *Volpone* (1945), and a mystery play, *The Miracle of Flanders* (1950).

After his First Symphony, Gruenberg composed four other Symphonies during the years 1942–48, as well as two Concertos for piano and orchestra and a Violin Concerto (1944), commissioned by Jascha Heifetz. *Serenade to a Beauteous Lady,* commissioned by the League of Composers, was introduced by the Chicago Symphony in 1935. Gruenberg's chamber works include two Violin Sonatas (1912 and 1914) and two Quintets (1929 and 1937), the second of which won a $1,000 prize awarded by the Lake Placid Club.

EMERSON WHITHORNE (1884–1958) was basically an Impressionist, though he sometimes showed himself a Romanticist, as in his *Dream Pedlar,* or a militant modernist, as Nicolas Slonimsky called him upon hearing his composition *The Aeroplane* (1920). Born in Cleveland, September 6, 1884, Whithorne studied there with James H. Rogers and later with Leschetizky and Robert Fuchs in Vienna. He was for a time music editor for publishing houses, but after 1922 devoted himself to composition.

Whithorne's works include the String Quartet *Greek Impressions;* a Suite of piano pieces, *New York Days and Nights* (1923), later orchestrated for large and small orchestras and played throughout the country; a ballet, *Sooner and Later* (1925); *Saturday's Child* (1926), a setting for tenor and orchestra of poems by Countee Cullen; *The Grim Troubadour,* for medium voice and string quartet, a setting of three more Cullen poems; a Piano Quintet (1926); *Poem* (1927), for piano and orchestra, introduced by Gieseking and the Chicago Symphony; *Fata Morgana,* a symphonic poem (1928); incidental music for the New York Theatre Guild's production of *Marco Millions* (1928), based on authentic Chinese themes and imitating Chinese instruments by means of an ingeniously selected orchestra; *The Dream Pedlar* (1931), a symphonic poem and a romantic, shimmering score; a Violin Concerto (1931); *Fandango* (1932), for orchestra; the tone poem *Moon Trail* (1933); the First Symphony (1934); the Second Symphony (1937); and *Sierra Morena* (1939), for orchestra. There are also a String Quartet (1930), a Violin Sonata, and numerous works for piano.

MARION BAUER (1887–1955) was born in Walla Walla, Washington, and studied music with her sister, Emilie Bauer, and in New York with Henry Holden Huss, Eugene Heffley, and Walter Henry Rothwell. In Paris she worked with Raoul Pugno, Nadia Boulanger, Campbell-Tipton, and André Gédalge. In her own music something of an Impressionist, she had a keen sympathy with and an understanding of modern composers, whose cause she helped further with the concertgoing public.

Miss Bauer's compositions include *Sun Splendor* for orchestra (1926); *Indian Pipes* for orchestra (1928); *Fantasia Quasi una Sonata* for violin and piano (1930); incidental music to *Prometheus Bound* (1930); a Viola Sonata (1932); *Symphony-Suite* for strings (1940); Concertino for oboe, clarinet, and string quartet (1940); Trio for flute, cello, and piano (1944); and *China* for chorus and orchestra (1945).

In addition to composing, Miss Bauer was active as a teacher and journalist, holding positions of associate professor of music at New York University and New York editor and critic of the *Musical Leader*. She wrote the book *Twentieth Century Music* and collaborated with Ethel Peyser on *How Music Grew, Music Through the Ages,* and *How Opera Grew*.

Though German by birth and training, WERNER JOSTEN (1888–1963) was more deeply influenced by the French Modernists and by exotic art than he was by the German Romanticists whom he followed in his early works. Born at Elberfeld, Germany, June 12, 1888, he studied with Rudolf Siegel in Munich, stayed in Paris until the outbreak of World War I, and returned to Germany after the war, serving as assistant conductor at the Munich Opera House till 1920, when he came to the United States to act as accompanist-assistant to various singers. In 1923 he was appointed professor of music at Smith College in Northampton, Massachusetts, where he was also conductor of the college orchestra.

Josten's orchestra works include a *Concerto Sacro,* completed in 1927, which, like his more recent music for the ballet *Joseph and His Brethren* (1936), unquestionably shows the influence of the severe religious atmosphere of his childhood. The two parts of the *Concerto Sacro* were introduced separately—No. 1 in 1933 and No. 2 in 1929— but they form a single work, inspired by a triptych painted for the

Isenheim altar at Colmar in Alsace by the sixteenth-century Rhenish master Mathias Grünewald. Josten's First Symphony was heard in 1936 and his Second, for strings alone, in 1946. *Jungle,* a symphonic movement inspired by Rousseau's painting *Forêt Exotique,* was introduced in 1929 and reveals Josten's interest in exotic art, an interest also apparent in his choreographic poem *Batouala* (1931). Josten's ballet *Endymion* was made into a concert Suite in 1933.

Several of Josten's major choral works were based on sacred subjects. *Crucifixion* (1915) was scored for bass solo and mixed chorus *a cappella,* while *Ode for St. Cecilia's Day* (1925) was written for voices and orchestra, and *A Une Madonne* (1929), after Baudelaire, called for tenor solo and orchestra. Secular choral works include *Hymnus to the Quene of Paradys* (1921) for women's voices, strings, and organ, and *Indian Serenade* (1922) for tenor and orchestra. For chamber combinations Josten composed a String Quartet (1934); a Violin Sonata (1936); a Cello Sonata (1938); a Sonatina for violin and piano (1939); a Trio for flute, clarinet, and bassoon (1941); a Trio for violin, viola, and cello (1942); a Trio for flute, cello, and piano (1943); a Sonata for horn and piano (1944); a *Canzona Seria,* for flute, oboe, clarinet, bassoon, and piano.

To return briefly to the avant-garde, there are three composers who seemed in the early 1960's as radical as they did when we first heard their music. EDGAR VARÈSE (1885——), who during the First World War announced himself an experimenter, has remained one ever since. Varèse himself says that he has been called a pioneer perhaps because he was "the first composer to explore, so to speak, outer musical space."

Varèse was born in Paris, December 22, 1885, and studied with Vincent d'Indy and Albert Roussel at the Schola Cantorum and with Charles Marie Widor at the Paris Conservatory. He was befriended by Debussy, which may account for the Romantic and Impressionist style of his early music. These works were either lost or destroyed by the composer. Varèse was also a protégé of Ferruccio Busoni, who no doubt was one of the influences which caused Varèse to work out an entirely new concept of composition in 1914. Varèse came to America in 1915 and in 1919 founded the New Symphony Orchestra for performance of new music. In 1926 he organized a Pan-American

Society for promoting the cause of music of the Americas, and with Carlos Salzedo he founded the International Composers' Guild in 1921.

Varèse's mature works date from 1922, with *Offrandes* for voice and small orchestra. Subsequent works include *Hyperprism* (1923), for wind instruments and percussion; *Octandre* (1924), for seven wind instruments and double bass; *Intégrales* (1925), for small orchestra and percussion; *Amériques* (1926), for large orchestra; *Ionisation* (1933), for forty-one percussion instruments of indefinite pitch and two sirens—composed, despite its radical sonorities, in sonata form with exposition, development, abridged recapitulation, and coda; *Equatorial* (1934), scored for theremin, bass voice, trumpets, trombone, organ, and percussion; *Density 21.5* (1935), for unaccompanied flute; and, to cite two works using electronic devices, *Deserts* (1954), utilizing wind instruments, five percussionists, and "one Ampex tape recorder model 3502 with two speakers faced toward the rear for indirect hearing," and *Poème Electronique* (1958), composed for the Philips Pavilion at the Brussels Exposition in 1958.

After a New York Town Hall concert of Varèse's works, Paul Henry Lang wrote in the New York *Herald Tribune* of May 2, 1961:

Of late we have seen many men who came to the arena after the war; engineers, scientists, and composers manqués rally behind the movement to adjust music to the machine age. Most of them are suspect, and in some instances I would even question their honesty, but last night we heard one of the real pioneers, who was at it when such things were not fashionable, when some of the much-publicized and well-supported heroes of machine-made music, both here and abroad, were in diapers or were just discovering that to compose with ordinary human means is beyond their powers.

In 1962 Varèse was awarded a Creative Arts Citation of $1,500 by Brandeis University.

CARLOS SALZEDO (1885–1961) was graduated from the Paris Conservatory with honors in harp and piano, and was known as a brilliant harpist and an apostle of advanced musical tendencies. Born in Archanon, France, April 6, 1885, he settled in this country and became an American citizen in 1924. He collaborated with Varèse in the 1921 founding of the International Composers' Guild, and he was a member of the Board of the United States Section of the International

Society for Contemporary Music. He founded the harp department at the Curtis Institute and also taught at the Juilliard School. He wrote numerous works for harp solo, for harp and orchestra, and for various combinations of instruments and voices including one or more harps. He enriched the composer's orchestral vocabulary by demonstrating numerous hitherto unexploited sounds and colors of which the harp is capable. His music has been heard in many performances and broadcasts and includes *The Enchanted Isle* (1919), for harp and orchestra; an untitled work for harp, brasses, and strings; a Concerto (1927) and a *Préambule et Jeux* for harp with several other instruments (1929); and a Sonata for harp and piano, published by the Society for the Publication of American Music (1922).

JOHN J. BECKER (1886–1961), a champion of musical radicalism, was born in Henderson, Kentucky, and was educated in the Middle West. He was for a time director of music at Notre Dame University; professor of fine arts at the College of St. Scholastica; conductor of two orchestras and of the St. Cloud (Minnesota) Civic Choir; and state director of the Federal Music Project for Minnesota. In 1943 he became director of music and composer-in-residence at Barat College of the Sacred Heart in Lake Forest, Illinois.

Becker composed seven Symphonies, the first in 1912 and the Seventh, based on the Sermon on the Mount, in 1947. The Second was performed at the Frankfurt Music Festival in Germany in 1932, and the Third was introduced by Leonard Bernstein in 1958, twenty-nine years after its composition. Reviewing this work, subtitled *Symphonia Brevis*, Wallingford Riegger wrote in an article in the *Bulletin of the American Composers' Alliance* (Volume X, No. 1, 1959):

This work demonstrates how completely the composer has shaken off the shackles of Europe and followed his own code. . . . The symphony is outstanding . . . in the realm of orchestral dynamics, from the tenderest passages in the woodwinds to the final cumulative series of Pelions on Ossa, so to speak, in the extraordinary orchestral weaving of dissonant blends into a mounting climax unparalleled in the annals of music-making. . . . It is typical of the contemporary scene that this notable work had to wait thirty years for performance.

In addition to the Symphonies, Becker has composed various Concertos for solo instruments with orchestra: for piano, for two flutes, for horn, and for viola; a number of so-called *Sound Pieces* for string combinations; a large number of choral and chamber works; several works for the stage, including *Dance Figure,* and *Obongo, Dance Primitive.* Becker experimented with new combinations of music, dance, and dramatic action in *A Marriage with Space* and in a work based on Andreiev's *The Life of Man.*

So much for the extreme radicals of the decade. Mention ought also to be made of a man who was considerably advanced in his musical thinking, though not actually a member of the avant-garde. EDWARD ROYCE (1886——), born at Cambridge, Massachusetts, December 25, 1886, graduated from Harvard in 1907 and from Stern Conservatory in Berlin in 1913. He founded the music department at Middlebury College, Vermont, and was head of the theory department at the Ithaca Conservatory of Music from 1916 to 1921; from 1923 to 1947 he was professor of composition at the Eastman School of Music in Rochester, where two of his tone poems were first performed: *The Fire Bringers* (1926) and *Far Ocean* (1929). He also composed a set of Piano Variations and numerous piano pieces and songs.

There were several other Harvard graduates born in this decade, three of whom achieved distinction and were somewhat conservative in their outlook. Boston-born PHILIP GREELEY CLAPP (1888–1954) studied not only at Harvard, but abroad with Max Schillings. Director of music at Dartmouth College from 1915 to 1918, band-leader in the American Expeditionary Forces during World War I, and from 1919 until his death professor and director of music at the State University of Iowa, he also served during leaves of absence as director of extension for the Juilliard Foundation and as guest conductor of the American Orchestral Society in New York and at concerts of the Cincinnati Orchestra in Birmingham, Alabama, and Knoxville, Tennessee. His works include six Symphonies; four symphonic poems; a Piano Concerto; a symphonic work for the Saxe-Alloo seven-valve independent trombone; a String Quartet; a Piano Sonata; and choral works. His earliest symphonic poem, *Norge,* was performed by the Pierian Sodality of Harvard and by the Boston Symphony in 1908; the Boston Symphony also introduced his First and Second Symphonies in 1914 and 1917 respectively. An orchestral prelude, *In Summer*, was heard in St. Louis, Minneapolis, and Chicago.

EDWARD BALLANTINE (1886——) became widely known for his Piano Variations in the style of ten different composers on *Mary Had a Little Lamb*, composed in 1924. In 1934 Ballantine issued a second series of Variations on the same tune, parodying the styles of Stravinsky, Gershwin, and other contemporaries. Born in Oberlin, Ohio, and educated in Springfield, Massachusetts, and at Harvard (where he took highest honors in music) and in Berlin with Schnabel, Ganz, and Rüfer, Ballantine joined the music faculty at Harvard in 1912, becoming assistant professor in 1927 and associate professor from 1932 until his retirement in 1947. His orchestra pieces include *Prelude to the Delectable Forest* (1914); *The Eve of St. Agnes* (1917); *The Awakening of the Woods*; and an *Overture to the Piper*.

CHALMERS CLIFTON (1889——), born in Jackson, Mississippi, April 30, 1889, studied in Cincinnati, at Harvard with E. B. Hill and Walter Spalding, and in Paris with Vincent d'Indy. In 1910 he was musical director of the first Peterborough (New Hampshire) Festival. From 1915 to 1917 he conducted the Cecilia Society of Boston, and from 1922 to 1930 he led the National Orchestral Association in New York City. From 1935 to 1939 he directed the Federal Music Project in New York. His compositions include *Adagio* for orchestra; *The Poppy* for baritone and orchestra; two Piano Sonatas; two pieces for clarinet and piano; a Violin Sonata; and a Suite for trumpet and orchestra.

While Harvard produced its Royce, Clapp, Ballantine, and Clifton, Yale produced its SETH BINGHAM (1882——), known to his fellow alumni as the composer of the stirring Yale song *Mother of Men*. Born in Bloomfield, New Jersey, April 16, 1882, he studied at Yale with Horatio Parker and during the years 1906–7 worked in Paris with Widor, d'Indy, and Guilmant. He held several positions as church organist in New York, and until his retirement in 1954 he was professor of organ and composition at Columbia University.

Bingham's organ works include *Harmonies of Florence, Pioneer America,* and a Suite. Among his numerous choral works is a folk cantata, *Wilderness Stone* (1933), based on a love episode from Stephen Vincent Benét's *John Brown's Body*. Bingham also composed a *Wall Street Fantasy* (1912, first performed 1916); *Tame Animal Tunes* (1918), for chamber orchestra; a Suite for wind instruments; a *Passacaglia* (1918); two Suites, *Memories of France* and *The Breton Cadence* (1926); a Concerto for organ and orchestra (1946); a *Connecticut Suite* for organ and strings (1954); and a Concerto for brass, snare drum, and organ (1954).

Another composer closely associated with the organ, ERIC DE LAMARTER (1880–1953) was born in Lansing, Michigan, February 18, 1880, and studied with Middelschulte in Chicago and with Widor in Paris. For many years a leading organist in Chicago, he played from 1914 to 1936 at the Fourth Presbyterian Church. He served as a music critic for the Chicago *Record-Herald* in 1908–9 and for the *Tribune* in 1909–10, and as assistant conductor with the Chicago Symphony from 1918 to 1936. His orchestral compositions include an Overture, *The Faun* (1914); *Serenade* (1915); *Masquerade*, an Overture (1916); *Fable of the Hapless Folktune* (1917); three Symphonies (1914, 1926, 1931); a ballet, *The Betrothal* (1918); two Organ Concertos (1920 and 1922); *Weaver of Tales* (1926), for organ and chamber orchestra; a ballet, *The Black Orchid* (1931); a ballet Suite, *The Dance of Life* (1931); and an Overture, *The Giddy Puritan*, on two early New England tunes, composed in 1921 and first performed in 1938.

Still another composer who was also a highly proficient organist, New York City–born JAMES PHILIP DUNN (1884–1936) studied at Columbia University with Edward MacDowell and Cornelius Ruber. Active as an organist and teacher as well as composer, he wrote *Overture on Negro Themes* for orchestra (1922); a *Passacaglia and Fugue* for orchestra; *We* (1927), a symphonic poem describing Lindbergh's flight; two String Quartets; a Piano Quintet; a Violin Sonata; and numerous songs.

A number of composers from the 1880's were associated primarily with the Midwest. Indiana-born CARL EPPERT (1882–1961), a native of Carbon City in Clay County, studied in Milwaukee and Germany and organized Milwaukee's Civic and Symphony orchestras, which for four seasons he conducted. Associated with several conservatories, he was active as conductor and teacher in Terre Haute, in Seattle, and in Berlin. His orchestra piece *Traffic,* actually the opening movement of *Symphony of the City,* won third prize in the National Broadcasting Company's 1932 contest. His *Symphonic Impressions* won a prize from the Chicago Symphony Orchestra in 1941. Others of his orchestral works include a fantasy, *The Argonauts;* a tone poem, *The Pioneer;* a *Little Symphony;* a Symphony in C Minor; a satirical portrait, *Escapade;* a Suite, *Vitamins;* and a *Concert Waltz Suite.* He also composed for symphonic bands and wrote a considerable amount of choral and chamber music.

MAX WALD (1889–1954), a pupil of Vincent d'Indy and chairman of the theory department of the Chicago Musical College from 1936 until his death, was born in Litchfield, Illinois. In 1932 his symphonic poem *The Dancer Dead* won second prize in the National Broadcasting Company competition. His works include *Retrospectives* for orchestra (1926); *Comedy Overture; In Praise of Pageantry* for orchestra (1946); chamber music; and piano music.

Although born and trained in New York, the son of the architect of Carnegie Hall, BURNET CORWIN TUTHILL (1888——) has lived his professional life in Cincinnati and Memphis. After a number of years in business he became manager of the Cincinnati Conservatory of Music, and in 1935 settled in Memphis, Tennessee, where he became director of the Memphis College of Music. With his father he founded the Society for the Publication of American Music. A clarinetist himself, Tuthill has devoted himself largely to music for wind combinations, such as his Scherzo, Opus 1, for three clarinets; an *Intermezzo* for two clarinets and basset horn; Variations on *When Johnny Comes Marching Home Again* for five wind instruments and piano; and the march *Dr. Joe,* for band, composed in honor of Joseph Maddy, founder of the National Music Camp. Others of his works include a Symphonic Overture; a Pastorale for orchestra, *Bethlehem* (1934); *Come Seven* (1935), a Rhapsody; a symphonic poem, *Laurentia* (1936); *Big River* for orchestra (1943); a Quintet for clarinet and strings (1936); a Sextet for strings (1937); and a Sonata for violin and piano (1937).

EDWARD KURTZ, born at New Castle, Pennsylvania, July 31, 1881, became head of the music department of the Iowa State Teachers'

College in 1940. His works include three Symphonies (1927, 1937, 1941); *La Charmante* for orchestra (1914); March in D for orchestra (1919); *Parthenope* (1922), tone poem for violin and orchestra; *The Daemon Lover* (1933), tone poem for orchestra; Scherzo for orchestra (1932); chamber music; instrumental pieces; and songs.

Several of the lesser composers from the decade were known chiefly for their operas. W. FRANKE HARLING (1887–1958), born in London, England, was brought to this country when he was a year old. He trained in Boston, London, and Brussels. For a number of years he was active as a church organist and conductor, but in the 1930's he went to Hollywood as an arranger and composer for pictures. Harling won high praise from critics and enthusiasm from audiences when his opera *A Light from St. Agnes* was produced by the Chicago Opera Company on Christmas, 1925. Based on a lyric tragedy written by the actress Minnie Maddern Fiske, the work was set in a village near New Orleans; the composer made of it a jazz opera, modernizing his orchestra with saxophones, banjo, and xylophone, and employed many jazz effects, a device he returned to in a second opera, *Deep River*. Set again in New Orleans, in the 1830's, the work combined voodoo meetings and quadroon balls, and was performed in Philadelphia and New York in 1926. Others of Harling's works include a *Jazz Concerto*; a *Venetian Fantasy*; a Suite, *Chansons Populaires*, based on themes by Berlin, Kern, and Gershwin; *The Miracle of Time*, a symphonic ballad for chorus and orchestra, which won a prize at the Newark (New Jersey) Festival in 1916; incidental music for plays; songs; and choral works.

CLARENCE LOOMIS (1889——), born in Sioux Falls, South Dakota, was educated in Chicago and Vienna and taught at the American Conservatory in Chicago. From 1930 to 1936 a faculty member at the Arthur Jordan Conservatory in Indianapolis, he became an instructor at Highlands University in Las Vegas, New Mexico, in 1945. Loomis' operas include *Yolando of Cyprus* (1929); *Susannah Don't You Cry* (1939), with score based on Stephen Foster melodies, commissioned by J. K. Lilly, founder of Foster Hall in Indianapolis; and *The Fall of the House of Usher*, of which three scenes were presented in Indianapolis in 1941. The librettos to *Susannah* and *Usher* were the work of Ethel Ferguson. Loomis' ballet *The Flapper and the Quar-*

terback was introduced in Kyoto, Japan, at the coronation of the Emperor Hirohito in 1928.

Francesco Bartholomeo de Leone (1887–1948) was born in Ravenna, Ohio, and died in Akron. His opera *Alglala,* produced in Akron and Cleveland, was awarded the David Bispham Memorial Medal in 1924 as well as the Medal of the National Federation of Music Clubs. His works include a light opera in Italian, *A Millionaire Caprice;* the operettas *Cave Man Stuff* and *Princess Ting-Ah-Ling;* four sacred music dramas: *Ruth, The Prodigal Son, The Golden Calf,* and *David;* an oratorio, *The Triumph of Joseph;* orchestral works (*Six Italian Dances, Italian Rhapsody, Gibraltar Suite*); more than four hundred songs and many piano pieces.

Paul Hastings Allen (1882–1952), born in Hyde Park, Massachusetts, composed twelve operas, including *O Munasterio* (1911); *Il Filtro* (1912); *Milda* (1913); *The Last of the Mohicans (L'Ultimo dei Moicani,* 1916); *Cleopatra* (1921); and *La Piccola Figaro* (1931), all produced in Italy. His other works include two Symphonies; *Serenade* (1928) and *Ex Hocte* (1930), for orchestra; for chamber orchestra, a Suite (1928), *Dans la nuit* (1928), and *Three Pieces* (1928); four String Quartets; a Quartet for two clarinets, basset horn, and bass clarinet; a Trio for oboe, clarinet, and bassoon; Three Women's Choruses; Seven Madrigals; *Left but the Power,* for chorus; several Piano Sonatas; and many songs and piano pieces.

Eugene Bonner (1889————), born in Washington, North Carolina, composed four operas: *Barbara Frietchie, Celui qui epousa une femme muette, The Venetian Glass Nephew,* and *The Gods of the Mountain;* as well as *White Nights* for orchestra; *Whispers of Heavenly Death* for soprano and orchestra; and some chamber music.

Theodore Stearns (1880–1935), born in Berea, Ohio, was a music critic in New York from 1922 to 1926, went to Germany in 1927 on a Guggenheim fellowship, and for three years preceding his death was a member of the faculty of the University of California in Los Angeles. His opera-ballet *Snowbird* (1923) was awarded the David Bispham Medal. He also composed a lyric drama, *Atlantis* (1926); a symphonic poem, *Tiberio;* and two orchestral Suites, *Caprese* and *Before the Door of the Wigwam.* The latter work was performed in Würzburg, Germany, when the sixteen-year-old composer was studying at the Würzburg Conservatory.

Two women deserve inclusion in this chapter. The elder of them, MARY HOWE (1882——), was born in Richmond, Virginia, April 4, 1882, and studied in this country with Ernest Hutcheson, Harold Randolph, and Gustav Strube, and in Germany with Richard Burmeister. Her orchestral works include *Sand* (1928); a *Dirge* (1931); *Pastoral* (1936); *Stars* (1937); *Whimsy* (1937); *Coulennes; American Piece; Castellano* (1935), for two pianos and orchestra; *Spring Pastoral* (1936), for solo violin and thirteen instruments; *Potomac* (1949), an orchestral Suite; a *Passacaglia and Fugue* (1954); and *Rock,* a symphonic poem. Mrs. Howe's chamber music includes a Sonata for violin and piano (1922); a Suite for string quartet and piano; a String Quartet (1940); and a Fugue for string quartet. Among her choral works are a *Chain Gang Song* (1925); *Prophecy, 1792* (1943); *Song of Palms;* and for men's voices, *Robin Hood's Heart.*

The younger of these two women, ETHEL GLENN HIER (1889 ——), was born in Cincinnati and studied with Stillman Kelley, Percy Goetschius, and Ernest Bloch. In addition to numerous shorter works for voice and piano, including her *A Day in the Peterboro Woods,* she has written several Quartets for voice, violin, cello, and piano; a Suite for string quartet; a Sextet for flute, oboe, violin, viola, cello, and piano; a setting of *America the Beautiful* for chorus and orchestra; and a ballet for orchestra, *Choréographe.* She was awarded a Guggenheim fellowship in 1930.

To return to the male members of the profession, ALBERT ELKUS (1884–1962), born in Sacramento, California, studied piano with Harold Bauer and Josef Lhévinne and with Robert Fuchs in Germany. He taught in various capacities at Mills College, the San Francisco Conservatory of Music, where he was head of the theory department, and the University of California in Berkeley, where he was chairman of the music department. His compositions include a *Concertino on Lezione III of Ariosto* for cello and string orchestra (1917); *Impressions from a Greek Tragedy* for orchestra (1920); and a chorus for men's voices, *I Am the Reaper* (1921).

GEORGE FOOTE (1886–1956) was born of American parents in Cannes, France. His works include *Variations on a Pious Theme* (1931), for orchestra; a symphonic Suite, *In Praise of Winter* (1940); a setting of the *98th Psalm* for chorus and orchestra (1934);

a religious pantomime, *We Go Forward* (1943); a Trio for flute, harp, and violin; and other chamber works.

FREDERICK PRESTON SEARCH (1889——), born in Pueblo, Colorado, 1889, was a member of the Leipzig Gewandhaus Orchestra from 1910 to 1912 and first cellist of the American Symphony Orchestra in Chicago from 1915 to 1916. His compositions include *The Bridge Builders*, for soloists, chorus, and orchestra; the symphonic poem *The Dream of McCorkle;* Rhapsody for orchestra; *Festival Overture;* eight String Quartets; two Cello Sonatas; a Cello Concerto; a Piano Quintet; a Piano Septet; and a Sextet in F.

The eminent American violinist ALBERT SPALDING (1888–1953) had numerous compositions to his credit. Born in Chicago, August 15, 1888, he made his debut in Paris in 1905. His works include two Violin Concertos; a String Quartet; a Sonata for violin and piano; Theme and Variations for orchestra; and numerous shorter pieces.

Like his colleague Spalding, the violinist EFREM ZIMBALIST (1889——) is also a composer. Born in Rostov on the Don in Russia, he immigrated to the United States in 1911, making his American debut as soloist with the Boston Symphony. In 1941 he became director of the Curtis Institute of Music in Philadelphia. His compositions include an opera, *Landura* (1956); an *American Rhapsody* (1956); a symphonic poem, *Portrait of an Artist* (1945); a Violin Concerto; a String Quartet; and a Violin Sonata.

There were a number of others, born abroad, who came here to live and to do their most important work. Among them, LAZARE SAMINSKY (1882–1959) became one of the leaders in Jewish musical circles, both as director of music at New York's Temple Emanu-El and as a composer who believed in the freshness of the racial element in art. Born near Odessa, Russia, he was first trained in languages, higher mathematics, and political economy. He did not start to study music seriously until he was fifteen. When he was twenty, his family met financial ruin, and he became a tutor in Latin and mathematics. He received a scholarship at the Moscow Conservatory, but was expelled in 1906 for joining a revolutionary group and taking part in political demonstrations. He moved to the Conservatory of Petrograd and continued his studies. He began to compose and gradually acquired a reputation as his pieces were performed. After the armistice he left Russia, went to Paris and then to London, and finally came to America in 1920.

Before coming to this country he had composed two Symphonies, a number of orchestral works, some chamber music, a four-act opera, and some ballet music. In America he added to his list three Symphonies; an opera-ballet, *Gagliarda of the Merry Plague* (1925), based on Poe's *Mask of the Red Death*; several large choral works; a Suite for orchestra, *Ausonia*; "poems" for orchestra: *Stilled Pageant, Three Shadows, Pueblo—a Moon Rhapsody, To a Young World*; and a Rhapsody, *Dunlap's Creek*, for chamber orchestra. In addition to composing, Saminsky contributed articles on music to current magazines and to a number of books, including *Music of Our Day* and *Music of the Ghetto and the Bible*.

JOSEPH ACHRON (1886–1943) was born in Lithuania and died in Hollywood. He composed three Violin Concertos; two Sonatas for violin and piano; a *Children's Suite* for piano, clarinet, and string quartet; a *Golem Suite* for chamber orchestra; and numerous other orchestral and chamber works.

GEORGE FREDERICK BOYLE (1886–1948) was born in Sydney, Australia, came to America in 1910, and taught at the Peabody Conservatory in Baltimore from 1910 to 1912 and at the Curtis Institute in Philadelphia from 1924 to 1926. His compositions include a *Symphonic Fantasy* for orchestra; *Slumber Song and Aubade* for orchestra; Concerto for cello and orchestra; Concerto for piano and orchestra; Sonata for piano; a cantata, *The Pied Piper of Hamelin*; a Viola Sonata (1918); a Cello Sonata (1928); a Suite for two pianos (1932); a Violin Sonata (1934); a Trio for piano, violin, and cello (1934); a *Concertino* for piano and orchestra (1935); and about fifty songs and one hundred piano pieces.

Two of our foreign-born composers came from Central Europe and began as string players, later becoming conductors. VICTOR KOLAR (1888–1957), born in Budapest, February 12, 1888, came to America in 1900 and five years later became a violinist in the Pittsburgh Orchestra. From 1908 to 1920 he played with the New York Symphony, of which he was appointed assistant conductor in 1914; and in 1920 he was appointed associate conductor of the Detroit Symphony, later becoming full-ranking conductor; he resigned in 1941. His works include a symphonic poem, *Hiawatha* (1908); a *Slovakian Rhapsody* (1922); and three works that he conducted himself while associated with the New York Symphony: *A Fairy Tale* (1912); a symphonic Suite, *Americana* (1914); and Symphony No. 1 (1916).

Born in Prague, the cellist ALOIS REISER (1887——) studied with Dvořák and came to America in 1905. A cellist with the Pittsburgh Symphony and the New York Symphony, he conducted the orchestra at the Strand Theatre, New York, from 1918 to 1929. He subsequently went to Hollywood, conducting in the motion picture studios. Reiser's works include an opera, *Gobi* (1912); several tone poems: *A Summer Evening* (1907), *From Mount Rainier* (1926), *Erewhon* (1931); a *Slavic Rhapsody* (1927); two Trios (1910 and 1931); and a Sonata for violin and piano. In 1918 Reiser won the E. S. Coolidge Prize with his First String Quartet; in 1931 he won second prize in the Hollywood Bowl competition with his Cello Concerto; and in 1936 he won second prize in the National Broadcasting Company Music Guild competition with his Second String Quartet.

3. FROM THE 1890's

As we come further into the twentieth century there is a wider diversity of styles, but it is interesting to note that the decade of the 1890's produced no composers who were more venturesome and revolutionary than Charles Ives and Carl Ruggles of the 1870's or than Edgar Varèse and Wallingford Riegger of the 1880's.

In spite of the small number of major works he composed, the outstanding figure of the decade was undoubtedly GEORGE GERSHWIN (1898–1937). Reared in the music publishing houses of Broadway, he evolved an idiom of his own that is unmistakably American, even though it represents only one phase of American life. In his music Gershwin merged American popular music with that of the concert hall and opera house. Opinions may vary as to the success of the merger—some say that he was primarily a composer of musical comedy tunes and that his symphonic works were merely extensions of something better adapted to the dance hall and operetta stage, while others have held that he is the most important of any American composer who has yet lived, regardless of the origin of his inspiration.

One fact is clear: Gershwin's works are played more frequently, at home and abroad, than those of any of his contemporaries. Since the *Rhapsody in Blue* was first performed at Paul Whiteman's Aeolian Hall concert, it has become the most widely and often played orchestral work by any American; *Porgy and Bess*, first produced in 1935, revived in 1942 and again in 1953, produced for an epoch-making tour of Europe in 1955–56 that included sensationally triumphant performances in Moscow, has been heard and seen by more people than any other American opera.

Gershwin was born in Brooklyn, New York, September 26, 1898. He received musical training from Charles Hambitzer and Edward Kilenyi from the age of thirteen, and at sixteen he became demonstration pianist for J. H. Remick & Company in New York, plugging the house's new songs. He soon began to write songs of his own, revealing a spontaneity, a gift for the unexpected twist of rhythm, tune, or harmony that attracted immediate attention and soon had everybody whistling. His first song was *When You Want 'Em, You Can't Get 'Em; When You Got 'Em, You Don't Want 'Em*. His first success was *I Was So Young, You Were So Beautiful*, interpolated in a musical comedy called *Good Morning, Judge!*, produced in 1919. His first show was produced that year—*La, La, Lucille*.

Swanee, interpolated by Al Jolson in *Sinbad*, was the song that brought Gershwin his first real fame. Then came a succession of musical comedies containing songs that have almost become American folk songs, among them *That Certain Feeling; Fascinating Rhythm; Do, Do, Do; Fidgety Feet; Maybe; Sweet and Lowdown; The Man I Love; 'S Wonderful; Embraceable You;* and many others, generally with words by Gershwin's brother Ira. Gershwin's musical comedies are more fully described in our chapter on the Musical Theatre.

Gershwin had ambitions as a composer of serious music early in his career, and at one time he studied orchestration with Rubin Goldmark. His opportunity came in 1924, when Paul Whiteman asked him to compose an original piece for his "Experiment in Modern Music" concert at Aeolian Hall, February 12. Whiteman was faced with a difficult problem in planning this concert. It was all right to ask music critics to listen to his arrangements of pretty little tunes and his jazzing of the classics, but there had to be a climax, some reason for the band's being in the concert hall at all—something new, written especially for the event. Gershwin hit upon the idea of writing a piano piece which he himself could play with the orchestra, a sort of concerto. In ten days he completed the *Rhapsody in Blue*, and Ferde Grofé, confronted with a task for which there was no precedent in musical history, orchestrated the piece for Whiteman's band, and thereby taught a few things to musical theorists in the way of tone coloring.

I remember the dress rehearsal of the concert, held in the Palais-Royal at midafternoon when the heavy drapes looked gloomy and the tables bare. The audience stood or sat in groups on the scattered chairs. Victor Herbert was there to conduct the *Serenades* he had written for the program. Carl Van Vechten and Gilbert Seldes drifted in to see what it was all about. The music critics came for an advance hearing, and of course many Broadway friends of the composer were present. Things were interesting right along through the afternoon, but the climax came when Ross Gorman's clarinet started to laugh in the opening bars of *Rhapsody*. And how it did chuckle. Here was something new—the syncopations of the jazz artist given development and symphonic treatment. Real Broadway tunes, blues and all, and a warm and compelling Tchaikovskian theme, woven together. The success of the piece was immediate; it established Gershwin's fame overnight. And it did as much for Whiteman as it did for Gershwin, for as Henry O. Osgood remarked in his book *So This is Jazz*,[1] the *Rhapsody in Blue* was the first work "that allowed jazz to stick its head outside the cabaret door."

In 1925 Walter Damrosch commissioned Gershwin to compose a piano concerto for performance with the New York Symphony Society. The piece was to be for symphony orchestra, not for the jazz band of which Grofé was a master instrumentator, so Gershwin decided to do his own orchestration, for which he sought the counsel of Rubin Goldmark. When he had finished the score, Gershwin hired the Globe Theatre and an orchestra of sixty musicians to play the piece over for an hour to be sure it sounded as he had intended. After a few changes in the string parts, he took the score to Damrosch.

[1] Boston, Little, Brown & Co., 1926.

On December 3, 1928, Dr. Damrosch prefaced the concerto's first performance with these remarks:

Various composers have been walking around jazz like a cat around a plate of hot soup, waiting for it to cool off, so that they could enjoy it without burning their tongues, hitherto accustomed only to the more tepid liquid distilled by cooks of the classical school. Lady Jazz, adorned only with her intriguing rhythms, has danced her way around the world, even as far as the Eskimos of the North and the Polynesians of the South Sea Isles. But for all her travels and her sweeping popularity, she has encountered no knight who could lift her to a level that would enable her to be received as a respectable member in musical circles.

George Gershwin seems to have accomplished this miracle. He has done it boldly by dressing this extremely independent and up-to-date young lady in the classic garb of a concerto. Yet he has not detracted one whit from her fascinating personality. He is the Prince who has taken Cinderella by the hand and openly proclaimed her a princess to the astonished world, no doubt to the fury of her envious sisters.

Some feel that the Concerto in F is Gershwin's finest orchestral work, yet there are others who believe that in writing it the composer was a little too mindful of his musical manners, that his desire to compose a real symphonic work took away much of the natural charm and exuberance of the *Rhapsody in Blue*. Nevertheless, the Concerto is still played often, and repeated hearings have increased rather than diminished its popularity.

Gershwin's next symphonic piece was *An American in Paris*, which was also composed for Damrosch, and was performed first by the New York Symphony, December 13, 1928. In this musical picture Gershwin found a subject perfectly suited to his style, and he created a charming and relaxed bit of writing. It had humor and gaiety, two of the things that jazz could handle best. And its program—the adventures of an American (recognizably the composer himself) three thousand miles from home, opened the door to a "blue" mood and a blues theme that is one of Gershwin's happiest inspirations.

Four years later Gershwin offered a Second Rhapsody for piano and orchestra, which he introduced with himself as pianist with the Boston Symphony Orchestra under Koussevitzky, February 5, 1932. This work was an expansion of a five-minute sequence which Gershwin had composed for a motion picture, *Delicious*. Olin Downes described the piece in the New York *Times* (February 6, 1932): "This rhapsody has more orchestration and more development than the *Rhapsody in Blue*. Its main motive is reasonably suggestive of rivets and racket in the streets of the metropolis; also, if you like, of the liveliness and bonhomie of its inhabitants. There is a second theme, built into a contrasting section. Thus jazz dance rhythm and sentimental song are opposed and juxtaposed in this score. The conception is wholly orchestral." Downes then concluded his review with this opinion: "But with all its immaturities, the *Rhapsody in Blue* is more individual and originative than the piece heard last night . . . we have had better things from Mr. Gershwin, and we expect better in time to come." This was a sound verdict, for the Second Rhapsody has not been often performed.

It was about this time (1931) that the satirical musical comedy *Of Thee I Sing* was produced. This work, which won the Pulitzer Prize for the best play of the season, poked fun at government officialdom, and its opening song, *Wintergreen for President*, has become a classic. The sequel to *Of Thee I Sing*, *Let 'Em Eat Cake*, was not a success.

It was perhaps inevitable that Gershwin should turn to the grand opera stage, and he did so with great distinction, even though there was much discussion as to whether *Porgy and Bess* was a high-class musical comedy or a low-class grand opera. As a matter of fact, it was neither. It was nearest, perhaps, to a folk-opera; but however classified, it is, to date, the most individual American opera that has been successfully produced, and it may very well be a pioneer in establishing a native school of American opera.

Porgy and Bess was based on the play *Porgy* by Du Bose and Dorothy Heyward. It was produced by the Theatre Guild and was first performed in Boston, September 30, 1935. Then it was taken to Broadway, where it enjoyed a run at the Alvin Theatre. To gather material on the Negroes around Charleston, South Carolina, and to study the "Gullah" dialect, Gershwin spent some considerable time in the South. There is no doubt that he produced something highly authentic, for the Negro-like music he composed made the audience feel that they were actually sitting in Catfish Row, rather than in a theatre.

Opinion was divided at the time of the original production as to whether Gershwin had produced a unified score for the entire dramatic work, or whether he had supplied merely a succession of appropriate hit songs: *Summertime, I Got Plenty of Nuthin', It Ain't Necessarily So, Bess, You Is My Woman Now,* and the others. Brooks Atkinson remarked in the New York *Times* (October 11, 1935) that "Mr. Gershwin is still easiest in mind when he is writing songs with choruses."

For the 1942 production of *Porgy and Bess* a number of cuts were made in the score and in the action, and the result was a far more unified whole, and one of the most touching creations in the theatre. The songs were still there, and they charmed the audience just as they did in the original production. But this time the action and the accompanying score had been tightened; they did not have a chance to wander from their main course, and as a consequence the song-hits became an integrated part of the drama.

Following the 1953 revival and the 1955–56 world tour, *Porgy and Bess* was made in 1959 into a motion picture that gave thousands who would probably never have seen it in theatres or opera houses a chance to see and hear the work.

The year 1937 found Gershwin in the prime of his career. His musical comedy songs were counted in the hundreds, and dozens of them showed enduring vitality. In the recital field his three Preludes for piano were becoming part of the standard repertory. His symphonic works were relatively few in number, but these were being performed so often that he was more frequently heard than his colleagues. His works in lighter fields had brought him a large fortune, and he was adding to it each season. In the summer of that year he was in Hollywood working on the score of *The Goldwyn Follies.* He collapsed one day at the film studios, and two weeks later, on July 11, 1937, he died of a brain tumor which was discovered too late for the attempted operation to be successful.

The following August 9 a memorial concert was given in the Lewisohn Stadium, New York, and since that time an all-Gershwin program during the Stadium season of the New York Philharmonic-Symphony has become an annual event which surpasses all other concerts in attendance records.

Turning from Broadway to the concert hall, we come to HOWARD HANSON (1896——), one of our leading composers. Contemporary critics' emphasis upon Hanson's eclecticism and conservatism is somewhat misleading. Admittedly a Romanticist, Hanson nonetheless employed advanced tonal combinations, polytonality, and powerful, asymmetrical rhythms when such devices were still considered modernisms. The influence of Sibelius is apparent in Hanson's broad, lyrical passages, a kinship no doubt explicable by Hanson's Scandinavian ancestry. Hanson occupies an honored position among American composers—both for his own compositions, which are distinguished and many, and for the training which he has given to many of our younger composers at the Eastman School of Music; he has been an ardent and effective champion of his fellow composers.

Hanson was born in Wahoo, Nebraska, October 28, 1896, of Swedish parents. He was educated at Luther College, Nebraska, at Northwestern University, and at the Institute of Musical Art in New York. At the age of twenty he was appointed professor of theory at the Music Conservatory of the College of the Pacific, and in 1919 he became its dean. In 1921 he was awarded a fellowship in the American Academy in Rome, and upon his return to America in 1924 he accepted the directorship of the Eastman School of Music at Rochester, a position that he has held ever since. Besides carrying on his administrative and teaching work, he inaugurated the American Composers' Concerts. Through these and the annual Festival of American Music at Rochester, Hanson has done more to encourage his fellow composers and to give new talent a hearing than any other individual or group in the country.

Hanson's orchestral works include five Symphonies: the *Nordic* (1922), the *Romantic* (1930), the Third (1937), the Fourth (1943), and *Sinfonia Sacra* (1955); five symphonic poems: *Before the Dawn* (1920), *Exaltation* (1920), *North and West* (1923), *Lux Aeterna* (1923), *Pan and the Priest* (1926); a *Symphonic Prelude* (1916); a *Symphonic Legend* (1917); a Symphonic Rhapsody (1919); a Concerto for organ and orchestra based on themes from *North and West* (1926); a Piano Concerto (1948); an *Elegy in Memory of My Friend Serge Koussevitzky* (1956); *Mosaics* (1958); *Summer Seascape* (1959); and *Bold Island* (1962). Hanson's chamber music includes a Quintet in F Minor for piano and strings (1916); a String Quartet (1923); and a Pastorale for oboe, harp, and strings (1956). His choral works include *The Lament for Beowulf* (1925); *Heroic Elegy* (1927); *Three Poems from Walt Whitman* (Songs from *Drum Taps*, 1925); and *Song of Democracy* (1957).

The most widely performed of the orchestral works have been the *Nordic* and *Romantic* Symphonies, the latter commissioned by Serge Koussevitzky for the fiftieth anniversary of the Boston Symphony Orchestra, and the two symphonic poems *Lux Aeterna* and *Pan and the Priest*. The Fourth Symphony was first performed by the Boston Symphony December 3, 1943, the composer conducting. The following April it won for its composer the Pulitzer Prize for musical composition. The work is dedicated to the memory of the composer's father and consists of four separate movements which follow the plan of the Requiem Mass: *Kyrie, Requiescat, Dies Irae,* and *Lux Aeterna*. The Symphony departs from the Romanticism of Hanson's early works and in structure and idiom is the most compact and direct of his compositions.

Sinfonia Sacra, the Fifth Symphony, was first performed by the Philadelphia Orchestra, February 18, 1955. Robert Sabin, writing in *Musical America* of March, 1955, remarked that "for all its brevity (fifteen minutes), the music has the effect of spaciousness and completion. . . . It is a pleasure to observe Hanson moving away from subjective sentimentality and the musical rhetoric of Sibelius toward a more intellectual, independent style."

Hanson's opera *Merry Mount* was performed by the Metropolitan Opera Company, New York, February 10, 1934, and given nine performances that season. The work had been heard in concert form at the Ann Arbor Festival the preceding May 20. The libretto, by Richard L. Stokes, tells a tragic and violent tale of Puritans in Colonial Massachusetts. According to newspaper reports, the Metropolitan première aroused such applause that composer, librettist, and performers were called back for fifty curtain calls. But in spite of the public acclaim, the critics were somewhat reserved in their praise. Lawrence Gilman, in the New York *Herald Tribune* (February 11, 1934), wrote that "as a whole, Mr. Hanson's score is impressive in its security and ease of workmanship, its resourcefulness and maturity of technique. It is unequal in musical value. But at its best, as in the more puissant choruses, it is moving and individual and expressive." An orchestra Suite from *Merry Mount* is occasionally performed, but the opera itself has only had an occasional revival.

The *Elegy in Memory of My Friend, Serge Koussevitzky* was commissioned by the Koussevitzky Music Foundation for the Boston Symphony's seventy-fifth anniversary and was first played in Boston, January 20, 1956. Cyrus Durgin, writing in *Musical America* of February 1, 1956, hailed the piece as "real music, neither of funereal cast nor intellectual dryness, but of full-throated emotion. . . . I think Serge Koussevitzky would have liked it, for it is the sort of music in which he, as interpreter, excelled. . . . It 'sings' rhapsodically from start to finish."

While Hanson may be regarded as a Romanticist, his colleague VIRGIL THOMSON (1896——) is in his own words a neo-Romanticist. For many years Thomson was a resident of Paris, and our knowledge of him came principally from other American composers who had studied there. We heard from them of this young American who had come under the influence of Satie and Cocteau and who had made a setting of Gertrude Stein's *Capitals Capitals*. He had, it was said, a long list of unpublished compositions which included a *Sonata da Chiesa* for wind instruments and viola, two Piano Sonatas, and a *Symphony on a Hymn Tune*, as well as a three-act opera on a text adapted from Gertrude Stein, entitled *Four Saints in Three Acts*. This legendary figure returned to America and eventually became one of the most powerful figures of our musical life—as composer and critic.

It was *Four Saints in Three Acts* that established Thomson. This work had been produced largely as an experiment by the Friends and Enemies of Modern Music in Hartford, Connecticut, February 8, 1934, and was brought to New York later in the same month. In spite of the fact that the words meant absolutely nothing to anyone in the audience, people flocked to a Broadway theatre to hear the all-Negro cast sing such sentences as: "Pigeons on the grass alas. Pigeons on the grass alas. Short longer grass short longer shorter yellow grass," set to music which Lawrence Gilman in the New York *Herald Tribune* (February 21, 1934) called "deceptively simple, a little self-consciously candid and naive, actually very wily and deft and slick, often subtly and wittily elusive, distinguished in its artful banality."

Gilman's phrase "artful banality" describes what is perhaps one of the pleasantest features of Thomson's music. He never hesitates to introduce familiar and often sentimental American tunes into such works as the ballet *Filling Station* and the *Symphony on a Hymn Tune*. An early set of Variations and Fugue for organ used the hymn tunes *Come Ye Disconsolate, There's Not a Friend Like the Lowly Jesus, Will There Be Any Stars in My Crown?*, and *Shall We Gather at the River?*

Thomson was born in Kansas City, Missouri, November 25, 1896. He studied music at Harvard with Hill, Davison, Gebhard, and Goodrich and graduated in 1922. While in college he supported himself accompanying singers, playing the piano in theatres and the organ in churches. He interrupted his Harvard studies for a year in Paris, where he studied organ and composition with Nadia Boulanger. From 1920 to 1925 he was an assistant instructor at Harvard; he then returned to Paris until the outbreak of the war, coming to the United States only for the original production of *Four Saints in Three Acts*.

In 1940 Thomson succeeded the late Lawrence Gilman as music critic of the New York *Herald Tribune*. He became widely read, for his reviews were informal and direct. Sometimes his terse comments were devastating for what they left unsaid. He resigned from the *Herald Tribune* in 1954 so that he could devote all his time to composing. Selections from his criticism were collected into three volumes: *The State of Music* (1939), *The Musical Scene* (1945), and *The Art of Judging Music* (1948).

Thomson's *Symphony on a Hymn Tune* was composed in Paris in 1928, but it was not until February 28, 1945, that it had its première performance in New York, the composer conducting. In an article on Thomson in the *Musical Quarterly* of April, 1949, Peggy Glanville-Hicks wrote: "It is impossible to listen to the Hymn Symphony without a smile, and it is unlikely that anyone will listen to the end without a lump in his throat. Common chords and major scales are the materials, and an American classic the result. The idiom is the musical terminology of the man in the street, and the sophistication implicit in the objective arrangement of such materials is the sophistication that has traveled full circle—back to the utmost simplicity."

A Second Symphony, composed in 1931, waited until November 17, 1941, for its première, in reorchestrated form, in Seattle. *Three Pieces for Orchestra* comprise works introduced on different occasions: *The Seine at Night* (1948), composed for the fifteenth anniversary of the Kansan Philharmonic Orchestra; *Wheatfield at Noon* (1948), first heard in Louisville; and *Sea Piece with Birds* (1952), introduced in Dallas. Thomson's Cello Concerto (1950) was introduced by the Philadelphia Orchestra; writing in the New York *Herald Tribune* (March 28, 1950), Jerome D. Bohm found the work "a thoroughly engaging product . . . [one that] seeks to evoke the American scene of past days and does so with eminent success; exuberantly in the corner movements, nostalgically in the central slow movement." *Five Songs after William Blake* for soprano and orchestra (1952), introduced in Louisville, were described by Jay S. Harrison in the same paper (October 14, 1952) as "music as simple as it is tender. . . . Serenity is the rule, understatement the technique." A Concerto for flute, strings, and percussion was introduced in Venice in 1954. Several of Thomson's orchestra works are Suites from music composed as background scores for documentary films: *The Plough that Broke the Plains* (1936), *The River* (1937), and *Louisiana Story* (1948). Thomson also composed the score for Paddy Chayefsky's film *The Goddess.*

Thomson tried his hand a second time at composing an opera to a text by Gertrude Stein, this one called *The Mother of Us All* and dealing with the suffragette leader Susan B. Anthony. The work was introduced in New York, May 7, 1947, but it did not capture the public fancy as its predecessor had. Another stage work, the ballet *Filling Station*, was first performed in Hartford in 1938.

Thomson's chamber music includes the early *Sonata da Chiesa* (1926); a Violin Sonata (1930); two String Quartets (1931 and 1932); four Piano Sonatas (1929, 1929, 1930 and 1940); a Sonata for flute alone (1943); and Ten Etudes for piano (1940). *A Solemn Music* (1949), originally composed for band, has been scored for orchestra by the composer. In addition Thomson has written numerous works for organ and choral pieces for church use, including a *Stabet Mater* for voice and string quartet (1962) and a Mass for unison voices. In 1960 Thomson was elected to the American Academy of Arts and Letters.

When ROY HARRIS (1898——) returned from his studies in

Europe late in the 1920's Paul Rosenfeld wrote [2] that "very few American composers, indeed very few composers throughout the world, give greater promises of growth than does this awkward, serious young plainsman. . . . And it is doubtful whether if he does fill in the rugged outline of a composer he has drawn, any other American composer, original or traditional, will bulk larger than himself."

It cannot be denied that Harris has been one of the most prolific of our composers. By 1962 his list of Symphonies had reached number eight, and his other orchestra works, major choral pieces, and chamber compositions form a catalogue as large as, if not larger than that of almost any of his contemporaries. He has, moreover, developed a style and idiom that are distinctively his own and easily recognizable as belonging to Roy Harris. Nicolas Slonimsky writes of Harris's style: [3] "He has developed a strikingly individual type of composing technique, broadly diatonic in essence, often derived from modal progressions; his harmony is polytonal; he has elaborated a special theory of kinship of major and minor chords."

In spite of Harris's eminence as one of the leaders among our composers and despite the number of "first" performances his works receive by our major symphony orchestras, his compositions, with few exceptions, do not remain in the repertory as do those of Aaron Copland, Samuel Barber, Howard Hanson, and others of his colleagues. The outstanding exception is his Third Symphony, first performed by the Boston Symphony in 1939, a work that was hailed by Francis D. Perkins, writing in the New York *Herald Tribune* of March 18, 1940, as "one of the most significant contributions to native orchestral repertoire, in breadth and scope, consequentiality of ideas and emotional force." This estimate has not been diminished with the passage of years, and the Third Symphony is still frequently played. In January of 1962, when Harris's Eighth Symphony had its première in San Francisco, Jack Loughner wrote in the San Francisco *News-Call Bulletin* that Harris had done little since his Third Symphony "but rewrite it and reissue it under different titles."

It may be that Harris's facility for mass production has prevented

[2] In *An Hour with American Music*, Philadelphia, J. B. Lippincott Co., 1929.
[3] In *Baker's Biographical Dictionary of Musicians*, New York, G. Schirmer, 1959.

his achieving the greatness that his unquestioned talent should have attained for him. His aggressiveness has led him to become a super-promoter of his own works, and his own estimate of his talents has led to a self-identification with Beethoven that even his admirers do not concur with. In his eagerness to express the spirit of America, Harris is given to attaching lengthy explanations to his works. Thus the *American Overture,* based on *When Johnny Comes Marching Home,* bears with it a programmatic outline that reads in part: "The work should express a gamut of emotions particularly American and in an American manner. . . . The moods which seem particularly American to me are a certain noisy ribaldry, a sadness, a groping earnestness which amounts to suppliance toward those deepest spiritual yearnings within ourselves; and finally a fierce struggle of will for power, sheer power in itself. There is little grace and mellowness in our midst. That will probably come after we have passed the high noon of our growth as a people." In fairness it should be added that this *American Overture,* commissioned for recording by the RCA-Victor Company and first performed in its final form by the Minneapolis Symphony in 1935, is another of Harris's works that has enjoyed continued popularity.

For his *Symphony 1933,* the first in his list of symphonies and first performed by the Boston Symphony in 1934, Harris explained: "In the first movement I have tried to capture the mood of adventure and physical exuberance; in the second, the pathos which seems to underlie all human existence; in the third, the mood of a positive will to action." In his eagerness to establish the atmosphere of the first movement, Harris reiterates a short rhythmic motive so insistently that it reminds one of a broken phonograph record. At any rate, the "positive will to action" that Harris regards as a fundamental American trait is certainly part of his own nature and is reflected in nearly all of his works.

Harris was born in Lincoln County, Oklahoma, February 12, 1898, of pioneer parents who staked a claim and tilled a farm. Malaria drove the family to California where they continued farming in the Gabriel Valley. Here Harris spent his youth and early manhood and had his grammar and high school education. When he was

eighteen he started a farm of his own and spent his leisure time studying Greek philosophy.

When America entered the First World War, Harris served as a
private in the army. After a year he returned to Southern California
and gave himself largely to study. He entered the Southern Branch
of the University of California, began to study harmony, and delved
into Hindu theology. In the daytime he drove a truck and in the
evenings attended classes.

During his boyhood he had played a little on the piano, clarinet,
and organ, but it was not until after the war that his real interest in
music grew. While studying harmony and theory, he approached
Arthur Farwell, still in California, and asked to become his pupil.
Farwell taught him for two years and later remarked, "I was convinced that he would one day challenge the world."

While he was studying with Farwell, Harris composed a Suite for
string quartet and an Andante for orchestra that was chosen from a
mass of submitted manuscripts for performance by the New York
Philharmonic-Symphony at the Stadium Concerts. Shortly thereafter
Harris went abroad to study in Paris with Nadia Boulanger, where
he composed his Concerto for string quartet, piano, and clarinet
(1927) and his Piano Sonata (1928). These works represented a
tremendous advance over the somewhat groping Andante and were
instrumental in winning him a Guggenheim fellowship. In 1929
Harris suffered an accident which fractured his spine. He partially
recovered in a Paris hospital and then returned to New York for an
operation. During his six months' convalescence he composed a String
Quartet, and he believes that it was the enforced absence from a
piano which freed him from the restrictions of the keyboard and
rendered his technique more fluent.

Harris's vogue dates from these years and from the early American
performances of the Concerto and the Piano Sonata, which brought
him recognition and commissions for new works. In 1931 the Pasadena Music and Arts Association awarded him a fellowship providing
him leisure for creative work; there were no conditions except that
he produce according to his capacity and ability. Since the Second
World War, when he was chief of the Office of War Information

Music Section's Radio Program Bureau, Harris has held a number of distinguished academic positions for varying periods of time, most of which carried with them the title composer-in-residence or the equivalent.

After the early Andante (1926), Harris's major orchestral works include a Toccata (1931); an *Andantino* (1931); the First Symphony (1934); the *American Overture* (1935); the Second Symphony (1936); a Prelude and Fugue for string orchestra (1936); a symphonic Elegy, *Farewell to Pioneers* (1936); *Time Suite* (1937), commissioned by the Columbia Broadcasting System; the Third Symphony (1939); the Fourth Symphony (1940), a "folksong symphony" for chorus and orchestra; *American Creed* (1940), commissioned by the Cleveland Orchestra for its fiftieth anniversary, a diptych for orchestra and chorus intended by the composer as a reply to the questions "What do we believe? What do we want? What is the American way?"; *Cimarron* (1941), a symphonic Overture for band composed for the tri-state festival at Enid, Oklahoma; the Fifth Symphony (1943); the Sixth Symphony (the *Gettysburg Address Symphony*, 1944); the Seventh Symphony (1953), intended by the composer "to communicate the spirit of affirmation as a declaration of faith in mankind," found by the New York *Herald Tribune* reviewer to contain "endlessly fascinating harmonies, though they never suggest a destination," and to be reminiscent of "a new-model auto, with shiny chromium trimmings and a roaring engine, which moves on square wheels"; an Overture, *Kentucky Spring* (1959); *Reverie and Dance* (1958), written for student orchestra; the Eighth Symphony (1962), written on a commission commemorating the fiftieth anniversary of the San Francisco Symphony; the Ninth Symphony, subtitled *1963*, commissioned by Eugene Ormandy for the Philadelphia Orchestra and "dedicated to the City of Philadelphia as the cradle of American Democracy."

Harris's concertos include a Concerto for accordion and orchestra (1946); a Concerto for two pianos and orchestra (1947); and a Concerto for piano and orchestra (1953). A *Fantasy* for piano and orchestra appeared in 1955. His choral works include *Songs for Occupations* (1934) and a *Symphony for Voices* (1935), both eight-part *a cappella* settings of texts by Walt Whitman. The three-movement Symphony makes cruel demands of the singers, and the triple fugue in the last movement is harshly unvocal. The *Festival Folk Fantasy* for chorus was first performed at the Juilliard Festival in New York, 1956. *Give Me the Silent Sun,* a cantata for baritone and orchestra, was composed in 1959.

Harris's chamber music includes a Suite for string quartet (1925); a Concerto for piano, clarinet, and string quartet (1927); three String Quartets (1929, 1933, 1938); a Sextet for flute, oboe, clarinet, bassoon, horn, and piano (1932); a Quintet for piano, flute, oboe, horn, and bassoon (1932); a String Sextet (1932); a Trio (1934); a *Poem* for violin and piano (1935); a Piano Quintet (1937); a String Quartet (1940); and a Violin Sonata (1941).

Although DOUGLAS MOORE (1893——) first attracted attention with his widely played orchestral Suite *The Pageant of P. T. Barnum,* it is by his operas, with their unique combination of folk elements and Broadway directness, that he has become best known: two of the operas have enjoyed a success comparable to that of the best works of Gian-Carlo Menotti. The first was a setting of Stephen Vincent Benét's allegorical story *The Devil and Daniel Webster,* with a libretto prepared by Benét himself. It tells the story of a New Hampshire farmer who has sold his soul to the Devil for the material prosperity he needs in order to marry. The Devil, disguised as a Boston attorney, breaks in upon the wedding festivities to claim the bridegroom's soul, but is thwarted by the legal skill and eloquence of Webster, who wins a verdict in favor of the farmer in a remarkable plea (based on a speech actually delivered by Webster) to a jury composed of famous traitors and scoundrels summoned from the infernal regions by the Devil. To this fantasy Moore brought a characteristic New England atmosphere, taking Yankee fiddle tunes and ballad-like melodies for his set numbers and alternating dialogue with singing. Since its 1939 première the opera has had numerous productions by companies in our large cities as well as in universities and opera workshops, and in 1958 it entered the repertory of the New York City Opera Company.

The second of Moore's operas to reach a large audience was *The Ballad of Baby Doe,* commissioned by the Koussevitzky Foundation to honor the bicentennial of Columbia University. It was first produced at the Central Opera Festival in Colorado in 1956, an appropriate locale for the première, since John La Touche's libretto dealt with real characters who have become a Colorado legend—Horace Tabor, the silver king who was at one time the richest man in the state, and Baby Doe, for whom he divorced his wife. The opera was presented in condensation over network television the next season and in 1958 was included in the New York City Opera's American Season, remaining several years in the repertory. Jay S. Harrison remarked in the New York *Herald Tribune* (April 4, 1958) that

apart from *Porgy and Bess* and *The Mother of Us All*, no single American work has mirrored so clearly the way of life and the era of a people. . . . As to its musical style, *Baby Doe* is in no way problematical, and it should, for this reason, serve as an ideal music-theater introduction for those who regard opera as a torture instrument on a par with the rack. The airs are all floated on an ingenious and easily accessible orchestral base and even the recitative has a willowy suppleness to make it communicate with pace and power. The scoring, as ever with Moore, is appropriate and fresh as the open air it depicts, and the composer's sense of prosody enlivens every syllable and word.

In 1958 the opera was given the New York Music Critics' Circle Award.

Several years before *Baby Doe* Moore wrote the music for the three-act *Giants in the Earth*, to a libretto by Arnold Sundgaard, from the novel by Ole Rölvaag. Awarded a Pulitzer Prize after its first production in 1951, the opera was nonetheless felt by some critics to lack sufficient characterization in book or music, and in 1963 Moore undertook a revision of the work. In *The Wings of the Dove*, written to a libretto by Ethan Ayer from Henry James's novel and composed in response to a Ford Foundation commission for the New York Opera Company, Moore treated a cosmopolitan theme within the framework of a grand opera, and for the moment abandoned regional nostalgia and folk idioms. Critical reaction was mixed in the extreme: Robert Sabin of *Musical America* called the work a "turkey," while Winthrop Sargeant of the *New Yorker* found it "the most artistically successful American opera thus far written."

Moore was born in Cutchogue, Long Island, August 10, 1893. He studied music with Horatio Parker and David Stanley Smith at Yale and, after service in the Navy during the First World War, with d'Indy and Nadia Boulanger in Paris and with Ernest Bloch in Cleveland. From 1922 to 1925 he was music curator of the Cleveland Art Museum, a position he held until receiving a Pulitzer fellowship for study abroad. After working with Boulanger he returned to America and joined the music faculty of Columbia University, of which he remained a member for thirty-six years and of which he became head in 1940. In 1934 he received a Guggenheim fellowship. From 1945 to 1953 Moore was president of the National Institute of Arts and Letters, and in 1951 he was elected to membership in the American Academy of Arts and Letters, serving as president for the years 1959–62. From 1957 to 1960 he was a director of the American Society of Composers, Authors, and Publishers (ASCAP).

Moore's first important work was a set of *Four Museum Pieces*, composed in 1923 for organ and later arranged for orchestra. *A Pageant of P. T. Barnum* (1924) consisted of five episodes: *Boyhood at Bethel*, with country fiddles, bands, early Connecticut hymnology, the sort of music that was probably familiar to the young Barnum; *Joice Heth*, depicting the one-hundred-and-sixty-one-year-old Negro who was Barnum's first exhibit, supposedly the first person to put clothes on the infant George Washington; *General and Mrs. Tom Thumb*, the midgets; *Circus Parade*, the finale, depicting Barnum's greatest triumph, his circus—animals, wagon wheels, calliope, and the great Barnum himself.

In 1928 Moore produced the symphonic poem *Moby Dick* and in 1930 a Sonata for violin and piano. His *Symphony of Autumn* (1930) is a short, three-movement work that follows classical outlines. The *Overture on an American Theme* (1932) was originally named for its inspiration—*Babbitt*—and attempted a tonal portrait of Sinclair Lewis's hero. Other works include a Quartet for strings (1936); *Village Music* (1942), a Suite of four dances designed for small school orchestra; a Quintet for winds (1944); *In Memoriam* (1944), an orchestral work in honor of the soldiers who fell in World War II; the Symphony in A (1946); a Quintet for clarinet and strings (1946); a Piano Trio (1953); *Cotillion Suite* for orchestra (1959); the Second String Quartet (1959), found by Jay S.

Harrison in the New York *Herald Tribune* of March 30, 1959, to evidence "a lovely sense of tune, technical expertness, and an easy-going and conservative harmonic point of view."

Some of the happiest expressions of Moore's genial gifts are found in the operettas and short operas he has composed for production in schools and colleges and by opera workshops: *The Headless Horseman* (1937); *White Wings* (1949), from a play by Philip Barry; *The Emperor's New Clothes* (1949); the "soap opera" *Gallantry* (1959), spoofing soap-sponsored radio and television melodramas, with "commercials" to interrupt the action; and the Christmas opera *The Greenfield Christmas Tree* (1962). Moore also provided music for the films *Youth Gets a Break* and *Power and the Land*.

RANDALL THOMPSON, born April 21, 1899, in New York City, studied under Spalding and Hill at Harvard, graduating in 1920 and receiving his master's degree two years later, and subsequently had lessons with Ernest Bloch. From 1922 to 1925 he was a fellow of the American Academy in Rome, and in 1929 and 1930 he was granted a Guggenheim fellowship. He was at different times assistant professor of music at Wellesley College, lecturer at Harvard, professor of music and director of the University Chorus at the University of California, director of the Curtis Institute in Philadelphia, head of the music division of the School of Fine Arts at the University of Virginia, and assistant professor of music at Princeton University. In 1948 he was appointed to the music faculty of Harvard.

Thompson's Second Symphony (1932) is one of the high marks of American music. Though the work is highly rhythmic, Thompson has not used the obvious percussion devices but, limiting his battery to cymbals and kettledrums, has produced music that is itself intrinsically rhythmic. As Lawrence Gilman wrote of this symphony in the New York *Herald Tribune* of November 3, 1933, "He [Thompson] has not hesitated at times to be obvious; he has not strained, he has not constricted his fancy and his feeling; he has not been afraid to sound quite different from Schoenberg. His music has humor, and warmth and pleasantness; many will find it agreeable and solacing."

Thompson's orchestral works include a tone poem, *Pierrot and Cothurnus* (1922); a *Jazz Poem* (1928) for piano and orchestra; a

First Symphony (1930); a Symphonic Prelude, *The Piper at the Gates of Dawn* (1924); and the Third Symphony, commissioned by the Alice M. Ditson Fund (1949). Virgil Thomson, writing in the New York *Herald Tribune* of May 15, 1949, found the Symphony "both grateful and gracious to the ear," and Henry Cowell, in the *Musical Quarterly* of July, 1949, remarked on Thompson's "freshness and ease in handling of folklike material in the last two movements. . . . Thompson never spoils such material by over-sophistication. . . . He is expertly simple." An orchestra fantasy, *The Trip to Nahant* (1955), was introduced by the Philadelphia Orchestra. In *Musical America* of May, 1955, Joseph Sneller wrote, "The music is genuinely evocative and American in spirit. . . . Two of its subjects derive from square dance patterns and the shaped-note phrases of early American hymn-singing. . . . It is traditional in the best sense." Thompson's chamber works include *The Wind in the Willows* (1924), for string quartet; a Suite for oboe, clarinet, and viola (1940); and a String Quartet (1941).

Even perhaps more than by his orchestral works, Thompson has earned distinction with his major choral pieces, which include *The Peaceable Kingdom* (1936), for mixed voices *a cappella*, subtitled *A Sequence of Sacred Choruses—Text from Isaiah*. The opposed choirs of the double chorus carry out the dual idea which was suggested to the composer by a painting, *The Peaceable Kingdom*, of Edward Hicks, an American painter of the eighteenth century. The picture shows on one side William Penn making peace with the Indians and on the other Daniel in the midst of a group of lions. As the composer remarked, "The lions in this part look as though they were trying to make peace with Daniel; they appear to be succeeding."

Satire is often the basis for Thompson's choral music, sometimes gentle and occasionally slapstick, as in *Americana*, which uses as a text excerpts from H. L. Mencken's articles in the old *American Mercury*. Here burlesque oratorio music matches the inanities of the items Mencken chose from the newspapers of the nation. In *Rosemary*, for women's voices, the four divisions are entitled *Chemical Analysis, A Sad Song, A Nonsense Song*, and *To Rosemary, on the methods by which she might become an angel*. Other choral works include *The Testament of Freedom* (1943), for men's chorus and orchestra, composed in honor of the two hundredth anniversary of Thomas Jefferson's birth, with text drawn from his writings; *Ode to the Virginian Voyage* (1957), to a text by the seventeenth-century English poet Michael Drayton, composed for the three hundred and fiftieth anniversary of the Jamestown, Virginia, colony; a *Requiem* for double chorus *a cappella* (1959); and *Frostiana,* a setting for chorus of seven poems by Robert Frost.

Thompson has also composed a radio opera commissioned by the Columbia Broadcasting Company in association with the League of Composers, *Solomon and Balkis,* to a libretto adapted by the composer from Kipling's "The Butterfly that Stamped," one of the *Just So Stories.* In 1941, with Benjamin Britten and Alexander Tansman, Thompson was awarded a Coolidge Medal for distinguished service to chamber music.

WALTER PISTON (1894——), like Roy Harris, Virgil Thomson, and Aaron Copland, studied with Nadia Boulanger in Paris in the 1920's. He has often been called a twentieth-century classicist, for he adheres to traditional forms and is a master contrapuntist. His consummate technique is revealed in his three books, *Harmony* (1941), *Counterpoint* (1947), and *Orchestration* (1955). There are those who consider Piston's music somewhat conventional, but his harmonic structures are inventive and advanced, his rhythms are intricate and occasionally syncopated with a flavor of American jazz patterns.

Piston was born in Rockland, Maine, January 20, 1894, the grandson of the Italian-born Antonio Pistone, who Americanized his name by dropping the final *e* after he came to this country. The young Piston intended to become an artist and was graduated from the Massachusetts School of Art in 1914. He then went to Harvard and became interested in music. After his graduation in 1924 he went abroad to study with Nadia Boulanger. Upon his return he became an assistant professor at Harvard, and from 1948 until his retirement in 1960 he was the university's Naumburg Professor of Music.

Piston first gained prominence when Koussevitzky conducted his *Symphonic Piece* with the Boston Symphony in 1928. A Suite for Orchestra was composed in 1929 and introduced in Boston the following year. It was followed by a Concerto for Orchestra (1934), a Prelude and Fugue for orchestra (1934), and a *Concertino* for piano and chamber orchestra (1937), commissioned by the Columbia Broad-casting Company. Piston's First Symphony was commissioned by the League of Composers in 1936 and given its première by the Boston Symphony in 1938.

After these works came the music for a ballet, *The Incredible Flutist*, that was for many years Piston's most widely known work. Composed in the spring of 1938 for the Boston "Pops" Orchestra, it was performed as a ballet in November of the same year by the Hans Wiener Ballet in Providence, Rhode Island. Piston arranged the ballet as a concert Suite which has become a standard item in the orchestral repertory.

Piston's later works include the Concerto No. 1 for violin and orchestra (1940); the Second Symphony (1944), winner of the New York Music Critics' Circle Award, and in which Virgil Thomson felt (New York *Herald Tribune*, June 3, 1945) that "formalities about workmanship, rather than the immediacies of personal feeling, are the main preoccupation"; the Third Symphony (1948), awarded the Pulitzer Prize; the Symphony No. 4 (1951), a romantic work with an almost Sibelian mood; the Fifth Symphony (1956), com-missioned for the fiftieth anniversary of the Juilliard School of Music, hailed by Robert Sabin in *Musical America* of March, 1956, as "deeply moving . . . the work of a master"; the Sixth Symphony (1955), commissioned for the Boston Symphony's seventy-fifth anni-versary; the Seventh Symphony (1961), commissioned by the Phila-delphia Orchestra and, like the Third, winner of a Pulitzer Prize.

Other orchestral works include a Prelude and Allegro for organ and strings (1943); a Second Suite for Orchestra (1948); a Toccata for orchestra (1948); a *Fantasy* for English horn, harp, and strings (1954); *Serenata* (1956), commissioned by the Louisville Orchestra; a Concerto for viola and orchestra (1958), winner of the New York Music Critics' Circle Award; *Three New England Sketches* (1959); the Concerto No. 2 for violin (1960), commissioned by the Ford Foundation and described by Donald G. Wilkins in *Musical America* (December, 1960) as "a work of lasting beauty, beautifully made by a composer whose craft is complete. As we have come to expect from Mr. Piston, this is no revolutionary statement or experimental path-finding; here is mastery of an idiom in which the composer obviously

feels perfectly at home, and of which he has command at all times";
a *Symphonic Prelude* (1961), composed for the Convention of the
Association of Symphony Orchestra Women's Committees; and a
Lincoln Center Festival Overture (1962), commissioned by the Phila-
delphia Orchestra for its first concert in New York's Philharmonic
Hall at Lincoln Center.

Piston's chamber music includes four String Quartets; *Three Pieces*
for flute, clarinet, and bassoon (1926); a Sonata for flute and piano
(1930); a Suite for oboe and piano (1931); a Trio for violin, cello,
and piano (1935); a Sonata for violin and piano (1939); a Quintet
for piano and strings (1942); a *Partita* for violin, viola, and organ
(1944); a Sonatina for violin and harpsichord (1945); a *Divertimento* for nine instruments (1946); a Piano Quintet (1949); a
Quintet for wind instruments (1956); and a Nonet (1962), described by Ronald Eyer in the New York *Herald Tribune* of April 7,
1962, as a "conservative, completely tonal work with no obeisances
to 'the music of the future.' "

BERNARD ROGERS (1893———), another composer who leans toward
classicism, was born in New York, February 4, 1893. He studied in
this country with Ernest Bloch and abroad with Frank Bridge and
Nadia Boulanger. In 1918 he was awarded a Pulitzer traveling
scholarship and in 1927–28 a Guggenheim fellowship. In 1929 he
joined the faculty of the Eastman School of Music, where he has
been composition teacher to many of our outstanding composers.

Rogers first came to the attention of concertgoers with his tone
poem *To the Fallen* (1919), composed in memory of those who had
died in the First World War. *The Faithful* was performed in New
York in 1924, followed by a *Soliloquy* for flute and string orchestra
(1925) and *Fuji in the Sunset Glow* (1926), introduced by Damrosch
and the New York Symphony Society. All four of Rogers's Symphonies were introduced by the Rochester Philharmonic under Howard Hanson: the First, subtitled *Adonais*, in 1926; the Second, 1930;
the Third, 1938; and the Fourth in 1948.

Rogers's other orchestra works include the Prelude to *Hamlet*
(1926); *Three Japanese Dances* (1928); two *American Frescoes*
(1935); *The Supper at Emmäus* (1935); *Five Fairy Tales* (1935),
drawn from Andrew Lang; a *Fantasy* for flute, viola, and orchestra

(1937); a second *Soliloquy* (1938), for bassoon and string orchestra; *Dance of Salomé* (1938); *The Colors of War* (1939); *The Song of the Nightingale* (1940); *The Plains* (1940), for small orchestra; three orchestral works inspired by World War II: *Sailors of Toulon* (1943), *Invasion* (1943), and *In Memory of Franklin D. Roosevelt* (1947); *Characters from Hans Christian Andersen* (1945), for a small orchestra; the Overture *Amphitryon* (1947); *Leaves from the Tale of Pinocchio* (1950), for small orchestra; *The Silver World* (1950), for flute, oboe, and strings; *Dance Scenes* (1953), inspired by Japanese art concepts; a *Fantasia* for solo horn, string orchestra, and kettledrums (1954); *The Portrait*, for violin and orchestra (1956); *Variations on a Song by Mussorgsky* (1960); and *New Japanese Dances* (1962).

Rogers's operas include *The Marriage of Aude* (1931), to a libretto by Charles Rodde; *The Warriors* (1947), a one-act treatment of the Samson and Delilah story, with libretto by Norman Corwin, produced by the New York Metropolitan Opera Company; *The Veil* (1950), another one-act opera, with libretto by Robert Lawrence; and *The Nightingale* (1955). Rogers has also composed a number of significant choral works, including *The Raising of Lazarus* (1930), a cantata; *The Exodus* (1933), also a cantata; *The Passion* (1944), an oratorio; and *The Prophet Isaiah* (1962), for soloists, chorus, and large orchestra.

ALBERT STOESSEL (1894–1943) was born in St. Louis, Missouri, and had his musical training from local teachers and at the Royal Hochschule in Berlin. He made his debut in Berlin as a violinist, playing three concertos with orchestra. He returned to America in 1915, appeared as soloist with the St. Louis Symphony Orchestra, and toured the country as assisting artist with Enrico Caruso. In 1922 Stoessel became conductor of the Oratorio Society of New York and music director of the Chatauqua Institution; in 1923 he was appointed head of the music department of New York University, but resigned in 1930 to become director of the orchestra and opera departments of the Juilliard Graduate School. All these duties proved too much for his strength: he fell dead of a heart attack while conducting a performance of Walter Damrosch's *Dunkirk* at the American Academy of Arts and Letters, May 12, 1943.

One of Stoessel's earliest compositions was his *Suite Antique* (1922) for two violins and piano, a work in more or less conventional style. In his *Concerto Grosso* (1936) for strings he became a neo-classicist, using traditional forms and patterns in the spirit and musical speech of the twentieth century. In the fall of 1936 Stoessel completed an opera to a libretto by Robert A. Simon, and *Garrick* was first produced by the opera department of the Juilliard School of Music in 1937. Stoessel's earlier works include a *Hispania Suite* for orchestra (1921) and a symphonic poem, *Cyrano de Bergerac* (1922). He published a Sonata for violin and piano, numerous pieces and songs, and a number of choruses.

From a radical experimenter whose innovations were considered by many outlandish and unworthy of serious consideration, HENRY COWELL (1897——) has developed into one of our most substantial composers. Born at Menlo Park, California, March 11, 1897, he began the study of the violin at the age of five but three years later gave the instrument away and decided to become a composer, working out his own principles. He found that simple concords expressed simple thoughts and that dissonance reflected anger and strong emotions. Later, when he studied music at the University of California with Charles Seeger and at the Institute of Applied Music in New York and became acquainted with the rules of musical theory, he was shocked to find that these rules played favorites and were partial to concords.

Cowell first attracted attention with his so-called "tone-clusters," with which he had experimented even earlier than the "note-clusters" with which Leo Ornstein astounded the public in 1915. Both devices were simply the simultaneous sounding of whole blocks of adjacent tones, though Ornstein would use his fists to achieve the cluster and Cowell the palm of his hand, his entire forearm, and in some cases a ruler. (It will be noted that Charles Ives wrote chords that required a ruler or board.) In the book *New Musical Resources* which he published in 1919 [4] Cowell explained that since, when a tone is sounded, the ear actually hears not only the tone but its natural overtones, the composer is merely following acoustic principles in playing all the overtones simultaneously with the note; he may, in effect, secure a

---

[4] Revised edition, 1930.

"clouded sonority" not realizable any other way. The theory, of course, ignores the fact that while tone-clusters give all the notes equal volume of sound, the overtones of a single note are in fact subsidiary in volume to their fundamental tone. In later years Cowell has come to call his tone-clusters "secundal chords," arguing that just as traditional harmony builds chords on intervals of the third and atonal harmony on fourths, they might also be built on seconds. The result, naturally, is indistinguishable from a "cluster."

Cowell's early experimental works include tone poems with the titles *Vestiges; Some Music; Some More Music; Communication.* There are in addition a Concerto for piano and orchestra (1930); a Concerto "for piano strings"; *Symphonietta; Polyphonica;* a ballet, *Atlantis,* the last-named three all scored for chamber orchestra; a *Quartet Pedantic; Movement; Quartet Romantic;* and *Quartet Euphometric,* all for string quartet. The titles of some of Cowell's experimental piano pieces are *Six Ings (Floating, Frisking, Fleeting, Scooting, Wafting,* and *Seething); Advertisements; Amiable Conversation; Antimony; Dynamic Motion; Fabric; What's This?; Sinister Resonance;* and *Four Casual Developments.* In addition to tone combinations, Cowell experimented with rhythmic patterns, particularly polyrhythms, impossible for a single player or even a group of players to perform. With Leon Theremin, inventor of the electronic instrument that bears his name, Cowell developed an instrument called the Rhythmicon, capable of performing multiple rhythms, each devised according to the vibration of the pitch of each tone in a composition. Experiments in this direction led to the composition of *Rhythmicana* (1931), for Rhythmicon and orchestra.

In the mid-30's Cowell began writing in a far more conservative style, revealing many of the elements that have marked his more mature works. Chief among these was an affinity for Celtic and Gaelic traditions, not only for Celtic folk music, but for the Celtic love of the weird and the whimsical. Almost simultaneously came an interest in American subjects, followed a number of years later by a fascination for the Orient. The Celtic influence was apparent in *Shoontree (Sleep Music,* 1940); in the widely-played *Tales of the Countryside* (1941), for piano and orchestra; in a *Celtic Set* (1943), originally for orchestra and later scored for band; and in a *Gaelic Symphony* (1943).

Interest in American subjects was evident in the *Old American Country Set* (1937), its four movements subtitled *Blarneying Lilt, Comallye, Charivari (Shivaree), Meeting House,* and *Cornhuskers' Hornpipe;* in *Pastoral* and *Fiddler's Delight* (1940), and in the series of works based on the fuguing tunes of William Billings. By 1962 there were thirteen of these, written for combinations ranging from large symphony orchestra to three solo recorders.

Cowell has composed an impressive number of Symphonies. No. 1, a student work (1916–17), shows the influence of Mahler. No. 2 (1938–39) is subtitled *Anthropos (Mankind).* No. 3, subtitled *Gaelic,* is scored alternately for band with strings or for orchestra with saxophones. The Fourth Symphony incorporates material from the *Hymn and Fuguing Tune No. 6.* Subsequent Symphonies are No. 5 (1948); No. 6 (1950–55); No. 7 (1952), for small orchestra; No. 8 (1953), for chorus and orchestra; No. 9 (1953) and No. 10 (1953–54), both using material from the *Hymn and Fuguing Tunes,* the latter commissioned by the Vienna State Orchestra for its tour of Israel; No. 11 (1954), subtitled *The Seven Rituals of Music* and including dance rhythms, the sounds of Balinese orchestras, and bits of early Americana; No. 12 (1955–56); No. 13 (1959), subtitled the *Madras Symphony* and first performed in that city by the Little Orchestra Society of New York with Indian artists playing the jalatarang and the tablatarung; the score specifies three Indian instruments or their equivalents, and ingeniously develops Indian themes, often according to Western compositional precepts. Symphonies No. 14 and No. 15 were first performed in 1961, the latter, subtitled *Thesis,* commissioned by Broadcast Music, Inc., and originating in a set of movements for string quartet written twenty-five years earlier. The glissandoing violin effects in two of the movements are reminiscent of similar eerie effects in Cowell's *Banshee,* a piano piece played directly upon the piano strings.

Cowell's interest in the Near East dates from 1956–57, when he and his wife embarked on a world-tour sponsored by the Rockefeller Foundation and the United States Information Service. *Persian Set,* a five-movement orchestral work employing native instruments though avoiding folk melodies, resulted from an invitation of the Iranian government to study Persia's ancient and modern music, and was performed in 1958, the year that saw the première of Cowell's

Ongaku, a work flavored with the sonorities of early Japanese court music. Another Orient-inspired work, *Mela and Fair,* composed for the United States exhibit at the World Agricultural Fair at New Delhi, had its first performance at the Fair in 1959; it was scored for interchangeable combinations of Eastern and Western instruments; Cowell explained that the music of East and West in this work "meet on equal terms."

The Variations for Orchestra (1959) proved to be something of a virtuoso concerto for orchestra; *Variations on Thirds,* for two solo violas and string orchestra, appeared in 1962, the same year that a concert of Cowell's works was given at the Juilliard School in New York in honor of his sixty-fifth birthday. Cowell recalled the past with a piece in which he had fifty years earlier shocked a San Francisco audience by using his entire forearm and fist to produce tone-clusters; he also reminded his audience of the sensation he had once caused by sweeping his fingers across the piano strings and then plucking them.

Cowell has taught at Stanford University, at the New School for Social Research in New York, at the University of California, at Mills College, at the Peabody Conservatory of Music in Baltimore, at Columbia University, and in other institutions. In 1930–31 he was awarded a Guggenheim fellowship. In 1927 he established the *New Music Quarterly* for the publication of ultramodern music, acting as its editor until 1936. In 1951 he was elected a member of the American Academy of Arts and Letters. In addition to his first book, *New Musical Resources* (1919 and 1930), he edited an illuminating book entitled *American Composers on American Music* (1933) and collaborated with his wife, Sidney Cowell, on the book *Charles Ives and His Music* (1955).

In his article on "The Music of Henry Cowell" in the *Musical Quarterly* of October, 1959, Hugo Weisgall describes Cowell as "a kind of Paul Bunyan in music . . . a figure a little larger than life. . . . One cannot point to another composer on the American scene who has submitted himself with such confidence to the entire gamut of musical experience and who has created such an impressive amount of work embodying so many different kinds of musical ideas, techniques, and sounds."

There are of course some composers who not only started as

radicals but have remained representatives of the avant-garde. For many years the austere idiom of ROGER SESSIONS (1896——) was so forbidding that performances of his works were rare. In commenting on the première of Sessions' Second Symphony (1947), Nicolas Slonimsky remarked [5] that the work was appropriately dedicated to the memory of Franklin D. Roosevelt, since it "was as much a challenge to untutored ears as Roosevelt's political ideas were a challenge to horse-and-buggy minds."

Sessions was born in Brooklyn, New York, December 28, 1896, of a long line of New England ancestors. In 1911 he was graduated from the Kent School in Connecticut and in 1915 from Harvard. During the following two years he studied at the Yale School of Music under Horatio Parker, and from 1917 to 1921 taught music theory at Smith College. He had meanwhile met Ernest Bloch, who encouraged his early efforts at composition and took him as assistant to the Cleveland Institute of Music. When Bloch resigned in 1925, Sessions also left, spending two years abroad on a Guggenheim fellowship, three as a fellow of the American Academy in Rome, and two on a Carnegie fellowship. Upon his return to America Sessions joined with Aaron Copland in presenting in New York a series of modern music concerts, the Copland-Sessions Concerts. He taught in New York at the Dalcroze Institute; from 1944 to 1952 at the University of California; and after 1952 as a professor of music at Princeton University.

As the ears of the public have caught up with our more venturesome composers, the respect that music-lovers and critics have held for Sessions has developed into a better understanding of his remarkable and complex idiom. Performers too have been able to master the difficulties of his scores, and with the passage of time his works have had more frequent hearings. Commenting on Sessions' First Symphony (1927) in the January, 1950, issue of the *Musical Quarterly*, Henry Cowell wrote that

the first movement combines Stravinskian elements with more formal symphonic development, including even some of the polyphonic devices of Schoenberg. . . . The standard American repertory should certainly include this symphony. Its dissonant gaiety and polytonal melodiousness would make it really popular with music lovers. In the 20's a dash of Schoenberg with

[5] In *Music Since 1900* (3d ed.), New York, Coleman-Ross Co., 1949.

one's Stravinsky was too much to be borne. But today this seems to be an added attraction, an enhancement of formal values that give solidity to a work of great clarity and charm.

Apart from the First Symphony, the two works for which Sessions was best known during the 1920's were an orchestral Suite from the incidental music he composed in 1923 for Leonid Andreiev's play *The Black Maskers* and *Three Chorale Preludes* for organ, written in Florence in 1928. These works were followed by a Piano Sonata (1930) and a Violin Concerto (1940). In an article on the Concerto in the *Musical Quarterly* of July, 1959, Elliott Carter pointed out that the Concerto was finished just before Alban Berg's Violin Concerto, but "under cultural conditions so vastly different that the achievement of such an outstanding work represents an even more remarkable artistic triumph—a triumph over the apathy, cultural confusion, and uncertainty that caused its subsequent neglect." Carter characterized the Concerto as a "work whose main feature is a wealth of long, beautifully shaped singing or rhythmic lines and figurations that move in very broad sweeps." The accompaniment is scored for an unusual orchestra that includes no violins.

Subsequent works include *Idyll of Theocritus*, for soprano and orchestra, composed on a Louisville commission (1956); a Concerto for piano and orchestra (1956), commissioned for the fiftieth anniversary of the Juilliard School of Music; and the Third Symphony (1957), commissioned for the seventy-fifth anniversary of the Boston Symphony. Of this work P. J. Lang wrote in the New York *Herald Tribune* (December 12, 1957), "The first impression this music creates in the listener is that of a profound conviction in the composer's high office. There lives in Mr. Sessions the ancient pride of the old craftsmen of music who believed that a score must be fitted, joined and polished until it acquires the proportions and finish of a beautiful piece of cabinet work." In the Fourth Symphony (1960), composed for the Minnesota centennial, Sessions employed atonal patterns and entitled the three movements after the "ancient categories of drama": *Burlesque, Elegy,* and *Pastorale.*

Sessions' chamber music includes a Duo for violin and piano (1942); a Second Piano Sonata (1946); a Sonata for violin alone

(1953); a String Quintet (1958), employing the twelve-tone technique; and a Sonata for violin and piano (1961).

Sessions' opera *The Trial of Lucullus,* first produced at the University of California in Berkeley in 1947, was characterized by Ronald Eyer in *Musical America* as "difficult to sing, difficult to play, difficult to produce." The text of the opera was a radio play by Bertolt Brecht depicting the defeated pride of a dictatorial aggressor. Commenting on the work in the *Musical Quarterly* of July, 1961, Benjamin Boretz noted that "the words are, in truth, dreadful, but blissfully without importance." Another opera, *Montezuma,* presented at the Deutscher Oper in Berlin, April 29, 1964, was composed to a libretto by Antonio Borghese based on Bernard Diaz del Castillo's chronicle of the Spanish conquest of the Aztecs in the sixteenth century. Reviewing the work in the New York *Times* of April 21, 1964, Peter Maxwell Davies commented that "Mr. Sessions is at his best as a melodist—although his melodies are still problematic to many ears. . . . There is little doubt that this is Sessions' masterpiece; it is also his most problematic and difficult work. One can only hope that Americans will be given a chance to hear it, as *Montezuma* marks such a huge step in the history of American music and probably the biggest single step, so far, in the history of American opera."

Among the radicals from this decade there are several who are definitely atonalists. ADOLPH WEISS (1891——), a disciple of Arnold Schoenberg, has worked along lines similar to those laid down by the Viennese atonalists, though Schoenberg is said to have considered Weiss too independent a personality to be called his pupil. But like Schoenberg, Weiss works with twelve-tone rows; he also builds up an entire composition on the basis of one or two intervals.

The son of a piano pupil of Busoni, Weiss was born September 12, 1891, in Baltimore, Maryland. He played bassoon professionally in New York, Hollywood, and elsewhere, and studied composition with Adolf Weidig in Chicago, with Cornelius Rybner in New York, and with Schoenberg in Vienna. In 1932 he won a Guggenheim fellowship.

Weiss's works include a *Ballade;* a *Kammersymphonie* (1927); a Scherzo, *American Life* (1930); and *Five Pieces;* these works are all for orchestra. His chamber works include three String Quartets (1925, 1926, and 1932); a Quintet for wind instruments (1931);

Chamber Music for woodwinds; a Trio for clarinet, flute, and bassoon; a Violin Sonata; a Piano Sonata (1932); a Sextet for woodwinds and piano (1947); a Trio for clarinet, viola, and cello (1948); a Concerto for bassoon and string quartet (1949); a Trio for flute, violin, and piano (1955); a tone poem for brass and percussion (1957); a Rhapsody for four French horns (1957); and *Vade Mecum* for wind instruments (1958).

RICHARD DONOVAN (1891——) began his composing career as something of an Impressionist, influenced by the French school, but in later life he developed a more biting style verging on atonality. Born in New Haven, Connecticut, November 29, 1891, he studied at the Yale School of Music, at the Institute of Musical Art in New York, and with Charles Widor in Paris. He has been active as organist and choirmaster in New York and New Haven and as a teacher at the Institute of Musical Art in New York, at Smith College, and since 1938 at Yale University. His works include a *Serenade* for flute, violin, and cello; a symphonic poem, *Smoke and Steel* (1932); *Wood-Notes* (1926); a Symphony for chamber orchestra (1937); a Sextet for wind instruments and piano (1932); *Four Songs* for soprano and string quartet (1933); a Suite for piano (1933); a Trio for violin, cello, and piano (1937); a Suite for string orchestra and oboe (1944–45); *Design for Radio* (1945), for orchestra; an Overture, *New England Chronicle* (1945); *Passacaglia on Vermont Folk Tunes* (1949), for orchestra; Quartet for woodwinds (1953); *Soundings* (1953), for trumpet, bassoon, and sixteen percussion instruments; a Symphony in D; and many choral works and pieces for organ.

While he can scarcely be called a radical, BERNARD WAGENAAR (1894——) has experimented with atonality. Born in Arnheim, Holland, July 18, 1894, he first came to this country in 1921 when his fellow Hollander, Willem Mengelberg, was conducting the New York Philharmonic. He joined the orchestra as violinist, doubling as harpsichordist, pianist, organist, and, upon occasion, celesta player. Two years later he began his teaching career in New York, first at the Master Institute of the Roerich Museum, then at the Institute of Musical Art (1926–27) and since 1927 at the Juilliard Graduate School.

Wagenaar's First Symphony was introduced by the Philharmonic-

Symphony Society of New York in 1928 under Mengelberg; the Second, one of the few American works performed by the same orchestra while Toscanini was its conductor, was introduced in 1932; the Third in 1937 at the Juilliard School, the composer conducting; and the Fourth in 1949 by the Boston Symphony. Wagenaar's Triple Concerto for flute, harp, cello, and orchestra was introduced by the Philadelphia Orchestra in 1938. An "operatic comedy," *Pieces of Eight*, was presented by the Columbia Theatre Associates and the music department of Columbia University in 1944. The libretto, by Edward Eager, concerned the attempt of a pirate to find Captain Kidd's hidden treasure on Long Island.

Other orchestral works include a *Divertimento* (1929); a Sinfonietta (1930); a *Concertino* for strings and wind instruments (1942); *Five Tableaux* for cello and orchestra (1955); and a *Preamble for Orchestra*, introduced at the fiftieth anniversary concert of the Juilliard School in New York, 1956. Wagenaar's chamber music includes three String Quartets, a Sonata for violin and piano, and a Sonatina for cello and piano.

QUINCY PORTER (1897———) was born in New Haven, Connecticut, February 7, 1897, the son of a professor at the Yale Divinity School. He was graduated from Yale in 1919 and two years later from the Yale School of Music, where he was a pupil of Horatio Parker and David Stanley Smith. He later went to Paris to study with d'Indy and returned to America for further work with Ernest Bloch. In 1928 he went to Paris again on a Guggenheim fellowship. He taught for seven years at the Cleveland Institute of Music and for several years was professor of music at Vassar College. In 1938 he was appointed dean of the faculty at the New England Conservatory of Music in Boston, and from 1942 to 1946 directed the Conservatory. In 1946 he became a professor at Yale University.

Porter's orchestral works include a *Ukrainian Suite* for strings (1925); a Suite in C Minor (1926); a *Poem and Dance* (1932); a First Symphony (composed in 1934, introduced in 1938, the composer conducting the New York Philharmonic-Symphony); *Two Dances for Radio* (1938), commissioned by the Columbia Broadcasting System; a *Fantasy* for cello and small orchestra (1942); a Viola Concerto (1948); *The Desolate City* (1950), for baritone and orchestra; a *Concerto Concertante* for two pianos and orchestra (1954), introduced in Louisville, Kentucky, and subsequently awarded a Pulitzer Prize; a symphonic Suite, *New England Episodes* (1958); a Concerto for harpsichord (1960); and a Concerto for wind symphony (1960).

Porter has specialized in string quartets, of which he had composed eight by 1950. Everett Helm wrote in *Musical America* of September, 1962, that "it would be no exaggeration to consider his [Porter's] quartets an American counterpart to Bartók's." Porter's chamber works also include two Violin Sonatas (1925 and 1929); a Suite for viola alone (1930); a Piano Sonata (1930); a Quintet for clarinet and strings (1940); a Sonata for French horn and piano (1946); and a String Sextet (1947).

JOSEPH SCHILLINGER (1895–1943) was born in Kharkow, Russia, August 31, 1895, and studied at the Conservatory and the State University in Petrograd. From 1922 to 1926 he was music consultant to the Soviet Union's board of education. In November 1928 he came to New York as a lecturer, and in 1930 he settled here permanently, becoming a citizen the same year. He taught at Teachers College, Columbia University; at New York University; and at the New School for Social Research.

Although he achieved a limited reputation as a composer of somewhat experimental music—an *Airphonic Suite* played by the Cleveland Orchestra and a *Symphonic Rhapsody* commissioned by the Soviet government, while he still lived in Russia, to commemorate the twelfth anniversary of the Revolution—it was as a teacher of composers, with a unique system of instruction, that Schillinger was best known. He devised a system which applied scientific formulae to harmonic, contrapuntal, and melodic construction. His pupils included such composers of popular songs as Mark Warnow, Hal Kemp, Oscar Levant, Benny Goodman, and Tommy Dorsey, and a number of serious composers as well, including George Gershwin, who is said to have written the entire score of *Porgy and Bess* under his supervision.

In 1933 Schillinger published a book called *The Mathematical Basis of the Arts*. It did not achieve general circulation, but after his death a more detailed work, *The Schillinger System of Musical Composition*, was widely distributed.

Another Russian-born American, LEO ORNSTEIN (1895——) astonished the concert world during the early years of the First World War as the bad boy of American music, as an impish youngster out to punish our ears with clusters of notes that took the place of single tones, somewhat like Cowell's tone-clusters. (In printing Ornstein's music the engraver had to invent new stems at crazy angles to show what notes should be struck together.) Later, Ornstein had plenty of company, but he stood almost alone when he started.

Born in southwest Russia, December 11, 1895, Ornstein was a musical prodigy and enjoyed an excellent education that finally led to work with Alexander Glazounov at the Petrograd Conservatory. But with revolutions and pogroms Russia was unsafe for Jews, and the Ornstein family fled to America in 1907, living on New York's lower East Side. Leo attended the Institute of Musical Art and became a favorite pupil of Mrs. Thomas Tapper. He spent several years in Europe before making his New York debut as concert pianist in 1911.

Ornstein remained a curious contradiction, for there were two distinct sides to his nature: one the barbaric urge of his own *Wild Men's Dance*—the steely, stony feeling for the strings of the piano, and the other an extreme sentimentalism, most apparent when he played Chopin or Liszt. When he performed the Chopin *Nocturnes* or Liszt's *Liebestraum,* the syrup almost dripped from them. Eventually Ornstein almost dropped from view; he ceased to be the revolutionary, perhaps because so many of his successors and colleagues have been far more advanced than he ever thought of being. He achieved a highly respected place as piano teacher in Philadelphia, where he taught at the Musical Academy, and in 1940 became director and head of the piano department at the Ornstein School of Music.

In addition to such pieces as *Wild Men's Dance* and *A la Chinoise,* which attracted the most attention on his recital programs, Ornstein composed a Piano Concerto (1923); a Quintet (1929); a Quartet (1929); two Sonatas for violin and piano; a Cello Sonata; and a Piano Sonata. In 1935 he was commissioned by the League of Composers to write an orchestral work; he responded with *Nocturne and Dance of the Fates,* introduced in 1937 by Vladimir Golschmann and the St. Louis Orchestra.

Passing from one extreme to another, we come to a composer who is decidedly a Romantic. HAROLD MORRIS (1890–1964), born in San Antonio, Texas, March 17, 1890, graduated from the University of Texas and studied music at the Cincinnati Conservatory of Music. From 1922 to 1939 he was a faculty member of the Juilliard School of Music in New York and from 1939 to 1946 he taught at Teachers College, Columbia University.

Morris's compositions include a *Poem* for orchestra (1918), after Rabindranath Tagore's *Gitanjali;* a Piano Concerto (1931) with a slow movement based on the Negro spiritual *I Am a Poor Wayfarin' Stranger,* which the composer himself introduced as soloist with the Boston Symphony; a Violin Concerto; an *American Epic* (1942); a *Heroic Overture* (1943); and a Suite for orchestra, premièred in 1962, which the New York *Herald Tribune* critic described as "a lush, large-scale, thoroughly sentimental exercise in musical retrospections." Morris's chamber music includes four Piano Sonatas; two Sonatas for violin and piano; two String Quartets; two Quintets for strings and piano; a Quartet for piano, violin, cello, and flute; and two Piano Trios.

A number of composers from the decade may be considered nationalists, either because they used native material or subjects or because they espoused nationalism as a viewpoint. FREDERICK JACOBI (1891–1952) achieved distinction as a young man of thirty-three with his *String Quartet on Indian Themes* (1924) and shortly afterwards with his *Indian Dances* for orchestra (1927–28). These were so widely played that they attached to him the label of composer of American Indian music, but the diverse nature of his later work shows that this was but a passing phase of his career. Jacobi did not believe in a consciously sought musical nationalism but rather—though he was thoroughly contemporary—in "line"—melody, which is at once an idea and its development.

Born in San Francisco, California, May 4, 1891, Jacobi was educated largely in New York, where he attended the Ethical Culture School and studied music with Paolo Gallico and Rubin Goldmark. He subsequently studied in Berlin with Paul Juon at the Hochschule für Musik. When he returned to America he became assistant conductor at the Metropolitan Opera House from 1914 to 1917, and then went west to study the life and music of the Pueblo Indians in New

Mexico and Arizona. After the First World War, in which he served as a saxophone player in army bands, he made his home at Northampton, Massachusetts; after 1936 he taught composition at the Juilliard School in New York.

Jacobi's orchestral works include a symphonic poem, *The Pied Piper* (1915); a *California Suite* (1917); *The Eve of St. Agnes* (1919); Symphony No. 1, "Assyrian" (1924); *Ode for Orchestra* (1943); *Two Pieces in Sabbath Mood* (1947); and a Second Symphony (1948). A number of orchestral works feature solo instruments: *Three Psalms* for cello and orchestra (1933); a Piano Concerto (1934); a Violin Concerto (1939); and a *Concertino* for piano and string orchestra (1946). Jacobi also composed String Quartets and a Piano Quintet, *Hagiographa* (1938).

Jacobi was an important composer of Jewish sacred music. His *Sabbath Evening Service* (1931), for baritone solo and mixed voices *a cappella,* is patterned melodically after Hebrew hymns, and contains poignant passages of passionate intensity. In 1944 Jacobi was awarded the David Bispham Memorial Award for his opera *The Prodigal Son.*

Robert Russell Bennett (1894———) was born June 15, 1894, in Kansas City, Missouri, the son of musical parents. His mother taught him to play the piano; from his father, who led a band and orchestra, he learned to play many of the instruments of the orchestra. When he was fifteen he began formal musical study in harmony with Carl Busch. Before the First World War he was in New York as copyist and arranger; for a year he served in the army, and then he was back, this time on Broadway, where he began his very successful career as an orchestrator of musical comedy scores.

Anyone who wants to become closely acquainted with Bennett's consummate technique and exquisite taste need only listen to the phonograph recordings of the Rodgers and Hammerstein operettas. Through almost four decades Bennett has been the most sought-after of all orchestral arrangers for musical comedies, and the audiences who attended Broadway shows heard not only the sparkling melodies of Jerome Kern, Richard Rodgers, Harold Arlen, and others, but also the masterful counterpoint and the rich, luxurious instrumentation of a truly great craftsman.

Bennett's serious work as a composer began when he went to Paris to study with Nadia Boulanger. While abroad in 1927 he won a Guggenheim fellowship which was renewed the following year, enabling him to turn out a considerable number of works, including a Symphony which won honorable mention in the *Musical America* contest that produced Bloch's *America*. His works from this period include *Paysage* for orchestra; a one-act opera, *An Hour of Delusion*; *Endymion*, "an operetta-ballet à l'antique" (1926); *Sights and Sounds*, an orchestra entertainment; *Abraham Lincoln, a Likeness in Symphonic Form*, composed in Berlin in 1926—the two last-named pieces winning two of the five prizes into which the judges of the 1929 RCA-Victor contest split the $25,000 award; and numerous songs, choruses, and chamber works.

Bennett had a chance to use his theatrical experience in an original work when the Juilliard School presented his opera *Maria Malibran*, with a libretto by Robert A. Simon, then music critic of the *New Yorker*, in 1935. The plot of the opera concerns the famous singer, daughter of Manuel García, during the two-year visit she paid to American shores.

Bennett's purely orchestral works include a *Charleston Rhapsody* (1926); a March for two pianos and orchestra; a *Concerto Grosso* using a dance band as the *concertino* (1932); an *Adagio Eroico* (1935); *Eight Etudes for Orchestra* (1942), bearing dedications, respectively, to Walter Damrosch, Aldous Huxley, Noel Coward, "King" Carl Hubbell (a baseball pitcher), "to all dictators," to the Grand Lama, to the painter Eugene Speicher, and "to the ladies"; *The Four Freedoms*, inspired by four paintings of Norman Rockwell (1943); a Concerto for violin and orchestra (1944); a *Classic Serenade* for strings (1946); a Second Symphony (1946); *Overture to an Imaginary Drama* (1946); *Dry Weather Legend* (1947); a Piano Concerto (1948); a *Concerto Grosso* (1958), for orchestra and woodwind quintet; and a Symphony (1963), dedicated to Fritz Reiner. *Trackmeet*, a Suite for symphonic band, was published in 1960. Bennett has also composed a String Quartet (1956) and a Suite of short pieces for violin and piano, *Hexapoda, Five Studies in "Jitteroptera"* for violin and piano: the individual sections are entitled *Gut-Bucket Gus; Jane Shakes Her Hair; Betty and Harold Close Their Eyes; Jim Jives;* and *Till Dawn Sunday.*

WILLIAM GRANT STILL (1895——), born in Woodville, Mississippi,

May 11, 1895, has become one of the most widely recognized of our Negro composers. He was trained at the Oberlin Conservatory in Ohio and studied in Boston with George W. Chadwick, later working with Edgar Varèse. In his early years he arranged for jazz orchestras and subsequently orchestrated for Hollywood motion pictures. In the early 20's Still arranged for such clients as W. C. Handy, Paul Whiteman, and Don Voorhees, and for such musical shows as Earl Carroll's *Vanities, Rain or Shine*, and the unforgettable *Shuffle Along*.

Toward 1925 Still decided to devote himself to the development of the Negro idiom and the treatment of Negro subjects in his major works, which include *From the Black Belt* (1926); *Darker America* (1924); *From the Journal of a Wanderer* (1925); three works forming a trilogy, *Africa* (1930), *Afro-American Symphony* (1931), and *Symphony in G Minor* (1937); *Kaintuck* (1935), for piano and orchestra, commissioned by the Columbia Broadcasting System; a cantata, *And They Lynched Him on a Tree* (1940), with text by Katherine Garrison Chapin, wife of former Attorney General Biddle, scored for two choruses, contralto solo, and orchestra; *Plain Chant for America* (1941), a setting for baritone and orchestra of another poem by Miss Chapin; *Pages from Negro History* (1943); and *In Memoriam* (1944), an orchestra work in honor "of the colored soldiers who died for democracy."

Still's other orchestral works include *Old California* (1944), written for the one hundred and sixtieth anniversary of the city of Los Angeles; a Third and a Fourth Symphony, dated 1945 and 1949 respectively; a *Festive Overture* (1945); *Wood Notes* (1948); and *The Peaceful Land* (1961), winning work in a contest sponsored by the National Federation of Music Clubs and awarded the $1,500 prize donated by the Aeolian Music Foundation. Still has composed two works for symphonic band, *From the Delta* (1945) and *To You, America* (1952). His stage works include five operas: *Blue Steel* (1935); *Troubled Island* (1938); *A Bayou Legend* (1940); *A Southern Interlude* (1942); and *Costaso* (1949); and the ballets *La Guiablesse* (1927) and *Sahdji* (1930). Still has received the Harmon Award, the Rosenwald fellowship, and three Guggenheim fellowships.

HARL McDONALD (1899–1955), prominent not only as a composer

but as an educator and as the manager of the Philadelphia Orchestra, was born July 27, 1899, on his father's cattle ranch in the high Rockies above Boulder, Colorado. He started to compose at the age of seven, and some of his earliest pieces were published. While a young man he toured as accompanist with several well-known concert artists, and in 1921 he played his First Piano Concerto with the San Francisco Symphony. He studied in Germany; his symphonic fantasy *Mojave* was performed by the Berlin Philharmonic and by Albert Coates in London in 1922. In the same year he taught at the Académie Tournefort in Paris, returning to the United States to teach privately and to appear in recital. During the 1925–26 season he taught at the Philadelphia Academy of Music, and in 1927 he was appointed to the faculty of the University of Pennsylvania. In 1939 he became manager of the Philadelphia Orchestra, a position that he held until his death.

McDonald's orchestral works include four Symphonies: *Santa Fe Trail* (1934); a *Rhumba Symphony* (1935), whose scherzo movement, a rhumba, proved popular on phonograph records; *Lamentations of Fu Hsuan* (1936), a work calling for a chorus and soprano soloist and based on a series of Chinese poems; and the Fourth Symphony (1938), which is untitled and which employs a cakewalk in the scherzo movement. He also composed an orchestral Suite, *Festival of the Workers* (1934); a Concerto for two pianos and orchestra (1937); a *Tragic Cycle*, for orchestra; the choral *Songs of Conquest* (1937); a Suite, *From Childhood*, for harp and orchestra (1941); a set of *Orchestral Variations* (1942); a symphonic poem, *Bataan* (1942); a Violin Concerto (1943); two String Quartets; two Trios; and a rather curious *Lament for the Stolen* (1938), a tonal elegy for orchestra and chorus on the Lindbergh kidnaping.

GEORGE FREDERICK McKAY (1899——), born in Harrington, Washington, June 11, 1899, studied at the University of Washington and with Selim Palmgren and Christian Sinding at the Eastman School in Rochester. He graduated from Eastman in 1923 and became a member of the University of Washington's music faculty in 1941.

McKay's works include four Sinfoniettas; *Fantasy on a Western Folk Song* (1933); a Quintet for winds and piano entitled *American Street Scenes* (1935); *Bravura* (1939), for brass ensemble; *Port Royal, 1861*, a Suite for strings on Negro folk songs (1939); a Violin

Concerto (1940); *To a Liberator* (1940), a symphonic poem; *Introspective Poem* for strings (1941); a *Prairie Portrait* (1941); *Pioneer Epic* (1942); a Cello Concerto (1942); two Organ Sonatas; and *Six Songs on Poems of Robert Frost* for chorus.

WERNER JANSSEN (1899——) was born in New York, June 1, 1899, and was educated at the Phillips Exeter Academy and at Dartmouth College. After graduation he became a writer of popular songs, played the piano in a variety of places, and used every possible moment to study symphonic scores. In 1930 he became a fellow of the American Academy in Rome.

While Janssen was in Italy, the Rome String Quartet played his *Miniature Fantasy on American Popular Melodies* (1932). Then came several years of conductorial success abroad and the pronouncement by Sibelius that Janssen was the greatest interpreter of his music. All of this led to Janssen's appointment as one of the regular conductors of the New York Philharmonic-Symphony during the 1934–35 season. Unfortunately, the talented young man became the victim of his friends and admirers. No living creature could have lived up to the advance reports of his prowess as a conductor. He remained with the Philharmonic for his first season's engagements and then departed for other fields. From 1937 to 1939 he was conductor of the Baltimore Symphony, and in 1940 he organized an orchestra of his own in Hollywood, California. Between 1946 and 1954 he conducted successively the Utah Symphony Orchestra, the Portland (Oregon) Orchestra, and the San Diego Philharmonic. In Hollywood he composed background music for pictures, most notably *The General Died at Dawn*.

Janssen's music is often American in its choice of subject. *New Year's Eve in New York* (1929) uses jazz instruments in addition to the symphony orchestra; *Louisiana Suite* (1930) has a *Dixie Fugue* that has often been played as a separate piece. A *Foster Suite* (1937) is based on Stephen Foster melodies. Janssen has also composed two String Quartets and *Kaleidoscope*, for string quartet.

LAMAR STRINGFIELD (1897–1959), born in Raleigh, North Carolina, October 10, 1897, studied at the Institute of Musical Art in New York, played the flute in New York orchestras and chamber ensembles, and at various times conducted the North Carolina Symphony Orchestra, the Radio City Music Hall Symphony, the Knoxville Symphony Orchestra, and the Charlotte Symphony. He based his compositions on our Anglo-American folk music heritage. His works include a symphonic poem, *Indian Legend* (1923); *From the Southern Mountains* (1928), winner of a Pulitzer award; *Negro Parade* (1931); *The Legend of John Henry*, a symphonic ballad; *Moods of a Moonshiner* (1934); *Mountain Dew and Mountain Dawn* (1945); *About Dixie* (1950); and a number of other orchestral compositions with an Appalachian background.

WILLIAM LEVI DAWSON (1899——), born in Anniston, Alabama, September 26, 1899, studied at Tuskegee Institute, in Kansas City under Busch, and with Weidig and Otterstrom in Chicago. He played trombone in the Chicago Civic Orchestra and became director of the School of Music and of the choir at Tuskegee in 1931. In 1930 and 1931 he won the Rodman Wanamaker Contest in Composition. His works include a *Negro Folk Symphony No. 1* (1934), a Scherzo for orchestra; several choral works; a Trio for violin, cello, and piano; and a Sonata for violin and piano.

Although at the age of nineteen ERNST BACON (1898——) published a brochure, entitled *Our Musical Idiom*, devoted to new harmonic systems, he has not abandoned tradition in his own compositions. Born in Chicago, May 26, 1898, he studied at the University of Chicago and at Northwestern and in Germany and Austria; Ernest Bloch was one of his teachers. His activities have covered a wide field: he founded and conducted the Carmel (California) Bach Festival; he supervised the Federal Music Project and conducted the Federal Symphony Orchestra in San Francisco; he was acting professor of music at Hamilton College and was in charge of the Music School of Converse College in Spartanburg, North Carolina. In 1932 he was awarded a Pulitzer scholarship and in 1939 a Guggenheim fellowship. He later became director of the music department of Syracuse University. In 1962 he was awarded a $2,000 grant by the National Institute of Arts and Letters.

Bacon's orchestral works include two Symphonies (1932 and 1937); two Suites, *From These States* and *Ford's Theatre* (1940), portraying in twelve successive movements the events leading up to Lincoln's assassination; *Tree on the Plains* (1942), an "American music-play"; incidental music for Shakespeare's *The Tempest;* a musical adaptation of Paul Horgan's book *Great River: The Rio Grande* (1957); *The Enchanted Isle,* composed on a Louisville commission; and *Erie Waters* (1961), a poem for orchestra. Several of his works are for soloist with orchestra: *The Postponeless Creature,* for baritone or contralto, on poems by Whitman and Emily Dickinson; *Whispers of Heavenly Death,* on poems of Whitman, for baritone or contralto; *Midnight Special,* for mezzo-soprano; *Black and White Songs,* for baritone; *My River,* for mezzo-soprano, on poems by Emily Dickinson. He has also written humorous songs; a Suite, *To the Children,* for two pianos; several piano pieces in lighter vein: *Wastin' Time, Kankakee River,* and, with Luenning, *Coal Scuttle Blues.* He has also composed *By Ontario's Shore* (1958), for chorus and orchestra.

CHARLES VARDELL (1893——), born in Salisbury, North Carolina, trained at the Eastman School of Music and is best known for his racy orchestral piece *Joe Clark Steps Out* (1937), based on an American folk tune. Vardell has also composed a Symphony, subtitled *A Folk Symphony from the Carolina Hills* (1938); and *Shelf Behind the Door* (1942).

Other composers have followed in Gershwin's path, among them the man who arranged *Rhapsody in Blue* for Paul Whiteman's orchestra. FERDE GROFÉ (1892——), a distinguished arranger and a master of instrumentation, did more than any other musician to develop the sweet type of jazz for which Paul Whiteman became famous. Grofé was born in New York, March 27, 1892. His mother's father had shared first cello desk with Victor Herbert at the Metropolitan; his uncle was concertmaster of the Los Angeles Orchestra; his father had been a singer with the original Bostonians. So it was agreed that the young Ferde should *not* be a professional musician. But the jobs he tried as bank clerk, bookbinder, printer, were not so interesting, and he drifted back to music, playing the violin, viola, or piano for dances, traveling with a patent medicine vendor and playing in a saloon or at a mining camp. Finally he got to Los Angeles and landed a job with Whiteman's band at the Hotel Alexandria in 1920.

Whiteman was interested in developing new instrumental effects, and Grofé was interested, too. So they talked things over and started to make their own arrangements. Before that, dance orchestras had borrowed the huddle system from football games and had everything and everybody playing all the time. But Grofé conceived the idea of instrumental contrast and the "harmony chorus" where some solo instrument played the melody against subdued choral accompaniment in the brass. This was one of the first departures from noisy jazz. Grofé retired as pianist of the orchestra to devote himself to arranging. It was with *Rhapsody in Blue* that Grofé made his reputation—and Gershwin's, too, for that matter, for if the scoring had not been right, the piece itself would have fallen flat and Gershwin might never have had his day as a composer of serious music.

Grofé has many original compositions to his credit, of which the *Grand Canyon Suite* (1931) is probably the most widely known. His other orchestral works include *Tabloid Suite* (1933); *Symphony in Steel* (1937); *Mississippi Suite; Knute Rockne; Three Shades of Blue; Ode to the Star-Spangled Banner; Wheels* (a "transportation suite"); *Hollywood Suite; Broadway at Night; New England Suite; Metropolis; Aviation Suite; Symphonic Serenade; Hudson River Suite; San Francisco Suite* (1960); *Niagara Falls Suite* (1961), commissioned by the New York State Power Authority and played by the Buffalo Symphony Orchestra at the ceremonies opening the Niagara River Power Project; and a *World's Fair Suite*, commissioned for the 1964 New York World's Fair.

OTTO CESANA (1899——), an arranger for Hollywood, Radio City Music Hall, and several radio programs, has produced six Symphonies; a symphonic poem, *Negro Heaven*; six Concertos for various solo instruments with orchestra; *Three Moods* for orchestra (1939); *Ali Baba and the Forty Thieves*, a ballet; and a *Swing Sextet* (1942). Born in Brescia, Italy, Cesana came to this country as a child. A dance-band flavor permeates much of his work. He is the author of several theoretical books, including *Course in Modern Harmony* (1939); *Course in Counterpoint* (1940); and *Voicing the Modern Dance Orchestra* (1946).

THOMAS GRISELLE (1891–1955), one of the first to realize the artistic possibilities of jazz, was born at Upper Sandusky, Ohio, January 10, 1891; studied at the Cincinnati College of Music and in Paris with Nadia Boulanger; and worked as a radio conductor and arranger, settling in Hollywood in 1939. Griselle won the Victor Talking Machine Company's first prize of $10,000 in 1928 with his *Two American Sketches*. His orchestral compositions include *Cubist*, a "classical jazz" work which was played in the Cohan *Revue* of 1918; *Two Pieces from the Olden Times* (1921); a *Keyboard Symphony* for six pianos (1928); *Program Music* (1937), a satirical sketch; two tone poems; a *Dance Suite*; two Sinfoniettas; and considerable chamber music.

Many of our composers have studied with Rosario Scalero, an Italian who first taught in his native Italy and France, came to this country in 1919, and for nine years taught at the Mannes School in New York, later joining the faculty of the Curtis Institute in Philadelphia.

PHILIP JAMES (1890———), born in Jersey City, May 17, 1890, studied with Scalero and Rubin Goldmark. During the First World War he served for two years in the infantry, and after the armistice he became commanding officer of General Pershing's Band. He subsequently played organ in churches in and around New York; conducted theatrical productions, Victor Herbert operettas, the New Jersey Orchestra, which he helped to found, the Brooklyn Symphony Orchestra, and the Bamberger Little Symphony on radio station WOR, New York; and appeared as guest conductor with several of the country's leading orchestras. He was chairman of the music department at New York University from 1933 until his retirement in 1955.

Known equally as a composer, conductor, and music educator, James has had notable success winning prizes in contests. In 1932 his *Station WGZBX* for orchestra won the first prize of $5,000 in a contest sponsored by the National Broadcasting Company; in 1936 his Overture *Bret Harte* was awarded honorable mention in a contest conducted by the Philharmonic-Symphony Society of New York, for which no one was given the cash prize; in 1937 his *Suite for Strings* was chosen for publication by the Juilliard School in New York; and in 1938 his orchestral *Song of Night* won the $500 prize in a contest fostered by the New York Women's Symphony. His works also include an *Overture on French Noëls*; a *Sea Symphony*; an orchestral tone poem, *Judith*; a Suite for chamber orchestra; choral pieces, among them a setting of Vachel Lindsay's *General William Booth Enters Heaven*; several organ works; and many secular and sacred songs.

CHARLES HAUBIEL (1894――――) was born in Delta, Ohio, January 30, 1894, and studied music in New York—composition with Rosario Scalero and piano with Rudolph Ganz and the Lhévinnes. For eight years he was a piano teacher at the Institute of Musical Art in New York and a member of the music faculty of New York University. Haubiel first came into prominence when his symphonic work *Karma* won the first prize in the Schubert Centennial Contest. His other works include the symphonic compositions *Mars Ascending* (1923); *Pastoral* (1935); *Ritratti* (*Portraits*, 1935), winner of second prize in a contest sponsored by Swift and Company, the Chicago meat packers; *Suite Passecaille* (1936); *Symphony in Variation Form* (1936); *Vox Cathedralis* (1938); *Passacaglia in A Minor* (*The Plane Beyond*, 1938); and *Miniatures* for string orchestra (1939).

LEOPOLD DAMROSCH MANNES (1899――――), grandson of Leopold Damrosch and son of the noted violinist and teacher David Mannes, was born in New York, December 26, 1899, and studied with Goetschius and Rosario Scalero. He won a scholarship from the Walter Scott Foundation in 1924 which enabled him to study in Paris with Alfred Cortot; the Pulitzer Prize for composition in 1925; and the Guggenheim fellowship to study abroad in 1926. He taught composition at the David Mannes School and at the Institute of Musical Art in New York, but later abandoned music as a profession to enter the research laboratory of the Eastman Kodak Company. With Leopold Godowsky (son of the pianist) he was co-inventor of the Kodachrome process of color photography.

Mannes's compositions include a set of Variations for piano (1920); a Suite for two pianos (1922); a Suite for orchestra (1924); a String Quartet (1927); incidental music for Shakespeare's *Tempest;* and a number of songs and choral works.

CARL ERNEST BRICKEN (1898――――), born in Shelbyville, Kentucky, December 28, 1898, studied at Yale University and with Rosario Scalero. His teaching positions have included member of the faculty of the Mannes School in New York, teacher of theory at the Institute of Musical Art, professor of music and chairman of the music department at the University of Chicago, and professor of music at the University of Wisconsin. He has conducted the Seattle Symphony and guest-conducted the Chicago Symphony. His works include a Suite for Orchestra (1931); a Symphony (1935); a Prelude for orchestra; and considerable chamber music. He received a Guggenheim fellowship in 1930–31.

The name of ELIOT GRIFFIS (1893——) may be added to those who studied with Horatio Parker at Yale. Born in Boston, January 28, 1893, he also studied with Stuart Mason at the New England Conservatory. He attracted attention in 1919 with the publication of an atmospheric Piano Sonata which enjoyed a number of performances. His works include a Symphony; two symphonic poems, *A Persian Fable* and *Colossus;* a set of Variations for strings; three String Quartets, one of which won him a Pulitzer scholarship; a Trio, *To the Sun;* a Suite for trio; an operetta; a Sonata for violin and piano; and numerous piano pieces and songs.

In addition to those already mentioned, Harvard is represented by three others who had a part of their training with E. B. Hill. CARL McKINLEY (1895——), born in Yarmouth, Maine, October 9, 1895, studied also with Nadia Boulanger and established a reputation as an educator and composer. In 1929 he joined the New England Conservatory of Music, teaching organ, composition, and history of music. He won a number of awards: the Boott Prize in 1916; a Naumburg traveling fellowship in 1917; the Flagler Prize of the New York Symphony in 1921; and two Guggenheim fellowships in 1927 and 1928. From 1928 to 1929 he acted as stage assistant at the Munich Opera.

His orchestral compositions include *Indian Summer Idyl* (1917); *The Blue Flower* (1924); *Masquerade, an American Rhapsody* (1926); Chorale, Variations, and Fugue (1941); and *Caribbean Holiday* (1948). He has also composed a cantata, *The Kid* (1955); a String Quartet, dated 1941; a Cello Sonata (1953); and numerous organ pieces and songs.

TIMOTHY MATHER SPELMAN (1891——), born in Brooklyn, New York, January 21, 1891, studied with Harry Rowe Shelley, at Harvard with W. R. Spalding and E. B. Hill, and at the Munich Conservatory with Courvoisier. After 1920 he lived in Italy, except during the period of Fascism and the war, when he lived in the United States. His works include a setting of Turgeniev's poem *How Fair, How Fresh Were the Roses;* a four-act pantomime, *Snowdrop* (1916); a Prelude for string orchestra, *In the Princess' Garden;* a wordless one-act fantasy, *The Romance of the Rose;* two one-act operas: *La Mag-nifica,* to a libretto by his wife, Leolyn Louise Everett, and *The Sunken City,* to his own libretto; a three-act opera, *The Sea Rovers; Pervigilium Veneris* for soli, chorus, and orchestra (1934); Symphony in G Minor (1936); a Rhapsody, *Homesick Yankee in North Africa* (1944); *Jamboree* (1945), a "pocket ballet"; a Suite, *Sunday Paper* (1946); a String Quartet (1953); and an Oboe Concerto (1954).

DONALD TWEEDY (1890–1948), born at Danbury, Connecticut, was educated at Harvard, where he studied with E. B. Hill, and at the Institute of Musical Art, with Percy Goetschius. His compositions include *L'Allegro,* a symphonic study; *Three Dances for Orchestra;* incidental music for Sidney Howard's play *Swords;* and chamber music.

LORRAINE NOEL FINLEY (1899———), born in Montreal, Canada, December 24, 1899, is known as a poet and translator of song texts as well as a composer in her own right. She studied in Canada, Switzer-land, Germany, and at the Institute of Musical Art in New York, where she was a composition pupil of Percy Goetschius and Rubin Goldmark. She settled in the United States and became an American citizen, presenting her works, together with those of her husband, Theodore F. Fitch, on the radio program *Mr. and Mrs. Composer.* She has composed *Three Theatre Portraits* for orchestra; a Clarinet Sonata; a Violin Sonata; numerous choral pieces; and songs.

LEROY ROBERTSON (1896———), born in Fountain Green, Utah, December 21, 1896, won what may be the largest sum ever awarded in a composition contest when his *Trilogy* for orchestra was given a first prize of $25,000 in a composition sponsored by Henry A. Reich-hold of Detroit. The work was first performed by the Detroit Sym-phony, December 11, 1947, and as so often happens in the case of prize-winning compositions, has had few later performances.

Robertson studied at the New England Conservatory in Boston with George W. Chadwick and Frederick Converse and in Switzerland with Ernest Bloch. He became instructor of music at Brigham Young University and in 1948 was appointed head of the music department at the University of Utah. His works include a Piano Quintet (1933); a *Prelude, Scherzo, and Ricercare* for orchestra (1940); a String Quartet (1940) that won the New York Music Critics' Circle

Award in 1944; a Rhapsody for piano and orchestra (1944); *American Serenade* for string quartet (1944); *Punch and Judy Overture* (1945); a Violin Concerto (1948); an oratorio, *The Book of Mormon* (1953); a *Passacaglia* for orchestra (1955), composed to commemorate the Battle of Thermopylae and introduced by the Greek State Orchestra; and a Cello Concerto (1956).

PAUL WHITE (1895——), born in Bangor, Maine, August 22, 1895, studied at the New England Conservatory and for a number of years played first violin in the Cincinnati Symphony before becoming a teacher at the Eastman School in Rochester. He is best known for his work for chorus and orchestra, *The Voyage of the Mayflower* (1935), and for his orchestral Suite *Five Miniatures* (1934). His other orchestral works include a Symphony in E Minor (1934); a *Pagan Festival Overture; Feuilles Symphoniques; Sea Chanty;* and *To Youth.* He has in addition composed a Sonata for violin and piano and a Sinfonietta for string orchestra or string quartet.

SAMUEL BARLOW (1892——), WALTER HELFER (1896–1959), and EDWIN STRINGHAM (1890——) supplemented their American training by studying with Ottorino Respighi in Rome. Born in New York City, June 1, 1892, Barlow was educated in music at Harvard and later studied piano with Isidor Philipp in Paris. He studied theory with Franklin Robinson in New York and orchestration with Respighi. His works include a symphonic poem, *Alba* (1928); a Piano Concerto (1931); a one-act opera, *Mon ami Pierrot* (1935), the first work by an American composer to be produced at the Opéra Comique in Paris; two other operas, *Eugénie* and *Amanda;* a symphonic work, *Babar;* a set of *Biedermeier Waltzes* (1935); *For Strings* (1935); and *Sousa and Parnassum* (1939), for orchestra.

Walter Helfer was born in Lawrence, Massachusetts, September 30, 1896. He was a fellow of the American Academy in Rome in 1925, where he studied with Respighi, and from 1928 until his death a faculty member of Hunter College, New York. His works include a *Symphony on Canadian Airs;* Concert Overture in D Major; *Overture in Modo Giocoso; Water Idyl* for orchestra; Prelude, Intermezzo, and Fugue for orchestra; choral works; and chamber music.

Edwin John Stringham, born in Kenosha, Wisconsin, July 11, 1890, was dean of the Denver College of Music from 1920 to 1928.

In the years following 1930 he taught composition at Union Theological Seminary and acoustics at the Institute of Musical Art and joined the faculty of Teachers College of Columbia University. From 1930 to 1933 he was music editor for Carl Fischer, Inc., and in 1933 became general music editor for the American Book Company. In 1936 he went to Germany on a Cromwell traveling fellowship, and from 1938 to 1946 he was chairman of the music department at Queens College.

His works include a set of *Three Pastels* (1928); three symphonic poems; a Symphony (1929); a Concert Overture; a Nocturne for orchestra (1935); a *Notturno* for winds and harp; a fantasy on *American Folk Tunes* for violin and orchestra (1942); a String Quartet; miscellaneous works for chorus; instrumental pieces; and songs.

HERBERT ELWELL (1898——) and QUINTO MAGANINI (1897 ——) may be added to the long list of Nadia Boulanger pupils. Born in Minneapolis, Minnesota, May 10, 1898, Elwell was a fellow of the American Academy in Rome in 1926 and a pupil of Ernest Bloch as well as of Boulanger. He is best known for *The Happy Hypocrite*, originally music for a ballet and subsequently arranged as a Suite for orchestra. In the latter form it won the Eastman Publication award. In 1932 he became music critic for the Cleveland *Plain Dealer* and program annotator for the Cleveland Symphony. In 1935 he was appointed assistant director of the Cleveland Institute of Music, where he headed the theory and composition department. His works include a String Quartet; a Quintet; a Piano Sonata; a Sonata for violin and piano; an Introduction and Allegro for orchestra (1942); a cantata for male chorus, *I Was with Him* (1942); a *Blue Symphony* (1945), for voice and string quartet; Pastorale for voice and orchestra (1948); a work for chorus and orchestra, *Lincoln, Requiem Aeternam* (1947); an *Ode* for orchestra (1950); *The Forever Young* (1953), for voice and orchestra; and a Concert Suite for violin and orchestra (1958).

Quinto Maganini combines in his activities the roles of composer, conductor, educator, and music patron. Born in Fairfield, California, November 30, 1897, he studied the flute with Georges Barrère in New York and composition with Nadia Boulanger in Paris. He started his professional career as a flutist in the San Francisco Orchestra in 1917. Two years later he became a member of the New York Symphony Orchestra under Walter Damrosch and remained with that organization until it was merged with the Philharmonic Society in 1928. In 1927 he was awarded the Pulitzer scholarship in music, and in 1928 and 1929 a Guggenheim fellowship.

Maganini made guest appearances conducting leading orchestras in New York, Paris, and San Francisco, and for a number of seasons conducted the New York Sinfonietta. In 1932 he founded the Maganini Chamber Symphony Orchestra, with which he made several national tours. In the summer of 1938 he alternated with Eugene Ormandy and José Iturbi as conductor of the New York Philharmonic-Symphony in a series of concerts at Silvermine, Connecticut. He later became the regular conductor of symphony concerts in Norwalk and Stamford, Connecticut, of the Danbury (Connecticut) Festival, and of children's concerts in Greenwich, Connecticut, and Scarsdale, New York. Maganini has taught counterpoint and orchestration at Columbia University, and in the role of music patron he has given his fellow-composers the most practical form of assistance: playing their works at his concerts and publishing their music at Edition Musicus, a publishing firm of which he was founder, director, and administrator.

The Argonauts, an opera-cycle dealing with California history on which Maganini worked for fourteen years, has been published but not performed in its entirety; it was awarded the Bispham Medal. California is also the subject of *Tuolumne,* a Rhapsody for orchestra (1924). *South Wind* for orchestra (1931) is described by the composer as "decorative music" seeking merely to picture a sunrise over the Mediterranean. It was originally entitled *Night on an Island of Fantasy.* Some of Maganini's best work has been written for small orchestra: *Ornithological Suite* (with cuckoos, hummingbirds, and mockingbirds); the *Sylvan Symphony* (1932); and *Cuban Rhapsody.* He has also made arrangements of early American music.

MARK WESSEL (1894——) was born in Coldwater, Michigan, March 26, 1894, and was graduated from the Northwestern University School of Music. He taught piano and theory at Northwestern and became professor of piano and composition at the University of Colorado. Although not himself an atonalist, he studied with Arnold Schoenberg and was awarded a Pulitzer scholarship and two Guggenheim fellowships. His works include a *Concertino* for flute and chamber orchestra (1928); a Sextet for woodwinds and piano (1928); a *Symphony Concertante* (1929), for piano, horn, and orchestra; a Violin Sonata (1930); a *Ballade* for violin, oboe, and string orchestra (1931); a Piano Trio (1931); a String Quartet (1931); an orchestral piece entitled *Holiday* (1932); a Symphony (1932); *Song and Dance* for orchestra (1932); *Plains and Mountains* (1937), for piano and string quartet; *The King of Babylon* (1938), a symphonic poem for chorus, mimers, and orchestra; two Cello Sonatas (1937 and 1943; a Sonatina for trumpet and piano (1942); and numerous piano pieces.

WESLEY LA VIOLETTE (1894————), a product of the Midwest both by birth and by training, was born in St. James, Minnesota, January 4, 1894, and educated at Northwestern University and the Chicago School of Music. He headed the theory department of the De Paul University from 1933 to 1940 and began teaching at the Los Angeles Conservatory of Music in 1946. His orchestral works include a *Requiem* (1925); *Penetrella* (1928), for eighteen-part string orchestra; *Osiris* (1929); two Violin Concertos (1929 and 1938), the first subtitled *Dedications; Nocturne* (1932); *Collegiana* (1936); two Symphonies (1936 and 1942); a *Chorale* (1936); a Piano Concerto; a Concerto for string quartet and orchestra (1937); *San Francisco Overture* (1941); a *Concertino* for flute and orchestra; and a choral Symphony, *The Song of the Angels* (1952). He has written two operas: *Shylock*, winner of the Bispham Medal in 1930, and *The Enlightened One* (1955). His chamber works include several String Quartets; a Piano Quintet; an Octet; and two Violin Sonatas.

CARL HUGO GRIMM (1890————) is also from the Midwest. Born in Zanesville, Ohio, October 31, 1890, he was educated in Cincinnati and studied composition with his father and with Frank van der Stucken. In 1927 he was awarded a $1,000 prize by the National Federation of Music Clubs for his *Erotic Poem*, and in 1930 he won another $1,000 prize from the MacDowell Club of New York for his choral work, *The Song of Songs*. Fond of harmonic combinations which grow out of Oriental and other exotic scale forms, Grimm has composed four symphonic poems; a Suite for orchestra; a Suite for chamber orchestra; a String Quartet; a *Fantasia* for two clarinets, cello, and piano; a *Serenade* for wind instruments; choral works; and numerous songs.

Born in Keene, New Hampshire, AVERY CLAFLIN (1898————) has composed an opera, *Hester Prynne;* a Symphony; a *Moby Dick Suite* for orchestra; *Recitativo, Aria, and Stretto* for orchestra; a one-act opera, *The Fall of Usher;* and chamber music.

Several others remain to be added to the list of foreign-born composers. DANE RUDHYAR (1895————), whose real name was Daniel Chennevière, was born in Paris, March 23, 1895. His music derives from Scriabin, particularly in its cosmic-philosophical underpinnings. He has written several books on mysticism and astrology and was led by his theosophical interests to adopt the Hindu name Rudhyar. Trained at the Sorbonne and the Paris Conservatory, he came to America in 1916 for the performance of his *Poèmes Ironiques* and *Vision Végétale* at a dance recital at the Metropolitan Opera House. He remained and later became a citizen. His orchestral works include *The Surge of Fire* (1921); *To the Real* (1923); *Ouranos* (1924); a Symphony (1928); *Hero Chants* (1930); and a Sinfonietta (1931). In 1934 he completed the piano score of a symphonic poem with recitation, *Paean to the Great Thunder,* the first part of a trilogy called *Cosmophony.*

AURELIO GIORNI (1895–1938), widely known as the pianist of the Elshuco Trio, was born in Perugia, Italy, September 15, 1895, and came to the United States in 1915. At the time of his death he was teaching at Smith College. His Sonata for cello and piano was one of the early works chosen for publication by the Society for the Publication of American Music (1924). He also composed a symphonic poem, *Orlando Furioso* (1926); a Symphony in D (1936); a *Sinfonia Concertante* for piano with orchestra; a String Quartet (1936); a Piano Quintet (1926); a Piano Quartet (1927); a Piano Trio (1934); Sonatas for flute and piano (1932), for violin and piano (1924), and for clarinet and piano (1933); and numerous other works.

ARCADY DUBENSKY (1890————) was born in Viatka, Russia, October 3, 1890. At the age of eight he sang in the cathedral choir and at thirteen he played the violin in a theatre orchestra. In 1909 he graduated from the Moscow Conservatory, a pupil in violin of Hřimaly and in counterpoint of Iljinsky. In 1911 he became a member of the Moscow Imperial Opera Orchestra, where he remained until 1919. Since 1921 he has lived in New York, becoming a violinist with the New York Philharmonic-Symphony in 1922.

Dubensky's works include an opera-miniature, *Romance with Double Bass* (1916); a Fugue for eighteen violins (1932); a symphonic poem, *Russian Bells;* two Suites for orchestra; a *Fantasy* for tuba and orchestra; a "melodeclamation," *The Raven* (1932), based on Poe's poem; a *Tom Sawyer Overture,* composed for the Mark Twain anniversary in 1935; a Suite, *Anno 1600,* for strings (1937); and *Stephen Foster: Theme, Variations, and Finale* (1940), one of the few successful and satisfying symphonic treatments of Foster songs, revealing to advantage his highly developed technique in instrumentation; a *Concerto Grosso* for three trombones, tuba, and orchestra (1953); a Trombone Concerto (1953); a Violin Concerto; and a *Capriccio* for piccolo and orchestra.

Louis Cheslock (1899———), born in London, came to the United States in 1901 and has been active as a violinist, teacher, and composer. His works include a Symphony; a Violin Concerto; a Horn Concerto; a String Quartet; a Violin Sonata; several tone poems for orchestra; and choral music.

Isidor Achron (1892–1948) was born in Warsaw and came to America in 1919. His works include a Concerto for piano and orchestra (1937); *Suite Grotesque* for orchestra (1942); *Nocturne Fantasia,* for violin and piano; and solo pieces for piano.

Alexander Tcherepnin (1899———), son of the composer Nicholas Tcherepnin, was born January 21, 1899, in St. Petersburg, Russia, where he made his debut as a pianist at the age of fourteen. He went to Paris to study piano with Isidor Philipp and composition with Paul Vidal. After establishing an international reputation as a pianist and as a composer, he came to this country, teaching at the San Francisco Music and Art Institute in 1948 and at De Paul University, Chicago, since 1949. His music, recognizably Russian in flavor, often combines eclectic modernism with buoyant good humor in a way which is uniquely the composer's. His piano works include *Bagatelles,* a favorite in recitals; a Sonata; a *Sonatine Romantique; Arabesques;* three

Concertos for piano and orchestra, and one *Concerto da Camera*, winner of Schott's international prize; his orchestral works include four Symphonies, Russian Dances, and the ballets *Le Gouffre*, *Colline des Fantomes*, and *La Femme et son ombre*. His opera, *The Farmer and the Fairy*, won the David Bispham Award in 1960.

DIMITRI TIOMKIN (1899——), born in Russia, May 10, 1899, studied at the Conservatory of Music in St. Petersburg and in 1919 began his European career as a conductor and concert pianist, introducing, among other works, Gershwin's Concerto in F to continental audiences. He came to this country in 1925 and twelve years later became a naturalized citizen. Though as a performer Tiomkin has been responsible for introducing many French and Russian compositions to American concertgoers, he is far better known for his work in motion pictures, which has won him nine Academy Award nominations and three Academy Awards. One of the most prolific and versatile of all Hollywood composers, Tiomkin has written background music ranging from the Wagnerian and symphonic to the light and folkloric, as in his theme song for *High Noon* (1952). He reveals a chameleon-like mastery of techniques, styles, mannerisms, and colorist inflections which enables him to capture the flavor of any regional background and to write scores suitable to melodrama (*Dial M for Murder*), fantasy (*Portrait of Jenny*), epic (*Duel in the Sun*), and Western (*The Alamo*). Tiomkin has scored over one hundred and twenty films, among them some of Hollywood's largest-grossing. During World War II he conducted the scores for the orientation and training films of the Signal Corps of the United States Army.

4. FROM THE 1900'S

It was in the first year of the new century that AARON COPLAND (1900——) was born, a man who without question has become the most important of living American composers, and one of the outstanding composers of the world. Though his style has ranged from an early preoccupation with jazz to a late use of serialism and atonalism, his music is always the music of Aaron Copland, stamped with its own sparse and lean character rather than with any borrowed style or technique.

Copland was born in Brooklyn, November 14, 1900, of Russian-

Jewish parents. The family name was originally Kaplan, but his father, on landing in England in 1876, was supplied by an immigration official with an impromptu spelling of his name as it sounded when he pronounced it. So Copland it has been ever since.

After his graduation from the Boys' High School in Brooklyn, Copland started the study of harmony and composition with Rubin Goldmark in 1917. After four years he went to Paris and to the American School at Fontainebleau and studied with Nadia Boulanger. It is claimed that he was her first American pupil. Copland returned to New York in 1924.

His first work of distinction had its initial performance at Fontainebleau—a "Scherzo Humoristique" for piano, *The Cat and the Mouse*. While abroad he also wrote a one-act ballet named *Grohg;* though it was never performed in its original form, Howard Hanson conducted an excerpt from it, the *Cortège Macabre*, in 1925. That same year, Copland became the first composer to win a Guggenheim fellowship. When the RCA-Victor Company announced a $25,000 prize for a symphonic work in 1929, Copland set to work on a *Symphonic Ode*, but about a month before the competition was to close he realized that he could not finish it in so short a time. As a last resort he took *Grohg* from his shelves, extracted a set of three dances from it, called them a *Dance Symphony*, and mailed them to the judges. The work was one of five which won $5,000 each. The other awards went one each to Ernest Bloch and Louis Gruenberg, and two to Robert Russell Bennett. *Dance Symphony* was first performed by the Philadelphia Orchestra under Stokowski April 15, 1931.

Copland's First Symphony, originally performed by Walter Damrosch and the New York Symphony in 1925, was scored for organ and orchestra. It was later extensively revised by the composer and in its new form introduced in Berlin in 1932. A Suite, *Music for the Theatre*, for small orchestra, was composed at the Peterboro Colony in the summer of 1925 and had its first performance in November of the same year, at a New York concert of the League of Composers under Koussevitzky. This was Copland's first orchestral work to be widely performed, and it was also one of his earliest attempts to employ jazz patterns.

Copland himself was soloist when the Boston Symphony introduced his Piano Concerto in 1927. In spite of the fact that he used jazz formulas so naturally in this work that they ceased to be formulas, the Concerto was Copland's last attempt at using them. He decided that they were limiting, and perhaps agreed with those of his critics who found more animal excitement than spiritual content in the Concerto. In 1931 Copland finished the *Symphonic Ode* which he had started in 1929; it was ready for the fiftieth anniversary of the Boston Symphony, and was played in 1932 on February 19. A quarter of a century later Copland revised it for the seventy-fifth anniversary of the orchestra, and rededicated it to the memory of Serge Koussevitzky. It was performed February 3, 1956.

Copland's next orchestral work, a *Short Symphony*, was first played in Mexico by the Orquesta Sinfónica, conducted by Carlos Chávez, in 1934. Copland later arranged this work as a Sextet for clarinet, piano, and string quartet, in which form it was introduced in New York in 1939. A Suite in six movements, entitled *Statements*, was composed in 1935 but did not receive its first complete performance until it was played by the Philadelphia Orchestra in 1942. Meanwhile Chávez introduced another Copland work in Mexico, *El Salón México*. One of Copland's most popular compositions, the piece employs Mexican rhythms and folk tunes to create a vivid, colorful picture of a smoke-filled dance hall typical of the places visited by tourists. *El Salón México* was first performed in Mexico City in 1937.

Commissioned by the Columbia Broadcasting System to compose an orchestral piece, Copland responded with a work which he called *Music for Radio*, feeling unable to give it a more specific title. The broadcasters accordingly asked members of the radio audience to suggest names. From over a thousand replies, *Saga of the Prairie* was selected. Copland's only description of the piece was that "it lasts about ten minutes, starting allegro vivace, forte, and ending quietly." It was first performed in 1937 on the CBS network.

With the writing of this piece Copland revealed his growing interest in what the Germans call *Gebrauchmusik*, a term that may be translated as "music for everyday use." In his book *Our New Music*, published in 1941, Copland wrote:

I began to feel an increasing dissatisfaction with the relations of the music-loving public and the living composer. The old "special relation" of the modern music concerts had fallen away, and the conventional concert public continued apathetic or indifferent to anything but the established classics. It seemed to me that we composers were in danger of working in a vacuum. Moreover, an entirely new public for music had grown up around the radio and the phonograph. It made no sense to ignore them and to continue writing as if they did not exist. I felt it was worth the effort to see if I couldn't say what I had to say in the simplest possible terms.

Continuing to seek this "new public," Copland composed an operetta for school children, *The Second Hurricane*. It was first performed in New York in 1937. Since that time it has been given in schools throughout the country, and when Leonard Bernstein presented it at one of the Young People's Concerts of the New York Philharmonic in 1960, television viewers the nation over were able to judge for themselves how up-to-date and fresh it sounded almost a quarter of a century after it was written. Copland followed the work with another piece written for school use—*An Outdoor Overture*. First performed in New York in 1938, the Overture has come to be one of Copland's most widely-played works.

In writing music for motion pictures, Copland set a wholesome and salutary example for film composers. Instead of the high-flown bombastic flamboyant accompaniments that Hollywood had considered essential to mammoth productions, Copland composed sincere, restrained, sparse underlinings of dramatic action that by their very economy of means do more to accent the emotions and atmosphere of the films than whole regiments of trumpets and trombones could. The first of Copland's film scores, *The King's Men*, was composed in 1939. It was followed by a score for *The City*, produced in the spring of 1939 by American Documentary Films; the score was later arranged as a concert Suite entitled *Quiet City*, for trumpet, English horn, and strings; in that form it was first played in New York in 1941. Copland's next film score was for the film adaptation of John Steinbeck's *Of Mice and Men*. In the spring of 1940 Copland provided the score for the film version of Thornton Wilder's *Our Town*. Two concert Suites were made from this score, one for orchestra and the other for piano. The orchestral Suite was first played by the CBS orchestra in 1940.

During the following years Copland composed film scores for *North Star* (1942), *The Cummington Story* (1945), and *The Red Pony*

(1947), based on John Steinbeck's story. Copland arranged some of the *Red Pony* music as a *Children's Suite* for orchestra, which was first played in Houston, Texas, in 1948. During the same year Copland composed the music for the film *The Heiress*, based on Henry James's novel *Washington Square*.

Copland's success in writing for mass audiences has led some critics to speak of his *Gebrauchmusik* as a commercialized, "popular" part of his output, in contrast to his purely concert music. In an article in the *Musical Quarterly* of July, 1954, Israel Citkowitz commented that, in writing music for the mass media, particularly for motion pictures, Copland simplified his style drastically, to the point where he developed a lean, sparse idiom that was relatively easily grasped. "The lighter, translucent style that resulted," Citkowitz explained, "was more or less written off as 'popular' Copland—music trimmed down to the demands of commercial media. Serious consideration was still reserved for his 'serious' music: which is to say, music in the abstract forms and for the concert hall. Copland's work outside these sacred precincts was regarded with a vague moralizing kind of suspicion, not on the composer's musical motives, but on his extra-musical ones."

Citkowitz goes on to explain what he feels really happened:

A musical phenomenon realized itself. What seemed to have been fashioned *ad hoc*, strictly determined by motives of practical expedience, developed an intensely personal character of its own. By an attitude of 'intellectual innocence,' to use W. B. Yeats's phrase, Copland could see afresh the most conventional aspects of musical syntax. The simplicity of rhetoric must have echoed some fundamental resonance of his sensibilities. For, behind the 'folksy' Copland that is still patronizingly referred to, there was always a folk-like Copland, adumbrated here and there in his prior work; particularly in the exquisitely fresh character he could elicit out of the simplest intervals and tunes.

Copland has also composed highly effective and individual music for the ballet. His first dance score, *Billy the Kid*, was presented by the Ballet Caravan Company in Chicago, October 16, 1938, and contributed a fresh impetus to the development of a typically American ballet. The choreography was the work of Eugene Loring, who danced the title role. Copland's score established a Western atmosphere through the fragmentary use of cowboy songs. An orchestral Suite from the work was first played by the Boston Symphony in 1942. Copland's next ballet, *Rodeo,* was first presented in New York by the Ballets Russes de Monte Carlo, October 16, 1942. The choreographer Agnes de Mille gained her first recognition through her work for this ballet. Again, Copland drew on regional folk tunes for his score.

Copland's most widely heard ballet score is *Appalachian Spring.* Martha Graham first presented the ballet, which had been composed for her, in Washington, D.C., October 30, 1944. An orchestral Suite from the score, presented by the New York Philharmonic-Symphony, October 4, 1945, was awarded the Pulitzer Prize of that year. The score draws on country/fiddler tunes, square-dance rhythms, revivalist hymns, and a lovely Shaker melody, *Simple Gifts.* Some fifteen years later Copland used this tune and some of the material from the last part of the ballet in a work for concert band, *Variations on a Shaker Melody,* first performed by the Goldman Band in New York, June 23, 1961.

Copland's other stage works include a grand opera, *The Tender Land,* commissioned by Richard Rodgers and Oscar Hammerstein II and given its first performance at New York's City Center by the New York City Opera Company, April 1, 1954. The libretto by Horace Everett tells the story of a young farm girl who falls in love with a drifter and leaves her home to join him. In the *Musical Quarterly* article cited above, Israel Citkowitz summarized his estimate of the work: "*The Tender Land* reaps the harvest of Copland's long and serious concern with the possibilities of this style. At every point the work manifests the ripeness of his technique. The simplest touch is telling." Nevertheless, *The Tender Land* has never proved as successful as others of Copland's works. For its second season at the City Center the composer made extensive revisions, particularly in the second act, where the dramatic impact of the libretto was felt to be weak.

In addition to his operas, Copland's vocal works include two major compositions for chorus: *In the Beginning* (1947), for mezzo-soprano and chorus, and *Canticle of Freedom* (1955), for chorus and orchestra. Copland's settings for solo voice of *Five Poems by Emily Dick-*

inson were composed in the years 1948–50 and have been heard frequently on recital programs.

To return to Copland's orchestral works, the composer's "railroad ballad" *John Henry* was first performed by the CBS orchestra in 1940. Two years later the subscribers of the Cincinnati orchestra heard the première of a work that was perhaps the most poignantly effective piece he had yet written. *A Lincoln Portrait* (1942) was commissioned by André Kostelanetz, who at the time asked several composers to write works descriptive of great Americans which would "mirror the magnificent spirit of our country." In choosing Lincoln as his subject, Copland stated that he wanted to suggest "something of the mysterious sense of fatality that surrounds Lincoln's personality," as well as "something of his gentleness and simplicity of spirit." These aspects of Lincoln's character are dramatically set forth in the rugged simplicity of the opening section. The second part of the piece established the background of Lincoln's era with brief suggestions of songs of the day: Foster's *Camptown Races* and the folk-ballad *Springfield Mountain*. The concluding section brings Lincoln's own words, ending with the closing lines of the Gettysburg Address, spoken by a narrator over a sparsely scored orchestral background. Of all the pieces devoted to Abraham Lincoln, Copland's *Portrait* is without question the most moving.

During the Second World War Copland produced several orchestral works: *Music for the Movies* (1943), an instrumental Suite; *Fanfare for the Common Man* (1943), for brass and percussion; *Letter from Home* (1944); and *Variations on a Theme by Eugene Goossens* (written with nine other composers and performed in Cincinnati in 1945). In 1946 Copland's *Danzón Cubano*, an orchestral version of a two-piano piece he had written in 1942, was introduced in Baltimore.

Copland's Third Symphony, commissioned by the Koussevitzky Foundation and dedicated to the memory of Natalie Koussevitzky, the conductor's first wife, was introduced by the Boston Symphony in its home city in 1946. Following a later performance in New York, Virgil Thomson wrote in the *Herald Tribune* that the work was "at once a pastoral and heroic symphony . . . the reflected work of a mature artist, broadly conceived and masterfully executed." Olin Downes wrote in the New York *Times* that it had "moments of rare beauty

. . . akin to the atmosphere of mountain heights and silences of nature." In the spring of 1947 the Third Symphony received the New York Music Critics' Circle Award.

In May of 1947 Copland's *Preamble to the Charter of the United Nations* was performed in New York, and three years later his Concerto for clarinet, string orchestra, harp, and piano, commissioned by Benny Goodman, who was soloist at the première, was introduced by the NBC orchestra under Fritz Reiner. The work was later used as a score for the ballet *The Pied Piper*, performed by the New York City Ballet.

Copland has composed a number of works for chamber combinations. Among the earliest is a piece written in 1928 and scored for soprano, flute, and clarinet—*As It Fell upon a Day*. *Vitebsk* is a Trio for violin, cello, and piano based on a Jewish theme; it was first played in New York in 1929 at a League of Composers Concert. We have already learned of the Sextet for clarinet, piano, and string quartet that Copland arranged from his *Short Symphony*. A Violin Sonata was composed in 1943.

Copland's Quartet for piano and strings, first played by the Coolidge Quartet in the Library of Congress in Washington (1950), is important principally because it constitutes the composer's first attempt in the twelve-tone technique. Virgil Thomson wrote in the New York *Herald Tribune* (November 5, 1950): "The work shows the composer at fifty working with compositional methods that are, for him, a new path. If he is not yet free and bold with these, he has nevertheless made with them a piece that is musically impressive." Copland's Nonet for solo strings was commissioned by the Dumbarton Oaks Research Library in honor of the golden wedding anniversary of Mr. and Mrs. Robert Woods Bliss. It received its première at the library in 1961.

Copland's piano music, pianistically grateful for performers and distinguished by its musical content, includes the *Scherzo Humoristique* mentioned previously and a *Passacaglia* dedicated to Mlle. Boulanger and published in Paris in 1922. In 1930 Copland composed a set of Piano Variations; twenty-eight years later, receiving a commission from the Louisville Orchestra, he orchestrated them and retitled the work *Orchestral Variations*. In their new form they were introduced in Louisville in 1958. Copland has composed a Piano

Sonata, which he himself played for the first time in Buenos Aires in 1941. In 1957 Copland attempted what might be described as a compromise between the dodecaphonic technique and the orthodox tonal system. *Piano Fantasy*, the work embodying this experiment, was composed for the fiftieth anniversary of the Juilliard School of Music and was played by William Masselos at the school in 1957.

Five years later Copland went all the way and wrote a completely twelve-tone work, *Connotations for Orchestra* (1962). The first orchestral piece that Copland had written since 1947, it was commissioned by the New York Philharmonic for the special opening concert at the new Philharmonic Hall at the Lincoln Center for the Performing Arts. In the New York *Times* of September 24, 1962, Harold C. Schonberg described *Connotations* as "a nineteen-minute work in a very personalized twelve-tone idiom. . . . In a way the music is a reversion to early Copland—the austere composer of jagged lines and sparse harmonies; except, however, that some long-breathed lines demonstrate a type of melodic writing not conventionally melodic but ever so typically Copland." *Music for a Great City*, based on Copland's music for the film *Something Wild*, was introduced by the London Symphony in 1964.

Copland has been active in fields other than composing. He has been the teacher of a number of our younger composers, particularly at the Berkshire Music Center at Tanglewood, Massachusetts. He has lectured extensively and has conducted courses at the New School for Social Research in New York and at Harvard. In 1951–52 he was the Charles Eliot Norton lecturer at Harvard, and his lectures on that occasion were published as *Music and Imagination* (1952). Others of his books include *What to Listen for in Music* (1939) and *Our New Music* (1941). In 1955 he was elected to the American Academy of Arts and Letters, and in 1956 he received an honorary degree of Doctor of Music from Princeton University.

At the time of Copland's sixtieth birthday (November 14, 1960), Richard Franko Goldman wrote a tribute in the *Musical Quarterly* of January, 1961.

The historian of American music may run through his list . . . of the other good and respectable composers; but none of these men of earlier generations comes up to our expectations of what a major composer really is. Copland does. We can now see what his contribution to this date has been, and can recognize that he stands almost alone in this generation, as Ives stood completely alone in his. A decade or so ago, one thought of Copland and perhaps a quartet of others as our "representative" or "leading" composers, but the last ten or fifteen years have separated this group in more ways than one. And it is Copland's music that has most effectively remained with us.

Although the works of ELLIOTT CARTER (1908——) date from 1934, it was in the 1950's that he gained recognition and was hailed as "the most original and daring musical mind at work in the United States today."[1] Carter's innovation has not been the invention of new harmonic combinations or serial techniques, but rather a vigorous, novel, and asymmetrical use of rhythm. For several years he had been working out a rhythmic principle which he called "metrical modulation," the passing from one metrical speed to another by lengthening or shortening the value of the basic unit note: in 1948, with his Sonata for cello and piano, Carter introduced the device. It has since become the trademark of his mature scores. In his String Quartet of 1951 he carried the "metrical modulation" even further with changes of speed occurring unsimultaneously in the four instruments. This produced what Richard Franko Goldman termed[2] "superinvertible counterpoint, to which a new element of absolute and independent speeds has been added."

When Carter was questioned at the Princeton Seminar in Advanced Musical Studies he explained his "metrical modulation":[3]

If you will listen to or look at any part of the first or last movement of my First String Quartet, you will find that there is a constant change of pulse. This is caused by an overlapping of speeds. Say, one part in triplets will enter against another part in quintuplets and the quintuplets will fade into the background and the triplets will establish a new speed that will become the springboard for another such operation. The structure of such speeds is correlated throughout the work and gives the impression of varying rates of flux and change of material and character, qualities I seek in my recent works.

In the same report Carter expressed his reservations on the use of formulas:

[1] "The Music of Elliott Carter," *Musical Quarterly*, April, 1957.
[2] *Ibid*.
[3] Proceedings printed in *Musical Quarterly*, April 1960.

There is the danger of rapid and wide dissemination of oversimplified formulas that shortens their life. It is obvious that one technical fad after another has swept over twentieth century music as the music of each of its leading composers has come to be intimately known. Each fad lasted only a few years, only to be discarded by succeeding generations of composers, then by the music profession, and finally by certain parts of the interested public. . . . I do not consider my rhythmic procedures a trick or a formula. . . . All aspects of a composition are closely bound together.

Carter was born in New York City, December 11, 1908. A man of wide interests, he did not decide upon a musical career until the latter part of his six years at Harvard, four of them spent as an undergraduate and two as a graduate student in English. He attended Walter Piston's composition courses at Harvard and also a course with Gustav Holst, at the time a visiting professor. For the next three years, from 1932 to 1935, he lived in Paris and studied with Nadia Boulanger. The awards and honors he has received include Guggenheim fellowships in 1945 and 1950, a grant from the National Institute of Arts and Letters in 1950, and the Prix de Rome in 1953. In 1956 he was elected to the National Institute of Arts and Letters, and at present he is a professor of music at Yale University.

Carter's early works, composed before he had worked out his original rhythmic patterns, include a comic opera, *Tom and Lily* (1934); two ballets, *The Ballroom Guide* (1937) and *Pocahontas* (1939); an oratorio, *The Bridge* (1937); *Prelude, Polka, and Fanfare* for small orchestra (1938); a Suite for four alto saxophones (1939); Pastorale for viola and piano (1940); *The Defense of Corinth* (1942), after Rabelais, for speaker, men's chorus, and piano four hands; and the Symphony No. 1, composed in 1942 and played in Rochester in 1944.

With the completion of his Piano Sonata (1945–46), a work marked by ingenious rhythmic patterns, Carter began to fuse into a mature and highly individual style the different compositional elements with which he had been experimenting. A ballet, *The Minotaur,* was performed in New York by the Ballet Society in 1947. The year 1948 heard the first performance of Carter's *Holiday Overture* for orchestra and was also the year that Carter composed the Woodwind Quintet which was to have its première in 1949. In 1950 Carter composed *Eight Etudes and a Fantasy* for flute, oboe, clarinet, and bassoon, and *Two Pieces* for kettledrums. A Sonata for flute, oboe, clarinet, and harpsichord, written in 1952, made liberal use of metrical modulation. In the same year Carter composed a Sonata for harp, flute, oboe, and cello, which had its première in 1958. During the 1950's Carter rewrote two of his earlier works: an *Elegy* (1952) for string orchestra was arranged from an Adagio for viola and piano composed in 1943, and a *Canonic Suite* for four clarinets (1956) was a reworking of the 1939 saxophone Suite.

When Carter accepted a commission to write an orchestral piece for the Louisville Orchestra, he used fewer of his metric modulations, feeling that they would be exceedingly difficult for an orchestra to play effectively. Nevertheless, the Variations for Orchestra (1956) that he composed for Louisville employ an infinite variety of contrapuntal, structural, and rhythmic devices to alter a lengthy and complex theme. In his article on Carter in the *Musical Quarterly* of April, 1957, Richard Franko Goldman wrote, "In the Variations Carter has stunningly summed up all of his experience and produced an orchestral masterpiece that is constantly stimulating, marvelously sonorous, and kindling to the imagination. . . . The shadows of Berg, Bartók and Schoenberg are dissolved into the background and indistinguishable; they are now a point of departure for a new, dominant, strong and sure personality."

Carter's First String Quartet, composed in 1951, was first performed in 1958. His Second String Quartet was introduced by the Juilliard Quartet in 1960, and reviewing the piece for the *Musical Quarterly* of July, 1960, Goldman wrote, "The Second Quartet . . . is the work of an assured master who has created an idiom entirely his own, in which passion, intelligence, and taste unite to form an expression of power, intensity, and lucidity." The Second Quartet was awarded the New York Music Critics' Circle Award in the spring of 1960. Carter's Double Concerto for piano, harpsichord, and two chamber orchestras (1961), commissioned by the Fromm Foundation, won its composer a second New York Music Critics' Circle Award in the spring of 1962. In the field of vocal music, Carter has composed numerous short choral works and several songs to poems of Robert Frost.

Had Henry Cowell and GEORGE ANTHEIL (1900–1959) both been born in the same decade, they might well have been placed together in this book, for they both started their careers as shocking radicals. Antheil's *Ballet mécanique* was first heard in Paris on June 19, 1926, and in New York, April 10, 1927, the latter performance causing a near-riot. In his lively autobiography [4] Antheil explains that the New York performance was far more avant-garde than the Paris one. The sponsor, an enterprising piano manufacturer, insisted that there be eight, rather than four, pianos in the orchestra; that instead of merely the simulated sound of an airplane propeller, an actual propeller be set in motion on the stage and that a gigantic curtain depicting a 1927 jazz-mad America be hung against the back wall of the stage. "The curtain," wrote Antheil, "single-handedly accomplished two things: it sent me back to Europe broke—and gave an aura of complete charlatanism to the whole proceedings."

When *Ballet mécanique* was performed twenty-seven years later by the League of Composers at the New York Museum of Modern Art, Henry Cowell wrote in the *Musical Quarterly* of April, 1954:

My memory of the first performance is of great noise and excitement and a propulsive rhythmic energy. . . . After having heard many other percussion works in the meantime, I still find the work exciting, if less productive of noisy confusion than I thought; and it emerged as a piece of very good musical craftsmanship. It was written about 1924, at a time when Stravinsky was having great influence on the youthful American; the relationship of this work to the *Sacre* is fairly obvious, although the brash attempt to out-Stravinsky Stravinsky is equally evident.

Antheil was born in Trenton, New Jersey, July 8, 1900. He studied piano with Constantin von Sternberg in Philadelphia and composition with Ernest Bloch. In 1920 he went to Europe, appearing for six years in various countries as a concert pianist and including in his programs a number of his ultramodern piano pieces—*Airplane Sonata*, *Mechanisms*, and *Sonate Sauvage*. During these years he composed *Zingareska* for orchestra (1921); a *Jazz Symphony* (1921), for chamber orchestra; the Symphony Number 1 in F Major, first performed by the Berlin Philharmonic in 1930; and the opera

[4] *Bad Boy of Music*, New York, Doubleday, Doran & Co., 1945.

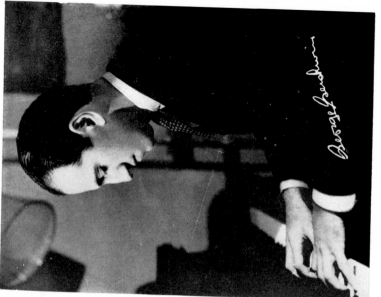

George Gershwin
(See pages 446–452)

Howard Hanson
(See pages 452–456)

Aaron Copland

Virgil Thomson

(See page 167-68)

Transatlantic. The opera employed old-fashioned jazz in the service of a libretto written by the composer and caricaturing American life. The plot chronicled the attempts of the beautiful Helen to decoy Hector, candidate for the presidency. There were feverish struggles for power and for love, dances, booze parties, political meetings, attempted murders, until finally Hector rescued Helen from suicide on Brooklyn Bridge and was elected president.

In 1932 and again in 1933 the Guggenheim fellowship jury took Antheil seriously enough to include him on their list of beneficiaries. John Erskine collaborated with him on an opera, *Helen Retires,* produced by the Juilliard School in 1934. In 1936 Antheil settled in Hollywood, where he composed background music for films, a profession that gave him sufficient security to enable him to devote the major part of his time to composition for the concert hall and opera house; he also wrote magazine articles and a syndicated newspaper column for the lovelorn.

In all, Antheil wrote six Symphonies. The Second, entitled *American Symphony,* is dated 1937; the Third was composed in 1942; the Fourth was premièred by Stokowski in 1944; the Fifth was performed first in 1948, and the Sixth in 1949. Antheil's stage works include the operas *Volpone* (1953); *The Brothers* (1954); and *The Wish* (1955), composed on a Louisville commission; and the ballet, *The Capital of the World* (1953). A Suite from the last-named score was played in New York in 1955. Orchestra works include a Suite, *Decatur at Algiers; Capriccio* (1930); *Archipelago* (1933); and a Violin Concerto (1937). Chamber works include a Suite for twenty instruments (1926); *Crucifixion* for string orchestra (1927); *Course* for five instruments (1935); three String Quartets; two Violin Sonatas; four Piano Sonatas; and a Concerto for flute, bassoon, and piano.

Antheil died in New York, February 12, 1959. His cantata *Cabeza de Vaca* was posthumously performed on the CBS television network in 1962. Reviewing the performance for the New York *Herald Tribune* of June 11, 1962, Francis D. Perkins observed that "in this score, which occupies forty-three minutes, Antheil has turned far away from his early days as a musical radical. It has a persuasive melodic simplicity and directness along with color and warmth and salient musical ideas; it is skilfully wrought both for the orchestra and the choral and solo voices. . . . It projects the emotions of the text with sincerity and conviction."

In contrast to Carter and to the early Antheil, PAUL CRESTON (1906——) is decidedly not an experimentalist; although he uses rhythms ingeniously and though his harmonic combinations are contemporary, the form and construction of his works move along conservative lines. Creston's real name was Joseph Guttoveggio, and he was born in New York City, October 10, 1906. His boyhood friends gave him the nickname "Cress" which was to develop into the Paul Creston that he adopted as his legal name. Self-taught in composition, he studied piano and organ with Giuseppe Randegger, Gaston Déthier, and Pietro Yon; for many years he has been organist at St. Malachy's Church in New York. In 1938 and 1939 he was awarded Guggenheim fellowships; in 1943 he received a $1,000 award from the American Academy of Arts and Letters, and in 1945 a grant for the same amount from the Alice M. Ditson Fund. In 1956 he was elected president of the National Association for American Conductors and Composers, and in 1960 he succeeded Douglas Moore as a director of the American Society of Composers, Authors, and Publishers.

Creston's orchestral works include a *Threnody* for orchestra (1938); *Choric Dances* (1940); a *Concertino* for marimba and orchestra (1940); a *Prelude and Dance* for piano, percussion, and strings (1941); a symphonic sketch, *A Rumor* (1941); the First Symphony, introduced in 1941 and given the New York Music Critics' Circle annual award the same year; a set of *Dance Variations* for soprano and orchestra; *Pastorale and Tarantella* (1942); *Fantasy* for piano and orchestra (1942); *Chant of 1942* (1943), for percussion, piano, and strings; *Frontiers* (1943); a Saxophone Concerto (1944); a *Poem* for harp and orchestra (1945); the Second Symphony (1945); a *Fantasia* for trombone and orchestra (1948); a Piano Concerto (1949); the Third Symphony (1950); a Concerto for two pianos and orchestra (1951); the symphonic poem *Walt Whitman* (1952); the Fourth Symphony (1952); *Invocation and Dance* (1954), commissioned by the Louisville Orchestra; a *Celebration Overture* (1955), commissioned by the Goldman Band of New

York; *A Dance Overture* (1955), commissioned by the National Federation of Music Clubs and in four successive movements applying the bolero, country dance, loure, and American square dance rhythms to the same basic theme, the work being among Creston's most popular; *Lydian Ode* (1956), for piano, percussion, and strings; the Fifth Symphony (1956); *Fanfare for Paratroopers* (1956); Toccata for Orchestra (1957), devoted to the rhythms possible in ¾ meter, of which there are, according to the composer, more than a hundred, and found by *Musical Quarterly* (January, 1958) to be "brilliant, jubilant music, superbly scored to display the virtuosity of a first-class orchestra"; a *Pre-Classic Suite* for strings (1957); a Concerto for accordion and orchestra (1958); the symphonic poem *Janus* (1959), commissioned by the Association of Women's Committees for Symphony Orchestras; and two Concertos for violin, both introduced in 1960. Of the Second *Musical America* (January, 1961) commented, "Unlike most modern concertos it is written *for* the instrument rather than *against* it. The violin part is idiomatic and abounds in graceful technical and melodic passages. The orchestra is treated in modern style and never overwhelms the soloist." Ronald Eyer, writing in the New York *Herald Tribune* of March 20, 1962, found the work's conservatism a little hard to take: "There was nothing in what I was able to hear of Creston's Concerto that could not have been written fifty years ago. . . . It is a lush, vernal growth which lifts ideas and idioms indiscriminately from any number of composers of the late Romantic and Impressionist periods."

Creston has composed a number of major chamber works, among them a Suite for saxophone and piano (1935); a String Quartet (1936); a Suite for viola and piano (1937); a Suite for violin and piano (1939); a Sonata for saxophone and piano (1939); a Suite for flute, viola, and piano (1952); a *Partita* for flute, violin, and strings (1957); and a Suite for cello and piano (1961). Creston's choral works include *Three Chorales from Tagore* (1936); *Missa pro Defunctis* (1938); *Dirge* (1940); *Missa Solemnis* (1949); and numerous shorter works. There are also a number of songs, as well as pieces for piano and for organ. Creston composed the score for the documentary film *The Frozen War*, which was shown on CBS-TV in 1959.

VITTORIO GIANNINI (1903——), resembling Creston in being a conservative of Italian extraction, was born in Philadelphia, October 19, 1903. From 1929 he studied at the Juilliard School of Music, where he was a pupil of Rubin Goldmark. Graduating in 1931, he won the Grand Prix de Rome the following year and for four years was a fellow of the American Academy in Rome. In 1939 he was appointed teacher of composition and orchestration at the Juilliard School and at the Manhattan School of Music.

Giannini has attracted attention principally as a composer of operas. His first opera, *Lucedia*, was produced in Munich in 1934; the second, *Flora*, is dated 1937; the third, *The Scarlet Letter*, based on Nathaniel Hawthorne's novel, had its première in Hamburg in 1938. Two of his operas were first performed on the radio: *Beauty and the Beast* (1938), commissioned by the Columbia Broadcasting System, and *Blennerhassett* (1939). Giannini's setting of Shakespeare's *The Taming of the Shrew* has been widely performed; introduced in concert form by the Cincinnati Symphony in 1953, it was produced on color television by the NBC Opera Theatre in 1954. Virgil Thomson, writing in the New York *Herald Tribune*, commented of the opera that there was not "one musical idea in it that can be called original or personal." Yet, he found the opera "a strong work, a highly professional achievement." P. H. Lang, also writing in the *Herald Tribune*, found that the work showed "remarkable skill and innate feeling for the medium; the vocal writing is expert, and the orchestra sparkles."

The Medead (1960), described as a "monodrama" for soprano and orchestra, was composed under a Ford Foundation grant to the composer's own libretto, which deals with Medea's emotions at four pivotal points in Euripides' drama. *The Harvest*, an opera with text by the composer and Karl Fleister and also commissioned by the Ford Foundation, was introduced in 1961 by the Chicago Lyric Opera. Again, critics were impressed with Giannini's conservatism. *Rehearsal Call*, a comic opera, was produced at the Juilliard School of Music in 1962.

Giannini's orchestral works include a Prelude and Fugue for string orchestra (1926); a Suite for Orchestra (1931); a Symphony *In Memoriam Theodore Roosevelt* (1936), commissioned by the New

York State Theodore Roosevelt Commission; two Concertos (1937), one for piano and orchestra and the other for organ and orchestra, the latter commissioned by the Vienna Gesellschaft der Musikfreunde; an orchestral *Triptych* (1937); a Symphony (1939), commissioned by International Business Machines for performance at the New York World's Fair; a Concerto for two pianos and orchestra (1940); a Symphony (1957), composed on commission from the Music Educators' National Conference to mark its fiftieth anniversary and found by one critic to be "ultra-conservative"; and the Fourth Symphony (1960). A String Bass Concerto, subtitled *Psalm 130* (*Out of the Depths My Soul Cries Out*), was introduced in 1963 at the Composers' Symposium at the Brevard (North Carolina) Music Center, Giannini being dean of the center's advanced division. A reviewer for *Musical America* (September, 1963) found the Concerto "a rather unusual but highly appealing addition to the string bass repertoire."

Giannini's choral works include a *Stabat Mater* (1919); a Madrigal for vocal quartet (1930); *Primavera* (1933), a cantata; a *Requiem* (1936); a cantata, *Lament for Adonis* (1940); and *Canticle of the Martyrs* (1957), commissioned for the 500th anniversary of the Moravian Church. Chamber works include a String Quartet (1930); a Piano Quintet (1931); a Woodwind Quintet (1933); a Piano Trio (1933); a Piano Sonata (1934); and two Violin Sonatas (1926 and 1945).

MARC BLITZSTEIN (1905–1964) also composed operas, though of a different sort from Giannini's. During the 1930's Blitzstein was deeply concerned with the march of political and social events. He cast his lot with the political left, and whatever the effect on politics, the effect on his music was to give it a function and a direction which until then it had seemed to lack. *The Cradle Will Rock*, a play with music (originally written for the W.P.A. Theatre, and later produced in 1937 by the Mercury Theatre with Blitzstein himself presiding as pianist and narrator), was a powerful and biting allegory. It made a deep impression on its audiences and achieved a Broadway run of several months. However, when the work was revived on Broadway ten years later, the plot had lost its emotional and political impact, and the play had only a short run.

Blitzstein was born in Philadelphia, March 2, 1905. He studied at the University of Pennsylvania and at the Curtis Institute—piano with Siloti and composition with Scalero, Boulanger, and Schoenberg. His early works include a Concerto for piano and orchestra (1931); a set of Variations for orchestra (1934); and numerous pieces of chamber music which were played at the Copland-Sessions concerts, at the League of Composers Concerts, and at the first Yaddo Festival. A sketch, *Triple Sec*, was included in the *Garrick Gaieties*, and then came *The Cradle Will Rock*.

In 1940 Blitzstein composed a "radio song play" on commission from the Columbia Broadcasting System. Its title was *I've Got the Tune*, and it proved to be an allegory on Blitzstein's own career as a composer; its moral was that the modern composer's mission is to write music for the masses. In 1940 Blitzstein was awarded a Guggenheim fellowship, and the following year he was ready with another opera, which, like *The Cradle Will Rock*, was concerned with the class struggle, trade-unionism, and social injustice. Entitled *No for an Answer* and depicting love, a labor-party meeting, arrest, a fight, a fire, and the death of a union organizer, it was produced at the Mecca Auditorium in New York in 1941.

For his next major stage work Blitzstein composed a Broadway show based on Lillian Hellman's play *The Little Foxes;* as usual, he wrote his own libretto. Entitled *Regina*, the work opened in New York in 1949 and ran fifty-six performances. In his book on the *American Musical Theater* [5] David Ewen wrote of *Regina* that it was "effective theater. . . . It provides the proof of how far Blitzstein can progress in the theater when he abandons the soapbox and becomes concerned with the forces motivating the lives and actions of his characters." Blitzstein subsequently revised *Regina* to make it suitable for opera houses. In its new form it was produced by the New York Opera Company at City Center in 1950.

After a ballet, *The Guest*, produced by the New York City Ballet in 1953, Blitzstein's next major work for the stage was a musical adaptation of Sean O'Casey's *Juno and the Paycock*. Entitled *Juno*, it opened at the Winter Garden in New York, March 9, 1959, and closed after two weeks. The reasons for the short run may be found in the review that appeared in *Musical America* of April, 1959. "It must

[5] New York, 1958.

be admitted," the critic wrote, "that Blitzstein's version dilutes and prettifies the original, and the whole lacks continuity of style. . . . Blitzstein appropriately bases his musical style on Irish folksongs and dances. He captures the firm and lively rhythms easily; he is less successful in evoking the wistful charm of Irish melodies, and the romantic songs are neither good imitations nor straightforward show tunes."

Blitzstein composed a number of major vocal works. *Gods*, for mezzo-soprano and orchestra, is dated 1926, and an oratorio, *The Condemned*, 1930. *The Airborne*, a lengthy cantata, was first performed on the radio on March 23, 1946. Another cantata, *This Is the Garden*, commissioned by the Interracial Fellowship Chorus, was presented in New York in 1957. The work was an idiomatic tribute to New York, and the various movements, with text by Blitzstein, depict the rush-hour on the Lexington Avenue subway; the daydreams of a boy in the slums; a murder; a couple of street scenes; and finally the festival of San Gennaro in Little Italy on the lower East Side of the city.

In addition to the orchestral works already mentioned, a symphonic poem, *Freedom Morning*, was introduced in London in 1953, and *Lear*, a "study," had its première with Dmitri Mitropoulos and the New York Philharmonic in 1958. Reviewing the performance for the New York *Herald Tribune* (February 28, 1958), Jay S. Harrison wrote that "Mr. Blitzstein has . . . produced a first-rate piece of music, a work of vigorous imagination, bold color, and strong contrasts."

Blitzstein's chamber works include a String Quartet (1932) and a *Serenade* for string quartet (1932), as well as *Percussion Music* for piano (1929) and a Piano Sonata. He also composed incidental music for Orson Welles's production of *Julius Caesar* and background music for the documentary film *Valley Town*. In 1954 Blitzstein translated and adapted Bert Brecht's book and lyrics to Kurt Weill's *Three-Penny Opera*, and the work was produced off-Broadway and had a phenomenal record-breaking run. In 1946 Blitzstein won the composition prize of the National Institute of Arts and Letters, of which he became a member. At the time of his death he left several operas incomplete: *Sacco and Vanzetti*, commissioned by the New York Metropolitan Opera, and *The Magic Barrel* and *Idiots First,* both based on short stories of Bernard Malamud.

Ross Lee Finney (1906——) was born at Wells, Minnesota, and studied at the University of Michigan, in Europe with Nadia Boulanger and Alban Berg, and in the United States with Roger Sessions and E. B. Hill. He was awarded Guggenheim fellowships in 1937 and 1947. After teaching at Smith College in Northampton, Massachusetts, and at nearby Mount Holyoke College, he became in 1948 a faculty member of the University of Michigan.

His works include a Piano Concerto (1934); a Violin Concerto (1936); a *Barber Shop Ballad* for orchestra (1940); *Overture for a Drama* (1941); *Trail to Mexico* (1941); *Communiqué* (1943); and *Pilgrim Psalms* (1945). His chamber music includes eight String Quartets; a Piano Trio; a *Fantasy in Two Movements* for solo violin, commissioned by Yehudi Menuhin; a Viola Sonata; a Cello Sonata; and five Piano Sonatas. Finney has also composed several song cycles and a dance drama, *Masse Mensch* (1936).

Reviewing a performance of Finney's Second Symphony (1959), Paul H. Lang remarked in the New York *Herald Tribune* of November 25, 1959, "It was only a day ago that I heard a distinguished American work in which the twelve-tone technique, so feared by audiences, was put to imaginative uses, entirely free of the grimness that so often accompanies it." Pointing out that during the performance "no one ran for the exits," and that the composer received a genuine ovation, Lang continued, "I am afraid that the ovation he received was mainly owing to his expert orchestral writing rather than for the music itself."

Louis Gesensway (1906——), born in Dvinsk, Latvia, moved to Canada with his family as a child and studied in Toronto; he became a violinist with the Philadelphia Orchestra in 1926. He has achieved what he calls a system of "color harmony" by expanding and developing the diatonic scale into new intervallic progressions. His works include a Suite for strings and percussion (1946); A Flute Concerto (1946); a *Double Portrait for Orchestra* (1952); an orchestra sketch, *The Four Squares of Philadelphia* (1955); a tone poem, *Now Let the Night Be Dark for All of Me* (1957); and an *Ode to Peace* (1960). He has also composed an opera, *Buffo,* and a number of chamber works.

HARRY PARTCH (1901————), born in Oakland, California, June 24, 1901, utilizes microphones, new divisions of the scale, and instruments of his own invention and construction. Metropolitan music-lovers and critics had a chance to see and hear a typical Partch work when his dance-satire, *The Bewitched,* was produced by Columbia University in cooperation with the University of Illinois at the Juilliard Concert Hall in New York, April 10, 1959. The dance critic of the New York *Herald Tribune,* Walter Terry, confessed that it was almost an impossible task to describe the work. "The point that Mr. Partch and Joyce Trisler (the choreographer) make is that catharsis through irreverent laughter is quite as cleansing to the mind and soul (and probably nerves) as heroic tragedy." Terry remarked that he would like to describe the "both wise and slightly mad humor" as "sophisticated primitivity," but he was not sure that the reader would know what he meant. Some of the titles of the dance episodes are: *The Romancing of a Pathological Liar Comes to a Fascinating End; A Soul Tormented by Contemporary Music Finds a Humanizing Alchemy; Visions Fill the Eyes of a Defeated Basketball Team in the Shower Room; Two Detectives on the Tail of a Tricky Culprit Turn in Their Badges.*

Jay S. Harrison reviewed Partch's music for the ballet, composed for instruments of Partch's own invention, in the same issue of the *Herald Tribune* (April 11, 1959): "Mr. Partch's instruments give off a rainbow luminosity. . . . The score itself is mainly incantational, an effect close to hypnosis being Mr. Partch's ultimate aim." The effect of rhythmic counterpoint given out by bizarre instruments and the composer's predilection for divisions of the octave into forty-three equal intervals, gave an effect "quite unlike any other music associated with the Western world. . . . Surprisingly, it all works, all comes off with remarkable vibrancy. . . . In the final analysis it makes an authentic communication."

Partch is almost entirely self-taught, having done his own research in public libraries. From 1923 to 1928 he formulated the ideas which he set forth in a book, *Genesis of a Music,* published in 1949 by the University of Wisconsin Press. Subsidies and fellowships have been awarded to Partch by the Carnegie Corporation (1934), by the Guggenheim Foundation (1943, 1945, 1950), by the University of Wisconsin (1944–47), and by the Fromm Foundation (1956). Among the instruments that Partch has invented are the Kithara, a lyre-type instrument with seventy-two strings in chords of six each; Harmonic Canons, a set of three instruments, each with forty-four strings, with a movable bridge on each string to alter the pitch; Diamond Marimba, a set of thirty-six blocks with bamboo resonators; Chromelodeon, a reed organ capable of playing forty-three microtones to the octave; Cloud-Chamber Bowls, made from the tops and bottoms of carboys, the large glass bottles used for acids. Partch's works include *U.S. Highball, a Musical Account of a Transcontinental Hobo Trip* (1943); *Oedipus* (1951); *Plectra and Percussion Dances* (1952); and three satyr plays: *Ring around the Moon; Castor and Pollux;* and *Dance Music for an Absent Drama.*

Another member of the avant-garde of this decade, RUTH PORTER CRAWFORD (1901–1953), a graduate of the American Conservatory of Chicago and a pupil of Adolf Weidig and Heniot Levy, received a Guggenheim fellowship in 1930 for study in Berlin and Paris, and during the late thirties settled in Washington, where the work of her husband Charles Seeger in the Resettlement Administration and in the Federal Music Project of the WPA brought her into contact with American folk music. In this connection she collaborated with John and Alan Lomax in the editing of the second volume of *American Folk Songs and Ballads.* Miss Crawford's works include *Three Songs* for contralto, oboe, piano, and percussion, with orchestral *ostinato;* a Violin Sonata; a String Quartet; *Three Movements* for wind instruments and piano; *Two Movements* for chamber orchestra; four *Diaphonic Suites* for flute, oboe, clarinet, and celli; two works for chorus performed at the Workers' Olympiad in 1933: *Sacco-Vanzetti* and *Chinaman Laundryman;* and *Rissolty Rossolty* for ten wind instruments, drums, and strings.

EDWARD GERSHEFSKI (1909——), born in Meriden, Connecticut, studied at Yale with David Stanley Smith and Richard Donovan, at the Tobias Mathay School in London, with Arthur Schnabel in Italy, and with the mathematician Joseph Schillinger, who was undoubtedly the most potent factor in the composer's development. Gershefski's compositions include *Half Moon Mountain* (1948), a folk ballad for women's chorus, baritone, and orchestra, that takes its text from an article by Robert Hagy in *Time* magazine; a cantata, *The Lord's*

Controversy with His People, based on a modernized version of a passage in the book of Micah concerning world brotherhood; a work for chorus and orchestra, *There Is a Man upon the Cross* (1951), composed for the state convention of the South Carolina Federation of Music Clubs; *Fanfare, Fugato, and Finale* (1937), for orchestra; Concerto for violin and orchestra (1952); Toccata and Fugue for orchestra (1953); a *Guadalcanal Fantasy* for band (1943); *Streamline* (1935), for band; *Processional March* (1940), for chamber ensemble; *Workout* (1933), for two violins and two violas; a Piano Quintet (1935); a Trio for violin, cello, and piano (1956); *100 Unaccompanied Variations* for violin, cello, and piano (1953); a *Classical Symphony,* written at Yale, and a series of Piano Preludes which later became an orchestral *Saugatuck Suite.* In 1940 Gershefski was appointed instructor at Converse College in Spartanburg, South Carolina, and in 1947 he became dean of the college's School of Music.

Discussion of the radical composers from this decade brings us to a man who has been an undisputed leader in the search for new sounds —Otto Luening (1900——), and to his partner, Vladimir Ussachevsky (1913——). Born in Milwaukee, Wisconsin, June 15, 1900, Luening studied in Munich from 1914 to 1917 and, when America entered World War I, went to Switzerland where he attended the Zurich Conservatory. Ferruccio Busoni, with whom he studied privately, is said to have remarked upon learning that his pupil was to return to America, "Too bad! You have talent." As Jack Beeson observed in an article on Luening,[6] "For a time it seemed that there might have been some sense to the remark, for the contrapuntal wunderkind (upon his return to America) was reduced to arranging for export the gospel hymns of Homer Rodeheaver."

In Europe the teenage Luening had made his living playing the flute and conducting the local Swiss orchestras. While in Zurich he worked as stage manager in a local theatre and played juvenile leads and character parts in James Joyce's English Players Company. His early stage and conducting experience stood him in good stead when he returned to America, for in 1920 he co-founded, coached, and conducted the America Grand Opera Company in Chicago, and in 1925 he became executive director of the opera department of the Eastman

[6] *Bulletin of the American Composers' Alliance,* Vol. III, No. 3.

School of Music in Rochester. In 1930 he held a Guggenheim fellowship, and from 1932 to 1934 he was an associate professor at the University of Arizona. In 1934 he became professor of music at Bennington College, a position that he held for ten years; he inaugurated the Bennington School of Arts as well as festivals of dance, opera, and old and new chamber music. In 1944 he went to New York to teach at Barnard College, and from 1944 to 1958 he was musical director at the Brander Matthews Theatre at Columbia University, where he conducted the first performances of Menotti's *The Medium*, Thomson's *The Mother of Us All*, and his own *Evangeline*.

As regards Luening's idiom, the composer himself once stated that he has been called in turn "conservative, ultramodern, a stylist, vulgar, imposing, a melodist, folksy, and insane," mostly, he is careful to add, by critics familiar with one or two of his works. His instrumental compositions include two symphonic poems (composed 1921 and 1924); *Concertino* for flute and orchestra (1923); *Symphonic Fantasia* (1924); Symphonietta (1933); *Concertino* for flute, harp, celesta, and strings (1935); *Americana*, for orchestra (1936); *Prelude to a Hymn Tune* (after William Billings), for piano and small orchestra (1937); Suite for String Orchestra (1937); *Fantasia Brevis*, for strings (1939); *Fuguing Tune*, for flute, oboe, clarinet, bassoon, and horn; *Pilgrim's Hymn* for chamber orchestra (1947); Prelude for chamber orchestra (1947); *Symphonic Fantasy* No. 2 (begun 1939 but finished 1949); *Louisville Concerto* (1952); *Legend* for oboe and strings (1951); *Music for Orchestra* (1952); and a *Wisconsin Suite* for orchestra (1955), subtitled *Suite of Childhood Tunes Remembered*. In addition to chamber music, piano works, and choral pieces, Luening has composed the opera *Evangeline* (1932, performed 1948), as well as numerous songs to poems of Shelley, William Blake, Walt Whitman, Byron, and Emily Dickinson. When the *Dickinson Song Cycle* was sung in New York, Jay S. Harrison wrote in the *Herald Tribune* of December 13, 1951, "It is eloquent of line, poised of harmony. Neither dissonant pressure nor rhythmic contortion disturb its serenity. It is, in sum, gentle, sophisticated, moving song."

The most recent of Luening's "careers," that of experimenter with new sounds, began in the early 1950's. His preoccupation has been chiefly with electronic music, and specifically with music for tape recorder. In association with his colleague at Columbia, Vladimir Ussachevsky,[7] he has been a leader in developing various types of electronic music, as well as instruments to produce it. At the Columbia University Studio Luening and Ussachevsky have established a library of "sound on tape," available to composers interested in using it.

Electronically produced music is, of course, of earlier origin. Edgar Varèse was probably the pioneer in its use when he included a Theremin in the score of his *Ecuatorial* in 1934. The introduction of the tape recorder made possible the modern developments in this type of music. In writing of his piece, *Sonic Countours* (first played at the Museum of Modern Art in New York in 1952), Ussachevsky explained:

In magnetic tape we have, for the first time, I believe, the multiple means of magnifying musical sounds after they have been recorded, or while they are being recorded. This is possible because of the flexibility with which tape can be cut up, spliced in any order, reversed for playing backward, sped up or slowed down or erased at any point. . . . My own experiments at this time have been restricted to the use of sounds well below the conventional piano range; to modification of the tone quality of the sounds with conventional piano range; and to electronic repetition of any such sound by means of a specially designed gadget. The sounds produced by the latter create a peculiarly dimensional effect, and permit many individual variations in dynamic level, in notes sounding simultaneously. . . .

In describing his composition *A Piece for Tape Recorder*,[8] Ussachevsky explained that the tape medium includes both electronically produced and nonelectronically produced sounds. For *Piece* Ussachevsky restricted his nonelectronic sounds to those of a gong, a piano, a cymbal stroke, a kettledrum note, the noise of a jet plane, and a few

---

[7] Ussachevsky was born in China, of Russian parents, November 3, 1913. He came to the United States in 1930 and was educated in California and at the Eastman School. In 1947 he joined the Columbia faculty. His compositions for traditional media include a *Jubilee Cantata* (1938); *Theme and Variations* for orchestra (1935); *Miniatures for a Curious Child* for orchestra (1950); a Piano Concerto (1951); and a Piano Sonata (1952).

[8] In a paper read to the Princeton Seminar in Advanced Musicological Studies. Reprinted in *The Musical Quarterly*, April, 1960.

organ chords. The electronic sounds consisted of four pure tones, produced on an oscillator, and a tremolo, produced by the stabilized reverberation of a click from a tape recorder. Ussachevsky explained:

The sounds of the piano and of the jet noise are used in episodic manner, and serve to impart dynamic punctuation to otherwise evolving sound texture. The remaining sounds are used in a secondary role of background accompaniment, sometimes obviously as plain old-fashioned sustained tones, sometimes with more subtle variations of timbre. The over-all structure seeks to effect a gradual transition from a type of sound material that possessed a certain clearly recognizable musical quality to the type of sound that is more closely identified with a complex noise spectrum.

Critics' reactions toward this new sound-producing medium are mixed. Some are dismayed if not outraged. One went so far as to call it "the strangest music this side of paranoia. . . . Bebop is old hat compared with this music. Schoenberg never had it so good and wild." Other commentators have been more judicious, even though they have had reservations. Reviewing Luening and Ussachevsky's *Rhapsodic Variations for Tape Recorder and Orchestra,* William Mootz wrote in the Louisville (Kentucky) *Courier-Journal:*

The composers have electronically distorted and mixed their original sound track to arrive at different orchestral colors in much the same way a painter mixes his colors on a palette. The initial impact of the work gives one the impression of opposing and merging strata of sound, ingeniously worked out with strikingly rhythmic pliability. A basic weakness of the work, however, is that the hearer cannot help identifying some of the emanations from the speaker with more mundane associations. You hear roars from an air terminal, background effects from a cheap radio thriller, the staccato click of rolling dice, screeching brakes, or the unpleasant vibrato of an electric organ.

Then Mootz asked the most pertinent question:

What value does such a work have as music? Your guess is as good as mine. One thing I do know. Luening and Ussachevsky cannot be dismissed as playboy pranksters.

There were others who had a higher opinion of the *Rhapsodic Variations.* Lester Trimble wrote in the New York *Herald Tribune* of December 4, 1955:

The two composers in this joint avant-garde venture . . . have created a substantial work of music . . . experimental as to means, but fully formed and expressive in its final product. It is full of the newest sounds, of great enveloping winds and other-worldly chirps, often tremblingly brilliant, and continuously integrated with orchestral textures of the most forthright clarity. It has an expressive life, too, strangely evocative of emotional states in the past tense. They are like profound experiences relived in one's memory —a remembered happiness, or a half-forgotten tragedy. It is provocative music and amazingly secure with its new materials.

It is not unexpected that scientists are enthusiastic about the possibilities of electronic music. One distinguished physicist, Dr. Harry F. Olson,[9] director of the RCA Acoustical Laboratories, has gone so far as to condemn all "conventional" musical instruments as primitive and outmoded. According to Dr. Olson, only electronic instruments deserve to be considered in our modern age. Under such a premise, the physicist would become the arbiter of the arts.

Paul Henry Lang commented on Dr. Olson's statement in the New York *Herald Tribune* at the end of the 1955–56 season:

We may be indulgent toward the scientist. He is carried away by his technological miracles, and in his zeal reaches out into territories that are not within his competence. What is deplorable is that he has been joined by musicians. . . . It is entirely legitimate and desirable to search for new sounds, and some remarkable developments have taken place in the last few years—the novel use of percussion instruments is a case in point. But to experiment to enrich music is one thing; it is quite another to substitute for works of art experiments which by their nature are lacking in musical organization in the artistic and human sense. The very moment when the active functioning of the creative mind is supplanted by happenings beyond its control, we are no longer within the domain of art.

I am glad to report that the American representatives of *Musique concrète* frankly state that what they are doing is experimentation with a view to possible further use for *musical composition*. Whether they will succeed remains to be seen, but in the meantime let us play the piano as Mr. Steinway made it, blow into the front end of a clarinet, run the tape recorder at its normal speed and just compose music as it was conceived by the human brain; it is a difficult enough task.

In addition to the *Rhapsodic Variations* Luening has collaborated

[9] In his book *Musical Engineering*, Prentice-Hall.

with Ussachevsky on *A Poem in Cycles and Bells* for tape recorder and orchestra, commissioned by the Los Angeles Philharmonic Orchestra; a Suite from *King Lear,* incidental music written for the Orson Welles production at New York's City Center; a *Ballet of Identity* composed in 1955 for the American Mime Theatre; *Incantation for Tape Recorder* (1955); and music for Shaw's *Back to Methuselah,* composed in 1958 for Margaret Webster's New York Theatre Guild production.

Alone, Luening has composed several works for tape recorder, including *Fantasy in Space, Low Speed,* and *Invention,* all three for flute on tape, and all composed in 1952; *Theater Piece No. 2,* a ballet composed in 1956 for Doris Humphrey and José Limón; *Dynamophonic Suite* (1958); and *Gargoyles* for violin solo and synthesized sound.

Returning to those who use conventional instruments and who do not attempt to break altogether with tradition, we come to NIKOLAI LOPATNIKOFF (1903———). Born in Estel, Estonia, March 10, 1903, he studied music at the St. Petersburg and Helsinki Conservatories and with Ernest Toch and Hermann Grabner in Karlsruhe, Germany, where in 1927 he graduated from the Technological College as a civil engineer. After living five years in London, he moved to New York in 1939 and became an American citizen in 1944; the following year he became professor of music at the Carnegie Institute of Technology in Pittsburgh.

Lopatnikoff's compositions are generally neoclassic in texture, tonal in harmonic vocabulary, and characterized by the composer's strong rhythmic sense and feeling for form and clear melodic outline. They include the *Introduction and Scherzo* for orchestra (1928); the First Symphony (1930); the First Piano Concerto (1932); the Second Symphony (1939); a Violin Concerto (1942); *Opus Sinfonicum* (1943), winner of first prize in the Cleveland Orchestra's twenty-fifth anniversary contest; *Concertino for Orchestra* (1945); the Second Piano Concerto (1946); the Third Symphony (1954); two String Quartets; a Duo for violin and cello (1926); a Cello Sonata (1928); a Piano Trio (1938); a Piano Sonata (1944); and *Variations and Eclogue,* for cello and piano, composed in 1946. A *Festival Overture* has figured in New York concert programs in 1961 and 1963.

Critics have often commented upon the deeply Russian flavor of Lopatnikoff's work, as well as on a colorful use of dissonance in the later compositions. Lopatnikoff has received two Guggenheim fellowships, a commission from the Koussevitzky Foundation, and a grant from the National Institute of Arts and Letters. In addition he has received commissions from the Musical Arts Society of La Jolla, California, and from the Louisville Orchestra.

Another neoclassicist, GERALD STRANG (1908———) was born in Claresholm, Alberta, and was graduated from Leland Stanford University. He has interested himself in comparative musicology, an avocation which he shares with Henry Cowell, with whom he was associated in 1933 as director of the New Music Workshops, and whom he succeeded in 1936 as director of the New Music Society and managing editor of New Music Editions. Strang served as assistant to Arnold Schoenberg in the music department of the University of California in Los Angeles from 1936 to 1938. In composition Strang has confined himself largely to chamber music, much of it based on elaborate canonic devices. His works include Intermezzo for orchestra (originally the second movement of a symphony; 1937); *Three Pieces* for flute and piano (1933); *Percussion Music* for three players (1935); a Quintet for clarinet and strings; two String Quartets and a *Passacaglia* for string quartet; a choral work, *Vanzetti in the Death House; Incidental Music for a Satirical Play;* and a piano piece, *Mirror-rorrim.*

While we are using the prefix "neo," we would probably call Philadelphia-born PAUL NORDOFF (1909———) a neo-Romanticist. Nordoff studied at the Philadelphia Conservatory of Music and at the Juilliard School of Music in New York; he was head of the composition department of the Philadelphia Conservatory from 1938 to 1943. He was awarded Guggenheim fellowships in 1933 and 1935; in 1933 his Prelude and Variations for piano won him the Bearns prize from Columbia University, and in 1940 he received a Pulitzer scholarship.

Nordoff's works include his First Piano Concerto (1934); *Triptych* (1934), three songs with Dryden texts; *Prelude and Three Fugues* (1933), originally written for piano and later performed in orchestral form (1937); a Concerto for two pianos and orchestra (1939); three operas: *Through a Glass Darkly, Nebrahma,* and *The Masterpiece;* a *Secular Mass* (1934), for chorus and orchestra; a Suite for Orchestra (1940); a Violin Concerto (1940); *The Sun* (1945), a cantata with eurhythmic ballet; *Little Concerto* (1950), for violin, viola, cello, bass, and small orchestra; *Dance Sonata,* for flute and piano; two String Quartets (1932 and 1935); a Piano Quintet (1936); a Sonata for violin and piano (1932); a Sonata for cello and piano; incidental music to *Romeo and Juliet* and to *Saint Joan;* a Concerto for violin, piano, and orchestra (1934); a *Winter Symphony* (1954), commissioned by the Louisville Orchestra; and an orchestral piece, *The Frog Prince* (1955).

MIRIAM GIDEON (1906——), another neo-Romanticist, was born in Greeley, Colorado, and studied composition with Lazare Saminsky and Roger Sessions. Her works include *Three-Corner Pieces* for flute, clarinet, and piano (1936); *Incantation on an Indian Theme* for viola and piano (1940); *Epigrams* for chamber orchestra (1941); *Lyric Pieces* for string orchestra (1942); Sonata for flute and piano (1943); *The Hound of Heaven* (1945), for baritone, oboe, and string trio; *Fantasy on a Javanese Motif* (1949); *Five Shakespearean Sonnets* for voice, string orchestra, and trumpet (1951); *Two Movements* for orchestra (1953); a *Lyric Piece* for strings (1956); a Sonata for viola and piano; and *The Condemned Playground,* a song cycle to poems of Horace, Gary Spokes, and Baudelaire, scored for soprano, tenor, string quartet, flute, and bassoon.

There are a number of composers from this decade who may be called nationalists. ARTHUR KREUTZ (1906——), who has chosen American subjects for a number of his works, studied violin with Cecil Burleigh in Madison, Wisconsin, and composition with Roy Harris, Edwin Stringham, and Sigrid Prager. In 1940 he became instrumental director and conductor of the orchestra at the Georgia State College for Women, and in 1946 he was appointed an instructor at the Rhode Island State College. Kreutz's First String Quartet was published in 1935. A Symphony in three movements entitled *Music for Symphony Orchestra* was played by the NBC Symphony in 1940, and his *Paul Bunyan Suite* was awarded the Prix de Rome in 1940. A *Study in Jazz* (*To a Jitterbug*) was composed in 1943, the year he won a Guggenheim fellowship. Others of Kreutz's works include

American Dances for chamber orchestra (1941); *Winter of Blue Snow,* a symphonic poem (1942); *Symphonic Sketch on Three American Folktunes* (1942); a Violin Concerto (1942); *Triumphal Overture* (1944); *Symphonic Blues* (1945); two Symphonies (1945 and 1946); *New England Folksing* for chorus and orchestra (1948); *Mosquito Serenade* for orchestra (1948); a ballad opera, *Acres of Sky* (1952); and *The University Greys* (1961), another opera.

BURRILL PHILLIPS (1907———) was born in Omaha, Nebraska, and was graduated from the Eastman School in 1932. He then took a master's degree at Eastman and became a member of the school's faculty. He held a Guggenheim fellowship in 1942 and in 1944 was given a $1,000 award by the American Academy of Arts and Letters; the same year, he received a commission from the Koussevitzky Foundation.

In his works based on native subjects Phillips exploits typically American rhythms, handling them with neoclassic methods. His orchestral compositions include *Selections from McGuffey's Readers* (1934), based on three American poems: *The One Hoss Shay, The Courtship of Miles Standish,* and *The Midnight Ride of Paul Revere; The Courthouse Square,* another American-inspired work, portraying various phases of small town life (1936); a *Sinfonia Concertante* (1935); an *American Dance* for bassoon and strings (1940); *Satiric Fragments* (1941); a Piano Concerto (composed 1937, introduced in 1943); a Scherzo (1944); and a *Tom Paine Overture.*

An orchestral piece, *Perspectives in a Labyrinth,* was composed for the 1963 Festival of Contemporary Arts at the University of Illinois. The reviewer Robert Shallenberg, writing in the *Musical Quarterly* of July, 1963, found the work:

. . . a relatively new facet of the continuing growth of this widely respected composer. It is scored for three string orchestras, each of which is divided into three groups—of high, middle, and low pitch. The work utilizes a type of twelve-tone procedure, perhaps with more than one set, or perhaps with permutations other than the ordinary ones of transposition, inversion, and retrogression. At any rate, the treatment seems quite free, with many returns of pitch and both melodic and harmonic octave relations, and since the rhythmic treatment is generally not dissimilar to his past rhythmic practices, most of the work has a sound that is unmistakably Phillips's own.

For the stage Phillips has composed several ballets: *Grotesque Dance from a Projected Ballet* (1932); *Princess and Puppet* (1935); *Play Ball* (1938); *Step into My Parlor* (1944); an opera buffa, *Don't We All?* (1949). *The Return of Odysseus* (1957), for baritone, narrator, chorus, and orchestra, was commissioned by the Fromm Music Foundation. Phillips's chamber music includes a Trio for trumpets (1937); a String Quartet (1939); a Violin Sonata (1942); a Cello Sonata (1946); and a *Partita* for violin, viola, cello, and piano (1948).

Like Douglas Moore, ALEC WILDER (1907——) has composed operas with a typically American background. His stage works, however, are more in the field of *Gebrauchmusik:* they are generally short, and are scored for a few singers and require only a small orchestra, or, if desirable, merely a piano accompaniment. Wilder was born in Rochester, New York, February 7, 1907, and trained at the Eastman School of Music. His short operas include *The Lowland Sea* (1951); *Sunday Excursion* (1953); and *Kittiwake Island* (1955), the latter two with librettos by Arnold Sundgaard. Wilder has also composed music for a ballet, *Juke Box* (1942). His purely instrumental works include a Concerto for oboe and string orchestra (1950); a Horn Concerto (1955); a *Carl Sandburg Suite;* and a Quintet for French horn and strings (1960).

Reviewing the Quintet for *Musical America* (November, 1960), Ralph Kammerer noted that the composer "in attempting to cast music of instantaneous appeal into a classical mold relies chiefly on . . . jazz rhythms and some lush melodies. . . . Like all such attempts, this seems by its very nature foredoomed to failure or, at best, partial success." Wilder has also composed three Woodwind Quintets; a Woodwind Octet; numerous piano pieces, some of which bear such descriptive titles as *A Debutante's Diary, Neurotic Goldfish, Walking Home in the Spring;* and songs, including one which has become a popular standard, *While We're Young*. Wilder has written incidental music for the theatre and background music for films; one of his outstanding film scores was composed for the widely shown documentary, *Albert Schweitzer*.

THEODORE F. FITCH (1900——), born in Rochester, New York, February 17, 1900, trained at the Eastman School while Christian

Sinding headed the composition department, and later taught at the Universities of North Carolina, Rochester, and Minnesota, and at the Eastman School itself. His orchestral works include *Terra Nova*, played by the New York Philharmonic under Stokowski in 1949; *Two New England Fancies; Divertimento* for chamber orchestra; *Sestina* for clarinet and strings. His chamber works include a *Montana Sonata* for cello and piano, and he has also written many choral pieces.

A list of other Eastman graduates, if we take them according to age, would start with Pennsylvania-born IRVINE MCHOSE (1902——), for many years a member of the composition faculty at the Eastman School. His works include a Concerto for oboe and orchestra, first performed at the Eastman Festival in 1932 and repeated ten years later.

HERBERT INCH (1904——), a fellow of the American Academy in Rome in 1931, was born in Missoula, Montana, November 25, 1904, and after 1931 taught at Hunter College, New York. His works include a Symphony (1932); an orchestral piece, *To Silvanus* (1933); a Piano Concerto (1937); a *Serenade* for woodwinds and strings (1936); *Answers to a Questionnaire* (1944); *Northwest Overture* (1943); a Violin Concerto; and a *Concertino* for string orchestra (1955). His chamber music includes a Quintet (1930); *Mediterranean Sketches* for string quartet (1933); a Sonata for cello and piano (1934); a *Divertimento* for brass instruments (1934); a Piano Sonata (1935); a String Quartet (1936); and *Three Conversations* for string quartet (1944).

HUNTER JOHNSON (1906——), born in Benson, North Carolina, April 14, 1906, was a fellow of the American Academy in Rome in 1933 and received Guggenheim fellowships in 1941 and 1954. From 1929 to 1933 he was head of the composition department of the University of Michigan. His works include a Prelude for orchestra (1929); a Symphony (1931); a Concerto for piano and small orchestra (1935); an Andante for flute and strings (1939); an *Elegy* for clarinet and strings (1937); a Sonatina for violin and piano (1937); and a Piano Sonata (1934). In 1940 Johnson composed a ballet for Martha Graham, *Letter to the World*. In 1952 he arranged the score as a Suite for chamber orchestra.

FREDERICK WOLTMANN (1908——) was born in Flushing, New

York, May 13, 1908. As a child he sang for a season in the boys' chorus of the Metropolitan Opera House. He entered Columbia University and received a scholarship to the Eastman School, where he obtained his bachelor of music degree. In 1937 he received a fellowship at the American Academy in Rome, where he studied with Ildebrando Pizzetti. His works include a *Poem* for eight instruments (1933); a Symphony, *Songs for Autumn* (1937); a Piano Concerto (1937); a tone poem, *The Pool of Pegasus* (1937); a Scherzo for eight instruments (1937); *Songs from a Chinese Lute* (1937), for voice and thirty-three instruments; *From Dover Beach* (1938), for orchestra; *Variations on an Old English Folk Tune* (1939); and *From Leaves of Grass* (1946), after Walt Whitman, for voice and orchestra; there are also a number of highly expressive songs.

ANTHONY DONATO (1909———), born in Prague, Nebraska, March 8, 1909, studied at the Eastman School with Howard Hanson, Bernard Rogers, and Edward Royce. He has taught at Drake University, at Iowa State Teachers' College, and at the University of Texas; in 1947 he became professor of composition at Northwestern University. In 1951 he received a Fulbright grant to live in England for a year. Donato's orchestral works include two Symphonies (1944 and 1945); an Overture, *Prairie Schooner* (1947); *March of the Hungry Mountains* (1949), for chorus and orchestra; *The Plains* (1953); *Solitude in the City* (1954), for narrator and orchestra; a Sinfonietta (1959); and a *Serenade* for small orchestra (1962). Donato's chamber works include three String Quartets; two Violin Sonatas; a Sonatina for three trumpets (1949); and a Sonata for horn and piano (1950). He has also written numerous choral works and teaching pieces for piano.

There are a number of composers from this decade—we have already mentioned some of them—who have had part of their training with Nadia Boulanger. Anyone listing the major influences that have shaped American music will do well to include Nadia Boulanger, for, with the possible exception of Ernest Bloch, she has trained and influenced more of our composers than any other teacher. Perhaps the highest testament to her teaching skill is that each of her pupils has developed his own individuality in his own way. There is no Boulanger identification and certainly no common idiom, or even purpose, that stamps the music of such of her pupils as Virgil Thomson, Roy Harris, and Aaron Copland, for there are wide gaps between the quasi-Romantic, often sentimental, and sometimes impishly satirical music of Thomson, the savage intensity and extroversion of Harris's symphonic works, and the sparse, lean, economical writing of Copland.

LOUISE TALMA (1906———) was born in Arnachon, France, October 31, 1906, of American parents. She studied theory with George Wedge, counterpoint with Percy Goetschius, and composition with Howard Brockway, receiving a bachelor of music degree from New York University in 1931 and her master's from Columbia in 1933. Since 1926 she has spent seventeen summers studying with Nadia Boulanger at the Fontainebleau school, and since 1928 has taught music at Hunter College in New York, attaining the rank of professor in 1952. An impressive collector of awards and prizes, Miss Talma won the Joseph E. Bearns Prize in composition in 1932 and the Juilliard Publication Award in 1946 for her Toccata for orchestra. She won Guggenheim fellowships in 1946 and 1947, and in 1959 was given a Koussevitzky Foundation commission that resulted in her Cantata for tenor, clarinet, violoncello, piano, and percussion (1963). The National Institute of Arts and Letters bestowed the Marjorie Peabody Waite Award upon her in 1960, and in 1963 she was thrice honored—with an award from the National Federation of Music Clubs, another award from the National Association for American Composers and Conductors, and the Sibelius Medal for Composition from Harriet Cohen International Awards, London.

Miss Talma's most discussed work to date has been her opera *The Alcestiad*, a setting of a Thornton Wilder libretto, first performed at Frankfurt-am-Main in 1962. The day after the première the critic of the *Hanauer Anzeiger* wrote, "Louise Talma . . . is everywhere at home, in tonal as well as atonal practice; she makes use of twelve-tone rows, and shows herself at times inspired by the late impressionism of Stravinsky, also of Bartók. Clearly visible are her abhorrence of every melodic banality and the refinement of her orchestration."

Miss Talma's choral works include *In Principio Erat Verbum* (composed 1939), for mixed chorus and organ; *The Divine Flame* (composed 1946–48), an oratorio for mixed chorus and orchestra, text from the Bible and Missal; *The Leaden Echo and the Golden Echo* (1950), a setting of a Gerard Manley Hopkins text for double chorus, soprano, and piano; *Let's Touch the Sky* (composed 1953–54), a setting of an e. e. cummings poem for mixed chorus, flute, oboe, and clarinet; and *La Corona* (composed 1954–55), a setting of seven Donne sonnets for *a cappella* chorus. Miss Talma's chamber works include a String Quartet (1954) and a Sonata for violin and piano (1962); her piano compositions include two Sonatas; *Alleluia in the Form of a Toccata*; *Six Etudes*; *Passacaglia and Fugue*; and *Four-Handed Fun*. She has composed a song cycle, *Terre de France*, dated 1943–45.

ELIE SIEGMEISTER (1909———), born in New York City, January 15, 1909, studied with Seth Bingham at Columbia University, with Wallingford Riegger, and with Nadia Boulanger in Paris. He became a teacher in New York and in 1940 organized the American Ballad Singers, whom he conducted for five years. In 1949 he joined the faculty of Hofstra College. Siegmeister has composed several works for the stage: a play with music, *Doodle Dandy of the U.S.A.* (1942); *Sing Out, Sweet Land*, a musical show based on folk songs, produced in New York in 1944; a one-act opera, *Darling Corie* (1952); an opera, *Miranda and the Dark Young Man* (1955). His orchestral works include a *Walt Whitman Overture* (1940); *Ozark Set* (1944); *Wilderness Road* (1945); *Western Suite* (1945); *Sunday in Brooklyn* (1946); *Lonesome Hollow* (1948); *From My Window* (1949); *Summer Night* (1952); *Divertimento* (1953); a Clarinet Concerto (1956); and *Prairie Legend* (1957). Siegmeister's first three Symphonies were introduced in 1947, 1952, and 1959, respectively.

For chamber combinations Siegmeister has composed a Woodwind Quintet (1932); a String Quartet (1936); an *American Sonata* for piano (1944); and two Violin Sonatas. His choral works include *Abraham Lincoln Walks at Midnight* (1937); *Eight American Folksongs* (1940) and *Freedom Train* (1943), for men's voices. He has composed an American Suite, entitled *Hootenanny*, for band. In 1944 Siegmeister edited *A Music Lover's Handbook*, an anthology; and with Olin Downes he compiled and edited *A Treasury of American Song*, first published in 1940 and revised and enlarged in 1943.

NORMAND LOCKWOOD (1906———) was born in New York City, March 19, 1906, and studied at the University of Michigan School of Music and in Europe with Nadia Boulanger and Ottorino Respighi. In 1930 he was awarded a fellowship at the American Academy in Rome, and in 1932 he became a faculty member of the Oberlin Conservatory of Music. He was awarded Juilliard fellowships in 1943 and 1944. After lecturing at Columbia University and teaching at Trinity University in San Antonio, Texas, he joined the faculty of the University of Wyoming in 1955.

Lockwood is best known as the composer of such major choral works as *Drum Taps* (1930); *Requiem* (1931); *The Hound of Heaven* (1937); and *Out of the Cradle Endlessly Rocking*, which was dedicated to the New York World's Fair and which won a $500 prize awarded by G. Schirmer in 1938. In 1945 the Experimental Theatre of Columbia University produced Lockwood's opera *The Scarecrow*, based on Percy MacKaye's play.

Others of Lockwood's works include *Mary Who Stood in Shadow* (1945), for soprano and orchestra; *Prairie* (1952), a setting for chorus and orchestra of selections from Carl Sandburg's poems; *Children of God* (1957), an oratorio; *Light out of Darkness* (1957), a cantata; *The Birth of Moses*, for women's voices, flute, and piano; a setting of *Psalm 112* for mixed voices and orchestra; *Four Songs from James Joyce's Chamber Music* for medium voice and string quartet (1948); and a *Carol Fantasy* for mixed chorus and orchestra (1962). A second opera, *Early Dawn*, was presented by the Denver University School of the Theatre and the Lamont School of Music in 1961. Lockwood's instrumental works include *A Year's Chronicle* (1935), winner of the Swift $1,000 award; *Moby Dick* (1946), for small orchestra; *A Ballad of the North and South* (1961), for band; a Sonata for three cellos (1935); *Dichromatic Variation* for piano (1935); six String Quartets, all dated 1937; a Piano Quintet (1940); a Trio for flute, viola, and harp (1940); a Piano Sonata (1944); and a group of *Serenades* for string quartet (1945).

JOSEPH WAGNER (1900———), born in Springfield, Massachusetts, January 9, 1900, trained at the New England Conservatory and studied conducting with Weingartner and Monteux and composition with Nadia Boulanger. He was for more than twenty years assistant director of music in the Boston public schools, and was the founder, and for nineteen years the conductor, of the Boston Civic Orchestra. He has taught in Boston, at Hunter College in New York, and at Brooklyn College; from 1947 to 1950 he conducted the Duluth Symphony, and from 1950 to 1954 the Orquesta Sinfónica Nacional de Costa Rica. He has appeared as guest conductor in Havana, Helsinki, Stockholm, Washington, and Buffalo.

Wagner's compositions include the music for three ballets: *The Birthday of the Infanta* (1935); *Dance Divertissement* (1937); and *Hudson River Legend* (1941). His orchestral works include three Symphonies (1944, 1946, and 1951); two Sinfoniettas (1931 and 1942); *Variations on an Old Form* (1941); *Four Miniatures* (1941); *A Fugal Triptych* for piano, percussion, and strings (1941); *From the North Shore* (1942), two pieces for string orchestra; *American Jubilee* (1946), scored both for orchestra and for band; *Northern Saga* (1949), a "landscape" for orchestra; and *Concerto Grosso,* for three cornets and baritone. A number of Wagner's works are scored for solo instrument and orchestra: a *Miniature Concerto* (1919), later revised as a Concerto in G Minor (1930); a Rhapsody for clarinet, piano, and strings (1926); a Concerto for harp and orchestra (1946); a *Fantasy in Technicolor* for piano and orchestra (1948); and an *Introduction and Scherzo* for bassoon and strings (1951). Wagner has composed numerous piano pieces, including the Suite *From the Monadnock Region* (1942); *Radio City Snapshots* (also scored for orchestra; 1945); Sonata in B Minor (1946); *Pastoral and Toccata* (1948); and an *After Dinner Sonata* for two pianos (1949). He has also composed chamber music and a number of choral works, including a *Psalm of Faith* (from *Psalm XXIV*) for voice and orchestra.

HOWARD SWANSON (1909———), another remarkable Boulanger pupil, was born in Atlanta, Georgia, August 18, 1909. His First Symphony was composed in 1945, and a group of songs performed in 1949 caused Virgil Thomson [10] to note "a delicate elaboration of thought and an intensity of feeling that recall Fauré." In a later issue of the same paper Peggy Glanville-Hicks hailed Swanson's talent as "a real creative gift, a lyric, dramatic sense that evokes its own spontaneous form." But it was Swanson's Second Symphony, entitled *A*

---

[10] New York *Herald Tribune*, November 16, 1949.

Short Symphony, that brought him to the attention of the public. The work was composed in 1948 and first performed by the New York Philharmonic in 1950, Mitropoulos conducting. Swanson immediately became headline news: conductors in other cities played the work, and it was given the New York Music Critics' Circle Award. Virgil Thomson wrote [11] that the piece was characterized by "elegance, sincerity and grace."

Swanson's background may have helped to make him newsworthy. A Negro, he was taken as a child to Cleveland, where he earned a living by manual labor and as a postal clerk. He studied with Herbert Elwell at the Cleveland Institute of Music and subsequently won a Rosenwald fellowship for study in Europe. He worked with Nadia Boulanger in Paris, and upon returning to the United States in 1940 worked with the Internal Revenue Department until 1945. He continued to compose during these years and attracted the attention of Marian Anderson, who sang a group of his songs at a New York recital. In addition to the Symphonies, Swanson's works include *Night Music* (1950), for small orchestra; *Music for Strings* (1952), a short lyrical work that brings reminders of Schoenberg's *Verklaerte Nacht;* a Concerto for orchestra, composed on a Louisville commission and performed in the 1956–57 season; a Suite for cello and piano; and a number of songs and piano pieces.

MARK BRUNSWICK (1902——), born in New York City January 6, 1902, studied theory and composition with Rubin Goldmark, Ernest Bloch, and Nadia Boulanger, living for several years in Vienna where he studied further with Anton Webern. He returned to New York in 1937 to teach at the Studios of Musical Education; in 1946 he became chairman of the music department of the College of the City of New York. His works include a ballet, *Lysistrata;* a *Fantasia* for viola solo (1933); a String Quartet (1936); two *Chorale Preludes* for organ; and a Symphony in B-flat (1947).

ROBERT MILLS DELANEY (1903–1956), born in Baltimore, Maryland, July 24, 1903, studied at the University of Southern California, and with Nadia Boulanger and Lucien Capet, the violinist, at the Ecole Normale Supérieure de Musique in Paris, where he was a Guggenheim fellow. After completing his training, he became a theory

[11] New York *Herald Tribune,* November 24, 1950.

instructor at the School of Music in Concord, Massachusetts, and later was music director at the Santa Barbara School in California. His works include a *Don Quixote Symphony* (1930); Symphonic Piece No. 1 (1935); Symphonic Piece No. 2 (1937); *John Brown's Body*, a choral setting of Stephen Vincent Benét's poem; choral works; String Quartets; and an early Violin Sonata (1927). His *Work 22* was performed by the New York City Symphony, a unit of the WPA Federal Music Project, in 1940.

ULRIC COLE (1905——), another of Boulanger's women pupils, was born September 9, 1905, in New York, where she studied with Lhévinne, Goldmark, and Goetschius; she subsequently studied in Paris with Boulanger. Her works include two Sonatas for violin and piano; two Concertos for piano and orchestra; a Suite for orchestra; a Piano Quintet; a Suite for trio; and a *Fantasy Sonata* for piano. One of the more widely played of her works is the *Divertimento* for string orchestra and piano, which she herself introduced as soloist with the Cincinnati Symphony in 1939.

RAY GREEN (1909——) and HALSEY STEVENS (1908——) may be numbered among Ernest Bloch's pupils. Green was born September 13, 1909, in Cavendish, Missouri, and received his first musical training from Albert Elkus in San Francisco. He later studied with Bloch and in 1935 received a two-year fellowship for study in Italy. He was made director of the Federal Music Project in California after teaching at the University of California in 1937 and 1938. In 1943 he entered the armed forces and was chief of music from 1946 to 1948 for the Veterans Administration. In 1948 he became executive secretary of the American Music Center.

American subjects have provided Green with material for a number of his compositions. An early work for percussion instruments is entitled *Three Inventories of Casey Jones* (1936); *Sunday Sing Symphony* (1946) uses early American hymns and fuguing tunes; and his pieces for band include *Kentucky Mountain Running Set* and *Jig Theme and Six Changes*. His orchestra works include *The Birds* (1934); a *Concertino* for piano and orchestra (1937); *Concertante* for viola and orchestra (1948); *Three Pieces for a Concert* (1948); Rhapsody for harp and orchestra (1950); a Violin Concerto (1952); Symphony No. 1 (1953); and *Five Epigrammatic Portraits* for strings (1954). His choral compositions include two Madrigals to Whitman texts (1933); *Sea Calm* (1934), for men's voices; and *Westron Wind* (1946). His chamber music includes *Duo Concertante* for violin and piano (1950) and a *Concertante* for viola and piano. For two pianos he has written a *Jig for a Concert* (1948) and *Dance Sonata* (1950). He has composed several ballet scores and music for plays.

HALSEY STEVENS was born in Scott, New York, December 3, 1908. His early musical training was gained at the University of Syracuse, and he later studied with Ernest Bloch at the University of California. He has taught at several universities: Dakota Wesleyan, Bradley, Redlands, and the University of Southern California, where he became chairman of the department of composition. His interest in the music of Bartók culminated in a book, *The Life and Music of Béla Bartók* (1953).

When Stevens conducted his First Symphony with the San Francisco Symphony Orchestra, Alfred Frankenstein wrote in *Modern Music* (Spring, 1946) that it was "one of the most dynamic, compactly meaningful, and finely-shaped scores of the year." Stevens's Second Symphony appeared a little over a year later. Stevens has been fortunate in the number of commissions he has received. The Louisville orchestra commissioned *Triskelion* (1953), a three-movement composition in *concerto grosso* style. In 1954 the University of Redlands commissioned Stevens's Trio No. 3, and in 1955 the University of California invited him to compose a work for its seventy-fifth anniversary. Stevens filled the commission with *The Ballad of William Sycamore,* a setting for mixed chorus and small orchestra of a poem by Stephen Vincent Benét.

In 1957 the Fromm Foundation commissioned Stevens's Septet for wind and string instruments. In 1958 the American Music Center, under a grant from the Ford Foundation, commissioned a set of *Symphonic Dances* for the San Francisco Symphony. Arthur Bloomfield, writing in *Musical America* of July 15, 1959, stated: "The best thing about this piece is its delicately scored and beautifully touching slow movement." Stevens's orchestral compositions include a *Green Mountain Overture* (1948); an *Adagio and Allegro* for strings (1955; actually a transcription of the composer's 1949 String Quartet No. 3);

Music for String Orchestra (1957); and a Concerto for piano and orchestra (1957). For chamber combinations Stevens has composed a Sonatina for flute and piano (1943); a Suite for clarinet (or viola) and piano (1945); a Sonata for violin and piano (1947); a Sonata for bassoon and piano (1949); a Sonata for horn and piano (1953); a *Sonatina Giocosa* for double-bass and piano (1954); and a Suite for violin solo (1954). Stevens has also composed, under a commission from the North Texas State University, a Magnificat for mixed voices, trumpet, and string orchestra.

OSCAR LEVANT (1906——), born in Pittsburgh, Pennsylvania, December 27, 1906, studied piano with Stojowski and composition with Schoenberg and Joseph Schillinger. Before establishing himself as a serious composer he wrote successful popular songs and was a pianist in jazz bands. His major works include a Piano Concerto (1936); an *Overture 1912* and a *Dirge* (1942); a Sinfonietta (1943); a *Nocturne* for orchestra (1936); and a String Quartet (1937). He has also composed music for films and has written a book, *A Smattering of Ignorance*, which made the best-seller list of 1940.

Several of the composers of this decade are products of the Midwest, some by birth as well as by training. ROBERT L. SANDERS (1906 ——), born in Chicago, July 2, 1906, studied at the Bush Conservatory and in Europe with Ottorino Respighi. From 1925 to 1929 he was a fellow at the American Academy in Rome, and in 1954 he held a Guggenheim fellowship. He has taught music at the University of Chicago, at the Chicago Conservatory of Music, at the School of Music at Indiana University, where he was dean, and at Brooklyn College. He came first into prominence when his *Little Symphony in G* was co-winner of the New York Philharmonic's 1938 contest for a short symphonic work. Other orchestral works include a *Suite for Large Orchestra* (1928); *Saturday Night* (1934), a "barn dance"; a Violin Concerto (1935); *Scenes of Poverty and Toil* (1935); a *Second Little Symphony* (1954); and a Symphony in A (1954). There is also a Symphony for band (1943).

Sanders's chamber music includes a Trio (1926); a Violin and Piano Sonata (1929); a String Quartet (1929); a Cello and Piano Sonata (1932); *The Imp* (1941), for clarinet quartet or for clarinet and piano; a Quintet for brass (1942); a Rhadsody for woodwind quartet (1943); a Sonata for trombone and piano (1945); a Suite for brass quartet (1949); a *Scherzo and Dirge* for four trombones (1949); and a *Fugue on a Noel* (1949), for woodwind quartet. Sanders's choral compositions include a cantata for soprano, chorus, and chamber orchestra, *A Celebration of Life* (1956); a setting of the *23rd Psalm* for soprano and organ; and a *Recessional* for mixed voices and organ.

FLORENCE GRANDLAND GALAJIKIAN (1900———), born in Maywood, Illinois, July 19, 1900, graduated from the Northwestern University School of Music in 1918 and from the Chicago Musical College in 1920, touring extensively as a concert pianist for many years. Her compositions include a *Fantasie* for violin and piano; *Symphonic Intermezzo* (winner of fourth prize, NBC orchestral contest, 1932); *Tragic Overture* (1934); a ballet, *Transitions* (1937); Andante and Scherzo for string quartet; and choral works.

DOROTHY JAMES (1901———), born in Chicago, December 1, 1901, studied at the Chicago Musical College and at the American Conservatory in Chicago. She was appointed to the music faculty of the Michigan State Normal College in 1929. Her compositions include *Paolo and Francesca* (1931), an opera; *Three Orchestral Fragments* (1932); *Three Pastorales* for clarinet, harp, and strings (1933); *The Jumblies* (1935); *The Little Jesus Come to Town* (1935); *Paul Bunyan* (1938); *Niobe* (1941); *Mary's Lullaby* (1942); and *Recitative and Air* for viola, two violins, and two cellos (1943).

RADIE BRITAIN (1903———), born in Amarillo, Texas, March 17, 1903, studied piano at the American Conservatory in Chicago and with Albert Noelte in Munich. Her works include *Light* (1938), dedicated to Thomas Edison; *Southern Symphony* (1940); *Fantasy* for oboe and orchestra (1941); *Heroic Poem* (1942), based on Lindbergh's flight to Paris; *Cactus Rhapsody* for orchestra (1945); two String Quartets; and numerous choral works.

RUDOLF FORST (1900———), born in New York City, October 20, 1900, trained at Columbia University under Daniel Gregory Mason. He was for a time violinist in the Radio City Music Hall orchestra and a violin instructor at the New York College of Music. His works include a Sonata for cello and piano (1932); a Symphonietta for strings (1936); a *Sonata da Camera* (1937); a Symphony (1937);

and a *Symphonic Rhadsody* based on two Ozark folk tunes (1937). He won third prize in the NBC chamber music contest of 1937 with the first of his two String Quartets.

PARKER BAILEY (1902——), a lawyer practicing in New York and a nephew of Horatio Parker, studied with David Stanley Smith at Yale and with Ernest Bloch in Cleveland. He was born in Kansas City, Missouri, March 1, 1902, and has served as legal adviser to the Society for the Publication of American Music and to the Edward MacDowell Association. His compositions include a Flute Sonata (1929); *Variations Symphoniques* for orchestra (1930); *Toccata-Ricercare-Finale* on a Bach chorale (1933); and a number of choruses and songs.

DANTE FIORELLO (1905——) was born July 4, 1905, in New York City. He studied the cello at the Greenwich House Music Settlement and was largely self-taught in composition. He received a Guggenheim fellowship in 1935 which was renewed for three successive seasons. In 1939 he won a Pulitzer Prize of $1,500 "on the basis of eight of the twelve symphonies" he had composed. The long list of his works includes *Music for Chamber Orchestra*; Concerto for harpsichord and strings; Concerto for oboe, horn, piano, strings, and timpani; eleven String Quartets; several *Partitas* for orchestra; Concertos for various instruments with orchestra; Piano Quintets and Trios; instrumental Sonatas; a Horn Quintet; songs and choruses.

Born in Cairo, Egypt, CHARLES NAGINSKI (1909–1940) came to America in 1927, where he studied with Rubin Goldmark and Roger Sessions. In 1938 he was awarded a fellowship at the American Academy in Rome. He became an American citizen and was just gaining recognition when he was drowned in a lake near Lenox, Massachusetts. Naginski's orchestral works include a Suite (1931); two Symphonies (1935 and 1937); a *Poem* (1936); a Sinfonietta (1937); *Three Movements* for chamber orchestra (1937); a ballet, *The Minotaur* (1938); *Nocturne and Pantomime* (1938); *Children's Suite* (1940); and *Movement* for strings. He also composed two String Quartets (1933) and a number of highly individual songs.

JOHN VERRALL (1908——), another composer who received part of his training at the Juilliard School, was born in Britt, Iowa, July 17, 1908. Verrall attended the Royal College of Music in London

Paul Creston
(See pages 515–516)

William Schuman
(See pages 539–540)

Morton Gould

ASCAP

Leonard Bernstein

Henz H. Weissenstein

and the Liszt Conservatory of Music in Budapest, where he studied composition with Zoltan Kodály. Returning to the United States, he studied at the University of Minnesota and subsequently with Aaron Copland, with Roy Harris, and at Juilliard with Frederick Jacobi. In 1946 he was awarded a Guggenheim fellowship, and in 1948 he became an instructor at the University of Washington in Seattle.

Verrall has composed three operas, all performed in Seattle: *The Cowherd and the Sky Maiden* (1952); *The Wedding Knell* (1952); and *Three Blind Mice* (1955). His First Symphony was performed in Minneapolis in 1940, and his Second was composed three years later. Others of his orchestral works include *Portrait of Man* (1940), a symphonic Suite; a *Symphony for Young Orchestras* (1948); *Dark Night of Saint Joan* (1949); *Variations on an Ancient Tune* (1955); a symphonic poem, *Portrait of Saint Christopher* (1956); and a Prelude and Allegro for string orchestra (1956). Verrall has composed works for band and six String Quartets in addition to numerous chamber works, choral works, and piano pieces.

Harvard may lay claim to ALEXANDER STEINERT (1900———), born September 21, 1900, in Boston, who graduated in 1922 and studied with Charles Martin Loeffler and abroad with Vincent d'Indy, Charles Koechlin, and André Gédalge. Awarded the American Prix de Rome in 1927, he spent three years at the American Academy in Rome, and upon his return to America conducted opera in New York and Los Angeles and became interested in directing and arranging music for films. His orchestral works include *Southern Night* (1926); *Leggenda Sinfónica* (1931); *Three Poems by Shelley* (with soprano solo; 1932); *Concerto Sinfónico* for piano and orchestra (1934); *Air Corps Suite* (1942); *Flight Cycle* (1944); Rhapsody for clarinet and orchestra (1945); and *The Nightingale and the Rose* (1950), for speaker and orchestra, after Oscar Wilde. His chamber music includes a Sonata for violin and piano (1925); a Trio (1927); and a Sonata for piano (1929).

DAVID VAN VACTOR (1906———), born in Plymouth, Indiana, March 8, 1906, studied at Northwestern University and with Paul Dukas in Paris and Louis Niedermeyer in Berlin. From 1931 to 1943 he doubled as flutist with the Chicago Symphony Orchestra and teacher at the Northwestern University School of Music. From 1943 to 1945 he was assistant conductor of the Kansas City Philharmonic and in 1947 he became conductor of the Knoxville (Tennessee) Symphony Orchestra.

Van Vactor's orchestral compositions include a *Chaconne* for strings (1928); an Overture, *Cristobal Colón* (1930); a symphonic Prelude, *Masque of the Red Death* (1932), winner of honorable mention in a contest sponsored by Swift and Company, the meat packers; a Concerto for flute and twenty-one instruments (1931); a *Passacaglia and Fugue in D Minor* (1933); a *Concerto Grosso* for three flutes, harp, and orchestra (1935); an *Overture to a Comedy* (1935); a Symphony in D (1937), awarded first prize in the New York Philharmonic contest; a *Divertimento for Chamber Orchestra* (1938); a *Symphonic Suite in Four Movements* (1938); *Five Bagatelles for Strings* (1938); Concerto for Viola (1940); *Overture to a Comedy No. 2* (1941); *Variazioni Solenne* (1941); *Music for the Marines* (1943); *Pastoral and Dance* for flute and strings (1947); *Introduction and Presto* for strings (1954); *Introduction, Chaconne, and Allegro* (1957), written on a Louisville commission; Symphony No. 2 in C Major; and a Violin Concerto.

Van Vactor's chamber music includes a String Quartet (1940); a Suite for two flutes (1942); a String Trio (1942); a Quintet for flute and strings; and a Flute Sonata (1945). His vocal works include a Cantata for three treble voices and orchestra, and *Credo*, a secular cantata for mezzo-soprano, chorus, and orchestra.

JOHN VINCENT (1902——), born in Birmingham, Alabama, May 17, 1902, studied at the New England Conservatory with George W. Chadwick and at Harvard with Walter Piston and Hugo Leichtentritt, the musicologist; a John Knowles Paine traveling fellowship from the latter institution enabled him to study two years in Paris with Nadia Boulanger. He has held teaching positions at George Peabody College in Nashville, Tennessee, at the Western Kentucky State College, and at the University of California at Los Angeles; during a year's leave of absence from teaching in 1941–42 he studied composition with Roy Harris and musicology with Otto Kinkeldey at Cornell University. In 1952 he became director of the Huntington Hartford Foundation.

Vincent's compositions include a ballet, *Three Jacks* (1954); a Symphony in D, subtitled *A Festival Piece in One Movement,* composed in 1955 on a Louisville commission and revised a year later; *La Jolla Concerto* (1959), for chamber orchestra; a Suite for orchestra; and a *Serenade* for string orchestra. Vincent's chamber works include a Piano Quintet and a String Quartet in G (1936). He has written choral works and a theoretical book, *The Diatonic Modes in Modern Music.*

NICOLAI BEREZOWSKY (1900–1953) stands out prominently among the foreign-born from this decade. Born in St. Petersburg, Russia, May 17, 1900, he was first violinist at the Moscow Bolshoi Theatre and music director of the School for Modern Art. For several years after his arrival in this country he was a first violinist of the New York Philharmonic-Symphony and a member of the Coolidge String Quartet. In 1944 he won a $1,000 grant from the Americal Academy of Arts and Letters, and in 1948 he was awarded a Guggenheim fellowship. Until his death he was active as a radio conductor and violinist in the CBS symphony orchestra.

Berezowsky's compositions, nearly all of them Russian in flavor, include four Symphonies (1931, 1934, 1937 and 1943); a Violin Concerto (1930); a *Sinfonietta* (1932); a *Concerto Lirico* for cello and orchestra (1935); a Viola Concerto (1942); a *Christmas Festival Overture* (1943); *Soldiers on the Town* (1943); a Harp Concerto (1945); and a *Passacaglia* for theremin and orchestra (1948). A cantata, *Gulgamesh,* was introduced in New York in 1947, and a children's opera, *Babar the Elephant,* was first performed in New York in 1947. Berezowsky's chamber works include two String Quartets; two Woodwind Quintets; a String Sextet; a Suite for brass instruments; and a Piano Sonata. His first wife, Alice Berezowsky, wrote an entertaining book about her husband and herself—*Duet with Nicky,* published in New York in 1953.

Another of our Russian-born composers, VERNON DUKE (1903 ——), whose real name is Vladimir Dukelsky, might conceivably belong in the chapter on "Our Lighter Musical Moments." Under his pen name (which was suggested by George Gershwin) he composed some charming popular songs for Broadway and Hollywood, including the score to *Cabin in the Sky,* songs for such Broadway shows as *The Show is On, Garrick Gaieties, Walk a Little Faster,*

Three's a Crowd, Americana, and *Ziegfeld Follies.* Until 1955 Duke used his real name, Dukelsky, for his symphonic compositions, but after that he dropped it and used the name Vernon Duke for all his works.

Born in Pskoff, Russia, October 10, 1903, Duke studied with Reinhold Glière. After the revolution he lived in Paris, settling in the United States in 1929 and subsequently becoming a naturalized citizen. Duke's compositions include three Symphonies (1928, 1930, and 1947); a Piano Concerto (1924); *Dédicaces* (1938), for soprano, piano, and orchestra; an oratorio, *The End of St. Petersburg* (1938); and a Violin Concerto (1943). His stage works include two operas, *Demoiselle Paysanne* (1928) and *Mistress into Maid* (1959). Among his chamber works are a String Quartet (1956); a Sonata for violin and piano; and *Souvenir de Venise,* a Sonata for piano or harpsichord. When the two sonatas were issued on an LP recording together with Duke's *Parisian Suite* for piano and an Etude for violin and bassoon, a reviewer for *Musical America* (October, 1961) wrote of the music and its composer: "If you want to hear a fine technique applied to a barrage of Continental small talk, . . . try this. Mr. Duke has a basically witty and entertaining mind. But, like the late Mr. Rachmaninoff, he can be a musical chatterbox." Other of Duke's piano works include *Barrel Organ Barcarolle* (1943); *Brooklyn Barcarolle* (1943); *Homage to Boston,* suite (1943); *Surrealist Suite* (1944); and *Serenade to San Francisco* (1956).

Born March 26, 1900, in Brest Litovsk, Russia, Isadore Freed (1900–1960) was brought to America at the age of three and studied at the Philadelphia Conservatory of Music, at the University of Pennsylvania, and privately with Ernest Bloch and Vincent d'Indy. After holding various teaching positions, he was appointed in 1944 to the faculty of the Hartt College of Music in Hartford, Connecticut.

Freed composed several works for the stage, including a ballet, *Vibrations* (1928), and three operas: *Homo Sum* (1930), *The Princess and the Vagabond* (1948), and a work based on *The Taming of the Shrew.* Freed's orchestral works include a *Ballad* for piano and orchestra (1925); a symphonic Rhapsody, *Pygmalion* (1926); three Suites: *Jeu de Timbres* (1931), *Triptyque* (1932), and *Pastorales* (1936); two Symphonies (1937 and 1951), the second of which is scored for brass instruments; *Appalachian Mountain Sketches* (1946); a *Festival Overture* (1946); a Rhapsody for trombone and orchestra (1951); a Violin Concerto (1951); a Cello Concerto (1952); a *Concertino* for English horn and orchestra (1953); and an *Improvisation and Scherzo* for horn, oboe, and strings, posthumously performed in 1962. Freed's chamber music includes three String Quartets (1931, 1932, and 1937); a Trio for flute, viola, and harp (1940); *Triptych* for violin, viola, cello, and piano (1943); *Passacaglia* for cello and piano (1947); Quintet for woodwinds and horn (1949); and a Sonatina for oboe and piano (1954). He also composed piano and organ pieces, songs, and a number of choral works.

Born April 2, 1900, on the island of Cyprus, ANIS FULEIHAN (1900——), a piano pupil of Alberto Jonas but largely self-taught in composition, came to the United States in 1915; before becoming a professor at the University of Indiana in 1947, he toured the United States and the Near East and settled briefly in Cairo. In 1953 he went abroad again to become director of the Beirut Conservatory in Lebanon.

Fuleihan's compositions include *Mediterranean,* a Suite for orchestra (1922); a Violin Concerto (1930); *Preface to a Child's Storybook* (1936), for orchestra; a First Symphony (1936); Concerto No. 1 for piano and string orchestra; Concerto No. 2 for piano and full orchestra (1938); *Fiesta* (1939), for orchestra; *Symphonie Concertante* for string quartet and orchestra (1940); Concerto for two pianos and orchestra (1940); *Epithalamium* (1941), for piano and strings; *Invocation to Isis* (1941), for orchestra; Concerto for theremin and orchestra (1945); Rhapsody for cello and string orchestra (1946); *Cyprus Serenades* for orchestra (1946); *Overture* for five winds (1947); a symphonic poem, *The Pyramids of Giza* (1952); four String Quartets; a *Divertimento* for string quartet; four Piano Sonatas; choral music; songs; and numerous short piano pieces.

COLIN MCPHEE (1901——), born in Montreal, Canada, March 15, 1901, studied composition with Strube, LeFlem, and Varèse, and piano with Friedheim and Philipp. He was at one time known principally as a member of the experimentalist group. Following a visit to Bali in 1931, which was extended from the originally planned six months to six years, he became a specialist in Balinese music. In 1942 and 1943 he was granted a Guggenheim fellowship to pursue his researches and to prepare a book, *A House in Bali*. The years in Bali gave new impetus to McPhee's music, and directed his talent into fresh channels. In 1936 he produced a symphonic work, Bali, and later transcribed a set of three pieces of *Balinese Ceremonial Music* for two pianos. In response to a League of Composers' commission he wrote *From the Revelation of St. John the Divine*, for men's chorus, two pianos, three trumpets, and timpani. In the summer of 1940 he furnished incidental music for Paul Robeson's production of Eugene O'Neill's *The Emperor Jones*.

McPhee's earlier works include a Concerto for piano and orchestra; a *Sarabande* for orchestra; a Concerto for piano and eight wind instruments; a Sonatina for two flutes, trumpet, clarinet, and piano; and scores for two films: *Mechanical Principles* and *H_2O*. McPhee's later works include *Tabuh-Tabuhan* (1936); *Transitions* for orchestra; three Symphonies, the second of which was commissioned by the Louisville Orchestra; *Four Iroquois Dances;* and a Concerto for wind symphony. McPhee's piano compositions include *Inventions and Kineses*.

DAVID BROKEMAN (1902———), born in Leyden, Holland, May 13, 1902, studied at the Conservatory of the Hague and came to the United States in 1924. After acting as editor for a New York music publisher, he went to Hollywood, where he composed film music. He eventually settled in New York and was active in organizing and conducting concerts of contemporary music. His compositions include two Symphonies (1934 and 1947); a String Quartet (1954); and an opera, *Barbara Allen* (1954). His film scores include *All Quiet on the Western Front* and *The Phantom of the Opera*. In 1948 he published a book, *The Shoestring Composer*, describing the life of a composer in Hollywood.

BORIS KOUTZEN (1901———), born in Uman, Southern Russia, April 1, 1901, studied with Glière and was a member of the Moscow Symphony Orchestra under Koussevitzky before coming to America in 1923, where he played violin with the Philadelphia and NBC orchestras. In 1930 he became head of the violin department of the Philadelphia Conservatory, and he was later appointed associate professor of music at Vassar College. His orchestral works include a poem-nocturne, *Solitude* (1927); a *Symphonic Movement* for violin and orchestra (1929); a symphonic poem, *Valley Forge* (1931); a Concerto for five solo instruments (1934); a Symphony (1937); a Concert Overture, *From the American Folklore* (1943); a Violin Concerto (1952), introduced in Philadelphia by the composer's daughter, Nadia Koutzen; a *Concertino* for piano and strings; and an orchestral *Fanfare, Prayer, and March* (1962). Koutzen has also composed three String Quartets; a Sonata for violin and piano; a Trio for flute, cello, and harp; a Sonata for violin and cello; and a one-act opera based on Balzac's *La Grande Bretêche* (1955).

TIBOR SERLY (1900———), born in Losanc, Hungary, November 25, 1900, was brought to America as a child. After returning to Budapest in 1922 to study composition with Kodály and Bartók and violin with Hubay, he played viola with the Cincinnati Symphony, the Philadelphia Orchestra, and the NBC Symphony. His works include a Sonata for violin and piano (1923); a String Quartet (1924); a Viola Concerto (composed 1929, introduced in 1961 in Amsterdam); a Symphony (1935); *American Elegy* (dated 1945, introduced 1961 in Amsterdam); a Rhapsody for viola and orchestra (1948); and a Trombone Concerto (1952). In 1945 Serly completed and orchestrated Bartók's unfinished Viola Concerto.

Although FRANZ WAXMAN (1906———), born in Königshütte, Germany, December 24, 1906, was twenty-eight years old when he came to America and had been trained in Dresden and Berlin, it was in Hollywood that he studied with Arnold Schoenberg and found a field well suited to his talents. As a composer of film scores he has earned an enviable distinction, and in 1950 his music for *Sunset Boulevard* won an Academy Award. Waxman has also composed for the concert hall. His Sinfonietta for strings and timpani was written in 1955 for his appearance as a conductor in Zurich, and had its American première in Los Angeles in 1956. Critics were agreed that the score was constructed with craftsmanship and that it was distinguished by its slow movement, a threnody for cellos and violas over a steady drumbeat. An oratorio, *Joshua*, had its première in Dallas, Texas, in the sanctuary of Temple Emanu-El. The work has a libretto by the English playwright John Forsyth.

AMADEO DE FILIPPI (1900———) was born in Ariano, Italy, and

came to America in 1905. His works include an Overture to Shake-speare's *Twelfth Night; Medieval Court Dances* for orchestra; *Diversions* for string orchestra; Concerto for flute, bassoon, horn, trumpet, and strings; *Raftsman's Dance* for orchestra (based on Mississippi folk tunes and commissioned by CBS); Suite for brass quartet; *Music for Recreation*, for string orchestra; a Piano Quintet; a String Quartet; and a Sonata for violin and piano.

Hungarian-born ZOLTAN KURTHY (1902——) had his first lessons with his father, Sandor Kurthy. At nine he entered the Royal Academy of Music at Budapest, where he studied violin with Mambriny, Memeny, and Hubay; organ with d'Antalffy; conducting with Weiner; and composition with Kodály. Kurthy came to America in 1923 and became a violinist with the New York Philharmonic. His principal works are a *Passacaglia* for organ; a *String Quartet on American Indian Themes;* a symphonic Rhapsody, *Puszta;* a six-minute Overture scored for two of every woodwind; and a Scherzo for orchestra.

Russian-born ISRAEL CITKOWITZ (1909——) studied with Copland, Sessions, and Boulanger. His compositions, chiefly for chamber combinations, with and without voices, include a sensitive setting of William Blake's poem *The Lamb* for chorus; a String Quartet; a *Sonatine* for piano; and a *Song Cycle to Words of Joyce.*

5. FROM THE 1910's

It would be tempting to divide the composers from this decade into two general groups: those who compose by the twelve-tone and serial systems, and those who adhere to tonality and achieve their contemporary flavor through a free use of dissonance and linear counterpoint or by a stylistic neoclassicism. Nevertheless, the composers of the 1910's, like those of other periods, cannot easily be classed under any specific label.

For example, the music of SAMUEL BARBER (1910——) has passed from a lyric neo-Romanticism, through a Stravinskian neoclassicism, to an occasional use of atonality. In the 1958 edition of *Baker's Biographical Dictionary of Music and Musicians*, Nicolas Slonimsky summed it up, "Barber's music is distinguished by striking lyricism;

his melodies are basically tonal, but he makes free use of chromatic techniques verging on atonality in his later works. His harmonic textures are often polytonal while his contrapuntal writing contains strong canonic and fugal elements."

Born in West Chester, Pennsylvania, March 9, 1910, Barber studied at the Curtis Institute, where his composition teacher was Rosario Scalero. He won two Bearns prizes from Columbia University: the first in 1928, and the second, for his Overture to *The School for Scandal*, in 1933. Composed in 1932, the Overture was first performed a year later by the Philadelphia Orchestra. In 1935 Barber won the American Prix de Rome with his Cello Sonata (composed 1932) and *Music for a Scene from Shelley* (1935), inspired by certain lines in *Prometheus Unbound*. While a fellow at the American Academy in Rome, Barber composed his First Symphony, the *Symphony in One Movement*, first performed in Rome by the Augusteo Orchestra in 1936. Two years later, in 1938, Arturo Toscanini selected Barber's *Adagio for Strings* and *Essay for Orchestra* as the first American works to be played by the NBC Symphony under his leadership. Barber's Concerto for Violin and Orchestra was introduced by Albert Spalding in 1941; writing in the New York *Herald Tribune* of February 12, 1941, Virgil Thomson found the work "tenderly poetic in melody and disarmingly straightforward in its general make-up. . . . It cannot fail to charm by its gracious lyrical plenitude and its complete absence of tawdry swank."

A *Second Essay for Orchestra* was introduced by the New York Philharmonic in 1942. Though perhaps rooted in Barber's reactions to the war, it is less specifically military than such works as the Second Symphony (1944), commissioned by and dedicated to the Army Air Force and including in its instrumentation an electronic instrument to imitate radio signals, or the *Commando March* (1943), or *A Stop-Watch and an Ordnance Map* (1944), for chorus and orchestra. While Barber experimented with Stravinskian rhythms and colors in the *Capricorn Concerto* (1944), for flute, oboe, trumpet, and strings, his music showed a temporary return to the lyric spirit of his earlier works following his 1945 discharge from the Air Force, when he took up residence in Mount Kisco, New York, in a house that he had purchased with a former schoolmate at Curtis, Gian-Carlo Menotti.

The Cello Concerto (1946) particularly exemplifies the lyricism of this period.

One of Barber's most effective orchestral works originated in a score composed for Martha Graham, *The Serpent Heart* (1946), later retitled *Cave of the Heart*. Barber recast some of the material, and in its new form it was introduced by the Philadelphia Orchestra in 1947, entitled *Medea's Meditation and Dance of Vengeance*. Another stage work, *Souvenirs*, originated in a series of piano duets evoking a *divertissement* in the Palm Court of the Hotel Plaza in New York around the year 1914. First produced as a ballet in 1943, *Souvenirs* became an orchestral ballet suite and was played seventeen years later, in 1960, by the Boston Symphony.

Two of Barber's piano works seem pivotal in his development. Although as early as 1944 his Second Symphony had indicated a change in his idiom, it was not until his Piano Sonata, introduced by Vladimir Horowitz in 1950, that Barber actually broke with neo-Romanticism and employed a twelve-tone technique. Twelve years later, when John Browning introduced Barber's First Piano Concerto (1962), commissioned for the hundredth anniversary of the publishing firm of G. Schirmer, Inc., Barber seemed almost to have returned to neo-Romanticism. Reviewing the Concerto for the *Musical Quarterly* (January, 1963), Nathan Broder was able to write, "In Barber's Canzona . . . we have a lyric poem as fresh as it is lovely. It is the most consistently tonal of the three movements, departing only once from C-sharp minor." To describe the Concerto, Broder used the word "enchantment." In the spring of 1963 the work was awarded the Pulitzer Prize for that year.

There was similarly little atonality in Barber's opera *Vanessa*, first produced at New York's Metropolitan Opera in 1958. The work had the advantage of an eminently stageworthy libretto by Gian-Carlo Menotti, and Barber's music was so dramatically effective that Paul Henry Lang exclaimed in his review, "It is almost unbelievable that this should be (Barber's) first opera. . . . His mastery of the operatic language is remarkable and second to none now active. . . . [His] vocal writing is impeccable and his handling of the orchestra virtuoso to a Straussian degree." Menotti was again librettist for Barber's short chamber-opera, *A Hand of Bridge* (1960). Lasting only nine or ten minutes, the opera deals with two couples playing bridge: none of the players really has his mind on the game, and the text reveals what each is really thinking about. In the fall of 1960 the Philadelphia Orchestra introduced Barber's *Toccata Festiva* for organ and orchestra, and two months later the Boston Symphony introduced *Die Natalis (Christmastide)*, a sequence of chorale preludes based on Christmas carols.

In addition to his operas, Barber's vocal works include *Dover Beach* (1931), for voice and string quartet; *A Stop-Watch and an Ordnance Map*, mentioned above; *Knoxville: Summer of 1915* (1948), for soprano and orchestra, a setting of a text by James Agee; *Prayers of Kierkegaard* (1954), for soprano, mixed chorus, and orchestra, a work whose harmonic style ranges easily from the modal to the classical to the atonal; and *Andromache's Farewell* (1963), for soprano and orchestra, commissioned for the New York Philharmonic's first season at Lincoln Center. Barber's songs include the ten *Hermit Songs* (1953), to anonymous texts, commissioned by the Elizabeth Sprague Coolidge Foundation. Barber's chamber music includes a *Serenade* for string quartet (1929); a String Quartet (1936), from which he drew his Adagio for Strings; and *Summer Music* (1956), for wind quintet.

WILLIAM SCHUMAN (1910——) started his musical career as a song writer, arranger, and song-plugger for Tin-Pan Alley. Born in New York City, August 4, 1910, he organized a jazz band in high school but, becoming interested in symphonic music, took up the serious study of harmony (with Max Persin) and counterpoint (with Charles Haubiel). He took a bachelor's and a master's degree in music at Columbia, and in 1935 went to Salzburg to study conducting. He became an instructor at Sarah Lawrence College in Bronxville, New York, the same year. In 1939 and 1940 he was awarded a Guggenheim fellowship, and from 1945 to 1952 he was publication director for the firm of G. Schirmer, Inc. In 1952 he left Sarah Lawrence to become president of the Juilliard School of Music, where he was responsible for numerous innovations in the curriculum. In 1962 he left Juilliard to become president of the Lincoln Center for the Performing Arts in New York.

Unlike George Gershwin, Schuman made a complete break with

popular songs in order to devote himself exclusively to serious works. He has returned to Broadway on occasion (he wrote the music for a sketch in Billy Rose's review *The Seven Lively Arts,* 1944), but not as a Tin-Pan Alley composer. The influence of jazz can be felt in his major works, as can that of Roy Harris, who was Schuman's adviser and candid critic for a number of years.

In his article on "The Music of William Schuman" in the *Musical Quarterly* of January, 1945, Nathan Broder wrote:

> There is little of what the average listener would be inclined to regard as grace or charm, but humor may be found, either of the burlesque sort . . . or of a subtler kind. . . . The melodies are often combined in a contrapuntal texture that employs the time-honored devices of imitation, augmentation, diminution, and so on. The resulting harmonies are usually dissonant, by textbook standards. . . . His harmony is not . . . a mere haphazard result of the combination of melodic lines. Instead the counterpoint is carefully planned, not to proceed from one harmony to another, as in older music, but to result in a definite kind of harmonic texture, which is maintained consistently for the length of the passage in question.

Schuman's Symphonies constitute an important body of his work. The First (1936), scored for eighteen instruments, and the Second (1938) were withdrawn by the composer for revision. The Third (1941) won the New York Music Critics' Circle Award and demonstrated what Robert Lawrence, writing in the New York *Herald Tribune* of November 23, 1941, called "superb rhythmical equipment. . . . One had only to hear the subject of his fugue to recognize a composer who can accomplish anything he wants in the field of technique." Schuman's Fourth Symphony was introduced in 1942 and the Fifth, for strings, in 1943. Reviewing Schuman's Sixth, first heard in 1949, Paul Henry Lang wrote in the New York *Herald Tribune* of April 28, 1958, "Mr. Schuman has a 'reputation' for music that exudes power, austerity, ruggedness, and even harshness. Yet what I have found most attractive in this work were the portions that conveyed just the opposite: softness, melody, and a flowing line."

The Seventh Symphony was first played in 1960, and the Eighth, commissioned by the New York Philharmonic for its first season in its new hall in Lincoln Center, in 1962. Reviewing the latter work in the *Musical Quarterly* of January, 1963, Richard Franko Goldman wrote:

It is rather surprising to realize how fundamentally conservative Schuman's Eighth proves to be, not only in its evident concern with tonality and its handling of melodic ideas, but in its structural concepts and its implicit esthetic. It is a big, romantic work, not unlike a Tchaikovskian symphony, having many of the same virtues and possibly a few of the same faults. . . . Technically, the Eighth reveals little change from Schuman's work of other years. The basic harmonic trade-mark is still the major-minor triad in wide-open position; the melodies are still more notable as "tunes" than as themes or motifs; and the rhythmic bounce and restlessness, the energetic punctuation of brass and percussion are still characteristic. In the Eighth Symphony, one feels this latter element of the Schuman style to be more of an overlay than it has appeared to be previously.

Schuman's other orchestra works include the *American Festival Overture* (1939), built on a three-note street call used by New York boys; a Concerto for piano and small orchestra (1943); *Prayer in Time of War* (1943), winner of the first Pulitzer Prize given for a musical work; a *William Billings Overture* (1944), based on tunes of our pioneer composer; a Violin Concerto (1947), twice revised; *Credendum* (1955), composed at the invitation of the United States Commission for UNESCO; *New England Triptych* (1956), based on three anthems of William Billings and commissioned by André Kostelanetz; and *A Song of Orpheus* (1962), commissioned by the Ford Foundation for the cellist Leonard Rose. Schuman's works for band include *Newsreel in Five Shots* (1941), also scored for orchestra; *Sideshow* (1944), using music composed for *The Seven Lively Arts*; *George Washington Bridge* (1950); and *Chester* (1957), based on William Billings's revolutionary hymn.

Schuman's stage works include the ballets *Undertow* (1945), "a psychological murder story"; *Night Journey* (1948); and *Judith* (1950), the two latter works composed for Martha Graham; and the opera *Casey at the Bat* (1953), based on Ernest L. Thayer's popular ballad and later retitled *The Mighty Casey*. Harold Schonberg, writing in the New York *Times*, found much of the opera "lively, amusing, tongue-in-cheek," but questioned the suitability of Schuman's jerky melodies, austere harmonies, and rhythmic intensity to "this pleasant little fable." Schuman has also composed four String Quartets, the First and Second dated 1936 and 1937, respectively, the Third introduced in 1940, and the Fourth in 1950.

Although GIAN-CARLO MENOTTI (1911———) has been hailed as the successor of Puccini in writing operas of the "verismo" school, it is perhaps significant that his first opera, *Amelia al Ballo* (*Amelia Goes to the Ball*), was not filled with grim realism, but was a gay and sparkling specimen of the traditional *opera buffa*.

Menotti was born in Milan, Italy, July 7, 1911. At the age of seventeen he reversed the nineteenth-century custom of American composers going to Europe for teachers by coming to America to study composition with Rosario Scalero at the Curtis Institute in Philadelphia. He has lived principally in this country ever since, though he has not become an American citizen. *Amelia al Ballo*, begun in 1933 when the composer was twenty-two and finished two and a half years later, was first produced by the opera department at the Curtis Institute, and subsequently by the New York Metropolitan in 1938.

The success of *Amelia* led to a commission from the National Broadcasting Company, and *The Old Maid and the Thief* was first broadcast in April, 1939. Again Menotti demonstrated sparkling humor, skill, and craftsmanship, and again the libretto was his own work. His next work, *The Island God*, produced by the Metropolitan in 1942, proved to be a one-act tragedy with so little action that it could almost be considered a cantata. Virgil Thomson remarked in the New York *Herald Tribune* of February 21, 1942, that Menotti "proved in *Amelia at the Ball* his sense of theatrical values, but he has not proved in *The Island God* that he can do without a plot."

Menotti's next production, a pair of operas for which he as usual wrote both libretto and music, consisted of *The Telephone*, an ingenious and funny curtain-raiser, and *The Medium*, a two-act tragedy that demonstrated for the first time Menotti's gift for gripping drama. This tale of a fraudulent medium and her deaf-mute confederate remains one of the composer's most striking contributions to the stage. The two operas were first produced at Columbia University in 1946, and the next year they enjoyed a successful run on Broadway. *The Consul*, first produced in Philadelphia in 1950, was also successfully produced on Broadway; in this work Menotti depicted the plight of political refugees who cannot obtain visas to a free country.

In his next work Menotti temporarily turned his back on tragedy and composed a Christmas play suffused with charm and feeling. Commissioned by the National Broadcasting Company, *Amahl and the Night Visitors* was first presented on television Christmas Eve, 1951, and has become an annual production ever since. Modestly scored, as are most of Menotti's works, *Amahl* has had many productions by colleges and opera workshops; in fact, because of the accessibility and generally modest demands of his operas, Menotti can claim to be the most widely known and performed of our opera composers, both at home and abroad.

The Saint of Bleecker Street (1954), a tragedy set in New York's "Little Italy," did not enjoy as long a run as *The Consul*, though it won the Drama Critics' Circle Award as the best musical play of 1954 and the Pulitzer Prize for 1955. Menotti's next stage work, described as a "Madrigal Fable" for chorus, ten dancers, and nine instruments, was entitled *The Unicorn, the Gorgon and the Manticore, or Three Sundays of a Poet*. It was commissioned by the Elizabeth Sprague Coolidge Foundation and first performed in the Library of Congress in Washington in 1956.

Maria Golovin, commissioned by the National Broadcasting Company for television, was first produced at the International Exposition at Brussels in 1958. Its failure on Broadway may perhaps be blamed on the fact that the producer presented it as a drama with music rather than as an opera: the New York drama critics found the work melodramatic. Later produced on television and by the New York City Opera, the work won more enthusiastic notices from music critics. Paul Henry Lang, writing in the New York *Herald Tribune* of March 31, 1959, found that *Maria Golovin* "makes for good, efficient, and entertaining musical theater."

In 1963 the National Broadcasting Company presented the fifty-five-minute *Labyrinth*, a work written expressly for television and employing dissolves and trick photography that would have been impossible in a conventional theatre or opera house. Menotti himself admitted that *Labyrinth*, with its highly surrealistic plot, was "more of a riddle than an opera." Reviewing the work in *Musical America* of March 6, 1963, John Ardoin wrote, "Menotti took a giant step forward in his development as a composer in 1954 with *The Saint of Bleecker Street*. It was not a total success, but it seemed to indicate a greater substance and depth in Menotti's talent than had been there previously. In 1958 Menotti emerged as an impresario with his Festival of Two Worlds in Spoleto. Only two works have been heard since: *Maria Golovin* and *Labyrinth*. Both are regressions from the promise *The Saint* held, and make me wonder if Menotti has the time or the calm to pursue his craft in a way that would pay him musical dividends, by allowing time for reflection and growth."

In 1963 Menotti's *L'Homme Sauvage* was premièred at the Paris Opera, and the following year it was presented at the New York Metropolitan under the title *The Last Savage*. Critics found the work undeniably entertaining but expressed disappointment at its derivative and often superficial score. Ironically, one of the loveliest moments in the opera was a twelve-tone interlude intended by the composer to burlesque twentieth-century musical modernism, with which he professes little sympathy.

Other works for stage and concert hall include *Sebastian* (dated 1944) and *Errand into the Maze* (1947), both ballets; a Concerto for piano and orchestra (1945); *Apocalypse* (1951), a symphonic poem; and a Concerto for violin and orchestra (1952). *The Death of the Bishop of Brindisi*, a cantata for soli, chorus, children's chorus, and orchestra, had its première in 1963. Henry Humphreys, writing in the New York *Herald Tribune* of May 20, 1963, had the impression "that this dramatic and colorful cantata will be a permanent and valuable addition to the choro-orchestral repertory." Menotti's short opera *Martin's Lie* was introduced in England in 1964.

A newspaper columnist once called LEONARD BERNSTEIN (1918—) "a national asset," a title he fully deserves, for he has reached, and continues to reach, more people with good music, excellently played and clearly and simply explained, than any other musical missionary in history; availing himself of the opportunities offered by television, radio, and recordings, he has used these media with a showmanship and salesmanship approaching genius.

Born August 25, 1918, in Lawrence, Massachusetts, Leonard Bernstein at first intended to be a pianist, but studied composition with Walter Piston and Edward Burlingame Hill at Harvard. He then spent two years at the Curtis Institute in Philadelphia and his summers at Tanglewood in the Berkshires, where he studied conducting with Koussevitzky. In 1942 he settled in New York, gave music lessons at small fees, and did arrangements for a music publisher. Then came an appointment as assistant conductor of the Philharmonic-Symphony. In November of 1943, Bruno Walter fell ill during his term as guest conductor, and Bernstein was called upon to take his place. With little preparation he led the concert so well that he received not only an ovation from the audience but praise from the critics, and Artur Rodzinski, permanent conductor of the orchestra, immediately assigned him several further concerts.

Since Bernstein's substitute conducting had been broadcast over the Columbia network, the young man's success became a national rather than a local event, and within a short time the Bernstein career took on the look of a Horatio Alger novel. After serving two seasons as conductor of the New York City Center Orchestra, guest-conducting leading orchestras in the United States and abroad, and touring Europe and Palestine, Bernstein was appointed permanent conductor of the New York Philharmonic. The appointment proved beneficial to the orchestra, which profited from Bernstein's expert leadership; to audiences, who filled the concerts to capacity and listened avidly to Bernstein's comments and talks during performances, and, most important, to the musical public of the nation.

Although conducting has proved to be the most important of Bernstein's activities, it is as a composer that this book is chiefly concerned with him. Bernstein has composed in two fields: concert music and Broadway shows. At a Philharmonic-Symphony concert in 1944 Bernstein conducted a performance of his Symphony *Jeremiah*, a work that had been premièred earlier the same year by the Pittsburgh Symphony. Based on the Book of Lamentations, the symphony requires a soprano soloist to sing the Hebrew text. The following spring, the Symphony received the Music Critics' Circle Award as the best orchestral work by an American composer heard in New York that season.

Bernstein was piano soloist in 1949 when Serge Koussevitzky conducted the Boston Symphony in the first performance of his Second Symphony, entitled *The Age of Anxiety*. This programmatic work, based on a poem by W. H. Auden, passes from religious moods to an ultramodern idiom that includes a spectacular episode in jazz style.

Writing in the New York *Herald Tribune* of February 23, 1950, Virgil Thomson found the Symphony "picturesque and expressive . . . its form improvisatory, its melodic content casual, its harmony stiff, its contrapuntal tension weak. . . . As a ballet it may support choreographic fantasy. As a concert piece it is lacking in the chief elements . . . that make for survival in the repertory." *The Age of Anxiety* has in fact survived better in the ballet than in concert.

Trouble in Tahiti, a one-act opera combining the popular idiom with the operatic, composed to Bernstein's own libretto, was first performed at Brandeis University in 1952 and later put into the repertory of the New York City Opera at City Center. The composer himself conducted his *Serenade* for violin solo, strings, and percussion (after Plato's *Symposium*) at the Venice Festival in 1954.

A Third Symphony, *Kaddish,* based on the traditional prayer for the dead in Jewish liturgy, was played by Charles Munch and the Boston Symphony in 1964; it had earlier been introduced in Tel Aviv under the composer's baton. The work combined a soprano soloist, chorus chanting the Aramaic text, orchestra, and narrator. Though the work delighted American audiences, critics questioned the unorthodox alternation of spoken text and music. Among Bernstein's shorter works are a Clarinet Sonata (1943), and the song cycles *Five Kid Songs* (1943), *I Hate Music* (1943), and *La Bonne Cuisine* (1947).

It was through ballet that Bernstein first established himself on Broadway. When produced by the Ballet Theatre at the Metropolitan Opera House in New York in 1944, Bernstein's *Fancy Free* proved so entertaining that it achieved the status of a hit, and the house was sold out whenever the work was announced on the company's bill. For the following season Bernstein incorporated some of the material from *Fancy Free* into a score for the musical comedy *On the Town* (1944), and added to it a number of gay, sparkling songs. The show was one of the most popular musical comedies of the year. In 1953 *Wonderful Town,* book and lyrics again by Betty Comden and Adolf Green and music by Bernstein, opened to glowing reviews and ran for 556 performances.

Bernstein's next Broadway show, *Candide,* was a critical rather than a popular success. Though Brooks Atkinson noted in the New York

Times that none of Bernstein's previous theatre music "has had the joyous variety, humor, and richness of this score," the show suffered from an untheatrical book adapted by Lillian Hellman from Voltaire's satirical novel and closed after a short run.

Of completely different character were both book and music of Bernstein's next show. *West Side Story*, which opened in New York in 1957, had a book by Arthur Laurents, who had updated the Romeo and Juliet plot, substituting warring teen-age gangs for the Montagues and Capulets. Walter Kerr, reviewing the show in the New York *Herald Tribune* of September 27, 1957, described the production vividly:

Director, choreographer, and idea-man Jerome Robbins has put together, and then blasted apart, the most savage, electrifying dance patterns we've been exposed to in a dozen seasons. . . . He was almost sacrificially assisted in this macabre and murderous onslaught of movement by composer Leonard Bernstein. Mr. Bernstein has permitted himself a few moments of graceful, lingering melody . . . but for the most part he has served the needs of the on-stage threshing machine, setting the fierce beat that fuses a gymnasium dance, putting a mocking insistence behind taunts at a policeman, dramatizing the footwork rather than lifting the emotions into song.

A brilliant success in the United States and on its tour abroad, *West Side Story* was made into a spectacular motion picture.

Another composer who has not been afraid to communicate with a broad, contemporary public, NORMAN DELLO JOIO (1913——) was born in New York City, January 24, 1913. From hearing his father, a church organist, play accompaniments to chants, he gained a feeling for Gregorian music that has played an important part in his later works. The Gregorian element is particularly apparent in the Third of his four Piano Sonatas (dated 1943, 1944, 1947, and 1949, respectively) and in his *Variations, Chaconne, and Finale* for orchestra (1948), where he develops the Gregorian-derived material by a variety of means and does not hesitate to clothe the themes in jazz rhythms, thereby reversing Bach's procedure of converting traditional dance tunes into stately chorales.

After studying at the Institute of Musical Art, Dello Joio earned a scholarship to the Juilliard Graduate School, and in 1940 and 1941 he studied with Paul Hindemith, who encouraged him to let his natural lyricism assert itself. Dello Joio was granted a Guggenheim fellowship in 1944 and 1945. He then succeeded William Schuman as head of the composition department of Sarah Lawrence College, a position that he held until 1950, when he resigned to devote himself to composition.

Dello Joio's long list of orchestral works includes a *Concertino* for piano and orchestra, composed in 1938 before he entered Juilliard; three works composed at Juilliard, a *Concertino* for flute and strings (1939), a Concerto for two pianos and orchestra (1941), and a rather neoclassic Sinfonietta for piano and orchestra (1941); a Concerto for harp and orchestra (composed 1942); *To a Lonely Sentry* (composed 1943); a Concerto for clarinet and orchestra (composed 1943); *Concert Music* (1946); *Ricercari* for piano and orchestra (1946); *Three Symphonic Preludes*, later retitled *New York Profiles* (1948); a *Serenade* for orchestra (1948); a *Concertante* for clarinet and orchestra (1949); *Psalm of David* (composed 1950); a symphonic cantata, *Song of Affirmation* (1952); *Epigraph* (1952), composed in memory of the Philadelphia philanthropist A. Lincoln Gillespie; a dramatic cantata, *The Lamentation of Saul* (1954), composed to a text adapted from D. H. Lawrence's play *David*, originally scored for baritone, flute, oboe, clarinet, viola, cello, and piano, but later expanded by an orchestral accompaniment; *Meditations on Ecclesiastes* (1957); and *Fantasy and Variations* for piano and orchestra (1962), commissioned by a piano manufacturer and making bravura use of the technical resources of the solo instrument.

Dello Joio's chamber music includes a Sonata for cello and piano (1937); a Sonata for violin and piano (1938); a Sextet for three recorders and strings (1941); *Fantasia on a Gregorian Theme* (1943), for violin and piano; a Trio for flute, violoncello, and piano (1944); and an *Aria and Toccata* for two pianos (1953).

Much of Dello Joio's best-known music has been written for the stage. His first opera, *The Triumph of St. Joan*, has had an interesting career. Introduced in its original version at a concert of the League of Composers in New York in 1950, it was found lacking in dramatic pace, though full of effective music. Dello Joio took a number of the opera's themes and used them in a Symphony, also entitled *The Triumph of St. Joan*, performed in 1951 in Louisville.

The dramatic effect of the music was enhanced by the miming of Martha Graham, who subsequently danced the piece under the title *Seraphic Ode*. During the next five years, drawing from the actual proceedings of Joan's trial, the composer created an almost new work, entitled *The Trial at Rouen*, in which the dramatic faults of the original were overcome and the drama moved swiftly and decisively. *The Trial at Rouen* was performed on television by the NBC-TV Opera Theatre in 1956, and three years later was presented on the stage by the New York City Opera Company under its original title, *The Triumph of St. Joan*. The opera was given the New York Music Critics' Circle Award in 1960.

A second opera, *The Ruby*, was first performed at the University of Indiana in 1955. The one-act work was drawn from Lord Dunsany's play *A Night at the Inn*, and the musical treatment was unashamedly theatrical. In keeping with the ominous plot, the orchestration was colorful and exciting, and critics noted touches of Puccini in the melodic lines.

Dello Joio's third opera, *Blood Moon*, was commissioned by the Ford Foundation as part of its plan to encourage American composition. It was first performed in San Francisco in 1961. The libretto, based by Gale Hoffman upon the composer's scenario, dealt with interracial love in the ante-bellum South. Critical opinion agreed that the work was dramatically weak, and some critics found the music banal. Dello Joio himself stated that he wanted to write music accessible to the public, and *Blood Moon* is frankly melodic, with dramatic climaxes, arias, ensembles, and a lilting waltz.

Other stage works include music for the ballets *The Duke of Sacramento* (composed 1940); *On Stage!* (1946); and *There Is a Time* (1956). The *Serenade* for orchestra was used as music for the ballet *Diversion of the Angels*. In addition, Dello Joio has composed incidental music for the plays *The Tall Kentuckian* (played by the Louisville Orchestra in 1953) and Shakespeare's *Antony and Cleopatra* (1960). He has also written scores to accompany the CBS television programs *Air Power* (1956–57) and *Vanity Fair* (1961), a dramatization of Thackeray's novel.

Dello Joio's choral works include a setting of Walt Whitman's *The Mystic Trumpeter* for mixed chorus and French horn (composed

1943); *A Fable,* to a Vachel Lindsay text, and *A Jubilant Song,* adapted from Walt Whitman, both for mixed chorus and piano and both composed in 1946; and *Prayer of Cardinal Newman,* for mixed chorus and organ, composed in 1960. His songs include *There Is a Lady Sweet and Kind,* composed 1946; *Lament,* composed 1947; and *Six Love Songs,* composed 1949.

Initially complex to the point of atonality, the music of DAVID DIAMOND (1915——) developed in the direction of neo-Romanticism, with straightforward melodies supported by essentially tonal harmony, until his Eighth Symphony, which used a twelve-tone technique. Born in Rochester, New York, July 9, 1915, Diamond studied at the Cleveland Institute of Music, at the Eastman School with Bernard Rogers, and at the New School with Roger Sessions and Paul Boepple; he also studied with Nadia Boulanger in Paris. His numerous prizes include an Elfrida Whiteman scholarship in 1935, Guggenheim fellowships in 1938 and 1941, the Paderewski Prize in 1943, and a $1,000 award from the American Academy of Arts and Letters in 1944.

Diamond's orchestral compositions include a Sinfonietta (1936); a *Psalm* for orchestra (1937); the First Violin Concerto (1937); *Heroic Piece* (1938); a Cello Concerto (composed 1938, first performed 1942); *Concert Piece* (1940); a Concerto for chamber orchestra (1940); the First Symphony, introduced in a major performance by the New York Philharmonic in 1941; *Rounds for String Orchestra* (1944), commissioned by Dmitri Mitropoulos for the Minneapolis Symphony, a skillful, lyrical score that has proved to be Diamond's most popular to date; the Second Symphony (1944), introduced by the Boston Symphony and admitted by critics to be of high workmanship, though they questioned its distinction; the Second Violin Concerto (1948); *Music for Shakespeare's Romeo and Juliet* (1947), a terse and vivid score commissioned by Thomas Scherman for the Little Orchestra Society of New York; *Timon of Athens, a Symphonic Portrait after Shakespeare* (1949), written in fulfillment of a Louisville commission; *The Enormous Room* (1949), after e. e. cummings; a Piano Concerto (1949); the Third Symphony (1950); the Fourth Symphony (1948), which in spite of its numbering was heard more than two years before the Third, was another of

Diamond's lyrical works and was commissioned by the Koussevitzky Foundation; *Ahavah* (1954) for narrator and orchestra, commissioned by the National Jewish Music Council; *Diaphony* (1956), scored for brass, two pianos, timpani, and orchestra; *Sinfonia Concertante*, introduced during the Rochester Philharmonic's 1956–57 season; the Sixth Symphony (1957), a powerful work which the *Musical America* critic (April, 1957) nonetheless felt "lacking in the craftsmanship which has distinguished other—and better—of Diamond's music."

Diamond's *The World of Paul Klee* (1958), commissioned through a grant by the Rockefeller Foundation, was intended to "bring contemporary music within the reach of superior student orchestras." Inspired by paintings of the Swiss artist, the piece was divided into four sections: *The Dance of the Grieving Child; The Black Prince; Pastorale;* and *The Twittering Machine*. Though technically easy to play, the composition was in no sense simplified music, but a substantial work which the critic of the *Herald Tribune* (February 20, 1960) found to be "composed with notable persuasiveness and . . . lucid and delicately hued orchestration."

The reviewer for the same paper (January 31, 1962) found that Diamond's Seventh Symphony (1962) suffered from the composer's "old-fashioned modernism." The Eighth Symphony (performed in 1961, the year preceding the first performance of the Seventh), constructed by means of an unorthodoxly free twelve-tone technique, moved the New York *Times* critic (October 28, 1961) to characterize the work as "dissonant; busy; complicated; highly rhythmic; melodically dry; has twelve-tone aspects; snarling brasses; makes plenty of noise; has a slow movement with determinedly melodic figurations that sound more calculated than natural. . . . Plenty of energy coupled to almost a total lack of charm or relaxation; neuroticism unreined." In 1962 the Buffalo *Evening News* commissioned Diamond to set Lincoln's Gettysburg Address for chorus, children's chorus, baritone solo, and orchestra. Entitled *This Sacred Ground*, the work was performed the same year by the Buffalo Philharmonic under Lukas Foss.

Diamond's lengthy list of chamber works includes four String Quartets (1940, 1943, 1946, 1951); a *Partita* for oboe, bassoon, and piano (1935); a Concerto for string quartet (1936); a Quintet for flute, string trio, and piano (1937); a String Trio (1937); a Piano Quartet (1938); a Cello Sonata (1938); a Violin Sonata (1945); a *Canticle for Perpetual Motion* (1947), for violin and piano; a *Chaconne* for violin and piano (1947); a Quintet for clarinet, two violas, and two cellos (1951); *Night Music* (1962), for accordion and string quartet; and a second Concerto for string quartet (1962). For piano Diamond has composed a Sonatina (1935), an *Album for Young People* (1946), and a Sonata (1947), as well as a Concerto for two pianos (1941). His vocal music consists of numerous short choral pieces and a cycle of solo songs.

LEON KIRCHNER (1919———), born in Brooklyn, New York, January 24, 1919, abandoned a premedical course to study composition with Arnold Schoenberg at the University of California in Los Angeles, thereafter studying with Albert Elkus, Edward Strickland, Ernest Bloch, and Roger Sessions. After spending the years 1943–46 in the army, he returned to the University of California to receive his M.A. After lecturing a year at the University, he received a Guggenheim fellowship and in 1950 became an associate professor of music at the University of Southern California. In 1954 he was appointed a professor at Mills College, California.

In an article on Kirchner in the January, 1957, issue of the *Musical Quarterly*, Alexander L. Ringer admitted that his subject was an eclectic, "but only in the sense in which the United States as a whole is an eclectic nation whose roots draw strength from many soils." Ringer noted that "Kirchner's remarkable sense of form comes to expression mainly in his treatment of rhythm and tempo. . . . [His music] thrives upon temporal fluctuations punctuated by changes in volume and intensity. There is nothing special about his melodic and harmonic procedures as such. They remain consistently dissonant and chromatic. But when related to the surging rhythms and ever changing tempos, they, too, assume unsuspected expressive powers."

Kirchner's works include a Duo for violin and piano (1947); a Piano Sonata (1948); a String Quartet, composed in 1949 and performed the following year; a *Little Suite* for piano (1949); a *Sinfonia in Two Parts* (1952), written on a commission from Richard Rodgers and Oscar Hammerstein II awarded through the League of Composers and first performed by the New York Philharmonic under

Mitropoulos; a Piano Concerto, a bravura work composed in 1953 and first performed in 1956; a Trio for violin, cello, and piano (1954); a Toccata for strings, solo winds, and percussion, composed in 1955 and first heard in 1956; and the Second String Quartet, composed in 1958, of which Richard Franko Goldman wrote in the *Musical Quarterly* of January, 1960, "It . . . uses no serial techniques at all. . . . [Kirchner] achieves delicate and beautiful sounds, created by rather subtle melodic lines in a carefully balanced polyphony. The harmonic calculation is curious and original, and is unsystematic enough to include even major triads."

A Concerto for violin, ten winds, and percussion, first performed in 1961, struck Goldman (*Musical Quarterly*, January, 1962) as possessing the strengths of Kirchner's best work, which he enumerated as "powerful, almost 'romantic' drive, independence of direction, and a fine sense of sound. . . . [Kirchner] appears to be a composer who is able, even when it is no longer fashionable, to laugh and to weep, show anger and joy." Kirchner has also composed two settings of poems by Walt Whitman for soprano and piano: *Of Obedience* and *The Runner*.

VINCENT PERSICHETTI (1915——) and William Schuman would seem to have formed a mutual admiration society. Persichetti and his wife published a book entitled *William Schuman* in 1954, and when Persichetti published another book in 1961,[1] Schuman reviewed it for the *Musical Quarterly*, entitling his article "The Compleat Musician: Vincent Persichetti and Twentieth-Century Harmony." The characterization is perhaps justifiable in view of the fact that Persichetti began studying piano and organ at the age of five and counterpoint, score-reading, transposition, and composition at the age of nine, playing the piano at weddings and on local radio stations at six, performing on the organ in church at fifteen, and giving piano recitals as a child prodigy.

Persichetti was born in Philadelphia June 6, 1915. He studied piano with Olga Samaroff and Alberto Jonas, composition with Paul Nordoff and Roy Harris, and conducting with Fritz Reiner. In 1942 he became head of the composition department of the Philadelphia

---

[1] *Twentieth-Century Harmony, Creative Aspects and Practice*, New York, W. W. Norton, Inc.

Conservatory, and in 1948 he was appointed to the staff of the Juilliard School of Music in New York. In 1958–59 he had a Guggenheim fellowship.

Like much modern music, Persichetti's is essentially eclectic, deriving from a variety of sources. Some critics have felt that he does not fuse the elements in his compositions sufficiently to sustain his own individuality. Reviewing an early Piano Sonata, Arthur Berger remarked in the New York *Herald Tribune* of December 27, 1949, that the work was indicative of "a tendency to take material fresh from the pens of composers like Copland and Hindemith without remolding it to a sufficiently personal shape." Another critic discerned Tchaikovskian moments in Persichetti's Fourth Symphony five years later, while others have remarked an episodic quality in some of his work, a characteristic that may be traced to the composer's fondness for compactness. In the 1958 edition of *Baker's Biographical Dictionary of Musicians* Nicolas Slonimsky offered this précis of Persichetti's music: "The basis is tonal, but the component parts often move independently; the rhythmic element is always strong and emphatic; the melody is more frequently diatonic than chromatic or atonal."

Persichetti's orchestral compositions include the First and Second Symphonies, both composed in 1942; a *Concertino* for piano and orchestra (1945); *Fables* (1945), for orchestra with narrator; *The Hollow Men* (1946), for trumpet and string orchestra; the Third Symphony (1947); *Dance Overture* (1948); *Fairy Tale* (1950); the Fourth Symphony (1954); the Fifth Symphony (1954), scored for strings alone and composed on a Louisville commission; the Sixth Symphony (1956), commissioned by the Washington University Band of St. Louis and scored for wind instruments alone; and the Seventh Symphony (1957), described by the composer as "liturgic" and scored for full orchestra. In addition to the Sixth Symphony, Persichetti's band works include *Psalm; Bagatelles; Divertimento* (1950); and *Pageant* (1953).

The long list of Persichetti's chamber works includes three String Quartets; *King Lear,* a septet for woodwind quintet, timpani, and piano; Sonatas for solo violin (1940), for violin and piano (1941), and for unaccompanied cello (1952); and two quintets for piano and strings (1940 and 1950). Persichetti has also composed a series of

Serenades for various instrumental groups. No. 1 and No. 2, both composed in 1929 when the composer was fourteen, are scored respectively for ten wind instruments and for piano solo; No. 3 (1941) for violin, cello, and piano; No. 4 (1945) for violin and piano; No. 5 (1950) for orchestra; No. 6 (1950) for trombone, cello, and piano; No. 7 (1952) for piano; No. 8 (1954) for piano, four hands. The Ninth, Tenth, Eleventh, and Twelfth *Serenades* are scored for soprano and alto recorders, for flute and harp, for band, and for solo tuba, respectively. Persichetti's keyboard music includes ten Sonatas and six Sonatinas for solo piano; occasional pieces, such as the *Little Piano Book*, intended for teaching the piano; a Sonata for organ; a Sonatina for organ pedals alone; a Sonata for two pianos (1940); a Sonata for harpsichord (1951); and a Concerto for piano, four hands (1952).

Persichetti's vocal works include songs to texts by a variety of modern poets, including Sara Teasdale, Carl Sandburg, James Joyce, Hilaire Belloc, Robert Frost, Emily Dickinson, and e. e. cummings. Most of his choral music has been written for church, including the Magnificat (composed 1940) for chorus and organ, *Hymns and Responses for the Church Year* (composed 1955), and a Mass for mixed chorus *a cappella* (1961). Of his *Stabat Mater* (1964) the New York *Times* critic commented (May 2, 1964), "It uses more or less conventional harmonic language in a way that shows that, in Mr. Persichetti's case, conventional harmonic language is not all used up. *Stabat Mater* is a combination of starkness and warmth, boldness and ease."

According to a report by Broadcast Music, Inc., there were a total of 1,080 performances of works by ALAN HOVHANESS (1911——) during the period June 1961–July 1962 alone, a remarkable record equaled by few living American composers and a testament to the extraordinary favor which this composer has won with the public. Born March 8, 1911, in Somerville, Massachusetts, of an Armenian father and a Scottish mother, Hovhaness was christened Haroutin Hovhaness Chakmakjian, but decided to adopt his middle name as a surname and Alan for his given name.

His early musical training consisted of piano lessons with Heinrich Gebhard and studies in composition with Frederick Converse. At the age of thirty-one he was given a scholarship to study with Bohuslav Martinu at Tanglewood. In 1940, having decided that the compositions of his youth and early manhood were undistinguished, he burned them all—nearly a thousand pieces, including two symphonies, several operas, and many smaller works. About this time he became organist of the Armenian Cathedral in Boston and became deeply interested in the modes and patterns of Hebraic and Aramaic as well as Ambrosian and Gregorian chants.

Nicolas Slonimsky [2] has described the process by which Hovhaness developed his idiom: "He gradually evolved an individual type of art, in which quasi-Oriental cantillation and a curiously monodic texture became the mainstay. By dint of ceaseless repetition of themes and relentless dynamic tension, a definite impression is created of originality; the atmospheric effect often suggests Impressionistic exoticism."

Writing in the *Musical Quarterly* of July, 1951, Henry Cowell has characterized Hovhaness's music as "moving, long-breathed . . . splendidly written and unique in style. It is a contemporary development of the archaic spirit and sounds like the music of nobody else at all." In the same article, describing Hovhaness's Symphony *Saint Vartan* (1951), which was composed for the celebration of the 1,500th anniversary of the Armenian warrior-saint Vartan Marmikonian, Cowell wrote: "Of the [symphony's] twenty-four movements, twelve are canons, for the most part in several keys or tonalities at once. This is because Hovhaness usually has his canonic voices enter on different degrees of the scale or mode and then imitate the intervals exactly, with no change to bring the melody lines within the key or mode of the first entrance. The result, of course, is a constant polytonality."

Others of Hovhaness's Symphonies include No. 6, *Celestial Gate* (1960); No. 7, *Nanga Parvat* (1960); No. 8, *Arjuna* (1960); No. 10, *Dawn* (1961); No. 11 (1961); No. 12 (1961), for chamber orchestra and chorus, based on the *23rd Psalm*; and No. 13 (1961), scored for single winds and strings. Other orchestral works include three *Armenian Rhapsodies;* a Prelude and Quadruple Fugue

<hr>

[2] *Baker's Biographical Dictionary of Musicians,* 5th ed., G. Schirmer, New York, 1958.

(1955); *Vision from the Rock* (1955); *The Mysterious Mountain* (1957); and *Mountain of Prophecy* (1961). Reviewing *The Mysterious Mountain*, Anne Holmes wrote in the Houston *Chronicle* of November 1, 1957, that the work's "long-phrased themes seemed to pour through the orchestral choirs like molten gold," while Hubert Rousel of the Houston *Post* exclaimed: "Tonality . . . was back again —and how good, how wonderfully good it did sound!" Hovhaness's *Meditations of Orpheus*, for dancer and orchestra, and Variations and Fugue for orchestra were both introduced in 1964.

There are also a number of Concertos, scored for a variety of large and small instrumental combinations. No. 1 (1952), subtitled *Arevakal*, and No. 7 (1954) are scored for orchestra, while No. 5 (1954) is scored for piano and strings. Others bear subtitles: *Sivas* is scored for solo violin and strings; *Khaldis* for piano, any multiple of four trumpets, and percussion; *Talin*, for solo viola and strings; *Ardos*, for piano, timpani, and orchestra; *Artik*, for piano and strings; and *Sosi—Forest of Prophetic Sounds*, for violin, piano, percussion, and strings. Hovhaness has also composed a Concerto for Accordion (1960).

His choral works include *The Thirteenth Ode of Solomon; Ad Lyram; The Stars;* and a *Triptych*, consisting of *Ave Maria* and *As on the Night, The Beatitudes*, and *Easter Cantata*. Hovhaness's stage works include a ballet, *Wind Drum;* incidental music for Clifford Odets's play *The Flowering Peach;* and the operas *The Blue Flame* (1959), *The Burning House* (1962), and *Pilate* (1962). He has also a long list of chamber works to his credit.

ALVIN ETLER (1913——) was born at Battle Creek, Iowa, on February 19, 1913, and studied with Arthur Shepherd at Western Reserve University and with Paul Hindemith at Yale. From 1938 to 1940 he was oboist with the Indianapolis Symphony, and from 1940 to 1942 he was a Guggenheim fellow. He taught from 1942 to 1946 at Yale and from 1946 to 1947 at Cornell. In 1947 he joined the staff of the University of Illinois and in 1949 became a professor at Smith College.

Etler's early work shows the influence of Hindemith, but after the early 1950's he integrated into his style elements of the idioms of composers as diverse as Schoenberg and Bartók. His orchestral works include two Suites (1936 and 1939); *Music for Chamber Orchestra* (1938); two Sinfoniettas (1940 and 1941); a Concerto for wind quintet and string orchestra (1946); *Passacaglia and Fugue* (1947); a Concerto for string quartet and string orchestra (1948); the Symphony No. 1, composed in 1951 and in 1953 awarded a prize in the Queen Elizabeth of Belgium Competition; a *Dramatic Overture*, composed in 1956; a *Concerto in One Movement*, commissioned by the Cleveland Orchestra for its fortieth anniversary and introduced in 1957; and an *Elegy* for small orchestra, dated 1959. Etler's chamber works include a Sonata for oboe, clarinet, and viola (1944); a Sonata for bassoon and piano (1951); two Quintets for woodwinds; a Quartet for strings (1955); a Sonata for cello and piano (1956); a Sonata for viola and harpsichord; a Concerto for violin and woodwind quintet; and a Suite for flute, oboe, and clarinet.

When Etler's Concerto for wind quintet and orchestra had its first New York performance by the New York Philharmonic under Leonard Bernstein in 1962, Ronald Eyer wrote in the New York *Herald Tribune* of October 27, 1962: "With its bright-hued sonorities and carefully calculated contrasts, it is a bang-up piece of show music. I particularly liked the last movement of the three with its jazzy syncopations tossed airily from plucked basses to bongo drums and xylophone in the extra-large battery section and the final concussion with a rearing-back glissando on the harp which couldn't really be heard but looked like fun."

MORTON GOULD (1913――) brings to his symphonic scores a flavor of the American popular idiom that is simultaneously Broadway and concert hall. His product is often theatrical and sometimes slick in the Hollywood manner, but it has proved immensely popular. Gould was born in Richmond Hill, New York, December 10, 1913. He was a child prodigy and started to compose at the age of four. When he was fifteen he was graduated from New York University. He studied music privately and enjoyed amazing his friends by being an "elbow pianist." Economic reverses made it necessary for him to earn his living in Tin-Pan Alley; he eventually found a place as arranger on the music staff of Radio City Music Hall, and later with the National Broadcasting Company. An able conductor, he had his own radio program for a number of years, performing mostly light music; has made guest appearances with major symphony orchestras; and leads his own orchestra on phonograph records. In 1959 he succeeded the author of this book as a director of the America Society of Composers, Authors, and Publishers.

Ever since his First *American Symphonette* (1933), which contained the widely-known *Pavane*, Gould has produced compositions that strike the public fancy. The Second and Third *American Symphonettes* followed in 1935 and 1937 respectively, and in 1936 Stokowski introduced the *Chorale and Fugue in Jazz* for two pianos and orchestra. Subsequent orchestral works include a Piano Concerto (1937) and a Violin Concerto (1937); *A Foster Gallery* (1940), based on melodies of Stephen Foster and commissioned by Fritz Reiner; the widely played *Latin-American Symphonette* (1941); *A Lincoln Legend* (1941); *Spirituals* for string choir and orchestra (1942); *Interplay* (1943), an "American concertette" for piano and orchestra, later used by the choreographer Jerome Robbins for a ballet of the same title; *American Salute*, based on Gilmore's famous song *When Johnny Comes Marching Home*; *Harvest* (1945), for harp, vibraphone, and strings; *Minstrel Show* (1946); *Philharmonic Waltzes* (1948), composed at the request of the Philharmonic League of New York; a Concerto for Orchestra (1948), characterized by Virgil Thomson in the *Herald Tribune* as "neatly and noisily orchestrated throughout, though its musical matter is a little thin"; *Inventions* (1953), for four pianos and orchestra; *Dance Variations* (1953), for two pianos and orchestra; the score for the film *Cinerama Holiday* (1954); *Showpiece* (1954), for timpani, percussion harp, piano, and strings; *Derivations* (1956), for clarinet and brass band, introduced by Benny Goodman in Washington, D.C.; *Declaration* (1957), composed in honor of President Eisenhower's second inauguration; *Jekyll and Hyde Variations* (1957); *Dialogues* (1958), for piano and strings; and *Rhythm Gallery* (1958).

Gould has also composed Symphonies: the First was introduced in 1943; the Second, a *Symphony on a Marching Tune*, in 1944; the Third in 1944; and the Fourth, for marching band, at West Point. *Fall River Legend*, a ballet with scenario and choreography by Agnes de Mille, was first produced by the Ballet Theatre in New York in 1948. Though Lizzie Borden was acquitted of the crime, the work twists history and deals with the psychological motivations that allegedly led Lizzie Borden to murder her stepfather; the score is flavored with New England hymn tunes and dances. Gould has prepared a six-movement concert Suite from the score. The unusual Concerto for tap dancer and orchestra (1952) was composed for the dancer Danny Daniel and uses the rhythmic patter of the dancer's feet in contrast to the orchestral ensemble just as the traditional concerto uses the solo instrument.

BERNARD HERRMANN (1911——) attracted wide attention when his dramatic cantata *Moby Dick*, for male chorus, soloists, and orchestra, was first performed by the New York Philharmonic Society, April 11, 1940. Writing in the New York *Herald Tribune* of April 12, 1940, Francis D. Perkins announced that the work "reveals a remarkable command of the resources of instrumental coloring and timbre, an exceptional ability to depict with convincing vividness a wide variety of emotional hues and atmospheres," qualities which have placed Herrmann in the top rank of film composers.

Born in New York City, June 29, 1911, Herrmann studied with Albert Stoessel, Philip James, and Bernard Wagenaar at the Juilliard Graduate School. He became a staff conductor for the Columbia Broadcasting Company in 1938 and five years later was appointed symphonic director. In 1942 he received a $1,000 award from the National Academy of Arts and Letters. His compositions include a String Quartet (1932); an *Aubade* for fourteen instruments (1933); orchestral variations on *Deep River* and *Water Boy* (1933); a symphonic poem, *The City of Brass* (1934); a Sinfonietta for strings (1935); a *Currier and Ives Suite* (1935), for orchestra; Nocturne and Scherzo for orchestra (1936); a Violin Concerto (1937); a Fiddle Concerto (1940); a cantata, *Johnny Appleseed* (1940); the First Symphony (1941); and a brief orchestra work, *To the Fallen*, played by the New York Philharmonic in 1943.

When live music ceased being a major concern of the radio networks, Herrmann moved to Hollywood to compose and conduct scores for motion pictures. He wrote the music to *Citizen Kane* (1940), *The Devil and Daniel Webster* (1941), and *Anna and the King of Siam* (1947); and his scores for the films of Alfred Hitchcock have set and maintained a high standard of craft, imagination, and taste.

GAIL KUBIK (1914——) won a $1,000 prize offered in 1941 by Jascha Heifetz for a new Violin Concerto and in addition received $500 for his work from the RCA-Victor Company. Eleven years later, in 1952, his *Symphonie-Concertante* was awarded a Pulitzer Prize following its performance by the Little Orchestra Society of New York.

Born in South Coffeyville, Oklahoma, September 5, 1914, Kubik studied at the American Conservatory in Chicago and at the Eastman School of Music. During the Second World War he served as music consultant for the Motion Pictures Bureau of the Office of War Information and composed the score for the documentary *The World at War*. As corporal in the Army Air Force he composed scores for Air Force films, and his music for the United States Maritime Commission's documentary *Men and Ships* has been heard as a concert piece on the radio. In 1946 Kubik taught at the University of Southern California, and in 1948 he received a Guggenheim fellowship.

Kubik's orchestral compositions include an *American Caprice* for piano and chamber orchestra (1936); a Violin Concerto (1938); *Paratroops* (1941), a suite for small orchestra; two works inspired by folk songs, *Camptown Races* (1946) and *Erie Canal* (1947); *Bachata* (1956); and *A Festival Opening* (1957). Kubik's works for band include *Stewball Variations* (1941); *Fanfare and March* (1946); and an Overture (1946). For chamber combinations he has written *Trivialities* (1934), for flute, horn, and strings; a Piano Trio (1934); *Puck, a Christmas Score* (1940), for speakers, winds, and strings; a Suite for three recorders (1941); a Sonatina for violin and piano (1944); a Toccata for organ and strings (1946); and a *Little Suite* for flute and two clarinets (1947). Kubik's stage works include incidental music for *They Walk Alone* (1941); a ballet for dance band and folk singer, based on *Frankie and Johnny* (1946); *Mirror for the Sky*, a folk opera on the life of Audubon, from which excerpts were performed in New York in 1947 and which was performed in its entirety in Oregon in 1958; and *Boston Baked Beans*, a one-act operatic farce about a Harvard graduate who goes west to make his fortune and who is captured by a girl named Clementine, who cooks beans exquisitely.

A. LEHMAN ENGEL (1910——) is best known as a conductor. He

organized and directed the Madrigal Singers, a unit of the WPA Music Project in New York, and conducted the premières of numerous modern works under other auspices. In recent years he has been much in demand as conductor for Broadway shows.

Born in Jackson, Mississippi, September 14, 1910, Engel studied at the Cincinnati College, the Cincinnati Conservatory, and the Juilliard School, as well as working with Roger Sessions. His works include the orchestral pieces *Jungle Dance* (1930); *Introduction and Allegretto* (1932); *Scientific Creation* (1935); and *Traditions* (1935). He has written a number of choral pieces; a String Quartet (1934); a Piano Sonata (1936); incidental music to Eliot's *Murder in the Cathedral* (1936), O'Casey's *Within the Gates* (1934), Aristophanes' *The Birds* (1935), and Shakespeare's *Macbeth* (1941), among other plays; the operas *Pierrot of the Minute* (1927), *Medea* (1935), and *The Soldier* (1956); and a ballet, *Phobias* (1933).

HERSHY KAY (1919———), a composer and a skilled orchestrator of other composers' scores, is a younger counterpart of Robert Russell Bennett, with whom he has in fact collaborated. Kay has written scores for the New York City Ballet; prepared works for nightclub acts, concert singers, and recordings; worked on the music of numerous television specials; and orchestrated Broadway shows, including Marc Blitzstein's *Juno;* Leonard Bernstein's *On the Town* and *Candide; Once upon a Mattress; The Happiest Girl in the World;* and *Milk and Honey.*

Kay was born in Philadelphia, November 17, 1919. He entered the Curtis Institute of Music with a cello scholarship and claims that he is altogether self-taught in composition and orchestration. Unlike Bennett, Kay does not take himself seriously as a composer of original works, though he has a number of them to his credit, notably ballet scores. While these are generally based on folk music or on the music of older composers, the development and treatment which Kay brings to his borrowed material entitle these works to consideration as original compositions. In an article in *Musical America* of October, 1961, Michael Sonini quotes Kay on the use of traditional material: "Composing with a good foundation in folk elements is what makes a good composer. Not that he should quote his source elements literally. But he must assimilate them into his work—almost unconsciously. This is what Bach, Mozart, Beethoven and Haydn did, and in our own day, Bartók, Prokofieff, and Stravinsky. . . ."

Cakewalk, commissioned by the New York City Ballet, is based on music by Louis Moreau Gottschalk; while *Western Symphony* and *Stars and Stripes,* both composed for George Balanchine, are based respectively on cowboy songs and on John Philip Sousa marches. *The Concert,* written for Jerome Robbins's *Ballets USA,* is a free treatment of Chopin works. Among Kay's few nontheatrical compositions are *Saturday Night* (1955), for orchestra; *Water Music,* for band; and a highly effective orchestration of Gottschalk's *Grand Tarantella* for piano and orchestra, made for Eugene List, who found a piano score of the piece in the British Museum.

JEROME MOROSS (1913———), born in New York, April 1, 1913, is perhaps best known for his ballets, which include *Paul Bunyan* (1936), *Memorials* (1935), *American Pattern* (1936), *Frankie and Johnny* (1938), *Guns and Castanets* (1939), *Robin Hood* (1939), as well as the "ballet operas" *Susanna and the Elders* (1940), *Willie the Weeper* (1945), and *The Eccentricities of Davy Crockett* (1946), and the "ballet ballads" *Judgment* and *Red Riding Revisited* (1948). Moross's musical play *The Golden Apple,* with book and lyrics by John La Touche, had a run of 125 performances on and off Broadway, and Moross enjoyed a Guggenheim fellowship while composing the score.

His orchestral works include *Beguine* (1934); *A Tall Story* (1938), commissioned by the Columbia Broadcasting System; and a Symphony, introduced in Seattle in 1943. Moross's film work in Hollywood kept him so busy that no stage or concert works were heard from him for a number of years, but in 1963 the New York City Opera announced that it had commissioned an opera from him under a Ford Foundation grant. Entitled *Gentlemen Be Seated* and patterned after a minstrel show, the opera, with libretto and lyrics by Edward Eager, was given its première in 1963. Critics conceded that the work had good tunes, but found it closer to musical comedy than opera.

DANA SUESSE (1911———), at one time an arranger for the publishers T. B. Harms and Famous Music, has composed numerous popular songs; a *Concerto in Three Rhythms* for piano and orchestra

(1932), commissioned by Paul Whiteman; scores for two of Billy Rose's *Casa Mañana Revues*; a Concerto for two pianos and orchestra (1943); a Suite for orchestra entitled *Three Cities: Vienna, Warsaw, and Paris*; a Suite for harp and orchestra, originally entitled *Young Man with a Harp*; a *Concertino* for piano and orchestra; and a *Cocktail Suite* for piano. Miss Suesse was born in Kansas City, Missouri, December 3, 1911, and has composed since childhood. Largely self-taught, she studied briefly with Siloti and Rubin Goldmark. Though her earlier works are in the commercial jazz idiom, she later decided not to restrict herself to its limitations.

SAM RAPHLING (1910——), born in Fort Worth, Texas, March 19, 1910, trained in Chicago and in Germany as an exchange student. His compositions include *Cowboy Rhapsody* (1946), for violin and orchestra; *Abraham Lincoln Walks at Midnight* (1946), an orchestral piece inspired by Vachel Lindsay's poem; an *American Album* (1946), for two pianos; a *Dance Suite* (1950), for two trumpets; a Concerto for trombone, oboe, and strings (1953); an opera, *Tin Pan Alley* (1954); a Pastorale (1955), for oboe and strings; and Variations for two flutes, or for flute and clarinet unaccompanied; a Sonatina for two trombones or bassoons; *Sonata, Variations, and Introduction and Workout* for French horn unaccompanied; Duograms for two oboes; and a Trio for three oboes, all dated 1955. Raphling has also written a Suite for string orchestra.

Though a traditionalist, GARDNER READ (1913——) is also enough of an eclectic to ensure his music's sounding thoroughly contemporary. Born in Evanston, Illinois, January 2, 1913, Read studied composition with Howard Hanson and Bernard Rogers and conducting with Vladimir Bakalenikof. A Cromwell fellowship for 1938–39 enabled him to study with Pizetti in Rome and with Sibelius in Helsinki. After returning to the United States, he studied composition at the Berkshire Music Center with Aaron Copland, and from 1943 to 1945 he was head of the composition department at the Kansas City Conservatory of Music. He subsequently taught at the Cleveland Institute of Music and in 1948 became professor of composition and music theory at the School of Fine and Applied Arts at Boston University.

Read's orchestral music includes *The Lotus Eaters* (1932);

Sketches of the City (1933), a symphonic Suite after Carl Sandburg; *The Painted Desert* (1933); *Fantasy* for viola and orchestra (1935); Prelude and Toccata (1937); Suite for string orchestra (1937); the First Symphony (1937), winner of the New York Philharmonic $1,000 prize and, like Read's other three symphonies, composed at the MacDowell Colony in Peterborough, New Hampshire; *Passacaglia and Fugue* (1936); *American Circle* (1941); First Overture (1943); *Night Flight* (1941); the Second Symphony (1943), winner of the Paderewski Prize and introduced by the Boston Symphony; Concerto for cello and orchestra (1945); *Music for Piano and Strings* (1946); *Threnody* for flute and strings (1946); *Partita* for small orchestra (1946); *Pennsylvania Suite* (1947); *Dance of the Locomotives* (1948); *Quiet Music* (1948), for strings; the Third Symphony, composed in 1948 but not performed till 1962; *Sound Piece* for brass and percussion (1949); *Arioso Elegiaco* for strings (1951); *Chorale and Fughetta* for strings (1951); *The Temptation of St. Anthony, Dance Symphony after Flaubert* (1953); *Toccata Giocosa* (1954), a Louisville commission; *Vernal Equinox* (1955); the Fourth Symphony, composed in 1958; and the symphonic poem *Pan e Dafni*.

Read's chamber compositions include a Suite for string quartet (1936); a Piano Quintet (1945); *Sonata Brevis* (1948), for violin and piano; *Nine by Six* (1951), for wind sextet; a String Quartet (1957); and a *Sonoric Fantasia*, for celesta, harp, and harpsichord (1958). Works for voice and orchestra include *Four Nocturnes* (1935); *From a Lute of Jade* (1936); *Songs for a Rainy Day* (1942); and *The Golden Journey to Samarkand* (1939), scored for soloists, mixed chorus, and orchestra. Read's piano works include a *Driftwood Suite* (1942), a *Sonata da Chiesa* (1945), and numerous short pieces. There are in addition numerous organ works, solo songs, and choral pieces. Read has written the technical treatises *Thesaurus of Orchestra Devices* (1953); *Orchestral Style* (1961); and *Music Notation* (1962).

ROBERT WARD (1917——) believes that a reaction against the great musical revolution is in order, and he has had the courage to use harmonic combinations as simple as the common triad, to write in a diatonic language that recalls the nineteenth century, to shape a symphony in traditional sonata form, and to bring to his works reminders of American folk song and jazz, and sometimes even of Broadway. The result is a music that pleases audiences without sacrificing the respect of the critics.

When he was thirty years old, Ward expressed his credo in these words:

The composer of my generation is working during the aftermath of a great musical revolution, a period in which the apple cart of the past has been magnificently spilled by such men as Varèse, Bartók, Schoenberg, Stravinsky, and Ives. Slowly, however, since the first World War, those principles which are of perhaps eternal value have reasserted themselves, stripped of all the nonsense in which they were already buried by the pedants and unventuresome at the turn of the century. Hence, whether we like it or not, my generation will have the task of reworking materials which the revolution has given us, while at the same time reapplying the basic principles which have again been clarified.

Ward was born in Cleveland, Ohio, September 13, 1917. He studied composition with Howard Hanson, Bernard Rogers, and Frederick Jacobi and conducting with Albert Stoessel; he also worked with Aaron Copland at the Berkshire Music Center. In 1949, after serving as bandleader for the Seventh Infantry Division during the war, he received a Guggenheim fellowship; two years later he received another, and in 1955 he became president of the American Composers' Alliance. In 1956 he became managing director of the Galaxy Music Corporation.

Ward's orchestral compositions include an Andante and Scherzo for strings (1938); an *Ode* (1939); *Yankee Overture* (1940); the First Symphony (1941), in which the composer's interest in American folk song and jazz and his fondness for austere counterpoint, simple melodies, and rhythmic dance tunes are fully in evidence; an *Adagio and Allegro* (1943); the boisterous, extroverted *Jubilation Overture* (1946); *Concert Music* (1948); the Second Symphony (1948); *Night Music* (1949); the Third Symphony (1950), the unusual second movement of which introduces a solo piano as well as other featured instruments; *Jonathan and the Gingery Snare* (1950), composed for the Young People's Concerts of the New York Philharmonic-Symphony; *Euphony* (1954), commissioned by the Louisville Orchestra; and the frankly melodic Fourth Symphony (1959). Other compositions include a Sonata for violin and piano (1950) and *Night Fantasy* (1962), for band.

Ward has had two operas produced by the New York City Opera Company. *He Who Gets Slapped,* with libretto by Bernard Stambler adapted from Leonid Andreyev's play, was produced in 1956 by the Columbia University Workshop under the title *Pantaloon,* and in 1959 was produced at New York City Center under its original title. The vocal writing, as is typical in Ward's music, was melodious and natural. *The Crucible,* with libretto again by Mr. Stambler from Arthur Miller's play, was commissioned by the New York Opera under a Ford Foundation grant and was given its first performance in 1961. The following spring it was awarded a Pulitzer Prize and the New York Music Critics' Circle Award.

When a piano concerto by ALEXEI HAIEFF (1914——) was given its première performance in 1952 under the auspices of Columbia University and the Columbia Broadcasting Company, Henry Cowell commented in the *Musical Quarterly* of July, 1962, that "the effect of so many exclamations and explosions, kept up for so long that no possible resolution of the forces involved could give proportionate relief, is exhausting; one leaves the concert hall feeling somewhat bruised and battered, if respectful." Lest it be assumed that Haieff is an *enfant terrible,* his *Ballet in E* (1955), an orchestra suite in three movements, moved Jay S. Harrison to characterize the piece (New York *Herald Tribune,* January 13, 1958) as "simple, diatonic, charming, and in its non-aggressive way, rather expressive. . . . The *Ballet in E* is a chipper work, and, despite its larking quality, a substantial one. What a joy to hear music that is sturdily made . . ."

Haieff was born in Siberia, August 25, 1914, and received his early education at Harbin, Manchuria. In 1931 he came to the United States, where he studied with Frederick Jacobi and Rubin Goldmark at the Juilliard School of Music. In 1938 and 1939 he studied with Nadia Boulanger in Paris, and in 1946 and 1949 he was awarded Guggenheim fellowships. In 1947 and 1948 he was a fellow at the American Academy in Rome, and in 1952 and 1953 he was a composer-in-residence at the Academy. His works include a Sonatina for string quartet (1937); the First Symphony (1942); a Sonata for two pianos (1945); three ballets: *Divertimento* (1944), *The Princess Zondilda and Her Entourage* (1946), and *Beauty and the Beast* (1947); a Violin Concerto (1948); the Second Symphony (1958); and the Third Symphony (1961), of which Paul H. Lang commented in the *Herald Tribune* of November 17, 1962, "Mr. Haieff is an accomplished orchestrator and is well-equipped with compositional skills. But the slow movement immediately betrays the real defects of that too-conscious mild modernism that has sprouted all over the West as a result of Stravinsky's tremendous attraction."

WALTER MOURANT (1910——) was born in Chicago, Illinois, August 29, 1910. When a recording of three of his works—*Valley of the Moon, Sleepy Hollow*, and *Air and Scherzo*—was issued by Composers' Recordings, Inc., Wilfred Willers expressed his dissatisfaction in a review in the *Musical Quarterly* of January, 1963: "Mourant so debilitates us with chronic chromatics, synthetic sentiment, and syrupy strings that we grow panicky, fearing that we're glued to our cinema seats for bad and all. I don't know how these expertly concocted bonbons found their way into the CRI series, except as evidence of the variety of American production (rather than creativity); surely it would have been better to leave a recording to the cocktail lounge." Mourant's other works include *Five Inhibitions* (1937); *Three Dances* (1939); a Quintet for strings (1942); and a String Quartet (1957).

NORMAN CAZDEN (1914——), born in New York City, September 23, 1914, has composed a String Quartet; a Sonata for flute and piano; *Three Ballads from the Catskills*, for orchestra; a Suite for brass sextet; and a Concerto for ten instruments that was performed by the New Century Players in New York, February 10, 1958.

HOMER KELLER (1915——), born in Oxnard, California, has composed three Symphonies: the First, in A Minor, was awarded $500 in the 1939 Henry Hadley Foundation contest, and the Third was performed in Honolulu on December 9, 1956. Keller has also composed a *Serenade* for clarinet and strings (1939); a *Chamber Symphony* (1941); an Overture, 1947; a *Little Suite* for violin and orchestra; and a number of piano pieces.

ARTHUR BERGER (1912——), born in New York City, May 15, 1912, leaned toward atonalism in his early works but later developed a neoclassic style somewhat in the manner of Stravinsky. A modified hybrid idiom is apparent in the orchestral piece *Ideas of Order* (1953), in which a three-tone motif is treated in the manner of a twelve-tone row. Henry Cowell summarized Berger's method in a review in the July, 1943, *Musical Quarterly:* "His style is diatonic with some excursions into familiar modes, and with sparing use of a few chromatic tones that resolve into the nearest neighbor as advised by the harmony books, so that it is not allied to free chromaticism as practiced by the neo-Viennese school." Jay S. Harrison, writing in the New York *Herald Tribune* of April 12, 1953, found that *"Ideas of Order,* despite the complexity with which it is made, is as simple and charming as a Haydn symphony."

Berger studied under Walter Piston at Harvard and from 1937 to 1939 studied with Darius Milhaud and Nadia Boulanger in Paris. After returning to New York he taught at Mills College, at Brooklyn College, and at the Juilliard School of Music. From 1943 to 1946 he was music critic for the New York *Sun,* and from 1946 to 1953, when he became associate professor of music at Brandeis, he was on the music staff of the New York *Herald Tribune.*

Berger's orchestra works include a *Serenade Concertante* for violin, woodwind quartet, and small orchestra (1945); *Three Pieces* for string orchestra (1946); and *Polyphony for Orchestra* (1956), composed on a Louisville commission. Berger's chamber music includes *Chamber Music for Thirteen Players;* a Woodwind Quartet (1941); two Duos for violin and piano (1948 and 1950); a Duo for cello and piano (1951); a Duo for oboe and clarinet (1952); and a String Quartet, composed in 1958, which won the 1961–62 New York Music Critics' Circle Award. A *Chamber Concerto,* commissioned by the Fromm Foundation, was introduced in New York in 1962. Berger has also composed a *Fantasy* (1942), a *Capriccio* (1945), and a *Partita* (1947) for solo piano, as well as a number of songs.

ULYSSES SYMPSON KAY (1917——), born in Tucson, Arizona, January 7, 1917, received his bachelor's degree at the University of Arizona and studied with Bernard Rogers and Howard Hanson at the Eastman School in Rochester and with Paul Hindemith at Yale. He spent the years 1942 to 1945 in the navy, where he played piccolo and saxophone in bands, and the years 1949 to 1952 at the American

Academy in Rome as winner of the Prix de Rome and a Fulbright scholarship.

While studying at Eastman, Kay composed an Oboe Concerto (1940); *Five Mosaics* (1940), for chamber orchestra; and a ballet, *Danse Callinda* (1941). In 1944 his Overture *Of New Horizons* was played at the Lewisohn Stadium in New York. In 1947 Kay won a Broadcast Music, Inc., award for his Suite for Orchestra, composed in 1945, and the third annual George Gershwin Memorial Award for *A Short Overture*, written in 1946. A *Portrait Suite* for orchestra is dated 1948, and a Suite for Strings was first performed in 1949. Reviewing this work in the New York *Herald Tribune* of October 10, 1952, Virgil Thomson described it as "a warm and appealing piece . . . full of depths . . . spontaneous, gracious, and of evident sincerity."

Though the Suite for Strings is rather neo-Romantic in spirit, generally Kay's music is neoclassic. When his Sinfonia in E was introduced in Rochester in 1951, George H. Kimball wrote in the Rochester *Times-Union* of May 3, 1951, that the piece "demonstrated what can be done by an expert in combining the familiar diatonic harmonies with the modernist's chromatic dissonances to achieve lucidly expressive music." The year 1954 saw two important Kay premières: a Concerto for Orchestra was performed in New York, and a *Serenade* for orchestra in Louisville, Kentucky. Reviewing the latter composition in *High Fidelity Magazine*, September, 1955, Alfred Frankenstein wrote, "The composer is modest in the title of his Serenade. . . . The work is actually a symphony of remarkable eloquence, energy, and integrity; it is one of the very finest of the many works commissioned by the Louisville Orchestra."

Kay's *Music for Wind Choir* was first performed in Pittsburgh in 1961, and another work for wind instruments, *Forever Free: A Lincoln Chronicle*, was introduced by the United States Marine Band in 1962 during a hundredth anniversary program commemorating the Emancipation Proclamation. Kay's chamber music includes a Piano Sonata (1940); a Quintet for flute and strings (1947); a Piano Quintet (1959); a *Partita* for violin and piano (1950); and three String Quartets, the first two dated 1953 and 1958, respectively, and the Third first performed in 1962. Kay's vocal works include a cantata,

Song of Jeremiah (1945); *Three Pieces after Blake* (1955), for soprano and orchestra; and two one-act operas, *The Boor* (1955), after Chekhov, and *The Juggler of Our Lady,* first performed at Xavier University in New Orleans in 1962. Kay composed the score to the film *The Quiet One* (1956), from which he drew a concert suite.

CHARLES MILLS (1914——), born in Asheville, North Carolina, January 8, 1914, studied with Aaron Copland, Roy Harris, and Roger Sessions. In 1952 he held a Guggenheim fellowship. His works include three Symphonies; a Flute Concerto (1948); a Piano Concerto (1948); *Crazy Horse Symphony;* Prelude and Fugue for orchestra; Toccata for orchestra; *Prologue and Dithyramb* for strings; *The Dark Night,* for mixed chorus and orchestra; a *Chamber Concerto* for ten instruments; three String Quartets; a Piano Trio; a Sonata for flute and piano; five Sonatas for unaccompanied flute; two Cello Sonatas; a Violin Sonata; an Oboe Sonata; a *Concerto Sereno* for woodwind octet; two Piano Sonatas; and a Sonatina, composed in neoclassic style.

INGOLF DAHL (1912——) was born of Swedish parents in Hamburg, Germany, June 9, 1912. He was trained at the Conservatory of Cologne and at the University of Zurich and came to the United States in 1935. He was assistant professor at the University of Southern California in 1945, and from 1952 to 1955 he taught summers at the Berkshire Music Center. In 1952 and 1962 he was awarded Guggenheim fellowships.

An advanced polyphonist who employs free dissonant counterpoint, Dahl has composed an *Andante and Ariso* for woodwinds (1942); *Music for Brass Instruments* (1944); *Concerto a Tre* for clarinet, violin, and cello (1946); *Divertimento* for viola and piano (1948); a Concerto for saxophone and wind orchestra; *Symphony Concertante* for two clarinets and orchestra (1953); *Sonata Seria* for piano (1953); a symphonic legend, *The Tower of Saint Barbara* (1955), commissioned by the Louisville orchestra; and a Sinfonietta for concert band (1962).

Three composers from this decade have specialized in opera. Two of them, HUGO WEISGALL (1912——) and PEGGY GLANVILLE-HICKS (1912——) were born abroad and in the same year. Born in Ivancice, Czechoslovakia, October 13, 1912, Weisgall was brought to Baltimore,

Maryland, when he was eight years old. He had his early training at the Peabody Conservatory and studied composition with Roger Sessions in New York and with Rosario Scalero at the Curtis Institute in Philadelphia. His operas include *Night* (1932); *Lillith* (1934); *The Tenor* (1952), based on a play of Frank Wedekind's, *Der Kammersänger; The Stronger* (1952); *Six Characters in Search of an Author* (1959), based on the Pirandello play; a one-act opera, *Purgatory* (1962); and *Athaliah* (1963). Weisgall's nonoperatic works include the ballets *Quest* (1938), *One Thing Is Certain* (1939), and *Outpost* (1947); an Overture in F (1943); the cantata *A Garden Eastward* (1953); and *Soldier Songs* (1946), for baritone and orchestra.

Peggy Glanville-Hicks was born in Melbourne, Australia, December 29, 1912, and before coming to the United States in 1939 she studied with Ralph Vaughan Williams in London, with Egon Wellesz in Vienna, and with Nadia Boulanger in Paris. Her operas include *The Transposed Heads* (1954), *The Glittering Gate* (1959), and *Nausicaä* (1961). In 1963 she was commissioned by the Ford Foundation to compose *Sappho*, to a text by Lawrence Durrell. Her instrumental works include a Concertino da Camera (1945); a Harp Sonata (1950); a Sonata for Piano and Percussion (1951); *Letters from Morocco* (1953); an *Etruscan Concerto* (1956) for piano and orchestra; and a *Concerto Romantico* (1957) for viola and orchestra. In 1957 Miss Glanville-Hicks was awarded a Guggenheim fellowship.

IRVING MOPPER (1914——), born in Savannah, Georgia, December 1, 1914, studied composition with Julius Herford and Olivier Messiaen and orchestration with Frederick Prausnitz. He is perhaps most noted for his vocal music. *The Door* (1955), a one-act opera, won a competition sponsored by the National Federation of Music Clubs, and after its New York première was taken on a transcontinental tour under the sponsorship of Boosey and Hawkes and Willard Matthews. *The Creation,* a cantata for bass solo, chorus, and orchestra to a text by James Weldon Johnson, was first performed in New York in 1957. In 1961 the Orchestra Association of America presented the dramatic scene *Nero's Daughter,* based on a Stephen Phillips play. Ronald Eyer, writing in the New York *Herald Tribune* of February 23, 1961, commented that "Mr. Mopper is a young man who has the courage to write in a tonal idiom in a day when tonality is the music equivalent of leprosy, but he is here trying to achieve a Straussian effect similar in intensity to *Elektra* without Strauss's ability to translate literary and visual horror into aural horror. It does not quite come off, perhaps because he tries to sustain it too long, but it is a good try."

Mopper's works include another opera, *George;* a *Passacaglia and Fugue* for piano; *Patterns,* for soprano and orchestra; a Trio for strings; a Concerto for clarinet and orchestra; three Sonatinas for piano; *The Wondrous Works of God,* a cantata for soloists, chorus, and orchestra; chamber works; songs; short choral pieces; and piano music.

GEORGE ROCHBERG (1918——) is distinctly a twelve-tone composer, but he has developed a serial system that differs considerably from orthodox dodecaphony. Born in Patterson, New Jersey, July 15, 1918, he studied in New York with George Szell and Leopold Mannes and at the Curtis Institute in Philadelphia with Rosario Scalero and Gian-Carlo Menotti. A Fulbright fellowship enabled him to spend the year 1950–51 at the American Academy in Rome, and while in Italy he gained the friendship of Luigi Dallapiccola, who proved a wise mentor to him. Rochberg's subsequent teaching activities have included an instructorship at the Curtis Institute and the chairmanship of the music department of the University of Pennsylvania. In 1955 he became music director of the Theodore Presser Company, publishers of *The Hexachord and Its Relation to the Twelve-Tone Row* (1955), a treatise setting forth his compositional methods. Rochberg's Second Symphony (1959) exemplifies his hexachordal procedure: by breaking his row into halves, or hexachords, Rochberg is able to create motifs which he uses in such a freely melodic way as to create a genuinely lyric impression.

Others of Rochberg's compositions include a *Capriccio* for two pianos (1949); *Cantio Sacra* for chamber orchestra (1953); *Night Music* (1953), a symphonic poem that won the George Gershwin Memorial Award; a *Fantasia* for violin and piano (1955); a *Waltz Serenade* for orchestra (1958); *Serenata d'Estate* (1958); the First Symphony (1958); Sonata for clarinet and piano (1958), commissioned by the Koussevitzky Foundation; *Time Span* (1960), for orchestra, commissioned by the Junior Division of the Women's Association of the St. Louis Symphony Society, funds for the purpose being raised by an auction sale of art by the city's painters and sculptors. Reviewing the work in the *Musical Quarterly* of January, 1961, Alexander Ringer commented that "Rochberg's outlook is essentially monophonic declamatory," and that the almost Webernian *Time Span* "adds to the contemporary repertoire of shorter orchestral compositions a little masterpiece, carefully planned, deeply felt, and brilliantly executed." Rochberg has also composed two String Quartets, the Second of which features a soprano solo; *David the Psalmist*, a lyrical work for tenor and orchestra; two Piano Sonatas; smaller piano pieces; and songs. In 1962 Rochberg was awarded a $2,000 grant by the National Institute of Arts and Letters.

BEN WEBER (1916——) is a largely self-taught atonalist who has independently developed a serial technique characterized by such traditional devices as recurring themes, recapitulation, and canon. Born in St. Louis, Missouri, July 23, 1916, he has won two Guggenheim fellowships, an award and citation from the National Institute of Arts and Letters, and two awards from the Fromm Foundation. Many of Weber's works are scored for chamber combinations: these include a *Symphony in Four Movements on Poems of William Blake* (1952), for baritone and chamber orchestra; two Sonatas for violin and piano; Variations for violin, clarinet, cello, and piano; a *Concertino* for violin, clarinet, and cello; a *Sonata da Camera* for violin and piano; a Concerto for piano, cello, and woodwind quartet; two String Quartets; *Colloquy* for brass septet; a *Concertino* for flute, oboe, and cello that Jay S. Harrison, writing in the New York *Herald Tribune* of January 27, 1954, called "a hale and jolly four-movement piece . . . neither agonizingly atonal nor harmonically complex. . . . It has gumption and it has charm, and it makes a lovely sound." When Weber's *Chamber Fantasia* was played in New York in 1959, William Flanagan wrote in the *Herald Tribune* of November 20 that "Mr. Weber has never been known to compose a piece either dull or uninspired." *Three Songs* for soprano and string quartet were premièred in 1962.

In addition to a *Serenade for Strings*, Weber's works for small orchestra include *Two Pieces for String Orchestra* (1952), composed not in Weber's usual twelve-tone idiom but based on a single line described as "motivic in structure"; the work is one of Weber's most expressive. He has also composed a *Rhapsodie Concertante* for viola and small orchestra. Weber's comparatively few works for large orchestra include a Concerto for violin and orchestra (1954), a *Prelude and Passacaglia* (1955), and a Piano Concerto (*In Memoriam Dmitri Mitropoulos;* 1960), composed for William Masselos under a Ford Foundation grant.

JULIA SMITH (1911———), born in Denton, Texas, January 25, 1911, studied in Dallas and at the Institute of Musical Art in New York. In 1933 she was awarded a fellowship in composition at the Juilliard Graduate School, where she studied with Rubin Goldmark and Frederick Jacobi. *Cynthia Parker*, the opera which first brought her into prominence, was produced in her home town in 1939. Her other operas include *The Stranger of Manzano, The Gooseherd and the Goblin,* and *Cockcrow* (1964).

Her orchestral works include *American Dance Suite; Episodic Suite;* Concerto in E Minor for piano and orchestra; and a *Folkways Symphony* based on American folk tunes and cowboy songs. She has also written for piano a *Characteristic Suite* in twelve-tone technique. Virgil Thomson once wrote of Miss Smith (New York *Herald Tribune,* May 15, 1950), "Her music is jolly, and even in twelve-tone syntax, easy to take." Miss Smith has been awarded a citation of merit from the Texas Club of New York for outstanding attainment in the field of creative music.

ELLIS KOHS (1916———), born in Chicago, Illinois, May 12, 1916, studied with Carl Bricken at the University of Chicago, with Bernard Wagenaar at the Juilliard School of Music, and with Walter Piston at Harvard. He has taught at Wesleyan University, at the Conservatory of Kansas City, and at the University of Southern California, where he was appointed chairman of the theory department.

When Kohs's First Symphony, commissioned by Pierre Monteux for the San Francisco Symphony, was introduced in 1950, Alfred Frankenstein described it in the San Francisco *Chronicle* as "remarkable for its high-spirited humor, its melodiousness, and its lithe, sparkling texture, both harmonic and orchestral." Kohs's Second Symphony, commissioned by the Fromm Foundation and scored for chorus and orchestra, was introduced by Robert Shaw in 1957. Nicolas

Slonimsky has explained [3] that Kohs "attempts to unify a given work by emphasizing the pervading melodic and rhythmic line, in accordance with [Heinrich] Schenker's theories. . . . He pursues the aim of classical clarity. . . . In some works he applies a modified dodecaphonic technique [and] employs asymmetrical rhythms in the manner of Béla Bartók."

Other of Kohs's orchestral works include a Concerto for Orchestra (1941); *Passacaglia* for organ and strings (1946); *Legend* for oboe and string orchestra (1947); a Concerto for cello and orchestra (1947); incidental music for *Macbeth* (1947); a *Chamber Concerto* for viola and string nonet (1949); *Lord of the Ascendant* (1955), for chorus, dancers, and orchestra; and *Four Orchestral Songs* (1959), for voice and orchestra.

Kohs's chamber works include a String Quartet (1942); *Night Watch* (1943), for flute, horn, and kettledrums; Sonatina for bassoon and piano (1944); Sonatina for violin and piano (1948); *Short Concert* for string quartet (1948); and a Clarinet Sonata (1951). He has also written many choral pieces, a set of Variations, a Toccata (1948), and numerous shorter works for the piano. In 1955 he completed a four-volume set of *Syllabi in Music Theory* for use in his classes at the University of Southern California.

IRVING FINE (1914–1962), born in Boston, December 3, 1914, studied with Walter Piston and Nadia Boulanger and, not surprisingly, showed traces of the influence of Stravinsky and Hindemith in his early works; he later wrote in a highly rhythmic, contrapuntal manner and ultimately evolved a style which Arthur Berger, writing in the New York *Herald Tribune* of February 18, 1953, termed "amiable and melodious." In several late works he experimented with a serial method quite close to orthodox twelve-tone composition.

In 1946 Fine served on the faculty of the Berkshire Music Center at Tanglewood, Massachusetts, and from 1947 to 1950 he was assistant professor of music at Harvard; in 1950 he became composer-in-residence at Brandeis University, and at the time of his death he was chairman of the Brandeis School of Creative Arts.

Fine's compositions include incidental music to *Alice in Wonderland* (1942); a cantata, *The Choral New Yorker* (composed in 1944

---

[3] *Baker's Biographical Dictionary of Musicians*, New York, 1958.

to a text consisting of short verses from *The New Yorker magazine*); a Violin Sonata (1946); a *Toccata Concertante* (1948), for orchestra; a *Partita* for wind quintet (1948); *The Hour Glass* (1949), a choral cycle; a String Quartet (1950), marking Fine's entry into the field of atonality; *Serious Song* (1956), scored for strings, a grave, diatonic work; and a Symphony (1962), commissioned by the Boston Symphony and the American Music Center under a Ford Foundation grant.

In contrast to Fine, who, like Copland and Barber, came to grips with atonality in his later works, GORDON BINKERD (1916——) started his career as an atonalist and then thought better of it. In the *American Composers' Alliance Bulletin* of September, 1962, Dorothy Veinus Hagen wrote, "Binkerd's Cello Sonata (1952) is completely a twelve-tone piece. The first two movements of the First Symphony (1955) . . . employ rows. . . . From the beginning, [Binkerd] says, the technique worked for him like a charm. But between the second and third movements of his first symphony he experienced an intense revulsion away from the system. He gave it up and has returned to it only briefly, and in a sense casually."

Born in Lynch, Nebraska, May 22, 1916, Binkerd studied composition with Bernard Rogers and Walter Piston and became a member of the music faculty of the University of Illinois. His first two Symphonies, commissioned for the University of Illinois Festivals of Contemporary Arts, were first performed in 1955 and 1957, respectively. The slow movement of the Second includes a two-note motto taken from a bird song heard in the woods near the MacDowell Colony in Peterborough, where Binkerd began the work. *Studenten-schmauss*, for organ solo and double brass choir, was premièred at the University of Illinois in 1962. The String Quartet No. 2, a freely and perhaps complexly tonal piece, was performed the same year at Kansas State College, during the eleventh Annual Festival of University Composers Exchange.

JOHN CAGE (1912——), born in Los Angeles, California, September 5, 1912, studied composition with Adolph Weiss, Henry Cowell, Arnold Schoenberg, and Edgar Varèse. A seeker of new sounds not so much through novel systems of tone combination as through manipulation of instrumental resources, Cage has experimented in three broad areas. He has first of all made use of what he calls the "prepared piano." Preparation of the instrument calls for small pieces of leather and metal and rubber bands which, placed between the strings, cause them to produce the rather tinkling sounds that resemble Oriental or primitive instruments. Secondly, Cage has relied upon electronic instruments, such as radios and tape recorders. And thirdly, he has attempted to introduce an element of chance into music by casting Chinese dice or coins, the *I-Ching*, to determine the pitch, note values, and instrumentation of a composition.

The prepared piano technique was demonstrated in a piece entitled *34'46,766*, played at a Composer's Showcase concert in New York in 1961. Alan Rich described the piece in *Musical America* in June of that year:

Two pianists at prepared pianos hit the keys, the strings and the case, blew whistles and rang bells. A violinist extracted notes, sweet and sour, from an instrument under his chin, took occasional swipes with his bow at a second instrument on a stool in front of him, and kicked a wastebasket. This was music largely written out and therefore planned, but indeterminate in not prescribing the method of preparing pianos or giving definite instructions for use of noisemakers.

Cage's *Imaginary Landscape* (1951) employed radios. Henry Cowell described the first performance in the *Musical Quarterly* of January, 1952: "On the stage were twelve radios, with two players at each, and the composer-conductor—twenty-five people in all. The score calls for one performer to manipulate the dial that selects the various stations desired by the composer to be heard in the course of the work, and another performer for the dial that regulates the dynamics. The composer's directions for tuning the various stations in and out use notes and rests; the wavelength for each station is indicated in kilocycles." Reviewing the performance in the New York *Herald Tribune* of May 11, 1951, Arthur Berger wrote, "It would be nice to report a sensation or a side-splitting joke. If anything was amusing it was merely the sight of Mr. Cage earnestly conducting an ensemble of some of our finest musicians in a series of embarrassing silences, and, at best, the shreds of broadcasts you get at home when you turn the dial rapidly."

Cage claims that the purpose of composing music by casting dice is to eliminate the subjective element in composition. In the article already quoted, Cowell points out that Mozart is said to have composed a set of contra-dances in which dice are to be thrown to determine the order of the measures, though, unlike many of Cage's, the measures are composed and set down in full.

Cage has also explored the possibilities of silence in his compositions. In 1954 he introduced his perhaps most widely-known piece, *4 Minutes and 33 Seconds,* in which a pianist sits at the piano for this length of time without playing. Others of Cage's many compositions include a Concerto for piano and orchestra, a work employing such devices as free choice of notes, indeterminacy, and improvisation; *Forever and Sunsmell,* for voice and percussion; and *Aria with Fontana Mix,* which Richard Franko Goldman, in the *Musical Quarterly* of July, 1962, labeled "truly intolerable, a scrap heap of taped sounds, with gurgles and grunts. . . . At one time, it might have been said that Cage had at least the merit of having restored a kind of gaiety to contemporary music (a quality it sadly lacks), but *Fontana Mix* is drably depressing."

In the article already referred to, Alan Rich stated that

the time has passed when Mr. Cage's curious efforts on behalf of the Muse can be ridiculed or dismissed. His influence on a wide generation of important young avant-garde composers is enormous; his works and philosophy seem, if anything, better known and respected abroad than here. Today he obtains grants and serious academic posts, and concerts such as this [Composer's Showcase concert dedicated to Cage's works] draw crowds in New York and Europe. He is, in short, to be reckoned with. . . . In the very worst sense, the music of Cage is, for these ears, excruciatingly uneventful. This extremely basic consideration cannot be nullified by any musical defense, however belligerent.

Mr. Rich quotes Cage as saying, "My music is a process, not an object. I am interested in letting sounds be themselves instead of reflecting my ideas and feelings." To which Mr. Rich replies, "Very well, Mr. Cage, but I fear very deeply that you have talked yourself right out of music."

Henry Cowell, generally sympathetic to new ideas and to independence of musical thought, concluded his *Musical Quarterly* review of *Imaginary Landscape* with words which might be applied to all of the Cage *oeuvres:* "If one must decide what genuine value is, or is not, to be found in this music, a last throw of the coins of I-Ching will have to determine that for us, too." When Cage's *Atlas Eclipticalis,* a score which, according to the composer, "may be performed in whole or in part, for any duration, by any ensemble," was performed by the New York Philharmonic in 1964, many listeners made up their minds without consulting *I-Ching.* Harold C. Schonberg described the performance in the New York *Times* of February 7, 1964, in these words:

[Cage] used an orchestra of more than eighty players, and each instrument was equipped with a contact microphone that led into a little preamplifier on the floor. The preamplifier led into an electronic mixer, which fed into six amplifiers, which went to six loudspeakers scattered through the hall. The piano was amplified, and on the podium was, instead of a conductor, a mechanical affair with a spoke that slowly revolved. When eight minutes were up, the piece was over. . . . One might think that Mr. Cage's piece . . . would have caused some kind of demonstration. What happened was that during the progress of the work, people walked out. When it was over, there was a more general exodus. There were a few lusty boos, a few counter-cheers. But on the whole the music fell flat.

MILTON BABBITT (1916———), born in Philadelphia, Pennsylvania, May 10, 1916, studied at Princeton University and in 1938 became an instructor there, teaching mathematics as well as music. After 1948 Babbitt extended the dodecaphonic organization of his music and not only gave each note of his twelve-note themes to one of twelve different instruments, but organized his rhythm in terms of twelve basic rhythmic values. Critics have viewed Babbitt's work with mixed opinions. Following a performance of Babbitt's *Composition for Viola and Piano,* Harold Schonberg wrote in the New York *Times* of February 1, 1953, that there were "long stretches where the music seems to be pushed along by its theories rather than by any motor source." Arthur Berger wrote in the New York *Herald Tribune,* "With enormous erudition and skill [Babbitt] has extended Webern's contribution. There is quiet sensitivity in his textures, and no sound or pattern ever abuses the ears."

Commenting on Babbitt's Woodwind Quintet, critic James Lyon

stated that the work was as absorbing "as a new mathematical formulation, and just about as communicative." Babbitt's *Composition for Four Instruments,* performed in 1959, eleven years after it was written, puzzled the critics. Writing in the *Musical Quarterly* of January, 1960, Richard Franko Goldman stated that "one would need a careful study to pretend to understand more than the general principles involved in [the piece's] construction," and went on to raise the point whether "such study would be worthwhile," and whether "increased familiarity with the composition would be rewarding."

Babbitt has also experimented with electronic music. Reviewing his *Composition for Synthesizer,* written for the RCA Mark 11 Synthesizer, Alan Rich wrote in the *Musical America* of June, 1961: "From the instrument Mr. Babbitt has drawn a fascinating spectrum of sound, some of it sounding amazingly like conventional music-making apparatus, but much of it a logical extension of these sounds into new realms. . . . This is a difficult fugal ostinato work in Babbitt's well-known post-Webern language, for an instrument on which all of its performance problems can be solved." Babbitt has also written *Vision and Prayer,* a setting of a Dylan Thomas text for human voice and a "synthesized" accompaniment.

HENRY BRANT (1913——), born September 15, 1913, in Montreal, Canada, has been an experimentalist throughout his career. He studied at McGill University's School of Music, at the Juilliard School, and with Wallingford Riegger, Aaron Copland, and George Antheil, whom he acknowledges as his principal teacher. He has worked as an arranger for Benny Goodman and André Kostelanetz, and has composed and arranged for radio and for films.

In the New York *Herald Tribune* of February 11, 1958, Jay S. Harrison vividly described a performance of Brant's *Mythical Beasts,* one of the composer's experiments in "directional sound." Mr. Harrison wrote:

There was a bassoonist in one aisle, a cellist in another. At the rear of the auditorium was a trombone player and in a corner a tympanist and a row of tubular chimes. There was a mezzo in the balcony and a double bass and fiddle on stage. The conductor raised his hand, dropped it slowly, and the whole bewildered pack of musicians began to play one after another in a fashion describable only as desultory. . . . The result was a disaster.

Brant has composed, in addition to chamber works, two Symphonies (1931 and 1937); *Gallopjig Colloquy*, a ballad for orchestra (1934); a Concerto for saxophone (1940); *Music for an Imaginary Ballet* (1947); *Spanish Underground* (1947), a cantata; *Millennium No. 2*, for thirty brass instruments and four percussion; *Variations in Oblique Harmony*, to be played "by any four instruments"; *Miss O'Grady*, an opera; *Entente Cordiale*, a satire with music; a *Lyric Cycle*, for soprano, three violas, and piano; *Crying Jag*, for military band; a Symphony in B-flat Minor; a Quintet for oboe and strings; a Concerto for eleven flutes; a Concerto for double bass and orchestra; a *Sonata Sacra* for hardware and piano; a Violin Concerto; a Clarinet Concerto; a *Whoopee Overture*; and a ballet, *The Great American Goof*. Like various other composers, notably Scriabin, Brant has experimented with colored lights in association with music. His *Concerto with Lights*, for violin and ten instruments "with projected lights" was introduced in 1961.

When Brant's *Voyage Four*, "a spatial concert piece for eighty-three instrumentalists and one singer led by three conductors," was introduced in 1964, Howard Klein wrote in the New York *Times* of January 16 that, though "there were occasional snickers at the groaning double basses in the rear under the balcony and at the rattling banjo and harpsichord on stage, the work contained moments of extraordinary beauty. Not only did the shimmering conglomerations of sound ravish the ear with beauty of sensuous orchestral coloring, but some of the melodic fragments that emerged from the rich sounds also had the warmth and subjective power of romantic themes."

Critics have used such words as lovely, delicate, simple, and unafraid to describe the music of LOU HARRISON (1917——), a man whose music has ranged from the relatively conservative to the polytonal and atonal. Born in Portland, Oregon, May 14, 1917, Harrison studied with Henry Cowell and Arnold Schoenberg and has taught at Mills College, at the University of California in Los Angeles, and at the Black Mountain College in North Carolina. He has worked on the music staff of the New York *Herald Tribune* and has received grants from the American Academy of Arts and Letters, as well as Guggenheim fellowships in 1952 and 1954. In 1955 Harrison was given the Fromm Foundation Award for his Mass; scored for mixed choir, trumpet, harp, and strings, the work derives from the unique variety of plainsong sung by Indians in the California missions.

Indicative of Harrison's fascination with esoteric sounds, an interest which he shares with his colleague John Cage, are such works as *Canticle No. 3*, scored for percussion ensemble consisting of ocarina, six muted iron pipes, three wood blocks, five muted brake drums, three suspended brake drums, five dragon's mouths, six water buffalo bells, sistrums, five tongued teponaztli, grand tam-tam, five muted cowbells, snare drum, bass drum, and five tom-toms; the Suite for solo violin, solo piano, and a small orchestra that includes a tack-piano (1951); a *Recording Piece* (1955), for concert boobams, talking drums, and percussion; *Simfony in Free Style* (1956), for flutes, viols, bells, tack-piano, harps, drums, maracas, and trombone; and the Concerto (1959), for violin with percussion orchestra—the percussion including a double bass struck like a drum, flower pots, and several washtubs. It should be noted that, unlike the similarly experimental music of many of his colleagues, Harrison's rarely sounds freakish or silly.

Like another colleague, Harry Partch, Harrison has also been interested in dividing the scale into tones smaller than the semitone and in retuning instruments to play in pure intonation according to various original scale patterns. The *Strict Songs* (1956), written on a Louisville commission, are scored for eight baritones accompanied by two trombones, piano, harp, percussion, and strings; the piano is specially tuned, and the other instruments take their intonation from it. Harrison has also tried his hand at instrument-making and has built a Phrygian aulos as well as pioneering new principles in clavichord construction. He has developed a process for direct composition for phonograph and has elaborated theories of interval and rhythm controls.

Harrison has also composed an *Alleluia* for orchestra; a Suite, subtitled *Seven Pastorales;* a Concerto for flute and percussion ostinati; a *Symphony in G;* a *Concerto in Slendro for Violin,* the orchestra of which includes a celesta and garbage pails; a *Nokturno* for violins, violas, and two solo cellos; *Solstice,* for chamber orchestra; *Song of Quextecoatl,* for percussion orchestra; and *Double Music,* on which he collaborated with John Cage. His works in more traditional media include three Suites for strings; a *Motet for the Day of Ascension;* an opera, *Rapunzel,* to a text by William Morris; incidental music to plays; and many ballets, including *The Only Jealousy of Emer.*

ARTHUR COHN (1910——), born in Philadelphia, Pennsylvania, November 6, 1910, received a fellowship in composition from the Juilliard School of Music in 1933 and studied there with Rubin Goldmark. His orchestral works include *Four Symphonic Documents; Variations on a Theme by Paganini,* for cello and orchestra; *Five Nature Studies* (1932); *Retrospections* (1935), for strings; a Suite for viola and orchestra (1937); Four Preludes for string orchestra (1937); Quintuple Concerto (1940); Variations for clarinet, saxophone, and string orchestra (1945); *Quotations in Percussion* (1959); and three Symphonies. His chamber works include *Music for Ancient Instruments* (1938); *Music for Bassoon,* unaccompanied (1947); four String Quartets; and a Violin Sonata.

WAYNE BARLOW (1912——), born in Elyria, Ohio, September 6, 1912, studied with Arnold Schoenberg and at the Eastman School, where in 1937 he became a faculty member. His compositions include *Three Moods for Dancing* (1940), for orchestra; *De Profundis,* a poem for orchestra; *Lyrical Piece* for clarinet and strings (1945); *Nocturne for Eighteen Instruments* (1946); Mass in G (1951); Sinfonia in C; *Lento for Orchestra* (1958); a String Quartet; a Sonata for violin and piano; a Piano Quintet (1951); a choral ballet, *False Faces;* and a cantata, *Zion in Exile.* Barlow's most widely played work, *The Winter's Past,* for oboe and strings, is based on an Appalachian mountain tune. It was first heard in Rochester in 1938.

HERBERT OWEN REED (1910——), born in Odessa, Missouri, June 17, 1910, was educated at the Universities of Missouri, Louisiana State, and Rochester, and was appointed instructor at Michigan State College in 1939, subsequently becoming chairman of the theory and composition department of that institution. His teachers included Howard Hanson, Bernard Rogers, Bohuslav Martinu, and Roy Harris. In 1948 he was awarded a Guggenheim fellowship which enabled him to spend six months in Mexico composing and studying native folk music.

Reed's works include the ballet-pantomime *The Masque of the*

Red Death (1936); a symphonic poem, *Evangeline* (1938); Symphony No. 1 (1939); an Overture for orchestra (1941); a *Symphonic Dance* for orchestra (1942); an Overture for band (1947); *Missouri Shindig* (1951), for band; a folk symphony for band, *La Fiesta Mexicana* (1954); a folk opera, *Michigan Dream* (1955, revised 1959); *Renascence* (1959), for band; and an Overture for Strings (1961). Reed's chamber music includes a Piano Sonata (1934); a String Quartet (1937); a Scherzo for clarinet and piano (1947); and a *Symphonic Dance* for piano and woodwind quintet. There are also several vocal works and occasional piano pieces.

ROBERT PALMER (1915———), born in Syracuse, New York, June 2, 1915, studied with Howard Hanson and Bernard Rogers at the Eastman School and with Roy Harris and Aaron Copland. From 1940 to 1943 he taught at the University of Kansas, and in 1943 he became an instructor at Cornell University. His works, written mostly for chamber combinations, include the First String Quartet (1940); a *Concerto for Five Instruments,* composed 1943; the Second String Quartet (1946), commissioned by the Koussevitzky Foundation; a Quartet for piano and strings (1949); a Quintet for piano and strings (1951), commissioned by Elizabeth S. Coolidge; a Sonata for viola and piano (1951); a Quintet for winds (1952); a Quintet for piano, clarinet, and strings; and the Third String Quartet (1955), commissioned by the Stanley Quartet of the University of Michigan.

Palmer's comparatively few orchestral works include a *Poem* for violin and chamber orchestra (1938); a *Concerto for Small Orchestra* (1941), commissioned by the Columbia Broadcasting System and the League of Composers; a Concerto for Orchestra, dated 1943; *K 19, Symphonic Elegy for Thomas Wolfe* (1945); *Variations, Chorale, and Fugue* (1954), commissioned by Dmitri Mitropoulos; the First Symphony (1954), written while the composer was enjoying a Guggenheim fellowship; and *Memorial Music* (1958), for orchestra.

Reviewing a recording of the last-mentioned work for the *Musical Quarterly* of January, 1963, Wilfred Mellers wrote:

Robert Palmer's music was always remarkable for a slightly grim integrity, but its pioneering modal melody, its rugged, Harris-like evolutionary polyphony, and its preoccupation with rhythmic contrariety seemed to have reached a technical and emotional impasse. In *Memorial Music* there is a hint that Palmer is finding a way out . . . through a bolder exploration of Ivesian heterophony and polyrhythm, combined with a formal discipline more suggestive of Copland than of Harris.

Palmer's piano works include two Sonatas (1940 and 1942) for solo piano; a Sonata (1944) for two pianos; and a Sonata (1953) for piano four hands. Palmer's major choral works are *Abraham Lincoln Walks at Midnight* (1948), for chorus and orchestra, and *The Trojan Women* (1955), for women's chorus, winds, and percussion.

KENT KENNAN (1913——), born in Milwaukee, Wisconsin, April 18, 1913, attended the University of Michigan, received his master's degree from the Eastman School in 1936 and, receiving the Prix de Rome, was a fellow of the American Academy in Rome until 1939, when he returned to the United States to teach at Kent State University in Ohio. In 1957 he took a teaching position at the University of Texas. A pupil of Ildebrando Pizetti, Kennan has composed *Night Soliloquy* (1937), for flute and strings, his best-known work; a *Promenade* for orchestra (1938); a Symphony (1939); an Andante for oboe and small orchestra (1947); and a *Concertino* for piano and orchestra. He is the author of two textbooks which are standard works in their field, *Technique of Orchestration* (1952) and *Counterpoint* (1959).

GRANT FLETCHER (1913——), born in Hartsburg, Illinois, October 25, 1913, studied at the Eastman School with Bernard Rogers and Howard Hanson and with Herbert Elwell in Cleveland. Three of his major orchestral works were first performed in Rochester: *Song for Warriors* (1945); *Panels from a Theater Wall* (1949); and the First Symphony (1951). His *American Overture* was premièred in Duluth in 1948. Others of his works include *The Crisis* (1945), for chorus and orchestra; five String Quartets; choral works; piano pieces; and songs.

To the list of Boulanger pupils may be added ROGER GOEB (1914——) and CECIL EFFINGER (1914——). Born in Cherokee, Iowa, October 9, 1914, Roger Goeb learned during his childhood and youth to play a variety of instruments—trumpet, horn, viola, violin, and all of the woodwinds. He attended the University of Wisconsin, and for two years played in jazz bands to earn enough money to study with Nadia Boulanger in Paris. In 1939 he returned to New York and worked with Otto Luening, earning an M.A. degree at New York University and, in 1945, a Ph.D. at the State University of Iowa. In 1950 he was awarded a Guggenheim fellowship. He subsequently taught at the University of Oklahoma, the State University of Iowa, Bard College, the Juilliard School of Music, Columbia University, and Stanford University.

Goeb's First and Second Symphonies are dated 1942–45 and 1946 respectively. The Third Symphony was presented in 1952 during a Festival of Music sponsored jointly by Columbia University and the Columbia Broadcasting Company, Leopold Stokowski conducting. Reviewing the piece for the *Musical Quarterly* of July, 1962, Henry Cowell wrote: "The work is a dynamo of activity; it is entirely free of sentimentality and pretentiousness. It has what is the most valuable expressive quality in any art; it betrays the personality of its maker directly and quite unintentionally. One hears in the music the speech of an honest, serious and talented person whose only vital lack— surely a temporary one—is that of inner repose." Goeb's Fourth Symphony was introduced in 1956 by the Pittsburgh Symphony under William Steinberg.

Others of Goeb's orchestra works include *Five American Dances* for strings (1952); a Violin Concerto (1954); *Concertinos* for orchestra, the Second (1956) commissioned by the Louisville Orchestra; a *Fantasy* for two pianos and orchestra (1958); and *Iowa Concerto* (1960), for orchestra. Goeb's chamber music includes four *Concertantes* for various combinations of winds and strings; two Wind Quintets; a Sonata for viola solo (1942); three String Quartets; a String Trio (1945); a Suite for four clarinets (1946); a Suite for woodwind trio (1946); *Prairie Songs* for woodwind quintet (1947); a Quintet for trombone and string quartet (1950); and two Clarinet Quartets.

Cecil Effinger, born in Colorado Springs, Colorado, July 22, 1914, studied composition with Nadia Boulanger and Bernard Wagenaar and from 1935 to 1941 was oboist with the Detroit Symphony Orchestra. During the Second World War he was a U.S. Army bandmaster in France, and later became head of the theory department of the University of Colorado. His works include two Symphonies

(1947 and 1949); a *Western Overture* (1942); *Variations on a Cowboy Tune* (1946); *Tennessee Variations* (1946); a *Choral Symphony* (1952); *Tone Poem on the Square Dance* (1955); a Concerto for piano and chamber orchestra (1948); four String Quartets; a Viola Sonata (1944); a *Pastoral* for oboe and strings (1948); a *Chorale and Fugue* for band (1949); and numerous choral works, including a *Christmas Cantata* (1953). His *Little Symphony*, first performed in St. Louis in 1945, was given the annual music award of the Walter W. Naumburg Foundation fourteen years later.

ALAN SHULMAN (1915———), born in Baltimore, Maryland, June 14, 1915, studied at the Peabody Conservatory and at the Juilliard School of Music, and played cello with the NBC Symphony and with the Stuyvesant Quartet. His works include *Theme and Variations* for viola and orchestra (1941); *Pastorale and Dance* for violin and orchestra (1944); *Rendezvous* for clarinet and strings (1946); a Cello Concerto (1948); *Waltzes for Orchestra* (1949); *Threnody* for string quartet (1950); a *Laurentian Overture* for orchestra (1952); *Popocatepetl* (1952), a symphonic picture; *Suite Miniature* for eight cellos (1956); and *Top Brass*, a piece for brass instruments that bears the subtitle *Six Minutes for Twelve* (1958).

PAUL BOWLES (1910———), born in New York, December 30, 1910, studied composition with Aaron Copland and Virgil Thomson, but since the publication of his first novel in 1949 has become better known as a writer than as a composer. For several years he was a music critic for the New York *Herald Tribune;* in 1941 he was awarded a Guggenheim fellowship and in 1959 a Rockefeller grant. His interest in exotic music has taken him to Spain, North Africa, the Antilles, and South and Central America.

Bowles's score *Yankee Clipper* was played by the Philadelphia Orchestra in 1937, and a year later the work was presented in its full form by the Ballet Caravan in New York. Others of Bowles's ballets are *The Ballroom Guide* (1937), *Sentimental Colloquy* (1944), and *Pastorales* (1947). He has composed two operas, *Denmark Vesey* (1937) and *The Wind Remains* (1943), as well as incidental music for numerous plays. His orchestral works include a Suite (1933) and *Danza Mexicana* (1941). His chamber works include *Anabase* (1932), for voice, oboe, and piano; a Trio (1936); *Melodia* for nine instruments (1937); *Prelude and Dance* for wind instruments, percussion, double bass, and piano (1947); and *Picnic Cantata* (1954), for four women's voices, two pianos, and percussion.

EDMUND HAINES (1914——), another of Copland's pupils, was born in Ottumwa, Iowa, December 15, 1914, and was educated at Kansas City and at the University of Rochester. Besides Copland, his teachers included Roy Harris and Otto Luening. He subsequently became a faculty member of Sarah Lawrence College. In 1941 his First Symphony won the Pulitzer Prize; in 1947 he received an award from the American Guild of Organists, and in 1957 an award from the Guggenheim Foundation. His works include *Three Dances* for orchestra; *Informal Overture*; a *Symphony in Miniature*; a *Poem* for violin and orchestra; *Interludes for Strings*; two String Quartets; two Sonatas for piano; and shorter pieces for various combinations of instruments and voices; a Rondino and Variations (1957) was composed under commission from the Muncie (Indiana) Symphony Orchestra, and a *Concertino* for seven solo instruments and orchestra (1959), written on a commission from the American Music Center, was assigned to the Oklahoma Symphony Orchestra.

EDWARD T. CONE (1917——), born May 4, 1917, in Greensboro, North Carolina, studied with Roger Sessions at Princeton, whose faculty he joined after graduating in 1939. In 1947 he was given a Guggenheim fellowship. His works include a Symphony; a cantata, *The Lotus Eaters*; two String Quartets; choral and chamber works; and piano pieces.

VIVIAN FINE (1913——), born in Chicago, September 28, 1913, also studied with Roger Sessions. Associated at various times with modern music societies, she is fond of complex harmonies and highly dissonant linear counterpoint. Her works include a Suite for oboe and piano (1939); *Opus 51*, a ballet for piano and percussion (1941); a Piano Concerto (1944); and a stage work commissioned by the Rothschild Foundation for the Arts and Sciences, *A Guide to the Life Expectancy of a Rose* (1956).

EVERETT HELM (1913——), born in Minneapolis, Minnesota, July 17, 1913, graduated from Harvard in 1935 and with a John Knowles Paine scholarship from that institution studied in Europe with Gian Francesco Malipiero and Vaughan Williams. In 1943 and

1944 he taught at Western College in Ohio, and from 1948 to 1959 he was theatre and music officer under the Military Government in Germany. In 1960 Helm became chief of the European bureau of *Musical America*.

When Helm's First Piano Concerto was introduced in New York, Noel Strauss declared in the New York *Times* of April 16, 1954, that it "at once established Mr. Helm as one of the best trained and most competent of the younger generation of American composers. The work has a vividness and power quite its own." In 1956 Helm's Second Piano Concerto was introduced by the Louisville Orchestra, which had commissioned it: the work is scored for a reduced orchestra, and the solo part is relatively undemanding. Its third movement is in the vein of a Saturday night barn dance, with a jaunty fiddler's tune that clashes with a jazz rhythm; this conflict leads to a fugue that is developed against a tinkling waltz rhythm in the piano.

Helm's other works include a Concerto for string orchestra (1950); a Concerto for five instruments, percussion, and string orchestra (1953); *Three Gospel Hymns for Orchestra* (1956); *Divertimento* for string orchestra (1957); *String Symphony* (1961); *The Siege of Tottenburg* (1956), a three-act opera; a ballet, *Le Roy fait battre tambour* (1956); and a singspiel, *500 Dragon Thalers* (1956). His chamber works include a Woodwind Quartet, a String Quartet, and two Piano Sonatas. He has also written songs and choral pieces.

WILLIAM D. DENNY (1910——), born in Seattle, Washington, July 2, 1910, studied at the University of California and in Paris with Paul Dukas. From 1939 to 1941 he held the Horatio Parker scholarship at the American Academy in Rome, and from 1942 to 1945 he was an instructor at Harvard and an assistant professor at Vassar. In 1945 he joined the faculty of the University of California. His works include a *Concertino* for orchestra (1939); two Symphonies (1939 and 1951); a Sinfonietta for Strings (1940); an Overture for Strings (1945); a Praeludium for orchestra (1947); a Viola Sonata; numerous choral works; and three String Quartets, the Second of which received a Fromm Foundation Award.

DON GILLIS (1912——), born in Cameron, Missouri, June 17, 1912, played the trumpet and trombone in school bands, graduating from Christian University at Fort Worth, Texas. Largely self-taught, he has composed eight Symphonies, Numbers 1 to 7 inclusive. One of them, bearing the number 5½, falls between 5 and 6. It is subtitled *Symphony for Fun*. When Toscanini performed it with the NBC Symphony in 1947, Noel Straus, writing in the New York *Times*, called it "democriteanly cachinnigenous." Gillis's orchestral works include *Portrait of a Frontier Town; The Panhandle; Thoughts on Becoming a Prospective Papa;* and others with equally unconventional titles. He has composed six String Quartets and a cantata, *Crucifixion*. An opera, *The Libretto*, was introduced at the National Opera Convention in Dallas, Texas, 1960.

JAN MEYEROWITZ (1913——), born in Breslau, Germany, studied with Casella, Respighi, and Molinari, and came to the United States in 1946, where he has taught at the Berkshire Music Center at Tanglewood, Massachusetts, and at Brooklyn College; in 1956 he received a Guggenheim fellowship. His works, composed in a complex and chromatic, though not atonal style, include a *Short Suite for Brass* (1954); a Symphony, *Midrash Esther*, composed 1954 and first performed by the New York Philharmonic in 1957; *Flemish Overture* (1957); *Silesian Symphony* (1957), for strings; the operas *The Barrier* (1949), *Eastward in Eden* (1951), and *Esther* (1956); choral works, among them *Ave Maris Stella* (1954), *Missa Rachel Plorans*, and *Stabat Mater* (1957); cantatas for solo voices and orchestra on poems of Cummings, Dickinson, Herrick, and Mallarmé; keyboard works, songs, and chamber music.

Boston-born FRANK WIGGLESWORTH (1918——) devoted himself to the violin and viola as a child and later studied composition with Otto Luening. He has taught at Columbia University, at Queens College, and at the New School for Social Research in New York; he received an Alice M. Ditson fellowship in 1944 and, in 1951, an award from the National Institute of Arts and Letters and the Prix de Rome. His compositions include a *New England Concerto* for violin and orchestra (1941); a Suite for Strings (1947); *Three Movements for String Orchestra* (1949); *Telesis* (1950), for small orchestra; a ballet, *Young Goodman Brown* (1951); *Summer Scenes* (1951), for flute, oboe, and strings; two Symphonies (1953 and 1958); *Lake Music* (1947), for solo flute; a Trio Sonata for two trumpets and trombone (1953); a Brass Quintet (1956); Trios for three bassoons and for three flutes (1958); a Sonata for viola and piano; songs; choral works; and keyboard music.

JACOB AVSHALOMOV (1919——) was born of an American mother and a Siberian father in Tsingtao, China, March 28, 1919, and came in 1937 to this country, where his teachers included Jacques Gershkovitch and Bernard Rogers; he subsequently taught at Columbia University, Reed College, and the University of Washington. He received an Alice M. Ditson fellowship in composition in 1945, a Guggenheim fellowship in 1951, and a Naumburg Recording Award in 1956. In 1953 his choral work, *Tom o' Bedlam*, received a New York Music Critics' Circle award. His orchestral compositions include *Slow Dance* (1942); *The Taking of T'ung Kuan* (1943, revised 1947); Sinfonietta (1946, revised 1952); *Evocations* for clarinet and chamber orchestra (1952, revised 1957); a Suite from the film score *The Plywood Age* (1955); and incidental music for *The Little Cart*. His choral works include *Two Pensive Songs* (1952); *Prophecy* (1947); a cantata, *How Long, O Lord* (1950); *Of Man's Mortalitie* (1952); *Proverbs of Hell* (1956); *Threnos* (1956); *Inscriptions at the City of Brass* (1956), scored for large chorus, female narrator, and a large orchestra without strings augmented by five percussion, piano, harp, and banjo; *Make a Joyful Noise unto the Lord* (1956); *Whimsies* (1956), to texts from *The New Yorker*; *Now Welcome Summer* (1957), for chorus and solo flute. Avshalomov has also composed chamber music, keyboard music, and numerous songs.

GEORGE BARATI (1913——), born April 3, 1913, in the town of Gyor, Hungary, was first cellist of the Budapest Symphony Orchestra before coming to this country and embarking upon a distinguished career as composer and conductor. He has taught at Princeton University, New Jersey Teachers' College, and the Westminster Choir School, and in 1959 he won the Naumburg Recording Award for his *Chamber Concerto* (1952). His other orchestral works include *Fever Dreams* (1938); Introduction and Allegro (1939); *The Cloud* (1940), for mixed chorus and strings; *Two Symphonic Movements* (1944); *Lamentoso* (1945); Scherzo (1946); *Configuration for Orchestra* (1947); Concerto for cello and orchestra (1954); and *The Dragon and the Phoenix* (1960). He has also written numerous chamber works and piano pieces.

Ethelbert Nevin
(See pages 559–563)

Albert Hay Malotte

Oley Speaks

HERMAN BERLINSKI (1910———), born in Leipzig, Germany, fled to France after the rise of Nazism, studying with Nadia Boulanger and Alfred Cortot; during World War II he volunteered in the French Foreign Legion, and after the fall of France found his way to this country. Like Ernest Bloch, Berlinski has taken his point of musical departure from the Hebraic tradition. His works include *David and Goliath* (1946), for baritone and orchestra; *Symphonic Visions for Orchestra* (1949); *Concerto da Camera* (1951), for woodwinds, timpani, piano, and strings; *For the Peace of Mind* (1952), for oboe, piano, and strings; *Kiddush Ha-Shem* (1958), an oratorio for chorus, solo vocal quartet, and large orchestra; *Avodat Shabbat* (1961), the Friday Evening Service, scored for tenor or baritone solo, chorus, and orchestra without violins; chamber music; piano works; organ works, mostly liturgical in character; choral works for the synagogue; and songs.

BERNARD HEIDEN (1910———), born August 24, 1910, in Frankfurt, Germany, studied at the Hochschule für Musik in Berlin and for five years with Paul Hindemith, whom he considers his principal teacher. He won the highly sought Mendelssohn Prize in 1933, two years before he emigrated to America, where he supported himself as a teacher, pianist, harpsichordist, organist, and radio arranger. During the Second World War he was assistant bandmaster of the 445th Armed Forces Services Band, writing for it over a hundred arrangements. In 1946 he joined the faculty of the University of Indiana, where he became professor of music in charge of the composition department. Heiden's orchestral works include two Symphonies, the Second dated 1954; *Euphorion* (1949), a "scene for orchestra"; and *Memorial for Orchestra* (1955), commissioned by the Fromm Foundation. He has also composed a Sinfonia for woodwind quintet (1949); a Quintet for horn and strings; Sonatas for saxophone and piano (1937), for horn and piano (1939), for violin and piano (1954), for piano (1952), and for piano four hands (1946); Sonatinas for clarinet and piano (1955) and for violin, first position, and piano (1956); and *Divine Poems* (1953), for four-part mixed chorus *a cappella*, to texts by John Donne.

EMANUEL LEPLIN (1917———), born October 3, 1917, in San Francisco, California, studied violin with Georges Enesco, composition with Roger Sessions and Darius Milhaud, and conducting with Pierre

Monteux; he was active as a composer, violinist and violist, and conductor before being stricken with poliomyelitis in 1954. Despite this handicap, he has produced an impressive body of work. Commenting on two of Leplin's compositions in the San Francisco *Chronicle* of May 6, 1960, Alfred Frankenstein wrote, "Serenity, clarity, richness of color, and strength of substance were the keynote in *Landscapes,* and *Skyscrapers* added great excitement of rhythm, a grand gesture, a sense of the epical and the monumental." Others of Leplin's orchestral works include *Rustic Dance* (1941), for two pianos, horn, and strings; *Prelude and Dance* (1941); an orchestral Suite, *Iphigenia* (1941); *Galaxy* (1942), for two celli and orchestra; *Three Dances for Small Orchestra* (1942); *Two Pieces for Chorus and Orchestra* (1942), after poems of Elizabeth Barrett Browning; *Comedy* (1946); *Birdland* (1948), a children's Suite; *Cosmos* (1949), for violin and orchestra; *Overture to the Gettysburg Address* (1959); *Prologue for Orchestra* (1960); Symphony No. 1 (1961); and *Elegy* for Albert Elkus (1962). Leplin has also written prolifically in the field of chamber music, and has several vocal and piano works to his credit.

6. COMPOSERS BORN AFTER 1920

While we shall find a number of the composers in this section writing fiercely dissonant music, there are no straight serialists. The avant-garde composers, as well as their more conservative colleagues, are for the most part eclectic in their idioms. The first three composers we shall consider are all Eastman graduates: LOUIS MENNINI (1920——), PETER MENNIN (1923——), and WILLIAM BERGSMA (1921——).

The brothers Mennini were born in Erie, Pennsylvania—Louis on November 18, 1920, and Peter on May 17, 1923. Each entered the Oberlin Conservatory in Ohio, and in 1942 they both joined the Army Air Force, serving for three years. They subsequently enrolled in the Eastman School of Music in Rochester, studying composition with Howard Hanson and Bernard Rogers.

Louis received his bachelor and master of music degrees in 1947, and after a year as assistant professor at the University of Texas returned to the Eastman School to teach orchestration and composition. After earning his master's degree from Eastman, Peter—who had by now shortened the family name to Mennin—received a Ph.D. from the University of Rochester in 1947, the same year that he won a Guggenheim fellowship. For the next eleven years he taught at the Juilliard School in New York, and in 1958 he was appointed director of the Peabody Conservatory of Music in Baltimore. In 1962 he accepted an appointment as president of the Juilliard School of Music, succeeding William Schuman.

Louis Mennini's compositions include a ballet, *Allegro Energico*, performed in 1948, and two chamber operas: *The Well* (1951), and *The Rope* (1955), based on a play by Eugene O'Neill and commissioned by the Berkshire Music Center. His orchestral works include an Andante and Allegro (1946); *Andante and Allegro Energico* (1947); *Arioso for Strings* (1948); *Canzona* for chamber orchestra (1949); *Cantilena* (1950); an *Overtura Breve* (1952); and a Symphony (1963), commissioned by Duke University. He has also composed a Violin Sonata (1947) and a Sonatina for cello and piano (1952), commissioned by the Serge Koussevitzky Foundation in the Library of Congress; the latter was characterized by a reviewer in the October, 1957, issue of *Musical America* as "a clean and straightforward work with a clear harmonic palette, rhythmic drive, and a lyrical flow. Though not profound, it is a well-made piece, direct and musical." For chorus Mennini has written *Tenebrae* (*a cappella*, 1948), and a Proper of the Mass (1953).

By the time Peter Mennin was thirty-three years old, he had composed seven Symphonies. The First was composed in 1942, when he was nineteen, and the Second, composed in 1944, won the George Gershwin Memorial Award in 1945. The Third Symphony, composed in 1946, was performed in New York in 1947, and Virgil Thomson took the occasion to write in the New York *Herald Tribune* that he was aware "of being in the presence of talent and some kind of strength." The Fourth Symphony, *The Cycle*, for chorus and orchestra, was commissioned by the Collegiate Chorale of New York; introduced in 1949, it won the Naumburg Recording Award. When the Fifth Symphony was introduced in New York in 1951 by the Boston Symphony Orchestra, Henry Cowell wrote in the *Musical*

Quarterly of April, 1951, that the work "maintains a convincing feeling of dignity, musicality, skill, unity, and melodic breadth. . . . There is little tonic-dominant-tonic key sense but instead we have here a modern revival of the ecclesiastical modes, with rapid changes from one to the other. . . . One gathers that neither key, mode, nor atonality is a main point of interest to the composer, whose style seems to draw from all these elements without seeming to care particularly about any of them." The Sixth Symphony, commissioned by the Louisville Orchestra, was first performed by that organization in 1953; the Seventh, introduced by the Cleveland Orchestra in 1964, is in one movement, and is subtitled *A Variation Symphony*; its theme consists of fourteen notes, the first twelve of which could be construed as a twelve-tone row, though the music is far from dodecaphonic.

Mennin's other orchestral works include a *Folk Overture* (1945); a Sinfonia (1947); a Concerto for violin and orchestra (1950); a *Concertante* (1952), subtitled *Moby Dick*, a ten-minute work related to Herman Melville's novel emotionally rather than descriptively; a Concerto for cello (1950), composed for the fiftieth anniversary of the Juilliard School; *Canto* (1957), commissioned by the National Federation of Music Clubs for its biennial convention; and a Concerto for piano (1958), commissioned by the Cleveland Orchestra for its fortieth anniversary. Mennin has written a *Canzona* for band (1951); a *Sonata Concertante* for violin; and several String Quartets. His cantata *The Christmas Story* (1949) was commissioned by the Protestant Radio Commission and was first performed over the ABC Network by the Robert Shaw Chorale.

William Bergsma, born in Oakland, California, April 1, 1921, studied at the Eastman School of Music with Howard Hanson and Bernard Rogers and after receiving a Guggenheim fellowship in 1946 joined the faculty of the Eastman School in New York, where he became associate dean and chairman of the departments of composition, literature, and materials of music. In 1963 he was appointed director of the School of Music of the University of Washington.

Bergsma's orchestral works include a Symphony for chamber orchestra (1943); *Music on a Quiet Theme* (1943); *Suite from a Children's Film* (1945); *The Fortunate Islands* (1946); Symphony No. 1 (1950); *A Carol for Twelfth Night* (1954), commissioned by the Louisville Orchestra; *Chameleon Variations* (1960); and a work commissioned by the Juilliard Orchestra, *In Celebration: Toccata for the Sixth Day* (1962), described by Richard Franko Goldman in the *Musical Quarterly* of January, 1963, as "frankly a bright and cheerful piece for a program opener . . . rhythmically lively, neatly scored, and tightly constructed on a main motif of twelve notes. It is always pleasant to hear an allegro that is really an allegro." Bergsma's stage works include two ballets, *Paul Bunyan* (1939) and *Gold and the Señor Commandante* (1942). An opera, *The Wife of Martin Guerre*, was premièred at the Juilliard School Festival of Music in 1956; critics felt that Bergsma was handicapped by Janet Helm's difficult, monochrome libretto, though Everett Helm noted in *Musical America* of February 15, 1956, that the opera "is a thoroughly serious work . . . which eschews gimmicks and remains on a high esthetic plane."

Bergsma's chamber works include three String Quartets, a Suite for brass quartet (1942), and a Concerto for wind quartet (1959), commissioned by the Coolidge Foundation. Reviewing the Concerto for the *Musical Quarterly* of January, 1960, Irving Lowens commented that "with the Andante the work comes alive. . . . There is about this movement a curiously moonlit aspect, a lonely out-of-doors feeling reminiscent of the mood so exquisitely captured by Aaron Copland in *Quiet City*." Bergsma's *Fantastic Variations* for viola and piano was commissioned by the Harvard Musical Association and first performed in 1961.

LUKAS FOSS (1922——) was born in Berlin, Germany, August 15, 1922, and in 1933 moved with his parents to Paris, where he studied at the Conservatoire with Ernst Levy and Noel Gallon. In 1937 he came to the United States and worked with Rosario Scalero and Fritz Reiner at the Curtis Institute and with Paul Hindemith and Serge Koussevitzky at the Berkshire Music Center in Tanglewood. In 1943 he became an American citizen. He was awarded a Guggenheim fellowship in 1945 and a Prix de Rome in 1950. He joined the faculty of the University of California, Los Angeles, and in 1963 was appointed music director and conductor of the Buffalo (New York) Philharmonic.

Foss's works are marked by the musical enthusiasm of the composer's own personality and by a natural melodic instinct so strong that some critics have felt it overpowers his structures. His orchestra works include two *Symphonic Pieces* (1939 and 1940); a Piano Concerto (1942); *The Tempest* (1942), a Suite for chamber orchestra that won him a Pulitzer scholarship; an *Ode* for orchestra (1944); a Symphony in G (1945); and a *Symphony of Chorales* (1959), based on four Bach chorales, of which Francis D. Perkins commented in the *Herald Tribune* of April 17, 1959, "Emotional force is one of the work's strong points. There is also much ingenuity in [Foss's] blending of his musical material, although a more frequent emergence of the chorales from the skilfully wrought musical complex might have been welcome."

It was the Columbia Broadcasting System's radio performance of Foss's cantata, *The Prairie* (1943), that first brought him wide attention. His subsequent choral works include two cantatas for solo voice, chorus, and orchestra: *Song of Anguish*, unusual among Foss's works in its grim bitterness, with text drawn from Isaiah telling of "woe, of the mourning of earth, of the confusion of good and evil, of the anger of the Lord, of the wasting of cities, and the desolation of the land"; and *The Song of Songs*, commissioned by the Kulas Foundation and introduced in 1947 by the Boston Symphony. *Song of Anguish*, though composed in 1945, was not performed until the Boston Symphony's 1949–50 season. Foss composed another choral work, *Behold I Build a House*, in 1951; and his *Parable of Death* was first performed in New York in 1953. Formally a short oratorio, the composition is based on poems of Rainer Maria Rilke and is fashioned after the manner of Bach's *Passions*. In his program notes for the oratorio Foss wrote that he found in Bach's insight into the nature of story-telling in music "an ideal reconciliation of the conflicting claims of music and narrative." As a result, *A Parable of Death* employs a narrator, large polyphonic choruses, tenor soli, figured chorales, and several melodramas combining the vocal and instrumental elements with narration. *Psalms*, for chorus and orchestra, was first performed by the New York Philharmonic and the Schola Cantorum in 1957.

Foss has composed several short operas, which by their novelty show the enthusiastic, youthful side of the composer's nature. *The Jumping Frog of Calaveras County* (1942), based on Mark Twain's short story, delighted critics and audiences, while *Griffelkin* (1955), first performed on NBC television, caused Robert Sabin to comment in *Musical America:* "Perhaps the most notable characteristics of this score are its rhythmic ingenuity and transparence of texture. Foss has absorbed the bounce, the syncopation and dance impulse of the popular music of our day into his bloodstream and his music reflects them in ways that are natural, unforced, and delightful."

Introductions and Goodbyes, to a libretto by Gian-Carlo Menotti, was commissioned by Menotti for the Festival of Two Worlds and had its first stage performance at Spoleto in 1960. The composer characterizes the nine-minute work as "an aria accompanied by small orchestra and a vocal quartet (or small chorus) in the pit." Writing in the New York *Herald Tribune* of May 18, 1962, Martin Bernheimer described the piece as "nothing more than a witty pantomime with vocal narration in which a host greets a motley assembly of visitors, watches them get tangled up, and bids them a not too fond adieu. It was small-scale fun, well suited to its environment in terms both of the clever score and of Gian-Carlo Menotti's libretto."

While in previous works he had employed neo-Baroque and neo-Romantic styles which sometimes led him into musical garrulity, with *Time Cycle* (1960) Foss ventured into atonality and produced a work of condensation, discipline, and clarity of thought. Commissioned by the Ford Foundation, *Time Cycle* is scored for soprano and orchestra and is based on four poems by Auden, Housman, Kafka, and Nietzsche, each dealing with time, clocks, or bells. The *Herald Tribune* reviewer (October 22, 1960) observed that "Mr. Foss has treated his orchestra like a giant though delicately made mechanism, in which flecks of percussion are combined with taut strands of string and wood tone. To this is added the measured lines of the voice which lights, almost like an insect, on wildly different levels of pitch." *Time Cycle* was given the New York Music Critics' Circle Award for the year.

The initial performance of *Time Cycle* was accompanied, or more accurately, interrupted by a demonstration of Foss's Improvisation Chamber Ensemble, a small group consisting of piano, cello, percussion, and clarinet. Between the numbers of *Time Cycle*, the ensemble improvised on the thematic material of the song just heard. Organized by Foss late in the 1950's, the ensemble improvised in a manner analagous to the jam sessions of jazz players. Foss explained, "In our improvised chamber music, system and chance act as partners: a musical vision (texture and formal development) is conceived and recorded on paper—not, however, in notes, rhythms, etc., but in the form of directions to the players, symbols, letters, numbers. One can call this a score, but it is actually a mere blueprint, a type of instruction sheet, an order." When the ensemble played its *Concerto for Five Improvising Instruments* with the Philadelphia Orchestra in 1960, the orchestral accompaniment was written out by Foss and his colleagues, who improvised within the orchestral framework.

In *Musical America* of November of that year, Max de Schaunsee described the performance as "beguiling for its air of improvisation, its tripping rhythms, its unusual bits of orchestral coloring and provocative figuration." Not unexpectedly, after several performances the pattern may become so firmly established that a permanent piece will have been developed; in fact, when Foss's *Studies in Improvisation* was played in New York in 1962, Everett Helm wrote in *Musical America* of May, 1962, that the performance did not sound improvised: he suggested that "the members of the Improvisation Chamber Ensemble have improvised so often together that regular patterns have been established."

The decade has produced its share of opera composers. CARLISLE FLOYD (1926——) was born at Latta, South Carolina, June 11, 1926, and studied at Converse College in Spartanburg, where he was a pupil of Ernest Bacon. He subsequently received his master's degree from Syracuse University, and in 1947 joined the music faculty of Florida State University at Tallahassee. In 1956 he was awarded a Guggenheim fellowship.

Composed in 1949, Floyd's one-act opera *Slow Dusk* was not performed until 1957, when it was presented by the Opera Workshop of Augustana College. *Slow Dusk* is a tale of Carolina folk, and at its climax a young lass must be told that her lover has been drowned: this information is delivered without music, in slow monotone. Some might feel that the composer surrendered his rights as a musician at this point, but it might be argued with equal logic that he was being a good dramatist.

Susannah, the work which established Floyd as one of our most effective operatic composers, was first produced at Florida State University in 1955. Floyd based his libretto on the Apocryphal tale of Susannah and the Elders, setting it among the present-day mountain people of Tennessee. The story of the beautiful and innocent Susannah, suspected of immorality and condemned by her neighbors and ultimately seduced by the itinerant preacher who imagines that he is trying to save her soul, is made dramatic and moving with the hymn-singing of the congregation, the frenzied exhortations of the preacher, and Susannah's own lyric arias.

Produced by the New York Opera Company in 1956, the work was hailed by critics and music-lovers as an almost perfectly integrated musical drama. Robert Eyer, editor of *Musical America,* described it as "gripping, flesh and blood drama. . . . The score is unself-conscious and unstylized in any particular way. While cognizant of contemporary harmonic and rhythmic devices, it is not widely dissonant and depends frequently upon frank lyricism and reminiscences of hymn-tunes and folksongs, the latter sometimes in Elizabethan tonalities reflective of the still-remembered heritage of many of our mountain people."

Floyd's next dramatic work, *Wuthering Heights,* was commissioned by the Santa Fe Opera Association and first performed at that organization's festival in 1958. Setting a libretto which he had fashioned from Emily Brontë's novel, Floyd again faced the problem of spoken word *versus* recitative and song, and his solution was not in fact an opera in the traditional sense. Reviewing the work in *Musical America* of September, 1958, Martin David Levy remarked that Floyd "seems to be trying to forge a new form of lyric theater from a combination of popular theater and music without the traditions associated with opera. . . . The declamation of the word setting begins to fall into a kind of hurried rhythmic rigidity that does not always exploit the dramatic possibilities of the words themselves. Only occasionally does Floyd compose a line that is beautiful in the voice as well as moving emotionally. But when he does, it is warm and effective."

Floyd revised the opera after the Santa Fe production: feeling that the third act had been overly symphonic, he gave the voices as much to sing as possible and varied the texture with frequent orchestral silences. In its new version *Wuthering Heights* was produced by the New York City Opera Company in 1959. Paul Henry Lang remarked in the New York *Herald Tribune* of April 10, 1959, that Floyd had ratified the promise he gave in the earlier *Susannah*, and "at the same time shows a maturity that promises still further." Lang noted that the new opera "no longer presents a medley, it no longer uses folkish tunes, and the continuity is far more ambitiously carried out than in the earlier work."

Floyd's next opera, *The Passion of Jonathan Wade*, was commissioned by Julius Rodel for the New York City Opera under a Ford Foundation grant and was presented at City Center in 1962. The libretto, again by Floyd himself, tells of an occupation officer wanting to bring peace to the Civil War–prostrated town of Columbia, North Carolina, but caught between Northern carpetbaggers and defeated Southerners, who in their frustration and intolerance turn against him. Having stated his "abiding faith" in Giuseppe Verdi, Floyd constructed the work out of duets, trios, ensembles, arias, ariettas, scenas, and accompanied recitatives. There is little that is avant-garde about the work's musical idiom, though Floyd claims to have used more polytonality than in his earlier operas.

The Sojourner and Mollie Sinclair, commissioned by the Carolina Tercentenary Commission and composed for television, was premièred in Raleigh, North Carolina, in 1964. Again, Floyd wrote his own libretto.

Floyd's work has not been limited to opera. Among his earliest works are a *Theme and Variations* for piano and a Nocturne for soprano and orchestra. He has also composed *Lost Eden* (1951), for solo piano; *Pilgrimage* (1956), a solo cantata for voice and orchestra on a Biblical text; a Piano Sonata (1959) dedicated to Rudolf Firkusny, who introduced it; and *The Mystery*, subtitled *Five Songs of Motherhood* (1960), for soprano and orchestra, commissioned by the Ford Foundation.

MARK BUCCI (1924——), born in New York City, February 26, 1924, has composed principally for the theatre. Trained at the Juilliard School of Music under Tibor Serly, Frederick Jacobi, and Vittorio Giannini, he studied with Aaron Copland at Tanglewood and in 1953 was awarded a Guggenheim fellowship. Since 1946, when his incidental music to a YMHA production of *Death Takes a Holiday* was performed in New York, Bucci has written a widely performed score to Brecht's *Caucasian Chalk Circle* (1948); a one-act opera, *The Boor* (1949), based on Chekhov's comedy; and music and lyrics to two plays: Paula Jakobi's *The Adamses* (1952) and James Thurber's *The Thirteen Clocks* (1952).

In 1953 two short operas by Bucci were performed at the Kaufmann Auditorium in New York: *The Dress*, "written and dress-designed" by the composer, and *Sweet Betsy from Pike*, a satire based on American folk songs and scored for soprano, mezzo, baritone, guitar, and piano. Bucci's *Tale for a Deaf Ear* was produced in 1957 at Tanglewood and a year later included in the spring repertory of the New York City Opera Company. Bucci himself wrote the libretto of this one-act opera, based on Elizabeth Enright's story of two unhappily-married people hurling oaths and insults at one another. Bucci has also written a *Concerto for a Singing Instrument* (1962). Reviewing three of Bucci's short operas in the New York *Herald Tribune* of November 22, 1958, Judith Crist commented on his "ability to provide . . . so true a balance of word and music and action that an effect of true theater is achieved."

The death of ROBERT KURKA (1921–1957) brought to a close a career that showed great promise, even though the young man's talent had not yet reached its full development. Born in Cicero, Illinois, December 22, 1921, Kurka received his bachelor's and master's degrees from Columbia University and studied at the Berkshire Music Center. After serving in the armed forces he attended Otto Luening's composition seminar at Columbia, and in 1951 enjoyed a Guggenheim fellowship; he was also awarded a grant by the National Institute of Arts and Letters.

Three of Kurka's important works were performed posthumously. *The Good Soldier Schweik*, an opera based on Jaroslav Hašek's novel, was introduced by the New York Opera Company at City Center in 1958. Writing in the New York *Herald Tribune* of April 24, 1958, Jay S. Harrison commented that "the opera . . . is the work of a man whose foot was on the threshold but who was cut down before he passed it. For *The Good Soldier Schweik* is a sung play written by a musician who still had to consolidate an avalanche of gifts." A Suite for wind orchestra drawn from the opera had been performed in New York in 1952.

Kurka's Second Symphony was introduced to New York in 1959; a highly professional work, it revealed a certain kinship to, and perhaps a too great influence of, Prokofieff's Fifth Symphony. Kurka's Concerto for marimba and orchestra was introduced by the Orchestra of America the same year; Jay Harrison, in the *Herald Tribune* of November 12, found the concerto "everywhere lively and zestful . . . filled with leaping tunes. . . . It exploits the agility of its soloist to the limit."

Kurka's *Ballad* for French horn and strings was posthumously premièred at Fort Wayne, Indiana, in 1961. Kurka's other works include a Concerto for violin and chamber orchestra; a *Serenade* for small orchestra; a *Concertino* for two pianos and string orchestra; a Symphony for strings and brass; chamber works; and choral music.

Ezra Laderman (1926———), born June 29, 1926, studied composition at Columbia University with Otto Luening and Douglas Moore and in 1958 received a Guggenheim fellowship. His television opera *Sarah* was produced the same year on CBS-TV, and the reviewer for *Variety* (December 3, 1958) described the work as "a vibrant, sweeping score . . . a music that is modern and yet ancient with its overtones of the East." Another opera, *Goodbye to the Clown,* presented in New York in 1960, drew an unfavorable comment from Robert Sabin in *Musical America* of June, 1960: "a patchy, clumsily fashioned score with scarcely a trace of thematic invention, dramatic color, or ingenuity." *Hunting of the Snark,* a little opera based on Lewis Carroll's nonsense poem and described as an "entertainment," was introduced by the Little Orchestra Society of New York in 1961.

Laderman's output is not limited to dramatic works. He has composed a Trio for violin, cello, and piano (1955), a Sonata for violin and piano (1959), and a String Quartet (1959), of which Allen Hughes commented in the New York *Herald Tribune*, "if [the piece] is related to Bartók's monumental essays in this form, it need not apologize. Better parents would be hard to find." Laderman's Violin Concerto was introduced by the CBS Concert Orchestra in 1963, Geoffrey Horne reading the poetic prefaces which Norman Rosten had written to each of the four movements. The work won Laderman the Prix de Rome, enabling him to study at the American Academy in Rome.

LEE HOIBY (1926———), born in Madison, Wisconsin, February 27, 1926, was educated at the University of Wisconsin, at Mills College, and at the Curtis Institute in Philadelphia, where he studied composition with Gian-Carlo Menotti. In 1952 he received a Fulbright grant which enabled him to live in Italy, and in 1957 the National Institute of Arts and Letters awarded him $1,000.

Hoiby's one-act opera *The Scarf*, based on a short story by Chekhov, was introduced at the Spoleto Festival in 1958 and testified to the composer's talent, flair for the lyric stage, and ability to project the emotional and dramatic elements of a libretto with effect and conviction. Although the vocal line of *The Scarf* consists for the most part of lyric recitation, there are also arioso episodes to prevent the submerging of the singers by the vigorous orchestral background.

Another opera, *Beatrice*, based on Maeterlinck's play about a nun who finds redemption through the purity of her love, was produced in Louisville, Kentucky, in 1959, first on television and subsequently in full stage production. The *Musical America* reviewer (November 15, 1959) felt that the first act was merely tentative, but added that "once it is out of the way, however, Hoiby's imagination takes fire. The opera becomes a work of mounting power and emotional perspective." In 1964 the New York City Opera produced another opera by Hoiby, *Natalia Petrovna*, based on Turgenev.

Hoiby's other works include a Toccata for piano (1950); *Noctambulations* (1952); and a Suite, *Hearts, Meadows, and Flowers* (1952), for orchestra; Five Preludes for piano (1952); *Design for Strings* (1953); *Diversions* (1954), for woodwind quintet; *Pastoral Dances* (1956), for flute and orchestra; *The Witch* (1956), a one-act opera; incidental music to *The Duchess of Malfi* (1957); a Second Suite for orchestra (1960); and a *Hymn of the Nativity* (1961), for chorus, orchestra, and soloists, set to lines by the seventeenth-century mystical poet Richard Crabshaw.

STANLEY HOLLINGSWORTH (1924———), born in Berkeley, California, August 27, 1924, studied with Darius Milhaud at Mills College and with Gian-Carlo Menotti at the Curtis Institute. During the year 1955–56 he was resident in the American Academy in Rome, where his opera *The Mother* had been produced in 1954. His television opera *La Grande Bretêche,* based on Balzac's tale, was commissioned by the NBC Television Theater in 1954 and presented on the NBC network in 1957. Hollingsworth's nonoperatic works include a *Dumbarton Oaks Mass* for chorus and string orchestra; a Sonata for oboe and piano; a Quintet for harp and woodwinds; and a *Stabat Mater* for chorus and orchestra (1957).

When *The Mother* was introduced to New York in 1960, Robert Sabin noted in *Musical America* of June, 1960, that the opera was "a work of notable musical beauty and poetic imagination that would be enough in itself to mark [Hollingsworth] as a major talent among young American composers. . . . He follows traditional paths of melody and harmony, but he spins lovely and dramatically expressive tunes and he sets them with a keen sense of atmosphere and theater. When one is as gifted as he is, one does not need to worry about being called old-fashioned."

JACK BEESON (1921——) was born in Muncie, Indiana, July 25, 1921; he trained at the Eastman School and studied privately with Béla Bartók. He enjoyed a Prix de Rome from 1948 to 1950 and a Fulbright scholarship from 1949 to 1950, and in 1951 he became an assistant professor of music at Columbia University. His opera *Sweet Bye and Bye,* with libretto by Kenward Elmslie, was presented by the Juilliard School of Music in 1957; William Bergsma, writing in the *Musical Quarterly* of January, 1958, found the work "directly theatrical, blessedly free from musical ideologies." Beeson's one-act opera *Hello Out There,* to a text by William Saroyan, was composed in 1953 and recorded by Columbia in 1958. Reviewing the recording, the *Musical America* critic (July, 1958) found the opera "a far more persuasive theater piece" than *Sweet Bye and Bye,* and felt that it was "a pretty good example of contemporary chamber opera, particularly through its use of 'sung speech.' "

Returning to the nonoperatic composers, we come to BENJAMIN LEES (1924——), who was born in Harbin, China, January 8, 1924, and studied in Los Angeles with various teachers, including George Antheil and Ingolf Dahl. In 1956 he was awarded a Fulbright scholarship that enabled him to visit Finland. Lees's First String

Quartet, composed in 1952, won a Fromm Foundation Award. Reviewing a recording of the work in the *Musical Quarterly* of January, 1958, Halsey Stevens remarked, "It is difficult to persuade oneself that the Benjamin Lees Quartet could have been written in the second half of the 20th century by a composer who had attained the age of twenty-eight. It is anachronistic from beginning to end. . . . Thematically, Lees deals in platitudes; harmonically he meanders. . . . Structurally all the seams show."

Lees composed his Second String Quartet in Vienna, while he was enjoying a Guggenheim fellowship. In the April, 1956, issue of the *Musical Quarterly* the always broad-minded Henry Cowell noted the piece's conservatism, but added that while "neither the many short motifs nor the structural patterns are very original, the total impression is one of a fully developed 20th-century composition in which old materials are placed in new juxtapositions. The result has a great deal of personal style. . . . It ranks among the best music written by the younger middle-of-the-road Americans."

Lees's Second Symphony, composed on a Louisville commission, was introduced in that city in 1958; a Concerto for orchestra was introduced in Rochester in 1962 and a Piano Concerto in Paris the same year; the Violin Concerto was first played in Boston in 1963, and Robert Taylor, writing in the Boston *Post* of February 9, 1963, termed the work "a modern extension of romanticism." Lees has also composed a *Profile* for orchestra; *Declamations* for string orchestra and piano; *Divertimento Burlesca* for orchestra; *Three Contrasts* for winds and piano; a Sonata for two pianos; a Sonata for violin and piano; four Piano Sonatas; a one-act opera, *The Oracle*; and various shorter works.

ROBERT MOEVS (1920——), born at La Crosse, Wisconsin, December 2, 1920, received his bachelor's and master's degrees in music from Harvard, and studied principally with Walter Piston and Nadia Boulanger. From 1952 to 1955 he was a Rome prize fellow in music at the American Academy in Rome; in 1956 he received an award from the National Institute of Arts and Letters, and in 1963 he received a Guggenheim fellowship. He has taught at Harvard and Rutgers Universities. The first performance by the Boston Symphony of his *Attis* (1959), for tenor solo, mixed chorus, percussion, and orchestra, to a gory Latin text by Catullus, occasioned front-page articles in the Boston newspapers; one critic asserted that the work's impact exceeded that of Stravinsky's *Rite of Spring.*

Others of Moevs's compositions include *Youthful Songs* (1951), for voice and piano; *Sonatina per pianoforte* (1947); *Endymion* (1948), a ballet in three scenes; *Sonata per pianoforte* (1950); *Pan: Music for Solo Flute* (1951); *Cantata Sacra* (1952), for baritone solo, men's chorus, flute, four trombones, and timpani, to a Latin text from the Easter liturgy; *Fourteen Variations for Orchestra,* commissioned by the Koussevitzky Foundation and introduced by Leonard Bernstein and the Symphony of the Air in 1956; a Duo for oboe and English horn (1953); *Three Symphonic Pieces,* commissioned by the League of Composers for the fortieth anniversary of the Cleveland Orchestra and introduced in 1957 by George Szell; a Sonata for solo violin (1956); a String Quartet (1957); a Concerto for piano, orchestra, and percussion (1960); *In Festivate* (1962), for wind instruments and percussion; and *Improvisations for Orchestra* (1964).

HAROLD SHAPERO (1920——), born in Lynn, Massachusetts, April 29, 1920, studied with Nicolas Slonimsky and Ernst Křenek. He majored in music at Harvard, and later worked with Piston, Hindemith, Copland, and Nadia Boulanger. In 1941 he won the Prix de Rome with his *Nine-Minute Overture,* which was performed by the CBS Symphony Orchestra the same year. He won the Gershwin Prize in 1946 and held a Guggenheim fellowship in 1946 and 1947; in 1951 he was a fellow of the American Academy in Rome, and in 1952 he became a professor of music at Brandeis University in Waltham, Massachusetts.

Shapero's orchestra works include a *Serenade in D* for strings (1945) and a *Symphony for Classical Orchestra* (1948), of which Leonard Burkat wrote in the *Musical Quarterly* of April, 1958, "Shapero does not try to say the old things in a new way. He says new things in the old way. He uses much of the musical vocabulary of the late 18th and early 19th centuries and arrives at completely new musical locutions, a new expression." An Overture, *The Travellers,* is dated 1948, while *Credo,* commissioned by the Louisville Orchestra, was introduced in 1955. The Concerto for orchestra, completed in 1958, was eight years in the composing; the *Partita in C* for piano and orchestra was introduced in 1961.

Shapero's chamber works include a String Quartet, of which Virgil Thomson, writing in the New York *Herald Tribune* of February 23, 1948, noted, "its distinction lies in the elevation of its thought rather than in its intrinsic interest, musical or expressive." Shapero has also composed *Three Pieces for Three Pieces* (1938); a Trumpet Sonata (1939); a Violin Sonata (1942); three Piano Sonatas (1944); a set of Piano Variations in C Minor (1955); as well as a four-hand Piano Sonata and three *Amateur Sonatas* for piano. *Until Night and Day Shall Cease* (1955), a cantata, was composed for the National Jewish Music Council.

Although MEYER KUPFERMAN (1926——) first attracted attention with his twelve-tone work, he has shown an increasing tendency toward neoclassicism and even neo-Romanticism. Born in New York City, July 3, 1926, he was educated at the New York High School of Music and Art and at Queens College. He played clarinet with the American Youth Orchestra, was a co-founder of the New Chamber Society, and has taught at Sarah Lawrence College. His works include a *Divertimento* for chamber orchestra, performed in New York in 1950; a *Little Symphony* (1953); a *Chamber Concerto*, performed in 1956, which Ezra Laderman in *Musical America* of March, 1956, termed "a big, romantic concerto, replete with lush sounds, jazz rhythms, virtuoso cadenzas . . ."; four Symphonies, the Fourth of which (1957) was commissioned by the Louisville Orchestra; and a Sonata for two pianos (1958). Kupferman's stage works include a ballet, *Electra*, and the operas *In a Garden, Doctor Faustus Lights the Lights, Voices for a Mirror* (1957), and *The Curious Fern* (1957). He composed a highly-praised score for the experimental film *Hallelujah the Hills* (1963).

JOHN LESSARD (1920——), born in San Francisco, California, July 3, 1920, studied in Paris with Nadia Boulanger; he received a Guggenheim fellowship in 1946 and a grant from the National Institute of Arts and Letters in 1952. His works include a Violin Concerto (1941); a Quintet for violin, viola, cello, flute, and clarinet (1943); two Piano Sonatas (1944 and 1945); *Box Hill Overture* (1946), for orchestra; *Cantilena* (1947), for oboe and strings; a Concerto for twelve winds (1951), which Arthur Berger, writing in the New York *Herald Tribune* of January 29, 1951, termed "uncommonly clean, lucid, contemporary writing"; a Toccata for harpsichord and cello, of which Virgil Thomson commented in the *Herald Tribune* of January 16, 1952, that "all four movements bear a spiritual (and formal) resemblance to the improvisatory speech freedoms and virtuosities of the Baroque organ toccatas . . . not in a long time have I heard contemporary music of such unashamed nobility and fervor"; *Three Movements* for violin and piano; a Concerto for flute, clarinet, bassoon, and strings; an Octet for flute, clarinet, bassoon, two trumpets, two horns, and trombone; a Sonata for cello and piano (1955); and a Trio for flute, violin, and piano that was first performed in New York in 1960.

Louis Calabro (1926———), born in Brooklyn, New York, November 1, 1926, attended the Juilliard School of Music, where he studied with Vincent Persichetti. In 1952 and 1953 he was winner of the Elizabeth S. Coolidge Chamber Music Award; in 1954 and 1959 he was given Guggenheim fellowships, and in 1955 he joined the music faculty of Bennington College. Calabro's compositions, generally neoclassic in style, include a Violin Sonata written in 1953; String Quartet No. 1, composed in 1954; the First Symphony, composed in 1956 and first performed five years later under an Alice Ditson grant to the composer and to the Jacksonville (Florida) Symphony; the Second Symphony (1957); a Sonata for viola (1958), subtitled *Dynamogeny*; a Motet in forty-two parts (1958); *Processional* (1958), for brass and percussion; a Piano Sonata; *Rain Has Fallen* (1960), for four-part women's chorus; *Bodas de Sangre* (1961), for violin, clarinet, cello, piano, timpani, and guitar; and the Third Symphony (1962).

Leo Smit (1921———), born in Philadelphia, Pennsylvania, January 12, 1921, won a scholarship to the Curtis Institute of Music at the age of nine, and in 1950 won both a Guggenheim fellowship and a Fulbright scholarship that enabled him to spend several years in Rome. His orchestral works include *Joan of Arc* (1942); *Hymn and Toccata-Breakdown* (1945); a ballet, *Virginia Sampler* (1947); *The Parcae*, an Overture composed in 1951 and first performed in 1953; the First Symphony (1957), commissioned by the Koussevitzky Foundation and winner of the New York Music Critics' Circle Award, a work which, Robert Sabin observed in *Musical America* of March, 1957, "owes much to Stravinsky, with lesser echoes from Mahler and others," though "its frank eclecticism does not obscure Mr. Smit's own personality." Smit's *Capriccio* for string orchestra was introduced in 1958; he has also written works for violin and piano, for chorus, for piano, and for voice.

EASLEY BLACKWOOD (1933——), son of the inventor of the Blackwood Convention used in contract bridge bidding, was born in Indianapolis, Indiana, April 21, 1933. He appeared at the age of fourteen as soloist with the Indianapolis Symphony, and studied composition with Olivier Messiaen at the Berkshire Music Center and with Paul Hindemith at Yale. He subsequently studied two years in Paris with Nadia Boulanger, for whom he edited a remarkable collection of figured basses, and in 1958 was appointed to the music faculty of the University of Chicago.

In the *Musical Quarterly* of April, 1960, Irving Lowens wrote that "to some extent, Easley Blackwood is the Van Cliburn of American composers. His gifts are just as real, and he too has been set apart from his confrères by an external event, that is, by the uproar in the press over the Symphony No. 1" (1958). The "uproar" consisted of largely divergent opinions which agreed only in recognizing Blackwood's talent and his promise for the future. In the New York *Herald Tribune* of November 13, 1958, Jay S. Harrison found the Symphony "first and foremost extraordinary for its gravity of utterance, for its absolute refusal to indulge in the kind of instrumental or expressive monkeyshines that is said to curry favor with audiences and make for easy listening . . . Mr. Blackwood has a great many substantial things to say and speaks in a dissonant language that is severe, austere, and not a little forbidding." Disagreeing, Winthrop Sargent, in *The New Yorker* of November 22, labeled the Symphony "foundation music . . . that has no meaning for audiences, and is not, in fact, designed to have any such meaning, but, on the contrary, has as its sole purpose the winning of prizes, scholarships, and grants-in-aid dispensed by various worthy and wealthy organizations."

Blackwood's Second Symphony, commissioned by the firm of G. Schirmer for the 100th anniversary of its founding, was introduced in 1961 by the Cleveland Orchestra; the work caused Paul H. Lang, writing in the New York *Herald Tribune,* to comment that Blackwood's "orchestral texture is heavy, he is curiously untouched by either Vienna or Paris, in fact he often sounds like a latter-day Russian composer. He has good ideas but also a tendency to hold onto them and to their orchestral timbers a little too long."

Blackwood's other works include a Chamber Symphony, Opus 2, composed in 1954, which when introduced to New York in 1960 caused Robert Sabin of *Musical America* to exclaim, "The sheer sound of it is voluptuous; Mr. Blackwood is a Romantic! (At least he was in Opus 2.)"; the First String Quartet (1957), commissioned by the Fromm Foundation; the Second String Quartet (1960), commissioned by the Koussevitzky Foundation; a *Concertino* for five instruments (1960), of which Paul H. Lang remarked in the *Herald Tribune* of April 20, "Easley Blackwood is at the neo-classic stage; however, this is normal; composers like children must go through 'stages.' Mr. Blackwood, too, will be heard from in the future." Blackwood has also composed a Sonata, Opus 1, for viola and piano; a Sonata, Opus 7, for violin and piano; a *Fantasy, Opus 8,* for cello and piano; and a Concerto for clarinet and orchestra.

ANDREW IMBRIE (1921———), born in New York City, April 6, 1921, studied piano with Leo Ornstein and with Robert Casadesus. He received an A.B. degree from Princeton University in 1941 and an M.A. from the University of California in 1947, to whose faculty he was subsequently appointed. In 1947 he was awarded the American Prix de Rome, spending the following two years and the years 1953–55 at the American Academy in Rome; he received a Guggenheim fellowship in 1953.

Imbrie's works include a String Quartet No. 1, written as his senior thesis at Princeton and awarded the New York Music Critics' Circle Award in 1944 following its New York première; a Piano Trio (1946); a Piano Sonata (1947); a *Ballad* for orchestra, composed in 1947 and introduced in Florence, Italy, in 1949; a *Divertimento* for six instruments (1948); *On the Beach at Night* (1948), for mixed chorus and orchestra; a *Serenade* for flute, viola, and oboe (1952); the Second and Third String Quartets (1953 and 1957), which caused Ingolf Dahl, writing in the *Musical Quarterly* of January, 1960, to remark upon Imbrie's "lyrical orientation," his "clear, classically oriented form," and his ability to "speak the language of chromatic Expressionism naturally and with authority"; *Legend* (1959), for orchestra; and a Concerto for violin and orchestra. While in Japan on a Guggenheim commission in 1960–61, Imbrie composed *Drum Taps*, a work for four-part chorus and orchestra, and completed all but the orchestration of an hour-long opera entitled *Three Against Christmas*.

MELVIN POWELL (1923———), born in New York City, February 13, 1923, became known as "Mel" Powell when he played piano in dance bands. At heart a musician with serious intentions, he entered the Yale School of Music in 1948 and studied composition with Paul Hindemith, receiving his B.M. degree in 1952 and subsequently teaching at the Mannes School in New York and at Queens College. During the 50's Powell received two important commissions: one from the Louisville Orchestra in 1954 for his Suite for Orchestra, and another from the Koussevitzky Foundation in 1958 for a work for piano and string quartet. Powell's *Divertimento* for five wind instruments won the 1956–57 award of the Society for the Publication of American Music.

Powell has composed a String Quartet (1955); a *Divertimento* for violin and harp (1955); a Sonata for harpsichord (1956); a Trio (1957); and *Stanzas* (1959), for chamber orchestra, a work which Paul Henry Lang described in the New York *Herald Tribune* of May 4, 1959, as "a lean piece, stripped of non-essential detail. Mr. Powell picked up from Webern the admirable barrenness and coolness of the expression and his music bears the stamp of the inimitable daintiness and elegance of his master's voice." Reviewing Powell's Quintet for piano and strings (1959), the outcome of the Koussevitzky commission, Irving Lowens remarked in the *Musical Quarterly* of July, 1959, that "the organization of the piece is not dodecaphonic, but it does bring to mind Schoenberg's special blend of forbidding intellectuality and uneasy passion. . . . Its idiom can certainly not be termed ingratiating. It is too cerebral—tart, bitter, almost medicinal in flavor. I have a hunch that in years to come, Powell will learn to simplify. And to sugarcoat." Powell has also composed *Eight Miniatures for Baroque Ensemble* (1960), two Sonatos for piano; and music for documentary films.

DANIEL PINKHAM (1923———), born in Lynn, Massachusetts, June 5, 1923, attended Harvard College, where he studied composition with Walter Piston and choral conducting with Archibald Davison, receiving his bachelor's degree in 1943 and his master's in 1944. He subsequently studied harpsichord with Wanda Landowska, organ with E. Power Biggs, and composition at Tanglewood with Aaron Copland, Arthur Honegger, and Nadia Boulanger. He has taught music history at Simmons College and harpsichord at Boston University and has served as visiting lecturer at Harvard, faculty member of the New England Conservatory, and music director of King's Chapel in Boston. He received a Fulbright fellowship in 1950 and in 1962 was one of eleven choral conductors to receive awards from the Ford Foundation, in his case to enable him to produce a series of radio programs featuring commissioned works.

Pinkham's orchestral works include a *Concertino in A* (1950); *Five Short Pieces for Orchestra* (1952); *Concertante* No. 1, for violin and harpsichord soli and string orchestra (1954); a Violin Concerto (1956); a *Divertimento* for oboe and strings (1958); *Concertante* No. 2, for violin and strings (1958); Symphony No. 1 (1961), commissioned by Broadcast Music, Inc., on the occasion of its twentieth anniversary, a work in which Carl Sigman, writing in *Musical America* of May, 1962, noted "relaxed dissonance softened by lush rhythms . . . in characteristic Pinkham style; tone-rows are here added without real textural significance"; a *Concertante* for organ and percussion (1962); a *Fanfare, Aria, and Echo* for orchestra (1962); an *Emily Dickinson Mosaic* for chorus and orchestra (1962); and *Catacoustical Measures* (1962), commissioned by the architectural firm of Bolt, Beranek and Newman to test the acoustics of the new Philharmonic Hall at Lincoln Center in New York City.

In an article in the *American Composers' Alliance Bulletin* (Volume X, No. 1, 1961), Warren Storey Smith commented on Pinkham's approach in general, "Pinkham is no manipulator of tones in the sense of Augenmusik (music for the eyes), though when it serves his purpose, he is capable of using a modified form of serial technique. He is not the first to discover that a twelve-tone row can be harmonized tonally, and that such a series of tones can be generally expressive."

NED ROREM (1923———), born in Richmond, Indiana, October 23, 1923, trained at the Curtis Institute in Philadelphia, at the Berkshire

Music Center in Tanglewood, and at the Juilliard School in New York, where he studied with Bernard Wagenaar, receiving his master's degree in 1949. He also studied privately with Aaron Copland and Virgil Thomson. He received the George Gershwin Memorial Award in 1948, the Lili Boulanger Award in 1950, and a Fulbright fellowship in 1951. During the year 1949–50 he served as Slee Professor at the University of Buffalo (New York).

Rorem's orchestral works include the First Symphony, composed in 1949 and introduced two years later in Vienna; two Piano Concertos, composed in 1950 and 1951, respectively; *Design for Orchestra* (1955), commissioned by the Louisville Orchestra; the Second Symphony (1956); a Sinfonia for woodwinds and percussion (1957); *The Poet's Requiem*, for soprano solo, chorus, and orchestra (1957); the Third Symphony (1959), which Howard Taubman reviewed in the New York *Times* of April 19, 1959, commenting, "Mr. Rorem's style is conventional. He writes gracefully, sweetly, and cheerfully. His aim is to divert, and this symphony is a crowd-pleaser. The second movement, with its mild jazz rhythms, evoked a burst of applause. The trouble with Mr. Rorem's music is that it is predictable, and its emotion is on the surface."

Rorem has also composed *Eagles* (1959), for orchestra, and *Eleven Studies for Eleven Instruments*. His operas include *A Childhood Miracle* (1955) and *The Robbers* (1958). Rorem's setting of the play *Mamba's Daughter*, written under a Ford Foundation commission for an opera to be produced by the New York City Opera Company, had to be put aside because of copyright complications, and in 1962 he started work on a replacement opera, *Charade*, to a libretto by Jascha Kessler. In 1964 he was working on another opera, *Miss Julie*, to a libretto by Kenward Elmslie.

It is as a composer of songs that Rorem has won the highest critical acclaim. Reviewing in the New York *Herald Tribune* of February 25, 1959, a recital that had included Rorem's *Cycle of Holy Songs* and *Songs of Solitude and Pleasure*, Jay S. Harrison stated that the art-song is a medium which Rorem "has nurtured and developed since childhood and one in which he has no equal to my knowledge among his immediate contemporaries. . . . He has an uncanny knack of distilling into tone—limpid or dramatic—the essence of a poem, its inner meaning as well as its outer verbal surface." A more recently composed song-cycle, in effect a miniature opera, *King Midas,* was performed in 1962. Rorem has also composed two String Quartets and two Piano Sonatas.

WILLIAM SYDENAM (1928——), born in New York City, May 8, 1928, studied at the Mannes College and privately with Roger Sessions, earning his master's degree at the Hartt College in Hartford, where he studied with Arnold Franchetti. In 1958 he served as a faculty member at Hartt College, and the following year as instructor in theory and composition at Mannes. He was winner of the Pacifica Foundation's composition competition and in 1962 was given an award of $2,000 by the National Institute of Arts and Letters.

Among Sydenam's works are several *Concerti da Camera,* two of them for violin with woodwinds and strings. Reviewing a performance of the Second of these by the Carnegie Chamber Players in 1962, the critic of the New York *Times* (May 12, 1962) wrote that the work had "a certain sense of grand gesture that was dissonant yet suggestive of tonal impulses . . . elaborately worked out, jagged and driving, using repetition and insistence in a fresh and inventive way." The other *Concerti da Camera* are scored for viola and for piano, respectively. Reviewing a recording of Sydenam's *Seven Movements for Seven Instruments,* Thomas F. Johnson wrote in *Musical America* of September, 1962, that "William Sydenam's pieces are as brainy as anything the serialists can muster, but warmer, more alive, less arid than much of the music in this genre."

Others of Sydenam's works include a *Divertimento* for flute, clarinet, and string quartet; a Chamber Symphony; a *Concert Piece* for French horn and string orchestra; a Largo for cello and strings; a *Concertino* for oboe, piano, and strings; a *Study* for orchestra; *Orchestral Abstracts* (1962); *Hommage to L'Histoire du soldat* (1962); *Music for Flute, Viola, Guitar, and Percussion* (1963); and Trio for contrabassi (1963).

LESTER TRIMBLE (1923——), born in Bangor, Wisconsin, August 29, 1923, studied under Nicolai Lopatnikoff at the Carnegie Institute in Philadelphia and subsequently with Darius Milhaud and Arthur Honegger in Paris. He served as music critic for *The Nation* and for the New York *Herald Tribune,* and for a time taught at Bennington

College. In 1961 he became general manager of the American Music Center, a post he held until the fall of 1963, when he became professor of music at the University of Maryland.

Trimble's music, which generally eschews fashionable avant-gardisms, includes a Concerto for winds and strings (1956); *A Night View of Pittsburgh* (1958), commissioned for the Pittsburgh Symphony and stressing the percussive resources of the orchestra in order to depict the steel industries of that city; a Symphony in Two Movements (1959); *Four Fragments from the Canterbury Tales* (1959), a cantata for soprano, harpsichord, flute and clarinet; and *Five Episodes* (1962), commissioned by the Florida Symphony Orchestra. Trimble has composed a Duo for viola and piano and two String Quartets, as well as background music for the play, *The Little Clay Cart*, and a three-act opera, *Boccaccio's Nightingale*, to a libretto by George Maxim Ross based on a story from the *Decameron*. In 1961 Trimble received an award from the National Institute of Arts and Letters.

PAUL NELSON (1929——), born in Phoenix, Arizona, January 26, 1929, studied with Walter Piston, Randall Thompson, Paul Creston, Paul Hindemith, and Lukas Foss. He has worked as a dance-band arranger, first trumpeter with the Phoenix (Arizona) Symphony, staff arranger-composer for the U.S. Military Band at West Point, New York, director of the West Point Post Chapel Choir, and instructor of music theory and composition at the University of Louisville. Nelson lived in Europe under the auspices of a Harvard University John Knowles Paine traveling fellowship, and spent three years at the American Academy in Rome as a fellow in musical composition, subsequently joining the faculty of the music department of Brown University in Providence.

Among Nelson's orchestral works are *Variations on a Western Folksong* (1950); *Theme and Passacaglia* (1954), winner of a Louisville Orchestra award; *Symphonic Thesis* (1956); *Narrative for Orchestra* (1956); *Two Contrasts for Orchestra* (1962), winner of the Arizona Anniversary Music Project Competition; and a Sinfonietta (1962) introduced by the Rome Radio Orchestra. Nelson has also composed two Suites for concert band, a *Divertimento* for clarinet and six instruments (1961), commissioned by Leopold Stokowski, a Trio for Strings, and a Horn Sonata. His choral works include *The Crea-*

tion (1950), for mixed chorus, narrator, piano, and percussion; *Christmas Cantata* (1950); *Easter Cantata* (1952); *Dedication and Praise* (1953), for mixed chorus and two brass choirs; *Songs of Life* (1957), for mixed chorus and piano; and numerous works for solo voice, in conjunction with piano and with small instrumental groups.

CHARLES WUORINEN (1938——), born in New York City June 8, 1938, studied privately with Vladimir Ussachevsky and Jack Beeson and at Columbia with Beeson and Otto Luening. In 1958 he won the Bearns Prize and a fellowship at the MacDowell Colony, and in 1959 was an Alice M. Ditson fellow at Columbia. In 1961 and 1962 he won the Lili Boulanger Prize.

Reviewing Wuorinen's Third Symphony in the *Herald Tribune* of November 12, 1959, Jay S. Harrison termed the work a "hulking blockbuster of a piece." Reviewing a recording of the same work for the *Musical Quarterly* of July, 1962, Kurt Stone remarked that "we get a roaring piece for full orchestra, which shouts and drums and rises to ecstasies, taps mysteriously, exhibits an indiscriminate but relentless procession of musical expressions, and occasionally steps on quite a number of esthetic toes. . . . The Symphony commands considerable respect. . . . It has genuinely emotional drive, it contains fine, strong, musical ideas, and the composer undoubtedly has real talent and a natural feeling for form and proportion."

Wuorinen's *Evolutio Transcripta* was given its first New York performance in 1962. He has also composed a number of pieces for chamber orchestra and smaller groups, including two Trios for flute, cello, and piano. Reviewing the Second of these, John Gruen wrote in the New York *Herald Tribune* of May 22, 1963, that "Wuorinen's musical vocabulary is deeply avant-garde, steeped in the latest, most complex techniques, yet brimming with individuality and invention." In addition to four Symphonies, Wuorinen's orchestral works include a *Concert Piece* for piano and string orchestra; *Music for Orchestra; Summer Music,* for solo violin and orchestra; and a Concerto for Violin and Orchestra. Wuorinen has composed music for the theatre, as well as small instrumental pieces and vocal compositions, including a *Symphonia Sacra* (1961), for voices, instruments, and electronic sounds.

JOHN LA MONTAINE (1920——), born in Chicago, Illinois, March

17, 1920, studied at the Eastman School and at Juilliard. The success of his song-cycle *Songs of the Rose of Sharon,* performed in 1956 by Leontyne Price with the National Symphony Orchestra in Washington, led to a commission through the American Music Center for an orchestral work. La Montaine responded with a Concerto for Piano and Orchestra (1958), of which Irving Lowens wrote in the *Musical Quarterly* of April, 1959, "it would be hard to point to a better piano concerto written by an American since World War II." The Concerto won the Pulitzer Prize for 1958.

In 1961 La Montaine won the Rheta A. Sosland Award of $1,000 for his First String Quartet, and on Christmas Eve his short opera, *Novellis, Novellis (News, News)* was presented at the Washington, D.C., Cathedral. The libretto, by the composer himself, tells the story of the Annunciation, the Journey to Bethlehem, and the Birth of the Christ Child. La Montaine's other works include Canons for Orchestra; *Jubilant Overture; Ode* for oboe and orchestra; and a Rondo for piano and orchestra. He has also composed Sonatas for piano and for cello and piano, and his vocal works include *Five Sonnets of Shakespeare* and *Songs of the Nativity.* In 1962 La Montaine was awarded a $2,000 grant by the National Institute of Arts and Letters.

JULIA PERRY (1927——), born in Lexington, Kentucky, March 25, 1927, attended the University of Akron for a year, received her bachelor's and master's degrees from the Westminster Choir School at Princeton, and studied at the Juilliard School, with Luigi Dallapiccola in Florence, and at the Berkshire Music Center. Her *Stabat Mater* for solo voice and string orchestra, composed 1951, is undoubtedly her most widely performed major work. Miss Perry has also composed *Episode,* a short piece for orchestra; *Fragments of Letters of Saint Catherine,* for solo voice, chorus, and chamber orchestra; *Requiem* for orchestra; two operas, *The Bottle* and *The Cask of Amontillado;* a String Quartet; a Woodwind Trio; and *Seven Contrasts* for baritone and chamber ensemble. In addition to a Fontainebleau Award, Miss Perry has received a Grand Prix from Nadia Boulanger for her Violin Sonata.

HALL OVERTON (1920——), born in Bangor, Michigan, February 23, 1920, studied with Vincent Persichetti, Wallingford Riegger, and Darius Milhaud. In 1955 he enjoyed a Guggenheim award. Active both as a composer and as a jazz musician, Overton feels that jazz has influenced his compositional style, though on a subconscious level; in his concert works, his chief aim has been "the exploration of non-systematic, intuitive harmony, both tonal and dissonant, from which other elements—melody, counterpoint, and form—can be derived."

Overton's orchestral works include a *Symphonic Movement* (1950); a *Symphony for Strings* (1955), commissioned by the Koussevitzky Foundation; a *Concertino* for violin and strings (1958); and a Second Symphony, commissioned by the Louisville Orchestra. His chamber music includes two String Quartets (1950 and 1954), the second of which won the 1959 publication award of the Society for the Publication of American Music; a *Fantasy* for five brass, piano, and percussion (1957); a String Trio (1957); a Sonatina for violin and harpsichord (1956); Sonatas for viola and piano and for cello and piano (both 1960); and a Sonata (1953) and *Polarities* (1959) for piano. His stage works include two operas, *The Enchanted Pear Tree* (1950) and *Pietro's Petard* (1963), and *Nonage* (1951), a ballet suite. His *Dialogues,* for chamber orchestra, were introduced in 1964.

LOCKREM JOHNSON (1924———), born in Davenport, Iowa, March 15, 1924, studied at the Cornish School of Music in Seattle and at the University of Washington, where he subsequently taught. He has appeared as pianist with chamber groups throughout the Northwest. In 1952 he was awarded a Guggenheim fellowship, and in 1954 he became editor of a music publishing house in New York. His works include six Piano Sonatas; three Violin Sonatas; two Cello Sonatas; and a chamber opera, *A Letter To Emily,* produced at the Provincetown Playhouse in New York in 1955.

ROBERT EVETT (1922———), born November 30, 1922, in Loveland, Colorado, studied many years with Roy Harris. His love of the Baroque is evident in many of his works, and despite his highly complex contrapuntal idiom, he considers himself fundamentally a "IV-V-I" composer. His orchestral works include a Concerto for small orchestra (1952); a *Concertino for Orchestra* (1952); a Concerto for cello and orchestra (1954); Variations for clarinet and orchestra (1955); Concerto for piano and orchestra (1957); Symphony No. 1 (1960); and a Concerto for harpsichord and orchestra. His chamber works include Sonatas for clarinet and piano (1948), for cello and harpsichord (1955), for viola and piano (1958), and for violin and piano (1960); a Quintet for piano and strings (1954); a Duo for violin and cello; and a Quartet for piano and strings. He has also composed keyboard, choral, and solo vocal music.

ROBERT PARRIS (1924———), born May 21, 1924, in Philadelphia, Pennsylvania, writes a highly chromatic and tonally elusive music which nonetheless is marked by strong thematicism. His most publicized work, the virtuoso Concerto for five kettledrums and orchestra, was composed in 1955 and first performed in 1958; his other orchestral compositions include *Harlequin's Carnival* (1948); two *Symphonic Movements;* the First Symphony (1952); a Concerto for piano and orchestra (1954); a Concerto for viola and orchestra (1956); and a Violin Concerto (1959). Parris has also composed an impressive body of chamber music for combinations as diverse as brass sextet and recorder quartet; keyboard music; and vocal works.

New York–born GUNTHER SCHULLER (1925———) coined the term "third stream" in reference to music which combines modern jazz and contemporary concert procedures. In addition to concert works and jazz works, Schuller has composed an impressive amount of "third stream" music himself. An accomplished horn player, he left the Manhattan School of Music, where he had studied theory and counterpoint, to play in the orchestras of the Ballet Theatre, the Cincinnati Symphony, and the Metropolitan Opera. In 1959 he resigned as solo horn player at the Metropolitan in order to devote himself more completely to composition. In 1960 he received awards from the National Institute of Arts and Letters and from Brandeis University, and in 1962 the Oxford University Press published his book *Horn Technique.*

In the New York *Times* of January 21, 1962, Eric Salzman commented, "Schuller's various musical activities are not unconnected with his creative work. In his music one can hear the instrumental knowhow of the wind player; the idiomatic and finely calculated orchestral sensibility of the conductor; the technical mastery and brilliant eclecticism of the modern music expert, and the controlled freedom and invention of a creative personality that knows and understands jazz." Schuller's orchestral compositions include a Concerto for horn and orchestra (1944); a Concerto for cello and orchestra (1945); a *Fantasia Concertante* for three trombones and orchestra (1947); a *Symphonic Study* for orchestra (1948); a Symphony for brass and percussion (1950); *Dramatic Overture* (1951); *Recitative and Rondo* for violin and orchestra (1954); *Spectra* (1958), commissioned by the New York Philharmonic and Dmitri Mitropoulos; *Contours* (1958); *Concertino* for jazz quartet and orchestra (1959); *Seven Studies on Themes of Paul Klee* (1959), commissioned by the Ford Foundation in conjunction with the American Music Center; *Capriccio* for tuba and orchestra (1960); and *Contrasts* (1961) for solo woodwind quintet and orchestra.

Much of Schuller's prolific work in the chamber music field is scored for jazz groupings or reflects the influence of contemporary jazz; this is not surprising, since Schuller is a leading jazz performer and composer, and has been associated closely with the Modern Jazz Quartet; he is also editor and director of MJQ Music, Inc., a firm specializing in jazz editions. Examples of his imaginative scoring can be seen in such works as the Quartet for four contrabasses (1947); *Variants on a Theme of John Lewis* (1960), for flute, alto saxophone, vibraphone, guitar, string quartet, two basses, and drums; and *Lines and Contrasts* (1960), for sixteen horns.

SEYMOUR SHIFRIN (1926——) was born in Brooklyn, New York, February 28, 1926, and studied with William Schuman, Otto Luening, and Darius Milhaud. His String Quartet (1949) was awarded the Bearns Prize, and he has received two Guggenheim fellowships. In the *Musical Quarterly* of July, 1958, Andrew Imbrie wrote that Shifrin's "chromaticism and transparency of texture might at first recall Webern; yet the impulse is predominantly melodic—almost melismatic—rather than motivic in the miscroscopic sense. One is fascinated by the highly expressive and exposed melodic shapes, interrelated in a supple and elastic rhythmic context. The music is not twelve-tone, but organized on broadly tonal principles." Shifrin's compositions include a Sonata for cello and piano (1948); a Chamber Symphony (1953); *Serenade* for five instruments (1954); *Three Pieces* for orchestra (1958); and *Concert Piece* for solo violin (1959). He has composed piano music and choral works, including the *Cantata to the Text of Sophoclean Choruses* (1958), for mixed chorus and large orchestra.

EARL BROWN (1926——), born in Lunenberg, Massachusetts, December 26, 1926, majored in engineering and mathematics at Northeastern University and later studied composition with Dr. Roslyn Brogue Henning and the Schillinger techniques of composition and orchestration with Dr. Kenneth McKillop. However, Brown differs from Schillinger in being a pioneer in music which has been variously described as "random" or "aleatory." Brown claims to owe the aesthetic orientation of his music to the organizational precision of the sculpture of Alexander Calder and to the intensified spontaneous dynamism of the painting of Jackson Pollock. Concerning his piano composition *Synergy* (1952), the composer offers this information: ". . . to have elements exist in space . . . space as an infinitude of directions from an infinitude of points in space. To work from right to left, back, forward, up, down and all points in between. The score is a picture of this space at one instant which the performer must set in motion, which is to say, realize that it *is* in motion and step into it. Either sit and let it move or move through it at all speeds." *Synergy* is one of several pieces collectively called *Folio Pieces*, differently notated "graphic events" to be performed however the performer wishes.

Brown's compositions include *Available Forms 1*, for eighteen musicians, commissioned by the city of Darmstadt; *Available Forms 11*, commissioned by the Rome Radio Orchestra, for large orchestra "four hands," i.e., two conductors and ninety-eight musicians; *Four Systems*, "for any number of any instruments for indefinite time"; *From Here*, for four-part chorus and twenty instruments; *Indices*, a ballet; *Times Five*, for flute, trombone, harp, violin, cello, and four channels of tape; *Four More* and *Four Systems* for one or more pianos; *Home Burial*, for piano solo; *Twenty-five Pages*, for one to twenty-five pianos; *Octet I* and *Octet II*, both for eight magnetic tapes.

RUSSELL SMITH (1927——) born in Tuscaloosa, Alabama, April 23, 1927, studied with Otto Luening, Douglas Moore, William Mitchell, Aaron Copland, and Bernard Rogers. He has won numerous awards: the John Hancock Fellowship in Composition at the Berkshire Music Center (1947), the Seidl Fellowship in Theatrical Composition at Columbia (1950), the George Gershwin Memorial Award (1954), and a Guggenheim fellowship (1955). His orchestral works include a Sinfonietta (1947), for timpani and strings; *Music in Concerto Style* (1951); two Piano Concertos (1952 and 1956); *Tetrameron* (1957); *Divertimento* (1958), for two oboes, two horns, and strings; and *Can-Can and Waltz* (1959). Smith has also composed chamber music, works for the organ, a *Piece for Ondes Martenot* (1952), and a choral Anglican Mass (1954).

DAVID AMRAM (1930——), born November 17, 1930, studied at the Oberlin Conservatory of Music, at George Washington University, and at the Manhattan School of Music, where Vittorio Giannini was his teacher of composition. Amram's varied interests encompass the French horn, of which he is an accomplished player; jazz—he has worked with Charlie Mingus, with Oscar Pettiford, and with his own group; dramatic music—he had by July, 1964, written scores for close to forty plays, six films, and five television shows; and concert music, of which he has an impressive list to his credit. Jack Diether, who has stated that "Amram is very close to a perfect modern musician of the theater," commented of Amram in *Musical America* of June, 1960:

Personally, I am delighted in these tense, overwrought days that someone with original musical ideas is able to convey them in such a relaxed and humorous fashion as this. It seems to be assumed that the ideal theater composer, with faculty for pithy, self-contained effects, must lack the sustaining power for concert building, and therefore is not worth considering in that regard, while on the other hand we are repeatedly being told, by established concert composers, that thematic development is just what they are now deliberately avoiding in favor of unrelated juxtaposition! Here, however, was a generous and syntactic flow of music, notably capricious, but quite free of the boredom of dutifully labored contrivance.

In addition to the incidental music which constitutes a large body of his work, Amram's compositions include a Trio for tenor saxophone, horn, and bassoon (1958); *Autobiography for Strings* (1959); *Shakespearean Concerto* (1959), for oboe, two horns, and strings, based on material from the many scores composed for New York Shakespeare Festival productions; a Piano Sonata (1960); *Lysistrata* (1960), for unaccompanied flute; a Sonata for violin and piano (1960); *The Wind and the Rain* (1960), for viola and piano; a String Quartet (1961); *Discussion* for flute, cello, piano, and per-

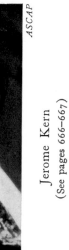

Jerome Kern
(See pages 666–667)

Victor Herbert
(See pages 653–654)

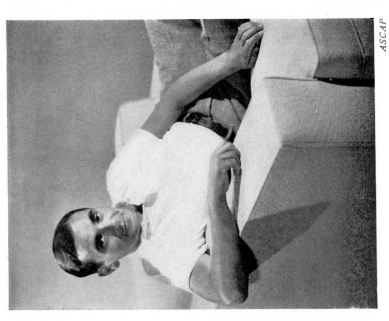

Irving Berlin

Richard Rodgers

cussion (1961); *Shir L'Erev Shabbat* (1961), a Sacred Service for the Sabbath Eve, for tenor solo, mixed chorus, and organ, commissioned by the Park Avenue Synagogue in New York; *The American Bell* (1962), for narrator and orchestra, composed for the Luma-drama lighting of Independence Hall in Philadelphia; *Dirge and Variations* (1962), for violin, cello, and piano; an opera, *Twelfth Night* (1964); and a cantata, *A Year in Our Land,* on texts by Wolfe, Steinbeck, Baldwin, and Kerouac. In 1963 Amram was appointed musical director of the Lincoln Center Repertory Theater, and was also commissioned by the Jewish Theological Seminary and the ABC television network to compose a Passover opera for television, *The Final Ingredient.*

There are three more foreign-born composers from the decade of the 20's to be considered. HALIM EL-DABH (1921————), born in Cairo, Egypt, March 4, 1921, graduated from Cairo University as an agricultural engineer but in 1949 decided to make music his career and came to the United States, where he studied at Brandeis and New Mexico Universities, at the New England Conservatory and the Berkshire Center in Tanglewood, and with Irving Fine, Francis Cooke, and Aaron Copland. El-Dabh's first major success in this country was the 1958 performance of his dance epic *Clytemnestra,* commissioned by Martha Graham for her company. A year later he received a Guggenheim fellowship in composition. Reviewing *Clytemnestra* in the Jerusalem *Post* of September 26, 1958, Y. Boehm commented that "the impression that it successfully transmits to the listeners is that this is archaic Oriental music, functional, effective, a good blend of modern technique in composition with an ancient heritage, creating something timeless with an authentic ring."

Others of El-Dabh's compositions include three Symphonies (1951, 1952, and 1955); a Concerto and a *Fantasia-Tahmeel* for derabucca (or timpani) and strings (1954); *Symphonic Eclogue* (1956); *Bacchanalia* (1958), for orchestra; two ballet suites for orchestra, *Agamemnon* and *Furies in Hades* (1958); *House of Atreus* (1958), for dramatic soprano and baritone, chorus, and orchestra; three *Juxtapositions* for percussion ensemble; and a large number of works for piano and for small instrumental ensembles.

ROBERT STARER (1924————), born in Vienna, January 8, 1924,

studied at the Jerusalem Conservatory and, after serving in the British Royal Air Force during the war, came to New York in 1947 and studied at the Juilliard School, where he later became a teacher. Starer has composed two Symphonies, dated 1948 and 1951; a Piano Concerto, in which he appeared as soloist in New York in 1949; a *Concerto a Tre* for clarinet, trumpet, trombone, and strings (1954), which the reviewer for *Musical America* of December 15, 1954, found "a vigorous, well-constructed score . . . written with a bright, pungent style of orchestration. . . . The thematic substance is animated . . . and generally of a dance-like propulsion and heartiness"; a *Prelude and Rondo Giocoso* (1956), for orchestra; a *Ballade* for violin and orchestra (1957); and a Concerto for viola, strings, and percussion (1959), of which the *Musical America* critic remarked that, while "Starer is no stranger to Bartók . . . this influence never degenerates into stylistic aping. Starer speaks with the true ring of individualism."

Starer's chamber music includes a *Concertino* for two voices or instruments (1948), a String Quartet, and a *Serenade* for woodwind quintet. His one-act opera *The Intruder* was produced by the Punch Opera in New York in 1956. For Martha Graham and her dance company he has composed the ballets *Secular Games, Samson Agonistes,* and *Phaedra.*

PETER JONA KORN (1922———) received his training in Berlin, where he was born, in Jerusalem and, after coming to the United States, in Los Angeles, where in 1948 he founded the New Orchestra. His orchestral works, a number of which have been introduced abroad, include a *Concertino* for horn and strings; *Variations on a Theme from The Beggar's Opera;* two Symphonies; Rhapsody for oboe and strings; a Concerto for Orchestra; and *Tom Paine,* a symphonic portrait. His chamber works include a String Quartet; a *Passacaglia and Fugue* for horns; a Wind Octet; a Brass Quintet; a *Serenade* for flute, viola, and cello; and Sonatas for cello, for oboe, for horn, and for piano. He has also composed choral works; songs; and piano pieces.

CHAPTER THIRTEEN

Composers Best Known for Their Shorter Works

1. COMPOSERS OF SONGS AND SHORT PIECES

At this point we present those composers who are most widely known for short works—songs, instrumental pieces, and, in some cases, teaching material. Many of them have composed also in the larger forms, but they are best known to the public for their briefer compositions.

Perhaps the artistic parent of all our present-day song composers was ETHELBERT NEVIN (1862–1901), who left us *The Rosary* and *Mighty Lak' a Rose*. Nevin was born November 25, 1862, at "Vineacre," his father's country place near Pittsburgh. When he was five he used to sit on the piano stool and improvise accompaniments to the songs he knew. When he was eight he began his study of the piano, and in 1881 he went to Boston to study with B. J. Lang and took harmony lessons from Stephen A. Emery. In 1884 he went to Klindworth in Berlin, and after a year graduated with highest honors from the Klindworth School. He studied theory with Carl Bial, who encouraged him to give more time to writing. Nevin had not undertaken music with the idea of composing: it was only after some of his little pieces became popular that he realized he would do best to concentrate on composition.

He returned to America in 1886, and went to live in Boston, where his songs were warmly received by the Manuscript Club. Some of his best songs came from this period: *Herbstgefühl; Wynken, Blynken, and Nod; Oh, That We Two Were Maying;* and *Little Boy Blue.* His piano suite *Water Scenes* was published in 1891; the fourth of these five pieces, *Narcissus,* was destined to be his most popular piano work.

The years 1891–1897 were spent mostly in Europe. In 1892 Nevin wrote his piano suite *In Arcady,* and in 1895 he and his wife settled in Italy, where he composed the piano suites *May in Tuscany* and *A Day in Venice.* In 1897 Nevin returned to America, and the following year wrote *The Rosary;* ill health overcame him, and in 1901 he passed quietly away. His music was performed at the funeral service: *The Rosary; Jesu, Jesu, Miserere;* and the *Ave Maria* from *A Day in Venice.* His life was done, and his work was finished; he died not a master of great things, but a poet of beautiful little verses.

Like Nevin, ADOLPH M. FOERSTER (1854–1927) was born in Pittsburgh. His songs reveal the influence of Robert Franz and of his own German ancestry; they include *The Daisy, At Night, Love Seemeth Terrible,* and *The Robin's Lullaby.* He also wrote orchestral and instrumental works.

ARTURO BUZZI-PECCIA (1854–1943) was born in Milan, studied with Massenet and Saint-Saëns in Paris, and came to the United States in 1898, where his pupils included Alma Gluck and Sophie Breslau. He wrote an opera, *Forza d'Amore;* an orchestral *Saturnale;* many songs, including *Lolita, Gloria,* and *Faith;* and chamber music and choral works.

JOHN W. METCALF (1856–1926) is said to have been the first music instructor at Stanford University in California. His songs include *Absent,* the beloved ballad of the early twentieth century so popularized in concert and on acoustical recordings by the tenor Evan Williams; *Persian Serenade; Hark, as the Twilight Fades; O Sing Ye Birds; The Cares of Yesterday; Love and Springtime; The Sunset Glow; Watching;* and *Niawasa: an American Indian Idyll.*

MARY TURNER SALTER (1856–1938), the wife of Sumner Salter, made successful appearances in oratorio and church concerts and published nearly a hundred songs, duets, part-songs, and church music, including *The Pine Tree, The Cry of Rachel,* and *A Christmas Song.*

WILLIAM ARMS FISHER (1861–1948) studied with Horatio Parker and Dvořák, whose Largo (from the *New World* Symphony) he adapted as *Goin' Home.* Fisher made many settings of Negro spirituals, as well as writing original songs.

When publishers consistently rejected the songs of CARRIE JACOBS BOND (1862–1946), she established her own printing press and achieved enormous popularity with her first printed song, *A Perfect Day;* later works, particularly *I Love You Truly,* had an almost equal success. In 1927 Mrs. Bond published *The Roads of Melody,* an autobiography.

Jessie L. Gaynor (1863–1921) specialized in children's songs. In addition to the widely sung *Slumber Boat,* a setting of Alice C. D. Riley's verses, she published the collections *Songs to Little Folks, Songs and Scissors,* and *Mother Goose Songs,* as well as operettas, entertainments, and songs for adults. Her daughter Dorothy Gaynor Blake also composed.

Frederick Field Bullard (1864–1904) studied with Rheinberger and taught in Boston. Of his forty songs, the best known are *The Stein Song, A June Lullaby,* and *From Dreams of Thee.*

Sidney Homer (1865–1953), another Rheinberger pupil, composed numerous songs, including *Banjo Song; The Song of the Shirt; Sing to Me, Sing;* and *Songs from Mother Goose,* as well as organ, chamber, and piano works. Frederick Stock scored several of his songs for orchestra, including the lovely *Sweet and Low.* Homer's wife was Louise Homer, the eminent contralto.

Robert Huntington Terry (1867–1953) composed many well-known songs, including *The Answer; At Twilight; Song Is So Old;* and *Which Flower I Love.*

Mabel Wood Hill (1870–1954) studied with Walter Rothwell and Cornelius Rayber. In addition to orchestral works, she composed the songs *Ebb Tide; The Song of Capri; The Gull;* and a collection of twelve songs entitled *Calliope, or the Vocal Enchantress.*

English-born Bruno Huhn (1871–1950) came to New York at the age of twenty. A self-taught organist, he wrote many songs and choral works, including *Te Deum Laudamus; Blest Pair of Sirens; The Message; Christ Triumphant; Meditation; Jubilate Deo.* His setting of Henley's *Invictus* is well known. He also composed the cycle *The Divan,* for mixed quartet, as well as organ and piano pieces.

Charles Fonteyn Manney (1872–1951), a vocal pupil of William Arms Fisher, studied with Wallace Goodrich and Percy Goetschius. He composed an opera, three cantatas, piano pieces, and songs, including *At Evenfall, And Let Me the Canakin Clink,* and the cycle *A Shropshire Lad.*

Before becoming a novelist, RUPERT HUGHES (1872–1956) composed several songs, including *Tears, Idle Tears,* and *In a Gondola.* His writings on musical subjects include *Contemporary American Composers; The Music Lover's Encyclopedia;* and *Love Affairs of Great Musicians.*

GEORGE ALFRED GRANT-SCHAEFER (1872–1939) composed, in addition to that favorite encore song *Cuckoo Clock,* many other songs, some moderately difficult piano works, and some unusual arrangements of French-Canadian folk songs.

EDWARD HORSMAN (1873–1918) is perhaps best remembered for the rare talent he demonstrated in *Bird of the Wilderness* and the few songs which he left us.

OSCAR G. SONNECK (1873–1928) was in charge of the Music Division of the Library of Congress from 1902 to 1917, and he developed what had been a mere accumulation of music deposited for copyright into one of the great music libraries of the world. From 1917 until his death he was music editor of the publishing house of G. Schirmer in New York, and he founded *The Musical Quarterly* in 1915. His highly original, thoughtful and scholarly songs include *To Helen* and *Studies in Song, Opus 19,* which were frankly experiments in the use of flexible rhythms in setting poems.

CHARLES GILBERT SPROSS (1874–1961), a well-experienced concert accompanist and church organist, published cantatas, anthems, a Sonata for violin and piano, and piano pieces. Among his well-known songs are the beloved *Abide with Me; The Conquest; I Do Not Ask, O Lord; Forever and a Day; When Winds Are Raging;* and *Asleep.*

The songs of OLEY SPEAKS (1876–1948) rivaled those of Carrie Jacobs Bond in popularity, though they were less sentimental and better suited to men singers than to women. His first popular success was his setting of Kipling's *On the Road to Mandalay,* followed by *Sylvia,* to words by Clinton Scollard, and *Morning.* His sacred song *The Prayer Perfect* was widely used in churches. A student of Emma Thursby, he was himself a singer, and published altogether over two hundred songs.

CLIFFORD DEMAREST (1874–1946) was known chiefly for his songs, anthems, and organ pieces. His organ works include a *Pastoral Suite in F; Rip van Winkle;* Prelude on *Materna; Rustic Song;* and

Festival Postlude. For organ and piano he composed a *Fantaisie in C Minor;* a *Grand Aria;* and a Rhapsody. He also composed two cantatas, *The Cross Victorious* and *The Shepherds of Bethlehem.*

HALLETT GILBERTÉ (1875——) composed several choral works, piano and violin compositions, and about two hundred and fifty songs. His setting of Browning's *Ah, Love But a Day* rivaled Mrs. Beach's in popularity.

PEARL CURRAN (1875–1941) did not begin to write music until she was thirty-five. Her songs include *Life,* first sung by Caruso; *Dawn; Rain; Nocturne; The Best Is Yet to Come;* sacred songs; and children's songs written for her grandchildren.

HENRY PURMONT EAMES (1875–1950) studied with Clara Schumann and Paderewski. His songs include *Sweetest and Dearest* and *Irish Croon-song.* He also composed some choral and orchestral works and a light opera that won the David Bispham Medal in 1925.

JAMES MACDERMID (1875–1960) called himself a writer of "plain songs." Among the fifty or more of these are *If I Knew You and You Knew Me; Fulfillment;* and *The Song My Heart Is Singing.* A skilled accompanist, he made a number of tours with his wife, Sybil Sammis MacDermid.

FREDERICK VANDERPOOL (1877–1947) wrote many lyric ballads, including *If; I Did Not Know; Values;* and *Ma Little Sunflower.*

JOHN PRINDLE SCOTT (1877–1932) wrote the words to nearly all his songs, which included *The Secret; Wind's in the South; A Sailor's Love Song; Nocturne;* and *The Old Road.* His church songs include *The Voice in the Wilderness* and *He Maketh Wars to Cease.* He also wrote quartets and piano music, including *Three Irish Sketches.*

HARRIET WARE (1877–1962) studied with William Mason in New York and with Sigismund Stojowski in Paris. Her *Women's Triumphal March* was made the national song of the Federation of Women's Clubs in 1927, and her tone poem *The Artisan* was performed by the New York Symphony Orchestra in 1929. She also composed a one-act opera, *Undine;* two cantatas; a choral cycle, *Trees;* and numerous songs, including *Joy of the Morning; Stars; Sunlight; Hindu Slumber Song; The Boat Song;* and a setting of Edwin Markham's *The Cross.*

CLAUDE WARFORD (1877–1950), a singing teacher, published more than forty songs, including *Pietà; Earth Is Enough; Dream Song;* and *Three Ghosts.*

HEINRICH GEBHARD (1878——), born in Germany, came to America as a boy and became a talented pianist and composer. His works include a *Fantasy* for piano and orchestra (1925); a *Divertimento* for piano and chamber orchestra (1927); a String Quartet; a *Waltz Suite* for two pianos; a song cycle, *The Sun, the Cloud, and the Flower;* a Sonata for violin and piano; and many piano pieces. He played the piano part of Loeffler's *A Pagan Poem* when it was first performed in Boston and arranged the work, of which he was considered the foremost interpreter, for two pianos.

FRANK LA FORGE (1879–1953), a gifted accompanist, wrote brilliant and stunningly effective songs, including *Song of the Open Hills; I Came with a Song;* and others. He was one of the first accompanists to play from memory. His arrangements include a version of Alabieff's *Nightingale* and *Fledermaus Fantasy* for voice and flute.

JOHN DENSMORE (1880–1943) studied composition and orchestration at Harvard and composed a cantata for chorus and orchestra, *Hail, Ceres, Hail,* as well as many choral works and the songs *All to Myself; Roadways; I Must Down to the Sea Again; A Village Romance;* and others.

GEOFFREY O'HARA (1882——), born in Canada, was active as instructor of native Indian music for the government, song leader in army camps, and entertainer. His songs include the dramatic narratives *Leetle Bateese* and *The Wreck of the Julie Plante; Give a Man a Horse He Can Ride;* and the stuttering song, *K-K-K-Katy,* which he adapted from an obscure folk song during the First World War.

ARTHUR BERGH (1882——), born in Saint Paul, Minnesota, composed about eighty songs, including the cycle *The Congo;* a choral setting of Whitman's *O Captain, My Captain;* as well as a number of violin pieces. In larger forms he composed two melodramas with orchestra: *The Raven* and *The Pied Piper of Hamelin;* a symphonic chorale, *The Unnamed City;* a romantic opera, *Niorada;* the marches for orchestra *Honor and Glory* and *Festival March;* and two operettas, *In Arcady* and *The Goblin Fair.*

FAY FOSTER (1886–1960) won a prize at the International Waltz Competition in Berlin in 1910 and first prize in the American Composers contest in 1913. She made her reputation when she published

The Americans Come in 1918, precisely the number for singers who needed a timely song on their programs. She composed three operettas; over a hundred songs, including *My Menagerie, Maria Mia,* and *Your Kiss;* choral works; chamber music; and piano pieces.

LILY STRICKLAND (1887–1958) lived in many parts of the world, including India, and was always successful in catching the spirit of native melodies and carrying their idiom into her own tunes. Her songs include the famed *Lindy Lou; Bayou Songs;* the cycles *From a Sufi's Tent, Songs of India,* and *A Beggar at Love's Gate.* She also wrote piano pieces; a symphonic Suite, *Carolina;* and a piano Concerto.

CLARA EDWARDS (1887——), born in Minnesota, was first an accompanist and then a composer. She wrote children's music, incidental music to *Alice in Wonderland,* and many songs—*By the Bend of the River, Into the Night, The Fisher's Widow,* and others. In 1940 an early song, *With the Wind and the Rain in Her Hair,* was made into a popular song and for several weeks held top place on the "Hit Parade."

KATHLEEN LOCKHART MANNING (1890–1951), a pupil of Moszkowski, Eichelberger, and de Sales, wrote two song cycles—*Sketches of Paris* and *Sketches of New York,* as well as *Autumn Leaves, Nostalgia, The Truant,* and *Chinois.*

OSCAR RASBACH (1888——) studied piano with Leschetizky and later taught in San Marino, California. His piano compositions include Scherzo; *Valse Charlene; You and You*—a transcription of a waltz from Strauss's *Die Fledermaus;* and three unusual *Folksong Sonatinas,* entitled *Early California, From Dixieland,* and *In Colonial Days.* Rasbach's songs include *April, The Look,* and *Mountains,* as well as the widely sung *Trees.*

HOWARD MCKINNEY (1890——), an organist, teacher, and co-author of a music appreciation book as well as editor for a music publishing house, achieved greatest renown with his whimsical composition *Crumbs from Peacock Pie.*

MANA-ZUCCA (1891——) studied under Alexander Lambert, Max Vogrich, Godowsky, and Busoni. She published a Piano Concerto as well as such songs as *Rachem; If Flowers Could Speak; The Big Brown Bear; Mirror of My Soul; Memory; What Is a Kiss; Retribution;* and over a hundred others.

CLARENCE OLMSTEAD (1892——) was for many years in charge of

radio programs for advertising agencies. His songs include *Deep in My Heart; Tears; Thy Sweet Singing; I Am Thy Harp; The Ladies of St. James's; Pirate Song; Today;* and *Until the Day.*

HORACE JOHNSON (1893——) was a music journalist in New York for many years, managing editor of the *Musical Courier,* and New York City director of the WPA Federal Music Project. He composed many songs, including *The Pirate; When Pierrot Sings; Three Cherry Trees;* and *Thy Dark Hair.* His orchestral works include *Imagery* and *Streets of Florence;* a tone poem, *Astarte;* and *Joyance,* for strings.

MARIA GREVER (1894——), born in Mexico City, was educated in a Spanish convent, studied with Debussy, and made her home in New York. Her works, many of them prize winners, include the songs *Júrame, Lamento Gitano, Make Love with a Guitar,* and *Tipitín.*

ALBERT HAY MALOTTE (1895——) was a theatre organist and worked several years on Walt Disney's music staff, composing "Silly Symphony" scores. His setting of *The Lord's Prayer* has been phenomenally successful, its sales surpassing those of any other item in its publisher's catalogue, it is said. He has also made settings of the *23rd Psalm* and other scriptural texts.

RICHARD KOUNTZ (1896–1956) composed pieces for organ and for piano, as well as songs, including *The Sleigh, Lili, Cossack Love Song,* and *Prayer of the Norwegian Child.* He also wrote radio scripts and managed standard and educational publications for M. Witmark and Sons.

MARY WEAVER (1906——), wife of the organist-composer Powell Weaver, studied in Kansas City with Molly Margolies and at the Curtis Institute with Wanda Landowska and Rosario Scalero, where she acted as accompanist in orchestral solfege classes for Marcel Tabuteau, the great oboist. Mrs. Weaver has brought her gifts to bear on the writing of songs, poetry, radio scripts, and advertising copy. Her works include choral pieces; the songs *Cradle Song, The Heart of Heaven,* and *Songs of the Self; Festival Sonata* and *Triptych* for piano; *Patterns after the Zodiac,* an unusual collection of piano preludes, sonnets, and drawings; three volumes of poetry; and the novels *Hasty Waters* and *Standing in the Need.* A noted piano teacher, she has instructed such award winners as Albertine Baumgartner, Leona Rae Peltzman, and Phyllis Pehr.

EARL ROBINSON (1910——), a pupil of Aaron Copland, achieved prominence with his *Ballad for Americans,* scored for chorus, solo, and orchestra, with a text by John La Touche, first introduced in 1939 in the WPA production *Sing for Your Supper.* Following the success of the work when broadcast by Paul Robeson, Robinson composed several other works in a similar vein. In 1940 and 1941 he was awarded a Guggenheim fellowship to work on a musical setting of Carl Sandburg's *The People, Yes.* Among numerous other works, Robinson has composed the cantatas *The Lonesome Train* and *The Tower of Babel;* the songs *The House I Live In; Joe Hill; Abe Lincoln; Free and Equal Blues; Same Boat, Brother;* the ballet *Bouquet for Molly;* the opera *Sandhog;* the symphonic poem *A Country They Call Puget Sound;* and the musical *One Foot in America.*

2. ART SONGS

In this century men like Samuel Barber and Aaron Copland have, as we have seen, written beautiful and highly sensitive recital songs; but in addition to such composers, there are also men who have either specialized in or are known chiefly for their art songs. However, as we look over the lists of song composers we find few writing that type of ballad that Oley Speaks, Carrie Jacobs Bond, Lily Strickland, and countless others were writing in the early decades of the century. There are "pop" songs in superabundance, but between that extreme and the art song there no longer seems to be a real middle ground.

RICHARD HAGEMAN (1882——), born in Holland, settled in this country in 1907 and was appointed assistant conductor at the Metropolitan Opera House, where his opera *Caponsacchi* was performed in 1937. Head of the voice department at Chicago Musical College for a number of years, he has written film music, piano pieces, and many songs, including *At the Well; May Night; Do Not Go, My Love; Lift Thou the Burdens, Father;* and *Miranda.*

Paris-born CARL ENGEL (1883–1944) was educated at the universities of Strassburg and Munich, and came to America in 1905, where from 1909 to 1921 he was editor and musical adviser of the Boston Music Company. In 1922 he was appointed chief of the Music Division of the Library of Congress, and in 1929 he became president of G. Schirmer, Inc., and editor of the *Musical Quarterly*. He was instrumental in establishing the Archives of American Folksong at the Library of Congress, and he was one of the founders of the American Musicological Society. His compositions include a *Triptych* for violin and piano; a number of piano pieces; and many songs, including *The Sea-Shell, The Trout,* and *The Conspirator*.

BAINBRIDGE CRIST (1883——) wrote a number of instrumental works and experimented with songs to Oriental texts. He was particularly happy in his songs *Chinese Mother Goose Rhymes, Drolleries from an Oriental Doll's House, Colored Stars, Into a Ship Dreaming, April Rain,* and *Queer Yarns*.

WINTTER WATTS (1884–1962) won the $1,000 Morris Loeb Prize in 1919 with his symphonic poem *Young Blood,* and in 1923 won the Pulitzer Prize and a Prix de Rome that enabled him to spend the next two years at the American Academy in Rome. His larger works include a *Bridal Overture;* a Suite, *Etchings;* and three songs with string orchestra. Possibly his best known songs are *The Poet Sings, Wings of Night,* the cycle of *Vignettes of Italy, The Little Page's Song, Wild Tears, Alone, With the Tide,* and *Joy*.

WARREN STOREY SMITH (1885——) held the post of professor of theory and composition at the New England Conservatory from 1922 to 1958, while acting as music critic for various Boston papers. His songs include *Four Songs from Tennyson's In Memoriam* (1930); *To Helen* (1914); *The Gift of Pan; Faith; I Know a Trail* (1915); and a setting of Richard Le Gallienne's *A Caravan from China Comes* (1916), a work rivaled by perhaps only one other setting, that of ALICE BARNETT (1888——), who has also to her credit a setting of Scollard's *Serenade;* a cycle after Browning, *In a Gondola;* and a setting of Cale Young Rice's *Chanson of the Bells of Osenèy,* a remarkable, almost mystic song in which each bell has its own carillon-like motive. Miss Barnett was a pupil of Weidig, Borowski, Middelshulte, Ganz, and Kaun.

LOUIS EDGAR JOHNS (1886——) wrote piano pieces, chamber music, orchestral works, and *Lyrics from the German,* five volumes of songs in the German Romantic style.

WALTER GOLDE (1887–1963) studied at the Imperial Conservatory of Vienna and became a singers' accompanist. His songs include a setting of Rossetti's *Sudden Light* and the lyrical *To an Invalid* and *A Lad Went a-Wooing*.

A. WALTER KRAMER (1890———) worked on the staff of *Musical America*, which he eventually edited, and served as a director of the Galaxy Music Corporation in New York and of the American Society of Composers, Authors, and Publishers. His orchestral works include a *Symphonic Rhapsody* for violin and orchestra; *In Elizabethan Days*, for strings; two *Symphonic Sketches*; a *Gavotte*; a *Night Song*; and a transcription of Bach's *Chaconne*. He has also composed an *Eklog* for violin and piano; a choral cycle, *In Normandy*; and numerous songs, the form in which he achieved the widest distinction: these last include *Beauty of Earth*; *Swans*; *Pleading*; *Before the Paling of the Stars*; *The Faltering Dusk*; and *The Last Hour*.

ERNEST CHARLES (1895———) composed piano pieces and songs which proved popular in concert and on the radio. They include *Clouds*; *The House on the Hill*; *Spendthrift*; *Sweet Song of Long Ago*; *When I Have Sung My Songs*. From 1945 to 1947 he was producer of a radio program, "Great Moments in Music."

JOHN DUKE (1899———) studied with Artur Schnabel and Nadia Boulanger and in 1923 became an instructor at Smith College. His instrumental works include a Concerto for piano and orchestra (1938) and a *Carnival Overture* (1942). In addition to a String Quartet, a String Trio, and a Piano Trio, he has produced over a hundred songs, many to texts by noted poets, including *I've Dreamed of Sonnets*; *Loveliest of Trees*; *Wild Swans*; *Luke Havergal*; *Bells in the Rain*; and *There Will Be Stars*. He has also composed the chamber operas *Captain Lovelace*; *The Sire of Maledroit*; and *The Yankee Pedlar*.

THEODORE WARD CHANLER (1902–1961) wrote chiefly in the smaller forms, particularly songs. A student of Arthur Shepherd, Percy Goetschius, Ernest Bloch, and Nadia Boulanger, he served for a number of years as music critic for the Boston *Herald*, and in 1944 was granted a Guggenheim fellowship. Chanler's songs, characterized by their lyric melody and mildly polytonal textures, include two series of *Epitaphs*; a song cycle, *The Children*; and a choral work, *Ann Gregory*, commissioned jointly by Town Hall and by the League of Composers. Others of his works include a Sonata for violin and piano;

Five Short Colloquies, a Suite for piano; a Mass for two women's voices; a ballet, *Pas de Trois;* a Fugue for two pianos, *Joyful Mystery;* and a chamber opera, *The Pot of Fat.*

Like many of our composers of effective art songs, CELIUS DOUGHERTY (1902——) has profited from his wide experience as a singers' accompanist. His sensitive and deeply-moving songs include *Hushed Be the Camps Today; Loveliest of Trees; Madonna of the Evening Flowers; Children's Letter to the U. N.,* and the whimsical *Love in the Dictionary.* His instrumental works include a Piano Concerto; a two-piano Sonata on nautical themes; a Piano Sonata; and a Sonata for violin and piano.

JOHN EDMUNDS (1913——) studied with Scalero, Piston, Roy Harris, and Otto Luening, and has attracted attention as a writer of songs. While at Columbia he was awarded the 1937 Bearns Prize for a group of forty songs, and in 1940 he received a Seidl traveling fellowship. A 1951 Fulbright grant enabled him to edit a hundred songs by Purcell, and from 1954 to 1956 he held an Italian government fellowship for studying the solo cantatas of Alessandro Scarlatti and Benedetto Marcello. In 1956 Edmunds succeeded the author of this volume as curator of the Americana Collection of the New York Public Library, a position he held until 1961.

Though he has composed in larger forms, WILLIAM FLANAGAN (1926——), born September 14, 1926, in Detroit, has won recognition chiefly as a composer of highly effective songs. Reviewing Flanagan's narrative for coloratura soprano and baritone, *The Lady of Tearful Regret,* Jay S. Harrison commented in the New York *Herald Tribune* of February 26, 1959, that Flanagan "writes with exceeding grace, much vitality and an ear all enlightened in the matter of delicate sonority." Others of Flanagan's works include a cycle, *The Weeping Pleiades; Billy Budd;* a set of Five Songs for soprano; a song-cycle, *Moss;* and a dramatic work, *Horror Movie,* which John Ardoin of *Musical America* (May, 1962) found a mélange of Ives and Richard Rodgers. Flanagan has also written three Piano Sonatas; *By the Waters of Babylon* (1959), for orchestra; a *Divertimento for Classical Orchestra* (1960); a *Concert Ode* (1960); incidental music to James Albee's play *The Ballad of the Sad Café;* and a four-scene opera, *Bartleby,* with libretto by Albee and James Hinton, Jr., based on

Melville's story. In 1963 the Ford Foundation gave Albee and Flanagan a grant to compose an opera, tentatively entitled *The Ice Age,* for the New York City Opera.

3. CHORAL PIECES AND PART-SONGS

One group of our composers has specialized in choral writing. ELMER SAMUEL HOSMER (1862–1945), a pupil of J. C. D. Parker and Percy Goetschius, composed anthems, solos and duets for church use, as well as three cantatas: *The Man Without a Country; Columbus;* and *Pilgrims of 1620.* He taught at the Rhode Island College of Education.

NATHANIEL CLIFFORD PAGE (1866–1956) made arrangements of other composers' music for chorus and for orchestra, but was also a composer in his own right. He composed light operas, incidental music for plays, cantatas, orchestral music, songs, and pieces.

DANIEL PROTHEROE (1866–1934) was born in Wales and came to America in 1886. A talented choral conductor, he wrote many choral works, as well as cantatas, a symphonic poem, and two String Quartets. He compiled the *Hymnal* for the Welsh Presbyterian Church and four books of music for the Scottish Rite.

WILLIAM RHYS-HERBERT (1868–1921) was also born in Wales, but was identified with music in this country for many years. Though his specialty was school operettas, he also published part-songs, cantatas, and a number of songs.

SAMUEL RICHARDS GAINES (1896–1945) is probably best known for his *Salutation* for chorus. He also composed an oratorio, *The Vision,* and a *Fantasy on Russian Folk Songs.* For years he was organist and choirmaster of the Old Shawmut Church in Boston.

HENRY CLOUGH-LEIGHTER (1874–1956) was active as a choral composer and as an editor. His works include the cantatas *The Righteous Branch* and *Christ Triumphant;* a symphonic ode, *Christ of the Andes,* for double chorus, soli, and orchestra; several songs and song cycles for solo voice and orchestra, some hundred shorter choral works, and an equal number of songs.

F. FLAXINGTON HARKER (1876–1936) came to this country from Scotland when he was twenty-five, and from 1914 was a choral conductor and organist in Richmond, Virginia. He wrote cantatas, anthems, choruses, sacred and secular songs, and organ pieces.

GENA BRANSCOMBE (1881——), born in Canada, was educated in the United States, which she made her home. Her choral works include *Pilgrims of Destiny; The Phantom Caravan; Youth of the World; Mary at Bethlehem;* and other works. Her numerous songs include *Songs of the Unafraid* and the delightful *Unimproving Songs for Enthusiastic Children.* She has composed a *Procession* for orchestra, as well as a *Festival Prelude* and a symphonic Suite, *Quebec.* She has also written a String Quartet, a number of piano pieces, and several violin pieces.

KURT SCHINDLER (1882–1935) came to New York in 1905 from Germany to be assistant conductor at the Metropolitan. He founded the MacDowell Chorus in 1909; in 1912 it became the Schola Cantorum. A specialist in the choral arrangement of folk songs, he also composed many original choruses and songs himself.

WILLIAM LESTER (1889——), born in England, came to America when he was thirteen. His works include the oratorios *Everyman, The Manger Babe, The Coming of the King,* and *The Golden Legend;* a grand opera on an Iroquois theme, *Manabozo;* part-songs; songs; Suites for piano, for organ, and for chamber combinations; a String Quartet; and a Violin Sonata.

JOSEPH WADDELL CLOKEY (1890——) is known principally for his choral works, which include highly effective transcriptions of early American songs: a Billings anthem, Stephen Foster melodies, and two choice gutter-ballads: *Cocaine Lil* and *Frankie and Johnnie.* His works include a Symphony, five operas, part-songs, cantatas, sacred choruses, organ music, and an orchestral *Ballet Suite.* He is skillful in using sharp contrasts, sudden changes of tonality, and cannily planned dissonance.

JOHN TASKER HOWARD (1890–1964), the author of this volume, was known more widely for his books on American music than as a composer, but he has nevertheless about one hundred and fifty published compositions to his credit. These are written for various mediums, but those that have gained the widest circulation and performance are short choral pieces, some secular and some sacred. Among the former are *Oh! Did You Hear the Meadow Lark!*

(originally published as a solo song); *The Little Bay Mare; The Smart Red Fox; The Old School Bus;* and a number of others. The most widely used of his anthems are *St. Augustine's Prayer; God Who Made the Earth;* and *The Virgin's Cradle Hymn.* His other works include *Fantasy on a Choral Theme* for piano and orchestra; *From Foster Hall,* for string quartet; a *Foster Sonatina* for violin and piano (also scored as a Sinfonietta for orchestra); numerous piano pieces; songs and choral works; and a number of settings of Stephen Foster songs and works by early American composers. Brooklyn-born, John Tasker Howard received his education at Williams College, and studied music privately with Paul Tidden, Howard Brockway, and Mortimer Wilson. His books, in addition to *Our American Music,* include *Stephen Foster, America's Troubadour; Ethelbert Nevin; Our Contemporary Composers;* and *This Modern Music.* From 1940 to 1945 he was curator of the Americana Collection at the New York Public Library. From 1945 to 1959 he was a member of the board of directors of the American Society of Composers, Authors, and Publishers, and from 1953 to 1958 he was secretary of the society.

FRANCES MCCOLLIN (1892–1960) achieved distinction in spite of the handicap of blindness. Her works, traditional rather than contemporary in style, include part-songs; choral works; a Scherzo for strings, *Heavenly Children at Play;* a String Quartet; a Piano Quintet; an *Adagio* for string orchestra; and a Trio for organ (or piano), violin, and cello.

4. FOLK SONG SETTINGS

A number of our composers have made effective concert settings of folk songs. HARVEY WORTHINGTON LOOMIS (1865–1930), a pupil of Dvořák, was a specialist in catching the spirit of Indian music and preserving it in his arrangements of the melodies. His *Lyrics of the Red Man,* settings for piano first issued by Wa-Wan Press, are altogether remarkable in the way they emphasize native, primitive traits. Loomis also composed an opera, *The Traitor Mandolin;* four comic operas; a number of musical pantomimes; incidental music to plays; a Piano Sonata; and a Sonata for violin.

THURLOW LIEURANCE (1878–1963) was known to the public primarily for his song *By the Waters of Minnetonka,* an adapted Indian melody. Lieurance trained at the Cincinnati College of Music and spent some twenty years in research work among the Indians, studying their life and recording their songs. He composed an opera, *Drama of the Yellowstone.*

Among the composers who have specialized in Negro music, the name of HENRY THACKER BURLEIGH (1866–1949) is prominent, since he was a pioneer in arranging spirituals for concert use and also since, as a singer, himself a Negro, he performed the songs of his people throughout the country. A pupil of Dvořák, Burleigh made arrangements of dozens of spirituals, sophisticated in harmonic treatment, though generally without alteration or development of the melodies. His setting of *Deep River* has enjoyed great popularity.

CLARENCE CAMERON WHITE (1880——) was principally active as a violinist, but his *Bandanna Sketches,* for violin and piano, attracted attention to his gifts as a composer. Kreisler, Spalding, and other famous violinists found his setting of *Nobody Knows the Trouble I've Seen* a highly effective program number. White published a book of *Forty Negro Spirituals,* and he composed a *String Quartet on Negro Themes* and a *Negro Rhapsody* for orchestra.

WILLIAM J. REDDICK (1890——) first came to the attention of the public through his characteristic settings of Negro spirituals—*Standin' in the Need of Prayer; Leanin' on de Lawd;* and *Wait Till I Put on My Crown.* Reddick's major works include *Espanharlem* for orchestra; *Armistice Day* for orchestra, men's chorus, tenor, and baritone soli; the songs *Velvet Darkness; Red Bombay; Since You Are Gone; Your Love and Mine; In the Darkness of Night;* and *I'm Goin' to Hitch My Mule.* He also compiled and edited an album of *Roustabout Songs of the Ohio River.*

DAVID GUION (1895——) classified his piano pieces into several groups: "Cowboys' and Old Fiddlers' Breakdowns," such as *Turkey in the Straw; Sheep and Goat Walkin' to Pasture;* and *Arkansas Traveler;* and "Alley Tunes," such as *Brudder Sinkiller and His Flock of Sheep; The Lonesome Whistler;* and *The Harmonica Player.* He has made piano settings of traditional Mother Goose tunes, as well as arranging a number of spirituals and cowboy tunes. His original works include a *Negro Lament;* a *Pickaninny Dance; The Scissors Grinder;* and a *Jazz Scherzo,* all for piano; a group of

Imaginary Early Louisiana Songs of Slavery; a Suite for Orchestra; and a primitive African ballet, *Shingandi.*

JACQUES WOLF (1896——), born in Roumania in 1896, came to this country as a small boy and made a specialty of songs remarkable for their Negro flavor, including *De Glory Road, Gwine to Hebb'n, Betsy's Boy,* and *God's World.* He composed the music for the play *John Henry,* starring Paul Robeson, and an opera, *The Trysting Tree.* His setting of the song *Shortnin' Bread* has been a great favorite.

The songs of ROBERT MACGIMSEY are so adroitly composed in the idiom of the Louisiana Negro that it is difficult to distinguish between them and his settings of Negro folk songs. His original compositions include *Shadrach; Daniel in the Lion's Den; The Old Home; To My Mother; Roofs; The Old Slave; Sweet Little Jesus Boy; Jonah and the Whale;* and *Abraham.*

JOHN JACOB NILES (1892——), a collector and arranger of both Negro folk songs and the Anglo-American ballads of the Southern Appalachians, constructed his own instruments for accompanying his singing (traditional dulcimers and lutes) and concertized extensively, both alone and in collaboration with Marion Kirby. Niles's publications include *Singing Soldiers* (1927); *Seven Kentucky Mountain Songs* (1929); *Seven Negro Exaltations* (1929); *Ten Christmas Carols* (1935); *More Songs of the Hill-Folk* (1936); and *Ballads and Tragic Legends* (1937).

JOSEPHINE MCGILL (1877–1919), one of the first collectors of Appalachian Mountain ballads, also composed several original songs, among them the lovely *Duna.* She published *Folk Songs of the Kentucky Mountains* and wrote a number of articles on American music.

VICTOR YOUNG (1889——) composed the highly successful settings of the Appalachian Mountain songs *The Red Rosey Bush* and *The Unconscious Lover,* among others; he also arranged and conducted orchestral accompaniments for singers on many of the early Edison records. His works include operettas; orchestra compositions, such as *In the Great Smokies, Arizona Sketches, Jeep, Charm Assembly Line* (a ballet), and *A Fragment* for string orchestra; and numerous songs, including *Flowers and You.*

OSCAR J. FOX (1879——) was one of the first to make concert

arrangements of cowboy songs, chiefly those found in the Lomax collections. He set *Whoopee Ti Yi Yo, Old Paint, Old Chisholm Trail, Rounded Up in Glory,* and others, as well as three desperado songs—*Sam Bass, Prisoner for Life,* and *Jesse James.*

5. INSTRUMENTAL PIECES

A large group of our composers, even though they composed in various forms, have been most widely known for their short instrumental pieces. A number of the older ones came from abroad. JOHN ORTH (1850–1932) was born in Bavaria and was brought to America as an infant. He taught in Boston and was an authority on Liszt, with whom he had studied; he wrote many piano pieces, and did considerable editorial work. CONSTANTIN VON STERNBERG (1852–1924) came here from Russia in 1880 and in 1886 became a citizen. He founded the Sternberg School of Music in Philadelphia and wrote over a hundred works for piano. RICHARD BURMEISTER (1860–1944) was born in Germany and settled in America when he was twenty-five. In 1903 he returned to Europe. During his eighteen years in America he taught at the Peabody Conservatory in Baltimore and was director of the Scharwenka Conservatory in New York. Probably the best known of his many piano pieces was the *Persian Song* for piano. He wrote an impressive Piano Concerto.

GIUSEPPE FERRATA (1865–1928) was born in Italy and came to America when he was twenty-seven. He wrote piano pieces, works for violin and piano, songs, organ pieces, a String Quartet, a Piano Concerto, a Symphony for orchestra and chorus, and some Catholic church music: a *Messe Solennelle,* a *Missa in G Major,* and other works. THORVALD OTTERSTRÖM (1868–1942) was born in Denmark and came to America when he was twenty-four. A Chicago professor of composition and theory, he was an active composer and wrote pieces for piano and orchestra. CHARLES BOCHAU (1870–1932) was born in Germany and brought to this country in his youth. From 1912 he taught at the Peabody Conservatory in Baltimore. He composed principally violin music, also songs and a number of church anthems.

Perhaps the best known of this foreign-born group was FELIX BOROWSKI (1872–1956), composer of the famous *Adoration* for violin.

Borowski was born in England and, after he had established a reputation abroad, was invited to head the theory and composition department of the Chicago Musical College. He became a newspaper critic and wrote program notes for the Chicago Symphony Orchestra. He wrote much in the larger forms, composing a Piano Concerto, tone poems, Overtures, Rhapsodies, ballets and pantomimes for orchestra, three Organ Sonatas, a Piano Sonata, and many pieces in smaller forms.

Returning to the native-born, we come to CLAYTON JOHNS (1857–1932), who studied architecture before deciding on a musical career. He studied in Boston with John K. Paine and in Berlin with Rummel and Kiel. In 1912 he joined the staff of the New England Conservatory. He left many pieces for piano and some for violin, among them *Melody, Berceuse, Intermezzo, Romance,* and *Scherzino.* He wrote books on music and published his *Reminiscences of a Musician.*

GUSTAV SAENGER (1865–1935), a music editor, violinist, and conductor, was editor of the *Musical Observer* from 1904 to 1929. He arranged standard works for the violin and wrote many original pieces as well, including a Concertino for violin. CAMILLE ZECKWER (1875–1924) studied with Dvořák and Scharwenka and later co-directed the Philadelphia Academy with Frederick E. Hahn. He composed songs, pieces, and many works in larger forms—a symphonic poem, a Piano Concerto, cantatas, an opera, and some chamber music. ANNA PRISCILLA RISHER (1875——) studied with Goetschius and Chadwick. Her published compositions number some three hundred, many of them for teaching: piano pieces; Trios for piano, violin, and cello; and songs. Her *Indian Lament* for piano won one of the Presser prizes.

JAMES FRANCIS COOKE (1875——), known chiefly as editor of *The Etude,* was for many years in charge of the publications of the Presser firm in Philadelphia. He wrote many piano pieces, including the popular *Sea Gardens.* LOUIS CAMPBELL-TIPTON (1877–1921) taught theory at the Chicago Musical College before settling in Paris in 1901. He was known chiefly for piano pieces and songs, but had in manuscript two operas and a number of orchestral works. EASTWOOD LANE (1879–1951) prided himself on his lack of musical training and was content to let his natural talent find its own outlet; some of his short pieces, consequently, have enough ideas for a symphony. His several sets of piano pieces include *Sleepy Hollow, Five American Dances, Adirondack Sketches,* and others. Ferde Grofé scored several of them for Paul Whiteman.

ALEXANDER MACFAYDEN (1879–1936) was trained principally at the Chicago Musical College; he taught in New York and Milwaukee. He published about a hundred piano pieces and songs, including the widely sung *Cradle Song* and *Inter Nos.* ALEXANDER RUSSELL (1881–1953) was widely known as a concert organist, pianist, and choral conductor; he also composed organ works, choral works, and a number of charming songs. FANNIE CHARLES DILLON (1881–1947) studied with Godowsky, Kaun, and Rubin Goldmark. For many of her piano works she took her inspiration from the birds, as in *Melodic Poems of the Mountains,* with two of its movements entitled *Birds at Dusk* and *Birds at Dawn.* Her orchestral works include *Celebration of Victory, A Letter of the Southland,* and *Chinese Symphonic Suite.* She also wrote songs and chamber music.

FRANK H. GREY (1883–1951) was a New York radio director and a Broadway musical comedy conductor. He composed orchestral works, songs, and piano pieces, including *Ten Aquarelles* and *Winter Scenes.* His musical comedies include *Sue, Dear* (1922), *Matinee Girl* (1926), and *Happy* (1927). CECIL BURLEIGH (1885——) wrote principally for his own instrument, the violin. His teaching pieces have been much used, for they are distinguished by the combination of practical usefulness and real musical interest. His concert pieces are also well known, including his three Violin Concertos and his two Violin Sonatas, *The Ascension* and *From the Life of St. Paul.* He also wrote a number of piano pieces and many songs.

LEE PATTISON (1890——) studied with Chadwick, Baermann, Juon, and Schnabel. Though best known as a pianist and music educator, he also composed piano pieces, including *Florentine Sketches* and a Suite, *Told in the Hills.* In 1937 he joined the faculty of Columbia University. SAMUEL GARDNER (1891——) was born in Russia and was brought to this country when he was six. He studied with Franz Kneisel and Percy Goetschius and began his career as a concert violinist. Though widely known to the concert public for his racy little violin piece *From the Canebreak,* he also composed works of larger dimensions: *Broadway*, a tone poem; a Violin Concerto; a String Quartet; a symphonic poem, *New Russia*; a Quintet, *To the Fallen*; a Prelude and Fugue for string quartet; and a set of Variations for string quartet.

NICOLAS SLONIMSKY (1894——) was born in St. Petersburg, Russia, where he studied at the Conservatory. He came to the United States in 1923 and in 1931 became a citizen. His compositions include *A Study in Black and White* and *Four Russian Melodies* for clarinet and piano. Slonimsky is widely known as a musicologist and author. His books include *Music Since 1900* (1937); *The Music of Latin America* (1945); *The Road to Music* (1947); *Thesaurus of Scales and Melodic Patterns* (1947); *A Thing or Two About Music* (1948); and *Lexicon of Musical Invective* (1953); he edited editions of the *International Cyclopedia of Music and Musicians* and *Baker's Biographical Dictionary of Musicians*.

ERIK LEIDZEN (1894–1962) was born in Sweden and came to the United States in 1915. He was for many years arranger for the Goldman Band and composed many original works, most of them for band: *Springtime Overture, Autumn Overture, Holiday Overture, Nordic March, Storm King Overture,* and others. For orchestra he composed an *Irish Symphony* and a *Swedish Rhadsody*. CECIL COWLES (1901——) made her piano debut at six. Her piano compositions include *Arabesque, In a Ricksha, Song of Persia, Lotus Flower, The Ocean,* and others. Her song *Hey Nonny, Oh* has been popular.

Born in New York, August 17, 1903, ABRAM CHASINS (1903——) studied piano with Josef Hofmann and composition with Rubin Goldmark. He became the first American composer to have his music conducted by Arturo Toscanini when in 1931 the Maestro led the New York Philharmonic-Symphony in an orchestral version of his *Three Chinese Pieces*, originally composed for piano in 1925. Chasins also composed twenty-four Preludes for piano and two Piano Concertos. In the Second Concerto he departed from the usual structural conventions and employed such smaller forms as waltz and fugue. In 1943 Chasins was appointed music consultant of radio station WQXR (New York), and in 1947 he became its director. He has written many lively and penetrating articles as well as the books *Speaking of Pianists* (1958) and *The Van Cliburn Legend* (1959).

LEROY ANDERSON (1908——) was born in Cambridge, Massachusetts, June 29, 1908. He graduated from Harvard in 1929 and while studying there for his master's degree was director of the university band. From 1929 to 1935 he was organist and choirmaster of the East Congregational Church in Milton, Massachusetts. During the same period and later, he was active as conductor and arranger in Boston and New York, doing much of his arranging for the Boston "Pops" Orchestra. His light instrumental pieces have delighted audiences at "pop" concerts, on phonograph records and on radio and television. The music is invariably descriptive of the fanciful titles—*Fiddle Faddle, Sleigh Ride, The Syncopated Clock, Jazz Pizzicato, A Trumpeter's Lullaby*, and dozens of others. One of his pieces, *Blue Tango*, achieved international hit-parade status; Anderson also wrote the score for the Broadway show *Goldilocks*.

RICHARD FRANKO GOLDMAN (1910——), son of Edwin Franko Goldman, was born in New York City, December 7, 1910. He studied piano with Ralph Leopold and composition with Pietro Floridia and Nadia Boulanger. In 1937 he became assistant conductor of the Goldman Band, and upon his father's death in 1956 he became director of the band. By performing and commissioning new pieces, he has exerted a wide influence on the modern development of the concert band repertory, and in 1961 he received an Alice M. Ditson award for his contribution to American music. Goldman taught at the Juilliard School of Music from 1946 to 1960. His compositions include *A Curtain Raiser and Country Dance* and *A Sentimental Journey*, for band; *Hymn for Brass Choir*; an orchestral setting of the old American tune *The Lee Rigg*; a Sonatina for piano; a Violin Sonata; a *Divertimento* for flute and piano; *Two Monochromes* for flute alone; Three Duets for clarinets; and a Duo for tubas. Goldman is the compiler of *Landmarks of Early American Music* and author of two textbooks, *The Band's Music* (1938) and *The Concert Band* (1946). He wrote the libretto of Hugo Weisgall's opera *Athaliah*. In 1962 he was awarded a Guggenheim fellowship to enable him to make "a critical study of the nature and function of music in the middle of the twentieth century."

ROBERT GUYN MCBRIDE (1911——) was born in Tucson, Arizona, February 20, 1911, studied music at the University of Arizona, and joined the faculty of Bennington College in Vermont, where he taught until 1946. In 1951 he received a Guggenheim fellowship. It is high praise to say that his compositions are as entertaining as their titles; his works include *Depression* (1934), a Sonata for violin and piano; *Mexican Rhapsody* (1934), for orchestra; *Prelude to a Tragedy* (1935); *Go Choruses* (1935); *Fugato on a Well-Known Theme* (1937); a ballet, *Show Piece* (1937); *Swing Stuff* (1938), for clarinet and piano; *Jam Session* (1941), for wind quintet; *Strawberry Jam (Home Made)* (1942), for orchestra; *Side Show* (1944), for orchestra; *Popover* (1945), originally for clarinet and piano and later scored for orchestra; *Sherlock Holmes*, a Suite for military band; a Violin Concerto (1954), and *Sunday in Mexico* (1960), for orchestra.

GEORGE KLEINSINGER (1914———), born in San Bernardino, California, February 13, 1914, studied with Philip James, Frederick Jacobi, and Bernard Wagenaar. His works include a Symphony (1942); a Cello Concerto (1946); a Violin Concerto (1955); a Trio for clarinet, cello, and piano (1955); *Dawn to Dawn*, a Suite for piano and orchestra; an *Overture on American Folk Themes* (1955); *Coney Island Overture* (1955); and *The Tree That Found Christmas* (1955). But Kleinsinger is probably best known for such delightfully descriptive orchestral pieces as *Tubby the Tuba* (1942); *Pan the Piper* (1946); *Pee-Wee the Piccolo* (1946); and *Street Corner Concerto* (1947), for harmonica and orchestra. He has also written a *Brooklyn Baseball Cantata* (1948); *archy and mehitabel*, a comic opera based on Don Marquis's stories (1954); and *Adventures in a Zoo*, for young people's concerts.

CHAPTER FOURTEEN

Latter-Century and Present-Day Religious Music

1. DUDLEY BUCK (1839–1909) AND HIS SUCCESSORS

In previous chapters the growth of religious music has been traced from colonial days, through the works of Lowell Mason and his colleagues in the first half of the nineteenth century. The first psalmodists and hymn-tune writers were succeeded by men of better training, some of whom studied in Europe. Many wrote tunes which are still in wide use. Few of them, however, attempted the larger forms of choral writing. In this field the name of Dudley Buck stands out as a pioneer, just as John K. Paine rises above his colleagues as the first of our symphonists to achieve success.

In many ways Buck's missionary work in giving organ recitals was as educational as that of Theodore Thomas with his orchestra. His musicianship was combined with the ability to catch and hold popular attention. As a choir director and composer he helped to develop our literature for the church, and since he was fond of the mixed quartet which has become a feature of American worship, and sometimes its curse, he had a profound influence upon our choir music. In his larger choral works he had due regard for the requirements of the text he chose, and he was inventive and versatile in obtaining appropriate effects. As a teacher he trained many church composers of the next generation—Harry Rowe Shelley, John Hyatt Brewer, Frederick Grant Gleason, and others.

Dudley Buck was born in Hartford, Connecticut, March 10, 1839. His father was a shipping merchant, and even though the son showed an early taste for music, his father intended that he should become a businessman. He had no music lessons until he was sixteen, but he made up for lost time and became so ardent a pupil that his father relented, allowed his son to become a musician, and determined that he should have the best possible training for his profession. Dudley went to Leipzig in 1858, where he studied with Hauptmann, Richter, Plaidy, and Moscheles. Then he went to Dresden to take organ lessons with Friedrich Schneider. He later spent a year in Paris, coming home in 1862 to become the organist of Hartford's Park Church.

In 1864 he published his first *Motette Collection*, at a time when such motets were much needed. In 1869 he was called to Chicago to be organist of St. James's. When the church burned in the great fire of '71, many of his manuscripts were lost, including a setting of Drake's poem *The Culprit Fay*. He then went to Boston to take charge of the music at St. Paul's, and in 1872 he composed a *Festival Hymn* for Gilmore's second jubilee; a year later his setting of the *46th Psalm* was performed by the Handel and Haydn Society. In 1874 he published *The Legend of Don Munio*, a setting of a metrical version of Irving's *Alhambra*, for small chorus and orchestra. The work was well adapted to the choral resources of small cities and became very popular.

Theodore Thomas invited Buck in 1875 to go to New York to act as assistant conductor of the Central Park Garden Concerts; Thomas also appointed him assistant conductor of the Cincinnati Festival. Buck moved his family to Brooklyn, where he became organist of Holy Trinity after a short term at St. Ann's in New York. In 1876 Buck composed the *Centennial Meditation of Columbus*, to a poem written for the occasion by the poet-musician Sidney Lanier. The work was performed under Thomas at the inaugural ceremonies of the centennial in Philadelphia.

In 1877 Buck published a work which has been of great help to organists and choirmasters: *Illustration in Choir Accompaniment, with Hints on Registration*. This handbook enjoyed many editions, and it is still in use. In the same year Buck published his Second Organ Sonata. *The Nun of Nidaro* (1879) was from Longfellow's poems, as were the *Scenes from the Golden Legend*, the symphonic cantata that won the $1,000 prize at the Cincinnati Festival in 1880. That same year Theodore Thomas introduced Buck's symphonic Overture to Scott's *Marmion* at one of the concerts of the Brooklyn Philharmonic.

In 1881 Buck published settings of more of Longfellow's *Saga of King Olaf*, from which he had taken *The Nun of Nidaro*. The later work was *King Olaf's Christmas*. Like *The Nun*, it was scored for male chorus with solos, to the accompaniment of piano obbligato, reed organ, and string quartet ad lib. The composer knew what was practical in the way of accompaniment in his day.

Buck's reputation abroad was strengthened in 1885 by the London performance of his dramatic cantata, *The Light of Asia*. For the text of *The Voyage of Columbus*, Buck again turned to Washington Irving and adapted a libretto from the *Life of Columbus*. Buck's cantata presented six scenes: *The Chapel of St. George at Palos*, *On the Deck of the Santa Maria*, *The Vesper Hymn*, *Mutiny*, *In Distant Andalusia*, and *Land and Thanksgiving*. The work has had frequent performances in America and in Germany. Buck made his own German translation of the libretto.

Of all Buck's works, church choirs have found most useful the series of short cantatas depicting the prophecy, birth, death, resurrection, and ascension of Christ. There are three works in the cycle: *The Coming of the King*, *The Story of the Cross*, and *Christ the Victor*, all suited to performance in connection with a Christmas or Easter service. *A Midnight Service for New Year's Eve* has seen many an old year out and a new year in.

Buck wrote a number of shorter songs and ballads, both sacred and secular. Some are a trifle cloying in their sweetness. He also made organ transcriptions of such familiar songs as *Home Sweet Home* and *The Last Rose of Summer*, for many congregations would rather hear these as an offertory than the music of Bach or Handel. Buck wrote for his market, and his work as a whole represents a compromise between the public's taste and the composer's own ideals. Yet undeniably he worked to raise standards, and to a degree his constant efforts succeeded.

Many of Buck's pupils made names for themselves. CHARLES BEACH HAWLEY (1858–1915), son of a Massachusetts farmer who appreciated good music, had been a church organist and had directed music at the Cheshire Military Academy before he came to Buck to study composition. For many summers he took charge of the music at St. James's chapel in Elberon, New Jersey. Hawley's principal compositions were songs, for he had a pretty gift for lyric melody; he wrote many part-songs for men's voices, many of them of a "bull-frog on the bank" variety. Male quartets of several generations sang *They Kissed! I Saw Them Do It.* There were sacred songs, too—no pupil of Dudley Buck could have avoided writing them. Hawley's *Trisagion and Sanctus* was perhaps the best known.

WILLIAM HAROLD NEIDLINGER (1863–1924) was an organist and conductor, but he specialized in child psychology and wrote many delightful songs for children. Born in Brooklyn, he had his musical training with Dudley Buck. In addition to songs, he wrote the cantata *Prayer, Promise, and Praise,* as well as two comic operas.

Three of Buck's most prominent pupils lived in and were principally active in Brooklyn. JOHN HYATT BREWER (1856–1931) was organist at Lafayette Avenue Presbyterian Church from 1881. He had become organist of the City Park Chapel in Brooklyn at the age of fifteen, and was prominent as a choral conductor. He was one of the founders of the American Guild of Organists, and in 1916 New York University made him a Doctor of Music. Brewer wrote over two hundred compositions, many of them for chorus, including *Up with the Flag* (1894); *Lord of the Dunderberg* (1905), a cantata for men's voices and orchestra; and *Bedouin Love-Song* (1906), for mixed voices *a cappella.* He wrote much instrumental music, including a String Quartet, a Suite for orchestra, an orchestra *Fantaisie,* and some pieces for string quartet and flute.

New Haven-born HARRY ROWE SHELLEY (1858–1947) studied with Dudley Buck and with Dvořák. He lived in Brooklyn and was organist of its leading churches—Plymouth Church and the Church of the Pilgrims. For many years he was the organist at the Fifth Avenue Baptist Church in New York. His sacred oratorios and cantatas include *The Inheritance Divine; Death and Life; Vexilla Regis;* and *Lochinvar's Ride.* His anthems are singable and effective, for he knew his church choir from experience. His orchestral works include two Symphonies; a *Santa Claus Overture;* an orchestral Suite, *Souvenir de Baden-Baden;* a Violin Concerto; and a *Fantasia* for piano and orchestra.

Brooklyn-born RAYMOND HUNTINGTON WOODMAN (1861–1943) studied with Dudley Buck and in Paris with César Franck. His works include anthems and cantatas, a few works for organ, and many songs. He was for over five decades organist of the First Presbyterian Church in Brooklyn.

Among the many others who have contributed to American church music we must include HOMER NEWTON BARTLETT (1846–1920), organist of the Madison Avenue Baptist Church in New York for thirty-three years. He studied with S. B. Mills and O. F. Jacobsohn and wrote over two hundred and fifty compositions. His organ works include a Toccata, a Suite, a *Festival Hymn, De Profundis,* and a *Méditation Sérieuse.* He composed an opera and an operetta; a symphonic poem and a *Legende* for orchestra; a Concerto and a *Ballade* for violin and orchestra. Bartlett was one of the founders of the American Guild of Organists. Rupert Hughes termed Bartlett's Opus One, the *Grande Polka de Concert,* "one of the most outrageously popular piano pieces ever published in America"—which indeed it was.

LUCIEN GATES CHAFFIN (1846–1927) was born in Worcester, Massachusetts, and graduated from Brown University. He devoted himself to teaching, to composing, and to work as a concert organist, music critic, and editor. His compositions include a setting of the *23rd Psalm;* a cantata, *Holy Night;* many anthems, organ pieces, and songs.

EDWARD JULIUS BIEDERMANN (1849–1933) was chiefly concerned with music for the Catholic church. The son of the piano teacher and composer A. J. Biedermann, he wrote several Masses and considerable choral music.

EDUARDO MARZO (1852–1929), another composer of Catholic church music, was an Italian who came to New York in 1867 as a prodigy pianist. For several years he served as accompanist for soloists, and from 1878 he lived in New York as a vocal teacher, as organist at the Church of the Holy Name, and as a music editor and composer. He wrote nine Masses, four Vespers, forty songs and anthems for the Catholic service, as well as three *Te Deums,* forty anthems, and sacred solos for the Protestant church. He also wrote secular music, including operettas, cantatas, and songs.

SUMNER SALTER (1856–1944) was one of the most prolific of our church composers. He studied with Eugene Thayer, J. C. D. Parker, and J. K. Paine, and began his career as an organist while a student at Amherst College. For nearly twenty years choirmaster at Williams

College, he wrote many anthems for men's voices. *Tarry with Me, O My Saviour* has long been a favorite. He made hundreds of vocal arrangements for various combinations; he knew what voices could do and how they would blend effectively. His responses and choir services are both musical and devotional.

HAMILTON CRAWFORD MACDOUGALL (1858–1945), a pupil of Sherwood, Lang, and J. C. D. Parker, was organist, choirmaster, and professor of music at Wellesley College for almost thirty years. He published music for the Masonic ritual and made a setting of the *85th Psalm* for tenor, bass, chorus, and organ. He wrote many articles and several books on organ technique and church music.

PETER CHRISTIAN LUTKIN (1858–1931), from 1897 dean of the School of Music of Northwestern University, was an active composer of church music. He wrote a Communion Service, several *Te Deums,* a number of settings of the Magnificat and *Nunc Dimittis,* and many anthems.

JAMES HOTCHKISS ROGERS (1857–1940) was born in Connecticut but from 1883 was identified with the musical life of Cleveland, where he was organist of the Euclid Avenue Temple and the First Unitarian Church. Rogers studied with Towne, Clarence Eddy, with Haupt and Loeschorn in Germany, and with Guilmant and Widor in Paris. Rogers's organ works include a Sonata, two Suites, a Concert Overture, a *Christmas Pastorale,* and a *Processional March.* He composed morning and evening services, two cantatas, and many anthems. Among his songs the best known are *The Star* and *Wind Song.* He was an able teacher, and for many years he served as music critic of the Cleveland *Plain Dealer.*

GEORGE WARING STEBBINS (1869–1930) was the son of George C. Stebbins, the singing evangelist, but his love for good music and his training with Guilmant and Henschel made him a respectable musician. He was one of the founders of the American Guild of Organists and was organist at several Brooklyn churches, including Emmanuel Baptist and Plymouth. His compositions number many organ pieces, anthems, choruses, and songs.

GEORGE BALCH NEVIN (1859–1933), a cousin of Ethelbert Nevin, was long known as a composer of church music. He wrote several cantatas, including *The Crown of Life* and *The Incarnation.* Like Chadwick he made a setting of Lanier's *Into the Woods My Master Went*. For nearly thirty years he divided his time between music and a wholesale paper business.

His son, GORDON BALCH NEVIN (1892–1943), a church organist, published a number of works, principally for the organ, including a *Sonata Tripartite* and a *Pageant Triumphale*. There are also a number of secular songs and concert versions of Stephen Foster's *I Dream of Jeanie, Carry Me 'Long,* and *De Camptown Races.*

CHARLES WHITNEY COOMBS (1859–1940) was prolific in both sacred and secular music. Born in Bucksport, Maine, of New England parentage, he went abroad in 1878 to study at Stuttgart and Dresden; in 1887 he became organist and choirmaster of the American Church at Dresden. He returned to America in 1891 to become organist of the Church of the Holy Communion in New York. He became organist at St. Luke's in 1908 and retired from professional life in 1928. Coombs's most important works are his cantatas: *The Vision of St. John, The First Christmas, Ancient of Days, Sorrows of Death,* and *Light Eternal.* He wrote many anthems and sacred and secular songs, of which *Her Rose* is perhaps the best known.

New York-born LOUIS RAPHAEL DRESSLER (1861–1932) was for many years organist at All Souls' in New York and was active as choral conductor, accompanist, composer of church music, and music editor for a publishing house.

English-born WALTER HENRY HALL (1862–1935) lived in this country after he was twenty-one years old. He was organist in Germantown, Pennsylvania, and Albany, New York, and after 1896 in New York City. In 1893 he founded the Brooklyn Oratorio Society. In 1913 he was made professor of choral and church music at Columbia University. His compositions include a Communion Service in G, a Magnificat and *Nunc Dimittis,* a *Festival Te Deum,* and many anthems, canticles, and hymn-tunes. In 1919 he was a member of the committee on the Episcopal *Hymnal.*

Born in Bath, England, T. TERTIUS NOBLE (1867–1953) was a scholarship pupil at the Royal Conservatory, where he studied organ with Parratt, harmony and counterpoint with Bridge, and composition with Stanford. He became the organist at All Saints' Church in Colchester in 1881, remaining until 1889. From 1890 to 1892 he was assistant organist at Trinity College, Cambridge. He was organist at Ely Cathedral from 1892 to 1898 and at York Minster from 1898 to 1913. In 1910 he revived the once-celebrated York Festival, after a lapse of seventy-five years.

Noble came to the United States in 1913 and centered his musical activities on St. Thomas's Church in New York, where he not only played the organ and directed the choir, but also established a choir school which has been training choristers since 1918. Noble concertized extensively in the United States, Canada, and England. He wrote orchestral works, services, hymns, choruses, songs, and pieces for piano and for violin. He composed a comic opera, *Killibegs* (1911); for orchestra he wrote *Introduction and Passacaglia* (1934) and a *Morris Dance;* for organ a Concerto in G Minor, Toccata and Fugue in F Minor, *Solemn March in E Minor, Theme in D-flat with Variations;* also a festival cantata, *Gloria Domini;* and songs, including *Winter; a Birthday Song;* and *Waiting for the May.*

Canon CHARLES WINFRED DOUGLAS (1867–1944) devoted much of his life to the restoration of plain chant in the Episcopal church. As one of the editors of the music edition of the 1940 *Hymnal* of the Episcopal church he introduced about forty tunes of plain song or polyphonic type. He composed a number of original hymn-tunes, notably one for John Bunyan's words, "He who would valiant be, let him come hither." After many years as organist in several churches, Canon Douglas became director of music for the Sisterhood of St. Mary and instructor in plain chant at the General Theological Seminary in New York. His works include a *Missa de Angelis, Asperges me, Cantica Eucharistica, Compline, Missa Marialis, Missa Penitentialis, Missa Paschalis, Canticles at Evensong, St. Dunstan Psalter and Kyrial,* and a Mass in G for women's voices and small orchestra.

2. TWENTIETH-CENTURY RELIGIOUS MUSIC

Since men born as early as the 1870's had hardly reached their maturity by the end of the nineteenth century, their works may be considered to belong to the twentieth, and we shall accordingly open this section with a man who was born in 1870.

WILLIAM CHARLES MACFARLANE (1870–1945) was born in London, England, and was brought to the United States at the age of four, where he held various positions as organist and choirmaster. He composed a cantata, *The Message of the Cross,* and numerous anthems, sacred songs, and organ pieces. He compiled *The Church Service Book* (1912) and composed *America First, A Boy Scout Operetta* (1917) and two light operas: *Little Almond Eyes* (1917) and *Swords and Scissors* (1918).

Born at Eidsvold, Norway, F. MELIUS CHRISTIANSEN (1871–1955) came to this country in 1888 and founded the influential St. Olaf's Lutheran Choir in Northfield, Minnesota. Christiansen's works include a *Reformation Cantata* (1917) and a cantata on the subject of *The Prodigal Son* (1918). He was also the compiler and editor of collections of choral works and hymns. Upon his retirement in 1914 his son Olaf Christian Christiansen (1901———), formerly choirmaster at Oberlin College, succeeded his father as director of the Music School of St. Olaf's College.

FRANK EDWIN WARD (1872———) was a pupil of MacDowell at Columbia University and from 1909 to 1919 was an associate professor of music there. From 1906 to 1940 he was organist and choirmaster of the Church of the Holy Trinity in New York. He composed many anthems, organ pieces, services, and part-songs, as well as a Symphony; an *Ocean Rhapsody;* and a Scherzo for orchestra, *Peter Pan;* two String Quartets, a Trio, and two Sonatas for violin and piano.

T. CARL WHITMER (1873–1959), an organist and choirmaster, considered that his life work had been the writing and composing of the *Spiritual Music Dramas* produced at Dramamount, an artistic colony which he founded near the Hudson River in New York State. His published works include songs, pieces for piano and for organ, anthems and choruses, a *Syrian Ballet* for orchestra, and a *Choral Rhapsody* for soli, chorus, and orchestra, to a text by Walt Whitman. Whitmer was organist of the Sixth Presbyterian Church of Pittsburgh from 1916 to 1932.

Tertius Noble's distinguished New York colleague CLARENCE DICKINSON (1873———) trained in Chicago and subsequently with Guilmant, Vierne, and Moszkowski in Paris. Until 1900 he was organist of Saint James's Church in Chicago and conductor of the English Opera Company and several choral societies. When he came to New York he was appointed organist of the Brick Presbyterian Church and of Temple Beth-El. He helped found the American Guild of Organists. Dickinson's compositions include vocal solos and choruses, a Symphony for organ, and shorter works for organ and stringed instruments. He edited a series of *Sacred Choruses, Ancient and Modern;* a *Book of Eighty Anthems;* and a *Book of Forty Antiphons.* In 1945 he published *90 Interludes for Organ.*

English-born MARK ANDREWS (1875–1939) studied music with Sir John Thomas Ruck at Westminster Abbey and came to America in 1902, settling in Montclair, New Jersey, where he was organist for several churches. His religious music includes a cantata, *Galilee;* religious songs, among them *Rock of Ages;* and many anthems. He also composed a setting for male voices of the folk song *John Peel,* as well as two Organ Sonatas, a String Quartet, and a secular cantata, *The Highwayman.*

ALEXANDER MATTHEWS (1879——) was born in Cheltenham, England; he studied music with his father, John Alexander Matthews, and in 1900 came to the United States and continued his studies with George A. A. Westward and William Wallace Gilchrist in Philadelphia. He became active in that city as an organist, choral conductor, teacher, and choirmaster. In addition to *The Story of Christmas,* one of the most widely used Christmas cantatas ever published in the United States, Matthews composed the cantatas *The Triumph of the Cross, The City of God, The Conversion, The Life Everlasting,* and *An Easter Pageant.*

Matthews also composed hundreds of separate anthems, including *Lord I Have Loved the Habitation,* a motet; *The Recessional,* for chorus and orchestra; *Sing We Then Those Glorious Strains,* a Christmas carol based on a Chinese melody; *Welcome Happy Morning,* an Easter anthem; and a setting of *By the Waters of Babylon.* His organ works include the volume *The Introits and Graduals of the Church Year* (1924) and the secular *Five Wayside Impressions of New England.* Matthews also composed secular choral works, including a pageant, *The Song of America,* and a comic opera, *Hades, Inc.*

Alexander Matthews's elder brother, JOHN SEBASTIAN MATTHEWS

(1870–1934), also born in Cheltenham, England, came to America early in his career and became active in Philadelphia and elsewhere as an organist and teacher. He composed a number of anthems and organ pieces.

HARVEY BARTLETT GAUL (1881–1945) studied with Widor, d'Indy, Guilmant, Dudley Buck, and Le Jeune. A resident of Pittsburgh from 1910, he was organist at Calvary Church, music teacher at Carnegie Institute of Technology, and music critic for the *Post* and *Sun*. He composed Overtures, Suites, and tone poems for orchestra, including *Père Marquette* and *New England Prelude*. His *Fosteriana* is a Suite for string orchestra on Foster melodies. Perhaps his best known choruses are *Prayer of Thanksgiving* and *Appalachian Mountain Melodies*. He published cantatas, oratorios, songs, and organ pieces.

EVERETT TITCOMB (1884——) spent virtually his entire life as a church organist, choirmaster, and prolific composer of music for the Protestant church. From 1910 to 1960 he was music director of the choir at the Church of Saint John the Evangelist in Boston. Titcomb composed six Communion Services, numerous motets, and works with Latin texts. In addition he wrote many anthems. His purely instrumental works include a Prelude for organ and brass ensemble, a *Rhapsody on Gregorian Motifs*, a Suite in E Major, *Improvisation* (on the *Tonus Peregrinus*) and *Festive Flutes*, the last-named composed for the flute stops alone and based on a theme from the Gregorian Introit for the Fifth Sunday after Easter. Titcomb has also published a Suite for flute and piano and a Christmas cantata, *The Story of Christmas*.

JAMES ROBERT GILLETTE (1886——), an organist and teacher of music, founded the Carleton Symphonic Band of Carleton College, Northfield, Minnesota, in 1923, and the Gillette Chamber Orchestra in 1937; he made several tours as organist and conductor of chamber music. He published two cantatas; two Symphonies for modern band; about forty organ pieces, including *Chanson de Matin*, *Toccatina*, Pastorale, and *Grand Choeur*; also band compositions and songs.

EDWIN SHIPPEN BARNES (1887–1958) studied with Horatio Parker at Yale and with d'Indy in Paris. He was organist at the Church of the Incarnation, at the Rutgers Presbyterian Church in New York, and at

St. Stephen's Church in Philadelphia. He also served as organist and choirmaster at the First Presbyterian Church in Santa Monica, California. His works include three cantatas, *The Comforter*, *Remember Now Thy Creator*, and *Christmas;* three Suites and two Symphonies for organ; *Fantasia* for chorus and organ; many organ solos and piano pieces; anthems and sacred and secular songs.

DAVID McK. WILLIAMS (1887——), a composer of anthems and of liturgical music for the Episcopal church, was born of American parents in Wales and spent his early life in Denver, Colorado, where he received his first musical training. He later studied in Paris with d'Indy, Widor, and Pierné. He taught at the David Mannes School in New York and headed the organ departments at Columbia University (1920–24) and at the Juilliard School of Music (1942–48). From 1920 till 1948 he was organist and choirmaster at St. Bartholomew's Church in New York. His most widely used anthems are *The King's Highway; Darest Thou Now, O Soul?; Whispers of Untimely Death; In the Year That King Uzziah Died;* and *Hymn of the Immortals*. He also composed an opera, *Florence Nightingale*, and an operetta, *Enchanted Waters*.

HAROLD VINCENT MILLIGAN (1888–1951), organist at many New York churches, composed a number of choral works, sacred and secular, some organ pieces, and two operettas; but he is perhaps best known to the general public for his arrangements of songs by Francis Hopkinson and other early American composers. Like the author of this book, he wrote a biography of Stephen Foster.

POWELL WEAVER (1890–1951) was widely known as an organist and composer of choral music, organ pieces, and songs. He studied organ with Pietro Yon in New York and composition with Ottorino Respighi in Rome. In addition to playing organ recitals he acted as accompanist for a number of prominent singers. His shorter works include the anthems *Now the Day Is Over*, *All Weary Men*, *Like the Young Sheep;* the sacred vocal solos *Build Thee More Stately Mansions*, *O Zion Haste*, and *Joy to the World;* the secular vocal solos *Moon-Marketing*, *My Garden*, and *The Abbot of Derry; Copper Country Suite*, for organ; and *The Squirrel*, an ever-popular encore number with organists; and several orchestral works: *Plantation Overture* (1925); *The Vagabond* (1931); *Dance of the Sand-*

Dune Cranes (1941), for piano and orchestra; and a Fugue for Strings, written for the Kansas City Philharmonic. His wife, Mary Weaver, the distinguished piano pedagogue, is also a well-known composer and poet.

CARL MUELLER (1892——), a skilled arranger of works for *a cappella* chorus, was educated at Elmhurst College in Illinois and at Westminster Choir College at Princeton, New Jersey. From 1927 to 1952 he was organist and choirmaster of the Central Presbyterian Church in Montclair, and organized there an excellent *a cappella* choir. He has composed more than a hundred works for voice, chorus, organ, and piano. He has also written *The Junior Chorister* and *The Junior Choir Anthem Book*.

T. FREDERICK H. CANDLYN (1892——), born in England, received his bachelor of music degree from the University of Durham in that country and completed his studies at the New York State University in Albany, where after receiving his doctorate he was appointed head of the department of music in 1923. From 1915 to 1943 he was organist and choirmaster at St. Paul's Episcopal Church in Albany and from 1934 to 1954 he was choirmaster of St. Thomas's Church in New York. Candlyn has composed more than two hundred published works, a number of which have won prizes. Among his many anthems, the most widely used are *Masters in This Hall; Thee We Adore; Ding, Dong, Merrily on High; Christ Whose Glory;* and *What Child Is This?*

Born in Grand Rapids, Michigan, May 1, 1895, LEO SOWERBY (1895——) received his musical education in Chicago, studying piano with Calvin Lampert and theory with Arthur Olaf Anders. There have been a number of "firsts" in Sowerby's career. He was the first composer to hold a fellowship in the American Academy at Rome, from 1921 to 1924; after serving thirty-five years as organist and choirmaster of St. James's (Episcopal) Cathedral in Chicago and thirty-seven years as teacher of composition at the American Conservatory of Music in Chicago, he became in 1962 the first director of the newly-formed College of Church Musicians at the Washington (D.C.) Cathedral, a unique organization operating on a master-pupil relationship somewhat akin to the apprentice system that existed in America until it was replaced by the "school of music"; and in 1963 he went to Surrey, England, where at Addington Palace, in the presence of Queen Elizabeth, he received an honorary diploma as a Fellow of the Royal School of Church Music, the first American to be so honored.

Sowerby's music is marked by freshness and vigor. His harmonic style is twentieth-century, but he adheres to strict formal design in his works and stays within the bounds of traditional tonality. He has composed in almost all forms, and his works have been widely performed. He has achieved his most lasting success in the field of church music, with his choral works and anthems and organ compositions. In addition to shorter anthems, his choral works include the *Canticle of the Sun,* after Saint Francis, first performed in New York in 1945 and awarded the Pulitzer Prize for that year; the oratorio *Christ Reborn* (1953); and *The Throne of God* (1957), a poem for mixed voices. Sowerby's major organ works include a Symphony in G (1930) and a Concerto for organ and orchestra (1938). He has also composed a *Pageant of Autumn* (1937), for organ.

In his early years Sowerby composed a wide variety of orchestral and chamber works, including the orchestral Suite *A Set of Four* (1918); an Overture, *Comes Autumn Time* (1918); a *Serenade* for string quartet (1918); a Trio for flute, viola, and piano (1919); a Quintet for wind instruments (1920); the First Piano Concerto (1920), introduced by the composer himself with the Chicago Symphony; a Suite for violin and piano (1921); the First Symphony (1922); *King Estmere* (1923), a ballad for two pianos and orchestra; the First String Quartet (1923); a Sonata for cello and piano (1924); *Money Musk* (1924), for orchestra; the cantata, *The Vision of Sir Launfal* (1926); *A Medieval Poem* (1926), for organ and orchestra; *From the Northland* (1927), an orchestral Suite; *Prairie* (1929), a symphonic poem; the Second Symphony (1929); the Second Piano Concerto (composed 1932, introduced 1936); *Passacaglia, Interlude, and Fugue* (1931); the Symphony No. 3 (1941), composed for the Golden Jubilee of the Chicago Symphony Orchestra; a Concert Overture (published 1941); a Sonata for clarinet (or viola) and piano (published 1944); the Violin Concerto (1943); the Fourth Symphony (1944); and *All on a Summer's Day,* introduced in Louisville in 1955.

Noble Cain (1896——), an *a cappella* specialist, studied with Allen Spencer, Adolf Weidig, and Leo Sowerby and graduated from Friends' University, the University of Chicago, and the American Conservatory, receiving an honorary music doctor's degree from Lawrence College. In 1930 he organized the Chicago A Cappella Choir, and presented the group in various parts of the country. He has conducted over NBC since 1933, specializing in arrangements of Negro spirituals. He has also made lecture tours for several years. Cain's cantatas include *The King and the Star*, *Evangeline*, and *Paul Revere's Ride*. Among his *a cappella* choruses are *Rarely Comest Thou*; *Watchers of the Stars*; *Offering of the Soul*; and *Wake Up, Sweet Melody*. He has written an oratorio, *Christ in the World*; he has composed more than a hundred part-songs and has written a textbook on choral music.

Garth Edmundson (1900——) studied with Harvey Gaul, Joseph Bonnet, and Isidor Philipp. For many years a church organist in western Pennsylvania, Edmundson has composed anthems and organ works. Among the latter are two Organ Symphonies; fifty-six *Chorale-Preludes*; a Suite, *In Modum Antiquum*; and Concert Variations.

John Holler (1904——), a church organist and choirmaster, has composed organ music and anthems, among the latter *The Risen Christ*; *Praise My Soul*; *Jesus Meek and Gentle*; *The Little Jesus*; *An Easter Carol*; *Saviour, Teach Me*; and *The Loving Saviour*. Chief music editor of the H. W. Gray Company, publishers of church music, he has compiled a series of *Junior Choir Anthem Books*.

Robert Leech Bedell (1909——), a prominent organist in New York City and the East, has written about fifty original organ numbers and more than a hundred organ transcriptions and arrangements. Perhaps his best known original composition is *Legende*, which he has also scored for full orchestra. Among his anthems are *Sing We This Day*, *'Tis Gladsome Easter*, and *March On, Ye Soldiers True*. He has made piano arrangements of the standard classics.

Robert Hall Elmore (1913——) was born of American parents in Ramapatnam, India, and was brought to America when he was a year old. He began studying the piano when he was six and the organ when he was nine. In 1933 he received the degree of Licentiate of the Royal Academy of Music, London, in three different subjects: organ, piano, and piano accompaniment. In the United States he studied organ under Pietro Yon and composition under Harl McDonald. He attended the University of Pennsylvania where he received his bachelor of music degree in 1937. In 1940 he began teaching composition at the University of Pennsylvania, and in 1942 he became organist of the Church of the Holy Trinity in Philadelphia. His works include a tone poem for orchestra, *Valley Forge—1777* (1937); *Three Colors, a Suite of Green, Blue, and Orange* (1941); and some songs. He has also written a choral work entitled *The Prodigal Son (A Sermon in Swing)*.

Trained as a child in piano and violin, HOWARD BOATWRIGHT (1918——) became an associate professor in violin at the University of Texas in 1943. In 1945 he decided to pursue his interest in composition and went to Yale to study with Paul Hindemith, receiving his bachelor's degree in 1947 and his master's in 1948. He joined the Yale faculty as assistant professor of music theory, and in 1954 was made an associate professor.

Boatwright has composed *Salutation, a Short Cantata on an Old Hymn* (1948), for mixed chorus and organ; a Communion Service in F (1955), for unison voices and organ; *Canticle of the Sun* (1963), to a text of St. Francis of Assisi, for full orchestra and chorus; and many shorter anthems as well as a number of sacred songs for solo voice and organ. Boatwright's chamber works include a Quartet for clarinet and strings; a String Quartet (1947); a Trio for two violins and viola (1948); a *Serenade* for violin, clarinet, horn, and cello (1952); and Canon for two violins and piano (1953). Boatwright has also composed a *Song for St. Cecilia's Day* (1948), for string orchestra; Variations for Small Orchestra (1949); and *The Woman of Trachis* (1955), for chamber orchestra and women's voices, a set of six choruses from Ezra Pound's translation of Sophocles's play. Boatwright has also written secular songs for solo voice and piano, and numerous settings of English-American folk songs. Discussing his composition, Boatwright has remarked to the author, "I would reserve the right to use any style or technique—archaic, conventional, or advanced—that seems appropriate for the work at hand." In 1949 Boatwright became director of music at Saint Thomas's Episcopal Church in New Haven, Connecticut.

A large group of composers has specialized in music for the Roman Catholic church. Among the older of them, NICOLA ALOYSIUS MONTANI (1880–1948) was influential in promoting the use of Gregorian music. In 1941 he founded the Society of St. Gregory of America for the restoration of Gregorian chant and the early polyphonic style recommended in the *Motu Proprio* of Pope Pius X. Born in Utica, New York, November 6, 1880, Montani studied under American teachers and in 1900 went to Rome to study with Lorenzo Perosi. During the years 1905 and 1906 he made an intensive study of Gregorian music under Dom Mocquereau and Dom Eudine on the Isle of Wight. On returning to the United States in 1908 he became organist and choirmaster at the Church of St. John the Evangelist; in 1924 he performed the same services at St. Paul's in New York. From 1925 until his death he was a school instructor in Philadelphia and New York. Montani's compositions include eight Masses; a *Stabat Mater*; motets; and songs. He compiled and edited the *St. Gregory Hymnal* and a *Catholic Choir Book*. He was the author of *Essentials of Sight Singing* and *The Art of A Cappella Singing*.

CASIMIRO DELLO JOIO (1881–1963) was born in Gragnano, Italy, and after joining the United States Navy came to this country at the age of seventeen. For twenty years until his death he was organist of Our Lady of Good Counsel Catholic Church in New York. He composed a number of Masses and smaller religious works. His son, Norman Dello Joio, is discussed elsewhere in this volume.

PIETRO ALESSANDRO YON (1886–1943), born in Settimo, Italy, studied at the Conservatories of Milan and Turin and in 1905 graduated with the first prize from the Santa Cecilia in Rome. He came to the United States, serving as organist at St. Francis Xavier's in New York from 1907 to 1919 and from 1921 to 1926. In 1921 he became an American citizen. He was organist at St. Patrick's Cathedral in New York from 1926 until his death. Most of Yon's compositions are for organ, including the *Concerto Gregoriano*; three Sonatas; two Rhapsodies; twelve *Divertimentos*; and a popular little Christmas piece published in 1917, *Gesù Bambino*, subsequently issued in various vocal and instrumental arrangements. Yon's choral works include a number of Masses; motets; and an oratorio, *The Triumph of St. Patrick*, that was heard first in New York in 1934.

PHILIP G. KRECKEL (1886———), born at Rochester, New York, studied organ and composition with Maz Reger in Munich, where his tone poem *Evangeline* was played in 1908 at the Conservatory. On his return to America Kreckel succeeded his father as organist of St. Boniface's church in Rochester. Kreckel's many works for the Catholic church include Masses in honor of Our Lady (male voices); St. Sebastian (unison); St. Boniface (mixed voices); St. Thomas Aquinas (mixed voices); St. Ann (unison voices); St. Bernard (male voices); St. Joseph (three-part women's or men's voices); and the Holy Name of Jesus (mixed voices). Kreckel has composed a number of Preludes and Fugues and numerous *Gregorian Improvisations* for the organ.

LEOPOLD SYRE (1887———), born at Bendorf Rhein, Germany, graduated from the Gregorian Institute at Aachen, Germany, and came to America in 1907. From that year until 1962 he was organist and choir director of St. Peter's Roman Catholic Church in Philadelphia as well as conductor of several choral organizations. His compositions include seven Masses and a number of motets.

JOSEPH J. MCGRATH (1889———), born in Oswego, New York, studied organ with Charles M. Courboin and William Berwald. He made an intensive study of church music with Monsignor Leo P. Manzetti in Baltimore, Maryland. For eight years McGrath was organist at the Church of St. John the Evangelist in Syracuse, and subsequently organist at the Immaculate Conception Cathedral in that city. His works include *Missa Regina Angelorum*, *Missa Cor Jesu*, and *Missa Rosa Mystica*.

The Reverend CARLO ROSSINI (1890———), born in Ancona, Italy, entered the Seminary of Panopesair at the age of nineteen and was ordained in 1913. He then entered the Pontifical School of Music in Rome and during World War I became an assistant chaplain. After coming to the United States in 1921 and associating himself with the Scalbrinian Fathers in New York, he moved in 1923 to Pittsburgh, where he became choir director of the Church of the Epiphany and conductor of the Pittsburgh Polyphonic Choir, more recently taking charge of the music at the Pittsburgh Cathedral. Father Rossini's compositions consist largely of Masses, including *Missa Adeste Fidelis*, *Missa Salve Mater*, *Missa Te Deum Laudamus*, *Missa Orbis Factor*,

Missa Salve Regina, Missa Solemnis Justus Florebit, Missa Victimae Paschali, Missa Benedicamus Domino, Missa Sinite Parvulos, Missa Ave Maria, Missa Choralis, and *Short Mass in Honor of St. Pius X.*

FRANK CAMPBELL-WATSON (1899———) was born in New York and studied music with Max Reger, Hans Sitt, Theodore Spiering, Walter Henry Rothwell, and Nicholas Eisenheimer. His compositions for the Catholic church include three Masses; Organ Preludes on Gregorian themes; and a number of anthems, among them *Alleluja, Christ Is Risen;* and *Christ Our Passover.* Others of his compositions include *Phantomesque* and *Chant de Nuit* for organ; a *Petite Suite* and *Fiddlers Four* for strings; *Cotton Moon,* an Overture for band; and a *Divertimento* for woodwinds. Campbell-Watson was editor of music publications for the University Society from 1923 to 1931 and since then has been editor-in-chief for the Standard and Educational Division of the Music Publishers' Holding Corporation, New York.

COSMO PUSA-TERI (1908———), born in New York, was a child prodigy who had piano lessons from his father at the age of three. After giving a farewell recital at the age of thirteen, he went to Italy, where he studied at the Royal Conservatory and toured as a pianist and organist. His compositions include *Missa Modo Dorico, Naval Mass, Missa Modo Frigio; Missa Ipodorico; Cathedral Mass;* and *Mass in Honor of Saint Christopher.*

A number of Jewish composers whose principal works are described elsewhere have added sacred works to the repertory of the Synagogue. Among these are Ernest Bloch with his Sacred Service, Frederick Jacobi with his Sabbath Evening Service, and Lazar Saminsky with his settings of *Psalms.* There are in addition several others, best known for their religious music.

GERSHON EPHROS (1890———) was born in Serotsk in Poland, where he served as choir leader of the Cantor of Sgerch. He was trained as a cantor at Professor Idelsohn's Institute of Jewish Music in Jerusalem, and came to the United States from Palestine in 1911, continuing his studies here with Herman Spileter and Joseph Achorn. He was appointed teacher at the Hebrew Union College and became Cantor of Temple Beth Mordecai, New Jersey. Ephros's works include three volumes of *Cantorial Anthology;* an *Album of Jewish Folksong; Priestly Benediction I and II;* a *Junior Service;* and a *Children's Suite* for voice and piano.

JAMES G. HELLER (1892———), a rabbi in Cincinnati, Ohio, was born in New Orleans; when he went to Cincinnati to study theology he became a composition pupil of Edgar Stillman Kelley as well as of other teachers. He is both composer and musicologist, having taught musicology at the Cincinnati College of Music and for twelve years having written the program notes of the Cincinnati Orchestra. His *New Union Hymnal* (1930–32) contains a number of Jewish Services. His compositions include *Three Aquatints* for string quartet (1929); *Four Sketches* for orchestra (1936); a Sonata for violin and piano; an *Elegy and Pastorale* for voice and string orchestra (1934); a Trio; *Four Solo Services for Friday Evening;* and an oratorio, *Watchman, What of the Night?*

ABRAHAM WOLFE BINDER (1895———) is a recognized authority on Jewish music and has written many articles on its history and development. He is the compiler of a *New Palestinian Songbook* and in 1931 edited the third edition of the *Union Hymnal*. Binder was born in New York, studied at the New York College of Music, and received his bachelor of music degree in 1926 at Columbia University. Since 1917 he has directed the music of the Young Men's Hebrew Association, and in 1923 he became the choirmaster of the Free Synagogue in New York. He was appointed professor of liturgical music at the Jewish Institute of Religion, New York, in 1937. In 1931 he was guest conductor of the Palestine Symphonic Ensemble in Palestine, and of the Manhattan Symphony Orchestra in New York. He has composed a number of works for orchestra, including an Overture, *Ha Chalutsim (The Pioneers,* 1931); *Holy Land Impressions* (1933); and a symphonic fantasy, *The Valley of Dry Bones,* 1936. He has also written a Sabbath Eve Service; a children's oratorio, *Judas Maccabäus;* songs; part-songs; anthems; and folk songs; as well as violin and piano pieces.

3. FOLK HYMNS AND THE GOSPEL SONG

Conservative churchgoers and members of liturgical congregations are apt to raise their eyebrows at the so-called "gospel songs," feeling that if religion is to be held as a noble part of our lives, music better fitted to the dance hall will hardly preserve its nobility. The gospel songs, of course, have an undeniable value in swaying crowds at revival meetings. Some of them have shown amazing endurance: we still "gather at the river, the beautiful, the beautifu-hul river," and some of our children, in Sunday School at least, continue to "fight with sin bravely," in waltz time. Basses and tenors still echo sopranos and altos in singing, "In the sweet—(in the sweet)—by and by—(by and by)," and for a full quarter-century, Billy Sunday brought the repentant up the sawdust trail to the strains of Homer Rodeheaver's *Brighten the Corner Where You Are.*

The gospel song actually has a long history. It has been perhaps the most stirring, even disturbing, phenomenon in religious music. It appeared as revival song, Sunday School song, or gospel hymn in the latter part of the nineteenth century, and its production line is still moving rapidly. A fact less widely recognized is that gospel songs are not an original growth, but a side sprout or "sucker growth" from an older, sturdier stem whose roots reach into the rich soil of American and British folk song. The musically literate person long remained unaware of this earlier music, since it was unwritten and purely "country," and hence strange to urban ears. The uncovering of this American folk song tradition is almost entirely the work of George Pullen Jackson, whose research was accomplished in the third and fourth decades of this century.

Dr. Jackson found that throughout the Gulf states there was still a hoary, rural community-singing activity kept alive by the Sacred Harp singers, who took their name from the title of a fat, oblong, hundred-year-old volume of part song—their sole musical manual. Jackson observed this folkway firsthand and described it in *White Spirituals in the Southern Uplands* (1933), coining the name as a temporary term to avoid confusion with the Negroes' spirituals. In two subsequent volumes—*Spiritual Folk Songs of Early America* (1937) and *Down East Spirituals and Others* (1942)—he edited and published the bulk of the tunes, five hundred and fifty from *The Sacred Harp* (first edition, 1844), *The Southern Harmony* (1835), and a score of other all-but-forgotten handbooks of a similar nature. Jackson's diggings into origins, nature, and habitat gradually lighted up the whole growth period of country religious song, a growth which began some two hundred years ago.

Gospel song accompanied or followed the religious outburst known as the "New Awakening" which began with Jonathan Edwards and other religious ecstatics. Since psalm-singing was too sedate to suit this fiery upheaval of hell-fire and heaven-storming, since the movement needed a type of song suited to the countryside and frontier and to the frontiersman, these religious enthusiasts (rural Baptists, chiefly, then Methodists, New Side Presbyterians, and others) began to sing their favorite folksy hymns (Watts, Newton, Stenett, Cennick), as well as many homemade religious lyrics, to the well-known tunes of the old secular ballads—*Barbara Allen, Little Hugh, Captain Kidd, Lord Lovel,* and scores of others.

This process went on briskly during the decades following the Revolutionary War. Jackson's five hundred and fifty songs just mentioned are the product, and his book *White and Negro Spirituals, Their Life Span and Kinship* tells the two hundred years' story in detail. The songs are a time-tested body of melody of, for, and by the very people who put these melodies to the new use of expressing religious folk emotions.

Around the year 1800 the all-denominational camp meetings took up these songs, livened them, filled out partially remembered texts with repetition, refrains, and choruses, and thus made them over into a rather roistering type of song which took its place by the side of the comparatively quieter variety and which went under the various names of spiritual songs, camp meeting songs, revival songs, and chorus songs.

Both of these closely related folk song types grew in popularity through the first half of the nineteenth century, despite the frowns (and worse) of the more cultured church folk and their musical mentors. While the songs grew, they remained for almost that whole period essentially "unwritten" music. When they gradually appeared in printed form during the 1830's to 1860's they were dressed up in a notation as different from the ordinary notation as were the tunes from those of ecclesiastic tradition. This unorthodox musical writing was a modification of the "shape notation" which we have noted in the opening pages of Chapter III as Andrew Law's experiment. This shape note music had become by mid-century the "God's music" of all pious rurals from Pennsylvania onward south and west, where it remains surprisingly widespread to this day.

To be sure, as early as 1805 one semiliterate enthusiast, Jeremiah Ingalls, had dared to publish a book of the tunes—*The Christian Harmony*—in New Hampshire. But the book was shunned in its region as illegitimate, and it had no progeny there. The really successful, and in time complete, recording of the unwritten songs first took place in Pennsylvania (*Beauties of Harmony*, 1813?), then in Virginia (*The Kentucky Harmony*, before 1815), and in still later books published farther south. In its old form, the tradition lives today only among the deep-Southern Sacred Harp singers.

This country music had hardly come into full light before what some have called the "religious section of Tin-Pan Alley" recognized it as a trend which could be capitalized upon. The result of this recognition was the personally fabricated and signed, and thus copyrightable, songs of the 1850's. The earliest of these publications showed the most obvious cribbing of folk-melody ideas. Dadmun's *Revival Melodies* (1859) is an example. Then the light gait, the refrain-and-chorus technique, and the textual repetitions of the earlier anonymous folk material flowed further and naturally, but mechanically, into the productions of the Sankeys and their kind.

There were, of course, men of lesser and greater gifts who contributed songs of corresponding quality. One of the oldest of the gospel song writers was CHARLES CROZAT CONVERSE (1832–1918), whose best-known hymn, *What a Friend We Have in Jesus*, is a pretty melody that has been widely used. He studied with Richter and Hauptmann in Germany before practicing both law and music in Erie, Pennsylvania. He wrote a song that he hoped would become a national hymn—*God for Us*. He composed an *American Concert Overture* based on *Hail Columbia* as well as a *Festouvertüre*, and he left in manuscript two Symphonies, two oratorios, several Overtures, String Quartets, and Quintets.

WILLIAM HOWARD DOANE (1832–1915) was one of the most prolific of the gospel hymn writers. A manufacturer of woodworking machinery and a pupil of B. F. Baker in Boston, he became active in music in his thirtieth year and was awarded the Doctor of Music degree by Denison University in 1875. Among Doane's most popular hymns are *Saved by the Blood*, *My Faith Still Clings*, *This I Know*, and *Sound the Alarm*.

WILLIAM GUSTAVUS FISCHER (1835–1912), a Philadelphia book-binder, was also a gifted teacher and choral leader. For thirty years from 1868 he was a successful piano dealer. He is best known to Sunday Schools through his ballad-hymn *I Love to Tell the Story* and the somewhat maudlin *Whiter than Snow*.

HART PEASE DANKS (1834–1903) is best known as the composer of *Silver Threads Among the Gold*, yet he, too, devoted his saccharine talents to the church. His first composition, the tune *Lake Street*, appeared in Bradbury's *Jubilee Collection*. He wrote a sacred song, *Not Ashamed of Christ*, and in 1892 he published a set of what he or his publishers termed *Superior Anthems for Church Choirs*. A carpenter at nineteen and an assistant in his father's building trade, he was largely self-taught in music. It is said that he published over 1,300 compositions, mostly songs. In its day, *Don't Be Angry with Me, Darling* ranked with *Silver Threads* in popularity.

THOMAS PHILANDER RYDER (1836–1887), a New Englander, made a name for himself as organist at Hyannis and later at the Tremont Temple in Boston. He was a popular teacher and choir leader, and his hymns were used considerably. He compiled *Golden Treasure*, "a collection of hymn tunes, anthems, chants, etc. for public worship, together with part-songs and glees, for mixed and male voices, for musical conventions."

PHILIP PAUL BLISS (1838–1876), a protégé of George F. Root, was connected in his later years with the gospel meetings of Major D. W. Whittle, it being his task to lead the singing and put life into it. *Hold the Fort, Only an Armor Bearer, Pull for the Shore*, and *Rescue the Perishing* were among his exhortations. He compiled many hymnbooks, including *The Joy* and *Sunshine for Sunday Schools*. He contributed to the standard Bigelow and Main collection of gospel hymns.

HUBERT PLATT MAIN (1839–1925) was a practical person who knew what people liked to sing. He spent much of his long life as a writer and compiler of hymns, meeting with great success. *Search Me, O Lord; Our Refuge;* and *Wonderful Love* are typical of his style.

IRA DAVID SANKEY (1840–1908), the best-known musical evangelist of the nineteenth century, was for years the music partner of Dwight L. Moody, one of the most famous of our revivalists. From

1871 till 1899 Sankey toured with Moody through the United States and Great Britain. "Moody and Sankey songs" became almost a generic term, representing to many musicians the lowest depths to which music could descend. Yet there is undeniably something moving and gripping in Sankey's tunes, in spite of their obvious banality and sentimentality. *Shine On, O Star!*; *He Is Coming*; *Not Far from the Kingdom*; *O Brother, Life's Journey Beginning*; *The Ninety and Nine*; and *A Soldier of the Cross* were among the hundreds of hymns that Sankey wrote.

Mention should be made of GEORGE C. STEBBINS (1846–1945) who composed until his death at the age of ninety-nine. He wrote over fifteen hundred hymn tunes.

The Reverend GEORGE BENNARD (1873–1958) became an officer of the Salvation Army in 1892 and after 1907 was an interdenominational evangelist in the United States and Canada. He wrote the words and music of *The Old Rugged Cross*, which since its first publication in 1913 has become a favorite among gospel hymns. In addition to composing, Reverend Bennard also compiled many song collections, including *Heart and Life Songs, Sweet Songs of Salvation, Full Redemption Songs, Revival Classics*, and others.

HOMER RODEHEAVER (1880–1955), a leader of singing at revival meetings, composer of gospel songs, and publisher of songbooks, has already been mentioned as the composer of *Brighten the Corner Where You Are*, which became famous as the theme song of Billy Sunday's mammoth tent sessions. From 1909 to 1931 Rodeheaver had charge of the music at Billy Sunday's revival meetings, playing trombone as well as singing. He made a tour of the world with the evangelist William Edward Biederwolf in 1923–24.

Rodeheaver led the singing of the largest community groups ever congregated in this country. He directed 62,000 people at the opening of the Atlantic City Auditorium; 85,000 at the Chicagoland Festival in Soldiers' Field; and 250,000 at Elwood, Indiana, for the Willkie notification. Over KDKA he presented the first gospel song program ever heard over the radio, when that station was a pioneer. In addition to composing hymn tunes and editing hymnbooks, he founded a school of evangelistic singing and was president of the Rodeheaver-Hall-Mack Publishing Company.

In view of the comments on the character of gospel songs which were made at the beginning of this chapter, it seems only fair to end with the words Rodeheaver once wrote in response to an invitation to defend these songs:

The gospel song is a declaration of God's plan of salvation and his promises, addressed to the people. We can bring you thousands of illustrations of individuals whose lives have actually been changed by the message of the gospel song, and who have become assets in their communities where they were liabilities before. These songs are not written for prayer meetings, but to challenge the attention of people on the outside who have not been interested in any form of church work or worship. If critics knew how some of these songs were loved by many people, they would never refer to the "saccharine talents" of great and good men who have blessed the world with their songs.

Another influence of the gospel songs is apparent: many of the older of these songs are reflected in the spirituals of the Negro, and it may be said that the writers of our gospel songs had far more to do with Negro spirituals than had African tribesmen. This matter is more fully discussed in the next chapter, under the heading "Negro Folk Music."

CHAPTER FIFTEEN

Our Folk Music

1. THE MUSIC OF THE NORTH AMERICAN INDIAN

I

THE folk music of the United States is a controversial topic among musicians. What is it? Where did it come from? Which part of it is truly American? These are matters that are easily decided by those who think superficially; but scholars hesitate to answer such questions. It all depends on what we consider to be American in our surroundings. If Americanism is a matter of geography, or residence, the distinction is clear. But if sources and distinguishing traits are to be considered, the subject of American folk song offers a puzzle that is not easy to solve.

There are many definitions of folk song. It is obviously a song of the people, not the street tune that is sung for a few months and then forgotten, but a song that lives for generations. Generally its origin is unknown, as far as the individual who composed it is concerned. To be a true folk song it must be typical of the people who sing it, part of their daily lives. Most important of all, the song itself must be more important than its composer. *Dixie* is better known than Dan Emmett; *Old Folks at Home*, than Stephen Foster.

We have many groups of folk songs in this country, yet few of them belong to the United States as a whole. The Negro songs are a characteristic utterance of those who were our slaves. The cowboy songs belong to the West; mountain ballads to the mountaineers; hillbilly songs come from the Ozarks; and the music of the American Indian is a primitive expression which has little to do with the art forms of a civilized people. There is folk music in America, but the overworked melting pot has much to do before any part of our folk song literature becomes a characteristic utterance of the entire nation.

The music of the Indians is a case in point. It is as far from our way of musical thinking as Chinese music. Although the Indians inhabited America for centuries before our ancestors came here, who are the Americans today: the white men or the red men? A brutally asked question, but pertinent. In their mode of life the primitive Indians who sang the songs that have since been collected from the remnants of the original tribes, are as foreign to the various white groups that compose America now as the Eskimos or South Sea Islanders. Can it then be said that primitive Indian music is American folk song?

Some say that Indian music is as much the heritage of Americans, as the music of the barbaric hordes of Russia is the heritage of cultured Russians. Not at all; the Russians of today are the descendants of those barbaric ancestors. Relatively few of us have Indian blood in our veins. Furthermore, as soon as composers attempt to idealize the songs of the Indian, and reduce them to a white man's harmonization, their whole character is lost in the process. For there is a long distance between savage music and folk music. Folk song is a relatively polished product, and while it may be composed of the same basic material, this material is presented in coherent sentences instead of in ejaculations and recurrence of unchanging rhythms.

Then, too, the term *Indian*, as applied to all primitive peoples who lived on the North American continent, is too general. There were over fifty basic linguistic stocks, all of whom were divided into separate tribes. At the present time the Office of Indian Affairs is dealing with three hundred and forty-two tribes, not including the subtribes and rancheria. These separate races all had different customs and ways of living. Some were highly organized socially and politically, while others were simply constituted. Each had its own legends, and presumably its own music. It is more exact, therefore, to speak of Chippewa, Hopi, or Blackfoot music, than Indian music, even though it all may sound the same to the novice. There are traits that all tribes seem to have in common musically, but these are probably characteristics that would be common to savage music in general.

II

It would be impossible in a chapter on the music of the American Indian to give anything approaching a comprehensive account of the songs of the many tribes. All that can be presented is a brief survey of the research that has been done in the field, and a short review of some of the things that these investigators have found. The earliest settlers in America spoke of the Indian's music, and there were many remarks on its peculiarities. When William Wood visited Plymouth and Massachusetts Bay he published an account of what he heard and saw. (London, 1634.)

Their musick is lullabies to quiet their children, who generally are as quiet as if they had neither spleene or lungs. To hear one of these Indians unseene, a good eare might easily mistake their untaught voyce for the warbling of a well tuned instrument. Such command have they of their voices.

Being unmusical themselves, the colonists made little attempt to study the music of the Indians, or to make any notation of their songs. In the latter eighteenth century there were several publications that attempted to reproduce occasional Indian songs in music notation. William Beresford printed an Indian tune when he published in 1789 his record of *A voyage around the world; but more particularly to the northwest coast of America.* Somewhere around 1800, George Gilfert published in New York, and P. A. Van Hagen in Boston, a song that purported to be a genuine Indian melody. This was *Alknomook, the Death Song of the Cherokee Indians.* It had been sung in Mrs. Hatton's *Tammany,* for which James Hewitt had arranged the music (1794). The song became very popular, and was known in almost every American drawing room in the early nineteenth century.

It was published in London first. It was issued there in 1784 under the title *Alknomook,* "The death song of the Cherokee Indians, An Original Air, brought from America by a gentleman long conversant with the Indian tribes, and particularly with the Nation of the Cherokees. The Words adapted to the Air by a Lady." Frank Kidson, in the *Musical Antiquary,* said that this "lady" was Anne Hone Hunter, the wife of a famous surgeon, and Haydn's hostess when he was in London. She wrote verses for a number of Haydn's settings, notably "My mother bids me bind my hair." Whatever Cherokee or primitive traits *Alknomook* may have had, it appeared in wholly conventional dress in both the English and American editions.

When George Catlin published the report of his "eight years travel [1832–39] amongst the wildest tribes of Indians in North America," he included a description of Indian music and dances. Henry Rowe Schoolcraft, in 1851, gave an account of the rites and symbolic notation of the songs of the Walbeno, and showed how these people used mnemonic symbols to refresh their memories for traditional songs.

The first serious attempt by a musician to make a scientific study of the music of the Indians was undertaken by THEODORE BAKER, in 1880. Baker, a German who later made his permanent residence in this country, was at the time a student at Leipzig University. He chose the music of the North American Indians as the subject of a thesis for his doctorate, and he visited the Seneca Reservation in New York State and the Indian school at Carlisle, Pennsylvania. He collected a number of songs, studied and analyzed them, but since his essay was published in Germany, it has had less influence than those by others which followed it.

ALICE C. FLETCHER came next. Her treatise on Omaha songs, various articles on the music of the Sioux and Pawnee Indians, and her book *The Indian in Song and Story*, were among the first authoritative works on the subject. Miss Fletcher was a Fellow in the Peabody Museum of Harvard University. Among her collaborators was Francis La Flesche, who made a study of the customs of the Osage and Omaha Indians. JOHN COMFORT FILLMORE assisted Miss Fletcher in harmonizing and analyzing the characteristics of the tunes she had collected. Fillmore was a well-trained musician, founder of the Milwaukee School of Music, and later director of music at Pomona College in California. His arrangements of the Omaha melodies are adequate from a musical standpoint, yet they are so conventional that they make the tunes seem not the real thing, even to the ears of the layman. He went so far as to state that the Indians have a subconscious sense of harmony and that their tunes are harmonic melodies.

When the Hemenway Southwestern Expedition was at work among the Zuñi, Hopi, and other Pueblo Indians, BENJAMIN IVES GILMAN had charge of the study of their music. Gilman was very scientific. He studied certain songs from the acoustic standpoint, and by using a mechanical device, sought to measure the exact intervals the Indians used in their songs. He invented a system of notation to show minute deviations from diatonic pitch.

Probably the first investigator to use the phonograph in recording the songs of the Indian was JESSE WALTER FEWKES, who first studied the songs of the Passamaquoddy Indians in Maine in 1889. He later joined the Hemenway Expedition, and it was from his records of Zuñi songs that Gilman made his analysis.

FREDERICK R. BURTON commenced his study of Ojibway music in 1901. While at Harvard in 1882 he wrote music for *Hiawatha*. This was later developed into a dramatic cantata and published in 1898. After this he lived among the Indians for long periods. His study of their music culminated in his book *American Primitive Music*, published shortly after his death in 1909.

NATALIE CURTIS started her work with the Hopis and Zuñis in the Southwest about the same time that Burton began his study of the Ojibways in Minnesota and Wisconsin. Miss Curtis, later Mrs. Burlin, published her observations of over eighteen tribes in *The Indian's Book*. She did not harmonize the songs, but offered them as faithfully to their original form as music notation could present them. Her work is especially valuable in showing the Indians' attitude toward their music.

FRANCES DENSMORE has for many years been collaborator of the Bureau of American Ethnology of the Smithsonian Institution. Her researches have led her to study the music and customs of many Indian tribes—Chippewa, Teton Sioux, Northern Ute, Mandan Hidatsa, and others. She has used the phonograph in recording native singing, and her records have been preserved for students. She is one of the outstanding authorities on the subject of Indian music, and her views are based on a common sense attitude that not only demands facts, but distinguishes between the logical and the purely romantic point of view.

III

Although it is rarely accurate to speak of Indian music and customs as such, there are a few traits common to all tribes. Few Indians make music for its own sake. Every song is associated with some tribal custom, and is used only for the performance of that custom. There is a song for almost everything—friends, enemies, gods, animals, forests, lakes, clothing, and sometimes whiskey. As Densmore puts it, "the Indians used song as a means of accomplishing definite results"—to treat the sick, to have success in war or in the hunt, to accomplish anything the Indian felt was beyond his power as an individual. Songs are so closely associated with the ceremonies they accompany that Indians do not like to sing them on other occasions, even when they are showing the white man the songs of their tribe. One old Indian refused to sing a hunting song for Burton because it was not hunting season at the time.

Indians sing differently from white men, and there has been much discussion of their relative musical abilities. Some hold that the Indian has a far greater developed sense of rhythm than the white man, shown by his ability to beat his drum in one rhythm while he sings his song in another. Some think that the Indian's scale is far in advance of ours; that his divisions into smaller intervals than we use give him far greater flexibility and expressiveness in his melodies. Yet there are cynics who say that these phenomena merely show that the Indian cannot keep time nor sing in tune. Maybe they are right, for it is but logical to believe that our musical scale, evolved through centuries, has been formalized by natural acoustic laws. Primitive music is no doubt an early groping for these natural effects.

Of course, it is often true that an Indian singer will render a song many times over in exactly the same way that he sang it first. Miss Densmore has had songs recorded in the summer and again in the following winter by the same singer. Comparison of the two records shows the performances to be exactly alike in melody, pitch, and tempo. Often a song has been sung eight or ten times on a single phonograph record and the repetitions have been uniform in every respect. Burton took issue with Gilman on the question of the Indian's intonation. Gilman devised an elaborate notation to show exactly what intervals the Indians sang. Burton believed that deviations from pitch were caused, not by the singers' instinctive feeling for smaller intervals than those of the diatonic scale, but by their inability to hold an accurate pitch. He pointed out that this inability was by no means confined to the Indian, and that if we were to make phonographic records of civilized chorus rehearsals, when the singers were unaccompanied, we would find many curious intervals, if we undertook to measure them accurately. Also records of opera singers. He cited an experience that Fillmore had had with the Indians: [1]

In one case, Mr. Fillmore observed that the second part of a song was sung in a key a semitone lower than the first part. There was an upward skip of an octave and the singers fell short of it. They proceeded, however, from their false start and sang the second part relatively like the first; but when Mr. Fillmore played the song to them on the pianoforte and carried through the second part, his Indian listeners were displeased. When he played the piece throughout in the same key, they were satisfied.

Many Indians sing with a vibrato, and one of their favorite tricks is to attack a tone by beginning it sharp and immediately sliding down to the sustained tone. Descending melodies are a characteristic of all savage music. Often an Indian tune will descend steadily from the first note to the last. Sometimes there is an ascent in the middle, but then it starts to go down again. Miss Densmore found that in eight hundred and twenty songs, 67 per cent began with a downward progression, and in 87 per cent, the last note was the lowest tone occurring in the melody.

Reduced to an approximation of the accepted scale, many Indian melodies are found to utilize the five-tone, or pentatonic, major and minor modes. This is true of much folk music, for these modes involve the most natural intervals. Many of the songs seem to be in no particular key, although Miss Densmore has found that the majority of them seem to end on a tone that proved a satisfactory keynote to the ear. She found this true of 67 per cent of three hundred and forty Chippewa songs.

Then there is the question of multiple rhythms. When a civilized musician sings a song, his audience expects that song and accompaniment shall have some relation to each other. When the Indian sings, the arm that wields his drumstick has never heard of his voice, even though they both belong to the same person. When Burton began to study Indian music he had the conviction that the Indian had de-

[1] Frederick R. Burton, *American Primitive Music*, Moffat, Yard & Co.

veloped rhythm more highly than the white man. Intensive study made him change his mind, and brought him to the conclusion that the Indian is not aware that his drum beat is in conflict with the scheme of accents he invents for his song.[2]

Both, drum beat and song, are ingenuous expressions of his nature. One is extremely primitive, the other comparatively advanced, and, as he is still primitive, he clings to his cheerful noise, understanding it, aroused by it, while his musical soul toils darkly on toward an expression that aims ever at, and sometimes attains, symmetry. All of which is to say that he drums as he does because he knows no better.

IV

The collector of Indian songs has to be a discriminating person, to choose between what is traditional and real and what is new and synthetic. Much passes for Indian music that is quite modern, composed by comparatively civilized Indians. There are three classes of songs, as far as collectors are concerned. First, the old songs, sung by the old singers. These are now growing scarce, but many have been preserved on records. Second, the old ceremonial and medicine songs belonging to men now dead, but which can still be sung with reasonable correctness by Indians who heard their owners sing them. Third, the comparatively modern songs, representing a transitional culture, and showing the influence of civilization.

There are many kinds of Indian songs, each tribe having not only its own songs, but its own types as well. Many of the tribes have lullabies and children's songs. Some have comparatively few of these, for the mothers were busy in the fields all day, and babies were left to lie in their hammocks. Yet the Chippewa, Yuma, Makah, Mandan, Ute, and Hopi tribes are notable for their children's songs. Many of them accompany games which teach the young how to do essential things.

Songs are often the property of individuals. Those received in dreams may generally be sung only by their owners. Some songs may be purchased from their owners, generally with magic power for heal-

[2] Frederick R. Burton, *American Primitive Music*, Moffat, Yard & Co.

ing the sick. There are songs praising a man's virtues, his success in war or in hunting, or maybe his generosity.

Miss Densmore claims that love songs were not sung by the old-time Indians except in working love charms. Marriages among Indians were usually arranged by parents, and were confined to groups who had no blood relationship. Except with the Makahs, love songs are modern, and generally associated with disappointments. Playing the flute at dusk is a custom common to nearly every tribe, although it may not always be for the romantic purpose that poets would have us believe. Yet no doubt it has often helped the bashful lover to say his little speech.

The musical instruments of the Indians were flutes, whistles, drums, and rattles. In some form these were common to all tribes in North America. Miss Densmore has said that the Tule Indians of Panama were the only Indians who did not use a drum or pound anything. Flutes were often played by the youth of the village to please the maidens, but sometimes they were used to warn against the approach of an enemy in wartime. Whistles were used by magicians and by doctors when attending patients.

The drum was essential to all Indian music. Many Indians could not sing without it. There were hand drums, big drums which took several men to play, and drums that looked like kegs and were partly filled with water. They accompanied ceremonial dances, religious rites, and the singing of all sorts of songs. Rattles were generally regarded as sacred objects to be used only on religious occasions. There were different kinds of rattles. Some were receptacles containing small objects that hit against each other; some were sticks with objects that hit together suspended from them; and some were wooden clappers. Then there was the notched stick, which was laid by one end on a hollow gourd, while the performer ran a smaller stick over the notches.

In the bulletins of the Bureau of American Ethnology, Miss Densmore has given a detailed account and analysis of Chippewa songs. There were the Mĭdè, or Medicine songs, for the expression of religious ideas. Some were for direct ceremonial use (initiations, to secure success in hunting, and so on), and others were connected with the use of medicine (for healing or working charms). Many of these songs were taught only to those who would pay for the privilege of learning them.

The Chippewas were firm believers in dream songs, learned in visions while fasting. Some of these were the songs of the doctor, which could never be bought or sold. There were also the songs of the juggler, who did a sort of Houdini act in freeing himself from all sorts of ropes and knots before the assembled tribe. There were of course the war songs—some to incite war, some, songs of the warpath, and others of the scalp dance. Many of them had a religious significance; the "God with us" idea is by no means the sole property of the white man in wartime.

Game songs were found in many tribes; often each side sang them to invoke victory. The Indians were great gamblers and the stakes sometimes ran high. In the moccasin game of the Chippewas, four bullets or balls were hidden under four moccasins. The man or side that guessed which bullet was marked got the jack pot. Some of the songs showed a true sporting instinct. One is translated—"I will go home if I am beaten, after more articles to wager."

There is indeed a rich literature in the traditional music of the various Indian tribes. Much of it is interesting and some of it is beautiful. As interpretations of the Indian the songs are invaluable. As specimens of primitive art they are choice. American composers (way back to the time of Father Heinrich) have given us interesting examples of what can be done with these songs in larger compositions. We have already heard of MacDowell's *Indian Suite*, and there are many others who have sought to tap the melodic source of the primitive savages. There is an exotic flavor about them that is tempting; there is a haunting loveliness in some of the melodies that is very beautiful. Yet not all of them can be reduced to our conception of harmony and survive the process with any degree of appropriateness.

To select Indian tunes because they are useful is one thing. To choose them for nationalistic purposes is a different matter entirely, for they are American in the geographic sense alone. Mrs. H. H. A. Beach commented on the matter with much common sense when I asked her what she thought of using Indian themes. "I see no harm in it, if you want to do it," she replied.

2. NEGRO FOLK MUSIC

I

The songs of the American Negro form one of the choicest groups of folk song found in this country. Whatever their origin, or their ultimate significance to us, they are as rich, as colorful, and as warm in their melodic phrases as any songs that have ever been born here, or have been brought to our shores from abroad. For the Negro likes to sing, and whether he is singing a tune he inherited from his ancestors, or something he has picked up from the white man, he puts all of himself into his performance, gay or sad.

The songs are vital because they are sincere—they speak the Negro's real nature. Some of them fervent, some superstitious, others shiftless and irresponsible, they all show some phase of the undeveloped black man's childlike temperament. And when songs truly reflect the character of the people who sing them, they are folk songs, beyond all question of their origin. Everything the Negro sings about —"Norah" and the Ark, Daniel in the Lion's Den, or the ribald tale of Frankie and Johnnie (*Albert* with the Negroes)—he invariably reduces to his own experience.

Negro music has probably made a deeper impression on American life than has any other class of songs. First, through its cousin the minstrel song, then by way of ragtime, and later through the blues and jazz, the Negroid manner has permeated our popular music. The intelligentsia has so glorified this element that serious composers have been able to stay respectable while they experiment with its idiom. Side by side has come our welcome to the "spirituals," the Negro's religious songs. They have been invited to our concert halls, whether clothed in the trappings of Debussy and sometimes of Stravinsky, or in more appropriate costumes.

General recognition of the artistic value of Negro songs is comparatively modern. Singing on the plantations has long been a tradition, but the vogue of the "spiritual" has come with the present century. Thomas Jefferson spoke of the natural musical talents of the Negro in his *Notes on Virginia*, way back in 1784, and there were some airs from Virginia, one a Negro Jig, in Aird's *Selection of Scotch, Eng*

lish, Irish and Foreign Airs, published in Glasgow in 1782. (It was
this collection that contained the first known printing of *Yankee
Doodle.*) We have seen how the minstrel shows, from the 1830's,
were direct imitations of Negro singing. But serious consideration of
Negro songs, as anything better than comedy dialect, did not come
until after the Civil War, and not too quickly even then.

Negro singing, somewhat formalized, first became known to the
country at large through the travels of Negro singers, first from Fisk
University, and then from Hampton, Tuskegee, and other industrial
schools. Fisk University was founded in Nashville, Tennessee in 1866,
a pioneer institution to educate the freed slaves. Its early years saw
bitter struggles; it was hard to raise money for a project not altogether
popular at the time. Finally George L. White, who had been in charge
of singing at the school, started on a concert tour with thirteen members
of his choir. This was in 1871, and, though the first months were discouraging, before the little band of singers had finished three years'
travel, they had raised $150,000 for the University—chiefly through
voluntary collections among their audiences. Moreover, they had been
a feature of Pat Gilmore's 1872 Jubilee in Boston, they had been
abroad, received by Queen Victoria in England, and by the Emperor
in Germany.

As other Negro institutes were founded, this became one of the
favorite ways of raising funds for their maintenance. The Hampton
and Tuskegee quartets have sung in churches in the winter, and at
resort hotels in the summer, and through their singing have gained
money for their cause, and have helped create the vogue of the Negro
spiritual.

At the end of the century a few serious composers experimented
with Negro music. Years before, Gottschalk had used Creole songs
from Louisiana (in his *Bananier, Bamboula,* and other piano pieces),
but it was not until our guest composer of the nineties, the Bohemian
Dvořák, wrote his *New World* Symphony, that the idea of using
Negro music took hold. At that, there is considerable dispute as to
whether Dvořák intended to use actual Negro tunes, or whether he
merely meant to catch their spirit. But what Dvořák accomplished
was to create our respect for the folk songs that existed in our own
country. Since then we have had hundreds of concert settings of Negro

songs, some sophisticated and others simple in treatment; choral arrangements; and developments and elaborations of Negro material in symphonic works.

II

The origin of these songs is a matter that has troubled many a student, and caused much discussion. The more seriously students study the question, the less they are inclined to venture dogmatic theories. One supposition is that their idiom is African; that the ancestors of the Negroes brought their songs with them in the slave ships. Their peculiarities were adapted to English words when the Negroes learned the language of their masters, and heard the Bible stories of the missionaries and evangelists. Comparisons are made between the music of African savages and that of the American Negro. The pentatonic scale is common to both; each has a decided tendency to syncopation. Both seem to have an instinct for part-singing. Specific songs are brought forth to prove a connection. One writer claimed that *Go Down, Moses* so resembles an old Jewish Chant *Cain and Abel,* that Hebrews think the Negro song is theirs, and that Negroes claim the Jewish song. This has led to a theory that there was an ancient relation between Negro and Semitic races on the African continent. And yet again it may only explain why the Jew becomes an expert at jazz.

Of course, the pentatonic scale is found in folk songs the world over, and syncopation is the exclusive property of no race in particular. Yet it is only logical to assume that there are the relics of an African background in the music of the American Negro. Disputes today center around the question of how much of the Negro music we hear is African, and how much is learned from the white man. Some say that none of the spirituals, or at least very few, really belong to the colored man. They are merely his version of songs he heard from revivalists and missionaries. Those who know the gospel songs of the white folk are in accord with this view. It is known that the Negro did adopt many scores of his religious tunes and texts from the white people especially the Baptist white people. He resang them with that perfect freedom which led to much unconscious revision according to his abilities, racial preferences, and individual hunches (just as all real folk singers do). The adoptive process was comparatively late, beginning not much before the middle of the nineteenth century.

Yet, even though gospel hymns are the parents of many of the spirituals, it may be admitted that the Negro has improved them musically, and has treated them according to his African heritage.

Testimony on the makings of many of these spirituals is forthcoming from those who have witnessed them. Baptisms, camp meetings, spiritual orgies are supposed to give birth to new songs. One starts to intone a phrase, another joins him, and soon the whole crowd is answering and swaying to the rhythm. A folk song is born, then and there. Natalie Curtis Burlin described such a scene in the *Musical Quarterly*, January, 1919:

On a suffocatingly hot July Sunday in Virginia, in a little ramshackle meeting-house that we had approached over a blinding road nearly a foot deep in dust, a number of rural Negroes had gathered from an outlying farm, dressed all in their dust-stained Sunday best for the never-to-be-omitted Sabbath service. . . . Service had already begun before we came and the congregation, silent and devout, sat in rows on the rough backless benches. The preacher now exhorted his flock to prayer and the people with one movement surged forward from the benches and down onto their knees, every black head deep-bowed in an abandonment of devotion. Then the preacher began in a quavering voice a long supplication. Here and there came an uncontrollable cough from some kneeling penitent or the sudden squall of a restless child; and now and again an ejaculation, warm with entreaty, "O Lord!" or a muttered "Amen, Amen"—all against the background of the praying, endless praying.

Minutes passed, long minutes of strange intensity. The mutterings, the ejaculations, grew louder, more dramatic, till suddenly I felt the creative thrill dart through the people like an electric vibration, that same half-audible hum arose—emotion was gathering atmospherically as clouds gather —and then, up from the depths of some "sinner's" remorse and imploring, came a pitiful little plea, a real Negro "moan," sobbed in musical cadence. From somewhere in that bowed gathering another voice improvised a response: the plea sounded again, louder this time and more impassioned: then other voices joined in the answer, shaping it into a musical phrase; and so, before our ears, as one might say, from this molten metal of music a new song was smithied out, composed then and there by no one in particular and by everyone in general.

Collectors of Negro songs tell of many individual bards who are reputed to have composed their songs. C. W. Hyne, in the introduction to *Utica Jubilee Singers Spirituals* [1] gives an account of "Singing" Johnson, who sang his way from community to community.

His coming was eagerly anticipated. The congregation hung on his voice, alert to learn a new song. As they listened, some would join in uncertainly, the keener ears soon catching the melody and words. The whole congregation easily learned the response, which is generally unvarying. Always the strong voice of the leader corrected errors until the song was learned perfectly. Singing Johnson undoubtedly derived his support in somewhat the same way as the preachers: part of a collection, food and lodging. He spent his leisure time in originating new words and melodies and new lines for old songs. A maker of songs and a man with a delicate sense of when to come to the preacher's support after a climax in the sermon, by breaking in with a line or two of a song that expressed a certain sentiment, often just a single line.

Odum and Johnson, in *Negro Workaday Songs,* [2] tell the story of "Left Wing" Gordon, of the *species hobo,* who never stayed in any place more than three weeks, "leastwise never mo' 'n fo'." Gordon was a great songster.

"Wing" claimed a blues for every state and more; if there was none already at hand, he would make one of his own. . . . Wing had practically no variation in his tunes and technique of singing. A high-pitched voice, varied with occasional low tones, was the most important part of his repertoire. But what variation in words and scenes, phrases and verses, the recording of which would exhaust the time and endurance of the listener and call for an ever-recording instrument!

It is not always safe to trust the Negro's claim to authorship. William Francis Allen and Lucy McKim Garrison, when they published their collection of *Slave Songs* in 1867, often found songs in Methodist Hymn Books, which Negroes said they had composed themselves. *Climb Jacob's Ladder* proved to be a song from a Northern book, as did *Give Me Jesus,* and *I'll Take the Wings of the Morning.*

Discussion regarding the origin of Negro songs is after all an aca-

---

[1] *Utica Jubilee Singers Spirituals,* taken down by J. R. Johnson, introduction by C. W. Hyne: Oliver Ditson Co.

[2] Odum and Johnson, *Negro Workaday Songs,* University of North Carolina Press.

demic matter. The important fact is that they are the Negro's interpretations of his surroundings, his superstitions, his beliefs, his
legendry. If he has derived, even copied, a small part or most of this
from the white man, it makes little difference. The songs are beautiful,
and there is a wealth of them. If they have been shaped by the Negro's
American surroundings and influences, they have far more claim to
being American than if they were pure importations from Africa.

III

In one respect, the singing groups from Fisk and Hampton have
given a false, or at least one-sided, emphasis to our idea of Negro music.
The traveling quartets, which have sung principally in churches, have
confined themselves to the spirituals, or religious songs. When a Negro "gets religion" he turns his back to his "wicked" secular songs. It
is largely through Tin-Pan Alley that the nonreligious type of Negro
song is generally known, and then largely formalized and stripped of
most of its native charm. For this reason some of the latest collections
of authentic Negro secular songs are most valuable.

Although all the songs of the colored man have much in common,
musically and temperamentally, his music may be separated into religious and secular groups. Of course, the religion of the Negro is partly
superstition. Also, in the slave days, he seized upon the idea of an
after life as his release from bondage. He interpreted many Bible
stories in terms of his own experience. The children of Israel were in
a predicament similar to his own; he looked to a black Moses for his
deliverance. If the Lord had delivered Daniel, he certainly wouldn't
forget the poor black man in America.

The religious songs include the spirituals and the shout songs. Allen
and Garrison claimed that the shout songs, or "Running Sper-chels"
were confined to the Baptists, and were to be heard mostly in South
Carolina and the states south of it. A typical "shout" was described by
a writer in the New York *Nation* in 1867.

The true "shout" takes place on Sundays or on "praise-nights" through
the week, and either in the praise-house or in some cabin in which a regular
religious meeting has been held. . . . The benches are pushed back to
the wall when the formal meeting is over, and old and young, men and
women, sprucely-dressed young men, grotesquely half-clad field-hands . . .

boys with tattered shirts and men's trousers, young girls barefooted, all stand up in the middle of the floor, and when the "sperchil" is struck up, begin first walking and by-and-by shuffling round, one after the other, in a ring. The foot is hardly taken from the floor, and the progression is mainly due to a jerking, hitching motion, which agitates the entire shouter, and soon brings out streams of perspiration. Sometimes they dance silently, sometimes as they shuffle they sing the chorus of the spiritual, and sometimes the song itself is also sung by the dancers. But more frequently a band, composed of some of the best singers and of tired shouters, stand at the side of the room to "base" the others, singing the body of the song and clapping their hands together or on the knees. Song and dance are alike extremely energetic, and often, when the shout lasts into the middle of the night, the monotonous thud, thud of the feet prevents sleep within half a mile of the praise house.

Some of the spirituals are sad, some are happy. Generally the sad ones express a hope for the future, or a childlike faith in the hereafter: "Nobody knows the trouble I see, Nobody knows but Jesus"; "Swing low, sweet chariot, Comin' for to carry me Home." Often lively rhythms and tunes were used for the most devout songs: "Couldn' hear nobody pray"; "Roll, Jordan, roll"; "I want to be ready."

The precentor idea was common among the Negroes. Hundreds of the spirituals, and the secular songs, too, had their verses lined out by the leader, while the congregation of worshipers waited to join in the oft-repeated refrain. The leader would start:

> I got a robe, you got a robe;

then the chorus:

> All God's chillun got a robe,
> When I get to heab'n, gonna put on my robe,
> Gonna shout all over God's heab'n.

In the next verse the leader had a harp, in the third, wings, and in the fourth, somewhat in anticlimax, shoes.

Obviously the spirituals may be subdivided into many smaller groups. Funeral songs and chants, songs of a semireligious nature, sung in a comic vein, but with Bible stories for their text. Slave songs and sorrow songs form a definite group, although many fall into several classifications.

IV

The secular songs cover a far greater field than is commonly appreciated. Not only are there the songs that date back to the slave days—plantation melodies and cabin songs—but many of more modern origin, which show outside influences, but nevertheless seem authentically of the Negro. Work songs, for cotton picking, corn shucking, stevedoring; railroad songs of the section gang; steamboat songs; prison songs of the chain gang and the rock pile; bad men's songs; devil songs (many unprintable); and then, of course, the "blues," which have been carried into our modern jazz.

The Negro has a love of balladry, of the true narrative type. Many of these songs are his versions of the white man's ballads—*Casey Jones,* and others of its kind; and some of the English ballads from the mountaineers in the Appalachians are sung by the Negroes. Yet many of them seem to be of his own making. He loves the bad-man ballads—the tale of the *Travelin' Man,* who made a "livin' stealin' chickens"; or *Bad Man Lazarus* (not the one of Bible fame), who "broke in de commissary" and finally was shot down with a forty-five. The Negro often violates the impersonal tradition of balladry by using the first person pronoun, thus injecting his imaginary self into the story. "I'm de hot stuff man from de devil's lan' "; or "I'm de rough stuff of dark-town alley."

In his music the Negro is often filled with self-pity. Like the white man, he loves to think how people will mourn for him after he is dead, maybe by his own hand, maybe by jumping into the sea, or by laying his head on a railroad track. Then he will be understood and appreciated, when it is too late. He sings "Ship my po' body home, if I die a long way from home"; or "I wish I was dead," in which he borrows a phrase from the white man—"Over de hill is de po' house."

This self-pity element has been partly responsible for the "blues," a type of sorrows song. This kind of song has forced its way into our modern jazz, and into polite musical circles. It was popularized largely through the efforts of WILLIAM CHRISTOPHER HANDY (1873–1958), the son of a Negro preacher of Florence, Alabama. Handy was born in Florence, November 16, 1873, but he seems to be always identified with Memphis, for it was there that he composed his first blues in 1909—the *Memphis Blues*, written to further the mayoralty campaign of a politician named Edward H. Crump. Next came the *St. Louis Blues*, the most popular of them all, destined to earn Handy the title of "the father of the blues." Then came *Beale Street Blues* and dozens of others, and Handy moved his headquarters to New York.

In spite of failing eyesight, he established and successfully developed a publishing house which became known as the "home of the blues." Recognition finally came to him, and he was invariably honored at all gatherings of musicians and song writers. He died March 28, 1958, in New York, at the age of eighty-four.

Handy once remarked on the fact that while the blues are based on self-pity, they often in happy-go-lucky fashion express the singer's knowledge, or hope, that maybe things are not so bad after all. Handy wrote, "Why the happy character in a plaintive mood? Why call it the blues when the music is joyous? It happens this way: Rastus owes his rent. He is going to be ejected tomorrow if he does not pay. He has part of the money. He tries in vain to get the rest. Defying his fate, he goes to a party—dances joyously, spends generously, camouflaging perfectly his heavy heart. That's why the blues are joyous."

Since Handy popularized the blues, they have been sung by whites as well as Negroes. Many have been written by sophisticated composers, yet the originals are no doubt genuine, and thoroughly characteristic of a predominant phase of the uneducated Negro's make-up. Odum and Johnson, in *Workaday Songs*, discuss at length the question of authentic and modern blues, especially in view of the millions of phonograph records that have been sold in the past ten or fifteen years. They have found a surprising similarity between the words and titles of recent popular blues, and those of the songs collected more than twenty-five years ago. Explaining the present relationship between folk blues and the formal, or composed variety, they write: [3]

When a blues (phonograph) record is issued it quickly becomes the property of a million Negro workers and adventurers who never bought it and perhaps never heard it played. Sometimes they do not even know that the song is from a record. They may recognize in it parts of songs long familiar

[3] Odum and Johnson, *Negro Workaday Songs*, University of North Carolina Press.

to them and think that it is just another piece which some songster has put together. Their desire to invent a different version, their skill at adapting stanzas of old favorites to the new music, and sometimes their misunderstanding of the words of the new song, result in the transformation of the song into many local variants. In other words, the folk creative process operates upon a song, the origin of which may already be mixed, and produces in turn variations that may later become the bases of other formal blues. . . .

Whether the formal blues have come to stay or not, it is impossible to tell at present. Possibly they will undergo considerable modification as the public becomes satiated and the Negro takes on more and more of the refinements of civilization. . . .

The folk blues will also undergo modification, but they will always reflect Negro life in its lower strata much more accurately than the formal blues can. For it must be remembered that these folk-blues were the Negro's melancholy song long before the phonograph was invented. Yet the formal songs are important. In their own way they are vastly superior to the cruder folk productions, since they have all of the advantages of the artificial over the natural. They may replace some of the simpler songs and thus dull the creative impulse of the common Negro folk to some extent, but there is every reason to suppose that there will be real folk blues as long as there are Negro toilers and adventurers whose naïveté has not been worn off by what the white man calls culture.

v

And now for the significance of all this Negro music to America. It has been protested that it is the song of the Negro alone, who represents but a single part of our population. Those of us who are not black cannot share the ownership of this literature with the Negro, because it is characteristic of him, and not of us. The Americanism of Negro song involves questions that are beyond the scope of a book on music; social and political questions, involving segregation of races, or admixtures not pleasant to discuss. In the case of mixtures, one Southern gentleman has said that the melting pot would become a witches' cauldron, and there are many Northerners who would sympathize with him. Obviously, the Negro songs are nearer our musical comprehension than the savage chants of the Indian. The Negro has been long enough in contact with the white man to acquire his musical scale.

There is a universality of appeal about the Negro music that makes it something more than the chant of a single race. The songs are so fundamentally human that they have already outlived the generation and conditions that produced the oldest of them. As Alain Locke writes in *The New Negro:* [4]

They have survived in turn the contempt of the slave owners, the conventionalizations of formal religion, the repressions of Puritanism, the corruptions of sentimental balladry, and the neglect and disdain of second-generation respectability. They have escaped the lapsing conditions and the fragile vehicle of folk art, and come firmly into the context of formal music.

We have seen in foregoing chapters how many of these Negro songs have been used by serious composers. Some have been treated in type, and some have been garbed in a dress that is incongruous. Though the Negro songs are nearer our own expression than the music of the Indians, they nevertheless have to be treated appropriately to preserve their native appeal, otherwise their original flavor is lost. As MacDowell said when discussing Indian music, the problem of Americanism in music is not so easily solved as by taking folk songs born in America and harmonizing them haphazardly.

3. OTHER SOURCES OF FOLK SONGS

I

Throughout America there are sources of folk songs that have been appreciated by collectors only in recent years. It is good for our literature that we have at last awakened to the fact that we have valuable folk songs in hitherto unsuspected places, for as primitive customs and manners disappear, the songs associated with these traditions will vanish also. Civilization—and especially its age of machinery—does not provide fertile soil for folk songs. With our modern standardization of living, and such mediums as the radio and the talking pictures setting artificial standards in even the remotest places, the most rural countryman may soon acquire the manners and speech of the city dweller. Then he will sing the latest jazz hits instead of his own songs.

Folk songs are generally common to people whom civilization has

[4] *The New Negro*, edited by Alain Locke: A. & C. Boni.

touched the least, where society and life in general is the least organized. Isolation from other people, hand labor, and lack of printed literature are factors that nourish and perpetuate folk music. A certain naïveté is essential to the true people's song; sophistication is its deadliest enemy. True folk music is found among the Negroes, the mountaineers in the Southeast Appalachians, the cowboys, the lumberjacks and shanty boys, in the New England farm districts, among the wandering tribe of hoboes, among sailors and longshoremen, and often in the jails.

Not that each group has an exclusive, individual literature. There is much interrelation of songs. The cowboy sings, "Bury me not on the lone prai-rie," and the sailor chants, "O bury me not in the deep, deep sea." *The Dying Hobo* is heard in West Virginia, among the Maine lumberjacks, and in Texas. *Turkey in the Straw*, originally known as *Zip Coon*, is native to the minstrel show, indigenous to the South and Southwest, it is the authentic accompaniment to the Virginia Reel, and it is used for barn dances in Maine. It is probably the nearest approach to a truly national folk tune that we have.

II

The mountain regions of Kentucky, Tennessee, the Carolinas, and Virginia offer a splendid example of preservation of folk song by isolation. British settlers came into these mountains in the latter eighteenth or early nineteenth century. The region is secluded and inaccessible. Few roads have been built into the mountains, and railroads are miles away. The people have been dependent on themselves alone. Each family has raised its own vegetables, and had its own cattle and sheep. Money was unnecessary; when they traded, the mountaineers bartered in kind. For liquor they had their own stills, and made their own moonshine; hence, the feuds with revenue officers of the government. When disputes arose with neighbors, justice was a private matter, often requiring a gun. Then revenge was in order, and blood feuds between families and clans were carried on for generations.

Otherwise, they are a leisurely people, sociable and kindly when they are not suspicious. Hospitable to anyone they are not afraid is a "revenoo-er," they are cordial to strangers, courteous and dignified. Cecil Sharp found them somewhat like English peasants, with one

servile
obsequish

essential difference. They had none of the obsequiousness common to the English villager.

Most of the mountain songs are traditional English ballads, brought from England by the ancestors of the present inhabitants. Civilization has not touched the singers or the songs, and even though those who sing today may understand little of what they are singing, they tell of knights and ladies, of courtships and tragedies, of a time and place far different from their own. Cecil Sharp, when he published his collection of *English Folk Songs from the Southern Appalachians,* included in his work an appendix that shows where various of the songs have been noted in England. Thirty-seven of the ballads are to be found, for example, in Child's *English and Scottish Ballads.* Among them are the tales of *Barbara Allen; The Maid Freed from the Gallows* (known also as *The Hangman's Song,* and sung in various forms in many corners of the globe); *The Two Brothers; Lord Randal; Earl Brand;* and many others. The songs include *My Boy Billy* (generally known as *Billie Boy); Sourwood Mountain; The Farmyard* (seemingly an ancestor of the Rotarians' *Old MacDonald Had a Farm); Frog Went a-Courtin';* and so on.

Other collectors have noted some of these and other songs. Josephine McGill published a collection, and Howard Brockway and Loraine Wyman gathered a number into their set of *Lonesome Tunes* and *Twenty Kentucky Mountain Songs.* In his *Folk Songs of the South,* John H. Cox presented songs he had collected in West Virginia.

While most of the songs were obviously brought by the first settlers from England, some of them make references to more modern events. *Brother Green* speaks of the "Southern foe," who "laid him low." The story evidently refers to the Civil War, though in its present form the song may be a variant of an older version. *The Wreck on the C. & O., The Boston Burglar,* and others of their kind are the mountaineers' versions of American ballads.

Generally the mountain people sing without accompaniment, in a straightforward manner, unconscious of an audience. The folk singer thinks of the story he is telling rather than the effect he is producing on a listener. In some quarters, visitors to the mountains have found instruments. Occasionally a fiddle, and sometimes a guitar. Some of the folk singers accompany themselves on the dulcimer, a shallow wooden box, with four sound-holes—a sort of elongated violin. Generally three strings are stretched over this box. Two are used as drones, and the third for the melody. The effect is either that of an ancient drone, or a sound like the twanging of a banjo or guitar.

III

The cowboys of the Southwest have had their song literature, some of it preserved by such ardent collectors as John A. Lomax. Railroads and other modern forms of transportation, and the cutting up of the huge ranches into small farms, have dimmed the romance of the time-honored profession of cow punching. The old-time roundup has almost disappeared, and the cattle trails to Kansas and to Montana are covered with grass. In the seventies and eighties large forces of men were needed to take care of the cattle in the winter season, to round them up in the spring and to brand the calves. Then they had to be driven to market, up the long trails from Texas, sometimes as far north as Montana, where the grass made better grazing.

The cowboys had to provide their own entertainment; so they sang, sometimes songs they had learned elsewhere, and often those they composed themselves. Many of their songs were useful—rhythmic yells to stir up lagging cattle, or cattle "lullabies" to quiet the restless animals at night. Sometimes the "dogie" songs were used to halt stampedes. Aside from songs connected with his business, the cowboy's taste ran to opposites. He liked songs and ballads of the desperado—*Jesse James* (found in many parts of the country); *Billy the Kid;* or the story of *The Hell-Bound Train.* He could grow sentimental and sing of *The Dying Cowboy;* his *Home on the Range;* or the religious *Rounded Up in Glory.* He also shared many ballads and songs with frontiersmen and ballad singers generally. Some of these were pretty much unchanged by the cowboy: *The Boston Burglar;* the tale of *MacAfee's Confession,* and others. Sometimes he adapted songs to his own surroundings, and occasionally he included in his song-words, stanzas that are found elsewhere. For example, the cowboy refrain

> Jack o' diamonds, Jack o' diamonds,
> I know you of old,
> You've robbed my pockets
> Of silver and gold,

is similar to the refrain of a totally different song—the Negro convict song *Water-Boy,* known chiefly through Avery Robinson's concert arrangement.

The cowboy literature is colorful; some of the melodies he sang are very beautiful. On the whole, his ballads are typical of himself, and like all folk-song literature they show the temperament and life of those who sing them. As Lomax has written in his volume of *Cowboy Songs:* [1]

The changing and romantic West of the early days lives mainly in song and story. The last figure to vanish is the cowboy, the animating spirit of the vanishing era. He sits his horse easily as he rides through a wide valley, enclosed by mountains, clad in the hazy purple of the coming night,—with his face turned steadily down the long, long road, "the road that the sun goes down." Dauntless, reckless, without the unearthly purity of Sir Galahad, though as gentle to a pure woman as King Arthur, he is truly a knight of the twentieth century. A vagrant puff of wind shakes a corner of the crimson handkerchief knotted loosely at his throat; the thud of his pony's feet mingling with the jingle of his spurs is borne back; and as the careless, gracious, lovable figure disappears over the divide, the breeze brings to the ears, faint and far yet cheery still, the refrain of a cowboy song:

> Whoopee ti yi yo, git along little dogies;
>   It's your misfortune and none of my own.
> Whoopee ti yi yo, git along little dogies;
>   For you know Wyoming will be your new home.

IV

Lumberjack songs from the woods of Michigan, Wisconsin, and Minnesota have been collected by Franz Rickaby, and published in a volume of *Ballads and Songs of the Shanty-Boy.*[2] Some of these seem to be original and others are adaptations. Rickaby found that the shanty boy makes no general use of his songs while he is actually at work. He is not by nature a gang worker, and so his songs do not have the place that other songs have had in labors where efforts are timed in unison, or the general rhythm of the work is maintained by the singing of the group, or an individual in the group. But, as Rickaby wrote,

---

[1] John A. Lomax, *Cowboy Songs and other Frontier Ballads,* Macmillan Co.
[2] Franz Rickaby, *Ballads and Songs of the Shanty-Boy,* Harvard University Press.

. . . back in the shanty, particularly on Saturday evenings, secure from the outer cold,—his supper stowed safely within him, the old iron stove throwing out its genial heat, and the mellowing ministrations of tobacco well begun,—the shanty-boy became story-teller and singer. The emotional thaw set in; and a great many of his songs were, in the words of an old shantyboy, "as fine as any you'll hear."

Many of his favorite songs tell of his own type of life:

> Oh, a shanty-man's life is a wearisome life,
>   Altho' some think it void of care.
> Swinging an axe from morning till night
>   In the midst of the forests so drear.

Or the *Shanty-man's Alphabet,* in which

> A is for axe as you all very well know,
> B is for boys that can use them just so.
> C is for chopping, and now I'll begin;
> And D is for danger we ofttimes run in.

Rickaby believes that the woods songs were composed by individuals who set out definitely to compose. There has been little communal writing of songs and ballads, similar to that attributed to the Negro. New stanzas might often have been added, but the songs themselves rarely if ever originated with the group. Generally the words were fitted to a tune the author had in mind when he wrote them.

Roland Palmer Gray collected the *Songs and Ballads of the Maine Lumberjacks.* His volume presents a number of the songs that Rickaby found in the Midwest: *The Alphabet Song,* and a version of the *Shanty Man's Life*—the *Lumberman's Life* in Maine. There are a few of the old English ballads—*The Twa Sisters, The Dark-Eyed Sailor,* and some historical ballads. Some of these, culled from broadsides, record local historical events of recent date—*The Bangor Fire,* of 1911. One is a tribute to President Wilson.

V

Origin of folk songs and ballads will always provide material for discussion and controversy, and it is difficult and dangerous to be arbitrary in such matters. Sometimes a publisher has issued a sheet music edition of a traditional ballad, and many people have thought it a new song. There was a recent vogue of *Ain' gonna rain no more,* and not all who heard it for the first time realized how old it really was. *Frankie and Johnny* has been attributed to various sources, and has known countless versions. The incident it relates has been credited to various localities—from New Orleans to the North. A certain story in the New York *World* stated positively that it occurred in St. Louis, as recently as 1889; that the man's name was Albert and that Frankie is still living. Moreover, that the actors in the tragedy were not white, but colored.

Sometimes a recently composed and published song achieves such currency that it is commonly considered a traditional ballad. *The Blue and the Gray* was issued before the Spanish War as coming from the pen of Paul Dresser, brother of Theodore Dreiser, the novelist, yet it is included in Louise Pound's *American Ballads and Songs,* with the meager information that the compiler found the text in a manuscript book.

The perpetuation of these songs is as interesting as their origin. Some were introduced into plays, and were sung nightly all over the country. *In the Baggage Coach Ahead* was used in vaudeville, its dreary story illustrated by lantern slides. Then there were broadsides, or song sheets (a relic of an English custom dating back to the time of Queen Elizabeth), which were sold at fairs and circuses, or by traveling sellers of patent medicines. Of course, in isolated sections, such as the mountain districts, songs were handed down from father to son by word of mouth, especially where the people were illiterate. Then there was another way in which families have helped to preserve songs through several generations—the manuscript books, into which were written the words of songs heard orally.

We have already learned something of the extent of the overlapping of songs in different sections of the country; how some lyrics and ballads are the common property of cowboys and lumberjacks, Negroes and mountain whites. The more general anthologies are valuable in showing types of songs which had had widespread use. In *The American Songbag,* Carl Sandburg groups the songs as "Dramas and Portraits," "Minstrel Songs," "The Ould Sod" (those of an Irish flavor), "Pioneer Memories," "Kentucky Songs," songs commemmorating "The Lincolns and Hankses," the "Great Lakes and Erie

Canal," "Hobo Songs," tales of "The Big Brutal City," "Prison and Jail Songs," "Blues, Mellows, and Ballets," songs of "The Great Open Spaces," "Mexican Border Songs," ballads and lyrics of the "Southern Mountains," "Picnic and Hayrack Follies, Close Harmony, and Darn Fool Ditties," "Railroad and Work Gangs," songs of "Lumberjacks," and of the "Sailorman," "Bandit Biographies," songs of the "Five Wars," about "Lovely People," and the "Road to Heaven."

VI

In recent years the vogue of the folk singer has grown tremendously. The decade of the fifties saw the emergence or the continued popularity of such guitar-playing singers as the Negro Huddie Ledbetter ("Leadbelly"), who sang his way out of a prison sentence for murder by writing a song for the governor of the state; the white, bearded Burl Ives, who dubbed himself the "Pore Wayfarin' Stranger"; the more polished Tom Scott, the older John Jacob Niles, and the West Indian Calypso-singing Harry Belafonte, all of whom gained wide popularity, reaching their audiences through phonograph recordings, radio, and television.

During the early sixties, the folk music craze had a strong effect on younger people, and groups of young folk singers gathered together for singing sessions, many of them in Washington Square, New York; these sessions, ranging in size from the intimate to the mammoth, became known as "hootenannies"—a sort of folk-singing round-robin, in which performers follow each other until the wee hours of the night. As has often happened in the past, folk music served the cause of social change and the voicing of grievances, and many folk singers and folk songs of the early sixties became identified, in part, with the civil rights movement of that period.

VII

What effect all our folk music, from different races and sources, will have on American music of the future is impossible to determine. It is hard to say which part of it is truly American. Some has been born here, and some brought from abroad. There are people who hold that transplanted folk songs of the European nationalities that make up the

American nation are legitimately to be considered as forming part of the body of American folk music. And there are others who say that nothing is American that does not have its origin in America.

Yet in folk music, as in the formal music of the concert hall, Americanism is a more subtle thing than a mere question of geographic origin. As in spoken or written language, there are certain habits of speech and certain points of view that are peculiar to us: not mere references to local events and scenes, but the manner of referring to them and looking at them. And so in music: it is a question of association and of traits inherent in the music itself.

In America, as elsewhere, some people say that a composer shows his poverty of ideas if he cannot invent his own tunes. Yet it is surely better to hear a good folk song, admirably handled, than a mediocre theme of the composer's own making. For even great composers sometimes write undistinguished melodies. Music makers the world over have made frequent use of folk tunes almost since music began, just as poets have based their poems on traditional legends, and painters have taken their subjects from life and nature. Haydn's music was filled with Croatian melodies; the first phrases of the *Austrian Hymn* were taken literally from a folk song. Weber, Brahms, Liszt, Grieg, the Russian nationalists since Glinka have drawn heavily on the songs of their people.

The American composers who have used the folk songs heard in this country have generally done so for one of two reasons—sometimes for both. Often they have had no purpose other than to take melodies, which they thought were beautiful, and treat them in a way that would emphasize their beauty or their native character. Sometimes they have aimed to make their compositions describe the people who sing the songs.

The other motive has been a desire to throw off the European yoke, to cease imitating the styles and traditions of the Old World. So much of our early music has been in imitation of foreign models that American musicians have developed an inferiority complex, which has made some of them take desperate measures to cut the cord as quickly as possible. Even though they must have known that such a condition was inevitable in a country that had been a nation for little more than a century, composed of people from all races, and of our composers who had gone to European masters for their training, they nevertheless grew self-conscious about our lack of nationalism in music, and took stern measures to acquire a native speech. They preferred provincialism to a diluted internationalism. Some of them used traditional musical formulae in handling the folk songs, and employed accepted forms and harmonies. Others made sincere attempts to devise a harmonic dress that would clothe primitive themes in robes to emphasize their native flavor.

Although the problem of musical nationalism is far too complex to solve by the use of such obvious devices, and though many of the ardent nationalists have shot wide of their mark, the interest in folk music has stimulated composition in this country. It has put into our music a more vital note than it had before. And the intense sincerity of the leaders in the movement has rendered it something that cannot be brushed aside by cynicism. Though we cannot admire all we hear, we must needs respect the pioneer spirit at the bottom of it all, and take off our hats to the man who wants to be himself and not a mere reflection of someone else.

We have learned that American composers experimented with folk music, Indian melodies, and the like, way back into the eighteenth century. Father Heinrich was the first to use Indian themes in orchestral works of the larger variety. But the idea never took strong hold or aroused much interest until Antonin Dvořák spent almost four years in this country, from 1892 to 1895. An intense nationalist, his work is filled with the folk spirit of his native Bohemia. In his work at the National Conservatory of Music in New York he tried to develop a nationalistic school of music among his American pupils. The works he wrote in this country were intended as examples of what our own composers could do with the material at hand. He expressed the impressions he received during his visits to various parts of the country. He studied the folk songs in America and used and imitated them in his works. The *New World* Symphony, played first by the New York Philharmonic in 1893, has the virtue of being the greatest of Dvořák's several symphonies; and because it is a great work, and a highly popular one, it focused attention on the use of American folk songs. Whether or not Dvořák actually used *Swing Low, Sweet Chariot*, or whether he himself composed Negro-like themes for his symphony, he did try to express America. He tried to embody the same spirit in a String Quartet and in a Quintet. Probably all he accomplished was to give a Bohemian's impression of America, and in plaintive moments to voice his own homesickness. But he started the vogue, and most of the serious effort to harness American folk song dates from the visit of the Bohemian Dvořák.

Arthur Farwell, Henry F. B. Gilbert, Harry Burleigh, Harvey Worthington Loomis, Charles Wakefield Cadman, Charles S. Skilton, Carl Busch, all were among the pioneers who turned to folk music of the North American continent around the turn of the century. Some of them lost their enthusiasm in later years, or at least decided that they did not care to limit themselves to folk material. They came to realize the subtlety of Americanism in art, and that while the essence of folk music is native, it alone cannot produce a nationalist idiom.

CHAPTER SIXTEEN

Our Lighter Musical Moments

1. YESTERDAY

MOST of the popular music of the day has been transitory; here today and gone tomorrow, with something new to take its place. And not always so new, either. Often the latest songs are old ideas rehashed and modernized. Yet with each generation the type of popular music changes; as people become sophisticated their songs do likewise. Of course, much of the music discussed in our early chapters has been popular music, especially the early balladry and minstrel songs. Stephen Foster's songs were, and still are, songs that people everywhere sing. The only difference has been that Foster's songs have been the real thing, and have endured. They have passed from the category of popular music into that of true folk songs.

In the middle of the nineteenth century, when Foster was writing his immortal songs, the minstrel shows were entering their prime. These entertainments naturally produced later composers, and the one whose name is best known today is JAMES A. BLAND (1854–1911), who has lived to our day, and perhaps for all time, through just one of the many songs he composed—*Carry Me Back to Old Virginny*. Bland was himself a Negro, and one of the ironic features of his career was the difficulty he had in realizing his ambition to become a minstrel performer. Minstrel companies were for the most part composed of white men who blacked their faces and imitated colored men. There was no place in these troupes for a genuine Negro, and it was not until a real "colored minstrel" company came along that Bland found his place in his chosen profession.

He was the son of a Charleston, South Carolina, father who was one of the first college-bred Negroes in America. James Bland was born in Flushing, New York, October 22, 1854. Then his parents moved to Washington, D.C. where his father was appointed examiner in the United States Patent Office—the first colored man to hold such a position.

James received his education in the Washington public schools, and later was graduated from Howard University, at the age of nineteen. He was not particularly brilliant in his academic subjects, but was considered a musical prodigy. He was always energetic, and his affability made friends for him wherever he went. As a boy he was a page in the House of Representatives. Then his talents became known, and he was frequently engaged to entertain prominent guests in Washington. He could sing, play the banjo, and compose songs for any occasion.

He was famous as a song writer before he was able to perform with minstrel troupes. He appeared first with a colored troupe in New York in 1879 and then toured the Pacific Coast with them. In 1882 he went to England and Scotland where he made a great success and remained for nearly twenty years. He is said to have earned ten thousand dollars a year in those days. King Edward, then Prince of Wales, attended his performances and honored him on several occasions.

Returning from England in 1901, Bland arrived in Washington, destitute. The only work he could find was a job in the office of a friend. He became discouraged and moved to Philadelphia, where he died May 5, 1911.

He wrote about seven hundred songs, of which not many are remembered today. Among them are *Christmas Dinner, Dem Golden Slippers* (which sold over 100,000 copies before 1888), *De Golden Wedding,* and *In the Evening by the Moonlight.*

During Stephen Foster's lifetime WILLIAM SHAKESPEARE HAYS (1837–1907), popularly known as "Will Hays," was one of his strongest rivals. Hays was the composer of one of the most maudlin self-pity songs ever written—*Driven from Home,* which is today revived by song antiquarians as a curiosity. The rivalry with Foster was so strong at one time that some of Hays's admirers claimed that he, and not Foster, was the real author of some of Foster's songs.

Hays wrote his first ballad when he was sixteen. After that he published nearly three hundred songs, which in their day had a sale total-ing several millions. He was born in Louisville, Kentucky, in 1837, and died there July 22, 1907. Some of his best-known songs were *Evangeline, My Southern Sunny Home, Mollie Darling,* and *Write Me a Letter from Home.*

There are others who contributed at least one significant song to our popular music (even if that significance rests chiefly on an unquestion-ably wide appeal), and their words and melodies are still remembered, although their names may be forgotten.

GEORGE COOPER (1840–1927) whose collaboration with Foster has been mentioned earlier, became one of our most important writers of lyrics that people love to sing. His best-known song text was that of *Sweet Genevieve,* inspired by his first and only love who died shortly after their marriage in 1869. Cooper wrote his poem from an aching heart, but during one of his habitual periods of financial diffi-culty he sold it for five dollars to HENRY TUCKER, who supplied the tune that has become a permanent favorite with informal harmoniz-ers. (Tucker has already received credit for the music of *Weeping Sad and Lonely or When This Cruel War Is Over.* He wrote many songs, among them a setting of Bret Harte's *The Heathen Chinee,* and was famous also as an editor and arranger of music, including the famous *Star of the Evening* by James M. Sayles.)

As a result of his association with Foster, George Cooper for many years remained the pet lyricist of our popular tunesmiths. His partner-ship with JOHN ROGERS THOMAS (1829–1896) was particularly fruit-ful, with *Rose of Killarney* as a climax (1876). With T. BRIGHAM BISHOP (1835–1925) he wrote *Pretty as a Picture* (1872), popu-larized by the minstrel Billy Emerson whose best-known song was *The Big Sunflower* (by Bobby Newcombe). As late as 1883, Cooper had an immense hit in *Strolling on the Brooklyn Bridge,* which he wrote with J. P. SKELLY. He lived until 1927, a gold mine of in-formation on American popular song writing from Foster to Tin-Pan Alley.

An earlier song, with a history similar to that of *Sweet Genevieve,* was *When You and I Were Young, Maggie,* published by its com-poser JAMES AUSTIN BUTTERFIELD (1837–1891) in 1866. The words were by a Canadian schoolteacher, George W. Johnson, who had fallen in love with one of his pupils, Maggie Clark. His poem was inspired by the actual scenes of their courting, and represented what he hoped would be the memories of their old age together. But, like Cooper's Genevieve, Maggie died soon after her marriage. Johnson's words were published in a collection called *Maple Leaves*, where they attracted the attention of Butterfield, a trained musician, who was born in England in 1837. For many years a musical leader in Chicago, Butterfield was active as a composer, publisher, teacher, singer, and conductor.

Both men live today in the one song *When You and I Were Young, Maggie*.

Many of America's most popular songs, both before and after Stephen Foster's day, came from England or were written by English composers in this country. A successful song writer of the 1860's was MRS. CHARLOTTE ALINGTON BARNARD (1830–1869) known by the pseudonym "Claribel," a woman of some musical education, who depended chiefly on her own reliable instinct for sentimentality. Claribel's *Take Back the Heart That Thou Gavest* (1864) is remembered today for its lush lines and solid waltz rhythm. But her best song was unquestionably *Come Back to Erin*, which has often been regarded as a piece of actual Irish folk music.

Far more important to America's popular music was the visit of WILLIAM HORACE LINGARD (1839–1927) who came here from London in 1868. He was an accomplished comedian, heading his own company on Broadway, and he wrote at least the words of a number of successful songs. Best remembered today is *Captain Jinks of the Horse Marines*, for which T. MACLAGAN supplied the tune. Lingard was also the lyricist of *Walking Down Broadway* (music by CHARLES E. PRATT, 1841–1902), which was honored by both imitations and parodies. (Its chorus contains an early example of the slang expression "O.K.") Another Lingard song, for which he seems to have written the music as well as the words, was *On the Beach at Brighton*, and this was immediately copied by American versions which substituted Cape May and Newport for the English resort.

Another Englishman to score an American success both as actor and as song writer was GEORGE LEYBOURNE, who deserves credit for the words of *The Flying Trapeze* (later prefixed by *The Man on*), with music by ALFRED LEE, also of English birth. This famous song, brought out piratically and anonymously by at least three publishers in 1868, has had the doubtful compliment of a modern revival in highly garbled form. The combination of Leybourne and Lee also produced the popular *Champagne Charlie*, with the former as its greatest interpreter.

Leybourne may have had a hand also in that early aviation song *Up in a Balloon*, which was introduced to New York by Mrs. Lingard, professionally known as Alice Dunning. The probable composer was G. W. HUNT (another Englishman), and, as usual, there were several American versions. Hunt was responsible for a number of other hits, including the utterly British *Awfully Clever* and *The Bell Goes a-Ringing for Sai-rah.*

The passage of time has had little effect on such a song as *Silver Threads Among the Gold*, written in 1872 by HART PEASE DANKS and EBEN E. REXFORD. It sold more than two million copies before the end of the century, and another million after its revival in 1907. Other popular songs of the early seventies were the still current *Reuben and Rachel*, by HARRY BIRCH and WILLIAM GOOCH (1871), WILLIAM SCANLAN's *Jim Fisk* (1872), which whitewashed one of the most notorious swindlers of the time, and *Bonnie Sweet Bessie, the Maid of Dundee* (1873), by BELLA ROOT and J. L. GILBERT.

I'll Take You Home Again, Kathleen, still appearing on our community song sheets, was written in 1876 by THOMAS PAINE WESTENDORF, a Viriginian, who had moved to Louisville, Kentucky, with his wife, after the death of their son. Mrs. Westendorf, prosaically christened Jane but nicknamed Kathleen, had been ill and unhappy in their new surroundings, and her husband realized that a change was needed. A poem by George Parsely, *Barney, I'll Take You Home Again*, gave him the idea for the song, and within an hour he had written both the words and the music of *I'll Take You Home Again, Kathleen.*

In 1877 the Reverend ROBERT LOWRY (1826–1899), composer of the successful hymn-tune *I Need Thee Every Hour*, created the words and music of *Where Is My Wandering Boy Tonight*, which millions of Americans have heard sung in *The Old Homestead*. The same year produced the contrastingly lively *Whoa, Emma*, of English origin.

The early eighties were not marked by many popular songs beyond those of Harrigan and Braham. A certain JENNIE LINDSAY wrote the moralizing *Always Take Mother's Advice* in 1884, and the same year saw the publication of BANKS WINTER's *White Wings,* whose lilting melody is still familiar. The perennial *Rock-a-bye, Baby,* by EFFIE I. CANNING (who died in 1940), is dated 1887. And in 1888, Frank Harding published the rousing *Drill, Ye Tarriers, Drill,* while Monroe H. Rosenfeld announced *With All Her Faults I Love Her Still.*

Then came those sturdy Irish ditties—*Down Went McGinty,* by JOSEPH FLYNN (1889), and J. W. KELLY's *Throw Him Down, McCloskey* (1890), popularized by the Amazonian Maggie Cline. When HENRY SAYERS (1854–1929) picked up the nonsensical *Ta-ra-ra-boom-deré* in a St. Louis brothel, turning the dusky Babe Connors into a "sweet Tuxedo girl," the Gay Nineties had definitely arrived.

There were, of course, thousands of songs of sentiment. They are always with us. As Sigmund Spaeth says in the title of his recent book, "They Still Sing of Love"; and they probably always will. It was in the nineties that the story-telling song came into its greatest vogue. CHARLES K. HARRIS (1865–1930) gave it a tremendous boost with *After the Ball.* His autobiography is one of the best accounts of the song-writing business in existence. It tells how a natural melodist thinks of his songs and then has an arranger write them down for him; and of how songs were promoted and made popular in the days before the radio and the sound pictures. Harris was smart enough to realize that the vogue of his songs depended on the popularity of the actors and singers who sang them in public, and he wrote songs to fit various situations in the plays they acted in. Among his best-known lyrics were *Break the News to Mother; Hello, Central, Give Me Heaven* (one of the first telephone songs); *Can You Pay for a Broken Heart; Kiss and Let's Make Up; Why Don't They Play with Me; No One to Kiss You Good-night; My Mother's Kiss (The Sweetest Kiss of All),* and many others. He was also influential in having the copyright bill of 1909 passed. This enabled song writers and composers to collect royalties from the sale of phonograph records and other reproducing devices.

PAUL DRESSER was an older man than Harris—he lived from 1857 to 1911—but his songs were of the same type. He was best known for a song that has been almost a folk song—*On the Banks of the Wabash,*

but no one seemed interested in singing them, least of all the troops in Korea. It seems that war, with its H-bomb threats, is not anything to sing about any more.

Recent years and crises have seen the publication and failure of more up-to-date songs: *The Berlin Wall; Castro Ain't Convertible; Castro's Got to Go, Cha-cha-cha;* and *Fidel Castro Rock.*

5. THE TWENTIETH-CENTURY MUSICAL THEATRE

Any consideration of the twentieth-century musical theatre in America might well begin with RUDOLF FRIML (1881———), born in Prague, Czechoslovakia, December 27, 1881. He was a pupil of Dvořák, and in 1901 came to America as accompanist for the violinist Jan Kubelik. He made frequent appearances as a concert pianist and played his own Piano Concerto with the New York Symphony Orchestra. He composed and published several thousand piano, violin, cello, and organ compositions, but is best known for his works for the operetta stage, which include *The Firefly* (1913); *High Jinks* (1913); *Katinka* (1915); *You're in Love* (1917); *Sometime* (1918); *Gloriana* (1918); *Tumble In* (1919); *June Love* (1921); *The Blue Kitten* (1922); and *Cinders* (1923).

It was in 1924 that Friml achieved his biggest hit, even though he had to share honors with Herbert Stothart for a few interpolated songs. The show was *Rose-Marie,* and the Friml numbers included *Rose-Marie, Indian Love Call,* and *Totem Tom Tom.* A year later Friml almost repeated his success with *The Vagabond King* (1925), with a libretto by Brian Hooker and W. H. Post loosely based on the career of François Villon. The score contained *Only a Rose* and the rousing *Song of the Vagabonds.* With one exception the subsequent Friml shows were failures, but *The Three Musketeers* (1928), with its stirring *March of the Musketeers,* achieved a distinguished run.

SIGMUND ROMBERG (1887–1951) was born in Hungary, July 29, 1887. He trained as an engineer to build bridges, but upon his arrival in this country decided to pursue music, which had hitherto been his hobby. After playing piano in light orchestras and writing songs for various revues, he supplied the score for *Hands Up* (1915), his first "book" show. *The Blue Paradise* (1915) contained several Romberg numbers, and *Maytime* (1917) had an all-Romberg score. Four years later, after numerous revues and shows to which Romberg contributed part or, in a few undistinguished cases, all of the music, there came to Broadway a Romberg triumph—*Blossom Time* (1921), based on the life of Franz Schubert. Romberg's adaptation of Schubert melodies caused much discussion, especially the waltz treatment of a theme from the *Unfinished Symphony*.

Romberg's warm melodic gift, used with taste and discretion, was again apparent in *The Student Prince* (1924), produced three years and ten shows later. The popularity of the frankly romantic operetta has scarcely waned down to this day, and songs like *Deep in My Heart* and *The Drinking Song* are still much sung. Romberg went on to write the scores to *Louis the 14th* (1925); *Princess Flavia* (1925); *The Desert Song* (1926); *Cherry Blossoms* (1927); *My Maryland* (1927); *Rosalie* (1928), which also included several songs by George Gershwin; and *The New Moon* (1928), a show which contained four of Romberg's most durable melodies: *Softly, as in a Morning Sunrise; Stouthearted Men; One Kiss;* and *Lover Come Back to Me.*

In the decade of the 1920's Romberg had over twenty-three shows produced on Broadway. He was less successful in the 1930's, producing only six shows—of which most were outright failures. Only *May Wine* (1935) achieved a creditable run. In the 1940's Romberg founded and organized the Song Writers' Protective Organization (now the American Guild of Composers and Authors), and in 1945 he returned to the theatre with one of his most successful shows—*Up in Central Park*. With a book set in the 1870's, the show might be called streamlined Romberg—not jazzy, and still highly romantic, but up-to-date in its adaptability to modern ballet techniques. Romberg's last show, *The Girl in Pink Tights* (1954), was produced three years after his death. In all, Romberg contributed music to more than seventy stage productions.

JEROME KERN (1885–1945) was fully as romantic as Friml and Romberg, but he was a distinctly American composer, and the tender tunefulness of his melodies and the sharpness of his rhythms bear little resemblance to the Continental inventions of his foreign-born colleagues. His masterpiece was undoubtedly the score of *Showboat* (1928). With a book by Oscar Hammerstein II based upon Edna

Ferber's novel, *Showboat* was almost a folk opera; seldom has any subject been treated with better musical and dramatic taste than in this unpretentious classic. It has been revived time and time again, and its songs have entered the permanent repertory of American ballads. Some have gone so far as to say that if there is ever to be an American school of opera, *Showboat* points the path which that school must take.

Born in New York on January 27, 1885, Kern first became known to Broadway by his music for *The Red Petticoat* (1912). Two years later he contributed a song to *The Girl from Utah* (1914)—entitled *They Didn't Believe Me,* the number has been sung, hummed, and whistled ever since it was first introduced on Broadway. A year later, Kern was engaged with librettist Guy Bolton to write shows for the tiny Princess Theatre in New York. The Princess musicals departed from convention in that the songs were integrated into the plots, and the story situations, while funny, were nonetheless logical. Produced during the war years when manpower was short, the shows got along with only two sets and a twelve-man band, helped out by the ingenious arrangements of Fred Saddler.

Kern and Bolton collaborated on numerous musicals, including *Nobody Home* (1915); *Very Good Eddie* (1915); *Have a Heart* (1917); *Oh, Boy!* (1917); *Leave It to Jane* (1917); and *Oh, Lady! Lady!* (1917), the last four written in collaboration with P. G. Wodehouse. When *Leave It to Jane* was revived off-Broadway in 1959 it ran longer than the original production. A torch song that was dropped from *Oh, Lady! Lady!* before the show reached New York was introduced by Helen Morgan a decade later in *Showboat*. The song, *Bill,* was the only number in the show with lyrics not by Hammerstein. *Miss 1917* (1917), a revue, had music by both Kern and Victor Herbert. *Love o' Mike* (1917) was written to a book by Thomas Sidney and lyrics by Harry B. Smith.

After three comparatively unsuccessful shows in 1918, Kern initiated a collaboration with Anne Caldwell that resulted in *She's a Good Fellow* (1919); *The Night Boat* (1920); *The Bunch and Judy* (1922); *Stepping Stones* (1923); and *Criss Cross* (1923). With Guy Bolton, Kern wrote a more traditionally-patterned musical, *Sally* (1920), in which the song *Look for the Silver Lining* was introduced.

Two of Kern's most popular songs, *Who?* and *Two Little Bluebirds,* made their appearance in *Sunny* (1925), a show with book and lyrics by Otto Harbach and Oscar Hammerstein.

In 1927 Florenz Ziegfeld agreed to produce *Showboat,* despite Hammerstein and Kern's revolutionary innovations in book and score. After the success of *Showboat* Kern worked almost exclusively with either Hammerstein or Harbach, both of whom now felt free to write believable books for Broadway musicals. *Sweet Adeline,* with book and lyrics by Hammerstein, appeared in 1929; *The Cat and the Fiddle,* book and lyrics by Harbach, in 1931—the score included the songs *The Night Was Made for Love* and *She Didn't Say Yes, She Didn't Say No. Music in the Air,* book and lyrics by Hammerstein, was produced in 1932—the score contained an unusually high percentage of hits: *I've Told Ev'ry Little Star; And Love Was Born; The Song Is You;* and *In Egern on the Tegern Sea. Roberta,* book and lyrics by Harbach, was produced in 1933; the score contained *Smoke Gets in Your Eyes* and *The Touch of Your Hand.* Kern's last show, *Very Warm for May* (1939), with book and lyrics by Hammerstein, was a failure, but it introduced one of Kern's most popular songs—*All the Things You Are.*

In 1941 Artur Rodzinski, then conductor of the Cleveland Symphony, asked Kern to prepare a symphonic version of the Showboat music. The *Scenario for Orchestra on Themes from Showboat* was accordingly arranged; Rodzinski introduced it the same year. The following year, André Kostelanetz commissioned three composers—Aaron Copland, Virgil Thomson, and Kern—each to compose an entirely original work. Kern responded with *A Portrait of Mark Twain for Orchestra,* which Kostelanetz introduced with the Cincinnati Symphony in 1942. Robert Lawrence, reviewing the piece in the New York *Herald Tribune* of June 8, 1942, wrote: " 'Twain' offered much that made for good basic listening. This seemed not to be music aimed at the intellect. It avoided contrapuntal forms, placing its reliance on melodic, harmonic and emotional appeal. . . . It is pleasant, once in a while, not to be fugally overwhelmed, and Mr. Kern's approach for its own purposes must be accounted a success."

A highly individual lyricist and melodist, IRVING BERLIN

(1888——) is actually a throwback to the sentimental songs of a past day, even though he is occasionally referred to as a composer of "jazz." His first hit-song, *Alexander's Ragtime Band* (1912), was one of the first numbers to be seized upon by jazz bands and made their own, but the song itself is distinctly not jazz—it is scarcely ragtime.

Berlin was born Izzy Baline in Russia, May 11, 1888, and was brought to America by his family when he was little more than a baby. He grew up on the lower East Side and the Bowery in New York and wrote his first song while he was a singing waiter at Nigger Mike's in Chinatown—reputed to be the gathering place of gangsters, thieves, and gunmen, but more likely a showplace for slumming parties from uptown. The song, *Marie from Sunny Italy,* had words by Berlin and music by N. Nicholson, the pianist at Nigger Mike's. At first Berlin wrote only the words of his songs: his melodic gift was not apparent till later. He played the piano a little himself, enough to piece together his tunes, and then an arranger took them down and fixed up their harmonies. Berlin eventually went uptown and got to know the song publishers. There soon appeared hundreds of songs, "words and music by Irving Berlin," which are virtually part of the folk literature of our country. Among them, to mention only a few, were *Alexander's Ragtime Band; Everybody's Doing It; When That Midnight Choochoo Leaves for Alabam'; A Pretty Girl Is Like a Melody; What'll I Do; Russian Lullaby; Always; Blue Skies; Remember;* and *Pack Up Your Sins.* Soon Berlin had his own publishing business; he became a theatrical producer and wrote the music for most of his revues. Eventually he was one of the highest-paid and most sought-after composers for motion pictures.

During World War I, as a private at Camp Upton, Berlin wrote and produced the soldier show *Yip! Yip! Yaphank,* containing the song *Oh, How I Hate to Get Up in the Morning.* At the beginning of World War II Berlin set to work writing and producing another soldier show—*This Is the Army.* It had a long Broadway run, toured the country, went abroad, and was made into a movie. His song *God Bless America* had been written and laid aside years earlier, but Kate Smith began singing it on the radio, and it became almost an unofficial national anthem. Berlin donated his royalties from the song to the

Boy and Girl Scouts of America. Many other topical songs came from his pen during the war years—songs devoted to the Bond Drives, to the Red Cross, and even to the paying of income taxes.

With the exception of his scores for *The Coconuts* (1925), with a libretto by George S. Kaufman, and *Face the Music* (1932), with a Moss Hart libretto, the majority of Berlin's theatre songs for a great many years were used in revues: four *Ziegfeld Follies* (1911, 1919, 1920, and 1927); Berlin's own *Music Box Revues* (1921, 1922, 1923, and 1924); and the memorable *As Thousands Cheer*, a show with sketches by Hart and a score that included the perennial *Easter Parade*. In 1940 Berlin provided the score for the musical comedy *Louisiana Purchase*, with book by Morrie Ryskind.

With his next musical, *Annie Get Your Gun*, Berlin reached the undoubted climax of his career. The show's producers, Rodgers and Hammerstein, had engaged Jerome Kern to provide the score for Herbert and Dorothy Fields' book, which was based on the career of Annie Oakley, the famous rifle shot of Buffalo Bill's Wild West Shows. When Kern died, Berlin was asked to take over; though at first reluctant, he finally agreed to do the score. It is fair to say that few musicals have contained such a concentration of hits, a doubly remarkable fact when we consider that Berlin supplied both music and words. *Annie Get Your Gun* (1946) included these song successes: *Doin' What Comes Naturally; The Girl that I Marry; You Can't Get a Man with a Gun; There's No Business Like Show Business; They Say It's Wonderful; My Defenses Are Down; I Got the Sun in the Morning and the Moon at Night; Anything You Can Do I Can Do Better*. All of them were marked with the characteristic warmth or the stirring lilt that are inherent in Berlin's best songs. They also demonstrated that unerring gift for matching words and music that Berlin shares with his illustrious predecessor from another century—Stephen Foster.

Three years later Berlin collaborated with Robert Sherwood on *Miss Liberty* (1949), and a little over a year later with Russell Crouse and Howard Lindsay on *Call Me Madam* (1950), which—like *Annie Get Your Gun*—starred Ethel Merman and enjoyed enormous success. The score included *You're Just in Love* and *It's a Lovely Day Today*. For the next ten years Berlin seemed to have gone into a well-earned retirement, but in the early 1960's announcement was made that he and the team of Lindsay and Crouse were getting together on another show. The resulting *Mr. President* (1962) opened to a record-breaking advance sale and, though it did not attain hit status, it enjoyed a creditable Broadway run.

GEORGE GERSHWIN, and his place in American music, are discussed at length in Chapter XII. Nevertheless, an examination of his musical comedies belongs here. The last of them, *Let 'Em Eat Cake,* was produced on Broadway in 1933, and they may now be regarded with a perspective which shows that as stage productions they were far less important than the delightful songs which George Gershwin and his brother Ira wrote for them. Only three of the twenty-two musical comedies for which Gershwin supplied all or part of the music ran for more than three hundred performances: *Lady Be Good* (1924), with book by Guy Bolton and Fred Thompson; *Rosalie* (1928), with book by William Anthony MacGuire and Guy Bolton (a show in which Gershwin shared composing honors with Romberg); and *Of Thee I Sing* (1931), the Pulitzer Prize–winning satire with book by George S. Kaufman and Morrie Ryskind. Though the book is unquestionably dated, the score to this show remains the most sophisticated and ingeniously contrived of any of Gershwin's for the light theatre.

Even though Gershwin's other shows had shorter runs, many of them were considered the hit shows of their seasons, and they all featured such leading players of the decade as Adele and Fred Astaire, Gertrude Lawrence, Victor Moore, Jimmy Durante, and Ethel Merman. They included *Oh, Kay* (1926); *Funny Face* (1927); *Treasure Girl* (1928); *Show Girl* (1929); *Strike Up the Band* (1929); *Girl Crazy* (1930); and *Let 'Em Eat Cake* (1933).

LOUIS HIRSCH (1887–1924) was born in New York City, where he had his schooling and first music lessons. Intending to become a concert pianist, he studied in Europe with Rafael Joseffy, but became more interested in popular music and from 1907 contributed songs to Broadway productions. He had his first success with the score to *Vera Violetta* (1917), the show that made Al Jolson a star. Hirsch composed scores for the *Ziegfeld Follies* of 1915, 1916, 1918, and 1922; for *Going Up* (1917); for George M. Cohan's *Mary* (1920); for *The O'Brien Girl* (1921); and for the *Greenwich Village Follies* of

1922 and 1923. Perhaps his best-known song is *The Love Nest*, written for *Mary*. In 1914 Hirsch was one of the nine original founders of ASCAP.

VINCENT YOUMANS (1898–1946) saw twelve shows with his music produced in the twelve years 1921–32. Three of them had runs exceeding three hundred performances: *Wildflower* (1923); *No, No, Nanette* (1925); and *Hit the Deck* (1927). His first show, *Two Little Girls in Blue*, had songs by another composer, and in *Wildflower*, his first hit, he shared composing honors with Herbert Stothart. After two more shows, *Mary Jane McKane* (1923) and *Lollipop* (1924), Youmans achieved his second real success with *No, No, Nanette*. Otto Harbach and Frank Mandel wrote the book, and the lyrics were the work of Harbach and Irving Caesar. Two of the songs were among Youmans's best: *Tea for Two* and *I Want to Be Happy*. Both, deceptively simple in their melodies, are typical of Youmans.

The next year Youmans had a comparative failure in *Oh, Please!* (1926). One of the songs in the score continued to be popular after the show was forgotten: *I Know That You Know*. The following spring *Hit the Deck* (1927) was produced on Broadway, a show that contained another of Youmans's simple-sounding melodies, *Sometimes I'm Happy*, and the effervescently buoyant *Hallelujah*. The remaining five shows with Youmans music had only short runs, but four of them contained songs of lasting popularity: *Great Day* (1929) had the title song and the haunting *Without a Song*, with lyrics by Billy Rose; *Smiles* (1930) had *Time on My Hands*; *Through the Years* (1932) had the title song and *Drums in My Heart*; *Take a Chance*, a show that had music by two other composers as well, was distinguished by Youmans's *Rise 'n' Shine*. After 1932 Youmans wrote no more Broadway shows, though in spite of ill health he wrote songs for a number of motion pictures. His score for *Flying Down to Rio* contained the title song, descriptive of the speed of the modern airplane, and *The Carioca*.

The work of lyricist-composer COLE PORTER (1892–1964) still represents the height of song-writing sophistication, dealing as it does with the primal instincts of love in typically twentieth-century fashion, with many-syllabled words and rhymes consisting of whole phrases like "a certain fear in me, waked the pioneer in me" or "under the hide of me, burning inside of me." Porter has had countless imitators, but no equals in his unique art. And being a versatile fellow, he wrote an authentic imitation of cowboy ballads in *Don't Fence Me In,* one of his most popular songs.

Porter was born in Peru, Indiana, June 9, 1892. As a Yale undergraduate he wrote two of the college songs: *Bingo Eli Yale* and the *Yale Bulldog Song.* He had already, at the age of seventeen, had a song issued by a Broadway publisher. To please his wealthy grandfather Porter entered Harvard Law School, but when the dean suggested that he might do better at the School of Music the grandfather gave his consent and the transfer was made. Porter was still at Harvard when he collaborated with a fellow-student on a show, *See America First,* which was produced on Broadway for a fifteen-performance run in 1916. Porter then went to Paris, studied at the Schola Cantorum, and joined the Foreign Legion. When the United States entered the war Porter was transferred to the French Artillery School at Fontainebleau.

On shipboard returning to the United States for a visit in 1919, Porter met Raymond Hitchcock, who commissioned him to write the songs for *Hitchy-Koo 1916.* The show ran for fifty-six performances. After two more indifferently successful shows, Porter collaborated with Herbert Fields on his first real success, *Fifty Million Frenchmen* (1929). After two less successful shows came *The Gay Divorcee* (1932), containing *Night and Day,* and *Anything Goes* (1934), containing the title song, *You're the Top, Blow, Gabriel, Blow,* and *The Gypsy in Me.* Moss Hart wrote the book for *Jubilee* (1935), which introduced one of Porter's most popular songs, *Begin the Beguine.* In 1939 came *Red, Hot, and Blue,* with a cast including Ethel Merman, Jimmy Durante, and Bob Hope and a score including *It's De-Lovely;* after *You Never Know* (1938) came *Leave It to Me* (1938), the show in which Mary Martin made her mark singing *My Heart Belongs to Daddy.* Porter went on to compose scores for *Du-Barry Was a Lady* (1939); *Panama Hattie* (1940); *Let's Face It* (1941); *Something for the Boys* (1943); and *Mexican Hayride* (1944). These were followed by two less successful shows, *Seven Lively Arts* (1944) and *Around the World in Eighty Days* (1946).

In 1948 Porter's most successful musical opened in New York: *Kiss Me, Kate*. The book, a play within a play based on Shakespeare's *Taming of the Shrew*, was written by Sam and Bella Spewack; the production ran for 1,077 performances and the score contained more hit songs than any earlier Porter show, among them: *Wunderbar* (a parody of the Romberg type of Viennese operetta song); *I Hate Men; So in Love; Always True to You Darling in My Fashion; Too Darn Hot; Why Can't You Behave;* and many others that are still heard. *Out of This World* (1950) had an only indifferent success, but was followed by *Can-Can* (1953), with a book by Abe Burrows, and *Silk Stockings* (1955), with a book based on the film *Ninotchka*. Both shows were popular successes. Porter also wrote scores to several Hollywood films, including *High Society* and *Les Girls*.

HARRY TIERNEY (1895——) was born in Perth Amboy, New Jersey, May 21, 1895. He studied at the Birgil Conservatory of Music in New York and for a time toured the country as a concert pianist. In 1915 he went to London and became a staff composer for a British publisher, writing music for stage productions. On his return to New York he decided that his future lay in the musical comedy field. Tierney composed the score for a musical that was claimed to have had the longest Broadway run of any show up to that time—670 performances. The show was *Irene* (1919), and the principal hit song was *Alice Blue Gown*, with lyrics provided by Joseph McCarty, who wrote most of Tierney's words. Tierney's later shows included *Up She Goes; Kid Boots* (1923); the *Ziegfeld Follies* of 1923 and 1924, and in 1927 the climax of his career, *Rio Rita*—the first show to occupy Ziegfeld's palatial Ziegfeld Theatre. It scored a huge success.

RAY HENDERSON (1896——), born in Buffalo, New York, December 1, 1896, received a formal musical training, principally at the Chicago Conservatory of Music, and went to New York and became a staff pianist for music publishers and an accompanist for vaudeville. It was not long before he was writing songs of his own, some of them achieving hit status: *That Old Gang of Mine* (1923); *Follow the Swallow* (1924); and in 1925 *Alabammy Bound, Bye Bye, Blackbird,* and *Five Foot Two, Eyes of Blue*. In 1925 Henderson formed a partnership with the lyricists Lew Brown and Buddy de Sylva which became in the next five years a veritable factory of motion picture and theatre music, producing such songs as *Black Bottom, The Birth of the Blues, The Girl Is You, Lucky Day,* and such shows as *Good News* (1927), containing the title song, *The Best Things in Life Are Free,* and *Varsity Drag; Hold Everything* (1928), containing *You're the Cream in My Coffee; Follow Through* (1929), containing *Button Up Your Overcoat* and *You Are My Lucky Star; Flying High* (1930); and such Hollywood films as *The Singing Fool, Sunny Side Up, Say It with Songs, Follow the Leader,* and *Manhattan Mary.*

ARTHUR SCHWARTZ (1900———), an ex-lawyer, is a member of Phi Beta Kappa, holds four university degrees, and has been an English teacher. But his erudition does not prevent him from writing songs which have a wide appeal. *Dancing in the Dark, You and the Night and the Music, Something to Remember You By* are typical of the hauntingly melodious tunes he has written for Broadway productions and for motion pictures. The first shows for which he provided music were *Grand Street Follies* of 1926 and 1929; *The New Yorkers* (1927); the *First* and the *Second Little Show* (1929 and 1930); and *Three's a Crowd* (1930). It was in the *Little Shows* that Schwartz began his partnership with Howard Dietz, who subsequently provided the lyrics for many of Schwartz's songs, as well as sketches for the reviews in which they appeared and in some cases the books for the story musicals they created together.

Schwartz's subsequent shows include *The Band Wagon* (1931); *Flying Colors* (1932); *Revenge with Music* (1934); *At Home Abroad* (1935); *Between the Devil and the Deep Blue Sea* (1937); *Stars in Your Eyes* (1939); *Inside U.S.A.* (1948); *A Tree Grows in Brooklyn* (1951); *By the Beautiful Sea; The Gay Life* (1961); and *Jennie* (1963).

RICHARD RODGERS (1902———) was born in New York City, June 28, 1902; his father was a physician and his mother an accomplished amateur pianist. When he was a student at Columbia he wrote music for the Varsity shows, and a producer included seven of his songs in the Broadway production *Poor Little Ritz Girl.* Rodgers wrote these numbers and all his early musical comedies with the same lyricist, Lorenz Hart, including *The Garrick Gaieties; Dearest Enemy; The Girl Friend; Peggy-Ann* (1926); *A Connecticut Yankee* (1927); *Present Arms* (1928); *America's Sweetheart* (1931); *Simple Simon;*

Spring Is Here; the score for Maurice Chevalier's motion picture *Love Me Tonight; Jumbo; On Your Toes,* with its famous ballet *Slaughter on Tenth Avenue,* integrated right into the action—an innovation for Broadway; *Babes in Arms* (1937); *I'd Rather Be Right* (1937); *I Married an Angel* (1938); *The Boys from Syracuse* (1938); *Higher and Higher* (1940); *Pal Joey* (1940), with book adapted by John O'Hara from his own grimly sordid *New Yorker* stories—probably the first Broadway show to combine musical numbers with a realistic, three-dimensional book, and as such a turning point in the development of American musicals; and *By Jupiter,* the last show on which Rodgers and Hart collaborated.

Shortly before Hart's death in 1943, Rodgers had started collaborating with Oscar Hammerstein II, the librettist who had furnished Jerome Kern, Sigmund Romberg, and other Broadway composers with some of their best lyrics. The first Rodgers and Hammerstein work was an adaptation of Lynn Riggs's play *Green Grow the Lilacs,* renamed *Oklahoma!* It opened on Broadway in 1943 and played for a run of 2,212 performances to sold-out houses. In a sense, *Oklahoma!* was epoch-making:. for the first time in operetta, the plot, dialogue, songs, ballet, and ensembles were united into a single, cohesive whole. After supplying the score for the motion picture *State Fair* (1944), Rodgers and Hammerstein collaborated on an adaptation of Ferenc Molnar's *Liliom,* entitled *Carousel.* The score was more ambitious than that of *Oklahoma!,* and Rodgers attempted near-operatic effects in such extended numbers as his hero's soliloquy; the orchestra required was one of the largest in the history of American musical theatre. *Carousel* had a successful run of 890 performances.

Rodgers and Hammerstein's next collaboration, *Allegro* (1947), ran for only 315 performances, but in 1949 they produced a show whose success almost rivaled that of *Oklahoma!* Adapted from a book by James A. Michener, *South Pacific* ran for 1,925 performances on Broadway and in 1950 became the second Broadway musical to win a Pulitzer Prize. As was now to be expected of Rodgers and Hammerstein, the musical was woven together with enormous skill; drama, action, and music flowed together completely naturally. *The King and I* (1951) followed *South Pacific* by two years and played

1,246 performances; the integration of music and plot was accomplished to a degree sometimes lacking in grand opera.

After composing music for the television documentary *Victory at Sea* (1952), from which Robert Russell Bennett arranged a successful and popular nine-movement Suite, Rodgers collaborated with Hammerstein on *Me and Juliet* (1953); *Pipe Dream* (1955), adapted from John Steinbeck's novel *Sweet Thursday*; *Flower Drum Song* (1958); and *The Sound of Music* (1959), based on the career of the Trapp Family Singers. This show was their last collaboration, for Hammerstein died in 1961. Rodgers wrote his own lyrics for his score to *No Strings* (1962), to general critical approval. In 1962 he was appointed director of the New York Music Theatre at the Lincoln Center of the Performing Arts.

HAROLD ARLEN (1905———) came to New York from Buffalo in 1925 to work as an arranger for a publishing house. From 1930 to 1934 he wrote music for eight Cotton Club shows; the most important song from these scores, *Stormy Weather*, was popularized by Ethel Waters and has become a classic. Undoubtedly it was Arlen's Cotton Club experience that helped him develop the understanding of the Negro folk-idiom which so characterizes his best music. Arlen began composing songs for the screen in 1933, and in 1939 he won an Academy Award for *Over the Rainbow*, a song sung by Judy Garland in *The Wizard of Oz*. The lyric was by E. Y. Harburg. For *Star-Spangled Rhythm* Arlen composed *That Old Black Magic*, and for *Here Come the Waves*, *Accentuate the Positive*—both songs with lyrics by Johnny Mercer, who also wrote the words to *Blues in the Night*, the Arlen song in the film of the same name.

Although his theatrical scores have not always met with the success of his film music, the blame may be placed partly on the books he has had to deal with. His Broadway record is as distinguished as many: he contributed three songs to *Earl Carroll Vanities* (1930); he wrote the scores for *You Said It* (1931); *Life Begins at 8:40* (1934); *Hooray for What!* (1937); *Bloomer Girl* (1944); *St. Louis Woman* (1946); *House of Flowers* (1954); *Jamaica* (1957); and *Saratoga* (1959), an adaptation of Edna Ferber's novel *Saratoga Trunk*.

While attending the High School of Commerce in New York,

BURTON LANE (1912——) became a staff composer at the Remick publishing house. A few of his songs were interpolated in such Broadway revues as *Three's a Crowd* (1930), *The Third Little Show* (1931), and *Earl Carroll Vanities* (1931). In 1933 Lane went to Hollywood to write numbers for motion pictures. He composed his first complete Broadway score, *Hold On to Your Hats*, in 1940. His next Broadway venture was the Olsen and Johnson show, *Laffing Room Only* (1944). Lane's most successful score was *Finian's Rainbow* (1947). In 1957 Lane was elected president of the American Guild of Authors and Composers.

When the original production of *My Fair Lady* finally closed in New York in 1962, it had achieved a record Broadway run of six and a half years; it continued to meet with spectacular popularity in tours around the country and in productions across the world. Probably the most successful and in the opinion of many critics the most perfect of American musicals to date, *My Fair Lady* was the work of two men: FREDERICK LOEWE (1904——), the composer, and ALAN JAY LERNER (1918——), the librettist and lyricist.

Born in Vienna, Loewe studied music with Ferruccio Busoni and Eugene D'Albert and at thirteen was piano soloist with the Berlin Symphony. In 1924 he came to the United States, where after stints as night club pianist, cafeteria busboy, riding instructor, and prize fighter, he provided songs for the musical *Salute to Spring*, produced by the St. Louis Opera Association in 1937, and for *The Great Lady*, produced on Broadway in 1938. After the failure of *Great Lady* Lerner went back to playing piano in restaurants, until he met Alan Jay Lerner in 1942. Lerner, Loewe's junior by fourteen years, was the son of the owner of a chain of clothes stores; he had studied music at the Juilliard School and had written lyrics and music for two Hasty Pudding shows while at Harvard and after graduation had become a radio-script writer.

Lerner and Loewe's collaboration began with the rather undistinguished *Life of the Party* (1942) and continued with *What's Up* (1943) and *The Day Before Spring* (1945). It was with *Brigadoon* (1947) that Lerner and Loewe achieved their first real success. The story was original with Lerner, based on the legend of a Scottish town that came to life every hundred years, and Loewe's score captured the fanciful Highland atmosphere, with several of the songs achieving hit status. *Brigadoon* was followed by *Paint Your Wagon* (1951), a lusty treatment of the gold-prospecting days in the American West, with songs that so skillfully caught the color of the period and locale that they hardly sounded like Broadway show tunes.

In 1954 the partners came together again and decided to work on an adaptation of George Bernard Shaw's comedy *Pygmalion*. The resulting *My Fair Lady* did full justice to Shaw and at the same time set a new standard in musical comedy craftsmanship. The songs, by turns melodious, witty, and lyric, were always in keeping with the action and grew out of Shaw's own characters and situations so perfectly that it was hard to imagine that the show was an adaptation at all. The show produced at least five hit songs: *With a Little Bit of Luck; Get Me to the Church on Time; Wouldn't It Be Loverly?; I Could Have Danced All Night;* and *On the Street Where You Live;* and its popularity appeared to be as long-lasting as any light opera's ever written.

Lerner and Loewe followed *My Fair Lady* with the motion picture *Gigi*, based on Colette's novel. Loewe's score again reflected the period and the locale of the story—in this case, Paris at the turn of the century—and the title song took its place among Lerner and Loewe hits. The Broadway successor to *My Fair Lady*, an adaptation of T. H. White's *The Once and Future King*, was an attempt to create musical comedy out of Arthurian legend. Entitled *Camelot* (1960), the show did not meet with as great critical approval as its predecessor, and to many ears the songs, while attractive, seemed to be rewrites of those in *My Fair Lady*. Nevertheless, *Camelot* enjoyed a successful run of 874 performances. Shortly after the closing of the show, Loewe announced that he was taking a leave from Broadway for reasons of health.

During the 1937–38 season, which saw such socially and politically significant musicals as Rodgers and Hart's *I'd Rather Be Right* and Marc Blitzstein's *The Cradle Will Rock*, the International Ladies' Garment Workers Union produced its own revue, *Pins and Needles*, at its own Labor Theatre (formerly the Princess) in New York. The cast, composed entirely of union members, rehearsed every night after their day's work for a year and a half; although the critics ignored

the revue, word-of-mouth reports began circulating, and the sma
theatre was soon filled to capacity every night. The show was move
to a larger theatre and altogether ran for 1,108 performances. *Pir
and Needles* not only demonstrated that light wit and humor could I
effective instruments of liberal propaganda, but also launched th
career of a young man who was to become a prominent figure on th
Broadway musical stage—HAROLD ROME (1908——).

Born in Hartford, Connecticut, May 27, 1908, Rome studied a
Yale, dabbled in law and architecture after graduation, and finall
joined the entertainment staff at an adult summer camp in th
Catskills. It was not a great leap from writing topical songs for th
camp revues to providing the songs for *Pins and Needles*. Followin
his debut with the garment workers, Rome went on to write the mus
for *Sing Out the News* and *Let Freedom Ring* (1942). While in th
army Rome occupied himself with soldier shows, and upon returnin
to civilian life wrote the score for *Call Me Mister* (1946).

In 1950 several of Rome's songs were included in *Alive and Kic*
ing and in Michael Todd's *Peep Show,* and during the same yea
Rome collaborated with Arnold Auerbach on a revue, *Bless You A*
Two years later Rome saw his first book musical produced. *Wish Yc*
Were Here, based on Arthur Kober's play *Having Wonderful Tim*
opened in 1952, and though lukewarmly reviewed enjoyed a goc
run. Rome's semi-operatic *Fanny* (1954) established itself in spite c
reviews, and ran for almost two years; the book, by S. N. Behrma
and Joshua Logan, was based on the French film trilogy of Marc
Pagnol. Rome's next show, *Destry Rides Again* (1959), had a rathe
undistinguished book by Leonard Gershe based on the film *Destr*
No doubt Rome recalled his experiences with the garment worker
union when he composed the music for his next show, *I Can Get It f*
You Wholesale. Jerome Weidman supplied the book, an adaptatic
of his own novel of cutthroat competition in the garment trad
Rome's score had bite and pace and matched the book admirabl

When one of the less successful of the Rodgers and Hammerste
shows had been produced a prominent musician and critic was aske
what he thought of it. "Well," he replied, "if Jule Styne had writte
it, we would say, 'How he has improved!' but for R. and H., it
decidedly not up to their standard." Nevertheless, JULE STYN

(1905———) had become a dominant figure on Broadway by the early 1960's, and although his scores may lie close to the formulas of old-fashioned musical comedy and lack the distinction of those of his colleagues, they have nevertheless met with gratifying success.

Styne was born in London, England, December 31, 1905, and was brought to this country at the age of eight. He studied music at the Chicago College of Music and as a child appeared as piano soloist with the Chicago and Detroit Symphony Orchestras. In the 1920's he became fascinated with popular music and became a pianist with a dance band, later organizing his own orchestra. He was soon writing songs of his own, many of them for movies of the 30's and 40's.

Styne's first show, written with lyricist Sammy Cahn, *Glad to See You*, closed in Boston without getting to Broadway. Styne and Cahn came into their own with *High Button Shoes* (1946), a show with book by Sydney Longstreet and with a score that included the captivating *Papa, Won't You Dance with Me*. *Gentlemen Prefer Blondes* (1949), an adaptation of Anita Loos's classic tale of the mercenary Lorelei Lee, had a book by Joseph Fields and Miss Loos and lyrics by Leo Robin; Styne's score included such popular numbers as *Diamonds Are a Girl's Best Friend* and *I'm Just a Little Girl from Little Rock*. Both *Shoes* and *Gentlemen* ran for over two years on Broadway.

Styne's next three shows had much shorter runs. *Two on the Aisle* (1951) was a revue with sketches and lyrics by Betty Comden and Adolf Green; *Hazel Flagg* (1953) had a book by Ben Hecht and lyrics by Bob Hilliard; *Peter Pan* (1954), a delightful musicalization of Barrie's fantasy, had half a dozen songs by Styne and half a dozen by Marc Charlap. *Bells Are Ringing* (1956), with book and lyrics by Comden and Green, ran 924 performances, longer than any of Styne's previous shows. *Say, Darling* (1958), an adaptation of Richard Bissell's novel about New York show business, had a book by Mr. and Mrs. Bissell and Abe Burrows and lyrics by Comden and Green.

Gypsy (1959), probably the most mature and well-integrated of all Styne's shows, had a libretto by Arthur Laurents drawn from Gypsy Rose Lee's autobiography, lyrics by Stephen Sondheim, and a dynamic performance by Ethel Merman as a stage mother driving her children to success. Styne and Sondheim created what Stanley Green called "a superbly congruous score that illuminated all the courage, misplaced ambition, and singleness of purpose of the central character." One of the cleverest devices of the show was the use of an exquisitely banal song (*May We Entertain You?*) as music for two little girls auditioning for a vaudeville show, later as a production number when the girls have become a more experienced duo, and finally as the vulgar accompaniment to Gypsy's first strip-tease.

Styne's next show, *Do Re Mi* (1960), with book by Garson Kanin and lyrics by Comden and Green, was a more conventional type of musical with a comic book about jukebox racketeers. Styne became more serious in *Subways Are for Sleeping* (1961), an adaptation by Comden and Green of Edmund Love's book about New York vagrants. In 1963 Styne supplied incidental music to a Broadway production of Bert Brecht's *Arturo Ui*, and in 1964 he wrote two scores: *Funny Girl*, a musical very loosely based on the life of the comedienne Fannie Brice, with lyrics by Bob Merrill and book by Isobel Lennart; and *Fade-out, Fade-in*, with book and lyrics by Comden and Green.

The musical theatre knows FRANK LOESSER (1910———) as a lyricist, composer, librettist, and producer. Born in New York City, June 29, 1910, Loesser began as a lyricist. In 1931 he published his first song, *In Love with a Memory*, with music by William Schuman, and after contributing lyrics to a number of songs in *The Illustrators' Show* (1936), he went to Hollywood and worked as a lyricist. Loesser entered the army at the outbreak of World War II, and during his service years he wrote both words and music to such songs as *Praise the Lord and Pass the Ammunition*; *What Do You Do in the Infantry?*; *Rodger Young*; and *Private Mary Brown*. In 1946 Loesser returned to Hollywood to write songs for pictures, winning an Academy Award in 1949 for the song *Baby, It's Cold Outside*. In 1952 he supplied the score to the film *Hans Christian Andersen*, which included *Wonderful, Wonderful Copenhagen*, one of Loesser's most delightful numbers.

Loesser's Broadway career may be said to have begun with his score to *Where's Charley?* (1948), a musical adaptation by George Abbott of the venerable farce *Charley's Aunt*. Loesser, as usual, supplied both music and lyrics. The score contained two of his most popular songs: *My Darling, My Darling,* and *Once in Love with Amy.* *Guys and Dolls* (1950), an adaptation by Abe Burrows of a Damon Runyon story, *The Idyll of Miss Sarah Brown,* contained such memorable Loesser numbers as *A Bushel and a Peck, Take Back Your Mink,* and *Sit Down, You're Rocking the Boat.* The phenomenally successful show ran for 1,200 performances and was later filmed.

For *The Most Happy Fella* (1956) Loesser not only composed the music and lyrics, but also wrote the libretto, which he based on Sidney Howard's play *They Knew What They Wanted.* Loesser worked on the job for four years, and the result was what Stanley Green has called "the most ambitiously operatic work ever created for the Broadway musical theater." Loesser, however, insisted that "all it has is a great frequency of songs. It's a musical with music." As the orchestrator, Don Walker, put it, "This is a musical comedy expanded. Not an opera cut down."

For his next show, *Greenwillow* (1960), Loesser turned to a folk-like background. The libretto, adapted from a novel by B. J. Chute, concerned the rural customs of an imaginary community located on the banks of a river. The show had only a short run. In 1961 Loesser returned to Broadway with *How To Succeed in Business Without Really Trying,* to which he contributed both music and lyrics, while Abe Burrows, Jack Weinstock, and Willie Gilbert collaborated on the book, a satirical picture of an opportunist climbing his way up the ranks of a corporation. Among the many delights of the production was the public reappearance of Rudy Vallee in a starring role.

MEREDITH WILLSON (1902———), born in Mason City, Iowa, May 18, 1902, learned to play the flute and piccolo while in high school. He studied with Georges Barrère at the Institute of Musical Art in New York and from 1921 to 1923 was a flutist in Sousa's band. After a year in the orchestra of New York's Rialto Theatre he became a flutist with the New York Philharmonic, a position he held from 1924 to 1929. During several years as a radio conductor, Willson composed a number of symphonic works: a First Symphony (1936), commemorating the thirtieth anniversary of the San Francisco earthquake; O. O. McIntyre Suite (1936); and a symphonic poem, *The Jervis Bay* (1942). While in Hollywood Willson composed scores for a number of motion pictures, among them Charlie Chaplin's *The Great Dictator* (1940) and *The Little Foxes* (1942). In 1942 he enlisted in the army and for the duration of the war had charge of the music division of the Armed Forces Radio Service.

The Music Man, Willson's first Broadway musical, opened in New York in 1957 and ran for 1,375 performances. It was later made into a film that was much less well-received than the original production. For this show and his second, *The Unsinkable Molly Brown* (1960), Willson wrote both music and lyrics. For his third show, *Here's Love* (1963), Willson wrote the book as well, adapting it from a Hollywood film of the 40's, *Miracle on 34th Street.*

The partnership of RICHARD ADLER (1923——) and JERRY ROSS (1926–1955) was unique in that both of them wrote both music and lyrics. Adler came from a musical family: his father, Clarence Adler, is a well-known pianist and teacher. Ross, a native of the Bronx, sang at the age of ten in a synagogue choir, later taking part in the plays of various Yiddish acting companies. He studied at New York University.

Neither Adler nor Ross had any success as a song writer until they collaborated, producing the hit song *Rags to Riches* and providing several songs for the revue *John Murray Anderson's Almanac.* They then collaborated on two highly successful Broadway shows, *The Pajama Game* (1954), with a book by George Abbott from Richard Bissell's novel about labor troubles in a pajama factory, *7½ Cents;* and *Damn Yankees* (1955), with a book by Abbott and Douglass Wallopp from the latter's novel *The Year the Yankees Lost the Pennant.* After Ross's death in 1955, Adler continued on his own, contributing the music and lyrics to *Kwamina* (1961), with a libretto by Robert Alan Arthur concerning the struggles of a newly independent African country.

JERRY BOCK (1928——), born in New Haven, Connecticut, began his career writing songs, continuity, dialogue, and special material for television during the early 50's. His first Broadway score, *Mr Wonderful* (1956), was followed by *The Body Beautiful* (1958) and *Fiorello!* (1959), a show about New York's Mayor La Guardia, his first big hit, with book by Jerome Weidman and George Abbott and lyrics by Sheldon Harnick. The same foursome collaborated on a second musical about New York life, *Tenderloin* (1960), from a book by Samuel Hopkins Adams. Working again with Harnick to a book by Joe Masterhoff, Bock produced the score to *The Shop Around the Corner* (1963). *Fiddler on the Roof*, a musical based on the stories of Sholem Aleichem, opened in 1964.

6. TWENTIETH-CENTURY POPULAR SONG COMPOSERS

As we move into the twentieth century we continue to find that many of the "pop" songs record current history. When the depression deepened, JAY GORNEY (1896——) teamed up with lyricist E. Y. Harburg to provide its theme song—*Brother, Can You Spare a Dime?* And Rudy Vallee introduced on the radio a song by Herman Hupfield that seemed to epitomize the fatalistic, what-do-we-care attitude, *Let's Put Out the Lights and Go to Sleep.*

Chicago-born MILTON AGER (1893——) wrote many popular songs, often to lyrics by Jack Yellen: *Who Cares?; Crazy World, Crazy Tune; Ain't She Sweet; I Wonder What's Become of Sally. Happy Days Are Here Again*, composed for a Jack Benny movie, was played at the 1932 Democratic convention and subsequently became the theme song of Franklin D. Roosevelt's campaigns.

RICHARD A. WHITING (1891–1938) composed one of the most celebrated ballads of World War I, *Till We Meet Again*, as well as such favorites as *Japanese Sandman, Sleepy Time Gal, Ain't We Got Fun?* and *Horses*. He settled in Hollywood in 1929, where he wrote numerous film scores. For Maurice Chevalier in *Innocents of Paris* he composed *Louise*, and for Shirley Temple in *Bright Eyes, On the Good Ship Lollipop.*

FRED E. AHLERT (1892–1953), a native of New York and for two years president of ASCAP, intended to be a lawyer but abandoned his law studies to compose such hits in their time as *I'll Get By, Mean to Me, I'm Going to Sit Right Down and Write Myself a Letter, Where the Blue of the Night Meets the Gold of the Day*, and others.

To HENRY CARROLL (1892–1962) belongs the dubious distinction of being one of the first to help himself to the classics for singable melodies. *I'm Always Chasing Rainbows*, his biggest success, was composed for a 1918 musical, *Oh, Look!* and lifted its melody from the middle section of Chopin's *Fantaisie-Impromptu*. Other tunes for which he did not consciously borrow melodies include *There's a Girl in the Heart of Maryland*, *The Trail of the Lonesome Pine*, and *By the Beautiful Sea.*

WALTER DONALDSON (1893–1947), a native of Brooklyn, New York, wrote the music to such immortal songs as *My Mammy* (introduced by Al Jolson in 1920), *Carolina in the Morning*, *My Blue Heaven*, *Little White Lies*, *On the 'Gin 'Gin 'Ginny Shore*, *Makin' Whooppee*, and, in 1919, *How You Gonna Keep 'Em Down on the Farm?*

HERMAN HUPFIELD (1894–1951), born in Montclair, New Jersey, of a musical mother who taught and played piano and organ, studied violin here and in Germany and played saxophone in the Newport Naval Reserve Band in World War I and piano at army camps in World War II. But it was not until he was more than thirty years old that his real talent was recognized, when in 1929 his song *Sing Something Simple* was interpolated into *The First Little Show.* Hupfield wrote words and music to hundreds of songs, including such favorites as *As Time Goes By*, *Let's Put Out the Lights and Go to Sleep*, *Are You Making Any Money*, *When Yuba Plays the Rhumba on the Tuba*, *Savage Serenade*, *My Little Dog Has Ego*, and others.

JOSEPH MEYER (1894——) was born in California, where he studied harmony and counterpoint and played the violin in a San Francisco café. He will perhaps always be known as the composer of *California, Here I Come*, with lyrics by Buddy De Sylva, interpolated by Al Jolson into his 1922 show *Bombo*. Among his other hits Meyer composed *If You Knew Susie* and *Crazy Rhythm.*

NACIO HERB BROWN (1896——), born in Deming, New Mexico, composed the music for what is said to have been Irving Thalberg's first all-talking, all-singing musical picture, *Broadway Melody* (1928). The score included the title song and another number that became popular, *The Wedding of the Painted Doll*. Brown's first hit dates from 1920, when Paul Whiteman popularized *Coral Sea*. Others of Brown's songs include *You Were Made for Me* and *The Pagan Love Song.*

The name MABEL WAYNE (1898——) is synonymous with her song *Ramona*, but she achieved an almost equal success with several

other songs, including *In a Little Spanish Town* and *Chiquita*. Born
in New York, she has been, in addition to song writer, a singer,
dancer, and vaudeville entertainer.

HARRY WARREN (1893——), a native of Brooklyn, N. Y., settled
in Hollywood in 1929 and for more than thirty years turned out
picture tunes, including *Shuffle Off to Buffalo; Forty-Second Street;
Lullaby of Broadway; On the Atchison, Topeka, and the Santa Fe;
Chattanooga Choo Choo;* and *I Found a Million Dollar Baby in a
Five-and-ten-cent Store.*

JIMMY McHUGH (1895——) was born in Boston and became a
song-plugger and pianist in local theatres and five-and-ten-cent stores.
In the 1920's he wrote songs for New York's Cotton Club, and in
collaboration with Dorothy Fields he wrote songs for *Blackbirds of
1928,* including *I Can't Give You Anything but Love, Baby.* He went
to Hollywood in 1930, where with Miss Fields and Harold Adamson
he produced numerous movie scores, including *Cuban Love Song.*
He composed scores for Deanna Durbin's pictures and contributed
songs to *The Helen Morgan Story* (1957); *Home Before Dark*
(1958) and *Let No Man Write My Epitaph* (1961).

HARRY RUBY (1895——), a native New Yorker, worked as a
publishing house pianist, song-plugger, and piano player in vaudeville
houses and nickelodeons, forming a partnership with lyricist Bert
Kalmar, who wrote the words for most of his best-known songs. Ruby
is perhaps best known for *Three Little Words,* composed for the
Amos 'n' Andy picture *Check and Double Check.* Ruby and Kalmar
wrote not only screen songs, but screenplays. After Kalmar's death in
1947 Ruby wrote most of his own lyrics.

FRANK E. CHURCHILL (1901–1942), who abandoned his medical
studies, spent the last twelve years of his life under contract to the
Walt Disney Studio. After *Who's Afraid of the Big Bad Wolf?* for
Three Little Pigs, he supplied the songs for all the Disney pictures
through the immortal *Snow White,* for which he composed the equally
immortal songs, *Some Day My Prince Will Come, With a Smile and
a Song, I'm Wishing, Heigh-Ho,* and *Whistle While You Work.*

SAMMY FAIN (1902——) composed music for Walt Disney's *Peter
Pan* and *Alice in Wonderland.* With lyricist Irving Kahal such num-

bers as *Let a Smile Be Your Umbrella; I Can Dream, Can't I?* and with Paul Francis Webster several songs, including *Love Is a Many-Splendored Thing.*

The husband-wife partnership of ALEX C. KRAMER (1903——) and JOAN WHITNEY (1914——) has produced such songs as *Far Away Places, High on a Windy Hill, My Sister and I, Candy, Comme Ci Comme Ça,* and *Dangerous Dan McGrew.* Each partner has a hand in music and words.

A native of Pennsylvania, JAY LIVINGSTON (1915——) studied theory and composition with Harl McDonald at the University of Pennsylvania. With lyricist Ray Evans he supplied songs for over a hundred Paramount pictures, including such numbers as *Buttons and Bows, Tammy,* and *Almost in Your Arms.* The team has made two attempts to write for Broadway: *Oh Captain* (1958), from the motion picture *The Captain's Paradise,* and *Let It Ride* (1961), from the play *Three Men on a Horse.*

Born in Syracuse, New York, JIMMY VAN HEUSEN (1913——) wrote music for Billy Rose's *Aquacade* at the 1939 World's Fair in New York and for Hollywood films, including over twenty Bing Crosby musicals. Many of his songs have become standards.

A number of our popular composers have specialized in novelty and instrumental pieces. FELIX ARNDT (1889–1918) is remembered chiefly for his piano piece *Nola.* A staff pianist and accompanist, Arndt made over a thousand player-piano rolls, as well as many phonograph records.

ZEZ CONFREY (1895——), a pioneer in developing piano jazz, composed *Kitten on the Keys* and the song *Stumbling,* an early popularization of cross rhythms. Moreover, he wrote and published an instruction book on "Novelty Piano Playing"—in other words, jazz piano. It told all the "tricks of the trade" and sold 150,000 copies in the first two months of publication. Born in Illinois, Confrey studied at the Chicago Musical College in order to become a concert pianist, but he found that jazz was easier for him—and more profitable!

PETER DE ROSE (1896–1953), born in New York, composed *Deep Purple,* an instrumental success even before words were added to it, and many sacred songs with an almost equal appeal. In 1923 he formed a professional partnership with May Singhi Breen, and the two became popular on the radio as the "Sweethearts of the Air." They were married in 1929. Among the De Rose songs which have enjoyed popularity are *Tiger Rose, Wagon Wheels, Somebody Loves You,* and *Muddy Water.*

Indiana-born HOAGY CARMICHAEL (1899——) gave up the law to compose. The song *Stardust,* initially written as an instrumental, brought him fame, and he continued his success with *Lazybones, Georgia on My Mind, Rockin' Chair,* and dozens of others in the hit class.

VICTOR YOUNG (1900–1956), born August 8, 1900, in Chicago, graduated from the Warsaw Conservatory in Poland in 1917 and made his debut as a violinist in Chicago at the age of twenty-one. He played violin in theatre orchestras, conducted and arranged music for radio programs, directed music for a recording company, and ultimately joined the music staff of Paramount Pictures. He is best known for his scores to motion pictures, which have included *For Whom the Bell Tolls, Love Letters, Frenchman's Creek, To Each His Own, Golden Earrings, Samson and Delilah,* and *Around the World in Eighty Days.* Theme-melodies and theme-songs drawn from his film scores have enjoyed wide popularity and often have achieved hit-parade status.

LOUIS ALTER (1902——) composed a type of instrumental piece in the popular idiom which is the modern type of salon music. *Manhattan Serenade* and *Metropolitan Nocturne* are perhaps the best known, and like the others they are marked by urban sophistication and make polite use of modern dissonance, often reflecting the influence of jazz and the blues. Alter has also written such popular songs as *Morning, Noon and Night; Twilight Trail;* and *Blue Shadows,* as well as contributing to Broadway and Hollywood musicals. Born in Haverhill, Massachusetts, he studied music at Boston's New England Conservatory.

RAYMOND SCOTT (1909——), who was born Harry Warnow, trained at the Institute of Musical Art in New York and has specialized in such instrumental novelties as *The Toy Trumpet, In an 18th Century Drawing-Room* (adapted from the main theme of

Mozart's C Major Piano Sonata), *Duet for Piano and Pistol, Square Dance for Eight Egyptian Mummies, Dinner for a Pack of Hungry Cannibals,* and many others.

DAVID ROSE (1910——) was born in London, and at the age of four was brought to Chicago, where he studied at the College of Music and played piano in dance bands. He became an arranger, radio conductor, and music director of a West Coast radio network before interrupting his musical activities in 1942 to join the armed forces. He was appointed composer and director of the Army Air Force show *Winged Victory.* His compositions include a collection of piano pieces, *Music for Moderns,* and the gay, sparkling *Holiday for Strings,* which established him.

Passing the half-century mark, we find that current history continues to be recorded in songs, even though the songs do not make much headway. E. Y. Harburg and Harold Arlen's protest song from the musical play *Jamaica, Leave the Atom Alone; The John Birch Society,* a song introduced in the revue *Seven Come Eleven;* the Kennedy songs in the film *P. T. 109;* Jimmy McHugh and Ned Washington's *First Lady Waltz;* such songs as the *Astronaut, Astronaut Count-Down, John Glenn March,* and *Help Me, Telstar,* have all failed to arouse public interest. Jule Styne's *Now,* a catchy up-dating of the traditional Hebrew melody *Hava Nagilah,* achieved brief popularity largely because of its well-timed tie-in with the civil rights movement of the early 60's, despite a radio and television ban which forbade the broadcasting of the "controversial" number.

CHAPTER SEVENTEEN

Conclusion

WE are at the end of our story. In the year 1964, with nearly three and a half centuries of our American music behind us. And much of it still with us. At a place where maybe we can have a bit of perspective, and take stock of what we have amassed in our musical inventory. Three and a half centuries—not a very long time as the world looks at things; but ages in terms of American history.

The three periods of our musical growth have been suggested by the divisions of our book. The first, from 1620 to 1800, produced very little that has lived to our day—Holden's *Coronation, Yankee Doodle,* and *Hail Columbia* are about the only bits of music that have preserved themselves, for Hopkinson's songs and Billings's anthems were discovered and revived. Yet these formative years produced the seeds of things that would bear fruit later.

The second period, 1800 to 1860, gave us Lowell Mason and the hymn writers, as well as Gottschalk and Stephen Foster, but it is only since 1860 that we have had our important serious composers, starting with John K. Paine and Dudley Buck. Yet the two hundred and forty years before their productive years must be known and understood if we are to know our present-day composers, even if it is only to appreciate them by contrast with what went before them. For composers rarely happen; they are generally produced by environment or heredity. Or in some cases by tradition.

Especially interesting have been our foreign relations. In art we were not able to sign a declaration of independence and to pursue a policy of isolation. It is doubtful if it would have been desirable anyway. We had to depend on Europe for culture until we had been here long enough to develop an art of our own. And that was not as easy as planting corn and watching it sprout in the same season. We have had to import before we could manufacture and export.

There have been three distinct periods of intensive immigration. The 1780's and 1790's, following our independence and the French Revolution; the influx of 1848, when there was unrest in Central Europe; and that of our own time, from the days of the First World War to the present. The first two periods of immigration had a profound effect on our few native composers. In the last quarter of the eighteenth century the foreigners took the center of the stage, and Billings and his colleagues retired to the background. After the turn of the century the native composer returned with Lowell Mason, but again in 1848 the foreigners, principally Germans, took matters into their own hands. There were few musicians here who could compare in ability with those from abroad. So most of the natives took a rear place. Some were a bit sensitive about foreign domination, and we met Fry and Bristow as early champions of the American composer. We started to grow self-conscious in the middle of the nineteenth century.

In the present century, particularly during the last decades, immigrations from Europe have had a different effect from those of the preceding centuries. In the late nineteenth century, or even in the early 1900's, we would have been completely overwhelmed by the arrival of so many hundreds of foreigners. When racial persecution menaced Central Europe in the early 1930's, and refugees packed every ship coming to our shores, we would no doubt have been forced to turn over to them the entire conduct of our music life, had our native musicians, particularly our composers, been in the same position, and as comparatively few in numbers, as their predecessors were a half, or even a quarter century before. But now the newcomers do not press our native composers into their own mold, and make our music little more than an imitation of their own. The Americans and the foreigners both realize that each has something important to learn from the other, and to teach to each other. American music is establishing itself, and the newcomers recognize the fact; many of them are as much influenced by their new environment as the nineteenth-century American composers were affected by European surroundings.

Obviously, this state of affairs did not just happen. Much conscious effort, and a great deal of propagandizing, some of it wise and some of it misguided, was necessary to gain for the American composer the three essentials of his existence: publication of his music, particularly of his larger compositions; performances of his important works; and adequate payment when his music is performed for profit.

As the second half of the century begins, the publishing of larger works by American composers is assuming major proportions. It has been materially aided by new methods of offset printing which have reduced the cost considerably. And in cases where the printing of orchestral parts is not warranted, publishers have instituted rental service of parts photographically duplicated from manuscript copies. Publishers have also been alert to develop new markets for orchestral music among amateur and school and college orchestras.

But even if the American publisher has done as much as and more than could have been expected of him, he has not been able to print or otherwise make available all that should be published. Many of the excellent scores that have been composed and performed have had to remain in manuscript form, simply because there has been a limit to what our publishers can handle.

Back in 1901, Arthur Farwell sensed this problem. He felt that publishers were interested only in works in conventional mold; that they were afraid of anything that seemed too new, especially if written by Americans who had not yet established their reputations. He felt that the only way to remedy the evil was to start a new publishing venture, and he founded the Wa-Wan Press, which was the first to introduce several talented composers to the music lovers of their own country. To secure regular distribution, subscribers were solicited who would receive in periodical form the publications of the Press as they were issued quarterly each year.

The Society for the Publication of American Music adopted a similar method of distribution when it was founded by Burnet Corwin Tuthill in 1919. In this case the object is to issue chamber music, which is published not only as a philanthropic gesture, but also is wisely put into the hands of musicians and music lovers who may play it at home and in public. Subscriptions are solicited and sold. The membership fee entitles the subscriber to the works issued each year by the society.

By this method the buyer agrees in advance to take what is published, and the society in turn is assured of a certain sale for the works it brings out. The Society for the Publication of American Music has achieved permanence, and in 1964 was forty-five years old.

Several philanthropists took an interest in the publication of orchestral works. George Eastman, of Kodak fame, who founded and endowed the Eastman School of Music at Rochester, established a fund for the annual publication of orchestral scores by American composers. The works published were selected from those performed at the American Composers' Concerts at the Eastman School. They were issued by a commercial publishing house and distributed through regular trade channels, but all costs of publication are paid by the Eastman Fund, and the commercial publisher took no risk.

The Juilliard Musical Foundation subsidized publication of orchestral works by Americans in a similar manner. The printing and distribution was attended to by a publishing house, but the Juilliard Foundation paid all the bills and got no return. Of the gross returns from the sale of printed copies and from performance fees, the composer received sixty per cent and the publisher forty.

Yet publication is not all of the problem. If printed music is never performed it remains just so much paper and ink. In the case of the Eastman publications, they had already had performance at Rochester before they were selected for publication, and the Juilliard Foundation undertook to secure major performances for the works issued under its subsidy. As far as our regular symphony orchestras are concerned, we still hear echoes of Fry's complaint against the New York Philharmonic almost eighty years ago. The situation has changed, however. Fifty years ago few American compositions were played by orchestras because there were few American compositions. Today there are so many that it would be impossible for our orchestras to give all the worthy ones an adequate hearing even if all the conductors wanted to. We have already learned that agitation for the American composer's rights began early in the nineteenth century. The Bohemian Heinrich felt himself entitled to recognition because he was an American, and a naturalized one at that. Fry and Bristow bewailed the plight of their fellows and themselves. With the turn of the century many more took up the cudgels, and by the time of the First World War, the thing became an organized propaganda with slogans—The American Composer First, and others.

Way back in 1856, Edward Jerome Hopkins started an American Music Association to promote works by American composers. There were several sporadic attempts after that to form organizations that would help our writers, for some people were beginning to realize that if we were to have serious composers, they must have their day in the concert hall. The Manuscript Society of New York was organized in 1889, to meet once a month for hearing compositions written by its members. In 1899 it was reorganized as the Society of American Musicians and Composers. The meetings introduced many interesting works, but the society was never successful in its ambition to interest the general public in its activities. A Manuscript Society was organized in Philadelphia in 1892, with William Wallace Gilchrist as its first president. Like the New York society, the Philadelphia group held monthly meetings for performances of original works by its members, and it also arranged public concerts with the Philadelphia Orchestra and the choral societies of the city. It held a number of prize contests for new works. In 1896 a Manuscript Society was organized in Chicago, and Frederick Grant Gleason was the first president. There have been similar organizations in other cities.

Arthur Farwell was interested in performances of American works as well as in their publication. He was one of the organizers of the American Music Society, and its moving spirit. The society was formed first in Boston, and by the time Farwell joined the staff of *Musical America* in New York (1910) and had to give up the traveling that was entailed in the activities of the organization, there were chapters, or centers, as they were called, in twenty cities. The objects of the society were the study and performance of the works of American composers; the study of all folk music touching the development of music in the United States; and the publication of articles, discussions, or any significant matter relative to American music. It disclaimed any intention of urging acceptance of American music simply because it is American; it must be good music.

The young American composer needs a laboratory for his experiments. The major symphony orchestras can play only his finished works, composed when he has gained a command of his technique.

Before that he needs to hear what he has written so that he will know what his ideas for instrumental combinations sound like. The growth of orchestras in smaller cities, of conservatory orchestras and amateur groups is helping to provide a workshop for our composers. When the short-lived State Symphony Orchestra was established in New York in 1923, one of its functions was to hold special rehearsals to which composers could bring their manuscripts and hear them performed. This was valuable, but of course a finished performance was not possible, as the works were merely read through by conductor and players.

The American Composers' Concerts at the Eastman School in Rochester overcame this difficulty. They have provided carefully rehearsed performances of works that for the most part have never been played in public before. The composer is invited to come to Rochester to hear the rehearsals and the performances. The League of Composers, established in New York in 1923, was concerned chiefly with the modernists of America and the world, but performed a similar service. And, of course, today even the major orchestras do not shy at performing a fair percentage of modern works by both American and foreign composers. In the 1963–64 season of the New York Philharmonic, Leonard Bernstein went so far as to present several avant-garde pieces for tape recorder. Numerically, the number of American works played by our major and our lower-budgeted orchestras is on the rise, approaching in recent years 15 per cent of the total number of works performed.

A number of organizations have been formed with the express purpose of giving hearings to American works. These include the Composers' Forums, formed by the WPA during the depression of the 1930's, where a composer's works are performed before a discriminating audience, and the composer is subsequently questioned or challenged by his listeners; the National Association for American Composers and Conductors, founded by Henry Hadley shortly before his death in 1937, which offers programs of American music, awards a medal and citation annually for distinguished service to American music, and sponsors the Henry Hadley Memorial Library in the Americana Music Room of the New York Public Library, where performers and conductors may examine scores; and the recording com-

nies, which we shall discuss presently. But perhaps as important a
velopment as any of these has been the growth of the performing
ghts societies, which protect the composer's interests and in many
ses make it materially possible for him to devote himself to his art.

Early in the century it was impossible for anyone in this country to
ake a living solely by composing so-called "serious" music. Even
lacDowell had to turn to concertizing and teaching. The composer
ot only received a meager return from the sale of his printed music,
generally had to provide at his own expense manuscript scores and
rts to any orchestra willing to perform his works. Conditions are
ill far from ideal in this regard, but there is a new conception of the
mposer's rights that has improved his economic status. Most of this
mprovement comes from the realization that the primary use of
usic is in performance, and that when players are paid for perform-
g it and listeners are paying to hear it, the composer himself is en-
tled to payment for the use of his product.

The copyright laws of most countries give to the owner of a copy-
ghted musical work (either the composer himself or his assignee)
e exclusive right to perform that work in public. Though in France
d the British Commonwealth and most foreign countries anyone
ho performs copyrighted music in public, even in schools and
urches, must have a license to do so, in the United States the right
control performance of one's music is limited to public performance
r profit. Under the American copyright laws of 1909, the copyright
wner is entitled to demand fees from such performances of his work.

To collect performance fees, performing rights societies have been
ganized in most of the countries of the world. In the United States
e leading societies are the American Society of Composers, Authors,
d Publishers (ASCAP), the only American performing rights so-
ety that is owned exclusively by its composer and publisher mem-
rs; Broadcast Music, Inc. (BMI), organized and owned by the
oadcasters themselves; and the Society of European Stage Authors
d Composers (SESAC), a privately owned corporation. These or-
nizations do far more than seek recognition and fame for the com-
ser and song writer: they provide for his material needs by collect-
g and turning over to him payment for the use and performance of
s music. With the coming of radio, ASCAP established through liti-

gation the fact that a radio performance was actually a performance for profit, even though the broadcasters claimed that it was not since the listener paid nothing for it—just as, in the second decade of the century, Victor Herbert, one of the founders of ASCAP, established through litigation the broader definition of the concept "performance for profit" which enabled the collecting societies to function. The collecting societies protect those who provide the music for radio, television, stage, and screen—as well as concert hall—by seeing to it that they are paid for their contribution. Today the societies collect from users of music, and distribute to their members, several millions of dollars annually.

A number of organizations and some individuals have devoted themselves to making the composer's lot a happier one, both creatively and economically. Among them are the MacDowell Colony at Peterborough, New Hampshire, already mentioned in the section on Edward MacDowell; the American Academy in Rome, which has for many years awarded three fellowships in music: one provided by the Frederick A. Juilliard Fund, another by the Walter Damrosch Fund, and the third by the Horatio Parker Fund; and the Huntington Hartford Foundation, an art colony in California established and maintained by the noted Great Atlantic and Pacific Tea Company heir and patron of the arts.

Prize contests open to American composers have included those administered by the Ignace Paderewski Fund; by the Hollywood Bowl Association; by Columbia University under the will of Lillia M. Bearns; by the RCA-Victor Company; by the broadcasting networks; by the symphony orchestras themselves; and by the National Federation of Music Clubs, which since 1909 has fostered contests open to American composers, the prizes ranging from $100 to the $10,000 that was awarded to Horatio Parker's opera *Fairyland* in 1915.

But there can be no doubt that commissions intelligently awarded to selected composers produce more enduring works than do prize contests. Among the most distinguished organizations commissioning American music are the Elizabeth Sprague Coolidge Foundation, administered by the Music Division of the Library of Congress; the Alice M. Ditson Fund of Columbia University; the John Simon Guggenheim Memorial Foundation, which grants highly-sought fellowships; the Rockefeller Foundation, which awards commissions through the Louisville Orchestra; the John Hay Whitney Foundation; the Lili Boulanger Memorial Fund; the Koussevitzky Music Foundation; and the Ford Foundation, which undertook perhaps the most far-reaching program, commissioning operas for selected opera houses, compositions for specific concert performers, and works for student orchestras in the secondary schools of the nation.

We have briefly summarized the aids to the American composer in widening his market and in providing a product for that market. A word remains to be said for the recording companies, which enable the music-lover and student to hear hundreds of American works in their own homes, at their own convenience. A number of companies should be singled out for special commendation: Columbia and Mercury, among the established labels, have been assiduous and discerning in their proselytization of the modern Americans, with Westminster and Capitol not far behind. Several of the smaller independents, notably Concert Hall Society, New Editions, Contemporary, Music Library, and the Society of Participating Artists, have shown remarkable enterprise.

The private subscription firms deserve an extra vote of thanks. One of them, the American Recording Society, has built up a substantial audience nationally with an all-domestic repertory that is about evenly distributed between nineteenth- and twentieth-century works. A grant from the Alice M. Ditson Fund helped to put this group on its feet; in turn thousands were introduced to such considerable achievements as the Carter Piano Sonata, the Haieff Piano Concerto, Piston's Symphony No. 2, Wagenaar's Symphony No. 4, Cowell's Symphony No. 5 and a good many others now available through commercial channels. Another house, the Concert Hall Society, has performed a meritorious service with its "Limited Edition" series. Its members were the first to know the Barber Violin Concerto, Copland's *Jazz Concerto*, and otherwise still unrecorded chamber music by such diverse eminences as Bloch and Bernstein.

Organizations like the American Composers Alliance and the variously interested foundations (Rockefeller, Koussevitzky, Naumburg, Fromm, *et al.*) have been munificent in their support of the commercially-released modern recorded repertory. Sudsidy is frankly welcome in any recording of a major contemporary work. None of the relatively new pieces is yet "box office," and the prestige of having an impressive few of them in one's catalogue is more than offset by the prohibitive costs involved in a full-scale (and union-scale) recording session.

That brings up a cruel irony that defines the plight of the instrumental musician today—a problem that is not out of place here because the preponderance of our young composers earn their bread and butter as instrumentalists, or as copyists or arrangers. All of these pursuits are dependent on "live" music, and the fact is that "live" music on the professional level has been disappearing from the American scene at a time when public interest in listening to music has been increasing beyond the most optimistic predictions of a decade ago. When the bottomless Pandora's box of the prospective long-playing repertory first sprang open in the late forties, economic imperatives induced all but the largest of the record companies—even those primarily concerned with American works—to make their recordings in Europe. This situation has continued; run your fingers across your record collection and see for yourself.

At the same time it has come to pass that the average music consumer, lured by the wonders of the record catalogues, has tended more and more to spend his money at the store counters and not at the ticket windows. Without going into the merits of the proposition that the record buyer ultimately will become a concert customer (the converse would be more like it), it is therefore reasonable to observe that the postwar decade marked a point of no visible return for the performing musician in our society. The manifest tragedy of this is that the whole cycle of the American musician's coming of age was traversed in such a frenetically short time. In 1946, just to pick one landmark at random, the Boston Symphony Orchestra appointed a native-born first-desk man for the first time in its long history. All over the country, in the four or five years that followed, talented young Americans were being installed in responsible positions formerly reserved for Europeans, and the birth rate of "serious" ensembles was steadily on the rise. And yet, by 1954, a pathetically small fraction of union musicians anywhere were making a living at their craft. A careful scrutiny of orchestra personnel lists showed that amateur or semi-amateur musicians were heavily in the majority. Even in New York City, thousands of violinists and pianists were driving taxicabs or selling insurance; the counsel of the American Federation of Musicians, Henry Kaiser, could report that 175,000 AFM members were employed *outside* the musical fields. At our finest schools, coveted scholarships were going a-begging. Juilliard, perhaps the finest of them, abolished its famous Summer Session altogether after two decades because there were not enough applicants to warrant the heavy operating loss.

So that new millions may have been stimulated to an intense love for good music—indeed there *were* new millions, on the face of it—but they were not populating the concert halls in the early fifties. Nor were the government-trained musicians finding anything but disillusionment in their expensively acquired skills. The future for composers, accordingly, was not roseate from any practical point of view. Nor was there any hope in sight that this absurd paradox would cancel itself out within the generation, especially with the prospects for federal subsidy as far away as ever. It is always possible, of course, that the production of new music will continue unabated without regard to these matters. Perhaps adversity, like criticism, discourages only the second-rate.

Be that as it may, a certain few of the trends since 1945 are patently beyond any valid critical comment. What is to be said of the atonal jazz *coterie*, for example, or of the experimenters in magnetic tape? All that can be said, actually, is that their activities are symptomatic of the prevailing impatience with rules and regulations as concomitants of the ideal form; symptomatic, that is, of the longing of every composer to be a creative entity unto himself. Unless he is an authentically great genius—and then only hypothetically because who of them is?—the composer of today can achieve an identity of his own in two ways only. One way is to invest nostalgia with exceptional craft, which usually means some sort of folkish end-product. This cross-pollination method is exemplified at the one extreme by Copland, at the other by the longhair jazz folk like Teo Macero. William Coss, writing in *Metronome*, implies that the "serious" works that incorporated jazz have been unsuccessful as art because all of the jazz in them was, and continues to be, *circa* 1920. The atonal jazz composers, on the other hand, feel that the evolution of their hybrid is "just around a not too square corner" because their raw material is up-to-the-minute direct expression of the unconscious, non-codified variety that preoccupies urban intellectuals. The second way, of course, is the way of gadgetry *à la* Ussachevsky and Luening, or Feldman, or Cage, all of whom have added refinements to the magnetic tape techniques evolved by Schaeffer and others in France.

With the didactic processes so highly formalized, it is a rare young composer these days who does not begin his career with a thorough knowledge of all the styles in vogue. So that everybody has been composing like somebody else, which is all right except that it does not help the abundantly facile to find themselves. Folklorism can create a demand, hence fame, but it poses no intellectual challenge. The electronic way is a hard one because there is presently no demand for it whatsoever, but we are assured by its disciples that its intellectual rewards *for the composer* are beyond measure. The question arises: To what avail is one hundred per cent personal expression if none of it be communicated artfully? The growing number of "tapesichordists" may have found a trap door in the ceiling insofar as their understandable impulse toward unfettered expressivity is concerned. If so, and their rapidly spreading movement gathers the momentum they anticipate, the sad estate of the working instrumentalist would be in even worse repair. That eventuality being implausible, we can afford the indulgence of conjecturing on the esthetic workability of the phenomenon.

Leopold Stokowski defines magnetic tape music as "music that is composed directly with sound instead of first being written on paper and later made to sound. Just as the painter paints his picture directly with colors, so the musician composes his music directly with tone. In classical orchestral music many instruments play different groups of notes which sound together. In tape music several or even many tapes are superimposed; the tapes sound together the groups of tones that are recorded on them. So, essentially, it is a new way of doing what has been done for centuries by old methods." This is far and away the most sensibly succinct statement that I have seen of the "tapesichordist's" *raison d'être*. It gives his approach a humanist aspect, and gives the carping critic pause. Mr. Stokowski's argument does not include a definition of "tone." Presumably he means for that term to cover any point in the audible spectrum. But is there not a "musical spectrum" that is circumscribed within that range? I do not insist that there is. But it would seem to be a dubious proposition to derive esthetic criteria from what engineers call "mismatched impedance" (a characteristic reverberation that audio engineers go to great lengths to *avoid* because it distorts true reproductive sound) rather than from the deep human experience that has, ostensibly, determined the anatomy of the musico-creative process these many centuries.

Back to less hypothetical matters, it remains to be noted that the postwar decade saw the demise of that estimable journal, *Modern Music.* The reason given was the usual one these days about increasing production costs. It is more likely that the magazine passed out of existence simply because it was suddenly seen to be tilting at windmills. Its long fight for the recognition of the contemporary composer had been won for some time; the dramatic advent of the long-playing record clinched a *fait accompli.* As if to sandbag the newly-taken citadel, however, a number of aggressively partisan organizations soon came into being with a view to providing an audition for the newest scores by their favored few. I shall not go into the complex politics of these determined little bands; suffice it to say that it existed and still does but not to the indefinite exclusion of any worthy young talents.

The prognosis, then, is not altogether pessimistic. If one were not preoccupied with the future, indeed, the picture is nothing if not bright. It is undoubtedly true that only a dozen or so of the newly-arrived composers will fulfill their current promise, and that prospect is not especially alarming in the light of history for all the shocking implications of publisher Leonard Feist's estimate of the number of working composers in the United States—none less than five thousand! For the public, at least, there is a certain consolation in the fact that the field never has been so crowded with competence: At random one thinks of Haieff, Shapero, Carter, Kirchner, Fine, Foss, Weber, Babbitt, Brant, Mennin, Imbrie, Calabro and uniquely Bernstein—these are gifted men, not uniformly secure in all departments but sufficiently well-trained to take their own direction when the impulse will be upon them. Aaron Copland reminded us a decade ago that Whitman's prophecy had come true, that there were scads of young composers about who rivaled their elders in technical dexterity. Today those "scads" are multiplied many times, and the survivors will have to be something far more than dextrous. To borrow a restatement of the obvious from Sean O'Casey, "only a few great souls come out of time to live beyond it." Lest the reader infer that this is to acknowledge the efficacy of the masterpiece theory, I hasten to close with this thought by Peggy Glanville-Hicks: "American [composition] is still at the beginning of the great curve of history; and as in earlier epochs of all things the fate is in the hands of the many rather than of the few. [In such an enterprise] much that is presented must of necessity fall back into obscurity and oblivion. But it is from just this humus that later the 'big trees' come." If I read that correctly, it is a plea for the right of every composer to be heard. It is good to be able to say that we are closer to that millennial realization than ever before. Ives may well have been the last of our musical giants, if not the first as well, for whom death was the price of recognition.

BIBLIOGRAPHY

Bibliography

Revised and brought up to date (1964) by Karl Kroeger

GENERAL BACKGROUND AND HISTORY

Alverson, Margaret Blake. *Sixty Years of California Songs*. San Francisco: Sunset Publishing House, 1913.

American Music Center. *American Music on Records, a Catalog of Recorded American Music Currently Available*. New York: American Music Center, 1957.

Andrus, Helen Josephine. *A Century of Music in Poughkeepsie, 1802–1911*. Poughkeepsie, New York: F. B. Howard, 1912.

Arditi, Luigi. *My Reminiscences*. New York: Dodd, Mead and Company, 1896.

Armstrong, W. G. *Record of the Opera at Philadelphia*. Philadelphia: Porter and Coates, 1884.

Art and Music in California. Reprinted from *News-Notes of California Libraries*. Sacramento: W. W. Shannon, Superintendent State Printing, 1908.

Barnes, Edwin N. C. *American Music: from Plymouth Rock to Tin Pan Alley*. Washington, D.C.: Music Education Publications, 1936.

Barton, E. M. *History of the Worcester Choral Union*. Worcester: West and See, 1875.

Barzun, Jacques. *Music in American Life*. Garden City, New York: Doubleday and Company, 1956.

Bauer, Marion. *Twentieth Century Music*. New York: G. P. Putnam's Sons, 1933.

—— and Ethel Peyser. *How Music Grew*. New York: G. P. Putnam's Sons, 1925.

Bio-Bibliographical Index of Musicians in the United States of America from Colonial Times. Washington, D.C.: Music Division,

Pan-American Union, 1941. (2nd edition, Washington, D.C.: Music Section, Pan-American Union, 1956.)

Bloom and Ewen. *The Year in American Music.* (1946–47 edited by Julius Bloom; 1948 edited by David Ewen.) New York: Allen, Towne & Heath, 1946–48.

Bloomfield, Arthur J. *The San Francisco Opera.* 1923–61. New York: Appleton-Century-Crofts, 1961.

Berry, Ira. *Sketch of the History of the Beethoven Musical Society of Portland, Maine (1819–1825).* Portland: S. Berry, 1888.

Bonner, Eugene. *The Club in the Opera House; the Story of the Metropolitan Opera Club.* Princeton, New Jersey: Princeton University Press, 1949.

Boston Academy of Music. *Annual Reports.* Boston: Perkins and Marvin, 1833–46.

Boston School Committee. *Report* upon the petition that instruction in vocal music be introduced into the public schools of the city. Boston, 1837.

Bottje, Will Gay. *A Catalog of Representative Works by Resident Living Composers of Illinois.* 1961.

Britton, Allen P. *Theoretical Introductions in American Tunebooks to 1800.* Ann Arbor, Michigan: University Microfilms (No. 1505), 1950. Dissertation: University of Michigan.

Brooks, Henry M. *Olden-Time Music.* A compilation from newspapers and books. Boston: Ticknor and Company, 1888.

Brown, Francis. *An Address on Music,* delivered before the Handel Society, Dartmouth College, August, 1809. Hanover, New Hampshire: C. and W. S. Spear, 1810.

Burnham, C. G. "Olden Time Music in the Connecticut Valley." *New England Magazine,* 1900.

Campbell, Jane. *Old Philadelphia Music.* Philadelphia: City History Society, 1926.

Carpenter, Paul S. *Music as Art and a Business.* Norman, Oklahoma: University of Oklahoma Press, 1950.

Carson, William G. B. *St. Louis Goes to the Opera, 1837–1941.* Missouri Historical Society, 1946.

Cartford, Gerhard M. *Music in the Norwegian Lutheran Church: A Study of Its Development and Transfer to America, 1825–1917.*

Ann Arbor, Michigan: University Microfilms (L.C. No. Mic. 62–1768), 1961. Dissertation: University of Minnesota.

Celebrities in Eldorado, 1850–1906. A biographic record of 111 prominent musicians who visited San Francisco. San Francisco: Work Projects Administration, 1940.

Chase, Gilbert. *America's Music, from the Pilgrims to the Present.* New York: McGraw-Hill, Inc., 1955.

Cheney, Simeon P. *The American Singing Book . . . The Biographical Department Containing Biographies of 40 of the Leading Composers, Book-makers, etc. of Sacred Music in America.* Boston: White-Smith, 1879.

Clarke, Eric. *Music in Everyday Life.* New York: W. W. Norton and Company, Inc., 1935.

Copland, Aaron. *Our New Music.* New York: McGraw-Hill, Inc., 1941.

—— "Serge Koussevitzky and the American Composer." *Musical Quarterly,* July, 1944.

Cotton, John. *Singing of Psalms a Gospel Ordinance: or a Treatise wherein are Handled these Four Particulars. I. Touching the Duty Itself. II. Touching the Matter to be Sung. III. Touching the Singers. IV. Touching the Manner of Singing.* Boston, 1647.

Crews, Emma K. *A History of Music in Knoxville, Tenn. 1791– 1910.* Ann Arbor: University Microfilms (L.C. No. Mic. 61– 5634), 1961. Dissertation: Florida State University.

Daniel, Ralph T. "English Models for the First American Anthems." *Journal of the American Musicological Society,* Vol. 12, No. 1 (Spring, 1959).

Da Ponte, Lorenzo. *Memoirs.* Boston: Houghton Mifflin Company, 1929.

Da Silva, Owen. *Mission Music of California.* Los Angeles, California: Warren & Lewis, 1941.

David, Hans T. *Musical Life in the Pennsylvania Settlements of the Unitas Fratrum* (Moravian Music Foundation Publication No. 6). Winston-Salem, North Carolina: Moravian Music Foundation, 1959. (Reprint from *Transactions of the Moravian Historical Society,* 1942.)

Despard, Mabel H. *The Music of the United States, Its Sources and*

Its History. A Short Outline. New York: J. H. H. Muirhead, 1936.

Dinneen, William. *Music in the Meeting House, 1775–1958.* Providence, Rhode Island: Privately printed for the First Baptist Church in America, 1958.

Directory of New York State Musicians. New York: New York Federation of Music Clubs, 1931.

Drummond, Robert Rutherford. *Early German Music in Philadelphia.* New York: D. Appleton and Company, 1910.

Dunlap, William. *A History of the American Theatre.* New York: J. and J. Harper, 1832.

Earle, Alice M. *The Sabbath in Puritan New England.* New York: Charles Scribner's Sons, 1896.

Eaton, Quaintance. *Musical U.S.A.* New York: Allen, Towne & Heath, 1949.

—— *Opera Caravan; Adventures of the Opera on Tour, 1883–1956.* New York: Farrar, Straus & Cudahy, 1957.

Edwards, George Thornton. *Music and Musicians of Maine.* Portland: The Southworth Press, 1928.

—— *Maine Musical Festivals: Programs, 1897–1928.*

Ellingwood, Leonard. *The History of American Church Music.* New York: Morehouse-Gorham, 1953.

Ellis, F. R. "Music in Cincinnati." *Music Teachers' National Association Proceedings, 1913.*

Elson, Arthur. *Music Club Programs from All Nations.* Boston: Oliver Ditson Company, 1928.

—— *Woman's Work in Music.* Boston: L. C. Page and Company, 1913.

Elson, Louis C. *The History of American Music.* New York: The Macmillan Company, 1904. (Revised to 1925 by Arthur Elson.)

Engel, Carl. *An Introduction to the Study of National Music.* London: Longmans, Green and Dyer, 1866.

——, compiler. *Music from the Days of George Washington.* Washington, D.C.: United States George Washington Bicentennial Commission, 1931.

Engelke, Hans. *A Study of Ornaments in American Tune Books, 1790–1800.* Ann Arbor: University Microfilms (L.C. No. Mic. 60–558), 1960. Dissertation: University of Southern California.

Erskine, John. *The Philharmonic-Symphony Society of New York.* New York: The Macmillan Company, 1943.

Ewen, David. *Music Comes to America.* New York: Thomas Y. Crowell Company, 1942.

Farwell, Arthur. *A Letter to American Composers.* Newton Center, Massachusetts: The Wa-Wan Press, 1903.

———— and W. Dermont Darby. *Music in America,* Vol. IV of *The Art of Music.* New York: The National Society of Music, 1915.

Fernald, John P. *History of the Salem Oratorio Society, 1868–91.* Salem, Massachusetts: Barry and Lufkin, 1891.

Ffrench, Florence. *Music and Musicians in Chicago.* Chicago: F. F. Ffrench, 1899.

Finck, H. T. *Songs and Song Writers.* New York: Charles Scribner's Sons, 1900.

Fischer, D. B. "The Story of New Orleans's Rise as a Music Center." *Musical America,* Vol. XIX, No. 19, 1914.

Fisher, William Arms. "The American Music Publisher and His Relationship to the Music Teacher and the Composers." *Music Teachers' National Association Proceedings, 1918.*

———— "The Great American Symphony." *Music Teachers' National Association Proceedings, 1929.*

———— *Notes on Music in Old Boston.* Boston: Oliver Ditson Company, 1918.

———— *Ye Olde New England Psalm Tunes (1620–1820),* with historical sketch. Boston: Oliver Ditson Company, 1930.

———— *One Hundred and Fifty Years of Music Publishing in the United States.* Boston: Oliver Ditson Company, 1933.

Foote, Henry Wilder. *Three Centuries of American Hymnody.* Cambridge, Massachusetts: Harvard University Press, 1940. (Reprint edition, Garden City, New York: Nelson Doubleday, 1961.)

———— *American Unitarian Hymn Writers and Hymns.* Cambridge, Massachusetts: Author, 1959.

———— *Catalog of American Universalist Hymn Writers and Hymns.* Cambridge, Massachusetts: Author, 1959.

Frank, Leonie C. *Musical Life in Early Cincinnati.* Cincinnati, Ohio: The author, 1932.

Fredericks, Jessica M. *California Composers*. San Francisco: California Federation of Music Clubs, 1934.

Gay, Julius. *Church Music in Farmington in the Olden Time*. Hartford, Connecticut: Lockwood and Brainard Company, 1891.

Gerson, Robert A. *Music in Philadelphia*. Philadelphia: Theodore Presser Company, 1940.

Gilbert, Henry F. "The American Composer." *Musical Quarterly*, April, 1915.

Gillis, Don. *A List of American Operas, Compiled for the American Opera Workshop*. . . . Ann Arbor, Michigan: Interlocken Press, 1959.

Goldman, Richard Franko. *Landmarks of Early American Music, 1760–1800*. A Collection of 32 Compositions. New York: G. Schirmer, Inc., 1943.

Good, Marian Bigler. *Some Musical Backgrounds of Pennsylvania*. Carrolltown, Pennsylvania: Carrolltown News Press, 1932.

Gould, Nathaniel D. *History of Church Music in America*. Boston: A. N. Johnson, 1853.

Graf, Herbert. *Opera for the People*. Minneapolis: University of Minnesota Press, 1951.

―――― *Producing Opera for America*. Zurich: Atlantis Books, 1961.

Graham, Alberta P. *Great Bands of America*. New York: Thomas Nelson & Sons, 1951.

Grider, Rufus A. *Historical Notes on Music in Bethlehem, Pennsylvania (1741–1871)*. Philadelphia: J. A. Martin, 1873. (Reprint edition, with foreword by Donald M. McCorkle, Moravian Music Foundation Publication No. 4. Winston-Salem, North Carolina: Moravian Music Foundation, 1957.)

Gruenberg, Louis. "For an American Gesture." *Modern Music*, June, 1924.

Hackett, Karleton. *The Beginning of Grand Opera in Chicago (1850–1859)*. Chicago: The Laurentian Press, 1913.

Hall, Jacob Henry. *Biography of Gospel Songs and Hymn Writers*. New York: Fleming H. Revell Company, 1914.

Hanson, Howard. "A Forward Look in American Composition." *Music Teachers' National Association Proceedings, 1925*. (Reprinted by the Eastman School of Music, Rochester, New York.)

—— *Music in Contemporary American Life*. Lincoln, Nebraska: University of Nebraska Press, 1951.

Harwell, Richard B. *Confederate Music*. Chapel Hill, North Carolina: University of North Carolina Press, 1950.

Hastings, Thomas. *The History of Forty Choirs*. New York: Mason Brothers, 1854.

Heimsheimer, H. W. "Opera in America Today." *Musical Quarterly*, Vol. 37, No. 3 (July, 1951).

Hewitt, John Hill. *Shadows on the Wall*. Baltimore: Trumbull Brothers, 1877.

Higginson, Vincent. *Hymnody in the American Indian Missions* (Papers of the Hymn Society, 18). New York: Hymn Society of America, 1954.

Hill, Double E. *A Study of Tastes in American Church Music as reflected in the Music of the Methodist Episcopal Church*. Ann Arbor, Michigan: University Microfilms (L.C. No. Mic. 63–3270). Dissertation: University of Illinois, 1962.

Hipsher, Edward Ellsworth. *American Opera and Its Composers*. Philadelphia: Theodore Presser Company, 1927.

History of Opera in San Francisco. San Francisco: Work Projects Administration, 1938.

Hoban, C. F. *Pennsylvania in Music*. Harrisburg, Pennsylvania: Public Instruction Department, 1926.

Hohmann, Rupert K. *The Church Music of the Old Order Amish of the United States*. Ann Arbor: University Microfilms (L.C. No. Mic. 60–436), 1959. Dissertation: Northwestern University.

Holde, Artur. *Metropolitan Opera House New York; die Geschichte eines Musikzentrums*. Berlin: Rembrandt Verlag, 1961.

Holderness, Marvin E. *Curtain in Forest Park; a Narrative of the St. Louis Municipal Opera, 1919–1958*. St. Louis, Missouri: St. Louis Municipal Theatre Association, 1960.

Hood, George. *History of Music in New England*. Boston: Wilkins, Carter and Company, 1846.

Hopkins, Edward Jerome. *Music and Snobs, or a Few Funny Facts Regarding the Disabilities of Music in America*. New York: R. A. Saalfield, 1888.

Horn, Dorothy D. *Quartal Harmony in the Pentatonic Hymns of the*

Sacred Harp. Indianapolis: Author, 1958. (Reprint from *Journal of American Folklore,* Oct./Dec. 1958.)

Howard, John Tasker. *The Music of George Washington's Time.* Washington, D.C.: United States George Washington Bicentennial Commission, 1931.

———— *A Program of Early American Piano Pieces.* (Works by Reinagle, Taylor, Pelissier, Carr, and others.) New York: J. Fischer and Brother, 1931.

———— *A Program of Early and Mid-Nineteenth Century American Songs.* New York: J. Fischer and Brother, 1931.

———— *Our Contemporary Composers: American Music in the Twentieth Century.* New York: Thomas Y. Crowell Company, 1941.

———— *A Program Outline of American Music.* New York: Thomas Y. Crowell Company, 1931.

———— *This Modern Music.* New York: Thomas Y. Crowell Company, 1942.

———— and George K. Bellows. *A Short History of Music in America.* New York: Thomas Y. Crowell Company, 1957.

———— and Eleanor S. Bowen. *Music Associated with the Period of the Formation of the Constitution and the Inauguration of George Washington.* Washington, D.C.: United States Constitution Sesquicentennial Commission, 1937.

Howe, Mabel Almy. *Music Publishers in New York City Before 1850.* New York: New York Public Library, 1917.

Howe, Mark Anthony De Wolfe. *The Boston Symphony Orchestra, An Historical Sketch.* Boston: Houghton Mifflin Company, 1914. (Sesquicentennial Edition, revised and extended by John N. Burk, 1931.)

Hubbard, W. L. *History of American Music,* Volume in the American History and Encyclopedia of Music. Toledo, Ohio: Irving Squire, 1908.

Hughes, Rupert. *American Composers.* Boston: The Page Company, 1900. (Revised to 1914 by Arthur Elson.)

Huneker, James Gibbons. *The Philharmonic Society of New York and Its 75th Anniversary.* New York: The Society, 1917.

Huntington, P. W. "Old-time Music of Columbus, Ohio." Columbus: *Old Northwest Genealogical Quarterly,* Vol. VIII, No. 2, 1905.

Ireland, J. N. *Records of the New York Stage, from 1750 to 1860.* New York: T. H. Marell, 1866–67.

Jackson, George P. "Pennsylvania Dutch Spirituals." *Musical Quarterly*, Vol. 38, No. 1 (January, 1952).

Jackson, George S. *Early Songs of Uncle Sam.* Boston: Bruce Humphries, Inc., 1933.

James-Reed, Mint O. *Music in Austin, 1900–1956.* Austin, Texas: Von Boeckmann-Jones Co., 1957.

Johnson, Frances Hall. *Musical Memories of Hartford.* Hartford, Connecticut: Witkower's, 1931.

Johnson, H. Earle. "The Adams Family and Good Listening." *Journal of the American Musicological Society*, Vol. 9, No. 2–3 (Summer-Fall, 1958).

——— "Early New England Periodicals Devoted to Music." *Musical Quarterly*, April, 1940.

——— *Musical Interludes in Boston, 1795–1830.* New York: Columbia University Press, 1943.

——— "Some 'First Performances' in America." *Journal of the American Musicological Society*, Vol. 6, No. 1 (Spring, 1953).

——— *Symphony Hall, Boston.* Boston: Little, Brown and Company, 1956.

Johnson, Thomas. "American Orchestras and American Music." *American Composers Alliance Bulletin*, Vol. 11, No. 1 (June, 1963).

Jones, Howard Mumford. *America and French Culture, 1750–1848.* (Chapter on French Music in America.) Chapel Hill, North Carolina: University of North Carolina Press, 1927.

Kaufmann, Helen L. *From Jehovah to Jazz; Music in America from Psalmody to the Present Day.* New York: Dodd, Mead and Company, 1937.

Keppel, Frederick P., and R. L. Duffus. *The Arts in American Life.* New York: McGraw-Hill, Inc., 1933.

Kinscella, Hazel Gertrude. *History Sings. Backgrounds of American Music.* Lincoln, Nebraska: The University Publishing Company, 1940.

Krehbiel, H. E. *Chapters of Opera.* New York: Holt, Rinehart and Winston, 1909.

—— *More Chapters of Opera*. New York: Holt, Rinehart an Winston, 1919.

—— *Notes on the Cultivation of Choral Music and the Orator Society in New York*. New York: Edw. Schuberth and Company 1884.

—— *The Philharmonic Society of New York*. New York an London: Novello, Ewer and Company, 1892.

—— *Review of the New York Musical Season, 1885–86 1889–90*. New York and London: Novello, Ewer and Company 1886–90.

Krohn, Ernest C. *A Century of Missouri Music*. St. Louis: Private printed, 1924.

—— "The Development of the Symphony Orchestra in St. Louis. *Music Teachers' National Association Proceedings, 1924*. (R printed, St. Louis, 1924.)

Krummel, Donald W. *Philadelphia Music Engraving and Publishin 1800–1820; a Study in Bibliography and Cultural History*. An Arbor, Michigan: University Microfilms (No. 58–7749), 195 Dissertation: University of Michigan.

Lahee, H. C. *Annals of Music in America*. Boston: Marshall Jon Company, 1922.

—— *Grand Opera in America*. Boston: L. C. Page and Company 1902.

Landowska, Wanda. *La Musique Américaine*. Paris: Pierre Hora 1952.

Lang, Paul Henry, editor. *One Hundred Years of Music in Americ a Centennial Publication*. New York: G. Schirmer, 1961.

Lavignac, Albert. *Music and Musicians*, with Chapters on Music i America by H. E. Krehbiel. New York: Holt, Rinehart an Winston, 1899.

Learned, Marion Dexter. *Life of Francis Daniel Pastorius, t Founder of Germantown*. Philadelphia: W. J. Campbell, 190

Lenhart, Charmenz. *Musical Influence on American Poetry*. Athen Georgia: University of Georgia Press, 1956.

Levant, Oscar. *A Smattering of Ignorance*. Garden City, New Yor Doubleday, Doran, 1940.

Ling, Louis. "Music in Detroit." *Music Teachers' National Association Proceedings, 1921.*

List of American Orchestral Works Recommended by WPA Music Project Conductors. Washington, D.C.: Work Projects Administration, 1941.

Loft, Abram. "Richard Wagner, Theodore Thomas and the American Centennial." *Musical Quarterly,* Vol. 37, No. 2 (April, 1951).

Lowens, Irving. "The Bay Psalm Book in 17th-Century New England." *Journal of the American Musicological Society,* Vol. 8, No. 1 (Spring, 1955).

―――― *The Easy Instructor (1798–1831); a History and Bibliography of the First Shaped Note Tune Book.* Ann Arbor, Michigan: Allen P. Britten, University [of Michigan] School of Music, 1953. (Reprint from *Journal of Research in Music Education,* Spring, 1953.)

―――― "John Wyeth's *Repository of Sacred Music, Part Second:* A Northern Precursor of Southern Folk Hymnody." *Journal of the American Musicological Society,* Vol. 5, No. 2 (Summer, 1952).

―――― "The Origins of the American Fuging Tune." *Journal of the American Musicological Society,* Vol. 6, No. 1 (Spring, 1953).

―――― "Writings about Music in the Periodicals of American Transcendentalism (1835–50)." *Journal of the American Musicological Society,* Vol. 10, No. 2 (Summer, 1957).

Lucas, G. W. *Remarks on the Musical Conventions in Boston.* Northampton, Massachusetts: For the author, 1844.

Luper, Albert T. "Civil War Music" (Special issue of *Civil War History*). Iowa City: Iowa State University, 1958.

MacDougall, Hamilton C. *Early New England Psalmody, 1620–1820.* Brattleboro, New Hampshire: Stephen Daye Press, 1940.

Madeira, L. C. *Annals of Music in Philadelphia.* Philadelphia: J. B. Lippincott Company, 1896.

Manchester, Arthur L. "Music Education; A Musical America; The American Composer." *Musical Quarterly,* October, 1928.

Manuscript Society of New York; Constitution and Bylaws. New York: The Lotus Press, 1895.

Maretzek, Max. *Crochets & Quavers; or Revelations of an Opera Manager in New York.* New York, 1855.

—— *Sharps & Flats; a Sequel to Crochets & Quavers.* New York: American Musician Publishing Company, 1890.

Marrocco, W. Thomas, and Harold Gleason. *Music in America, 1620 to 1865; an Anthology.* New York: W. W. Norton and Company, Inc., 1964.

Mason, Daniel Gregory. *The Dilemma of American Music.* New York: The Macmillan Company, 1928.

—— *Music in My Time.* New York: The Macmillan Company, 1938.

—— *Tune In, America!* New York: Alfred A. Knopf, 1931.

Mates, Julian. *The American Musical Stage Before 1800.* New Brunswick, New Jersey: Rutgers University Press, 1962.

Mather, Morey and Henderson. "The American Spirit in Art" (Vol. VI of *The Pageant of America*). New Haven, Connecticut: Yale University Press, 1927.

Mathews, W. S. B. "Art Music in the Middle West." *The Etude,* Vol. XXIII, No. 3, 1905.

——, associate editor. *A Hundred Years of Music in America.* Chicago: G. L. Howe, 1889.

Mattfield, Julius. *A Handbook of American Operatic Premieres.* Detroit, Michigan: Information Services, Inc., 1963.

—— *A Hundred Years of Grand Opera in New York (1825–1925).* New York: New York Public Library, 1927.

Maurer, Maurer. "A Musical Family in Colonial Virginia." *Musical Quarterly,* Vol. 34, No. 3 (July, 1948).

—— "The 'Professor of Musick' in Colonial America." *Musical Quarterly,* Vol. 36, No. 4 (October, 1950).

Maynard, Olga. *The American Ballet.* Philadelphia: Macrae, Smith, 1959.

McCarty, Clifford. *Film Composers in America; a checklist of their work.* Glendale, California: Distributed by John Valentine, 1953.

McCorkle, Donald M. *Moravian Music in Salem; a German-American Heritage.* Ann Arbor, Michigan: University Microfilms (L.C. No. Mic. 59–333), 1959. Dissertation: Indiana University.

McGee, Mrs. Curtis M. *Kentucky Composers and Compilers of Folk Music, Native and Adopted*. Frankfort, Kentucky: *The State Journal*, 1950.

Memoirs of a New England Village Choir. Atkinson, New Hampshire, 1829.

Metcalf, Frank J. *American Psalmody (1721–1820)*. New York: C. F. Heartmann, 1917.

—— *American Writers and Compilers of Sacred Music*. New York: The Abingdon Press, 1925.

—— *Stories of Hymn Tunes*. New York: The Abingdon Press, 1928.

Mendel, Henry M. *History of Milwaukee from Its First Settlement to the Year 1895*, edited by H. L. Conrad, Vol. II (Chapter on Music and Musical Societies). Chicago and New York: American Bibliographical Publishing Company, 1925.

Michigan Federation of Music Clubs: Year Book. Issued annually.

Michigan Library Bulletins, March and December, 1926 (Biographical Sketches of Michigan Composers with Lists of Their Works). Lansing: Michigan State Library.

Miller, Winifred V. "Wisconsin's Place in the Field of Music." *Wisconsin Blue Book*. Madison: State Printing Board, 1929.

Milligan, Harold V. *Pioneer American Composers*. A Collection of Early American Songs. Boston: The Arthur P. Schmidt Company, 1921.

Minnesota Music. Minneapolis: Publication of Minnesota State Music Teachers' Association, 1913–20.

Moore, John W. *A Dictionary of Musical Information and a List of Modern Musical Works Published in the United States from 1640 to 1875*. Boston: O. Ditson, 1876.

Morgan, James O. *French Comic Opera in New York, 1855–1890*. Ann Arbor, Michigan: University Microfilms (L.C. No. Mic. 60–219), 1959. Dissertation: University of Illinois.

Morris, Harold. *Contemporary American Music*. Rice Institute Pamphlets, Vol. XXI. Houston, Texas: Rice Institute of Liberal and Technical Learning, 1934.

Mueller, John H. *The American Symphony Orchestra; a Social*

History of Musical Taste. Bloomington, Indiana: Indiana University Press, 1951.

Musical Attractions at Willow Grove Park, with a Short History of Music's Development in Philadelphia, from Colonial Days Up to the Present Time. Philadelphia: John Winston Company, 1910.

Music by Indiana Composers and About Indiana. Indianapolis: State Library, 1942.

Music in Denver and Colorado. Denver: *The Lookout,* Vol. I, No. 1, 1927.

Music Teachers' National Association Proceedings, 1928, pp. 1–263, "Fifty Years of Music in America, 1876–1926."

Nathan, Hans. "Early Banjo Tunes and American Syncopation." *Musical Quarterly,* Vol. 42, No. 4 (October, 1956).

National Federation of Music Clubs Book of Proceedings, Vol. III. "American Composers' Forum." Ithaca, New York, 1939.

New York Philharmonic Journal (edited by Edward Jerome Hopkins). New York: The Society, 1868–1885.

Noble, Helen. *Life with the Met.* New York: G. P. Putnam's Sons, 1954.

Northern California Musicians' Directory. San Francisco: Donaldson Printing Company, 1916–17.

Odell, George C. D. *Annals of the New York Stage,* Vols. I–XIII. New York: Columbia University Press, 1927–40.

Offenbach, Jacques. *Offenbach in America.* New York: G. W. Carleton and Company, 1877.

Osburn, Mary. *Ohio Composers and Musical Authors.* Columbus, Ohio: Heer Printing Company, 1942.

Otis, Philo A. *The Chicago Symphony Orchestra (1891–1924).* Chicago: Clayton F. Summy Company, 1924.

―――― "The Development of Music in Chicago; an Historical Sketch." *Music Teachers' National Association Proceedings, 1920.*

Pacific Coast Musical Review. Panama-Pacific Exposition Souvenir and Historical Edition. San Francisco: September 25, 1915.

Pacific Coast Musical Review. 17th Anniversary Edition, Vol. XXXIII, No. 3, 1917.

Pacific Coast Musicians' Year Book. Los Angeles: F. H. Colby, 1926–27.

Pacific Northwest Musical Directory (Music and Musicians), annually since 1915. Seattle, Washington.

Paine, J. K., Theodore Thomas, and Karl Klauser. *Music in America*, Vol. II of *Famous Composers and Their Works*. Boston: J. B. Millet and Company, 1901.

Pannain, Guido. *Modern Composers*. London: J. M. Dent and Sons, 1932.

Parker, Mrs. A. A. *Church Music and Musical Life in Pennsylvania in the Eighteenth Century* (3 vols.). Philadelphia: Pennsylvania Society of the Colonial Dames in America, 1926–27.

Parker, John R. *A Musical Biography*. Boston: Stone and Farwell, 1825.

Pennsylvania in Music. Harrisburg, Pennsylvania: Department of Public Instruction, 1927.

Perkins, Charles C., and John S. Dwight. *History of the Handel & Haydn Society of Boston*. Boston: A. Mudge and Sons, 1883.

Pettis, Ashley. "The WPA and the American Composer." *Musical Quarterly*, January, 1940.

Pfleiderer, Elizabeth. *The Music of the United States—Guide Map to Its Sources and History*. New York: J. H. H. Muirhead, 1930.

Phillips, H. D. "The Musical Psychology of America." *Musical Quarterly*, October, 1923.

Pichierri, Louis. *Music in New Hampshire, 1623–1800*. New York: Columbia University Press, 1960.

———, editor. *Grove's Dictionary of Music and Musicians*. American Supplement, Vol. VI. New York: The Macmillan Company, 1920 and 1928.

Pierce, Edwin H. "Gospel Hymns and Their Tunes." *Musical Quarterly*, July, 1940.

——— "The Rise and Fall of the 'Fugue-Tune' in America." *Musical Quarterly*, April, 1930.

——— "United States Navy Bands, Old and New." *Musical Quarterly*, Vol. 33, No. 3 (July, 1947).

Pratt, Waldo Selden. *The Music of the Pilgrims*. Boston: Oliver Ditson Company, 1921.

Proceedings of the Musical Convention Assembled in Boston, August 16, 1838. Boston: Kidder and Wright, 1838.

Rau, Albert George, and Hans T. David. *A Catalogue of Music by American Moravians*. Bethlehem, Pennsylvania: The Moravian Seminary, 1938.

Redway, Virginia Larkin. *Music Directory of Early New York City*. A file of musicians, music publishers, and musical instrument makers . . . from 1786 through 1835. New York: New York Public Library, 1941.

—— "A New York Concert in 1736." *Musical Quarterly*, April, 1936.

Reinbach, Edna, compiler. *Music and Musicians in Kansas*. Topeka: Kansas State Historical Society, 1930.

Reis, Claire R. *Composers, Conductors and Critics*. New York: Oxford University Press, 1955.

Ritter, Frédéric Louis. *Music in America*. New York: Charles Scribner's Sons, 1884. (Revised, 1890.)

Rodríguez, José. *Music and Dance in California*. Hollywood, California: Bureau of Musical Research, 1940.

Rohrer, Gertrude Martin. *Music and Musicians of Pennsylvania*. Philadelphia: Theodore Presser Company, 1940.

Rosenfeld, Paul. *An Hour with American Music*. Philadelphia: J. B. Lippincott Company, 1929.

Russell, Charles Edward. *The American Orchestra and Theodore Thomas*. Garden City, New York: Doubleday, Page and Company, 1927.

Sachse, Julius Friedrich. *Music of the Ephrata Cloister*. Lancaster, Pennsylvania: For the author, 1903.

Saerchinger, César. "Musical Landmarks in New York." *Musical Quarterly*, 1920.

Salter, Sumner. "Early Encouragements to American Composers." *Musical Quarterly*, January, 1932.

Saunders, Richard Drake. *Music and Dance in California and the West*. Hollywood, California: Bureau of Musical Research, 1948.

Scharf, John Thomas. *History of Baltimore City and County* (chap. xxxviii). Philadelphia: L. H. Everts, 1881.

—— *History of St. Louis City and County* (Vol. II, chap. xxxviii). Philadelphia: L. H. Everts and Company, 1883.

—— and Thompson Wescott. *History of Philadelphia*. Philadelphia: L. H. Everts and Company, 1884.

Schiavo, Giovanni E. *Italian-American History*. New York: Vigo Press, 1947. (Vol. 1, Books I & II, contains Italian music and musicians in America.)

Schickel, Richard. *The World of Carnegie Hall*. New York: Julian Messner, Inc., 1960.

Scholes, Percy A. *The Puritans and Music in England and New England*. New York: Oxford University Press, 1934.

Schwartz, Harry W. *Bands of America*. Garden City, New York: Doubleday and Company, 1957.

Seebirt, Elizabeth E. Gunn. *Music in Indiana*. South Bend, Indiana: For the author, 1928.

Seilhamer, George O. *History of the American Theatre (1749–1797)*. Philadelphia: Globe Printing House, 1888–91.

Sessions, Roger. *Reflections on the Musical Life in the United States*. (Merlin Music Books, Vol. 6.) New York: Merlin Press, 1956.

Sewall, Samuel (1652–1730). *Diary*. Three-volume edition. Boston: Massachusetts Historical Society, 1878–82. One-volume edition, edited by Mark Van Doren, New York: Macy-Masius, 1927.

Sharp, Cecil. "American Music" in Bruce Bliven's *Twentieth Century Unlimited*. Philadelphia: J. B. Lippincott Company, 1950.

Shawn, Ted. *Thirty-three Years of American Dance, 1927–1959*. Pittsfield, Massachusetts: For the author, 1959.

Sherman, John K. *Music and Theater in Minnesota History*. Minneapolis: University of Minnesota Press, 1958.

Simkins, Francis B., editor. *Art and Music in the South*. (Institute of Southern Culture Lectures at Longwood College, 1960.) Farmville, Virginia: Longwood College, 1961.

Simpson, Eugene E. *America's Position in Music*. Boston: The Four Seas Company, 1920.

—— *A History of St. Olaf Choir*. Minneapolis, Minnesota: Augsburg Publishing House, 1921.

Slepian, Dorothy. "Polyphonic Forms and Devices in Modern American Music." *Musical Quarterly,* Vol. 33, No. 3 (July, 1947).

Slonimsky, Nicolas. *Music Since 1900.* New York: W. W. Norton and Company, 1937.

Smith, Carleton Sprague. "The 1774 Psalm Book of the Reformed Protestant Dutch Church in New York City." *Musical Quarterly,* Vol. 34, No. 1 (January, 1948).

Smith, Cecil. *Worlds of Music.* Philadelphia: J. B. Lippincott Company, 1952.

Smythe, J. Henry, editor. *The Amazing Benjamin Franklin* (Chapter on Franklin: The Patron Saint of the Music Industries, by Dewey Dixon). New York: Frederick A. Stokes and Company, 1929.

Sonneck, O. G. *Bibliography of Early Secular American Music.* Washington, D.C.: H. L. McQueen, 1905. (Revised and enlarged by William Treat Upton. Washington, D.C.: The Library of Congress, 1945.)

——— *Early Concert Life in America.* Leipzig: Breitkopf and Haertel, 1907.

——— *Early Opera in America.* New York: G. Schirmer, Inc., 1915.

——— *Miscellaneous Studies in the History of Music* (Chapter on Early American Operas). New York: The Macmillan Company, 1921.

——— *Suum Cuique* (Chapter on a Survey of Music in America). New York: G. Schirmer, Inc., 1916.

Southern California Musicians' Directory. Los Angeles: H. A. Horwitz, 1916.

Spaeth, Sigmund. *Music and Dance in Pennsylvania, New Jersey and Delaware.* New York: Bureau of Musical Research, 1954.

——— *Music and Dance in New York State.* New York: Bureau of Musical Research, 1952.

——— *Music and Dance in the New England States.* New York: Bureau of Musical Research, 1953.

——— *Music and Dance in the Southeastern States.* New York: Bureau of Musical Research, 1952.

Spalding, Walter R. "The War in Its Relation to American Music." *Musical Quarterly,* January, 1918.

Spell, Lota May. *Music in Texas.* Austin, Texas, 1936.

Standish, L. W. *The Old Stoughton Musical Society*. Stoughton, Mass., 1929.

Staples, Samuel E. *The Ancient Psalmody and Hymnology of New England*. Worcester, Massachusetts: C. Jillson, 1880.

Stearns, H. E., editor. *Civilization of the United States* (Chapter on Music by Deems Taylor). New York, 1922.

Stone, James H. "Mid-Nineteenth-Century American Beliefs in the Social Values of Music." *Musical Quarterly*, Vol. 43, No. 1 (January, 1957).

Stringfield, Lamar. *America and Her Music*. Chapel Hill, North Carolina: University of North Carolina Press, 1931.

Swan, Howard. *Music in the Southwest, 1825–1950*. San Marino, California: Huntington Library, 1952.

Swope, R. H. *Items of Music in the Annals of Harrisburg*. Paper read before Dauphin County (Pa.) Historical Society, 1928.

Thomas, Margaret F. *Musical Alabama*. Montgomery, Alabama: The Paragon Press, 1925.

Thorpe, H. C. "Interpretative Studies in American Songs." *Musical Quarterly*, January, 1929.

Thorson, Theodore W. *A History of Music Publishing in Chicago: 1850–1960*. Ann Arbor, Michigan: University Microfilms (L.C. No. Mic. 62–874). Dissertation: Northwestern University.

Tunison, Frank. *Presto! From the Singing School to the May Festival*. Cincinnati, Ohio: E. H. Beasley Company, 1888.

Upton, George P. *Musical Memories*. Chicago: A. C. McClurg and Company, 1908.

Upton, William Treat. *Art-Song in America*. Boston: Oliver Ditson Company, 1930.

—— *Art-Song in America. Supplement, 1930–38*. Boston: Oliver Ditson Company, 1930.

Vaill, J. H., compiler. *Litchfield County Choral Union (1900–1912)*. Norfolk, Connecticut: Litchfield County University Club, 1912.

Vernon, Grenville. *Yankee Doodle-Doo; A Collection of Songs of the Early American Stage*. New York: Payson and Clarke, 1927.

Wagenknecht, Edward Charles. *Jenny Lind*. Boston: Houghton Mifflin Company, 1931.

Walters, Raymond. *The Bethlehem Bach Choir*. Boston: Houghton Mifflin Company, 1918.

Warrington, James. *Short Titles of Books Relating or Illustrating the History and Practice of Psalmody in the United States*. Philadelphia: Privately printed, 1898.

Wascher, A. E., and T. C. Ingham. *Who's Who in Music and Dramatic Art in the Twin Cities* (containing histories of Minneapolis Symphony Orchestra and various St. Paul and Minneapolis musical organizations). Minneapolis: Associated Publishers' Bureau, 1925.

Weight, Newell B. *An Historical Study of the Origin and Character of Indigenous Hymn Tunes of the Latter-Day Saints*. Ann Arbor, Michigan: University Microfilms (L.C. No. Mic. 61–6310). Dissertation: University of Southern California.

Wells, L. Jeanette. *A History of the Music Festival at Chautauqua Institution from 1874 to 1957*. Washington, D.C.: The Catholic University of America Press, 1958.

White, G. H., editor. *The Boston Musical Year Book*. Boston: George H. Ellis, 1883–86.

White, William C. *A History of Military Music in America*. New York: Exposition Press, 1944.

Whitlock, E. Clyde, and Richard Drake Saunders, editors. *Music and Dance in Texas, Oklahoma and the Southwest*. Hollywood, California: Bureau of Musical Research, 1950.

Whitmer, T. Carl. "The Energy of American Crowd Music." *Musical Quarterly*, January, 1918.

Wiggin, Frances T. *Maine Composers and Their Music: A Biographical Dictionary*. Thomaston, Maine: Maine Federation of Music Clubs, 1959.

Williams, George. "Charleston Church Music, 1562–1833." *Journal of the American Musicological Society*, Vol. 7, No. 1 (Spring, 1954).

Winsor, Justin, editor. *The Memorial History of Boston, 1630–1880*, Vol. IV, chap. vii. Boston: J. R. Osgood and Company, 1880–81.

Wisconsin Music Teacher. Official Publication of Wisconsin Music Teachers' Association, quarterly since 1912. Madison.

Worcester County Musical Festival Programs. Worcester, Massachusetts, 1873.

COMPOSERS AND PERFORMERS
Individual Biography and Memoirs

Marian Anderson

> Albus, Harry J. *The 'Deep River' Girl; the Life of Marian Anderson in Story Form.* Grand Rapids, Michigan: Wm. B. Eerdmans Publishing Company, 1949.

> Anderson, Marian. *My Lord, What a Morning; an Autobiography.* New York: The Viking Press, 1956.

John Antes

> McCorkle, Donald M. "John Antes, American Dilettante." *Musical Quarterly,* Vol. 42, No. 4 (October, 1956).

George Antheil

> Antheil, George. *Bad Boy of Music.* Garden City, New York: Doubleday, Doran & Company, 1945.

> Copland, Aaron. "George Antheil." *Modern Music,* January, 1925.

> Glanville-Hicks, Peggy. "George Antheil." *Bulletin of the American Composers Alliance,* Vol. 4, No. 1, 1954.

> Thompson, Randall. "George Antheil." *Modern Music,* May–June, 1931.

Harold Arlen

> Jablonski, Edward. *Harold Arlen: Happy with the Blues.* Garden City, New York: Doubleday and Company, 1961.

Louis Armstrong

> Armstrong, Louis. *Satchmo; My Life in New Orleans.* Englewood Cliffs, New Jersey: Prentice-Hall, 1954.

> Goffin, Robert. *Horn of Plenty, the Story of Louis Armstrong.* New York: Allen, Towne & Heathe, 1947.

> —— *Louis Armstrong; le roi du jazz.* Paris: P. Seghers, 1947.

> McCarthy, Albert J. *Louis Armstrong.* New York: A. S. Barnes and Company, 1961.

> Panassié, Hugues. *Louis Armstrong.* Paris: Editions de Belvédère, 1947.

Jacob Avshalomov

> Bergsma, William. "The Music of Jacob Avshalomov." *American Composers Alliance Bulletin,* Vol. 5, No. 3, 1956.

Frederick Ayres
>   Upton, William Treat. "Frederick Ayres." *Musical Quarterly,* January, 1932.

Samuel Barber
>   Broder, Nathan. *Samuel Barber.* New York: G. Schirmer, Inc., 1954.
>   —— "The Music of Samuel Barber." *Musical Quarterly,* Vol. 34, No. 3 (July, 1948).
>   Horan, Robert. "Samuel Barber." *Modern Music,* March–April, 1943.

William "Count" Basie
>   Horricks, Raymond. *Count Basie and his Orchestra, Its Music and Its Musicians.* London: Victor Gollancz, Ltd., 1957.

Mrs. H. H. A. Beach
>   Tuthill, Burnet C. "Mrs. H. H. A. Beach." *Musical Quarterly,* July, 1940.

John J. Becker
>   Riegger, Wallingford. "John J. Becker." *American Composers Alliance Bulletin,* Vol. 9, No. 1, 1959.

Harry Belafonte
>   Shaw, Arnold. *Belafonte, an Unauthorized Biography.* Philadelphia: Chilton Company, 1960.

Nicolai T. Berezowsky
>   Berezowsky, Alice. *Duet with Nicky.* Philadelphia: J. B. Lippincott Company, 1943.

Arthur Berger
>   Glanville-Hicks, Peggy. "Arthur Berger." *American Composers Alliance Bulletin,* Vol. 3, No. 1 (Spring, 1953).

Irving Berlin
>   Ewen, David. *The Story of Irving Berlin.* New York: Holt, Rinehart and Winston, 1950.
>   Woollcott, Alexander. *The Story of Irving Berlin.* New York: G. P. Putnam's Sons, 1925.

Herman Berlinski
>   Kayden, Mildred. "The Music of Herman Berlinski." *American Composers Alliance Bulletin,* Vol. 8, No. 3, 1959.

Leonard Bernstein

>   Briggs, John. *Leonard Bernstein; the Man, His Work, and His World.* Cleveland, Ohio: World Publishing Company, 1961.
>
>   Ewen, David. *Leonard Bernstein, a Biography for Young People.* Philadelphia: Chilton Company, 1960.
>
>   Holde, Artur. *Leonard Bernstein.* Berlin: Rembrandt Verlag, 1961.
>
>   Schubart, Mark A. "Triple-Note Man of Music." *New York Times Magazine,* January 28, 1945.

William Billings

>   Barbour, James M. *The Church Music of William Billings.* East Lansing: Michigan State University Press, 1960.
>
>   Goldberg, Isaac. "The First American Musician." *American Mercury,* Vol. XIV, pp. 67–75.
>
>   Lindstrom, Carl E. "William Billings and His Times." *Musical Quarterly,* October, 1939.
>
>   Pierce, Edwin Hall. "The Rise and Fall of the 'Fugue-Tune' in America." *Musical Quarterly,* April, 1930.

Gordon Binkerd

>   Hagen, Dorothy V. "Gordon Binkerd." *American Composers Alliance Bulletin,* Vol. 10, No. 3 (September, 1962).

Arthur Bird

>   Loring, William C., Junior. "Arthur Bird, American." *Musical Quarterly,* January, 1943.

James Bland

>   Daly, John J. *A Song in his Heart.* Philadelphia: J. C. Winston Co., 1951.

Philip Paul Bliss

>   Whittle, Daniel W., editor. *Memoirs of Philip P. Bliss.* New York: A. S. Barnes and Company, 1877.

Marc Blitzstein

>   Blitzstein, Marc. "Towards a New Form." *Musical Quarterly,* April, 1934.

Ernest Bloch

>   Gatti, G. M. "Ernest Bloch." *Musical Quarterly,* January, 1921.

Rosenfeld, Paul. *Musical Chronicle*. New York: Harcourt, Brace and Company, 1923.

—— *Musical Portraits*. New York: Harcourt, Brace and Company, 1923.

Sessions, Roger. "Ernest Bloch." *Modern Music*, November, 1927.

Stackpole, Ralph. "Portraits of Ernest Bloch." *Modern Music*, November, 1927.

Carrie Jacobs Bond

Bond, Carrie Jacobs. *The Roads of Melody*. New York: D. Appleton and Company, 1927.

Dudley Buck

A Complete Bibliography of His Works. New York: G. Schirmer, Inc., (*ca.*) 1910.

Ole Bull

Bull, Sara Chapman. *Ole Bull, A Memoir*. Boston: Houghton Mifflin Company, 1883.

Smith, Mortimer B. *The Life of Ole Bull*. Princeton, New Jersey: Princeton University Press, 1943.

Cecil Burleigh

Howard, John Tasker. *Cecil Burleigh*. New York: Carl Fischer, Inc., 1929.

Charles Wakefield Cadman

Sanford-Tefft, Lulu. *Little Intimate Stories of Charles Wakefield Cadman*. Hollywood, California: David Graham Fischer Corporation, 1926.

John Cage

Henmar Press, Inc. *John Cage*. New York: Henmar Press, 1962.

Hoagy Carmichael

Carmichael, Hoagy. *The Stardust Road*. New York: Holt, Rinehart and Winston, 1946.

—— *Sometimes I Wonder*. New York: Farrar, Straus & Giroux, 1965.

John Alden Carpenter

Borowski, Felix. "John Alden Carpenter." *Musical Quarterly*, October, 1930.

Downes, Olin. "John Alden Carpenter." *Musical Quarterly*, October, 1930.

Howard, John Tasker. "John Alden Carpenter." *Modern Music*, November–December, 1931.

Rosenfeld, Paul. *Musical Chronicle*. New York: Harcourt, Brace and Company, 1923.

Benjamin Carr

Redway, Virginia Larkin. "The Carrs, American Music Publishers." *Musical Quarterly*, January, 1932.

Elliott Carter

Goldman, Richard F. "The Music of Elliott Carter." *Musical Quarterly*, Vol. 43, No. 2 (April, 1957).

Skulsky, Abraham. "Elliott Carter." *American Composers Alliance Bulletin*, Vol. 3, No. 2 (Summer, 1953).

Norman Cazden

Haufrecht, Herbert. "The Writings of Norman Cazden: Composer and Musicologist." *American Composers Alliance Bulletin*, Vol. 8, No. 2, 1959.

George W. Chadwick

Engel, Carl. "George W. Chadwick." *Musical Quarterly*, July, 1924. (Reprinted in pamphlet form by the New England Conservatory of Music, Boston.)

Langley, Allen Lincoln. "Chadwick and the New England Conservatory of Music." *Musical Quarterly*, January, 1935.

Chou Wen-chung

Slonimsky, Nicholas. "Chou Wen-chung." *American Composers Alliance Bulletin*, Vol. 9, No. 4, 1961.

F. Melius Christiansen

Bergmann, Leola. *Music Master of the Middle West; the Story of F. Melius Christiansen and the St. Olaf Choir*. Minneapolis: University of Minnesota Press, 1944.

Henry Leland Clarke

Verrall, John. "Henry Leland Clarke." *American Composers Alliance Bulletin*, Vol. 9, No. 3, 1960.

Van Cliburn

Chasins, Abram, and Villa Stiles. *The Van Cliburn Legend*. Garden City, New York: Doubleday and Company, 1959.

Aaron Copland

Berger, Arthur. *Aaron Copland*. New York: Oxford University Press, 1953.

French, Alfred. "Aaron Copland, a Portrait." *Modern Music*, March, 1926.

Goldman, Richard F. "Aaron Copland." *Musical Quarterly*, Vol. 47, No. 1 (January, 1961).

Hill, Edward Burlingame. "Copland's Concerto in Boston." *Modern Music*, May, 1927.

Kirkpatrick, John. "Aaron Copland's Piano Sonata." *Modern Music*, May–June, 1942.

Smith, Julia F. *Aaron Copland, His Work and Contribution to American Music*. New York: E. P. Dutton and Company, 1955.

Sternfeld, Frederick W. "Copland as a Film Composer." *Musical Quarterly*, Vol. 37, No. 2 (April, 1951).

Thomson, Virgil. "Aaron Copland." *Modern Music*, January–February, 1932.

Henry Cowell

Gerschefski, Edwin. "Henry Cowell." *American Composers Alliance Bulletin*, Vol. 3, No. 4 (Winter, 1953–54).

Harrison, Jay S. "Cowell: Peck's Bad Boy of Music." *American Composers Alliance Bulletin*, Vol. 3, No. 4 (Winter, 1953–54).

Weisgall, Hugo. "The Music of Henry Cowell." *Musical Quarterly*, Vol. 45, No. 4 (October, 1959).

Bainbridge Crist

Howard, John Tasker. *Bainbridge Crist*. New York: Carl Fischer, Inc., 1929.

Bing Crosby

Crosby, Bing, and Pete Martin. *Call Me Lucky*. New York: Simon and Schuster, 1953.

Crosby, Edward J. *The Story of Bing Crosby*. Cleveland, Ohio: World Publishing Company, 1946.

Mise, John T. H. *Bing Crosby and the Bing Crosby Style*. Chicago: Who's Who in Music, Inc., 1948.

Ulanov, Barry. *The Incredible Crosby*. New York: Whittlesey House, 1948.

Walter Damrosch

Damrosch, Walter. *My Musical Life.* New York: Charles Scribner's Sons, 1923.

Henderson, W. J. "Walter Damrosch." *Musical Quarterly,* January, 1932.

Miles Davis

James, Michael. *Miles Davis.* London: Cassell and Company, Ltd., 1961.

Reginald De Koven

De Koven, Mrs. Reginald. *A Musician and His Wife.* New York: Harper and Brothers, 1926.

Norman Dello Joio

Downes, Edward. "The Music of Norman Dello Joio." *Musical Quarterly,* Vol. 48, No. 2 (April, 1962).

Richard Donovan

Frankenstein, Alfred. "Richard Donovan." *American Composers Alliance Bulletin,* Vol. 5, No. 4, 1956.

Paul Dresser

Dreiser, Theodore, editor. *The Songs of Paul Dresser.* New York: Boni and Liveright, 1927.

Vernon Duke

Duke, Vernon. *Passport to Paris.* Boston: Little, Brown and Company, 1955.

James P. Dunn

Howard, John Tasker. *James P. Dunn.* New York: J. Fischer and Brother, 1925.

John Sullivan Dwight

Waters, Edward N. "John Sullivan Dwight, First American Critic of Music." *Musical Quarterly,* January, 1935.

Jacob Eckhard

Williams, George W. "Jacob Eckhard and his Choirmasters Book." *Journal of the American Musicological Society,* Vol. 7, No. 1 (Spring, 1954).

Duke Ellington

Gammon, Peter. *Duke Ellington and His Music.* New York: Roy Publishers, 1958.

Lambert, George E. *Duke Ellington.* New York: Barnes, 1961.

—— *Duke Ellington*. London: Cassell and Company, Ltd., 1959.

Ulanov, Barry. *Duke Ellington*. New York: Creative Age Press, 1946.

Daniel Decatur Emmett

Galbreath, Charles B. *Daniel Decatur Emmett, Author of Dixie*. Columbus, Ohio: F. J. Heer, 1904.

Vivian Fine

Riegger, Wallingford. "The Music of Vivian Fine." *American Composers Alliance Bulletin*, Vol. 8, No. 1, 1958.

Ella Fitzgerald

Jungermann, Jimmy. *Ella Fitzgerald; ein Porträt*. Wetzlar: Pegasus Verlag, 1960.

William Flanagan

Albee, Edward, and Ned Rorem. "William Flanagan." *American Composers Alliance Bulletin*, Vol. 9, No. 4, 1961.

Stephen Foster

Foster, Morrison. *My Brother Stephen*. Indianapolis, Indiana: Privately printed for the Foster Hall Collection, 1932.

—— *Songs and Musical Compositions of Stephen Collins Foster*. Pittsburgh, Pennsylvania, 1896.

Fuld, James. *A Pictorial Bibliography of the First Editions of Stephen C. Foster*. Philadelphia, Musical Americana, 1957.

Howard, John Tasker. "Newly Discovered Fosteriana." *Musical Quarterly*, January, 1935.

—— *Stephen Foster, America's Troubadour*. New York: Thomas Y. Crowell Company, 1934. (Reprint edition, New York: Tudor Publishing Company; reprint edition, New York: Thomas Y. Crowell Company, 1953; reprint edition, New York: Apollo, 1962.)

Jackson, George Pullen. "Stephen Foster's Debt to American Folk-Song." *Musical Quarterly*, April, 1936.

Milligan, Harold V. *Stephen Collins Foster, A Biography*. New York: G. Schirmer, Inc., 1920.

Morneweck, Evelyn Foster. *Chronicles of Stephen Foster's Family*. 2 volumes. Pittsburgh, Pennsylvania: Pittsburgh University Press, 1944.

Purdy, Claire Lee. *He Heard America Sing; the Story of Stephen Foster*. New York: Julian Messner, Inc., 1940.

Songs, Compositions and Arrangements by Stephen Collins Foster. Foster Hall Reproductions. Indianapolis: Privately printed, 1933.

Sonneck, O. G., and Walter Whittlesey. *Catalogue of the First Editions of Stephen C. Foster*. Washington, D.C.: Library of Congress, Government Printing Office, 1915.

Walters, Raymond W. *Stephen Foster: Youth's Golden Gleam; a Sketch of His Life and Background in Cincinnati, 1846–1850*. Princeton, New Jersey: Princeton University Press, 1936.

Johan Franco

Hoskins, William. "Johan Franco: the Music and the Man." *American Composers Alliance Bulletin*, Vol. 8, No. 3, 1959.

William Henry Fry

Upton, William Treat. *William Henry Fry, American Journalist and Composer-Critic*. New York: Thomas Y. Crowell Company, 1954.

—— *The Musical Works of William Henry Fry in the Collections of the Library Company of Philadelphia*. Philadelphia: 1946.

Edwin Gerschefski

McRae, Donald. "Edwin Gerschefski." *American Composers Alliance Bulletin*, Vol. 10, No. 1, 1961.

George Gershwin

Armitage, Merle. *George Gershwin*. New York: Longmans, Green and Company, 1938.

—— *George Gershwin, Man and Legend*. New York: Duell, Sloan and Pearce, 1958.

Ewen, David. *A Journey into Greatness; the Life and Music of George Gershwin*. New York: Holt, Rinehart and Winston, 1956.

—— *The Story of George Gershwin*. New York: Holt, Rinehart and Winston, 1943.

Gershwin, George. *George Gershwin's Song Book*. New York: Simon and Schuster, 1930.

Goldberg, Isaac. *George Gershwin, A Study in American Music.* New York: Simon and Schuster, 1931. (New edition, New York: Frederick Ungar Publishing Company, 1958.)

Jablonski, Edward, and Lawrence D. Stewart. *The Gershwin Years.* Garden City, New York: Doubleday and Company, 1958.

Jacobi, Frederick. "The Future of Gershwin." *Modern Music,* November–December, 1937.

Longolius, Christian. *George Gershwin.* Berlin: Max Hesses Verlag, 1959.

Payne, Pierre S. R. *Gershwin.* New York: Pyramid Books, 1960. (Reprint edition, London: Hale, 1962.)

Schipke, Brigitte. *George Gershwin und die Welt seiner Musik.* Freiburg im Breisgau: Drei Ringe Musikverlag, 1955.

Schoorl, Bob. *George Gershwin; van Broadway tot Carnegie-hall.* Amsterdam: A. J. G. Strengholt, 1952.

Schwinger, Wolfram. *Er komponierte Amerika; George Gershwin, Mensch und Werk.* Berlin: Der Morgen, 1960.

Thomson, Virgil. "George Gershwin." *Modern Music,* November–December, 1935.

Mariam Gideon

Perle, George. "The Music of Mariam Gideon." *American Composers Alliance Bulletin,* Vol. 7, No. 4, 1958.

Henry F. Gilbert

Carter, Elliott. "American Figure, with Landscape." *Modern Music,* May–June, 1943.

Downes, Olin. "An American Composer." *Musical Quarterly,* January, 1918.

Dizzy Gillespie

Götze, Werner. *Dizzy Gillespie, ein Porträt.* Wetzlar: Pegasus Verlag, 1960.

James, Michael. *Dizzy Gillespie.* London: Cassell and Company, Ltd., 1959.

Patrick Gilmore

Darlington, Marwood. *Irish Orpheus; the Life of Patrick S. Gilmore, Bandmaster Extraordinary.* Philadelphia: Maney-Klein, 1956.

Gilmore, P. S. *History of the National Peace Jubilee and Great Musical Festival*. Boston: For the author, 1871.

Roger Goeb

Luening, Otto. "Roger Goeb." *American Composers Alliance Bulletin*, Vol. 2, No. 2 (June, 1952).

Benny Goodman

Connor, Donald R. *B. G.—Off the Record; a Bio-discography of Benny Goodman*. Fairless Hills, Pennsylvania: Gaildonna Publishers, 1958.

Louis Moreau Gottschalk

Arpin, Paul. *Life of Louis Moreau Gottschalk*, translated from the French by H. C. Watson. New York, 1852.

Doyle, John G. *The Piano Music of Louis Moreau Gottschalk (1829–1869)*. Ann Arbor, Michigan: University Microfilms (L.C. No. Mic. 61–317), 1960. Dissertation: New York University.

Fors, Luis Ricardo. *Louis Moreau Gottschalk*. Havana, 1880.

Hensel, Octavia. *Life and Letters of Louis Moreau Gottschalk*. Boston: Oliver Ditson Company, 1870.

Howard, John Tasker. "Louis Moreau Gottschalk, as Portrayed by Himself." *Musical Quarterly*, January, 1932.

Loggins, Vernon. *Where the World Ends; the Life of Louis Moreau Gottschalk*. Baton Rouge: University of Louisiana Press, 1958.

Peterson, Robert Evans, translator. *Notes of a Pianist by Louis Moreau Gottschalk*. Philadelphia: J. B. Lippincott Company, 1881.

Percy Grainger

Hughes, Charles W. "Percy Grainger, Cosmopolitan Composer." *Musical Quarterly*, April, 1937.

Gottlieb Graupner

Stone, Mrs. George Whitefield. Manuscript *Biography of Graupner* in Public Library of the city of Boston.

Charles Tomlinson Griffes

Bauer, Marion. "Charles T. Griffes as I Remember Him." *Musical Quarterly*, July, 1943.

Howard, John Tasker. *Charles Tomlinson Griffes*. New York:
    G. Schirmer, Inc., 1923.

Maisel, Edward M. *Charles T. Griffes; The Life of an Ameri-
    can Composer*. New York: Alfred A. Knopf, 1943.

Upton, William Treat. "The Songs of Charles T. Griffes."
    Musical Quarterly, July, 1923.

Louis Gruenberg

Kramer, A. Walter. "Louis Gruenberg." *Modern Music*,
    November–December, 1930.

Woody Guthrie

Guthrie, Woody. *Bound for Glory*. New York: E. P. Dutton and
    Company, 1943.

Henry K. Hadley

Boardman, Herbert R. *Henry Hadley, Ambassador of Harmony*.
    Emory University, Georgia: Banner Press, 1932.

William C. Handy

Handy, William C. *Father of the Blues; An Autobiography*.
    New York: The Macmillan Company, 1941.

Howard Hanson

Alter, Martha. "Howard Hanson." *Modern Music*, January–
    February, 1941.

Tuthill, Burnet C. "Howard Hanson." *Musical Quarterly*, April,
    1936.

Charles K. Harris

Harris, Charles K. *After the Ball, Forty Years of Melody; An
    Autobiography*. New York: Frank-Maurice, Inc., 1926.

Roy Harris

Farwell, Arthur. "Roy Harris." *Musical Quarterly*, January,
    1932.

Piston, Walter. "Roy Harris." *Modern Music*, January–Febru-
    ary, 1934.

Slonimsky, Nicholas. "Roy Harris." *Musical Quarterly*, Vol. 33,
    No. 1 (January, 1947).

Lou Harrison

Yates, Peter. "Lou Harrison." *American Composers Alliance
    Bulletin*, Vol. 9, No. 2, 1960.

Herbert Haufrecht

Cazden, Norman. "Herbert Haufrecht: the Composer and the Man." *American Composers Alliance Bulletin,* Vol. 8, No. 4, 1959.

Roland Hays

Helm, MacKinley. *Angel Mo' and Her Son, Roland Hays.* Boston: Little, Brown and Company, 1942.

Anton Philip Heinrich

Upton, William Treat. *Anthony Philip Heinrich.* New York: Columbia University Press, 1939.

Victor Herbert

Kaye, Joseph. *Victor Herbert.* New York: G. H. Watt, 1931.

Purdy, Claire Lee. *Victor Herbert, American Music Master.* New York: Julian Messner, Inc., 1945.

Waters, Edward N. *Victor Herbert, His Life and Work.* New York: The Macmillan Company, 1955.

Edward Burlingame Hill

Smith, George H. L. "Edward Burlingame Hill." *Modern Music,* November–December, 1938.

Sidney Homer

Homer, Sidney. *My Wife and I; The Story of Louise and Sidney Homer.* New York: The Macmillan Company, 1939.

Thorpe, Henry Colin. "The Songs of Sidney Homer." *Musical Quarterly,* January, 1931.

Francis Hopkinson

Hastings, George E. *The Life and Works of Francis Hopkinson.* Chicago: The University Press, 1926.

Milligan, Harold V. *Colonial Love Lyrics: Six Songs by Francis Hopkinson.* Boston: The Arthur P. Schmidt Company, 1919.

————— *The First American Composer: Six Songs by Francis Hopkinson.* Boston: The Arthur P. Schmidt Company, 1918.

Sonneck, O. G. *Francis Hopkinson and James Lyon.* Washington, D.C.: H. L. McQueen, 1905.

Alan Hovhaness

Daniel, Oliver. "Alan Hovhaness." *American Composers Alliance Bulletin*, Vol. 2, No. 3 (October, 1952).

Hutchinson Family

Brink, Carol. *Harps in the Wind; the Story of the Singing Hutchinsons*. New York: The Macmillan Company, 1947.

Jordan, Philip D. *Singin' Yankees*. Minneapolis: University of Minnesota Press, 1946.

Charles Ives

Bellamann, Henry. "Charles Ives: The Man and His Music." *Musical Quarterly*, January, 1933.

——— "The Music of Charles Ives." *Pro-Musica Quarterly*, March, 1927.

Carter, Elliott. "Ives Today: His Vision and Challenge." *Modern Music*, May–June, 1944.

Cowell, Henry. "Charles Ives." *Modern Music*, November–December, 1932.

——— and Sidney R. Cowell. *Charles Ives*. New York: Oxford University Press, 1955.

Grunfeld, Frederic. "Charles Ives—Yankee Rebel." *American Composers Alliance Bulletin*, Vol. 4, No. 3, 1955.

Rosenfeld, Paul. "Ives' Concord Sonata." *Modern Music*, January–February, 1939.

Frederick Jacobi

Diamond, David. "Frederick Jacobi." *Modern Music*, March–April, 1937.

Hunter Johnson

Monaco, Richard A. *The Music of Hunter Johnson*. Ann Arbor, Michigan: University Microfilms (L.C. No. Mic. 61–6663), 1960. Dissertation: Cornell University.

Lochrem Johnson

Freed, Arnold. "Lochrem Johnson: Conservative Rebel." *American Composers Alliance Bulletin*, Vol. 8, No. 4, 1959.

Louis Antoine Jullien

Jullien's Concert Book. New York: J. Darcie, 1853.

Ulysses Kay

    Slonimsky, Nicholas. "Ulysses Kay." *American Composers Alliance Bulletin*, Vol. 7, No. 1 (Fall, 1957).

Jerome Kern

    Adams, Franklin P. "Words and Music." *The New Yorker*, February 8, 1930.

    Ewen, David. *The Story of Jerome Kern*. New York: Holt, Rinehart and Winston, 1953.

    —— *The World of Jerome Kern; a Biography*. New York: Holt, Rinehart and Winston, 1960.

    Simon, Robert. "Jerome Kern." *Modern Music*, January, 1929.

Harrison Kerr

    Ringer, Alexander. "Harrison Kerr: Composer and Educator." *American Composers Alliance Bulletin*, Vol. 8, No. 2, 1959.

Leon Kirchner

    Ringer, Alexander. "Leon Kirchner." *Musical Quarterly*, Vol. 43, No. 1 (January, 1957).

Ellis Kohs

    Kohs, Ellis B. "Thoughts from the Work Bench." *American Composers Alliance Bulletin*, Vol. 6, No. 1 (Autumn, 1956).

Serge Koussevitsky

    Leichtentritt, Hugo. *Serge Koussevitsky, the Boston Symphony Orchestra and the New American Music*. Cambridge, Massachusetts: Harvard University Press, 1946.

    Smith, Moses. *Koussevitsky*. New York: Allen, Towne and Heath, 1947.

A. Walter Kramer

    Howard, John Tasker. *A. Walter Kramer*. New York: J. Fischer and Brother, 1926.

Eastwood Lane

    Howard, John Tasker. *Eastwood Lane*. New York: J. Fischer and Brother, 1925.

Sidney Lanier

    Whittemore, Myrtle. *The Flute Concerto of Sidney Lanier*. New York: Pageant Press, 1953.

Oscar Levant

   Levant, Oscar. *A Smattering of Ignorance.* Garden City, New
      York: Doubleday and Company, 1940.

Jenny Lind

   Benét, Laura. *Enchanting Jenny Lind.* New York: Dodd, Mead
      and Company, 1939.
   Bulman, Joan. *Jenny Lind, a Biography.* London: Barrie, 1956.
   Shultz, Gladys. *Jenny Lind: the Swedish Nightingale.* Phila-
      delphia: J. B. Lippincott Company, 1962.
   Wagenknecht, Charles E. *Jenny Lind.* Boston: Houghton
      Mifflin Company, 1931.
   Werner, M. R. *Barnum.* New York: Harcourt, Brace and Com-
      pany, 1923.

Normand Lockwood

   Lynn, George. "Normand Lockwood and Choral Music." *Ameri-
      can Composers Alliance Bulletin,* Vol. 6, No. 4, 1957.
   McDowell, John. "A Note on Several Facets of Normand
      Lockwood's Music." *American Composers Alliance Bulletin,*
      Vol. 6, No. 4, 1957.

Charles Martin Loeffler

   Engel, Carl. "Charles Martin Loeffler." *Musical Quarterly,* July,
      1925.
   Gilman, Lawrence. *Phases of Modern Music.* New York: Harper
      and Brothers, 1904.
   Hill, Edward Burlingame. "Charles Martin Loeffler." *Modern
      Music,* November–December, 1935.
   Rosenfeld, Paul. *Musical Portraits.* New York: Harcourt, Brace
      and Company, 1923.

Otto Luening

   Beeson, Jack. "Otto Luening." *American Composers Alliance
      Bulletin,* Vol. 3, No. 3 (Autumn, 1953).

James Lyon

   Alexander, Samuel Davies. *Princeton College During the 18th
      Century.* New York: A. D. F. Randolph and Company,
      1872.
   Edwards, George Thornton. *Music and Musicians of Maine.*
      Portland, Maine: The Southworth Press, 1928.

Sonneck, O. G. *Francis Hopkinson and James Lyon.* Washington, D.C.: H. L. McQueen, 1905.

Robert McBride

McKelvey, Nat. "Robert McBride: Practical Music Maker." *American Composers Alliance Bulletin,* Vol. 8, No. 1, 1958.

Edward MacDowell

Brown, Abbie Farwell. *The Boyhood of Edward MacDowell.* New York: Frederick A. Stokes and Company, 1924.

Brown, Rollo Walter. *Lonely Americans.* New York: Coward-McCann, Inc., 1929.

Butler, Nicholas Murray. "Columbia and the Department of Music." New York: The University, 1904. (Reprinted from *The New York Times,* February 8, 1904.)

Currier, T. P. "MacDowell as I Knew Him." *Musical Quarterly,* January, 1915.

Erskine, John. "MacDowell at Columbia: Some Recollections." *Musical Quarterly,* October, 1942.

Garland, Hamlin. "Roadside Meetings of a Literary Nomad." *The Bookman,* March, 1930.

Gilbert, Henry F. "Personal Recollections of Edward MacDowell." *New Music Review,* Vol. II, No. 132, 1912.

Gilman, Lawrence. *Edward MacDowell, A Study.* New York: John Lane Company, 1908.

—— *Phases of Modern Music.* New York: Harper and Brothers, 1904.

Hier, Ethel G. *The Boyhood and Youth of Edward MacDowell.* Peterboro, New Hampshire: The Nubanusit Press, 1926.

Humiston, William H. *MacDowell.* New York: Breitkopf and Haertel, 1921.

MacDowell, Edward. *Critical and Historical Essays.* Boston: The A. P. Schmidt Company, 1912.

MacDowell, Marian. "MacDowell's 'Peterboro Idea.'" *Musical Quarterly,* January, 1932.

—— *Random Notes on Edward MacDowell and His Music.* Boston: A. P. Schmidt Company, 1957.

McWhood, Leonard. "Edward MacDowell at Columbia University." *Music Teachers' National Association Proceedings,* 1923.

Matthews, James Brander. *Commemorative Tributes to Edward MacDowell.* New York: American Academy of Arts and Letters, 1922.

Page, Elizabeth Fry. *Edward MacDowell, His Work and Ideals.* New York: Dodge Publishing Company, 1910.

Porte, John F. *Edward MacDowell, A Great American Tone Poet.* London: K. Paul, Trench, Trubner and Company, 1922.

Sinclair, Upton. "MacDowell." *American Mercury,* Vol. VII (1926), pp. 50–54.

Sonneck, O. G. *Catalogue of the First Editions of Edward MacDowell.* Washington, D.C.: Library of Congress, Government Printing Office, 1917.

———— *Suum Cuique (MacDowell vs. MacDowell).* New York: G. Schirmer, Inc., 1916.

Daniel Gregory Mason

Klein, Sr. Mary Justina. *The Contribution of Daniel Gregory Mason to American Music.* Washington, D.C.: Catholic University of America Press, 1957.

Tuthill, Burnet C. "Daniel Gregory Mason." *Musical Quarterly,* Vol. 34, No. 1 (January, 1948).

Lowell Mason

Birge, Edward Bailey. *History of Public School Music in the United States.* Boston: Oliver Ditson Company, 1928.

Boston Academy of Music. *Annual Reports.* Boston: Perkins and Marvin, 1833–46.

Boston School Committee. *Report* (upon the petition praying that music be introduced into the public schools of the city). Boston, 1837.

Lucas, G. W. *Remarks on the Musical Conventions in Boston.* Northampton, Massachusetts: The author, 1844.

Mason, Henry L. *Hymn-Tunes of Lowell Mason; A Bibliography.* Cambridge, Massachusetts: The University Press, 1944.

Proceedings of the Musical Convention Assembled in Boston, August 16, 1838. Boston: Kidder and Wright, 1838.

Rich, Arthur L. *Lowell Mason, "The Father of Singing Among the Children."* Chapel Hill, North Carolina: University of North Carolina Press, 1946.

Seward, T. F. *The Educational Work of Lowell Mason.* 1879.

William Mason

Mason, William. *Memories of a Musical Life.* New York: The Century Company, 1902.

Glenn Miller

Bedwell, Stephen F. *A Glenn Miller Discography and Biography.* Revised edition. London: Glenn Miller Appreciation Society, 1956.

Douglas Moore

Luening, Otto. "Douglas Moore." *Modern Music,* May–June, 1943.

Ferdinand "Jelly Roll" Morton

Williams, Martin T. *Jelly Roll Morton.* London: Cassell and Company, Ltd., 1962.

Ethelbert Nevin

Howard, John Tasker. *Ethelbert Nevin.* New York: Thomas Y. Crowell Company, 1935.

Rogers, Francis. "Some Memories of Ethelbert Nevin." *Musical Quarterly,* July, 1917.

Thompson, Vance. *The Life of Ethelbert Nevin.* Boston: Boston Music Company, 1913.

Dika Newlin

Wolff, Konrad. "Dika Newlin." *American Composers Alliance Bulletin,* Vol. 10, No. 4 (December, 1962).

Leo Ornstein

Buchanan, C. L. "Ornstein and Modern Music." *Musical Quarterly,* April, 1918.

Martens, Frederick L. *Leo Ornstein.* New York: Breitkopf and Haertel, 1918.

Rosenfeld, Paul. *Musical Chronicle.* New York: Harcourt, Brace and Company, 1923.

———— *Musical Portraits*. New York: Harcourt, Brace and Company, 1923.

Hall Overton

Cohen, David. "Hall Overton." *American Composers Alliance Bulletin*, Vol. 10, No. 4 (December, 1962).

Charles Theodore Pachelbel.

Redway, Virginia L. "Charles Theodore Pachelbel, Musical Emigrant." *Journal of the American Musicological Society*, Vol. 5, No. 1 (Spring, 1952).

John Knowles Paine

Howe, Mark Anthony De Wolfe. "John Knowles Paine." *Musical Quarterly*, July, 1939.

Robert Palmer

Austin, William. "The Music of Robert Palmer." *Musical Quarterly*, Vol. 42, No. 1 (January, 1956).

Charlie Parker

Harrison, Max. *Charlie Parker*. New York: A. S. Barnes and Company, 1961.

Reisner, Robert G. *Bird: the Legend of Charlie Parker*. New York: The Citadel Press, 1962.

Horatio Parker

A Brief Tribute to the Life and Work of Dr. Horatio Parker. New York: Silver, Burdett Company, 1925.

Chadwick, George W. *Horatio Parker*. New Haven, Connecticut: Yale University Press, 1921.

"Horatio Parker." *Musical Times*, London, September 1, 1902.

Krehbiel, H. E. "Parker's Hora Novissima and Bach's Magnificat in D." *New Music Review*, Vol. IX (1914), pp. 146–47.

Rosenfeld, Paul. *Musical Chronicle* ("The Fate of Mona") New York: Harcourt, Brace and Company, 1923.

Semler, Isabel Parker. *Horatio Parker*. New York: G. P. Putnam's Sons, 1942.

Smith, David Stanley. "A Study of Horatio Parker." *Musical Quarterly*, April, 1930.

George Perle

Weinberg, Henry. "The Music of George Perle." *American*

Composers Alliance Bulletin, Vol. 10, No. 3 (September, 1962).

Vincent Persichetti

Schuman, William. "The Compleat Musician: Vincent Persichetti and Twentieth-Century Harmony." *Musical Quarterly*, Vol. 47, No. 3 (July, 1961).

John Frederick Peter

Rau, Albert G. "John Frederick Peter." *Musical Quarterly*, July, 1937.

Daniel Pinkham

Smith, Warren S. "Daniel Pinkham." *American Composers Alliance Bulletin*, Vol. 10, No. 1, 1961.

Paul A. Pisk

Kennan, Kent. "Paul A. Pisk." *American Composers Alliance Bulletin*, Vol. 9, No. 1, 1959.

Walter Piston

Atkowitz, Israel. "Walter Piston, Classicist." *Modern Music*, January–February, 1936.

Quincy Porter

Boatwright, Howard. "Quincy Porter." *American Composers Alliance Bulletin*, Vol. 6, No. 3, 1957.

Silas G. Pratt

"Silas G. Pratt, American Composer." *American Art Journal*, Vol. LXVII, No. 6. New York: J. Fischer and Brother, 1925.

Alexander Reinagle

Krohn, Ernst C. "Alexander Reinagle as Sonatist." *Musical Quarterly*, January, 1932.

Wallingford Riegger

Becker, John J. "Wallingford Riegger." *American Composers Alliance Bulletin*, Vol. 9, No. 3, 1960.

Carter, Elliott. "Wallingford Riegger." *American Composers Alliance Bulletin*, Vol. 2, No. 1, 1952.

Goldman, Richard F. "The Music of Wallingford Riegger." *Musical Quarterly*. Vol. 36, No. 1 (January, 1950).

Ritchie Family

    Ritchie, Jean. *The Singing Family of the Cumberlands*. New York: Oxford University Press, 1955.

Richard Rodgers

    Ewen, David. *Richard Rodgers*. New York: Holt, Rinehart and Winston, 1957.

    Green, Stanley. *The Rodgers and Hammerstein Story*. New York: The John Day Company, 1963.

    Taylor, Deems. *Some Enchanted Evenings, the Story of Rodgers and Hammerstein*. New York: Harper and Brothers, 1953.

Bernard Rogers

    Diamond, David. "Bernard Rogers." *Musical Quarterly*, Vol. 33, No. 2 (April, 1947).

    Hanson, Howard. "Bernard Rogers." *Modern Music*, March–April, 1945.

Sigmund Romberg

    Arnold, Elliott. *Deep in My Heart, a Story Based on the Life of Sigmund Romberg*. New York: Duell, Sloan & Pearce, 1949.

George Frederick Root

    Root, George F. *The Story of a Musical Life*. Cincinnati, Ohio: The John Church Company, 1891.

Carl Ruggles

    Seeger, Charles. "Carl Ruggles." *Musical Quarterly*, October, 1932.

Alexander Russell

    Howard, John Tasker. *Alexander Russell*. New York: J. Fischer and Brother, 1925.

Henry Russell

    Russell, Henry. *Cheer! Boys, Cheer! Memories of Men and Music*. London: John MacQueen, 1895.

    —— *The Passing Show*. Boston: Little, Brown and Company, 1926.

Lazare Saminsky

    Lazare Saminsky. New York: Bloch Publishing Company, 1930.

    Saleski, Gdal. *Famous Musicians of a Wandering Race*. New York: Bloch Publishing Company, 1927.

Slonimsky, Nicolas. "Lazare Saminsky." *Modern Music,* January–February, 1935.

Ira D. Sankey

Sankey, Ira D. *My Life and Sacred Songs.* London: Hodder and Houghton, 1906.

Daniel Schlesinger

Biographical Notices of Daniel Schlesinger. Extracts from the *New York Mirror* (1839) in the New York Public Library.

William Schroeder

Schroeder, Nikita M. *Our American Composer, a Rhapsodic Biography.* New York: Vantage Press, 1958.

William Schuman

Bernstein, Leonard. "Young American—William Schuman." *Modern Music,* January–February, 1942.

Broder, Nathan. "The Music of William Schuman." *Musical Quarterly,* January, 1945.

Frankenstein, Alfred. "William Schuman." *Modern Music,* November–December, 1944.

Schreiber, Flora R. *William Schuman.* New York: G. Schirmer, 1954.

Tom Scott

Ringo, James. "Some Notes on Tom Scott's Music." *American Composers Alliance Bulletin,* Vol. 6, No. 2, 1957.

Roger Sessions

Brunswick, Mark. "Roger Huntington Sessions." *Modern Music,* May–June, 1933.

Welch, Roy D. "A Symphony Introduces Roger Sessions." *Modern Music,* May, 1927.

Oliver Shaw

Memorial of Oliver Shaw. Providence, Rhode Island: Veteran Citizens' Historical Association, 1884.

William, Thomas. *A Discourse on the Life and Death of Oliver Shaw.* Boston: C. C. P. Moody, 1851.

Arthur Shepherd

Leedy, Denoe. "Arthur Shepherd." *Modern Music,* January–February, 1939.

Newman, William S. "Arthur Shepherd." *Musical Quarterly,*
Vol. 36, No. 2 (April, 1950).

Charles Sanford Skilton
Howard, John Tasker. *Charles Sanford Skilton.* New York:
Carl Fischer, Inc., 1929.

David Stanley Smith
Tuthill, Burnet C. "David Stanley Smith." *Musical Quarterly,*
January, 1942.

O. G. Sonneck
Putnam, Herbert, and Rubin Goldmark. "Remarks at the
Funeral Services." *Musical Quarterly,* January, 1929.

John Philip Sousa
Berger, Kenneth W. *The March King and His Band; the Story
of John Philip Sousa.* New York: Exposition Press, 1957.
Lewiton, Mina. *John Philip Sousa, the March King.* New York:
Didier, 1944.
Lingg, Ann M. *John Philip Sousa.* New York: Holt, Rinehart
and Winston, 1954.
Sousa, John Philip. *Marching Along, An Autobiography.* Boston:
Hale, Cushman and Flint, 1928.

Leo Sowerby
Tuthill, Burnet C. "Leo Sowerby." *Musical Quarterly,* July,
1938.

Albert Spalding
Spalding, Albert. *Rise to Follow, an Autobiography.* New York:
Holt, Rinehart and Winston, 1943.

Halsey Stevens
Pisk, Paul A. "Halsey Stevens." *American Composers Alliance
Bulletin,* Vol. 4, No. 2, 1954.

William Grant Still
Arvey, Verna. *William Grant Still.* New York: J. Fischer and
Brother, 1939.

Deems Taylor
Howard, John Tasker. *Deems Taylor.* New York: J. Fischer and
Brother, 1927.

Jack Teagarden
Waters, Howard J. *Jack Teagarden's Music, His Career, and*

Recordings (Jazz Monographs No. 3). Stanhope, New Jersey: W. C. Allen, 1960.

Theodore Thomas

Rice, Edwin T. "Thomas and Central Park Garden." *Musical Quarterly*, April, 1940.

Russell, Charles Edward. *The American Orchestra and Theodore Thomas.* Garden City, New York: Doubleday, Page and Company, 1927.

Thomas, Rose Fay. *Memoirs of Theodore Thomas.* New York: Moffat, Yard and Company, 1911.

Thomas, Theodore. *A Musical Autobiography* (2 vols.), edited by G. P. Upton. Chicago: A. C. McClurg and Company, 1905.

Randall Thompson

Forbes, Elliot. "The Music of Randall Thompson." *Musical Quarterly*, Vol. 35, No. 1 (January, 1949).

Porter, Quincy. "Randall Thompson." *Modern Music*, May–June, 1942.

Virgil Thomson

Barlow, S. L. M. "Virgil Thomson." *Modern Music*, May–June, 1941.

Glanville-Hicks, Peggy. "Virgil Thomson." *Musical Quarterly*, Vol. 35, No. 2 (April, 1949).

Hoover, Kathleen O., and John Cage. *Virgil Thomson, His Life and Music.* New York: Thomas Yoseloff, Publisher, 1959.

Rudy Vallée

Vallée, Rudy. *Vagabond Dreams Come True.* New York: E. P. Dutton and Company, 1930.

Edgar Varèse

Cowell, Henry. "The Music of Edgar Varèse." *Modern Music*, January, 1928.

Hirsch, Stefan. "Portrait of Varèse." *Modern Music*, January, 1928.

John Verrall

Beale, James. "The Music of John Verrall." *American Composers Alliance Bulletin*, Vol. 7, No. 4, 1958.

Bernard Wagenaar

Fuller, Donald. "Bernard Wagenaar." *Modern Music*, May–June, 1944.

Robert Ward

Stambler, Bernard. "Robert Ward." *American Composers Alliance Bulletin*, Vol. 4, No. 4, 1955.

Ben Weber

O'Hara, Frank. "About Ben Weber." *American Composers Alliance Bulletin*, Vol. 5, No. 2, 1955.

Hugo Weisgall

Rochberg, George. "Hugo Weisgall." *American Composers Alliance Bulletin*, Vol. 7, No. 2, 1958.

Adolph Weiss

Cowell, Henry. "Adolph Weiss." *American Composers Alliance Bulletin*, Vol. 7, No. 3, 1958.

Emerson Whithorne

Hammond, Richard. "Emerson Whithorne." *Modern Music*, January–February, 1931.

Howard, John Tasker. *Emerson Whithorne*. New York: Carl Fischer, Inc., 1929.

Arthur Whiting

Mason, Daniel G. "Arthur Whiting." *Musical Quarterly*, January, 1937.

Septimus Winner

Claghorne, Charles Eugene. *The Mocking Bird; the Life and Diary of Its Author, Septimus Winner*. Philadelphia: The Magee Press, 1937.

Henry Clay Work

Work, Bertram G., compiler. *Songs of Henry Clay Work*. New York: J. J. Little and Ives Company, 1920.

COLLECTIVE BIOGRAPHY

Apthorp, William Foster. *Musicians and Music Lovers*. New York: Charles Scribner's Sons, 1908.

Aronson, Rudolph. *Theatrical and Musical Memoirs*. New York: McBride, Nast and Company, 1913.

Bakeless, Katharine. *Story-Lives of American Composers*. New York: Frederick A. Stokes, 1941.

—— *In the Big Time; Career Stories of American Entertainers*. Philadelphia: J. B. Lippincott Company, 1953.

Baker, Theodore, editor. *Biographical Dictionary of Musicians*. New York: G. Schirmer, Inc., 1919. (Revised edition, 1940.)

Barnes, Edwin N. C. *American Women in Creative Music*. Washington, D.C.: Music Education Publications, 1936.

Bispham, David. *A Quaker Singer's Recollections*. New York: The Macmillan Company, 1921.

Cowell, Henry, editor. *American Composers on American Music*. Stanford, California: Stanford University Press, 1933. (Reprint edition, New York: Frederick Ungar Publishing Company, 1962.)

Cuney-Hare, Maud. *Negro Musicians and Their Music*. Washington, D.C.: The Associated Publishers, 1936.

Edmunds, John. *Some Twentieth-Century American Composers; a Selective Bibliography*. 2 volumes. New York: New York Public Library, 1959–60.

Ewen, David. *American Composers Today*. New York: The H. W. Wilson Company, 1949.

Finck, Henry T. *My Adventures in the Golden Age of Music*. New York: Funk and Wagnalls Company, 1926.

Foote, Arthur. "A Bostonian Remembers." *Musical Quarterly*. January, 1937.

Franko, Sam. *Chords and Discords; Memoirs and Musings of an American Musician*. New York: The Viking Press, 1938.

Freer, Eleanor Everest. *Recollections and Reflections of an American Composer*. New York: Musical Advance Publishing Company, 1929.

Goss, Madeline. *Modern Music Makers: Contemporary American Composers*. New York: E. P. Dutton and Company, 1952.

Grove's Dictionary of Music and Musicians (American Supplement edited by W. S. Pratt). New York: The Macmillan Company, 1920 and 1928.

Handy, William C. *Negro Authors and Composers of the United States*. New York: Handy Brothers Music Company, 1938.

Hewitt, John Hill. *Shadows on the Wall*. Baltimore, Maryland: Trumbull Brothers, 1877.

Hoffman, Richard. *Some Musical Recollections of Fifty Years*. New York: Charles Scribner's Sons, 1910.

Hughes, Langston. *Famous Negro Music Makers*. New York: Dodd, Mead and Company, 1955.

Hurok, Solomon, and Ruth Goode. *Impresario, a Memoir*. New York: Random House, 1946.

Johns, Clayton. *Reminiscences of a Musician*. Cambridge, Massachusetts: Washburn and Thomas, 1929.

Johnson, Allen, and Dumas Malone, editors. *Dictionary of American Biography*. 20 volumes. New York: Charles Scribner's Sons, 1928–1936.

Jones, F. O. *A Handbook of American Music and Musicians*. Buffalo, New York: C. W. Moulton and Company, 1887.

Jordan, Jules. *The Happenings of a Musical Life*. Providence, Rhode Island: Palmer Press, 1922.

Key, Pierre, editor. *Pierre Key's Musical Who's Who*. New York: Musical Publications, Inc., 1930.

Knippers, Ottis J. *Who's Who Among Southern Singers and Composers*. Lawrenceburg, Tennessee: J. D. Vaughn, 1937.

Lomax, John A. *Adventures of a Ballad Hunter*. New York: The Macmillan Company, 1947.

Mannes, David. *Music is My Faith; an Autobiography*. New York: W. W. Norton and Company, 1938.

Maretzek, Max. *Crotchets & Quavers; or Revelations of an Opera Manager in America*. New York, 1855.

—— *Sharps & Flats; a Sequel to Crotchets & Quavers*. New York: American Musician Publishing Company, 1890.

McNamara, Daniel, editor. *The ASCAP Biographical Dictionary*. New York: Thomas Y. Crowell Company, 1952.

McPhee, Colin. *A House in Bali*. New York: John Day Company, 1946.

Pan Pipes of Sigma Alpha Iota (New York). (Since 1949, its Amer-Allegro section in December or January issue contains biographical information on contemporary American composers.)

Paris, Leonard A. *Men and Melodies*. New York: Thomas Y. Crowell Company, 1954.

Reis, Claire. *Composers in America, 1912–1937.* New York: The Macmillan Company, 1938. (Revised edition, New York: The Macmillan Company, 1947.)

Rogers, Clara Kathleen. *Memories of a Musical Career.* Boston: Little, Brown and Company, 1919.

Ryan, Thomas. *Recollections of an Old Musician.* New York: E. P. Dutton and Company, 1899.

Samaroff Stokowski, Olga. *An American Musician's Story.* New York: W. W. Norton and Company, 1939.

Schoen-René, Anna Eugenie. *America's Musical Inheritance; Memories and Reminiscences.* New York: G. P. Putnam's Sons, 1941.

Slonimsky, Nicolas. "Composers of New England" (principally Gilbert, Allen, Ruggles, Ives, Sessions). *Modern Music,* February–March, 1930.

Spaeth, Sigmund G. *Fifty Years with Music.* New York: Fleet Publishing Corp., 1959.

Stoddard, Hope. *Symphony Conductors of the U.S.A.* New York: Thomas Y. Crowell Company, 1957.

Thompson, Oscar, editor. *The International Cyclopedia of Music and Musicians.* New York: Dodd, Mead and Company, 1939.

Tiomkin, Dimitri, and Prosper Buranelli. *Please Don't Hate Me.* Garden City, New York: Doubleday and Company, 1959.

Trotter, James M. *Music and Some Highly Musical People: Containing . . . Sketches of the Lives of Remarkable Musicians of the Colored Race.* Boston: Lee and Shepard, 1878.

Upton, George P. *Musical Memories (1850–1900).* Chicago: A. C. McClurg and Company, 1908.

Upton, William Treat. "Our Musical Expatriates" (Strong, Fairchild, Campbell-Tipton, Spellman). *Musical Quarterly,* January, 1928.

Whittle Music Company. *Texas Composers.* Dallas, Texas: Whittle Music Company, 1955.

Wiggin, Frances T. *Maine Composers and Their Music: a Biographical Dictionary.* Thomaston, Maine: Maine Federation of Music Clubs, 1959.

Wisconsin Federation of Music Clubs. *Wisconsin Composers,* 1948.

POPULAR MUSIC AND JAZZ

American Society of Composers, Authors and Publishers. *Thirty Years of Motion Picture Music.* New York: American Society of Composers, Authors and Publishers, 1960.

Armstrong, Louis. *Swing That Music.* New York: Longmans, Green and Company, 1926.

Balliett, Whitney. *The Sound of Surprise; 46 Pieces on Jazz.* New York: E. P. Dutton and Company, 1959.

Berendt, Joachim E. *Blues.* München: Nymphenberger Verlagshandlung, 1957.

———— *The New Jazz Book; a History and Guide.* New York: Hill and Wang, 1962.

Blesh, Rudi. *Shining Trumpets; a History of Jazz.* New York: Alfred A. Knopf, 1946. (2nd edition, revised and enlarged, New York: Alfred A. Knopf, 1958.)

———— and Harriet Janis. *They All Played Ragtime; the True Story of an American Music.* New York: Alfred A. Knopf, 1950.

Borris, Siegfried. *Modern Jazz.* Berlin: Rembrandt Verlag, 1962.

Béchet, Sidney. *Treat It Gentle.* New York: Hill and Wang, 1960.

Brunn, H. C. *The Story of the Original Dixie Land Jazz Band.* Baton Rouge: Louisiana State University Press, 1960.

Burton, Jack. *The Blue Book of Broadway Musicals.* Watkins Glen, New York: Century House, 1952.

———— *The Blue Book of Hollywood Musicals.* Watkins Glen, New York: Century House, 1953.

———— *The Blue Book of Tin Pan Alley.* Watkins Glen, New York: Century House, 1950.

———— *The Index of American Popular Music.* Watkins Glen, New York: Century House, 1957.

Carey, David A. *The Directory of Recorded Jazz and Swing Music.* 6 volumes. Fordingbridge, New Hampshire: Delphic Press, 1949–57.

Charles, Norman. *Social Values in American Popular Songs (1890–1950).* Ann Arbor, Michigan: University Microfilms (L.C. No. Mic. 58–3313), 1958. Dissertation: University of Pennsylvania.

Charters, Samuel B. *The Country Blues*. New York: Holt, Rinehart and Winston, 1959.

Chipman, John H. *Index to Top-Hit Tunes (1900–1950)*. Boston: Bruce Humphries, 1962.

Condon, Eddie. *Eddie Condon's Treasury of Jazz*. New York: Dial Press, 1956.

—— *We Called It Music; a Generation of Jazz*. New York: Holt, Rinehart and Winston, 1947.

Copland, Aaron. "Jazz Structure and Influence." *Modern Music*, January, 1927.

Dance, Stanley, Yannick Bruynoghe, and others. *Jazz Era; the 'Forties*. London: MacGibbon and Kee, 1961.

De Toledano, Ralph. *Frontiers of Jazz*. New York: O. Durrell, 1947.

Dexter, Dave. *Jazz Cavalcade, the Inside Story of Jazz*. New York: Criterion Books, 1946.

Erlich, Lillian. *What Jazz Is All About*. New York: Julian Messner, Inc., 1962.

Ewen, David. *Men of Popular Music*. New York: Ziff-Davis, 1944.

—— *Popular American Composers from Revolutionary Times to the Present*. New York: The H. W. Wilson Company, 1962.

—— *The Story of America's Musical Theatre*. Philadelphia: Chilton Books, 1961.

Feather, Leonard. *The Book of Jazz; a Guide to the Entire Field*. New York: Horizon Press, 1957.

—— *The Encyclopedia of Jazz*. New York: Horizon Press, 1955. (new edition, New York: Horizon Press, 1960.)

—— *The Encyclopedia Year Book of Jazz*. New York: Horizon Press, 1956.

—— *Inside Be-bop*. New York: J. J. Robbins, 1949.

—— *The New Yearbook of Jazz*. New York: Horizon Press, 1958.

Finkelstein, Sidney. *Jazz: a People's Music*. New York: The Citadel Press, 1948.

Fox, Charles. *Jazz on Record; a Critical Guide*. London: Hutchinson and Company, 1960.

Francis, André. *Jazz*. Translated and revised by Martin Williams. New York: Grove Press, 1960.

Fredericks, Vic. *Who's Who in Rock 'n Roll; Facts, Fotos and Fan*

Gossip About Performers in the World of Rock 'n Roll. New York: Frederick Fell, Inc., 1958.

Freeman, Larry. *The Melodies Linger On; 50 Years of Popular Song.* Watkins Glen, New York: Century House, 1951.

Fuld, James J. *American Popular Music (Reference Book) 1875–1950.* Philadelphia: Musical Americana, 1955. (Supplement published in 1956.)

Gammon, Peter, and Peter Clayton. *Dictionary of Popular Music.* New York: Philosophical Library, 1961.

Gammon, Peter, editor. *The Decca Book of Jazz.* London: F. Muller, 1958.

Gentry, Linnell. *A History and Encyclopedia of Country, Western and Gospel Music.* Nashville, Tennessee: McQuiddy Press, 1961.

Gleason, Ralph J. *Jam Session; an Anthology of Jazz.* New York: G. P. Putnam's Sons, 1958.

Goffin, Robert. *Jazz, from the Congo to the Metropolitan.* Garden City, New York: Doubleday, Doran, 1944.

Goldberg, Isaac. *Tin Pan Alley.* New York: The John Day Company, 1930.

——— *Tin Pan Alley; a Chronicle of American Popular Music.* Supplement by Edward Jablonski. New York: Frederick Ungar Publishing Company, 1961.

Goodman, Benny, and Irving Kolodin. *The Kingdom of Swing.* New York: Stackpole Sons, 1939.

Graham, Alberta P. *Strike Up the Band; Band Leaders of Today.* New York: Thomas Nelson and Sons, 1950.

Green, Abel. *Show Biz from Vaude to Video.* New York: Holt, Rinehart and Winston, 1951.

Green, Benny. *Five Studies in the Growth of Jazz.* London: MacGibbon and Kee, 1962.

Green, Stanley. *The World of Musical Comedy.* New York: Ziff-Davis, 1960.

Grossman, William L. *The Heart of Jazz.* New York: New York University Press, 1956.

Guinle, Jorge. *Jazz Panorama.* Rio de Janeiro: Agir, 1953.

Handy, William C. *Blues; an Anthology.* New York: A. and C. Boni, 1926.

—— *Collection of Blues.* New York: Robbins-Engel, Inc., 1925.

Handy, William C., and E. A. Niles. *Blues; an Anthology of Jazz Music from the Early Negro Folk Blues to Modern Music.* New York: A. and C. Boni, 1926.

Hansen, Chadwick C. *The Ages of Jazz; a Study of Jazz in Its Cultural Context.* Ann Arbor, Michigan: University Microfilms (L.C. No. Mic. 59–6054), 1959. Dissertation: University of Minnesota.

Harris, Rex. *Jazz.* Harmondsworth: Penguin Books, 1952.

—— *The Story of Jazz.* New York: Grosset and Dunlap, 1955.

Haywood, Charles. *The James A. Bland Album of Outstanding Songs.* New York: Marks, 1946.

Heaps, Willard A. *The Singing Sixties; the Spirit of the Civil War Days Drawn from the Music of the Times.* Norman, Oklahoma: University of Oklahoma Press, 1960.

Hentoff, Nat. *The Jazz Life.* New York: Dial Press, 1961.

Hentoff, Nat, and McCarthy, A. J., editors. *Jazz; New Perspectives on the History of Jazz by 12 of the World's Foremost Jazz Critics & Scholars.* New York: Holt, Rinehart, and Winston, 1959.

Hobson, Wilder. *American Jazz Music.* New York: W. W. Norton and Company, 1939.

Hodier, André. *Jazz: Its Evolution and Essence.* New York: Grove Press, 1956.

—— *Toward Jazz.* New York: Grove Press, 1962.

Hopkins, John. *Hopkins' New Orleans 5-cent Songster* (Confederate Songs). New Orleans, 1861.

Hughes, Langston. *The First Book of Jazz.* New York: Franklin Watts, Inc., 1955.

James, Burnett. *Essays on Jazz.* London: Sidgewick and Jackson, 1961.

Johnson, Helen Kendrick. *Our Familiar Songs and Those Who Made Them.* New York: Holt, Rinehart and Winston, 1907.

Jordan, Phillip D., and Lillian Kessler. *Songs of Yesterday.* Garden City, New York: Doubleday, Doran, 1941.

Jubilee and Plantation Songs. Boston: Oliver Ditson Company, 1887.

Keepnews, Orvin, and Bill Grauer, Jr. *A Pictorial History of Jazz; People and Places from New Orleans to Modern Jazz.* New

York: Crown Publishers, 1956. (2nd edition, London: Spring Books, 1959.)

Landauer, Bella C. *My City 'Tis of Thee; New York City on Sheet Music Covers.* New York: New-York Historical Society, 1951.

—— *Striking the Right Note in Advertising; Selections from the Music Collection of Bella C. Landauer at the New-York Historical Society.* New York: New-York Historical Society, 1951.

Lang, Iain. *Background of the Blues.* London: Workers' Music Association, 1943.

—— *Jazz in Perspective; the Background of the Blues.* London: Hutchinson and Company, 1947.

Laubenstein, Paul Fritz. "Jazz—Debit and Credit." *Musical Quarterly,* October, 1929.

Levy, Newman. "The Jazz Formula." *Modern Music,* June, 1924.

Lewine, Richard, and Alfred Simon. *Encyclopedia of Theatre Music ... 1900–1960.* New York: Random House, 1961.

Loesser, Arthur. *Humor in American Song.* New York: Howell Soskin, Inc., 1942.

Longstreet, Stephen. *The Real Jazz, Old and New.* Baton Rouge: Louisiana State University Press, 1956.

—— and Alfons M. Dauer. *Knaurs Jazz Lexikon.* München: Droemersche Verlagsanstalt, 1957.

Lucas, John. *Basic Jazz on Long Play.* Northfield, Minnesota: Carleton College, 1954.

Luther, Frank. *Americans and Their Songs.* New York: Harper and Brothers, 1942.

Marks, Edward B. *They All Had Glamour. From the Swedish Nightingale to the Naked Lady.* New York: Julian Messner, Inc., 1944.

—— *They All Sang, from Tony Pastor to Rudy Vallée.* New York: The Viking Press, 1934.

Mattfield, Julius. *Variety Music Cavalcade, 1620–1950.* Englewood Cliffs, New Jersey: Prentice-Hall, 1952.

—— *Variety Music Cavalcade, 1620–1960.* (2nd edition, Englewood Cliffs, New Jersey: Prentice-Hall, 1962.)

McCarthy, Albert. *Jazzbook, 1955.* London: Cassell and Company, Ltd., 1955.

Mehegan, John F. *Jazz Improvisation; Tonal and Rhythmic Principles.* New York: Watson-Guptill Publications, 1959.

Merriam, Alan P. *A Bibliography of Jazz.* Philadelphia: American Folklore Society, 1954.

Meyer, Hazel. *The Gold in Tin Pan Alley.* Philadelphia: J. B. Lippincott Company, 1958.

Miller, Eduard Paul. *Miller's Year Book of Popular Music.* Chicago: Pen Publications, 1943.

Montgomery, Elizabeth R. *The Story Behind Popular Songs.* New York: Dodd, Mead and Company, 1958.

Morgan, Alun, and Raymond Horricks. *Modern Jazz; a Survey of Developments Since 1939.* London: Victor Gollancz, Ltd., 1956.

Morgan, Sophie. *That's an Old One; a Compilation of Song Titles and Their Copyright Dates.* Glendale, California: Morgan Mimeographing, 1949.

Newton, Francis. *The Jazz Scene.* London: MacGibbon and Kee, 1959.

Oliver, Paul. *Blues Fell This Morning; the Meaning of the Blues.* London: Cassell and Company, 1960.

Osgood, Henry O. *So This Is Jazz.* Boston: Little, Brown and Company, 1926.

Ostransky, Leroy. *The Anatomy of Jazz.* Seattle: University of Washington Press, 1960.

Panassié, Hugues. *Hot Jazz.* New York: M. Witmark and Sons, 1936.

—— *Jazz Panorama.* Paris: Deux Rives, 1950.

—— *The Real Jazz.* New York: Smith and Durrell, 1942. (Revised and enlarged edition, New York: A. S. Barnes and Company, 1960.)

Panassié, Hugues, and Madeline Gautier. *Guide to Jazz.* Boston: Houghton-Mifflin Company, 1956.

Paskman, Dailey, and Sigmund Spaeth. *Gentlemen, Be Seated; A Parade of the Old-time Minstrels.* Garden City, New York: Doubleday, Doran, 1928.

Paul, Elliot H. *That Crazy American Music.* Indianapolis, Indiana: The Bobbs-Merrill Company, 1957.

Ramsey, Frederic. *A Guide to Longplay Jazz Records*. New York: Long Player Publications, 1954.

———— and Charles Edward Smith, editors. *Jazzmen*. New York: Harcourt, Brace and Company, 1939.

Reisner, Robert G. *The Literature of Jazz; a Preliminary Bibliography*. New York: New York Public Library, 1954.

———— *The Literature of Jazz; a Selective Bibliography*. New York: New York Public Library, 1949.

A San Francisco Songster, 1849–1939. San Francisco: Work Projects Administration, 1939.

Sargeant, Winthrop. *Jazz: Hot and Hybrid*. New York: Arrow Editions, 1939. (New and enlarged edition, New York: E. P. Dutton and Company, 1946.)

Schwaninger, A. *Swing Discographie*. Genève: C. Grasset, 1945.

Shapiro, Nat, and Nat Hentoff. *Hear Me Talkin' to Ya; the Story of Jazz by the Men Who Made it*. New York: Holt, Rinehart and Winston, 1955.

———— *The Jazz Makers*. New York: Holt, Rinehart and Winston, 1957.

Shay, Frank. *My Pious Friends and Drunken Companions*. New York: The Macaulay Company, 1927.

———— *Drawn from the Wood; Consolations in Words and Music for Pious Friends and Drunken Companions*. New York: The Macaulay Company, 1929.

———— *More Pious Friends and Drunken Companions*. New York: The Macaulay Company, 1928.

Simon, George T. *The Feeling of Jazz*. New York: Simon and Schuster, 1961.

Smith, Cecil. *Musical Comedy in America*. New York: Theatre Arts Books, 1950.

Spaeth, Sigmund. *Read 'em and Weep*. Garden City, New York: Doubleday, Page and Company, 1926.

———— *Weep Some More, My Lady*. Garden City, New York: Doubleday, Page and Company, 1927.

———— *They Still Sing of Love*. New York: Horace Liveright, Inc., 1929.

——— *A History of Popular Music in America*. New York: Random House, 1948. (Reprint edition, New York: Theatre Arts Books, 1950.)

Specht, Paul L. *How They Became Name Bands; the Modern Technique of a Danceband Maestro*. New York: Fine Arts Publications, 1941.

Stearns, Marshall W. *The Story of Jazz*. New York: Oxford University Press, 1962.

Stock, Denis. *Jazz Street*. Garden City, New York: Doubleday and Company, 1960.

Stringham, E. J. "Jazz—An Educational Problem." *Musical Quarterly*, April, 1926.

Traill, Sinclair. *Concerning Jazz*. London: Faber and Faber, 1957.

——— *Play That Music; a Guide to Playing Jazz*. London: Faber and Faber, 1956.

——— and Gerald Lascelles. *Just Jazz*. London: Peter Davies, Ltd., 1957.

Ulanov, Barry. *A Handbook of Jazz*. New York: The Viking Press, 1957.

——— *A History of Jazz in America*. New York: The Viking Press, 1952.

Vallée, Rudy, and Gil McKean. *My Time Is Your Time; the Story of Rudy Vallée*. New York: Ivan Obolensky, Inc., 1962.

Whiteman, Paul, and Mary Margaret McBride. *Jazz*. New York: J. H. Sears and Company, 1926.

Williams, Martin T. *The Art of Jazz; Essays on the Nature and Development of Jazz*. New York: Oxford University Press, 1959.

Wilson, John S. *The Collector's Jazz: Traditional and Swing*. Philadelphia: J. B. Lippincott Company, 1958.

Witmark, Isidore. *The Story of the House of Witmark: from Ragtime to Swingtime*. New York: L. Furman, 1939.

Woodward, Woody. *Jazz Americana; the Story of Jazz and All-Time Jazz Greats from Basin Street to Carnegie Hall*. Los Angeles, California: Trend Books, 1956.

FOLK AND TRADITIONAL MUSIC

Allen, William Francis, Charles P. Ware, and Lucy McKim Garrison. *Slave Songs of the United States*. New York: A. Simpson and Company, 1867. (Reprinted 1929 by Peter Smith, New York.)

Andrews, Edward D. "Shaker Songs." *Musical Quarterly*, October, 1937.

Armour, Eugene. *The Melodic and Rhythmic Characteristics of the Music of the Traditional Ballad Variants Found in the Southern Appalachians*. Ann Arbor, Michigan: University Microfilms (L.C. No. Mic. 62–1409), 1961. Dissertation: New York University.

Armstrong, Mrs. F. W., and Helen W. Ludlow. *Hampton and Its Students*. New York: G. P. Putnam's Sons, 1875.

Baker, Theodore. *Über die Musik der nordamerikanischen Wilden*. Leipzig: Breitkopf and Haertel, 1882.

Ballanta, C. J. S. *St. Helena Spirituals*. New York: G. Schirmer, Inc., 1925.

Barry, Philips. *British Ballads from Maine*. New Haven, Connecticut: Yale University Press, 1929.

———— *The Maine Woods Songster*. Cambridge, Massachusetts: The Powell Printing Company, 1939.

Beck, Earl Clifton. *Lore of the Lumber Camps*. Ann Arbor, Michigan: University of Michigan Press, 1948.

———— *Songs of the Michigan Lumberjacks*. Ann Arbor, Michigan: University of Michigan Press, 1941.

———— *They Knew Paul Bunyan*. Ann Arbor, Michigan: University of Michigan Press, 1956.

Black, Eleanora, and Sidney Robertson. *The Gold Rush Song Book*. San Francisco: The Colt Press, 1940.

Blesh, Rudi. *O Susanna; a Sampler of the Riches of American Folk Music*. New York: Grove Press, 1960.

Boas, F. "The Central Eskimo." Washington, D.C.: Bureau of Ethnology, *6th Annual Report*, 1888.

Boyer, Walter E., Albert F. Buffington, and Don Yoder. *Songs Along the Mahantongo; Pennsylvania Dutch Folksongs.* Lancaster, Pennsylvania: Dutch Folklore Center, 1951.

Brand, Oscar. *The Ballad Mongers–Rise of the Modern Folk Song.* New York: Funk and Wagnalls, 1962.

Brawley, Benjamin. *The Negro in Literature and Art in the United States.* New York: Duffield and Company, 1929.

Brewster, Paul G. *Ballads and Songs of Indiana.* Bloomington, Indiana: Indiana University, 1940.

Bronson, Bertrand H. "Some Observations about Melodic Variation in British-American Folk Tunes." *Journal of the American Musicological Society,* Vol. 3, No. 2 (Summer, 1950).

Browne, C. A. *The Story of Our National Ballads.* New York: Thomas Y. Crowell Company, 1919. (Revised edition by Willard A. Heaps, New York: Thomas Y. Crowell Company, 1960.)

Buchanan, Annabel Morris. *Folk-Hymns of America.* New York: J. Fischer and Brother, 1938.

Burchenal, Elizabeth. *American Country Dances.* New York: G. Schirmer, Inc., 1918.

Burleigh, Harry T. *Negro Folk Songs.* New York: G. Ricordi and Company, 1921.

—— *Negro Spirituals.* 2 volumes. New York: G. Ricordi and Company, 1917–22.

Burlin, Natalie Curtis. "Black Singers and Players." *Musical Quarterly,* October, 1919.

—— *Hampton Series of Negro Folk-Songs* (4 books). New York: G. Schirmer, Inc., 1918–19.

—— "Negro Music at Birth." *Musical Quarterly,* January, 1919.

—— "A Plea for Our Native Art." *Musical Quarterly,* April, 1920.

Burton, Frederick R. *American Primitive Music.* New York: Moffat, Yard and Company, 1909.

Cadman, Charles Wakefield. "The Idealization of Indian Music." *Musical Quarterly,* July, 1915.

Campbell, Olive D., and Cecil J. Sharp. *English Folksongs from the Southern Appalachians.* New York: G. P. Putnam's Sons, 1917.

Carmer, Carl. *America Sings; Stories and Songs of America's Growing.* New York: Alfred A. Knopf, 1942.

—— *Songs of the Rivers of America*. New York: Holt, Rinehart and Winston, 1942.

Catlin, George. *Letters and Notes on the Manners, Customs, and Condition of the North American Indians*. London: For the author, 1841.

Chamber, H. A. *The Treasury of Negro Spirituals*. New York: Emerson Books, 1963.

Chase, Richard. *American Folk Tales and Songs*. New York: New American Library, 1956.

Check List of California Songs. Berkeley, California: University of California, 1940.

Check-List of Recorded Songs in the English Language in the Archive of American Folk Song, to July, 1940. Washington, D.C.: Library of Congress, Government Printing Office, 1942.

Check-List of the Literature and Other Material in the Library of Congress on the European War (List of Music prepared by Walter R. Whittlesey). Washington, D.C.: Library of Congress, Government Printing Office, 1918.

Christensen, Abigail M. H. "Spirituals and Shouts of Southern Negroes." *Journal of American Folk-Lore*, Vol. III, 1890.

Coffin, Tristram P. *The British Traditional Ballad in North America*. Philadelphia: The American Folklore Society, 1950.

Cohen, Lily Young. *Lost Spirituals*. New York: W. Neale, 1928.

Coleridge-Taylor, Samuel. *Twenty-four Negro Melodies*. Transcribed for the piano. Boston: Oliver Ditson Company, 1905.

Courlander, Harold. *Negro Folk Music, U.S.A.* New York: Columbia University Press, 1963.

Cox, John H. *Folk Songs of the South*. Cambridge, Massachusetts: Harvard University Press, 1925.

Cringan, Alexander T. *Iroquois Folk Songs*. Toronto: Toronto Educational Department, 1903.

Curtis, Natalie. "American Indian Cradle-Songs." *Musical Quarterly*, October, 1921.

—— *The Indian's Book*. New York: Harper and Brothers, 1907.

—— *Songs and Tales from the Dark Continent*. New York: G. Schirmer, Inc., 1920.

Dann, Hollis, and H. W. Loomis. *Fifty-eight Spirituals for Choral Use*. Boston: C. C. Birchard and Company, 1924.

Davis, Arthur K. *Traditional Ballads of Virginia*. Cambridge, Massachusetts: Harvard University Press, 1929.

—— *Folksongs of Virginia*. Durham, North Carolina: Duke University Press, 1949.

—— *More Traditional Ballads of Virginia*. Chapel Hill, North Carolina: University of North Carolina Press, 1960.

Davis, A. K., Junior. "Some Problems of Ballad Publication." *Musical Quarterly*, April, 1918.

Densmore, Frances. *The American Indians and Their Music*. New York: The Woman's Press, 1926.

—— "Chippewa Music" and "Chippewa Music No. 2." *Bulletins* 45 and 53 of the Bureau of American Ethnology. Washington, D.C., 1910 and 1913.

—— *Indian Action Songs*. Boston: C. C. Birchard and Company, 1921.

—— "Mandan and Hidatsa Music." *Bulletin 80* of the Bureau of American Ethnology. Washington, D.C., 1923.

—— "Music of the Acoma, Isleta, Cochiti and Zuni Indians." *Bulletin 165* of the Bureau of American Ethnology. Washington, D.C., 1957.

—— "Northern Ute Music." *Bulletin 75* of the Bureau of American Ethnology. Washington, D.C., 1922.

—— "The Study of Indian Music." *Musical Quarterly*, April, 1915.

—— "Teton Sioux Music." *Bulletin 61* of the Bureau of American Ethnology. Washington, D.C., 1918.

De Silva, Owen Francis. *Mission Music of California*. Los Angeles, California: W. F. Lewis, 1941.

Dett, R. Nathaniel. *Negro Spirituals*. 3 volumes. Cincinnati, Ohio: John Church Company, 1919.

Diton, Carl R. *Thirty-six South Carolina Spirituals*. New York: G. Schirmer, Inc., 1930.

Dobie, James Frank. *Texas and Southwestern Lore*. Austin, Texas: Texas Folk-Lore Society, 1927.

Dolph, Edward Arthur. *Sound Off! Soldier Songs from the Revolution to World War II*. New York: Holt, Rinehart and Winston, 1942.

Downes, Olin, and Elie Siegmeister. *A Treasury of American Song.* New York: Alfred A. Knopf, 1943.

Drake, F. S., editor. *The Indian Tribes of the United States.* Philadelphia, 1884.

Eckstorm, Fannie Hardy, and Mary Winslow Smyth. *Minstrelsy of Maine.* Boston: Houghton Mifflin Company, 1927.

Eddy, Mary Olive. *Ballads and Songs from Ohio.* New York: J. J. Augustin, 1939.

Edwards, Charles L. *Bahama Songs and Stories.* Boston: Houghton Mifflin Company, 1895.

Elson, Louis C. *The National Music of America.* Boston: The Page Company, 1899. (Revised to 1924 by Arthur Elson.)

Farwell, Arthur. *American Indian Melodies,* harmonized by Arthur Farwell. Newton Center, Massachusetts: The Wa-Wan Press, 1901.

—— *Folk-Songs of the West and South: Negro, Cowboy and Spanish California.* Newton Center, Massachusetts: The Wa-Wan Press, 1905.

—— *From Mesa and Plain; Indian, Cowboy and Negro Sketches.* Newton Center, Massachusetts: The Wa-Wan Press, 1905.

Fenner, T. P., and F. G. Rathbon. *Cabin and Plantation Songs as Sung by the Hampton Students.* New York: G. P. Putnam's Sons, 1874.

Fewkes, J. W. *Additional Studies of Zuñi Songs and Rituals with the Phonograph.* 1890.

—— "A Contribution to Passamaquoddy Folk-lore." *Journal of American Folk-Lore,* Vol. III, 1890.

—— *On the Use of the Phonograph Among the Zuñi Indians.* 1890.

Fillmore, John Comfort. *The Harmonic Structure of Indian Music.* New York: G. P. Putnam's Sons, 1899.

Finger, C. J. *Frontier Ballads.* Garden City, New York: Doubleday, Page and Company, 1927.

Fisher, Miles M. *Negro Slave Songs in the United States.* Ithaca, New York: Cornell University Press for the American Historical Association, 1953.

Fisher, William Arms, editor. *Seventy Negro Spirituals.* Boston: Oliver Ditson Company, 1926.

Flanders, Helen H. *Ancient Ballads Traditionally Sung in New England*. 3 volumes. Philadelphia: University of Pennsylvania Press, 1960–63.

——— *Ballads Migrant in New England*. New York: Farrar, Straus and Young, 1953.

——— *The New Green Mountain Songster; Traditional Folk Songs of Vermont*. New Haven, Connecticut: Yale University Press, 1939.

——— and George Brown. *Vermont Folk-Songs and Ballads*. Brattleboro, Vermont: Stephen Daye Press, 1931.

Fletcher, Alice C. "The Hako: A Pawnee Ceremony." Washington, D.C.: Bureau of American Ethnology, *22nd Annual Report*, 1904.

——— *Indian Games and Dances with Native Songs*. Boston: C. C. Birchard and Company, 1915.

——— *Indian Story and Song from North America*. Boston: Small, Maynard and Company, 1900.

——— with John Comfort Fillmore. *A Study of Omaha Indian Music*. Cambridge, Massachusetts: Peabody Museum of American Archæology and Ethnology, 1893.

——— with Francis La Flesche. "The Omaha Tribe." Washington, D.C.: Bureau of American Ethnology, *27th Annual Report*, 1911.

Ford, Ira W. *Traditional Music of America*. New York: E. P. Dutton and Company, 1940.

Gardner, Emelyn E., and Geraldine J. Chickering. *Ballads and Songs of Southern Michigan*. Ann Arbor, Michigan: University of Michigan Press, 1939.

Gellert, Lawrence. *Negro Songs of Protest*. New York: American Music League, 1936.

Gilman, Benjamin Ives. "Hopi Songs." *Journal of American Ethnology and Archæology*, Vol. V, 1908.

——— "Zuñi Melodies." *Journal of American Ethnology and Archæology*, Vol. I, 1891.

Gray, Robert P. *Songs and Ballads of the Maine Lumberjacks*. Cambridge, Massachusetts: Harvard University Press, 1924.

Greenway, John. *American Folksongs of Protest*. Philadelphia: University of Pennsylvania Press, 1953.

Griggs, John Cornelius. *Studien über die Musik in Amerika*. Leipzig: Breitkopf and Haertel, 1894.

Grissom, Mary Allen. *The Negro Sings a New Heaven*. Chapel Hill, North Carolina: University of North Carolina Press, 1930.

Gordon, R. W. "American Folk-Music"; series of eighteen articles in *New York Times Magazine*, 1926–27.

Guion, David. *Darkey Spirituals*. New York: M. Witmark and Sons, 1918.

Guthrie, Woody. *American Folksong; Woody Guthrie*. Edited by Moses Asch. New York: Oak Publications, 1961.

Hague, Eleanor. *Early Spanish-Californian Folk Songs*. New York: J. Fischer and Brother, 1922.

Hallowell, Emily. *Calhoun Plantation Songs*. Boston: C. W. Thompson and Company, 1901.

Handy, W. C. *A Treasury of the Blues*. New York: Simon and Schuster, 1949.

Harlow, Frederick P. *Chanteying Aboard American Ships*. Barre, Massachusetts: Barre *Gazette*, 1962.

Harwell, Richard B. *Songs of the Confederacy*. New York: Broadcast Music, Inc., 1951.

Hayes, Roland. *My Songs; Aframerican Religious Folk Songs*. Boston: Little, Brown and Company, 1948.

Haywood, Charles A. *A Bibliography of North American Folklore and Folksong*. New York: Greenberg, Publisher, Inc., 1951. (2nd revised edition, 2 volumes, New York: Dover Publications, 1961.)

Henry, Mellinger Edward. *Folk-Songs from the Southern Highlands*. New York: J. J. Augustin, 1938.

Higginson, Vincent. *Hymnody in the American Indian Missions* (Papers of the Hymn Society, 18). New York: Hymn Society of America, 1954.

Hoffman, Walter James. "The Mide'-wiwin or 'Grand Medicine Society' of the Ojibway." Washington, D.C.: Bureau of American Ethnology, 7th *Annual Report*, 1891.

Hubbard, Lester A. *Ballads and Songs from Utah*. Salt Lake City: University of Utah Press, 1961.

Hudson, Arthur P. *Folklore Keeps the Past Alive* (Eugenia Dorothy Blount Lamar Memorial Lectures, 1961, delivered at Mercer University . . .). Athens, Georgia: University of Georgia Press, 1962.

Ives, Burl. *The Burl Ives Song Book; American Song in Historical Perspective.* New York: Ballantine Books, 1953.

—— *Songs in America; Our Musical Heritage.* New York: Duell, Sloan and Pearce, 1962.

—— *Wayfaring Stranger.* New York: Whittlesey House, 1948.

Jackson, George Pullen. *A Directory of Sacred Harp Singers and Singing Conventions.* Nashville, Tennessee: Privately printed, 1945.

—— *Down-East Spirituals.* New York: J. J. Augustin, 1943.

—— *Spiritual Folk-Songs of Early America.* New York: J. J. Augustin, 1937 (Reissued in 1953 by J. J. Augustin).

—— *The Story of the Sacred Harp, 1844–1944.* Nashville, Tennessee: Vanderbilt University Press, 1944.

—— *White and Negro Spirituals, Their Life Span and Kinship.* New York: J. J. Augustin, 1944.

—— *White Spirituals in the Southern Uplands.* Chapel Hill, North Carolina: University of North Carolina Press, 1933.

Jameson, Gladys V. *Wake and Sing; a Miniature Anthology of the Music of Appalachian America.* New York: Broadcast Music, Inc., 1955.

Johnson, Guy B. *John Henry; Tracking Down a Negro Legend.* Chapel Hill, North Carolina: University of North Carolina Press, 1929.

Johnson, Hall. *The Green Pastures Spirituals.* New York, 1930.

Johnson, James Weldon, and J. Rosamond Johnson. *The Book of American Negro Spirituals.* New York: The Viking Press, 1940.

Johnson, J. Rosamond. *Rolling Along in Song; a Chronological Survey of American Negro Music.* New York: The Viking Press, 1937.

—— *Sixteen New Negro Spirituals.* New York: Handy Brothers Music Company, 1939.

—— *Utica Jubilee Singers' Spirituals,* taken down by J. Rosamond Johnson. Introduction by C. W. Hyne. Boston: Oliver Ditson Company, 1930.

Kennedy, Charles O. *A Treasury of American Ballads, Gay, Naughty and Classic*. New York: Robert M. McBride and Company, 1954.

Kennedy, R. Emmet. *Black Cameos*. New York: A. and C. Boni, 1924.

————— *Mellows: Negro Work Songs, Street Cries, and Spirituals*. New York: A. and C. Boni, 1925.

————— *More Mellows*. New York: Dodd, Mead and Company, 1931.

Kidson, Frank. "Some Guesses About Yankee Doodle." *Musical Quarterly*, January, 1917.

Kinsella, Hazel G. *Folksongs and Fiddle Tunes of the U.S.A.* New York: Carl Fischer, 1959.

Kirby, Percival R. "A Study of Negro Harmony." *Musical Quarterly*, July, 1923.

Kobbé, Gustav. *Famous American Songs*. New York: Thomas Y. Crowell Company, 1906.

Korson, George. *Coal Dust on the Fiddle; Songs and Stories of the Bituminous Industry*. Philadelphia: University of Pennsylvania Press, 1943.

————— *Minstrels of the Mine Patch; Songs and Stories of the Anthracite Industry*. Philadelphia: University of Pennsylvania Press, 1938.

————— *Pennsylvania Songs and Legends*. Philadelphia: University of Pennsylvania Press, 1949.

Krehbiel, Henry E. *Afro-American Folk Songs*. New York: G. Schirmer, Inc., 1914.

Kurath, Gertrude P. "Antiphonal Songs of Eastern Woodland Indians." *Musical Quarterly*, Vol. 42, No. 4 (October, 1956).

La Flesche, Francis. "The Osage Tribe." Washington, D.C.: Bureau of American Ethnology, *36th Annual Report*, 1921.

Laubenstein, Paul Fritz. "Race Values in Aframerican Music." *Musical Quarterly*, July, 1930.

Lawless, Ray M. *Folksingers and Folksongs in America; a Handbook of Biography, Bibliography, and Discography*. New York: Duell, Sloan and Pearce, 1960.

Laws, G. Malcolm. *American Balladry from British Broadsides; a Guide for Students and Collectors of Traditional Song*. Philadelphia: American Folklore Society, 1957.

Ledbetter, Huddie. *Leadbelly; a collection of World-famous songs.* New York: Folkways Music Publishers, 1959.

Lee, George W. *Beale Street, Where the Blues Began.* New York: R. O. Ballou, 1934.

Lieurance, Thurlow. *Songs of the North American Indians.* Philadelphia: Theodore Presser Company, 1920.

Lilje, Hanns, Kurt Hansen, and Siegfried Schmidt-Joss. *Das Buch der Spirituals und Gospel Songs.* Hamburg: Furche-Verlag, 1961.

Linscott, Eloise Hubbard. *Folk Songs of Old New England.* New York: The Macmillan Company, 1939. (2nd edition, Hamden, Connecticut: Anchor Book, Doubleday and Company, 1962)

Locke, Alain. *The Negro and His Music.* Washington, D.C.: The Associates in Negro Folk Education, 1936.

———, editor. *The New Negro.* New York: A. and C. Boni, 1927.

Logan, William A. *Road to Heaven.* University, Alabama: University of Alabama Press, 1955.

Lomax, Alan. *The Folksongs of North America in the English Language.* Garden City, New York: Doubleday and Company, 1960.

Lomax, John A. *Cowboy Songs and Other Frontier Ballads.* New York: The Macmillan Company, 1929.

——— *Folksong, U.S.A.* New York: Duell, Sloan and Pearce, 1947.

——— " 'Sinful Songs' of the Southern Negro." *Musical Quarterly,* April, 1934.

——— and Alan Lomax. *American Ballads and Folk Songs.* New York: The Macmillan Company, 1934.

——— *Negro Folk Songs as Sung by Leadbelly.* New York: The Macmillan Company, 1936.

——— *Our Singing Country; a Second Volume of American Ballads and Folk Songs.* New York: The Macmillan Company, 1941.

Loomis, Harvey Worthington. *Lyrics of the Red Man.* Newton Center, Massachusetts: The Wa-Wan Press, 1903–4.

Ludlow, Helen W. *Tuskegee Normal and Industrial Institute; Its Story and Songs.* Hampton, Virginia: Institute Press, 1884.

Lummis, Charles F. *Spanish Songs of Old California.* Los Angeles: The author, 1923.

Maginty, Edward A. "'America': The Origin of Its Melody." *Musical Quarterly*, July, 1934.

Mark, Jeffrey. "Recollections of Mountaineers." *Musical Quarterly*, April, 1930.

Marsh, J. B. T. *The Story of the Jubilee Singers, with Their Songs.* Boston: Houghton Mifflin Company, 1880.

Mason, Daniel Gregory. "The Folk-Songs and American Music." *Musical Quarterly*, July, 1918.

Mattfeld, Julius. *The Folk Music of the Western Hemisphere.* A List of References in the New York Public Library. New York: New York Public Library, 1925.

Matthews, Washington. *Navaho Legends.* Boston: Houghton Mifflin Company, 1897.

McCoy, William J. *Folk-Songs of the Spanish California.* San Francisco: Sherman Clay and Company, 1926.

McGill, Josephine. *Folk Songs of the Kentucky Mountains.* New York: Boosey and Company, 1917.

—— "Following Music in a Mountain Land." *Musical Quarterly*, July, 1917.

—— "Old Ballad Burthens." *Musical Quarterly*, April, 1918.

McIlhenny, Edward A. *Befo' de War Spirituals.* Boston: The Christopher Publishing House, 1933.

McMeekin, I. M. *Melodies and Mountaineers.* Boston: Stratford, 1921.

Merriam, Alan P. "Flathead Indian Instruments and Their Music." *Musical Quarterly*, Vol. 37, No. 3 (July, 1951).

Mitchell, Mrs. A. L. *Songs of the Confederacy and Plantation Melodies.* Cincinnati, Ohio: The G. B. Jennings Company, 1901.

Mitchell, Edwin Valentine. "Music on the Maine Coast." (In *Anchor to Windward*, pp. 87–101.) New York: Coward-McCann, Inc., 1940.

Monroe, Mina. *Bayou Ballads, Twelve Folk-Songs from Louisiana.* New York: G. Schirmer, Inc., 1921.

Moore, Frank. *Lyrics of Loyalty.* New York: G. P. Putnam, 1864.

—— *Rebel Rhymes and Rhapsodies.* New York: G. P. Putnam, 1864.

———— *Songs and Ballads of the American Revolution.* New York: D. Appleton and Company, 1856.

———— *Songs of the Soldiers.* New York: G. P. Putnam, 1864.

Morris, Alton Chester. *Folksongs of Florida.* Gainesville: University of Florida Press, 1950.

Muller, Joseph. *The Star-Spangled Banner; Words and Music Issued Between 1814–1864.* An annotated bibliographical list. New York: G. A. Baker and Company, 1935.

Music of the Gold Rush Era. San Francisco: Work Projects Administration, 1939.

Nason, Reverend Elias. *Our National Song, a Monogram.* Albany, New York: J. Munsell, 1869.

Nathan, Hans. "Two Inflation Songs of the Civil War." *Musical Quarterly,* April, 1943.

Neely, Charles. *Tales and Songs of Southern Illinois.* Menasha, Wisconsin: George Banta Publishing Company, 1938.

The Negro Singer's Own Book. Philadelphia: Turner and Fisher, 1846.

Nettl, Bruno. *American Indian Music North of Mexico; its Styles and Areas.* Ann Arbor, Michigan: University Microfilms (No. 5873), 1953. Dissertation: Indiana University. (Published as "North American Indian Musical Styles" in *Memoirs of the American Folklore Society,* Vol. XLV, No. 9, Philadelphia: American Folklore Society, 1954.)

———— *An Introduction to Folk Music in the United States.* Wayne State University Studies, Humanities, No. 7. Detroit: Wayne State University Press, 1960.

———— "Polyphony in North American Indian Music." *Musical Quarterly,* Vol. 47, No. 3 (July, 1961).

———— "Stylistic Variety in North American Indian Music." *Journal of the American Musicological Society,* Vol. 6, No. 2 (Summer, 1953).

Nevin, Arthur. "Two Summers with the Blackfeet Indians of Montana." *Musical Quarterly,* April, 1916.

Niles, John Jacob. *The Ballad Book.* Boston: Houghton Mifflin Company, 1961.

Niles, John J. *Seven Kentucky Mountain Songs*. New York: G. Schirmer, Inc., 1929.

—— *Seven Negro Exaltations*. New York: G. Schirmer, Inc., 1929.

—— "Shout, Coon, Shout!" *Musical Quarterly*, October, 1930.

—— *Singing Soldiers*. New York: Charles Scribner's Sons, 1927.

—— *Songs of the Hill-Folk; Twelve Ballads from Kentucky, Virginia, and North Carolina*. New York: G. Schirmer, Inc., 1934.

—— and Douglas Moore. *Songs My Mother Never Taught Me*. New York: The Macaulay Company, 1929.

Odum, H. W., and G. B. Johnson. *The Negro and His Songs*. Chapel Hill, North Carolina: University of North Carolina Press, 1925.

—— *Negro Workaday Songs*. Chapel Hill, North Carolina: University of North Carolina Press, 1926.

Owens, William A. *Texas Folk Songs*. Austin: Texas Folklore Society, 1950.

Palmer, Edgar A. *G.I. Songs*. New York: Sheridan House, 1944.

Parker, Priscilla Post. *California Song Book; a Brief History of California*. Lancaster, California: C. M. Parker, 1950.

Parrish, Lydia. *Slave Songs of the Georgia Sea Islands*. New York: Creative Age Press, 1942.

Parsons, Elsie Clews. *Folk-Lore of the Sea Islands, South Carolina*. Cambridge, Massachusetts: American Folk-Lore Society, 1923.

Peterson, Clara Gottschalk. *Creole Songs from New Orleans*. New Orleans: Gruenewald and Company, 1902.

Pike, G. D. *The Jubilee Singers and Their Campaign for Twenty Thousand Dollars*. Boston: Lee and Shepard, 1873.

Plantation Songs and Jubilee Hymns. Chicago: White, Smith and Company, 1881.

Posselt, Eric. *Give Out! Songs of, by, and for the Men in Service*. New York: Arrowhead Press, 1943.

Pound, Louise. *American Ballads and Songs*. New York: Charles Scribner's Sons, 1922.

Powell, John. *Twelve Folk Hymns*. New York: J. Fischer and Brother, 1934.

Preble, George Henry. *History of the Flag of the United States* (chapter on national and patriotic songs). Boston: A. Williams and Company, 1880.

Provisional Check List of Disks (excluding primitive music) in the Archive of American Folk Song in the Library of Congress. Washington, D.C.: Library of Congress, 1937.

Ramsey, Frederic. *Been Here and Gone.* New Brunswick, New Jersey: Rutgers University Press, 1960.

Randolph, Vance. *Ozark Folksongs.* 4 volumes. Columbia, Missouri: The State Historical Society of Missouri, 1946–50.

—— *Ozark Mountain Folks.* New York: The Vanguard Press, 1932.

Religious Folk-Songs of the Negro as Sung on the Plantations. Hampton, Virginia: Institute Press, 1909. (Revised and enlarged edition by R. Nathaniel Dett. New York: G. Schirmer, Inc., 1926.)

Richardson, Ethel Park, and Sigmund Spaeth. *American Mountain Songs.* New York: Greenberg, Publisher, 1927.

Rickaby, Franz. *Ballads and Songs of the Shanty Boy.* Cambridge, Massachusetts: Harvard University Press, 1926.

Ritchie, Jean. *A Garland of Mountain Song; Songs from the Repertoire of the Ritchie Family of Viper, Kentucky.* New York: Broadcast Music, Inc., 1953.

Robb, John Donald. *Hispanic folk songs of New Mexico.* Albuquerque: University of New Mexico Press, 1954.

Roberts, H. H. "Some Songs of the Puget Sound Salish." *Journal of American Folk-Lore,* Vol. XXXI, 1918.

Roberts, Helen M. "Possible Survivals of African Song in Jamaica." *Musical Quarterly,* July, 1926.

Rodeheaver, Homer A. *Rodeheaver's Spirituals.* Chicago: The Rodeheaver Company, 1923.

Salisbury, Stephen. *An Essay on the Star-Spangled Banner and National Songs.* Worcester, Massachusetts: C. Hamilton, 1873.

Sandburg, Carl. *New American Song Bag.* New York: Broadcast Music, Inc., 1950.

Scarborough, Dorothy. *On the Trail of Negro Folk-Songs.* Cambridge, Massachusetts: Harvard University Press, 1925.

—— *A Song Catcher in the Southern Mountains*. New York: Columbia University Press, 1937.

Scherpf, John C. *African Quadrilles, Selected from the Most Admired Negro Melodies and Arranged for the Pianoforte*. New York: E. Riley, 1844.

Schoolcraft, Henry Rowe. *Information Respecting the History, Condition, and Prospects of the Indian Tribes in the United States*. Philadelphia: Lippincott, Grambo and Company, 1851–57.

Seward, Theodore F. *Jubilee Songs, as Sung by the Jubilee Singers of Fisk University*. New York: Bigelow and Main, 1872.

Sharp, Cecil J. *American-English Folk-Songs*. New York: G. Schirmer, Inc., 1918.

—— *English Folksongs from the Southern Appalachians*. 2 volumes. London: Oxford University Press, 1932. (2nd edition, London: Oxford University Press, 1952.)

—— *Folk-Songs of English Origin from the Appalachian Mountains*. London: Novello and Company, 1921.

—— *Nursery Songs from the Appalachian Mountains*. London: Novello and Company, 1921–23.

Shearin, A. M., and J. H. Coombs. *Syllabus of Kentucky Folk-Songs*. Transylvania University Studies in English, 1911.

Shoemaker, Henry W. *Mountain Minstrelsy of Pennsylvania*. Philadelphia: J. F. McGirr, 1931.

—— *Music and Musical Instruments of Pennsylvania Mountaineers*. Altoona, Pennsylvania: Mountain City Press, 1924.

Silber, Irwin. *Songs of the Civil War*. New York: Columbia University Press, 1960.

Smith, C. Alphonso. "Ballads Surviving in the United States." *Musical Quarterly*, January, 1916.

Smith, N. Clark. *New Plantation Melodies as Sung by the Tuskegee Students*. Tuskegee, Alabama, 1909.

Smith, Nicholas. *Stories of Great National Songs*. Milwaukee, Wisconsin: The Young Churchman Company, 1899.

Smith, Reed. *American Anthology of Old World Ballads*. New York: J. Fischer and Brother, 1937.

—— *South Carolina Ballads*. Cambridge, Massachusetts: Harvard University Press, 1928.

Sonneck, O. G. *Miscellaneous Studies in the History of Music* (Chapter on the First Edition of *Hail Columbia*). New York: The Macmillan Company, 1921.

Speck, F. G., and J. D. Sapir. *Ceremonial Songs of the Creek and Yuchi Indians.* Philadelphia: University of Pennsylvania Anthropological Publications, Vol. I, 1911.

The Star-Spangled Banner. Revised and enlarged from the Report of 1909. Washington, D.C.: Library of Congress, Government Printing Office, 1914.

Report on *The Star-Spangled Banner, Hail Columbia, America, Yankee Doodle.* Washington, D.C.: Library of Congress, Government Printing Office, 1909.

Still, William Grant. *Twelve Negro Spirituals.* New York: Handy Brothers Music Company, 1937.

Stout, Earl J. *Folklore from Iowa.* New York: The American Folk-Lore Society, 1936.

Sturgis, Edith B., and Robert Hughes. *Songs from the Hills of Vermont.* New York: G. Schirmer, Inc., 1919.

Sulzer, Elmer G. *Twenty-five Kentucky Folk Ballads.* Lexington, Kentucky: Transylvania Printing Company, 1936.

Thomas, Jean. *Ballad Makin' in the Mountains of Kentucky.* New York: Holt, Rinehart and Winston, 1939.

—— *Devil's Ditties, Being Stories of the Kentucky Mountain People.* Chicago: W. W. Hatfield, 1931.

—— *The Singin' Fiddler of Lost Hope Hollow.* New York: E. P. Dutton and Company, 1938.

—— and Joseph A. Leeder. *The Singin' Gatherin'; Tunes from the Southern Appalachians.* New York: Silver Burdett Company, 1939.

Troyer, Carlos. *Indian Music Lecture: The Zuñi Indians and Their Music.* Philadelphia: Theodore Presser Company, 1913.

Turner, Harriet. *Folk Songs of the American Negro.* Boston: Boston Music Company, 1925.

Van Stone, Mary R. *Spanish Folk Songs of New Mexico.* Chicago: R. F. Seymour, 1926.

Wallaschek, Richard. *Primitive Music.* (Chap. I, "America"). London: Longmans, Green and Company, 1893.

Waterman, Richard A. " 'Hot' Rhythm in Negro Music." *Journal of the American Musicological Society*, Vol. 1, No. 1 (Spring, 1948).

The Weavers Song; Folk Songs of America and Other Lands. New York: Folkways Music Publishers, 1951.

Weedon, Miss Howard. *Songs of the Old South*. New York: Doubleday, Page and Company, 1900.

Wellman, Manly W. *The Rebel Songster; Songs the Confederates Sang*. Charlotte, North Carolina: Heritage House, 1959.

Weybright, Victor. *Spangled Banner; The Life of Francis Scott Key*. New York: Holt, Rinehart and Winston, 1935.

Wheeler, Mary. *Steamboatin' Days; Folksongs of the River Packet Era*. Baton Rouge: Louisiana State University Press, 1944.

—— and William J. Reddick. *Roustabout Songs; a Collection of Ohio River Valley Songs*. New York: Remick Music Corporation, 1939.

White, Clarence Cameron. *Negro Folk Melodies*. Philadelphia: Theodore Presser Company, 1927.

White, Newman I. *American Negro Folk-Songs*. Cambridge, Massachusetts: Harvard University Press, 1928.

White, Richard Grant. *National Hymns—How They Are Written, and How They Are Not Written*. New York: Rudd and Carleton, 1886.

White, William C. *A History of Military Music in America*. New York: Exposition Press, 1944.

Whitfield, Irène Thérèse. *Louisiana French Folk Songs*. University, Louisiana: Louisiana State University Press, 1939.

Wilgus, D. K. *Anglo-American Folksong Scholarship Since 1898*. New Brunswick, New Jersey: Rutgers University Press, 1959.

Work, Frederick Jerome. *Some American Negro Folk-Songs*. Boston, 1909.

Work, John Wesley. *American Negro Songs*. New York: Howell, Soskin and Company, Inc., 1940.

—— *Folk Song of the American Negro*. Nashville, Tennessee: Fisk University Press, 1915.

Wyman, Loraine, and Howard Brockway. *Lonesome Tunes; Folksongs from the Kentucky Mountains*. New York: H. W. Gray Company, 1916.

—— *Twenty Kentucky Mountain Songs.* Boston: Oliver Ditson Company, 1920.

Yoder, Don. *Pennsylvania Spirituals.* Lancaster, Pennsylvania: Pennsylvania Folklore Society, 1961.

MUSIC PERIODICALS

(Arranged in chronological order, according to their founding. Those still published are marked with an asterisk [*].)

Euterpeiad: or Musical Intelligencer. Devoted to the Diffusion of Musical Information and Belles Lettres. Boston, 1820 to 1823.

Lyre: The New York Musical Journal. New York, 1824 to 1825.

Euterpeiad, an Album of Music, Poetry and Prose. New York, 1830 to 1831.

The Musical Review and Record of Musical Science, Literature, and Intelligence. New York, 1838.

Boston Musical Gazette. Boston, 1838 to 1846.

Musical World. New York, 1849 to 1860.

Musical Magazine. Boston, 1839 to 1842.

American Monthly Musical Review. New York, 1851 to 1852.

The American Musical Almanac for 1852. New York, 1851.

Musical Review and Choral Advocate. New York, 1852 to 1853.

The Musical World and Journal of Fine Arts. New York, 1852 to 1856.

Dwight's Journal of Music. Boston, 1852 to 1881.

Boston Musical Journal. Boston, 1853 to 1854.

New York Musical Review and Choral Advocate. New York, 1854 to 1855.

New York Musical Pioneer and Chorister Budget. New York, 1855 to 1871.

New York Musical Review and Gazette. New York, 1855 to 1860.

American Art Journal. New York, 1863–1905.

Folio; a Journal of Music, Art, Drama and Literature. Boston, 1871 to 1895.

Ditson & Company's Musical Record. Boston, 1878 to 1903.

Musical Review. New York, 1879 to 1881.

Southern Musical Journal. 1879 to 1882.

Musical Courier. New York, 1880 to 1962.

The Etude. Philadelphia, 1883 to 1957.

The Boston Musical Year-Book. Boston, 1883 to 1886.

* *Metronome*. New York, 1885 to the present.

The Musical Year-Book of the United States. Boston, 1886 to 1893.

Music. Chicago, 1891 to 1902.

Music Review. Chicago, 1892 to 1894.

* *The Musical Leader*. Chicago, 1895 to the present.

The Musician. Boston (then New York), 1896 to 1948.

Concert-goer. New York, 1897 to 1903.

* *Musical America*. New York, 1898 to the present.

Pacific Coast Musical Review. San Francisco, 1901 to 1933.

New Music Review and Choral Advocate. New York, 1901 to 1935.

Music Teachers' National Association Book of Proceedings. 1906 to 1949.

The Musical Observer. New York, 1904 (absorbed by *Musical Courier* in 1933).

* *Music Supervisors' Journal:* official organ of the Music Supervisors' National Conference, 1914 to 1934; became *Music Educators' Journal*, 1934 to the present.

Music News. Chicago, 1908 to 1952.

The Musical Monitor. New York, 1912 to 1919; official organ of the National Federation of Music Clubs.

* *The Musical Quarterly*. New York, 1915 to the present.

Music and Musicians. Seattle, 1915 to 1937.

Pacific Coast Musician. Los Angeles, 1919 to 1937.

* *Official Bulletin of the National Federation of Music Clubs*. 1922 to 1928; became *Music Clubs' Magazine*, 1928 to 1960; became *Showcase*, 1960 to the present.

Musical Digest. New York, 1921 to 1947.

Pro-Musica Quarterly. New York, 1923 to 1929.

Modern Music. New York, 1924 to 1946.

Pierre Key's International Music Year Book. New York, 1925–26, 1926–27, 1929–30, 1935, 1938.

Singing. New York, 1926 to 1927; became *Singing & Playing*, New York, 1927 to 1930; became *Encore*, 1930 to 1933.

Northwest Musical Herald. Minneapolis, 1926 to 1934.

* *Downbeat*. New York, 1934 to the present.

American Record Guide. New York, 1935 to 1953.

* *American Composers Alliance Bulletin*. New York, 1938, 1952 to the present.

* *Music Publishers' Journal*. New York, 1943 to 1946; became *Music Journal*, 1946 to the present.

Music of the West. 1945 to 1962.

* *Instrumentalist*. 1946 to the present.

* *Pan Pipes of Sigma Alpha Iota. American Music Issue*. New York, 1947 to the present.

* *Journal of the American Musicological Society*. 1948 to the present.

* *The Hymn*, published by the Hymn Society of America, New York. 1949 to the present.

* *American Music Teacher*. 1951 to the present.

* *Moravian Music Foundation Bulletin*. Winston-Salem, North Carolina, 1956 to the present.

Jazz Review. 1958 to 1962.

* *Music Today*. New York, published by the American Music Center, 1958 to the present.

* *Perspectives of New Music*. Princeton, New Jersey, 1962 to the present.

INDEX

Index

(Compositions which bear merely the title of a musical form, such as Violin Concerto and Symphony No. 1, are not listed in the index.)

A

Abbot, Asahel (*The Waldenses*), 249
Abbot of Derry, The (Weaver), 655
Abbott, George, 746, 748
Abel, F. L., 138
Abe Lincoln (Robinson), 629
Abide with Me (Spross), 624
Aborn Opera Company, 717
About Dixie (Stringfield), 465
Abraham (MacGimsey), 637
Abraham Lincoln (Bennett), 461
Abraham Lincoln Song (Damrosch, W.), 352
Abraham Lincoln Walks at Midnight (Palmer), 580
Abraham Lincoln Walks at Midnight (Raphling), 558
Abraham Lincoln Walks at Midnight (Siegmeister), 514
Abrahams, Maurice (1883-1931), 709
Absent (Metcalf), 622
Abt, Franz, 297
Abt Male Singing Society, Philadelphia, 303
Academic Overture (Hadley), 377
Accentuate the Positive (Arlen), 741
Achron, Isidor (1892-1948), 477
Achron, Joseph (1886-1943), 423, 662
Acis and Galatea (Handel), 157
Adagio (McCollin), 635
Adagio and Allegro (Stevens), 519
Adagio and Allegro (Ward), 560
Adagio Eroico (Bennett), 461
Adagio for Orchestra (Clifton), 416
Adagio for Strings (Barber), 531
Adams, Samuel Hopkins, 749
Adams and Liberty (Paine), 126

Adams and Washington (Van Hagen, Jr.), 75
Adamses, The (Bucci), 597
Adamson, Harold, 751
Adding Machine, The, 402
Address to the Ladies of Charleston (Pownall), 108
Ade, George, 719
Adgate, Andrew (?-1793), 105-107, 136
Adirondack Sketches (Lane), 640
Adler, Richard (1923-), 748
Ad Lyram (Hovhaness), 551
Adonais (Chadwick), 309
Adonais (Rogers, B.), 446
Adopted Child (Van Hagen, P. A.), 74
Adoration (Borowski), 638
Adventures in a Perambulator (Carpenter), 371, 373
Adventures in a Zoo (Kleinsinger), 643
Advertisements (Cowell), 449
Advice to the Ladies of Boston (Pownall), 108
Aeolian Hall (New York), 722
Aeolian Music Foundation, 462
Aeroplane, The (Whithorne), 410
Africa (Still), 462
African Kraal (Freeman), 361
Afro-American Symphony (Still), 462
After Dinner Sonata (Wagner), 516
After the Ball (Harris), 705, 715
Agamemnon and Furies in Hades (El-Dabh), 619
Agee, James, 533
Age of Anxiety, The (Bernstein), 539-540
Ager, Milton (1893-), 749
Ahavah (Diamond), 545
Ahlert, Fred E. (1892-1953), 749

Ah, Love, But a Day (Beach), 322
Ah, Love, But a Day (Gilberté), 625
Ahner, Henry, 271
Ah, Why on Quebec's Bloody Plain (Pelissier), 95
Ah! Wilderness, 720
Ain' Gonna Rain No More, 696
Ainsworth, Henry, 4-5
Ain't She Sweet (Ager), 749
Ain't We Got Fun? (Whiting), 749
Air and Scherzo (Mourant), 562
Airborne, The (Blitzstein), 497
Air Corps Suite (Steinert), 523
Aird, James, 115
Airphonic Suite (Schillinger), 457
Airplane Sonata (Antheil), 490
Air Power (Dello Joio), 543
Akron, University of, 613
Alabama Minstrels, 178
Alabamy Bound (Henderson), 738
A la Chinoise (Ornstein), 458
Aladdin (Kelley), 345
Alamo, The, score for (Tiomkin), 478
Alba (Barlow, S. L. M.), 472
Albany State Register, 185
Albee, James, 632, 633
Albert, Eugene d', 742
Albini, Madame, 159
Album for Young People (Diamond), 546
Album of Jewish Folksong (Ephros), 662
Alcestiad, The (Talma), 513
Alcotts, The (Ives), 366
Aleichem, Sholem, 749
Alexander's Ragtime Band (Berlin), 733
Algerian, The (De Koven), 718
Alglala (De Leone), 420
Alhambra (Buck), 645
Ali Baba and the Forty Thieves (Cesana), 467
Alice Blue Gown (Tierney), 738
Alice in Wonderland (Edwards), 627
Alice in Wonderland (Kelley), 346
Alice in Wonderland, music for (Fain), 751
Alice in Wonderland, music for (Fine), 570
Alive and Kicking (Rome), 744
Alkmoonok, the Death Song of the Cherokee Indians, 672-673
Allah (Freeman), 361

Allan, Maud, 392
Alleghanians, 173
Allegro (Rodgers-Hammerstein), 740
Allegro Energico (Mennini), 589
Alleluia (Harrison), 577
Alleluia in the Form of a Toccata (Talma), 514
Alleluja, Christ is Risen (Campbell Watson), 662
Allen, Paul Hastings (1882-1952), 420
Allen, William Francis, 684, 685
All Hail the Power of Jesus' Name (Holden), 60
All on a Summer's Day (Sowerby), 65
All Quiet Along the Potomac (Hewitt, J. H.), 169
All Quiet on the Western Front, score for (Brokeman), 528
All the Things You Are (Kern), 732
All Things Bright and Fair Are Thine (Shaw), 135
All Things Love Thee, So Do I (Horn), 157
All to Myself (Densmore), 626
All Weary Men (Weaver), 655
Alma Mater (Hadley), 377
Almost in Your Arms (Livingston), 752
Alone (Watts, W.), 630
Along the Columbia River (Saar), 361
Alphabet Song, The, 695
Alpine songs and singers, 174-175
Alter, Louis (1902-   ), 753
Always (Berlin), 733
Always Take Mother's Advice (Lindsay), 706
Always True to You Darling in My Fashion (Porter), 738
Amahl and the Night Visitors (Menotti), 537
Amanda (Barlow, S. L. M.), 472
amateurs, in early concerts, 158
Amateur Sonatas (Shapero), 603
Amelia Goes to the Ball (Menotti), 536
America, 47, 126-128
America (Bloch), 393
America, Commerce and Freedom (Reinagle), 80
America First (MacFarlane), 652
Americana (Duke), 526
Americana (Kolar), 424
Americana (Luening), 502
Americana (Thompson, R.), 443

American Academy in Rome, 402, 430, 442, 452, 464, 473, 495, 511, 512, 515, 520, 522, 523, 531, 561, 563, 567, 580, 584, 599, 600, 601, 602, 606, 611, 630, 656, 762

American Academy of Arts and Letters, 377, 382, 402, 434, 441, 447, 451, 472, 486, 492, 509, 525, 544, 576

American Album (Raphling), 558

Americana Music Collection (*see under* New York Public Library)

American Antiquarian Society, Worcester, Massachusetts, 128

American Ballads and Songs (Pound), 696

American Ballad Singers, 514

American Beauty, The (Kerker), 714

American Bell, The (Amram), 619

American Book Company, 473

American Broadcasting Company, 590, 619

American Caprice (Kubik), 555

American Circle (Read), 559

American Company, 72

American Composers' Alliance, 560, 763

American Composers' Alliance Bulletin, 414, 571, 608

American Composers' Concerts (*see under* Eastman School of Music)

American Composers' Contest, 626

American Composers on American Music (Cowell, ed.), 451

American Concert Overture (Converse, C. C.), 666

American Conservatorio, 239

American Conservatory of Music, Chicago, 419, 500, 521, 555, 656, 658

American Creed (Harris), 438

American Dance (Phillips), 509

American Dances (Kreutz), 509

American Dance Suite (Smith), 569

American Documentary Films, 481

American Elegy (Serly), 528

American Epic (Morris), 459

Americanesque (Gilbert), 355

American Expeditionary Forces, 415

American Federation of Musicians, 765

American Festival Overture (Schuman), 535

American Folk Songs and Ballads, 500

American Folk Tunes (Stringham), 473

American Frescoes (Rogers), 446

American Glee Book, 144

American Grand Opera Company, 501

American Guild of Authors and Composers, 730, 742

American Guild of Organists, 311, 648, 649, 653

American Harmony, The (Holden), 61

American Hymn (Keller), 297, 709

American Idea, The (Cohan), 719

American Indian music (*see* Indian music)

American in Paris, An (Gershwin), 427

American Jubilee (Wagner), 516

American Life (Weiss), 454

American Magazine, 39

American Maid, The (Sousa), 715

American Musical Theatre (Ewen), 496

American Music Association, 759

American Music Center, 518, 519, 571, 583, 611, 613, 616

American Musicological Society, 630

American Music Society, 759

American Music Theatre, 506

American Opera Company, 286

American Opera Society of Chicago, 361

American Orchestra, New York, 368

American Orchestral Society, 415

American Overture (Fletcher), 580

American Overture (Harris), 436, 438

American Pattern (Moross), 551

American Piece (Howe), 421

American Polonaise (Riegger), 396

American Primitive Music (Burton), 674

American Quadrille (Jullien), 221, 222

American Recording Society, 763

American Rhapsody (Zimbalist), 422

American Romance (Freeman), 361

American Salute (Gould), 553

American Scenes (Ganz), 384

Americans Come, The (Foster), 627, 727

American Serenade (Robertson), 472

American Singing Book (Read), 63

American Sketches (Converse, F. S.), 381

American Sketches (Strong), 344

American Society of Composers, Authors, and Publishers (ASCAP), 402, 441, 492, 553, 631, 635, 709, 714, 761, 762

American Sonata (Siegmeister), 514

American Songbag, The (Sandburg), 696-697

American Street Scenes (McKay), 463

American Symphonette, 1, 2, and 3 (Gould), 553

American Symphony (Antheil), 491

American Symphony Orchestra, Chicago, 422

American Youth Orchestra, 603

America's Sweetheart (Rodgers-Hart), 739

America's Troubadour (Howard), 635

America the Beautiful, setting (Hier), 421

Amériques (Varèse), 413

Amiable Conversation (Cowell), 449

Amitié pour Amitié (Mason, W.), 280

Among the Garden Ways (Heilman), 389

Amphions, 173

Amphitryon (Rogers, B.), 447

Amran, David (1930-   ), 618-619

Anabase (Bowles), 582

Ancient of Days (Coombs), 650

Andante (Harris), 437

Andante (Kennan), 580

Andante and Allegro Energico (Mennini), 589

Andante and Ariso (Dahl), 565

Andantino (Harris), 438

Anders, Arthur Olaf, 656

An der See (Strong), 344

Anderson, Leroy (1908-   ), 642

Anderson, Marian, 517, 789

And Let Me the Canakin Clink (Manney), 623

And Love Was Born (Kern), 732

André, Major, 71

Andrews, Mark (1875-1939), 653

Andreyev, Leonid, 453, 561

Andromache's Farewell (Barber), 533

And They Lynched Him on a Tree (Still), 462

Angelo's Letter (Beach, J. P.), 370

Angels (Ruggles), 369

Animal Pictures (Ganz), 384

Anna (Van Hagen, Jr.), 75

Anna and the King of Siam, score for (Herrmann), 554

Ann Gregory (Chanler), 631

Annie Get Your Gun (Berlin), 734

Anno 1600 (Dubensky), 477

Anschütz, 283

Answer, The (Terry), 623

Answer of the Stars, The (Converse, F. S.), 382

Answers to a Questionnaire (Inch), 571

Antes, John, 29, 37, 789

Antheil, George (1900-1959), 490-492, 575, 600, 789

Antimony (Cowell), 449

Antitheatre law, 69-70, 72, 76

Antonio (Pratt), 305

Antony and Cleopatra, music for (Dello Joio), 543

Anxious Bugler, The (Carpenter), 373

Anything Goes (Porter), 737

Anything You Can Do I Can Do Better (Berlin), 734

Apocalypse (Menotti), 538

Apocalypse, The (Gallico), 361

Apollo (Selby), 68

Apollo Club, Boston, 293

Appalachian Mountain ballads, 405, 637, 687

Appalachian Mountain Melodies (Gaul), 654

Appalachian Mountain Sketches (Freed), 527

Appalachian Spring (Copland), 483

April (Rasbach), 627

April Rain (Crist), 630

Apthorp, William F., 217

Aquacade, Billy Rose's, 752

Arabesque (Cowles), 641

Arabesques (Tcherepnin), 477

Archdale (Law), 60

Archers, or Mountaineers, of Switzerland, The (Carr), 99

Archipelago (Antheil), 491

Archives of American Folksong, 630

archy and mehitabel (Marquis-Kleinsinger), 643

Ardoin, John, 537, 632

Ardos (Hovhaness), 551

Arevakal (Hovhaness), 551

Are You Making Any Money (Hupfield), 750

Argonauts, The (Eppert), 418

Argonauts, The (Maganini), 474

Aria and Toccata (Dello Joio), 542

Ariadne Abandoned by Theseus, in the Isle of Naxos (Pelissier), 95

Aria with Fontana Mix (Cage), 573

Arioso Elegiaco (Read), 559

Arioso for Strings (Mennini), 589

Arizona (Nevin, A.), 386

Arizona, University of, 502, 563, 642

Arizona Anniversary Music Project Competition, 611
Arizona Sketches (Young), 637
Arjuna (Hovhaness), 550
Arkansas Traveler (Guion), 406, 636
Arlen, Harold (1905-   ), 460, 741, 754, 789
Armenian Rhapsodies (Hovhaness), 550
Armistice Day (Reddick), 636
Armstrong, Louis (1900-   ), 724, 789
Army Air Force, symphony dedicated to, 531
Army Hymn (Dresel), 218
Arndt, Felix (1889-1918), 752
Arne, Thomas, 107
Arnheim (Holyoke), 62
Arnold, Samuel, 107, 124
Around the World in Eighty Days (Porter), 737
Around the World in Eighty Days, music for (Young), 753
Arrah Wanna (Morse), 707
Arrayed in Clouds of Golden Light (Shaw), 135
Arthur, Robert Alan, 748
Arthur Jordan Conservatory, 419
Artik (Hovhaness), 551
Artisan, The (Ware), 625
Artist's Wife, The (Hewitt, J. H.), 169
Art of A Cappella Singing, The (Montani), 660
Art of Judging Music, The (Thomson), 433
Art Thou Happy, Lovely Lady (Webb), 144
Arturo Ui (Brecht), 746
ASCAP (*see* American Society of Composers, Authors, and Publishers)
Ascension, The (Burleigh), 640
As Chloe Came into the Room, 31
As It Fell Upon a Day (Copland), 485
Asleep (Spross), 624
Asolani (Beach, J. P.), 370
As on the Night (Hovhaness), 551
Asperges me (Douglas), 651
Asra (Breil), 387-388
Assisi (Wetzler), 389
Association of Symphony Orchestras, 446, 493
Assyrian Symphony (Jacobi), 460
Astarte (Johnson, H.), 628
As Thousands Cheer (Berlin), 734
As Time Goes By (Hupfield), 750

Astronaut, Astronaut Count-Down, 754
As You Like It (Paine), 301
As You Like It (Wetzler), 389
At a Georgia Camp Meeting (Mills), 720
Atala, or the Love of Two Savages (Schoenefeld), 362
At Dawning (Cadman), 403
At Evenfall (Manney), 623
At Fox Meadow (Damrosch, W.), 353
Athalia (Freeman), 361
Athaliah (Weisgall), 566, 642
At Home Abroad (Schwartz), 739
Atkinson, Brooks, 429, 540
Atlanta Symphony Orchestra, 385
Atlantis (Cowell), 449
Atlantis (Stearns), 420
Atlas Eclipticalis (Cage), 574
At Night (Foerster), 622
At Night (Oldberg), 386
Atonement of Pan, The (Hadley), 376
At Sunset (Strong), 344
At the Fair (Powell), 406
At the Well (Hageman), 629
Attis (Moevs), 601-602
At Twilight (Terry), 623
Aubade (Herrmann), 554
Auditorium Festival Ode (Gleason), 304
Auer, Leopold, 363
Auerbach, Arnold, 744
Augustana College, 594
Augusteo Orchestra, 531
Auld Robin Gray, 80
A Une Madonne (Josten), 412
Au pays des Peaux-Rouges (Strong), 345
Aurora Borealis (Cadman), 404
Aurora Borealis (Hadley), 377
Ausonia (Saminsky), 423
Austrian Hymn, 698
Autobiography for Strings (Amram), 618
Autumn Leaves (Manning), 627
Autumn Overture (Leidzen), 641
Available Forms (Brown), 617
Ave atque Vale (Converse, F. S), 381
Ave Maria (Hovhaness), 551
Ave Maris Stella (Meyerowitz), 585
Aviation Suite (Grofé), 467
Avodat Shabbat (Berlinski), 587
Avshalomov, Jacob (1919-   ), 586, 789
Awakening of the Forest-Spirits (Strong), 344

Awakening of the Woods, The (Ballantine), 416
Awards (*see* names of specific funds, foundations, etc.)
Awfully Clever (Hunt), 705
Ayer, Ethan, 440
Ayres, Frederick (1876-1926), 364, 376, 790
Azara (Paine), 301
Azora (Hadley), 376

B

Babar (Barlow, S. L. M.), 472
Babar the Elephant (Berezowsky), 525
Babbitt, Milton (1916-   ), 574-575, 767
Babes in Arms (Rodgers-Hart), 740
Babes in Toyland (Herbert, V.), 717
Babies on Our Block, The (Braham), 713
Baby, It's Cold Outside (Loesser), 747
Babylon Is Fallen (Root), 267
Bacchanalia (El-Dabh), 619
Bach, Johann Sebastian, 67, 541, 557, 592
Bachata (Kubik), 555
Back, Back, Back to Baltimore (Van Alstyne), 708
Back to Methuselah, music for (Luening, 506
Bacon, Ernst (1898-   ), 393, 465-466, 594
Bad Man Lazarus, 687
bad men's songs, 687
Baermann, Carl, 321, 640
Bagatelles (Persichetti), 548
Bagatelles (Tcherepnin), 477
Bagatelles for Strings (Van Vactor), 524
Bailey, Parker (1902-   ), 522
Bakalenikof, Vladimir, 558
Baker, Benjamin Franklin (1811-1889), 147-148, 265
Baker, John C., 170-171
Baker, Theodore, 673
Bakers, The, 173
Balakovič, Zlato, 372
Balanchine, George, 557
Balinese Ceremonial Music (McPhee), 528
Ball, Ernest R. (1878-1927), 707
Ballad (Freed), 526

Ballad (Imbrie), 606
Ballad (Kurka), 598
Ballade (Bartlett), 648
Ballade (Brockway), 384
Ballade (Converse, F. S.), 382
Ballade (Foote), 312
Ballade (Mason, W.), 280
Ballade (Starer), 620
Ballade (Weiss), 454
Ballad for Americans (Robinson), 629, 727
Ballad of Baby Doe, The (Moore), 439-440
Ballad of the North and South, A (Lockwood), 515
Ballad of the Sad Cafe, music for (Flanagan), 632
Ballad of Trees and the Master (Chadwick), 310
Ballad of William Sycamore, The (Stevens), 519
Ballads and Songs of the Shanty-Boy (Rickaby), 694-695
Ballads and Tragic Legends (Niles), 637
Ballantine, Edward (1886-   ), 416
Ballet Caravan Company, 482, 582
Ballet in E (Haieff), 561
Ballet mécanique (Antheil), 490
Ballet of Identity (Luening-Ussachevsky), 506
Ballet Society, 488
Ballets Russe de Monte Carlo, 483
Ballet Suite (Clokey), 634
Ballets USA (Kay), 557
Ballet Theatre, 540, 553, 615
Ballet Viennoise (Barrymore), 389
Ballroom Guide, The (Bowles), 582
Ballroom Guide, The (Carter), 488
Baltimore *Evening Sun,* 388
Baltimore Symphony Orchestra, 362, 464, 484
Balzac, H., 600
Bamberger Little Symphony Orchestra, 468
Bamboula (Gottschalk), 205, 206, 681
Bananier, Le (Gottschalk), 205, 206, 681
band, minstrel, 177-178
Bandanna Sketches (White), 636
Band's Music, The (Goldman, R. F.), 642
Band Wagon (Schwartz), 749
Bangor Fire, The, 695
Bangor March (Shaw), 135

Banjo, The (Gottschalk), 206
banjo jigs, 181
Banjo Song, A (Homer), 623
Banshee (Cowell), 450
Barat College, 414
Barati, George (1913-   ), 586
Barbara Allen, 665, 692
Barbara Allen (Brokeman), 528
Barbara Frietchie (Bonner), 420
Barber, Samuel (1910-   ), 435, 530-533, 571, 629, 790
Barber Shop Ballad (Finney), 498
Barcarolle (Mills), 291
Barkers, The, 173
Barlow, Samuel L. M. (1892-   ), 472
Barlow, Wayne (1912-   ), 578
Barnard, Charlotte Alington (1830-1869), 704
Barnard, Ernst, 39
Barnard, John, 37, 47
Barnard College, 502
Barnes, Edwin Shippen (1887-1958), 654-655
Barnett, Alice (1888-   ), 630
Barney, I'll Take You Home Again (Parseby), 705
Barnum, P. T., 199, 202, 203
Barrel Organ Barcarolle (Duke), 526
Barrère, Georges, 380, 390, 473, 747
Barrier, The (Meyerowitz), 585
Barry, Philip, 442
Barrymore, Lionel (1878-1954), 389
Barth, Hans (1897-1956), 383, 384
Bartleby (Flanagan), 632
Bartlett, Homer Newton (1846-1920), 290, 648
Bartok, Bela, 513, 519, 529, 551, 557, 560, 570, 598, 600, 620
Barton, Andrew, 28, 115
Basie, William "Count" (1906-   ), 724, 790
Bataan (McDonald), 463
Batouala (Josten), 412
Battle Cry of Freedom (Root), 264, 265
Battle Hymn of the Republic, The, 255, 258-259
Battle of Hexham, The (Van Hagen, P. A.), 74
Battle of Manila (Pratt), 305
Battle of Prague (Kotzwara), 80-81
Battle of Prague (Schetky), 108
Battle of the Kegs (Hopkinson), 37

Battle of the Wabash, The, 126
Battle of Trenton (Hewitt), 88-89
Bauer, Emilie, 411
Bauer, Harold, 421
Bauer, Marion (1887-1955), 411
Baumgartner, Allbertine, 628
Bayley, Daniel, 48
Bayly, Thomas Haynes, 159, 160, 162
Bayou Legend, A (Still), 462
Bayou Songs (Strickland), 627
Bay Psalm Book, 5, 8-11, 15, 16
Bay State Glee Club, 148
Beach, Mrs. H. H. A. (1867-1944), 289, 319-323, 625, 679, 790
Beach, John Parsons (1877-1953), 370
Beale Street Blues (Handy), 688
Beals, John, 39
Beanes, Dr., 121-122
Bearns (Joseph E. and Lillia M.) Prize and Fund, 507, 513, 531, 612, 616, 632, 762
Beatitudes, The (Hovhaness), 551
Beatrice (Hoiby), 599
Beaubien, Mark, 270
Beauty and the Beast (Giannini), 494
Beauty and the Beast (Haieff), 562
Beauty of Earth (Kramer), 631
Beauty Spot, The (De Koven), 718
Because You're You (Herbert, V.), 717
Becker, John J. (1886-1961), 414-415, 790
Bedell, Robert Leech (1909-   ), 658
Bedouin Love Song (Brewer), 647
Beebe, Carolyn, 400
Beeson, Jack (1921-   ), 501, 600, 612
Beethoven, Ludwig van, 98, 217, 223, 237, 308, 557
Beethoven and His Forerunners (Mason, D. G.), 378
Before the Dawn (Hanson), 430
Before the Door of the Wigwam (Stearns), 420
Before the Paling of the Stars (Kramer), 631
Beggar at Love's Gate, A (Strickland), 627
Beggar on Horseback, 402
Beggar's Love (Patterson), 387
Beggar's Opera, The, 31, 69, 104
Begin the Beguine (Porter), 737
Begnis, Signor de, 150
Beguine (Moross), 557
Begum, The (De Koven), 718

Behold I Build a House (Foss), 592

Behrman, S. N., 744

Beirut Conservatory, 527

Beissel, Conrad, 26

Belafonte, Henry, 697, 790

Belle Dame sans Merci, La (Converse, F. S.), 382

Belle Dame sans Merci, La (Riegger), 396

Belle of New York, The (Kerker), 714, 716

Bell Goes a-Ringing for Sai-rah, The (Hunt), 705

Bell Ringers, 173

Bells, The (Taylor, R.), 93

Bells Are Ringing (Styne), 745

Bells in The Rain (Duke), 631

Belshazzar (Hadley), 377

Bendel, Franz, 305

Bendix, Max (1866-1945), 361

Beneath a Weeping Willow's Shade (Hopkinson), 42

Beneath the Honors (Holyoke), 63

Benét, Stephen Vincent, 417, 439, 518

Ben Hur (Kelley), 345, 347

Benkert, G. F., 710

Bennard, Rev. George (1873-1958), 668

Bennett, Robert Russell (1894-   ), 460-461, 479, 556, 741

Bennington College, 502, 604, 610, 643

Bentley, John, 71, 102, 103

Berceuse (Johns, C.), 639

Berceuse (Palmer), 389

Beresford, William, 672

Berezowsky, Alice, 525

Berezowsky, Nicolai (1900-1953), 379, 525, 790

Berg, Alban, 453, 498

Berger, Arthur (1912-   ), 562-563, 570, 572, 574, 603, 790

Berger Bell Ringers, 173

Bergh, Arthur (1882-   ), 548, 626

Bergmann, B., 81, 90

Bergmann, Carl (1821-1876), 214, 271, 279

Bergner, Frederick, 279

Bergsma, William (1921-   ), 540-591, 600

Berkenhead, John L., 68-69, 135

Berkshire Music Center and Festival, 392, 396, 486, 538, 558, 560, 563, 570, 585, 589, 591, 596, 597, 605, 608, 613, 617, 619

Berkshire Quartet, 359

Berlin Hochschule für Musik, 459, 581

Berlin, Irving (1888-   ), 719, 726, 733-735, 790

Berlin Philharmonic Orchestra, 384, 409, 463, 490, 742

Berlinski, Herman (1910-   ), 587, 790

Berlioz, Hector, 205, 242, 277

Bernheimer, Martin, 593

Bernstein, Leonard (1918-   ), 369, 414, 481, 538-541, 556, 760, 767, 791

Berwald, William Henry (1864-1948), 661

Bess, You Is My Woman Now (Gershwin), 429

Best Is Yet to Come, The (Curran), 625

Best Things in Life Are Free, The (Henderson), 739

Bethany (Mason), 137

Bethlehem, Pennsylvania, early music in, 24, 28-30

Bethlehem (Tuthill), 418

Betrothal, The (Delamarter), 417

Betty and Harold Close Their Eyes (Bennett), 461

Between the Devil and the Deep Blue Sea (Schwartz), 739

Bewitched, The (Partch), 499

Beyond (Daniels), 386

Beyond the Horizon (Barrymore), 389

Bial, Carl, 621

Bianca (Hadley), 376

Bibliography, 769-845
   collective biography, 814-817
   folk and traditional music, 826-843
   general, background and history, 769-788
   individual composers and performers, 789-814
   jazz and popular music, 818-825
   periodicals, 843-845
   popular music, 818-825

Biedermann, Edward Julius (1849-1933), 648

Biedermeier Waltzes (Barlow), 472

Biederwolf, William Edward, 668

Big Brown Bear, The (Mana-Zucca), 627

Biggs, E. Power, 608

Big River (Tuthill), 418

Big Sunflower, The (Newcombe), 703

Bill (Kern), 731

Billie (Cohan), 720
Billie Boy, 635, 692
Billings, William (1746-1800), 24, 49-57, 136, 366, 450, 502, 535, 634, 755, 791
Billy Budd (Flanagan), 632
Billy the Kid, 693
Billy the Kid (Copland), 482-483
Billy Patterson (Emmett), 181, 256
Binder, Abraham Wolfe (1895-), 663
Bingham, Seth (1882-), 416-417
Bingo Eli Yale (Porter), 737
Binkerd, Gordon (1916-), 571, 791
Biographical Dictionary of Musicians (Baker), 530, 548
biographies and autobiographies of composers and performers, 789-814
Birch, Harry, 705
Birchard, C. C., Company, 368
Bird, Arthur (1856-1923), 345, 791
Birdland (Leplin), 588
Bird of the Wilderness (Horsman), 624
Birds, The (Engel), 556
Birds, The (Green), 518
Birds at Dawn (Dillon), 640
Birds at Dusk (Dillon), 640
Birthday of the Infanta, The (Carpenter), 372
Birthday Song, A (Noble), 651
Birth of Moses, The (Lockwood), 515
Birth of the Blues, The (Henderson), 739
Biscaccianti, Eliza Ostinelli, 170
Bishop, T. Brigham (1835-1925), 703
Bispham, David, 371, 625
Bispham Memorial Medal, 380, 387, 420, 460, 474, 475, 478
Bissell, Richard, 745, 748
Black and White Songs (Bacon), 466
Blackbirds of 1928 (McHugh), 751
Black Bottom (Henderson), 739
Black Brigade (Emmett), 181
Black, Brown and Beige (Ellington), 724
Black Crook, The (Operti), 712
Blackmar, A. E., 262-263
Black Maskers, The (Sessions), 453
Black Mountain College, 576
Black Orchid, The (Delamarter), 417
Blackwood, Easley (1933-), 605-606
Blake, Dorothy Gaynor, 623
Blake, William, 502

Bland, James A. (1854-1911), 701-702, 791
Blennerhasset (Giannini), 494
Bless You All (Rome), 744
Blest Pair of Sirens (Huhn), 623
Blind King, The (Parker), 296
Blind Piper, The (Crouch), 172
Bliss, Philip Paul (1838-1876), 667, 791
Blithely and Gay (Horn), 158
Blitzstein, Marc (1905-1964), 495-498, 556, 791
Bloch, Ernest (1880-1959), 391-395, 421, 441, 442, 446, 452, 456, 465, 471, 473, 479, 490, 512, 517, 518, 522, 526, 546, 587, 631, 662, 791-792
Bloch Society, 394
Blood Moon (Dello Joio), 543
Bloomer Girl (Arlen), 741
Bloomfield, Arthur, 519
Blossom Time (Romberg), 730
Blow, Gabriel, Blow (Porter), 737
Blue and the Gray, The (Dresser), 696, 707
Blue Beard, 80
Blue Bell (Morse), 707
Blue Bird, The (Shaw), 136
Blue Danube (Strauss), 297
Blue Flame, The (Hovhaness), 551
Blue Flower, The (McKinley), 470
Blue Kitten, The (Friml), 729
Blue Paradise (Romberg), 729
blues, 687-689
Blue Shadows (Alter), 753
Blues in the Night (Arlen), 741
Blue Skies (Berlin), 733
Blue Steel (Still), 462
Blue Symphony (Elwell), 473
Blue Tango (Anderson), 642
Bluethner Orchestra, 396
'Bly the Colin (Pownall), 108
Boat Song, The (Ware), 625
Boatwright, Howard (1918-), 659
Boccaccio's Nightingale (Trimble), 611
Bochau, Charles (1870-1932), 638
Bock, Jerry (1928-), 748-749
Bodansky, Artur, 392
Bodas de Sangre (Calabro), 604
Body Beautiful, The (Bock), 748
Boehm, Y., 619
Boepple, Paul, 544
Bohannas family, 173
Bohm, Jerome D., 434
Böhme, F. M., 145

Boise, O. B., 359, 384, 386
Bold Island (Hanson), 430
Bolshoi Theatre, 525
Bolton, Guy, 731, 735
Bond, Carrie Jacobs (1862-1946), 622-623, 624, 629, 792
bones, 178
Bone Squash (Rice), 177
Bonja Song, 179
Bonne Cuisine, La (Bernstein), 540
Bonne Petite Fille (Taylor, R.), 94
Bonner, Eugene (1889-   ), 420
Bonnet, Jeseph, 658
Bonnie (Spencer), 714
Bonnie Blue Flag, The (McCarthy), 263
boogie-woogie, 724-725
Book of Eighty Anthems (Dickinson), 653
Book of Forty Antiphons (Dickinson), 653
Book of Mormon, The (Robertson), 472
Book of Psalmes (Ainsworth), 4-5
Boor, The (Bucci), 597
Boor, The (Kay), 565
Boott Prize, 470
Borden, Ann, 38
Borden, Lizzie, 553, 554
Boretz, Benjamin, 454
Borghese, Antonio, 454
Bornschein, Franz Carl (1879-1948), 388
Borowski, Felix (1872-1956), 630, 638-639
bossa-nova, 726
Boston, 23-24, 69-70, 214
Boston Academy Collection of Church Music (Mason, L.), 141
Boston Academy of Music, 139, 143, 146, 151, 275
Boston Anthem Book (Mason, L.), 141
Boston Baked Beans (Kubik), 555
Boston Burglar, The, 693
Boston Chamber Orchestra, 368
Boston Civic Symphony Orchestra, 516
Boston composers, 306-323
Boston Cotillons (Webb), 144
Boston Handel & Haydn Society's Collection of Sacred Music, 138, 141
Boston *Herald,* 631
Boston Jubilees, 645, 681, 709
Boston Musical Education Society's Collection of Church Music (Baker, Woodbury), 148
Boston Music Company, 629
Boston Music Hall, 295
Boston Music School, 147
Boston News-Letter, 22
Boston Peace Jubilee, 223
Boston Philharmonic Society, 131-132, 151
Boston "Pops" Orchestra, 445, 642
Boston *Post,* 601
Boston Public Library, 88, 93, 130
Boston Symphony Orchestra, 286, 300, 309, 349, 351, 354, 362, 372, 381, 382, 384, 385, 386, 390, 392, 409, 415, 416, 422, 427, 431, 432, 435, 436, 444, 445, 453, 456, 459, 479, 480, 483, 484, 532, 533, 539, 540, 544, 559, 571, 589, 592, 601, 764
Boston University, 296, 558, 608
Bottle, The (Perry), 613
Boulanger, Lilia, Prize and Fund, 609, 612, 763
Boulanger, Nadia, 411, 433, 437, 441, 444, 446, 461, 467, 470, 473, 479, 485, 488, 498, 512, 513, 514, 515, 516, 517, 518, 524, 530, 544, 561, 563, 566, 570, 581, 587, 601, 602, 603, 605, 608, 631, 642
Bouquet for Molly (Robinson), 629
Bourgeois, Louis, 6
Bowery, The (Gaunt), 715
Bowles, Paul (1910-   ), 582-583
Box Hill Overture (Lessard), 603
Boyle, George Frederick (1886-1948), 423
Boy Scout Operetta (MacFarlane), 652
Boys from Syracuse, The (Rodgers-Hart), 740
Bradbury, 146
Bradbury, William Batchelder (1816-1868), 140, 144-146, 667
Braham, David (1838-1905), 712-714
Braham, George, 714
Brahms, Johannes, 278
Brandeis University, 413, 540, 563, 570, 602, 615, 619
Branscombe, Gena (1881-   ), 634
Brant, Henry (1913-   ), 575-576, 767
Brattle, Thomas, 18
Brave Men, Behold Your Fallen Chief (Webster), 263
Brave Old Oak, The (Russell), 163

Bravura (McKay), 463
Bravura Variations on the Romance of Joseph (Herz), 204
Breaking Heart, The (Fry), 245
Break the News to Mother (Harris), 706
Brecht, Bertolt, 454, 497, 597, 746
Breen, May Singhi, 753
Breil, Joseph Carl (1870-1926), 387
Bremner, James, 39, 40, 43
Bremner, Robert, 40
Breslau, Sophie, 622
Bret Harte Overture (James), 468
Breton Cadence (Bingham), 417
Brevard (N. C.) Music Center, 490
Brewer, John Hyatt (1856-1931), 644, 647
Brice, Fannie, 746
Bricher, Thomas, 171
Bricken, Carl Ernest (1898-   ), 469-470, 569
Bridal Overture (Watts, W.), 630
Bride Elect, The (Sousa), 710, 715
Bride of the Gods, The (Gruenberg), 409
Bride's Tragedy, The (Grainger), 407
Bridge, Frank, 446, 650
Bridge, The (Carter), 488
Bridge Builders, The (Search), 422
Brigadoon (Loewe), 742, 743
Briggs House Concerts, 273
Brigham Young University, 471
Bright Jewels for the Sunday School (Bradbury), 145
Brighten the Corner Where You Are (Rodeheaver), 664, 668
Bristol (Shaw), 135
Bristol March (Shaw), 135
Bristow, George F. (1825-1898), 247-252, 756, 758
Bristow, William Richard, 249
Britain, Radie (1903-   ), 521
British Broadcasting Corporation, 395
British Museum, 557
Britten, Benjamin, 444
Broadcast Music, Inc., 450, 549, 564, 608, 761
Broadhurst, Miss, 87
Broadway (Gardner), 641
Broadway at Night (Grofé), 467
Broadway Melody (Brown), 750
Brockway, Howard (1870-1951), 384, 513, 635, 692
Broder, Nathan, 532, 534

Brokeman, David (1902-   ), 528
Broken Troth, The (Cole), 360
Bromfield, Edward, 18
Brook Farm, 218
Brooklyn Barcarolle (Duke), 526
Brooklyn Baseball Cantata (Kleinsinger), 643
Brooklyn College, 516, 520, 585
Brooklyn Oratorio Society, 650
Brooklyn Philharmonic Society, 216, 285, 645
Brooklyn Symphony Orchestra, 468
Brother, Can You Spare a Dime? (Gorney), 749
Brothers, The (Antheil), 491
Brother Soldiers All Hail (Hopkinson), 43
Brower, Frank, 178
Brown, Earl (1926-   ), 617
Brown, J. Appleton, 301
Brown, John, 258-259
Brown, Lew, 738
Brown, Nacio Herb (1896-   ), 750
Brown, Rollo Walter, 323, 335, 336
Brown, William, 71, 76, 102-103
Browne, Edmund, 21
Browne, Walter, 310
Browning, John, 532, 625
Browning, Robert, 369
Browns, The, 173
Brown University, 611
Bruckner, Dionys, 277
Brudder Sinkiller and His Flock of Sheep (Guion), 636
Brunswick, Mark (1902-   ), 517
Brussels Exposition, 413
Bryan, Vincent, 708
Bryant, William Cullen, 261
Bryant's Minstrels, 179, 257
Bucci, Mark (1924-   ), 596-597
Buck, Dudley (1839-1909), 289, 357, 365, 644-646, 647, 654, 755, 792
Buck, Gene, 708
Budapest Symphony Orchestra, 586
Buffalo, University of, 609
Buffalo *Evening News*, 545
Buffalo Philharmonic Orchestra, 545, 591
Buffo (Gesensway), 498
Build Thee More Stately Mansions (Weaver), 655
Bull, John (1563-1628), 127
Bull, Ole (1810-1880), 200-202, 214, 226, 792

Bullard, Frederick Field (1864-1904), 623
Bunch and Judy, The (Kern) 731
Bunyan, John, 651
Buonamici, Giuseppe, 388
Burdetts, The, 173
Burgomaster, The (Luders), 719
Burkat, Leonard, 602
Burleigh, Cecil (1885-   ), 508, 640
Burleigh, Henry Thacker (1866-1949) 636, 700, 792
Burlin, Natalie Curtis, 683
Burma (Eichheim), 382
Burmeister, Richard (1860-1944), 421, 638
Burning House, The (Hovhaness), 557
Burning Ship, The (Baker, B. F.), 148
Burrows, Abe, 745, 747
Burton Frederick R., 674, 675, 676-677
Busch, Carl   1862-1943), 358-359, 460, 465, 700
Busch, Fritz, 427, 383, 406, 409, 412
Bush Conservatory, 520
Bushel and a Peck, A (Loesser), 747
Busoni, Ferruccio, 501, 627, 742
Butler, Nicholas Murray, 338-342
Butterfield, James Austin (1837-1891) 703
Buttons and Bows (Livingston), 752
Button Up Your Overcoat (Henderson), 739
Buzzi-Peccia, Arturo (1854-1943), 622
Bye, Bye, Blackbird (Henderson), 738
By Jupiter (Rodgers-Hart), 740
By Ontario's Shore (Bacon), 466
Byrne, Flora, 263
By the Beautiful Sea (Carroll), 750
By the Beautiful Sea (Schwartz), 739
By the Bend of the River (Edwards), 627
By the Light of the Silvery Moon (Edwards), 708
By the Porta Catania (Heilman), 389
By the Rivers of Babylon (Loeffler), 351
By the Saskatchewan (Caryll), 716
By the Waters of Babylon (Flanagan), 632
By the Waters of Babylon (Hoffman), 290
By the Waters of Babylon (Matthews), 653

By the Waters of Minnetonka (Lieurance), 636

C

Cabeza de Vaca (Antheil), 491
Cabin in the Sky (Duke), 525
Cactus Rhapsody (Britain), 521
Cadets (Kerker), 714
Cadman, Charles Wakefield (1881-1946), 403-404, 700, 792
Cady, C. M., 265
Caesar, Irving, 1895-   ), 736
Cage, John (1913-   ), 571-574, 577, 766, 792
Cahn, Sammy, 745
Cain, Noble (1896-   ), 658
Cain and Abel, 682
Caira, 115
Cairo University, 619
Cakewalk (Kay), 557
Calabro, Louis (1926-   ), 604, 767
Caldwell, Anne, 731
California (Converse, F.), 381
California, Here I Come (Meyer), 750
California Suite (Jacobi), 460
California, University of, 375, 394, 395, 420, 421, 442, 448, 451, 452, 454, 507, 518, 519, 584, 606
California, University of, at Los Angeles, 524, 546, 576, 584, 591
Calliope (Hill), 623
Call Me Madame (Berlin), 734, 735
Call Me Mister (Rome), 744
Call of the Plains, The (Goldmark), 379
Calloway, Cab (1907-   ), 724
Calvin, John, 7
Camelot (Loewe), 743
Camillus the Conqueror (Baker, B. F.), 148
Campbell-Tipton, Louis (1877-1921), 411, 639
Campbell-Watson, Frank (1899-   ), 662
camp meeting songs, 665
Camptown Races (Foster), 181, 198, 484, 650
Camptown Races (Kubik), 555
Canary, The (Caryll), 716
Can-Can (Porter), 738
Can-Can and Waltz (Smith), 618
Candide (Bernstein), 540-541, 556

Candide (Riegger), 398
Candy (Kramer-Whitney), 752
Canning, Effie I., 706
Canon and Fugue (Riegger), 398
Canonic Suite (Carter), 489
Cantata (Talma), 513
Cantata Sacra (Moevs), 602
Cantata to the Text of Sophoclean Choruses (Shifrin), 616
Canterbury Pilgrims, The (De Koven), 718
Cantica Ecclesiastica, 144
Cantica Eucharista (Douglas), 651
Cantica Laudis (Mason, L.), 141
Canticle for Perpetual Motion (Diamond), 546
Canticle No. 3 (Harrison), 577
Canticle of Freedom (Copland), 483
Canticle of the Martyrs (Giannini), 495
Canticle of the Sun (Boatwright), 659
Canticle of the Sun (Sowerby), 657
Canticles at Evensong (Douglas), 651
Canticum Fratris Solis (Loeffler), 350
Cantilena (Lessard), 603
Cantilena (Mennini), 589
Cantio Sacra (Rochberg), 567
Canto (Mennin), 590
Cantorial Anthology (Ephros), 662
Can You Pay for a Broken Heart (Harris), 706
Canzona (Barber), 532
Canzona (Mennin), 590
Canzona (Mennini), 589
Canzona Seria (Josten), 412
Canzonet, 87
Capet, Lucien, 517
Capital of the World, The (Antheil), 491
Capitals Capitals (Stein, Thomson), 432
Capitol Records, 763
Capocchio and Dorinna (Taylor, R.), 91
Caponsacchi (Hageman), 629
Caprese (Stearns), 420
Capriccio (Antheil), 491
Capriccio (Berger), 563
Capriccio (Dubensky), 477
Capriccio (Rochberg), 567
Capriccio (Schuller), 616
Capriccio (Smit), 605
Capriccio Fantastico (Mason, W.), 280
Caprice de Concert (Hoffman), 290

Capron, Henri, 74, 76, 83, 102, 103-104
Captain Jinks of the Horse Marines (Lingard-MacLagan), 704
Captain Kidd, 665
Captain Lovelace (Duke), 631
Captain's Paradise, The, 752
Captain Stratton's Fancy (Taylor), 402
Captive, The (Strube), 363
Caravan from China Comes, A (Smith), 630
Cares of Yesterday, The (Metcalf), 622
Carey, Henry, 127
Caribbean Holiday (McKinley), 470
Carioca, The (Youmans), 736
Carleton Symphonic Band, 654
Carl Sandburg Suite (Wilder), 510
Carmagnole, La, 87, 115
Carmel Bach Festival, 465
Carmel Concerto (Carpenter), 373
Carmichael, Hoagy (1899-   ), 753, 792
Carnegie Chamber Players, 610
Carnegie Corporation, 499
Carnegie Fellowships, 452
Carnegie Hall, 352, 403
Carnegie Institute of Technology, 506, 654
Carnival Overture (Duke), 631
Carol, Jane, 361
Carol Fantasy (Lockwood), 515
Carol for Twelfth Night, A (Bergsma), 590
Carolina (Strickland), 627
Carolina in the Morning (Donaldson), 750
Carolina Tercentenary Commission, 596
Carolina, tribute to (Blackmar), 263
Carousel (Rodgers-Hammerstein), 740
Carpenter, John Alden (1876-1951), 302, 304, 371-373, 792-793
Carr, Benjamin (1768-1831), 43, 96-101, 115, 151, 793
Carr, Joseph, 123
Carr, Thomas, 123
Carroll, Earl, 462
Carroll, Henry (1892-1962), 749-750
Carroll, Lewis, 598
Carr's Musical Repository, 85, 97
Carry Me Back to Old Virginny (Bland), 701
Carry Me 'Long (Foster), 650
Carter, Elliott (1908-   ), 453, 487-489, 767, 793

Caruso, Enrico, 447, 625
Caryll, Ivan (1861-1921), 716
Casadesus, Robert, 606
Casanova Ballet Music (Taylor), 402
Case History (Riegger), 398
Casella, Alfredo, 585
Casey at the Bat (Schuman), 535
Casey Jones, 687
Cask of Amontillado, The (Perry), 613
Castellana (Howe), 421
Castle Garden, New York, 203
Castle of Andalusia, The, 78
Castle of Otranto (Pelissier), 96
Castles in the Air (Kerker), 714
Castor and Pollux (Partch), 500
Catacoustical (Pinkham), 608
Cat and the Fiddle, The (Kern), 732
Cat and the Mouse, The (Copland), 479
Cathedral Prelude (Smith), 380
Catholic Choir Book (Montani), 660
Catholic church music, 638, 660-662
Catlin, George, 673
Cato (Addison), 27
Catullus, 602
Caucasian Chalk Circle (Bucci), 597
Cave Man Stuff (De Leone), 420
Cave of Enchantment, The (Bentley), 102
Cave of the Heart (Barber), 532
Cazden, Norman (1914-), 562, 793
Caze, Mr., 33
Cecilia Society, Boston, 293, 301, 416
Celebration of Life, A (Sanders), 521
Celebration of Victory (Dillon), 640
Celebration Overture (Creston), 492
Celestial Gate (Hovhaness), 550
Celtic Set (Cowell), 449
Celui qui epousa une femme muette (Bonner), 420
Cennick, John, 665
Centennial Hymn (Paine), 299, 300
Centennial March (Wagner), 299
Centennial Meditation of Columbus (Lanier-Buck), 645
Centennial Overture (Pratt), 305
Central City Opera Festival, Color, 440
Central Park Garden concerts, 285, 645
Century of Negro Progress Exposition, 724
Cesana, Otto (1899-), 467
cha-cha-cha, 726
Chaconne (Diamond), 546

Chaconne (Van Vactor), 524
Chadwick, George Whitefield (1854-1931), 289, 306-310, 356, 374, 376, 378, 380, 385, 388, 462, 471, 524, 639, 640, 649, 793
Chaffin, Lucien Gates (1846-1927), 648
Chain Gang Song (Howe), 421
Chamber Concerto (Barati), 586
Chamber Concerto (Berger), 563
Chamber Concerto (Kohs), 570
Chamber Concerto (Kupferman), 603
Chamber Concerto (Mills), 565
Chambered Nautilus, The (Taylor), 400
Chamber Fantasia (Weber), 568
Chamber Music (Weiss), 455
Chamber Music for Thirteen Players (Berger), 563
Chamber Symphony (Keller), 562
Chameleon Variations (Bergsma), 591
Champagne Charlie (Leybourne-Lee), 705
Chanler, Theodore Ward (1902-1961), 631-632
Chanson de Matin (Gillette), 654
Chanson of the Bells of Osenèy (Barnett), 630
Chansons Populaires (Harling), 419
Chant de guerre (Strong), 345
Chant de Nuit (Campbell-Watson), 662
Chant from the Great Plains (Busch), 359
Chanticleer (Mason, D. G.), 378
Chant of 1942 (Creston), 492
Chapin, Katherine Garrison, 462
Chapin Library, Williams College, 128
Chappell, William, 124
Characteristic Suite (Smith), 569
Characters from Hans Christian Andersen (Rogers), 447
Charade (Rorem), 609
Chariot Jubilee (Dett), 408
Charlap, Marc, 745
Charlatan, The (Sousa), 715
Charles, Ernest (1895-), 631
Charles Ives and His Music (Cowell), 451
Charleston Is Ours, 263
Charleston Rhapsody (Bennett), 461
Charleston, South Carolina:
    City Theatre Orchestra, 109
    early music in, 30
Charlestown Collection (Holden), 61
Charley's Aunt, 746

Charlotte, (North Carolina) Symphony, 465
Charmante, La (Kurtz), 419
Charm Assembly Line (Young), 637
Charter Oak, The (Russell), 161
Chase dem Clouds Away (Gaunt), 715
Chasins, Abram (1903-   ), 641
Chasse, La, 87
Chattanooga Choo Choo (Warren), 751
Chautauqua Institution, 447
Chavez, Carlos, 480
Chayevsky, Paddy, 434
Check and Double Check, music for (Ruby), 751
Cheer, Boys, Cheer (Russell), 163
Chekhov, Anton, 565, 597, 599
Cheneys, The, 173
Cherry Blossoms (Romberg), 730
Cherry Ripe (Horn), 157
Cheslock, Louis (1899-   ), 477
Chester (Billings), 52-53
Chester (Schuman), 535
Chestnut Street Theatre, Philadelphia, 78
Cheyenne (Van Alstyne), 708
Chicago A Cappella Choir, 658
Chicago Civic Orchestra, 465
Chicago Conservatory of Music, 520, 738
Chicagoland Festival, 668
Chicago Musical College, 360, 382, 383, 384, 409, 418, 475, 521, 629, 639, 640, 745, 752, 754
Chicago music festivals, 286
Chicago North Shore Festival, 389
Chicago Opera Company, 372, 403, 419, 718
Chicago Philharmonic Orchestra, 286, 287
Chicago Philharmonic Society, 270-271
Chicago *Record-Herald,* 417
Chicago Sacred Music Society, 270
Chicago Symphony Orchestra, 360, 372, 382, 384, 410, 417, 418, 469, 523, 639, 657, 745
Chicago, University of, 465, 469, 520, 569, 605
Chicago Waltz (Lenssen), 271
Chicago World's Fairs, 287-289, 300, 377, 711, 720
Chickering, Jonas, 275
Child, F. J., 692
Childe Harold (Fry), 245
Childhood Miracle, A (Rorem), 609

Child of Earth with the Golden Hair (Horn), 158
children, music for, 139, 143
Children, The (Chanler), 631
Children of God (Lockwood), 515
Children's Letter to the U.N. (Dougherty), 632
Children's March (Grainger), 407
Children's Suite (Achron), 423
Children's Suite (Copland), 482
Children's Suite (Ephros), 662
Children's Suite (Naginski), 522
Child's Garden of Verses (Stevenson), 374
China (Bauer), 411
China (Swan), 63
Chinaman Laundryman (Crawford), 500
Chin-Chin (Caryll), 716
Chinese Honeymoon, A (Kerker), 714
Chinese Mother Goose Rhymes (Crist), 630
Chinese Symphonic Suite (Dillon), 640
Chinois (Manning), 627
Chiquita (Wayne), 751
Chopin, Frédéric, 206, 557, 749
Choral, The (Baker and Woodbury), 148
Chorale and Fughetta (Read), 559
Chorale and Fugue (Effinger), 582
Chorale and Fugue in Jazz (Gould), 553
Chorale on a Theme by Hassler (Strong), 345
Choral New Yorker, The (Fine), 570
Chorale Preludes (Brunswick), 517
Chorale-Preludes (Edmundson), 658
Chorale Symphony (Effinger), 582
Choral Rhapsody (Whitmer), 652
Choréographe (Hier), 421
Chorister's Companion (Jocelin), 48
Chou Wen-chung, 793
Chris and the Wonderful Lamp (Sousa), 715
Christ Church (Philadelphia), 18
Christian Harmonist (Holyoke), 62
Christian Harmony, The (Ingalls), 666
Christiansen, F. Melius (1871-1955), 652, 793
Christiansen, Olaf Christian, 652
Christian Watchman, 128
Christ in the World (Cain), 658
Christmas (Barnes), 655
Christmas Cantata (Effinger), 582

Christmas Cantata (Nelson), 612
Christmas Dinner (Bland), 702
Christmas Festival Overture (Berezowsky), 525
Christmas Oratorio (Gleason), 304
Christmas Overture (Taylor), 402
Christmas *Pastorale* (Rogers), 649
Christmas Song, A (Salter, M. T.), 622
Christmas Story, The (Mennin), 590
Christ of the Andes (Clough-Leighter), 633
Christ Our Passover (Campbell-Watson), 662
Christ Reborn (Sowerby), 657
Christ the Victor (Buck), 646
Christ Triumphant (Cough-Leighter), 633
Christ Triumphant (Huhn), 623
Christy, E. P., 188, 193, 194, 195
Christy Minstrels, 179
Chronicle (Riegger), 397
Chronicles of Stephen Foster's Family (Morneweck), 187
Churchill, Frank (1901-1942), 751
church music, 644-663
Church Service Book, The (MacFarlane), 652
Chute, B. J., 747
Cimarron (Harris), 438
Cincinnati College of Music, 285, 347, 360, 467, 556, 636, 663
Cincinnati Conservatory of Music, 418, 459, 556
Cincinnati Festival, 274, 285, 300, 318, 346, 348, 408, 645
Cincinnati Haydn Society, 270
Cincinnati Symphony Orchestra, 415, 472, 484, 494, 518, 529, 602, 615, 663, 732
Cinders (Friml), 729
Cinerama Holiday, score for (Gould), 553
Circus Day (Taylor), 401
Citizen Kane, score for (Hermann), 554
Citkowitz, Israel (1909-   ), 482, 530
City, The, score for (Copland), 481
City of Brass (Herrmann), 554
City of God, The (Matthews), 653
City of the Sea (Shepherd), 405
Civil War songs, 255-268
Claflin, Avery (1898-   ), 476

Clapp, Philip Greeley (1888-1954), 415-416
Clare de Kitchen, 181
"Claribel," 704
Clark, Grant, 709
Clark, James Freeman, 259
Clark, Maggie, 704
Clarke, Henry Leland, 793
Clarke, Hugh, 303, 387
Classical Chorus Book (Baker, B. F.), 147
Classical Symphony (Gershefski), 501
Classic Serenade (Bennett), 461
Cleopatra (Allen), 420
Cleopatra's Night (Hadley), 376
Cleveland Institute of Music, 392, 393, 452, 473, 517, 544, 558
Cleveland *Plain Dealer,* 473, 649
Cleveland *Press,* 404
Cleveland Symphony Orchestra, 394, 404, 405, 438, 456, 457, 473, 506, 552, 590, 605, 732
Cliburn, Van, 605, 793
Clifton, Chalmers (1889-   ), 416
Clifton, William, 171
Climb Jacob's Ladder, 684
Cline, Maggie, 706
Clokey, Joseph Waddell (1890-   ), 634
Cloud, The (Barati), 586)
Clouds (Charles), 631
Clough-Leighter, Henry (1874-1956), 633
Clytemnestra (El-Dabh), 619
Coal Black Rose, 179
Coal Scuttle Blues (Luening-Bacon), 466
Coates, Albert, 463
Cobham, William, 35
Cocaine Lil (Clokey), 634
Cockcrow (Smith), 569
Coconuts, The (Berlin), 734
Coerne, Louis Adolphe (1870-1922), 302
Cohan, George Michael (1878-1942), 468, 719-720
Cohan Revues (Cohan), 719
Cohen, Harriet, International Awards, 513
Cohn, Arthur (1910-   ), 578
Cole, Rossetter Gleason (1866-1952), 359-360
Cole, Ulric (1905-   ), 518
Colette, 743
Collection of Best Tunes and Anthems (Law), 60

Collection of Favorite Songs (Reinagle), 80

Collection of the Best Psalm Tunes, A (Flagg), 17, 64

College of Church Musicians, 656

College of St. Scholastica, 414

College of the City of New York, 379

College of the Pacific Music Conservatory, 430

Collegiana (La Violette), 475

Collegiate Chorale of New York, 589

Collegium Musicum, Moravians, 28

Collier, Constance, 401

Collier's Weekly, 400

Colline des Fantomes (Tcherepnin), 478

Colloquy (Weber), 568

Colorado, University of, 474, 581

Colorado College Conservatory, 379

Colors of War, The (Rogers, B.), 447

Colossus (Griffis), 470

Coloured Stars (Crist), 630

Columbia Broadcasting System, 402, 410, 438, 444, 445, 456, 462, 480, 481, 484, 491, 493, 494, 496, 525, 530, 539, 543, 554, 557, 561, 579, 581, 592, 598, 600, 602

Columbia Minstrels, 178

Columbian Centinel, 64, 69

Columbian Harmonist, The (Read), 63

Columbian Melodies (Pelissier), 95, 96

Columbian Repository of Sacred Harmony, The (Holyoke), 62

Columbia Records, 763

Columbia's Bold Eagle (Graupner), 131

Columbia University, 378, 416, 417, 441, 456, 457, 474, 499, 502, 503, 507, 513, 514, 515, 521, 531, 533, 536, 561, 581, 585, 586, 597, 598, 600, 612, 617, 632, 640, 650, 655, 739

Columbus (Hewitt), 89

Columbus (Hosmer), 633

Columbus (Reinagle), 80

Columbus (Van Hagen, P. A.), 74

Columbus March and Hymn (Paine), 300

Comden, Betty, 540, 745, 746

Come Back to Erin (Barnard), 704

Come Down My Evening Star (Stromberg), 715

Comedy (Leplin), 588

Comedy Overture (Wald), 418

Comedy Overture on Negro Themes (Gilbert), 354

Come, Fair Rosina, Come Away (Hopkinson), 42

Come Home, Father (Root), 267

Come, Josephine, in My Flying Machine (Fisher), 708

Comer, Tom, 143

Comes Autumn Time (Sowerby), 657

Come Seven (Tuthill), 418

"Come, Thou Almighty King," 47

Come Ye Disconsolate, 433

Comforter, The (Barnes), 655

Coming In on a Wing and a Prayer, 728

Coming of the King, The (Buck), 646

Coming of the King, The (Lester), 634

Commando March (Barber), 531

Comme Ci Comme Ça (Kramer-Whitney), 752

commissions for composers, 762-763

Communication (Cowell), 449

Communion Service (Hall), 650

Communiqué (Finney), 498

Complete Melody in Three Parts, A, 16

Compline (Douglas), 651

composers, biography, bibliography, 798-817

Composers' Forums, 760

composers, opportunities for publication and performance, 757-761

Composers' Recordings, Inc., 562

Composers' Showcase, 572, 573

Composition for Four Instruments (Babbitt), 575

Composition for Synthesizer (Babbitt), 575

Composition for Viola and Piano (Babbitt), 574

Concert, The (Kay), 557

Concertante (Dello Joio), 542

Concertante (Green), 518

Concertante (Mennin), 590

Concertantes (Goeb), 581

Concertantes (Pinkham), 608

Concert Band, The (Goldman), 642

Concert for Six Instruments (Beach, J. P.), 370

Concert Hall Society, 763

Concerti da Camera (Sydenam), 610

Concertino (Blackwood), 606

Concertino (Carpenter), 371

Concertino (Creston), 492

Concertino (Dello Joio), 542

Concertino (Denny), 584

Concertino (Freed), 527
Concertino (Green), 518
Concertino (Haines), 583
Concertino (Inch), 511
Concertino (Kennan), 580
Concertino (Korn), 620
Concertino (Koutzen), 529
Concertino (Kurka), 598
Concertino (Luening), 502
Concertino (Persichetti), 548
Concertino (Piston), 444-445
Concertino (Schuller), 616
Concertino (Starer), 620
Concertino (Suesse), 558
Concertino (Sydenam), 610
Concertino da Camera (Glanville-Hicks), 566
Concertino for Orchestra (Evett), 614
Concertino for Orchestra (Lopatnikoff), 506
Concertino in A (Pinkham), 608
Concertino on Lezione III of Ariosto (Elkus), 421
Concertinos (Goeb), 581
Concertinos (Hill), 374
Concertinos (Weber), 568
Concert Music (Dello Joio), 542
Concert Music (Ward), 560
Concerto a Tre (Dahl), 565
Concerto a Tre (Starer), 620
Concerto Concertanto (Porter, Q.), 457
Concerto da Camera (Berlinski), 587
Concerto da Camera (Tcherepnin), 478
Concert Ode (Flanagan), 632
Concerto for a Singing Instrument (Bucci), 597
Concerto for Five Improvising Instruments (Foss), 594
Concerto for Five Instruments (Palmer), 579
Concerto for Small Orchestra (Palmer), 579
Concerto Gregoriano (Yon), 660
Concerto Grosso (Bennett), 461
Concerto Grosso (Bloch), 392, 395
Concerto Grosso (Dubensky), 477
Concerto Grosso (Stoessel), 448
Concerto Grosso (Van Vactor), 524
Concerto Grosso (Wagner), 516
Concerto in F (Gershwin), 426-427
Concerto in One Movement (Etler), 552
Concerto in Slendro for Violin (Harrison), 577

Concerto in Three Rhythms (Suesse), 551
Concerto Lirico (Berezowsky), 525
Concerto on the Improved Pianoforte with Additional Keys (Reinagle), 80
Concerto on the Organ (Selby), 66
Concerto Romantico (Glanville-Hicks), 566
Concerto Sacro (Josten), 411-412
Concerto Sereno (Mills), 565
Concerto Sinfonica (Steinert), 523
Concert Overture (Sowerby), 657
Concerto with Lights (Brant), 576
Concert Piece (Diamond), 544
Concert Piece (Shifrin), 616
Concert Piece (Sydenam), 610
Concert Piece (Wuorinen), 612
concerts:
early, 22-23, 30-35
nineteenth-century, 150-158
Concert Waltz Suite (Eppert), 418
Concord, Massachusetts, 1840-60 (Ives), 365-366
Concordia, 151, 154
Concord School of Music, 518
Condemned, The (Blitzstein), 497
Condemned Playground, The (Gideon), 508
Cone, Edward T. (1917-   ), 583
Coney Island Overture (Kleinsinger), 643
Configuration for Orchestra (Barati), 586
Confrey, Zez (1895-   ), 752
Congo, The (Bergh), 626
Congo Minstrels, 178
Connecticut Suite (Bingham), 417
Connecticut Tercentenary (Hadley), 377
Connecticut Yankee, The (Rodgers-Hart), 739
Connors, Babe, 706
Connotations for Orchestra (Copland), 486
Conquest, The (Spross), 624
Conscious Lovers, 31
Conspirator, The (Engel, C.), 630
Conspirators, The (Stewart), 362
Conservatoire, Paris, 591
Conservatory of Cologne, 565
Conservatory of St. Petersburg, Russia, 641
Consul, The (Menotti), 536

Contemporary American Composers (Hughes), 624

Contemporary Composers (Mason, D. G.), 378

Contemporary Records, 763

Contours (Schuller), 616

contrast, instrumental, 467

Contrasts (Schuller), 616

Converse, Charles Crozat (1832-1918), 666

Converse, Frederick Shepherd (1871-1940), 302, 380-382, 471, 549

Converse College, 465, 501, 594

Conversion, The (Matthews), 653

Cooke, James Francis (1875-), 619, 639

Coolidge, Elizabeth Sprague, 351, 383, 579

Coolidge Foundation, 533, 537, 591

Coolidge Prize, 392, 396, 424, 444, 604, 762

Coolidge String Quartet, 485, 525

Coombs, Charles Whitney (1859-1940), 650

Coon, Oscar, 400

Cooper, George (1840-1927), 703

Copland, Aaron (1900-), 379, 435, 478-487, 513, 523, 530, 548, 558, 560, 565, 571, 575, 579, 580, 582, 583, 596, 602, 608, 609, 617, 619, 629, 732, 765, 767-768

Copland-Sessions Concerts, 452

Copley, John Singleton, 23

copyright law of 1909, 761

Coral Sea (Brown), 750

Cordelia's Aspirations, 714

Cornell, Katherine, 402

Cornell University, 375, 524, 551, 579

Cornemuse, La (Loeffler), 351

Cornish School of Music (Seattle), 614

Corona, La (Talma), 514

Coronation (Holden), 60, 755

Correct Method for the Banjo (Rice), 181

Cortège Macabre (Copland), 479

Cortot, Alfred, 469, 587

Corwin, Norman, 447

Cosmophony (Rudhyar), 476

Cosmos (Leplin), 588

Coss, William, 765

Cossack Love Song (Kountz), 628

Costaso (Still), 462

Cotillion Suite (Moore, D.), 441

Cottage Boy (Pownall), 108

Cotton, John, 10

Cotton, Seaborn, 21

Cotton Club Revues, 741, 751

Cotton Moon (Campbell-Watson), 662

Coudin, Mrs. V. G., 263

Coulennes (Howe), 421

Counterpoint (Kennan), 580

Counterpoint (Piston), 444

Country Gardens (Grainger), 406

Country Pictures (Mason, D. G.), 378

Country They Call Puget Sound (Robinson), 629

Country Wedding (Wilson), 385

Courboin, Charles M., 661

Course (Antheil), 491

Course in Counterpoint (Cesana), 467

Course in Modern Harmony (Cesana), 467

Courthouse Square, The (Phillips), 509

Court Jester, The (Freer), 361

Courtship of Miles Standish (Phillips), 509

Coward, Noel, 461

Cow-boy humoriste, Le (Strong), 345

Cowboy Rhapsody (Raphling), 558

cowboy songs, 636, 637, 638, 693-694

Cowboy Songs (Lomax), 694

Cowell, Henry Dixon (1897-), 370, 392, 393, 394, 443, 448-451, 452, 490, 507, 550, 561, 563, 571, 572, 573, 576, 581, 589, 601, 794

Cowell, Sidney, 451

Cowherd and the Sky Maiden (Verrall), 523

Cowles, Cecil (1901-), 641

Cox, John H., 692

Cradle Song (MacFadyen), 640

Cradle Song (Weaver), 628

Cradle Will Rock, The (Blitzstein), 495, 496, 743

Crawford, Ruth Porter (1901-1953), 500

Crazy Horse Symphony (Mills), 565

Crazy Rhythm (Meyer), 750

Crazy World, Crazy Tune (Ager), 749

Creation, The (Mopper), 566

Creation, The (Nelson), 611-612

Credendum (Schuman), 535

Credo (Shapero), 602

Credo (Smith), 380

Credo (Van Vactor), 524

Creston, Paul (1906-), 492-493, 611

Crisis, The (Fletcher), 580
Criss Cross (Kern), 731
Crist, Bainbridge (1883-   ), 630, 794
Crist, Judith, 597
Cristobal Colón (Van Vactor), 524
Cromwell Fellowship, 473, 558
Crosby, Bing, 752, 794
Crosby, Fanny, 265
Crosby, Uranus H., 272
Cross, Benjamin (1786-1857), 134, 151
Cross, The (Ware), 625
Cross of the South, 262
Cross Victorious, The (Demarest), 625
Crouch, Frederick William Nicholls (1808-1896), 172
Crouse, Russell, 734, 735
Crown of Life, The (Nevin, George B.), 649
Crucible, The (Ward), 561
Crucifixion (Antheil), 491
Crucifixion (Gillis), 585
Crucifixion (Josten), 412
Crumbs from Peacock Pie (McKinney), 627
Cry, The (Riegger), 398
Crying Jag (Brant), 576
Cry of Rachel, The (Salter, M. T.), 622
Crystal Palace, London, 305-306
Cuban Love Song (McHugh), 751
Cuban Rhapsody (Maganini), 474
Cubist (Griselle), 468
Cuckoo Clock (Grant-Schaeffer), 624
Culprit Fay, The (Buck), 645
Culprit Fay, The (Gleason), 304
Culprit Fay, The (Hadley), 377
Cullen, Countee, 410
Cummings, E. E., 549
Cummington Story, The, score for (Copland), 481
Cupid, 'mid the Roses Playing (Knight), 160
Curious Fern, The (Kupferman), 603
Curran, Pearl (1875-1941), 625
Currier, T. P., 330, 336
Currier and Ives Suite—The Skating Pond (Herrmann), 554
Curtain Raiser, A (Goldman, R. F.), 642
Curtis, Natalie, 674
Curtis Institute, 414, 422, 423, 442, 468, 496, 497, 531, 536, 538, 556, 566, 567, 591, 599, 604, 608, 628

Custis, Nelly, 43, 76
Cycle, The (Mennin), 589
Cycle of Holy Songs (Rorem), 609
Cynthia Parker (Smith), 569
Cyprus Serenades (Fuleihan), 527
Cyrano de Bergerac (Damrosch, W.), 352, 353
Cyrano de Bergerac (Stoessel), 448

D

Daemon Lover, The (Kurtz), 419
Dagger Dance (Herbert), 717
Dahl, Ingolf (1912-   ), 565, 600, 606
Daisy, The (Foerster), 622
d'Albert, Eugene (*see* Albert)
Dalcroze Institute, 452
Dallapiccola, Luigi, 567, 613
Daman and Phillida, 31
Dame Lillebule (Fairchild), 388
Damn Yankees (Adler-Ross), 748
Damrosch, Leopold (1832-1885), 287, 352-353
Damrosch, Walter (1862-1950), 287, 351-354, 371, 400-401, 406, 426-427, 446, 447, 461, 474, 479, 795
Damrosch Fund, 762
Danbury Festival, 474
Dance Divertissement (Wagner), 516
Dance Episodes on the Exotic Theme (Shepherd), 405
Dance Figure (Becker), 415
Dance for Eight Egyptian Mummies (Scott), 754
Dance in the Place Congo (Gilbert), 355
Dance Music for an Absent Drama (Partch), 500
Dance of Life, The (Delamarter), 417
Dance of Salome, The (Rogers, B.), 447
Dance of the Locomotives (Read), 559
Dance of the Sand-Dune Cranes (Weaver), 656
Dance of the Scarlet Sister Mary (Cadman), 404
Dance Ossianique (Gottschalk), 206
Dance Overture, A (Creston), 493
Dance Overture (Persichetti), 548
Dancer Dead, The (Wald), 418
Dance Scenes (Rogers, B.), 447
Dance Sonata (Green), 519
Dance Sonata (Nordhoff), 508
Dance Suite (Griselle), 468
Dance Suite (Raphling), 558

Dance Symphony (Copland), 479
Dance Symphony after Flaubert (Read), 559
Dance Variations (Creston), 492
Dancing in the Dark (Schwartz), 739
dancing schools, 20-21
Dandy Jim, 180
Dangerous Dan McGrew (Kramer-Whitney), 752
Daniel, Danny, 554
Daniel in the Lion's Den (MacGimsey), 637
Daniel Jazz, The (Gruenberg), 409
Daniels, Mabel Wheeler (1879-), 385-386
Daniel's Prediction (Horn), 156-157
Danks, Hart Pease (1834-1903), 667, 705
Danny by My Side (Braham), 714
Danny Deever (Damrosch, W.), 353
Danse Callinda (Kay), 564
Danse Suite (Griselle), 468
Dans la nuit (Allen), 420
d'Antalffy (*see* Antalffy)
Danza (Carpenter), 372
Danza Mexicana (Bowles), 582
Danzon Cubano (Copland), 484
Dardanella (Fisher), 708
Darest Thou Now, O Soul? (Williams), 655
Dark Dancers of the Mardi Gras (Cadman), 404
Darker America (Still), 462
Dark Eyed One (Horn), 157
Dark-Eyed Sailor, The, 695
Dark Night, The (Mills), 565
Dark Night of Saint Joan (Verrall), 523
Darling Corie (Siegmeister), 514
Darling Nelly Gray, 261
Dartmouth College, 415, 464
Daughter of the Forest, A (Nevin, A.), 386
David (De Leone), 420
David (Lawrence), 542
David and Goliath (Berlinski), 587
Davide Rizzio (Moore), 387
David the Psalmist (Rochberg), 568
Davies, Peter Maxwell, 454
Davies, Samuel, 16, 45
Davis, Miles, 795
Davis & Horn, 156
Davison, A. T., 433, 608
Dawn (Curran), 625

Dawn (Farwell), 375
Dawn (Hovhaness), 550
Dawning of Music in Kentucky (Heinrich), 227
Dawn to Dawn (Kleinsinger), 643
Dawson, William Levi (1899-), 465
Day (Converse, F. S.), 381
Day, John, 5, 6
Day Before Spring, The (Loewe), 742, 743
Daybreak (Daniels), 386
Daybreak (Smith), 380
Day in the Country (Fry), 245
Day in the Peterboro Woods, A (Hier), 421
Day in Venice, A (Nevin), 662
Day of Judgment (Fickenscher), 371
Dead March and Monody (Carr), 99
Dearest Enemy (Rodgers-Hart), 739
Dearest May, 355
Death and Life (Shelley), 647
Death of Commodore O. H. Perry (Shaw), 136
Death of the Bishop of Brindisi, The (Menotti), 538
Death Song of an Indian Chief, The (Gram), 63
Death Takes a Holiday, music for (Bucci), 597
Deblois, Samuel, 23
De Boatmen's Dance, 180
Debussy, Claude Achille, 333, 412, 628
Debutante's Diary, A (Wilder), 510
De Camptown Races (Foster), 181, 198, 484, 650
Decatur, Stephen, 124
Decatur at Algiers (Antheil), 491
Declamations (Lees), 601
Declaration (Gould), 553
DeClerque, Henri, 273
Decoration Day (Ives), 368
Dédicaces (Duke), 526
Dedication and Praise (Nelson), 612
Dedication Ode (Chadwick), 310
Dedications (La Violette), 475
Deep Forest (Daniels), 385-386
Deep in My Heart (Olmstead), 628
Deep in My Heart (Romberg), 730
Deep Purple (De Rose), 752
Deep River (Harling), 419
Deep River (Burleigh), 636
Deep River, variations on (Herrmann), 554

Deer Dance (Skilton), 358
Defense of Corinth, The (Carter), 488
De Glory Road (Wolfe), 637
D'Eissenburg, George, 39
De Koven, Reginald (1859-1920), 718, 719
Delacroix, Joseph, 84
Delamarter, Eric (1880-1953), 417
Delaney, Robert Mills (1903-1956), 517-518
De Leone, Francesco Bartholomeo (1887-1948), 420
Delia (Capron), 104
Delibes, Leo, 718
Dello Joio, Casimiro (1881-1963), 660
Dello Joio, Norman (1913-   ), 541-544, 660, 795
Demarest, Clifford (1874-1946), 624-625
Demarque, 109
De Meyer, Leopold, 290
Dem Golden Slippers (Bland), 702
de Mille, Agnes, 483, 553
Demoiselle Paysanne (Duke), 526
Demolition of the Bastile (Berkenhead), 68
Denison University, 666
Denmark Vesey (Bowles), 582
Denny, William D. (1910-   ), 584
Density 21.5 (Varèse), 413
Densmore, Frances, 674, 675, 676, 678
Densmore, John (1880-1943), 626
Denver College of Music, 472
Denver University School of the Theatre, 515
De Paul University, 475, 477
Depression (McBride), 643
De Profundis (Barlow, W.), 578
De Profundis (Bartlett), 648
Derivations (Gould), 553
De Rose, Peter (1896-1953), 752-753
Derry Down, 117
Derweis, Baron Paul von, 349
Descriptive Battle Symphony (Knaebel), 248
Deserter, The (Pelissier, Carr), 96
Deserts (Varèse), 413
Desert Song, The (Romberg), 730
Design for Orchestra (Rorem), 609
Design for Radio (Donovan), 455
Design for Strings (Hoiby), 599
Désirée (Sousa), 715
Desolate City, The (Porter, Q.), 456-457

Desolate Cry, The (Daniels), 385
Destry Rides Again (Rome), 744
de Sylva, Buddy, 738, 750
Déthier, Gaston Marie, 492
Detroit Symphony Orchestra, 423, 471, 581, 745
Dett, R. Nathaniel (1882-1943), 406, 407-408
Devil and Daniel Webster, The, score for (Herrmann), 554
Devil and Daniel Webster, The (Moore, D.), 439
Dewey, Admiral, 121
De Wild Goose Nation (Emmett), 182
Dial M for Murder, score for (Tiomkin), 478
Dialogues (Gould), 553
Dialogues (Overton), 614
Diamond, David (1915-   ), 544-546
Diamond, John, 177
Diamonds Are a Girl's Best Friend (Styne), 745
Diaphonic Suites (Crawford), 500
Diaphony (Diamond), 545
Diatonic Modes in Modern Music, The (Vincent), 525
Dichotomy (Riegger), 397
Dichromatic Variation (Lockwood), 515
Dickinson, Clarence (1873-   ), 652-653
Dickinson, Emily, 466, 483, 502, 549
Dickinson Song Cycle (Luening), 502
Dienval, Alexander, 32
Diether, Jack, 618
Dietz, Howard, 739
Dillingham, Charles, 399
Dillon, Fannie Charles (1881-1947), 640
d'Indy, Vincent (*see* Indy),
Dinner for a Pack of Hungry Cannibals (Scott), 754
Dipper, Thomas, 23
Dirge (Creston), 493
Dirge (Holden), 61
Dirge (Howe), 421
Dirge (Levant), 520
Dirge (MacDowell), 331
Dirge and Variations (Amram), 619
Disappointment, or the Force of Credulity, The, 28
Discussion (Amram), 618
Disney, Walt, 402, 628, 751
Ditson, Alice M., Fund, 397, 443, 492, 585, 586, 604, 612, 642, 762, 763

Ditson, Oliver, 219
Divan, The (Huhn), 623
Diversion of the Angels (Dello Joio), 543
Diversions (Filippi), 530
Diversions (Hoiby), 599
Divertimenti (Taylor, R.), 94
Divertimento (Campbell-Watson), 662
Divertimento (Cole), 518
Divertimento (Dahl), 565
Divertimento (Fitch), 511
Divertimento (Fuleihan), 527
Divertimento (Gebhard), 626
Divertimento (Goldman, R. F.), 642
Divertimento (Haieff), 562
Divertimento (Helm), 584
Divertimento (Imbrie), 606
Divertimento (Inch), 511
Divertimento (Kupferman), 603
Divertimento (Loeffler), 349
Divertimento (Mason, D. G.), 378
Divertimento (Nelson), 611
Divertimento (Persichetti), 548
Divertimento (Pinkham), 608
Divertimento (Siegmeister), 514
Divertimento (Smith), 618
Divertimento (Sydenam), 610
Divertimento (Taylor, R.), 93
Divertimento (Van Vactor), 524
Divertimento (Wagenaar), 456
Divertimento Burlesca (Lees), 601
Divertimentos (Powell), 607
Divertimentos (Yon), 660
Divertissement (Riegger), 397
Divine Flame, The (Talma), 513
Divine Poems (Heiden), 587
Dixie Fugue (Janssen), 464
Dixieland Jazz Band, 721
Dixie's Land (Emmett), 178, 181, 184, 255-258, 670
    anti-Southern words to, 257-258
    sources of, 256
Dixon, George Washington, 176
Doane, William Howard (1832-1915), 666
Doctor and the Apothecary, The (Bergmann), 90
Doctor Faustus Lights the Lights (Kupferman), 603
Dr. Joe (Tuthill), 418
Doctor of Alcantara, The (Eichberg), 218
Doctor of Music degree, first, 137

Do, Do, Do (Gershwin), 425
Dodsworth family, 249, 283
Dogie Song, 405
Doin' What Comes Naturally (Berlin), 734
Dolph, E. A., 726
Domain of Hurakan, The (Farwell), 375
Donaldson, Walter (1893-1947), 750
Donato, Anthony (1909-), 512
Donne, John, 514
Donne Secours, 7
Do Not Go, My Love (Hageman), 629
Do Not Grieve for Thy Dear Mother, 264
Donovan, Richard F. (1891-), 455, 500, 795
Don Quixote (De Koven), 718
Don Quixote (Neuendorf), 298
Don Quixote Symphony (Delaney), 518
Don't Be Angry with Me, Darling, (Danks), 667
Don't Be Foolish, Joe, 355
Don't Fence Me In (Porter), 737
Doodle, meaning of, 114-115
Doodle Dandy of the U.S.A. (Siegmeister), 514
Door, The (Mopper), 566
Do Re Mi (Styne), 746
Dorsey, Jimmy (1904-1957), 724
Dorsey, Tommy (1905-1956), 457, 724
Double Music (Harrison-Cage), 577
Double Portrait for Orchestra (Gesensway), 498
Dougherty, Celius (1902-), 632
Douglas, Charles Winfred (1867-1944), 651
Douglass, David, 27-28, 32
Dove of Peace, The (Damrosch, W.), 353
Dover Beach (Barber), 533
Down East Spirituals and Others (Jackson), 664
Downes, Olin, 354, 355, 395, 408, 428, 484
    Treasury of American Song, A (with Siegmeister), 514
Down Went McGinty (Flynn), 706
Down Where the Wurzberger Flows (H. Von Tilzer), 708
Doxology, 6
Do You Remember, Mary? (Horn), 157

Dragon and the Phoenix, The (Barati), 586

Drake University, 396

Drama Critics Circle Award, N. Y., 537

Drama of the Yellowstone (Lieurance), 636

Dramatic Overture (Etler), 552

Dramatic Overture (Schuller), 616

Drayton, Michael, 444

Dream King and His Love (Parker), 317

Dream of Jeanie, I (Foster), 650

Dream of McCorkle (Search), 422

Dream Pedlar (Whithorne), 410

Dream Song (Warford), 626

Dresel, Otto (1826-1890), 217-218, 320

Dress, The (Bucci), 597

Dresser, Paul (1857-1911), 696, 706-707, 795

Dressler, Louis Raphael (1861-1932), 650

Driftwood Suite (Read), 559

Drill, Ye Tarriers, Drill (Harding), 706

Drinking Song (Romberg), 730

Driven from Home (Hays), 702

Drolleries from an Oriental Doll's House (Crist), 630

Drummond, Robert R., 26

drums, 21

Drums in My Heart (Youmans), 736

Drum Taps (Imbrie), 607

Drum Taps (Lockwood), 515

Drum Taps (Whitman), 431

Dry Weather Legend (Bennett), 461

DuBarry Was a Lady (Porter), 737

Dubensky, Arcady (1890-   ), 476-477

Duchess of Malfi, music for (Hoiby), 599

Duel in the Sun, score for (Tiomkin), 478

Duet for Piano and Pistol (Scott), 754

Duetti (Moller), 104

Duet with Nicky (Berezowsky), 525

Dukas, Paul, 523, 584

Duke, John (1899-   ), 631

Duke, Vernon, formerly Vladimir Dukel-sky (1903-   ), 525-526, 795

Duke of Sacramento, The (Dello Joio), 543

Duke Street (Hatton), 17

Duke University, 589

Dulcimer, The (Woodbury), 148

Duluth Symphony, 516

Dumbarton Oaks Mass (Hollingsworth), 600

Dumb Wife (Gruenberg), 409

Duna (McGill), 637

Dundee, 6

Dunfermline, 6

Dunkirk (Damrosch, W.), 352, 447

Dunlap's Creek (Saminsky), 423

Dunn, James Philip (1884-1936), 417, 795

Dunsany, Lord, 543

Dunster, Henry, 8

Duo Concertante (Green), 519

Durante, Jimmie, 735, 737

Durgin, Cyrus, 432

Dvořák, Antonin (1841-1904), 315, 317, 378-379, 424, 622, 635, 636, 639, 681, 699-700

Dwight, John S. (1813-1893), 214, 218-219, 294, 295, 296, 297, 320, 795

Dwight's Journal of Music, 146-147, 153, 155, 163, 184, 201, 214, 215-216, 217, 218, 219, 236, 247, 249, 295

Dyer, Oliver, 278

Dyhrenfurth, Julius, 271

Dying Cowboy, The, 405, 693

Dying Hobo, The, 691

Dying Poet, The (Gottschalk), 206

Dynamic Motion (Cowell), 449

Dynamogeny (Calabro), 604

Dynamophonic Suite (Luening), 506

E

Eager, Edward, 456, 557

Eagle, The (MacDowell), 330

Eagles (Rorem), 609

Eames, Henry Purmont (1875-1950), 625

Earl and the Girl, The (Caryll), 716

Earl Brand, 692

Earl Carroll's Vanities, 462, 741, 742

Early California (Rasbach), 627

Early Dawn (Lockwood), 515

Earth is Enough (Warford), 626

East and West (Fairchild), 388

Easter Cantata (Hovhaness), 551

Easter Cantata (Nelson), 612

Easter Carol, An (Holler), 658

Eastern Song (Daniels), 385

Easter Pageant, An (Matthews), 653

Easter Parade (Berlin), 734

Eastman, George, 758

Eastman School of Music, 307, 415, 430, 446, 463, 466, 472, 501, 509, 510, 511, 512, 544, 555, 563, 564, 578,

579, 580, 588, 589, 590, 600, 613, 758
American Composers' Concerts at, 358, 387, 430, 758, 760
Eastward in Eden (Meyerowitz), 585
Ebb Tide (Wood-Hill), 623
Eberhart, Nellie Richmond, 403
Ecce jam Noctis (Chadwick), 310
Eccentricities of Davy Crockett, The (Moross), 557
Echo, The (Patterson), 387
Echo, The (Taylor), 399
Eckhard, Jacob, 795
Ecuatorial (Varèse), 503
Eddy, Clarence, 649
Edition Musicus, 474
Edmunds, John (1913-   ), 632
Edmundson, Garth (1900-   ), 658
Edwards, Clara (1887-   ), 627
Edwards, Gus (1879-1945), 708
Edwards, Jonathan, 16, 665
Edwin and Angelina (Pelissier), 94-95
Effinger, Cecil (1914-   ), 581-582
Ehlert, Louis, 334
Eichberg, Julius (1824-1893), 218
Eichelberger, Elizabeth, 627
Eight American Folksongs (Siegmeister), 514
Eight Etudes and a Fantasy (Carter), 489
Eight Miniatures for a Baroque Ensemble (Powell), 607
85th Psalm (MacDougall), 649
Eileen (Herbert, V.), 717
Eisfeld, Theodor (1816-1882), 216-217, 234, 284-285
Eisfeld Chamber Music Concerts, 273
Eklog (Kramer), 631
El Capitán (Sousa), 710-715
El-Dabh, Halim (1921-   ), 619
Electra (Damrosch, W.), 353, 358
Electra (Kupferman), 603
electronic music (*see* composers, *i.e.*, Cage, John; Luening, Otto; Ussachevsky, Vladimir; Varèse, Edgar; etc.
Elegiac Poem (Converse, F. S.), 381
Elegie (Barrymore), 389
Elegie (Palmer), 389
Elegie (Strong), 345
Elegy (Carter) 489
Elegy (Etler), 552
Elegy (Johnson), 511

Elegy (Leplin), 588
Elegy and Pastorale (Heller), 663
Elegy in Memory of My Friend Serge Koussevitzsky (Hanson), 430, 432
Eleven Studies for Eleven Instruments (Rorem), 609
Elgar, Edward, 371
Eliot, Charles, 302
Eliot, John, 7
Eliot, Samuel A., 139
Elizabeth Sprague Coolidge Foundation (*see* Coolidge Foundation; Library of Congress)
Elkus, Albert I. (1884-1962), 421, 518, 546, 588
Ellen, Arise (Carr), 100
Ellington, Duke (1899-   ), 724, 795-796
Elliott, Zo, 726
Elmslie, Kenward, 600, 609
Elopement, The (Demarque), 109
Elshuco Trio, 476
Elwell, Herbert (1898-   ), 473, 517, 580
Embraceable You (Gershwin), 425
Emerson, Billy, 703
Emerson, Ida, 708
Emerson (Ives), 366
Emerson, Luther Orlando (1820-1915), 261-262
Emery, Stephen A., 308, 311, 376, 621
Emily Dickinson Mosaic (Pinkham), 608
Emmett, Daniel Decatur (1815-1904), 181-184, 670, 796
Emperor Jones, The (Gruenberg), 408
Emperor Jones, The (McPhee), 528
Emperor's New Clothes, The (Moore, D.), 442
Enchanted Isle, The (Bacon), 466
Enchanted Isle, The (Gruenberg), 409
Enchanted Isle, The (Salzedo), 414
Enchanted Pear Tree, The (Overton), 614
Enchanted Waters (Williams), 655
End of St. Petersburg, The (Duke), 526
Endymion (Bennett), 461
Endymion (Josten), 412
Endymion (Moevs), 602
Endymion's Narrative (Converse, F. S.), 381
Enesco, Georges, 587
Engel, A. Lehman (1910-   ), 555-556
Engel, Carl (1883-1944), 351

English and Scottish Ballads (Child), 692
English Folk Songs from the Southern Appalachians (Sharp), 692
English Opera Company, 652
Enid (Oklahoma) Tri-State Festival, 438
Enlightened One, The (La Violette), 475
Enormous Room, The (Diamond), 544
Enraptur'd I Gaze, When My Delia Is By (Hopkinson), 42
Enright, Elizabeth, 597
Enstone, Edward, 22
Entente Cordiale (Brant), 576
Ephrata Cloister, 26
Ephros, Gerson (1890-   ), 662
Epic Poem (Smith), 380
Epigrams (Gideon), 508
Epigraph (Dello Joio), 542
Episcopal *Hymnal,* 650, 651
Episode (Perry), 613
Episodic Suite (Smith), 569
Epitaphs (Chanler), 631
Epithalaminum (Fuleihan), 527
Equatorial (Varèse), 413
Erewhon (Reiser), 424
Erie Canal (Kubik), 555
Erie Waters (Bacon), 466
Eroica Sonata (MacDowell), 327, 328
Erotic Poem (Grimm), 475
Errand Into the Maze (Menotti), 538
Erskine, John, 409, 491
Escapade (Eppert), 418
Espanharmlem (Reddick), 636
Esputa, John, 710
Essay for Orchestra (Barber), 531
Essay on Musical Taste (Hastings), 141
Essays on Music (Law), 59
Essentials of Sight Singing (Montani), 660
Essex Harmony (Kimball), 64
Esther (Meyerowitz), 585
Etchings (Watts, W.), 630
"Ethiopian opera," 177
Ethiopian Rhapsody (Hosmer), 388
Ethiopian Serenaders, 178
Etler, Alvin (1913-   ), 551-552
Etruscan Concerto (Glanville-Hicks), 566
Etude, The, 639
Etude Symphonique (Fairchild), 388
Eudine, Dom, 660

Eugénie (Barlow, S. L. M.), 472
Euphony (Ward), 560
Euphorion (Gallico), 361
Euphorion (Heiden), 587
Euphrosyne (Converse, F. S.), 381
Euterpe (Chadwick), 309
Euterpean Society, 151, 158, 170
Euterpeiad and Musical Intelligencer, 83, 85, 132, 170, 227, 228
Evangeline (Cain), 658
Evangeline (Hays), 703
Evangeline (Kreckel), 661
Evangeline (Luening), 502
Evangeline (Reed), 579
Evangeline (Rice-Goodwin), 712
Evans, Ray, 752
Eve of St. Agnes, The (Ballantine), 416
Eve of St. Agnes, The (Jacobi), 460
Everett, Horace, 483
Everett, Leolyn Louise, 471
Everybody's Doin' It (Berlin), 733
Everyman (Lester), 634
Everything Is Peaches Down in Georgia (Meyer), 709
Everywoman, 310
Evett, Robert (1922-   ), 614-615
Evocation (Loeffler), 351
Evocation (Riegger), 397
Evocations (Avshalomov), 586
Evocations (Bloch), 394
Evocations (Ruggles), 370
Evolutionary Quintet (Fickenscher), 371
Evolution Transcripta (Wuorinen), 612
Ewen, David, 496
Exaltation (Hanson), 430
Ex Hocte (Allen), 420
Exodus, The (Rogers, B.), 447
Experience (Bendix), 361
Experiment in Modern Music concert 425-426
Express, 240
Exultate Deo (Daniels), 385
Eyer, Robert, 595
Eyer, Ronald, 446, 454, 493, 552, 566

F

Fable, A (Dello Joio), 544
Fable of the Hapless Folktune (Delamarter), 417
Fables (Persichetti), 548
Fabric (Cowell), 449
Face the Music (Berlin), 734

Fade Out - Fade In (Styne), 746

Fain, Sammy (1902-   ), 751-752

Fairbanks, Douglas, 385

Fairchild, Blair (1877-1933), 388

Fair Co-ed, The (Luders), 719

Fairy Bridal, The (Hewitt, J. H.), 169

Fairy Fingers (Mills), 291

Fairyland (Parker), 319, 762

Fairy Scherzo (Daniels), 386

Fairy Tale (Kolar), 424

Fairy Tale (Persichetti), 548

Faith (Buzza-Peccia), 622

Faith (Smith), 630

Faithful, The (Rogers, B.), 446

Falckner, Justus, 25

Fall of the House of Usher, The (Hill), 374

Fall of the House of Usher, The (Loomis), 419

Fall of Usher, The (Claflin), 476

False Faces (Barlow, W.), 578

Faltering Dusk, The (Kramer), 631

Families, singing, 173-175

Fancy Free (Bernstein), 540

Fandango (Whithorne), 410

Fanfare and March (Kubik), 555

Fanfare, Aria, and Echo (Pinkham), 608

Fanfare for Paratroopers (Creston), 493

Fanfare for the People of Russia (Taylor), 402

Fanfare, Fugato, and Finale (Gershefski), 501

Fanfare, Prayer, and March (Koutzen), 529

Fanny (Rome), 744

Fantaisie Humoresque (Shepherd), 405

Fantaisie-Impromptu (Chopin), 749

Fantaisie in C Minor (Demarest), 625

Fantasia (Barnes), 655

Fantasia (Brunswick), 517

Fantasia (Converse, F. S.), 381

Fantasia (Creston), 492

Fantasia (Disney), 402

Fantasia (Grimm), 476

Fantasia (Rochberg), 567

Fantasia (Rogers, B.), 447

Fantasia (Shelley), 647

Fantasia Brevis (Luening), 502

Fantasia Concertante (Schuller), 616

Fantasia on a Gregorian Theme (Dello Joio), 542

Fantasia Quasi una Sonata (Bauer, M.), 411

Fantasia-Tahmeel (El-Dabh), 619

Fantasie (Brewer), 647

Fantasie (Galajikian), 521

Fantastic Concerto (Loeffler), 349

Fantastic Variations (Bergsma), 591

Fantasy (Berger), 563

Fantasy (Blackwood), 606

Fantasy (Britain), 521

Fantasy (Dubensky), 477

Fantasy (Gebhard), 626

Fantasy (Goeb), 581

Fantasy (Harris), 438

Fantasy (Overton), 614

Fantasy (Piston), 445

Fantasy (Porter, Q.), 456

Fantasy (Pratt), 305

Fantasy (Read), 559

Fantasy (Rogers, B.), 446

Fantasy and Variations (Dello Joio), 542

Fantasy in Delft (Gilbert), 356

Fantasy in Space (Luening), 506

Fantasy in Technicolor (Wagner), 516

Fantasy in Two Movements (Finney), 498

Fantasy on a Choral Theme (Howard), 635

Fantasy on a Javanese Motif (Gideon), 508

Fantasy on a Western Folk Song (McKay), 463

Fantasy on Down East Spirituals (Shepherd), 405

Fantasy on Russian Folk Songs (Gaines), 633

Fantasy Sonata (Cole), 518

Far Away Places (Kramer-Whitney), 752

Farewell of Hiawatha, The (Foote), 312

Farewell Symphony (Barrymore), 389

Farewell to Pioneers (Harris), 438

Far Horizon, The (Cadman), 404

Farmer and the Fairy, The (Tcherepnin), 478

Farmyard, The, 692

Far Ocean (Royce), 415

Farrel, Bob, 176

Farwell, Arthur (1872-1952), 375-376

Fascinating Rhythm (Gershwin), 425

Fata Morgana (Whithorne), 410

Father Abraham (Foster), 264

Father Abraham (Gibbons), 261

Father and Daughter (Grainger), 407

Father Kemp's Old Folks, 173
Father of Waters (Cadman), 404
Faun, The (Delamarter), 417
Feast of Tabernacles, The (Zeuner), 146
Federal Gazette, 41
Federal March (Reinagle), 81
Federal Music Project, 414, 416, 465, 500, 526
Federal Overture (Carr), 115
Federal Overture (Van Hagen), 75
Federal Street (Oliver), 147
Federal Street Theatre, Boston, 70
Federal Symphony Orchestra, 465
Federal Theatre (WPA), 495
Federation of Women's Clubs, 625
fellowships in music (*see also* names of individual foundations and funds), 762
Felsen von Plymouth, Der (Heinrich), 235, 237
Femme et son ombre, La (Tcherepnin), 478
Ferber, Edna, 731, 741
Ferguson, Ethel, 419
Ferrata, Giuseppe (1865-1928), 638
Festival (Oldberg), 386
Festival Flutes (Titcomb), 654
Festival Folk Fantasy (Harris), 439
Festival Hymn (Bartlett), 648
Festival Hymn (Buck), 645
Festival Hymn (Van der Stucken), 348
Festival Jubilate (Beach), 322
Festival March (Bergh), 626
Festival of Contemporary Arts, 509
Festival of Pan (Converse, F. S.), 381
Festival of the Workers (McDonald), 463
Festival of Two Worlds, Spoleto, 538, 593, 599
Festival of Youth (Shepherd), 405
Festival Opening, A (Kubik), 555
Festival Overture (Freed), 527
Festival Overture (Lopatnikoff), 506
Festival Overture (Riegger), 399
Festival Overture (Search), 422
Festival Overture (Severn), 362
Festival Piece in One Movement, A (Vincent), 525
Festival Postlude (Demarest), 625
Festival Prelude (Branscombe), 634
Festival Sanctus (Huss), 359
Festival Sonata (Weaver), 628

Festival Te Deum (Hall), 650
Festive Overture (Still), 462
Festouvertüre (Converse, C. C.), 666
Fête Galante (Smith), 380
Feuilles Symphoniques (White, P.), 472
Fever Dreams (Barati), 586
Fewkes, Jesse Walter, 674
Fickenscher, Arthur (1871-1954), 370-371
Fiddle-dee-dee (Stromberg), 715
Fiddle Faddle (Anderson), 642
Fiddler on the Roof (Bock), 749
Fiddler's Delight (Cowell), 450
Fiddlers Four (Campbell-Watson), 662
Fidgety Feet (Gershwin), 425
Fields, Dorothy, 734, 751
Fields, Herbert, 737
Fields, Joseph, 745
Fiesta (Fuleihan), 527
Fiesta Mexicana (Reed), 579
"Fifteen Men on a Dead Man's Chest,' 354
Fifth of November, The (Crouch), 172
Fifty Miles From Boston (Cohan), 719
Fifty Million Frenchmen (Porter), 737
Filippi, Amadeo de (1900-   ), 529-530
Filling Station (Thomson), 433, 434
Fillmore, John Comfort, 673, 676
Film music, 464, 467, 481, 484, 486, 491, 493, 497, 510, 529, 553, 554, 565, 738, 739, 740, 741, 742, 746, 748, 749, 750, 751, 752, 753, 754
Filtro, Il (Allen), 420
Final Ingredient, The (Amram), 619
Finck, Henry T., 332
Fine, Irving (1914-1962), 570-571, 619
Fine, Vivian (1913-   ), 583, 767, 796
Finian's Rainbow (Lane), 742
Finney, Ross Lee (1906-   ), 498
Fiorello! (Bock), 748
Fiorello, Dante (1905-   ), 522
Fire Bringers, The (Royce), 415
Firefly, The (Friml), 729
Firemen's Quadrille, 281
Fireside Tales (MacDowell), 330, 344
First American Symphonette (Gould), 553
First Christmas, The (Coombs), 650
First Gun Is Fired (Root), 265
First Lady Waltz (McHugh), 754
First Little Show, The (Hupfield), 750
First Modern Suite (MacDowell), 329, 334-335

Firth & Hall, 146
Firth, Pond & Company, 146, 196, 255
Fischer, Carl, Inc., 473
Fischer, William Gustavus (1835-1912), 667
Fisher, Fred (1875-1942), 708
Fisher, William Arms (1861-1948), 622
Fisher's Widow, The (Edwards), 627
Fiske, John, 117
Fiske, Minnie Maddern, 419
Fisk University singers, 681
Fitch, Theodore F. (1900-   ), 471, 510-511
Fitzgerald, Ella, 796
Five American Dances (Goeb), 581
Five American Dances (Lane), 640
Five Epigrammatic Portraits (Green), 518
Five Episodes (Trimble), 611
Five Fairy Tales (Rogers, B.), 446
Five Foot Two, Eyes of Blue (Henderson), 738
500 Dragon Thalers (Helm), 584
Five Inhibitions (Mourant), 562
Five Kid Songs (Bernstein), 540
Five Miniatures (White, P.), 472
Five Mosaics (Kay), 564
Five Nature Studies (Cohn), 578
Five Pieces (Weiss), 454
Five Poems by Emily Dickinson (Copland), 483
Five Shakespearean Sonnets (Gideon), 508
Five Short Colloquies (Chanler), 632
Five Short Pieces for Orchestra (Pinkham), 608
Five Songs after William Blake (Thomson), 434
Five Songs of Motherhood (Floyd), 596
Five Sonnets of Shakespeare and Songs of the Nativity (La Montaine), 613
Five Tableaux (Wagenaar), 456
Five Wayside Impressions of New England (Matthews), 653
Flagg, Josiah (1738-1794), 17, 64
Flagler Prize, 409, 470
Flanagan, William, 568, 796
Flapper and the Quarterback, The (Loomis), 419-420
Fledermaus Fantasy (La Forge), 626
Fleister, Karl, 494
Flemish Overture (Meyerowitz), 585

Fletcher, Alice C., 673
Fletcher, Grant (1913-   ), 580
Fleur, Baron Rudolph de, 159
Flight Cycle (Verrall), 523
Flight of the Eagle, The (Converse, F. S.), 382
Flitch of Bacon, The (Pelissier), 96
Flivver Ten Million (Converse, F. S.), 381
Flonzaley Quartet, 392
Flora (Giannini), 494
Floradora (Stuart), 716
Flora, or Hob in the Well, 30
Flora's Festival (Hewitt, J. H.), 169
Florence Nightingale (Williams), 655
Florentine Sketches (Pattison), 640
Florida State University (Tallahasee), 594, 595
Florida Symphony Orchestra, 611
Floridia, Pietro, 642
Flower Drum Song (Rodgers-Hammerstein), 741
Flowering Peach, The, music for (Hovhaness), 551
Flowers (Smith), 380
Flowers and You (Young), 637
Floyd, Carlisle (1926-   ), 594-596
Flute Serenade (Skilton), 358
Flying Colors (Schwartz), 739
Flying Down to Rio, score for (Youmans), 736
Flying High (Henderson), 739
Flying Trapeze, The (Leybourne, Lee), 704
Flynn, Joseph, 706
Flynt, Josiah, 21
Foerster, Adolph M. (1854-1927), 622
Folio Pieces (Brown), 617
folk music, 374-375, 405, 406-407, 725
    bibliography, 826-843
    cowboy songs, 636, 637, 638, 693-694
    lumberjack songs, 694-695
    mountain songs, 173-175, 725
    Negro, 407, 680-690
    North American Indian, 374, 670-679
    origin of, 695-696
Folk Overture (Mennin), 590
folk singers from European Alps, 174-175
folk singing, 597
Folk Song Fantasy on the English Air Fanny Blair (Mason, D. G.), 378
folk songs, settings of, 635-638

Folk Songs of the Kentucky Mountains (McGill), 637

Folk Songs of the South (Cox), 692

Folksong Sonatinas (Rasbach), 627

Folk Symphony from the Carolina Hills, A (Vardell), 466

Folkways Symphony (Smith), 569

Follow the Leader, score for (Henderson), 739

Follow the Swallow (Henderson), 738

Follow Through (Henderson), 739

Fontainebleau Award, 613

Foote, Arthur William (1853-1937), 289, 292, 302, 310-313, 376

Foote, George (1886-1956), 421

Ford Foundation, 440, 445, 488, 495, 519, 535, 543, 557, 561, 566, 569, 571, 593, 596, 608, 609, 616, 633, 742, 763

Ford's Theatre (Bacon), 465

Foret Noire, La (Pelissier), 80, 96

Forever and a Day (Spross), 624

Forever and Sunsmell (Cage), 573

Forever Free: A Lincoln Chronicle (Kay), 564

Forever Young, The (Elwell), 473

For Me and My Gal (Meyer), 709

For One Who Fell in Battle (Loeffler), 351

Forrage, Stephen, 39

For Strings (Barlow, S. L. M.), 472

Forst, Rudolf (1900-   ), 521-522

Forsyth, John, 529

For the Dear Old Flag I Die (Foster), 264

For the Gentlemen (Shaw), 136

For the Peace of Mind (Berlinski), 587

Fort McHenry, 126

Fortunate Islands, The (Bergsma), 590

Fortune Teller, The (Herbert, V.), 717

Forty Negro Spirituals (White), 636

Forty-Second Street (Warren), 751

46th Psalm (Buck), 645

For Whom the Bell Tolls, music for (Young), 753

Forza d'Amore (Buzzi-Peccia), 622

Foss, Lukas (1922-   ), 545, 591-594, 611

Foster, Fay (1886-1960), 626, 627, 727

Foster, Stephen Collins (1826-1864), 181, 184-198, 211, 264, 419, 553, 634, 635, 650, 655, 670, 755, 796-797

Foster Gallery (Gould), 553

Foster Hall, 186-187, 419

Fosteriana (Gaul), 654

Foster Sonatina (Howard), 635

Foster Suite (Janssen), 464

Four Casual Developments (Cowell), 449

Four Character Pieces after Omar Khayyám (Foote), 312, 313

Four Documents (Cohn), 578

Four Fragments from the Canterbury Tales (Trimble), 611

Four Freedoms, The (Bennett), 461

Four-Handed Fun (Talma), 514

Four Indian Tribal Melodies (Busch), 359

Four Indiscretions (Gruenberg), 409

Four Iroquois Dances (McPhee), 528

Four Miniatures (Wagner), 516

4 Minutes and 33 Seconds (Cage), 573

Four More (Brown), 617

Four Museum Pieces (Moore, D.), 441

Four Nocturnes (Read), 559

Four Orchestral Songs (Kohs), 570

Four Russian Melodies (Slonimsky), 641

Four Saints in Three Acts (Stein-Thomson), 432, 433

Four Seasons, The (Hadley), 377

Four Sketches (Heller), 663

Four Solo Services for Friday Evening (Heller), 663

Four Songs from James Joyce's Chamber Music (Lockwood), 515

Four Songs from Tennyson's In Memoriam (Smith), 630

Four Squares of Philadelphia, The (Gesensway), 498

Four Systems (Brown), 617

Fourteen Variations for Orchestra (Moevs), 602

4th of July, The (Hewitt), 88

Fourth of July (Ives), 368

Fourth of July, or Temple of American Independence (Pelissier), 96

Fox, George L., 712

Fox, Gilbert, 119-120

Fox, Oscar J. (1879-   ), 637-638

Fox family, The, 173

Fragment, A (Young), 639

Fragments of Letters of Saint Catherine (Perry), 613

Francesca da Rimini (Foote), 312

Franchetti, Arnold, 610

Franck, César, 360, 647
Franco, Johan, 797
Frankenstein, Alfred, 397, 519, 564, 569, 588
Frankfurt Music Festival, 414
Frankie and Johnny, 696
Frankie and Johnny (Clokey), 634
Frankie and Johnny (Kubik), 555
Frankie and Johnny (Moross), 557
Free and Equal Blues (Robinson), 629
Freed, Isadore (1900-1960), 526-527
Freedom Morning (Blitzstein), 497
Freedom Train (Siegmeister), 514
Free Lance, The (Sousa), 710, 715
Freeman, Henry Lawrence (1869-1954), 361
Freeman School of Grand Opera, 361
Freeman's Journal, 40
Freer, Eleanor Everest (1864-1943), 361
Free School for Spreading the Knowledgs of Vocal Music, 105
Free Synagogue, New York, 663
French, Jacob (1754-?), 64
French Genevan Psalter, 5, 6
Frenchman's Creek, music for (Young), 753
French Revolution, 118
Frenetic Rhythms (Riegger), 397
Friedheim, Arthur, 527
Friedman, Theodore Lewis (*see* Lewis, Ted)
Friends (*see* Quakers)
Friends and Enemies of Modern Music, 432
Friends of Music, 392
Fries, August, 215
Fries, Wulf, 215
Friml, Rudolf (1881-   ), 729
Frog Prince, The (Nordhoff), 508
Frog Went a-Courtin', The, 692
From a Log Cabin (MacDowell), 330
From a Lute of Jade (Read), 559
From a Sufi's Tent (Strickland), 627
From Childhood (McDonald), 463
From Dixieland (Rasbach), 627
From Dover Beach (Woltmann), 512
From Dreams of Thee (Bullard), 623
From Foster Hall (Howard), 635
From Greenland's Icy Mountains (Mason), 137
From Grieg to Brahms (Mason, D. G.), 378
From Here (Brown), 617

From Leaves of Grass (Woltmann), 512
Fromm Foundation, 398, 489, 499, 510, 519, 563, 568, 569, 576, 584, 587, 601, 606, 763
From Mount Rainier (Reiser), 424
From My Window (Siegmeister), 514
From My Youth (Wilson), 385
From Old New England (Severn), 362
From the American Folklore (Koutzen), 529
From the Black Belt (Still), 462
From the Canebreak (Gardner), 640
From the Delta (Still), 402
From the Journal of a Wanderer (Still), 462
From the Land of the Sky Blue Water (Cadman), 403
From the Life of St. Paul (Burleigh), 640
From the Monadnock Region (Wagner), 516
From the Mountain Kingdom of the Great North West, suite (Saar), 361
From the Northland (Sowerby), 657
From the North Shore (Wagner), 516
From the Plains (Ayres), 376
From the Revelation of St. John the Divine (McPhee), 528
From These States (Bacon), 465
From the Southern Mountains (Stringfield), 465
From Vernon's Mount Behold the Hero Rise (Holden), 61
Frontiers (Creston), 492
Frost, Robert, 444, 464, 489, 549
Frostiana (Thompson), 444
Frozen War, score for (Creston), 493
Fry, William Henry (1815?-1864), 238-247, 250, 756, 758, 797
Fuchs, Robert, 410, 421
Fugal Triptych, A (Wagner), 516
Fugato on a Well-known Theme (McBride), 643
Fugue Fantasia (Farwell), 375
Fugue for Eighteen Violins (Dubensky), 477
Fugue on a Noel (Sanders), 521
Fuguing pieces (Billings), 49, 55-57
Fuguing Tune (Luening), 502
Fuji in the Sunset Glow (Rogers, B.), 446

Fulbright Grants, 512, 564, 567, 599, 600, 604, 608, 609, 632
Fuleihan, Anis (1900-   ), 527
Fulfillment (MacDermid), 625
Full Redemption Songs (Bennard), 668
funds (*see* fellowships)
Funeral Dirge (Van Hagen, P. A.), 75
Funny Face (Gershwin), 735
Funny Girl (Styne), 746

G

Gade, Niels, 359
Gaelic Symphony (Beach), 321, 322
Gaelic Symphony (Cowell), 449, 450
Gagliarda of the Merry Plague (Saminsky), 423
Gaiety Girls, The, 716
Gaines, Samuel Richards (1869-1945), 633
Galajikian, Florence Grandland (1900-   ), 521
Galaxy (Leplin), 588
Galaxy Music Corporation, 560, 631
Galilee (Andrews), 653
Galimir Quartet, 398
Gallantry (Moore, D.), 442
Gallico, Paolo (1868-1955), 361, 459
Gallon, Noel, 591
Gallopjig Colloquy (Brant), 576
Gambling Song (Skilton), 358
Gamester, The, 72
Ganz, Rudolph (1877-   ), 383-384, 416, 469, 630
Garcia, Manuel, 204, 238-239
Garden Eastward, A (Weisgall), 566
Garden of Live Flowers, The (Taylor), 400
Garden of Mystery (Cadman), 403
Gardner, Mrs. Jack, 350
Gardner, Samuel (1891-   ), 640-641
Gargoyles (Luening), 506
Garland, Hamlin, 336-337
Garland, Judy, 741
Garland, The (Hopkinson), 41
Garrick (Simon, Stoessel), 448
Garrick Gaieties, 496, 525, 739
Garrison, Lucy McKim, 684, 685
Gaul, Harvey Bartlett (1881-1945), 654, 658
Gaunt, Percy (1852-1896), 715
Gavotte (Kramer), 631
Gay Divorcee (Porter), 737

Gay Life, The (Schwartz), 739
Gaynor, Jessie L. (1863-1921), 623
Gebhard, Heinrich (1878-   ), 433, 549, 626
Gebrauchmusik (music for use), 408, 480, 482, 510
Gédalge, André, 370, 411, 523
Geezer, The (Stromberg), 715
Gehot, Jean, 81-83
Geisha, The, 716
Genesis of a Music (Partch), 499
Geneva Conservatory, 392
Genevan Psalters, 6
General Died at Dawn, The, music for (Janssen), 464
General Theological Seminary, 651
General William Booth Enters Heaven (Lindsay, James), 468
Genii of the Rock (Bentley), 102
Gentle Annie (Foster), 196
Gentleman and Lady's Musical Companion (Stickney), 48
Gentleman's Magazine, The, 117
Gentlemen Be Seated (Moross), 557
Gentlemen Prefer Blondes (Styne), 746
Gentle Zephyr (Van Hagen, Jr.), 75
George (Mopper), 567
George Washington Bridge (Schuman), 535
George Washington, Jr. (Cohan), 719
George Washington University, 618
Georgia Camp Meeting, The (Mills), 657
Georgia on My Mind (Carmichael), 753
Georgia State College for Women, 508
Germania Orchestra, 273-274
Germania Society, 212-216, 273, 281
German ideas, 294
German Pietists, organ of, 17
German singing societies, 270, 272, 274
Germans, Pennsylvania (*see* Pennsylvania Germans)
Gerrard, Saida, 398
Gerschefski, Edward (1909-   ), 500-501, 797
Gershe, Leonard, 744
Gershkovitch, Jacques, 586
Gershwin, George (1898-1937), 353, 379, 424-429, 457, 466, 467, 525, 533, 722, 735, 797-798
Gershwin, Ira, 425
Gershwin Memorial Award, 564, 567, 589, 602, 609, 617

Gesensway, Louis (1906-   ), 498
Gesù Bambino (Yon), 660
Get Me to the Church on Time (Loewe), 743
Get Off the Track, 174
Gettysburg Address Symphony (Harris), 438
Giannini, Vittorio (1903-   ), 379, 494-495, 596, 618
Giants in the Earth (Moore), 440
Gibbons, James Sloan, 261
Gibraltar Suite (De Leone), 420
Gibsons, The, 173
Giddy Puritan, The (Delamarter), 417
Gideon, Miriam (1906-   ), 508, 798
Gieseking, Walter, 410
Gift of Pan (Smith), 630
Gigi, score for (Loewe), 743
Gilbert, Henry Franklin Belknap (1868-1928), 354-356, 700, 798
Gilbert, J. L., 705
Gilbert, Willie, 747
Gilberté, Hallett (1875-   ), 625
Gilchrist, William Wallace (1846-1916), 303, 653, 759
Gilfert, George, 672
Gillespie, Dizzy, 798
Gillespie, Lincoln A., 542
Gillette, James Robert (1886-   ), 654
Gillingham, George, 78, 85, 93, 97
Gillis, Don (1912-   ), 584-585
Gilman, Benjamin Ives, 673-674, 675
Gilman, Lawrence, 324, 366, 369, 382, 401, 431, 432, 433, 442
Gilmore, Patrick Sarsfield (1829-1892), 223, 297-298, 553, 681, 709, 798
Giorni, Aurelio (1895-1938), 476
Girl Behind the Gun, The (Caryll), 716
Girl Crazy (Gershwin), 735
Girl Friend, The (Rodgers-Hart), 739
Girl from Kays, The (Caryll), 716
Girl From Paris, The (Caryll), 716
Girl from Utah, The (Kern), 731
Girl in Pink Tights, The (Romberg), 730
Girl Is You, The (Henderson), 739
Girls, Les, score for (Porter), 738
Girl That I Marry, The (Berlin), 734
Gitanjali (Tagore), 373, 459
Give Me Jesus, 684
Give Me The Silent Sun (Harris), 439
Give My Regards to Broadway (Cohan), 720

Glad Hand, The (Stromberg), 715
Gladiator, The (Sousa), 710
Glad to See You (Styne), 745
Glanville-Hicks, Peggy (1912-   ), 395, 433, 516, 565, 566, 768
Glass Blowers, The (Sousa), 715
Glazounov, Alexander, 458
Gleason, Frederick Grant (1848-1903), 303-304, 385, 644, 759
Glière, Reinhold, 526, 528
Glittering Gate, The (Glanville-Hicks), 566
Gloria (Buzza-Peccia), 622
Gloria Dei Church, 17-18, 25, 31
Gloria Domini (Noble), 651
Gloriana (Friml), 729
Glory and Endless Years (Daniels), 386
Glory of Nature, The (Paine), 301
Glory Road, De (Wolfe), 637
Gluck, Alma, 622
Gobi (Reiser), 424
Goblin Fair, The (Bergh), 626
Go Choruses (McBride), 643
Godard, Benjamin Louis Paul, 359
God Bless America (Berlin), 733
Goddess, The, score for (Tiomkin), 434
God for Us (Converse, C. C.), 666
Go Down, Moses, 682
Godowsky, Leopold (1870-1938), 627, 640
Godowsky, Leopold, Jr., 469
Gods (Blitzstein), 497
God Save Great George Our King (Carey), 127
God Save the King, 47
Gods of the Mountain, The (Bonner), 420
Gods of the Mountain (Farwell), 375
God's World (Wolfe), 637
God Who Made the Earth (Howard), 635
Goeb, Roger (1914-   ), 580-581, ᵐᶜ ᵌ
Goetschius, Percy, 359, 378, 396, ⸱ ᶥ¹, 469, 471, 513, 518, 623, 631, 633, ϲ ᶽ9, 640
Going Up (Hirsch), 735
Goin' Home (Fisher), 622
Gold and the Senior Commandante (Bergsma), 591
Golde, Walter (1887-1963), 630-631
Golden Apple, The (Moross), 557
Golden Butterfly, The (De Koven), 718
Golden Cage, The (Whiting), 357

Golden Calf, The (De Leone), 420
Golden Earrings, music for (Young), 753
Golden Echo, The (Talma), 514
Golden Journey to Samarkand, The (Read), 559
Golden Legend, The (Lester), 634
Golden Series (Bradbury), 145
Golden Treasure (Ryder), 667
Golden Wedding, De (Bland), 702
Golden Wreath (Orlando), 261
Goldilocks (Anderson), 642
Goldman, Edwin Franko (1878-1956), 711
Goldman, Richard Franko (1910-), 396, 397, 486, 487, 489, 534, 547, 573, 575, 591, 642, 711
Goldman Band, 398, 483, 492, 641, 642, 711
Goldmark, Karl, 378
Goldmark, Rubin (1872-1936), 378-379, 425, 426, 459, 468, 471, 479, 494, 517, 518, 522, 561, 569, 578, 640, 641
Goldwyn Follies, The, 429
Golem Suite (Achron), 423
Golschmann, Vladimir, 458
Gooch, William, 705
Good-by Dolly Gray, 707
Goodbye, Mamma, I'm Off to Yokohama, 727
Goodbye to the Clown (Laderman), 598
Goodman, Benny (1900-), 457, 485, 553, 723, 799
Good Morning, Judge!, 425
Good News (Henderson), 739
Goodrich, Wallace, 433, 623
Good Soldier Schweik, The (Kurka), 597-598
Goodwin (Webb), 143
Goodwin, J. Cheever, 712
Gooseherd and the Goblin, The (Smith), 569
Gordon, "Left Wing," 684
Gorham, Joseph K., 721
Gorman, Ross, 426
Gorney, Jay (1896-), 749
gospel songs, 584, 663-669
    and Negro music, 682-683
Gottschalk, Louis Moreau (1829-1869), 205-210, 557, 681, 755, 799
Gouffre, Le (Tcherepnin), 478
Gould, Morton (1913-), 552-554
Gov. Arnold's March (Shaw), 135
Governor's Son, The (Cohan), 719

Grabner, Hermann, 506
Graham, Martha, 397, 483, 511, 532, 535, 543, 619, 620
Grainger, Percy Aldridge (1882-1961), 406-407, 799
Gram, Hans, 62, 63
Grand Aria (Demarest), 625
Grand Canyon Suite (Grofé), 467
Grand Choeur (Gillette), 654
Grande Bretêche, La (Hollingsworth), 600
Grande Bretêche, La (Koutzen), 528
Grande Polka de Concert (Bartlett), 648
Grandfather's Clock (Work), 267
Grand March to the Memory of Washington (Bull), 202
Grand Mogul, The (Luders), 719
Grandmother, My (Pelissier), 96
grand opera (*see* opera)
Grand Street Follies, The (Schwartz), 739
Grand Tarantella (Kay), 557
Grand Variations for harp and piano (Herz), 204
Granger, Thomas, 131, 151
Grant-Schaeffer, George Alfred (1872-1939), 624
Grattan, Mrs., 98
Graupner, Gottlieb (1767-1836), 129-133, 151, 176, 799
Graves, Juliette A. (*see* Adams, Mrs. Crosby
Gray, H. W., Company, 658
Gray, Roland Palmer, 695
Gray Mare's Best Horse, The (Taylor, R.), 91
Gray's Gardens, 107
Great American Goof, The (Brant), 576
Great Day (Youmans), 736
Great Dictator, The, music for (Willson), 748
Great Lady, The (Loewe), 742, 743
Great National Peace Jubilee, 297
Great River (Bacon), 466
Grecian Daughter, The (Knight), 160
Greek Impressions (Whithorne), 410
Greek State Orchestra, 472
Green, Adolf, 745, 746
Green, Joseph, 18
Green, Ray (1909-), 518-519
Greenaway, Kate, 314
Greenfield Christmas Tree, The (Moore, D.), 442

Green Grow the Lilacs (Riggs), 740
Green Mansions (Hudson), 410
Green Mountain Overture (Stevens), 519
Greenwich House Music School, 522
Greenwich Village Follies (Hirsch), 735
Greenwillow (Loesser), 747
Gregorian Improvisations (Kreckel), 661
Gregorian influence, 541
Gregorian Institute, 661
Grey, Frank H. (1883-1951), 640
Grieg, Edvard, 347, 407
  and MacDowell, 323, 325-326, 327-328
Griffelkin (Foss), 593
Griffes, Charles Tomlinson (1884-1920), 389-391, 799-800
Griffis, Eliot (1893-   ), 470
Grimm, Carl Hugo (1890-   ), 475-476
Grim Troubadour, The (Whithorne), 410
Griselle, Thomas (1891-1955), 467-468
Grofé, Ferde (1892-   ), 426, 466-467, 640
Grohg (Copland), 479
Grotesque Dance from a Projected Ballet (Phillips), 510
Grounds and Rules of Music Explained (Walter), 13
Gruen, John, 612
Gruenberg, Louis (1884-1964), 408-410, 479, 800
Grunewald, Mathias, 412
Guadalcanal Fantasy (Gershefski), 501
Guardian Angel, The (Skilton), 358
Guest, The (Blitzstein), 496
Guggenheim Memorial Fellowships, 421, 437, 441, 442, 446, 451, 452, 454, 456, 461, 462, 465, 469, 470, 474, 479, 488, 491, 492, 498, 499, 500, 502, 507, 508, 509, 511, 513, 517, 520, 522, 523, 525, 528, 533, 542, 544, 546, 548, 551, 555, 557, 560, 561, 565, 566, 568, 576, 578, 579, 581, 582, 583, 585, 586, 589, 590, 591, 594, 597, 598, 601, 602, 603, 604, 606, 607, 613, 614, 616, 617, 619, 629, 631, 642, 643, 762-763
Guiablesse, La (Still), 462
Guide to the Life Expectancy of a Rose, A (Fine), 583

Guilmant, Alexandre, 375, 416, 649, 652, 654
Guinevere (Levy), 401
Guion, David (1895-   ), 406, 636-637
Guiterman, Arthur, 352
Gulgamesh (Berezowsky), 525
Gull, The (Hill), 623
Gulliver (Kelley), 346-347
Gumbo Chaff, 256
Guns and Castanets (Moross), 557
Gur Amir (Shapleigh), 383
Gut-Bucket Gus (Bennett), 461
Guthrie, Woody, 800
Guttoveggia, Joseph (*see* Creston, Paul)
Guys and Dolls (Loesser), 747
Gwine Long Down, 181
Gwine to Hebb'n (Wolfe), 637
Gypsy (Styne), 745-746
Gypsy, The (Luders), 719
Gypsy in Me, The (Porter), 737

H

Ha Chalutsim (Binder), 663
Hackley School, 390
Hades, Inc. (Matthews), 653
Hadley, Henry Kimball (1871-1937), 376-377, 760, 800
Hadley Memorial Library, 376, 760
Hagar in the Desert (Converse, F. S.), 382
Hageman, Richard (1882-   ), 629
Hagen, Veinus, 571
Hagiographa (Jacobi), 460
Hahn, Frederick E., 639
Hahr, F. C., 405
Haieff, Alexi (1914-   ), 561-562, 767
Hail, Ceres, Hail (Densmore), 626
Hail Columbia (Phile), 107, 118-121, 666, 755
Hail, Hail, the Gang's All Here (Morse), 707
Hako, The (Farwell), 375
Hale, Edward Everett, 352
Hale, Philip, 307
Half Moon Mountain (Gershefski), 500
Hall, Walter Henry (1862-1935), 650
Hallam, Lewis, 27, 31
Hallelujah (Youmans), 736
Hambitzer, Charles, 425
Hamilton College, 465
Hamlet, 72
Hamlet (Maretzek), 298

Hamlet and Ophelia (MacDowell), 330, 335

Hamlet, Prelude to (Rogers, B.), 446

Hammerstein, Oscar, II, 483, 546, 730, 734, 740-741

Hampton Institute singers, 407, 681

Hanby, Benjamin Russell (1833-1867), 261

Hancock, John, 117

Hancock, John, Fellowship, 617

Hancock, Thomas, 23

Handel, George Frederick, 67, 105, 107, 127, 133, 214

Handel and Haydn Society, 67, 98, 133, 135, 137, 138, 141, 143, 146, 147, 151, 156, 170, 215, 293, 295, 296, 307, 318, 645

Handel in the Strand (Grainger), 407

Hand of Bridge, A (Barber), 532-533

Hands Up (Romberg), 729

Handy, William Christopher (1873-1958), 462, 687-688, 800

Hangman's Song, The, 692

Hanover (Crofts), 17

Hans Christian Andersen, score for (Loesser), 746

Hansen, F. G., 248

Hanson, Howard (1896-   ), 380, 430-432, 435, 446, 479, 512, 558, 560, 563, 578, 579, 580, 588, 590, 800

Happy (Grey), 640

Happy Days Are Here Again (Ager), 749

Happy Hypocrite, The (Elwell), 473

Harbach, Otto, 732, 736

Harburg, E. Y., 741, 749, 754

Harding, Frank, 706

Hark, as the Twilight Fades (Metcalf), 622

Harker, F. Flaxington (1876-1936), 633-634

Hark from the tombs (Holyoke), 63

Harlequin (Gallico), 361

Harlequin Pastry Cook (Pelissier), 96

Harlequin's Carnival (Parris), 615

Harlequin Shipwreck'd (Demarque), 80, 109

Harlequin's Invasion, 80

Harling, W. Franke (1887-1958), 419

Harmon Award, 462

Harmoneons, 173

Harmonia Americana (Holyoke), 62

Harmonica Player, The (Guion), 636

Harmonic Society, New York, 33

Harmonies of Florence (Bingham), 41?

Harmonious Blacksmith, Variations o? (Grainger), 407

Harmony (Piston), 444

harmony chorus, 467

Harmony Music (Phile), 107

Harmony of Harmony (French), 64

Harms, T. B., 557

Harnick, Sheldon, 748-749

Harrigan, Edward, 712, 713, 714

Harrigan and Hart, 712-713

Harris, Charles K. (1865-1930), 70?, 715, 800

Harris, Roy (1898-   ), 434-439, 508? 513, 523, 524, 534, 547, 565, 578? 579, 580, 583, 614, 632, 800

Harrison, Jay S., 398, 399, 434, 440, 441? 442, 497, 499, 502, 561, 563, 568? 575, 597, 598, 605, 609, 612, 63?

Harrison, Lou (1917-   ), 576-578, 80?

Hart, Lorenz, 739-740

Hart, Moss, 734, 737

Hart, Tony, 712, 713, 714

Hartford, Huntington, Foundation, 52?, 762

Hartmann, Johann Peter Emilius, 359

Hartt College of Music, 526, 610

Harvard Musical Association, 143, 21?, 218-219, 591

Harvard University, 300, 302, 374, 378? 380, 389, 415, 416, 433, 442, 444? 470, 472, 486, 488, 523, 524, 538? 555, 563, 569, 570, 583, 584, 60?, 602, 607, 608, 626, 642, 737, 74?

Harvest (Gould), 553

Harvest, The (Giannini), 494

Has Anybody Here Seen Kelly?, 707

Hasek, Jaroslav, 597

Haskell Institute, 357

Hastings, George E., 38

Hastings, Thomas (1784-1872), 141-14?

Hasty Waters (Weaver), 628

Hatton, Anne Julia, 89, 672

Haubiel, Charles (1894-   ), 469, 53?

Haufrecht, Herbert, 801

Haunted Tower, The (Pelissier), 96

Haupt, Karl August, 300, 308, 649

Hauptmann, Moritz, 145, 295, 64?, 666

Have a Heart (Kern), 731

Having Wonderful Time (Kober), 74?

Hawkins, Eric, 398

Hawley, Charles Beach (1858-1915), 646-647

Hawthorne (Ives), 366

Hawthorne, Alice (*see* Winner, Septimus)

Hawthorne, Nathaniel, 494

Haydn, Franz Josef, 81, 130, 131, 133, 214, 216, 557, 563, 672

Haydn Collection of Church Music (Baker, B. F.), 147

Haymarket, Boston, 70

Hays, Roland, 801

Hays, William Shakespeare (1837-1907), 702-703

Hazel Dell (Root), 265

Hazel Flagg (Styne), 745

Headless Horseman, The (Moore, D.), 442

Hear me crying, O God (Taylor, R.),

Hear, O Lord, and Consider My Complaint (Taylor, R.), 93 93

Heart and Life Songs (Bennard), 668

Heart of Darkness (Conrad), 406

Heart of Heaven, The (Weaver), 628

Heart of Maryland, The (Stromberg), 715

Hearts, Meadows, and Flowers (Hoiby), 599

Heathen Chinee (Harte-Tucker), 703

Heavenly Children at Play (McCollin), 635

Hebrew Union College, 662

Hecht, Ben, 745

Hector and Andromache (Hadley), 377

He'd Have to Get Under, Get Out and Get Under (Abrahams), 709

He Doeth All Things Well (Woodbury), 148

Heffley, Eugene, 411

Heiden, Bernard (1910-), 587

Heifetz, Jascha, 409, 555

Heigh-Ho (Churchill), 751

Heilman, William Clifford (1877-1946), 389

Heinrich, Anton Philip (1781-1861), 99, 226-238, 679, 758, 801

Heiress, The, score for (Copland), 482

He Is Coming (Sankey), 668

He Leadeth Me (Bradbury), 146

Helen Morgan Story, The, songs for (McHugh), 751

Helen Retires (Antheil), 491

Helfer, Walter (1896-1959), 472

Hell-Bound Train, The, 693

Heller, James G. (1892-), 663

Hello Broadway! (Cohan), 719

Hello, Central, Give Me Heaven (Harris), 706

Hello, Frisco, Hello (Hirsch), 708

Hello, My Baby (Howard), 708

Hello Out There (Beeson), 600

Helm, Everett (1913-), 457, 583-584, 591, 594

Helm, Janet, 591

Héloïse and Abélard (Severn), 362

Help Me, Telstar, 754

Helvetia (Bloch), 394

He Maketh Wars to Cease (Scott), 625

Henderson, Ray (1896-), 738-739

Henning, Roslyn Brogue, 617

Henschel, 649

Hensel, Octavia, 207

Herbert, Victor (1859-1924), 426, 716-718, 731, 762, 801

Herbstgefühl (Nevin), 621

Here Come the Waves (Arlen), 741

Herford, Julius, 566

Her Little Highness (De Koven), 718

Herman, Woody (1913-), 724

Hermit Songs (Barber), 533

Hero Chants (Rudhyar), 476

Herod Overture (Hadley), 377

Heroic Elegy (Hanson), 431

Heroic Overture (Morris), 459

Heroic Piece (Cole), 360

Heroic Piece (Diamond), 544

Heroic Poem (Britain), 521

Hero's Espousal, A (Bornschein), 388

Herrmann, Bernard (1911-), 554

Her Rose (Coombs), 650

Herz, Henri, 204

Hester Prynne (Claflin), 476

He Who Gets Slapped (Ward), 561

Hewitt, Eliza, 170

Hewitt, George Washington, 170

Hewitt, Herbert Doane (1852-1932), 170

Hewitt, Horatio Dawes, 169

Hewitt, Horatio Nelson, 170

Hewitt, James (1770-1827), 81-90, 98, 151, 672

Hewitt, James Lang (1807-1853), 86, 169-170

Hewitt, John Hill (1801-1890), 81, 161, 164-169

Hexachord and Its Relation to the Twelve-Tone Row, The (Rochberg), 567-568
Hexapoda (Bennett), 461
Heymann, Karl, 334
Hey Nonny, Oh (Cowles), 641
Heyward, DuBose and Dorothy, 428
Hiawatha (Burton), 674
Hiawatha (Kolar), 424
Hiawatha (Phelps), 296
Hiawatha Overture (Goldmark), 379
Hicks, Edward, 443
Hier, Ethel Glenn (1889-   ), 421
Higginson, Major, 286, 349
High Button Shoes (Styne), 745
High Daddy (Emmett), 181
Higher and Higher (Rodgers-Hart), 740
High Fidelity Magazine, 564
High Jinks (Friml), 729
High Noon, theme song for (Tiomkin), 478
High on a Windy Hill (Kramer-Whitney), 752
High School Cadets, The (Sousa), 710
High Society, score for (Porter), 738
Highwayman, The (Andrews), 653
Highwayman, The (De Koven), 718
Highwayman, The (Taylor), 400
Hill, Edward Burlingame (1872-1960), 364, 373-374, 416, 433, 442, 470, 471, 498, 538, 801
Hill, Junius, 321
Hill, Sumner, 145
Hill, Ureli Corelli (1802-1875), 151-153, 159
hillbilly songs (*see* mountain songs)
Hillegas, Michael, 44
Hiller, Ferdinand, 217, 279
Hilliard, Bob, 745
Hillier, Catherine Comerford, 130
Hill of Dreams (Gruenberg), 409
Hill Song No. 1 and No. 2 (Grainger), 407
Hindemith, Paul, 541, 548, 551, 554, 563, 570, 587, 591, 602, 605, 607, 611
Hindu Slumber Song (Ware), 625
Hinton, James, Jr., 632
His Majesty (Stewart), 362
Hispania Suite (Stoessel), 448
history of American music, bibliography, 769-788
History of a New Roof (Hopkinson), 37

History of England, The (Carr), 100
History of Music (Ritter), 291
History of Music in New England (Hood), 11
History of the Handel and Haydn Society (Perkins), 295
Hitchcock, Alfred, 554
Hitchcock, Raymond, 737
Hitchy-Koo 1916 (Porter), 737
Hit the Deck (Youmans), 736
Hoar, Leonard, 21
Hodges, Fletcher, Jr., 186
Hodgkinson, Mrs., 83
Hoffman, Gale, 543
Hoffman, Richard (1831-1909), 208, 209, 270, 290
Hofmann, Josef, 641
Hofstra College, 514
Hoiby, Lee (1926-   ), 599
Hoity-Toity (Stromberg), 715
Holden, Oliver (1765-1844), 60-62, 755
Hold Everything (Henderson), 739
Hold On to Your Hats (Lane), 742
Hold the Fort (Bliss), 667
Holiday (Wessel), 475
Holiday for Strings (Rose), 754
Holiday Overture (Carter), 488
Holiday Overture (Leidzen), 641
Holidays (Ives), 368
Holler, John (1904-   ), 658
Hollingsworth, Stanley (1924-   ), 599-600
Hollow Men, The (Persichetti), 548
Hollywood (*see* Film music)
Hollywood Bowl Association, 387, 424, 762
Hollywood Suite (Cadman), 404
Hollywood Suite (Grofé), 467
Holm, Hanya, 398
Holmes, Anne, 551
Holst, Gustav, 488
Holy Land Impressions (Binder), 663
Holy Night (Chaffin), 648
Holyoke, Samuel (1762-1820), 62-63
Holy Star, The (Daniels), 385
Homage to Boston (Duke), 526
Home Before Dark, songs for (McHugh), 751
Home Burial (Brown), 617
Home on the Range (Guion), 693
Homer, Sidney (1864-1953), 309, 623, 801

Homesick Yankee in North Africa (Spelman), 471
Home, Sweet Home (Buck), 646
Homeward Bound (Webb), 144
Hommage to L'Histoire du soldat (Sydenam), 610
Homo Sum (Freed), 526
Honegger, Arthur, 381, 608, 610
Honey Boy (A. Von Tilzer), 708
Honeymooners, The (Cohan), 719
Honor and Glory (Bergh), 626
Hood, George, 11
Hooker, Brian, 729
Hooray for What! (Arlen), 741
Hootenanny (Siegmeister), 514
Hoover, Herbert, 121
Hope, Bob, 737
Hope, gentle hope (Pelissier), 95
Hopkins, Edward Jerome, 759
Hopkins, Gerald Manley, 514
Hopkinson, Francis, 37-44, 102, 655, 755, 801
Hopkinson, Joseph, 107, 118-119
Hora Mystica (Loeffler), 350
Hora Novissima (Parker), 313, 317
Horgan, Paul, 466
Horizons (Shepherd), 404-405
Horn, Charles Edward (1786-1849), 153, 156-158, 159
Horne, Geoffrey, 598
Horn Technique (Schuller), 615
Horowitz, Vladimir, 532
Horror Movie (Flanagan), 632
Horses (Whiting), 749
Horsman, Edward (1873-1918), 624
Hosmer, Elmer Samuel (1862-1945), 633
Hosmer, Lucius (1870-1935), 388
Hot Time in the Old Town Tonight, A (Metz), 707
Hound of Heaven, The (Gideon), 508
Hound of Heaven, The (Lockwood), 515
Hound of Heaven, The (Stewart), 362
Hour Glass, The (Fine), 571
Hour of Delusion, An (Bennett), 461
House I Live In, The (Robinson), 629
House in Bali, A (McPhee), 528
House of Atreus (El-Dabh), 619
House of Flowers (Arlen), 741
House on the Hill, The (Charles), 631
Houston *Chronicle*, 551
Houston *Post*, 551
Hovhaness, Alan (1911-   ), 549-551, 802

Howard, John Tasker (1890-1964), 634-635
Howard, Joseph E. (1867-1961), 708-709
Howard, Sidney, 471, 747
Howe, Julia Ward, 259
Howe, Mary (1882-   ), 421
How Fair, How Fresh Were the Roses (Spelman), 470
How Happy Was My Humble Lot (Hewitt), 87
How Long, O Lord (Avshalomov), 586
How Music Grew (Bauer-Peyser), 411
How Opera Grew (Bauer), 411
How Roses Came Red (Horn), 158
How to Succeed in Business Without Really Trying (Loesser), 747
How to Write a Good Tune (Patterson), 387
How You Gonna Keep 'Em Down on the Farm? (Donaldson), 750
Hoyt, Charles, 715
H_2O (McPhee), 528
Hubay, Jeno, 529, 530
Hubbard, John, 59
Hubbell, Carl, 461
Huber, Hans, 383
Hudson River Legend (Wagner), 516
Hudson River Suite (Grofé), 467
Hughes, Allen, 598
Hughes, Rupert (1872-1956), 299, 624, 648
Hugo, John Adam (1873-1945), 387
Huhn, Bruno (1871-1950), 623
Hulett, William, 32
Humiston, W. H., 336
Humoresque, score for (Taylor), 402
Humperdinck, Engelbert, 375, 386, 390
Humphrey, Doris, 506
Humphreys, Henry, 538
Humphrey-Weidman Group, 397
Humpty-Dumpty (Operti), 712
Hunt, Arthur Billings, 99, 120
Hunt, G. W., 705
Hunter, Anne Hone, 672
Hunter College, 472, 511, 513, 516
Hunter in his Career, The (Grainger), 407
Hunting of the Snark (Laderman), 598
Hunting Song, A, 63
Huntley, Miss, 91, 93
Hupfield, Charles, 98, 151
Hupfield, Herman (1894-1951), 749, 750

Hurly-Burly (Stromberg), 715
Hushed Be the Camps Today (Dougherty), 632
Huss, Henry Holden (1862-1953), 359, 411
Hutcheson, Ernest (1871-1951), 421
Hutchinson Family, 173-174, 175, 266, 802
Hutton, Lawrence, 132
Huxley, Aldous, 461
Hymnal (Protheroe), 633
Hymn and Fuguing Tunes (Cowell), 450
Hymn and Toccata-Breakdown (Smit), 604
Hymn for Brass Choir (Goldman, R. F.), 642
Hymn of the Immortals (Williams), 655
Hymn of the Nativity (Hoiby), 599
Hymns (Watts), 15, 16
hymns, folk (*see* Gospel songs)
Hymns and Responses for the Church Year (Persichetti), 549
Hymn to the West (Paine), 300
Hymnus to the Queene of Paradys (Josten), 412
Hyne, C. W., 684
Hyperprism (Varèse), 413
Hypocrisie Unmasked (Winslow), 5

I

I Ain't Got Time to Tarry, 257
I Am a Poor Wayfarin' Stranger, 459
I Am The Reaper (Elkus), 421
I Am Thy Harp (Olmstead), 628
I Believe in Miracles (Meyer), 709
I Came with a Song (La Forge), 626
I Can Dream, Can't I? (Fain), 752
I Can Get It for You Wholesale (Rome), 744
I Can't Give You Anything but Love, Baby (McHugh), 751
Ice Age, The (Flanagan), 633
I Could Have Danced All Night (Loewe), 743
Ideas of Order (Berger), 563
I Did Not Know (Vanderpool), 625
Idiots First (Blitzstein), 498
I Do Not Ask, O Lord (Spross), 624
I'd Rather Be Right (Rodgers-Hart), 720, 740, 743

I Dream of Jeanie (Foster), 650
Idyll of Theocritus (Sessions), 453
If (Vanderpool), 625
If Flowers Could Speak (Mana-Zucca), 627
If I Knew You and You Knew Me (MacDermid), 625
If Maidens Would Marry (Horn), 158
I Found a Million Dollar Baby in a Five and Ten Cent Store (Warren), 751
If You Knew Susie (Meyer), 750
I Got Plenty of Nuthin' (Gershwin), 429
I Got the Sun in the Morning and the Moon at Night (Berlin), 734
I Hate Men (Porter), 738
I Hate Music (Bernstein), 540
I Have a Silent Sorrow (Reinagle), 80
I Know a Bank Whereon the Wild Thyme Grows (Horn), 158
I Know a Trail (Smith), 620
I Know That You Know (Youmans), 736
I Laugh, I Sing (Pelissier), 95
I'll Get By (Ahlert), 749
Illinois, University of, 499, 509, 551, 571
I'll Meet, Sweet Maid, with Thee (Webb), 144
I'll See You Home Again, Kathleen (Westendorf), 705
I'll Take the Wings of the Morning, 684
Illustration in Choir Accompaniment (Buck), 645
Illustrators' Show, The (Loesser), 746
I Love the Man with a Generous Heart (Russell), 163
I Love to Tell the Story (Fischer), 667
I Love You Truly (Bond), 623
I'm Afraid to Go Home in the Dark (Van Alstyne), 708
Imagery (Johnson, H.), 628
Imaginary Early Louisiana Songs of Slavery (Guion), 637
Imaginary Landscape (Cage), 572, 574
I'm Always Chasing Rainbows (Carroll), 749
I Married an Angel (Rodgers-Hart), 740
I'm a Yankee Doodle Dandy (Cohan), 720
Imbrie, Andrew (1921-   ), 606-607, 767

I'm Going Ober de Mountains (Emmett), 180, 181

I'm Going to Sit Down and Write Myself a Letter (Ahlert), 749

I'm Goin' to Hitch My Mule (Reddick), 636

I'm Just a Little Girl from Little Rock (Styne), 745

Immigrants, The (Converse, F. S.), 381

Imp, The (Sanders), 520

Imperial Conservatory, Vienna, 630

Impressions (Smith), 380

Impressions from a Greek Tragedy (Elkus), 421

Impressions from an Artist's Life (Schelling), 383

Impromptus (Hoffman), 290

Improving Songs for Anxious Children (Carpenter), 373

Improvisation (MacDowell), 330

Improvisation and Scherzo (Freed), 527

Improvisation on the Tonus Peregrinus (Titcomb), 654

Improvisations for Orchestra (Moevs), 602

I'm Seventeen Come Sunday (Grainger), 407

I Must Down to the Seas Again (Densmore), 626

I'm Wearing Awa' (Foote), 313

I'm Wishing (Churchill), 751

In a Garden (Kupferman), 603

In a Gondola (Barnett), 630

In a Gondola (Hughes), 624

In a Little Spanish Town (Wayne), 751

In an 18th Century Drawing-Room (Scott), 753

In Arcady (Bergh), 626

In a Ricksha (Cowles), 641

In Bohemia (Hadley), 377

Incantation for Tape Recorder (Luening-Ussachevsky), 506

Incantation on an Indian Theme (Gideon), 508

Incarnation (Nevin, George B.) 649

In Celebration: Toccata for the Sixth Day (Bergsma), 591

Inch, Herbert (1904-), 511

Incidental Music for a Satirical Play (Strang), 507

In Colonial Days (Rasbach), 627

Incredible Flutist, The (Piston), 445

In Deep Woods (Strong), 344

Indianapolis Symphony, 381, 389, 551, 605

Indiana University, 520, 527, 543, 587

Indian Carnival or The Indian's Festival of Dreams (Heinrich), 236

Indian Dances (Jacobi), 459

Indian Dances (Skilton), 357, 358

Indian Fanfares (Heinrich), 236

Indian in Song and Story, The (Fletcher), 673

Indian Lament (Risher), 639

Indian Legend (Stringfield), 465

Indian Love Call (Friml), 729

Indian March (Miguel), 248

Indian music, 670-679

Indian Pipes (Bauer, M.), 411

Indian Rhapsody (Miersch), 362

Indian's Book, The (Curtis), 674

Indian Serenade (Josten), 412

Indian's Lament, The (Woodbury), 148

Indian Suite (MacDowell), 327, 331, 334, 679

Indian Summer Idyl (McKinley), 470

Indian themes, 236, 357-359, 374-375, 386, 403, 459, 585, 636, 639, 699, 708, 717

Indices (Brown), 617

Indigent Female Assistance Society, 159, 161

Indy, Vincent, d', 378, 412, 416, 441, 456, 523, 526, 654, 655

I Need Thee Every Hour (Lowry), 705

In Egern on the Tegern Sea (Kern), 732

In Elizabethan Days (Kramer), 631

In Festivate (Moevs), 601

Informal Overture (Haines), 583

In Gay New York (Kerker), 714

In Flanders Fields (McRae), 726

Ingalls, Jeremiah, 666

In Georgia (Wilson), 385

Inheritance Divine, The (Shelley), 647

Inkle and Yarico (Pelissier), 96

In Love with a Memory of You (Schuman-Loesser), 746

In Memoriam (Dresel), 218

In Memoriam (Moore, D.), 441

In Memoriam (Still), 462

In Memoriam Dmitri Mitropoulos (Weber), 569

In Memoriam Theodore Roosevelt (Giannini), 494

In Memory of Franklin D. Roosevelt (Rogers, B.), 447
In Modern Antiquum (Edmundson), 658
In My Merry Oldsmobile (Edwards), 708
In October (MacDowell), 331
In Old Virginia (Powell), 406
In Praise of Pageantry (Wald), 418
In Praise of Winter (Foote), 421
In Principio Erat Verbum (Talma), 513
Inscriptions at the City of Brass (Avshalomov), 586
Inside U.S.A. (Schwartz), 739
Institute of Applied Music, N.Y., 448
Institute of Musical Art, 384, 396, 430, 455, 458, 464, 469, 471, 473, 541, 569, 747, 753
Institution for the Encouragement of Church Music, 105
Instrumental Assistant (Holyoke), 62
In Summer (Clapp), 416
Intégrales (Varèse), 413
Interludes for Strings (Haines), 583
Intermezzo (Johns, C.), 639
Intermezzo (Tuthill), 418
International Business Machines, 495
International Composers' Guild, 413
International Cyclopedia of Music and Musicians, 641
International Exposition, Brussels, 1958, 537
International Fellowship Chorus, 497
International Society for Contemporary Music, 413
International Waltz Competition, Berlin, 626
Inter Nos (MacFadyen), 640
Interplay (Gould), 553
In the Baggage Coach Ahead, 696
In the Beginning (Copland), 483
In the Bottoms (Dett), 407
In the Darkness of Night (Reddick), 636
In the Evening by the Moonlight (Bland), 702
In the Evening by the Moonlight (H. Von Tilzer), 708
In the Great Smokies (Young), 637
In the Greenwood (Daniels), 386
In the Mountains (Foote), 312
In the Mountains (Strong), 344
In the Princess' Garden (Spelman), 470

In the Shade of the Old Apple Tree (Van Alstyne), 708
In the South (Powell), 406
In the Year That King Uzziah Died (Williams), 655
Into a Ship Dreaming (Crist), 630
Into the Night (Edwards), 627
Into the Woods My Master Went (Nevin, George B.), 650
Introduction and Allegretto (Engel, A. L.), 556
Introduction and Allegro (Elwell), 473
Introduction and Fugue (Riegger), 399
Introduction and Passacaglia (Noble), 651
Introduction and Presto (Van Vactor), 524
Introduction and Scherzo (Lopatnikoff), 506
Introduction and Scherzo (Wagner), 516
Introduction, Chaconne, and Allegro (Van Vactor), 524
Introductions and Goodbyes (Foss), 593
Introits and Graduals of the Church Year, The (Matthews), 653
Introspective Poem (McKay), 464
Intruder, The (Starer), 620
Invasion (Rogers, B.), 447
Invention (Luening), 506
Inventions (Gould), 553
Inventions and Kineses (McPhee), 528
Invictus (Huhn), 623
Invocation and Dance (Creston), 492
Invocation to Isis (Fuleihan), 527
Ionisation (Varèse), 413
Iowa Concerto (Goeb), 581
Iowa, State University of, 415, 581
Iowa State Teachers' College, 418-419
Iphigenia (Leplin), 588
Irene (Tierney), 738
Irish Croon-song (Eames), 625
Irish Folk Song (Foote), 313
Irish jigs, 177
and minstrelsy, 179-180
Irish Sketches (Scott), 625
Irish Symphony (Leidzen), 641
Irish Tune from County Derry (Grainger), 406
Iron Chest, The (Taylor, R.), 94
Iroquois Indians, 634
Irving, Washington, 114, 645
Irwin, Wallace, 353

I'se G'wine to Alabammy, Oh (Gilbert), 354
Island Fantasy (Paine), 299, 301
Island God, The (Menotti), 536
Israel (Bloch), 392
It Ain't Necessarily So (Gershwin), 449
Italian Monk, The, 80
Italian Rhapsody (De Leone), 420
Italian Song (Pownall), 108
Italian Street Song (Herbert, V.), 717-718
Ithaca Conservatory of Music, 396, 415
It Happened in Nordland (Herbert, V.), 717
It's a Lovely Day Today (Berlin), 734
It's De-Lovely (Porter), 737
Iturbi, José, 474
It Was a Lover and His Lass (Foote), 313
I've Dreamed of Sonnets (Duke), 631
I've Got the Tune (Blitzstein), 496
Ives, Burl, 697
Ives, Charles E. (1874-1954), 364-368, 424, 448, 560, 632, 802
I've Told Every Little Star (Kern), 732
Ivy Green, The (Russell), 163
I Want to Be Happy (Youmans), 736
I Was So Young (Gershwin), 425
I Was With Him (Elwell), 473
I Will Be a Nun, 172
I Will Give Thanks unto the Lord (Taylor, R.), 93
I Wonder What's Become of Sally (Ager), 749

J

Jabberwocky (Taylor), 400
Jack and the Beanstalk (Gruenberg), 409
Jack o' diamonds, 693
Jack-O-Lantern (Caryll), 716
Jackson, George K. (1745-1823), 133-134, 138
Jackson, George Pullen, 57, 664-665
Jacksonville Symphony (Florida), 604
Jacobi, Frederick (1891-1952), 379, 459-460, 523, 560, 561, 569, 596, 643, 802
Jacobsohn, O. F., 648
Jadassohn, Salomon, 308
Jaell, Alfred, 214, 293

Jager's Adieu, The (Heinrich), 229
Jakobi, Penila, 597
Jamaica (Arlen-Harburg), 741, 754
Jamboree (Spelman), 471
James, Dorothy (1901-   ), 521
James, Harry (1916-   ), 724
James, Henry, 440, 482
James, Philip (1890-   ), 468, 554, 643
Jam Session (McBride), 643
Jane Shakes Her Hair (Bennett), 461
Janssen, Werner (1899-   ), 372, 464-465
Janus (Creston), 493
Japanese Nocturne (Eichheim), 383
Japanese Sandman (Whiting), 749
Java (Eichheim), 382
Jayhawker, The (Hewitt, J. H.), 169
Jazz, 720-726
  bibliography, 818-825
  "hot," 721
  "sweet," 721-722
  swing, 722-724
Jazz Concerto (Copland), 763
Jazz Concerto (Harling), 419
Jazzettes (Gruenberg), 409
Jazz Pizzicato (Anderson), 642
Jazz Poem (Thompson, R.), 442
Jazz Scherzo (Guion), 636
Jazz Suite (Gruenberg), 409
Jazz Symphony (Antheil), 490
Jeanne d'Arc (Converse, F. S.), 381
Jeep (Young), 637
Jefferson, Joseph, 270
Jefferson, Thomas, 42, 444
Jefferson Davis (Byrne), 263
Jekyll and Hyde Variations (Gould), 553
Jemmy of the Glen (Pownall), 108
Jennie (Schwartz), 739
Jenny Lind and the Septinarian (Heinrich), 233
Jenny Wade, the Heroine of Gettysburg, 263
Jephtha (Hewitt, J. H.), 169
Jeremiah (Bernstein), 539
Jerusalem Conservatory, 620
Jerusalem Post, 619
Jervis Bay, The (Willson), 748
Jesse James (Fox), 638, 693
Jesu, Jesu, Miserere (Nevin), 622
Jesus Meek and Gentle (Holler), 658
Jeux de Timbres (Freed), 526

Jewess (Halévy), 283
Jewish Institute of Religion, 663
Jewish religious music, 644-663, 682
Jewish Theological Seminary, 619
Jew's-harps, 21
Jig for a Concert (Green), 519
Jig Theme and Six Changes (Green), 518
Jim Crow song, 176, 179
Jim Fisk (Scanlan), 705
Jim Jives (Bennett), 461
Joachim, Joseph, 277, 349
Joan of Arc (Smit), 604
Job (Converse, F. S.), 382
Jocelin, Simeon, 48
Joe Clark Steps Out (Vardell), 466
Joe Hill (Robinson), 629
Johannes Kreisler (Bendix), 361
John Birch Society, The, 754
John Brown's Body (Benét), 417, 518
John Brown's Body (Delaney), 518
John Brown's Body Lies A-mouldering in the Grave, 259
John Glenn March, The, 754
John Henry (Copland), 484
John Henry, music for (Wolfe), 637
John Murray Anderson's Almanac (Adler-Ross), 748
Johnny Appleseed (Herrmann), 554
Johnny Dear (Barrymore), 389
Johnny Roach (Emmett), 181, 256
John Peel (Andrews), 653
Johns, Clayton (1857-1932), 302, 639
Johns, Louis Edgar (1886-   ), 630
Johnson, George W., 703
Johnson, Horace (1893-   ), 628
Johnson, Hunter (1906-   ), 511, 802
Johnson, James Weldon, 566
Johnson, John Rosamond (1873-1954), 684, 688-689
Johnson, Lockrem (1924-   ), 614, 802
Johnson, "Singing," 684
Johnson, Thomas, F., 610
John Street Theater, 32
Jolson, Al, 425
Jonah and the Whale (MacGimsey), 637
Jonas, Alberto, 527, 547
Jonathan and the Gingery Snare (Ward), 560
Jonny Boker, 180
Joplin, Scott (1868-1919), 720
Jordan, Arthur, Conservatory, 419

Jordan Is a Hard Road to Trabel (Emmett), 181, 182
Jornida and Jornidel (Beach, J. P.), 370
Joseffy, Rafael, 379, 735
Joseph and His Brethren (Josten), 411
Joshua (Waxman), 529
Josten, Werner (1888-1963), 411-412
Journal of Music, Dwight's (*see* Dwight's Journal of Music)
Joy (Watts, W.), 630
Joy, The (Bliss), 667
Joyance (Johnson, H.), 628
Joyce, James, 549
Joyful Mystery (Chanler), 632
Joy of the Morning (Ware), 625
Joy to the World (Weaver), 655
Juba Dance (Dett), 406, 407
Jubilant Overture (La Montaine), 613
Jubilant Song, A (Dello Joio), 544
Jubilate Deo (Huhn), 623
Jubilate Deo (Selby), 68
Jubilation Overture (Ward), 560
Jubilee (Heinrich), 230-231
Jubilee (Porter), 737
Jubilee, The (Pelissier), 96
Jubilee Collection (Bradbury), 667
Judas Maccabäus (Binder), 663
Judgment (Moross), 557
Judith (Chadwick), 310
Judith (James), 468
Judith (Schuman), 535
Juggler of Our Lady, The (Kay), 565
Juhan, Alexander (1765-1845), 76, 104-105, 106, 107
Juhan, James, 69
Juilliard Fellowships, 515
Juilliard Festival, 439
Juilliard Fund, 762
Juilliard Musical Foundation, 351, 409, 415, 758
Juilliard Orchestra, 591
Juilliard Publication Award, 513
Juilliard Quartet, 489
Juilliard School of Music, 351, 409, 414, 415, 445, 447, 448, 451, 453, 455, 456, 459, 460, 461, 468, 486, 491, 494, 507, 522, 523, 533, 540, 542, 548, 554, 556, 561, 563, 569, 575, 578, 581, 582, 589, 590, 591, 596, 600, 604, 609, 613, 620, 642, 742
Juke Box (Wilder), 510
Julius Caesar, music for (Blitzstein), 497

Jullien, Louis Antoine (1812-1860), 219-225, 283, 802
Jumbo (Rodgers-Hart), 740
Jump for Joy (Ellington), 724
Jumping Frog of Calaveras County, The (Foss), 591-592
June Love (Friml), 729
June Rhapsody (Daniels), 386
Jungle (Josten), 411
Juniata College, 402
Junior Choir Anthem Book (Mueller), 656
Junior Choir Anthem Books (Holler), 658
Junior Chorister (Mueller), 656
Junior Service (Ephros), 662
Juno (Blitzstein), 496, 556
Juno and the Paycock (O'Casey), 496
Juon, Paul, 459, 640
Jurame (Grever), 628
Jurgen (Taylor), 400-401
Just Before the Battle, Mother (Root), 266
Just Tell Them That You Saw Me (Dresser), 707
Juvenile Lyre (Mason, L.), 141
Juvenile Psalmodist (Mason, L.), 141
Juxtapositions (El-Dahb), 619

K

Kaddish (Bernstein), 540
Kahal, Irving, 751-752
Kaintuck (Still), 462
Kaiser, Henry, 765
Kaleidoscope (Janssen), 464
Kalmar, Bert, 751
Kalopin (Skilton), 358
Kammerer, Ralph, 510
Kammersymphonie (Weiss), 454
Kankakee River (Bacon), 466
Kansas, University of, 386, 579
Kansas City Conservatory of Music, 363, 558, 569
Kansas City Philharmonic Orchestra, 524, 656
Kansas Federation of Music Clubs, 358
Kansas Philharmonic Orchestra, 434
Kansas State College, 571
Karma (Haubiel), 469
Karnevalszene (Bird), 345
Kathleen Mavourneen (Crouch), 172
Katinka (Friml), 729

Kaufman, George S., 734, 735
Kaun, Hugo, 630, 640
Kay, Hershy (1919-), 556-557
Kay, Ulysses Simpson (1917-), 563-565, 803
Kaye, Sammy (1910-), 724
Kean and Murray Company, 27, 31
Keep the Home Fires Burning, 726
Keller, Homer (1915-), 562
Keller, Matthias (1813-1875), 296-297, 709
Kelley, Edgar Stillman (1857-1944), 345-347, 376, 421, 663
Kelley, Edgar Stillman, Society, 346
Kelly, J. W., 706
Kelpius, Johann, 25
Keltic Sonata (MacDowell), 327
Kemp, Hal, 457
Kemp's Old Folks, Father, 173
Kennan, Kent (1913-), 580
Kent State University, 580
Kentucky Harmony, The, 666
Kentucky Minstrels, 178
Kentucky Mountain Running Set (Green), 518
Kentucky Mountains, songs from, 384
Kentucky Rattlers, 178
Kentucky Spring (Harris), 438
Kerker, Gustave (1857-1923), 714, 716
Kern, Jerome (1885-1945), 460, 730-732, 734, 740, 803
Kerr, Harrison, 803
Kerr, Walter, 541
Kessler, Jascha, 609
Kethe, William, 6
Key, Francis Scott (1779-1843), 122-124
Keyboard Symphony (Griselle), 468
Khaldis (Hovhaness), 551
Kid, The (McKinley), 470
Kiddush Ha-Shem (Berlinski), 587
Kidson, Frank, 115, 672
Kiel, Friedrich, 305, 639
Kilenyi, Edward, 425
Killibegs (Noble), 651
Kimball, George H., 564
Kimball, Jacob (1761-1826), 64
King and I, The (Rodgers-Hammerstein), 740-741
King and the Star, The (Cain), 658
King Bibber's Army (Work), 267
King Dodo (Luders), 719
Kingdom Coming (Root), 267
King Estmere (Sowerby), 657

King Hal (Stewart), 362
King Lear (Persichetti), 548
King Lear, music for (Luening-Ussa-chevsky), 506
King Midas (Rorem), 610
King of Babylon, The (Wessel), 475
King Olaf's Christmas (Buck), 646
King's Henchman, The (Taylor), 401
King's Highway, The (Williams), 655
King's Men, The, score for (Copland), 481
Kinkeldey, Otto, 239, 524
Kipling, Rudyard, 444, 624
Kirby, Marion, 637
Kirchner, Leon (1919-   ), 546-547, 767, 803
Kirkpatrick, John, 366
Kiss and Let's Make Up (Harris), 706
Kiss Me Again (Herbert, V.), 717
Kiss Me, Kate (Porter), 737
Kiss Me Now or Never (Pownall), 108
Kitten on the Keys (Confrey), 752
Kittiwake Island (Wilder), 510
Kittredge, Walter, 263
K-K-K-Katy (O'Hara), 626, 726
Klauser, Karl, 280
Klein, Howard, 576
Kleinsinger, George (1914-   ), 643
Klemm, Johann Gottfried, 18
Klindworth, Karl, 277, 386, 621
Knaebel, *Descriptive Battle Symphony,* 248
Kneisel, Franz, 349, 359, 640
Knew Not the Sun (Heilman), 389
Knickerbocker, The, 179
Knickerbockers, The (De Koven), 718
Knight, Joseph Philip (1812-1887), 157, 159-160
Knight of the Raven Black Plume, The (Hewitt, J. H.), 168-169
K 19, Symphonic Elegy for Thomas Wolfe (Palmer), 579
Knoxville: Summer of 1915 (Barber), 533
Knoxville Symphony Orchestra, 465, 524
Knute Rockne (Grofé), 467
Kober, Arthur, 744
Kodaly, Zoltan, 523, 529, 530
Koechlin, Charles, 523
Kohs, Ellis (1916-   ), 569-570, 803
Kolar, Victor (1888-1957), 423
Konzertstück (Ganz), 384
Kootzen, Nadia, 529

Korean Sketch (Eichhorn), 383
Korean War, songs of, 728-729
Korn, Peter Jona (1922-   ), 620
Kostelanetz, André, 484, 535, 575, 732
Kotzschmar, Hermann, 300
Kountz, Richard (1896-1956), 628
Koussevitzky, Serge, 427, 431, 444, 479, 480, 528, 539, 591, 803
Koussevitzky Foundation, 432, 439, 484, 507, 509, 513, 545, 567, 579, 589, 602, 604, 606, 607, 614, 763
Koutzen, Boris (1901-   ), 528-529
Kramer, Alex C. (1903-   ), 752
Kramer, A. Walter (1890-   ), 631, 803
Krazy Kat (Carpenter), 371, 372
Kreckel, Philip G. (1886-   ), 661
Krehbiel, H. E., 151
Kreisler, Fritz, 636
Krenek, Ernst, 602
Kreutz, Arthur (1906-   ), 508-509
Kreutzer, Rodolphe, 349
Kubelik, Jan, 729
Kubik, Gail (1914-   ), 555
Kulas Foundation, 592
Kullak, Theodor, 292, 305
Kunitz, Luigi von, 403
Kupferman, Meyer (1926-   ), 603
Kurka, Robert (1921-1957), 597-598
Kurthy, Sandor, 530
Kurthy, Zoltan (1902-   ), 530
Kurtz, Edward (1881-   ), 418-419
Kwamina (Adler), 748

L

Labyrinth (Menotti), 537-538
Laderman, Ezra (1926-   ), 598-599, 603
Ladies of St. James, The (Olmstead), 628
Lad Went a-Wooing, A (Golde), 631
Lady Be Good (Gershwin), 735
Lady of Dreams (Daniels), 386
Lady of Lyons, The (Bulwer), 239
Lady of Tearful Regrets (Flanagan), 632
Lady of the Slipper, The (Herbert, V.), 717
Laffing Room Only (Lane), 742
La Flesche, Francis, 673
La Forge, Frank (1879-1953), 626
La Jolla Concerto (Vincent), 525

Lake at Evening, The (Griffes), 390
Lake Isle of Innesfree, The (Foote), 313
Lake Music (Wigglesworth), 585
Lake Placid Club chamber music contest, 410
Lake Street (Danks), 667
La, La, Lucille (Gershwin), 425
Lalla Rookh, 156
L'Allegro (Tweedy), 471
Lamb, The (Citkowitz), 530
Lambert, Alexander, 627
Lament (Dello Joio), 544
Lamentation of Saul, The (Dello Joio), 542
Lamentation over Boston (Billings), 53
Lamentations of Fu Hsuan (McDonald), 463
Lament for Adonis (Giannini), 495
Lament for Beowulf (Hanson), 431
Lament for the Stolen (McDonald), 463
Lament of the Alpine Shepherd Boy, The, 175
Lamento Gitana (Grever), 628
Lamentoso (Barati), 586
Lamia (MacDowell), 331, 335
La Montaine, John (1920-   ), 612-613
Lamont School of Music, 515
Lampert, Calvin, 656
Lancelot and Elaine (MacDowell), 331, 335
Lancelot and Elaine (Severn), 362
Landmarks of Early American Music (Goldman, R. F.), 642
Landowska, Wanda, 608, 628
Landscapes (Leplin), 588
Landura (Zimbalist), 422
Lane, Burton (1912-   ), 742
Lane, Eastwood (1879-1951), 639-640, 803
Lang, Andrew, 446
Lang, Benjamin James (1837-1909), 292-293, 301, 311, 621
Lang, Margaret Ruthven, 292
Lang, Paul Henry, 367, 399, 413, 453, 494, 498, 505, 532, 534, 537, 562, 596, 605, 606, 607
Lanier, Sidney, 310, 645, 650, 803
Laska, Edward, 728
Last Hope, The (Gottschalk), 206, 208
Last Hour, The (Kramer), 631
Last Link Is Broken, The (Clifton), 171
Last of the Hogans, The, 714
Last of the Mohicans, The (Allen), 420

Last Rose of Summer (Buck), 646
Last Savage, The (Menotti), 538
Lathrop, J., 63
Latin-American music, 726
Latin-American Symphonette (Gould), 553
La Touche, John, 440, 557, 629
Launch, The, or Huzza for the Constitution, The, 95
Laurentia (Tuthill), 418
Laurentian Overture (Shulman), 582
Laurents, Arthur, 541, 745
La Violette, Wesley (1894-   ), 475
Law, Andrew (1748-1821), 48, 59-60, 665
Lawlor, Charles B. (1852-1925), 708
Lawrence, D. H., 542
Lawrence, Robert, 447, 534, 732
Lawrence College, 658
Lazybones (Carmichael), 753
Leaden Echo, The (Talma), 514
League of Composers, 409, 410, 444, 445, 458, 479, 485, 490, 496, 528, 542, 546, 579, 602, 631, 760
Leah Kleschna (Freeman), 361
Leanin' on de Lawd (Reddick), 636
Lear (Blitzstein), 497
Leave it to Jane (Kern), 731
Leave It to Me (Porter), 737
Leaves from the Tale of Pinocchio (Rogers, B.), 447
Leave the Atom Alone (Arlen-Harburg), 754
LeBaron, William, 399
Ledbetter, Huddie ("Leadbelly"), 697
Lee, Alfred, 705
Lee, Gypsy Rose, 745
Lee Rigg, The (Goldman, R. F.), 642
Lees, Benjamin (1924-   ), 600-601
Leetle Bateese (O'Hara), 626
LeFlem, Paul, 527
Left but the Power (Allen), 420
Le Gallienne, Richard, 630
Legend (Imbrie), 606
Legend (Kohs), 570
Legend (Luening), 502
Legend (Skilton), 358
Legend, The (Breil), 387
Legende (Bartlett), 648
Legende (Bedell), 658
Legende Symphonique (Schelling), 383
Legend of Don Munio, The (Buck), 645

Legend of Hani, The (Hadley), 377

Legend of John Henry, The (String-field), 465

Legend of St. Christopher, The (Parker), 318

Legend of the Piper, The (Freer), 361

Leggenda Sinfonica (Steinert), 523

Lehmann, Edward, 215

Leichtentritt, Hugo, 524

Leidzen, Erik (1894-1962), 641

Leif Ericson (Bornschein), 388

Leipzig Gewandhaus Orchestra, 422

Le Jeune, L. Kendrick, 654

Lennart, Isobel, 746

Lenschow, Carl, 212, 214

Lenssen, Carlino, 271

Lento for Orchestra (Barlow), 578

Leone, Francesco Bartholomew de (*see* de Leone)

Leonora (Fry), 239-242, 250

Leopold, Ralph, 642

Leper, The (Moore), 387

Leplin, Emanuel (1917-   ), 587-588

Lerner, Alan Jay (1918-   ), 742-743

Le Roy fait battre tambour (Helm), 584

Leschetizky, Theodor, 383, 386, 405, 410, 627

Leslie, Edgar, 709

Lessard, John (1920-   ), 603-604

Lesson (Palma), 39

Lessons for the Uranian Society (Adgate), 107

Lester, William (1889-   ), 634

L'etang (Loeffler), 351

Let a Smile Be Your Umbrella (Fain), 752

Let 'Em Eat Cake (Gershwin), 428, 735

Let Freedom Sing (Rome), 744

Let It Ride (Livingston), 752

Let No Man Write My Epitaph, songs for (McHugh), 751

Let's Face It (Porter), 737

Let's Put Out the Lights and Go To Sleep (Gorney), 749

Let's Put Out the Lights and Go to Sleep (Hupfield), 750

Let's Touch the Sky (Talma), 514

Letter from Home (Copland), 484

Letter of the Southland, A (Dillon), 640

Letters from Morocco (Glanville-Hicks), 566

Letter That Never Came, The (Dresser), 707

Letter to Emily, A (Johnson), 614

Letter to the World (Johnson), 511

Let the Rest of the World Go By (Ball), 707

Levant, Oscar (1906-   ), 457, 520, 804

Levy, Ernest, 591

Levy, Heniot (1879-   ), 500

Levy, Martin David, 595

Lewis, John, 616

Lewis, Ted, 721

Lewisohn Stadium Concerts, New York, 363, 396, 429, 437, 564

Lexicon of Musical Invective (Slonimsky), 641

Leybourne, George, 704-705

Lhévinne, Josef, 421, 469, 518

Library of Classics, Schirmer, 155

Library of Congress (*see also* Coolidge Foundation), 88, 113, 227, 351, 373, 485, 537, 569, 589, 624, 629

Libretto, The (Gillis), 585

Lieurance, Thurlow (1878-1963), 635-636

Life (Curran), 625

Life and Music of Béla Bartók (Stevens), 519

Life Begins at 8:40 (Arlen), 741

Life Everlasting, The (Matthews), 653

Life of Man, The (Becker), 415

Life of Man, The (Parker), 296

Life of the Party (Loewe), 742, 743

Life on the Ocean Wave, A (Russell), 163

Lift Thou the Burden, Father (Hageman), 629

Light (Britain), 521

Light Eternal (Coombs), 650

Light from St. Agnes, A (Harling), 419

Light of Asia, The (Buck), 646

Light Out of Darkness (Lockwood), 515

Like the Young Sheep (Weaver), 655

Lilacs (Hill), 374

Lili (Kountz), 628

Liliom (Molnar), 402, 740

Lillith (Weisgall), 566

Lilly, Josiah K., 186, 419

Limón, José, 506

Lincoln, Abraham, 300, 352, 360, 368,

461, 473, 484, 514, 545, 558, 564, 580, 588,
Lincoln Center Festival Overture (Piston), 446
Lincoln Center for the Performing Arts, 446, 486, 533, 534, 608, 619, 741
Lincoln Legend, A (Gould), 553
Lincoln Portrait, A (Copland), 484
Lincoln, Requiem Aeternam (Elwell), 473
Lincoln Symphony (Pratt), 305
Lincoln Symphony, A (Mason, D. G.), 378
Lincoln, the Great Commoner (Ives), 368
Lind, Jenny (1820-1887), 199, 202-204, 214, 233, 804
Lindbergh, Charles E., 463, 521
Lindsay, Howard, 734, 735
Lindsay, Jennie, 706
Lindsay, Vachel, 468, 544, 558
Lindy Lou (Strickland), 627
Lines and Contrasts (Schuller), 616
Lingard, William Horace (1839-1927), 704
List, Eugene, 557, 638
Listemann, Bernhard, 349
Listen to the Mocking Bird (Winner), 264
Liszt, Franz von, 276, 277, 278, 290, 293, 335, 345, 348
Liszt Conservatory of Music, 523
Little Almond Eyes (MacFarlane), 652
Little Bay Mare, The (Howard), 635
Little Bit of Heaven, A (Ball), 707
Little Boy Blue (Nevin), 621
Little Cart, The (Avshalomov), 586
Little Cart, The, music for (Trimble), 611
Little Christopher Columbus (Caryll), 716
Little Concerto (Nordhoff), 508
Little Foxes, The (Hellman), 496
Little Foxes, The, music for (Willson), 748
Little Girl at Play, A (Patterson), 387
Little Hugh, 665
Little Jesus, The (Holler), 658
Little Jesus Come to Town, The (James), 521
Little Johnny Jones (Cohan), 719
Little Lost Child, The, 707
Little Mary Kelly (Cohan), 719

Little Millionaire, The (Cohan), 719
Little Nemo (Herbert, V.), 717
Little Orchestra Society of New York, 450, 544, 555, 598
Little Page's Song, The (Watts, W.), 630
Little Piano Book (Persichetti), 549
Little Robinson Crusoe (Luders), 719
Little Show, The (Schwartz), 739
Little Shows, 742, 750
Little Suite (Keller), 562
Little Suite (Kirchner), 546
Little Suite (Kubik), 555
Little Symphony (Effinger), 582
Little Symphony (Eppert), 418
Little Symphony (Kupferman), 603
Little Symphony in G (Sanders), 520
Little Tycoon, The (Spencer), 714
Little White Lies (Donaldson), 750
Liverpool (Tuckey), 35, 47
Livingston, Jay (1915-   ), 752
Lochinvar's Ride (Scott), 647
Lock and Key (Pelissier), 96
Lockwood, Normand (1906-   ), 515, 804
Loder, George, 248
Loeb, Morris, Prize, 630
Loeffler, Charles Martin (1861-1935), 348-351, 523, 626, 804
Loeschorn, Albert, 649
Loesser, Frank (1910-   ), 746-747
Loewe, Frederick (1904-   ), 742-743
Logan, Joshua, 744
Log Hut, The (Hewitt, J. H.), 169
Lolita (Buzza-Peccia), 622
Lollipop (Youmans), 736
Lomax, Alan, 500
Lomax, John A., 500, 693, 694
Lomax Collections, 638
Lombard brothers, 266
Londonderry Air, 406
London Symphony, 486
Lonely Americans (Brown), 323, 336
Lonesome Hollow (Siegmeister), 514
Lonesome Train, The (Robinson), 629
Lonesome Tunes (Brockway-Wyman), 384, 692
Lonesome Whistler, The (Guion), 636
Longfellow, Henry Wadsworth, 645
Long, Long Ago (Baylor), 160
Long, Long Trail (Elliott), 726
Longstreet, Sidney, 745
Look, The (Rasbach), 627

Look for the Silver Lining (Kern), 731
Looking Glass Insects (Taylor), 400
Loomis, Clarence (1889-   ), 419-420
Loomis, Harvey Worthington (1865-1930), 635, 700
Loos, Anita, 745
Lopatnikoff, Nikolai (1903-   ), 506-507, 610
Lord I Have Loved the Habitation (Matthews), 653
Lord Lovel, 665
Lord of All Being, Throned Afar (Holmes, O. W.), 147
Lord of the Ascendant (Kohs), 570
Lord of the Dunderberg (Brewer), 647
Lord Randal, 692
Lord's Controversy with His People, The (Gershefski), 501
Lord's Prayer, The (Malotte), 628
Loring, Eugene, 482
Lorna Doone Suite (Nevin, A.), 386
Los Angeles Conservatory of Music, 475
Los Angeles Philharmonic Orchestra, 466, 506
Lost Child, The (Shepherd), 405
Lost Eden (Floyd), 596
Lost Letter, The (Work), 267
Lotus Eaters, The (Cone), 583
Lotus-Eaters, The (Read), 558
Lotus Flower (Cowles), 641
Loughner, Jack, 435
Louise (Whiting), 740
Louisiana (Van der Stucken), 348
Louisiana Negroes, 355, 637
Louisiana Purchase (Berlin), 734
Louisiana Story (Thomson), 434
Louisiana Suite (Janssen), 464
Louis the 14th (Romberg), 730
Louisville (Ky.) *Courier-Journal*, 504
Louisville, University of, 611
Louisville Concerto (Luening), 502
Louisville Orchestra, 398, 399, 445, 485, 489, 491, 492, 508, 517, 519, 524, 525, 542, 543, 544, 548, 559, 560, 563, 564, 565, 577, 581, 584, 590, 591, 601, 602, 603, 607, 609, 611, 614, 763
Love, Charles, 32, 39
Love, Edmund, 746
Love Affairs of Great Musicians (Hughes), 624
Love and Springtime (Metcalf), 622
Love in a Village (Arne), 69, 97

Love in the Dictionary (Dougherty), 632
Love Is a Many-Splendored Thing (Fain), 752
Love Letters, music for (Young), 753
Loveliest of Trees (Dougherty), 632
Loveliest of Trees (Duke), 631
Lovely Alda, The (MacDowell), 331, 335
Lovely Lass, The (Selby), 68
Love Me Tonight, score for (Rodgers), 740
Love Nest, The (Hirsch), 736
Love o'Mike (Kern), 731
Lover, Come Back to Me (Romberg), 730
Lover's Melancholy, The, 114
Love Seemeth Terrible (Foerster), 622
Love's Last Words (Shaw), 136
Love's Sacrifice (Chadwick), 310
Love Verses from the Song of Solomon (Grainger), 407
Loving Saviour, The (Holler), 658
Low, Seth, 337, 338
Lowell, Amy, 374
Lowens, Irving, 591, 605, 607, 613
Lowland Sea, The (Wilder), 510
Lowry, Robert (1826-1899), 705
Low Speed (Luening), 506
Lucas, Alexander, 142
Lucedia (Giannini), 494
Lucifer (Hadley), 377
Lucille (Pratt), 305
Lucky Day (Henderson), 739
Lucrece Suite (Taylor), 402
Luders, Gustav (1865-1913), 718-719
Luening, Otto (1900-   ), 466, 501-506, 581, 583, 585, 587, 598, 612, 616, 617, 632, 766, 804
Luke Havergal (Duke), 631
Lullaby of Broadway (Warren), 751
Lully, Jean Baptiste, 127
Lumbard, Frank, 270
lumberjack songs, 694-695
Lumberman's Life, 695
Lutkin, Peter Christian (1858-1931), 649
Lux Aeterna (Hanson), 430, 431
Lydian Ode (Creston), 492
Lyon, James (1735-1794), 35, 37, 44-49, 574, 804-805
Lyon, Richard, 8
Lyra Sacra (Mason, L.), 141
Lyrical Piece (Barlow), 578

Lyric Cycle (Brant), 576
Lyric Pieces (Gideon), 508
Lyrics from the German (Johns), 630
Lyrics of the Red Man (Loomis), 635
Lysistrata (Brunswick), 517

M

Maas, Louis, 356
MacAfee's Confession, 693
Macbeth (Bloch), 391, 394
Macbeth (Engel), 556
Macbeth, music for (Kohs), 570
McBride, Robert Guyn (1911-   ), 642-643, 805
McCarthy, Henry, 263
McCarty, Joseph, 738
McCollin, Frances (1892-1960), 635
McCormack, John, 403
McCoy, Bessie, 399
McCoy, William J. (1848-1926), 361-362
MacDermid, James (1875-1960), 625
MacDermid, Sybil Sammis, 625
McDonald, Harl (1899-1955), 462-463, 752
MacDougall, Hamilton Crawford (1858-1945), 649
MacDowell, Edward (1861-1908), 323-344, 417, 652, 761, 805-806
McDowell, Jane Denny, 191
MacDowell, Mrs. Edward, 344
MacDowell Chorus (*see also* Schola Cantorum), 634
MacDowell Colony, Peterborough, N.H., 344, 762
Macero, Teo, 765
MacFadyen, Alexander (1879-1936), 640
MacFarlane, William Charles (1870-1945), 651-652
McGill, Josephine (1877-1919), 637, 692
McGill University, 575
MacGimsey, Robert, 637
McGrath, Joseph J. (1889-   ), 661
MacGuire, William Anthony, 735
Machine Ballet (Riegger), 398
McHose, Irving (1902-   ), 511
McHugh, Jimmy (1895-   ), 751
McKay, George (1899-   ), 463-464
MacKaye, Percy, 381, 515, 718
McKillop, Dr. Kenneth, 617
McKinley, Carl (1895-   ), 470
McKoy, William, 79, 120

MacLagan, T., 704
McPhee, Colin (1901-   ), 527-528
McRae, John, 726
Madcap Duchess, The (Herbert, V.), 717
Madden, Edward, 708
Maddy, Joseph, 418
Madeleine (Herbert, V.), 717
Madelon, 726
Mlle. Modiste (Herbert), 717
Madonna of the Evening Flowers (Dougherty), 632
Madras Symphony (Cowell), 450
Madrigal Singers, 556
Maeterlinck, Maurice, 599
Maganini, Quinto (1897-   ), 473-474
Maganini Chamber Symphony Orchestra, 474
Maggy Murphy's Home (Braham), 714
Magic Barrel, The (Blitzstein), 498
Magnifica, La (Spelman), 471
Magnificat (Hall), 650
Magnificat (Lutkin), 649
Magnificat (Persichetti), 549
Magnificat (Stevens), 520
Magnificat (Wetzler), 389
Mahler, Gustav, 604
Maid Freed from the Gallows, The, 692
Maid of the Mill (Pelissier), 96
Main, Hubert Platt (1839-1925), 667
Major, The (Harrigan-Hart), 713
Major Gilfeather (Braham), 713
Make a Joyful Noise unto the Lord (Avshalomov), 586
Make Love with a Guitar (Crever), 628
Makin' Whoopee (Donaldson), 750
Malibran, Maria, 204
Malipiero, Gian Francesco, 583
Ma Little Sunflower (Vanderpool), 625
Mallet, Francis, 131, 151
Malotte, Albert Hay (1895-   ), 628
Mamba's Daughter (Rorem), 609
mambo, 726
Manabozo (Lester), 634
Mana-Zucca, 627
Mandel, Frank, 735
Mandyczewski, Eusebius, 376
Manger Babe, The (Lester), 634
Manhattan Mary, score for (Henderson), 739
Manhattan School of Music, 494, 615, 618

Manhattan Serenade (Alter), 753
Manhattan Symphony Orchestra, 376, 663
Maniac, The (Russell), 161
Man I Love, The (Gershwin), 425
Manitou Mysteries (Heinrich), 236
Mann, Elias, 48
Männergesangverein Arion, 352
Mannes, David, 375, 469
Mannes, Leopold Damrosch (1899-   ), 469, 567
Mannes School, 384, 392, 468, 469, 607, 610, 655
Manney, Charles Fonteyn (1872-1951), 623
Manning, Kathleen Lockhart (1890-1951), 627
Man on the Flying Trapeze, The (Leybourne-Lee), 704
Manuscript Club, 621
Manuscript Society of Chicago, 759
Manuscript Society of New York, 759
Manuscript Society of Philadelphia, 759
Man Who Owns Broadway, The (Cohan), 719
Man Without a Country, The (Damrosch, W.), 352
Man Without a Country, The (Hosmer), 633
Manzetti, Monsignor Leo P., 661
Maple Leaf Rag (Joplin), 720
Marcelle (Luders), 719
March (Bennett), 461
Marching Song of Democracy (Grainger), 407
Marching Through Georgia (Work), 266, 267
Marching Tune (Grainger), 407
March of the Hungry Mountains (Donato), 512
March of the Musketeers, The (Friml), 729
March of the Toys (Herbert), 718
March On, Ye Soldiers True (Bedell), 658
Marco Millions (Whithorne), 410
Marco Takes a Walk (Taylor), 402
Mardi Gras (Beach, J. P.), 370
Maretzek, Max (1821-1897), 272, 298
Margolies, Molly, 628
Maria Golovin (Menotti), 537
Maria Malibran (Bennett), 461
Maria Mia (Foster), 627

Marie from Sunny Italy (Berlin), 733
Marine Band, U. S., 710
Markham, Edwin, 368, 625
Marmion (Buck), 645
Maroncelli, Signora, 159
Marquis, Don, 643
Marquis in Petticoats, The (Hewitt, J. H.), 169
Marriage Hymn, A (Lyon), 48
Marriage of Aude, The (Rogers, B.), 447
Marriage with Space, A (Becker), 415
Mars Ascending (Haubiel), 469
Marschner, Heinrich, 235
Marseillaise Hymn, 115
Martin, Mary, 737
Martin's Lie (Menotti), 538
Martinu, Bohuslav, 550, 578
Martyr, The (Freeman), 361
Mary (Cohan), 720, 735, 736
Mary at Bethlehem (Branscombe), 634
Mary Had a Little Lamb (Ballantine), 416
Mary Jane McKane (Youmans), 736
Maryland, University of, 611
Maryland, My Maryland (Ryder), 260
Mary's Lullaby (James), 521
Mary's Tears (Shaw), 135
Mary Who Stood in Shadow (Lockwood), 515
Mary Will Smile (Carr), 100
Marzo, Eduardo (1852-1929), 648
Mason, Daniel Gregory (1873-1953), 138, 302, 377-378, 521, 806
Mason, Henry, 138
Mason, Lowell (1792-1872), 133-134, 136-141, 143, 145, 151, 211, 265, 378, 755, 756, 806-807
Mason, Lowell, Jr., 138
Mason, Stuart, 470
Mason, William (1829-1908), 138, 208, 209, 232, 249, 274-280, 625, 807
Masonic Overture (Reinagle-Taylor), 80
Mason-Thomas chamber concerts, 283
Mason-Thomas Quartet, 279-280
Mason-Thomas recitals, 273
Masque of the Red Death, The (Reed), 578-579
Masque of the Red Death (Van Vactor), 524
Masquerade (Delamarter), 417
Masquerade (McKinley), 470

Massachusetts Charitable Fire Society, 126
Massachusetts Collection of Psalmody, 144
Massachusetts collection of sacred harmony (Mann), 48
Massachusetts Compiler, The, 62
Massachusetts Gazette, 67
Massachusetts Journal, 166
Massachusetts Musical Magazine, The, 61, 63
Massachusetts Spy, 61
Massart, Joseph Lambert, 349
Masselos, William, 486, 569
Masse Mensch (Finney), 498
Massenet, Jules, 622
Masses (Kreckel), 661
Masses (McGrath), 661
Masses (Pusa-Teri), 662
Masses (Rossini), 661-662
Masses (Syre), 661
Masses (Yon), 660
Masterhoff, Joe, 749
Masterpiece, The (Nordhoff), 508
Mastodon, The (Heinrich), 236
Materna (Demarest), 624
Mathematical Basis of the Arts, The (Schillinger), 457
Mather, Cotton, 7-8, 16
Mather, Increase, 23-24
Mather, Richard, 7, 8
Mathews, William Smith Babcock (1837-1912), 280, 291-292
Mathias, Georges Amandée St. Claire, 383
Matthews, Alexander (1879-   ), 653
Matthews, John Sebastian (1870-1934), 653-654
Matzka, George, 279, 298
Maybe (Gershwin), 425
May Day Carol (Taylor), 403
May in Tuscany (Nevin), 622
May Morning (Van Hagen, Jr.), 75
May Night (Hageman), 629
May Night Fantasy, The (Paine), 301
Maypole Lovers, The (Cole), 360
Maytime (Romberg), 730
May We Entertain You? (Styne), 746
May Wine (Romberg), 730
Mazurka (Volpe), 363
Me and Juliet (Rodgers-Hammerstein), 741
Mean to Me (Ahlert), 749

Mear (Barnard), 37, 47
Mechanical Principles (McPhee), 528
Mechanisms (Antheil), 490
Medea (Damrosch, W.), 353
Medea (Engel, A. L.), 556
Medead, The (Giannini), 494
Medea's Meditation and Dance of Vengeance (Barber), 532
Medieval Court Dances (Filippi), 530
Medieval Poem (Sowerby), 657
Meditation (Huhn), 623
Méditation sérieuse (Bartlett), 648
Meditations of Orpheus (Hovhaness), 551
Meditations on Ecclesiastes (Dello Joio), 542
Mediterranean (Fuleihan), 527
Mediterranean Sketches (Inch), 511
Medium, The (Menotti), 502, 536
Meeta (Horn), 157
Meet Me in St. Louis (Mills), 720
Meignen, Leopold, 238
Meisel, Carl, 215
Mela and Fair (Cowell), 451
Mellers, Wilfred, 579
Melodia (Bowles), 582
Melodia sacra (Shaw), 135
Melodic Poems of the Mountains (Dillon), 640
Melody (Johns, C.), 639
Melody on the Death of the Late Lieutenant-General of the Armies of the United States (Reinagle-Taylor), 80
Melmoth, Mrs., 84
Melpomene (Chadwick), 309
Melt the Bells, 262
Melville, Herman, 590
Memorial for Orchestra (Heiden), 587
Memorial Music (Palmer), 579
Memorials (Moross), 557
Memories of France (Bingham), 417
Memories of My Childhood (Loeffler), 351
Memory (Mana-Zucca), 627
Memphis Blues (Handy), 688
Memphis College of Music, 418
Memphis Five, 721
Men and Mountains (Ruggles), 369
Men and Ships, score for (Kubik), 555
Mencken, H. L., 443
Mendelssohn Prize, 587

Mendelssohn-Bartholdy, Felix, 214, 217, 223

Mendelssohn Club, Philadelphia, 303

Mendelssohn Glee Club, New York, 303

Mendelssohn Quintette Club, 215, 216, 273

Menel, 97

Mengelberg, Willem, 455, 456

Menie (MacDowell), 330, 332

Mennin, Peter (1923-   ), 589-590, 767

Mennini, Louis (1920-   ), 588-589

Menotti, Gian-Carlo (1911-   ), 531, 532, 536-538, 567, 593, 599

Mercer, Johnny, 741

Mercury Records, 763

Mercury Theatre, 495, 496

Merman, Ethel, 735, 737, 745

Merrill, Bob, 746

Merry Malones, The (Cohan), 719

Merrymount (Cole), 360

Merry Mount (Hanson), 431-432

Merrymount (Smith), 380

Merry Piping Lad, The (Taylor, R.), 93

Merry Wedding, The (Grainger), 407

Message, The (Huhn), 623

Message of the Cross, The (MacFarlane), 652

Messe Solenelle (Ferrata), 638

Messiaen, Olivier, 566, 605

Messiah, The (Handel), 34, 151

Metcalf, Frank J., 149

Metcalf, John W. (1856-1926), 622

Metronome, The, 765

Metropolis (Grofé), 467

Metropolitan Nocturne (Alter), 753

Metropolitan Opera Company, 318, 352, 353, 360, 372, 376, 377, 380, 387, 401, 403, 431, 447, 459, 476, 497, 512, 532, 536, 538, 615, 629, 634, 711

Metz, Theodore (1848-1936), 708

Mexican Hayride (Porter), 737

Mexican Rhapsody (McBride), 643

Meyer, George W. (1884-1959), 709

Meyer, Joseph (1894-   ), 750

Meyerowitz, Jan (1913-   ), 585

Miami, University of, Symphony Orchestra, 363

Michael, David Moritz, 29

Michener, James, 740

Michigan, University of, 399, 498, 511, 515, 579, 680

Michigan, University of, Music Festival, 431

Michigan Dream (Reed), 579

Michigan State College, 375

Michigan State Normal College, 521

Middelschulte, Wilhelm, 385, 417, 630

Middlebury College, 415

Midnight Ride of Paul Revere, The (Phillips), 509

Midnight Service for New Year's Eve (Buck), 646

Midnight Special (Bacon), 466

Midrash Esther (Meyerowitz), 585

Miersch, Paul Friedrich Theodore (1868-1956), 362

Mighty Casey, The (Schuman), 535

Mighty Lak' a Rose (Nevin), 621

Miguel, F. E., 248

Milda (Allen), 420

Milhaud, Darius, 563, 587, 599, 610, 613, 616

Millay, Edna St. Vincent, 401

Millennium No. 2 (Brant), 576

Miller, Arthur, 561

Miller, Gilbert, 402

Miller, Glenn, 807

Miller's Daughter, The (Chadwick), 309

Milligan, Harold Vincent (1888-1951), 186, 655

Millionaire Caprice, A (De Leone), 420

Mills, Charles (1914-   ), 565

Mills, Kerry (1869-1948), 720

Mills, Sebastian Bach (1838-1898), 290-291, 648

Mills College, 421, 546, 563, 576, 599

Milwaukee Civic and Symphony Orchestras, 417

Milwaukee *Musikverein*, 270, 272

Minerva, 167

Mingus, Charlie, 618

Miniature Concerto (Wagner), 516

Miniature Fantasy on American Popular Melodies (Janssen), 464

Miniatures (Haubiel), 469

Miniature Suite (Nevin, A.), 386

Minneapolis Orchestra, 358, 544

Minnehaha's Vision (Busch), 359

Minnesota, University of, 511, 523

Minnesota Federal Music Project, 414

Minotaur, The (Carter), 488

Minotaur, The (Naginski), 522

Minstrel, The (Neuendorf), 298

minstrel band, first, 177-178
Minstrel Show (Gould), 553
minstrel songs, 176-184
Minstrel's Return from the War, The (Hewitt, J. H.), 166
Miracle of Flanders, The (Gruenberg), 410
Miracle of Time (Harling), 419
Miracle on 34th Street (Willson), 748
Miraculous Mill (Demarque), 109
Mirage (Shapleigh), 383
Miranda (Hageman), 629
Miranda and the Dark Young Man (Siegmeister), 514
Mirror for the Sky (Kubik), 555
Mirror of My Soul (Mana-Zucca), 627
Mirrorrorrim (Strang), 507
Mirtil in Arcadia (Hadley), 377
Miscellaneous Essays (Hopkinson), 43
Miscellaneous Quartette (Reinagle), 80
Missa in G Major (Ferrata), 638
Missa pro Defunctis (Creston), 493
Missa Rachel Plorans (Meyerowitz), 585
Missas (Douglas), 651
Missa Solemnis (Creston), 493
Missionary Angel (Shaw), 135
Missionary Chant (Zeuner), 146
Missionary Hymn (Mason), 137
Mission Road, The (Bornschein), 388
Mississippi Suite (Grofé), 467
Miss Julie (Rorem), 609
Miss Liberty (Berlin), 734
Miss 1917 (Kern), 731
Miss O'Grady (Brant), 576
Missouri Minstrels, 178
Missouri, Missouri, bright land of the West, 260
Missouri Shindig (Reed), 579
Missouri University, 578
Mr. and Mrs. Composer, 471
Mr. President (Berlin), 735
Mr. Wonderful (Bock), 748
Mistress into Maid (Duke), 526
Mitchell, William, 617
Mitropoulos, Dimitri, 497, 517, 544, 547, 569, 579, 616
MJQ Music, Inc., 616
Mlle. Modiste (Herbert), 717
Moby Dick (Lockwood), 515
Moby Dick (Moore, D.), 441
Moby Dick Suite (Claflin), 476
Moccasin Game (Skilton), 358

Mock Morris (Grainger), 406
Mocquereau, Dom, 660
Modern Music, 519, 767
Modern Music (Billings), 54
Moevs, Robert (1920-   ), 601-602
Mojave (McDonald), 463
Moller, Christopher, 104
Moller, J. C., 77
Moller and Capron, 97
Moller and Capron's Monthly Numbers, 104
Molly Darling (Hays), 703
Molly on the Shore, 406
Molnar, Ferenc, 740
Mona (Parker), 313, 314, 318-319
Mon ami Pierrot (Barlow, S. L. M.), 472
Monckton, Lionel, 716
Money Musk (Sowerby), 657
Monody on Death of Washington (Taylor-Reinagle), 94
Monroe, Harriet, 310
Montana Sonata (Fitch), 511
Montani, Nicola Aloysius (1880-1948), 660
Monteux, Pierre, 515, 569, 588
Montezuma (Gleason), 304
Montezuma (Sessions), 454
Montezuma (Stewart), 362
Montressor opera troupe, 239
Mood Indigo (Ellington), 724
Moods of a Moonshiner (Stringfield), 465
Moody, Dwight L., 667
Moonlight Bay (Weinrich), 709
Moon-Marketing (Weaver), 655
Moon Trail (Whithorne), 410
Moore, Douglas (1893-   ), 393, 439-442, 492, 598, 617, 807
Moore, Mary Carr (1873-1957), 387
Mootz, William, 504
Mopper, Irving (1914-   ), 566-567
Moravian Archives, 28
Moravians:
    music of, 24, 28-30
    singing family, 173
Morehouse, Ward, 719
More Songs of the Hill-Folk (Niles), 637
Morgan, Helen, 731
Morgan, W. S., 65
Morgan's Living Pictures, 65
Morneweck, Evelyn Foster, 187

Morning (Speaks), 624

Morning Light Is Breaking, The (Smith and Webb), 143

Morning, Noon and Night (Alter), 753

Morocco (Schelling), 383

Moross, Jerome (1913-   ), 557

Morris, George P., 157

Morris, Harold (1890-1964), 459

Morris, William, 578

Morris Dance (Noble), 651

Morrison, May T., Festival, 395

Morse, Theodore F. (1873-1924), 707

Morte de Tintagiles, La (Loeffler), 349

Morton, Ferdinand "Jelly Roll," 807

Mosaics (Hanson), 430

Moscheles, Ignace, 175, 275, 276, 290, 291, 295, 304, 645

Moscow Conservatory, 422, 477

Moscow Imperial Opera Orchestra, 477

Moscow Symphony Orchestra, 528

Mosenthal, Joseph, 279

Mosquito Serenade (Kreutz), 509

Moss (Flanagan), 632

Most Happy Fella (Loesser), 747

Moszkowski, Moritz, 383, 627, 652

Motet for the Day of Ascension (Harrison), 578

Motette Collection (Buck), 645

Mother, The (Hollingsworth), 600

Mother Goose, 117

Mother Goose rhyme tunes (Guion), 636

Mother Goose Songs (Gaynor), 623

Mother Machree (Ball, Olcott), 707

Mother of Men (Bingham), 416

Mother of Us All, The (Thomson), 434, 502

Mountain Blood (Patterson), 387

Mountain Bugle, The (Hewitt, J. H.), 169

Mountain Dew and Mountain Dawn (Stringfield), 465

Mountaineers, The (Pelissier), 80, 96

Mountains (Rasbach), 627

mountain singers, 173-175

Mountain Song (Farwell), 375

mountain songs, 691-693, 725

Mount Holyoke College, 498

Mount Oread (Skilton), 358

Mourant, Walter (1910-   ), 562

Movement (Cowell), 449

Movement (Fiorello), 522

Mozart, J. M., 271

Mozart, W. A., 557, 573

Mozart Society, Chicago, 270

Mrs. Pownall's Adres, 108

Muck, Karl, 384, 392

Muddy Water (De Rose), 753

Mueller, Carl (1892-   ), 656

Muhlen, Heinrich, 25

Muller, Joseph, 88, 124

Mulligan Guard, The (Braham), 712-713

Mulligan Guard Ball, The (Harrigan-Hart), 713

Multiplication Table, 172

Munch, Charles, 540

Muncie Symphony Orchestra, 583

Munich Conservatory, 470, 661

Munich Opera House, 411

Munro, Kathleen, 159

Murder in the Cathedral (Engel), 556

Murmuring Fountain, The (Mills), 291

Murphy, Stanley, 709

Museum of Modern Art, 490, 503

Musical America, 369, 375, 393, 401, 431, 432, 440, 443, 445, 454, 457, 461, 493, 495, 496, 510, 519, 526, 537, 545, 556, 572, 575, 584, 589, 591, 593, 594, 595, 598, 599, 600, 603, 606, 608, 610, 618, 620, 631, 632, 759

Musical Antiquary, 672

Musical Arts Society, LaJolla, California, 507

musical comedies and theatre, 425, 428, 711-720, 729-749

Musical Courier, 387, 628

Musical Education, Studios of, 517

Musical Enthusiast, The (Hewitt, J. H.), 169

Musical Fund Society, 92, 98, 101, 108, 134, 143, 151, 237

Musical Gems for School and Home (Bradbury), 145

Musical Journal for the Pianoforte, 97

Musical Leader, 411

Musical Miscellany, 97

Musical Observer, 639

Musical Quarterly, 330, 339, 370, 392, 393, 396, 397, 433, 443, 451, 452, 453, 454, 482, 486, 489, 490, 491, 532, 534, 546, 547, 550, 561, 562, 563, 568, 572, 573, 575, 579, 582, 589, 591, 600, 601, 602, 605, 606, 607, 612, 613, 616, 624, 630, 683

Musical Review, 158

Musical Review and Gazette, 241-242

Musical Scene, The (Thomson), 433

Musical Solemnity, 151

Musical Times, The, 315

Musical World, The, 243, 244, 246, 247-249, 250, 251

Music and Imagination (Copland), 486

Musica Sacra, 141

Music Box Reviews (Berlin), 734

music conventions, 139-140

Music Critics' Circle Award, 395, 397, 398, 440, 445, 471, 517, 534, 539, 543, 561, 563, 586, 593, 604, 606

music education, 302-303

Music Educators' National Conference, 495

Music for a Great City (Copland), 486

Music for Ancient Instruments (Cohn), 578

Music for an Imaginary Ballet (Brant), 576

Music for a Scene from Shelley (Barber), 531

Music for Bassoon (Cohn), 578

Music for Brass Choir (Riegger), 398

Music for Brass Instruments (Dahl), 565

Music for Chamber Orchestra (Etler), 552

Music for Chamber Orchestra (Fiorillo), 522

Music for English Horn and Orchestra (Hill), 374

Music for Flute, Viola, Guitar, and Percussion (Sydenam), 610

Music for Four String Instruments (Loeffler), 350

Music for Moderns (Rose), 754

Music for Orchestra (Luening), 502

Music for Orchestra (Riegger), 398

Music for Orchestra (Wuorinen), 612

Music for Piano and Strings (Read), 559

Music for Recreation (Filippi), 530

Music for Shakespeare's Romeo and Juliet (Diamond), 544

Music for String Orchestra (Stevens), 520

Music for Strings (Swanson), 517

Music for the Marines (Van Vactor), 524

Music for the Movies (Copland), 484

Music for the Theatre (Copland), 479

Music for Wind Choir (Kay), 564

music history, bibliography, 769-788

Musicians and Music Lovers (Apthorp), 217

Music in America (Ritter), 291

Music in Concerto Style (Smith), 617-618

Music in England (Ritter), 291

Music in the Air (Kern), 732

Music Library Records, 763

Music Lover's Encyclopedia, The (Hughes), 624

Music Lover's Handbook, A (Siegmeister), 514

Music Man, The (Willson), 748

Music Notation (Read), 559

Music of Latin America, The (Slonimsky), 641

Music of Our Day (Saminsky), 423

Music of the Ghetto and the Bible (Saminsky), 423

Music of the Harp of Love (Hewitt), 87

Music on a Quiet Theme (Bergsma), 590

music periodicals, bibliography, 843-845

Music Publishers' Holding Corporation, 662

Music School Settlement, New York, 375

Music Since 1900 (Slonimsky), 641

music societies, formation of, 151

Music Through the Ages (Bauer-Peyser), 411

Musikverein, Milwaukee, 270

My Beautiful Lady (Caryll), 716

My Best Girl's a Corker (Stromberg), 715

My Blue Heaven (Donaldson), 750

My Country (Wilson), 385

My Dad's Dinner Pail (Braham), 714

My Darling, My Darling (Loesser), 747

My Days Have Been So Wondrous Free, 37, 41, 43

My Defenses Are Down (Berlin), 734

My Fair Lady (Loewe), 743

My Faith Looks Up to Thee (Mason), 137

My Faith Still Clings (Doane), 666

My Garden (Weaver), 655

My Gen'rous Heart Disdains, the Slave of Love To Be (Hopkinson), 42

My Heart Belongs to Daddy (Porter), 737

My Little Dog Has Ego (Hupfield), 750

My Love Is Gone to Sea (Hopkinson), 42

My Love Is to the Greenwood Gone (Grainger), 407

My Mammy (Donaldson), 750

My Maryland (Romberg), 730

My Menagerie (Foster), 627

My Mother's Kiss (Harris), 706

My Mother Was a Lady, or If Jack Were Only Here, 707

My People (Ellington), 724

My Poll and My Partner Joe (Pownall), 108

My River (Bacon), 466

My Sister and I (Kramer-Whitney), 752

My Southern Sunny Home (Hays), 703

Mysterious Marriage, The Hewitt), 89

Mysterious Monk, The (Pelissier), 96

Mysterious Mountain, The (Hovhaness), 551

Mystery, The (Floyd), 596

Mystic Trumpeter, The (Converse, F. S.), 381

Mystic Trumpeter, The (Dello Joio), 543

Mythical Beasts (Brant), 575

N

Nacht, Die (Strong), 344, 345

Nada, The Lily (Freeman), 361

Naginski, Charles (1909-1940), 522

Nagy, C. J., 88

Najads Idyl, The (McCoy), 362

Nanga Parvat (Hovhaness), 550

Narcissa (Moore), 387

Narcissus (Nevin), 621

Narrative for Orchestra (Nelson), 611

Natalia Petrovna (Hoiby), 599

Natalis, Die (Barber), 533

Natchez on the Hill (Powell), 406

Nathan, Robert, 352

Nation, The, 610

National airs, 113-128

National Association for American Composers and Conductors, 376, 492, 513, 760

National Broadcasting Company, 347, 352, 358, 377, 404, 418, 424, 468, 485, 494, 508, 521, 522, 528, 529, 531, 536, 537, 541, 543, 552, 582, 585, 593, 600, 658

National Conservatory of Music, New York, 315, 362, 378-379, 699

National Federation of Music Clubs, 346, 347, 361, 376, 377, 385, 400, 405, 420, 462, 475, 493, 513, 566, 590, 762

National Gazette, 238

National Institute of Arts and Letters, 441, 465, 488, 497, 507, 513, 554, 568, 585, 597, 599, 601, 603, 610, 611, 613, 615

nationalism in music, 226-252, 326-327

National Jewish Music Council, 545, 603

National Lyre, The (Tuckerman-Bancroft-Oliver), 147

National Melodies of America (Horn), 157

National Memories, Grand British Symphony (Heinrich), 234

National Music Camp, 418

National Opera Convention, 585

National Orchestral Association, 416

National Symphony Orchestra, 398, 613

Native Landscapes (Beach, J. P.), 370

Natoma (Herbert, V.), 318, 717

Nature's Awakening (Paine), 301

Naughty Marietta (Herbert, V.), 717

Naumburg, Walter W., Foundation Fellowships, 470, 582, 586, 589, 763

Nausicaa (Glanville-Hicks), 566

Navajo (Van Alstyne), 708

Naval Mass (Pusa-Teri), 662

Naval Pillar, The, 80

Nearer My God to Thee (Mason), 137

Near the Lake, Where Droops the Willow (Horn), 157

Nebraska University, School of Music, 385

"Negro breakdown," 177

"Negro dancer," 177

Negro folk music, 407, 636, 637, 680, 690

blues, 687-689

origin of, 682-685

secular, 687-689

sources, 680-690

spirituals, 636, 665, 682-683, 685-686

Negro Folk Symphony, No. 1 (Dawson), 465

Negro Heaven (Cesana), 467

Negro Lament (Guion), 636

Negro minstrelsy, 132, 176
Negro Parade (Stringfield), 465
Negro Rhapsody (Gilbert), 355
Negro Rhapsody (Goldmark), 379
Negro Rhapsody (White), 636
Negro themes, 157, 378, 405, 462, 636, 725, 741
Negro WAC Chorus, 408
Negro Workaday Songs (Odum and Johnson), 684, 688-689
Neidlinger, William Harold (1863-1924), 647
Nelson, Paul (1929-   ), 611-612
Nero's Daughter (Mopper), 566
Neuendorf, Adolf (1843-1897), 298
Neurotic Goldfish (Wilder), 510
Nevin, Arthur (1871-1943), 386
Nevin, Ethelbert (1862-1901), 206, 292, 323, 621-622, 635, 649, 807
Nevin, George Balch (1859-1933), 649-650
Nevin, Gordon Balch (1892-1943), 650
Nevins, Marian, 335
New American Melody (French), 64
Newark Festival, 419
New Carmina Sacra (Mason, L.), 141
New Century Players, New York, 562
New Chamber Society, 603
Newcombe, Bobby, 703
New Contredance (Capron), 104
New Dance (Riegger), 397
New Editions, 763
New England:
  early secular music in, 20-24
  hymnology of, 136-138
  latter eighteenth century, 58-70
  psalmody, 3-17
New England academics, 306-323
New England Chronicle (Donovan), 455
New England Concerto (Wigglesworth), 585
New England Conservatory of Music, 296, 307, 308, 309, 370, 376, 380, 386, 404, 456, 470, 471, 472, 515, 524, 608, 619, 630, 639
New England Episodes (Porter, Q.), 457
New England Feast of Shells, The (Heinrich), 234
New England Folksing (Kreutz), 509
New England Idyls (MacDowell), 330, 344

New England Prelude (Gaul), 654
New England Psalm Singer, The (Billings), 49-51
New England Suite (Grofé), 467
New England Symphony (Kelley), 345, 347
New England Triptych (Schuman), 535
New Haven Symphony Orchestra, 315, 379
New Japanese Dances (Rogers, B.), 447
New Jersey Orchestra, 468
New Jersey Teachers' College, 586
Newlin, Dika, 807
New Mexico, University of, 619
New Minstrel, The, 66
New Moon, The (Romberg), 730
New Musical Resources (Cowell), 448, 451
New Music Quarterly, 451
New Music Quartet, 398
New Music Society, 507
New Music Workshops, 507
New Orchestra, 620
New Orleans, opera in, 238, 270
New Orleans Street Cries (Beach, J. P.), 370
New Overture (Taylor, R.), 93
New Palestinian Songbook (Binder), 663
New Russia (Gardner), 641
New School for Social Research, 451, 457, 486, 544, 555, 585
Newsreel in Five Shots (Schuman), 535
New Symphony Orchestra, 412
Newton, John, 665
New Union Hymnal (Heller), 663
New Universal Harmony (Bayley), 48
New World Symphony (Dvořák), 622, 647, 681, 699, 711, 729
New Year's Eve in New York (Janssen), 464
New York:
  early music in, 31-36
  theatre in, 31-32, 76
New York, College of the City of, 517
New York Academy of Music, 200, 298
New York *American,* 402
New York Chamber Music Society, 400
New York *Chronicle,* 276
New York City Ballet, 485, 496, 556, 557
New York City Center, 561, 596
New York City Center Orchestra, 539

New York City Opera Company, 439, 440, 483, 496, 537, 540, 543, 557, 561, 595, 596, 597, 599, 609, 633
New York City Symphony, 518
New York College of Music, 663
New York Community Chorus, 375
New York Courier and Enquirer, 222
New York *Daily Advertiser,* 79, 81
New York Days and Nights (Whithorne), 410
New Yorker, 440, 461, 571, 586, 605, 740
New Yorkers, The (Schwartz), 739
New York *Evening Post,* 339, 340
New York *Herald,* 150, 718
New York *Herald Tribune,* 366, 367, 372, 395, 398, 399, 401, 413, 431, 432, 433, 434, 435, 438, 440, 442, 445, 446, 453, 459, 484, 485, 491, 493, 494, 497, 499, 502, 504, 531, 534, 536, 537, 538, 540, 541, 542, 543, 544, 545, 548, 552, 553, 554, 561, 562, 563, 564, 566, 568, 569, 570, 572, 574, 575, 576, 582, 589, 592, 593, 596, 597, 598, 603, 604, 605, 606, 607, 609, 610, 612, 632, 655, 667
New York High School of Music and Art, 603
New York *Home Journal,* 157, 209
New York Magazine, 97-98
New York Mercury, 35
New York Musical Review, 148
New York Music Critics' Circle (*see also* Music Critics' Circle award), 395, 397, 398, 440, 445, 471, 485, 489, 492
New York music festivals, 286
New York Normal Institute, 140, 142, 145
New York Oratorio Society, 346, 408, 447
New York Orchestra, 404
New York Philharmonic Society Orchestra, 151, 216, 281-282, 287, 367, 369-370, 372, 376, 393, 409, 455, 477
criticism of, 246-249
merger with New York Symphony Society, 246-249
New York Philharmonic-Symphony Society, 216, 281, 282, 285, 287, 367, 369, 370, 372, 376, 379, 408, 409, 447, 455, 477, 497, 511, 517, 520, 524, 525, 529, 530, 531, 533, 534, 539, 544, 546, 552, 554, 559, 560,
574, 585, 592, 616, 641, 681, 747, 758, 760
New York Profiles (Dello Joio), 542
New York Public Library, 88, 98, 99, 100, 104, 109, 376
  Americana Collection, 632, 635, 760
New York Sacred Music Society, 150, 151, 159, 160
New York Shakespeare Festival, 618
New York Sinfonietta, 474
New York State Power Authority, 467
New York State Theodore Roosevelt Commission, 495
New York Symphony Orchestra, 352-353, 370, 371, 380, 390, 401, 406, 423, 424, 426, 427, 446, 470, 473-474, 479, 625
New York *Telegram,* 240
New York Times, The, 241, 276, 395, 408, 428, 429, 454, 484, 486, 535, 541, 545, 549, 574, 576, 584, 585, 609, 610, 615
New York Town Hall, 413
New York *Tribune,* 209, 212, 240, 242, 245, 250, 400
New York University, 402, 407, 411, 447, 457, 468, 469, 513, 552, 581, 596, 748
New York *Weekly Post Boy,* 35
New York Women's Symphony Orchestra, 468
New York *World,* 239, 340, 401, 696
Niagara (Bull), 202
Niagara Falls Suite (Grofé), 467
Niawasa: an American Indian Idyl (Metcalf), 622
Niblo, William, 212
Nicholson, N., 733
Niedermeyer, Louis, 523
Night (Converse, F. S.), 381
Night (Weisgall), 566
Night and Day (Porter), 737
Night Boat, The (Kern), 731
Night Fantasy (Ward), 561
Night Flight (Read), 559
Nightingale (Alabieff), 626
Nightingale, The (Rogers, B.), 447
Nightingale and the Rose, The (Steinert), 523
Night in Old Paris, A (Hadley), 377
Night Journey (Schuman), 535
Night Music (Diamond), 546
Night Music (Rochberg), 567
Night Music (Swanson), 517

Night Music (Ward), 560
Night on an Island of Fantasy (Maganini), 474
Night, or The Firemen's Quadrille (Julien), 223-224
Night Soliloquy (Kennan), 580
Night Song (Heilman), 389, 631
Night View of Pittsburgh, A (Trimble), 611
Night Was Made for Love, The (Kern), 732
Night Watch (Kohs), 570
Niles, John Jacob (1892-   ), 637, 697, 726
Nine by Six (Read), 559
Nine-Minute Overture (Shapero), 602
1929—A Satire (Smith), 380
Ninety and Nine, The (Sankey), 668
98th Psalm (Foote), 421
90 Interludes for organ (Dickinson), 653
Niobe (James), 521
Niorada (Bergh), 626
Noble, T. Tertius (1867-1953), 650-651
Nobody Knows the Trouble I've Seen (White, C. C.), 636
Noctambulations (Hoiby), 599
Nocturne (Curran), 625
Nocturne (Levant), 520
Nocturne (Scott), 625
Nocturne (Stringham), 473
Nocturne and Dance of the Fates (Ornstein), 458
Nocturne and Pantomime (Fiorello), 522
Nocturne Fantasia (Achron), 477
Nocturne for Eighteen Instruments (Barlow), 578
Noelte, Albert, 521
No for an Answer (Blitzstein), 496
Nokturno (Harrison), 577
Nola (Arndt), 752
Nonage (Overton), 614
Nonet (Copland), 485
Nonet (Piston), 446
No, No, Nanette (Youmans), 736
No One to Kiss You Good-night (Harris), 706
Nordic March (Leidzen), 641
Nordic Symphony (Hanson), 430, 431
Nordoff, Paul (1909-   ), 379, 507-508, 547
Norfolk Festival, 346

Norge (Clapp), 415
Norse Sonata (MacDowell), 327, 328-329
North American Indians (*see* Indian music)
North American *Saengerbund*, 274
North and West (Hanson), 430
North Carolina, University of, 511
North Carolina Symphony, 465
North, East, South, West (Hadley), 377
Northern Refrain (Horn), 157
Northern Rhapsody (Hosmer), 388
Northern Saga (Wagner), 516
North Texas State University, 520
Northwestern University School of Music, 386, 474, 475, 512, 523, 617
Northwest Overture (Inch), 511
Nostalgia (Manning), 627
No Strings (Rodgers), 741
Not Ashamed of Christ (Danks), 667
"Note-clusters," 448, 458
Not Far from the Kingdom (Sankey), 668
Notre Dame de Paris, 252
Notre Dame University, 414
Notturno (Stringham), 473
Novelette (MacDowell), 330
Novellis, Novellis (La Montaine), 613
Novelty Piano Playing (Confrey), 752
Now Let the Night Be Dark for All of Me (Gesensway), 498
Now the Day Is Over (Weaver), 655
Now the King Eternal (Selby), 68
Now Welcome Summer (Avshalomov), 586
Noyes, Alfred, 383
Nunc Dimittis (Hall), 650
Nunc Dimittis (Lutkin), 649
Nun of Nidaro, The (Buck), 645, 646

O

O Be Joyful in the Lord (Selby), 68
Oberlin Conservatory of Music, 462, 515, 588, 652
Obongo Dance Primitive (Becker), 415
O'Brien Girl, The (Hirsch), 735
O Brother, Life's Journey Beginning (Sankey), 668
O Captain, My Captain (Bergh), 626
O'Casey, Sean, 496, 768
Ocean (Swan), 63
Ocean, The (Cowles), 641

Ocean, The (Hadley), 377
Ocean Fantasy (Paine), 301
Ocean Rhapsody (Ward), 652
Octandre (Varèse), 413
Octets (Brown), 617
Octoroon, The (Freeman), 361
Ode (Dello Joio), 543
Ode (Elwell), 473
Ode (Foss), 592
Ode (Hill), 374
Ode (Monroe, H.), 310
Ode (Ward), 560
Ode for Orchestra (Jacobi), 460
Ode for St. Cecilia's Day (Josten), 412
Ode for the New Year (Selby), 68
Ode in Honor of General Washington (Selby), 68
Ode on Masonry, 35
Ode on Music (Hopkinson), 39
Ode on the Anniversary of Independence (Selby), 68
Ode to Music (Hadley), 377
Ode to Peace (Gesensway), 498
Ode to the Brave (Bornschein), 388
Ode to the 4th of July, 1832 (Webb), 144
Ode to the Memory of James Bremner (Hopkinson), 39, 43, 44
Ode to the New Year, An (Taylor, R.), 92
Ode to the Star-Spangled Banner (Grofé), 467
Ode to the Virginian Voyage (Thompson), 444
Odets, Clifford, 551
Odum, H. W., 684, 688-689
Oedipus (Partch), 500
Œdipus Tyrannus (Paine), 300
Oehmler, Leo, 403
O'er the Hills Far Away, at the Birth of the Morn (Hopkinson), 42
Offering of the Soul (Cain), 658
Offrandes (Varèse), 413
Of Man's Mortalitie (Avshalomov), 586
Of Men and Music (Taylor), 400, 402
Of Mice and Men, score for (Copland), 481
Of New Horizons (Kay), 564
Of Thee I Sing (Gershwin), 428, 735
O'Hara, Geoffrey (1882-), 626, 726
O'Hara, John, 740
Oh, a shanty-man's life, 695
Oh, Boy! (Kern), 731

Oh Captain (Livingston), 752
Oh Dear, What Can the Matter Be, 115
Oh! Did You Hear The Meadow Lark! (Howard), 634
Oh, Fly to the Prairie (Knight), 160
Oh, Go Not to the Field of War (Webb), 144
Oh! Home of My Boyhood (Bricher), 171
Oh, How I Hate to Get Up in the Morning (Berlin), 726, 733
O Hush, or The Virginny Cupids (Rice), 177
Oh, Kay (Gershwin), 735
Oh, Lady, Lady (Kern), 731
Oh, Look! (Carroll), 749
Oh Lord, I have Wandered (Knight), 159
Oh, No, We Never Mention Her (Bayly), 162
Oh! Oh! Delphine (Caryll), 716
Oh, Please! (Youmans), 736
Oh! Promise Me (De Koven), 718
Oh, Susanna (Foster), 181, 187, 198
Oh, That Navajo Rag (Van Alstyne), 708
Oh, That We Two Were Maying (Nevin), 621
Oh! Weep Not (Russell), 162
Oklahoma! (Rodgers-Hammerstein), 740
Oklahoma, University of, 581
Oklahoma Symphony Orchestra, 583
Olcott, Chauncey, 707
Old American Company, 96, 102, 104, 107
Old American Country Set (Cowell), 450
Old Arm Chair, The (Russell), 162
Old Bell, The (Russell), 163
Oldberg, Arne (1874-1961), 386-387
Old California (Still), 462
Old Chisholm Trail (Fox), 405, 638
Old Dan Tucker (Emmett), 180, 181
Old Dog Tray (Foster), 195
Old Folks at Home (Foster), 185, 186, 188, 193, 194, 195, 670
Old Gray Goose, 180
Old Home, The (MacGimsey), 651
Old Homestead, The, 705
Old Hundredth, 6
Old Lavender, 714
Old Louisiana (Bornschein), 388
Old MacDonald Had a Farm, 692

Old Maid and the Thief, The (Menotti), 536
Oldmixon, Mrs., 87
Old 120th, 6
Old Paint (Fox), 638
Old Road, The (Scott), 625
Old Rugged Cross, The (Bennard), 658
Old School Bus, The (Howard), 635
Old Settlers Harmonic Society, 270
Old Sexton, The (Russell), 163
Old Ship of Zion (Gilbert), 354
Old Slave, The (MacGimsey), 637
Old Uncle Ned (Foster), 185, 187
Old Year's Gone, and the New Year's Come, The (Knight), 160
Oleana, 201
Ole Bull and Old Dan Tucker, 180
Ole Dad, 180
Ole Pee Dee, 180
Oliver, Henry Kemble (1800-1885), 134, 147
Oliver's Collection of Hymn and Psalm Tunes, 147
Olivet (Mason), 137
Olmstead, Clarence (1892-   ), 627-628
Olson, Harry F., 505
O Lud Gals Gib Me Chaw Terbackur, 180
O Munasterio (Allen), 420
On by the Spur of Valeur (Pownall), *Once and Future King, The* (White), 743
Once in Love With Amy (Loesser), 747 108
One Foot in America (Robinson), 629
One Hoss Shay, The (Phillips), 509
100 *Unaccompanied Variations* (Gershefski), 501
One Hundred Years of Music in America (Mathews), 292
O'Neill, Eugene, 408, 528, 589, 720
One Kiss (Romberg), 730
One Thing is Certain (Weisgall), 566
Ongaku (Cowell), 451
Only an Armor Bearer (Bliss), 667
Only a Rose (Friml), 729
Only Jealousy of Emer, The (Harrison), 578
On Music (Selby), 68
On Stage! (Dello Joio), 543
On the Atchison, Topeka and the Santa Fe (Warren), 751

On the Banks of the Wabash (Dresser), 706
On the Beach at Brighton (Lingard), 704
On the Beach at Night (Imbrie), 606
On the 'Gin 'Gin 'Ginny Shore (Donaldson), 750
On the Good Ship Lollipop (Whiting), 749
On the Mall (Goldman), 711
On the Road to Mandalay (Speaks), 624
On the Street Where You Live (Loewe), 743
On the Town (Bernstein), 540, 556
On the Way to Kew (Foote), 313
On Wings of Song (Mendelssohn), 169
On Your Toes (Rodgers-Hart), 740
O. O. McIntyre Suite (Willson), 747
Open Thy Lattice, Love (Foster), 187
Opera, 238-242, 286
   early, 27-28, 30-32
   first American, 94, 99
Opera Cloak, The (Damrosch, W.), 352
Opéra Comique, Paris, 388, 391, 472
Operti, Giuseppe, 712
Opus 51 (Fine), 583
Opus Sinfonicum (Lopatnikoff), 506
Oracle, The (Lees), 601
Oracle, The (Moore), 387
Oratorio Society, 346, 408, 447
Orchestra Association of America, 566
Orchestra Hall, Chicago, 289
Orchestral Abstracts (Sydenam), 610
Orchestral Style (Read), 559
Orchestral Variations (Copland), 485
Orchestral Variations (McDonald), 463
Orchestra of America, 368
Orchestra of the Air, 368
Orchestration (Piston), 444
Orchid, The (Caryll), 716
Ordering of Moses, The (Dett), 408
organs:
   early church, 17-24
   Gloria Dei Church, 17-18, 25, 31
Organum (Ruggles), 370
Oriental Impressions (Eichheim), 382
Oriental Rhapsody (Cadman), 404
Oriental scale form, 475
Oriental Sketches (Eichheim), 382
Oriental themes, 382-383, 390-391, 450-451
Orlando Furioso (Giorni), 476

Ormandy, Eugene, 438, 474
Ormazd (Converse, F. S.), 381
Ornithological Suite (Maganini), 474
Ornstein, Leo (1895-), 448, 458, 606, 807-808
Ornstein School of Music, 458
Orpheans, 173
Orquesta Sinfonica, Mexico, 480
Orquesta Sinfonica Nacional de Costa Rica, 516
Orth, John (1850-1932), 638
Osgood, Henry O., 426, 722
O Sing Ye Birds (Metcalf), 622
Osiris (La Violette), 475
Ostinelli, Louis, 131, 151, 170
Ostinelli, Sophia Hewitt, 170
O Swallow, Flying South (Foote), 313
O Tannenbaum, 260
Othello Overture (Hadley), 377
Otho Visconti (Gleason), 304
Otterström, Thorvald (1868-1942), 465, 638
Our American Music (Howard), 635
Ouranos (Rudhyar), 476
Our Contemporary Composers (Howard), 635
Our Fathers' Old Halls (Bricher), 171
Our Home Is on the Mountain Brow, 173
Our Musical Idiom (Bacon), 465
Our Native Land (Hewitt, J. H.), 169
Our New Music (Copland), 486
Our Prayer (Barrymore), 389
Our Refuge (Main), 667
Our Town, score for (Copland), 481
Our Way Across the Mountain, Ho (Russell), 163
Outdoor Overture, An (Copland), 481
Out of the Cradle Endlessly Rocking (Lockwood), 515
Out of the Gay Nineties (Fickenscher), 371
Out of This World (Porter), 738
Outpost (Weisgall), 566
Ouverture Joyeuse (Shepherd), 405
Over the Pavements (Ives), 365
Over the Rainbow (Arlen), 741
Over There (Cohan), 719
Overton, Hall (1920-), 613-614, 808
Overtura Breve (Mennini), 589
Overture (Fuleihan), 527
Overture (Kubik), 555
Overture (Moller), 104

Overture (Saroni), 248
Overture, Six-minute (Kurthy), 530
Overture de Demophon (Hewitt), 87
Overture "1849" (Wilson), 385
Overture for a Drama (Finney), 498
Overture in F (Weisgall), 566
Overture in Modo Giocoso (Helfer), 472
Overture in 9 Movements, Expressive of a Battle (Hewitt), 81
Overture in 12 Movements, Expressive of a Voyage from England to America (Gehot), 82
Overture 1912 (Levant), 520
Overture on American Folk Themes (Kleinsinger), 643
Overture on an American Theme (Moore, D.), 441
Overture on French Noëls (James), 468
Overture on Negro Themes (Dunn), 417
Overture to a Comedy (Van Vactor), 524
Overture to a Drama (Shepherd), 405
Overture to an Imaginary Drama (Bennett), 461
Overture to Marmion (Loder), 248
Overture to Shakespeare's Twelfth Night (Filippi), 530
Overture to the Gettysburg Address (Leplin), 588
Overture to the Piper (Ballantine), 416
Ozarka (Busch), 359
Ozark folk tunes, 522
Ozark Set (Siegmeister), 514
O Zion Haste (Weaver), 655

P

Pachelbel, Karl Theodor, 23, 31, 808
Pacifica Foundation, 610
Pacific 231 (Honegger), 381
Pack Up Your Sins (Berlin), 733
Paddy Duffy's Cart (Braham), 714
Paderewski, Ignace, 383, 384, 625
Paderewski Prize and Fund, 345, 377, 396, 405, 544, 559, 762
Padrone, The (Chadwick), 310
Paean to the Great Thunder (Rudhyar), 476
Pagan Festival (White, P.), 472
Paganini's Incantation (Heinrich), 236

Pagan Love Song, The (Brown), 750
Pagan Poem, A (Loeffler), 350, 626
Page, Nathaniel Clifford (1866-1956), 633
Pageant (Persichetti), 548
Pageant of Autumn (Sowerby), 657
Pageant of P. T. Barnum, The (Moore, D.), 439, 441
Pageant Triumphale (Nevin, Gordon B.), 650
Pages from Negro History (Still), 462
Pagnol, Marcel, 744
Paine, John Knowles (1839-1906), 289, 298, 303, 306, 311, 369, 371, 373, 378, 380, 611, 639, 648, 755, 808
Paine, Robert Treat, 126
Paine Fellowships, 524, 583, 611
Painted Desert, The (Read), 559
Paint Your Wagon (Loewe), 742, 743
Pajama Game, The (Adler-Ross), 748
Palestine Symphonic Ensemble, 663
Pal Joey (Rodgers-Hart), 740
Palma, John, 27, 39
Palmer, Courtlandt (1872-1951), 389
Palmer, Robert (1915-   ), 579-580, 808
Palmgren, Selim, 463
Panama Hattie (Porter), 737
Panama Hymn (Beach), 322
Panama-Pacific Exposition, 322
Pan-American Society, 412-413
Pan and the Priest (Hanson), 430, 431
Pan e Dafni (Read), 559
Panels from a Theater Wall (Fletcher), 580
Panhandle, The (Gillis), 585
Pan: Music for Solo Flute (Moevs), 602
Pantaloon (Ward), 561
Pan the Piper (Kleinsinger), 643
Paola and Francesca (Oldberg), 386
Paolo and Francesca (James, D.), 521
Papa, Won't You Dance With Me (Styne), 745
Parable of Death (Foss), 592
Paratroops (Kubik), 555
Parcae, The (Smit), 604
Paris Conservatory, 383, 412, 413, 476
Parisian Suite (Duke), 526
Paris Opéra, 538
Paris Opéra Comique, 388, 391, 472
Parker, Charlie, 808
Parker, Horatio William (1863-1919), 309, 313, 319, 365, 378, 416, 440, 452, 456, 470, 522, 808
Parker, James Cutler (1828-1916), 295-296, 633, 648, 649
Parker Fund, 584, 762
Parratt, Sir Walter, 650
Parris, Robert (1924-   ), 615
Parsely, George, 705
Parsons, Albert Ross (1847-1933), 291
Partch, Harry (1901-   ), 499-500, 577
Parthenope (Kurtz), 419
Partita (Berger), 563
Partita (Creston), 493
Partita (Diamond), 545
Partita (Fine), 571
Partita (Kay), 564
Partita (Loeffler), 351
Partita (Phillips), 510
Partita (Piston), 446
Partita (Read), 559
Partita in C (Shapero), 602
Partitas (Fiorello), 522
Pasadena Music and Arts Association, 437
Pasdeloup's Orchestra, 349
Pas de Trois (Chanler), 632
Pasquinade (Gottschalk), 206
Passacaglia (Berezowsky), 525
Passacaglia (Bingham), 417
Passacaglia (Copland), 485
Passacaglia (Freed), 527
Passacaglia (Haubiel), 469
Passacaglia (Kurthy), 530
Passacaglia (Robertson), 472
Passacaglia (Strang), 507
Passacaglia and Fugue (Dunn), 417
Passacaglia and Fugue (Etler), 522
Passacaglia and Fugue (Howe), 421
Passacaglia and Fugue (Korn), 620
Passacaglia and Fugue (Mopper), 567
Passacaglia and Fugue (Read), 559
Passacaglia and Fugue (Riegger), 398
Passacaglia and Fugue (Talma), 514
Passacaglia and Fugue (Van Vactor), 524
Passacaglia, Interlude, and Fugue (Sowerby), 657
Passacaglia on Vermont Folk Tunes (Donovan), 455
Passing of Arthur, The (Busch), 359
Passing of Summer, The (Cole), 360
Passion, The (Rogers, B.), 447
Passione Instrumentale, 83

Passion of Jonathan Wade, The (Floyd), 596
Passion of Our Saviour (Haydn), 83
Pastoral (Cowell), 450
Pastoral (Effinger), 582
Pastoral (Haubiel), 469
Pastoral (Howe), 421
Pastoral and Dance (Van Vactor), 524
Pastoral and Toccata (Wagner), 516
Pastoral Dances (Hoiby), 599
Pastorale (Gillette), 654
Pastorale and Dance (Shulman), 582
Pastorales (Bowles), 582
Pastorales (Freed), 526
Pastoral Ode (Daniels), 386
Pastoral Suite in F (Demarest), 624
Patriot, The, or Liberty Asserted (Hewitt), 90
Patterns (Carpenter), 372
Patterns (Mopper), 567
Patterns after the Zodiac (Weaver), 628
Patterson, Frank (1871-   ), 387
Patti, Adelina, 200
Pattison, Lee (1890-   ), 640
Paul Bunyan (Bergsma), 591
Paul Bunyan (James), 521
Paul Bunyan (Moross), 557
Paul Revere's Ride (Cain), 658
Paul Revere's Ride (Pratt), 305
Paur, Emil, 331
Pavane (Gould), 553
Pavlova (Bendix), 361
Pax Triumphans (Van der Stucken), 348
Paysage (Bennett), 461
Peabody, Asa, 133, 151
Peabody, George, College, 524
Peabody Conservatory, 362, 384, 388, 423, 451, 589, 638
Peaceable Kingdom, The (Thompson, R.), 443
Peace Festival, Boston, 297
Peaceful Land, The (Still), 462
Peace Pipe, The (Converse, F. S.), 382
Peace with a Sword (Daniels), 385
Peak Bell Ringers, 173
Pearl of Pekin, The (Kerker), 714
Peasants' Battle March (Strong), 344
Peep Show (Rome), 744
Pee-Wee the Piccolo (Kleinsinger), 643
Peggy Ann (Rodgers-Hart), 739
Peg O' My Heart (Fisher), 708
Pehr, Phyllis, 628

Pelham, Dick, 178
Pelham, Peter, 22-23
Pelissier, Victor, 94-96
Peltzman, Rae, 628
Penetrella (La Violette), 475
Penn, John, 39
Pennsylvania (Cadman), 404
Pennsylvania, University of, 300, 303, 463, 496, 526, 567, 659, 752
Pennsylvania *Gazette*, 45
Pennsylvania Germans, early music of, 24-25
Pennsylvania Herald, 105
Pennsylvania Packet, 105, 106
Pennsylvania Suite (Read), 559
Pennypacker, Governor, 121
Pensive Shepherd, The (Holyoke), 63
People, Yes, The (Sandburg), 629
Perabo, Ernst, 321
Percussion Music (Blitzstein), 497
Percussion Music (Strang), 507
Père Marquette (Gaul), 654
Perfect Day, A (Bond), 623
Perfect Modernist, The (Patterson), 387
performance of music, 758-761
performers, biography, bibliography, 789-817
periodicals, bibliography, 843-845
Perkins, Charles Callahan (1823-1886), 294, 295-296
Perkins, Francis, 372, 435, 491, 554, 592
Perles de Rosée, Les (Mason, W.), 275
Perosi, Lorenzo, 660
Perry, Julia (1927-   ), 613
Persian Fable, A (Griffis), 470
Persian Serenade (Metcalf), 622
Persian Set (Cowell), 450
Persian Song (Burmeister), 638
Persichetti, Vincent (1915-   ), 547-549, 604, 613, 809
Persin, Max, 533
Perspectives in a Labyrinth (Phillips), 509
Pervigilium Veneris (Spelman), 471
Pestalozzian method, 140
Peter, John Frederick, 29, 809
Peterboro, New Hampshire:
  Festival, 416
  MacDowell Colony at, 344, 479, 539, 762
Peter Ibbetson (Taylor), 401
Peter Pan (Styne), 745
Peter Pan (Ward), 652

Peter Pan, music for (Fain), 751
Peters, W. C., 187
Petite Piedmontese, La (Taylor, R.), 94
Petite Suite (Campbell-Watson), 662
Petrograd Conservatory, 422, 458
Pettiford, Oscar, 618
Peyser, Ethel, 411
Pfitzner, Hans, 375
Phaedra (Starer), 620
Phantom Canoe, The (Bornschein), 388
Phantom Caravan, The (Branscombe), 634
Phantomesque (Campbell-Watson), 662
Phantom Footsteps (Work), 267
Phantom of the Opera, The, score for (Brokeman), 528
Phantom Satyr (Beach, J. P.), 370
Phelps, Ellsworth C. (1827-1913), 296
Philadelphia:
  early music in, 24-28
  theatre in, 27-28, 76, 78
Philadelphia Academy of Music, 383, 458, 463, 639
Philadelphia Centennial Concerts, 285, 286, 645
Philadelphia-Chicago Opera Company, 717
Philadelphia City Concerts, 77-78
Philadelphia Conservatory of Music, 507, 528, 547
Philadelphia Exposition, 299
Philadelphia Hymn, The (Taylor, R.), 93
Philadelphia Mendelssohn Club, 303
Philadelphia Opera Company, 401
Philadelphia Symphony Orchestra, 303, 375, 378, 382, 395, 396, 431, 434, 438, 443, 445, 446, 456, 463, 479, 480, 498, 528, 529, 531, 532, 533, 582, 594, 759
Phile, Philip (?-1793), 107, 121
Philharmonic Hall, New York City (*see* Lincoln Center)
Philharmonic League of New York, 553
Philharmonic Society of New York (*see* New York Philharmonic Society)
Philharmonic Waltzes (Gould), 553
Philipp, Isidor, 472, 477, 527, 658
Phillips, Burrill (1907-   ), 509-510
Phillips, Stephen, 566
Phobias (Engel, A. L.), 556
Phoenix (Arizona) Symphony, 611
Phoenix Expirans (Chadwick), 310

Piano Fantasy (Copland), 486
Piano Sonata (Bloch), 394
Piano Sonata (Griffes), 390
Picayune Butler, 181
Piccola Figaro, La (Allen), 420
Pickaninny Dance (Guion), 636
Picnic Cantata (Bowles), 583
Piece for Ondes Martenot (Smith), 618
Piece for Tape Recorder, A (Ussachevsky), 503-504
Pieces of Eight (Wagenaar), 456
Pied Piper, The (Copland), 485
Pied Piper, The (Jacobi), 460
Pied Piper of Hamelin, The (Bergh), 626
Pied Piper of Hamelin, The (Boyle), 423
Pierian Sodality of Harvard University, 415
Pierne, Henri C., 655
Pierre de Provence, 80
Pierrot and Cothurnus (Thompson, R.), 442
Pierrot of the Minute (Engel, A. L.), 556
Pieta (Warford), 626
Pietro's Petard (Overton), 614
Pike, Albert, 257
Pilate (Hovhaness), 551
Pilgrimage (Floyd), 596
Pilgrim Fathers, The (Heinrich), 234
Pilgrim Ode (Cole, R. G.), 360
Pilgrim Psalms (Finney), 498
Pilgrim's Hymn (Luening), 502
Pilgrims of Destiny (Branscombe), 634
Pilgrims of 1620 (Hosmer), 633
Pilgrim's Progress, The (Kelley), 346
Pilgrim's Progress (Riegger), 398
Pilgrim Vision (Carpenter), 372
Pinero, Sir Arthur Wing, 90
Pine Tree, The (Salter, M. T.), 622
Pinkham, Daniel (1923-   ), 607-608, 809
Pink Lady, The (Caryll), 716
Pins and Needles (Rome), 743-744
Pioneer (Cole), 360
Pioneer, The (Eppert), 418
Pioneer America (Bingham), 416
Pioneer Epic (McKay), 464
Pipe Dream (Rodgers-Hammerstein), 741
Pipe of Desire, The (Converse, F. S.), 318, 380, 381

Piper at the Gates of Dawn, The (Thompson, R.), 443

Pippa's Holiday (Beach, J. P.), 370

Pirandello, Luigi, 566

Pirate, The (Johnson, H.), 628

Pirate's Island (Daniels), 386

Pirate Song (Gilbert), 354

Pirates of Penzance, The (Sullivan), 707

Pirate Song (Olmstead), 628

Pisk, Paul A., 809

Piston, Walter (1894-   ), 444-446, 488, 524, 554, 563, 569, 570, 571, 601, 602, 608, 611, 632, 809

Pit and the Pendulum, The (Kelley), 346

Pittsburgh Evening Chronicle, 199-200

Pittsburgh Polyphonic Choir, 661

Pittsburgh *Post* and *Sun*, 654

Pittsburgh Symphony Orchestra, 423, 424, 581, 611, 717

Pittsfield Chamber Music Festival, 382

Pixley, Frank, 719

Pizarro (Kotzebue), 80

Pizarro (Taylor-Reinagle), 94

Pizarro, or The Spaniards in Peru (Hewitt), 90

Pizzetti, Ildebrando, 512, 558, 580

Placide, Alexander, 109

Plaidy, Louis, 645

Plain Chant for America (Still), 462

Plain Psalmody (Holden), 61

Plains, The (Donato), 512

Plains, The (Rogers, B.), 447

Plains and Mountains (Wessel), 475

Plains of Manassas (Hewitt, J. H.), 169

Plane Beyond, The (Haubiel), 469

Plantation, The (Freeman), 361

plantation walk-arounds, 181

Play Ball (Phillips), 510

Playford, John, 13

Pleading (Kramer), 631

Please Go 'Way and Let Me Sleep (H. Von Tilzer), 708

Pleasure Dome of Kubla Khan, The (Griffes), 390, 391

Plectra and Percussion Dances (Partch), 500

Pleyel, Ignaz, 81

Plössl, Anna, 317

Plough That Broke the Plains, The (Thomson), 434

Plywood Age, The (Avshalomov), 586

Pocahontas (Carter), 488

Pocahontas Waltz (Heinrich), 236

Poe, Edgar Allan, 164, 166-168, 374, 477

Poem (Beach, J. P.), 370

Poem (Creston), 492

Poem (Griffes), 390-391

Poem (Haines), 583

Poem (Whithorne), 410

Poem (Woltmann), 512

Poème d'Extase (Scriabin), 395

Poème Electronique (Varèse), 413

Poèmes Ironiques (Rudhyar), 476

Poem for Orchestra (Morris), 459

Poem in Cycles and Bells, A (Luening-Ussachevsky), 506

Poems for Violin and Chamber Orchestra (Palmer), 579

Poet Sings, The (Watts, W.), 630

Poet's Requiem, The (Rorem), 609

Poia (Nevin, A.), 386

Polacca Guerriera (Bull), 202

Poland (Swan), 63

Polarities (Overton), 614

Polonaise (MacDowell), 330

Polyphonica (Cowell), 449

Polyphonic Composition (Ruggles), 370

Polyphony for Orchestra (Berger), 563

Polytone, 370

Pond, Sylvanus Billings (1792-1871), 146

Ponte, Lorenzo da, 239

Pontifical School of Music, 661

Poor Little Ritz Girl, The (Rodgers-Hart), 739

Poor Tom Bowling (Pownall), 108

Poor Vulcan (Pelissier), 96

Popocatepetl (Shulman), 582

Popover (McBride), 643

Poppy, The (Clifton), 416

popular music, 701-754
    bibliography, 818-825

Porgy and Bess (Gershwin), 425, 428-429, 457

Portals (Ruggles), 369

Porter, Cole (1892-1964), 736-738

Porter, Quincy (1897-   ), 456-457, 809

Portland (Oregon) Orchestra, 464

Portrait, The (Rogers, B.), 447

Portrait of a Frontier Town (Gillis), 585

Portrait of a Lady (Taylor), 400

Portrait of an Artist (Zimbalist), 422

Portrait of Jenny, score for (Tiomkin), 478

Portrait of Man (Verrall), 523

Portrait of Mark Twain for Orchestra (Kern), 732

Portrait of Saint Christopher (Verrall), 523

Portrait Suite, A (Kay), 564

Port Royal (McKay), 463

Postponeless Creature, The (Bacon), 466

Pot of Fat, The (Chanler), 632

Potomac (Howe), 421

Pound, Ezra, 659

Pound, Louise, 696

Poverty's Tears Ebb and Flow (Braham), 714

Powell, John (1882-1963), 378, 405-406

Powell, Melvin (1923-   ), 607

Power and the Land (Moore, D.), 442

Pownall, Mary Ann (1751-1796), 83, 87, 108-109

Pownall (Swan), 63

Practical Instrumentation (Patterson), 387

Praeludium Salutorium (Shepherd), 405

Prager, Sigfrid, 508

Prairie (Lockwood), 515

Prairie (Sowerby), 657

Prairie, The (Foss), 592

Prairie Legend (Siegmeister), 514

Prairie Portrait (McKay), 464

Prairie Schooner (Donato), 512

Prairie Songs (Goeb), 581

Praise My Soul (Holler), 658

Praise the Lord and Pass the Ammunition (Loesser), 728, 746

Pratt, Charles E. (1841-1902), 704

Pratt, Silas Gamaliel (1846-1916), 305-306, 809

Prausnitz, Frederick, 566

Prayer for Poland (Stojowski), 384

Prayer in Time of War (Schuman), 535

Prayer of Cardinal Newman (Dello Joio), 544

Prayer of Thanksgiving (Gaul), 654

Prayer of the Norwegian Child (Kountz), 628

Prayer Perfect, The (Speaks), 624

Prayer, Promise and Praise (Neidlinger), 647

Prayers of Kierkegaard (Barber), 533

Preamble and Fugue (Riegger), 398

Preamble to the Charter of the United Nations (Copland), 485

Préambule et Jeux (Salzedo), 414

Pre-Classic Suite (Creston), 493

Preface to a Child's Storybook (Fuleihan), 527

Prelude and Dance (Bowles), 583

Prelude and Dance (Creston), 492

Prelude and Dance (Leplin), 588

Prelude and Fugue (Giannini), 494

Prelude and Fugue (Mason, D. G.), 378

Prelude and Fugue (Piston), 444

Prelude and Fugue for String Orchestra (Harris), 438

Prelude and Passacaglia (Weber), 569

Prelude and Rondo Giocoso (Starer), 620

Prelude and Three Fugues (Nordoff), 507

Prelude for Orchestra (Hill), 374

Prelude, Polka, and Fanfare (Carter), 488

Prelude, Scherzo, and Ricercare (Robertson), 471

Prelude to a Hymn-Tune (Luening), 502

Prelude to a Tragedy (McBride), 643

Prelude to *Hamlet* (Rogers, B.), 446

Preludes in three classes (Reinagle) 80

Prelude to the Delectable Forest (Ballantine), 416

Preludium and Fugue (Barrymore), 389

Present Arms (Rodgers-Hart), 739

President's March (Phile), 107

President's March (Taylor, R.), 94

Presley, Elvis, 725

Presser, Theodore, 170, 567

Presser, Theodore, Co., 639

Presser Prizes, 639

Pretty as a Picture (Cooper-Bishop), 703

Pretty Girl Is Like a Melody, A (Berlin), 733

Price, Leontyne, 613

Pride of Our Plains (Van Hagen, Jr.), 75

Priestly Benediction I and II (Ephros), 662

Prigmore, Mr., 83

Primavera (Giannini), 495

Primrose Girl, The, 87

Primroses, 109

Prince, Thomas, 10
Prince Hal Overture (Smith), 380
Prince of Pilsen, The (Luders), 719
Princess and Puppet (Phillips), 510
Princess and the Vagabond, The (Freed), 526
Princess Ting-Ah-Ling (De Leone), 420
Princess Zondilda and Her Entourage, The (Haieff), 562
Princeton University, 442, 452, 486, 487, 574, 583, 586, 606
Prince Woodruff (Neuendorf), 298
Prisoner for Life, 638
Prisoner of Monterey, The (Hewitt, J. H.), 169
Private Mary Brown (Loesser), 746
Prix de Rome, 488, 494, 508, 523, 531, 564, 580, 585, 591, 599, 600, 602, 606, 630
prize contests (*see also* names of awards and contests), 762
Procession (Branscombe), 634
Processional (Calabro), 604
Processional (Taylor), 402
Processional March (Gershefski), 501
Processional March (Rogers), 649
Processional of the Holy Grail (Gleason), 304
Proclamation (Bloch), 395
Proctor, Edna Dean, 259
Prodigal Son, The (Christiansen), 652
Prodigal Son, The (De Leone), 420
Prodigal Son, The (Jacobi), 460
Prodigal Son Symphony (Pratt), 305
Profile (Lees), 601
Program Music (Griselle), 468
Prokofieff, Sergei, 557, 598
Prologue and Dithyramb (Mills), 565
Prologue for Orchestra (Leplin), 588
Promenade (Kennan), 580
Prometheus Bound (Bauer, M.), 411
Promise of Spring, A (Paine), 301
Pro Musica Society, 239
Propert, David, 65
Prophecy (Avshalomov), 585
Prophecy (Howe), 421
Prophet Isaiah, The (Rogers, B.), 447
Protestant Church, American hymnology, 136-138
Protestant Radio Commission, 590
Proverbs of Hell (Avshalomov), 586
Pruckner, Dionys, 383
Pryor, Arthur (1870-1942), 711

Psallonian Society, 135
Psalm (Diamond), 544
Psalm (Persichetti), 548
Psalm 19 (Lyon), 48
Psalmodist's Companion (French), 64
psalmody, New England, 3-17
Psalm of David (Dello Joio), 542
Psalm of Faith (Wagner), 516
Psalm of Praise (Daniels), 386
Psalm 130 (Giannini), 495
Psalm 112 (Lockwood), 515
Psalms (Foss), 592
Psalms (Saminsky), 662
Psalm 17 (Lyon), 48
Psalms of David Imitated (Watt), 15
Psalter (Ainsworth), 4-5
Psalter (Ravenscroft), 6, 7, 9
Psaltery, The (Mason, L.), 141
Ptaloemon to Pastora (Selby), 68
P. T. 109, music for, 754
publication of music, 757-758
Puck (Kubik), 555
Pueblo—a Moon Rhapsody (Saminsky), 423
Pugno, Raoul, 411
Pulitzer Prize, 428, 431, 440, 445, 446, 469, 470, 474, 483, 522, 532, 537, 555, 561, 583, 613, 630, 657, 735, 740
Pull for the Shore (Bliss), 667
Punch and Judy Overture (Robertson), 472
Punch Opera, New York, 620
Punch's Dance, 31
Purgatory (Weisgall), 566
Puritania (Kelley), 346
Purse, The, 80
Pusa-Teri, Cosmo (1908-   ), 662
Pushmataha, a Venerable Chief of a Western Tribe of Indians (Heinrich), 236
Put on Your Old Gray Bonnet (Weinrich), 709
Put Your Arms Around Me, Honey (A. Von Tilzer), 708
Pygmalion (Freed), 526
Pygmalion (Shaw), 743
Pyramids of Giza, The (Fuleihan), 527

Q

Quakers, 72
    and music, 26-27

Quaker's Sermon, The, 32
Quartet Euphometric (Cowell), 449
Quartet Pedantic (Cowell), 449
Quartet Romantic (Cowell), 449
Quartets for Strings (Moore, D.), 441-442
Quartetto (Moller), 104
Quebec (Branscombe), 634
Queen Elizabeth, score for (Breil), 388
Queen Elizabeth of Belgium Competition, 552
Queen Helen (Gruening), 409
Queen of Hearts, The (Sousa), 715
Queens College, 473, 585, 603, 607
Quest (Weisgall), 566
Quiet City, The, score for (Copland), 481
Quiet Music (Read), 559
Quiet One, The, score for (Kay), 565
Quin, Mr., 158
Quincy, Josiah (*Journal*), 30
Quintets (Hill), 374
Quotations in Percussion (Cohn), 578

R

Rachem (Mana-Zucca), 627
Radcliffe Choral Society, 385, 386
Radio City Music Hall Symphony, 465, 467, 521, 552
Radio City Snapshots (Wagner), 516
Radio Program Bureau, OWI, 437-438
Raff, Joachim, 277, 326, 334-335
Raftsman's Dance (Filippi), 530
Rags to Riches (Adler-Ross), 748
Ragtime, 720-721
Railroad Gallop, 281
Rain (Curran), 625
Rainer Family, 175
Rain Has Fallen (Calabro), 604
Rain or Shine, 462
Raising of Lazarus, The (Rogers, B.), 447
Ramayana (Shapleigh), 383
Ramona (Wayne), 750
Ramuntcho (Taylor), 401
Randall, James Ryder, 260
Randegger, Giuseppe Aldo, 492
Randolph, Harold, 421
"random" music, 617
Raphling, Sam (1910-   ), 558
Rappaccini's Daughter (Hawthorne), 403

Rapunzel (Harrison), 578
Rarely Comest Thou (Cain), 658
Rasbach, Oscar (1888-   ), 627
Rastus on Parade (Mills), 720
Rat Charmer of Hamelin, The (Neuendorf), 298
Raven, The (Bergh), 626
Raven, The (Dubensky), 477
Raven, The (Shapleigh), 383
Ravenscroft, Thomas, 6, 7, 9
Rayber, Cornelius, 623
RCA-Victor Company, prizes, 409, 461, 467-468, 479, 762
Read, Daniel (1757-1836), 63
Read, Gardner (1913-   ), 558-559
Recessional (De Koven), 718
Recessional (Sanders), 521
Recessional, The (Matthews), 653
Recitative and Air (James), 521
Recitative and Rondo (Schuller), 616
Recitative, Aria, and Stretto (Claflin), 476
Recollections of Home (Mills), 291
Recording Piece (Harrison), 577
recordings, 763-764
Red Bombay (Reddick), 636
Reddick, William J. (1890-   ), 636
Redemption Hymn (Parker), 296
Red Feather (De Koven), 718
Red Hot and Blue (Porter), 737
Redlands, University of, 519
Red Mill, The (Herbert, V.), 717
Red Petticoat, The (Kern), 731
Red Pony, The, score for (Copland), 481, 482
Red Riding Revisited (Moross), 557
Red Rosey Bush (Young), 637
Redway, Virginia Larkin, 123
Red Wing (Joplin), 720
Reed, Herbert Owen (1910-   ), 578-579
Reed College, 586
Reformation Cantata (Christiansen), 652
Reger, Max, 385, 661, 662
Regina (Blitzstein), 496
Reichhold, Henry A., 471
Reilly and the Four Hundred, 714
Reinagle, Alexander (1756-1809), 75-81, 97, 809
Reinecke, Karl, 291, 347
Reiner, Fritz, 461, 485, 553
Reiser, Alois (1887-   ), 424

religious music (*see also* gospel songs), 644-669
Remember (Berlin), 733
Remember Now Thy Creator (Barnes), 655
Remick, J. H., & Company, 425
Remission of Sin, The (Horn), 156
Renascence (Reed), 579
Rendezvous (Shulman), 582
Requiem (Giannini), 495
Requiem (Goldmark), 379
Requiem (La Violette), 475
Requiem (Lockwood), 575
Requiem (Perry), 613
Requiem (Smith), 380
Requiem for Double Chorus (Thompson), 444
Rescue the Perishing (Bliss), 667
Respighi, Ottorino, 472, 515, 520, 585, 655
Resurgam (Hadley), 377
Retribution (Mana-Zucca), 627
Retrospections (Cohn), 578
Retrospectives (Wald), 418
Return of Odysseus, The (Phillips), 510
Reuben and Rachel (Birch-Gooch), 705
Reuben, Reuben (Gaunt), 715
Revellers, The (Hewitt, J. H.), 169
Revenge with Music (Schwartz), 739
Revere, Paul, 17, 509
Reverie and Dance (Harris), 438
Review (Rose), 534
Revival Classics (Bennard), 668
Revival Melodies (Dadmun), 666
Revolutionary War, 43, 113-118
   effect on music, 58
Rexford, Eben E., 705
Rhapsodic Variations for Tape Recorder and Orchestra (Luening-Ussachevsky), 504-505
Rhapsodie Concertante (Weber), 569
Rhapsodie Mondial (Gallico), 361
Rhapsodie Montereyan (Gallico), 361
Rhapsodie Nègre (Powell), 405, 406
Rhapsody (Demarest), 625
Rhapsody (Freed), 527
Rhapsody (Oldberg), 386
Rhapsody (Search), 422
Rhapsody (Wagner), 516
Rhapsody in Blue (Gershwin), 425, 426, 427, 428, 466, 467, 722
Rhapsody of St. Bernard (Smith), 380

Rhapsody on Gregorian Motifs (Titcomb), 654
Rhapsody on Old Hebrew Melodies (Fairchild), 388
Rheinberger, Joseph Gabriel, 308, 315, 356, 359, 380, 386, 387, 623
Rhode Island College of Education, 633
Rhode Island State College, 508
Rhumba Symphony (McDonald), 463
Rhys-Herbert, William (1868-1921), 633
Rhythm Gallery (Gould), 553
Rhythmicana (Cowell), 449
Rhythmicon, 449
Rice, Cale Young, 630
Rice, Edward E., 712
Rice, Phil, 181
Rice, Thomas Dartmouth ("Daddy"), 176
Ricercari (Dello Joio), 542
Richmond Is Ours, 263
Richter, E. F., 295, 304, 645, 666
Rickaby, Franz, 694-695
Riders to the Sea (Synge)), 356
Riegger, Wallingford (1885-1961), 395-399, 414, 424, 514, 575, 613, 809
Ries, Ferdinand, 154
Riggs, Lynn, 740
Righteous Branch, The (Clough-Leighter), 633
Rights of Woman, 127
Riha, Francis, 215
Rime of the Ancient Mariner, The (Bornschein), 388
Ring Around the Moon (Partch), 500
Ringling, Barnum and Bailey Circus, 402
Rio Rita (Tierney), 738
ripieno, 93
Rip Van Winkle (Bristow), 250-252
Rip Van Winkle (Chadwick), 307, 309
Rip Van Winkle (Demarest), 624
Rip Van Winkle (Hewitt, J. H.), 169
Risen Christ, The (Holler), 658
Rise 'n' Shine (Youmans), 736
Rise of Rosie O'Reilly, The (Cohan), 719
Risher, Anna Priscilla (1875-   ), 639
Rissolty Rossolty (Crawford), 500
Rita Coventry, score for (Taylor), 402
Ritchie Family, 810
Rite of Spring (Stravinsky), 602

Ritratti (Haubiel), 469
Ritter, Frédéric Louis (1834-1891), 48, 291
River, The (Thomson), 434
river boatmen, 178
Road to Music, The (Slonimsky), 641
Roadways (Densmore), 626
Robbers, The (Rorem), 609
Robbins, Jerome, 541, 553, 557
Roberta (Kern), 732
Robert Browning Overture (Ives), 368
Roberts, Lee, 726
Robert Shaw Chorale, 590
Robertson, Leroy, 471-472
Robeson, Paul, 528, 629, 637
Robin, Leo, 745
Robin Hood (De Koven), 718
Robin Hood (Moross), 557
Robin Hood, or Sherwood Forest (Hewitt), 80, 90
Robin Hood's Heart (Howe), 421
Robin's Lullaby, The (Foerster), 622
Robinson, Avery, 694
Robinson, Earl (1910-   ), 629, 727
Robinson, Franklin, 472
Robinson Crusoe (Pelissier), 96
Rochberg, George (1918-   ), 567-568
Rochester, University of, 511, 578, 583, 589
Rochester American Composers' Concerts (*see under* Eastman School of Music)
Rochester Festival of Music, 430
Rochester Philharmonic Orchestra, 446, 545
Rochester *Times Union*, 564
Rock (Howe), 421
Rock-a-bye, Baby (Canning), 706
Rocked in the Cradle of the Deep (Knight), 159
Rockefeller Foundation, 450, 545, 582, 763
Rockin' Chair (Carmichael), 753
Rockingham (Miller), 17
Rock Me to Sleep, Mother (Hewitt, J. H.), 169
Rock of Ages (Andrews), 653
Rock of Ages, Cleft for Me, 142
Rock of Liberty, The (Cole), 360
Rockwell, Norman, 461
Rocky Mountains, 376
Rococo Suite (Saar), 360-361
Rodda, Charles, 447

Rodeheaver, Homer (1880-1955), 501, 664, 668-669
Rodel, Julius, 596
Rodeo (Copland), 483
Rodgers, Richard (1902-   ), 460, 483, 546, 632, 739-741, 810
Rodgers and Hart, 739-740
Rodger Young (Loesser), 746
Rodzinski, Artur, 539, 732
Roerich Museum, 455
Rogers, Bernard (1893-   ), 446-447, 512, 544, 558, 560, 563, 571, 578, 579, 580, 586, 588, 590, 617, 810
Rogers, James Hotchkiss (1857-1940), 410, 649
Rogers, Nathaniel, 21
Roi Arthur, Le (Strong), 345
Rolvaag, Ole, 440
Roman Catholic church music, 660-62
Romance (Johns, C.), 639
Romance of the Rose, The (Spelman), 470-471
Romance with Double Bass (Dubensky), 477
Roman Sketches (Griffes), 391
Romantic Composers, The (Mason, D. G.), 378
Romantic Symphony (Hanson), 430, 431
Romany Life (Herbert), 718
Romberg, Sigmund (1887-1951), 727, 729-730, 735, 740, 744, 810
Rome, Harold J. (1908-   ), 744
Romeo and Juliet (Bendix), 361
Romeo and Juliet (Nordoff), 508
Rome Radio Orchestra, 611, 617
Rome String Quartet, 464
Ronald, Landon, 164
Rondo (Moller), 104
Rondo and Variations for Two Pianos (Herz), 204
Rondo Appassionato (Smith), 380
Roofs (MacGimsey), 637
Roosevelt, Franklin D., 447, 452, 719, 749
Roosevelt, Theodore, 386, 494-495
Root, Bella, 705
Root, George Frederick (1820-1895), 140, 264-266, 810
Root, Hog or Die, 181
Rope, The (Mennini), 589
Rorem, Ned (1923-   ), 608-610
Rosa (Reinagle), 80
Rosalie (Gershwin), 735

Rosalie (Romberg), 730
Rosalie, the Prairie Flower (Root), 265
Rosary, The (Nevin), 622
Rose, Billy, 558, 736
Rose, David (1910-   ), 754
Rose, Leonard, 535
Rose Marie (Friml), 729
Rosemary (Thompson, R.), 443
Rosenfeld, Monroe H., 706
Rosenfeld, Paul, 324, 327, 348, 435
Rosenwald Fellowship, 462, 517
Rose of Algeria, The (Herbert, V.), 717
Rose of Alhambra, The (Hosmer), 388
Rose of Arragon, The (Taylor R.), 93
Rose of Killarney (Cooper-Thomas), 703
Rose of Sharon, The (Billings), 54
Rosina (Pelissier), 96
Ross, George Maxim, 611
Ross, Jerry (1926-1955), 748
Rossini, Gioacchino, 160, 239
Rossini, Rev. Carlo (1890-   ), 661
Rosten, Norman, 598
Roth, Philip (?-1804), 107-108, 120
Rothschild Foundation for the Arts and
    Sciences, 583
Rothwell, Walter Henry (1872-1927),
    411, 623, 662
Rounded Up in Glory, 638, 693
Rounds for String Orchestra (Diamond),
    544
Rousel, Hubert, 551
Roussel, Albett, 412
Roustabout Songs of the Ohio River
    (Reddick), 636
Rowson, Mrs. S. H., 80
Royal Academy, Munich, 380
Royal Academy of Music, Budapest, 530
Royal Academy of Music, London, 658
Royal College of Music, London, 522
Royal Conservatory, England, 650
Royal Conservatory, Rome, 662
Royal Opera in Berlin, 386
Royal School of Church Music, London,
    657
Royal Vagabond, The (Cohan), 719
Royce, Edward (1886-   ), 415, 512
Ruber, Cornelius, 417
Rubinstein, Nicholas, 278, 290, 334
Rubios, Los (Moore), 387
Ruby, Harry (1895-   ), 751
Ruby, The (Dello Joio), 543
Ruck, Sir John Thomas, 653
Rudhyar, Dane (1895-   ), 476

Rudiments of Music (Law), 48
*Rudiments of the art of playing the
    pianoforte*, 131
Rüfer, Philippe Bartholomé, 390, 416
Ruggles, Carl (1876-   ), 368-370, 424,
    810
Rummel, Franz, 639
Rumor, A (Creston), 492
Runaway Girl, The (Caryll), 716
Running for Office (Cohan), 719
Runyon, Damon, 747
Rural Harmony (Kimball), 64
Rural Life, A (Hewitt), 87
Rural Retreat, The (Selby), 68
Rural Revels (Demarque), 109
Russell,   Alexander   (1881-1953),   640,
    810
Russell,   Henry   (1812-1900),   157,   159,
    160-164, 810
Russell, Lillian, 714, 715
Russian Bells (Dubensky), 477
Russian Dances (Barrymore), 389
Russian Lullaby (Berlin), 733
Russians (Mason, D. G.), 378
Russian Symphony Orchestra, 405
Rustic Dance (Leplin), 588
Rustic Song (Demarest), 624
Ruszta (Zoltan Kurthy), 530
Rutgers State University, 601
Ruth (De Leone), 420
Ryan, Thomas, 213, 215
Rybner, Cornelius, 454, 623
Ryder, Thomas Philander (1836-1887),
    667
Ryskind, Morrie, 734, 735

S

Saar, Louis Victor (1868-1937), 360-361
Sabbath Evening Service (Jacobi), 460,
    662
Sabbath Eve Service (Binder), 663
Sabbath School Songs (Mason, L.), 141
Sabin, Robert, 369, 395, 431, 440, 445,
    593, 598, 600, 603, 606
Sacco and Vanzetti (Blitzstein), 497
Sacco-Vanzetti (Crawford), 500
Sacred Choruses, Ancient and Modern
    (Dickinson), 653
Sacred Harp, The, 664
Sacred Harp singers, 56-57, 666
Sacred Melodies (Gardner), 138
Sacred Service (Bloch), 394, 662

Sacrifice, The (Converse, F. S.), 381
Saenger, Gustav. (1865-1935), 639
Safie (Hadley), 376
Saga of King Olaf (Buck), 646
Saga of the Prairie (Copland), 480
Sahdji (Still), 462
Sailor's Landlady, The, 80
Sailor's Love Song, A (Scott), 625
Sailors of Toulon (Rogers, B.), 447
St. *Anne* (Crofts), 17
St. Anne's Church (Annapolis), 91
St. *Augustine's Prayer* (Howard), 635
St. Cecilia Society, 30, 34
St. Cloud Civic Choir, 414
St. *Dunstan Psalter and Kyrial* (Douglas), 651
St. *Florian,* 6
St. *Francis of Assisi* (Wetzler), 389
St. *Gregory Hymnal* (Montani), 660
Saint Joan (Nordoff), 508
St. *John* (Parker), 296
St. *Louis Blues* (Handy), 688
St. Louis Institute of Music, 360
St. Louis Musical Fund Society, 270
St. Louis Opera Association, 742
St. Louis Symphony Orchestra, 383, 447, 458, 568
St. *Louis Woman* (Arlen), 741
St. Louis World's Fair, 300, 375, 720
St. *Michael,* 7
Saint of Bleecker Street, The (Menotti), 537
Saint Olaf Choir, 652, 793
St. Paul's Chapel (New York), 35
St. *Peter* (Paine), 300
St. Petersburg Conservatory of Music, 478, 641
Saint-Saëns, Camille, 622, 716
Saint Vartan (Hovhaness), 550
Salammbô's Invocation to Tanith (Gilbert), 355
Sales, Regina de, 627
Saliment, George, 74, 84
Sally (Kern), 731
Sally, a Pastoral (Holyoke), 63
Sally in our Alley (Carey), 127
Salome (Hadley), 377
Salón México, El (Copland), 480
Salter, Mary Turner (1856-1938), 622
Salter, Sumner (1856-1944), 622, 648-649
Salutation (Boatwright), 659
Salutation (Gaines), 633
Salute to Spring (Loewe), 742, 743

Salzburg Festival, 366
Salzedo, Carlos (1885-1961), 413-414
Salzman, Eric, 615
Samaroff, Olga, 547
Sam Bass (Fox), 638
Same Boat, Brother (Robinson), 629
Saminsky, Lazare (1882-1959), 422-423, 508, 662, 810-811
Samson Agonistes (Starer), 620
Samson and Delilah, music for (Young), 753
Sanctuary (Converse, F. S.), 381
Sand (Howe), 421
Sandburg, Carl, 510, 515, 549, 559, 629, 696-697
Sandby, Hermann, 407
Sandel, Andreas, 25
Sanders, Robert L. (1906-   ), 520-521
Sandhog (Robinson), 629
San Diego Philharmonic, 464
Sandy Gibson's, or Chaw Roast Beef (Emmett), 182-183
San Francisco *Chronicle,* 397, 569, 588
San Francisco Conservatory, 393, 421
San Francisco Music and Art Institute, 477
San Francisco *News-Call Bulletin,* 435
San Francisco Orchestra, 438, 463, 473, 519, 569, 721
San Francisco Overture (La Violette), 475
San Francisco Suite (Grofé), 467
San Juan Capistrano (McDonald), 463
Sankey, Ira David (1840-1908), 667-668, 811
Santa Barbara School, 518
Santa Claus Overture (Shelley), 647
Santa Claus Symphony (Fry), 245-247
Santa Fe Opera Association, 595
Santa Fe Trail (McDonald), 463
Sappho (Glanville-Hicks), 566
Sarabande (McPhee), 528
Saracens, The (MacDowell), 331, 335
Sarah (Laderman), 598
Sarah Lawrence College, 533, 542, 583, 603
Saratoga (Arlen), 741
Sargent, Winthrop, 440, 605
Saroni, H., 248
Saroyan, William, 600
Satan (Horn), 156
Satiric Fragments (Phillips), 509
Satter, Gustav, 293

Saturday Night (Kay), 557
Saturday Night (Sanders), 520
Saturday's Child (Whithorne), 410
Saturnale (Buzzi-Peccia), 622
Saugatuck Suite (Gershefski), 501
Savage Serenade (Hupfield), 750
Saved by the Blood (Doane), 666
Savior, Teach Me (Holler), 658
Saviour, Like a Shepherd Lead Me
　(Bradbury), 146
Savoyard, or the Repentant Seducer,
　songs for (Reinagle), 80
Sawyer, Charles Carroll, 264
Saxonia Band, 300
Say, Darling (Styne), 745
Sayers, Henry (1854-1929), 706
Say It with Songs, score for (Hender-
　son), 739
Sayles, James M., 703
Scalero, Rosario, 468, 469, 496, 531, 536,
　566, 567, 591, 628, 632
Scanlan, William, 705
Scarecrow, The (Lockwood), 515
Scarecrow Sketches (Converse, F. S.),
　382
Scarf, The (Hoiby), 599
Scarlet Letter, The (Damrosch, W.),
　351, 353
Scarlet Letter, The (Giannini), 494
Scenario (Kern), 732
Scenes from the Golden Legend (Buck),
　645
Scenes in California (Stewart), 362
Scenes of Poverty and Toil (Sanders),
　520
Schaffer, Louis, 131
Scharfenberg, William (1819-1895), 154-
　156, 159
Scharfenberg & Luis, 155
Scharwenka, Franz Xaver, 638, 639
Schaunsee, Max de, 594
Schelling, Ernest (1876-1939), 383
Schelomo (Bloch), 392
Scherman, Thomas, 544
Scherzino (Johns, C.), 639
Scherzo (Riegger), 397
Scherzo and Dirge (Sanders), 521
Scherzo Diabolique (Hadley), 377
Scherzo Fantastique (Bloch), 395
Scherzo Humoristique (Copland), 485
Schetky, George (1776-1831), 108
Schillinger, Joseph (1895-1943), 457, 500,
　520, 617

*Schillinger System of Musical Composi-
　tion, The,* 457
Schillings, Max, 415
Schindler, Kurt (1882-1935), 634
Schirmer, Gustave, Music Company, 155,
　375, 391, 515, 532, 533, 569, 605,
　624, 630
Schirmer-Mapleson Opera Company, 376
Schlesinger, Daniel (1799-1839), 151,
　154, 811
Schmidt, Arthur P., 301
Schmidt, Henry, 275
Schmidt, John Henry, 109
Schnabel, Artur, 416, 500, 631, 640
Schneider, Friedrich, 645
Schneider, John, 39
Schoenberg, Arnold, 396, 397, 474, 496,
　507, 520, 529, 546, 551, 560, 571,
　576, 578, 607
Schoenefeld, Henry (1857-1936), 362
Schola Cantorum, 592, 634, 737
Schola Cantorum, Paris, 412
scholarships (*see* fellowships)
Schonberg, Harold C., 486, 535, 574
Schoolcraft, Henry Rowe, 673
School Days (Edwards), 708
School for Modern Art, 525
School for Scandal, The, Overture (Bar-
　ber), 531
schools, music in, 139, 143
Schoontree (Cowell), 449
Schott International Prize, 478
Schroeder, Alvin, 396
Schroeder, William, 811
Schubert, Franz, 360, 730
Schubert Centennial Contest, 469
Schuberth, Julius, 275
Schuckburg, Dr., 116, 118
Schuller, Gunter (1925-　　), 615-616
Schultze, William, 215
Schuman, William (1910-　　), 533-535,
　542, 547, 589, 616, 746, 811
Schumann, Clara, 203, 625
Schumann-Heink, Ernestine, 371, 382
Schwartz, Arthur (1900-　　), 739
Scientific Creation (Engel, A. L.), 556
Scissors Grinder, The (Guion), 636
Scollard, Clinton, 624, 630
Scotch jigs, 177
　and minstrelsy, 179-180
Scotch Poem, The (MacDowell), 330
Scott, Cyril, 407
Scott, John Prindle (1877-1932), 625

Scott, Raymond (1909-), 753-754
Scott, Sir Walter, 645
Scott, Tom, 697, 811
Scott, Walter, Foundation, 469
Scottish Psalter, 10
Scouts, The (Hewitt, J. H.), 169
Scriabin, Alexander, 395, 476, 576
Sea, The (MacDowell), 332
Sea, The (Oldberg), 387
Sea Calm (Green), 19
Sea Chanty (White, P.), 472
Sea Drift (Carpenter), 372
Sea Gardens (Cooke), 639
Sea God's Daughter, The (Bornschein), 388
Sea Pieces (MacDowell), 326, 330
Sea Piece with Birds (Thomson), 434
Search, Frederick Preston (1889-), 422
Search Me, O Lord (Main), 667
Sea Rovers, The (Spelman), 471
Sea-Shell, The (Engel, C.), 630
Sea Symphony (James), 468
Sea Symphony (Williams), 372
Seattle Symphony Orchestra, 376, 469
Sebastian (Menotti), 538
Second Essay for Orchestra (Barber), 531
Second Hurricane, The (Copland), 481
Secret, The, 212
Secret, The (Scott), 625
Secular Games (Starer), 620
secular music, nineteenth-century, 150-210
See America First (Porter), 737
See, down Maria's blushing cheek (Hopkinson), 42
Seeger, Charles, 448, 500
Seeonee Wolves, The (Ayres), 376
Seidl, Anton, 287
Seidl Fellowship, 617, 632
Seine at Night, The (Thomson), 434
Seldes, Gilbert, 426
Select Harmony (Law), 60
Selection of Sacred Harmony (Adgate), 107
Selection of Scotch, English, Irish and Foreign Airs (Aird), 680-681
Selections from McGuffey's Readers (Phillips), 509
Select Number of Plain Tunes (Law), 60
Select Psalms and Hymns (Adgate), 107

Sentimental Colloquy (Bowles), 582
Sentimental Journey, A (Goldman), 642
Sentimental Sketches (Mason, D. G.), 378
Septet (Stevens), 519
Sequin, Arthur, 239
Sequin opera troupe, 239
Serenade (Allen), 420
Serenade (Barber), 533
Serenade (Bernstein), 540
Serenade (Blitzstein), 497
Serenade (Boatwright), 659
Serenade (Bucci), 598
Serenade (Delamarter), 417
Serenade (Dello Joio), 542
Serenade (Donato), 512
Serenade (Donovan), 455
Serenade (Foote), 312
Serenade (Grimm), 476
Serenade (Imbrie), 606
Serenade (Inch), 511
Serenade (Kay), 564
Serenade (Keller), 562
Serenade (Korn), 620
Serenade (Mason, D. G.), 378
Serenade (Mason, W.), 249
Serenade (Shifrin), 616
Serenade (Smith), 630
Serenade (Sowerby), 657
Serenade (Starer), 620
Serenade Concertante (Berger), 563
Serenade for Strings (Weber), 568
Serenade in D (Shapero), 602
Serenades (Herbert), 426
Serenades (Persichetti), 549
Serenade to a Beauteous Lady (Gruenberg), 410
Serenade to San Francisco (Duke), 526
Serenata (Piston), 445
Serenata d'Estate (Rochberg), 567
Serious Song (Fine), 571
Serly, Tibor (1900-), 529
Serpent Heart, The (Barber), 532
Sessions, Roger (1896-), 393, 452-454, 498, 508, 522, 530, 544, 546, 556, 565, 566, 583, 587, 610, 811
Sestina (Fitch), 511
Set of Four, A (Sowerby), 657
Set of Three, A (Powell), 406
Seven Ages, The (Carpenter), 373
7½ Cents (Bissell), 748
Seven Contrasts (Perry), 613

Seven Kentucky Mountain Songs (Niles), 637

Seven Lively Arts, The (Porter), 737

Seven Lively Arts, The (Schuman), 534

Seven Movements for Seven Instruments (Sydenam), 610

Seven Negro Exaltations (Niles), 637

Seven Pastorales (Harrison), 577

Seven Rituals of Music, The (Cowell), 450

Seven Songs (Hopkinson), 41-42

Seven Studies on Themes of Paul Klee (Schuller), 615-616

Seven Words, 83

Severn, Edmund (1862-1942), 362

Sewall, Samuel, 16, 20, 22, 24

Seze, Madame de, 83

Shadows on the Wall (Hewitt, J. H.), 161, 166, 169

Shadrach (MacGimsey), 637

Shah Geridoun (Fairchild), 388

Shakespearean Concerto (Amram), 618

Shakespeare Sonnet (Riegger), 399

Shallenberg, Robert, 509

Shall We Gather at the River?, 433

Shanewis (Cadman), 403

shanty boy songs, 694-695

Shanty-man's Alphabet, 695

Shanty Man's Life, 695

Shape Alone Let Others Prize, A (Gram), 63

Shapero, Harold (1920-   ), 602-603, 767

Shapleigh, Bertram (1871-1940), 383

Sharp, Cecil, 692

Shaw, Artie, (1910-   ), 724

Shaw, George Bernard, 743

Shaw, Oliver (1779-1848), 134-136, 811

Shaw, Robert, 569

Shaw, Robert, Chorale, 590

Sheafe, William, 23

She Didn't Say Yes (Kern), 732

Sheep and Goat Walkin' to Pasture (Guion), 636

Shelf Behind the Door (Vardell), 466

Shelley, Harry Rowe (1858-1947), 357, 365, 470, 644, 647

She Never Blamed Him, Never (Bayly), 162

Shepherd, Arthur (1880-1958), 404-405, 551, 631, 811-812

Shepherds of Bethlehem, The (Demarest), 625

Sherlock Holmes (McBride), 643

Sherwood, Robert, 734

Sherwood, William Hall (1854-1911), 280, 292, 356, 649

Sherwood Piano School, 292

She's a Good Fellow (Kern), 731

She's the Daughter of Mother Machree (Ball), 707

She Went to the City (Dresser), 707

She Wore a Wreath of Roses (Knight), 159

Shifrin, Seymour (1926-   ), 616

Shine on, O Star! (Sankey), 668

Shingandi (Guion), 637

Shining Shore, The (Root), 265, 266

Ship That Never Returned, The (Work), 267

Shipwrecked Mariner Preserved, The (Taylor, R.), 94

Shir L'Erev Shabbat (Amram), 619

Shoestring Composer, The (Brokeman), 528

Sho-Gun (Luders), 719

Shop Around the Corner, The (Bock), 749

Short Concert (Kohs), 570

Short Mass in Honor of St. Pius X (Rossini), 662

Shortnin' Bread (Wolfe), 637

Short Overture, A (Kay), 564

Short Suite for Brass (Meyerowitz), 585

Short Symphony (Swanson), 517

Showboat (Ferber-Kern), 730, 731, 732

Show Girl (Gershwin), 735

Show Is On, The (Duke), 525

Showpiece (Gould), 553

Shuffle Along, 462

Shuffle Off to Buffalo (Warren), 751

Shulman, Alan (1915-   ), 582

Shylock (La Violette), 475

Sibelius, Jean, 430, 431, 464, 558

Sibelius Medal, 513

Sich a Gitting Upstairs, 179

Sicilian Romance, 80

Side Show (McBride), 643

Sideshow (Schuman), 535

Sidewalks of New York, The (Lawlor), 708, 713

Sidney, Thomas, 731

Siegel, Rudolf, 411

Siege of Belgrade, The (Pelissier), 96

Siege of Tottenburg, The (Helm), 584

Siegmeister, Elie (1909-   ), 514

Sierra Morena (Whithorne), 410
Sights and Sounds (Bennett), 461
Sigman, Carl, 608
Silesian Symphony (Meyerowitz), 585
Silk Stockings (Porter), 738
Silly Symphonies, 628
Siloti, Alexander, 496
Silver Bell (Weinrich), 709
Silver Spring (Mason, W.), 280
Silver Threads Among the Gold (Danks-Rexford), 667
Silver World, The (Rogers, B.), 447
Simfony in Free Style (Harrison), 577
Simmons College, 608
Simon, Robert A., 448, 461
Simple Gifts, Shaker melody, 483
Simple Simon (Rodgers-Hart), 739
Sinbad, 425
Sinbad the Sailor (Converse, F. S.), 381
Since You Are Gone (Reddick), 636
Sinding, Christian, 463, 511
Sinfonia (Moller), 104
Sinfonia Breve (Bloch), 395
Sinfonia Concertante (Diamond), 545
Sinfonia Concertante (Giorni), 476
Sinfonia Concertante (Phillips), 509
Sinfonia in E (Kay), 564
Sinfonia in Two Parts (Kirchner), 546
Sinfonia Sacra (Hanson), 430, 431
Sinfonietta (Berezowsky), 525
Sinfonietta (Diamond), 544
Sinfonietta (Donato), 512
Sinfonietta (Herrmann), 554
Sinfonietta (Levant), 520
Sinfonietta (Naginski), 522
Sinfonietta (Riegger), 399
Sinfonietta (Rudhyar), 476
Sinfonietta (Smith), 618
Sinfonietta (Wagenaar), 456
Sinfonietta (Waxman), 529
Sinfoniettas (Hill), 374
Sing for Your Supper (Robinson), 629
singing families, 173-175
Singing Fool, The, score for (Henderson), 739
Singing Soldiers (Niles), 637, 726
Sing Out, Sweet Land (Siegmeister), 514
Sing Out the News (Rome), 744
Sing Something Simple (Hupfield), 750
Singstunde, Bethlehem, Pennsylvania, 28
Sing to Me, Sing (Homer), 623
Sing We Then Those Glorious Strains (Matthews), 653

Sing We This Day (Bedell), 638
Sinister Resonance (Cowell), 449
Sintram (Strong), 344
Siren Song, The (Taylor), 400
Sire of Maledroit, The (Duke), 631
Sir Roger de Coverley (Crouch), 172
Sisters, The (Bendix), 361
Sit Down, You're Rocking the Boat (Loesser), 747
Sitt, Hans, 385, 662
Six Characters in Search of an Author (Weisgall), 566
Six Etudes (Talma), 514
Six Ings—Floating, Frisking, Fleeting, Scooting, Wafting, Seething (Cowell), 449
Six Italian Dances (De Leone), 420
Six Love Songs (Dello Joio), 544
Six Minutes for Twelve (Shulman), 582
Six Songs on Poems of Robert Frost (McKay), 464
Six Symphonic Movements (Wetzler), 389
Skeleton in Armor, The (Foote), 312
Skelly, J. P., 703
Skeptic's Lament, The (Russell), 161
Sketches of New York (Manning), 627
Sketches of Paris (Manning), 627
Sketches of the City (Read), 589
Skidmore Fancy Ball (Braham), 713
Skilton, Charles Sanford (1868-1941), 357-358, 700, 812
Skinner, John S., 122
Skyscrapers (Carpenter), 371, 372
Skyscrapers (Leplin), 588
Slaughter on Tenth Avenue (Rodgers), 740
Slave, The (Freeman), 361
Slaves in Algiers, songs for (Reinagle), 80
Slave Songs (Allen-Garrison), 684
Slavic Rhapsody (Reiser), 424
Sleep Music (Cowell), 449
Sleepy Hollow (Lane), 640
Sleepy Hollow (Maretzek), 298
Sleepy Hollow (Mourant), 562
Sleepy Time Gal (Whiting), 749
Sleigh, The (Kountz), 628
Sleigh Ride (Anderson), 642
Slonimsky, Nicolas (1894-), 410, 435, 452, 530, 548, 550, 570, 602, 641
Slovakian Rhapsody (Kolar), 424

Slow Dance (Avshalomov), 586

Slow Dusk (Floyd), 594

Slumber Boat (Gaynor), 623

Smattering of Ignorance, A (Levant), 520

Smile From the Girl of My Heart, A (Pownall), 108

Smiles (Roberts), 726

Smiles (Youmans), 736

Smit, Leo (1921-   ), 604-605

Smith, David Stanley (1877-1949), 316, 379-380, 440, 456, 500, 522, 812

Smith, Elihu Hubbard, 94, 95

Smith, Harry B., 731

Smith, John Stafford, 124-125

Smith, Julia (1911-   ), 569

Smith, Kate, 733

Smith, Russell (1927-   ), 617-618

Smith, Samuel Francis (1808-1895), 127-128, 143

Smith, Warren Storey (1885-   ), 608, 630

Smith College, 411, 452, 455, 476, 498, 551, 631

Smoke and Steel (Donovan), 455

Smoke Gets in Your Eyes (Kern), 732

Smugglers, The (Sousa), 715

Sneller, Joseph, 443

Snowbird, The (Stearns), 420

Snowdrop (Spelman), 470

Snow White, music for (Churchill), 751

sob-song, beginnings of, 99

Social Sacred Melodist, The (Shaw), 135

Society for the Publication of American Music, 359, 378, 414, 418, 476, 518, 522, 548, 551, 607, 614, 680, 681, 757-758

Society of American Musicians and Composers, 759

Society of European Stage Authors and Composers (SESAC), 761

Society of Participating Artists, 763

Society Whirl, The (Kerker), 714

So Fades the Lovely Blooming Flower (Steele), 147

Softly, as in a Morning Sunrise (Romberg), 730

Softly as the Breezes Blowing (Capron), 104

So in Love (Porter), 738

Soirées Musicales, 157

Sojourner and Mollie Sinclair, The (Floyd), 596

Sokolow, Anna, 398

Soldier, The (Engel), 556

Soldier of the Cross, A (Sankey), 668

Soldier's Dream, The (Carr), 100

Soldier Songs (Weisgall), 566

Soldiers on the Town (Berezowsky), 525

Solemn March in E Minor (Noble), 651

Solemn Music, A (Thomson), 434

Soliloquy (Rogers, B.), 446, 447

Solitude (Koutzen), 529

Solitude in the City (Donato), 512

Solitude of the Prairie (Bull), 202

Solomon and Balkis (Thompson, R.), 444

Solstice (Harrison), 577

Somebody Loves You (De Rose), 753

Some Day My Prince Will Come (Churchill), 751

Some Music; Some More Music (Cowell), 449

Something for the Boys (Porter), 737

Something to Remember You By (Schwartz), 739

Something Wild, score for (Copland), 486

Sometime (Friml), 729

Sometimes I'm Happy (Youmans), 736

Somewhere Else (Luders), 719

Somnambula, La, 270

Sonata Brevis (Read), 559

Sonata Concertante (Mennin), 590

Sonata da Camera (Weber), 568

Sonata da Chiesa (Read), 559

Sonata da Chiesa (Thomson), 432, 434

Sonata for the Pianoforte (Taylor, R.), 93

Sonata Noble (Powell), 406

Sonatas (Hill), 374

Sonatas (Mason), 378

Sonata Sacra (Brant), 576

Sonata Seria (Dahl), 565

Sonatas for the Pianoforte (Reinagle), 80

Sonata Tripartite (Nevin, Gordon B.), 650

Sonata, Variations, and Introduction and Workout (Raphling), 558

Sonata Virginianesque (Powell), 406

Sonate Savage (Antheil), 490

Sonatina Giocosa (Stevens), 520

Sonatina per pianoforte (Moevs), 602

Sonatinas (Hill), 374
Sonatine (Citkowitz), 530
Sonatine Romantique (Tcherepnin), 477
Sondheim, Stephen, 745
Song and Dance (Wessel), 475
Song Cycle to Words of Joyce (Citkowitz), 530
Song for Occupations (Harris), 438
Song for St. Cecilia's Day (Boatwright), 659
Song for Warriors (Fletcher), 580
Song Garden, The (Mason, L.), 141
Song Is So Old (Terry), 623
Song Is You, The (Kern), 732
Song My Heart Is Singing, The (MacDermid), 625
Song of Affirmation (Dello Joio), 542
Song of America, The (Matthews), 653
Song of Anguish (Foss), 592
Song of a Thousand Years, The (Work), 267
Song of Capri, The (Wood-Hill), 623
Song of Death (Webb), 144
Song of Democracy (Hanson), 431
Song of Faith (Carpenter), 373
Song of Freedom (Carpenter), 373
Song of India (Rimsky-Korsakoff), 722
Song of Jael (Daniels), 386
Song of Jeremiah (Kay), 565
Song of Life (Gleason), 304
Song of Night (James), 468
Song of Orpheus, A (Schuman), 535
Song of Palms (Howe), 421
Song of Persia (Cowles), 641
Song of Promise (Paine), 300
Song of Quextecoatl (Harrison), 577
Song of Songs, The (Foss), 592
Song of Songs, The (Grimm), 475
Song of the Angels, The (La Violette), 475
Song of the Nightingale, The (Rogers, B.), 447
Song of the Open (La Forge), 626
Song of the Pilgrims (Shepherd), 405
Song of the Sea (Converse, F. S.), 381
Song of the Sea Wind (Shepherd), 405
Song of the Shirt (Homer), 623
Song of the South, 260-261
Song of the Vagabonds (Friml), 729
Song of the Waving Willow, 87
Song of Welcome (Beach), 322
Songs and Ballads of the Maine Lumberjacks (Gray), 695

Songs and Scissors (Gaynor), 623
Songs for a Rainy Day (Read), 559
Songs from a Chinese Lute (Woltmann), 512
Songs from Mother Goose (Homer), 623
Songs My Mother Never Taught Me (Niles), 726
Songs of Conquest (McDonald), 463
Songs of Elfland (Daniels), 385
Songs of India (Strickland), 627
Songs of Solitude and Pleasure (Rorem), 609
Songs of the Hill-Folk (Niles), 634
Songs of the Rose of Sharon (La Montaine), 613
Songs of the Sable Harmonists (Foster), 187
Songs of the Self (Weaver), 628
Songster's Assistant (Swan), 63
Songs to Little Folks (Gaynor), 623
song writers, early, 158
Song Writers' Protective Association, 727, 730
Sonic Countours (Ussachevsky), 503
Sonini, Michael, 556
Son-in-Law, The (Pelissier), 96
Sonneck, Oscar G. (1873-1928), 113, 116, 118, 124, 624, 812
Sonoric Fantasia (Read), 559
Sons of the South (Blackmar), 262
Sontag, Henriette, 204
Sooner and Later (Whithorne), 410
Sophia of Brabant (Pelissier), 96
Sophisticated Lady (Ellington), 724
Sorrows of Death (Coombs), 650
Sosi-Forest of Prophetic Sounds (Hovhaness), 551
Sosland, Rheta A., Award, 613
So This Is Jazz (Osgood), 426
Sound of Music, The (Rodgers-Hammerstein), 741
Sound Piece (Read), 559
Sound Pieces (Becker), 415
Sound the Alarm (Doane), 666
Sourwood Mountain (Farwell), 692
Sousa, John Philip (1854-1932), 557, 709-711, 715, 812
Sousa and Parnassum (Barlow, S.), 472
South Carolina Federation of Music Clubs, 501
Southern California, University of, 517, 519, 546, 555, 565, 569, 570
Southern Girl, The, 262

Southern Harmony, The (Jackson), 664
Southern Interlude, A (Still), 462
Southern Night (Steinert), 523
Southern Nights (Bornschein), 388
Southern Rhapsody (Hosmer), 388
Southern Symphony (Britain), 521
South Pacific (Rodgers-Hammerstein), 740
Southwark Theatre, Philadelphia, 71, 227
Southwest, music in, 270
South Wind (Maganini), 474
Souvenir de Baden-Baden (Shelley), 647
Souvenir de Venise (Duke), 526
Souvenirs (Barber), 532
Sowerby, Leo (1895-   ), 656-657, 658, 812
Spaeth, Sigmund, 158, 706, 707
Spalding, Albert (1888-1953), 422, 442, 812
Spalding, Walter Raymond, 369, 416, 470
Spanish-American War, 121, 707, 708
Spanish Barber, 80
Spanish Castle (Hewitt), 90
Spanish Underground (Brant), 576
Speaking of Pianists (Chasins), 641
Speaks, Oley (1876-1948), 624, 727
Spectra (Schuller), 616
Speicher, Eugene, 461
Spelman, Timothy Mather (1891-   ), 470-471
Spencer, Allen, 658
Spencer, Willard (1852-1933), 714
Spewack, Sam and Bella, 738
Spiering, Theodore, 360, 662
Spiritual Folk Songs of Early America (Jackson), 664
Spiritual Music Dramas (Whitmer), 652
spirituals, 636, 665, 682-683, 685-86
Spokes, Gary, 508
Spoleto Festival (*see* Festival of Two Worlds)
Spoon River (Grainger), 407
Spring (Paine), 301
Springfield Collection of hymns (Warriner), 141
Springfield Festival, 310
Springfield Mountain, 484
Spring Is Here (Rodgers-Hart), 740
Spring Pastoral (Howe), 421

Springs of Saratoga (Nevin, A.), 386
Springtime Overture (Leidzen), 641
Spross, Charles Gilbert (1874-1961), 624
Squatter Sovereignty (Harrigan-Braham), 713-714
Squirrel, The (Weaver), 655
Stabat Mater (Giannini), 495
Stabat Mater (Hollingsworth), 600
Stabat Mater (Meyerowitz), 585
Stabat Mater (Montani), 660
Stabat Mater (Perry), 613
Stabat Mater (Persichetti), 549
Stabat Mater (Thomson), 434
Stadium Concerts (*see* Lewisohn Stadium Concerts
Stadler, John, 39
Stadt Theatre of Mayence, 376
Stambler, Bernard, 561
Standing in the Need (Weaver), 628
Standin' in the Need of Prayer (Gruenberg), 408
Standin' in the Need of Prayer (Reddick), 636
Standish, Miles, 509
Stand Up for the Flag (Foster), 264
Stand Up, Stand Up for Jesus (Webb), 143
Stanford University, 451, 507, 581, 622
Stanley Quartet, 579
Stanzas (Powell), 607
Star, The (Rogers), 649
Stardust (Carmichael), 753
Starer, Robert (1924-   ), 619-620
Star of the Evening (Sayles), 703
Stars (Howe), 421
Stars (Ware), 625
Stars, The (Hovhaness), 551
Stars and Stripes (Kay), 557
Stars and Stripes Forever, The (Sousa), 710
Stars in Your Eyes (Schwartz), 739
Star Song (Parker), 318
Star-Spangled Banner, The (Hewitt), 88
    national anthem, 121-126
Star-Spangled Rhythm (Arlen), 741
State Fair, score for (Rodgers-Hammerstein), 740
Statements (Copland), 480
State of Music, The (Thomson), 433
State Symphony Orchestra (New York), 760

Station WGZBX (James), 468

Stearns, Theodore (1881-1935), 420

Stebbins, George C. (1846-1945), 649, 668

Stebbins, George Waring (1869-1930), 649

Steele, Anne, 147

Steffe, William, 255, 258

Stein, Gertrude, 432, 434

Steinbeck, John, 481, 482, 741

Steinberg, William, 581

Steinert, Alexander Lang (1900-   ), 523

Stein Song (Bullard), 623

Steinway & Sons, 288

Stennet, Samuel, 665

Stephen Foster, America's Troubadour (Howard), 187

Stephen Foster: Theme Variations, and Finale (Dubensky), 477

Step into My Parlor (Phillips), 510

Stepney, Francis, 20

Stepping Stones (Kern), 731

Sternberg, Constantin Von (1852-1924), 490, 638

Stern Conservatory, Berlin, 415

Sterne's Maria, or The Vintage (Pelissier), 95

Sternhold and Hopkins, 5-7, 10, 15, 16

Stevens, David, 310

Stevens, Halsey (1908-   ), 519-520, 601, 812

Stevensoniana Suites (Hill), 374

Stewart, Humphrey John (1856-1932), 362

Stewball Variations (Kubik), 555

Steyermark Orchestra, 215

Stickney, John, 48

Stiles, Ezra, 19

Still, William Grant (1895-   ), 461-462, 812

Stilled Pageant (Saminsky), 423

Stock, Frederick (1872-1942), 289, 623

Stoessel, Albert (1894-1943), 447-448, 554, 560

Stojowski, Sigismond (1870-1946), 384, 520, 625

Stokes, Richard L., 431

Stokowski, Leopold, 368, 369, 378, 396, 479, 491, 542, 553, 581, 611, 766-767

Stone, Kurt, 612

Stone, Malcolm N., 88

Stone, Mrs. George Whitefield, 130

Stop-Watch and Ordnance Map, A (Barber), 531

Storm King, The (Baker, B. F.), 148

Storm King Overture (Leidzen), 641

Stormy Weather (Arlen), 741

Story of Christmas, The (Matthews), 655

Story of Christmas, The (Titcomb), 654

Story of the Cross, The (Buck), 646

Stothart, Herbert, 729, 736

Stoughton Musical Society, 55, 133

Stouthearted Men (Romberg), 730

Strang, Gerald (1908-   ), 507

Stranger, The, 80

Stranger of Manzano, The (Smith) 569

Strauss, Johann, 297

Strauss, Noel, 584, 585

Stravinsky, Igor, 557, 560, 562, 563, 570, 602, 604

Strawberry Jam (Home Made) (McBride), 643

Streamline (Gershefski), 501

Street Corner Concerto (Kleinsinger), 643

Streets of Florence (Johnson, H.), 628

Streets of Pekin, The (Hadley), 377

Strickland, Edward, 546

Strickland, Lily (1887-1958), 627

Strict Songs (Harrison), 577

Strike Up the Band (Gershwin), 735

Stringfield, Lamar (1897-1959), 464-465

Stringham, Edwin John (1890-   ), 472-473, 508

String Quartet on American Indian Themes (Kurthy), 530

String Quartet on Indian Themes (Jacobi), 459

String Quartet on Negro Themes (Mason, D. G.), 378

String Quartet on Negro Themes (White), 636

String Symphony (Helm), 584

Strolling on the Brooklyn Bridge (Cooper-Skelly), 703

Stromberg, John ("Honey") (1853-1902), 715

Strong, C. A., 88

Strong, George Templeton (1856-1948), 344-345

Stronger, The (Weisgall), 566

Strube, Gustav (1867-1953), 362-363, 421, 527

Stuart, Leslie, 716
Studenten-schmauss (Binkerd), 571
Student Prince, The (Romberg), 730
Studies in Song (Sonneck), 624
Study (Sydenam), 610
Study in Black and White (Slonimsky), 641
Study in Sonority (Riegger), 396-397
Stumbling (Confrey), 752
Stuyvesant Quartet, 582
Styne, Jule (1905-   ), 744-746
Subways Are for Sleeping (Styne), 746
Sudden Light (Golde), 631
Sue, Dear (Grey), 640
Suesse, Dana (1911-   ), 557-558
Sugar Cane Rag (Joplin), 720
Suite Antique (Stoessel), 448
Suite Caractéristique (Schoenefeld), 362
Suite Fantastique (Schelling), 383
Suite for Large Orchestra (Sanders), 520
Suite for Strings (James), 648
Suite from a Children's Film (Bergsma), 590
Suite Grotesque (Achron), 477
Suite Hébraïque (Bloch), 395
Suite Miniature (Shulman), 582
Suite Modale (Bloch), 395
Suite of American Folk-Tunes (Cadman), 404
Suite of Childhood Tunes Remembered (Luening), 502
Suite Passecaille (Haubiel), 469
Suite Primeval (Skilton), 358
Suite Symphonique (Bloch), 395
Suite Symphonique (Chadwick), 309
Sullivan, Sir Arthur, 707
Summer Evening (Reiser), 424
Summer Music (Barber), 533
Summer Music (Wuorinen), 612
Summer Night (Siegmeister), 514
Summer Scenes (Wigglesworth), 585
Summer Seascape (Hanson), 430
Summertime (Gershwin), 429
Sun, The (Nordoff), 508
Sun Bride, The (Skilton), 358
Sun, Cloud and the Flower, The (Gebhard), 626
Sunday, Billy, 664, 668
Sunday Excursion (Wilder), 510
Sunday in Brooklyn (Siegmeister), 514
Sunday in Mexico (McBride), 643
Sunday Paper (Spelman), 471
Sunday School songs, 145, 146, 600

Sunday Sing Symphony (Green), 518
Sundgaard, Arnold, 440, 510
Sunflower Rag (Joplin), 720
Sunken Bell, The (Ruggles), 369
Sunken City, The (Spelman), 471
Sunlight (Ware), 625
Sunny (Kern), 732
Sunny Side Up, score for (Henderson), 739
Sunset Boulevard, score for (Waxman), 529
Sunset Glow, The (Metcalf), 622
Sunset Trail, The (Cadman), 403
Sunshine for Sunday Schools (Bliss), 667
Sun Splendor (Bauer, M.), 411
Sun Treader (Ruggles), 369
Superior Anthems for Church Choirs (Danks), 667
Supper at Emmäus, The (Rogers, B.), 446
Surge of Fire, The (Rudhyar), 476
Surrealist Suite (Duke), 526
Susanna and the Elders (Moross), 557
Susannah (Floyd), 595
Susannah, Don't You Cry (Loomis), 419
Swan, Timothy (1757-1842), 63
Swan Bent Low, The (MacDowell), 332
Swanee (Gershwin), 425
Swanee River (see *Old Folks at Home*)
Swans (Kramer), 631
Swanson, Howard (1909-   ), 516-517
Swedish Rhapsody (Leidzen), 641
Sweeny, Joe, 177
Sweet Adeline (Kern), 732
Sweet and Low (Homer), 623
Sweet and Lowdown (Gershwin), 425
Sweet Betsy from Pike (Bucci), 597
Sweet Bye and Bye (Beeson), 600
Sweetest and Dearest (Eames), 625
Sweet Genevieve (Cooper-Tucker), 703
"sweet" jazz, 722
Sweet Little Ann (Shaw), 136
Sweet Little Jesus Boy (MacGimsey), 637
Sweet Song of Long Ago (Charles), 631
Sweet Songs of Salvation (Bennard), 668
Sweet Thursday (Steinbeck), 741
Swift and Company, 515, 524
Swing Low, Sweet Chariot, 699
Swing Sextet (Cesana), 467
Swing Stuff (McBride), 643
'S Wonderful (Gershwin), 425

Sword of Robert E. Lee, The (Blackmar), 263

Swords (Howard-Tweedy), 471

Swords and Scissors (MacFarlane), 652

Sydenam, William (1928-   ), 610

Syllabi in Music Theory (Kohs), 570

Sylvan Suite (Brockway), 384

Sylvan Symphony (Maganini), 474

Sylvia (Speaks), 624

Symbolist Studies (Farwell), 375, 376

Symmes, Reverend Doctor, 13-14

Symphonia Sacra (Wuorinen), 612

Symphonic Blues (Kreutz), 509

Symphonic Brevis (Becker), 414

Symphonic Dance (Reed), 579

Symphonic Dance in Basque Style (Wetzler), 389

Symphonic Eclogue (El-Dabh), 619

Symphonic Fantasia (Luening), 502

Symphonic Fantasies (Luening), 502

Symphonic Fantasy (Boyle), 423

Symphonic Fantasy (Wetzler), 389

Symphonic Hymn on March! March! (Farwell), 375

Symphonic Impressions (Eppert) 418

Symphonic Intermezzo (Galajikian), 521

Symphonic Movement (Overton), 614

Symphonic Movements (Parris), 615

Symphonic Ode (Copland), 479, 480

Symphonic Piece (Piston), 444

Symphonic Pieces (Foss), 592

Symphonic Poem (Nevin, A.), 386

Symphonic Prelude (Cole), 360

Symphonic Prelude (Hanson), 430

Symphonic Prelude (Piston), 446

Symphonic Prelude (Shapleigh), 383

Symphonic Prelude to Riders to the Sea (Gilbert), 356

Symphonic Rhapsody (Forst), 522

Symphonic Rhapsody (Hanson), 430

Symphonic Rhapsody (Kramer), 631

Symphonic Rhapsody (Schillinger), 457

Symphonic Serenade (Grofé), 467

Symphonic Sketches (Kramer), 631

Symphonic Sketches on Three American Folktunes (Kreutz), 509

Symphonic Song on Old Black Joe (Farwell), 375

Symphonic Study (Schuller), 616

Symphonic Thesis (Nelson), 611

Symphonic Visions for Orchestra (Berlinski), 587

Symphonie Concertante (Wetzler), 389

Symphonietta (Cowell), 449

Symphonietta (Forst), 521

Symphonietta (Luening), 502

Symphony Concertante (Dahl), 565

Symphony Concertante (Fuleihan), 527

Symphony Concertante (Wessel), 475

Symphony for Classical Orchestra (Shapero), 602

Symphony for Fun (Gillis), 585

Symphony for Voices (Harris), 438, 439

Symphony in C Minor (Schelling), 383

Symphony in D (Brockway), 384

Symphony in E Minor (Cadman), 404

Symphony in E Minor (White), 472

Symphony in F (McCoy), 362

Symphony in Four Movements on Poems of William Blake (Weber), 568

Symphony in G (Sowerby), 657

Symphony in G Minor (Spelman), 471

Symphony in G Minor (Still), 462

Symphony in Miniature (Haines), 583

Symphony in One Movement (Barber), 531

Symphony in One Movement (Carpenter), 372

Symphony in Steel (Grofé), 467

Symphony in Variation Form (Haubiel), 469

Symphony, 1933 (Harris), 436

Symphony of Autumn (Moore, D.), 441

Symphony of Chorales (Foss), 592

Symphony of the Air, 602

Symphony of the City (Eppert), 418

Symphony on a Hymn Tune (Thomson), 432, 433

Symphony on Canadian Airs (Helfer), 472

Symphony on Marching Tunes (Gould), 553

Symphony Society of New York (*see* New York Symphony Society)

Symphony-Suite for Strings (Bauer), 411

Syncopated Clock, The (Anderson), 642

Synergy (Brown), 617

Syracuse University, 465, 519, 594

Syre, Leopold (1887-   ), 661

Syrian Ballet (Whitmer), 652

Szell, George, 567, 602

Szigeti, Joseph, 394

T

Tabasco (Chadwick), 310
Tabloid Suite (Grofé), 467
Tabuh-Tabuhan (McPhee), 528
Tabuteau, Marcel, 628
Tagore, Rabindranath, 373, 459
Take a Chance (Youmans), 736
Take Back the Heart That Thou Gavest (Barnard), 704
Take Back Your Mink (Loesser), 747
Take Me Home (Hewitt, J. H.), 169
Take Me Home to the Sunny South (Hewitt, J. H.), 169
Take Me Out to the Ball Game (A. Van Tilzer), 708
Taking of T'ung Kuan, The (Avshalomov), 586
Tale for a Deaf Ear (Bucci), 597
Tales of a Countryside (Cowell), 449
Talin (Hovhaness), 551
Talk of New York, The (Cohan), 719
Tall Kentuckian, The, music for (Dello Joio), 543
Tall Story (Moross), 557
Talma, Louise (1906-), 513-514
Tame Animal Tunes (Bingham), 417
Taminek (Fairchild), 388
Taming of the Shrew, The, 738
Taming of the Shrew, The (Giannini), 494
Tamiris, Helen, 398
Tammany (Edwards), 708
Tammany (Hatton), 672
Tammany (Hewitt), 88-89
Tammany Society, 89
Tammy (Livingston), 752
Tam o'Shanter (Chadwick), 309
Tanglewood, Lenox, Mass. (*see* Berkshire Music Center and Festival)
Tannhäuser, Overture to (Wagner), 211
Tans'ur, William, 16-17, 49, 56
tape music, magnetic (*see* electronic music)
Tapper, Mrs. Thomas, 458
Tarantelle (Hoffman), 290
Tarantelle (Mills), 291
Tarry with Me, O My Saviour (Salter, S.), 649
Tate and Brady, 5, 10, 15, 16
Taubman, Howard, 609
Taunton (Shaw), 135

Tausig, Karl, 291
Taylor, Deems (1885-), 399-403, 812
Taylor, Raynor (1747-1825), 75, 80, 90-94, 151
Taylor, Robert, 601
Tcherepnin, Alexander (1899-), 477-478
Tea for Two (Youmans), 736
Teagarden, Jack, 812-813
Tears (Olmstead), 628
Tears, Idle Tears (Hughes), 624
Teasdale, Sara, 549
Technique of Orchestration (Kennan), 580
Te Deum Laudamus (Huhn), 623
Te Deums (Lutkin), 649
Telephone, The (Menotti), 536
Telesis (Wigglesworth), 585
Tell Her She Haunts Me Yet (Horn), 157
Tempest (Van der Stucken), 348
Tempest, The (Bacon), 465
Tempest, The (Foss), 592
Tempest, The (Paine), 301
Tempest, The (Severn), 362
Tempest, The, music for (Mannes), 469
Temple Dancer (Hugo), 387
Temple Emanu-El, 380, 422
Temple of American Independence (Pelissier), 96
Temple of Minerva, The, 40, 43
Temptation of St. Anthony, The (Read), 559
Ten Aquarelles (Grey), 640
Ten Christmas Carols (Niles), 637
Tender Land, The (Copland), 483
Tenderloin (Bock), 748
Tenebrae (Mennini), 589
Tennessee Variations (Effinger), 582
Tenor, The (Weisgall), 566
Tenting on the Old Camp Ground (Kittredge), 263
Terraminta (Holyoke), 63
Terra Nova (Fitch), 511
Terre de France (Talma), 514
Terry, Robert Huntington (1867-1953), 623
Terry, Walter, 499
Testament of Freedom, The (Thompson, R.), 443-444
Tetrameron (Smith), 618
Texas, University of, 512, 580, 588

Texas Christian University, 585
Thackeray, William M., 543
Thalia (Chadwick), 309
Thanksgiving (Ives), 368
Thanksgiving Anthem (Tuckey), 35
That Certain Feeling (Gershwin), 425
That Old Black Magic (Arlen), 741
That Old Gang of Mine (Henderson), 738
Thayer, Ernest, L., 535
Thayer, Eugene, 648
Theater Piece (Riegger), 397
Theater Piece No. 2 (Luening), 506
theatre, 94
    after Revolution, 72
    in Boston, 23-24
    in New York, 31-32, 76
    in Philadelphia, 27-28, 76, 78
Theatre Guild, New York, 410, 428, 506
Theme and Passacaglia (Nelson), 611
Theme and Variations (Floyd), 596
Theme and Variations (Shulman), 582
Theme and Variations for Orchestra (Shepherd), 405
Theme in D flat with Variations (Noble), 651
Theremin, Leon, 449
There Is a Lady Sweet and Kind (Dello Joio), 544
There Is a Man upon the Cross (Gershefski), 501
There Is an Hour of Peace and Rest (Shaw), 135
There Is a Time (Dello Joio), 543
There Liv'd in Altdorf City Fair (Carr), 99
There's a Girl in the Heart of Maryland (Carroll), 750
There's Music in the Air (Root), 265
There's No Business Like Show Business (Berlin), 734
There's Not a Friend Like the Lowly Jesus, 433
There's Nothing True but Heaven (Shaw), 135
There Will Be Stars (Duke), 631
Thesaurus of Orchestra Devices (Read), 559
Thesaurus of Scales and Melodic Patterns (Slonimsky), 641
Thesis Symphony (Cowell), 450
Thespians, Howe's, 71
They Didn't Believe Me (Kern), 731

They Kissed! I Saw Them Do It (Hawley), 647
They Knew What They Wanted (Howard), 747
They Say It's Wonderful (Berlin), 734
They Still Sing of Love (Spaeth), 706
They Walk Alone (Kubik), 555
Thief of Bagdad, The, 385
Thing or Two About Music, A (Slonimsky), 641
Third Little Show, The (Lane), 742
Thirteen Clocks, The (Bucci), 597
34'46, 766 (Cage), 572
This I Know (Doane), 666
This Is the Army (Berlin), 733
This Is the Garden (Blitzstein), 497
This Modern Music (Howard), 635
This Sacred Ground (Diamond), 545
Thomas, Dylan, 575
Thomas, Isaiah, 62
Thomas, John Rogers (1829-1896), 703
Thomas, Katharine Elwes, 117
Thomas, Theodore (1835-1905), 272, 279, 280-289, 320, 349, 352, 354, 361, 382, 645, 813
Thompson, C. F. 264
Thompson, Fred, 735
Thompson, Randall (1899-   ), 393, 442-444, 611, 813
Thomson, Virgil (1896-   ), 372, 398, 432-434, 443, 445, 484, 485, 494, 513, 516, 517, 531, 536, 540, 553, 564, 569, 582, 589, 603, 604, 609, 732, 813
Thoreau (Ives), 366
Thorough Bass and Harmony (Baker, B. F.), 148
Thorp, Sara Chapman, 201
Those Locks, Those Ebon Locks (Russell), 163
Thoughts on Becoming a Prospective Papa (Gillis), 585
Three Against Christmas (Imbrie), 607
Three Aquatints (Heller), 663
Three Ballads from the Catskills (Cazden), 562
Three Blind Mice (Verrall), 523
Three Cherry Trees, The (Johnson, H.), 628
Three Chinese Pieces (Chasins), 641
Three Chorales from Tagore (Creston), 493
Three Choral Preludes (Sessions), 453

Three Contrasts (Lees), 601
Three Conversations (Inch), 511
Three-Corner Pieces (Gideon), 508
Three Dances (Haines), 583
Three Dances (Mourant), 562
Three Dances for Orchestra (Tweedy), 471
Three Dances for Small Orchestra (Leplin), 588
Three Ghosts (Warford), 626
Three Gospel Hymns for Orchestra (Helm), 584
Three Inventories of Casey Jones (Green), 518
Three Jacks (Vincent), 524
Three Japanese Dances (Rogers, B.), 446
Three Little Pigs, music for (Churchill), 751
Three Little Words (Ruby), 751
Three Men on a Horse, 752
Three Moods (Cesana), 467
Three Moods for Dancing (Barlow, W.), 578
Three Movements (Crawford), 500
Three Movements (Fiorello), 522
Three Movements (Lessard), 604
Three Movements for String Orchestra (Wigglesworth), 585
Three Musketeers, The (Friml), 729
Three New England Sketches (Piston), 445
Three Orchestral Fragments (James, D.), 521
Three Pastels (Stringham), 473
Three Pastorales (James), 521
Three-Penny Opera (Blitzstein), 497
Three Persian Dances (Bornschein), 388
Three Pieces (Allen), 420
Three Pieces (Berger), 563
Three Pieces (Piston), 446
Three Pieces (Shifrin), 616
Three Pieces (Strang), 507
Three Pieces after Blake (Kay), 565
Three Pieces for a Concert (Green), 518
Three Pieces for Orchestra (Thomson), 433-434
Three Pieces for Three Pieces (Shapero), 603
Three Places in New England (Ives), 368
Three Poems by Shelley (Steinert), 523

Three Poems from Walt Whitman (Hanson), 431
Three Psalms (Jacobi), 460
Three Rondos for the Pianoforte or Harpsichord (Brown), 102
Three's a Crowd (Duke), 526
Three's a Crowd (Schwartz), 739, 743
Three Shades of Blue (Grofé), 467
Three Shadows (Saminsky), 423
Three Sonatas for the Pianoforte (Hewitt), 88
Three Songs (Crawford), 500
Three Songs (Weber), 568
Three Symphonic Pieces (Moevs), 602
Three Symphonic Preludes (Dello Joio), 542
Three Theatre Portraits (Finley), 471
Three Tone Pictures (Griffes), 390
Threnody (Creston), 492
Threnody (Read), 559
Threnody (Shulman), 582
Threnos (Avshalomov), 586
Throne of God, The (Sowerby), 657
Through a Glass Darkly (Nordoff), 508
Through the Looking Glass (Taylor), 400, 402
Through the Years (Youmans), 736
Thru the Streets of New York (Horn), 158
Thuille, Ludwig, 379, 385, 387
Thunderbird Suite (Cadman), 404
Thurber, James, 597
Thursby, Emma, 203, 624
Thy Beaming Eyes (MacDowell), 332
Thy Dark Hair (Johnson, H.), 628
Thy Smiles are all Decaing, Love (Carr), 100
Thy Sweet Singing (Olmstead), 628
Tibbett, Lawrence, 408
Tiberio (Stearne), 420
Tidden, Paul, 635
Tiger Rose (De Rose), 753
Till Dawn Sunday (Bennett), 461
Till Noah's Time, 63
Till the Sands of the Desert Grow Cold (Ball), 707
Till We Meet Again (Whiting), 749
Time Cycle (Foss), 593-594
Time on My Hands (Youmans), 736
Times Five (Brown), 617
Time Span (Rochberg), 567
Time Suite (Harris), 438

Timm, Henry Christian (1811-1892), 153-154, 234, 248
Timon of Athens (Diamond), 544
Tin Pan Alley (Raphling), 558
Tiomkin, Dimitri (1899-   ), 478
Tipitin (Grevor), 628
Tipperary, 726
Tip Top (Caryll), 716
'Tis Gladsome Easter (Bedell), 658
Titanic, 305
Titcomb, Everett (1884-   ), 654
To a Liberator (McKay), 464
To a Lonely Sentry (Dello Joio), 542
To Anacreon in Heaven, 123-125
To an Invalid (Golde), 631
To a Nordic Princess (Grainger), 406
To Arms, Columbia (Van Hagen, Jr.), 75
Toast (Hopkinson), 43
To a Vanishing Race (Cadman), 404
To a Water Lily (MacDowell), 330
To a Wild Rose (MacDowell), 330
To a Young World (Saminsky), 423
Toccata (Talma), 513
Toccata Concertante (Fine), 571
Toccata Festiva (Barber), 533
Toccata Giocosa (Read), 559
Toccata-Ricercare-Finale (Bailey), 522
Toccatina (Gillette), 654
Toch, Ernest, 500
Today (Olmstead), 628
To Each His Own, music for (Young), 753
To Helen (Smith), 630
To Helen (Sonneck), 624
To Jesus the Crown of My Hope (Shaw), 135
Told in the Hills (Pattison), 640
Tom and Lily (Carter), 488
Tomb of Genius, The (Heinrich), 238
Tomlinson, Ralph, 124-125
Tom o' Bedlam (Avshalomov), 586
Tomorrow (Smith), 380
Tom Paine (Korn), 620
Tom Paine Overture (Phillips), 509
Tom Sawyer Overture (Dubensky), 477
To My Mother (MacGimsey), 637
"tone-clusters," 448-449
Tone Poem on the Square Dance (Effinger), 582
Too Darn Hot (Porter), 738
Top Brass (Shulman), 582
Toplady (Hastings), 142

Toscanini, Arturo, 456, 531, 585, 631
To Silvanus (Inch), 511
Totem Tom Tom (Friml), 729
To the Children (Bacon), 466
To Thee, O Country (Eichberg), 218
To the Fallen (Gardner), 641
To the Fallen (Hermann), 554
To the Fallen (Rogers, B.), 446
To the Real (Rudhyar), 476
To the Spirit of Beethoven (Heinrich), 237
To the Sun (Griffis), 470
Touch and Technique (Mason, W.), 280
Touchstone, The (Bentley), 102
touch system, 274, 275, 277
Toulon, 7
Toulumne (Maganini), 474
Tower of Babel, The (Robinson), 629
Tower of Babel, or Language Confounded, The (Heinrich), 234
Tower of Saint Barbara, The (Dahl), 565
Town Hall, 631
Toyland (Herbert, V.), 718
To You, America (Still), 462
To Youth (White, P.), 472
Toy Trumpet, The (Scott), 753
Trackmeet (Bennett), 461
Traditions (Engel, A. L.), 556
Traffic (Eppert), 418
Tragedy of the Deep (Pratt), 305
Tragica Sonata (MacDowell), 326, 328, 329
Tragic Cycle (McDonald), 463
Tragic Overture (Galajikian), 521
Trail of the Lonesome Pine, The (Carroll), 750
Trail to Mexico (Finney), 498
Traitor Mandolin, The (Loomis), 635
Trajetta, Filippo, 239
Tramp, Tramp, Tramp (Root), 264, 266
Transatlantic (Antheil), 491
Transitions (Galajikian), 521
Transitions (McPhee), 528
Trans-Mississippi Exposition, 322
Transposed Heads, The (Glanville-Hicks), 566
Trapp Family Singers, 741
Traveler Benighted and Lost, O'er the Mountains Pursues his Way, The (Hopkinson), 42
Travelin' Man, 687

Travellers, The (Shapero), 602
Travellers Preserved, The (Taylor R.), 94
Treasure Girl (Gershwin), 735
Treasury of American Song, A (Downes, Siegmeister), 514
Treatise on Practical Thorough Bass (Jackson), 133
Treaty of William Penn with the Indians, The (Heinrich), 237
Tree Grows in Brooklyn, A (Schwartz), 739
Tree on the Plains, A (Bacon), 465
Trees (Rasbach), 627
Trees (Ware), 625
Tree That Found Christmas, The (Kleinsinger), 643
Trelawney of the Wells (Pinero), 90
Trend (Riegger), 398
Trial at Rouen, The (Dello Joio), 543
Trial of Lucullus, The (Sessions), 454
Tribute to Stephen Foster (Grainger), 406
Trilogy (Robertson), 471
Trimble, Lester (1923-   ), 610-611
Trio in B Minor (Riegger), 396
Trio No. 3 (Stevens), 519
Triple Concerto (Wagenaar), 456
Triple Sec (Blitzstein), 496
Trip to Chinatown, A (Gaunt), 715
Trip to Nahant, The (Thompson), 443
Triptych (Engel, C.), 630
Triptych (Freed), 527
Triptych (Giannini), 495
Triptych (Hovhaness), 551
Triptych (Shepherd), 405
Triptych (Weaver), 628
Triptyque (Freed), 526
Trisagion and Sanctus (Hawley), 647
Triskelion (Stevens), 519
Trisler, Joyce, 499
Triumphal Overture (Kreutz), 509
Triumph of Columbus (Pratt), 305
Triumph of Joseph, The (De Leone), 420
Triumph of St. Joan, The (Dello Joio), 542-543
Triumph of St. Patrick, The (Yon), 660
Triumph of the Cross, The (Matthews), 653
Trivialities (Kubik), 555
Trois Poèmes Juifs (Bloch), 392
Trojan Incident (Riegger), 398

Trojan Women, The (Palmer), 580
Troubled Island (Still), 462
Trouble in Tahiti (Bernstein), 540
Trout, The (Engel, C.), 630
Truant, The (Manning), 627
Trumpeter's Lullaby (Anderson), 642
Tryst, The (Freeman), 361
Trysting Tree, The (Wolfe), 637
Tubby the Tuba (Kleinsinger), 643
Tucker, Henry, 703
Tuckey, William, 34-36, 136
Tuck Me to Sleep in My Old 'Tucky Home (Meyer), 709
Tufts, John, 12-13
Tumble In (Friml), 729
Tune In, America (Mason, D. G.), 378
Turkey in the Straw (Zip Coon), 177, 355, 691
Turkey in the Straw, Arrangement of (Guion), 406
Turner, William, 65
Tuskegee Institute Singers, 465, 681
Tuthill, Burnet Corwin (1888-   ), 418, 757
Twain, Mark, 592
Twa Sisters, The, 695
Tweedy, Donald (1890-1948), 471
Twelfth Night (Amram), 619
Twelve Variations (Oldberg), 386, 387
Twelve Virtuoso Studies (MacDowell), 330
Twentieth Century Club, Boston, 356
Twentieth Century Music (Bauer), 411
Twenty-five Pages (Brown), 617
Twenty Kentucky Mountain Songs (Brockway-Wyman), 384, 692
23rd Psalm (Chaffin), 648
23rd Psalm (Malotte), 628
23rd Psalm (Sanders), 521
Twenty Years Ago (Knight), 160
Twilight (Nevin, A.), 386
Twilight Trail (Alter), 753
'Twill Nebber Do to Gib It Up So (Emmett), 180, 181
Twirly-Whirly (Stromberg), 715
Two American Sketches (Griselle), 468
Two Brothers, The, 692
Two Contrasts for Orchestra (Nelson), 611
Two Dances for Radio (Porter, Q.), 456
Two Indian Legends (Schoenefeld), 362
Two Little Bluebirds (Kern), 732

Two Little Girls in Blue (Youmans), 736

Two Monochromes (Goldman), 642

Two Movements (Crawford), 500

Two Movements (Gideon), 508

Two New England Fantasies (Fitch), 511

Two on the Aisle (Styne), 745

Two Pensive Songs (Avshalomov), 586

Two Pieces for Chorus and Orchestra (Leplin), 588

Two Pieces for String Orchestra (Weber), 568

Two Pieces from the Olden Times (Griselle), 468

Two Pieces in Sabbath Mood (Jacobi), 460

Two Symphonic Movements (Barati), 586

U

Ukrainian Suite (Porter, Q.), 456

Uncle Remus, 354

Unconscious Lover, The (Young), 637

Under Cover (Braham), 714

Undertow (Schuman), 535

Undine (Strong), 344

Undine (Ware), 625

Unfinished Symphony (Schubert), 730

Unger, Julius, 271

Unicorn, the Gorgon and the Manticore, The (Menotti), 537

Unimproving Songs for Enthusiastic Children (Branscombe), 635

Union Harmony (Holden), 61

Union Hymnal, 663

Union Theological Seminary, 473

United States Commission for UNESCO, 535

United States George Washington Bicentennial Committee, 373

U. S. Highball (Partch), 500

United States Information Service, 450

United States Marine Band, 564

United States Military Academy, West Point, 611

United States Psalmody (Pond), 146

United States Veterans Administration, 518

Universities (*see under* individual names)

University Composers, Exchange of, 571

University Greys, The (Kreutz), 509

University Society, 662

Unnamed City, The (Bergh), 626

Unsinkable Molly Brown, The (Willson), 748

Until Night and Day Shall Cease (Shapero), 603

Until the Day (Olmstead), 628

Up in a Balloon, 705

Up in a Balloon (Weinrich), 709

Up in Central Park (Romberg), 730

Up She Goes (Tierney), 738

Upton, George P., 210

Up with the Flag (Brewer), 647

Urania (Lyon), 35, 37, 46, 47, 48

Uranian Academy, 105-107

Uranian Instructions (Adgate), 107

Ussachevsky, Vladimir (1913-   ), 503-506, 612, 766

Utah, University of, 471

Utah Symphony Orchestra, 464

Utica Collection of hymns (Hastings), 141

Utica Jubilee Singers Spirituals, 684

Uzziah (Freeman), 361

V

Vacant Chair, The (Root), 266

Vade Mecum (Weiss), 455

Vagabond, The (Weaver), 655

Vagabond King, The (Friml), 729

Vagrom Ballad, A (Chadwick), 309

Valdo (Freeman), 361

Vallee, Rudy, 747, 749, 813

Valley Forge (Koutzen), 529

Valley of Dry Bones, The (Binder), 663

Valley of the Moon (Mourant), 562

Valley Town, score for (Blitzstein), 497

Valse Charlene (Rasbach), 627

Values (Vanderpool), 625

Van Alstyne, Egbert (1882-1951), 708

Van Cliburn Story, The (Chasins), 641

Vanderpool, Frederick (1877-1947), 625

Van Der Stucken, Frank (1858-1929), 347-348, 475

Van Dyke, Henry, 377

Vanessa (Barber), 532

Van Hagen, Peter Albrecht, 73-75, 82, 83, 84, 98, 672

Van Hagen, Peter, Jr. (1781-1837), 73, 75, 82, 83, 84, 98, 104

Van Heusen, Jimmy (1913-   ), 752

Vanity Fair (Dello Joio), 543
Van Vactor, David (1906-   ), 523-524
Van Vechten, Carl, 426
Vanzetti in the Death House (Strang), 507
Vardell, Charles (1893-   ), 466
Varèse, Edgar (1885-   ), 412-413, 424, 462, 503, 527, 560, 571, 813
Variants on a Theme of John Lewis (Schuller), 616
Variations (Riegger), 398
Variations and Double Fugue (Powell), 406
Variations and Epilogue (Lopatnikoff), 506
Variations, Chaconne, and Finale (Dello Joio), 541
Variations, Chorale, and Fugue (Palmer), 579
Variations for Orchestra (Carter), 489
Variations for Orchestra (Cowell), 451
Variations in Oblique Harmony (Brant), 576
Variations on a Cowboy Tune (Effinger), 582
Variations on an Ancient Tune (Verrall), 523
Variations on an Old Form (Wagner), 516
Variations on a Pious Theme (Foote), 421
Variations on a Shaker Melody (Copland), 483
Variations on a Song by Mussorgsky (Rogers, B.), 447
Variations on a Theme by Eugene Goossens (Copland), 484
Variations on a Theme by Paganini (Cohn), 578
Variations on a Theme from the Beggar's Opera (Korn), 620
Variations on a Theme in Medieval Style (Fickenscher), 371
Variations on a Theme of John Powell (Mason), 378
Variations on a Western Folksong (Nelson), 611
Variations on Thirds (Cowell), 451
Variation Symphony, A (Mennin), 590
Variazioni Solenne (Van Vactor), 524
Varsity Drag (Henderson), 739
Vassar College, 456, 529, 584

Vaux Hall Gardens, 84, 85, 93, 156
Veil, The (Rogers, B.), 447
Vellani, Madame, 159
Velvet Darkness (Reddick), 636
Vendetta (Freeman), 361
Venetian Fantasy (Harling), 419
Venetian Glass Nephew, The (Bonner), 420
Venice Festival (1954), 540
Vera Violetta (Hirsch), 735
Vernal Equinox (Read), 558-559
Verrall, John (1908-   ), 522-523, 813
Very Good Eddie (Kern), 731
Very Warm for May (Kern), 732
Vestiges (Cowell), 449
Veteran, The (Knight), 159
Vexilla Regis (Shelley), 647
Vibrations (Freed), 526
Victor, H. B., 101-102
Victor Company (*see* RCA-Victor)
Victory (Sousa), 715
Victory at Sea (Bennett), 741
Victory at Sea, music for (Rodgers), 741
Victory Ball, A (Schelling), 383
Vidal, Paul, 477
Vienna Conservatory, 379, 409
Vienna Gesellschaft der Musikfreunde, 495
Vienna State Orchestra, 450
Vierne, Louis, 652
Vigil of St. Mark, The (Taylor R.), 93
Vignettes (Watts, W.), 630
Village Music (Moore, D.), 441
Village Romance, A (Densmore), 626
Villanelle du Diable, La (Rollinat), 350
Villa of Dreams (Daniels), 385
Vincent, John (1902-   ), 524-525
Violin Harmonika, 73
Viotti, Giovanni, 84
Virginia, University of, 371, 442
Virginia Minstrels, 177
Virginia Reel, 634
Virginia Sampler (Smit), 604
Virginia State Choral Festival, 405
Virgin of the Sun, The (Pelissier), 96
Virgin's Cradle Hymn (Howard), 635
virtuosi, mid-nineteenth century, 198-205
Vision, The (Gaines), 633
Vision and Prayer (Babbitt), 575
Vision from the Rock (Hovhaness), 551
Vision of Isaiah (Smith), 380
Vision of St. John, The (Coombs), 650

Vision of Sir Launfal, The (Cadman), 404
Vision of Sir Launfal, The (Sowerby), 657
Vision Végétale (Rudhyar), 476
Vitamins (Eppert), 418
Vitebsk (Copland), 485
Vivandière, The (Hewitt, J. H.), 169
Vocal Companion (Holyoke), 62
Vocal Enchantress (Hill), 623
Vocal Music Concerts, Adgate's, 105
Vogrich, Max Wilhelm Karl (1852-1916), 363, 627
Voice in the Wilderness, A (Bloch), 394
Voice in the Wilderness, The (Scott), 625
Voice of McConnell, The (Cohan), 719
Voice of My Beloved (Daniels), 385
Voices for a Mirror (Kupferman), 603
Voicing the Modern Dance Orchestra (Cesana), 467
Volpe, Arnold (1869-1940), 363
Volpe Symphony Orchestra, 363
Volpone (Antheil), 491
Volpone (Gruenberg), 410
Voltaire, 541
Volunteers (Reinagle), 80
Von Tilzer, Albert (1878-1956), 708
Von Tilzer, Harry (1872-1946), 708
Voodoo (Freeman), 361
Voorhees, Don, 462
Vox Cathedralis (Haubiel), 469
Voyage Four (Brant), 576
Voyage of Columbus, The (Buck), 646
Voyage of the Mayflower, The (White, P.), 472
Vulture of the Alps, The, 175

W

Wachicanta (Schoenfeld), 362
Wagenaar, Bernard (1894-), 379, 455-456, 554, 569, 581, 609, 643, 814
Wagner, Joseph (1900-), 515-516
Wagner, Richard, 212, 214, 291
Wagon Wheels (De Rose), 753
Waite, Marjorie Peabody, award, 513
Waiting for the May (Noble), 651
Wait till I Put on My Crown (Reddick), 636
Wake, Nicodemus (Root), 267
Wake Up, Sweet Melody (Cain), 658
Wald, Max (1889-1954), 418

Waldenses, The (Abbot), 249
Walk a Little Faster (Duke), 525
walk-arounds, plantation, 181, 182, 257
Walker, Don, 747
Walking Delegate, The (Hosmer), 388
Walking Down Broadway (Lingard-Pratt), 704
Walking Home in the Spring (Wilder), 510
Walking Tune (Grainger), 407
Wallopp, Douglass, 748
Wall Street Fantasy (Bingham), 417
Wall Street Rag (Joplin), 720
Walter, Bruno, 372, 539
Walter, Thomas, 13, 49
Walt Whitman (Creston), 492
Walt Whitman Overture, A (Siegmeister), 514
Waltzes for Orchestra (Shulman), 582
Waltz Serenade (Rochberg), 567
Waltz Suite (Gebhard), 626
Wanamaker, Rodman, Contest in composition, 465
Wanderer's Psalm (Parker), 318
Wandering Village Maid, The (Taylor, R.), 93
Ward, Frank Edwin (1872-), 652
Ward, Robert (1917-), 559-561, 814
Ware, Harriet (1877-1962), 625
Wareham (Knapp), 17
Warford, Claude (1877-1950), 625-626
Warnow, Mark, 457
Warren, Harry (1893-), 751
Warriner, Solomon, 141
Warriors, The (Rogers, B.), 447
Warrior's March to the Battlefield (Heinrich), 232
war songs (*see* Civil War; Revolutionary War; Spanish-American War; World War I; World War II)
Washington (Hewitt, J. H.), 169
Washington (Holyoke), 63
Washington (Pownall), 108
Washington, George, 31, 41-43, 61
Washington, Martha, 43
Washington, Ned, 754
Washington, University of, 463, 523, 586, 590, 614
Washington Bicentennial celebration, 373
Washington, D. C.:
    Cathedral, 613, 656
    National Symphony, 398
    Opera Company, 363

Washington Post, The (Sousa), 710
Washington's Birthday (Ives), 368
Washington University, St. Louis, 548
Was My Brother in the Battle? (Foster), 264
Wastin' Time (Bacon), 466
Watchers of the Stars (Cain), 658
Watching (Metcalf), 622
Watchman, What of the Night? (Heller), 663
Water Boy, 694
Water Boy (Herrmann), 554
Water Colors (Carpenter), 373
Waterfall, The (Daniels), 386
Water Idyl (Helfer), 472
Waterman, The (Pelissier), 96
Water Music (Kay), 557
Waters, Ethel, 741
Water Scenes (Nevin), 621
Watts, Isaac, 10, 15, 16, 17, 665
Watts, Wintter (1884-1962), 630
Wa-Wan Press, 374-375, 405, 635, 757
Waxman, Franz (1906-   ), 529
Wayne, Mabel (1898-   ), 750
We (Dunn), 417
We Are Coming, Father Abraham (Gibbons), 261
We Are Happy and Free, 175
Weaver, Mary (1906-   ), 628, 656
Weaver, Powell (1890-1951), 655-656
Weaver of Tales (Delamarter), 417
Webb, George James (1803-1887), 139, 142-144, 151
Webb, Thomas Smith, 133, 135, 151
Weber, Ben (1916-   ), 568-569, 767, 814
Weber, Carl Maria von, 234
Weber and Fields, 715
Webern, Anton, 370, 517, 574, 575, 607, 616
Webster, C. W., 271
Webster, Fletcher, 259
Webster, Joseph Philbrick, 263
Webster, Margaret, 506
Webster, Paul Francis, 752
Wedding Knell, The (Verrall), 523
Wedding of the Painted Doll, The (Brown), 750
Wedge, George, 513
Weekly Mirror, 164
Weekly Post Boy (New York), 33, 35
Weeping Pleiades, The (Flanagan), 632

Weeping Sad and Lonely, or When This Cruel War Is Over (Tucker), 264
We Go Forward (Foote), 422
We Have Fed Our Seas for a Thousand Years (Grainger), 407
Weidig, Adolf (1867-1931), 363, 454, 465, 500, 630, 658
Weidman, Charles, 397-398
Weidman, Jerome, 744, 748
Weill, Kurt, 497
Weinrich, Percy (1887-1952), 709
Weinstock, Jack, 747
Weisgall, Hugo (1912-   ), 451, 565-566, 814
Weiss, Adolph (1891-   ), 454-455, 571, 814
Welcome Happy Morning (Matthews), 653
Welde, Thomas, 7
Well, The (Mennini), 589
Welles, Orson, 497, 506
Wellesley College, 442, 649
Wellesz, Egon, 566
Well-Tempered Listener, The (Taylor), 402
Wenzl, 145
We're Coming, Sister Mary (Work), 267
Wesleyan Univeristy, 569
Wessel, Mark (1894-   ), 474-475
West, music in the, 270
Westendorf, Thomas Paine, 705
Western College, Ohio, 346
Western Electric News, 400
Western Kentucky State College, 524
Western Overture (Effinger), 582
Western Recorder, The, 141
Western Reserve University, 404, 551
Western Suite (Siegmeister), 514
Western Symphony (Kay), 557
Western Wind (Green), 519
Westminster Choir College, 586, 613, 656
Westminster Records, 763
West of the Great Divide (Ball), 707
West Side Story (Bernstein), 541
Westward, George A. A., 653
Westward expansion, 269-274
Wetzler, Herman Hans (1870-1943), 389
We've a Million in the Field (Foster), 264
We Want to Sing About Women (Laska), 728

Weybosset (Shaw), 135
What a Friend We Have in Jesus (Converse, C. C.), 666
What Do You Do in the Infantry (Loesser), 746
What Is a Kiss (Mana-Zucca), 627
What'll I Do (Berlin), 733
What o' Dat (Emmett), 181
What's This? (Cowell), 449
What's Up (Loewe), 742, 743
What to Listen For in Music (Copland), 486
Wheatfield at Noon (Thomson), 434
Wheels (Grofé), 467
When I Have Sung My Songs (Charles), 631
When I Seek My Pillow (Webb), 144
When Johnny Comes Marching Home (Gilmore), 553, 709
When Johnny Comes Marching Home (Harris), 436, 709
When Johnny Comes Marching Home, Variations (Tuthill), 418
When Pierrot Sings (Johnson, H.), 628
When That Midnight Choo-Choo Leaves for Alabam' (Berlin), 733
When the Boys Come Home (Speaks), 727
When the Grown-Up Ladies Act Like Babies (Abrahams), 709
When the Shades of Night Pursuing (Hewitt), 87
When Winds Are Raging (Spross), 624
When You and I Were Young, Maggie (Johnson-Butterfield), 703, 704
When You Want 'Em (Gershwin), 425
When You Wore a Tulip (Weinrich), 709
When Yuba Plays the Rhumba on the Tuba (Hupfield), 750
Where Can the Soul Find Rest? (Baker, J. C.), 170
Where Is My Wandering Boy Tonight (Lowry), 705
Where's Charley? (Loesser), 746
Where the Blue of the Night Meets the Gold of the Day (Ahlert), 749
Where the Sweet Magnolia Blooms (Hewitt, J. H.), 169
Which Flower I Love (Terry), 623
While We're Young (Wilder), 510
Whimsies (Avshalomov), 586
Whimsy (Howe), 421

Whirligig (Stromberg), 715
Whispering Hope (Winner), 264
Whispers of Heavenly Death (Bacon), 466
Whispers of Heavenly Death (Bonner), 420
Whispers of Untimely Death (Williams), 655
Whistler and His Dog, The (Pryor), 711
Whistle While You Work (Churchill), 751
Whistling Rufus (Mills), 720
White, Charles, 132
White, Clarence Cameron (1880-   ), 636
White, George L., 681
White, Paul (1895-   ), 472
White, T. H., 743
White and Negro Spirituals, Their Life Span and Kinship (Jackson), 665
Whitefield, George, 16
Whitefield's Tune, 47
White Knight, The (Taylor), 400
Whiteman, Elfrida, 544
Whiteman, Paul, 401, 425-426, 462, 466-467, 640, 721-722, 750
White Nights (Bonner), 420
Whiter than Snow (Fischer), 667
White Spirituals in the Southern Uplands (Jackson), 664
White's Serenaders, 179
White Top Mountain Folk Music Festival, 405
White Wings (Moore), 442
White Wings (Winters), 706
Whithorne, Emerson (1884-1958), 410, 814
Whiting, Arthur Batelle (1861-1936), 296, 309, 356-357, 814
Whiting, Richard A. (1891-1938), 749
Whitlock, Billy, 177, 178
Whitman, Walt, 372, 438, 466, 492, 502, 512, 514, 543, 544, 547, 626, 652
Whitmer, T. Carl (1873-1959), 652
Whitney, Joan (1914-   ), 752
Whitney Foundation, 763
Whittle, Maj. D. W., 667
Who? (Kern), 732
Whoa, Emma, 705
Who Cares? (Ager), 749
Whole Book of Psalms (Playford), 13
Whoopee Overture (Brant), 576
Whoopee ti yi yo (Fox), 694

Whoopee Ti-Yi-Yo (Kubik), 638
Who Paid the Rent for Mrs. Van Winkle When Rip Van Winkle Went Away (Fisher), 708
Who's Afraid of the Big Bad Wolf? (Churchill), 751
Who Will Care for Mother Now? (Sawyer), 264
Why Can't You Behave (Porter), 738
Why Don't They Play with Me (Harris), 706
Why, Huntress, Why (Carr), 99
Widor, Charles, 374, 379, 412, 416, 417, 455, 649, 654, 655
Widow Nolan's Goat, The (Braham), 714
Wie ein fahrender Hornist sich ein Land erblies (Strong), 345
Wiener, Hans, Ballet, 445
Wieniawski, Henri, 278
Wife of Martin Guerre, The (Bergsma), 591
Wigglesworth, Frank (1918-   ), 585-586
Wignell, Thomas, 75, 78
Wignell and Reinagle Company, 72
Wilde, Oscar, 523
Wilder, Alec (1907-   ), 510
Wilder, Thornton, 481, 513
Wilderness Road (Siegmeister), 514
Wilderness Stone (Bingham), 417
Wildflower (Youmans), 736
Wild Goose Chase, The (Hewitt), 90
Wild Men's Dance (Ornstein), 458
Wild Swans (Duke), 631
Wild Tears (Watts, W.), 630
Wild Wood Spirits' Chant, The (Heinrich), 237
Wildwood Troubadour, The; a Musical Autobiography (Heinrich), 234
Wilhelm Tell (Schiller), 99
Wilkins, Donald G., 445
Willers, Wilfred, 562
William Billings Overture (Schuman), 535
William Ratcliff (Van der Stucken), 348
Williams, Aaron, 105
Williams, David McK. (1887-   ), 655
Williams, Harry, 708
Williams, Vaughn, 372, 566, 583
Williamsburg, Virginia, early music in, 30-31
Williams College, 635

Willie Has Gone to the War (Foster), 264
Willie the Weeper (Moross), 557
Willie, We Have Missed You (Foster), 196
Willis, N. P., 157
Willis, Richard Storrs, 246
Willow Tree, The (Cadman), 404
Willowwave and Wellaway (Fickenscher), 371
Will Shakespeare, 402
Willson, Meredith (1902-   ), 747-748
Will There Be Any Stars in My Crown?, 433
Will You Come to My Mountain Home, 173
Wilson, Mortimer (1876-1932), 385, 635
Wilson, Woodrow, 695
Wind and the Rain, The (Amram), 618
Wind Drum (Hovhaness), 551
Wind in the Willows, The (Thompson), 433
Wind of the Winter's Night (Russell), 161
Wind Remains, The (Lorca-Bowles), 582
Wind's in the South (Scott), 625
Wind-Song (Rogers), 649
Winged Victory (Rose), 754
Wings of Night (Watts, W.), 630
Wings of the Dove, The (Moore), 440
Winner, Septimus (1827-1902), 264, 814
Winona Symphony Orchestra, 369
Winslow, Edward, 5
Winter (Noble), 651
Winter, Banks, 706
Wintergreen for President (Gershwin), 428
Winter of Blue Snow (Kreutz), 509
Winter Scenes (Grey), 640
Winter's Past, The (Barlow), 578
Winter Symphony, A (Nordhoff), 508
Wisconsin, University of, 469, 499, 580, 599
Wisconsin Suite (Luening), 502
Wish, The (Antheil), 491
Wish You Were Here (Rome), 744
Witch, The (Hoiby), 599
Witches of the Rocks, The, 80
Witch of Brocken, The (Gruening), 409
Witch of Salem (Cadman), 403
With a Little Bit of Luck (Loewe), 743

With All Her Faults I Love Her Still (Rosenfeld), 706
With a Smile and a Song (Churchill), 751
Within the Gates (Engel), 556
With My Red Fires (Riegger), 397
Without a Song (Youmans), 736
With Pleasure Have I Past My Days (Hopkinson), 41
With the Tide (Watts, W.), 630
With the Wind and the Rain in Her Hair (Edwards), 627
Witmark, M., & Sons, 628, 716
Witt, Dr. Christopher, 18
Wodehouse, P. G., 731
Wolfe, Jacques (1896-), 637
Wolfe, Thomas, 579
Woltmann, Frederick (1908-), 511-512
Woman of Trachis, The (Boatwright), 659
Women's Triumphal March (Ware), 625
Wonderful Love (Main), 667
Wonderful Town (Bernstein), 540
Wonderful, Wonderful Copenhagen (Loesser), 746
Wondrous Works of God, The (Mopper), 567
Wood, William, 672
Woodbridge, William C., 127-128, 139
Woodbury, Isaac Baker (1819-1858), 148-149
Woodbury's Self-Instructor in Musical Composition and Thorough Bass, 148
Wood-Hill, Mabel (1871-1954), 623
Woodland (Luders), 719
Woodland Sketches (MacDowell), 326, 330
Woodman, Raymond Huntington (1861-1943), 647-648
Woodman and the Elves, The (Barrymore), 389
Wood-Notes (Donovan), 455
Wood Notes (Still), 462
Woodworth (Bradbury), 146
Worcester Collection, 62
Worcester Festival, 310, 346, 408
Work, Henry Clay (1832-1884), 266-268, 814
Workaday Songs (Odum-Johnson), 688-689

Workout (Gershefski), 501
work songs, Negro, 687
Works Progress Administration (W.P.A.) (*see* Federal Music Project; Federal Theatre)
Work 22 (Delaney), 518
World at War, The, score for (Kubik), 555
World of Paul Klee, The (Diamond), 545
World Peace Jubilee, 297
World's Fair (1892), Chicago, 287-289, 300, 377
World's Fair Suite (Grofé), 467
World Turned Upside Down, The, 117
World War I, songs of, 726-727, 733
World War II, songs of, 555, 727-728, 733
Wouldn't It Be Loverly? (Loewe), 743
Wounded Hussar, The (Hewitt), 87
Wounded Sailor, The (Taylor, R.), 93
W.P.A. (Works Progress Administration) (*see* Federal Music Project; Federal Theatre)
WQXR, New York, 641
Wreck of the Hesperus, The (Foote), 312
Wreck of the Julie Plante, The (O'Hara), 626
Wreck of the Mexico, The (Russell), 163
Wreck on the C & O, The, 692
Wrighten, Mrs. (*see* Pownall, Mary Ann)
Write Me a Letter from Home (Hays), 703
Wunderbar (Porter), 738
Wuorinen, Charles (1938-), 612
Würzburg Conservatory, 420
Wuthering Heights (Foss), 595-596
Wyeth, Miss, 270
Wyman, Loraine, 384, 692
Wynken, Blynken and Nod (Nevin), 621
Wyoming, University of, 515

X

Xavier University, 565

Y

Yaddo Composers' Colony, 398
Yaddo Festivals, 496

Yale Bulldog Song (Porter), 737

Yale Library, 93

Yale University School of Music, 346, 365, 367, 379, 452, 455, 456, 470, 488, 500, 522, 551, 563, 605, 607, 654, 744

Yankee, meaning of, 114

Yankee Clipper (Bowles), 582

Yankee Doodle, 113-118, 681

Yankee Doodle Boy, The (Cohan), 719

Yankee Overture (Ward), 560

Yankee Peddlar, The (Duke), 631

Yankee Prince, The (Cohan), 719

Year in Our Land, A (Amram), 619

Year's at the Spring, The (Beach), 322

Year's Chronicle, A (Lockwood), 515

Year the Yankees Lost the Pennant, The (Wallopp), 748

Yellen, Jack, 749

Yes, I Would the Cruel War Were Over (Winner), 264

Yip! Yip! Yaphank (Berlin), 733

Yolanda of Cyprus (Loomis), 419

Yon, Pietro (1886-1943), 492, 655, 660

You and the Night and the Music (Schwartz), 739

You and You (Rasbach), 627

You Are My Lucky Star (Henderson), 739

You Can't Get a Man with a Gun (Berlin), 734

Youmans, Vincent (1898-1946), 736

You Never Know (Porter), 737

Young, Victor (1889-   ), 637

Young, Victor (1900-1956), 753

Young, William, 81, 83

Young Blood (Watts, W.), 630

Young Goodman Brown (Wigglesworth), 585

Young Men's Hebrew Association, 597, 663

Young Men's Symphony Orchestra, New York, 363

Young People's Concerts, 383, 384

You're in Love (Friml), 729

You're Just in Love (Berlin), 734

You're the Cream in My Coffee (Henderson), 739

You're the Top (Porter), 737

Your Kiss (Foster), 627

You Said It (Arlen), 741

Youth and Life (Hadley), 377

Youthful Songs (Moevs), 602

Youth Gets a Break (Moore, D.), 442

Youth of the World (Branscombe), 634

Youth Triumphant (Hadley), 377

You Were Made for Me (Brown), 750

You Will See Your Lord a-Coming, 174

Z

Zal (Fairchild), 388

Zeckwer, Camille (1875-1924), 639

Zerr, Anna, 223

Zerrahn, Carl (1826-1909), 143, 215, 297-298

Zeuner, Charles (1795-1857), 146-147

Ziegfeld Follies, 708, 734, 735, 738

Ziegfeld Follies (Duke), 526

Ziehn, Bernard, 371

Zimbalist, Efrem (1889-   ), 422

Zingareska (Antheil), 490

Zion in Exile (Barlow, W.), 578

Zip Coon, see Turkey in the Straw

Zorinski (Pelissier), 96

Zorinski (Van Hagen), 74

Zuluki (Freeman), 361

Zulu King, The (Freeman), 361

Zululand (Freeman), 361

Zurich Conservatory, 501

Zvonar, Joseph Leopold, 235